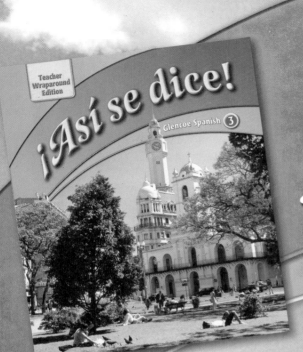

Teacher Wraparound Edition

¡Así se dice!

Glencoe Spanish 3

More than just a textbook!

W9-CIP-687

QuickPass

Use your chapter-specific Web code for quick and easy navigation. Access the Online Student Edition, extra practice, eFlashcards, eGames, and self-check quizzes with QuickPass at glencoe.com.

Students can download the entire audio program to their MP3 players for convenient practice anywhere, anytime.

Glencoe offers you an array of classroom tools on CD-ROM. Plan your days with TeacherWorks™. Present engaging lessons with PowerTeach. Interact with student materials including Student Edition, Audio and Video Programs, and workbooks with StudentWorks™ Plus. Assess with *ExamView® Assessment Suite*.

The Glencoe *¡Así se dice!* Video Program allows you to tailor learning to your students' needs. Enrich your instruction with our Vocabulario en vivo, Gramática en vivo, Diálogo en vivo, and Cultura en vivo DVDs.

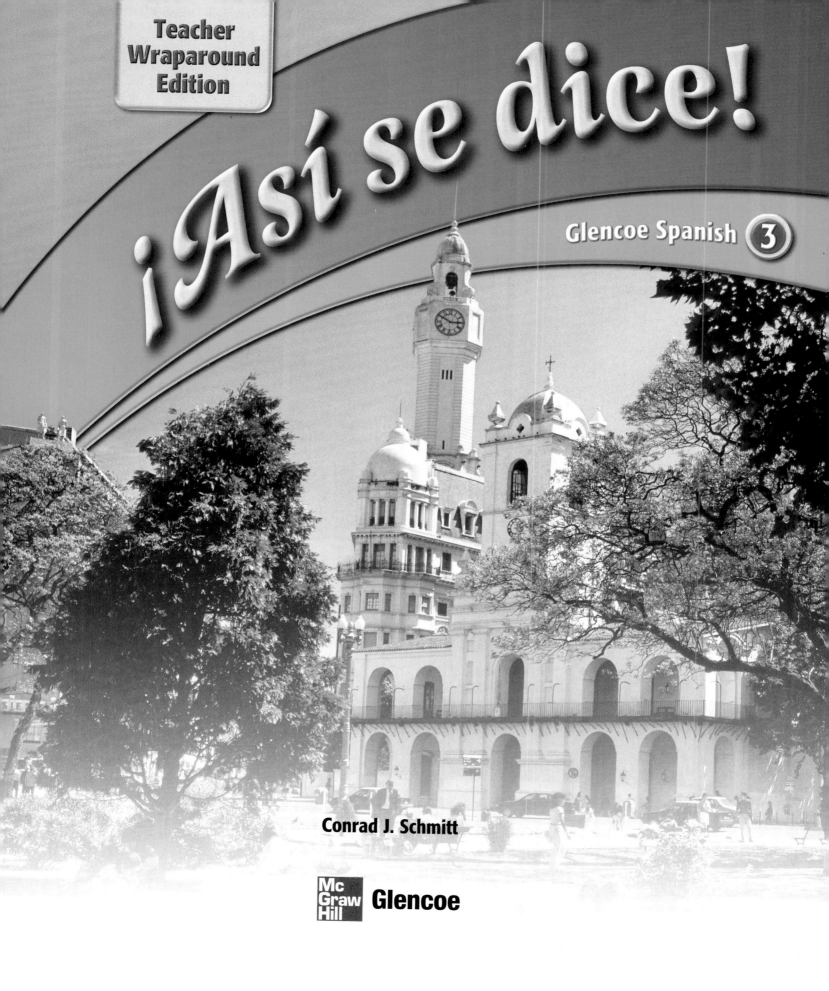

Teacher Wraparound Edition

¡Así se dice!

Glencoe Spanish 3

Conrad J. Schmitt

McGraw Hill Glencoe

The McGraw·Hill Companies

Glencoe

Send all inquiries to:
Glencoe/McGraw-Hill
8787 Orion Place
Columbus, OH 43240-4027

ISBN: 978-0-07-880499-1 *(Teacher Wraparound Edition)*
MHID: 0-07-880499-X *(Teacher Wraparound Edition)*
ISBN: 978-0-07-877784-4 *(Student Edition)*
MHID: 0-07-877784-4 *(Student Edition)*

Printed in the United States of America.

1 2 3 4 5 6 7 8 9 10   071/055   14 13 12 11 10 09 08

Dear Spanish Teacher,

Welcome to Glencoe's **¡Así se dice!** Spanish program. We hope that our presentation of the Spanish language and Hispanic cultures will make the Spanish language more teachable for you and more learnable for your students.

Upon completion of each chapter of **¡Así se dice!** your students will be able to communicate in Spanish in real-life situations. The high-frequency, productive vocabulary presented at the beginning of the chapter focuses on a specific communicative and cultural theme. The grammar points that follow the vocabulary section enable students to put their new words together to communicate coherently.

After students acquire the essential vocabulary and grammar needed to function in a given situation, we present a realistic conversation that uses natural, colloquial Spanish and, most importantly, Spanish that students can readily understand. To introduce students to the cultures of the Hispanic world, the chapter theme is subsequently presented in a cultural milieu in narrative form. The **Lectura cultural** recombines known language and enables students to read and learn—in Spanish—about the fascinating cultures of the people who speak Spanish.

Any one of us who has taught Spanish realizes the importance of giving students the opportunity to practice, a factor so often overlooked in many textbooks today. Throughout **¡Así se dice!** we provide students with many opportunities to use their Spanish in activities with interesting and varied, but realistic, formats. The activities within each chapter progress from simple, guided practice to more open-ended activities that may use all forms of the particular grammar point in question. Finally, activities that encourage completely free communication enable students to recall and reincorporate all the Spanish they have learned up to that point. Toward the end of each chapter, students are given ample opportunity to demonstrate both their oral and written proficiency. Since students need constant reinforcement of material to keep their language skills alive, each chapter includes both its own review and a cumulative review that covers all previously learned material.

We are aware that your students have varied learning styles and abilities. For this reason we have provided a great deal of optional material in **¡Así se dice!** to permit you to pick and choose material appropriate for the needs of your classes. In this Teacher Wraparound Edition we have clearly outlined the material that is required, recommended, or optional.

Many resources accompany **¡Así se dice!** to help you vary and enliven your instruction. We hope you will find these materials not only useful but an integral part of the program. However, we trust you will agree that the Student Edition is the lifeline of any program; the supporting materials can be used to reinforce and expand upon the themes of the main text.

We sincerely hope that you and your students experience much success and enjoyment using **¡Así se dice!**

Atentamente,

Conrad J. Schmitt

Contenido en breve

Teacher Edition

Student Edition

Scope and Sequence

TOPICS

Preliminary Lessons	Chapter 1	Chapter 2
• Greeting people • Saying good-bye • Speaking politely • Counting • Finding out the price • Days of the week • Months of the year • Finding out and giving the date • Asking and telling time • Seasons and weather	• Physical descriptions and personality traits • Nationalities • School subjects	• Families and pets • Houses and apartments • Rooms and furniture

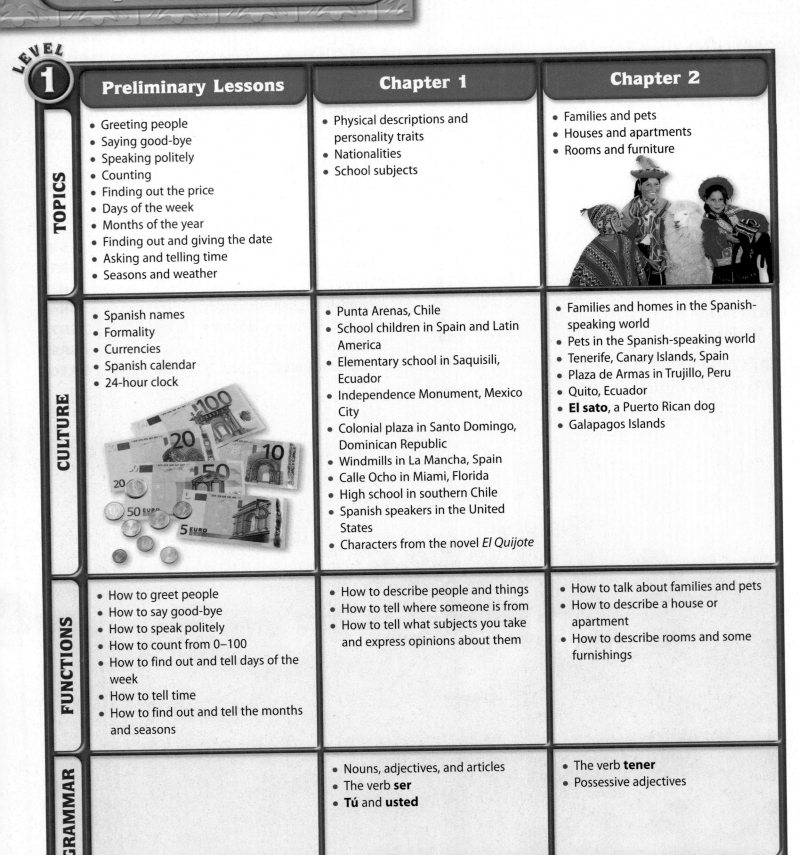

CULTURE

• Spanish names • Formality • Currencies • Spanish calendar • 24-hour clock	• Punta Arenas, Chile • School children in Spain and Latin America • Elementary school in Saquisilí, Ecuador • Independence Monument, Mexico City • Colonial plaza in Santo Domingo, Dominican Republic • Windmills in La Mancha, Spain • Calle Ocho in Miami, Florida • High school in southern Chile • Spanish speakers in the United States • Characters from the novel *El Quijote*	• Families and homes in the Spanish-speaking world • Pets in the Spanish-speaking world • Tenerife, Canary Islands, Spain • Plaza de Armas in Trujillo, Peru • Quito, Ecuador • **El sato**, a Puerto Rican dog • Galapagos Islands

FUNCTIONS

• How to greet people • How to say good-bye • How to speak politely • How to count from 0–100 • How to find out and tell days of the week • How to tell time • How to find out and tell the months and seasons	• How to describe people and things • How to tell where someone is from • How to tell what subjects you take and express opinions about them	• How to talk about families and pets • How to describe a house or apartment • How to describe rooms and some furnishings

GRAMMAR

	• Nouns, adjectives, and articles • The verb **ser** • **Tú** and **usted**	• The verb **tener** • Possessive adjectives

	Chapter 3	Chapter 4	Chapter 5
TOPICS	• In the classroom • School clothes and school supplies • After-school activities	• Foods and beverages • Eating at a café	• Soccer • Uniforms • Baseball • Colors • Basketball • Tennis
CULTURE	• Library in Barranco, Peru • School uniforms in Spain and Latin America • Barcelona, Spain, and its languages • Plaza de Armas in Arequipa, Peru • Home in Antigua, Guatemala • School and after-school activities in Spanish-speaking countries and the United States • Working habits of young people in the Spanish-speaking world	• Eating habits in the Spanish-speaking world compared to the United States • Eating times in the Spanish-speaking world compared to the United States • Spanish tapas • Cacao plant • Typical dishes from the Spanish-speaking world • Argentine beef • Popular beverages, such as Inca Cola and mate • Simón Bolívar, a Latin American hero	• Various soccer stadiums in Spain and Latin America • Copan, Honduras • Jai alai • San Pedro de Macoris, Dominican Republic • Nicaragua and the earthquake of 1972 • Sports in Spanish-speaking countries compared to the United States • Baseball player Roberto Clemente
FUNCTIONS	• How to talk about what you do in school • How to identify some school clothes and school supplies • How to talk about what you and your friends do after school	• How to identify food • How to describe breakfast, lunch, and dinner • How to find a table at a café • How to order in a café • How to pay the bill in a café	• How to talk about sports • How to describe a soccer uniform • How to identify colors
GRAMMAR	• Present tense of **-ar** verbs • The verbs **ir, dar,** and **estar** • The contractions **al** and **del**	• Present tense of **-er** and **-ir** verbs • Expressions with the infinitive—**ir a, tener que, acabar de**	• Present tense of stem-changing verbs • **Interesar, aburrir, and gustar**

LEVEL 1

	Chapter 6	Chapter 7	Chapter 8
TOPICS	• Personality, conditions, and emotions • A visit to the doctor's office • Illnesses	• Summer weather and activities • Winter weather and activities	• Celebrating a birthday • Attending concerts, movies, and museums
CULTURE	• Pharmacies in the Spanish-speaking world • Homes of the Embera people of Panama • Canary Islands • Bogota, Colombia • The Plaza Central in Merida, Mexico • Literary genre, the picaresque novel	• Iguazu Falls • Skiing in the Pyrenees Mountains • Beaches in Spain • Vacationing in Argentina • Summer and winter resorts in Spanish-speaking countries	• Mexican artist, Frida Kahlo • Andean musical instrument, **la zampoña** • La Boca, an artistic neighborhood of Buenos Aires • Museums throughout the Spanish-speaking world • El Museo del Barrio and the Hispanic Institute in New York • Shakira, a Colombian singer • *Zapatistas*, by José Clemente Orozco • Hispanic art and music • Art and music in Mexico City
FUNCTIONS	• How to describe people's personality, conditions, and emotions • How to explain minor illnesses • How to talk about a doctor's appointment	• How to talk about summer and winter weather • How to talk about summer and winter activities	• How to talk about a birthday party • How to discuss concerts, movies, and museums
GRAMMAR	• **Ser** and **estar** • Indirect object pronouns	• Preterite tense of regular **-ar** verbs • Preterite of **ir** and **ser** • Direct object pronouns	• Preterite tense of **-er** and **-ir** verbs • The verbs **oír** and **leer** • Negative expressions

	Chapter 9	Chapter 10*	Chapter 11*
TOPICS	• Shopping for clothes • Shopping for food	• Packing for a trip • Getting to the airport • At the airport • On board an airplane	• Parts of the body • Daily routine • Backpacking and camping
CULTURE	• Shopping centers, markets, and food stands in Spain and Latin America • Shopping in Spanish-speaking countries compared to the United States • Musical groups throughout the Spanish-speaking world • Indigenous open-air markets • Moorish influence in Spanish architecture	• Airports in Spain and Latin America • Air travel in South America • Nazca lines in Peru • Aqueduct of Segovia, Spain • A beach in Palma de Mallorca • **Casa Rosada** in Buenos Aires	• Backpackers in the Spanish-speaking world • Camping in the Spanish-speaking world • Nerja Beach, Spain • Petrohue Falls, Chile • Aconcagua Mountain, Chile
FUNCTIONS	• How to talk about buying clothes • How to talk about buying foods	• How to talk about packing for a trip and getting to the airport • How to speak with a ticket agent • How to buy an airplane ticket • How to talk about being on an airplane	• How to talk about your daily routine • How to talk about camping • How to talk about the contents of your backpack
GRAMMAR	• Numbers over 100 • The present tense of **saber** and **conocer** • Comparatives and superlatives • Demonstrative adjectives and pronouns	• Verbs that have **g** in the **yo** form of the present tense • The present progressive tense	• Reflexive verbs • Commands with **favor de**

Nota * Chapters 10 and 11, Level 1, repeat as Chapters 1 and 2, Level 2.

LEVEL 2

	Repaso	Chapter 1*	Chapter 2*
TOPICS	• Friends, students, and relatives • At home and at school • Personality and health • Sports • Shopping for food and clothing • Summer and winter vacations and activities	• Packing for a trip • Getting to the airport • At the airport • On board an airplane	• Parts of the body • Daily routine • Backpacking and camping
CULTURE	• Plaza Mayor, Antigua, Guatemala • School in Cartegena, Colombia • San Miguel de Allende, Mexico • Shopping in Lima, Peru • Lake Villarrica in Chile	• Airports in Spain and Latin America • Air travel in South America • Nazca lines in Peru • Aqueduct of Segovia, Spain • A beach in Palma de Mallorca • **Casa Rosada** in Buenos Aires	• Backpackers in the Spanish-speaking world • Camping in the Spanish-speaking world • Nerja Beach, Spain • Petrohue Falls, Chile • Aconcagua Mountain, Chile
FUNCTIONS	• How to talk about friends, family, and home • How to talk about activities at home and at school • How to talk about personality, health, and general well-being • How to talk about sports • How to describe food and clothing • How to talk about vacations	• How to talk about packing for a trip and getting to the airport • How to speak with a ticket agent • How to buy an airplane ticket • How to talk about being on an airplane	• How to talk about your daily routine • How to talk about camping • How to talk about the contents of your backpack
GRAMMAR	• The verb **ser** • Nouns, articles, and adjectives • The verb **tener** • Possessive adjectives • The present tense of verbs • The present tense of **ir, dar, estar** • Contractions • Uses of **ser** and **estar** • The verbs **aburrir, interesar, gustar** • The verbs **saber** and **conocer** • Comparatives and superlatives • The preterite of regular verbs • The preterite of **ir** and **ser** • Direct and indirect object pronouns	• Verbs that have **g** in the **yo** form of the present tense • The present progressive tense	• Reflexive verbs • Commands with **favor de**

MOCHILEROS BACKPACKERS HOSTEL

Nota *Chapters 1 and 2, Level 2, repeat Chapters 10 and 11, Level 1.

	Chapter 3	Chapter 4	Chapter 5
TOPICS	• Train travel • Train trips to Spain, Peru, and Mexico	• Restaurants and types of food • Utensils	• Various festivals • Traditional carnival costumes
CULTURE	• El AVE • Train station in Atocha, Madrid • Plaza de la Independencia in Montevideo, Uruguay • Indigenous market in Peru • Cordoba and the Guadalquivir River • Plaza de Armas in Cuzco, Peru • Machu Picchu • The Barranca del Cobre • Panama Canal and the Panama Canal Railway • Atacama Desert	• Restaurants in Spain and Latin America • **Paella,** a typical Spanish dish • **El casado,** a typical Costa Rican dish • San Telmo and Recoleta, unique neighborhoods of Buenos Aires • Sidewalk cafés in the Spanish-speaking world • Fruit stand in Tepoztlan, Mexico • Famous Argentine beef • Spanish tapas	• Patron saints • **Papel picado** • The use of the piñata in Hispanic celebrations • **Sagrada Familia** in Barcelona, Spain • **El Día de Independencia** in Puebla, Mexico • **El Día de San Juan** • **Día de los Muertos** • **La Navidad** and **Hanuka** • New Year's Eve in Madrid • Parade in Mexico City
FUNCTIONS	• How to use vocabulary related to train travel • How to discuss interesting train trips in Spain, Peru, and Mexico	• How to order and pay for a meal at a restaurant • How to identify more foods • How to identify eating utensils and dishes • How to discuss restaurants in Spain and Latin America	• How to talk about several Hispanic holidays • How to compare holidays in the U.S. with those in some Spanish-speaking countries
GRAMMAR	• The preterite of irregular verbs • The verb **decir** • Prepositional pronouns	• Stem-changing verbs in the present and preterite • Adjectives of nationality • The passive voice with **se**	• Regular and irregular forms of the imperfect tense

LEVEL 2

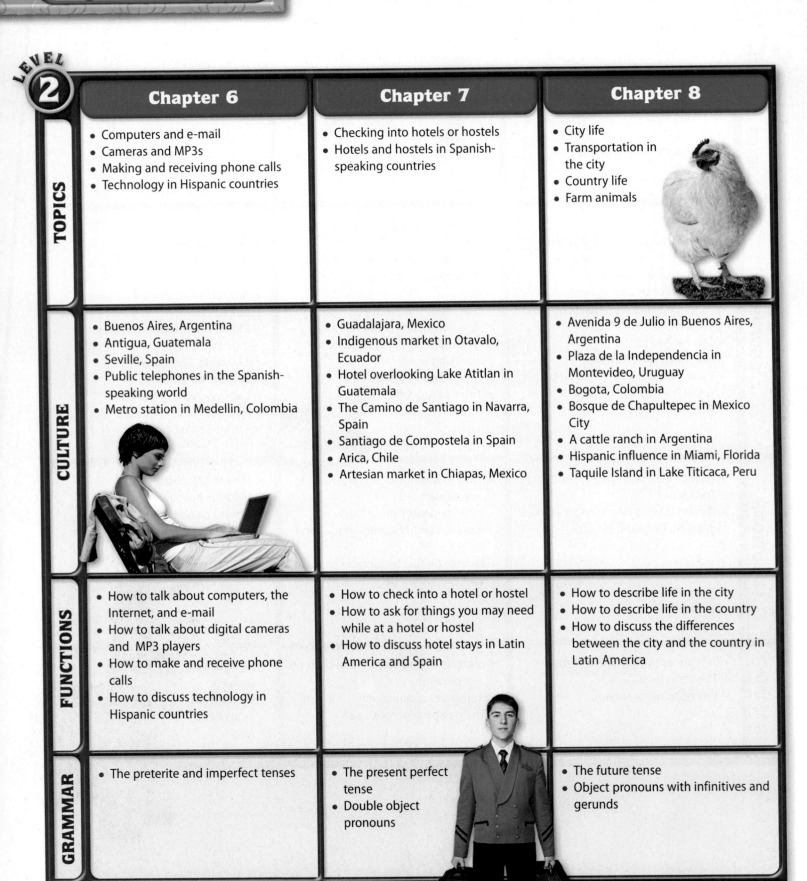

	Chapter 6	Chapter 7	Chapter 8
TOPICS	• Computers and e-mail • Cameras and MP3s • Making and receiving phone calls • Technology in Hispanic countries	• Checking into hotels or hostels • Hotels and hostels in Spanish-speaking countries	• City life • Transportation in the city • Country life • Farm animals
CULTURE	• Buenos Aires, Argentina • Antigua, Guatemala • Seville, Spain • Public telephones in the Spanish-speaking world • Metro station in Medellin, Colombia	• Guadalajara, Mexico • Indigenous market in Otavalo, Ecuador • Hotel overlooking Lake Atitlan in Guatemala • The Camino de Santiago in Navarra, Spain • Santiago de Compostela in Spain • Arica, Chile • Artesian market in Chiapas, Mexico	• Avenida 9 de Julio in Buenos Aires, Argentina • Plaza de la Independencia in Montevideo, Uruguay • Bogota, Colombia • Bosque de Chapultepec in Mexico City • A cattle ranch in Argentina • Hispanic influence in Miami, Florida • Taquile Island in Lake Titicaca, Peru
FUNCTIONS	• How to talk about computers, the Internet, and e-mail • How to talk about digital cameras and MP3 players • How to make and receive phone calls • How to discuss technology in Hispanic countries	• How to check into a hotel or hostel • How to ask for things you may need while at a hotel or hostel • How to discuss hotel stays in Latin America and Spain	• How to describe life in the city • How to describe life in the country • How to discuss the differences between the city and the country in Latin America
GRAMMAR	• The preterite and imperfect tenses	• The present perfect tense • Double object pronouns	• The future tense • Object pronouns with infinitives and gerunds

	Chapter 9	Chapter 10*	Chapter 11*
TOPICS	• Driving on the highway • Driving in the city • Cars • Gas stations	• The kitchen • Cooking • Types of food • Using a recipe	• Parts of the body • Exercise and physical activity • Minor medical problems • The emergency room
CULTURE	• The Bridge of the Americas in Panama • Avenida Bolívar • Traffic signs • Independence Monument in Mexico City • Pan American Highway • Traffic in Spanish-speaking countries	• Recipe for **paella** and paella utensils • Various foods from Spanish-speaking countries • Recipe for **sopa de pollo** • The metric system • Good nutrition • Recipe for **arroz con pollo** • Recipe for **la ropa vieja**	• Hospitals in the Spanish-speaking world • Physical activity and good health • Doctors Without Borders
FUNCTIONS	• How to talk about cars and driving • How to give directions • How to discuss the Pan American Highway **VIA PANAMERICANA QUITO →**	• How to talk about foods and food preparation • How to talk about a Spanish recipe	• How to identify more parts of the body • How to talk about exercise • How to talk about having a minor accident and a trip to the emergency room • How to discuss physical fitness
GRAMMAR	• **Tú** affirmative commands • The conditional	• The subjunctive • Formal commands • Negative informal commands	• The subjunctive with impersonal expressions • **Ojalá, quizás, tal vez** • The subjunctive of stem-changing verbs • The comparison of like things

Nota *Chapters 10 and 11, Level 2, repeat as Chapters 1 and 2, Level 3.

LEVEL 3

	Repaso	Chapter 1*	Chapter 2*
TOPICS	• At home and at school • Sports and daily routine • Vacations • Shopping and celebrations • City and country • Hotels and restaurants	• The kitchen • Cooking • Types of food • Using a recipe	• Parts of the body • Exercise and physical activity • Minor medical problems • The emergency room
CULTURE	• School in Cienfuegos, Cuba • Davis Cup tennis match in Palma de Mallorca, Spain • A ski resort near Santiago, Chile • Christmas lights in Medellín, Colombia • Plaza del estudiante in La Paz, Bolivia • Restaurant Tabacon in Alajuela, Costa Rica	• Recipe for **paella** and paella utensils • Various foods from Spanish-speaking countries • Recipe for **sopa de pollo** • The metric system • Good nutrition • Recipe for **arroz con pollo** • Recipe for **la ropa vieja**	• Hospitals in the Spanish-speaking world • Physical activity and good health • Doctors Without Borders
FUNCTIONS	• How to discuss home and school • How to discuss sports and daily routine • How to discuss vacations and summer and winter activities • How to discuss shopping and celebrations • How to discuss city and country life • How to discuss hotels and restaurants	• How to talk about foods and food preparation • How to talk about a Spanish recipe	• How to identify more parts of the body • How to talk about exercise • How to talk about having a minor accident and a trip to the emergency room • How to discuss physical fitness
GRAMMAR	• Present tense of regular and irregular verbs • The verbs **ir, dar, estar** • Preterite and imperfect of regular and irregular verbs • The verbs **interesar, aburrir, gustar** • Indirect and direct object pronouns • Uses of the preterite and imperfect • The present perfect tense • Regular and irregular past participles • Double object pronouns	• The subjunctive • Formal commands • Negative informal commands	• The subjunctive with impersonal expressions • **Ojalá, quizás, tal vez** • The subjunctive of stem-changing verbs • The comparison of like things

Nota ▸ * Chapters 1 and 2, Level 3, repeat Chapters 10 and 11, Level 2.

	Chapter 3	Chapter 4	Chapter 5
TOPICS	• Weddings • Baptisms • Birthdays • Funerals	• The hair salon • Washing clothes • Mailing letters and packages • The bank	• Courtesies • Manners
CULTURE	• **Quinceañera** celebrations • Wedding ceremonies and customs throughout the Spanish-speaking world • Cemetery of Old San Juan • Cathedral in Jerez de la Frontera, Spain • Atacama Desert • Mariachis • Madrid, Spain • *El hermano ausente en la cena de Pascua* by Abraham Valdelomar	• Palacio de Telecomunicaciones in Madrid, Spain • European currency • ATMs in Spanish-speaking countries • Police officers in Málaga, Spain • Hair salons, laundromats, and banks in Spanish-speaking countries • Baños, Ecuador • Puerto Banús beach in Marbella, Spain • Architectural influence of the Moors in Spain • *El mensajero de San Martín* • General José de San Martín • Torres del Paine National Park in Chile • Santiago, Chile • Plaza de España, Seville, Spain	• Typical greetings throughout Spanish-speaking countries • Typical gestures used among many Spanish speakers • Traditional wedding in Ibiza, Spain • Gardens at the Royal Palace in Madrid, Spain • Zaragoza, Spain • Cadaqués, Spain • *El conde Lucanor* by Don Juan Manuel • El AVE at the train station in Seville
FUNCTIONS	• How to talk about passages of life: weddings, baptisms, birthdays, and funerals • How to read a poem by the Peruvian writer Abraham Valdelomar	• How to talk about errands • How to discuss preparing for a trip through Andalusia • How to read a short story from Argentina	• How to discuss manners • How to compare manners in Spanish-speaking countries to manners in the U.S.
GRAMMAR	• The subjunctive to express wishes • The subjunctive to express emotions • Possessive pronouns	• The subjunctive with expressions of doubt • The subjunctive with adverbial clauses • The pluperfect, conditional perfect, and future perfect tenses	• The imperfect subjunctive • The subjunctive vs. the infinitive • Suffixes

NO SE PEMITE EL USO DEL MOVIL

LEVEL 3

	Chapter 6	Chapter 7	Chapter 8
TOPICS	• Air travel • Train travel • Car travel and rental	• Art • Literature	• History of Latinos in the United States • Spanish speakers in the United States • Spanish television and press in the United States
CULTURE	• Various airports throughout the Spanish-speaking world • The Panama Canal Railway • Atocha train station in Madrid • Lake Titicaca in Bolivia • Exotic bird in the Ecuadoran jungle • A trip to Bolivia • La Paz, Bolivia, and Plaza Murillo • *Temprano y con sol* by Emilia Pardo Bazán • La Coruña, Spain • Avila, Spain • Copacabana, Bolivia	• Frida Kahlo home and museum in Coyoacan, Mexico • Fernando Botero • Las Fallas in Valencia, Spain • Federico García Lorca • Mayan ruins in Copán, Honduras • Joan Miró Foundation in Barcelona • *Las meninas* by Diego Velázquez • *El oso y el madroño* in Madrid, Spain • Costa Brava, Spain • Guggenheim Museum in Bilbao, Spain • Don Quijote and Sancho Panza • La Boca, an artistic neighborhood in Buenos Aires • *La liberación del peón* by Diego Rivera • *No sé por qué piensas tú* by Nicolás Guillén • Havana, Cuba	• Street festivals in the U.S. honoring Latino heritage and culture • Jaime Escalante • Baseball player Alex Rodríguez • Univisión and Telemundo • Hernán Cortés, conqueror of Mexico • Francisco Pizarro, conqueror of Peru • Ibiza, Balearic island in the Mediterranean • Sandra Cisneros • *A Julia de Burgos* by Julia de Burgos • University of Puerto Rico • Capitolio Nacional in Havana, Cuba • A plaza in Guadalajara, Mexico • Arch of the Revolution, Mexico City
FUNCTIONS	• How to discuss several modes of travel • How to talk about a trip to Bolivia • How to read a short story by the Spanish author Emilia Pardo Bazán	• How to discuss fine art and literature • How to talk about a mural by the Mexican artist Diego Rivera • How to read a sonnet by the Spaniard Federico García Lorca • How to read a poem by the Cuban poet Nicolás Guillén	• How to talk about the history of Spanish speakers in the U.S. • How to discuss the experience of Latinos in the U.S. • How to read a poem by the Puerto Rican poet Julia de Burgos
GRAMMAR	• The subjunctive with conjunctions of time • The subjunctive to express commands and advice • Irregular nouns	• The present perfect and pluperfect subjunctive • **Si** clauses • Adverbs ending in **-mente**	• The subjunctive with **aunque** • The subjunctive with **-quiera** • Definite and indefinite articles (special uses) • Apocopated adjectives

LEVEL 3

	Chapter 9	**Chapter 10**
TOPICS	• Food and food preparation • History of food	• Careers • Job applications and interviews • Second languages and the job market
CULTURE	• Various foods popular throughout Spain and Latin America • Olive groves in Andalusia • History of the potato and the tomato • Taco de carne • History of spices • Arabic influence in Latin cuisine • *Oda a la alcachofa* by Pablo Neruda	• Antonio Villaraigosa • Calella de Palafrugell, Spain • Plaza de Armas in Quito, Ecuador • Shopping on Calle Florida in Buenos Aires • Mezquita de Córdoba and other Arabic influences throughout Spain • *Un día de éstos* by Gabriel García Márquez • Plaza Mayor in Cuenca, Ecuador • Cartagena, Colombia
FUNCTIONS	• How to identify more foods • How to describe food preparation • How to discuss the history of foods from Europe and the Americas • How to read a poem by the Chilean poet Pablo Neruda	• How to talk about professions and occupations • How to have a job interview • How to discuss the importance of learning a second language • How to read a short story by the Colombian novelist Gabriel García Márquez
GRAMMAR	• Passive voice • Relative pronouns • Expressions of time with **hace** and **hacía**	• **Por** and **para** • The subjunctive with relative clauses

LEVEL 4

	Chapter 1	Chapter 2
TOPICS	• The geography of Spain • The history of Spain • Spanish culture	• The geography of Ecuador, Peru, and Bolivia • The history of Ecuador, Peru, and Bolivia • The culture of Ecuador, Peru, and Bolivia
CULTURE	• The invasion of the Moors • Basque country • The Catholic Kings • Christopher Columbus • Roman influence and architecture • Spanish foods • Spanish Civil War, 1936–1939 • Extremadura, Spain • Valencia, Spain • Survivors of the Guernica bombing • *Guernica* by Pablo Picasso • Immigrants on the coast of Tarifa • *Canción del pirata* by José de Espronceda • *La primavera besaba* by Antonio Machado • *El niño al que se le murió el amigo* by Ana María Matute	• Quipu, an Incan accounting system • Geography of Peru and Ecuador • Land-locked Bolivia • The Andes Mountains • The Incas • Machu Picchu • Francisco Pizarro, conqueror of the Incan Empire • South American liberators Simón Bolívar and José de San Martín • Otavalo market in Ecuador • Food in Ecuador, Peru, and Bolivia • Tungurahua Volcano, Ecuador • *¡Quién sabe!* by José Santos Chocano • *Nostalgia* by José Santos Chocano • *Los comentarios reales* by el Inca Garcilaso de la Vega
FUNCTIONS	• How to express past actions • How to refer to specific things 	• How to describe habitual past actions • How to talk about past events • How to describe actions in progress • How to make comparisons
GRAMMAR	• Preterite of regular verbs • Preterite of stem-changing verbs • Preterite of irregular verbs • Nouns and articles • Feminine nouns beginning in **a** and **ha**	• The imperfect of regular and irregular verbs • The imperfect and the preterite to describe the past and to indicate past actions • The progressive tenses • The comparative and superlative • Comparison of equality

	Chapter 3	Chapter 4
TOPICS	• The geography of Chile, Argentina, Paraguay, and Uruguay • The history of Chile, Argentina, Paraguay, and Uruguay • The culture of Chile, Argentina, Paraguay, and Uruguay	• The geography of Central American countries • The history of Central American countries • The culture of Central American countries
CULTURE	• Atacama Desert • Patagonia and Tierra del Fuego • Guarani • Argentine gauchos and the pampas • Evita and Juan Perón • Ushuaia, Argentina • Argentine beef, Chilean seafood • Avenida 9 de Julio, Buenos Aires • Weather in Buenos Aires • *Martín Fierro* by José Hernández • *Los niños lloraban* by Pablo Neruda • *Historia de dos cachorros de coatí y dos cachorros de hombre* by Horacio Quiroga • *Continuidad de los parques* by Julio Cortázar	• The Central American isthmus • The Mayans • Capital cities of Central America • Tikal, Guatemala, largest ancient ruined city of the Maya civilization • Copan, Honduras, and its famous stelaes • Islas de San Blas in Panama • Central American cuisine • Rigoberta Menchú and los quichés, an indigenous group of Guatemala • *Lo fatal* by Rubén Darío • *Canción de otoño en primavera* by Rubén Darío • *me llamo Rigoberta Menchú y así me nació la conciencia* by Rigoberta Menchú
FUNCTIONS	• How to describe actions in the present • How to state location and origin • How to refer to people and things already mentioned • How to express surprise, interest, and annoyance • How to express affirmative and negative ideas	• How to form the present subjunctive • How to express necessity, possibility, and doubt using the subjunctive • How to express emotion using the subjunctive • How to give commands
GRAMMAR	• The present tense of regular and irregular verbs • **Ser** and **estar** • Object pronouns • **Gustar** and verbs like **gustar** • Affirmative and negative expressions	• The present subjunctive • Uses of the subjunctive • Direct and indirect commands

LEVEL 4

	Chapter 5	Chapter 6
TOPICS	• The geography of Mexico • The history of Mexico • The culture of Mexico	• The geography of Cuba, Puerto Rico, and the Dominican Republic • The history of Cuba, Puerto Rico, and the Dominican Republic • The culture of Cuba, Puerto Rico, and the Dominican Republic
CULTURE	• Indigenous civilizations • Hernán Cortés and the conquest of the Aztec Empire • September 16, Mexican Independence Day • **Cinco de Mayo** • Mexican Revolution of 1910 • El Zócalo • Tenochtitlán • Chichén Itzá • Mexican cuisine • Bosque de Chapultepec • Mexican film synopses • *En paz* by Amado Nervo • *Aquí* by Octavio Paz • *Malinche* by Laura Esquivel	• Mountain ranges in Cuba, Puerto Rico, and the Dominican Republic • The climate of the Greater Antilles • The exploration of Christopher Columbus • The Taino culture • Fidel Castro • José Martí • Santo Domingo • Havana, Cuba • Caribbean food • Caves of Camuy • *Búcate plata* by Nicolás Guillén • *Sensemayá* by Nicolás Guillén • *El ave y el nido* by Salomé Ureña • *Mi padre* by Manuel del Toro
FUNCTIONS	• How to express what people do for themselves • How to tell what was done or what is done in general • How to express what you have done recently • How to describe actions completed prior to other actions • How to express opinions and feelings about what has happened • How to place object pronouns in a sentence	• How to express future events • How to express what you will have done and what you would have done • How to refer to specific things • How to express ownership
GRAMMAR	• Reflexive verbs • Passive voice (with **se**) • Present perfect • Pluperfect • Present perfect subjunctive • Object pronouns	• The future and conditional • The future perfect and conditional perfect • Demonstrative pronouns • Possessive pronouns • Relative pronouns

	Chapter 7	**Chapter 8**
TOPICS	• The geography of Venezuela and Colombia • The history of Venezuela and Colombia • The culture of Venezuela and Colombia	• Latinos in the United States, past and present • Your own ethnicity 
CULTURE	• Angel Falls in Venezuela • Orinoco River • Petroleum industry • Four geographic regions of Colombia • Simón Bolívar and the fight for independence • Typical foods of Venezuela and Colombia • Cartagena, Colombia • *Cien años de soledad* by Gabriel García Márquez • *Los maderos de San Juan* by José Asunción Silva • *Vivir para contarla* by Gabriel García Márquez	• Various street festivals and parades celebrating Latinos in the U.S. • History of the term **hispano** • Hispanic celebrities in the U.S. • Hispanic cuisine in the U.S. • Latin and Spanish architectural influences • Mariachi music • **Cinco de Mayo** • *Desde la nieve* by Eugenio Florit • *El caballo mago* by Sabine Ulibarrí
FUNCTIONS	• How to form the imperfect subjunctive • How to use the subjunctive in adverbial clauses • How to express *although* and *perhaps* • How to use **por** and **para**	• How to form the pluperfect subjunctive • How to discuss contrary-to-fact situations • How to use definite and indefinite articles
GRAMMAR	• The imperfect subjunctive • The subjunctive with adverbs of time • The subjunctive with **aunque** • The subjunctive with **quizá(s), tal vez, ojalá (que)** • **Por** and **para**	• Pluperfect subjunctive • Clauses with **si** • Subjunctive in adverbial clauses • Shortened forms of adjectives • Definite and indefinite articles

The What, Why, and How of Reading

Reading is a learned process. Your students have been reading in their first language for a long time and now their challenge is to transfer what they know to enable themselves to read fluently in Spanish. Reading will help them improve their vocabulary, cultural knowledge, and productive skills in Spanish. Students are probably familiar with the reading strategies in the chart. Have students review these strategies and apply them as they continue to improve their Spanish reading skills.

What Is It?	Why It's Important	How To Do It
Preview Previewing is looking over a selection before you read.	Previewing lets you begin to see what you already know and what you'll need to know. It helps you set a purpose for reading.	Look at the title, illustrations, headings, captions, and graphics. Look at how ideas are organized. Ask questions about the text.
Skim Skimming is looking over an entire selection quickly to get a general idea of what the piece is about.	Skimming tells you what a selection is about. If the selection you skim isn't what you're looking for, you won't need to read the entire piece.	Read the title of the selection and quickly look over the entire piece. Read headings and captions and maybe part of the first paragraph to get a general idea of the selection's content.
Scan Scanning is glancing quickly over a selection in order to find specific information.	Scanning helps you pinpoint information quickly. It saves you time when you have a number of selections to look at.	As you move your eyes quickly over the lines of text, look for key words or phrases that will help you locate the information you're looking for.
Predict Predicting is taking an educated guess about what will happen in a selection.	Predicting gives you a reason to read. You want to find out if your prediction comes true, don't you? As you read, adjust or change your prediction if it doesn't fit what you learn.	Combine what you already know about an author or subject with what you learned in your preview to guess at what will be included in the text.
Summarize Summarizing is stating the main ideas of a selection in your own words and in a logical sequence.	Summarizing shows whether you've understood something. It teaches you to rethink what you've read and to separate main ideas from supporting information.	Ask yourself: What is this selection about? Answer who, what, where, when, why, and how? Put that information in a logical order.

What Is It?	Why It's Important	How To Do It
Clarify Clarifying is looking at difficult sections of text in order to clear up what is confusing.	Authors will often build ideas one on another. If you don't clear up a confusing passage, you may not understand main ideas or information that comes later.	Go back and reread a confusing section more slowly. Look up words you don't know. Ask questions about what you don't understand. Sometimes you may want to read on to see if further information helps you.
Question Questioning is asking yourself whether information in a selection is important. Questioning is also regularly asking yourself whether you've understood what you've read.	When you ask questions as you read, you're reading strategically. As you answer your questions, you're making sure that you'll get the gist of a text.	Have a running conversation with yourself as you read. Keep asking yourself: Is this idea important? Why? Do I understand what this is about?
Visualize Visualizing is picturing a writer's ideas or descriptions in your mind's eye.	Visualizing is one of the best ways to understand and remember information in fiction, nonfiction, and informational texts.	Carefully read how a writer describes a person, place, or thing. Then ask yourself: What would this look like? Can I see how the steps in this process would work?
Monitor Comprehension Monitoring your comprehension means thinking about whether you understand what you are reading.	The whole point of reading is to understand a piece of text. When you don't understand a selection, you're not really reading it.	Keep asking yourself questions about main ideas, characters, and events. When you can't answer a question, review, read more slowly, or ask someone to help you.

The What, Why, and How of Reading

What Is It?	Why It's Important	How To Do It
Identify Sequence Identifying sequence is finding the logical order of ideas or events.	In a work of fiction, events usually happen in chronological order. With nonfiction, understanding the logical sequence of ideas in a piece helps you follow a writer's train of thought. You'll remember ideas better when you know the logical order a writer uses.	Think about what the author is trying to do. Tell a story? Explain how something works? Present information? Look for clues or signal words that might point to time order, steps in a process, or order of importance.
Determine the Main Idea Determining an author's main idea is finding the most important thought in a paragraph or selection.	Finding main ideas gets you ready to summarize. You also discover an author's purpose for writing when you find the main ideas in a selection.	Think about what you know about the author and the topic. Look for how the author organizes ideas. Then look for the one idea that all of the sentences in a paragraph or all of the paragraphs in a selection are about.
Respond Responding is telling what you like, dislike, or find surprising or interesting in a selection.	When you react in a personal way to what you read, you'll enjoy a selection more and remember it better.	As you read, think about how you feel about story elements or ideas in a selection. What's your reaction to the characters in a story? What grabs your attention as you read?
Connect Connecting means linking what you read to events in your own life or to other selections you've read.	You'll "get into" your reading and recall information and ideas better by connecting events, emotions, and characters to your own life.	Ask yourself: Do I know someone like this? Have I ever felt this way? What else have I read that is like this selection?
Review Reviewing is going back over what you've read to remember what's important and to organize ideas so you'll recall them later.	Reviewing is especially important when you have new ideas and a lot of information to remember.	Filling in a graphic organizer, such as a chart or diagram, as you read helps you organize information. These study aids will help you review later.
Interpret Interpreting is using your own understanding of the world to decide what the events or ideas in a selection mean.	Every reader constructs meaning on the basis of what he or she understands about the world. Finding meaning as you read is all about interacting with the text.	Think about what you already know about yourself and the world. Ask yourself: What is the author really trying to say here? What larger idea might these events be about?
Infer Inferring is using your reason and experience to guess what an author does not come right out and say.	Making inferences is a large part of finding meaning in a selection. Inferring helps you look more deeply at characters and points you toward the theme or message in a selection.	Look for clues the author provides. Notice descriptions, dialogue, events, and relationships that might tell you something the author wants you to know.

What Is It?	Why It's Important	How To Do It
Draw Conclusions Drawing conclusions is using a number of pieces of information to make a general statement about people, places, events, and ideas.	Drawing conclusions helps you find connections between ideas and events. It's another tool to help you see the larger picture.	Notice details about characters, ideas, and events. Then make a general statement of the basis of these details. For example, a character's actions might lead you to conclude that he or she is kind.
Analyze Analyzing is looking at separate parts of a selection in order to understand the entire selection.	Analyzing helps you look critically at a piece of writing. When you analyze a selection, you discover its theme or message, and you learn the author's purpose for writing.	To analyze a story, think about what the author is saying through the characters, setting, and plot. To analyze nonfiction, look at the organization and main ideas. What do they suggest?
Synthesize Synthesizing is combining ideas to create something new. You may synthesize to reach a new understanding or you may actually create a new ending to a story.	Synthesizing helps you move to a higher level of thinking. Creating something new of your own goes beyond remembering what you learned from someone else.	Think about the ideas or information you've learned in a selection. Ask yourself: Do I understand something more than the main ideas here? Can I create something else from what I now know?
Evaluate Evaluating is making a judgment or forming an opinion about something you read. You can evaluate a character, an author's craft, or the value of the information in a text.	Evaluating helps you become a wise reader. For example, when you judge whether an author is qualified to speak about a topic or whether the author's points make sense, you can avoid being misled by what you read.	As you read, ask yourself questions such as: Is this character realistic and believable? Is this author qualified to write on this subject? Is this author biased? Does this author present opinions as facts?

Plan for teaching the chapter.

Preview tells you the theme and content of the chapter.

Spotlight on Culture expands on the comparison presented in Aquí y Allí.

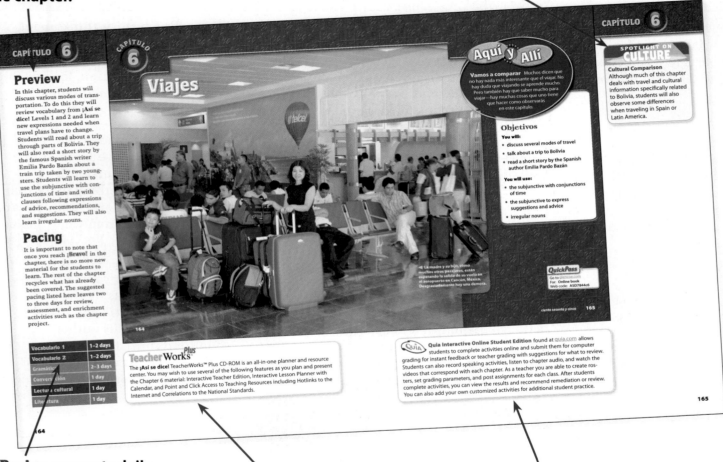

Pacing suggests daily scheduling options to help you budget your time.

TeacherWorks™ Plus is your complete lesson planner and resource center correlated to the National Standards.

The Quia Interactive Online Student Edition provides the Workbook and Audio Activities online with a customizable gradebook to disaggregate data.

Introduce the chapter theme.

Present provides suggestions about how you can make the most out of the photographs and information in Introducción al tema.

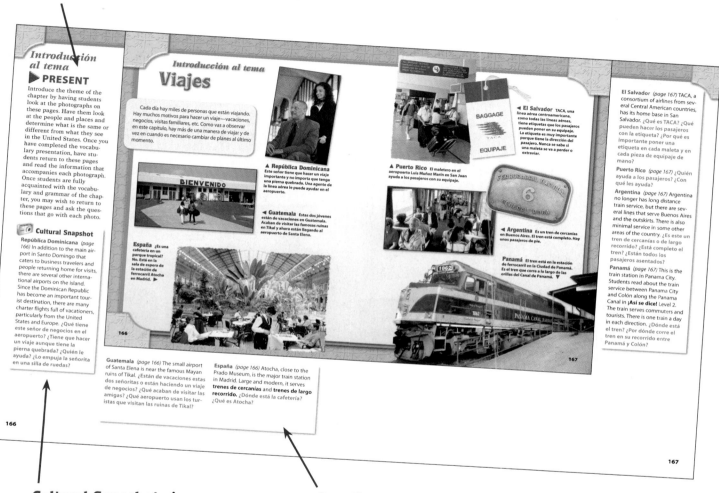

Cultural Snapshot gives you additional information about the cultural photos.

Questions are suggested to increase students' cultural awareness and to give them practice speaking.

Use helpful suggestions to present and practice the new vocabulary.

Quick Start (also available as Transparencies) provides a brief check of previously taught material as a way to begin the class session.

Resources lists the tools you will need to teach, practice, and assess each section of the chapter.

Tips for Success presents ideas that will help students master the activities.

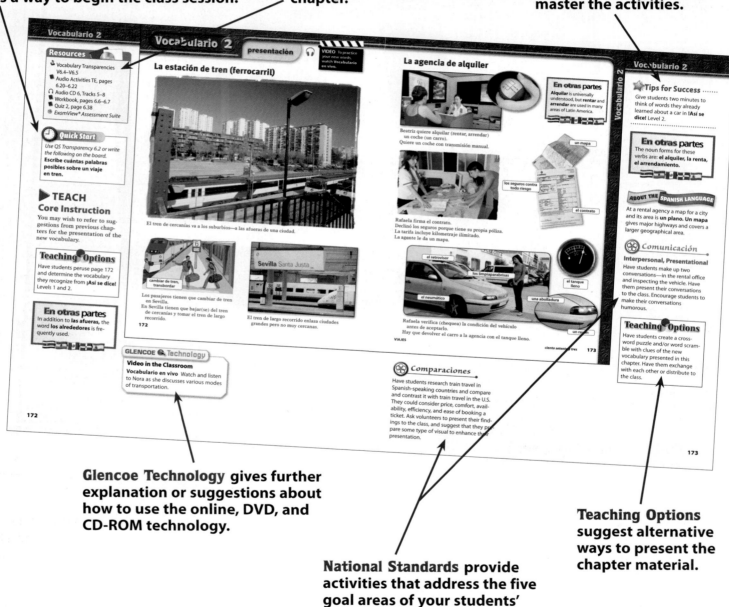

Glencoe Technology gives further explanation or suggestions about how to use the online, DVD, and CD-ROM technology.

National Standards provide activities that address the five goal areas of your students' learning needs.

Teaching Options suggest alternative ways to present the chapter material.

Reach your students through clear presentation of grammar.

Core Instruction offers a clear, step-by-step guide for your presentation of the lesson.

Differentiation offers alternate activities to meet the diverse learning styles and needs of your students.

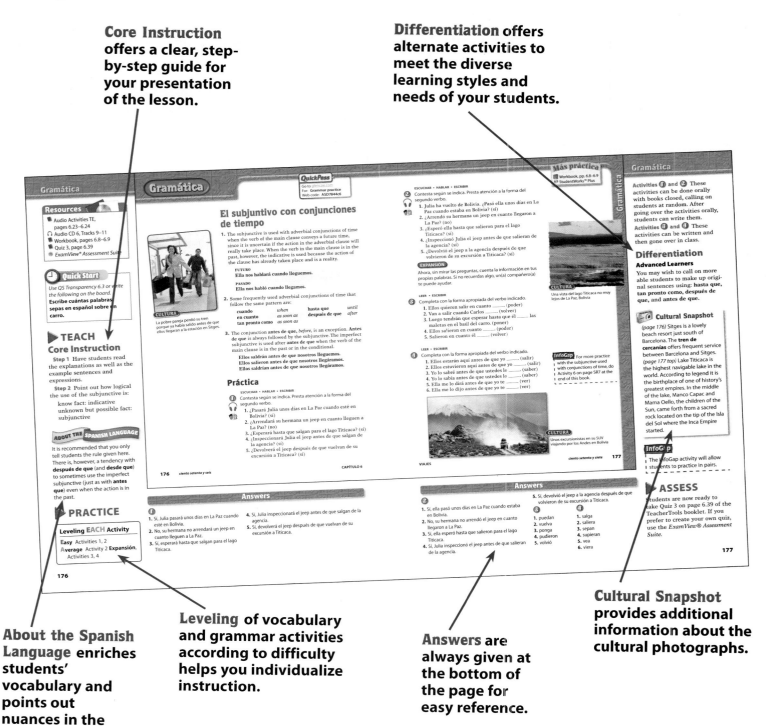

About the Spanish Language enriches students' vocabulary and points out nuances in the Spanish language.

Leveling of vocabulary and grammar activities according to difficulty helps you individualize instruction.

Answers are always given at the bottom of the page for easy reference.

Cultural Snapshot provides additional information about the cultural photographs.

Help your students feel confident about their speaking and writing skills.

Tips for Success presents ideas that will help students master the activities.

Pre-AP explains how activities offer students practice for different portions of the AP exam.

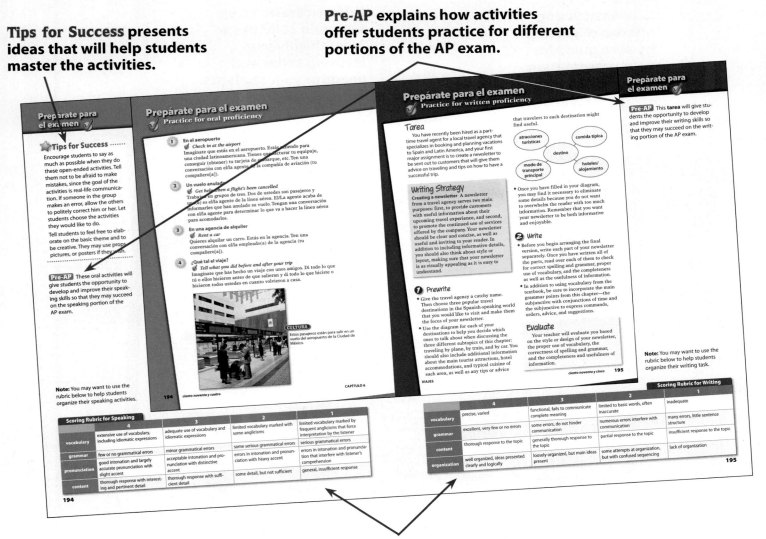

Rubrics not only help you evaluate your students' work, but also serve as a guide to help students with their preparation, organization, and presentation.

Help your students review what they have learned.

Audio Script is a quick reference at point of use for the listening activities. This gives you the option of reading the script yourself or using the audio CD.

References to activities tell you what is being reviewed and the pages where the information is taught.

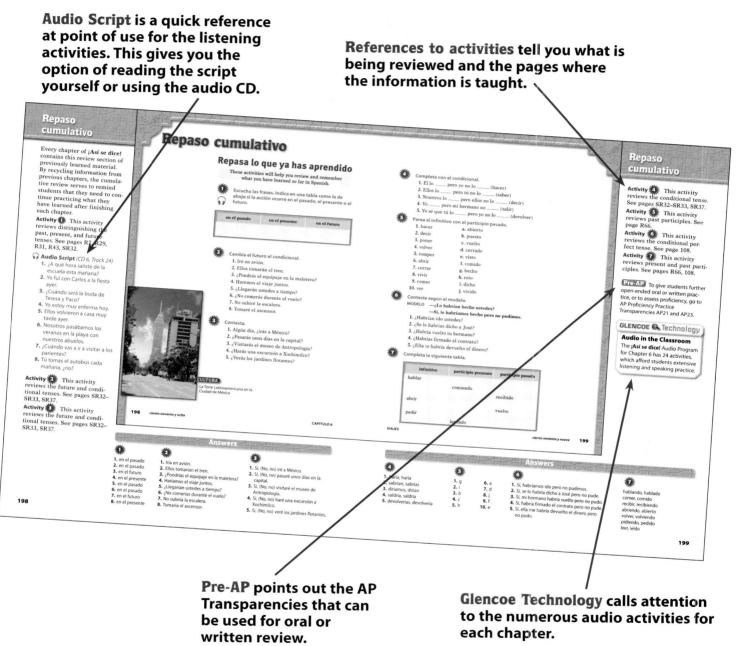

Repaso cumulativo

Every chapter of ¡Así se dice! contains this review section of previously learned material. By recycling information from previous chapters, the cumulative review serves to remind students that they need to continue practicing what they have learned after finishing each chapter.

Activity 1 This activity reviews distinguishing the past, present, and future tenses. See pages R7, R29, R31, R43, SR32.

Audio Script (CD 6, Track 24)
1. ¿A qué hora saliste de la escuela esta mañana?
2. Yo fui con Carlos a la fiesta ayer.
3. ¿Cuándo será la boda de Teresa y Paco?
4. Yo estoy muy enferma hoy.
5. Ellos volvieron a casa muy tarde ayer.
6. Nosotros pasábamos los veranos en la playa con nuestros abuelos.
7. ¿Cuándo vas a ir a visitar a los parientes?
8. Tú tomas el autobús cada mañana, ¿no?

Activity 2 This activity reviews the future and conditional tenses. See pages SR32–SR33, SR37.

Activity 3 This activity reviews the future and conditional tenses. See pages SR32–SR33, SR37.

Repaso cumulativo

Repasa lo que ya has aprendido

These activities will help you review and remember what you have learned so far in Spanish.

1 Escucha las frases. Indica en una tabla como la de abajo si la acción ocurre en el pasado, el presente o el futuro.

en el pasado	en el presente	en el futuro

2 Cambia el futuro al condicional.
1. Iré en avión.
2. Ellos tomarán el tren.
3. ¿Pondrás el equipaje en la maletera?
4. Haremos el viaje juntos.
5. ¿Llegarán ustedes a tiempo?
6. ¿No comerás durante el vuelo?
7. No subiré la escalera.
8. Tomaré el ascensor.

3 Contesta.
1. Algún día, ¿irás a México?
2. ¿Pasarás unos días en la capital?
3. ¿Visitarás el museo de Antropología?
4. ¿Harás una excursión a Xochimilco?
5. ¿Verás los jardines flotantes?

CULTURA
La Torre Latinoamericana en la Ciudad de México

198 ciento noventa y ocho
CAPÍTULO 6

4 Completa con el condicional.
1. Él lo _____ pero yo no lo _____ (hacer)
2. Ellos lo _____ pero tú no lo _____ (saber)
3. Nosotros lo _____ pero ellos no lo _____ (decir)
4. Yo _____ pero mi hermano no _____ (salir)
5. Yo sé que tú lo _____ pero yo no lo _____ (devolver)

5 Parea el infinitivo con el participio pasado.
1. hacer   a. abierto
2. decir   b. puesto
3. poner   c. vuelto
4. volver   d. cerrado
5. romper   e. visto
6. abrir   f. comido
7. cerrar   g. hecho
8. vivir   h. roto
9. comer   i. dicho
10. ver   j. vivido

6 Contesta según el modelo.
MODELO —¿Lo habrían hecho ustedes?
—Sí, lo habríamos hecho pero no pudimos.
1. ¿Habrían ido ustedes?
2. ¿Se lo habrías dicho a José?
3. ¿Habría vuelto tu hermano?
4. ¿Habrías firmado el contrato?
5. ¿Ella te habría devuelto el dinero?

7 Completa la siguiente tabla.

infinitivo	participio presente	participio pasado
hablar		
	comiendo	
abrir		recibido
pedir		vuelto
	leyendo	

VIAJES
ciento noventa y nueve **199**

Repaso cumulativo

Activity 4 This activity reviews the conditional tense. See pages SR32–SR33, SR37.

Activity 5 This activity reviews past participles. See page R66.

Activity 6 This activity reviews the conditional perfect tense. See page 108.

Activity 7 This activity reviews present and past participles. See pages R66, 108.

Pre-AP To give students further open-ended oral or written practice, or to assess proficiency, go to AP Proficiency Practice Transparencies AP21 and AP23.

GLENCOE Technology
Audio in the Classroom
The ¡Así se dice! Audio Program for Chapter 6 has 24 activities, which afford students extensive listening and speaking practice.

Answers

1
1. en el pasado
2. en el pasado
3. en el futuro
4. en el presente
5. en el pasado
6. en el pasado
7. en el futuro
8. en el presente

2
1. Iría en avión.
2. Ellos tomarían el tren.
3. ¿Pondrías el equipaje en la maletera?
4. Haríamos el viaje juntos.
5. ¿Llegarían ustedes a tiempo?
6. ¿No comerías durante el vuelo?
7. No subiría la escalera.
8. Tomaría el ascensor.

3
1. Sí, (No, no) iré a México.
2. Sí, (No, no) pasaré unos días en la capital.
3. Sí, (No, no) visitaré el museo de Antropología.
4. Sí, (No, no) haré una excursión a Xochimilco.
5. Sí, (No, no) veré los jardines flotantes.

198

Answers

4
1. haría, haría
2. sabrían, sabrías
3. diríamos, dirían
4. saldría, saldría
5. devolverías, devolvería

5
1. g   6. a
2. i   7. d
3. b   8. j
4. c   9. f
5. h   10. e

6
1. Sí, habríamos ido pero no pudimos.
2. Sí, se lo habría dicho a José pero no pude.
3. Sí, mi hermano habría vuelto pero no pude.
4. Sí, habría firmado el contrato pero no pude.
5. Sí, ella me habría devuelto el dinero pero no pudo.

7
hablando, hablado
comer, comido
recibir, recibiendo
abriendo, abierto
volver, volviendo
pidiendo, pedido
leer, leído

199

Pre-AP points out the AP Transparencies that can be used for oral or written review.

Glencoe Technology calls attention to the numerous audio activities for each chapter.

Reach All Students

Save planning time!
TeacherTools—FastFile booklets by chapter

Workbook Teacher Edition In your version of the student workbook, activities are leveled according to difficulty and answers are provided for all activities.

Audio Program Teacher Edition The Audio Program includes the scripts and answers for the audio activities. The activities found on these pages are recorded on the ¡Así se dice! Audio Program CDs and are available online for download.

TPR Storytelling We have written stories using the vocabulary and grammar learned in each chapter. Each story is accompanied by illustrations to allow you to implement TPR Storytelling in your classroom.

Quizzes Quizzes are provided to assess the vocabulary and grammar taught in each chapter. These quizzes give you immediate feedback about your students' progress.

Tests So you can be sure that you are assessing your students' achievement and proficiency in each of the skill areas, we include five kinds of tests for each chapter: Reading and Writing, Listening Comprehension, Speaking (Achievement), Oral and Writing Proficiency, and Reading Comprehension. In addition, the Reading and Writing Tests are leveled, meaning that there is a separate test for average students and another more challenging test for more able students.

Performance Assessment The Performance Assessment Task allows students to show you what they can do with their language skills at the end of each chapter.

Scoring Guidelines Guidelines help you evaluate students' work on the two Speaking Tests, on the Writing Proficiency Test, and on the Performance Assessment Task.

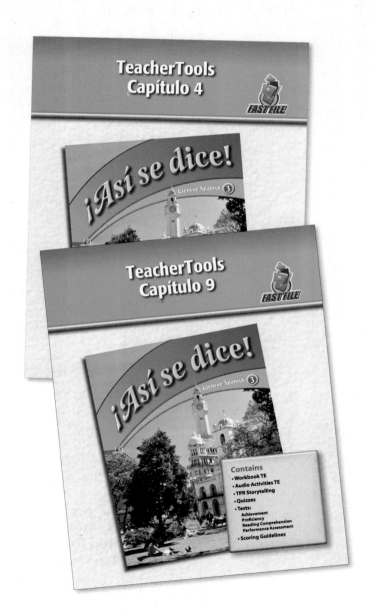

Provide leveled practice!

Reading and Writing Practice

The Workbook includes numerous activities to reinforce all the vocabulary and grammar presented in the Student Edition. Varied activities provide several ways for students to practice and apply the material you have presented in class. **Integración** activities give students additional practice with reading comprehension, and the **Tarea** offers opportunities for students to practice guided writing.

Listening and Speaking Practice

The Audio Activities target both listening and speaking skills. They include the vocabulary presentations, some activities, the Conversation, and Cultural Readings from the Student Edition. There are also additional activities to reinforce and expand upon what students have learned. **Integración** activities give students further listening practice. The audio activities are available on CD and online for convenient download to MP3 players.

Enhance your lessons visually!

Transparencies—visual tools to enrich your chapter presentations

Vocabulary transparencies include the photos and art of the **Vocabulario** section of the Student Edition along with overlays of the Spanish words and Spanish/English vocabulary lists for chapter vocabulary.

Maps help you illustrate and present the geography of the Hispanic world.

Quick Start transparencies serve as a brief review activity to begin each lesson.

Pronunciation transparencies provide a visual for pronunciation practice.

AP Proficiency Practice transparencies illustrate some chapter themes and conversations. They provide excellent oral and/or written practice for the AP exam and can also be used for assessment.

Assessment transparencies replicate the Self-Check for Achievement pages of the Student Edition. Assessment Answer transparencies allow you to easily review the answers with your students in class.

Museo de Arte fine art transparencies are for use with the Connection to Fine Art activities in the Interleaf pages preceding each chapter.

Increase success on the AP exam!

The **AP Prep Workbook** addresses the types of activities students will face when taking the Spanish AP exam. Students will know what to expect and will be better prepared.

PLAN with TeacherWorks!

TeacherWorks™ Plus is your all-in-one planner and resource center correlated to the National Standards. This convenient tool will help you reduce the time you spend planning for classes. Simply populate your school year calendar with customizable lesson plans. This program will also allow you to easily view your resources, such as Student and Teacher Editions and all print ancillaries, without carrying around a heavy bag of books.

PRESENT with PowerTeach!

Glencoe PowerTeach provides ready-made, customizable, PowerPoint® presentations with sound, interactive graphics, additional activities, and video. This presentation tool, available on CD and online, will help you vary your lessons and reach all students in your classroom.

INTERACT with StudentWorks!

StudentWorks™ Plus contains the Student Edition with links to the Internet, videos, and audio program; Workbook and Audio Activities; and AP Prep Workbook. This is a convenient alternative to the textbook.

ASSESS with ExamView!

ExamView®Assessment Suite helps you make a test in a matter of minutes by choosing from existing banks of questions, editing them, or creating your own test questions. You can also print several versions of the same test. The clip art bank allows you to create a test using visuals from the text.

Make Spanish come alive!

Glencoe Video Program on DVD is an entertaining and effective way to give students additional practice with vocabulary and grammar, while at the same time sharpening their listening skills and broadening their understanding of culture in the Spanish-speaking world.

- **Vocabulario en vivo** reinforces and contextualizes chapter vocabulary as students accompany Nora, an Argentine student, on her many interesting adventures in the Spanish-speaking world.
- **Gramática en vivo** allows students to practice and review grammar points in this fun, interactive, animated video.
- **Diálogo en vivo** gives students the opportunity to listen to native speakers in authentic settings as they enjoy conversations related to the chapter theme.
- **Cultura en vivo** takes students on fascinating field trips throughout the Spanish-speaking world.

Access the ¡Así se dice! Level 3 OLC!

The Online Learning Center gives students many opportunities to review, practice, and explore. Students can access chapter-related activities, eFlashcards, self-check quizzes, eGames, WebQuest activities, and links to Web sites throughout the vast Hispanic world.

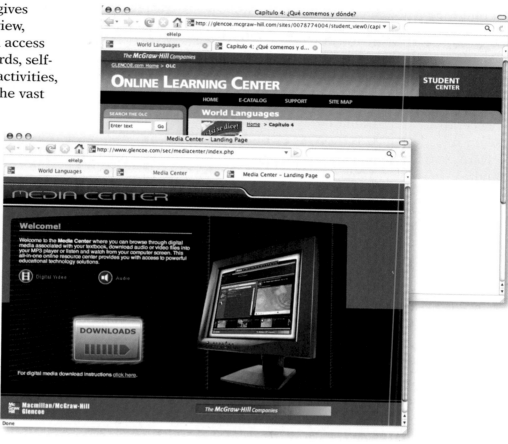

The Media Center, accessible from the OLC links, allows students to view and listen to, as well as download, audio and video files. Teachers can access all online student materials, answers for online activities, and Vocabulary PuzzleMaker.

QuickPass
makes it easy!

Go to glencoe.com, click on *QuickPass*, and use your chapter-specific Web code to access all our exciting online activities!

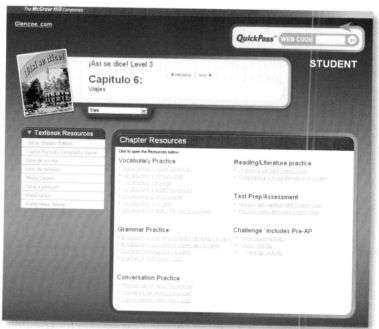

Spanish Names

The following are some Spanish boys' and girls' names that you may wish to give to your students.

Chicos			Chicas		
Adán	Julio	Patricio	Adela	Luisa	Pilar
Alberto	Justo	Pedro	Alejandra	Lupe	Raquel
Alejandro	Leonardo	Rafael	Alicia	Luz	Rosa
Alfonso	Luis	Ramón	Ana	Margarita	Rosalinda
Álvaro	Manuel	Raúl	Andrea	María	Rosana
Andrés	Marcos	Ricardo	Anita	Mariana	Rosario
Antonio	Mateo	Roberto	Bárbara	Marilú	Sandra
Armando	Miguel	Rubén	Beatriz	Marisa	Sara
Arturo	Nicolás	Santiago	Carlota	Marisol	Silvia
Benito	Octavio	Teodoro	Carmen	Marta	Sofía
Benjamín	Omar	Timoteo	Carolina	Mercedes	Susana
Camilo	Óscar	Tomás	Catalina	Micaela	Teresa
Carlos	Pablo	Vicente	Cecilia	Mónica	Verónica
César	Paco	Víctor	Claudia	Natalia	Victoria
Cristóbal		Wilfredo	Consuelo	Nidia	Yolanda
Daniel			Cristina	Olivia	
David			Diana	Patricia	
Diego			Dolores		
Eduardo			Dulce		
Efraín			Elena		
Emilio			Elisa		
Enrique			Emilia		
Ernesto			Estefanía		
Esteban			Estela		
Federico			Eva		
Felipe			Evangelina		
Fernando			Felicia		
Francisco			Francisca		
Gabriel			Gabriela		
Gerardo			Gloria		
Gilberto			Graciela		
Guillermo			Guadalupe		
Gustavo			Inés		
Héctor			Isabel		
Ignacio			Juana		
Jaime			Juanita		
Javier			Julia		
Jorge			Laura		
José			Lucía		
Juan					

Classroom Expressions

Below is a list of words and expressions frequently used when conducting a Spanish class.

Useful Verbs and Commands		
Ven.	Vengan.	Come.
Ve.	Vayan.	Go.
Entra.	Entren.	Enter.
Sal.	Salgan.	Leave.
Espera.	Esperen.	Wait.
Pon.	Pongan.	Put.
Dame.	Denme.	Give me.
Dime.	Díganme.	Tell me.
Repite.	Repitan.	Repeat.
Practica.	Practiquen.	Practice.
Estudia.	Estudien.	Study.
Contesta.	Contesten.	Answer.
Aprende.	Aprendan.	Learn.
Escoge.	Escojan.	Choose.
Prepara.	Preparen.	Prepare.
Mira.	Miren.	Look at.
Describe.	Describan.	Describe.
Empieza.	Empiecen.	Begin.
Pronuncia.	Pronuncien.	Pronounce.
Escucha.	Escuchen.	Listen.
Habla.	Hablen.	Speak.
Lee.	Lean.	Read.
Escribe.	Escriban.	Write.
Pregunta.	Pregunten.	Ask.
Sigue el modelo.	Sigan el modelo.	Follow the model.
Abre.	Abran.	Open.
Cierra.	Cierren.	Close.
Continúa.	Continúen.	Continue.
Siéntate.	Siéntense.	Sit.
Levántate.	Levántense.	Get up.
Cállate.	Cállense.	Be quiet.
Presta atención.	Presten atención.	Pay attention.

Classroom Supplies	
el papel	paper
la hoja de papel	sheet of paper
el cuaderno	notebook, workbook
el libro	book
el diccionario	dictionary
la regla	ruler
la cinta	tape
el bolígrafo, la pluma	pen
el lápiz	pencil
el sacapuntas	pencil sharpener
la goma	eraser
la tiza	chalk
la pizarra, el pizarrón	chalkboard
el borrador	chalkboard eraser
el escritorio, el pupitre	desk
la silla	chair
la fila	row
el CD	CD
la computadora, el ordenador	computer
el DVD	DVD
la pantalla	screen
el video	video

Su atención, por favor.	Your attention, please.
Silencio.	Quiet.
Otra vez.	Again.
Todos juntos.	All together.
En voz alta.	Out loud.
Más alto, por favor.	Louder, please.
En español, por favor.	In Spanish, please.
En inglés, por favor.	In English, please.

National Standards

¡Así se dice! has been written to help you meet the ACTFL Standards for Foreign Language Learning. Elements throughout the book, identified by the National Standards icon, address all the National Standards. The text also provides students with the interpersonal, interpretive, and presentational skills they need to create language for communication. Culture is integrated throughout the text, from the basic introduction of vocabulary, to the authentic photographs, to the cultural readings. Connections to other disciplines are addressed, not only in the GeoVista and Introduction to Theme pages, but also in the readings and project suggestions. Linguistic and cultural comparisons are made throughout the text. Suggestions are made for ways students may use their language skills in the immediate and more distant communities. Students who complete the ¡Así se dice! series are prepared to participate in the Spanish-speaking world. Specific correlations to each chapter are provided on the pages preceding each chapter in the Teacher Edition.

Communication

Communicate in Languages Other than English	Standard 1.1	Students engage in conversations, provide and obtain information, express feeling and emotions, and exchange opinions.
	Standard 1.2	Students understand and interpret written and spoken language on a variety of topics.
	Standard 1.3	Students present information, concepts, and ideas to an audience of listeners or readers on a variety of topics.

Cultures

Gain Knowledge and Understanding of Other Cultures	Standard 2.1	Students demonstrate an understanding of the relationship between the practices and perspectives of the culture studied.
	Standard 2.2	Students demonstrate an understanding of the relationship between the products and perspectives of the culture studied.

Connections

Connect with Other Disciplines and Acquire Information	Standard 3.1	Students reinforce and further their knowledge of other disciplines through the foreign language.
	Standard 3.2	Students acquire information and recognize the distinctive viewpoints that are only available through the foreign language and its cultures.

Comparisons

Develop Insight into the Nature of Language and Culture	Standard 4.1	Students demonstrate understanding of the nature of language through comparison of the language studied and their own.
	Standard 4.2	Students demonstrate understanding of the concept of culture through comparisons of the cultures studied and their own.

Communities

Participate in Multilingual Communities at Home and Around the World	Standard 5.1	Students use the language both within and beyond the school setting.
	Standard 5.2	Students show evidence of becoming life-long learners by using the language for personal enjoyment and enrichment.

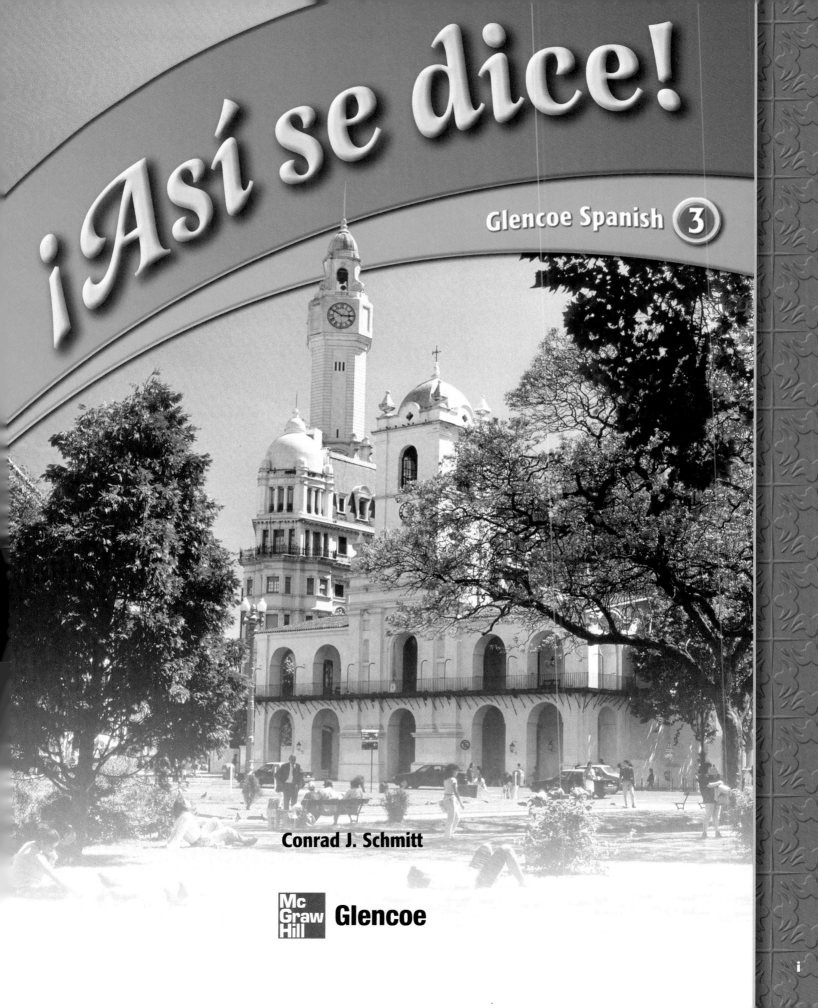

¡Así se dice!

Glencoe Spanish **3**

Conrad J. Schmitt

Mc Graw Hill
Glencoe

Information on featured companies, organizations, and their products and services is included for educational purposes only and does not present or imply endorsement of the **¡Así se dice!** program. Permission to use all business logos has been granted by the businesses represented in this text.

The **McGraw-Hill** Companies

 Glencoe

Copyright © 2009 The McGraw-Hill Companies, Inc. All rights reserved. No part of this publication may be reproduced or distributed in any form or by any means, or stored in a database or retrieval system, without the prior written consent of The McGraw-Hill Companies, Inc., including, but not limited to, network storage or transmission, or broadcast for distance learning.

Send all inquiries to:
Glencoe/McGraw-Hill
8787 Orion Place
Columbus, OH 43240-4027

ISBN: 978-0-07-877784-4
MHID: 0-07-877784-4

Printed in the United States of America.

1 2 3 4 5 6 7 8 9 10   071/055   15 14 13 12 11 10 09 08

About the Author

Conrad J. Schmitt

Conrad J. Schmitt received his B.A. degree magna cum laude from Montclair State University, Upper Montclair, New Jersey. He received his M.A. from Middlebury College, Middlebury, Vermont, and did additional graduate work at New York University. He also studied at the Far Eastern Institute at Seton Hall University, Newark, New Jersey.

Mr. Schmitt has taught Spanish and French at all academic levels—from elementary school to graduate courses. He served as Coordinator of Foreign Languages for the Hackensack, New Jersey, public schools. He also taught courses in Foreign Language Education as a visiting professor at the Graduate School of Education at Rutgers University, New Brunswick, New Jersey.

Mr. Schmitt has authored or co-authored more than one hundred books, all published by The McGraw-Hill Companies. He was also editor-in-chief of foreign languages, ESL, and bilingual education for The McGraw-Hill Companies.

Mr. Schmitt has traveled extensively throughout Spain and all of Latin America. He has addressed teacher groups in all fifty states and has given seminars in many countries including Japan, the People's Republic of China, Taiwan, Egypt, Germany, Spain, Portugal, Mexico, Panama, Colombia, Brazil, Jamaica, and Haiti.

Contributing Writers

Louise M. Belnay
Teacher of World Languages
Adams County School District 50
Westminster, Colorado

Reina Martínez
Coordinator/Teacher of World Languages
North Rockland Central School District
Thiells, New York

Contenido

Student Handbook

Repaso

CONTENIDO

Capítulo 1 Cocina hispana

Objetivos

You will:
- talk about foods and food preparation
- talk about a Spanish recipe

You will use:
- the subjunctive
- formal commands
- negative informal commands

Capítulo 2 ¡Cuídate bien!

Objetivos

You will:
- identify more parts of the body
- talk about exercise
- talk about having a little accident and a trip to the emergency room
- discuss physical fitness

You will use:
- the subjunctive with impersonal expressions
- **ojalá, quizás, tal vez**
- the subjunctive of stem-changing verbs
- the comparison of like things

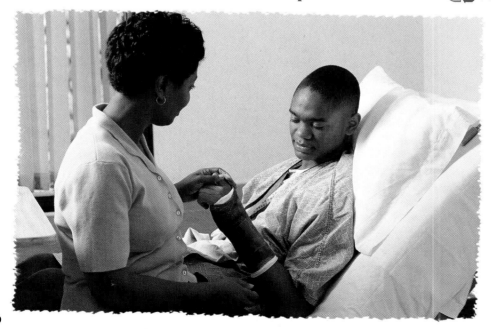

CONTENIDO

Contenido

Capítulo 3 Pasajes de la vida

Objetivos

You will:
- talk about passages of life: weddings, baptisms, birthdays, and funerals
- read a poem by the Peruvian writer Abraham Valdelomar

You will use:
- the subjunctive to express wishes
- the subjunctive to express emotions
- possessive pronouns

Capítulo 4 Quehaceres

Objetivos

You will:
- talk about errands
- discuss preparing for a trip through Andalusia
- read a short story from Argentina

You will use:
- the subjunctive with expressions of doubt
- the subjunctive with adverbial clauses
- the pluperfect, conditional, and future perfect tenses

Capítulo 5 ¿Buenos o malos modales?

Objetivos

You will:
- discuss manners
- compare manners in Spanish-speaking countries to manners in the United States
- read a famous episode from *El conde Lucanor* by Don Juan Manuel

You will use:
- the imperfect subjunctive
- the subjunctive vs. the infinitive
- suffixes

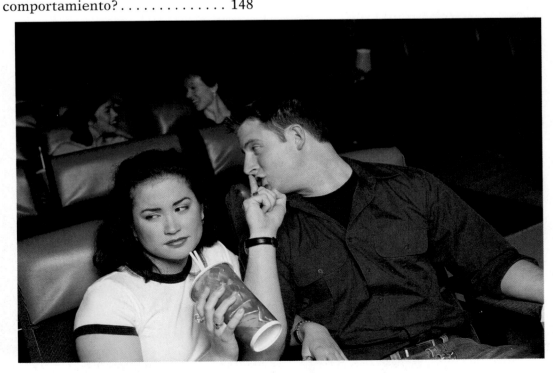

Capítulo 6 Viajes

Objetivos

You will:
- discuss several modes of travel
- talk about a trip to Bolivia
- read a short story by the Spanish author Emilia Pardo Bazán

You will use:
- the subjunctive with conjunctions of time
- the subjunctive to express suggestions and advice
- irregular nouns

Capítulo 7 Arte y literatura

Objetivos

You will:
- discuss fine art and literature
- talk about a mural by the Mexican artist Diego Rivera
- read a sonnet by the Spaniard Federico García Lorca
- read a poem by the Cuban poet Nicolás Guillén

You will use:
- the present perfect and pluperfect subjunctive
- **si** clauses
- adverbs ending in **-mente**

Capítulo 8 Latinos en Estados Unidos

Objetivos

You will:
- talk about the history of Spanish speakers in the United States
- read a poem by the Puerto Rican poet Julia de Burgos

You will use:
- the subjunctive with **aunque**
- the subjunctive with **-quiera**
- definite and indefinite articles (special uses)
- apocopated adjectives

Capítulo 9 Historia de la comida latina

Objetivos

You will:
- identify more foods
- describe food preparation
- discuss the history of foods from Europe and the Americas
- read a poem by the famous Chilean poet Pablo Neruda

You will use:
- the passive voice
- relative pronouns
- expressions of time with **hace** and **hacía**

Capítulo 10 Carreras

Objetivos

You will:
- talk about professions and occupations
- have a job interview
- discuss the importance of learning a second language
- read a short story by the famous Colombian writer Gabriel García Márquez

You will use:
- **por** and **para**
- the subjunctive in relative clauses

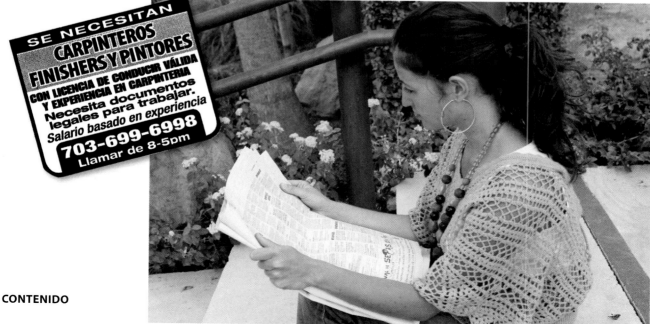

SE NECESITAN
CARPINTEROS
FINISHERS Y PINTORES
CON LICENCIA DE CONDUCIR VÁLIDA
Y EXPERIENCIA EN CARPINTERÍA
Necesita documentos legales para trabajar.
Salario basado en experiencia
703-699-6998
Llamar de 8-5pm

Contenido

Student Resources

Guide to Symbols

Throughout **¡Así se dice!** you will see these symbols, or icons. They will tell you how to best use the particular part of the chapter or activity they accompany. Following is a key to help you understand these symbols.

Audio link This icon indicates material in the chapter that is recorded on compact disk.

Recycling This icon indicates sections that review previously introduced material.

Paired activity This icon indicates activities that you can practice orally with a partner.

Group activity This icon indicates activities that you can practice together in groups.

Critical thinking This icon indicates activities that require critical thinking.

InfoGap **InfoGap** This icon refers to additional paired activities at the end of the book.

¡Bravo! **¡Bravo!** This icon indicates the end of new material in each chapter. All remaining material is recombination and review.

Why Learn Spanish?

¡Viva el español!

Spanish is currently the fourth-most-spoken language in the world. Studying Spanish will help you explore other cultures, communicate with Spanish speakers, and increase your career possibilities.

It's fascinating!

Culture Hispanic culture is full of diverse expressions of music, art, and literature. From dancing the tango or salsa to admiring a modern painting by Salvador Dalí, your studies will introduce you to an array of what the culture has to offer. You'll learn about the various customs, traditions, and values in Latin America and Spain. From food and family to school and sports, you'll learn all about life in the Hispanic world.

▲ **Dancers of the tango on the streets of Argentina**

It's all around us!

Communication The United States is home to more than forty-four million Hispanics or Latinos. Whether on the radio, in your community or school, or in your own home, the Spanish language is probably part of your life in some way. Understanding Spanish allows you to sing along with Latin music on the radio or chat with Spanish speakers in your school, community, or family. No matter who you are, Spanish can enrich your life in some way.

If you plan to travel outside the United States, remember that Spanish is the official language of twenty-one countries. Experiencing another country is more fun and meaningful when you can understand restaurant menus, read newspapers, follow street signs, watch TV, and better yet converse with the locals.

◄ **Singer Shakira performs.**

DENTISTA
Dra. Juana Ramos
741 – 8887

▲ A Spanish-speaking dentist

It's a lifelong skill!

Career Do you know what career you plan to pursue? Medicine, business, social work, teaching? What will you do if you have a Spanish-speaking patient, client, or student? Speak Spanish, of course! Whatever your career, you will be able to reach more people if you are able to converse in Spanish. After all, it's spoken by 13 percent of the U.S. population. You will also be open to many more career opportunities if you know Spanish. Businesses, government agencies, and educational institutions are always looking for people with the ability to speak and read more than one language.

It's an adventure!

Challenge When you study a language, you not only learn about the language and its speakers but also about yourself. Studying a language requires that you challenge yourself and more fully develop your skills. When you know about the customs and values of another culture, you are better able to reflect upon your own. Language is a means of self-discovery. Enjoy!

▼ Fans of Enrique Iglesias

Reading in a New Language

Following are skills and strategies that can help you understand what you read in a language you have just begun to learn. *Reading and Succeeding* will help you build skills and strategies that will make it easier to understand what you are reading in your exciting new language.

The strategies you use frequently depend on the purpose of your reading. You do not read a textbook or standardized testing questions the same way you read a novel or a magazine article. You read a textbook for information. You read a novel or magazine article for fun.

In the early stages of second-language learning, your vocabulary is, of course, very limited in comparison to the vast number of words you already know in English. The material presented to you to read in the early stages must accommodate this reality. Your limited knowledge of the language does not have to deter you from enjoying what you are reading. Most of what you read, however, will come from your textbook, since original novels and magazine articles are not written for people who have limited exposure to the language.

As you develop your reading ability in Spanish, you will encounter basically two types of readings.

Intensive Readings

These readings are short. They are very controlled, using only language you have already learned. You should find these readings easy and enjoyable. If you find them difficult, it means you have not sufficiently learned the material presented in the chapter of the textbook. The vast majority of these informative readings will introduce you to the fascinating cultures of the Spanish-speaking world.

A very important aspect of reading in Spanish is to give you things to "talk about" in the language. The more you read, speak, and use the language, the more proficient you will become. Whenever you finish reading one of the intensive reading selections, you should be able to talk about it; that is, you should be able to retell it in your own words.

Extensive Readings

Since it is unrealistic to assume that you will never encounter new words as you branch out and read material in Spanish, you will also be presented with extensive readings. The goal of these extensive readings is to help you develop the tools and skills you need in order to read at some future date an original novel or magazine article. They do indeed contain some words and structures that are unfamiliar to you. In this *Reading and Succeeding* section, you will learn to develop many skills that will enable you to read such material with relative ease.

Use *Reading and Succeeding* to help you:

- adjust the way you read to fit the type of material you are reading
- identify new words and build your vocabulary
- use specific reading strategies to better understand what you read
- improve your ability to speak by developing strategies that enable you to retell orally what you have read
- use critical thinking strategies to think more deeply about what you read

Identifying New Words and Building Vocabulary

What do you do when you come across a word you do not know as you read? Do you skip the word and keep reading? You might if you are reading for fun. If it hinders your ability to understand, however, you might miss something important. When you come to a word you don't know, try the following strategies to figure out what the word means.

Reading Aloud

In the early stages of learning a second language, a good strategy is to sit by yourself and read the selection aloud. This can help you understand the reading because you once again hear words that you have already practiced orally in class. Hearing them as you read them can help reinforce meaning.

Identifying Cognates

As you read you will come across many cognates. Cognates are words that look alike in both English and Spanish. Not only do they look alike

but they mean the same thing. Recognizing cognates is a great reading strategy. Examples of cognates are:

cómico	nacionalidad	entra
popular	secundaria	clase
cubano	matemática	prepara
video	blusa	televisión

Identifying Roots and Base Words

The main part of a word is called its root. From a root, many new words can be formed. When you see a new word, identify its root. It can help you pronounce the word and figure out its meaning.

For example, if you know the word **importante,** there is no problem determining the meaning of **importancia.** The verb **importar** becomes a bit more problematic, but with some intelligent guessing you can get its meaning. You know it has something to do with importance so it means *it is important,* and by extension it can even carry the meaning *it matters.*

Identifying Prefixes

A prefix is a word part added to the beginning of a root or base word. Spanish as well as English has prefixes. Prefixes can change, or even reverse, the meaning of a word. For example, the prefixes **in-, im-,** and **des-** mean *not.*

estable/inestable   posible/imposible
honesto/deshonesto

Using Syntax

Like all languages, Spanish has rules for the way words are arranged in sentences. The way a sentence is organized is called its syntax. Spanish syntax, however, is a bit more flexible than English. In a simple English sentence someone or something (its subject) does something (the predicate or verb) to or with another person or thing (the object). This word order can vary in Spanish and does not always follow the subject/verb/object order.

Because Spanish and English syntax vary, you should think in Spanish and not try to translate what you are reading into English. Reading in Spanish will then have a natural flow and follow exactly the way you learned it. Trying to translate it into English confuses the matter and serves no purpose.

Example

English always states: *John speaks to me.*
Spanish can state: *John to me speaks. or*
                    To me speaks John.

The latter leaves the subject to the end of the sentence and emphasizes that it is John who speaks to me.

Using Context Clues

This is a very important reading strategy in a second language. You can often figure out the meaning of an unfamiliar word by looking at it in context (the words and sentences that surround it). Let's look at the example below.

Example

The glump ate it all up and flew away.

You have no idea what a *glump* is. Right? But from the rest of the sentence you can figure out that it's a bird. Why? Because it flew away and you know that birds fly. In this way you guessed at the meaning of an unknown word using context. Although you know it is a bird, you cannot determine the specific meaning such as a robin, a wren, or a sparrow. In many cases it does not matter because that degree of specificity is not necessary for comprehension.

Let's look at another example:
The glump ate it all up and phlumped.

In this case you do not know the meaning of two key words in the same sentence—*glump* and *phlumped*. This makes it impossible to guess the meaning and this is what can happen when you try to read something in a second language that is beyond your proficiency level. This makes reading a frustrating experience. For this reason all the readings in your textbook control the language to keep it within your reach. Remember, if you have studied the vocabulary in your book, this will not happen.

Understanding What You Read

Try using some of the following strategies before, during, and after reading to understand and remember what you read.

Previewing

When you preview a piece of writing, you are looking for a general idea of what to expect from it. Before you read, try the following.

- Look at the title and any illustrations that are included.
- Read the headings, subheadings, and anything in bold letters.
- Skim over the passage to see how it is organized. Is it divided into many parts? Is it a long poem or short story?
- Look at the graphics—pictures, maps, or diagrams.
- Set a purpose for your reading. Are you reading to learn something new? Are you reading to find specific information?

Using What You Know

Believe it or not, you already know quite a bit about what you are going to read. Your own knowledge and personal experience can help you create meaning in what you read. There is, however, a big difference in reading the information in your Spanish textbook. You already have some knowledge about what you are reading from a United States oriented base. What you will be reading about takes place in a Spanish-speaking environment and thus you will be adding an exciting new dimension to what you already know. Comparing and contrasting are important critical skills to put to use when reading material about a culture other than your own. This skill will be discussed later.

Visualizing

Creating pictures in your mind about what you are reading—called visualizing—will help you understand and remember what you read. With the assistance of the many accompanying photos, try to visualize the people, streets, cities, homes, etc., you are reading about.

Identifying Sequence

When you discover the logical order of events or ideas, you are identifying sequence. Look for clues and signal words that will help you find how information is organized. Some signal words are **primero, al principio, antes, después, luego, entonces, más tarde, por fin, finalmente.**

Determining the Main Idea

When you look for the main idea of a selection, you look for the most important idea. The examples, reasons, and details that further explain the main idea are called supporting details.

Reviewing

When you review in school, you go over what you learned the day before so that the information is clear in your mind. Reviewing when you read does the same thing. Take time now and then to pause and review what you have read. Think about the main ideas and organize them for yourself so you can recall them later. Filling in study aids such as graphic organizers can help you review.

Monitoring Your Comprehension

As you read, check your understanding by summarizing. Pause from time to time and state the main ideas of what you have just read. Answer the questions: **¿Quién?** *(Who?)* **¿Qué?** *(What?)* **¿Dónde?** *(Where?)* **¿Cuándo?** *(When?)* **¿Cómo?** *(How?)* **¿Por qué?** *(Why?)*. Summarizing tests your comprehension because you state key points in your own words. Remember something you read earlier: reading in Spanish empowers your ability to speak by developing strategies that enable you to retell orally what you have read.

Thinking About Your Reading

Sometimes it is important to think more deeply about what you read so you can get the most out of what the author says. These critical thinking skills will help you go beyond what the words say and understand the meaning of your reading.

Compare and Contrast

To compare and contrast shows the similarities and differences among people, things, and ideas. Your reading experience in Spanish will show you many things that are similar and many others that are different depending upon the culture groups and social mores.

As you go over these culturally oriented readings, try to visualize what you are reading. Then think about the information. Think about what you know about the topic and then determine if the information you are reading is similar, somewhat different, or very different from what you know.

Continue to think about it. In this case you may have to think about it in English. Determine if you find the similarities or the differences interesting. Would you like to experience what you are reading about? Analyzing the information in this way will most certainly help you remember what you have read.

- Signal words and phrases that indicate similarity are **similar, semejante, parecido, igual.**
- Signal words and phrases that indicate differences are **diferente, distinto, al contrario, contrariamente, sin embargo.**

Cause and Effect

Just about everything that happens in life is the cause or the effect of some other event or action. Writers use cause-and-effect structure to explore the reasons for something happening and to examine the results of previous events. This structure helps answer the question that everybody is always asking: Why? Cause-and-effect structure is about explaining things.

- Signal words and phrases are **así, porque, por consiguiente, resulta que.**

Using Reference Materials

In the early stages of second-language learning, you will not be able to use certain types of reference materials that are helpful to you in English. For example, you could not look up a word in a Spanish dictionary as you would not be able to understand many of the words used in the definition.

You can, however, make use of the glossary that appears at the end of your textbook. A glossary includes only words that are included in the textbook. Rather than give you a Spanish definition, the glossary gives you the English equivalent of the word. If you have to use the glossary very frequently, it indicates to you that you have not studied the vocabulary sufficiently in each chapter. A strategy to use before beginning a reading selection in any given chapter is to quickly skim the vocabulary in the **Vocabulario 1** and **Vocabulario 2** sections of the chapter.

Expand your view of the Spanish-speaking world.

¡Así se dice! will show you the many places where you will be able to use your Spanish.

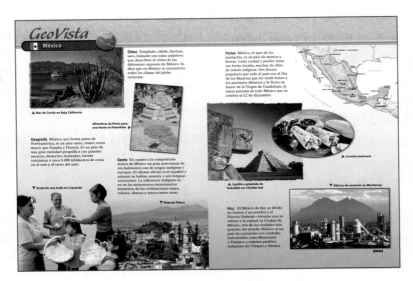

Cultural and geographic information is at your fingertips with **GeoVistas**, your virtual field trip to the Spanish-speaking countries.

Start your journey into language and culture.

Opening photo provides a cultural backdrop for the chapter.

Aquí y Allí introduces you to the chapter theme and invites you to make connections between your culture and the cultures of Spanish-speaking countries.

Objectives let you know what you will be able to do by the end of the chapter.

Access your eBook with QuickPass at glencoe.com.

Get acquainted with the chapter theme.

Explore each chapter's theme with vivid cultural photos and informative captions.

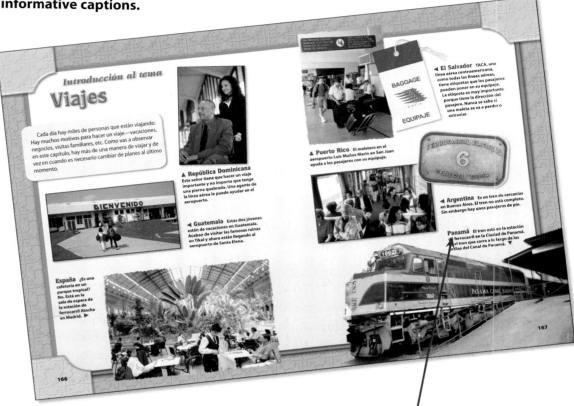

See how the theme relates to different countries in the Spanish-speaking world.

Talk about the chapter theme with your new vocabulary.

Learn colloquial phrases to make conversation easy.

Vocabulary is introduced and practiced in two manageable sections.

Recorded presentation ensures proper pronunciation.

Watch video clips to experience the diversity of the Spanish-speaking world while reinforcing the language you have learned and improving your listening and viewing skills.

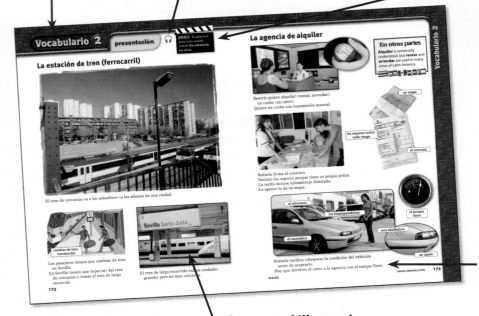

New words are used in a meaningful context.

Photos and illustrations aid comprehension and vocabulary acquisition.

Practice and master new vocabulary.

Graphic organizers make practice clear and easy.

Use QuickPass to easily access additional vocabulary practice at glencoe.com.

Practice and master your new vocabulary with your Workbook and StudentWorks™ Plus.

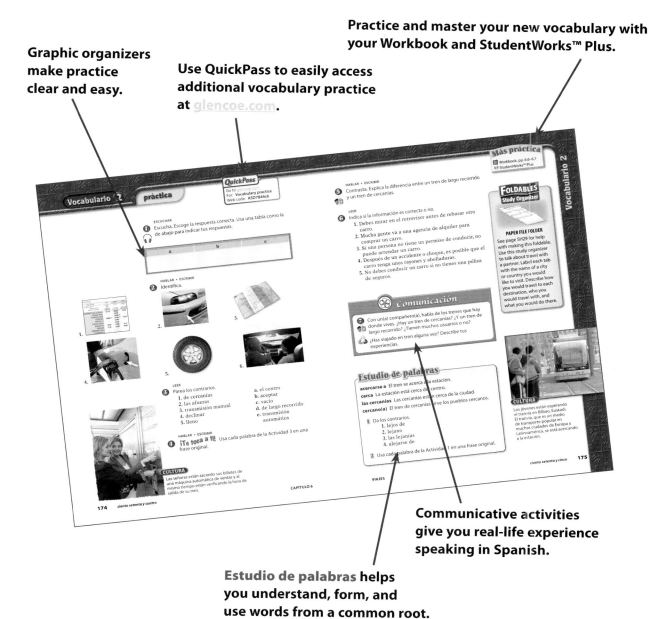

Communicative activities give you real-life experience speaking in Spanish.

Estudio de palabras helps you understand, form, and use words from a common root.

Learn grammar within the context of the chapter theme.

Use QuickPass to access additional grammar practice at glencoe.com.

Expansión enables you to tell and retell a story, using your new words.

Reinforce pronunciation and aural comprehension with audio activities.

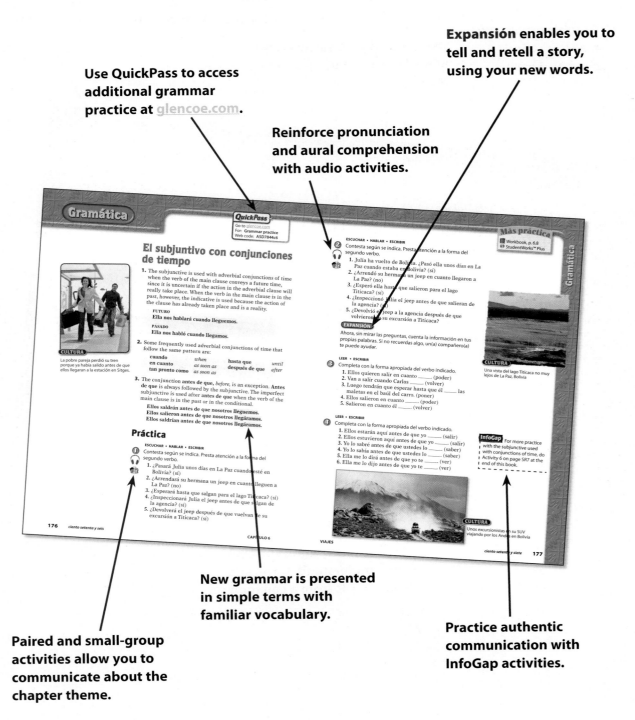

New grammar is presented in simple terms with familiar vocabulary.

Paired and small-group activities allow you to communicate about the chapter theme.

Practice authentic communication with InfoGap activities.

Build on what you already know.

Use your new vocabulary as you practice the new grammar points.

Have fun using your Spanish to figure out the meaning of Spanish proverbs.

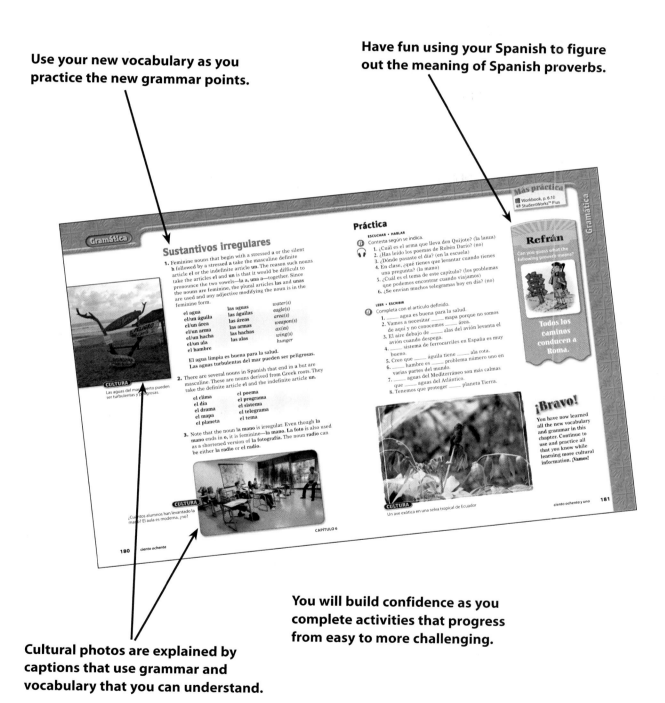

You will build confidence as you complete activities that progress from easy to more challenging.

Cultural photos are explained by captions that use grammar and vocabulary that you can understand.

Engage classmates in real conversation.

Use QuickPass to access the Conversation online at glencoe.com.

You will have a sense of accomplishment when you are able to comprehend the conversation.

Look for this symbol to find additional information to help you meet the National Standards for Foreign Language Learning.

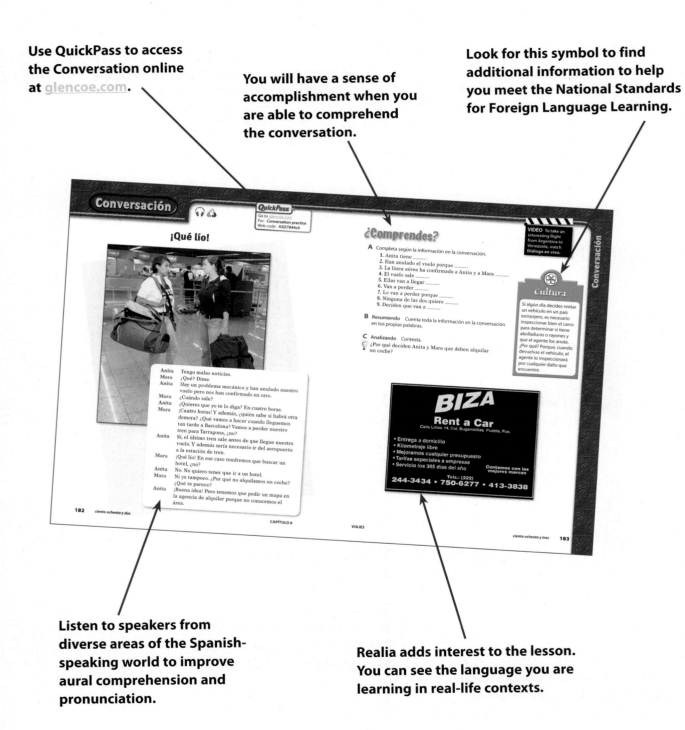

Listen to speakers from diverse areas of the Spanish-speaking world to improve aural comprehension and pronunciation.

Realia adds interest to the lesson. You can see the language you are learning in real-life contexts.

Heighten your cultural awareness.

Lectura cultural uses learned language to reinforce the chapter theme and to expand your understanding of the Spanish-speaking world.

Recorded reading online and on CD provides options for addressing various skills and learning styles.

Questions follow the reading to check comprehension.

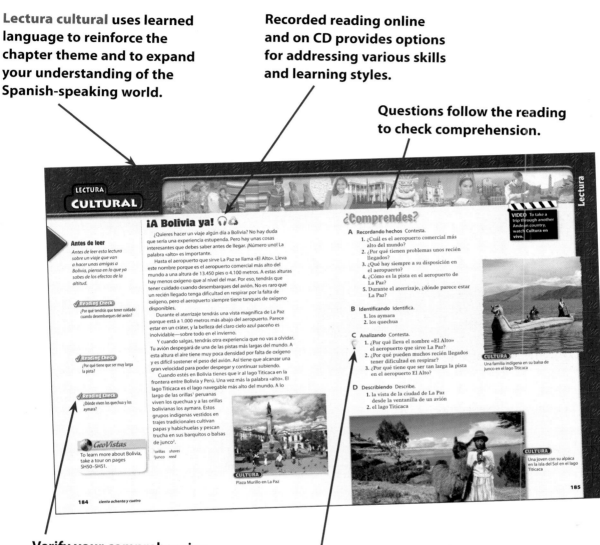

LECTURA CULTURAL

¡A Bolivia ya!

Antes de leer

Antes de leer esta lectura sobre un viaje que van a hacer unas amigas a Bolivia, piensa en lo que ya sabes de los efectos de la altitud.

✓ Reading Check
¿Por qué tendrás que tener cuidado cuando desembarques del avión?

✓ Reading Check
¿Por qué tiene que ser muy larga la pista?

✓ Reading Check
¿Dónde viven los quechua y los aymara?

GeoVistas
To learn more about Bolivia, take a tour on pages SH50–SH51.

¿Quieres hacer un viaje algún día a Bolivia? No hay duda que sería una experiencia estupenda. Pero hay unas cosas interesantes que debes saber antes de llegar. ¡Número uno! La palabra «alto» es importante.

Hasta el aeropuerto que sirve La Paz se llama «El Alto». Lleva este nombre porque es el aeropuerto comercial más alto del mundo a una altura de 13.450 pies o 4.100 metros. A estas alturas hay menos oxígeno que al nivel del mar. Por eso, tendrás que tener cuidado cuando desembarques del avión. No es raro que un recién llegado tenga dificultad en respirar por la falta de oxígeno, pero el aeropuerto siempre tiene tanques de oxígeno disponibles.

Durante el aterrizaje tendrás una vista magnífica de La Paz porque está a 1.000 metros más abajo del aeropuerto. Parece estar en un cráter, y la belleza del claro cielo azul paceño es inolvidable—sobre todo en el invierno.

Y cuando salgas, tendrás otra experiencia que no vas a olvidar. Tu avión despegará de una de las pistas más largas del mundo. A esta altura el aire tiene muy poca densidad por falta de oxígeno y es difícil sostener el peso del avión. Así tiene que alcanzar una gran velocidad para poder despegar y continuar subiendo.

Cuando estés en Bolivia tienes que ir al lago Titicaca en la frontera entre Bolivia y Perú. Una vez más la palabra «alto». El lago Titicaca es el lago navegable más alto del mundo. A lo largo de las orillas¹ peruanas viven los quechua y a las orillas bolivianas los aymara. Estos grupos indígenas vestidos en trajes tradicionales cultivan papas y habichuelas y pescan trucha en sus barquitos o balsas de junco².

¹orillas shores
²junco reed

Plaza Murillo en La Paz

¿Comprendes?

A Recordando hechos Contesta.
1. ¿Cuál es el aeropuerto comercial más alto del mundo?
2. ¿Por qué tienen problemas unos recién llegados?
3. ¿Qué hay siempre a su disposición en el aeropuerto?
4. ¿Cómo es la pista en el aeropuerto de La Paz?
5. Durante el aterrizaje, ¿dónde parece estar La Paz?

B Identificando Identifica.
1. los aymara
2. los quechua

C Analizando Contesta.
1. ¿Por qué lleva el nombre «El Alto» el aeropuerto que sirve La Paz?
2. ¿Por qué pueden muchos recién llegados tener dificultad en respirar?
3. ¿Por qué tiene que ser tan larga la pista en el aeropuerto El Alto?

D Describiendo Describe.
1. la vista de la ciudad de La Paz desde la ventanilla de un avión
2. el lago Titicaca

VIDEO To take a trip through another Andean country, watch *Cultura en vivo*.

CULTURA
Una familia indígena en su balsa de junco en el lago Titicaca

CULTURA
Una joven con su alpaca en la isla del Sol en el lago Titicaca

184 *ciento ochenta y cuatro*

185

Verify your comprehension throughout the selection with Reading Checks.

The lightbulb icon indicates a critical thinking activity.

Enhance your appreciation of Hispanic literature and culture.

Literatura gives you another opportunity to apply your reading skills in Spanish and to further acquaint you with authentic prose and poetry of the Spanish-speaking world.

Literatura

Temprano y con sol
de Emilia Pardo Bazán

▲ La Coruña, la provincia natal de Pardo Bazán en Galicia

Vocabulario

la manía   preocupación exagerada; deseo desordenado

la criada   señora que trabaja haciendo tareas domésticas por dinero

el oído   el aparato que sirve para la audición, que nos permite oír

el/la novio(a)   amigo con quien uno sale con frecuencia y a quien le expresa cariño

el mozo   el joven, el muchacho

el reloj   aparato que nos indica la hora

entregar   dar

echar   empezar a, ponerse a

avisar   informarle a alguien de algo; dejarle a uno saber algo

Práctica

❶ Completa con una palabra apropiada.
1. No sé la hora porque mi _____ no anda.
2. No quería que nadie oyera lo que me decía. Así es que lo murmuró en mi _____
3. Él tiene muchas _____. A veces yo no comprendo lo que hace.
4. Hace tiempo que los _____ están saliendo. Creo que se están enamorando.
5. Mucha gente de las clases altas pagan a una _____ para limpiar la casa.
6. El hijo de los López es un buen _____.

❷ Expresa de otra manera.
1. Lo necesitan. ¿Cuándo se lo vas a *dar*?
2. El niño tenía miedo y *se puso a* correr.
3. Es necesario que lo sepan. ¿Por qué no les *informan* de lo que está pasando?
4. Es *un muchacho* inteligente y simpático.
5. Es *una obsesión* que tiene.

¿Comprendes?

▲ Emilia Pardo Bazán (1852–1921), una ilustre autora española

INTRODUCCIÓN

Emilia Pardo Bazán, la condesa de Pardo Bazán, es considerada una de los novelistas más importantes de la literatura española. Nació en La Coruña, Galicia, de una familia aristócrata. Fue una mujer culta de gran curiosidad intelectual y talento creativo.

Su obra incluye varias novelas psicológicas y regionales. En dos de sus novelas importantes estudia y describe la decadencia de la aristocracia gallega.

Pardo Bazán cultivó el cuento también y se considera una maestra de este género literario.

186   ciento ochenta y seis   CAPÍTULO 6   VIAJES   ciento ochenta y siete   187

... y uno   191

Show what you know.

Review what you have learned and prepare for your chapter test.

Reference notes direct you to the correct pages for review.

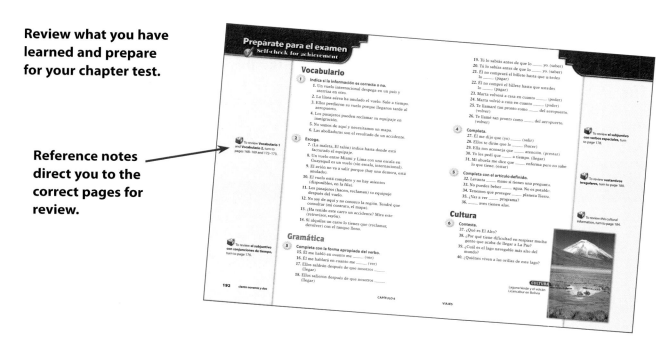

Apply what you have learned.

Use your new skills to communicate orally in meaningful, open-ended activities.

Practice what you have learned while improving your written Spanish.

Writing Strategy gives you the tools you need to develop better writing skills.

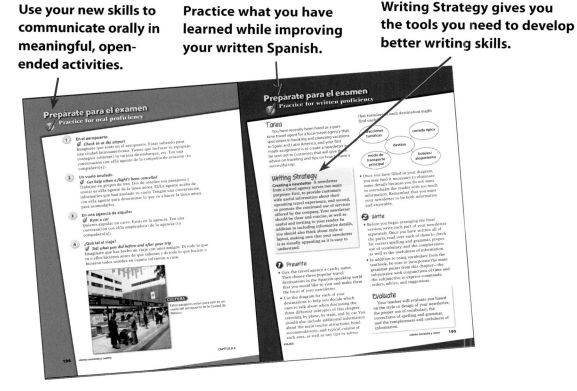

Review grammar and vocabulary at a glance.

Succinct grammar notes help you efficiently review chapter material.

Use this vocabulary list to review the vocabulary you have learned in this chapter.

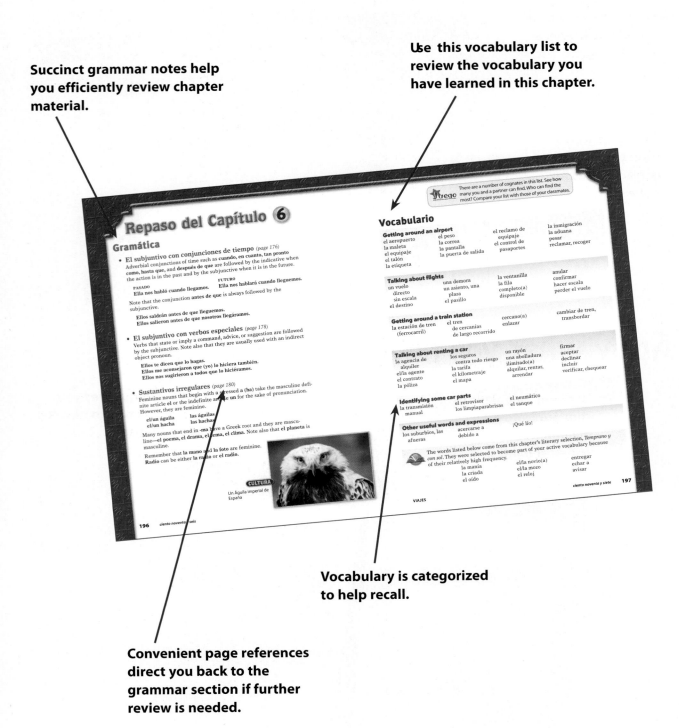

Repaso del Capítulo 6

Gramática

- **El subjuntivo con conjunciones de tiempo** *(page 176)*
  Adverbial conjunctions of time such as **cuando, en cuanto, tan pronto como, hasta que,** and **después de que** are followed by the indicative when the action is in the past and by the subjunctive when it is in the future.

  PASADO
  Ella nos habló cuando llegamos.

  FUTURO
  Ella nos hablará cuando lleguemos.

  Note that the conjunction **antes de que** is always followed by the subjunctive.

  Ellos saldrán antes de que lleguemos.
  Ellos salieron antes de que nosotros llegáramos.

- **El subjuntivo con verbos especiales** *(page 178)*
  Verbs that state or imply a command, advice, or suggestion are followed by the subjunctive. Note also that they are usually used with an indirect object pronoun.

  Ellos te dicen que lo hagas.
  Ellos me aconsejaron que (yo) lo hiciera también.
  Ellos nos sugirieron a todos que lo hiciéramos.

- **Sustantivos irregulares** *(page 180)*
  Feminine nouns that begin with a stressed **a (ha)** take the masculine definite article **el** or the indefinite article **un** for the sake of pronunciation. However, they are feminine.

  el/un águila   las águilas
  el/un hacha   las hachas

  Many nouns that end in -ma have a Greek root and they are masculine—**el poema, el drama, el tema, el clima.** Note also that **el planeta** is masculine.

  Remember that **la mano** and **la foto** are feminine. **Radio** can be either **la radio** or **el radio.**

CULTURA
Un Águila imperial de España

196   ciento noventa y seis

Vocabulario

Getting around an airport
el aeropuerto
la maleta
el equipaje
el talón
la etiqueta
el peso
la correa
la pantalla
la puerta de salida
el reclamo de equipaje
el control de pasaportes
la inmigración
la aduana
pesar
reclamar, recoger

Talking about flights
un vuelo
  directo
  sin escala
el destino
una demora
un asiento, una plaza
el pasillo
la ventanilla
la fila
completo(a)
disponible
anular
confirmar
hacer escala
perder el vuelo

Getting around a train station
la estación de tren (ferrocarril)
el tren
  de cercanías
  de largo recorrido
cercano(a)
enlazar
cambiar de tren, transbordar

Talking about renting a car
la agencia de alquiler
el/la agente
el contrato
la póliza
los seguros
  contra todo riesgo
la tarifa
el kilometraje
el mapa
un rayón
una abolladura
ilimitado(a)
alquilar, rentar, arrendar
firmar
aceptar
declinar
incluir
verificar, chequear

Identifying some car parts
la transmisión manual
el retrovisor
los limpiaparabrisas
el neumático
el tanque

Other useful words and expressions
los suburbios, las afueras
acercarse a
debido a
¡Qué lío!

The words listed below come from this chapter's literary selection, *Temprano y con sol.* They were selected to become part of your active vocabulary because of their relatively high frequency.
la manía
la criada
el oído
el/la novio(a)
el/la mozo
el reloj
entregar
echar a
avisar

VIAJES

ciento noventa y siete   197

There are a number of cognates in this list. See how many you and a partner can find. Who can find the most? Compare your list with those of your classmates.

Vocabulary is categorized to help recall.

Convenient page references direct you back to the grammar section if further review is needed.

Practice what you have learned so far in Spanish.

A wide variety of activities allow you to practice what you have learned so far in Spanish class.

The Cumulative Review always begins with an audio activity to give you more listening practice.

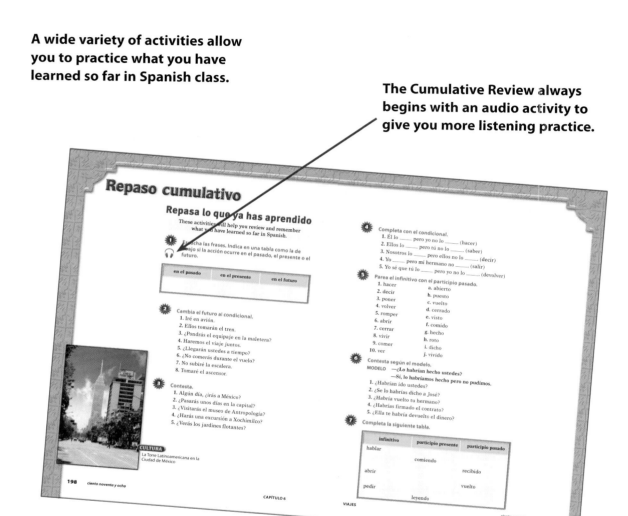

Repaso cumulativo

Repasa lo que ya has aprendido

These activities will help you review and remember what you have learned so far in Spanish.

1 Escucha las frases. Indica en una tabla como la de abajo si la acción ocurre en el pasado, el presente o el futuro.

en el pasado	en el presente	en el futuro

2 Cambia el futuro al condicional.
1. Iré en avión.
2. Ellos tomarán el tren.
3. ¿Pondrás el equipaje en la maletera?
4. Haremos el viaje juntos.
5. ¿Llegarán ustedes a tiempo?
6. ¿No comerás durante el vuelo?
7. No subiré la escalera.
8. Tomaré el ascensor.

3 Contesta.
1. Algún día, ¿irás a México?
2. ¿Pasarás unos días en la capital?
3. ¿Visitarás el museo de Antropología?
4. ¿Harás una excursión a Xochimilco?
5. ¿Verás los jardines flotantes?

CULTURA
La Torre Latinoamericana en la Ciudad de México

4 Completa con el condicional.
1. Él lo _____ pero yo no lo _____ (hacer)
2. Ellos lo _____ pero tú no lo _____ (saber)
3. Nosotros lo _____ pero ellos no lo _____ (decir)
4. Yo _____ pero mi hermano no _____ (salir)
5. Yo sé que tú lo _____ pero yo no lo _____ (devolver)

5 Parea el infinitivo con el participio pasado.
1. hacer	a. abierto
2. decir	b. puesto
3. poner	c. vuelto
4. volver	d. cerrado
5. romper	e. visto
6. abrir	f. comido
7. cerrar	g. hecho
8. vivir	h. roto
9. comer	i. dicho
10. ver	j. vivido

6 Contesta según el modelo.
MODELO   —¿Lo habrían hecho ustedes?
         —Sí, lo habríamos hecho pero no pudimos.
1. ¿Habrían ido ustedes?
2. ¿Se lo habrías dicho a José?
3. ¿Habría vuelto tu hermano?
4. ¿Habrías firmado el contrato?
5. ¿Ella te había devuelto el dinero?

7 Completa la siguiente tabla.

infinitivo	participio presente	participio pasado
hablar		
	comiendo	
abrir		recibido
pedir		vuelto
	leyendo	

198 ciento noventa y ocho
CAPÍTULO 6   VIAJES
ciento noventa y nueve **199**

Foldables

Dear Student,

Foldables are interactive study organizers that you can make yourself. They are a wonderful resource to help you organize and retain information. Foldables have many purposes. You can use them to remember vocabulary words or to organize more in-depth information on any given topic, such as keeping track of what you know about a particular country.

You can write general information, such as titles, vocabulary words, concepts, questions, main ideas, and dates, on the front tabs of your Foldables. You view this general information every time you look at a Foldable. This helps you focus on and remember key points without the distraction of additional text. You can write specific information—supporting ideas, thoughts, answers to questions, research information, empirical data, class notes, observations, and definitions—under the tabs. Think of different ways in which Foldables can be used. Soon you will find that you can make your own Foldables for study guides and projects. Foldables with flaps or tabs create study guides that you can use to check what you know about the general information on the front of tabs. Use Foldables without tabs for projects that require information to be presented for others to view quickly. The more you make and use graphic organizers, the faster you will become able to produce them.

To store your Foldables, turn one-gallon freezer bags into student portfolios which can be collected and stored in the classroom. You can also carry your portfolios in your notebooks if you place strips of two-inch clear tape along one side and punch three holes through the taped edge. Write your name along the top of the plastic portfolio with a permanent marker and cover the writing with two-inch clear tape to keep it from wearing off. Cut the bottom corners off the bag so it won't hold air and will stack and store easily. The following figures illustrate the basic folds that are referred to throughout this book.

Good luck!

Dinah Zike

Dinah Zike
www.dinah.com

Category Book

Los números Use this *category book* organizer as you learn dates and numbers.

Step 1 **Fold** a sheet of paper (8½" x 11") in half like a *hot dog*.

Step 2 On one side, **cut** every third line. This usually results in ten tabs. Do this with three sheets of paper to make three books.

Step 3 **Write** one Arabic number on the outside of each of the tabs. On the inside write out the respective number. As you learn more numbers, use *category books* to categorize numbers in this way.

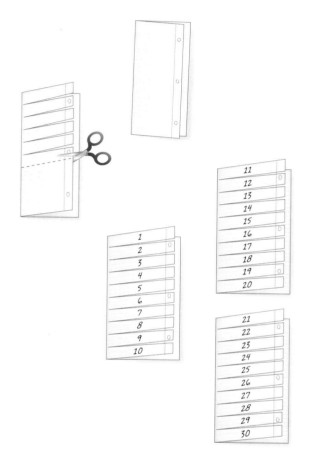

Other Suggestions for a *Category Book* Foldable

You may wish to use *category book* foldables to help remember numbers. As you learn numbers, make two *category book* foldables. One will have the numerals on the outside and the numbers written out on the inside. The other will have the numbers written out on the outside and the numerals on the inside. This is a good way for you to practice your numbers on your own. You may also wish to make one foldable containing even numbers and one containing odd numbers.

A *category book* foldable may be used to practice conjugating Spanish verbs. On the top tab, write the infinitive form of a verb. On the following tabs, write the subject pronouns: **yo, tú, él, ella, Ud., nosotros(as), ellos, ellas, Uds.** Then open each tab and write the corresponding form of the verb.

Forward-Backward Book

Las estaciones Use this *forward-backward book* to compare and contrast two seasons of your choice.

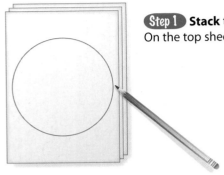

Step 1 **Stack** three sheets of paper. On the top sheet, trace a large circle.

Step 2 With the papers still stacked, **cut out** the circles.

Step 3 **Staple** the paper circles together along the left-hand side to create a circular booklet.

Step 4 **Write** the name of a season on the cover. On the page that opens to the right list the months of the year in that particular season. On the following page draw a picture to illustrate the season.

front

El invierno

inside

Step 5 **Turn the book upside down** and write the name of a season on the cover. On the page that opens to the right list the months of the year in that particular season. On the following page draw a picture to illustrate the season.

back

El verano

inside

Other Suggestions for a *Forward-Backward Book* Foldable

You may wish to use a *forward-backward book* foldable to organize vocabulary pertaining to the city and the country. On the front cover write **la ciudad.** Open your book. On the right-hand page list words you have learned that pertain to the city. On the next right-hand page, draw a picture illustrating the words on your list. Close your book and flip it over. On the back cover write **el campo** and do the same.

It may be helpful to use a *forward-backward book* foldable to organize the food groups. You could use the name of a food group in Spanish (meat, vegetable, fruit, etc.) as the title. On the inside, list as many foods in this food group as you can on the right-hand page and illustrate these foods on the opposite page. Give the same information for a second food group by reversing the book.

Pocket Book

La geografía Use this *pocket book* organizer in your ongoing study of all the countries in the Spanish-speaking world.

Step 1 **Fold** a sheet of paper (8½" x 11") in half like a *hamburger*.

Step 2 **Open** the folded paper and fold one of the long sides up two inches to form a pocket. Refold the *hamburger* fold so that the newly formed pockets are on the inside.

Step 3 **Glue** the outer edges of the two-inch fold with a small amount of glue.

Step 4 **Make a multipaged booklet** by gluing six pockets side-by-side. Glue a cover around the multipaged *pocket book*.

Step 5 **Label** five pockets with the following geographical areas: **Europa, la América del Norte, la América del Sur, la América Central,** and **Islas del Caribe.** Use index cards inside the pockets to record information each time you learn something new about a specific country. Be sure to include the name of the country (in Spanish, of course) and its capital.

Other Suggestions for a *Pocket Book* Foldable

You may wish to use a *pocket book* foldable to organize masculine and feminine nouns or singular and plural forms. You can make an index card to put in the correct pocket each time you learn a new word.

A *pocket book* foldable may be used to organize information about several subjects. For example, to organize information about airplane travel, label pockets with topics such as *preparing for a trip, getting to the airport, at the airport,* and *on the airplane* in Spanish.

Make cards for all the words and phrases you know that go with each topic.

If you wish to organize what you are learning about important people, works of art, festivals, and other cultural information in countries that speak Spanish, a *pocket book* foldable may be helpful. You can make a card for each person, work of art, or event that you study, and you can add cards and even add categories as you continue to learn about cultures that speak Spanish.

FOLDABLES

Tab Book

Preguntas Use this *tab book* to practice asking and answering questions.

Step 1 **Fold** a sheet of paper (8½" x 11") like a *hot dog* but fold it so that one side is one inch longer than the other.

Step 2 On the shorter side only, **cut** five equal tabs. On the front of each tab, **write** a question word you have learned. For example, you may wish to write the following.

Step 3 On the bottom edge, **write** any sentence you would like.

Step 4 Under each tab, **write** the word from your sentence that answers the question on the front of the tab.

Other Suggestions for a *Tab Book* Foldable

You may also use a *tab book* foldable to practice verb conjugations. You would need to make six tabs instead of five. Write a verb and a tense on the bottom edge and write the pronouns on the front of each tab. Under each tab, write the corresponding verb form.

You may wish to use a *tab book* foldable to practice new vocabulary words. Leave extra space on the bottom edge. Choose five or six vocabulary words and write each one on a tab.

You may also use a *tab book* to practice the subjunctive. On the top of each tab, write an expression that requires the subjunctive, for example **Es imposible que...** . Then open each tab and write a sentence using that expression with the subjunctive.

Single Picture Frame

Dibujar y escribir Use this *single picture frame* to help you illustrate the stories you write.

Step 1 **Fold** a sheet of paper (8½" x 11") in half like a *hamburger*.

Step 2 **Open** the *hamburger* and gently roll one side of the *hamburger* toward the valley. Try not to crease the roll.

Step 3 **Cut** a rectangle out of the middle of the rolled side of paper, leaving a ½" border and forming a frame.

Step 4 **Fold** another sheet of paper (8½" x 11") in half like a *hamburger*.

Step 5 **Apply** glue to the picture frame and place it inside the *hamburger* fold.

Variation:
• Place a picture behind the frame and glue the edges of the frame to the other side of the *hamburger* fold. This locks the picture in place.
• Cut out only three sides of the rolled rectangle. This forms a window with a cover that opens and closes.

Other Suggestions for a *Single Picture Frame* Foldable

You may wish to write about a shopping trip using a *single picture frame* foldable. Before you begin, organize what you will say by drawing your path through the shops at the market, through the supermarket, or through the mall. You can then write about the shopping trip using your drawings as a guide.

Work in small groups. Each student should create a *single picture frame* foldable with a picture glued into it. You may either cut out a magazine picture or draw your own, although it should be fairly complex. Then give your foldable to another member of the group who will write sentences about what is in the picture and what people in the picture are doing. That student will pass it on to a third student who will write sentences about what is not in the picture and what people in the picture are not doing. The foldables can be passed to additional students to see if they can add more sentences.

FOLDABLES

Minibook

Mi autobiografía Use this *minibook* organizer to write and illustrate your autobiography. Before you begin to write, think about the many things concerning yourself that you have the ability to write about in Spanish. On the left pages, draw the events of your life in chronological order. On the right, write about your drawings.

Step 1 **Fold** a sheet of paper (8½" x 11") in half like a *hot dog*.

Step 2 **Fold** it in half again like a *hamburger*.

Step 3 Then **fold** in half again, forming eight sections.

Step 4 **Open** the fold and **cut** the eight sections apart.

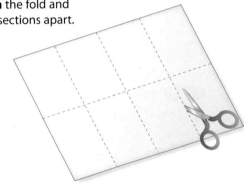

Step 5 **Place** all eight sections in a stack and fold in half like a *hamburger*.

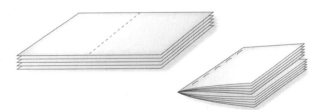

Step 6 **Staple** along the center fold line. **Glue** the front and back sheets into a construction paper cover.

Other Suggestions for a *Minibook* Foldable

Work in pairs to practice new verbs and verb forms using a *minibook* foldable. Illustrate different verbs on the left pages. If it is not clear what pronoun is required, you should write the pronoun under the drawing, for instance to differentiate between *we* and *they*. Then trade *minibooks* and write sentences to go with each picture on the right pages, using the new verb and the pronoun illustrated or indicated.

A *minibook* foldable can be used to help practice the imperfect tense. On each page, draw a picture of an activity that you enjoyed doing frequently. Below each picture, write a sentence describing what was happening. Remember to use the imperfect and to stick to the words you already know in Spanish.

Paper File Folder

Las emociones Use this *paper file folder* organizer to keep track of happenings or events that cause you to feel a certain way.

Step 1 **Fold** four sheets of paper (8½" x 11") in half like a *hamburger*. Leave one side one inch longer than the other side.

Step 2 On each sheet, **fold** the one-inch tab over the short side, forming an envelope-like fold.

Step 3 **Place** the four sheets side-by-side, then move each fold so that the tabs are exposed.

Step 4 Moving left to right, **cut** staggered tabs in each fold, 2⅛" wide. Fold the tabs upward.

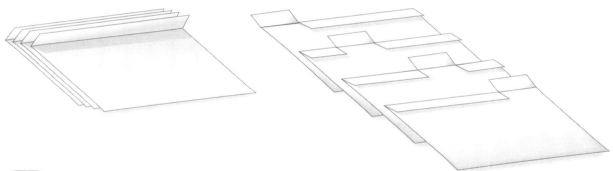

Step 5 **Glue** the ends of the folders together. On each tab, write an emotion you sometimes feel. Pay attention to when it is that you feel happy, sad, nervous, etc. Describe the situation in Spanish and file it in the correct pocket.

Other Suggestions for a *Paper File Folder* Foldable

You may use a *paper file folder* organizer to keep track of verbs and verb forms. You should make a folder for each type of regular verb and for each type of irregular verb. Write the conjugations for some important verbs in each category and file them in the *paper file folder* organizer. Add new tenses to the existing cards and new verbs as you learn them.

A *paper file folder* organizer can be useful for keeping notes on the cultural information that you will learn. You may wish to make categories for different types of cultural information and add index cards to them as you learn new facts and concepts about the target cultures.

Envelope Fold

Un viaje especial Use this *envelope fold* to make a hidden picture or to write secret clues about a city in the Spanish-speaking world you would like to visit.

Step 1 **Fold** a sheet of paper into a *taco* to form a square. Cut off the leftover piece.

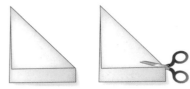

Step 2 **Open** the folded *taco* and refold it the opposite way, forming another *taco* and an X-fold pattern.

Step 3 **Open** the *taco fold* and fold the corners toward the center point of the X, forming a small square.

Step 4 **Trace** this square onto another sheet of paper. Cut and glue it to the inside of the envelope. Pictures can be drawn under the tabs.

Step 5 Use this foldable to **draw** a picture of the city you would like to visit. Or if you prefer, **write** clues about the city and have your classmates raise one tab at a time until they can guess what city the picture represents. Number the tabs in the order in which they are to be opened.

Other Suggestions for an *Envelope Fold* Foldable

An *envelope fold* can be useful for practicing vocabulary related to airports, trains, technology, or driving. Draw a scene that depicts many of the vocabulary words. Then write on each of the four flaps the new words that are represented under that flap. You could also give the picture to a partner and have the partner fill in the words.

You may want to use an *envelope fold* to review a selection you have read. Depict a scene from the selection on the paper covered by the tabs. Number the tabs in the order they are to be opened and have a partner open the tabs one at a time to guess what scene is illustrated. The partner should then write a description of the scenes.

Large Sentence Strips

El presente y el pasado Use these *large sentence strips* to help you compare and contrast activities in the past and in the present.

Step 1 Take two sheets of paper (8½" x 11") and **fold** into *hamburgers*. Cut along the fold lines, making four half sheets. (Use as many half sheets as necessary for additional pages to your book.)

Step 2 **Fold** each half sheet in half like a *hot dog*.

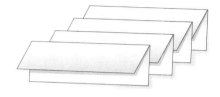

Step 3 Place the folds side-by-side and **staple** them together on the left side.

Step 4 About one inch from the stapled edge, **cut** the front page of each folded section up to the top. These cuts form flaps that can be raised and lowered.

Step 5 To make a half-cover, use a sheet of construction paper one inch longer than the book. **Glue** the back of the last sheet to the construction paper strip, leaving one inch on the left side to fold over and cover the original staples. Staple this half-cover in place.

Step 6 With a friend, **write** sentences on the front of the flap, either in the present tense or in the past tense. Then switch your books of sentence strips and write the opposite tense inside under the flaps.

Other Suggestions for a *Large Sentence Strips* Foldable

You may work in pairs to use *large sentence strips* to practice using direct and/or indirect object pronouns. On the front of each flap, write full sentences that have direct or indirect objects or both. Then trade sentence strips. You and your partner will each write sentences under the flaps replacing the direct or indirect objects with object pronouns.

Large sentence strips can help you contrast summer and winter activities. On the front of each flap, write sentences about activities that you do in either summer or winter. Under each flap, you should write that in the other season you do not do that activity, and you should tell what you do instead. This may be done as an individual or a partner activity.

You may use *large sentence strips* to practice using verbs that can be used reflexively and nonreflexively. Write a sentence using a reflexive verb on the outside of each flap. Under the flap, write a sentence using the same verb nonreflexively.

FOLDABLES

Project Board With Tabs

Diversiones favoritas Use this *project board with tabs* to display a visual about your favorite movie or event. Be sure to make it as attractive as possible to help convince others to see it.

Step 1 **Draw** a large illustration, a series of small illustrations, or write on the front of a sheet of paper.

Step 2 **Pinch** and slightly fold the sheet of paper at the point where a tab is desired on the illustrated piece of paper. Cut into the paper on the fold. Cut straight in, then cut up to form an L. When the paper is unfolded, it will form a tab with the illustration on the front.

Step 3 After all tabs have been cut, **glue** this front sheet onto a second sheet of paper. Place glue around all four edges and in the middle, away from tabs.

Step 4 **Write** or draw under the tabs. If the project is made as a bulletin board using butcher paper, tape or glue smaller sheets of paper under the tabs.

Think of favorite scenes from a movie or cultural event that you enjoyed and draw them on the front of the tabs. Underneath the tabs write a description of the scene or tell why you liked it. It might be fun to not put a title on the project board and just hang it up and let classmates guess the name of the movie or event you are describing.

Other Suggestions for a *Project Board With Tabs* Foldable

You may wish to use a *project board with tabs* to practice your formal commands. Think of the food words you know in Spanish and use them to create a recipe of your own. Draw a small picture of each ingredient in the order you will use it in your recipe. Next, lift each tab and write instructions about how to prepare each ingredient for your recipe using formal commands. For a more complex recipe, combine two or more *project boards with tabs.*

You may also use a *project board with tabs* to illustrate a party, museum, sport, or concert. Draw one aspect of it on the outside of the tab and write a description of your drawing under the tab.

You may work in pairs to practice the comparative and superlative. Each of you will make a *project board with tabs.* On the outside of each tab, draw a different comparison or superlative. Then trade with your partner and under each tab write a sentence describing the other's illustrations.

You may also wish to use a *project board with tabs* to practice the use of object pronouns. Draw a series of scenes involving two or more people on the outside of the tabs. Write sentences using object pronouns describing the people's conversations.

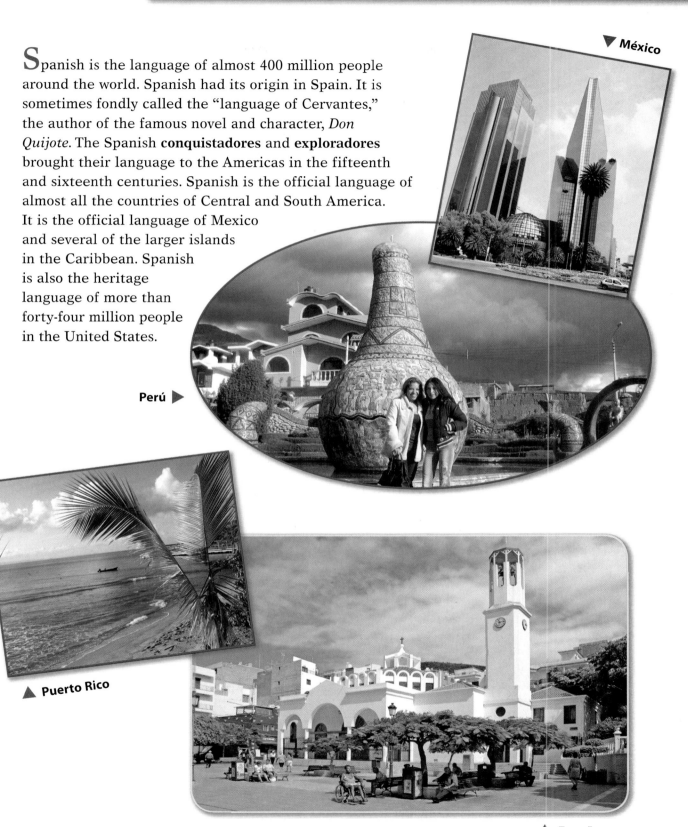

Spanish is the language of almost 400 million people around the world. Spanish had its origin in Spain. It is sometimes fondly called the "language of Cervantes," the author of the famous novel and character, *Don Quijote.* The Spanish **conquistadores** and **exploradores** brought their language to the Americas in the fifteenth and sixteenth centuries. Spanish is the official language of almost all the countries of Central and South America. It is the official language of Mexico and several of the larger islands in the Caribbean. Spanish is also the heritage language of more than forty-four million people in the United States.

▼ **México**

Perú ▶

▲ **Puerto Rico**

▲ **España**

OCÉANO ÁRTICO

Mar de Beaufort

Bahía de Baffin

Mar de Bering

Golfo de Alaska

CANADÁ

Mar del Labrador

AMÉRICA DEL NORTE

ESTADOS UNIDOS

OCÉANO ATLÁNTICO

MÉXICO

Golfo de México

Bahía de Hudson

OCÉANO PACÍFICO

MAR CARIBE

VENEZUELA

GUYANA
SURINAM
GUAYANA FRANCESA

COLOMBIA

ECUADOR

AMÉRICA DEL SUR

PERÚ

BRASIL

SAMOA

POLINESIA FRANCESA

BOLIVIA

PARAGUAY

TONGA

URUGUAY

CHILE   ARGENTINA

GOLFO DE MÉXICO

BAHAMAS

TURCAS Y CAICOS (R.U.)

OCÉANO ATLÁNTICO

CUBA

PUERTO RICO (EE.UU.)

ISLAS VÍRGENES (EE.UU. y R.U.)

MÉXICO

HAITÍ

REPÚBLICA DOMINICANA

ANTIGUA Y BARBUDA

BELICE

JAMAICA

SAN CRISTÓBAL-NEVIS

GUADALUPE (FR.)

GUATEMALA

DOMINICA

MARTINICA (FR.)

HONDURAS

MAR CARIBE

SANTA LUCÍA

EL SALVADOR

SAN VICENTE Y GRENADINES

NICARAGUA

ARUBA

GRANADA

BARBADOS

TRINIDAD Y TOBAGO

COSTA RICA

PANAMÁ

VENEZUELA

OCÉANO PACÍFICO

COLOMBIA

GUYANA

SURINAM

EL MUNDO HISPANOHABLANTE

España

OCÉANO ATLÁNTICO

FRANCIA

MAR CANTÁBRICO

Golfo
de Vizcaya

La Coruña

Santander

San
Sebastián

Oviedo

Asturias

Cantabria

Bilbao

Roncesvalles

ANDORRA

Santiago de
Compostela

CORDILLERA CANTÁBRICA

*País
Vasco*

Pamplona

LOS PIRINEOS

Galicia

León

Burgos

Navarra

Rioja

Río Ebro

Cataluña

Castilla y León

Zaragoza

Barcelona

Valladolid

Río Duero

Aragón

Salamanca

Segovia

Río Tajo

Ávila

SIERRA DE GUADARRAMA

Madrid

PORTUGAL

Madrid

E S P A Ñ A

*Comunidad
Valenciana*

Islas baleares

Menorca

Palma

Mallorca

Castilla-la Mancha

Valencia

Ibiza

Río Guadiana

Formentera

Lisboa

Extremadura

Alicante

**MAR
MEDITERRÁNEO**

Murcia

Murcia

Río Guadalquivir

Cartagena

Córdoba

Sevilla

Granada

Andalucía

SIERRA NEVADA

Jerez de la
Frontera

Málaga

COSTA DEL SOL

Cádiz

Marbella
Estepona

Gibraltar (R.U.)

Estrecho de Gibraltar

Ceuta (Esp.)

Tánger

Melilla (Esp.)

OCÉANO
ATLÁNTICO

ARGELIA

Islas Canarias

La Palma

Santa Cruz
de Tenerife

Lanzarote

Gomera

Fuerteventura

Tenerife

Las Palmas

Hierro

*Gran
Canaria*

MARRUECOS

MARRUECOS

ÁFRICA

OCÉANO ATLÁNTICO

SAHARA
OCCIDENTAL

MAR CARIBE

OCÉANO ATLÁNTICO

Barranquilla
Cartagena
Maracaibo
Caracas
Lago de Maracaibo
Río Orinoco
VENEZUELA
GUYANA
SURINAM
GUAYANA FRANCESA
Medellín
Río Magdalena
Santafé de Bogotá
COLOMBIA
Cali

Ecuador
Otavalo
Quito
ECUADOR
Guayaquil
Cuenca
Islas Galápagos (Ecuador)

Río Amazonas

PERÚ
El Callao
Lima
Cuzco
Lago Titicaca
La Paz
Cochabamba
Santa Cruz
Sucre
BOLIVIA

BRASIL
Brasília

Trópico de Capricornio

CORDILLERA DE LOS ANDES

PARAGUAY
Asunción

CHILE
Vicuña
Córdoba
Río Paraná
Valparaíso
Santiago
Rosario
URUGUAY
Montevideo
Buenos Aires
La Plata
Río de la Plata
ARGENTINA
Mar del Plata

OCÉANO PACÍFICO

OCÉANO ATLÁNTICO

Puerto Montt

PATAGONIA

Estrecho de Magallanes
Islas Malvinas (R.U.)
Tierra del Fuego
Punta Arenas
Cabo de Hornos

EL MUNDO HISPANOHABLANTE

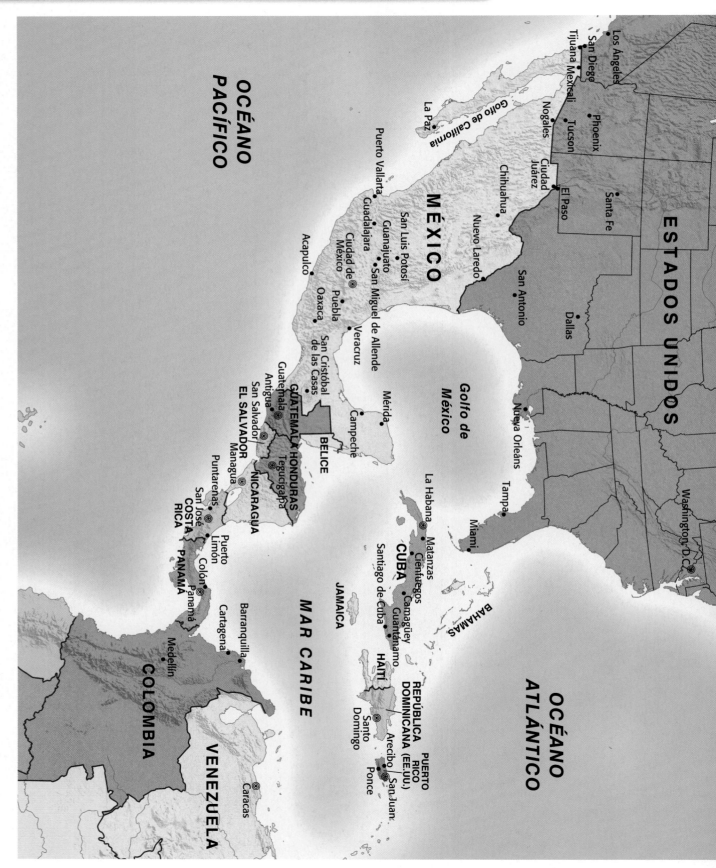

OCÉANO PACÍFICO

Los Angeles
San Diego
Tijuana Mexicali
La Paz
Nogales
Tucson
Phoenix
Ciudad Juárez
Chihuahua
Santa Fe
El Paso
Nuevo Laredo
Puerto Vallarta
San Luis Potosí
Guanajuato
Guadalajara
San Antonio
Dallas
Acapulco
Ciudad de México
San Miguel de Allende
Oaxaca
Puebla
Veracruz
MÉXICO
ESTADOS UNIDOS
San Cristóbal de las Casas
Guatemala
Antigua
San Salvador
EL SALVADOR
GUATEMALA
HONDURAS
BELICE
Campeche
Mérida
Golfo de México
Nueva Orleáns
Tampa
Miami
Managua
Tegucigalpa
NICARAGUA
Puntarenas
San José
COSTA RICA
PANAMÁ
Puerto Limón
Colón
Panamá
Cartagena
Barranquilla
Medellín
COLOMBIA
VENEZUELA
Caracas
MAR CARIBE
JAMAICA
La Habana
Matanzas
Cienfuegos
Santiago de Cuba
Camagüey
Guantánamo
CUBA
BAHAMAS
HAITÍ
REPÚBLICA DOMINICANA
Santo Domingo
Arecibo
PUERTO RICO (EE.UU.)
San Juan
Ponce
OCÉANO ATLÁNTICO
Washington, D.C.
Golfo de California

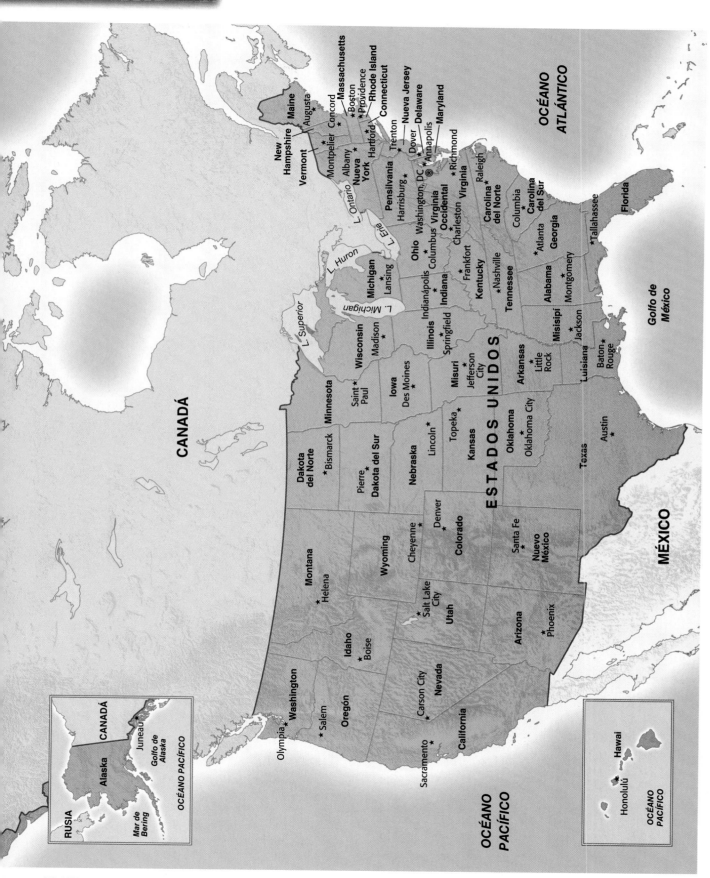

Massachusetts
Rhode Island
New Hampshire
Maine
Augusta
Concord
Boston
Providence
Connecticut
Montpelier
Albany
Hartford
Nueva Jersey
Vermont
Nueva York
Trenton
Dover
Delaware
Maryland
Pensilvania
Harrisburg
Annapolis
Richmond
L. Ontario
Washington, DC
Virginia
Raleigh
OCÉANO
ATLÁNTICO
L. Erie
Ohio
Columbus
Virginia
Occidental
Charleston
Carolina
del Norte
Columbia
Florida
Tallahassee
L. Huron
Michigan
Lansing
Indianápolis
Frankfort
Carolina
del Sur
Atlanta
Georgia
Illinois
Indiana
Kentucky
Nashville
Tennessee
Alabama
Montgomery
L. Superior
L. Michigan
Springfield
Misisipi
Jackson
Golfo de
México
Wisconsin
Madison
Iowa
Des Moines
Misuri
Jefferson
City
Arkansas
Little
Rock
Luisiana
Baton
Rouge
Minnesota
Saint
Paul
CANADÁ
Dakota
del Norte
Bismarck
Dakota del Sur
Pierre
Nebraska
Lincoln
Topeka
Kansas
Oklahoma
Oklahoma City
ESTADOS UNIDOS
Texas
Austin
MÉXICO
Denver
Colorado
Cheyenne
Santa Fe
Nuevo
México
Wyoming
Montana
Helena
Salt Lake
City
Utah
Arizona
Phoenix
Idaho
Boise
Washington
Salem
Oregón
Carson City
Nevada
OCÉANO
PACÍFICO
Olympia
California
Sacramento

Hawai
Honolulú
OCÉANO
PACÍFICO

EL MUNDO HISPANOHABLANTE

GeoVistas

Un excursionista mira la majestuosa vista del Fitz Roy y del Cerro Torre en el Parque Nacional de los Glaciares en la Patagonia, Argentina.

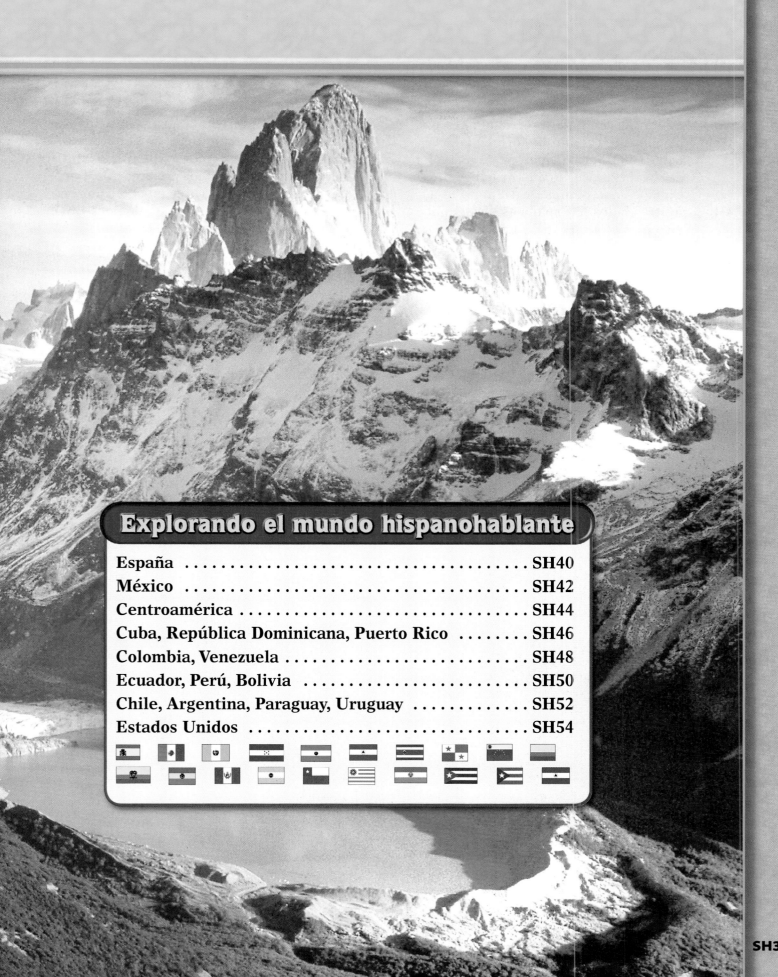

Explorando el mundo hispanohablante

GeoVista

Geografía España y Portugal en el sudoeste de Europa forman la Península Ibérica, nombre que viene de los iberos, sus primeros habitantes. Como es una península, tiene agua a los tres lados. Y España es el segundo país más montañoso de Europa después de Suiza.

Clima España tiene una variedad de climas. Hay mucha lluvia en el nordeste donde todo es de color verde. En el centro donde todo es de color oro-amarillo, hace mucho frío en invierno y mucho calor en verano. El sur es una región de poca lluvia y mucho calor (aunque los picos de la Sierra Nevada están cubiertos de nieve).

Picos de Europa, Asturias ▲

Playa de Nerja ▲

Gente El español es una mezcla de las muchas razas que han habitado la península. En Galicia, la gente tiene el pelo rubio o rojo con ojos azules o verdes—influencias de los celtas. En el sur hay gente morena con el pelo negro y ojos castaños—influencias de los árabes.

Alcázar de Segovia ▼

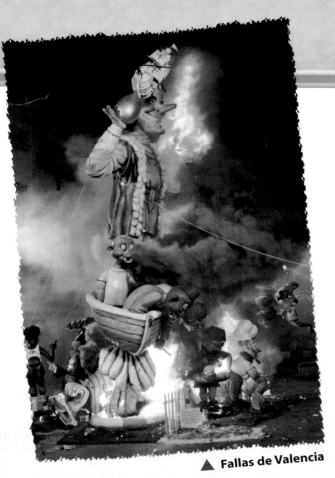

▲ Fallas de Valencia

Ferias España es famosa por sus ferias. En Valencia se celebran las Fallas en el mes de marzo. Los valencianos hacen fallas o sea figuras cómicas. Las exhiben por toda la ciudad y a la medianoche del 19 de marzo se queman, iluminando toda la ciudad.

El AVE—El tren de alta velocidad española en Zaragoza ▼

Museo Guggenheim en Bilbao ▼

Hoy España se ha modernizado mucho en los últimos cincuenta años. Tiene uno de los trenes y aeropuertos más modernos del mundo. Las ciudades de Madrid y Barcelona figuran entre las más sofisticadas de Europa. Y el nuevo museo Guggenheim en la ciudad industrial de Bilbao se considera una joya artística y arquitectónica.

Políticamente España se divide en diecisiete comunidades autónomas.

GeoVista

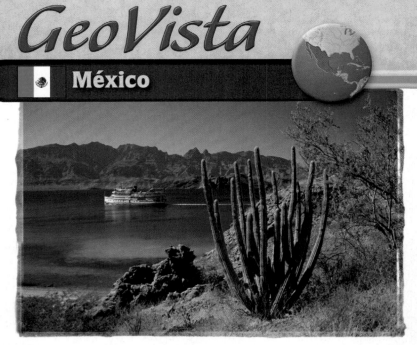

▲ **Mar de Cortés en Baja California**

Clima Templado, cálido, lluvioso, seco, húmedo son todos adjetivos que describen el clima de las diferentes regiones de México. Se dice que en México se encuentran todos los climas del globo terrestre.

Alfombras de flores para una fiesta en Patambán ▶

Geografía México, que forma parte de Norteamérica, es un país vasto, cuatro veces mayor que España y Francia. Es un país de una gran variedad geográfica con grandes mesetas, desiertos, montañas, sierras volcánicas y unos 8.000 kilómetros de costa en el este y el oeste del país.

Gente En cuanto a la composición étnica de México un gran porcentaje de sus habitantes son de origen indígena y europeo. El idioma oficial es el español y además se hablan sesenta y seis lenguas autóctonas. La influencia indígena se ve en los majestuosos monumentos históricos de las civilizaciones maya, tolteca, olmeca y azteca entre otras.

▼ **Antes de una boda en Coyoacán**

▼ **Vista de Toluca**

Ferias México, el país de los mariachis, es un país de música y fiestas. Cada ciudad y pueblo tiene sus ferias locales, muchas de ellas de índole religiosa. Dos fiestas populares por todo el país son el Día de los Muertos que les rinde honor a los parientes difuntos y la fiesta en honor de la Virgen de Guadalupe, la santa patrona de todo México que se celebra el 12 de diciembre.

▲ **Comida mexicana**

▲ **Castillo o pirámide de Kukulkán en Chichén Itzá**

▼ **Fábrica de cemento en Monterrey**

Hoy El México de hoy se divide en treinta y un estados y el Distrito Federal—término que se refiere a la capital, la Ciudad de México, una de las ciudades más grandes del mundo. México es un país de contrastes con ciudades industriales como Monterrey y Tampico y remotos pueblos indígenas en Chiapas y Oaxaca.

GeoVista

▲ **Una joven indígena de Guatemala**

Gente Hay una gran diversidad de gente en Centroamérica. La población de la mayoría de los países es de origen indígena y europeo. Los muchos grupos indígenas que habitan Centroamérica no comparten todas las mismas costumbres ni tradiciones. Costa Rica es el país que más europeos tiene; muchos son del norte de España. En la costa oriental de Costa Rica hay gente de ascendencia africana. Panamá es el país de mayor influencia africana.

Estela maya en Copán, Honduras ▼

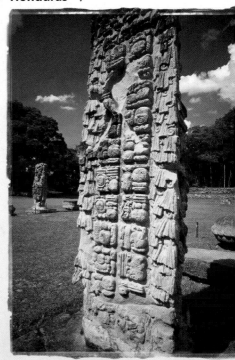

Geografía Centroamérica es un istmo que fusiona Norte y Sudamérica. Tiene una gran variedad de geografía con montañas que corren del norte al sur en el centro del istmo, selvas tropicales de una vegetación densa a lo largo de la costa del Caribe y en la costa del Pacífico playas de arena volcánica negra.

Cataratas del río Azul en Costa Rica ▼

La isla de Ometepe y el volcán de la Concepción, Nicaragua ▼

▲ **Avenida Balboa en la ciudad de Panamá**

Clima Los centroamericanos dividen su año en dos estaciones—el invierno, la estación calurosa y lluviosa, y el verano—la estación caliente y seca. El invierno es por lo general de mayo a noviembre. Muchas de las ciudades más importantes de Centroamérica como Tegucigalpa y San José son conocidas como ciudades de «primavera eterna».

Hoy Al hablar de Centroamérica es imposible generalizar. La situación económica y política es diferente en cada país y cada país tiene su propia atracción—pueblos coloniales e indígenas en Guatemala; lagos y volcanes en Nicaragua; parques nacionales de interés ecológico en Costa Rica; empresas bancarias y nuevos rascacielos en Panamá. Cada país tiene algo suyo.

▼ **Barcos haciendo la travesía del canal de Panamá**

GEOVISTA

GeoVista

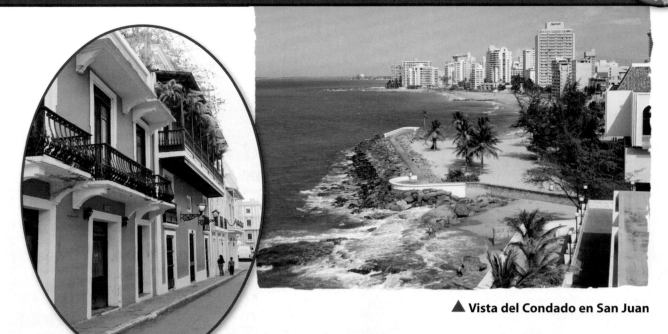

▲ Vista del Condado en San Juan

▲ Callecita típica del Viejo San Juan de Puerto Rico

◄ Estatua de Cristóbal Colón en Santo Domingo

Geografía Las islas llamadas las Grandes Antillas se encuentran en el mar Caribe al este de Estados Unidos. Tres de ellas son hispanohablantes y la más cercana de Estados Unidos es Cuba a solo 90 kilómetros de Cayo Cabo. La Española se divide en dos naciones—la República Dominicana de habla española y Haití de habla criolla. Más al este está Puerto Rico, un estado asociado de Estados Unidos. Las tres islas son montañosas y en Puerto Rico, por ejemplo, en un pico del centro del país se puede ver el Atlántico mirando hacia el norte y el Caribe hacia el sur.

▲ Escena montañosa de Puerto Rico

Clima Las tres islas tienen un clima tropical. Hace calor durante todo el año con la sola excepción de algunas bajas de temperaturas en las montañas sobre todo de noche. Suele llover más de junio a septiembre. Como son regiones tropicales cultivan una gran variedad de productos agrícolas tropicales como el azúcar, el coco, la banana y muchas otras frutas tropicales.

▲ Castillo del Morro a la entrada del puerto de La Habana

Gente En las tres islas se ve mucha influencia africana. Aunque hay africanos y europeos un gran porcentaje de la población tiene en sus venas sangre africana y europea. Hay poquísima influencia indígena porque la población indígena fue diezmada poco después de la llegada de los conquistadores. Murieron del trabajo forzado y de muchas enfermedades traídas por los europeos. Cada isla se conoce por sus sonidos y ritmos del tambor, la guajira y las marimbas. La gente es conocida por su viva personalidad «de sal y pimienta».

Estatua de José Martí, el gran poeta y héroe cubano ▼

Una de las muchas playas de la República Dominicana ▶

GEOVISTA

GeoVista

▲ **Vista panorámica de Bogotá**

Geografía Colombia y Venezuela en el norte del continente de Sudamérica tienen en común una variedad de características geográficas. Cada país tiene una costa larga; Colombia es el único país sudamericano con costa en el Pacífico y en el Caribe. Tienen también sierras andinas, grandes extensiones de llanos y sabanas y selvas tropicales en la cuenca del río Amazonas y sus tributarios.

Ciclistas en la Candelaria—el casco antiguo de Bogotá donde se prohíbe el tráfico vehicular los domingos. ▼

◀ **Medellín, ciudad colombiana famosa por sus flores**

Clima Como ambos países están cerca del ecuador, son cálidos y no hay mucha variación de temperatura durante todo el año—con una excepción. La temperatura cambiará según la altitud. Puede hacer mucho calor al nivel del mar mientras hace mucho frío en las montañas. Hay dos estaciones—el verano o la estación seca y el invierno o la estación lluviosa. Las estaciones varían según la región y están cambiando debido a la influencia de «El Niño».

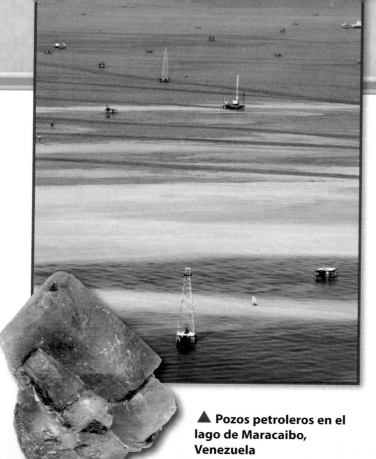

Hoy Más del 90 por ciento de los 46 millones de colombianos viven en la parte occidental del país que incluye la región andina y las dos costas. De los 26 millones de venezolanos, la mayoría vive en Caracas y en las ciudades de la costa.

Venezuela es un gran productor de petróleo y también de oro y diamantes. Colombia es famosa por la calidad de sus esmeraldas y café y Medellín, la segunda ciudad del país, se conoce como la «capital mundial de orquídeas». La tierra de los dos países es rica en una variedad de minerales.

▲ Pozos petroleros en el lago de Maracaibo, Venezuela

▲ Esmeralda preciosa de Colombia

Gente En cada país entre el 70 y el 75 por ciento de la población es una mezcla de indígenas, europeos y africanos. Se ve mayor influencia africana en las regiones litorales que en las montañas. Si lees un libro de turismo, leerás que los venezolanos y colombianos son gente simpática, cortés y abierta y no les molesta nada entablar una conversación con extranjeros.

▲ Turistas en una excursión en una canoa en la cuenca del Orinoco en Venezuela

Salto Ángel en Venezuela, dieciséis veces más alto que los saltos de Niágara ▼

GeoVista

Geografía Aunque no son los únicos países con majestuosos picos andinos, son Ecuador, Perú y Bolivia los países que se consideran la región andina. Los Andes corren del norte al sur. Ecuador y Perú tienen tres zonas geográficas—la costa en el oeste, la sierra o cordillera en el centro y la selva tropical en el este. Bolivia es el único país de la región que no tiene costa. Se divide en dos cordilleras separadas por un altiplano ventoso. Como sus vecinos, Perú y Ecuador, tiene selvas tropicales en el este.

Universitarios en Pichincha, Ecuador ▲

Paseo a orillas del río Guayas en Guayaquil, Ecuador ▼

Flamencos en la laguna Hedionda en Bolivia ▼

Clima Al mirar el mapa verás que el ecuador cruza el país de Ecuador y no queda muy lejos de Perú. Sin embargo en la costa de Ecuador y Perú no hace mucho calor y no llueve mucho. Una corriente fría llamada la corriente Humboldt pasa por la costa bajando la temperatura y la precipitación. En la sierra hay un clima más templado. La temperatura suele variar de unos 40 a 70 grados aunque unos picos andinos se ven cubiertos de nieve durante todo el año. En las selvas del este el clima es tropical y hace mucho calor.

◀ **Músicos tocando la zampoña en Cuzco**

Gente En cada uno de los países andinos un 50 por ciento de la población total vive en la sierra. Ecuador, Perú y Bolivia son los países de mayor población indígena pura o una mezcla de indígenas y europeos.

▲ **Plaza de Armas en Lima**

Hoy Los tres países son productores de petróleo pero no en cantidad tan grande como en Venezuela. Bolivia produce gas natural y estaño; Perú, hierro y fosfatos. Aunque La Paz es la capital de Bolivia y Quito es la capital de Ecuador, Sucre en Bolivia y Guayaquil en Ecuador son centros de gran importancia comercial y financiero.

◀ **Paceños admirando la vista de su capital, La Paz.**

GeoVista

Geografía La geografía de Chile, Argentina, Uruguay y Paraguay, los países del Cono sur, varía mucho. Chile, un país largo y estrecho, es conocido por sus picos andinos y el Atacama—el desierto más seco del mundo. Argentina es un país de llanuras y pampas donde pace el mejor ganado del mundo. Argentina y Chile comparten la Patagonia que se extiende desde el estrecho de Magallanes hasta la famosa región de los lagos. Uruguay, el país más pequeño de Sudamérica, es también una tierra de llanos conocidos por sus estancias grandes. Paraguay, como su vecino andino—Bolivia— no tiene costa. En el este, Paraguay tiene un bosque tropical y en el oeste el Chaco, una zona árida.

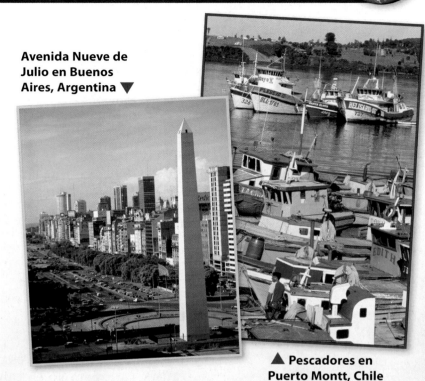

Avenida Nueve de Julio en Buenos Aires, Argentina ▼

▲ Pescadores en Puerto Montt, Chile

Clima La mayor parte del Cono sur goza de un clima templado con cuatro estaciones. Pero la Patagonia tiene un clima frío, lluvioso y ventoso durante casi todo el año. La tierra y el clima de una gran parte de Argentina, Chile y Uruguay son propicios para la agricultura. En el Chaco, la región seca de Paraguay, se explota mucha madera.

Pingüinos en Patagonia ▼

Vista del Fitz Roy al amanecer en el Parque Nacional de los Glaciares en la Patagonia argentina ▼

▲ Vista de Punta del Este, Uruguay

Gente De todas las regiones de Latinoamérica la que tiene la menor influencia indígena es el Cono sur con la excepción de Paraguay. Igual que a Estados Unidos emigraron muchos europeos a Argentina, Chile y Uruguay. Hay mucha gente de ascendencia española, italiana, británica, alemana y en menor grado del este de Europa. En Paraguay, siguen viviendo muchos guaraníes, los indígenas de la región. Paraguay tiene dos idiomas oficiales—el español y el guaraní, y la moneda del país se llama el guaraní.

Gauchos en las pampas argentinas ▼

▲ Valle de la Luna en el desierto de Atacama en Chile

GEOVISTA

GeoVista

Estados Unidos

Gente Es posible que Estados Unidos sea el país de población más heterogénea del mundo. Hay indígenas americanos, gente que ha emigrado de todas partes de Europa, grandes grupos de asiáticos y mucha gente de ascendencia africana cuyos antepasados llegaron en gran parte como gente esclavizada. Actualmente hay más de cuarenta y cuatro millones de latinos de todas partes de España y Latinoamérica. El grupo latino mayoritario son los mexicanoamericanos y sigue llegando gente sobre todo de La República Dominicana, Centroamérica, Ecuador y Perú, entre otros. En algunos lugares de Estados Unidos se oye más español, o por lo menos tanto español como inglés.

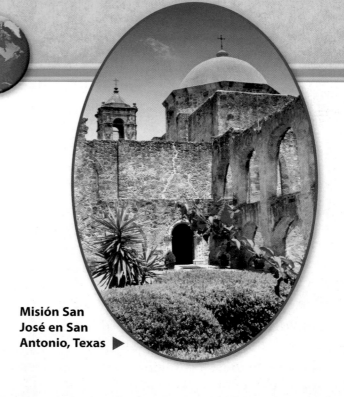

Misión San José en San Antonio, Texas ▶

Washington Heights en el norte de Manhattan ▼

▼Librería en Miami, Florida

Desfile en la calle 18 en Chicago para celebrar el día de la Independencia de México ▶

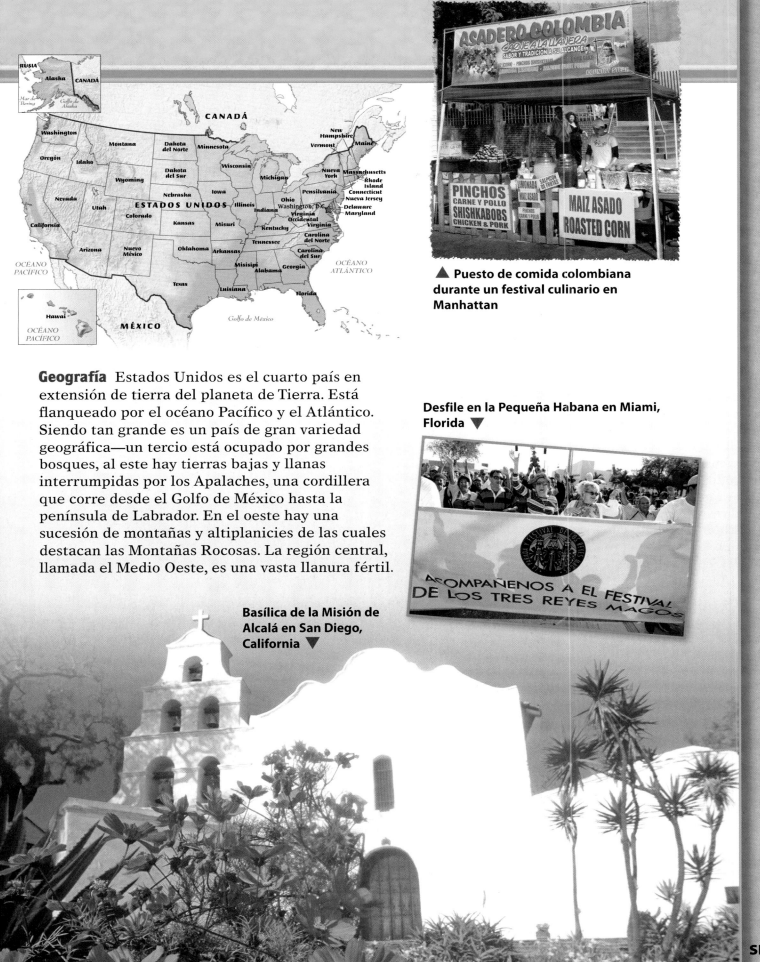

Puesto de comida colombiana durante un festival culinario en Manhattan

Geografía Estados Unidos es el cuarto país en extensión de tierra del planeta de Tierra. Está flanqueado por el océano Pacífico y el Atlántico. Siendo tan grande es un país de gran variedad geográfica—un tercio está ocupado por grandes bosques, al este hay tierras bajas y llanas interrumpidas por los Apalaches, una cordillera que corre desde el Golfo de México hasta la península de Labrador. En el oeste hay una sucesión de montañas y altiplanicies de las cuales destacan las Montañas Rocosas. La región central, llamada el Medio Oeste, es una vasta llanura fértil.

Desfile en la Pequeña Habana en Miami, Florida ▼

Basílica de la Misión de Alcalá en San Diego, California ▼

Preview

In Repaso A, students will review vocabulary associated with home and school. They will also review the present tense of regular verbs, the verbs **ir, dar,** and **estar,** and verbs with an irregular **yo** form in the present tense.

Leveling EACH Activity

The vocabulary and grammar activities within each chapter are marked according to level of difficulty. **E** indicates easy. **A** indicates average. **CH** indicates challenging. Some activities cover a range of difficulty. For example, advanced students will be able to produce more extensive responses while students who learn at a different rate may give less detailed responses. The leveling indicators will help you individualize instruction to best meet your students' needs.

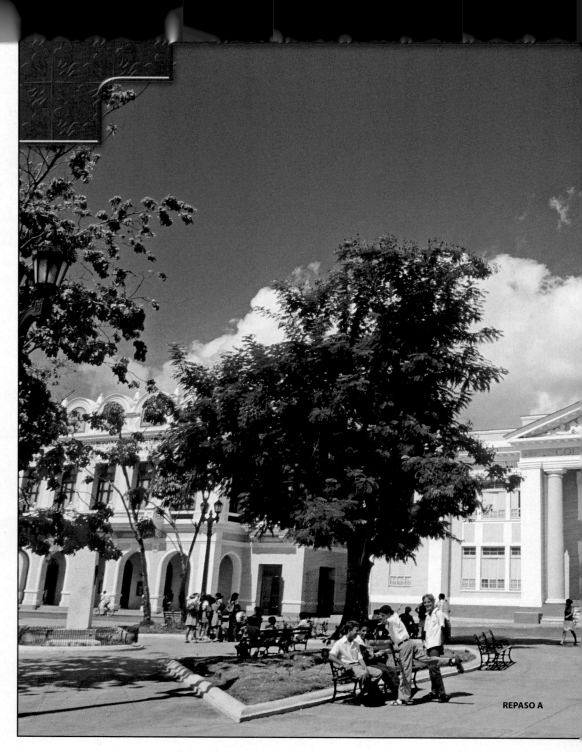

REPASO A

TeacherWorks *Plus*

The **¡Así se dice!** TeacherWorks™ Plus CD-ROM is an all-in-one planner and resource center. You may wish to use several of the following features as you plan and present the Repaso A material: Teacher Edition, Interactive Lesson Planner with Calendar, and Point and Click Access to Teaching Resources including Hotlinks to the Internet.

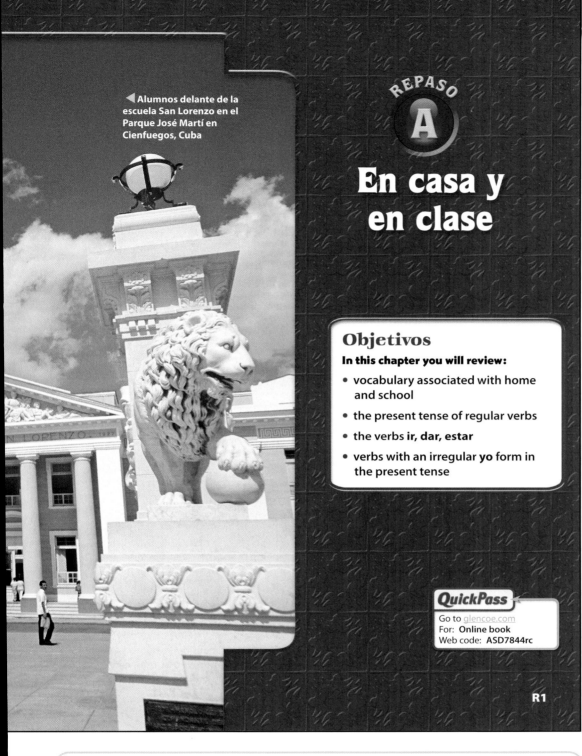

◀ Alumnos delante de la escuela San Lorenzo en el Parque José Martí en Cienfuegos, Cuba

REPASO A

En casa y en clase

Objetivos

In this chapter you will review:

- vocabulary associated with home and school
- the present tense of regular verbs
- the verbs **ir, dar, estar**
- verbs with an irregular **yo** form in the present tense

QuickPass

Go to glencoe.com
For: **Online book**
Web code: **ASD7844rc**

R1

Quia Interactive Online Student Edition found at quia.com allows students to complete activities online and submit them for computer grading for instant feedback or teacher grading with suggestions for what to review. Students can also record speaking activities, listen to chapter audio, and watch the videos that correspond with each chapter. As a teacher you are able to create rosters, set grading parameters, and post assignments for each class. After students complete activities, you can view the results and recommend remediation or review. You can also add your own customized activities for additional student practice.

Repaso A

QuickPass
Go to glencoe.com
For: Vocabulary practice
Web code: ASD7844rc

Resources

- Audio Activities TE, pages R.41–R.42
- Audio CD RC1, Tracks 1–3
- Workbook, pages R.3–R.5
- ExamView® Assessment Suite

Quick Start

Use QS Transparency R.1 or write the following on the board.

Contesta.
1. ¿Estudias español en la escuela?
2. ¿Hablas con tus amigos después de las clases?
3. ¿Escuchas al profesor?
4. ¿Compras un pantalón en la tienda?
5. ¿Miras a la profesora cuando ella habla?

► TEACH
Core Instruction

Step 1 Have students look at pages R2 and R3 as you point to each item and have students repeat.

Step 2 Intersperse your presentation with questions such as ¿Quién prepara la comida? ¿Dónde? ¿Quién pone la mesa? ¿Dónde come la familia? Después de la comida, ¿adónde va la familia? ¿Qué ven? ¿Qué hace papá?

Step 3 Call on students to give additional vocabulary they know related to the topics **en casa** and **en clase.**

Vocabulario 🎧

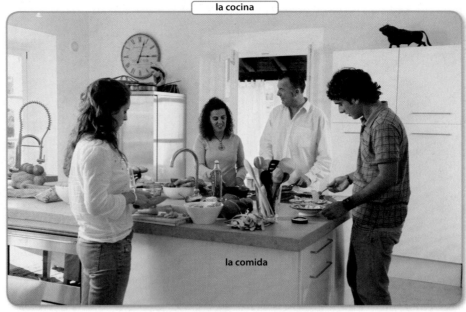

la cocina

la comida

La familia prepara la comida.

el comedor

José pone la mesa.
La familia come en el comedor.

la sala

Después de la comida la familia va a la sala.
En la sala algunos ven la televisión.
Y papá lee una revista.

R2

REPASO A

GLENCOE 🖱 Technology

Online Learning in the Classroom

Have students use QuickPass code ASD7844rc for additional vocabulary practice. They can download audio files of all vocabulary to their computer and/ or MP3 player. They will also have access to a self-check quiz and eGames.

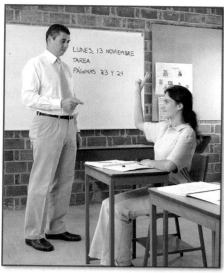

En la escuela los alumnos aprenden
mucho.
El profesor enseña.
Una alumna levanta la mano.
Hace una pregunta.
El profesor contesta la pregunta.

Las hermanas salen de casa.
Van a la escuela.
Van a la escuela a pie.

la computadora

Elena está en su cuarto (de dormir).
Recibe unos correos electrónicos.
Envía correos también.

Differentiation

Multiple Intelligences

You may wish to have **bodily-kinesthetic** learners act out the review vocabulary.
Prepara la comida.
Pone la mesa.
Come.
Va a la sala.
Ve la televisión.
Lee una revista.
Va a la escuela a pie.
Enseña.
Levanta la mano.
Envía un correo electrónico.

Advanced Learners

You may wish to have advanced learners use the vocabulary words in original sentences.

Writing Development

You may wish to have students draw a picture of something happening at home or at school. Then have them write a paragraph about it.

▶ PRACTICE

Leveling EACH Activity

Easy Activities 1, 4
Average Activities 2, 3, 5

Activity ❶ After going over this activity, you may wish to have students make up additional statements.

Activity ❷ This activity can be done orally in class with books closed calling on students at random to answer. It can also be done as a group activity.

Activity ❸ This activity can be done as a game.

Práctica

LEER

❶ Indica en una tabla como la de abajo donde se hace todo.

	en casa	en clase	en casa y en clase
1. Ellos preparan la comida.			
2. Ellos hacen muchas preguntas.			
3. Él enseña.			
4. Usan la computadora.			
5. Reciben y envían correos electrónicos.			
6. Habla en su móvil.			
7. Él lee el periódico después de la comida.			
8. Comen en el comedor.			
9. Ven la televisión en la sala.			
10. Toman apuntes y aprenden mucho.			

HABLAR • ESCRIBIR

❷ Contesta.
1. ¿Dónde prepara la familia la comida?
2. ¿Dónde comen ellos?
3. ¿Adónde van después de la comida?
4. ¿Qué hacen en la sala?
5. ¿A qué hora salen los hermanos para la escuela?
6. ¿Cómo van a la escuela? ¿En el bus escolar, en carro o a pie?
7. ¿Quiénes enseñan en la escuela?
8. ¿Quiénes estudian y aprenden mucho?

❸ **Rompecabezas**

Cambia una letra en cada palabra para formar una palabra nueva.
1. usa
2. todo
3. casa
4. ve
5. son

Answers

❶
1. en casa
2. en clase
3. en clase
4. en casa y en clase
5. en casa
6. en casa
7. en casa
8. en casa
9. en casa
10. en clase

❷
1. La familia prepara la comida en la cocina.
2. Ellos comen en el comedor.
3. Después de la comida van a la sala.
4. En la sala ven la televisión.
5. Los hermanos salen para la escuela a las ____.
6. Van a la escuela en el bus escolar (en carro, a pie).
7. Los profesores enseñan en la escuela.
8. Los alumnos estudian y aprenden mucho.

❸ *Answers will vary but may include:*
1. una, uso, esa, uva
2. tomo, toco, toro
3. cama, caso, cara, cosa
4. va, vi, me, te
5. sin, con, sol

Más práctica

■ Workbook, pp. R3–R5
● StudentWorks™ Plus

LEER • ESCRIBIR

4 Identifica.

1. las tres comidas
2. algunos vegetales
3. algunas frutas
4. algunas carnes
5. lo que lleva una ensalada
6. tu comida favorita
7. lo que pones en la mesa antes de comer
8. a tus parientes
9. la ropa que llevas
10. los cursos que tomas

LEER • HABLAR

5 Parea.

1. dar
2. tomar
3. prestar
4. leer
5. escribir
6. vivir
7. salir
8. conocer
9. asistir

a. atención
b. en la calle Bolívar
c. una fiesta
d. una composición
e. notas (apuntes) en clase
f. a muchos amigos
g. una novela
h. por la mañana
i. a clase

¡Ojo!

Ya sabes que las palabras afines son palabras que se parecen en dos o más idiomas y tienen el mismo significado. Ejemplos son **importante, atleta.** Hay también lo que llamamos «amigos falsos». Son palabras que se parecen en dos idiomas pero no tienen el mismo significado. Ejemplos son **pariente** *(relative)* y **asistir** *(to attend).*

CULTURA
Estos jóvenes de ascendencia maya estudian en una escuela secundaria en el estado de Chiapas, México.

REPASO A

R5

QuickPass

Go to glencoe.com
For: **Conversation practice**
Web code: ASD7844rc

Conversación 🎧

La escuela Abraham Lincoln

Antonio	¡Oye, Roberto! ¿A qué escuela asistes ahora?
Roberto	Asisto a la escuela Abraham Lincoln.
Antonio	¿Llevan los alumnos uniforme a la escuela?
Roberto	¡Uniforme! De ninguna manera. No estamos en Latinoamérica.
Antonio	¿Cómo vas a la escuela? ¿Tomas el bus?
Roberto	No, voy a pie. Salgo de casa muy temprano por la mañana.
Antonio	¿Cuántos cursos tomas este semestre?
Roberto	Cinco. Y algunos son bastante difíciles.

¿Comprendes?

A Contesta según la información en la conversación.

1. ¿A qué escuela asiste Roberto?
2. ¿Asisten Roberto y Antonio a la misma escuela?
3. ¿Sabe Antonio mucho sobre la escuela de Roberto?
4. ¿Cómo va Roberto a la escuela?
5. ¿Cuándo sale de casa?
6. ¿Cuántos cursos toma este semestre?
7. ¿Cómo son algunos de sus cursos?

B Analizando Contesta.

💡 ¿Asiste Roberto a una escuela norteamericana o latinoamericana? Defiende tu respuesta.

▶ TEACH
Core Instruction

Step 1 You may wish to have the students listen to the conversation once using Audio CD RC1.

Step 2 Since this is all review, call on two students to read aloud. Intersperse the reading with the questions from Activity A.

Differentiation
Multiple Intelligences

To engage **bodily-kinesthetic** learners, call on students to come to the front of the room and dramatize the conversation for the class. They should use appropriate gestures, facial expressions, and intonation.

Pre-AP Listening to this conversation on audio CD will help students develop the skills that they need to be successful on the listening portion of the AP exam.

Answers

A

1. Roberto asiste a la escuela Abraham Lincoln.
2. No, Roberto y Antonio no asisten a la misma escuela.
3. No, Antonio no sabe mucho de la escuela de Roberto.
4. Roberto va a la escuela a pie.
5. Sale de casa muy temprano por la mañana.
6. Toma cinco cursos este semestre.
7. Algunos de sus cursos son bastante difíciles.

B *Answers will vary.*

Gramática
Presente de los verbos regulares e irregulares

1. Review the forms of regular **-ar**, **-er**, and **-ir** verbs in the present tense.

	hablar	comer	vivir
yo	hablo	como	vivo
tú	hablas	comes	vives
Ud., él, ella	habla	come	vive
nosotros(as)	hablamos	comemos	vivimos
vosotros(as)	*habláis*	*coméis*	*vivís*
Uds., ellos, ellas	hablan	comen	viven

2. Most irregular verbs are irregular in the **yo** form only. Note that the verbs **ir, dar,** and **estar** are like an **-ar** verb in all forms except **yo.**

	ir	dar	estar
yo	voy	doy	estoy
tú	vas	das	estás
Ud., él, ella	va	da	está
nosotros(as)	vamos	damos	estamos
vosotros(as)	*vais*	*dais*	*estáis*
Uds., ellos, ellas	van	dan	están

3. The following verbs have an irregular **yo** form. All other forms are those of a regular **-er** or **-ir** verb.

hacer	→	hago	saber	→	sé
poner	→	pongo	conocer	→	conozco
traer	→	traigo	producir	→	produzco
salir	→	salgo	conducir	→	conduzco

4. Review the forms of the important irregular verb **ser.**

ser			
yo	soy	nosotros(as)	somos
tú	eres	*vosotros(as)*	*sois*
Ud., él, ella	es	Uds., ellos, ellas	son

REPASO A

R7

Resources

- Audio Activities TE, pages R.43–R.45
- Audio CD RC1, Tracks 6–9
- Workbook, pages R.6–R.7
- Test, pages R.75–R.76
- ExamView® Assessment Suite

Quick Start

Use QS Transparency R.2 or write the following on the board.
Parea los verbos para formar una expresión con los sustantivos.

hablar	música
levantar	uniforme
contestar	inglés
sacar	la pregunta
escuchar	notas buenas
llevar	la mano

▶ TEACH
Core Instruction

Step 1 Have students review the forms of the regular verbs. You may wish to write the verbs on the board and underline their endings.

Step 2 Have students read these verbs across. Only one form is irregular and it follows a pattern: **voy, doy, estoy.**

Step 3 You may wish to have students conjugate these verbs.

Step 4 Have students read the verb **ser.**

 Tips for Success ·······

You may wish to point out to students that most irregular verbs in the present tense are irregular in the **yo** form only.

► PRACTICE

Leveling EACH Activity

Average Activities 1, 2, 3
CHallenging Activities 4, 5, 6

⭐Tips for Success ·······

It is recommended that you go over the grammar activities once in class before they are assigned for homework.

Activity ① This activity can be done orally with books closed calling on students at random.

Differentiation

Advanced Learners

After going over Activity 1, have advanced learners retell as much information as they can in their own words.

Activity ② Go over this activity with students and then have them write it for homework.

CULTURA

Los padres de estos niños venden mantas en el mercado en Sololá, Guatemala. Los niños ayudan de vez en cuando pero ahora les ha captado el interés el móvil.

Práctica

ESCUCHAR • HABLAR

① Personaliza. Da respuestas personales.
1. ¿Cuántas lenguas hablas?
2. ¿A qué escuela asistes?
3. ¿Cómo vas a la escuela?
4. ¿Cuántos cursos tomas este semestre?
5. ¿Cómo son tus cursos?
6. ¿Quién es tu profesor(a) de español?
7. ¿Haces muchas preguntas en clase?
8. ¿Aprendes mucho en la escuela?
9. ¿Llevas tus materiales escolares en una mochila?
10. ¿Conoces a muchos alumnos en tu escuela?

Cultura

Casi todos los aparatos tecnológicos se ven y se usan hasta en zonas muy remotas.

LEER • ESCRIBIR

② Completa.
1. Yo voy y él _____ también.
2. Yo lo sé y ellos lo _____ también.
3. Yo lo pongo aquí y tú lo _____ allí.
4. Yo leo mucho y ustedes _____ mucho también.
5. Yo vivo en California y ellos _____ en Texas.
6. Yo conozco a mucha gente y tú _____ a mucha gente también.
7. Yo conduzco un carro viejo y ella _____ un carro nuevo.
8. Yo hago mucho trabajo y ellos _____ mucho trabajo también.
9. Yo soy alumno(a) y ellas _____ alumnas también.

R8

Answers

①
1. Hablo _____ lenguas.
2. Asisto a la escuela _____.
3. Voy a la escuela en el bus escolar (en carro, a pie).
4. Tomo _____ cursos este semestre.
5. Mis cursos son fáciles (difíciles, interesantes, aburridos).
6. Mi profesor(a) de español es _____.

7. Sí, (No, no) hago muchas preguntas en clase.
8. Sí, (No, no) aprendo mucho en la escuela.
9. Sí, (No, no) llevo mis materiales escolares en una mochila.
10. Sí, (No, no) conozco a muchos alumnos en mi escuela.

②
1. va
2. saben
3. pones
4. leen
5. viven

6. conoces
7. conduce
8. hacen
9. son

HABLAR • ESCRIBIR

3 Contesta.

1. ¿Dónde viven ustedes?
2. ¿A qué escuela asisten ustedes?
3. ¿Cómo van a la escuela?
4. ¿Qué hacen ustedes en la clase de español?
5. ¿A qué hora salen ustedes de la escuela?

LEER • ESCRIBIR

4 Forma frases con los siguientes verbos.

mirar   ver   vivir

comprar   leer   **ir**

escribir

conocer   **poner**   ser   estar

Comunicación

5 Con un compañero(a) de clase discute todas las cosas que haces en casa. Luego tu compañero(a) te va a decir lo que él o ella hace. Comparen sus actividades.

6 Trabaja con un(a) compañero(a). Describe tu día típico en la escuela. Luego tu compañero(a) va a hacer lo mismo. Comparen sus actividades.

CULTURA
Estas muchachas van a una escuela en Buenos Aires, Argentina. ¿Lo pasan bien después de las clases?

REPASO A

R9

Activity 3 Note that this activity has students use the **-amos, -emos,** and **-imos** endings.

Activity 4 Call on several students to read their sentences. The more students hear the verb forms, the better they will be at using them.

Activities 5 and 6 When having students do an open-ended activity with no learning prompts, they are communicating as if they were in a real-life situation. In such a situation, it is normal for learners to make a few mistakes. For this reason, you may decide not to interrupt and correct each error a student makes. This is up to your discretion.

Comparaciones

Have students look at the picture at the bottom of page R9. Have them compare these students from Buenos Aires with themselves and their friends. How are they the same? How are they different?

Answers

3
1. Nosotros vivimos en ____.
2. Nosotros asistimos a la escuela ____.
3. Vamos a la escuela en el bus escolar (en carro, a pie).
4. En la clase de español hablamos español (escribimos en español, aprendemos español).
5. Nosotros salimos de la escuela a las ____.

4 *Answers will vary.*

5 *Answers will vary.*

6 *Answers will vary.*

Preview

In Repaso B, students will review vocabulary related to sports and daily routine. To be able to talk about these activities, they will also review the present tense of stem-changing verbs and the present tense of reflexive verbs.

R10

TeacherWorks*Plus*™

The **¡Así se dice!** TeacherWorks™ Plus CD-ROM is an all-in-one planner and resource center. You may wish to use several of the following features as you plan and present the Repaso B material: Teacher Edition, Interactive Lesson Planner with Calendar, and Point and Click Access to Teaching Resources including Hotlinks to the Internet.

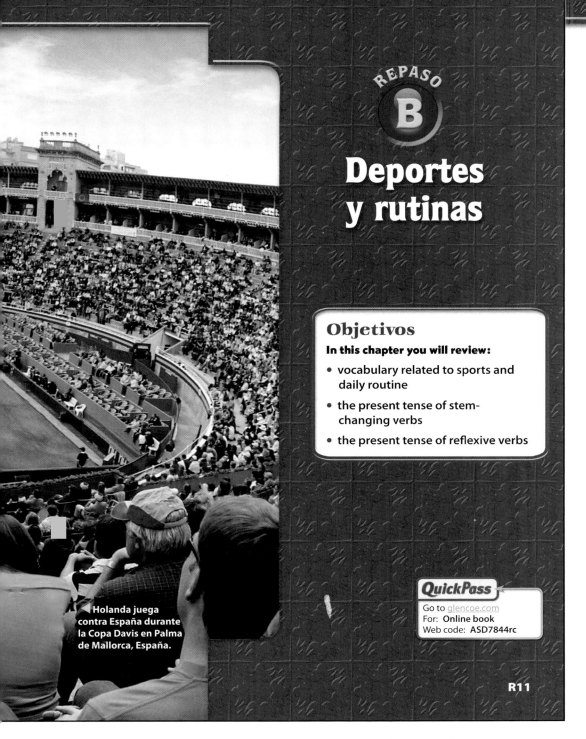

REPASO B

Deportes y rutinas

Objetivos

In this chapter you will review:

- vocabulary related to sports and daily routine
- the present tense of stem-changing verbs
- the present tense of reflexive verbs

QuickPass

Go to glencoe.com
For: **Online book**
Web code: **ASD7844rc**

Holanda juega contra España durante la Copa Davis en Palma de Mallorca, España.

R11

Quia Interactive Online Student Edition found at quia.com allows students to complete activities online and submit them for computer grading for instant feedback or teacher grading with suggestions for what to review. Students can also record speaking activities, listen to chapter audio, and watch the videos that correspond with each chapter. As a teacher you are able to create rosters, set grading parameters, and post assignments for each class. After students complete activities, you can view the results and recommend remediation or review. You can also add your own customized activities for additional student practice.

QuickPass
Go to glencoe.com
For: **Vocabulary practice**
Web code: **ASD7844rc**

Resources

- Audio Activities TE, pages R.46–R.48
- Audio CD RC1, Tracks 10–13
- Workbook, pages R.10–R.11
- ExamView® Assessment Suite

Quick Start

Use QS Transparency R.3 or write the following on the board.

Completa con la forma correcta del presente de ser.

1. Los jugadores ____ buenos.
2. Nuestro equipo ____ muy bueno.
3. Yo ____ jugador(a) en el equipo.
4. Y tú, ¿____ jugador(a) de béisbol o fútbol?

▶ TEACH
Core Instruction

Step 1 Call on students to read the sentences that accompany the presentation photos. Ask questions about the sentences.

Step 2 Have students make up additional questions about what they see in the photos and call on other students to respond.

 Comunicación

Interpersonal

Since this is all review material, separate students into small groups and have them talk as much as they can about sports and their own daily routines.

Vocabulario 🎧

> Hola. Me llamo Felipe. Y tú, ¿cómo te llamas? Soy jugador de fútbol. ¿Juegas fútbol también?

Los jugadores se acuestan temprano.
Mañana juegan (tienen) un partido (juego) importante.

el tanto

el balón

Es el campo de fútbol.
Empieza el segundo tiempo.
Los dos equipos vuelven al campo.

La muchacha se despierta temprano.
Va al cuarto de baño.
Se lava la cara.

R12

REPASO B

Total Physical Response (TPR)

(Student 1), **toma el guante**.
(Student 1), **ponte el guante**.
(Student 2), **toma el bate**.
(Student 2), **batea**.
(Student 2), **corre a la primera base**.
(Student 1), **atrapa la pelota**.

el guante

Es un equipo de béisbol.
El jugador (beisbolista) corre
de una base a otra.

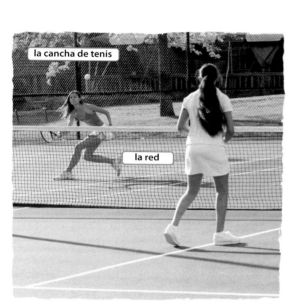

la cancha de tenis

la red

Las tenistas juegan individuales.
La pelota tiene que pasar por encima de la red.
Una jugadora devuelve la pelota.

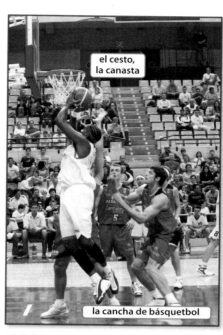

el cesto,
la canasta

la cancha de básquetbol

El balón entra en el cesto.
Cuando el muchacho encesta, marca
un tanto.

Nota

The contexts in which
campo and **cancha** are used
here is the most common.
However, their use can vary.
Most countries, for example,
use **un campo de fútbol,**
but you will sometimes hear
la cancha de fútbol.

Differentiation

Multiple Intelligences

Have bodily-kinesthetic learners come to the front of the
class. Have other classmates
call out the names of sports
they know in Spanish. The
bodily-kinesthetic learners will
act out the sport and say a
sentence about what they are
doing.

GLENCOE Technology

Online Learning
in the Classroom

Have students use QuickPass
code ASD7844rc for additional
vocabulary practice. They can
download audio files of all
vocabulary to their computer
and/or MP3 player. They will also
have access to a self-check quiz
and eGames.

Total Physical Response (TPR)

(Student 1), **ven acá.**
(Student 1), **toma el balón.**
(Student 1), **dribla con el balón.**
(Student 2), **ven acá.**
(Student 1), **pasa el balón a** *(Student 2).*
(Student 2), **dribla con el balón.**
(Student 2), **tira el balón para encestar.**

PRACTICE

Repaso B

Leveling EACH Activity

Easy Activities 1, 4
Average Activities 2, 3
CHallenging Activities 5, 6

Activity ❶ If possible, have students make up additional statements to be categorized.

Activity ❷ Go over this activity calling on students to answer at random.

Differentiation

Advanced Learners

Call on more advanced learners to redo the questions in Activity 2 using a different sport. They can call on other classmates to answer.

Práctica

LEER

❶ Categoriza indicando el deporte.

	el béisbol	el baloncesto	el fútbol	el tenis
1. El lanzador lanza la pelota al bateador.				
2. Driblan con el balón.				
3. Hay once jugadores en el equipo.				
4. Hay que tirar el balón con los pies, las piernas, las espaldas o la cabeza.				
5. La jugadora atrapa la pelota con un guante.				
6. Es posible jugar dobles o individuales.				
7. Corren de una base a otra.				
8. La pelota pasa por encima de una red.				
9. El portero guarda la portería y bloquea el balón.				
10. Cada vez que un jugador encesta marca un tanto.				

ESCUCHAR • HABLAR • ESCRIBIR

❷ Personaliza. Da respuestas personales.

1. ¿Tiene tu escuela un equipo de fútbol?
2. ¿Siempre quiere ganar el equipo?
3. ¿Gana siempre o pierde a veces?
4. ¿Juegan tus amigos fútbol?
5. ¿Cómo se llama el capitán del equipo?

Answers

❶

1. el béisbol
2. el baloncesto
3. el fútbol
4. el fútbol
5. el béisbol
6. el tenis
7. el béisbol
8. el tenis
9. el fútbol
10. el baloncesto

❷

1. Sí (No), mi escuela (no) tiene un equipo de fútbol.
2. Sí, el equipo siempre quiere ganar.
3. Gana siempre. (Pierde a veces.)
4. Sí (No), mis amigos (no) juegan fútbol.
5. El capitán del equipo se llama ____.

LEER • ESCRIBIR

3 Escoge la respuesta.

| en la cocina | a las once | enseguida | Pepe |
| para desayunar | a las seis y media | cepillarse los dientes | en el cuarto de baño |

1. ¿Cómo se llama el joven?
2. ¿A qué hora se despierta?
3. ¿Cuándo se levanta?
4. ¿Dónde se lava la cara y los dientes?
5. ¿Por qué se sienta a la mesa?
6. ¿Qué tiene que hacer antes de acostarse?
7. ¿A qué hora se acuesta?

No, no. No quiero levantarme. Tengo sueño y quiero dormir más.

ESCRIBIR

4 Identifica las partes del cuerpo en español.

LEER • ESCRIBIR

5 Forma frases con las palabras.

la pasta dentífrica   el jabón   el champú

el peine   el cepillo para los dientes

 Comunicación

6 Trabaja con un(a) compañero(a). Piensa en un(a) atleta que consideras héroe. Describe a la persona. Tu compañero(a) tratará de adivinar de quién hablas. Túrnense.

 CULTURA

Los jóvenes juegan fútbol delante de la iglesia de la Sagrada Familia en Barcelona, España.

REPASO B

R15

Activity **3** Have students go over this activity in class and then write it for homework.

Activity **4** Have several students respond to give as many answers as possible.

Activity **5** Have students read their sentences aloud.

Activity **6** When having students do an open-ended activity with no learning prompts, they are communicating as if they were in a real-life situation. In such a situation, it is normal for learners to make a few mistakes. For this reason, you may decide not to interrupt and correct each error a student makes. This is up to your discretion.

Differentiation

Multiple Intelligences

Have **verbal-linguistic** learners partner with **bodily-kinesthetic** learners. Ask **verbal-linguistic** learners to make up short conversations such as the one the young man in the photograph at the top of page R15 is having with himself. Then have the **bodily-kinesthetic** learners act out the conversation as the **verbal-linguistic** learners narrate.

Cultural Snapshot

(page R15 bottom) The beautiful Sagrada Familia church is still undergoing construction.

Answers

3
1. El joven se llama Pepe.
2. Se despierta a la seis y media.
3. Se levanta enseguida.
4. Se lava la cara y los dientes en el cuarto de baño.
5. Se sienta a la mesa para desayunar.
6. Antes de acostarse tiene que cepillarse los dientes.
7. Se acuesta a las once.

4 *Answers will vary but may include:* la cabeza, los dientes, la espalda, el brazo, el codo, el dedo, la rodilla, la pierna, el pie, la frente, el cuello, el hombro, el pecho, la muñeca, el tobillo, el dedo del pie

5 *Answers will vary.*

6 *Answers will vary.*

Repaso B

Resources

- Audio Activities TE, page R.48
- Audio CD RC1, Tracks 14–15

▶ TEACH

Core Instruction

Since this is all review material, call on the students to read the conversation aloud.

Differentiation

Multiple Intelligences

Visual-spatial learners might enjoy creating their own cartoon strip that uses the chapter's vocabulary and grammar. They can either imitate these characters or create new ones. They may want to share their cartoons with others in the class.

GLENCOE Technology

Online Learning in the Classroom

Have students use QuickPass code ASD7844rc for additional conversation practice. Students can download audio files for the conversation to their computer and/or MP3 player.

▶ PRACTICE

¿Comprendes?

A You may wish to have students do this as a factual recall activity.

B You may want students to write their summary.

Conversación

Un partido

¿Comprendes?

A Contesta.
1. ¿Cuándo va a acostarse Daniel esta noche?
2. ¿Por qué quiere dormir bien?
3. ¿Contra qué equipo juega?
4. ¿Pierden ellos mucho?
5. ¿Qué tienen?

B **Resumiendo** Relata toda la información en la conversación en tus propias palabras.

Answers

A
1. Daniel va a acostarse muy temprano esta noche.
2. Quiere dormir bien porque mañana tiene un partido importante.
3. Juega contra los Osos.
4. No, ellos no pierden casi nunca.
5. Tienen un portero fabuloso.

B *Answers will vary.*

Repaso

Gramática

Presente de los verbos de cambio radical

1. Many Spanish verbs have a stem change in the present tense. Review the forms of verbs that change their stem from **e** to **ie**.

	empezar	querer	preferir
yo	empiezo	quiero	prefiero
tú	empiezas	quieres	prefieres
Ud., él, ella	empieza	quiere	prefiere
nosotros(as)	empezamos	queremos	preferimos
vosotros(as)	empezáis	queréis	preferís
Uds., ellos, ellas	empiezan	quieren	prefieren

2. Review the forms of verbs that change their stem from **o** to **ue**.

	volver	poder	dormir
yo	vuelvo	puedo	duermo
tú	vuelves	puedes	duermes
Ud., él, ella	vuelve	puede	duerme
nosotros(as)	volvemos	podemos	dormimos
vosotros(as)	volvéis	podéis	dormís
Uds., ellos, ellas	vuelven	pueden	duermen

3. Remember that the verb **jugar** changes the **u** to **ue**.

juego   juegas   juega   jugamos   *jugáis*   juegan

4. Note that in all cases the only forms that do not have the stem change are **nosotros** and **vosotros**.

Resources

- Audio Activities TE, pages R.49–R.50
- Audio CD RC1, Tracks 16–18
- Workbook, page R.12
- ExamView® Assessment Suite

▶ TEACH
Core Instruction

Step 1 Write the verb forms from page R17 on the board and have students repeat them after you. Have students pronounce each form carefully and accurately. Show students that if they pronounce the form correctly, they will write it correctly. Pronounce **o → ue** verbs separately.

Step 2 To reinforce spelling visually, use different colored chalk or marker when writing the **nosotros** (and **vosotros**) forms on the board.

GLENCOE SPANISH

Why It Works!

In **¡Así se dice!** stem-changing verbs are not presented in isolation. They are taught together to show students that they all follow the same pattern.

GLENCOE 🖱 Technology

Online Learning in the Classroom

Have students use QuickPass code ASD7844rc for additional grammar practice. They can review each grammar point with an eGame or a self-check quiz.

Repaso B

PRACTICE

Leveling EACH Activity

Easy Activity 1
Average Activities 2, 3
CHallenging Activities 4, 5

GLENCOE SPANISH

Why It Works!

It is often suggested that you go over activities orally in class with books closed and then open books and go over them again. Going over activities first orally enables students to hear the stems and endings without reliance on the written form. This is a very important step for building oral (listening-speaking) competency.

Activity ❶ This activity encourages students to focus on the vowel changes between **ustedes** and **nosotros.**

Activity ❷ You may wish to have students write the sentences before going over them in class.

Activity ❸ This activity is more difficult as it makes students use all verb forms.

 Cultural Snapshot

(page R18 top) This scene of youngsters playing ball in small groups is very typical in many Latin American towns and cities.

CULTURA

Los amigos juegan fútbol en la Ciudad de México.

R18

Práctica

HABLAR

① Contesta.

  1. ¿Quieren ustedes ganar el partido?
  2. ¿Pueden ustedes ganarlo?
  3. ¿Juegan ustedes bien?
  4. ¿Pierden ustedes a veces?
  5. Tú y tus amigos, ¿prefieren ustedes participar en el partido o ser espectadores?

HABLAR • ESCRIBIR

② Forma frases.
  1. el segundo tiempo / empezar
  2. los jugadores / volver al campo de fútbol
  3. cada equipo / querer ganar
  4. los dos equipos / no poder ganar
  5. un equipo / perder
  6. los Osos / perder

LEER • ESCRIBIR

③ Completa.
  Yo __1__ (jugar) mucho (al) fútbol y Diana __2__ (jugar) mucho también, pero ahora ella no __3__ (poder).
  —Diana, ¿por qué no __4__ (poder) jugar ahora?
  —No __5__ (poder) porque __6__ (querer) ir a casa.
  Sí, Diana __7__ (querer) ir a casa porque ella __8__ (tener) un amigo que __9__ (volver) hoy de Puerto Rico y ella __10__ (querer) estar en casa. Pero mañana todos nosotros __11__ (ir) a jugar. Y el amigo puertorriqueño de Diana __12__ (poder) jugar también. Su amigo __13__ (jugar) muy bien.

Diana tiene un amigo que vuelve hoy de Puerto Rico y todos van a jugar fútbol. ¿Quieres también?

Answers

①
1 Sí, nosotros queremos ganar el partido.
2. Sí (No), nosotros (no) podemos ganarlo.
3. Sí (No), nosotros (no) jugamos bien.
4. Sí, nosotros perdemos a veces. (No, nosotros nunca perdemos.)
5. Nosotros preferimos participar en el partido (ser espectadores).

②
1. El segundo tiempo empieza.
2. Los jugadores vuelven al campo de fútbol.
3. Cada equipo quiere ganar.
4. Los dos equipos no pueden ganar.
5. Un equipo pierde.
6. Los Osos pierden.

Comunicación

4 ¿Cuál es tu deporte favorito? Descríbelo. Explica por qué lo consideras tu deporte favorito.

5 Habla con un(a) compañero(a) de clase sobre todos los equipos deportivos que hay en su escuela. Decidan cuáles son sus equipos favoritos y cuáles consideran los mejores. ¿Por qué?

Verbos reflexivos

1. A reflexive construction is one in which the subject both performs and receives the action of the verb. A reflexive verb in Spanish is accompanied by a pronoun called a reflexive pronoun. Review the forms of some reflexive verbs. Note too that some reflexive verbs also have a stem change.

	lavarse	levantarse	acostarse (o → ue)
yo	**me** lavo	**me** levanto	**me** acuesto
tú	**te** lavas	**te** levantas	**te** acuestas
Ud., él, ella	**se** lava	**se** levanta	**se** acuesta
nosotros(as)	**nos** lavamos	**nos** levantamos	**nos** acostamos
vosotros(as)	*os laváis*	*os levantáis*	*os acostáis*
Uds., ellos, ellas	**se** lavan	**se** levantan	**se** acuestan

2. In sentences where one person performs the action and another person or thing receives the action, a verb is not reflexive. It is only reflexive when the same person performs and receives the action of the verb. Review the following.

Federico lava el carro.   Federico se lava.
Patricia mira a su amigo.   Patricia se mira en el espejo.

3. When you refer to parts of the body or articles of clothing with a reflexive verb, you use the definite article rather than the possessive adjective.

Él se lava las manos.
Me pongo la camisa.
Ellas se lavan la cara.

La muchacha tiene frío por la mañana y se pone la bata mientras toma su desayuno. ▶

R19

Answers

1. juego
2. juega
3. puede
4. puedes
5. puedo
6. quiero
7. quiere
8. tiene
9. vuelve
10. quiere
11. vamos
12. puede
13. juega

4 *Answers will vary.*

5 *Answers will vary.*

Resources

- Audio Activities TE, page R.51
- Audio CD RC1, Tracks 19–20
- Workbook, pages R.13–R.14
- Test, pages R.77–R.79

Quick Start

Use QS Transparency R.4 or write the following on the board.

Completa en el presente.

1. Yo ___ a las seis y media. (despertarse)
2. Yo ___ enseguida. (levantarse)
3. Yo ___ la cara. (lavarse)
4. Yo ___ los dientes. (cepillarse)
5. Yo ___ a las once de la noche. (acostarse)

▶ TEACH
Core Instruction

Step 1 Have students open their books to page R19 and look over the chart.

Step 2 Explain to students that **se** is a reflexive pronoun and refers to the subject.

Step 3 Read Item 1 aloud.

Step 4 Read the verb paradigms in Item 1 aloud and have the class repeat after you. Then write the verbs **lavarse** and **levantarse** on the board. After you say **me lavo,** have students supply **me levanto.** Do the same with each subject.

Step 5 Explain Items 2 and 3 and have the class read the model sentences aloud.

► PRACTICE

Leveling EACH Activity

Easy Activity 6
Average Activities 7, 8
CHallenging Activities 9, 10

Activity ⑥ Do this activity orally with books closed calling on students at random to respond. You may also wish to do it as a paired activity.

Activity ⑦ Have students read their sentences aloud.

Práctica

ESCUCHAR • HABLAR

⑥ Personaliza. Da respuestas personales.

1. ¿Cómo te llamas?
2. ¿A qué hora te despiertas?
3. Cuando te despiertas, ¿te levantas enseguida o pasas un rato más en la cama?
4. ¿Te sientas a la mesa para tomar el desayuno?
5. ¿Cuándo te lavas los dientes, antes o después de tomar el desayuno?
6. Cuando hace frío, ¿te pones un suéter antes de salir de casa?
7. ¿A qué hora te acuestas?
8. Cuando te acuestas, ¿te duermes enseguida o pasas tiempo dando vueltas en la cama?

LEER • ESCRIBIR

⑦ Completa según las fotos.

1. Yo _____.
   Él _____.
   Tú _____.
   Usted _____.

2. Nosotras _____.
   Ellas _____.
   Ustedes _____.
   Ella y yo _____.

Answers

⑥ *Answers will vary but may include:*
1. Me llamo _____.
2. Me despierto a las _____.
3. Cuando me despierto, me levanto enseguida (paso un rato más en la cama).
4. Sí, (No, no) me siento a la mesa para tomar el desayuno.
5. Me lavo los dientes antes (después) de tomar el desayuno.

6. Cuando hace frío, (no) me pongo un suéter antes de salir de casa.
7. Me acuesto a las _____.
8. Cuando me acuesto, me duermo enseguida (paso tiempo dando vueltas en la cama).

8 Completa con un pronombre reflexivo cuando necesario.
1. ¿A qué hora _____ levantas?
2. Ana _____ pone su traje de baño en la mochila.
3. Ellos _____ divierten mucho en la fiesta.
4. Julia _____ cepilla al perro.
5. Nosotros _____ acostamos temprano.

Comunicación

9 Describe un día típico para los miembros de tu familia.

10 Compara con un(a) compañero(a) de clase la rutina que ustedes siguen de lunes a viernes y su rutina típica durante el fin de semana. ¿Hay diferencias?

Más práctica

■ Workbook, pp. R12–R14
● StudentWorks™ Plus

Comunidades

¿Hay muchos gimnasios privados donde vives? ¿Son tú y tus amigos socios de tal gimnasio o usan mayormente el gimnasio de su escuela?

Repaso

Activity 8 Remind students that the reflexive pronoun is not always necessary.

Activities 9 and 10 When having students do an open-ended activity with no learning prompts, they are actually communicating as if they were in a real-life situation. In such a situation, it is normal for learners to make a few mistakes. For this reason, you may decide not to interrupt and correct each error a student makes. This is up to your discretion.

CULTURA
Un joven anda en bici en un parque de Santiago de Chile.

REPASO B

R21

Answers

7
1. me lavo la cara, se lava la cara, te lavas la cara, se lava la cara
2. nos cepillamos (lavamos) los dientes, se cepillan (lavan) los dientes, se cepillan (lavan) los dientes, nos cepillamos (lavamos) los dientes

8
1. te
2. –
3. se
4. –
5. nos

9 Answers will vary.

10 Answers will vary.

Preview

In Repaso C, students will review vocabulary related to summer and winter activities, vacations, and traveling by plane and train. In order to be able to discuss these topics in Spanish, they will review the preterite of regular and irregular verbs.

R22

REPASO C

TeacherWorks^{Plus}

The **¡Así se dice!** TeacherWorks™ Plus CD-ROM is an all-in-one planner and resource center. You may wish to use several of the following features as you plan and present the Repaso C material: Teacher Edition, Interactive Lesson Planner with Calendar, and Point and Click Access to Teaching Resources including Hotlinks to the Internet.

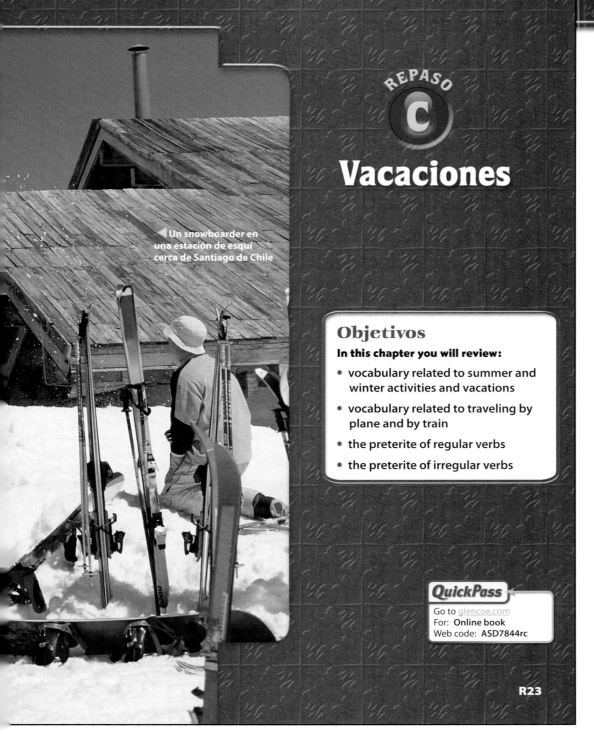

REPASO

C

Vacaciones

◄ Un snowboarder en una estación de esquí cerca de Santiago de Chile

Objetivos

In this chapter you will review:

- vocabulary related to summer and winter activities and vacations
- vocabulary related to traveling by plane and by train
- the preterite of regular verbs
- the preterite of irregular verbs

QuickPass

Go to glencoe.com
For: **Online book**
Web code: ASD7844rc

R23

Quia Interactive Online Student Edition found at quia.com allows students to complete activities online and submit them for computer grading for instant feedback or teacher grading with suggestions for what to review. Students can also record speaking activities, listen to chapter audio, and watch the videos that correspond with each chapter. As a teacher you are able to create rosters, set grading parameters, and post assignments for each class. After students complete activities, you can view the results and recommend remediation or review. You can also add your own customized activities for additional student practice.

Quick Start

Use QS Transparency R.5 or write the following on the board.

Completa en el presente.
1. Ellos ___ en avión. (viajar)
2. Yo ___ un vuelo de Miami. (tomar)
3. El avión ___ a Lima a tiempo. (llegar)
4. Nosotros ___ una merienda durante el vuelo. (tomar)
5. Los asistentes de vuelo me ___ en español. (hablar)
6. Y tú, ¿___ a Perú? (viajar)

▶ TEACH
Core Instruction

Step 1 Ask questions about each image on pages R24–R25.

Step 2 Since this is all review, have students give other words or expressions related to the photos that they have already learned.

Vocabulario 🎧

el aeropuerto

el billete, el boleto

la tarjeta de embarque

las maletas

el equipaje

José y sus amigos hicieron un viaje.
Fueron a Puerto Rico.
Fueron en avión.

las gafas (los anteojos) para el sol

el traje de baño, el bañador

una crema solar, una loción bronceadora

la playa

la piscina, la alberca

La familia pasó un mes en la playa.
Todos tomaron el sol y nadaron.

los esquís acuáticos (náuticos)

la arena

Maricarmen esquió en el agua.
Ella alquiló (rentó) los esquís acuáticos.

Total Physical Response (TPR)

(Student 1), **ven acá.**
Toma la cámara digital.
Toma una foto con la cámara.
Dame la cámara.
Toma la crema solar.
Ponte la crema solar.
(Student 2), **ven acá.**
Imagínate que estás en la playa.

Siéntate en la arena.
Toma la toalla.
Usa la toalla para quitarte la arena.
Ve al mar.
Nada.
Esquía en el agua.
Bucea.

la estación de tren (ferrocarril)

la boletería, la ventanilla

Elena y un grupo de amigos estuvieron en Perú.
Decidieron visitar Machu Picchu.
Tomaron el tren de Cuzco a Machu Picchu.

el telesilla

Los esquiadores subieron
la montaña en el telesilla.

el pico de la montaña

Anita bajó una pista avanzada.
Ella esquía bien.
Es muy aficionada al esquí.

la pista

R25

Differentiation

Multiple Intelligences

- Have **bodily-kinesthetic** learners pantomime packing a suitcase and say what they are putting in the suitcase.
- Have **bodily-kinesthetic** learners stand up while you recite sentences related to either summer or winter. Students should respond in unison with **durante el verano** or **durante el invierno** while gesturing the meaning of each sentence. After you've led several rounds, call on individual students to take over your part.

Comunicación

Interpersonal, Presentational

Have students make up and present short conversations that take place at a train station or at an airport.

Cultura

Have students tell what they remember about each of the following: **el viaje en tren de Cuzco a Machu Picchu, Machu Picchu, la Barranca del Cobre, los Tarahumara, el vuelo sobre las líneas de Nazca.**

Total Physical Response (TPR)

(Student), **levántate y ven acá, por favor.**
Imagínate que vas a esquiar.
Siéntate.
Ponte las botas.
Ponte los esquís.
Ahora levántate.
Ponte el anorak.
Ponte el gorro y los guantes.

Toma los bastones en las manos.
Ahora empieza a esquiar.
Baja la pista.
Gracias, *(Student)*. **Ahora puedes volver a tu asiento.**

▶ PRACTICE

Leveling EACH Activity

Easy Activities 1, 2
Average Activity 3
CHallenging Activity 3
Expansión, Activity 4

Differentiation

Advanced Learners

Have advanced learners categorize each word in Activity 1 and then use it in a complete sentence.

Activity ② Encourage students to be as complete as possible in giving their answers.

 Learning from Realia

(page R26) You may wish to have students look at the realia and identify all the parts of the body they can. Also have them identify any safety equipment they can.

Práctica

HABLAR

① Categoriza. Pon cada palabra o expresión en el lugar apropiado.

	la playa	una estación de esquí	un camping	más de uno
1. las botas				
2. el bañador				
3. los esquís acuáticos				
4. los bastones				
5. la carpa, la tienda de campaña				
6. la pista				
7. el telesilla				
8. la plancha de vela				

ESCUCHAR • HABLAR • ESCRIBIR

② Contesta.
1. ¿Qué tiempo hace en el verano donde vives?
2. ¿Qué tiempo hace en el invierno?
3. ¿Cuál de las dos estaciones prefieres? ¿Por qué?

CULTURA
Hay muchas actividades de verano y de invierno en La Angostura, Argentina.

Answers

①
1. una estación de esquí
2. la playa
3. la playa
4. una estación de esquí
5. un camping
6. una estación de esquí
7. una estación de esquí
8. la playa

② *Answers will vary but may include:*
1. En el verano donde vivo hace calor. Hace buen tiempo. Hace sol. Llueve a veces.
2. En el invierno hace frío. Hace viento. Nieva.
3. Prefiero el verano (el invierno). Lo prefiero porque ___.

LEER

3 ¿Sí o no?

1. Es necesario tener una tarjeta de embarque antes de poder embarcar (abordar) un avión.
2. En el aeropuerto los pasajeros esperan en el andén.
3. En la estación de ferrocarril se venden los boletos en una boletería (ventanilla) o en un distribuidor automático.
4. Antes de ir a la puerta de salida en el aeropuerto es necesario pasar por el control de seguridad.
5. Abordo de un avión es posible dejar el equipaje de mano en los pasillos del avión.
6. El revisor revisa los boletos en el tren.
7. Los aviones despegan de una vía.
8. Por lo general, los aeropuertos están en el centro de la ciudad y las estaciones de ferrocarril están en las afueras.

EXPANSIÓN

Corrige las frases falsas.

Comunicación

4 Describe el dibujo. Di todo lo que puedes. Trabaja con un(a) compañero(a) si quieres.

REPASO C

R27

Activity 3 You may wish to have students correct the false statements.

Activity 4 Have students identify things they see in the illustration. Then have them make up questions about it and ask them of their class-mates. You may also wish to have students make up true/false statements about the illustration and present them to their classmates.

Writing Development

You may wish to have students write a complete story about the illustration in Activity 4 in their own words.

Answers

3
1. sí
2. no
3. sí
4. sí
5. no
6. sí
7. no
8. no

4 *Answers will vary.*

QuickPass
Go to glencoe.com
For: Conversation practice
Web code: ASD7844rc

Resources

- Audio Activities TE, page R.55
- Audio CD RC1, Tracks 25–26

▶ TEACH
Core Instruction

Step 1 Have students close their books. Read the conversation to them or play Audio CD RC1.

Step 2 Have the class repeat the conversation once or twice in unison.

Step 3 Call on pairs of students to read the conversation. Encourage them to be as animated as possible.

Step 4 After presenting the conversation, go over the **¿Comprendes?** activity. If students can answer the questions with relative ease, move on. Students should not be expected to memorize the conversation.

GLENCOE Technology

Online Learning in the Classroom

Have students use QuickPass code ASD7844rc for additional conversation practice. Students can download audio files for the conversation to their computer and/or MP3 player.

Conversación

La plancha de vela

CULTURA

Los jóvenes hicieron la plancha de vela en el lago Nahuel Huapi en Argentina y no se cayeron.

R28

¿Comprendes?

A Completa según la información en la conversación.

1. Anita llegó al balneario _____.
2. Ella vino _____.
3. Vino en _____ porque su padre _____.
4. Su amiga Sandra llegó al balneario _____.
5. Ayer ella hizo _____.
6. Ella se cayó _____.
7. Lo que dijo José fue _____.
8. Ayer fue la primera vez que Sandra _____.

Answers

A
1. ayer
2. en tren
3. tren, no le permitió tener el carro
4. el miércoles
5. la plancha de vela
6. muchas veces (mucho)
7. que ella supera en todos los deportes
8. intentó hacer la plancha de vela

Gramática

Pretérito de los verbos regulares

1. Review the forms of the preterite tense of regular verbs.

	mirar	comer	subir
yo	miré	comí	subí
tú	miraste	comiste	subiste
Ud., él, ella	miró	comió	subió
nosotros(as)	miramos	comimos	subimos
vosotros(as)	*mirasteis*	*comisteis*	*subisteis*
Uds., ellos, ellas	miraron	comieron	subieron

2. Review the following spelling changes.

jugué → jugó   empecé → empezó   busqué → buscó
leí → leyó   caí → cayó

3. Note that in the preterite the verb **dar** is conjugated like an **-er** or **-ir** verb.

di   diste   dio   dimos   *disteis*   dieron

4. Remember that you use the preterite to express an action or event that started and ended at a specific time in the past.

Llegué ayer.
Lo estudiamos el año pasado.
Ellos me invitaron el viernes pasado.
Él salió hace un año.
Ella vendió su carro ayer y enseguida compró otro.

CULTURA
Este pavo real dio un gran *show* en un jardín en Cotacachi, Ecuador.

REPASO C

R29

ABOUT THE SPANISH LANGUAGE

Have students look at the photo at the bottom of page R29 and guess the meaning of **pavo real.**

QuickPass
Go to glencoe.com
For: **Grammar practice**
Web code: **ASD7844rc**

Resources

- Audio Activities TE, page R.56
- Audio CD RC1, Tracks 27–28
- Workbook, pages R.18–R.19
- *ExamView®* Assessment Suite

 Quick Start

Use QS Transparency R.6 or write the following on the board.
Contesta.
1. ¿Te gusta la playa?
2. ¿Juegas en la arena?
3. ¿Nadas mucho?
4. A veces, ¿son grandes las olas?
5. ¿Corres las olas?

▶ TEACH
Core Instruction

Step 1 Have students open their books to page R29. Read Item 1 aloud.

Step 2 Write the verbs **mirar, comer,** and **subir** on the board. Before you write the ending to each verb, prompt students to see if they can give it to you.

Step 3 Read the information in Item 2. You may wish to review the following spelling sequences:

ga, gue, gui, go, gu
ca, que, qui, co, cu
za, ce, ci, zo, zu

GLENCOE Technology

Online Learning in the Classroom

Have students use QuickPass code ASD7844rc for additional grammar practice. They can review each grammar point with an eGame or a self-check quiz.

▶ PRACTICE

Leveling EACH Activity

Easy Activity 1
Average Activity 2
CHallenging Activity 3

Activity ① You can present this activity orally with books closed calling on students to respond at random. Students can also write the answers for homework.

Activity ② You may wish to have students prepare this activity first and then go over it in class.

Práctica

HABLAR • ESCRIBIR

① Contesta.

1. ¿A qué hora saliste anoche?
2. ¿Te acompañaron unos amigos?
3. ¿Comieron ustedes en un restaurante mexicano?
4. ¿Vieron ustedes un filme en el cine o alquilaron un DVD?
5. ¿Quién volvió a casa a pie?
6. ¿Quién o quiénes tomaron el autobús?
7. ¿A qué hora volviste a casa?
8. Al volver a casa, ¿te acostaste enseguida?

LEER • ESCRIBIR

② Cambia al pretérito.

1. Esquío en las montañas.
2. Mi amigo Carlos compra los tickets para el telesilla.
3. Tomamos el telesilla para subir la montaña.
4. Yo pierdo mi casco.
5. Elena y Carlos bajan una pista avanzada.
6. Daniel baja una pista más fácil.

CULTURA

Las tarifas para usar las pistas en la estación de esquí Cerrobayo en Argentina

Comunicación

③ Trabaja con un(a) compañero(a). Van a hablar de un día que pasaron en la playa la semana pasada.

Answers

①

1. Salí a las ____.
2. Sí, me acompañaron unos amigos. (No, nadie me acompañó.)
3. Sí, (No, no) comimos en un restaurante mexicano.
4. Nosotros vimos un filme en el cine (alquilamos un DVD).

5. ____ volvió a casa a pie. (Yo volví / Tú volvíste a casa a pie.)
6. ____ tomó (tomaron / tomamos) el autobús.
7. Volví a casa a las ____.
8. Al volver a casa, (no) me acosté enseguida.

②
1. Esquié en las montañas.
2. Mi amigo Carlos compró los tickets para el telesilla.

3. Tomamos el telesilla para subir la montaña.
4. Yo perdí mi casco.
5. Elena y Carlos bajaron una pista avanzada.
6. Daniel bajó una pista más fácil.

③ *Answers will vary.*

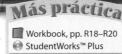
Pretérito de los verbos irregulares

1. Many verbs have an irregular root in the preterite. Review the following.

hacer	→ hic-	poner	→ pus-
querer	→ quis-	poder	→ pud-
venir	→ vin-	saber	→ sup-

tener	→ tuv-
andar	→ anduv-
estar	→ estuv-

	hacer	poner	tener
yo	hice	puse	tuve
tú	hiciste	pusiste	tuviste
Ud., él, ella	hizo	puso	tuvo
nosotros(as)	hicimos	pusimos	tuvimos
vosotros(as)	hicisteis	pusisteis	tuvisteis
Uds., ellos, ellas	hicieron	pusieron	tuvieron

2. Note the ending **-eron**, not **-ieron**, for verbs with a **j** or **y**.

decir	→ dijeron	leer	→ leyeron
traer	→ trajeron	construir	→ construyeron
conducir	→ condujeron		

decir			
yo	dije	nosotros(as)	dijimos
tú	dijiste	vosotros(as)	dijisteis
Ud., él, ella	dijo	Uds., ellos, ellas	dijeron

3. Review the forms of **ser** and **ir**. Remember that they are the same in the preterite.

ir, ser			
yo	fui	nosotros(as)	fuimos
tú	fuiste	vosotros(as)	fuisteis
Ud., él, ella	fue	Uds., ellos, ellas	fueron

Una muchacha patinó en línea y otra anduvo a bicicleta en el Parque Palermo en Buenos Aires, Argentina.

CULTURA

- Audio Activities TE, page R.57
- Audio CD RC1, Track 29
- Workbook, pages R.19–R.20
- Test, pages R.80–R.82

Quick Start

Use QS Transparency R.7 or write the following on the board.

1. Escribe tres cosas que hiciste ayer.

2. Escribe tres cosas que le dijiste a tu amigo(a) ayer.

▶ **TEACH**

Core Instruction

Step 1 It is suggested that you have students read these verb forms in unison.

Step 2 In Item 1, note that the verbs have been grouped: **i, u, uv.**

Step 3 In item 2, note that the **j** and **y** verbs are separated because of the spelling.

Step 4 Remind students that if they pronounce the verb forms correctly, they will write them correctly.

▶ PRACTICE

Leveling EACH Activity

Easy Activity 5
Average Activities 4, 6
CHallenging Activities 7, 8

Activity ④ You can do this activity orally with books closed calling on students at random to respond.

Differentiation

Advanced Learners

Call on advanced learners to retell all the information in Activity 4 in their own words.

 Cultural Snapshot

(page R32) This photo was taken in the beautiful lake region of Argentina. The world's smallest river, el Cruce, is found here. The river connects two lakes—Nahuel Huapi and Correntoso.

Práctica

HABLAR

④ Contesta.

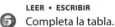

1. ¿Hiciste un viaje una vez?
2. ¿Cuándo hiciste el viaje?
3. ¿Adónde fuiste?
4. ¿Fuiste solo(a) o estuviste acompañado(a) de unos amigos o parientes?
5. ¿Fueron ustedes en carro?
6. ¿Quién condujo?
7. ¿Pusieron ustedes sus maletas en la maletera del carro?
8. En la autopista, ¿tuvieron que pagar un peaje?

CULTURA

Los jóvenes fueron a admirar la vista bonita en El Cruce en el distrito de los lagos en Argentina.

LEER • ESCRIBIR

⑤ Completa la tabla.

	querer	estar	saber	decir	ir
yo		estuve		dije	
nosotros	quisimos		supimos		fuimos
tú		estuviste		dijiste	fuiste
ustedes	quisieron		supieron		
él			supo		fue
ellos	quisieron	estuvieron			

Answers

④

1. Sí, hice un viaje una vez. (No, nunca hice un viaje.)
2. Hice el viaje ____.
3. Fui a ____.
4. Fui solo(a). (Estuve acompañado[a] de unos amigos.)
5. Sí (No), nosotros (no) fuimos en carro.
6. ____ condujo. (Yo conduje.)
7. Sí (No), nosotros (no) pusimos nuestras maletas en la maletera del carro.
8. En la autopista, (no) tuvimos que pagar un peaje.

LEER • ESCRIBIR

6 Lee. Luego cambia **En este momento** a **Ayer** y haz todos los cambios necesarios.

En este momento estoy en el mercado de Otavalo en Ecuador. Mi amigo Ramón está conmigo. Andamos por el mercado pero no podemos comprar nada. Qué lástima porque vemos muchas cosas que queremos comprar pero no podemos. ¿Por qué no? Porque vamos al mercado sin un peso.

Comunicación

7 En tus estudios del español leíste sobre unos viajes interesantes en tren: el viaje de Cuzco a Machu Picchu, el viaje por el Cañón del Cobre en México, el viaje a lo largo del canal de Panamá. Imagínate que hiciste uno de estos viajes y cuenta todo lo que «hiciste» y «viste».

8 Mira este dibujo de una escena que tuvo lugar en un aeropuerto ya hace algunos años. Relata todo lo que hicieron los pasajeros en el aeropuerto.

REPASO C R33

Answers

5
yo: quise, supe, fui
nosotros: estuvimos, dijimos
tú: quisiste, supiste
ustedes: estuvieron, dijeron, fueron
él: quiso, estuvo, dijo
ellos: supieron, dijeron, fueron

6
Ayer estuve en el mercado de Otavalo. Mi amigo Ramón estuvo conmigo. Anduvimos por el mercado pero no pudimos comprar nada. Qué lástima porque vimos muchas cosas que quisimos comprar pero no pudimos. ¿Por qué no? Porque fuimos al mercado sin un peso.

7 *Answers will vary.*

8 *Answers will vary.*

Preview

In Repaso D, students will review the vocabulary they learned in Level 2 associated with shopping and celebrations. They will also review the imperfect of regular and irregular verbs, the verbs **interesar, aburrir,** and **gustar,** and indirect object pronouns.

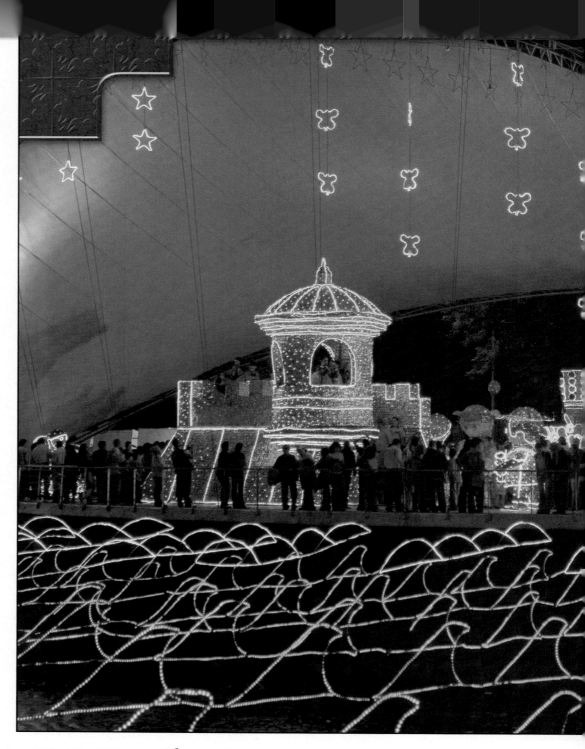

Teacher Works Plus™

The **¡Así se dice!** TeacherWorks™ Plus CD-ROM is an all-in-one planner and resource center. You may wish to use several of the following features as you plan and present the Repaso D material: Teacher Edition, Interactive Lesson Planner with Calendar, and Point and Click Access to Teaching Resources including Hotlinks to the Internet.

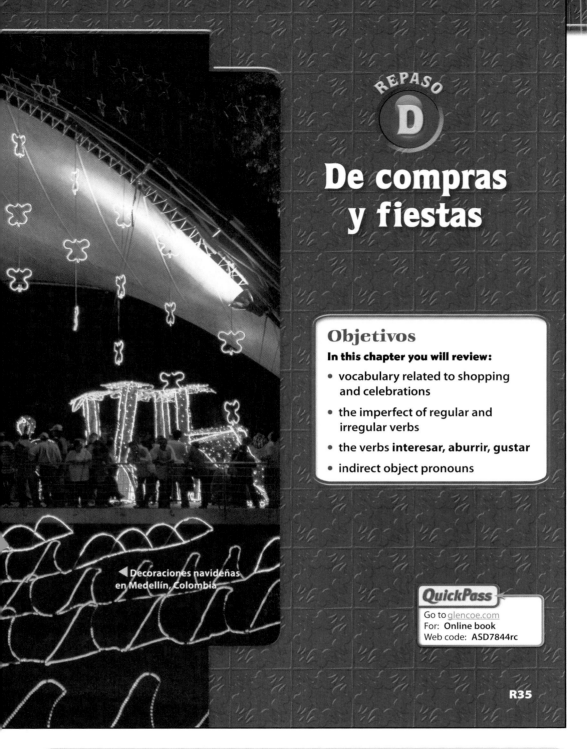

REPASO

D

De compras y fiestas

Objetivos

In this chapter you will review:

- vocabulary related to shopping and celebrations
- the imperfect of regular and irregular verbs
- the verbs **interesar, aburrir, gustar**
- indirect object pronouns

◀ Decoraciones navideñas en Medellín, Colombia

QuickPass

Go to glencoe.com
For: **Online book**
Web code: **ASD7844rc**

R35

QUIA **Quia Interactive Online Student Edition** found at quia.com allows students to complete activities online and submit them for computer grading for instant feedback or teacher grading with suggestions for what to review. Students can also record speaking activities, listen to chapter audio, and watch the videos that correspond with each chapter. As a teacher you are able to create rosters, set grading parameters, and post assignments for each class. After students complete activities, you can view the results and recommend remediation or review. You can also add your own customized activities for additional student practice.

QuickPass

Go to glencoe.com
For: Vocabulary practice
Web code: ASD7844rc

Resources

- Audio Activities TE, pages R.58–R.60
- Audio CD RC2, Tracks 1–3
- Workbook, pages R.22–R.23
- ExamView® Assessment Suite

Quick Start

Use QS Transparency R.8 or write the following on the board.
Escribe en español las comidas que recuerdas.

▶ **TEACH**

Core Instruction

Step 1 Have students open their books to page R36. As you review the vocabulary, have students repeat the words and sentences after you or Audio CD RC2.

Step 2 Ask questions using the words being reviewed such as **¿Dónde vivía Guadalupe cuando era joven? ¿Adónde iba el primero de noviembre? ¿Qué día celebra? ¿En honor de quienes? ¿Cómo andaba la gente al cementerio? ¿Qué llevaban algunos?** If students can answer these questions with relative ease, it indicates that they recall much of this material that was presented in Level 2.

Step 3 Once you have asked your questions about the photographs, have students say whatever they can about them. They may also want to ask one another questions.

Vocabulario 🎧

el camposanto
la tumba

Cuando Guadalupe era niña, vivía en México.
El primero de noviembre siempre iba al cementerio.
Celebraba el Día de los Muertos en honor de sus parientes difuntos.

un disfraz
el hueso
un cráneo
una máscara

La familia desfilaba hacia el cementerio.
Algunos llevaban máscaras o disfraces.
A veces todos comían en el cementerio.

un bizcocho

A los niños les gustaba comer bizcochos en forma de cráneos o esqueletos.

R36

un puesto

Antes del Día de los Muertos, Guadalupe iba al mercado con su abuela.
Iban de un puesto a otro.
Su abuela compraba todo lo que necesitaba para preparar la comida para la fiesta.

el cordero

la carne de res

el jamón

los huevos, los blanquillos

el pan

el jugo de naranja

la naranja

las uvas

la manzana

la leche

la mantequilla

el yogur

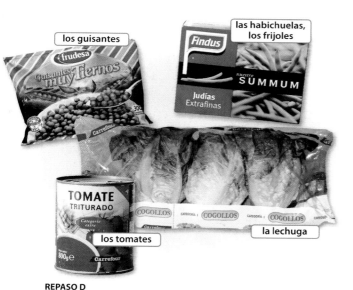

los guisantes

las habichuelas, los frijoles

SUMMUM

Judías Extrafinas

TOMATE TRITURADO

los tomates

la lechuga

el flan

FLAN Huevo al Baño maría

las galletas

LLETAS MARÍA INTEGRAL

REPASO D

R37

Differentiation

Multiple Intelligences

You may wish to have **bodily-kinesthetic** learners dramatize the following.

comer bizcochos, ponerse una máscara, ir de un puesto a otro

▶ TEACH
Core Instruction

Step 1 Since this is all review vocabulary, have students read the callout words and sentences on this page.

Step 2 Have them give additional words or expressions they know that are related to the topic of shopping for clothing.

Step 3 Have students make up questions about the photographs. Let them call on other students to answer the questions.

⭐Tips for Success · · · · · ·

To give students more practice reviewing this vocabulary, you may wish to have them describe one another's clothing.

Los amigos de José están en el centro comercial.
Hay muchas tiendas en el centro comercial.

Felipe está en la tienda de ropa.
Se pone una chaqueta.
No le queda bien.
Necesita una talla más grande.

Práctica

 1 ¿Sí o no?

1. Cuando Guadalupe era niña, vivía en Perú.
2. El primero de noviembre la familia de Guadalupe celebraba el Día de los Muertos.
3. En ese día rendían honor a sus parientes difuntos (muertos).
4. Todos los parientes iban al centro comercial.
5. La familia desfilaba hacia el camposanto.
6. Ellos comían en el camposanto.
7. Algunos llevaban disfraces.
8. Los niños comían bizcochos en forma de cráneos y esqueletos.

Comunicación

2 Has aprendido como se celebran otras fiestas en el mundo hispanohablante. Trabaja con un(a) compañero(a). Cada uno va a describir una fiesta diferente.

 3 Identifica.

1. tantas frutas posibles
2. tantas legumbres posibles
3. tantas carnes posibles
4. tantos postres posibles
5. tantas bebidas posibles

CULTURA

Un joven llevaba disfraz mientras celebraba el Día de los Muertos.

▶ PRACTICE

Leveling EACH Activity

Easy Activities 1, 3
CHallenging Activity 2

Activity 1 After going over this activity, have one student give all the information in his or her own words.

Activity 2 Other fiestas students may discuss are **el Cinco de Mayo, el día de San Juan, Navidad, el Día de los Reyes, el Año Nuevo, la vispera del Año Nuevo.**

Activity 3 You may wish to do this activity as a game and set a time limit. You may also separate the class into teams and have each team compete. You may want to write all words on the board and have students repeat them as a general review.

Teaching Options

Go over the **Práctica** activities as quickly as possible. If students appear to have a good command of the vocabulary, it is not necessary that they write their answers.

If, however, you believe students need additional reinforcement of the vocabulary, have them write the activities after you go over them orally in class.

Answers

1
1. no
2. sí
3. sí
4. no
5. sí
6. sí
7. sí
8. sí

2 *Answers will vary.*

3 *Answers will vary but may include:*
1. la naranja, la manzana, las uvas, la piña, el plátano
2. el pepino, la zanahoria, la cebolla, el pimiento, la lechuga, la papa, los guisantes, las judías verdes, el maíz

3. el jamón, el tocino (el bacón), el cerdo, la carne de res, el cordero
4. el flan, el helado, la torta, el bizcocho, la galleta
5. el café, el agua (mineral, con gas), el batido, la leche, el jugo (de naranja), la gaseosa, el chocolate, la cola

▶ PRACTICE (continued)

Leveling EACH Activity

Average Activity 4
CHallenging Activity 5

Activity ❹ As an expansion, you may wish to have students make up sentences using the options that were not correct.

Activity ❺ When having students do a completely open-ended activity with no learning prompts, they are actually functioning as if they were communicating in a real-life situation. In such a situation, it is normal for learners to make a few mistakes. For this reason, you may decide not to interrupt and correct each error a student makes. This is up to your discretion.

⭐Tips for Success ·······

Before having students do Activity 5 in groups, you may wish to have the class give some words, expressions, or even sentences about each one of the locales in this activity.

📷 Cultural Snapshot

(page R40) The Otavalo market in northern Ecuador is one of the most well-known in all of Latin America. The **otavaleños** are famous for their weavings and they can be seen selling them in cities worldwide.

R40

LEER
❹ Escoge.
1. Teresa quiere comprar una blusa verde.
   a. Va al mercado.
   b. Va a la verdulería.
   c. Va a la tienda de ropa.
2. ¿Dónde hay muchos puestos diferentes?
   a. en el mercado
   b. en el camposanto
   c. en el centro comercial
3. ¿Dónde hay muchas tiendas diferentes?
   a. en los tenderetes
   b. en el mercado
   c. en el centro comercial
4. ¿Dónde ponía la gente coronas de flores?
   a. en la florería
   b. en los puestos del mercado
   c. en las tumbas en el camposanto
5. ¿Qué bebías cuando eras bebé?
   a. mucha leche
   b. mucho café
   c. muchas bebidas diferentes
6. No me queda bien.
   a. Es verdad. Necesitas una talla más grande.
   b. ¿No? Lo siento mucho.
   c. Es tu talla.

CULTURA
Mucha gente hizo sus compras en el famoso mercado indígena en Otavalo, Ecuador.

🌸 Comunicación

❺ Trabajen en grupos de tres a cuatro. Imaginen que fueron a uno o más de los siguientes tipos de tiendas para hacer las compras. Preparen una conversación entre ustedes y no olviden que uno(a) será el/la empleado(a) o el/la vendedor(a).
un mercado indígena
un mercado municipal
una bodega o un colmado
una tienda en un centro comercial

Answers

❹
1. c
2. a
3. c
4. c
5. a
6. a

❺ *Answers will vary.*

Conversación

De compras

Felipe	Quiero comprarme una camisa nueva para la fiesta de Maricarmen.
José	Y yo necesito un pantalón. ¿Por qué no vamos juntos a la tienda?
Felipe	Buena idea. ¡Vamos!
	(En la tienda de ropa)
Empleada	¿En qué puedo servirles, señores?
Felipe	Yo estoy buscando una camisa.
Empleada	¿Qué talla usa usted?
Felipe	36.
Empleada	¿Por qué no se pone usted esta?
Felipe	José, ¿qué piensas? ¿Te gusta?
José	Pues, me gusta la camisa pero me parece que no te queda bien. Te queda grande.
Empleada	Sí, sí. Necesita usted una talla más pequeña.
	(Felipe se pone otra camisa y la compra.)
Empleada	Y usted, señor. ¿Quiere un pantalón largo o corto?
José	Largo, por favor. Uso la talla 40.
Empleada	¿Le gusta más un pantalón azul o beige?
José	Beige.
	(José se pone un pantalón beige que le gusta. Le queda bien y lo compra.)

QuickPass

Go to glencoe.com
For: **Conversation practice**
Web code: ASD7844rc

Repaso

Repaso **D**

Resources

- Audio Activities TE, page R.61
- Audio CD RC2, Tracks 4–5

▶ TEACH
Core Instruction

Step 1 Have students close their books. Read the conversation to them or play Audio CD RC2.

Step 2 Have the class repeat the conversation once or twice in unison.

Step 3 Call on pairs of students to read the conversation as a dramatization, using the proper intonation and gestures. Encourage them to be as animated as possible.

Step 4 After presenting the conversation, go over the **¿Comprendes?** activities. If students can answer the questions with relative ease, move on. Students should not be expected to memorize the conversation.

Differentiation
Multiple Intelligences

To engage **visual-spatial** learners, have students look at the details in the photo that accompanies the conversation. Ask them what kind of story they think the photo tells.

Pre-AP Listening to this conversation on audio CD will help students develop the skills that they need to be successful on the listening portion of the AP exam.

GLENCOE Technology

Online Learning in the Classroom

Have students use QuickPass code ASD7844rc for additional conversation practice. Students can download audio files for the conversation to their computer and/or MP3 player.

Why It Works!

Students can carry on a realistic conversation when buying clothing just as the young man is doing here. The conversation, as always in **¡Así se dice!**, uses only Spanish that students have already learned and can use in real-life situations.

▶ PRACTICE

¿Comprendes?

A Do this activity orally in class.

C Separate the class into groups of three, with different paced students in each group. Ask for groups to volunteer to present their conversation to the class.

¿Comprendes?

A Contesta.

1. ¿Adónde van los dos muchachos?
2. ¿Con quién hablan?
3. ¿Qué necesita cada uno?
4. ¿Cuál es el problema que tiene Felipe con la camisa que se prueba?
5. El pantalón que compra José, ¿cómo es?

B ¿Quién lo dice?

	José	Felipe	la empleada
1. ¿En qué puedo servirles?			
2. Quiero una camisa, talla 36.			
3. Me gusta más el beige.			
4. Necesito un pantalón.			
5. Me gusta la camisa pero esta no te queda bien.			
6. Quiero un pantalón largo.			

C **Resumiendo** Resume la conversación entre José, Felipe y la empleada en tus propias palabras.

chandals

P 48	M 52	G 54	XG 56	XXG 58	TALLAS ESPAÑOLAS
P	M	L	XL	XXL	TALLAS INGLESAS

Answers

A
1. Los dos muchachos van a la tienda de ropa.
2. Hablan con la empleada.
3. Felipe necesita una camisa y José necesita un pantalón.
4. La camisa que se prueba Felipe le queda grande.
5. El pantalón que compra José es beige.

B
1. la empleada
2. Felipe
3. José
4. José
5. José
6. José

C *Answers will vary.*

Gramática

El imperfecto

1. Review the forms of the imperfect tense of regular verbs. Note that the endings of **-er** and **-ir** verbs are the same.

	hablar	comer	vivir
	habl-	com-	viv-
yo	hablaba	comía	vivía
tú	hablabas	comías	vivías
Ud., él, ella	hablaba	comía	vivía
nosotros (as)	hablábamos	comíamos	vivíamos
vosotros (as)	hablabais	comíais	vivíais
Uds., ellos, ellas	hablaban	comían	vivían

2. The following are the only verbs that are irregular in the imperfect.

	ir	ser	ver
yo	iba	era	veía
tú	ibas	eras	veías
Ud., él, ella	iba	era	veía
nosotros(as)	íbamos	éramos	veíamos
vosotros(as)	ibais	erais	veíais
Uds., ellos, ellas	iban	eran	veían

CULTURA

Mucha gente patinaba en línea y disfrutaba del buen tiempo que hacía en el Parque Palermo en Buenos Aires.

QuickPass

Go to glencoe.com
For: **Grammar practice**
Web code: **ASD7844rc**

GLENCOE Technology

Online Learning in the Classroom

Have students use QuickPass code ASD7844rc for additional grammar practice. They can review each grammar point with an eGame or a self-check quiz.

Resources

- Audio Activities TE, page R.62
- Audio CD RC2, Tracks 6–7
- Workbook, page R.24
- ExamView® Assessment Suite

Quick Start

Use QS Transparency R.9 or write the following on the board.

Completa en el presente.
1. Nosotros ___ mucho. (aprender)
2. Tú ___ en la cafetería de la escuela. (comer)
3. ¿___ ustedes español con el profesor? (hablar)
4. Yo ___ cerca de Nueva York. (vivir)
5. Ella ___ a casa después de las clases. (ir)

▶ TEACH

Core Instruction

Step 1 Have students open their books to page R43. Read Item 1 to them aloud.

Step 2 Write the **-ar** imperfect verb forms on the boards. Underline the endings and have students read all forms aloud.

Step 3 Write the infinitives of the verbs **leer** and **escribir** on the board. Cross out the infinitive endings, leaving just the stems. Write the forms of **leer** and **escribir** in the imperfect on the board. Underline the endings.

Step 4 Now read Item 2 aloud.

Step 5 Write the infinitives of the verbs **ser** and **ir** on the board.

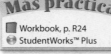
▶TEACH (continued)

Core Instruction

Step 6 When going over the verbs **ser** and **ir,** stress the importance of learning these verbs since they are used very often.

Step 7 Have students read the forms of **ver** once. Students very seldom have a problem with this verb.

Step 8 Have students read all the verb forms aloud.

Step 9 Now go over Item 3. Explain to students that the form **había** never changes.

Step 10 Have students read the time expressions that often accompany the imperfect. Have them read the model sentences aloud.

 Cultural Snapshot

(page R44) Cotacachi is a small town north of Otavalo known for its excellent leather goods.

3. The imperfect of **hay** is **había.**

   Había fuegos artificiales durante la fiesta.

4. The imperfect is used to express repeated, habitual actions or events in the past.

   Él lo hacía con frecuencia.
   Abuelita iba al mercado todos los días.
   Celebrábamos la fiesta cada año.

CULTURA

Los niños se divertían con sus caras pintadas durante una fiesta en Cotacachi, Ecuador.

Comunidades

¿Cuáles son unas fiestas que se celebran cerca de donde tú vives? ¿Te gusta tomar parte en las festividades? Describe una de las fiestas.

5. The imperfect is also used to describe persons, places, events, weather, and time in the past. It is also used to describe mental processes such as **creer, querer, saber.**

   La muchacha era alta y fuerte.
   Tenía dieciséis años.
   Siempre estaba contenta.
   Ella jugaba fútbol y siempre quería ganar.

Answers

 1

1. Sí, Isabel vivía en México cuando era niña.
2. Sí, su familia celebraba el Día de los Muertos.
3. La familia iba al cementerio (camposanto) para celebrar el Día de los Muertos.
4. Todos desfilaban.
5. Algunos llevaban disfraces (máscaras).
6. Los niños comían bizcochos en forma de cráneos o esqueletos.

 2

1. Vivía en ___ cuando era niño(a).
2. Mis abuelos vivían en ___.
3. Sí, (No, no) visitaba con frecuencia a mis abuelos.
4. Sí, estaban contentos cuando los visitaba.
5. Asistía a la escuela ___ cuando tenía ocho años.
6. Sí, (No, no) participaba en un equipo deportivo con mis amigos.

Práctica

Repaso

HABLAR

1 Contesta.

1. ¿Vivía Isabel en México cuando era niña?
2. ¿Celebraba su familia el Día de los Muertos?
3. ¿Adónde iba la familia para celebrar el Día de los Muertos?

4. ¿Cómo iban todos?
5. ¿Qué llevaban algunos?
6. ¿Qué comían los niños?

HABLAR • ESCRIBIR

2 Personaliza. Da respuestas personales.

1. ¿Dónde vivías cuando eras niño(a)?
2. ¿Dónde vivían tus abuelos?
3. ¿Visitabas con frecuencia a tus abuelos?
4. ¿Estaban contentos cuando los visitabas?
5. ¿A qué escuela asistías cuando tenías ocho años?
6. ¿Participabas en un equipo deportivo con tus amigos? *¿Como se llamaba? el equipo?*
7. ¿Qué deporte jugaban?
8. ¿Siempre querían ganar?

LEER • ESCRIBIR

3 Completa.

Cuando Ramona __1__ (tener) cuatro años, ella __2__ (vivir) en el campo. Los padres de Ramona __3__ (tener) una hacienda con muchos animales. Ramona __4__ (divertirse) mucho en el campo. Ella __5__ (tener) muchas amiguitas imaginarias. Ella les __6__ (servir) café a sus amiguitas. Las amigas la __7__ (querer) mucho a Ramona. Los padres no __8__ (poder) ver a las amiguitas, pero ellos __9__ (saber) que, para Ramona, las amiguitas sí __10__ (existir). Y Ramona nunca __11__ (aburrirse).

CULTURA

Un gaucho contemporáneo en su caballo en las pampas argentinas

Comunicación

4 Trabaja con un(a) compañero(a) de clase. Dile todo lo que hacías con frecuencia cuando eras muy joven. Luego tu compañero(a) te dirá lo que él o ella hacía. Comparen sus actividades.

5 Describe una fiesta que tu familia celebraba cuando eras niño(a). ¿Te gustaba? ¿Por qué?

REPASO D

R45

PRACTICE

Leveling EACH Activity

Easy Activities 1, 2
Average Activity 3
CHallenging Activities 4, 5

Activities 1 and 2 These activities can be done with books closed as oral activities, calling on students at random to respond.

Activity 3 You may wish to have students prepare this activity before going over it in class.

Activities 4 and 5 When having students do a completely open-ended activity with no learning prompts, they are actually functioning as if they were communicating in a real-life situation. In such a situation, it is normal for learners to make a few mistakes. For this reason, you may decide not to interrupt and correct each error a student makes. This is up to your discretion.

Cultural Snapshot

(page R45) Although the old lifestyle of the gaucho is a thing of the past, there are still young gauchos such as the one seen here working on the **estancias** of the **pampas,** some of which are not very far from Buenos Aires.

Answers

7. Jugábamos ____. (No jugábamos un deporte.)
8. Sí, siempre queríamos ganar.

3

1. tenía
2. vivía
3. tenían
4. se divertía
5. tenía
6. servía

7. querían
8. podían
9. sabían
10. existían
11. se aburría

4 *Answers will vary.*

5 *Answers will vary.*

Quick Start

Use QS Transparency R.10 or write the following on the board.
Escribe frases sobre las comidas que te gustan y que no te gustan.

GLENCOE SPANISH

Why It Works!

English-speaking students often have a problem grasping the concept of **gustar.** Introducing **interesar** and **aburrir** in conjunction with **gustar** makes it much easier for students, since we do have a parallel construction for these two verbs in English.

Note that **gustar** is presented after **me interesa/aburre** so that in using the important **me gusta** construction students do not get the idea that **me** means "I" and that "I" takes an **-a** or **-an** ending. Showing parallel constructions makes learning easier.

▶ TEACH
Core Instruction

Step 1 As you go over the explanation and **Práctica** activities, have students point to themselves as they say **me** and have them look at a friend as they say **te.**

Step 2 Go over Items 1–4.

Step 3 Since this is all review, you may wish to ask

Interesar, aburrir, gustar

1. The verbs **interesar** and **aburrir** function the same in English and Spanish.

> ¿Te aburre el béisbol?
> No, el béisbol me interesa.
> La verdad es que me interesan todos los deportes.

2. The verb **gustar** functions the same as **interesar** and **aburrir.** **Gustar** conveys the meaning *to like* but its true meaning is *to please.* Note that these verbs are used with an indirect object pronoun.

> Me gusta el helado.
> Te gustan las legumbres, ¿no?
> A José le gustan las frutas.
> Nos gustan los postres.
> A ellos les gusta el café.

3. The indirect object pronouns are:

me	nos
te	os
le (a usted, a él, a ella)	les (a ustedes, a ellos, a ellas)

> A él le gusta hablar y yo le hablo mucho.

4. **Gustar** is often followed by an infinitive.

> Me gusta nadar.
> A todos mis amigos les gusta nadar.

CULTURA

La gente toma refrescos y meriendas en este café típico en la plaza Dorrego en San Telmo en Buenos Aires, Argentina.

---

students questions to determine how much they remember. You may also want to review expressions such as: **¿Te duele la cabeza? ¿Te duele el estómago? ¿Te duele la pierna? ¿Le explica tus síntomas al médico? ¿Te examina la garganta el médico? ¿Te da una receta? ¿Le das la receta al farmacéutico?**

Answers

6
1. Sí, me gustan y como muchas.
2. Sí, me gusta y como mucha.
3. Sí, me gustan y como muchos.
4. Sí, me gusta y como mucho.
5. Sí, me gustan y como muchas.
6. Sí, me gusta y como mucho.

Práctica

ESCUCHAR • HABLAR

6 Contesta según el modelo.

 MODELO —¿Te gusta la ensalada?
—Sí, me gusta y como mucha.

1. ¿Te gustan las hamburguesas?
2. ¿Te gusta la carne?
3. ¿Te gustan los cereales?

4. ¿Te gusta el helado?
5. ¿Te gustan las frutas?
6. ¿Te gusta el arroz?

HABLAR • ESCRIBIR

7 Crea una conversación.

MODELO la gorra →
—¿Te gusta mi gorra?
—Sí, a mí me gusta. La verdad es que te
queda bien.

1. la camisa
2. la blusa
3. los tenis
4. el pantalón

5. la camiseta
6. la falda
7. los zapatos
8. el suéter

HABLAR • ESCRIBIR

8 Contesta con pronombres.
1. ¿Les enseña la empleada las camisas a los clientes?
2. ¿Le dice un cliente la talla que lleva?
3. ¿Le da el cliente el dinero a la empleada en la caja?
4. ¿Les da buen servicio a sus clientes la cajera?

Comunicación

 9 Trabaja con un(a) compañero(a) de clase. Discutan
algunas cosas que les gustan y que no les gustan.
Pueden incluir las siguientes categorías. Luego
comparen sus gustos.

comida   ropa   cursos
deportes   actividades

▶ PRACTICE

Leveling EACH Activity

Easy Activities 6, 7
Average Activity 8
CHallenging Activity 9

Differentiation

Advanced Learners
Have advanced learners make
up many additional questions
with **gustar,** etc., using more
foods, clothes, and sports.

⭐Tips for Success ·······

Activities such as these are useful for diagnostic purposes. If
you find that students need any
additional help with **interesar,
aburrir,** and **gustar,** you may
refer them to the original presentation in **¡Así se dice!** Level 1.

·······································

Answers

7
1. ¿Te gusta mi camisa? / Sí, a mí me gusta.
La verdad es que te queda bien.
2. ¿Te gusta mi blusa? / Sí, a mí me gusta.
La verdad es que te queda bien.
3. ¿Te gustan mis tenis? / Sí, a mí me gustan.
La verdad es que te quedan bien.
4. ¿Te gusta mi pantalón? / Sí, a mí me gusta.
La verdad es que te queda bien.

5. ¿Te gusta mi camiseta? / Sí, a mí me gusta. La
verdad es que te queda bien.
6. ¿Te gusta mi falda? / Sí, a mí me gusta. La verdad
es que te queda bien.
7. ¿Te gustan mis zapatos? / Sí, a mí me gustan. La
verdad es que te quedan bien.
8. ¿Te gusta mi suéter? / Sí, a mí me gusta. La verdad
es que te queda bien.

8
1. Sí, la empleada les enseña las camisas. (Sí, la
empleada se las enseña.)
2. Sí, un cliente le dice la talla que lleva. (Sí, un
cliente se la dice.)
3. Sí, el cliente le da el dinero. (Sí, el cliente se
lo da.)
4. Sí, la cajera les da buen servicio. (Sí, la cajera
se lo da.)

9 Answers will vary.

Preview

In Repaso E, students will review vocabulary related to city and country. They will also review direct object pronouns and the uses of the preterite and imperfect.

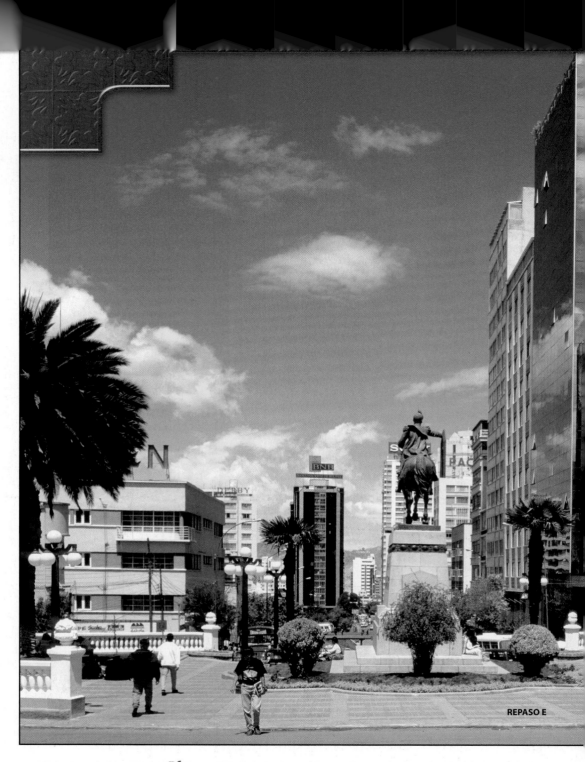

REPASO E

TeacherWorks™ Plus

The **¡Así se dice!** TeacherWorks™ Plus CD-ROM is an all-in-one planner and resource center. You may wish to use several of the following features as you plan and present the Repaso E material: Teacher Edition, Interactive Lesson Planner with Calendar, and Point and Click Access to Teaching Resources including Hotlinks to the Internet.

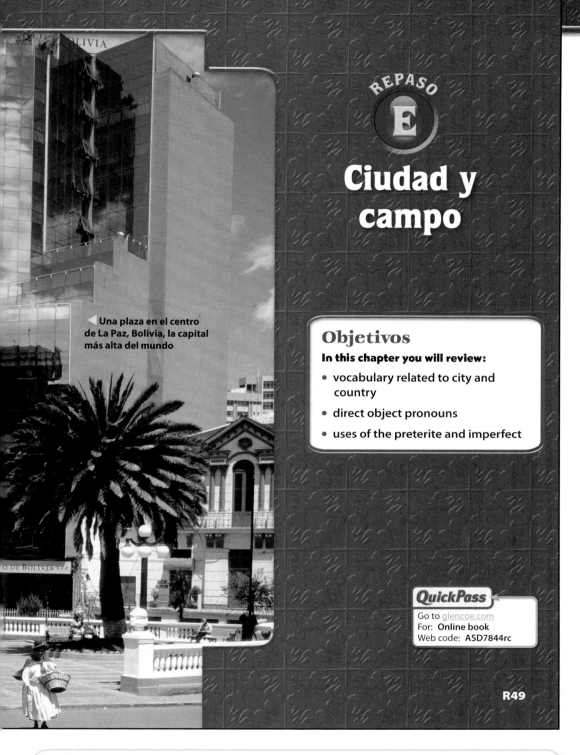

Una plaza en el centro de La Paz, Bolivia, la capital más alta del mundo

REPASO **E**

Ciudad y campo

Objetivos

In this chapter you will review:

- vocabulary related to city and country
- direct object pronouns
- uses of the preterite and imperfect

QuickPass

Go to glencoe.com
For: **Online book**
Web code: **ASD7844rc**

R49

Quia Interactive Online Student Edition found at quia.com allows students to complete activities online and submit them for computer grading for instant feedback or teacher grading with suggestions for what to review. Students can also record speaking activities, listen to chapter audio, and watch the videos that correspond with each chapter. As a teacher you are able to create rosters, set grading parameters, and post assignments for each class. After students complete activities, you can view the results and recommend remediation or review. You can also add your own customized activities for additional student practice.

QuickPass

Go to glencoe.com
For: **Vocabulary practice**
Web code: ASD7844rc

Resources

- Audio Activities TE, pages R.64–R.65
- Audio CD RC2, Tracks 10–12
- Workbook, pages R.27–R.28
- ExamView® Assessment Suite

Quick Start

Use QS Transparency R.11 or write the following on the board.

Contesta.

1. ¿Te gusta más la ciudad o el campo? ¿Por qué?
2. ¿Te prefiere ir en carro, en autobús o a pie?
3. ¿Hay una cola larga cuando esperas el autobús?
4. ¿Dónde está el centro comercial—en la ciudad o en el campo?
5. Hay mucha gente en el campo, ¿no?

▶ TEACH
Core Instruction

Step 1 Have students open their books to page R50. As you review the words and sentences, have students repeat after you or Audio CD RC2.

Step 2 Then have individuals read aloud all the sentences that accompany each photo.

Step 3 Ask questions to have students use the words.

Step 4 Have students tell other things they see in the photos.

Step 5 Have students make up additional questions about what they see in each photo.

Step 6 Call on students to give additional vocabulary they know related to **la ciudad** and **el campo.**

R50

Vocabulario 🎧

la ciudad
el semáforo
la esquina
el cruce de peatones

Los peatones cruzaban la calle. Empezaron a correr porque cambió el semáforo.

la parada de autobús

Había una cola larga en la parada de autobús.
Mucha gente esperaba.
Cuando llegó el autobús estaba completo y nadie pudo subir.

cultivar la tierra

el campo
una finca, una granja

Cuando José era joven, sus primos vivían en el campo.
Tenían una finca.
José los visitó dos veces.

R50

la autopista, la autovía
el carril

En la autopista hay varios carriles en cada sentido (dirección).
Un carro pasó (adelantó) otro que andaba más despacio.
Lo rebasó en el carril izquierdo.

REPASO E

Differentiation

Advanced Learners

Have advanced learners use the words and expressions in original sentences. You may want to have them put the sentences in the form of questions so other students can answer.

GLENCOE 🖲 Technology

Online Learning in the Classroom

Have students use QuickPass code ASD7844rc for additional vocabulary practice. They can download audio files of all vocabulary to their computer and/or MP3 player. They will also have access to a self-check quiz and eGames.

Práctica

HABLAR

 Indica si describe la ciudad o el campo.

	la ciudad	el campo
1. Hay muchas calles peatonales.		
2. Los campesinos cultivan el trigo.		
3. Hay una parada de autobús en casi cada esquina.		
4. Los caballos corren por el corral.		
5. Las gallinas ponen huevos.		
6. Es muy difícil encontrar un lugar donde se puede estacionar (aparcar) el carro.		

HABLAR • ESCRIBIR

 Contesta.

1. ¿Cruzaba la gente la calle en el cruce de peatones?
2. ¿Por qué empezaron a correr mientras cruzaban la calle?
3. ¿Qué había en la parada de autobús?
4. ¿Por qué no pudo nadie subir al autobús?
5. ¿Se permite el tráfico vehicular en una calle peatonal?
6. Cuando José era joven, ¿vivía en la ciudad? ¿Dónde vivían sus primos?
7. ¿Qué tenían ellos en el campo?
8. ¿Cuántas veces los visitó José?

CULTURA
Un pueblo en el campo cerca de Mérida, Venezuela

R51

▶ PRACTICE

Leveling EACH Activity

Easy Activity 1
Average Activity 2

Activity ① This activity can be done orally in class with books closed, calling on students at random to answer.

 Cultural Snapshot

(page R51) Mérida has grown a great deal in the twentieth century. It now has some three hundred thousand inhabitants and the best infrastructure for tourists. Tourism is its main source of income. Have students describe what they see in the photo.

Answers

①
1. la ciudad
2. el campo
3. la ciudad
4. el campo
5. el campo
6. la ciudad

②
1. Sí, la gente cruzaba la calle en el cruce de peatones.
2. Empezaron a correr mientras cruzaban la calle porque cambió el semáforo.
3. Había una cola larga en la parada de autobús.
4. Nadie pudo subir al autobús porque estaba completo.
5. No, no se permite el tráfico vehicular en una calle peatonal.
6. Sí, cuando José era joven, vivía en la ciudad. Sus primos vivían en el campo.
7. Ellos tenían una finca en el campo.
8. José los visitó dos veces.

Repaso E

Resources

■ Audio Activities TE, page R.66
🎧 Audio CD RC2, Tracks 13–14

▶ TEACH
Core Instruction

Step 1 Have students listen to the conversation using Audio CD RC2.

Step 2 Call on two students to read the conversation aloud with as much expression as possible.

Step 3 Go over the **¿Comprendes?** activity.

Differentiation

Advanced Learners

Call on an advanced learner to give a review of the conversation in his or her own words.

Slower Paced Learners

Call on a slower paced learner to repeat some of what the other said.

Writing Development

You may want students to write a paragraph summarizing the conversation. They can use their answers to the **¿Comprendes?** activity as a guide.

GLENCOE 🖱 Technology

Online Learning in the Classroom

Have students use QuickPass code ASD7844rc for additional conversation practice. Students can download audio files for the conversation to their computer and/or MP3 player.

Conversación 🎧

El otro día en la ciudad

Elena	El otro día estuve en la ciudad y no sé lo que pasaba pero el tráfico era horrible.
Teresa	¿Qué hacías en la ciudad?
Elena	Leí en el periódico que había una exposición de arte latinoamericano en el Museo Metropolitano y la quería ver.
Teresa	¿La viste?
Elena	Sí, pero como había tanto tráfico no pude tomar el bus. Tomé el metro.
Teresa	¿Qué tal te gustó la exposición?
Elena	Me gustó mucho. Había muchos cuadros con escenas rurales.

¿Comprendes?

A Contesta.
1. ¿Cuándo estuvo Elena en la ciudad?
2. ¿Qué había?
3. ¿Qué leyó Elena en el periódico?
4. ¿Qué quería ver?
5. ¿La vio?
6. ¿Le gustó?
7. ¿Qué había en muchos de los cuadros en la exposición?

R52

Answers

A
1. Elena estuvo en la ciudad el otro día.
2. Había mucho tráfico.
3. Elena leyó que había una exposición de arte latinoamericano en el Museo Metropolitano.
4. Quería ver la exposición.
5. Sí, la vio.
6. Sí, le gustó mucho.
7. Había escenas rurales en muchos de los cuadros.

Pre-AP Listening to this conversation on audio CD will help students develop the skills that they need to be successful on the istening portion of the AP exam.

QuickPass

Go to glencoe.com
For: **Grammar practice**
Web code: ASD7844rc

Repaso

Repaso **E**

Gramática

Pronombres de complemento directo

1. The direct object is the direct receiver of the action of the verb.

¿El peaje?	Ella lo pagó.
¿Los boletos?	Los compraron.
¿La llave?	La tengo.
¿Te vio?	Sí, me vio.

2. Review the forms of the direct object pronouns.

me	nos
te	*os*
lo	los
la	las

Práctica

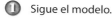

HABLAR • ESCRIBIR

1 Sigue el modelo.

MODELO el ticket para el autobús →
Aquí lo tienes.

1. el ticket para el metro
2. las entradas para el museo
3. el dinero para el peaje
4. la llave del carro
5. las fotografías de su finca
6. los boletos para el avión

LEER • ESCRIBIR

2 Completa las conversaciones.

1. —Teresa, ¿_____ invitó Elena a su fiesta?
   —Claro que _____ invitó. Ella y yo somos muy buenas amigas. ¿_____ invitó a ti también?
   —No, no _____ invitó porque sabe que tengo que trabajar.

2. —José, ¿viste a Luisa en el concierto?
   —Sí, _____ vi pero ella no _____ vio.
   —¿Cómo es que tú _____ viste pero ella no _____ vio?
   —Pues, no _____ pudo ver porque estaba sentada unas veinte filas delante de nosotros.

REPASO E

R53

⏱ **Quick Start**

Use QS Transparency R.12 or write the following on the board.

Emplea un pronombre directo.

1. Los peatones cruzaban *la calle.*
2. Pedro visita *sus abuelos* en el campo.
3. Ella no tiene *dinero* para el autobús.
4. El campesino cultiva *la tierra.*
5. Me gustan *las ciudades* porque hay museos y conciertos.

▶ **TEACH**

Core Instruction

Step 1 Go over Item 1 with the class. Ask if they have any questions. Point out that direct objects can refer to things or people.

Step 2 Have students open their books to page R53. Instead of providing or having students read the information in Item 2, you may wish to have students answer the following questions: Does **lo** replace a masculine or feminine noun? What pronoun replaces a feminine noun?

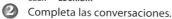

Answers

1
1. Aquí lo tienes.
2. Aquí las tienes.
3. Aquí lo tienes.
4. Aquí la tienes.
5. Aquí las tienes.
6. Aquí los tienes.

2
1. te, me, Te, me
2. la, me, la, te, me

Differentiation

Multiple Intelligences

To engage **bodily-kinesthetic** learners, call on them to come to the front of the class and dramatize the conversations in Activity 2. Encourage them to use proper intonation, facial expressions, and gestures.

Quick Start

Use QS Transparency R.13 or write the following on the board.

Escribe las frases en el pretérito.
1. Yo voy a la ciudad y veo una película.
2. Él habla con los otros peatones.
3. Mis primos viven en el campo.
4. Tú comes mucha pizza.
5. Usted lee un libro y yo oigo un CD.

▶ TEACH
Core Instruction

Step 1 Have students open their books to page R54. Lead them through Items 1–3.

Step 2 As you go over the model sentences in Item 1, draw a timeline on the board. Each time you give a verb in the preterite, draw an abrupt slash through the timeline to indicate completion or termination of the action in the past.

Step 3 As you go over the model sentences in Item 2, draw another timeline on the board. Each time you give a verb in the imperfect, draw a long shaded box alongside it to indicate duration.

Step 4 When explaining the difference between the preterite and the imperfect, you may wish to have students think of a play. Explain that the scenery, props, and the

---

El pretérito y el imperfecto

1. Remember that you use the preterite to express actions or events that began and ended at a specific time in the past.

   Carlos fue a la ciudad ayer.
   En la ciudad vio una exposición de arte.

2. You use the imperfect to talk about a continuous, habitual, or frequently repeated action in the past.

   Carlos iba a la ciudad con mucha frecuencia.
   Casi cada vez que estaba en la ciudad iba al museo donde veía una exposición de arte.

CULTURA

El joven admiraba un cuadro abstracto en el museo de la Fundación Joan Miró en Barcelona, España.

3. Often a sentence will have two or more verbs in the past. Quite often one verb indicates what was going on when something happened or took place. What was going on—the background—is expressed by the imperfect. What happened or took place is in the preterite.

   Un carro iba muy despacio y José lo rebasó.
   Los peatones cruzaban la calle cuando cambió el semáforo.

---

description are in the imperfect. What the actors and actresses actually do on stage is in the preterite.

Step 5 Give some examples and show the difference between background information and acting. Background: **Él era muy guapo. Había una fiesta. Había una mesa en la sala. Todo el mundo se divertía. José y Elena bailaban.** Acting: **En ese** momento Carlos entró. Dijo «Buenos días» a todo el mundo. Saludó a todos.

Step 6 Now use two verbs in one sentence to contrast the background information with the actions on stage. For example: **Ana y Paco bailaban cuando Carlos entró.**

Práctica

ESCUCHAR • HABLAR

3 Contesta.

1. ¿Visitaste a tus abuelos la semana pasada?
   ¿Cuándo visitaste a tus abuelos?
   ¿Visitabas a tus abuelos cada semana?
   ¿Cuándo visitabas a tus abuelos?
2. ¿Fuiste al campo el año pasado?
   ¿Cuándo fuiste al campo?
   ¿Ibas al campo muy a menudo?
   ¿Cuándo ibas al campo?

LEER • ESCRIBIR

4 Completa.

1. Una vez ellos _____ al campo y _____ a caballo.
   (ir, andar)
2. Ellos siempre _____ al campo donde _____ a caballo.
   (ir, andar)
3. Yo _____ el invierno pasado pero Elena _____ todos
   los inviernos. (esquiar, esquiar)
4. Los turistas _____ una semana en la capital y _____
   el casco antiguo. (pasar, visitar)

CULTURA

Una estancia en las pampas argentinas

▶ PRACTICE

Leveling EACH Activity

Easy Activity 3
Average Activity 4

Activity 3 You may want students to do this activity in pairs, taking turns asking and answering the questions.

Activity 4 Go over this activity in class and then have students write it for homework.

Cultural Snapshot

(page R54) Joan Miró himself founded this foundation.

(page R55) Many of the **estancias** on the **pampas** still have beautiful manor houses. Some are used as hotels and others are strictly for the family.

Answers

3

1. Sí, (No, no) visité a mis abuelos la semana pasada.
   Visité a mis abuelos ____.
   Sí, (No, no) visitaba a mis abuelos cada semana.
   Visitaba a mis abuelos ____.
2. Sí, (No, no) fui al campo el año pasado.
   Fui al campo ____.
   Sí, (No, no) iba al campo muy a menudo.
   Iba al campo ____.

4

1. fueron, anduvieron
2. iban, andaban
3. esquié, esquiaba
4. pasaron, visitaron

► PRACTICE (continued)

Leveling EACH Activity

Easy Activities 5, 7
Average Activity 6
CHallenging Activities 8, 9

Activity 6 Have students read their sentences to the class.

HABLAR • ESCRIBIR
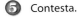

5 Contesta.
1. ¿Esperaba mucha gente en la parada cuando llegó el autobús?
2. ¿Cruzaban la calle los peatones cuando la luz del semáforo cambió?
3. ¿Vivían los primos de José en el campo cuando él los visitó?
4. ¿Conducía Elena el coche cuando ocurrió el accidente?

CULTURA
Aquí ves un rótulo en una esquina de Quito, Ecuador. ¿Cómo se dice «sentido único» en Ecuador?

LEER • ESCRIBIR
6 Completa para formar frases completas.

1.

Yo estudiaba cuando
a.
b.
c.
d.
e.

2.

Mis amigos	cuando yo llegué.
a.	
b.	
c.	
d.	
e.	

Answers

5
1. Sí (No), mucha gente (no) esperaba en la parada cuando el autobús llegó.
2. Sí, (No), los peatones (no) cruzaban la calle cuando la luz del semáforo cambió.
3. Sí, (No), los primos de José (no) vivían en el campo cuando él los visitó.
4. Sí, (No), Elena (no) conducía el coche cuando ocurrió el accidente.

6 *Answers will vary.*

HABLAR • ESCRIBIR

7 Contesta según se indica.

1. ¿Qué enviaba Manuel cuando sonó su móvil? (un correo electrónico)
2. ¿Quién lo llamó? (un amigo que tiene una finca en el campo)
3. ¿Qué estaba pasando mientras hablaban? (estaba cortando)
4. Por fin, ¿se les cortó la línea? (sí)
5. ¿Qué hizo el amigo de Manuel? (volvió a llamar)
6. ¿Sonó el móvil de Manuel? (no)
7. ¿Por qué no sonó? (él también trataba de llamar)

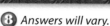 Comunicación

 8 Cuando eras niño(a), ¿vivías en una ciudad, un suburbio o en el campo? Describe la ciudad o el pueblo donde vivías. Habla de todo lo que hacías allí. ¿Te divertías?

9 ¿Cuántas veces en un solo día estás haciendo algo cuando algo o alguien te interrumpe? Piensa en algunas cosas que hacías ayer cuando algo te interrumpió. Cuenta lo que estabas haciendo y lo que pasó.

CULTURA
A estos dos niños les encanta vivir en el campo en Argentina. Un pasatiempo favorito es el de subir árboles.

Activity 7 This activity can be done as a paired activity.

Writing Development
You may wish to have students write their answer to Activity 8 in paragraph form as homework.

Activity 9 You may wish to ask volunteers to answer these questions in class.

Cultural Snapshot
(page R57) These youngsters live on an **estancia** not too far from Buenos Aires.

GLENCOE Technology

Online Learning in the Classroom
Have students use QuickPass code ASD7844rc for additional grammar practice. They can review each grammar point with an eGame or a self-check quiz.

Answers

7

1. Manuel enviaba un correo electrónico cuando sonó su móvil.
2. Un amigo que tiene una finca en el campo lo llamó.
3. Mientras hablaban estaba cortando.
4. Sí, por fin se les cortó la línea.
5. El amigo de Manuel volvió a llamar.
6. No, el móvil de Manuel no sonó.
7. No sonó porque él también trataba de llamar.

8 *Answers will vary.*

9 *Answers will vary.*

Preview

In Repaso F, students will review vocabulary related to hotels and restaurants. They will also review double object pronouns, the present perfect tense, and regular and irregular past participles.

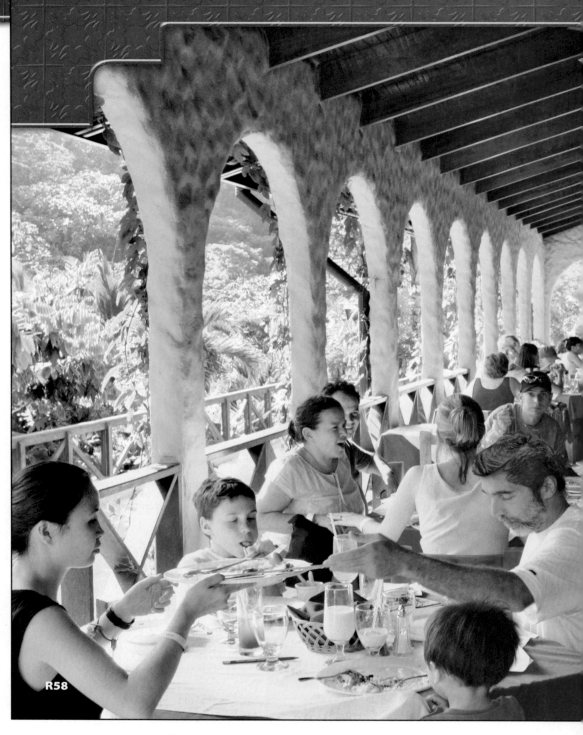

R58

TeacherWorks™ *Plus*

The **¡Así se dice!** TeacherWorks™ Plus CD-ROM is an all-in-one planner and resource center. You may wish to use several of the following features as you plan and present the Repaso F material: Teacher Edition, Interactive Lesson Planner with Calendar, and Point and Click Access to Teaching Resources including Hotlinks to the Internet.

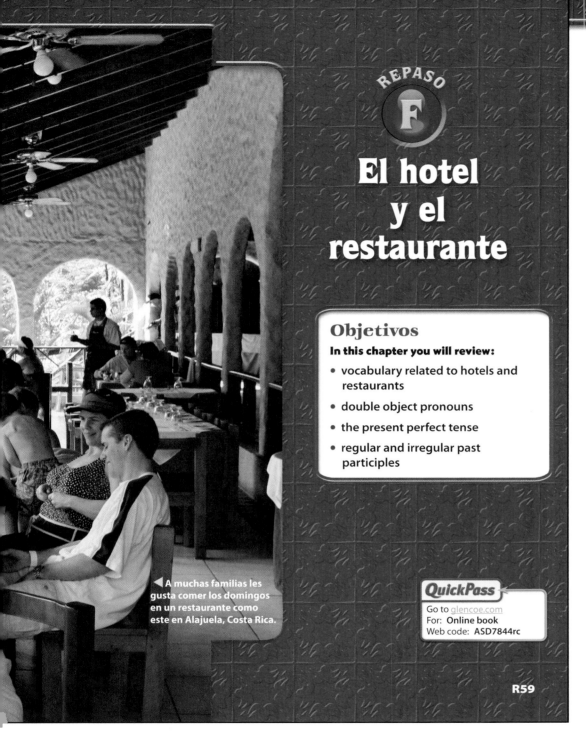

REPASO

F

El hotel y el restaurante

Objetivos

In this chapter you will review:

- vocabulary related to hotels and restaurants
- double object pronouns
- the present perfect tense
- regular and irregular past participles

◀ A muchas familias les gusta comer los domingos en un restaurante como este en Alajuela, Costa Rica.

QuickPass

Go to glencoe.com
For: **Online book**
Web code: **ASD7844rc**

R59

Quia Interactive Online Student Edition found at quia.com allows students to complete activities online and submit them for computer grading for instant feedback or teacher grading with suggestions for what to review. Students can also record speaking activities, listen to chapter audio, and watch the videos that correspond with each chapter. As a teacher you are able to create rosters, set grading parameters, and post assignments for each class. After students complete activities, you can view the results and recommend remediation or review. You can also add your own customized activities for additional student practice.

Resources

- Audio Activities TE, pages R.69–R.70
- Audio CD RC2, Tracks 19–20
- Workbook, pages R.32–R.33
- ExamView® Assessment Suite

Quick Start

Use QS Transparency R.14 or write the following on the board.

Completa.

1. En el hotel el mozo sube nuestro ___.
2. En el cuarto duermo en la ___.
3. Después de la ducha, uso una ___ limpia.
4. En el restaurante, el ___ escribe la orden.
5. Me gusta beber los batidos, pero leo el ___ y no hay nada.

▶ TEACH

Core Instruction

Step 1 Have students look at page R60 as you point to each item and have students repeat.

Step 2 Go over the sentences and ask students questions at random that elicit the new words.

Step 3 Ask if students recognize the verb tense in the sentences.

Vocabulario 🎧

Las amigas han llegado al hotel.
Están en la recepción.
El recepcionista les ha dado sus llaves.

Anita ha colgado su ropa en el armario.

La camarera ha limpiado el cuarto.
Ha hecho la cama.

El padre y su hija están en el restaurante.
Han leído el menú y han escogido lo que van a comer.
¿Le ha devuelto el señor el menú al mesero?
No, no, se lo ha devuelto pero se lo va a devolver.

Teaching Options

- Have students give you all the words and expressions they remember related to a hotel stay.
- Have students give all the words and expressions they remember about an experience at a restaurant or café.

- The amount of vocabulary students can give serves a diagnostic purpose. You can judge the amount of vocabulary they remember about these topics.

Práctica

LEER • ESCRIBIR

1 Escoge.

1. (Los huéspedes / Los recepcionistas) han llegado al hotel.
2. El recepcionista les ha dado (sus maletas / sus llaves).
3. Los amigos han subido a (su cuarto / su armario).
4. La camarera ha hecho (la cama / la almohada).
5. Ella ha cambiado las toallas (limpias / sucias).
6. El mesero les ha traído (la mesa / el menú).
7. La ducha y la bañera están en el cuarto de (baño / lavabo).
8. El cliente va a salir y ha (abandonado / reservado) su cuarto.

[Handwritten notes:]
1. Dónde han llegado las amigas?
2. ¿Cómo se llama el hotel?
3. Dónde están?
4. Quién trabaja en la recepción?
5. Qué les ha dado?
6. Dónde ha colgado su ropa Anita?
7. Quién ha limpiado el cuarto?
8. Qué ha hecho?
9. ¿Dónde están el padre y su hija?
10. Qué han leído?
11. Qué han escogido?

CULTURA
Un hotel bonito en el centro de la Ciudad de México

Differentiation

Slower Paced Learners

Have slower paced learners make up a simple sentence about what they see in one of the photos.

Advanced Learners

Have advanced learners tell all they can about the photos.

Multiple Intelligences

Have **visual-spatial** learners draw a picture of a scene in a hotel or restaurant and describe what they have drawn.

 **PRACTICE**

> **Leveling EACH Activity**
>
> **Easy** Activity 1

Activity 1 Do this activity orally in class. As an expansion, you may want to have students do the activity again, changing the sentences to the present tense.

Teaching Options

Ask for volunteers to imagine the inside of the luxurious hotel in the photo and describe it to the class.

Answers

1
1. Los huéspedes
2. sus llaves
3. su cuarto
4. la cama
5. sucias
6. el menú
7. baño
8. abandonado

▶ PRACTICE

Leveling EACH Activity

Average Activities 2, 3
CHallenging Activity 4

Activity ② Allow students to look at the photos as they do this activity. Have them first identify the **desayuno continental** and the **desayuno americano**.

Activity ③ This can be either an oral or written activity.

✿ Comunicación

Interpersonal, Presentational, Interpretive

Activity ④ Verbal-linguistic and **interpersonal** learners will enjoy collaborating to say or write an interpretation of the picture in the form of a story. **Bodily-kinesthetic** learners may want to work in pairs or small groups to present a skit based on the picture.

GLENCOE ⬚ Technology

Online Learning in the Classroom

Have students use QuickPass code ASD7844rc for additional vocabulary practice. They can download audio files of all vocabulary to their computer and/or MP3 player. They will also have access to a self-check quiz and eGames.

Repaso F

Más práctica
▪ Workbook, pp. R32–R33
◉ StudentWorks™ Plus

HABLAR • ESCRIBIR

② Describe.
1. un desayuno continental
2. un desayuno americano

HABLAR • ESCRIBIR

③ Contesta.
1. Vas a poner la mesa. ¿Qué necesitas?
2. Vas a hacer la cama. ¿Qué necesitas?
3. Llegas a un hotel. ¿Qué le dices a la recepcionista?
4. Estás en un restaurante y quieres comer tu comida favorita. ¿Qué vas a pedir?
5. Has terminado la comida. ¿Qué le pides al mesero?

✿ Comunicación

④ Describe el dibujo.

Answers

② *Answers will vary but may include:*
1. Un desayuno continental incluye el pan dulce, el panecillo, la mantequilla, la mermelada y el café o el jugo (de naranja).
2. Un desayuno americano incluye los huevos (revueltos), el tocino (el bacón, el lacón) y el café o el jugo (de naranja).

③
1. Necesito mantel, servilletas, platos, tenedores, cuchillos, cucharas, cucharitas, platillos y tazas.
2. Necesito sábanas, manta (frazada) y almohadas.
3. Le digo que he reservado un cuarto.
4. *Answers will vary.*
5. Le pido la cuenta.

④ *Answers will vary.*

Conversación

QuickPass

Go to glencoe.com
For: **Conversation practice**
Web code: **ASD7844rc**

Al café

¿Comprendes?

A Corrige.
1. Los amigos de José han llegado.
2. José los ha llevado a su hotel.
3. Ellos no han reservado un cuarto en ningún hotel.
4. Los amigos tienen sueño después de su viaje pero no tienen hambre.
5. Ya han comido.
6. José y Beatriz han estado en el nuevo Rincón Argentino.

B Analizando Contesta.
Si José y Beatriz nunca han comido en el Rincón Argentino, ¿por qué han decidido ir a comer allí con los amigos de Beatriz?

REPASO F

R63

Answers

A
1. Los amigos de Beatriz han llegado.
2. Beatriz los ha llevado a su hotel.
3. Ellos han reservado un cuarto un el Nacional.
4. Los amigos tienen sueño y hambre después de su viaje.
5. No han comido.
6. José y Beatriz no han estado en el nuevo Rincón Argentino.

B *Answers will vary but may include:* Han decido ir a comer allí con los amigos de Beatriz porque José ha oído que la comida es muy buena y bastante económica.

Resources

■ Audio Activities TE, pages R.70–R.71
🎧 Audio CD RC2, Tracks 21–22

▶ TEACH
Core Instruction

Step 1 Have students close their books and listen to the conversation using Audio CD RC2.

Step 2 Call on two students with good pronunciation to read the conversation aloud while students follow along in their books. You may wish to interrupt occasionally to ask questions.

Step 3 Do the **¿Comprendes?** activities.

Differentiation
Multiple Intelligences

You may wish to ask **bodily-kinesthetic** or **advanced** learners to act out the conversation without using the book. Suggest that they follow the same idea as the conversation in the book, but encourage them to ad-lib and say as much as they can. If necessary, allow them to use the present tense. Then ask the rest of the class whether they understood what was said.

GLENCOE SPANISH

Why It Works!

In Repaso F, students will review object pronouns and the present perfect tense. Have students find how many times these points are reinforced in the short conversation. Pronouns—4 times; Present perfect—8 times

Repaso F

Resources

- Audio Activities TE, page R.71
- Audio CD RC2, Track 23
- Workbook, page R.34
- ExamView® Assessment Suite

Quick Start

Use QS Transparency R.15 or write the following on the board.

Contesta con pronombres.
1. ¿Te subió las maletas?
2. ¿Te dio la llave el mozo?
3. ¿Te abrió la puerta?
4. ¿Te prendió el aire acondicionado?

▶ TEACH

Core Instruction

Step 1 Have students open their books. Lead them through Items 1–3 on page R64.

Step 2 Call on volunteers to read the model sentences aloud.

Step 3 You may wish to write the model sentences on the board. Highlight the objects as is done on page R64. Draw an arrow from the pronoun to the noun it replaces. Have students note that the second pronoun comes after the one that was already there.

ABOUT THE SPANISH LANGUAGE

You may wish to explain to students that **le** changes to **se** strictly for the sake of pronunciation. It would be both difficult and awkward to say **le lo, le la.**

CULTURA
Muchos hoteles de lujo ofrecen servicio a cuartos. Aquí el mozo va a servir el desayuno en el cuarto de los huéspedes.

Gramática

Dos complementos en una frase

1. Many sentences have both a direct and an indirect object pronoun. The indirect object pronoun always precedes the direct object and both objects precede the conjugated form of the verb.

¿Quién les ha servido el postre?
El mesero nos lo ha servido.

¿Quién te dio las llaves?
El recepcionista me las dio.

2. The indirect object pronouns **le** and **les** change to **se** when used with **lo, la, los,** or **las.**

El mozo le subió el equipaje.
El mozo se lo subió.

El mesero les sirvió la comida.
El mesero se la sirvió.

3. **Se** is often clarified with a prepositional phrase.

Yo se lo di
- a él.
- a ella.
- a usted.
- a ellos.
- a ellas.
- a ustedes.

Práctica

HABLAR • ESCRIBIR

① Sigue el modelo.

MODELO la percha →
—¿Quién te dio la percha?
—La camarera me la dio.

1. la almohada
2. la manta
3. el jabón
4. las toallas
5. el papel higiénico
6. las perchas

Answers

①
1. ¿Quién te dio la almohada? / La camarera me la dio.
2. ¿Quién te dio la manta? / La camarera me la dio.
3. ¿Quién te dio el jabón? / La camarera me lo dio.
4. ¿Quién te dio las toallas? / La camarera me las dio.
5. ¿Quién te dio el papel higiénico? / La camarera me lo dio.
6. ¿Quién te dio las perchas? / La camarera me las dio.

GLENCOE ✎ Technology

Online Learning in the Classroom

Have students use QuickPass code ASD7844rc for additional grammar practice. They can review each grammar point with an eGame or a self-check quiz.

LEER • ESCRIBIR

2️⃣ Contesta con **la camarera** o **el mesero** usando pronombres.
1. ¿Quién te ha dado el menú?
2. ¿Quién te ha cambiado las toallas?
3. ¿Quién te ha servido el desayuno?
4. ¿Quién te ha traído la manta?

LEER • ESCRIBIR

3️⃣ Cambia los sustantivos (nombres) a pronombres.
1. Abordo del avión el asistente de vuelo les sirvió la comida a los pasajeros.
2. En clase la profesora les explicó las reglas a los alumnos.
3. En la tienda de ropa el empleado le vendió el pantalón a José.
4. En el restaurante el mesero les trajo los platos a los clientes.
5. Elena le dejó la propina para el mesero.

CULTURA

El mesero ha servido un gran plato de mariscos en este restaurante en Punta Cana en la República Dominicana.

▶ PRACTICE

Leveling EACH Activity

Easy Activity 1
Average Activity 2
Average–**CH**allenging
Activity 3

Activity ① Students may want to do this activity with a partner.

Differentiation

Multiple Intelligences
You may wish to have **bodily-kinesthetic** learners make up an original conversation at a restaurant and present it to the class. Encourage them to use as many direct and indirect object pronouns as possible.

 Cultural Snapshot

(page R65) Punta Cana is a very popular resort on the northern coast of the Dominican Republic. There are many flights directly from the United States to Punta Cana, which is also popular with European tourists.

Answers

2️⃣
1. El mesero me lo ha dado.
2. La camarera me las ha cambiado.
3. El mesero me lo ha servido.
4. La camarera me la ha traído.

3️⃣
1. Abordo del avión el asistente de vuelo se la sirvió.
2. En clase la profesora se las explicó.
3. En la tienda de ropa el empleado se lo vendió.
4. En el restaurante el mesero se los trajo.
5. Elena se la dejó.

Quick Start

Use QS Transparency R.16 or write the following on the board.

Completa con haber.

1. Tú ___ hablado con el mesero.
2. Diego ___ tenido hambre.
3. Ellos ___ leído el menú.
4. Usted ___ limpiado el cuarto.
5. Nosotros ___ buscado una mesa libre.

▶ TEACH

Step 1 Go over the presentation of the past participle as you write the examples on the board. Have students repeat them.

Step 2 As you go over the conjugations, you may wish to give students just the forms of the verb **haber.** Then go over the present perfect forms presented here and have the students repeat them in unison.

Step 3 Have students repeat the irregular past participles several times. Ask them to use them in sentences.

CULTURA

Es tarde y mucha gente ya ha terminado de comer en este restaurante en la Ciudad de México.

R66

El presente perfecto

1. The present perfect tense is formed by using the present tense of the verb **haber** and the past participle. Review the forms of the present perfect.

	hablar	comer	subir
yo	he hablado	he comido	he subido
tú	has hablado	has comido	has subido
Ud., él, ella	ha hablado	ha comido	ha subido
nosotros(as)	hemos hablado	hemos comido	hemos subido
vosotros(as)	*habéis hablado*	*habéis comido*	*habéis subido*
Uds., ellos, ellas	han hablado	han comido	han subido

2. Review the following verbs that have an irregular past participle.

decir	→	dicho	abrir	→ abierto
hacer	→	hecho	cubrir	→ cubierto
escribir	→	escrito	poner	→ puesto
freír	→	frito	morir	→ muerto
romper	→	roto	volver	→ vuelto
ver	→	visto	devolver	→ devuelto

3. The present perfect tense describes an action completed in the very recent past. Review some expressions that are frequently used with the present perfect.

> ya
> todaviá no
> hasta ahora
> jamás
> nunca
>
> —En tu vida, ¿has estado en México?
> —No, no he ido nunca a México.
> —Yo, sí. Ya he estado tres veces.

Práctica

Más práctica
Workbook, pp. R35–R36
StudentWorks™ Plus

ESCUCHAR • HABLAR

4 Contesta con **sí.**

1. ¿Han llegado los amigos al hotel?
2. ¿Han ido a la recepción?
3. ¿Les ha ayudado el recepcionista?
4. ¿Han reservado ellos un cuarto?
5. ¿Les ha dado sus llaves el recepcionista?
6. ¿Han subido los amigos a su cuarto?
7. ¿Han subido en el ascensor?

HABLAR • ESCRIBIR

5 Personaliza. Da respuestas personales.

1. ¿Has comido en un restaurante mexicano?
2. ¿Jamás has comido tacos y enchiladas?
3. En tu vida, ¿has viajado en avión?
4. ¿Cuántos vuelos has tomado?
5. ¿Te has hospedado en un albergue juvenil?

ESCUCHAR • LEER • ESCRIBIR

6 Sigue el modelo.

MODELO —¿Van a verlo?
—**Pero, ya lo hemos visto.**

1. ¿Van a abrirlo?
2. ¿Van a hacerlo?
3. ¿Van a devolverlo?
4. ¿Van a escribirlo?
5. ¿Van a decirlo?

TACOS	
CARNE ASADA	2.80
POLLO ASADO	2.49
CARNITAS	2.49
3 CARNE ASADA	4.25
3 POLLO ASADO	3.71
3 ADOVADA	3.71
3 CABEZA	3.71
3 BUCHE	3.71

TORTAS	
CARNE ASADA	4.25
POLLO ASADO	3.71
MACHACA	3.50
CHORIZO	3.50

BURRITOS	
CARNE ASADA	4.25
POLLO ASADO	3.71
CARNITAS	3.71
MACHACA	3.50
CHORIZO	3.50
CHILE RELLENO	3.50
PANCHOS BURRITO	4.50

QUESADILLAS	
CARNE ASADA	4.25
POLLO ASADO	3.71

🏵 Comunicación

7 ¿Te has hospedado o has pasado unas vacaciones en un hotel? ¿En qué hotel? Describe tu experiencia.

8 ¿Has tenido una experiencia buena en un restaurante? Describe la experiencia.

9 Discute con un(a) amigo(a) las cosas que todavía no han hecho pero que quieren hacer algún día.

▶ PRACTICE

Leveling EACH Activity

Easy Activities 4, 5
Average Activity 6
CHallenging Activities 7, 8, 9

📰 Learning from Realia

(page 67) **Machaca** in Mexico is a dish of fried meat with eggs and onion. **Adovada** can also be written **adobada.**

Activities ⑦, ⑧, ⑨ When having students do a completely open-ended activity with no learning prompts, students are actually functioning as if they were communicating in a real-life situation. In such a situation, it is normal for learners to make a few mistakes. For this reason, you may decide not to interrupt and correct each error a student makes. This is up to your discretion.

Answers

④
1. Sí, los amigos han llegado al hotel.
2. Sí, han ido a la recepción.
3. Sí, el recepcionista les ha ayudado.
4. Sí, ellos han reservado un cuarto.
5. Sí, el recepcionista se las ha dado.
6. Sí, los amigos han subido a su cuarto.
7. Sí, han subido en el ascensor.

⑤
1. Sí, (No, no) he comido en un restaurante mexicano.
2. Sí, (No, no) he comido (nunca) tacos y enchiladas.
3. Sí, (No, no) he viajado en avión.
4. He tomado ___ vuelos. (No he tomado un vuelo.)
5. Sí, (No, no) me he hospedado en un albergue juvenil.

⑥
1. Pero, ya lo hemos abierto.
2. Pero, ya lo hemos hecho.
3. Pero, ya lo hemos devuelto.
4. Pero, ya lo hemos escrito.
5. Pero, ya lo hemos dicho.

⑦ *Answers will vary.*

⑧ *Answers will vary.*

⑨ *Answers will vary.*

Chapter Overview
Cocina hispana

● Scope and Sequence

Topics
- The kitchen
- Cooking
- Types of food
- Using a recipe

Culture
- Various foods from Spanish-speaking countries
- The metric system
- Good nutrition

Functions
- How to talk about foods and food preparation
- How to talk about a Spanish recipe

Structure
- The subjunctive
- Formal commands
- Negative informal commands

● Planning Guide

	required	recommended	optional
Vocabulario (pages 4–7) La cocina	✔		
Gramática (pages 8–13) El subjuntivo El imperativo formal El imperativo familiar—formas negativas	✔		
Conversación (pages 14–15) ¿Yo? ¿En la cocina?		✔	
Lectura cultural (pages 16–17) Una receta latina		✔	
Lectura Un poco más (pages 18–19) Una receta para «la ropa vieja»			✔
Prepárate para el examen (pages 20–23)			✔
Repaso cumulativo (pages 26–27)			✔

● Correlations to National Foreign Language Standards

Page numbers in light print refer to the Student Edition. Page numbers in bold print refer to the Teacher Edition.	
Communication Standard 1.1 Interpersonal	pp. **2–3, 4,** 7, **7,** 10, 13, 22
Communication Standard 1.2 Interpretive	pp. **4,** 6, **6,** 9, **9,** 10, 11, 12, 13, **14,** 15, 16, 17, **18,** 19, 21, **21,** 26, **27**
Communication Standard 1.3 Presentational	pp. **1C, 1D,** 4, **5,** 6, **7,** 11, **12, 16, 20,** 22, 23, **23, 24, 25**
Cultures Standard 2.1	pp. **1D, 14, 18**
Cultures Standard 2.2	pp. **1C, 1D, 1,** 2–3, **2–3,** 7, **7, 9, 10,** 12, 13, 15, **15,** 16, **16,** 17, 18, **19,** 21, 22, 23, 27
Connections Standard 3.1	pp. **1C, 1D,** 6, 10, **10**
Connections Standard 3.2	pp. 5, **5, 11,** 13, **13,** 15, **15,** 16, 17, 18, 19, **19,** 21
Comparisons Standard 4.1	pp. **1C,** 5, 8, **13, 19, 24,** 25
Comparisons Standard 4.2	pp. **1D,** 1, **1, 2,** 19
Communities Standard 5.1	pp. **1C, 15, 16, 20, 22, 24**
Communities Standard 5.2	pp. 5, **5,** 15, **15,** 19, **19**

To read the ACTFL Standards in their entirety, see the front of the Teacher Edition.

● Student Resources

Print

Workbook *(pp. 1.3–1.16)*
Audio Activities *(pp. 1.17–1.21)*
Pre-AP Workbook, Chapter 1

Technology

- StudentWorks™ Plus
- ¡Así se dice! Vocabulario en vivo
- ¡Así se dice! Gramática en vivo
- ¡Así se dice! Diálogo en vivo
- ¡Así se dice! Cultura en vivo
- Vocabulary PuzzleMaker
- **QuickPass** glencoe.com

● Teacher Resources

Print

TeacherTools, Chapter 1
   Workbook TE *(pp. 1.3–1.16)*
   Audio Activities TE *(pp. 1.19–1.32)*
   TPR Storytelling *(pp. 1.35–1.38)*
   Quizzes 1–4 *(pp. 1.41–1.45)*
   Tests *(pp. 1.48–1.71)*
   Performance Assessment, Task 1 *(pp. 1.73–1.74)*

Technology

- Quick Start Transparencies 1.1–1.5
- Vocabulary Transparencies V1.1–V1.3
- Museo de Arte Fine Art Transparencies F 54
- Audio CD 1
- *ExamView®* Assessment Suite
- TeacherWorks™ Plus
- PowerTeach
- ¡Así se dice! Video Program
- Vocabulary PuzzleMaker
- **QuickPass** glencoe.com

Chapter Project

Un programa de cocina

Students will prepare and present a Hispanic dish as if they were on a cooking show.

1. Pair students up to conduct preliminary research on Hispanic cuisine and to select a recipe to prepare and present—or have them choose from a predetermined list of recipes. Each pair should pick a name for their show, make a list of the ingredients they will need, and schedule a time outside of class to practice their presentation.

2. Each pair will draft a script in Spanish to use as a guideline for the presentation. You may wish to provide the class with a short list of cooking vocabulary and to encourage students to use a dictionary to find any additional words for utensils, measurements, or other cooking terms required to present their dish.

3. Although it is important for students to prepare for their episode in advance, students should not memorize their scripts word for word. You might allow them to use note cards as prompts—but remind them that reading their note cards and failing to maintain eye contact with the audience will result in a lower score.

4. In order to avoid mess and waste, or if you do not have cooking facilities available, you may want students to pantomime the preparation of their dish without using real ingredients. Have students gather props to use while presenting their cooking show to the class: bowls, utensils, measuring cups and spoons, etc. Each presentation should incorporate several visual aids in addition to the kitchen items. Students can use visuals or gestures to illustrate meaning of any new cooking vocabulary. Encourage students to be creative.

5. Have each pair submit a draft of their script to be checked or peer edited and corrected accordingly. Each pair should turn in their original draft along with the final corrected version, as well as a copy of the recipe they followed, when they present their show to the class. For additional cultural enrichment, you may wish to have students share actual dishes they have prepared in class or at home with the rest of the class.

Technology Expansion: If you are able, record the students' presentations with a digital video camera and then allow the students to edit their video clips. Using video editing software, they can add Spanish titles, credits, and music to make their video more like an actual television show. Post the video clips to the class Web site to share them with Spanish-speaking members of the community and student key pals.

Scoring Rubric for Project

	1	3	5
Evidence of planning	Draft of script is not provided.	Draft of script is provided but is not corrected.	Corrected draft of script is provided.
Use of visual aids	Cooking show contains no visual aids.	Cooking show contains few visual aids.	Cooking show contains several visual aids.
Presentation	Cooking show contains little of the required elements.	Cooking show contains some of the required elements.	Cooking show contains all the required elements.

Culture

● Recipe

▰▰▰▰▰▰▰▰▰▰▰ DULCE DE LECHE ▰▰▰▰▰▰▰▰▰▰▰

This delicious sauce is popular throughout Latin America and is used in various desserts as flavoring or filling. You may wish for students to research recipes that call for the use of **dulce de leche** so they can use this recipe to create another dish.

Ingredients:
4 cups whole milk
1⅓ cup sugar
1 vanilla bean
½ teaspoon baking soda

Combine all the ingredients in a large saucepan and bring to a boil over high heat. Stir to dissolve the sugar. Simmer over medium heat, stirring often, until the milk begins to thicken and turns a caramel color (about 45 minutes). Once the mixture has reached the consistency of condensed milk, remove and discard the vanilla bean. Transfer the mixture to a serving bowl or jar and allow to cool.

● La dieta

How we cook and what we cook is a reflection of our diet. The kinds of food one family eats may not be the same as those eaten by another family, especially if they live in another region or country. Diet is very much influenced by the surrounding culture and environment and often reflects the types of products found in a certain region of the world. The following is a list of foods that are part of a typical diet of inhabitants of Spain and Latin America.

Meat	• very little red meat • more chicken, lamb, veal, fish, and shellfish • fish and shellfish three to four times a week, perhaps
Vegetables	• beans, chickpeas, lentils • fresh vegetables such as peppers, tomatoes, and onions
Fruit	• as dessert and throughout day
Dairy	• no butter in cooking • no milk as adult beverage (babies and small children only) • much cheese, often at meal's end
Grains	• much unbuttered bread with meals • bread for breakfast, not cereal • rice

After sharing this chart with your students, have them come up with a typical diet for someone living in North America. How do the two diets differ? Which typical diet do students think is healthier, North American or Hispanic? Have students give reasons to support their responses.

● Connection to Fine Art

Show the students Glencoe *Museo de Arte* Fine Art Transparency F 54, *Preparando tortillas*, painted in 1926 by Diego Rivera. The tortilla maker boils corn with lime to make **nixtamal,** grinds that mixture into **masa** dough using a stone **mano** and **metate,** pats the dough into tortillas, and bakes the tortillas on a dish called a **comal.** Encourage students to investigate modern issues affecting these traditional techniques (such as alternative technology design) and to share their report with their social studies class.

50-Minute Lesson Plans

	Objective	Present	Practice	Assess/Homework
Day 1	Talk about foods and food preparation	Chapter Opener, p. 1 (5 min.) Introducción al tema, pp. 2–3 (10 min.) Core Instruction/Vocabulario, pp. 4–5 (20 min.)	Activities 1–4, pp. 6–7 (15 min.)	Student Workbook Activities A–D, pp. 1.3–1.4 **QuickPass** Vocabulary Practice
Day 2	Talk about foods and food preparation	Quick Start, p. 4 (5 min.) Review Vocabulario, pp. 4–5 (10 min.) Video, Vocabulario en vivo (10 min.)	Activities 5–7, p. 7 (10 min.) Total Physical Response, p. 5 (5 min.) Audio Activities A–E, pp. 1.19–1.22 (10 min.)	Student Workbook Activities E–G, pp. 1.5–1.6 **QuickPass** Vocabulary Practice
Day 3	The subjunctive	Core Instruction/Gramática, El subjuntivo, pp. 8–9 (20 min.)	Activities 1–2, pp. 9–10 (10 min.) Audio Activities A–B, p. 1.23 (10 min.)	Quiz 1, p. 1.41 (10 min.) Student Workbook Activities A–B, p. 1.7 **QuickPass** Grammar Practice
Day 4	The subjunctive	Quick Start, p. 8 (5 min.) Review Gramática, El subjuntivo, pp. 8–9 (15 min.)	Activities 3–5, p. 10 (20 min.) InfoGap, p. SR2 (10 min.)	Student Workbook Activities C–D, pp. 1.7–1.8 **QuickPass** Grammar Practice
Day 5	Formal commands	Quick Start, p. 11 (5 min.) Core Instruction/Gramática, El imperativo formal, p. 11 (10 min.)	Activities 6–10, pp. 11–12 (10 min.) Foldables, p. 11 (5 min.) Audio Activities C–F, pp. 1.24–1.25 (10 min.)	Quiz 2, p. 1.42 (10 min.) Student Workbook Activities A–E, pp. 1.9–1.10 **QuickPass** Grammar Practice
Day 6	Negative informal commands	Quick Start, p. 13 (5 min.) Core Instruction/Gramática, El imperativo familiar—formas negativas, p. 13 (15 min.)	Activities 11–13, p. 13 (10 min.) Audio Activities G–J, pp. 1.26–1.27 (10 min.)	Quiz 3, p. 1.43 (10 min.) Student Workbook Activities A–C, pp. 1.11–1.12 **QuickPass** Grammar Practice
Day 7	Develop reading and listening comprehension skills	Quick Start, p. 14 (5 min.) Core Instruction/Conversación, p. 14 (15 min.) Video, Diálogo en vivo (10 min.)	¿Comprendes? A–B, p. 15 (10 min.)	Quiz 4, p. 1.44 (10 min.) ¿Comprendes? C–D, p. 15 **QuickPass** Conversation
Day 8	Talk about a Spanish recipe	Core Instruction/Lectura cultural, p. 16 (20 min.)	¿Comprendes? A–C, p. 17 (15 min.)	Listening Comprehension Test, pp. 1.63–1.65 (15 min.) **QuickPass** Reading Practice
Day 9	Develop reading comprehension skills	Core Instruction/Lectura Un poco más, p. 18 (15 min.) Video, Cultura en vivo (10 min.)	¿Comprendes?, p. 19 (5 min.) Prepárate para el examen, pp. 20–21 (20 min.)	Prepárate para el examen, Practice for written proficiency, p. 23 **QuickPass** Reading Practice
Day 10	Chapter review	Repaso del Capítulo 1, pp. 24–25 (15 min.)	Prepárate para el examen, Practice for oral proficiency, p. 22 (20 min.)	Test for Writing Proficiency, p. 1.68 (15 min.) Review for chapter test

Day 11	Chapter 1 Tests (50 min.)
	    Reading and Writing Test, pp. 1.53–1.62
	    Speaking Test, p. 1.66
	    Test for Oral Proficiency, p. 1.67
	    Test for Reading Comprehension, pp. 1.69–1.71			

90-Minute Lesson Plans

	Objective	Present	Practice	Assess/Homework
Block 1	Talk about foods and food preparation	Chapter Opener, p. 1 (5 min.) Introducción al tema, pp. 2–3 (10 min.) Quick Start, p. 4 (5 min.) Core Instruction/Vocabulario, pp. 4–5 (20 min.) Video, Vocabulario en vivo (10 min.)	Activities 1–7, pp. 6–7 (20 min.) Total Physical Response, p. 5 (5 min.) Audio Activities A–E, pp. 1.19–1.22 (15 min.)	Student Workbook Activities A–G, pp. 1.3–1.6 **QuickPass** Vocabulary Practice
Block 2	The subjunctive	Quick Start, p. 8 (5 min.) Core Instruction/Gramática, El subjuntivo, pp. 8–9 (20 min.)	Activities 1–5, pp. 9–10 (25 min.) InfoGap, p. SR2 (10 min.) Audio Activities A–B, p. 1.23 (20 min.)	Quiz 1, p. 1.41 (10 min.) Student Workbook Activities A–D, pp. 1.7–1.8 **QuickPass** Grammar Practice
Block 3	Formal commands Negative informal commands	Quick Start, p. 11 (5 min.) Core Instruction/Gramática, El imperativo formal, p. 11 (10 min.) Quick Start, p. 13 (5 min.) Core Instruction/Gramática, El imperativo familiar—formas negativas, p. 13 (10 min.)	Activities 6–10, pp. 11–12 (15 min.) Activities 11–13, p. 13 (10 min.) Foldables, p. 11 (5 min.) Audio Activities C–J, pp. 1.24–1.27 (20 min.)	Quiz 2, p. 1.42 (10 min.) Student Workbook Activities A–E, pp. 1.9–1.10 Student Workbook Activities A–C, pp. 1.11–1.12 **QuickPass** Grammar Practice
Block 4	Talk about a Spanish recipe	Quick Start, p. 14 (5 min.) Core Instruction/Conversación, p. 14 (20 min.) Video, Diálogo en vivo (10 min.) Core Instruction/Lectura cultural, p. 16 (20 min.)	¿Comprendes? A–B, p. 15 (5 min.) ¿Comprendes? A–C, p. 17 (10 min.)	Quizzes 3–4, pp. 1.43–1.44 (20 min.) ¿Comprendes? C–D, p. 15 Prepárate para el examen, Practice for written proficiency, p. 23 **QuickPass** Conversation, Reading Practice
Block 5	Develop reading comprehension skills	Core Instruction/Lectura Un poco más, p. 18 (15 min.) Video, Cultura en vivo (10 min.)	¿Comprendes?, p. 19 (10 min.) Prepárate para el examen, pp. 20–21 (20 min.) Prepárate para el examen, Practice for oral proficiency, p. 22 (20 min.)	Listening Comprehension Test, pp. 1.63–1.65 (15 min.) Review for chapter test **QuickPass** Reading Practice

Block 6	Chapter 1 Tests (50 min.)
	    Reading and Writing Test, pp. 1.53–1.62
	    Speaking Test, p. 1.66
	    Test for Oral Proficiency, p. 1.67
	    Test for Writing Proficiency, p. 1.68
	    Test for Reading Comprehension, pp. 1.69–1.71
	Chapter Project, p. 1C (40 min.)			

Preview

In this chapter, students will learn the way in which several popular Latino dishes are prepared. They will also read a recipe for the popular **arroz con pollo**. In order to do this, students will learn the command forms of the verbs. They will also be introduced to the subjunctive.

Pacing

It is important to note that once you reach **¡Bravo!** in the chapter, there is no more new material for the students to learn. The rest of the chapter recycles what has already been covered. The suggested pacing listed here leaves two to three days for review, assessment, and enrichment activities such as the chapter project.

Vocabulario	1–2 days
Gramática	2–3 days
Conversación	1 day
Lectura cultural	1 day
Lectura Un poco más	1 day

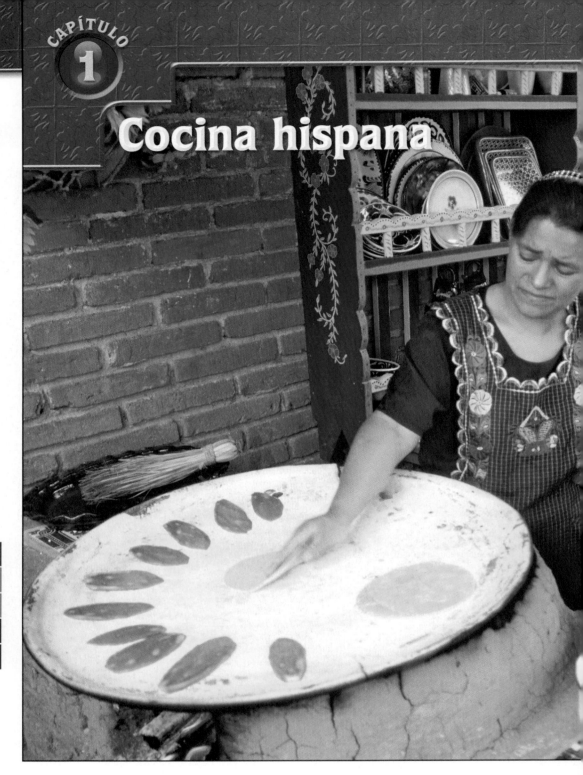

Cocina hispana

TeacherWorks*Plus*

The **¡Así se dice!** TeacherWorks™ Plus CD-ROM is an all-in-one planner and resource center. You may wish to use several of the following features as you plan and present the Chapter 1 material: Interactive Teacher Edition, Interactive Lesson Planner with Calendar, and Point and Click Access to Teaching Resources including Hotlinks to the Internet and Correlations to the National Standards.

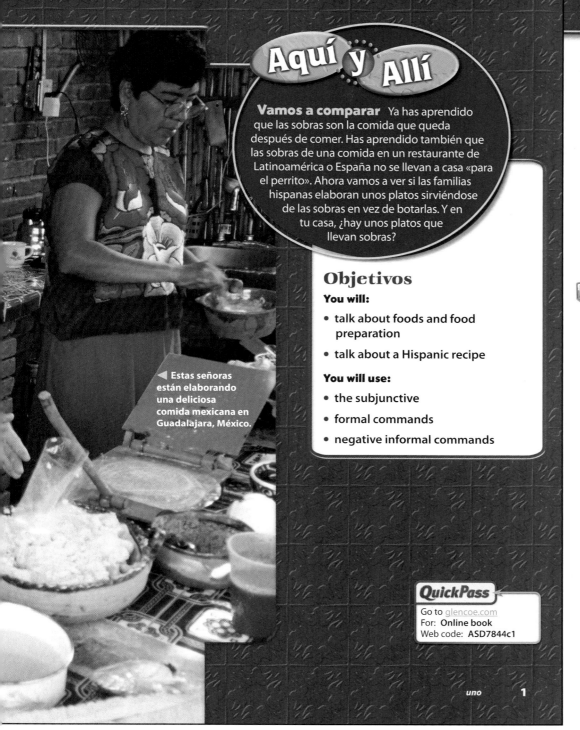

Aquí y Allí

Vamos a comparar Ya has aprendido que las sobras son la comida que queda después de comer. Has aprendido también que las sobras de una comida en un restaurante de Latinoamérica o España no se llevan a casa «para el perrito». Ahora vamos a ver si las familias hispanas elaboran unos platos sirviéndose de las sobras en vez de botarlas. Y en tu casa, ¿hay unos platos que llevan sobras?

Objetivos

You will:

- talk about foods and food preparation
- talk about a Hispanic recipe

You will use:

- the subjunctive
- formal commands
- negative informal commands

◄ Estas señoras están elaborando una deliciosa comida mexicana en Guadalajara, México.

QuickPass

Go to glencoe.com
For: **Online book**
Web code: **ASD7844c1**

SPOTLIGHT ON CULTURE

Cultural Comparison
As students go through this chapter, they will be able to make comparisons between the preparation of foods in Spain, Latin America, and the United States. They will also learn some interesting information about leftovers and doggie bags.

Cultural Snapshot
In many types of restaurants the wood-burning stove or oven is very common. The cook uses the little straw "broom," seen at the left of the picture, to fan the flames. The woman in the photograph is preparing **nopales,** a dish made with cactus.

Quia Interactive Online Student Edition found at quia.com allows students to complete activities online and submit them for computer grading for instant feedback or teacher grading with suggestions for what to review. Students can also record speaking activities, listen to chapter audio, and watch the videos that correspond with each chapter. As a teacher you are able to create rosters, set grading parameters, and post assignments for each class. After students complete activities, you can view the results and recommend remediation or review. You can also add your own customized activities for additional student practice.

1

Introducción al tema

▶ PRESENT

Introduce the theme of the chapter by having students look at the photographs on these pages. Have them look at the young people and determine if there is anything they see them doing that is the same or different from what they do with their own friends. Once you have completed the vocabulary presentation, have students return to these pages and read the information that accompanies each photograph. Once students are fully acquainted with the vocabulary and grammar of the chapter, you may wish to come back to these pages and ask the questions that go with each photo.

 Cultural Snapshot

México *(page 2)* Mexico is considered by many to be the culinary capital of Latin America. It has a rich cuisine that uses many indigenous products and varies greatly from region to region. The tortilla, however, is a basic component of many regional dishes. **¿Qué está preparando la señora? ¿Qué acompaña las tortillas? ¿Qué hay en el plato de chiles rellenos?**

(page 2 bottom left) **¿Cuál es un producto que se usa mucho en la cocina latina? ¿Son diferentes los pimientos los unos de los otros?¿Cuál es una característica de unos pimientos? Y, ¿cuál es una característica de otros? ¿Cuáles son unos nombres que se les dan a los pimientos?**

Introducción al tema
Cocina hispana

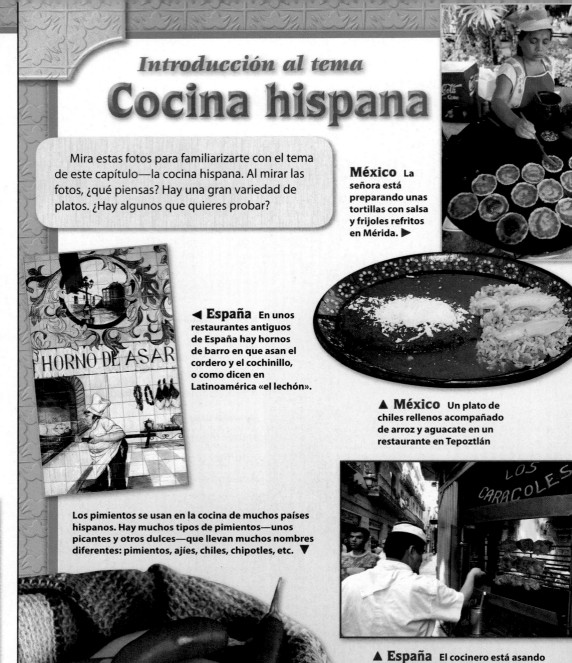

Mira estas fotos para familiarizarte con el tema de este capítulo—la cocina hispana. Al mirar las fotos, ¿qué piensas? Hay una gran variedad de platos. ¿Hay algunos que quieres probar?

México La señora está preparando unas tortillas con salsa y frijoles refritos en Mérida. ▶

◀ **España** En unos restaurantes antiguos de España hay hornos de barro en que asan el cordero y el cochinillo, o como dicen en Latinoamérica «el lechón».

HORNO DE ASAR

▲ **México** Un plato de chiles rellenos acompañado de arroz y aguacate en un restaurante en Tepoztlán

Los pimientos se usan en la cocina de muchos países hispanos. Hay muchos tipos de pimientos—unos picantes y otros dulces—que llevan muchos nombres diferentes: pimientos, ajíes, chiles, chipotles, etc. ▼

LOS CARACOLES

▲ **España** El cocinero está asando pollos en una parrilla a la entrada de un restaurante en Barcelona.

España *(page 2)* Spain is another country with a cuisine that varies from region to region. **Arroces,** or rice dishes, are typical in Andalusia, **asados** are found in the central regions, and haute cuisine is prevalent in Euskadi, or the Basque countries. Rich local stews, or **guisados,** are popular throughout the country. **¿De qué es el horno en la foto a la izquierda? ¿Cómo se dice «el cochinillo» en Latinoamérica? ¿Qué está asando el cocinero en la parrilla? ¿Dónde está la parrilla?**

THE BEST OF SPAIN

LA PAELLA

INGREDIENTES

3 tomates
2 cebollas grandes
2 pimientos (uno verde y uno rojo)
4 dientes de ajo
1/2 kilo de camarones

4 calamares
12 almejas
12 mejillones
langosta (opcional)
1 pollo en partes
3 chorizos

1 paquete de guisantes congelados
1 bote de pimientos morrones
1 1/2 tazas de arroz
3 tazas de consomé de pollo
4 pizcas de azafrán
1/4 taza de aceite de oliva

PREPARACIÓN

1. Pique los tomates, los pimientos, las cebollas y el ajo.
2. Lave las almejas y los mejillones en agua fría.
3. Limpie y pele los camarones.
4. Limpie y corte en rebanadas los calamares.
5. Corte en rebanadas los chorizos.
6. Fría o ase el pollo aparte.

▲ **España** Una receta para la paella en un libro de cocina española

▲ **Estados Unidos** El señor prepara pinchos y maíz en una parrilla durante el festival cubano de la Calle Ocho en la Pequeña Habana de Miami.

◄ **Argentina** El cocinero asa el famoso bife argentino en un restaurante de Buenos Aires.

Puerto Rico La señora vende empanadas, piononos, alcapurrias y pescado frito en su restaurante en San Juan. ▼

España *(page 3)* Students will learn about a paella from the conversation in this chapter. Since paella started out as **una comida casera,** it has many variations.

Estados Unidos *(page 3)* Mexican restaurants, including Tex Mex and southwestern varieties, have been popular all over the United States for many years. In addition, one can occasionally find a Spanish restaurant in some of the larger cities. With the arrival of the Cubans in the early sixties, Cuban restaurants started to become popular. Recently there has been a proliferation of restaurants serving dishes from many Latin American countries. **¿Qué está preparando este señor? ¿Has comido el maíz a la parrilla? ¿Lo comes generalmente hervido? ¿Dónde está el señor?**

Argentina *(page 3)* There is no doubt that Argentina is world renowned for its beef. Lesser known may be the fact that Argentine restaurants are famous for their large portions. **¿Qué está preparando el cocinero? ¿Cómo lo está cocinando? ¿Dónde está el restaurante?**

Puerto Rico *(page 3)* The foods seen here are served in many food stalls and **restaurantes económicos** throughout Puerto Rico. All of these foods are fried, often in lard. The empanadas are similar to those served in many areas of Latin America. The round items on the tray are made from slivers of ripe plantain wrapped around a ball of meat or cheese. The **alcapurrias** are banana-shaped pockets of mashed plantain (sometimes cassava) stuffed with meat or **jueyes,** which are land crabs. **¿Qué vende la señora? ¿Dónde? ¿Qué piensas—está orgullosa la señora de sus frituras?**

Vocabulario presentación

🕐 Quick Start

Use QS Transparency 1.1 or write the following on the board.
In Spanish, write the names of the rooms of a house. Add to this list any items you would find in each room.

▶ TEACH
Core Instruction

Step 1 Present the vocabulary first with books closed using Vocabulary Transparencies V1.2–V1.3.

Step 2 Have students repeat each word two or three times. You may wish to use some of your own props such as photos of kitchens and actual kitchenware.

Step 3 Intersperse the presentation with questions.

Step 4 Have students open their books and read the new vocabulary.

Differentiation
Multiple Intelligences

Call on **bodily-kinesthetic** learners to read aloud and dramatize the **Para conversar** sections.

La cocina

el congelador · el refrigerador, la nevera · el horno · el horno de microondas · la estufa, la cocina · el lavaplatos

freír las papas · el/la sartén

hervir el agua · la tapa · la olla, la cacerola

asar la carne · la parrilla

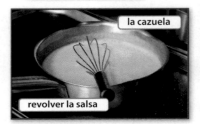
la cazuela · revolver la salsa

Para conversar

¿Quiere usted que yo ase el pollo o que lo fría?

Fríalo, por favor. Me gusta el pollo frito.

4 cuatro · CAPÍTULO 1

⭐ Tips for Success ··········

- As soon as students are familiar with the new vocabulary, have them read again the captions of the **Introducción al tema** on pages 2–3.

- After going over the **Práctica** activities, have students return to pages 4–5 and make up statements and questions about the photos.

4

SOPA DE POLLO · una receta

INGREDIENTES
1 taza de cebolla picada
1 taza de apio
1 taza de zanahorias
   cortadas en rebanadas
3 dientes de ajo machacados
½ cucharadita de
   pimienta negra
10 tazas de caldo de pollo
1½ tazas de pollo cortado
   en cubitos (¾ de una libra)

RECETA
Poner la cebolla, el apio, las zanahorias, el ajo y el caldo de pollo en un horno holandés. Poner a hervir; remover una o dos veces. Baje el fuego y déjelo cocer a fuego lento sin tapar por 15 minutos. Añadir el pollo; dejar cocer a fuego lento de 5 a 10 minutos.

VIDEO To practice your new words, watch Vocabulario en vivo.

los pimientos · la cebolla · el aguacate · el pepino · el ajo · las zanahorias

 cortar en pedacitos
 cortar en rebanadas
 picar
 pelar

Pique usted el ajo. Pele usted las zanahorias.

la chuleta de cerdo · el muslo de pollo · las alitas · el escalope de ternera · la pechuga de pollo

Para conversar

¿Quiere usted que yo ponga la cacerola al fuego?

Sí, póngala, por favor. Pero, cocínela (cuézala) a fuego lento. No quiero que se queme.

Cuando el cocinero cocina algo tiene que añadir condimentos.
Los condimentos le dan sabor a la comida.

COCINA HISPANA

En otras partes
- **El aguacate** is **la palta** in Chile.
- There are many terms that mean *slice*. Some general guidelines are:
  rebanada (de pan, pastel)
  tajada (de carne)
  lonja, loncha (de jamón)
  rodaja (de limón, pepino)
  raja (de melón)
- **Pedazos** and **trozos (trocitos)** refer to pieces.

⭐ **Tips for Success** ·······
Some students are motivated by competition. Have students work in small teams. Give them a time limit to write the names of as many foods as they can. The team that writes the largest number in the time limit wins.

GLENCOE Technology
Video in the Classroom
Vocabulario en vivo Watch and listen to Nora as she discusses cooking in the Spanish-speaking world.

GLENCOE Technology
You may wish to use the editable PowerPoint® presentation on PowerTeach for additional vocabulary instruction and practice.

cinco **5**

Total Physical Response (TPR)

(Student 1) y *(Student 2)*, **vengan acá.**
Imagínense en una cocina. Están preparando una comida.
Aquí tienen unas papas. Córtenlas en rebanadas.
Pongan las papas en una sartén y fríalas.
Ahora están haciendo una salsa. No quieren que se queme.

Revuelven la salsa.
¡Cuidado! Quiten la cacerola del fuego.
Bajen el fuego.
Pongan la cacerola en la estufa.
Revuélvanla de nuevo.
Añadan un poco de sal a la salsa.
Gracias, *(Student 1)* y *(Student 2)*.

QuickPass
Go to glencoe.com
For: **Vocabulary practice**
Web code: **ASD7844c1**

PRACTICE

Leveling EACH Activity

Easy Activities 1, 2, 4, 5
Average Activity 3
CHallenging Activities 6, 7

Activity ❶

🎧 **Audio Script**

1. Se puede freír el agua.
2. Se puede freír las papas.
3. Se puede freír o asar el pollo.
4. Se puede pelar la lechuga.
5. Se puede pelar las zanahorias y las papas.
6. Se puede asar la carne a la parrilla.
7. Se debe poner la carne cruda en el refrigerador.
8. Si se cocina algo a fuego lento se quema.
9. La sal y la pimienta son frutas.
10. Los condimentos dan sabor a una comida.

Activity ❷ Call on students to read the answers aloud.

GLENCOE ❋ Technology

Online Learning in the Classroom

Have students use QuickPass code ASD7844c1 for additional vocabulary practice. They can download audio files of all vocabulary to their computer and/or MP3 player. They will also have access to online flashcards and eGames.

Conexiones

Las matemáticas

Si lees una receta en español tienes que comprender los pesos métricos. La onza, la libra y la tonelada no existen en el sistema métrico que es un sistema decimal. Las medidas para el peso se basan en el kilogramo o kilo. Hay mil gramos en un kilo. El kilo es igual a 2,2 libras. Una libra inglesa o estadounidense es un poco menos de medio kilo.

ESCUCHAR

❶ Escucha cada frase y decide si la información es correcta o no. 🎧 Usa una tabla como la de abajo para indicar tus respuestas.

correcta	incorrecta

LEER

❷ Escoge.

1. Antes de hervirlas, debes (freír, pelar) las zanahorias.
2. Puedes freír las pechugas de pollo en (una cacerola, una sartén).
3. Tienes que (revolver, asar) la salsa.
4. Favor de poner los vasos sucios en (la nevera, el lavaplatos).
5. Si lo quieres cocinar rápido lo debes poner en (el horno, el horno de microondas).
6. ¿Quiere usted que yo ponga la olla (al agua, al fuego)?
7. ¿Quiere usted que yo pele (las zanahorias, los pimientos)?
8. Voy a cortar el pan en (rebanadas, pedacitos).

ESCRIBIR

❸ 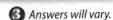 Good nutrition is an important part of staying healthy. Working in groups, use a piece of poster board and markers to make a food pyramid. Label the pyramid with each of the food groups: grains, vegetables, fruits, oils, milk, and meat/beans. Within each food group, write the names of foods that you know. Then present your pyramid to the class and suggest a healthy meal based on the foods you listed in each group.

Answers

❶

1. incorrecta   9. incorrecta
2. correcta   10. correcta
3. correcta
4. incorrecta
5. correcta
6. correcta
7. correcta
8. incorrecta

❷

1. pelar
2. una sartén
3. revolver
4. el lavaplatos
5. el horno de microondas
6. al fuego
7. las zanahorias
8. rebanadas

❸ *Answers will vary.*

❹

1. Cuando como pollo, prefiero el muslo (la pechuga).
2. Me gusta más una chuleta de cerdo (un escalope de ternera).
3. Prefiero el pescado asado (frito).
4. Prefiero mis legumbres muy cocidas (casi crudas).
5. Me gusta la carne con una salsa (sin salsa).
6. Sí, (No, no) me gusta la comida salada. Sí, (No, no) añado mucha sal.

HABLAR • ESCRIBIR

4 Personaliza. Da respuestas personales.

1. Cuando comes pollo, ¿prefieres el muslo o la pechuga?
2. ¿Te gusta más una chuleta de cerdo o un escalope de ternera?
3. ¿Prefieres el pescado asado o frito?
4. ¿Prefieres tus legumbres muy cocidas o casi crudas?
5. ¿Te gusta la carne con una salsa o sin salsa?
6. ¿Te gusta la comida salada o no? ¿Añades mucha sal?

LEER

5 Usa una tabla como la de abajo para indicar si se puede poner los siguientes ingredientes en una ensalada.

sí	no

1. la lechuga
2. el ajo
3. la carne cruda
4. el aguacate
5. las zanahorias
6. el aceite
7. el café
8. una cebolla

HABLAR • ESCRIBIR

6 Describe.

1. tu comida favorita
2. las legumbres que te gustan
3. los ingredientes de una buena ensalada
4. algunos alimentos que pones en el refrigerador
5. unas cosas que se preparan a la parrilla
6. una cocina moderna

Comunicación

7 Trabajen en grupos de cuatro y discutan sus platos o comidas favoritas. ¿Tienen ustedes los mismos gustos o no?

COCINA HISPANA

Más práctica

Workbook, pp. 1.3–1.6
StudentWorks™ Plus

CULTURA

El señor está asando carne en un puesto de comida en una calle de la Ciudad de Panamá.

▲ Unos platos populares ▼

siete 7

Vocabulario

Activity 4 This activity can also be done as a paired activity.

Activity 5 Students can make up additional foods and decide whether or not they can be used in a salad.

Comunicación

Interpersonal

Activity 7 As students do this activity extemporaneously, it is suggested that you not correct all errors since students are speaking and improvising on their own. This, however, is up to your own discretion or preference.

Tips for Success ....

Humor is an excellent way to engage students. Have them work in small groups to create recipes for ridiculous sandwiches, salads, or meals. Have them share their "inventions" with the class.

▶ ASSESS

Students are now ready to take Quiz 1 on page 1.41 of the TeacherTools booklet. If you prefer to create your own quiz, use the *ExamView*® *Assessment Suite*.

Cultural Snapshot

(page 7 top) **Puestos** or **tenderetes de comida** are very popular in almost all areas of Latin America. Some of them have a little stand-up counter and many have some tables and chairs. People use them most frequently for a snack or lunch. *(page 7 bottom)* Hamburgers with french fries as well as pizza are popular foods throughout the Spanish-speaking world.

Answers

5
1. sí
2. no (sí)
3. no
4. sí
5. sí
6. no (sí)
7. no
8. no (sí)

6 *Answers will vary but may include:*
1. Mi comida favorita es _____.
2. Las legumbres que me gustan son _____.
3. Los ingredientes de una ensalada buena son _____.
4. Algunos alimentos que pongo en el refrigerador son _____.
5. Unas cosas que se preparan a la parrilla son _____.
6. Una cocina moderna tiene _____.

7 *Answers will vary.*

7

QuickPass

Go to glencoe.com
For: **Grammar practice**
Web code: ASD7844c1

Resources

- Audio Activities TE, page 1.23
- Audio CD 1, Tracks 6–7
- Workbook, pages 1.7–1.8
- Quiz 2, page 1.42
- ExamView® Assessment Suite

Quick Start

*Use QS Transparency 1.2 or write the following on the board. Complete with the correct form of **querer** in the present.*
1. Yo ___ salir.
2. Pero ellos no ___ ir.
3. ¿Tú ___ ir o quedarte aquí?
4. ¿Por qué no ___ (nosotros) hacer la misma cosa?

▶ TEACH
Core Instruction

Step 1 Have students open their books to page 8. Have them read aloud the information in Items 1 and 2. It is important for students to understand this basic concept. You may also wish to present this information using the PowerPoint® presentation on PowerTeach.

Step 2 Go over the formation of the subjunctive. Point out to students that the vowel is the opposite of what they are familiar with in the indicative.

Step 3 Have students read the verb forms in Item 3 aloud.

Step 4 Have students read the verb conjugations in Items 4 and 5 aloud.

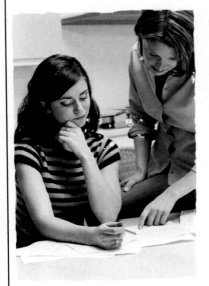

La profesora ayuda a una alumna porque quiere que salga bien en su examen y que tenga éxito.

El subjuntivo

1. All verbs you have learned so far are in the indicative mood. The indicative mood is used to express actions that actually do, did, or will take place. The indicative is used to express real events.

   Juan es un alumno bueno.
   Estudia mucho.
   Recibe buenas notas.

   All the preceding information is factual.

   John is a good student, he studies a lot, and he gets good grades.

2. You are now going to learn the subjunctive mood. The subjunctive is used to express something that is not necessarily factual or real. It expresses things that might happen. Compare the following.

   Juan estudia mucho y recibe buenas notas.
   Los padres de Juan quieren que él estudie mucho y que reciba buenas notas.

   The first sentence tells you that Juan studies a lot and gets good grades. The information is factual, and for this reason you use the indicative. The second sentence states that Juan's parents want him to study a lot and get good grades, but that doesn't mean that Juan will actually do it even though his parents want him to. The second sentence tells what may happen. It does not present facts, and for this reason you must use the subjunctive in the clause that depends upon **quieren.** Such a clause is called a dependent clause.

3. To form the present tense of the subjunctive of regular verbs, you drop the **o** ending of the **yo** form of the present indicative. This is also true for verbs that have an irregular form in the present tense of the indicative. Add **e** endings to all **-ar** verbs and **a** endings to all **-er** and **-ir** verbs.

INFINITIVE	PRESENT (YO)	STEM	PRESENT SUBJUNCTIVE (YO)
1. mirar	miro	mir-	mire
2. comer	como	com-	coma
3. vivir	vivo	viv-	viva
4. salir	salgo	salg-	salga
5. hacer	hago	hag-	haga
6. decir	digo	dig-	diga
7. conducir	conduzco	conduzc-	conduzca

⭐ Tips for Success

The basic concept for students to understand is that the subjunctive is used when we do not know if the action will take place. If we know that it is or will be a reality, the indicative is used. If students understand this, it will not be necessary for them to memorize lists of phrases that are followed by the subjunctive. You may give students the following simple outline:

Indicative: indicates or points something out; is factual; is objective; stands alone; is independent.

Subjunctive: is subjective; is not objective; is not factual; cannot stand alone; is dependent on something else; may or may not happen.

4. Study the forms for the present tense of the subjunctive.

	mirar	comer	vivir	salir
yo	mire	coma	viva	salga
tú	mires	comas	vivas	salgas
Ud., él, ella	mire	coma	viva	salga
nosotros(as)	miremos	comamos	vivamos	salgamos
vosotros(as)	miréis	comáis	viváis	salgáis
Uds., ellos, ellas	miren	coman	vivan	salgan

5. The following are the only verbs that do not follow the regular pattern for the formation of the present subjunctive.

	dar	estar	ir	saber	ser
yo	dé	esté	vaya	sepa	sea
tú	des	estés	vayas	sepas	seas
Ud., él, ella	dé	esté	vaya	sepa	sea
nosotros(as)	demos	estemos	vayamos	sepamos	seamos
vosotros(as)	deis	estéis	vayáis	sepáis	seáis
Uds., ellos, ellas	den	estén	vayan	sepan	sean

Práctica

ESCUCHAR • HABLAR • ESCRIBIR

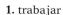 Sigue el modelo.

MODELO   estudiar mucho →
      Los padres de Mateo quieren que
          él estudie mucho.

1. trabajar
2. leer mucho
3. comer bien
4. aprender mucho
5. asistir a la universidad
6. recibir buenas notas
7. hacer el trabajo
8. poner todo en orden
9. salir bien en todo
10. ir a clase
11. estar aquí
12. ser bueno

CULTURA
Los señores están preparando una paella grande en Tenerife, España. Quieren que salga deliciosa y que a todos les guste.

COCINA HISPANA

GLENCOE SPANISH

Why It Works!

In this chapter, students are introduced to the subjunctive. As an introduction they will use the subjunctive after the verb **querer** only. This allows students to focus on the subjunctive verb forms themselves. Since the affirmative of formal commands and the negative of informal commands are all subjunctive forms, they are presented at the same time.

GLENCOE Technology

Online Learning in the Classroom

Have students use QuickPass code ASD7844c1 for additional grammar practice. They can review each grammar point with an eGame. They can also review all grammar points by doing the self-check quiz, which integrates the chapter vocabulary with the new grammar.

PRACTICE

Leveling EACH Activity

Easy Activity 1

Activity ① Have students read the sentences aloud to accustom their ears to hearing the subjunctive forms.

 Cultural Snapshot

(page 9) Large paellas such as the one seen here are made at some fairs and beachside restaurants.

Answers

1. Los padres de Juan quieren que él trabaje.
2. Los padres de Juan quieren que él lea mucho.
3. Los padres de Juan quieren que él coma bien.
4. Los padres de Juan quieren que él aprenda mucho.
5. Los padres de Juan quieren que él asista a la universidad.
6. Los padres de Juan quieren que él reciba buenas notas.
7. Los padres de Juan quieren que él haga el trabajo.
8. Los padres de Juan quieren que él ponga todo en orden.
9. Los padres de Juan quieren que él salga bien en todo.
10. Los padres de Juan quieren que él vaya a clase.
11. Los padres de Juan quieren que él esté aquí.
12. Los padres de Juan quieren que él sea bueno.

▶ PRACTICE (continued)

Leveling EACH Activity

Easy Activity 2
Average Activities 3, 5
CHallenging Activity 4

Activities ② and ③ It is suggested that you go over these activities orally in class and then have students write them.

Activity ④ This activity can be prepared as homework and then gone over in class.

▶ ASSESS

Students are now ready to take Quiz 2 on page 1.42 of the TeacherTools booklet. If you prefer to create your own quiz, use the *ExamView® Assessment Suite*.

 GeoVistas

Have students locate San Salvador on the maps on pages SH36 and SH45.

 Cultural Snapshot

(page 10) The **pupusa** is one of the most typical Salvadoran foods. The **pupusa** is a fried tortilla filled with beans, cheese, or **chicharrón** *(pork skin)*. A **pupusa revuelta** contains all of these fillings, and in **pupuserías** they are served with tomato sauce or **curtido,** a type of pickled cabbage.

10

CULTURA

La señora está haciendo pupusas en un restaurante en San Salvador, El Salvador.

Omit

 GeoVistas

To learn more about El Salvador, take a tour on pages SH44–SH45.

InfoGap For more practice with the subjunctive, do Activity 1 on page SR2 at the end of this book.

10 *diez*

LEER • ESCRIBIR

② Forma una frase completa usando el subjuntivo.

Yo quiero que Luis…

1. preparar la comida
2. cortar las cebollas
3. asar la carne
4. leer la receta
5. pelar los tomates
6. picar el ajo
7. poner la mesa
8. hacer una ensalada

HABLAR • ESCRIBIR

③ Completa la frase con tus propias ideas usando los siguientes nombres y pronombres.

Yo quiero que…

1. tú
2. Justina y Roberto
3. todos ustedes
4. ella
5. todos nosotros
6. mi profesor

LEER • ESCRIBIR

④ Completa con la forma apropiada del verbo.

1. Yo quiero que tú le _____ y ellos quieren que nosotros le _____. (hablar)
2. Yo quiero que él _____ el postre y él quiere que yo lo _____. (comer)
3. Ellos quieren que yo _____ el paquete y yo quiero que ellos lo _____. (abrir)
4. Tú quieres que yo lo _____ y yo quiero que tú lo _____. (hacer)
5. Ellos quieren que nosotros _____ la mesa y nosotros queremos que ellos la _____. (poner)
6. Él quiere que yo lo _____ pero no quiere que tú lo _____. (saber)
7. Ellos quieren que tú _____ pero no quieren que yo _____. (ir)
8. Yo quiero que ustedes se lo _____ y ellos quieren que nosotros se lo _____. (dar)

✿ Comunicación

⑤ Trabajen en grupos y discutan todo lo que tu profesor(a) de español quiere que ustedes hagan.

CAPÍTULO 1

Answers

②
1. Yo quiero que Luis prepare la comida.
2. Yo quiero que Luis corte las cebollas.
3. Yo quiero que Luis ase la carne.
4. Yo quiero que Luis lea la receta.
5. Yo quiero que Luis pele los tomates.
6. Yo quiero que Luis pique el ajo.
7. Yo quiero que Luis ponga la mesa.
8. Yo quiero que Luis haga una ensalada.

③ *Answers will vary.*

④
1. hables, hablemos
2. coma, coma
3. abra, abran
4. haga, hagas
5. pongamos, pongan
6. sepa, sepas
7. vayas, vaya
8. den, demos

⑤ *Answers will vary.*

El imperativo formal

1. The formal commands (**usted, ustedes**), both affirmative and negative, use the subjunctive form of the verb.

(no) **prepare** usted	(no) **preparen** ustedes
(no) **lea** usted	(no) **lean** ustedes
(no) **sirva** usted	(no) **sirvan** ustedes
(no) **haga** usted	(no) **hagan** ustedes
(no) **salga** usted	(no) **salgan** ustedes
(no) **conduzca** usted	(no) **conduzcan** ustedes
(no) **vaya** usted	(no) **vayan** ustedes
(no) **sea** usted	(no) **sean** ustedes

2. You have already learned that object pronouns can be attached to an infinitive or gerund or come before the helping verb. In the case of commands, the object pronouns must be added to the affirmative command, as you already know from the **tú** commands. They must come before the negative command.

AFFIRMATIVE	NEGATIVE
Háblele.	**No le hable usted.**
Démelo.	**No me lo dé usted.**
Levántense.	**No se levanten ustedes.**

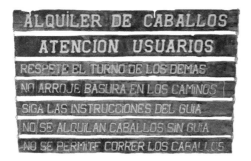

Más práctica

■ Workbook, pp. 1.9–1.10
◉ StudentWorks™ Plus

CULTURA
En un parque en San Pablo, Ecuador

Práctica

ESCUCHAR • HABLAR • ESCRIBIR

6 Contesta según el modelo.

MODELO —¿**Preparo la comida?**
—**Sí, prepare usted la comida.**

1. ¿Preparo el postre?
2. ¿Aso la carne?
3. ¿Pelo los tomates?
4. ¿Pico el ajo?
5. ¿Frío el pollo?
6. ¿Pongo la mesa?
7. ¿Hago la ensalada?
8. ¿Pongo la cacerola al fuego?

COCINA HISPANA

once **11**

FOLDABLES®
Study Organizer

PROJECT BOARD WITH TABS
See page SH32 for help with making this foldable. Think of the food words you know in Spanish and use them to create a recipe of your own. Draw a small picture of each ingredient on the front of each tab in the order you will use it. Next, lift each tab and write instructions about how to prepare your recipe using formal commands.

Answers

6
1. Sí, prepare usted el postre.
2. Sí, ase usted la carne.
3. Sí, pele usted los tomates.
4. Sí, pique usted el ajo.
5. Sí, fría usted el pollo.
6. Sí, ponga usted la mesa.
7. Sí, haga la ensalada.
8. Sí, ponga la cacerola al fuego.

Differentiation
Slower Paced Learners

Since slower paced learners tend to find the imperative in Spanish quite difficult, you may wish to present this point more for recognition than production. Students can avoid the active use of the commands by using the polite **favor de + infinitive**.

Resources

■ Audio Activities TE, pages 1.24–1.26
🎧 Audio CD 1, Tracks 8–13
■ Workbook, pages 1.9–1.10
■ Quiz 3, page 1.43
◉ *ExamView® Assessment Suite*

🕐 Quick Start

Use QS Transparency 1.3 or write the following on the board. Complete with as many foods as you can think of.
Ase usted _____.
Pele usted _____.
Fría usted _____.
Hierva usted _____.

▶ TEACH
Core Instruction

Although students have not yet actively used formal commands, they have heard the **ustedes** formal command many times when the teacher has given instructions to the entire class or groups.

Step 1 Have students repeat the verb forms aloud. Point out that they are the same subjunctive forms that they just learned.

Step 2 There is no doubt that students find the placement of pronouns with commands very tricky. Even when they understand the concept, they tend to get confused when trying to use them. Students need a lot of practice with this and most will take time before mastering this concept.

📰 Learning from Realia

Have students find the command forms on the sign on page 11.

Gramática

PRACTICE (continued)

Leveling EACH Activity

Easy–Average Activity 6
Average Activities 7, 9
CHallenging Activities 8, 10

Note: Because of the nature of this grammatical point, no activity is rated easy.

Activity ⑥ Have students present this activity as a short conversation.

Activities ⑦, ⑧, and ⑨ Have students present these activities as short conversations.

GLENCOE SPANISH

Why It Works!

Note that these forms reinforce and give students additional practice with the subjunctive forms they just learned in the previous section.

GLENCOE Technology

You may wish to use the editable PowerPoint® presentation on PowerTeach for additional grammatical instruction and practice.

ASSESS

Students are now ready to take Quiz 3 on page 1.43 of the TeacherTools booklet. If you prefer to create your own quiz, use the *ExamView® Assessment Suite*.

CULTURA

El señor está asando carne en Tikal, Guatemala. ¿Quieres que él te prepare la carne bien hecha o a término medio?

¿Te acuerdas?

Remember other polite ways you learned to express a command.
Favor de pasarme la sal.
¿Me pasaría usted la sal, por favor?

ESCUCHAR • HABLAR • ESCRIBIR

⑦ Contesta según el modelo.

MODELO —¿Preparamos la comida?
—No, no preparen ustedes la comida. Yo la voy a preparar.

1. ¿Preparamos el postre?
2. ¿Lavamos la lechuga?
3. ¿Pelamos las papas?
4. ¿Cortamos el pepino?
5. ¿Hacemos la ensalada?
6. ¿Ponemos la mesa?

ESCUCHAR • HABLAR • ESCRIBIR

⑧ Contesta según el modelo.

MODELO —¿Quiere usted que yo ase la chuleta?
—No, no la ase usted. Fríala.

1. ¿Quiere usted que yo ase el pollo?
2. ¿Quiere usted que yo ase las papas?
3. ¿Quiere usted que yo ase las chuletas de cordero?
4. ¿Quiere usted que yo ase los pimientos?
5. ¿Quiere usted que yo ase el pescado?
6. ¿Quiere usted que yo ase los camarones?

ESCUCHAR • HABLAR • ESCRIBIR

⑨ Sigue el modelo.

MODELO Páseme la sal, por favor. →
Pásemela, por favor.

1. Páseme la pimienta, por favor.
2. Páseme el pan, por favor.
3. Páseme la ensalada, por favor.
4. Páseme los platos, por favor.
5. Páseme el tenedor, por favor.
6. Páseme las zanahorias, por favor.

LEER • ESCRIBIR

⑩ Completa la tabla.

sí	no
Démelo.	
	No me lo diga usted.
Cocínelo a fuego lento.	
	No la revuelva usted.
Léamela.	

12 *doce*

CAPÍTULO 1

Answers

⑦
1. No, no preparen ustedes el postre. Yo lo voy a preparar.
2. No, no laven ustedes la lechuga. Yo la voy a lavar.
3. No, no pelen ustedes las papas. Yo las voy a pelar.
4. No, no corten ustedes el pepino. Yo lo voy a cortar.
5. No, no hagan ustedes la ensalada. Yo la voy a hacer.
6. No, no pongan ustedes la mesa. Yo la voy a poner.

⑧
1. No, no lo ase usted. Fríalo.
2. No, no las ase usted. Fríalas.
3. No, no las ase usted. Fríalas.
4. No, no los ase usted. Fríalos.
5. No, no lo ase usted. Fríalo.
6. No, no los ase usted. Fríalos.

⑨
1. Pásemela, por favor.
2. Pásemelo, por favor.
3. Pásemela, por favor.
4. Pásemelos, por favor.
5. Pásemelo, por favor.
6. Pásemelas, por favor.

⑩
sí: Dígamelo. / Revuélvala.
no: No me lo dé usted. / No lo cocine a fuego lento. / No me la lea usted.

El imperativo familiar—formas negativas

1. The negative **tú** or informal command uses the **tú** form of the verb in the subjunctive.

No hables más.	No salgas.
No comas más.	No vayas.
No sirvas más.	No conduzcas.

2. As with the formal commands, object pronouns are added to the affirmative command and come before the negative command.

Háblame.	No me hables.
Dímelo.	No me lo digas.

Práctica

 ESCUCHAR • HABLAR • ESCRIBIR

11 Contesta según el modelo.

 MODELO —¿Miro ahora o no?
—No, no mires ahora.

1. ¿Hablo ahora o no?
2. ¿Como ahora o no?
3. ¿Subo ahora o no?
4. ¿Sirvo ahora o no?
5. ¿Salgo ahora o no?
6. ¿Voy ahora o no?

LEER • ESCRIBIR

12 Completa la tabla.

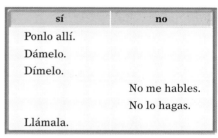

sí	no
Ponlo allí.	
Dámelo.	
Dímelo.	
	No me hables.
	No lo hagas.
Llámala.	

🌸 Comunicación

13 Acabas de recibir un gatito para tu cumpleaños. Como todos los gatitos, es muy curioso. Dale un nombre al gatito y dile que no haga cosas peligrosas y destructivas.

COCINA HISPANA

trece **13**

 ¿Te acuerdas?

You have already learned the familiar **tú** command in the affirmative.

Refrán

Can you guess what the following proverb means?

Espinacas, cómelas a sacas.

¡Bravo!

You have now learned all the new vocabulary and grammar in this chapter. Continue to use and practice all that you know while learning more cultural information. ¡Vamos!

Resources

- 📕 Audio Activities TE, page 1.27
- 🎧 Audio CD 1, Tracks 14–15
- 📘 Workbook, pages 1.11–1.12
- 📗 Quiz 4, page 1.44
- 💿 *ExamView® Assessment Suite*

🕐 Quick Start

Use QS Transparency 1.4 or write the following on the board.
Answer.
1. ¿Quién te prepara la cena, tu mamá o tu papá?
2. ¿Quién te sirve la comida en el restaurante?
3. ¿Te la sirve pronto el mesero?
4. ¿Le das la propina al mesero?
5. ¿Se la das antes o después de comer?

▶ TEACH
Core Instruction

You may wish to follow the same suggestions as given for the formal commands on page 11.

▶ PRACTICE

Leveling EACH Activity

Easy–Average Activity 11
Average Activities 12, 13

▶ ASSESS

Students are now ready to take Quiz 4 on page 1.44 of the TeacherTools booklet. If you prefer to create your own quiz, use the *ExamView® Assessment Suite*.

Refrán

Have students recite the proverb aloud. Then see if they can figure out its meaning and give an equivalent expression in English such as "Eat your spinach."

Answers

11
1. No, no hables ahora.
2. No, no comas ahora.
3. No, no subas ahora.
4. No, no sirvas ahora.
5. No, no salgas ahora.
6. No, no vayas ahora.

12
sí: Háblame. / Hazlo.
no: No lo pongas allí. / No me lo des. / No me lo digas. / No la llames.

13 *Answers will vary.*

Conversación

Quick Start

Use QS Transparency 1.5 or write the following on the board. Write the names of a few Latino dishes you are familiar with.

▶ **TEACH**

Core Instruction

Step 1 You may wish to have students listen to the conversation on Audio CD 1.

Step 2 Call on pairs of students to read the conversation aloud. Insist that they use proper intonation and expression.

Step 3 You may wish to ask the questions from Activity A on page 15 as you are going over the **Conversación.**

🌸 *Cultura*

You may wish to point out that, historically, chefs were men. Today, however, there are many well-known female chefs in the kitchens of renowned restaurants. This is true in Spain and Latin America as well as in the United States. Have students who watch cooking programs on television talk to the class about any chefs they know and what type of cuisine they are famous for.

¿Yo? ¿En la cocina?

Alicia, ¿te gusta cocinar?

A mí, ¿cocinar? ¿Hablas en serio, Jorge? En la cocina soy un desastre. ¿A ti te gusta cocinar?

Sí, bastante. La verdad es que algún día me gustaría ser cocinero.

Muchas cosas, pero mi plato favorito es la paella.

¿De veras? Dame una idea de lo que sabes preparar.

La paella, dices. ¿Qué es?

Pues, es una especialidad española, de Valencia. Lleva muchos ingredientes—mariscos, arroz. Algún día, ¿quieres que yo te prepare una paella?

Sí, pero no sé si me gustarán los mariscos.

Pues, nosotros los españoles comemos mucho pescado y mariscos. Pero ahora se están poniendo muy caros.

CAPÍTULO 1

¿Comprendes?

A Contesta según la informacíon en la conversación.
1. ¿A quién le gusta cocinar?
2. ¿Quién es un desastre en la cocina?
3. Algún día, ¿qué quiere ser Jorge?
4. ¿Cuál es el plato que más le gusta preparar?
5. ¿De qué región de España es la paella una especialidad?
6. ¿A Alicia le va a gustar una paella?
7. ¿Son caros los mariscos?

B Identifica quien lo dice.

	Jorge	Alicia
1. Le gusta cocinar y sabe cocinar.		
2. No sabe si le gustan los mariscos.		
3. Es un desastre en la cocina.		
4. Come mariscos.		

C Analizando Contesta.
1. ¿De qué país es Jorge? ¿Cómo lo sabes?
2. ¿Es Alicia de España?

D Personalizando ¿Qué piensas? ¿A ti te gustaría la paella o no? ¿Por qué?

CULTURA
En esta tienda en Valencia, España, se venden utensilios para elaborar una buena paella.

COCINA HISPANA

quince **15**

VIDEO To prepare an Argentine meal, watch **Diálogo en vivo.**

Conversación

 PRACTICE

¿Comprendes?

A and **B** You may wish to do Activity A as a factual recall activity and permit students to look up the information for Activity B.

Comunidades

There are many cooking shows on the Spanish-speaking TV channels in the United States. You may wish to have students view one at home and present what they learned to the class.

Cultural Snapshot

(page 15) You may wish to point out to students that the large hanging vessels in varying sizes are **paelleras.**

GLENCOE Technology

Video in the Classroom
Diálogo en vivo In this episode, Vicky and Alejandra prepare an Argentine meal. Ask students to note what time dinner will be served. How does this compare with typical dinnertimes in the United States?

GLENCOE Technology

You may wish to use the editable PowerPoint® presentation on PowerTeach to have students listen to and repeat the conversation. Additional activities are also provided.

Answers

A
1. A Jorge le gusta cocinar.
2. Alicia es un desastre en la cocina.
3. Algún día, Jorge quiere ser cocinero.
4. La paella es el plato que más le gusta preparar.
5. Es una especialidad de Valencia.
6. Alicia no sabe si le va a gustar la paella.
7. Sí, son caros los mariscos.

B
1. Jorge
2. Alicia
3. Alicia
4. Jorge

C
1. Jorge es de España. Dice que en España «comemos» muchos mariscos.
2. No.

D *Answers will vary.*

15

► TEACH
Core Instruction

You may wish to have students read this selection silently. When going over the **Preparación** section in the recipe, you may wish to have students read aloud since there are many examples of the command form.

Heritage Speakers

If you have heritage speakers in class, have them tell if they have ever had **arroz con pollo.** Ask them if they are familiar with the ingredients. If so, ask them if they are the same as those listed in the recipe. If not, what are the differences?

Cultural Snapshot

(page 16 right) **Azafrán** is now reported to be the most expensive spice in the world.

GLENCOE Technology

Online Learning in the Classroom

You may wish to have students use QuickPass code ASD7844c1 to develop their reading comprehension and writing skills. Students will be able to take a self-check quiz, which includes an essay.

LECTURA
CULTURAL

Antes de leer

Dale una ojeada a la receta para familiarizarte con los ingredientes y la preparación.

Durante la lectura

Al leer asegúrate que comprendes el orden de cada procedimiento durante la elaboración del plato.

✓ Reading Check

¿Por qué es amarillo el arroz?

CULTURA
Los ingredientes para hacer arroz con pollo

Después de leer

Trata de contar la receta de la manera más detallada posible a un(a) compañero(a) de clase.

Una receta hispana ♻

Otro plato delicioso y muy apreciado en España y otros países hispanohablantes es el arroz con pollo. Hay muchas variaciones en las recetas para elaborar un buen arroz con pollo pero aquí tiene usted una receta bastante sencilla. Decida si a usted le gustaría comer este plato delicioso.

Antes de leer la receta hay que saber algo más. El arroz en el arroz con pollo igual que el arroz en una paella es amarillo. Es el azafrán, una hierba de origen árabe, que le da al arroz el color amarillo. Pero el azafrán es muy caro y como colorante se puede usar bujol. El bujol se vende en muchos supermercados.

Arroz con pollo

Ingredientes
- 3 tomates
- 2 cebollas grandes
- 2 pimientos (uno verde y uno rojo)
- 4 dientes[1] de ajo
- 1 pollo en partes
- 3 chorizos[2]
- 1 paquete de guisantes congelados
- 1 frasco de (pimientos) morrones (rojos)
- 1 ½ tazas de arroz
- 3 tazas de consomé de pollo
- unas pizcas[3] de azafrán o bujol
- ¼ (una cuarta) taza de aceite de oliva
- una pizca de sal y pimienta

Preparación
1. Pique los tomates, pimientos, cebollas y ajo.
2. Corte en rodajas los chorizos.
3. Fría o ase el pollo aparte (se puede preparar el pollo en partes [muslos, media pechuga, piernas] o se puede cortarlo en pedazos deshuesados[4]).

Elaboración
Se usa una sartén o una olla grande.
1. Fría ligeramente[5] en el aceite los pimientos y las cebollas picadas.
2. Agregue (Añada) a la misma sartén el ajo y los tomates y fría ligeramente a fuego lento unos dos o tres minutos.
3. Agregue el arroz.
4. Revuelva el arroz con los tomates, cebollas, morrones y ajo.
5. Añada el pollo.
6. Agregue el consomé de pollo y llévelo a la ebullición[6].
7. Agregue el azafrán o bujol.
8. Ponga sal y pimienta a su gusto.
9. Tape[7] la sartén o la olla y cocine a fuego lento encima de la estufa unos treinta minutos.
10. Al final agregue los guisantes y pimientos morrones.

[1]dientes *cloves*
[2]chorizos *Spanish sausage*
[3]pizcas *pinches*
[4]deshuesados *deboned*

[5]ligeramente *lightly*
[6]a la ebullición *to a boil*
[7]tape *cover*

¿Comprendes?

Más práctica

Workbook, pp. 1.13–1.14
StudentWorks™ Plus

A Buscando palabras específicas ¿Cuál es la palabra?
Completa según la receta.

1. una _____ para hacer (elaborar) arroz con pollo
2. un _____ de guisantes congelados
3. cuatro _____ de ajo
4. una _____ de sal
5. tres _____ de consomé de pollo

B Recordando detalles importantes Lee la receta una vez más.
Luego, sin consultar la receta, escribe una lista de todos los
ingredientes necesarios. Luego consulta la receta para verificar
si has omitido algo.

C Confirmando información Verifica. ¿Sí o no?

	sí	no
1. Se puede cocinar el arroz con pollo encima de la estufa.		
2. El arroz con pollo lleva muchas papas.		
3. Hay muchos mariscos en un arroz con pollo.		
4. El arroz se pone amarillo.		
5. El chorizo es un tipo de salchicha española.		

COCINA HISPANA

▶ PRACTICE

Pre-AP These cultural readings
will develop the skills that students
need to be successful on the reading and writing sections of the AP
exam.

Answers

A
1. receta
2. paquete
3. dientes
4. pizca
5. tazas

B
3 tomates, 2 cebollas grandes, 2 pimientos (uno verde y
uno rojo), 4 dientes de ajo, 1 pollo en partes, 3 chorizos, 1
paquete de guisantes congelados, 1 frasco de (pimientos)
morrones (rojos), 1 ½ tazas de arroz, 3 tazas de consomé
de pollo, unas pizcas de azafrán o bujol, ¼ taza de aceite
de oliva, una pizca de sal y pimienta

C
1. sí
2. no
3. no
4. sí
5. sí

Lectura

▶ **TEACH**
Core Instruction

You may wish to have students read this selection on their own and do the ¿**Comprendes?** activities. Before having them read it, you may ask them if they remember what they have already learned about **sobras.** In Chapter 4 of Level 2, students learned that it is definitely not a custom in Spanish-speaking countries to ask to take your leftovers home.

Teaching Options

Call on some students to read aloud individually. After a student has read three or four sentences, ask questions of other students to check comprehension.

GLENCOE 🖰 Technology

Online Learning in the Classroom

You may wish to have students use QuickPass code ASD7844c1 to develop their reading comprehension and writing skills. Students will print and complete a review worksheet.

Una receta para «la ropa vieja» ♻

Antes de leer

A veces no podemos comer todo lo que está en nuestro plato. Lo que no comemos y dejamos en el plato son «las sobras». Piensa en unas recetas que tiene tu familia en que se usan las sobras.

Aquí tienes otra receta para un plato que es popular en muchas partes de Latinoamérica—sobre todo en Cuba. Se llama «ropa vieja»—un nombre divertido, ¿no? Se llama «ropa vieja» porque se puede elaborar con muchas sobras. Este plato tan conocido se originó en las islas Canarias.

Ropa vieja

Ingredientes
½ kg de carne (de ternera, bife) picada
1 cebolla
1 pimiento verde y un pimiento rojo
3 dientes de ajo
1 cucharadita de orégano

una pizca de pimienta
½ taza de tomate cocido (o enlatado)
3 cucharadas de aceite de oliva
½ taza de caldo (consomé de pollo)

Preparación o cocción
Corte los pimientos, las cebollas y los ajos en trocitos. Fría los pimientos, las cebollas y los ajos en el aceite de oliva con una pizca de pimienta y el orégano. Añada la carne picada y revuelva todos los ingredientes (unos dos minutos). Añada el caldo y cueza (cocine) a fuego mediano hasta que se evapore el caldo. Sirva con arroz blanco.

¿Comprendes?

Escoge o completa.

1. La ropa vieja viene de _____.
   a. Latinoamérica
   b. Cuba
   c. las islas Canarias

2. Se llama «ropa vieja» porque se puede elaborar (hacer) con _____.
   a. ropa
   b. comida que queda
   c. ingredientes divertidos

3. _____ es una cantidad muy pequeña.

4. Hay que _____ los pimientos verdes y rojos, la cebolla y los dientes de ajo en trocitos.
   a. cortar
   b. picar
   c. freír

5. Dos especias que lleva el plato son _____ y _____.

6. Cueza los ingredientes hasta que se evapore _____.
   a. el aceite
   b. el tomate
   c. el caldo

7. La ropa vieja se sirve acompañada de
   a. caldo
   b. azafrán
   c. arroz blanco

8. Un amigo vegetariano comerá la ropa vieja si no pones _____.

VIDEO To learn more about a staple of Mexican cuisine, watch **Cultura en vivo.**

TOMATE TRITURADO

800g

ACEITE DE OLIVA Y YBARRA

CONT. 1 L e

¡Más sabor!

COCINA HISPANA

diecinueve **19**

Lectura

Cultura

You may wish to have students look for Latino recipes online. They can share them and decide if there is one they would like to try. If you have any students interested in cooking, they may want to prepare the dish.

GLENCOE Technology

Video in the Classroom

Cultura en vivo In this episode, students visit a **tortillería** in Mexico. Ask students if there are any food products that they regularly purchase outside of a supermarket.

ABOUT THE SPANISH LANGUAGE

The word **triturado,** meaning *crushed,* appears on the **lata (el bote) de tomates** on page 19. A *garbage disposal unit* is **el triturador de basura** in many areas of Latin America.

Tips for Success

The multiple-choice comprehension activities that accompany the second reading selection have a format that will help students prepare for standarized tests.

Answers

1. c
2. b
3. Una pizca
4. a
5. orégano y pimienta
6. c
7. c
8. carne

el examen

Resources

- TPR Storytelling, pages 1.37–1.38
- Tests, pages 1.53–1.71
- Performance Assessment, Task 1, pages 1.73–1.74
- *ExamView® Assessment Suite*

✓ Self-check for achievement

This is a pre-test for students to take before you administer the chapter test. Note that each section is cross-referenced so students can easily find the material they feel they need to review. You may wish to use Self-Check Worksheet Transparency SC1 to have students complete this assessment in class or at home. You can correct the assessment yourself, or you may prefer to project the answers on the overhead in class using Self-Check Answers Transparency SC1A.

Differentiation

Slower Paced Learners

Have students work in pairs to complete the Self-Check in class. Once they have finished, call on individuals to give the correct answers as you review together.

Multiple Intelligences

To engage **visual-spatial** and **bodily-kinesthetic** learners, number from 1 to 40 on the board and call on a student to go to the board and write the correct answer (this may be done chronologically or you may allow students to choose the one they answer). Then have the student who wrote the first answer decide who will write the second, and so on, making sure to remind them not to pick the same person again.

20

Vocabulario

1 **Parea.**

 To review **Vocabulario,** turn to pages 4–5.

1. hervir	a. la salsa
2. freír	b. el pan
3. revolver	c. las zanahorias
4. pelar	d. el agua
5. cortar en rebanadas	e. sal y pimienta
6. añadir	f. el pollo

2 **Identifica.**

7.

8.

9.

10.

11.

12.

Answers

1

1. d
2. f
3. a
4. c
5. b
6. e

2

7. el lavaplatos
8. la estufa (la cocina, el horno)
9. el aguacate
10. el horno de microondas
11. las chuletas de cerdo
12. el ajo

Gramática

3 **Completa.**

13–14. Él quiere que yo _____ y yo quiero que él _____. (hablar)

15–16. Tú quieres que nosotros lo _____ y nosotros queremos que tú lo _____. (leer)

17–18. Yo quiero que tú lo _____ y tú quieres que yo lo _____. (escribir)

19–20. Tú quieres que yo lo _____ y él quiere que tú lo _____. (hacer)

21–22. Nosotros queremos que ellos _____ y ellos quieren que nosotros _____. (ir)

4 **Completa con el imperativo formal.**

23. _____ usted la comida. (preparar)

24. _____ usted la receta. (leer)

25. _____ usted la lata. (abrir)

26. _____ usted ahora. (salir)

27. Y _____ usted mañana. (regresar)

28. No me lo _____ usted. (decir)

29. No _____ usted más. (añadir)

5 **Escribe con el pronombre.**

30. Prepare usted *la ensalada*.

31. No prepare usted *el postre*.

32. Déme *las direcciones*.

6 **Escribe en la forma negativa.**

33. Luis, habla.

34. Jacinta, come más.

35. Carlos, levántate.

36. Teresa, ven.

Cultura

7 **Contesta.**

37–40. ¿Cuáles son algunos ingredientes que lleva el arroz con pollo?

COCINA HISPANA

To review **el subjuntivo,** turn to pages 8–9.

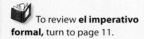
To review **el imperativo formal,** turn to page 11.

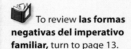
To review **las formas negativas del imperativo familiar,** turn to page 13.

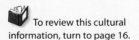
To review this cultural information, turn to page 16.

veintiuno **21**

Differentiation
(continued)

This type of review activity is particularly appealing to **inter-personal** learners but will also benefit the class on the whole by promoting an inclusive, student-centered learning environment.

Slower Paced Learners

Encourage students who need extra help to refer to the book icons and review any section before answering the questions.

Pre-AP Students preparing for the AP exam may benefit from a set time limit when completing this Self-Check. This may also help to identify students with learning difficulties or slower paced students who need extra help.

GLENCOE Technology

Online Learning in the Classroom

You may wish to have students use QuickPass code ASD7844c1 for additional test preparation. They will be able to complete a self-check quiz for chapter review.

Answers

3

13. hable
14. hable
15. leamos
16. leas
17. escribas
18. escriba
19. haga
20. hagas
21. vayan
22. vayamos

4

23. Prepare
24. Lea
25. Abra
26. Salga
27. regrese
28. diga
29. añada

5

30. Prepárela.
31. No lo prepare.
32. Démelas.

6

33. Luis, no hables.
34. Jacinta, no comas más.
35. Carlos, no te levantes.
36. Teresa, no vengas.

7

37–40. *Answers will vary but may include:* el pollo, el arroz, los tomates, las cebollas, los pimientos, el ajo, los chorizos, los guisantes congelados, los morrones, el consomé, el azafrán, el aceite de oliva, la sal, la pimienta.

Prepárate para el examen

⭐ Tips for Success ·······

Encourage students to say as much as possible when they do these open-ended activities. Tell them not to be afraid to make mistakes, since the goal of the activities is real-life communication. If someone in the group makes an error, allow the others to politely correct him or her. Let students choose the activities they would like to do.

Tell students to feel free to elaborate on the basic theme and to be creative. They may use props, pictures, or posters if they wish.

·······························

Pre-AP These oral activities will give students the opportunity to develop and improve their speaking skills so that they may succeed on the speaking portion of the AP exam.

Note: You may want to use the rubric below to help students prepare their speaking activities.

Prepárate para el examen
✔ Practice for oral proficiency

1 **Yo en la cocina**
✔ *Talk about cooking*
Habla con un(a) compañero(a) de clase. Dile si te gusta cocinar o no. Explícale por qué. Luego verifica si tu compañero(a) tiene las mismas opiniones que tú.

2 **Comidas étnicas**
✔ *Discuss and describe a restaurant and the food it serves*
¿Hay restaurantes étnicos, restaurantes que sirven comida de otras partes del mundo, en tu comunidad? Si hay, con un(a) compañero(a) preparen una lista de estos restaurantes y el tipo de comida que sirven. Luego describan un plato típico de uno de los restaurantes que les gusta.

3 **¡Qué comida más deliciosa!**
✔ *Describe a delicious meal*
Estás viajando por México. Anoche fuiste a cenar en un restaurante y pediste algo que salió delicioso, muy rico. Te gustó mucho. Llama a tus padres y descríbeles el restaurante y el plato que te gustó tanto. Si puedes, explícales como crees que el cocinero preparó el plato.

CULTURA
La gente está sentada en la terraza de un café en Puebla, México.

4 **Simón dice**
✔ *Give and receive commands*
Trabajen ustedes en grupos de cinco. Van a jugar «Simón dice». Cada líder dará cinco órdenes a todos los miembros del grupo y luego escogerá a otro líder.

5 **Mis padres**
✔ *Discuss what your parents want you to do*
Tus padres quieren que hagas muchas cosas, ¿no? Dile a un(a) compañero(a) todo lo que quieren tus padres que hagas. Tu compañero(a) te dirá si sus padres quieren que él o ella haga las mismas cosas.

22 *veintidós*

CAPÍTULO 1

Scoring Rubric for Speaking				
	4	**3**	**2**	**1**
vocabulary	extensive use of vocabulary, including idiomatic expressions	adequate use of vocabulary and idiomatic expressions	limited vocabulary marked with some anglicisms	limited vocabulary marked by frequent anglicisms that force interpretation by the listener
grammar	few or no grammatical errors	minor grammatical errors	some serious grammatical errors	serious grammatical errors
pronunciation	good intonation and largely accurate pronunciation with slight accent	acceptable intonation and pronunciation with distinctive accent	errors in intonation and pronunciation with heavy accent	errors in intonation and pronunciation that interfere with listener's comprehension
content	thorough response with interesting and pertinent detail	thorough response with sufficient detail	some detail, but not sufficient	general, insufficient response

22

Tarea

Your teacher wants to know the recipe for the warm quesadillas and chilled fresh tomato salsa that you brought to the last Spanish Club meeting. Use the ingredients listed below and additional vocabulary from the chapter to give your teacher instructions on how to make this delicious, easy-to-prepare Mexican snack.

Quesadillas	Salsa de tomate
unas tortillas de harina	tomates
queso triturado	pimientos verdes
(shredded cheese)	cebolla
aceite de oliva	chiles jalapeños
	ajo
	cilantro
	jugo de lima

Writing Strategy

Giving Instructions When giving instructions, it is important to present the details accurately, clearly, and in logical order. This is especially true when writing a recipe because directions that are incorrect, unclear, or out of order could cause the dish to taste bad or be ruined altogether.

① Prewrite

Make a list of the steps for completing the recipe and put them in chronological order. Also think about what utensils and/or appliances will be used, and remember that timing and presentation are very important. What should be prepared first? What should be prepared last? How will the dish be served?

② Write

- Use formal commands since this is a recipe for your teacher.
- Make sure all of the steps follow a logical order.
- Use transition words to help you present your information in an organized way.
- Remember to stick to vocabulary you already know and don't attempt to translate from English to Spanish.

Evaluate

Your teacher will evaluate you on accurate and logical presentation of details, correct use of vocabulary and grammar, and completeness of information.

Scoring Rubric for Writing

	4	3	2	1
vocabulary	precise, varied	functional, fails to communicate complete meaning	limited to basic words, often inaccurate	inadequate
grammar	excellent, very few or no errors	some errors, but do not hinder communication	numerous errors interfere with communication	many errors, little sentence structure
content	thorough response to the topic	generally thorough response to the topic	partial response to the topic	insufficient response to the topic
organization	well organized, ideas presented clearly and logically	loosely organized, but main ideas present	some attempts at organization, but with confused sequencing	lack of organization

Resources

- Audio Activities TE, pages 1.29–1.31
- Audio CD 1, Tracks 18–20
- Workbook, pages 1.15–1.16

Grammar Review

This page provides a quick "at a glance" summary of the grammar points students have learned in this chapter. The corresponding page numbers are also listed so that students can easily find each grammar point as it was presented.

Differentiation

Multiple Intelligences

You may want to call on **verbal-linguistic** and **logical-mathematical** learners for whom grammar often comes easily to explain the main concepts to their classmates in their own words. Having students explain the concepts in different ways may also help slower paced learners or students with learning difficulties.

Repaso del Capítulo ①

Gramática

- **El subjuntivo** *(pages 8–9)*
  The subjunctive expresses that which is not necessarily factual or real. It expresses things that might happen.

  El profesor quiere que los alumnos lean el libro.

  Review the following forms of the present subjunctive.

hablar	beber	escribir	poner
hable	beba	escriba	ponga
hables	bebas	escribas	pongas
hable	beba	escriba	ponga
hablemos	bebamos	escribamos	pongamos
habléis	*bebáis*	*escribáis*	*pongáis*
hablen	beban	escriban	pongan

  Review the following irregular verbs in the present subjunctive.

dar	estar	ir	saber	ser
dé	esté	vaya	sepa	sea
des	estés	vayas	sepas	seas
dé	esté	vaya	sepa	sea
demos	estemos	vayamos	sepamos	seamos
deis	*estéis*	*vayáis*	*sepáis*	*seáis*
den	estén	vayan	sepan	sean

- **El imperativo** *(pages 11 and 13)*
  The affirmative and negative formal commands and the negative familiar commands use the subjunctive form of the verb.

(no) mire usted	(no) miren ustedes	no mires
(no) coma usted	(no) coman ustedes	no comas
(no) asista usted	(no) asistan ustedes	no asistas
(no) salga usted	(no) salgan ustedes	no salgas
(no) vaya usted	(no) vayan ustedes	no vayas

  Object pronouns are attached to affirmative commands but must come before negative commands. Review the following sentences.

Mírelo.	No lo mire usted.	No lo mires.
Démelas.	No me las dé usted.	No me las des.
Levántenlas.	No las levanten ustedes.	No las levantes.

There are a number of cognates in this list. See how many you and a partner can find. Who can find the most? Compare your list with those of your classmates.

Vocabulario

Talking about some kitchen appliances and utensils

la cocina	el horno	la olla, la cacerola
el refrigerador, la nevera	el horno de microondas	la tapa
el congelador	el lavaplatos	la cazuela
la estufa, la cocina	el/la sartén	la parrilla

Talking about food preparation

la receta	cortar	quemarse
el/la cocinero(a)	en pedacitos	hervir
el sabor	en rebanadas	freír
pelar	añadir	asar
picar	poner al fuego	revolver
	cocinar, cocer a fuego lento	

Identifying more foods

la chuleta de cerdo	la pechuga de pollo	el aguacate
el escalope de ternera	la cebolla	el ajo
el muslo de pollo	la zanahoria	el condimento
las alitas de pollo	el pepino	
	el pimiento	

COCINA HISPANA

veinticinco **25**

Vocabulary Review

The words and phrases in the **Vocabulario** section have been taught for productive use in this chapter. They are summarized here as a resource for both student and teacher. This list also serves as a convenient resource for the **Prepárate para el examen** activities on pages 20–23.

Don't forget the chapter project and cultural activities found on pages 1C–1D. Students have learned all the information that they will need to complete these engaging enrichment tasks.

 The cognates in this list are: **el refrigerador, el escalope, el condimento.**

Differentiation

Slower Paced Learners

Slower paced learners may benefit from creating their own visual dictionary of words in this list. They can either draw their own depictions or use images from the Internet or magazines.

Every chapter of ¡Así se dice! contains this review section of previously learned material. By recycling information, the cumulative review serves to remind students that they need to continue practicing what they have previously learned.

Activity 1 This activity reviews comparatives and superlatives. See page SR16.

 Audio Script *(CD 1, Track 21)*

1. Miguel tiene ocho años. Su hermana tiene diez años. Miguel es mayor que su hermana.

2. La blusa cuesta veinte pesos. La falda cuesta treinta pesos. La falda cuesta más que la blusa.

3. Tú recibiste una A en español, una B en inglés y una D en matemáticas. Tú recibiste la mejor nota en inglés.

4. Un carro es rápido, un avión es más rápido, pero el tren es el más rapido de todos.

5. Mi casa tiene ocho cuartos. La casa de Elena tiene catorce cuartos. Mi casa es más pequeña que la casa de Elena.

Activity 2 This activity reviews vocabulary related to foods. For help, see the dictionaries at the end of this book.

Repaso cumulativo

Repasa lo que ya has aprendido

These activities will help you review and remember what you have learned so far in Spanish.

 1 Escucha las frases. Indica en una tabla como la de abajo si la información en cada frase es correcta o no.

sí	no

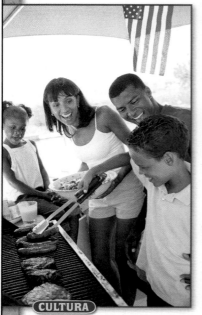

CULTURA
Una barbacoa para celebrar el Cuatro de Julio en Estados Unidos

 2 Identifica.

1. todas las legumbres que ya conoces en español
2. todas las carnes que ya conoces en español
3. todo lo que necesitas para poner la mesa
4. la diferencia entre un desayuno continental y un desayuno americano

 3 Completa en el presente.

1. Yo _____ bife y Anita _____ pescado y nosotros dos _____ flan. (pedir)
2. Nosotros no nos _____. El mesero nos _____. (servir)
3. Yo _____ esto y él _____ el otro. Nosotros nunca _____ la misma cosa. (preferir)

4 Describe las siguientes fiestas.

1. el Día de los Muertos
2. el Día de los Reyes
3. el Cuatro de Julio en Estados Unidos

5 Completa con el imperativo.

1. José, _____ más. (comer)
2. Rosario, _____ el correo electrónico. (leer)
3. Manuel, _____ tu regalo. (abrir)
4. Adela, _____ acá. (venir)
5. Alberto, _____ pronto. (volver)
6. Federico, _____ la mesa. (poner)
7. Magda, _____ la verdad. (decir)
8. Gabriel, _____ la comida. (servir)

Answers

 1

1. no
2. sí
3. no
4. no
5. sí

2 *Answers will vary but may include:*

1. la lechuga, los tomates, las papas (las patatas), los guisantes, las judías verdes, las zanahorias, las cebollas, los pimientos, el maíz, el pepino, el aguacate
2. el tocino (el bacón, el lacón), el pollo, el jamón, el biftec, la carne de res, el cerdo, el cordero, la ternera

3. los platos, el tenedor, la cuchara, la cucharita, el cuchillo, la taza, el platillo, el vaso, el mantel, la servilleta
4. **un desayuno continental:** panecillos, panes dulces, mermelada, mantequilla y café
   un desayuno americano: los huevos revueltos, el bacón (el tocino, el lacón), el pan tostado, la mantequilla, la mermelada, el café

 3

1. pido, pide, pedimos
2. servimos, sirve
3. prefiero, prefiere, preferimos

4 *Answers will vary.*

 5

1. come
2. lee
3. abre
4. ven
5. vuelve
6. pon
7. di
8. sirve

26

6 Categoriza según el deporte.

el fútbol

el básquetbol   el béisbol

deportes

el voleibol   el tenis

1. Un jugador lanza el balón y quiere que entre en la portería.
2. El portero no pudo bloquear el balón y el balón entró en la portería.
3. Un jugador corre de una base a otra.
4. Para marcar un tanto hay que meter el balón en el cesto.
5. El jugador corre y dribla con el balón.
6. La jugadora atrapa la pelota con el guante.
7. El balón o la pelota tiene que pasar por encima de la red.
8. Podemos jugar dobles o individuales.
9. Los jugadores juegan con un balón.
10. Los jugadores juegan con una pelota.

 7 Usa las siguientes palabras en frases originales.

el campo   la cancha   el balón

la pelota   el segundo tiempo   marcar

el tanto   lanzar   devolver

 8 Prepara una lista de lo que tienes que comprar para preparar un plato favorito. Da las cantidades también.

COCINA HISPANA

CULTURA
Un mercado en Tepoztlán, México

Repaso cumulativo

Activity 3 This activity reviews stem-changing verbs. See page R17.

Activity 4 This activity reviews vocabulary related to holidays. See page R36 and the dictionaries at the end of this book.

Activity 5 This activity reviews familiar commands. See page SR30.

Activity 6 This activity reviews vocabulary related to sports. See pages R12–R13.

Activity 7 This activity reviews vocabulary related to sports. See pages R12–R13.

Activity 8 This activity reviews vocabulary related to food. For help, see the dictionaries at the end of this book.

GLENCOE Technology

Online Learning in the Classroom
You may wish to have students use QuickPass code ASD7844c1 for additional cumulative review. They will be able to complete a self-check quiz.

GLENCOE Technology

Audio in the Classroom
The ¡Así se dice! Audio Program for Chapter 1 has 21 activities, which afford students extensive listening and speaking practice.

Answers

 6

1. el fútbol
2. el fútbol
3. el béisbol
4. el básquetbol
5. el básquetbol

6. el béisbol
7. el voleibol y el tenis
8. el tenis
9. el fútbol, el voleibol, el básquetbol
10. el béisbol

7 *Answers will vary.*

8 *Answers will vary.*

Pre-AP To give students further open-ended oral and written practice, or to assess proficiency, go to AP Proficiency Practice Transparency AP28.

Chapter Overview
¡Cuídate bien!

● Scope and Sequence

Topics
- Parts of the body
- Exercise and physical activity
- Minor medical problems
- The emergency room

Culture
- Hospitals in the Spanish-speaking world
- Physical activity and good health
- Doctors Without Borders

Functions
- How to identify more parts of the body
- How to talk about exercise
- How to talk about having a minor accident and a trip to the emergency room
- How to discuss physical fitness

Structure
- The subjunctive with impersonal expressions
- **Ojalá, quizás, tal vez**
- The subjunctive of stem-changing verbs
- The comparison of like things

● Planning Guide

	required	recommended	optional
Vocabulario 1 (*pages 32–35*) Más partes del cuerpo	✓		
Vocabulario 2 (*pages 36–39*) Unos accidentes En la sala de emergencia	✓		
Gramática (*pages 40–45*) El subjuntivo con expresiones impersonales **¡Ojalá! ¡Quizás! ¡Tal vez!** El subjuntivo de los verbos de cambio radical Comparación de igualdad	✓		
Conversación (*pages 46–47*) Un accidente		✓	
Lectura cultural (*pages 48–49*) Vida activa y buena salud		✓	
Lectura Un poco más (*pages 50–51*) Médicos Sin Fronteras			✓
Prepárate para el examen (*pages 52–55*)			✓
Repaso cumulativo (*pages 58–59*)			✓

● Correlations to National Foreign Language Standards

Page numbers in light print refer to the Student Edition. Page numbers in bold print refer to the Teacher Edition.	
Communication Standard 1.1 Interpersonal	pp. **28C, 28D, 30–31, 33, 34,** 35, **39,** 41, 42, 45, 54
Communication Standard 1.2 Interpretive	pp. **32,** 34, **34, 35, 36,** 38, 39, **39,** 40, **41,** 42, **45, 46,** 47, **48,** 50, **50,** 51, 53, **53,** 58, **59**
Communication Standard 1.3 Presentational	pp. **28C, 28D, 32, 33, 36, 37,** 41, **41,** 47, **47, 48, 52,** 54, 55, **56, 57**
Cultures Standard 2.1	pp. **28D,** 30–31, **30–31, 39,** 47, 48, 48–49, 49, 55
Cultures Standard 2.2	pp. **28D,** 40, 45, 48, 48–49, 49, 50, 51, 53
Connections Standard 3.1	pp. **28C, 28D,** 34, 44, 47, **47, 50, 59**
Connections Standard 3.2	pp. 36, 37, **37,** 38, 44, **44,** 45, **45,** 47, **47**
Comparisons Standard 4.1	pp. 37, **55, 56,** 57
Comparisons Standard 4.2	pp. **28D,** 29, **29, 30,** 48–49
Communities Standard 5.1	pp. **28C,** 38, 41, **41, 52, 54,** 55, **56**
Communities Standard 5.2	pp. 36, **37,** 44, **44,** 47, **47**

To read the ACTFL Standards in their entirety, see the front of the Teacher Edition.

● Student Resources

Print

Workbook *(pp. 2.3–2.20)*
Audio Activities *(pp. 2.21–2.26)*
Pre-AP Workbook, Chapter 2

Technology

- StudentWorks™ Plus
- ¡Así se dice! Vocabulario en vivo
- ¡Así se dice! Gramática en vivo
- ¡Así se dice! Diálogo en vivo
- ¡Así se dice! Cultura en vivo
- Vocabulary PuzzleMaker

QuickPass glencoe.com

● Teacher Resources

Print

TeacherTools, Chapter 2
  Workbook TE *(pp. 2.3–2.20)*
  Audio Activities TE *(pp. 2.23–2.28)*
  TPR Storytelling *(pp. 2.41–2.44)*
  Quizzes 1–6 *(pp. 2.47–2.53)*
  Tests *(pp. 2.56–2.78)*
  Performance Assessment, Task 2 *(pp. 2.79–2.80)*

Technology

- Quick Start Transparencies 2.1–2.5
- Vocabulary Transparencies V2.1–V2.5
- Museo de Arte Fine Art Transparencies F 7
- Audio CD 2
- *ExamView® Assessment Suite*
- TeacherWorks™ Plus
- PowerTeach
- ¡Así se dice! Video Program
- Vocabulary PuzzleMaker

QuickPass glencoe.com

Chapter Project

Un programa de entrevistas (Un talkshow)

Students will work in groups to plan and perform a talk show based on healthy living or other health-related issues.

1. Each group should pick a name for their show and choose a theme or topic to discuss. The group will then assign each member a role, as **el/la presentador(a)/conductor(a)** (host), **los invitados** (guests), **los expiertos** (experts), or **miembros del auditorio/del público** (audience members).

2. Students will work together to create an outline of their show and to develop a draft of the show's script. You may wish to establish a minimum number of lines that each group member must have. Then, each member should submit a draft of his or her part to be checked or peer edited and revised accordingly. Corrected drafts should be turned in on the day of the group's performance.

3. Each group should include all members in the discussion and should incorporate several props or visual aids related to the topic of the show. In addition to the interviews between the host and the guests and experts, each program should close with a question-and-answer session in which audience members participate. To add an element of improvisation and to check for comprehension, ask additional follow-up questions or have classmates who are not in the group do so.

4. You may wish to give students a minimum and/or maximum time for each show so that performances can be completed within a few class periods. Encourage students to have fun and be creative with this project, since talk shows are often full of excitement and sometimes controversial.

Scoring Rubric for Project

	1	3	5
Evidence of planning	Draft of script is not provided.	Draft of script is provided but is not corrected.	Corrected draft of script is provided.
Use of props or visual aides	Talk show contains no props or visual aids.	Talk show contains few props or visual aids.	Talk show contains several props or visual aids.
Presentation	Talk show contains little of the required elements.	Talk show contains some of the required elements.	Talk show contains all the required elements.

Culture

● Recipe

▼▼▼▼▼▼▼▼▼▼▼▼▼▼▼▼▼▼ GUACAMOLE ▼▼▼▼▼▼▼▼▼▼▼▼▼▼▼▼

Ingredients:
2 medium, ripe avocados
1 small onion, finely chopped

1 clove garlic, minced
1 tomato, chopped
2 tablespoons lime juice

Peel and mash avocados with a fork in a medium bowl. Stir in onion, garlic, tomato, and lime juice. Salt and pepper to taste. Chill for 30 minutes before serving. Can be served with tortilla chips as a dip or as a garnish for other dishes.

● ¿Caminar o conducir?

In this chapter, students will talk about exercise and fitness activities that can contribute to a healthy lifestyle. While the desire to be fit and healthy is equally evident in the United States and Spanish-speaking countries, getting exercise may be less of a challenge for those who live in Spain and Latin America. In Spain and Latin America, people walk more than we do in the United States, not for recreational or fitness purposes, but as a means of transportation. Because businesses are in close proximity to residences in Hispanic cities, people do not drive to shop and do errands—they walk or ride bikes. Even in the country, it is not unheard of to walk miles to the market or even a friend's home. Ask students to compare how things are done in the United States. How often do they walk instead of going by car? For one week have students keep track of how often they use a vehicle. Then have them try to reduce that frequency the following week by walking or biking more. Students can share this project with other appropriate classes.

● Connection to Fine Art

Show the students Glencoe *Museo de Arte* Fine Art Transparency F 7, *The Enchanted Crystal*, by Chilean artist Gonzalo Cienfuegos. Ask students to identify elements of the painting in Spanish. Students can discuss whether or not they like this painting and what they think it means. Elicit their opinions in Spanish.

50-Minute Lesson Plans

	Objective	Present	Practice	Assess/Homework
Day 1	Identify more parts of the body and talk about exercise	Chapter Opener, pp. 28–29 (5 min.) Introducción al tema, pp. 30–31 (10 min.) Core Instruction/Vocabulario 1, pp. 32–33 (20 min.)	Activities 1–4, p. 34 (15 min.)	Student Workbook Activities A–D, pp. 2.3–2.4 *QuickPass* Vocabulary Practice
Day 2	Identify more parts of the body and talk about exercise	Quick Start, p. 32 (5 min.) Review Vocabulario 1, pp. 32–33 (10 min.)	Activities 5–8, p. 35 (15 min.) Total Physical Response, pp. 32–33 (5 min.) Audio Activities A–D, pp. 2.23–2.25 (15 min.)	Student Workbook Activities E–G, pp. 2.4–2.5 *QuickPass* Vocabulary Practice
Day 3	Talk about having a minor accident and a trip to the emergency room	Core Instruction/Vocabulario 2, pp. 36–37 (20 min.) Video, Vocabulario en vivo (10 min.)	Activities 1–3, p. 38 (10 min.)	Quiz 1, p. 2.47 (10 min.) Student Workbook Activities A–C, pp. 2.6–2.7 *QuickPass* Vocabulary Practice
Day 4	Talk about having a minor accident and a trip to the emergency room	Quick Start, p. 36 (5 min.) Review Vocabulario 2, pp. 36–37 (10 min.)	Activities 4–6, p. 39 (10 min.) Total Physical Response, p. 36 (5 min.) InfoGap, p. SR3 (5 min.) Audio Activities E–H, pp. 2.25–2.27 (15 min.)	Student Workbook Activities D–F, pp. 2.7–2.8 *QuickPass* Vocabulary Practice
Day 5	The subjunctive with impersonal expressions	Quick Start, p. 40 (5 min.) Core Instruction/Gramática, El subjuntivo con expresiones impersonales, p. 40 (10 min.)	Activities 1–6, pp. 40–41 (15 min.) Audio Activities A–C, pp. 2.28–2.29 (10 min.)	Quiz 2, p. 2.48 (10 min.) Student Workbook Activities A–E, pp. 2.9–2.10 *QuickPass* Grammar Practice
Day 6	**Ojalá, quizás, tal vez** The comparison of like things	Quick Start, p. 42 (5 min.) Core Instruction/Gramática, **¡Ojalá! ¡Quizás! ¡Tal vez!**, p. 42 (5 min.) Core Instruction/ Gramática, Comparación de igualdad, p. 44 (5 min.)	Activities 7–9, p. 42 (10 min.) Activity 15, p. 45 (5 min.) Audio Activities D–H, pp. 2.29–2.31 (10 min.)	Quiz 3, p. 2.49 (10 min.) Activities 13–14, p. 45 Student Workbook Activities A–C, pp. 2.11–2.12 Student Workbook Activities A–C, p. 2.14 *QuickPass* Grammar Practice
Day 7	The subjunctive of stem-changing verbs	Core Instruction/Gramática, El subjuntivo de los verbos de cambio radical, p. 43 (10 min.) Video, Gramática en vivo (10 min.)	Activities 10–12, pp. 43–44 (10 min.)	Quizzes 4 and 6, pp. 2.50 and 2.52 (20 min.) Student Workbook Activities A–C, pp. 2.12–2.13 *QuickPass* Grammar Practice
Day 8	Develop reading and listening comprehension skills	Quick Start, p. 46 (5 min.) Core Instruction/Conversación, p. 46 (15 min.) Video, Diálogo en vivo (10 min.)	¿Comprendes? A–B, p. 47 (10 min.)	Quiz 5, p. 2.51 (10 min.) ¿Comprendes? C, p. 47 *QuickPass* Conversation
Day 9	Discuss physical fitness	Core Instruction/Lectura cultural, pp. 48–49 (20 min.)	¿Comprendes? A–C, p. 49 (15 min.)	Listening Comprehension Test, pp. 2.71–2.72 (15 min.) *QuickPass* Reading Practice
Day 10	Develop reading comprehension skills	Core Instruction/Lectura Un poco más, p. 50 (15 min.)	¿Comprendes?, p. 51 (10 min.) Prepárate para el examen, pp. 52–53 (25 min.)	Prepárate para el examen, Practice for written proficiency, p. 55 *QuickPass* Reading Practice
Day 11	Chapter review	Repaso del Capítulo 2, pp. 56–57 (15 min.)	Prepárate para el examen, Practice for oral proficiency, p. 54 (20 min.)	Test for Writing Proficiency, p. 2.75 (15 min.) Review for chapter test

Day 12	Chapter 2 Tests (50 min.)
	  Reading and Writing Test, pp. 2.61–2.70
	  Speaking Test, p. 2.73
			Test for Oral Proficiency, p. 2.74
			Test for Reading Comprehension, pp. 2.76–2.78	

90-Minute Lesson Plans

	Objective	Present	Practice	Assess/Homework
Block 1	Identify more parts of the body and talk about exercise	Chapter Opener, pp. 28–29 (5 min.) Introducción al tema, pp. 30–31 (10 min.) Quick Start, p. 32 (5 min.) Core Instruction/Vocabulario 1, pp. 32–33 (20 min.)	Activities 1–8, pp. 34–35 (20 min.) Total Physical Response, pp. 32–33 (10 min.) Audio Activities A–D, pp. 2.23–2.25 (20 min.)	Student Workbook Activities A–G, pp. 2.3–2.5 **QuickPass** Vocabulary Practice
Block 2	Talk about having a minor accident and a trip to the emergency room	Quick Start, p. 36 (5 min.) Core Instruction/Vocabulario 2, pp. 36–37 (20 min.) Video, Vocabulario en vivo (10 min.)	Activities 1–6, pp. 38–39 (20 min.) Total Physical Response, p. 36 (5 min.) InfoGap, p. SR3 (5 min.) Audio Activities E–H, pp. 2.25–2.27 (15 min.)	Quiz 1, p. 2.47 (10 min.) Student Workbook Activities A–F, pp. 2.6–2.8 **QuickPass** Vocabulary Practice
Block 3	The subjunctive with impersonal expressions **Ojalá, quizás, tal vez**	Quick Start, p. 40 (5 min.) Core Instruction/Gramática, El subjuntivo con expresiones impersonales, p. 40 (10 min.) Quick Start, p. 42 (5 min.) Core Instruction/Gramática, **¡Ojalá! ¡Quizás! ¡Tal vez!**, p. 42 (10 min.)	Activities 1–6, pp. 40–41 (20 min.) Activities 7–9, p. 42 (10 min.) Audio Activities A–F, pp. 2.28–2.30 (20 min.)	Quiz 2, p. 2.48 (10 min.) Student Workbook Activities A–E, pp. 2.9–2.10 Student Workbook Activities A–C, pp. 2.11–2.12 **QuickPass** Grammar Practice
Block 4	The subjunctive of stem-changing verbs The comparison of like things	Core Instruction/Gramática, El subjuntivo de los verbos de cambio radical, p. 43 (10 min.) Video, Gramática en vivo (10 min.) Core Instruction/Gramática, Comparación de igualdad, p. 44 (10 min.)	Activities 10–12, pp. 43–44 (10 min.) Activities 13–15, p. 45 (15 min.) Audio Activities G–H, p. 2.31 (15 min.)	Quizzes 3–4, pp. 2.49–2.50 (20 min.) Student Workbook Activities A–C, pp. 2.12–2.13 Student Workbook Activities A–C, p. 2.14 **QuickPass** Grammar Practice
Block 5	Discuss physical fitness	Quick Start, p. 46 (5 min.) Core Instruction/Conversación, p. 46 (15 min.) Video, Diálogo en vivo (10 min.) Core Instruction/Lectura cultural, pp. 48–49 (20 min.)	¿Comprendes? A–C, p. 47 (10 min.) ¿Comprendes? A–C, p. 49 (10 min.)	Quizzes 5–6, pp. 2.51–2.52 (20 min.) Prepárate para el examen, Practice for written proficiency, p. 55 **QuickPass** Conversation, Reading Practice
Block 6	Develop reading comprehension skills	Core Instruction/Lectura Un poco más, p. 50 (15 min.)	¿Comprendes?, p. 51 (10 min.) Prepárate para el examen, pp. 52–53 (25 min.) Prepárate para el examen, Practice for oral proficiency, p. 54 (25 min.)	Listening Comprehension Test, pp. 2.71–2.72 (15 min.) Review for chapter test **QuickPass** Reading Practice

Block 7	Chapter 2 Tests (50 min.)
	   Reading and Writing Test, pp. 2.61–2.70
	   Speaking Test, p. 2.73
	   Test for Oral Proficiency, p. 2.74
	   Test for Writing Proficiency, p. 2.75
	   Test for Reading Comprehension, pp. 2.76–2.78
	Chapter Project, p. 28C (40 min.)			

Preview

In this chapter, students will discuss some exercises and other physical activities to stay in shape. They will also learn some vocabulary they may need to discuss and get emergency medical attention in the event of an accident. Students will also learn some more uses of the subjunctive.

Pacing

It is important to note that once you reach **¡Bravo!** in the chapter, there is no more new material for the students to learn. The rest of the chapter recycles what has already been covered. The suggested pacing listed here leaves two to three days for review, assessment, and enrichment activities such as the chapter project.

Vocabulario 1	1–2 days
Vocabulario 2	1–2 days
Gramática	2–3 days
Conversación	1 day
Lectura cultural	1 day
Lectura Un poco más	1 day

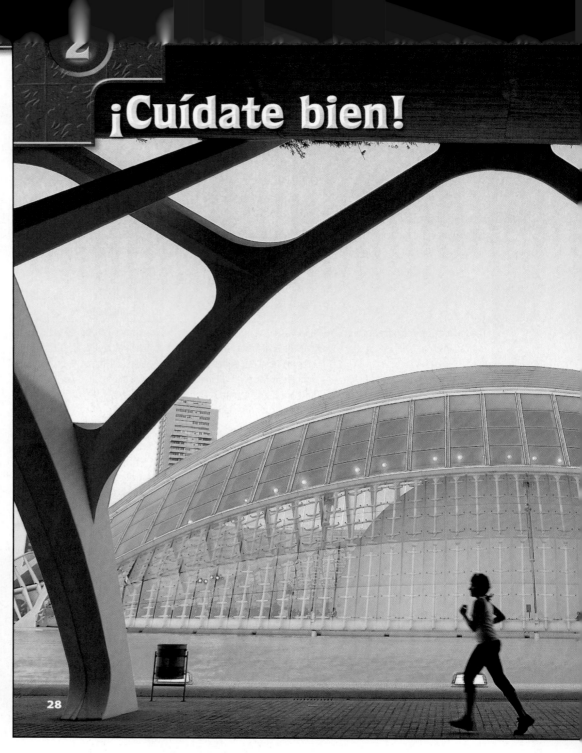

¡Cuídate bien!

28

TeacherWorks^Plus

The **¡Así se dice!** TeacherWorks™ Plus CD-ROM is an all-in-one planner and resource center. You may wish to use several of the following features as you plan and present the Chapter 2 material: Interactive Teacher Edition, Interactive Lesson Planner with Calendar, and Point and Click Access to Teaching Resources including Hotlinks to the Internet and Correlations to the National Standards.

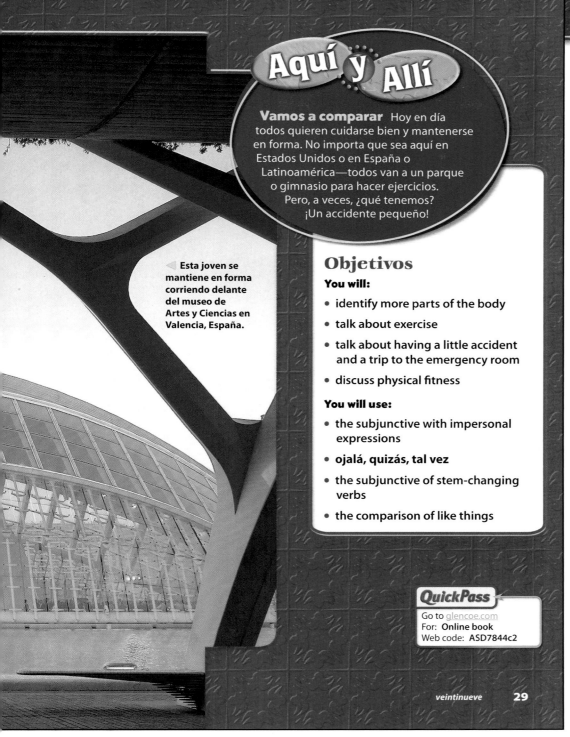

Aquí y Allí

Vamos a comparar Hoy en día todos quieren cuidarse bien y mantenerse en forma. No importa que sea aquí en Estados Unidos o en España o Latinoamérica—todos van a un parque o gimnasio para hacer ejercicios. Pero, a veces, ¿qué tenemos? ¡Un accidente pequeño!

◄ Esta joven se mantiene en forma corriendo delante del museo de Artes y Ciencias en Valencia, España.

Objetivos

You will:

- identify more parts of the body
- talk about exercise
- talk about having a little accident and a trip to the emergency room
- discuss physical fitness

You will use:

- the subjunctive with impersonal expressions
- ojalá, quizás, tal vez
- the subjunctive of stem-changing verbs
- the comparison of like things

QuickPass

Go to glencoe.com
For: **Online book**
Web code: **ASD7844c2**

SPOTLIGHT ON CULTURE

Cultural Comparison
In the United States, there is significant interest in health and well-being. Students will learn that many people in Spain and Latin America are equally interested in physical activities and keeping in shape. Just as in towns and cities across the United States, there are marathons in the cities of Spain and Latin America, the proceeds of which often benefit a particular health cause or concern.

Cultural Snapshot
The City of Arts and Sciences in Valencia is a museum campus that spans nearly 2 kilometers. It is home to **L'Hemisfèric,** a planetarium, the **Museu de les Ciències Príncipe Felipe,** a science museum, **L'Oceanogràfic,** an aquarium, and the **Palau de les Arts,** an opera house. The building featured in the picture is **L'Hemisfèric.** You may wish to mention to students that the official names of these museums are in Valencian, a regional variation of Catalan.

QUIA **Quia Interactive Online Student Edition** found at quia.com allows students to complete activities online and submit them for computer grading for instant feedback or teacher grading with suggestions for what to review. Students can also record speaking activities, listen to chapter audio, and watch the videos that correspond with each chapter. As a teacher you are able to create rosters, set grading parameters, and post assignments for each class. After students complete activities, you can view the results and recommend remediation or review. You can also add your own customized activities for additional student practice.

Introducción al tema

▶ PRESENT

Introduce the theme of the chapter by having students look at the photographs on these pages. Have them look at the young people and determine if there is anything they see them doing that is the same or different from what they do with their own friends. Once you have completed the vocabulary presentation, have students return to these pages and read the information that accompanies each photograph. Once students are fully acquainted with the vocabulary and grammar of the chapter you may wish to come back to these pages and ask the questions that go with each photo.

Cultural Snapshot

Chile *(page 30)* ¿Anda el joven en bici o en moto? ¿Por dónde anda? ¿Qué lleva? ¿Por qué lo lleva?

Argentina *(page 30)* ¿Por qué toma mucha gente agua mineral?

Ecuador *(page 30)* ¿Dónde están los jóvenes? ¿Qué van a jugar?

México *(page 30)* ¿Dónde está haciendo ejercicios la muchacha?

Introducción al tema
¡Cuídate bien!

Mira estas fotos para familiarizarte con el tema de este capítulo—cuídate bien. ¿Qué haces para cuidarte? ¿Hay algunas actividades que ves aquí que tú también practicas o que te gustan? Y, ¿puedes simpatizar con el joven ecuatoriano que ha tenido un accidente?

▲ **Chile** El joven anda en bici por las montañas. Nota que él también lleva casco. La seguridad siempre es importante, ¿no?

▲ **Argentina** Mucha gente toma agua mineral porque la consideran buena para la salud.

Ecuador Estos jóvenes van a jugar fútbol en un parque en Quito. ▼

◀ **México** La muchacha hace ejercicios en un gimnasio en la Ciudad de México.

30

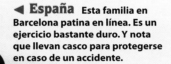

▲ **España** El joven está practicando el monopatín en Barcelona. ¿Qué piensas? ¿Debe llevar casco?

▲ **Guatemala** Una ambulancia en Antigua, Guatemala

◀ **Ecuador** Uno de estos estudiantes de la Universidad Católica en Quito ha tenido un accidente y tiene que andar con muletas. Pero no es nada serio. No se ha hecho mucho daño.

▲ **México** Un hospital privado en Oaxaca, México

◀ **España** Esta familia en Barcelona patina en línea. Es un ejercicio bastante duro. Y nota que llevan casco para protegerse en caso de un accidente.

España *(page 31 top)* ¿Qué está practicando el joven? ¿Dónde? ¿Qué debe hacer que no está haciendo?

Ecuador *(page 31)* ¿Dónde son estudiantes estos jóvenes? ¿Qué ha tenido uno de ellos? ¿Cómo tiene que andar? ¿Se ha hecho mucho daño o no?

España *(page 31 bottom)* ¿Qué está haciendo esta familia? ¿Es un ejercicio fuerte el patinaje en línea? ¿Qué están llevando todos?

31

Quick Start

Use QS Transparency 2.1 or write the following on the board. Write a list in Spanish of the parts of the body.

▶ TEACH

Core Instruction

Step 1 As you teach these parts of the body you may wish to have students point to themselves.

Step 2 If the pronunciation of the class is quite good, students do not have to repeat the sentences after you. Have them read them aloud or silently and intersperse the presentation with questions such as ¿Qué están practicando los amigos? Cuando practican yoga, ¿qué tipo de ejercicios hacen? ¿Cómo son los movimientos? ¿Qué efecto tienen estos ejercicios?

Differentiation

Multiple Intelligences

You can have **bodily-kinesthetic** learners dramatize the meaning of many of the expressions in this vocabulary section.

Más partes del cuerpo

la frente
el cuello
el pecho
el hombro
la muñeca
el dedo del pie
el tobillo

Los amigos están practicando yoga.
Hacen ejercicios de respiración.
Hacen movimientos lentos.
Liberan su espíritu de tensiones.

En el gimnasio

estirarse los brazos
hacer planchas
levantar pesas

La muchacha está haciendo ejercicios.
El señor anda en bicicleta.
El muchacho levanta pesas.
Es necesario que él tenga cuidado.
Es importante que todos hagamos ejercicios.

32 *treinta y dos* CAPÍTULO 2

Total Physical Response (TPR)

(Student), **ven acá, por favor.**
Vas a hacer unos ejercicios.
Estírate los brazos.
Estírate las piernas.

Levanta una pesa.
Acuéstate en el suelo.
Haz planchas—uno, dos, tres. Muy bien, *(Student).*

el casco
las rodilleras

el monopatín

un buzo
descansar
hacer jogging

Las jóvenes están patinando en línea.
Es importante que lleven casco y rodilleras.

Los corredores participan en un maratón.

Están corriendo una carrera de relevos.
Cada corredora corre una vuelta.

Es una carrera a campo traviesa.
Una carrera a campo traviesa es de larga distancia.

¡CUÍDATE BIEN!

treinta y tres **33**

Vocabulario 1

Vocabulario ① practica

 QuickPass
Go to glencoe.com
For: **Vocabulary practice**
Web code: **ASD7844c2**

► PRACTICE

Leveling EACH Activity

Easy Activities 1, 2, 4
Average Activities 3, 5, 7
CHallenging Activities 6, 8

Activity ①

🎧 **Audio Script**
1. Están en el gimnasio.
2. Están corriendo.
3. Están levantando pesas.
4. Se están estirando.
5. Están haciendo ejercicios de respiración.

Activity ② This activity can be done as an entire class activity or you may wish to have students work in pairs.

Activity ③ This activity can be prepared in advance and then gone over in class.

Activity ④ This activity can be done in small groups as a game.

34

ESCUCHAR

① Escucha las frases. Parea cada frase con la foto que describe.

🎧

a.   b.   c.

ESCUCHAR • HABLAR

② Personaliza. Da respuestas personales.
🎧
1. ¿Haces muchos ejercicios?
2. ¿Haces ejercicios aeróbicos o abdominales?
3. ¿Te estiras los brazos y las piernas?
4. ¿Levantas pesas?
5. ¿Andas en bicicleta?
6. ¿Haces jogging?
7. ¿Participas en carreras?
8. ¿Corres vueltas?
9. ¿Practicas yoga?
10. ¿Has participado en un maratón?

LEER • ESCRIBIR

③ Completa con una palabra apropiada.
1. Uno se pone _____ cuando va al gimnasio o cuando hace jogging.
2. Es importante ponerse _____ para proteger el cráneo al andar en bicicleta.
3. Es importante llevar _____ al patinar en línea.
4. ¿Cuántas _____ puedes correr sin descansar?
5. El yoga ayuda a liberar el espíritu de _____.
6. Muchas ciudades y organizaciones tienen _____ que son carreras de muy larga distancia.
7. Dos tipos de carreras son _____ y _____.

LEER • ESCRIBIR

④ Pon las siguientes partes del cuerpo en orden desde la parte más alta del cuerpo hasta la más baja.

el pecho   la mano   el dedo del pie
la frente
el tobillo   el cuello   el hombro   la rodilla

Conexiones

La anatomía
La anatomía es el estudio de la estructura del cuerpo de un ser viviente y de sus órganos. Ya sabemos las partes del cuerpo humano pero son aun más importantes los órganos vitales—el corazón, los pulmones, los riñones, el hígado y el páncreas.

Answers

①
1. c
2. a
3. c
4. b
5. b

②
1. Sí, (No, no) hago muchos ejercicios.
2. Hago ejercicios aeróbicos (abdominales).
3. Sí, (No, no) me estiro los brazos y las piernas.
4. Sí, (No, no) levanto pesas.

5. Sí, (No, no) ando en bicicleta.
6. Sí, (No, no) hago jogging.
7. Sí, (No, no) participo en carreras.
8. Sí, (No, no) corro vueltas.
9. Sí, (No, no) practico yoga.
10. Sí, (No, no) he participado en un maratón.

③
1. un buzo
2. un casco
3. rodilleras
4. vueltas
5. tensiones
6. maratones
7. una carrera de relevos, una carrera a campo traviesa (un maratón)

④ *Answers will vary.*

HABLAR

5 Dramatiza. Trabajen en grupos. Escojan a un líder. El líder va a dramatizar un ejercicio o un deporte. Los otros miembros del grupo adivinarán la actividad. Cambien de líder.

HABLAR • ESCRIBIR

6 Usa las siguientes expresiones en frases originales.

hacer ejercicios	patinar en línea	hacer jogging
practicar yoga	correr vueltas	hacer planchas

CULTURA
Equipo para hacer ejercicios en un gimnasio en un hotel en Montelimar, Nicaragua

ESCRIBIR

7 Completa con lo que falta.

1. el cue_o
2. las rodi_eras
3. el tobi_o
4. el _imnasio

5. los _óvenes
6. un bu_o
7. el bra_o

Comunicación

8 Trabajen en grupos y discutan las actividades que practican en su clase de educación física. Indiquen las actividades que les gustan y que no les gustan. Expliquen por qué.

¡CUÍDATE BIEN!

treinta y cinco **35**

Differentiation

Multiple Intelligences

Activity 5 This activity is particularly beneficial for **bodily-kinesthetic** learners.

Activity 6 This activity should be prepared in advance and then gone over in class.

Activity 7 You may also wish to give students a dictation with these words.

Activity 8 Depending upon your preference, you may or may not wish to correct all errors as students speak in this open-ended activity.

 **Cultural Snapshot**

(page 35) Montelimar is a resort area on the Pacific coast of Nicaragua.

▶ **ASSESS**

Students are now ready to take Quiz 1 on page 2.47 of the TeacherTools booklet. If you prefer to create your own quiz, use the *ExamView®* *Assessment Suite*.

Answers

5 *Answers will vary.*

6 *Answers will vary.*

7
1. el cuello
2. las rodilleras
3. el tobillo
4. el gimnasio
5. los jóvenes
6. un buzo
7. el brazo

8 *Answers will vary.*

Vocabulario 2 presentación

VIDEO To practice your new words, watch **Vocabulario en vivo.**

Quick Start

Use QS Transparency 2.2 or write the following on the board.
Complete in the present.

1. Él _____ una pierna quebrada. (tener)
2. Le _____ mucho. (doler)
3. No _____ andar. (poder)
4. _____ que usar muletas. (tener)
5. ¡Qué lástima! _____ jugar fútbol. (querer)
6. Y no _____ jugar. (poder)

▶ TEACH

Core Instruction

You may wish to use some suggestions given in previous vocabulary sections for the presentation of these new words.

Differentiation

Multiple Intelligences

Have **bodily-kinesthetic** learners make up and present little skits about these emergency procedures.

Slower Paced Learners

After the presentation of the new vocabulary show Vocabulary Transparencies V2.4–V2.5 again. Allow slower paced learners to give isolated words indicating what they see in each illustration.

36

Unos accidentes

una herida

Pilar se cortó el dedo.
Tiene una herida.
Pero no es seria. No se ha hecho mucho daño.

José corría y se torció el tobillo.
El tobillo está hinchado.
Le duele mucho.

El joven se cayó.
¿Se rompió (Se quebró) la pierna?

la camilla   los socorristas   la ambulancia

Total Physical Response (TPR)

(Student), **ven acá, por favor.**
Dramatiza los siguientes accidentes.
Te cortaste el dedo.
Se te torció el tobillo.
Andas con muletas.
Te duele mucho la muñeca.
Tienes el dedo muy hinchado.

Do as a group TPR activity.
Dramaticen lo siguiente.
Me duele el dedo.
Me duele el pie.
Me duele la cabeza.
Me duele la garganta.
Me duele el estómago.

En la sala de emergencia

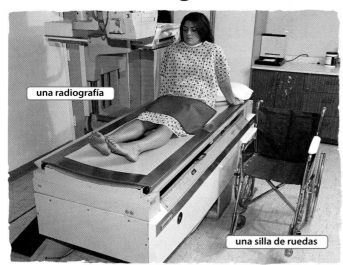

una radiografía

una silla de ruedas

Le toman (hacen) una radiografía.

Nota

In addition to **hacerse daño,** you will hear **lastimarse.** Another term for **radiografía** is **rayos equis.**

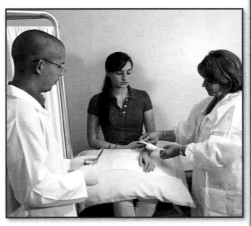

La cirujana ortopédica le ha reducido (acomodado) el hueso.
Le ha puesto la pierna en un yeso.
Paula tendrá que andar con muletas.

Es necesario que el médico cierre la herida.
El médico pone unos puntos (unas suturas).
La enfermera le va a poner una venda.

Differentiation

Advanced Learners

Have advanced learners look at Vocabulary Transparencies V2.4–V2.5 and make up sentences about what they see.

⭐Tips for Success ·······

- As soon as students are familiar with the new vocabulary, have them read again the captions of the **Introducción al tema** on pages 30–31.
- After going over the **Práctica** activities, have students return to pages 36–37 and make up statements and questions about the photos.

·······················

GLENCOE 🖱 Technology

Video in the Classroom
Vocabulario en vivo Watch and listen to Nora as she discusses exercise and staying in shape.

GLENCOE 🖱 Technology

You may wish to use the editable PowerPoint® presentation on PowerTeach for additional vocabulary instruction and practice.

QuickPass
Go to glencoe.com
For: **Vocabulary practice**
Web code: ASD7844c2

▶ PRACTICE

Leveling EACH Activity

Easy Activities 1, 2, 3
Average Activities 4, 5,
   Activity 2 **Expansión,**
   Activity 3 **Expansión**
CHallenging Activity 6

Activity ❶

🎧 Audio Script

1. Un tobillo torcido se hincha.
2. Si tienes un brazo quebrado tienes que andar con muletas.
3. El cirujano ortopédico le ha puesto la pierna en un yeso porque tiene una fractura.
4. Han puesto al herido en una camilla porque no puede levantarse.
5. Lo han puesto en una silla de ruedas porque no puede sentarse.
6. Le van a suturar porque se cortó el pie.

Activities ❷ and ❸ These activities should be done orally before they are written.

Cultural Snapshot

(page 38) This hospital is typical of the many modern, new hospitals throughout Spain.

 Escucha cada frase y decide si la información es correcta o no. Usa una tabla como la de abajo para indicar tus respuestas.

correcta	incorrecta

 Contesta sobre un accidente que tuvo Mariana.

   1. Mariana ha tenido un accidente. ¿Se cayó ella?
   2. ¿Se torció el tobillo?
   3. ¿Le duele mucho el tobillo?
   4. ¿Está hinchado el tobillo?
   5. ¿Le duele mucho cuando anda a pie?
   6. ¿Tendrá que andar con muletas?
   7. ¿Se ha hecho mucho daño o no?

EXPANSIÓN

Ahora, sin mirar las preguntas, cuenta la información en tus propias palabras. Si no recuerdas algo, un(a) compañero(a) te puede ayudar.

 Contesta según se indica.

   1. ¿Qué tuvo Tomás? (un accidente serio)
   2. ¿Qué le pasó? (se quebró la pierna)
   3. ¿Qué le causó la pierna quebrada? (mucho dolor)
   4. ¿Adónde fue? (a la sala de emergencia)
   5. ¿Cómo fue? (en ambulancia)
   6. ¿Quiénes lo ayudaron? (los socorristas)
   7. ¿En qué lo pusieron? (una camilla)
   8. ¿Qué le tomaron en el hospital? (radiografías)
   9. ¿A qué médico llamaron? (al cirujano ortopédico)
   10. Al salir del hospital, ¿qué necesitará Tomás? (una silla de ruedas)

EXPANSIÓN

Ahora, sin mirar las preguntas, cuenta la información en tus propias palabras. Si no recuerdas algo, un(a) compañero(a) te puede ayudar.

CULTURA
Un hospital grande y moderno en Barcelona, España

Answers

❶
1. correcta
2. incorrecta
3. correcta
4. correcta
5. incorrecta
6. correcta

❷
1. Sí, se cayó.
2. Sí, se torció el tobillo.
3. Sí, (No, no) le duele mucho el tobillo.
4. Sí (No), el tobillo (no) está hinchado.
5. Sí, (No, no) le duele mucho cuando anda a pie.
6. Sí, (No, no) tendrá que andar con muletas.
7. Sí, (No, no) ha hecho mucho daño.

❸
1. Tomás tuvo un accidente serio.
2. Se quebró la pierna.
3. La pierna quebrada le causó mucho dolor.
4. Fue a la sala de emergencia.
5. Fue en ambulancia.
6. Los socorristas lo ayudaron.
7. Lo pusieron en una camilla.
8. Le tomaron radiografías en el hospital.
9. Llamaron al cirujano ortopédico.
10. Al salir del hospital, Tomás necesitará una silla de ruedas.

Más practica
Workbook, pp. 2.6–2.8
StudentWorks™ Plus

HABLAR • ESCRIBIR

4 Trabajen en grupos. Describan unas actividades que tienen lugar en esta sala de emergencia.

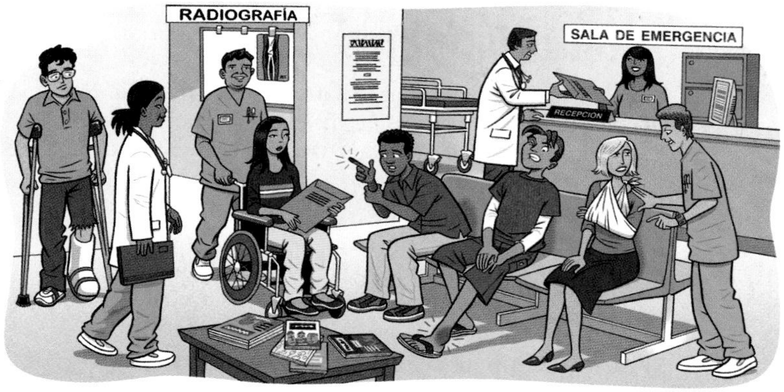

ESCRIBIR

5 Completa con lo que falta.

1. una _erida
2. un tobi_o _inchado
3. el _ospital
4. la cami_a y la si_a de ruedas
5. se ca_ó
6. el _eso
7. el _ueso
8. una _enda

CULTURA
Los socorristas ayudan a un herido en una ambulancia en Madrid.

ESCRIBIR

6 **Rompecabezas**

Pon las palabras en orden para formar frases. Luego, pon las frases en orden para crear una historia.

1. dijo no que le la necesitaba enfermera suturas
2. corrió la de cerca bicicleta perro muy un
3. calle la andaba por en Catalina bicicleta
4. de sala fue la a emergencia
5. rodilla enfermera venda la le en la puso una
6. ella perro a le cayó el se sorprendió y Catalina
7. rodilla cayó cortó se se la cuando

InfoGap For more practice with your new vocabulary, do Activity 2 on page SR3 at the end of this book.

Answers

4 *Answers will vary.*

5

1. una herida
2. un tobillo hinchado
3. el hospital
4. la camilla y la silla de ruedas
5. se cayó
6. el yeso
7. el hueso
8. una venda

6 *Correct order of sentences:* 3, 2, 6, 7, 4, 1, 5

1. La enfermera le dijo que no necesitaba suturas.
2. Un perro corrió muy cerca de la bicicleta.
3. Catalina andaba en bicicleta por la calle.
4. Fue a la sala de emergencia.
5. La enfermera le puso una venda en la rodilla.
6. El perro le sorprendió a Catalina y ella se cayó.
7. Cuando se cayó se cortó la rodilla.

Vocabulario 2

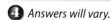

Tips for Success

It is important that all students hear the answers to these activities. The answers give them the opportunity to hear their new words in context, thus reinforcing meaning and helping to make the new words an active part of the students' vocabulary.

Activity 4 This activity can be done as a group activity.

Comunicación

Interpersonal

Have students use the illustration that accompanies Activity 4 to make up conversations.

Activity 5 You may also wish to use these words in a dictation.

Cultura

Spain is currently known for its excellent medical services. Its services are reported to have surpassed those of several other countries in the European Union.

GLENCOE Technology

Online Learning in the Classroom

Have students use QuickPass code ASD7844c2 for additional vocabulary practice. They can download audio files of all vocabulary to their computer and/or MP3 player. They will have access to online flashcards and eGames. Students can print and complete the **Vocabulario 1** and **2** Review Worksheet.

ASSESS

Students are now ready to take Quiz 2 on page 2.48 of the TeacherTools booklet. If you prefer to create your own quiz, use the *ExamView® Assessment Suite.*

Gramática

QuickPass

Go to glencoe.com
For: Grammar practice
Web code: ASD7844c2

Resources

- Audio Activities TE, pages 2.28–2.29
- Audio CD 2, Tracks 9–11
- Workbook, pages 2.9–2.10
- Quiz 3, page 2.49
- ExamView® Assessment Suite

Quick Start

Use QS Transparency 2.3 or write the following on the board.
Rewrite with **nosotros.**
1. Me acuesto.
2. Me despierto.
3. No quiero.
4. Me siento aquí.
5. No puedo.
6. No vuelvo.
7. No pierdo.

▶ TEACH
Core Instruction

Step 1 As you go over the use of the subjunctive in impersonal expressions, point out that the subjunctive is used because it is not known if the information in the clause will actually take place or not. Indicate to students that the rationale for using the subjunctive with these expressions is the same as the rationale for using the subjunctive after **querer,** which they learned in Chapter 1.

Step 2 Have students read the expressions aloud as well as the example sentences.

▶ PRACTICE

Leveling EACH Activity

Easy Activities 1, 4
Average Activities 2, 3, Activity 4 **Expansión**
CHallenging Activities 5, 6

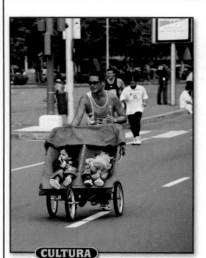

CULTURA
Papi corre en un maratón con sus dos niños en Tenerife en las islas Canarias. Es posible que ganen, ¿no?

CULTURA
¿Es posible que el cocinero esté aprendiendo a cocinar algo en esta escuela culinaria en España?

40 *cuarenta*

CAPÍTULO 2

El subjuntivo con expresiones impersonales

The subjunctive is used after each of the following impersonal expressions because it is not known if the information in the clause that follows will actually take place. It may or may not.

es importante	es fácil
es necesario	es difícil
es imposible	es bueno
es posible	es probable
es mejor	es improbable

Es probable que él esté bien.
Pero es necesario que vea al médico.
Es importante que sepa lo que tiene.

Práctica

ESCUCHAR • HABLAR • ESCRIBIR

1️⃣ Sigue el modelo.

MODELO   **Tú haces ejercicios.** →
   Es necesario que tú hagas ejercicios.

1. Hablas con el entrenador.
2. Vas al gimnasio.
3. Haces jogging.
4. Corres por lo menos cinco vueltas.
5. Participas en el maratón.

HABLAR • ESCRIBIR

2️⃣ Prepara una lista de cosas que es probable que tú hagas con frecuencia porque es fácil hacerlas. Prepara otra lista que indica lo que es difícil que tú hagas. Luego compara tus listas con las listas que ha preparado un(a) compañero(a).

LEER • ESCRIBIR

3️⃣ Sigue el modelo.

MODELO   **es necesario / saber la receta** →
   Es necesario que el cocinero sepa la receta.

1. es importante / lavar las ollas
2. es fácil / pelar las papas
3. es probable / freír el pescado
4. es mejor / asar el cordero
5. es posible / servir la comida

Answers

1️⃣
1. Es necesario que tú hables con el entrenador.
2. Es necesario que tú vayas al gimnasio.
3. Es necesario que tú hagas jogging.
4. Es necesario que tú corras por lo menos cinco vueltas.
5. Es necesario que tú participes en el maratón.

2️⃣ *Answers will vary.*

3️⃣
1. Es importante que el cocinero lave las ollas.
2. Es fácil que el cocinero pele las papas.
3. Es probable que el cocinero fría el pescado.
4. Es mejor que el cocinero ase el cordero.
5. Es posible que el cocinero sirva la comida.

HABLAR

④ Contesta.

1. ¿Es importante que los jóvenes de Estados Unidos estudien una lengua?
2. ¿Es necesario que ellos sepan hablar otra lengua?
3. ¿Es bueno que ellos hablen otra lengua?
4. ¿Es necesario que ellos conozcan otra cultura?
5. ¿Es posible que algún día ellos tengan la oportunidad de visitar otros países?
6. ¿Es probable que ellos vayan a otros países?

EXPANSIÓN

Ahora, sin mirar las preguntas, cuenta la información en tus propias palabras. Si no recuerdas algo, un(a) compañero(a) te puede ayudar.

LEER • ESCRIBIR

⑤ Completa.

Abuelito está un poco nervioso. Es posible que sus nietos __1__ (llegar) mañana por la mañana. Es importante que abuelito __2__ (saber) cuándo van a llegar. Pero es difícil que abuelita le __3__ (decir) la hora precisa de la llegada de los nietos. Es posible que mañana __4__ (hacer) mal tiempo. Como los nietos vienen en carro será necesario que __5__ (conducir) despacio y con mucho cuidado si hay nieve. Es mejor que ellos __6__ (llegar) un poco tarde. Abuelito no quiere que ellos __7__ (tener) un accidente. Es mejor que __8__ (llegar) tarde pero sanos y salvos.

Comunicación

⑥ Trabaja con un(a) compañero(a) de clase. Dile cosas que haces. Tu compañero(a) te dará su opinión sobre las cosas que haces usando las siguientes expresiones: **es importante, es bueno, es necesario, es mejor.**

¡CUÍDATE BIEN!

cuarenta y uno **41**

Más práctica

Workbook, pp. 2.9–2.10
StudentWorks™ Plus

FOLDABLES®
Study Organizer

TAB BOOK
See page SH25 for help with making this foldable. Use this study organizer to help you practice the subjunctive. On the top of each tab, write an expression that requires the subjunctive, for example **Es imposible que...** Then open each tab and write a sentence using that expression with the subjunctive.

Gramática

Activity ① Have students use the correct intonation as they give the sentence with **es necesario.** The proper intonation can indicate that it is necessary but maybe it won't happen.

Activity ② After students read their lists, you may wish to expand the activity by having them make up additional sentences such as: ____ **y yo hemos decidido que es difícil que (nosotros) ____.**

Activity ③ This activity can be prepared in advance and then gone over orally in class.

⭐Tips for Success ·······

Have students read the captions that accompany the photographs since they reinforce the grammar point they are learning.

·····································

Activity ④ This activity can be done orally in class.

Activity ⑤ This activity can be prepared before being gone over in class.

Differentiation

Advanced Learners
Slower Paced Learners

Have students make up sentences telling what they think is important, necessary, etc., for others to do. For example: **Es necesario que tú (yo, ustedes)...** After a student gives his or her sentence to the class, he or she will call on classmates to indicate whether or not they agree. Advanced learners will be capable of making up many sentences while slower paced learners will make up just a few. The important point is that all students will be working to capacity.

41

Answers

④

1. Sí, (No, no) es importante que los jóvenes de Estados Unidos estudien una lengua.
2. Sí, (No, no) es necesario que ellos sepan hablar otra lengua.
3. Sí, (No, no) es bueno que ellos hablen otra lengua.
4. Sí, (No, no) es necesario que ellos conozcan otra cultura.
5. Sí, (No, no) es posible que algún día ellos tengan la oportunidad de visitar otros países.
6. Sí, (No, no) es probable que ellos vayan a otros países.

⑤

1. lleguen
2. sepa
3. diga
4. haga
5. conduzcan
6. lleguen
7. tengan
8. lleguen

⑥ *Answers will vary.*

Resources

- Audio Activities TE, pages 2.29–2.30
- Audio CD 2, Tracks 11–14
- Workbook, pages 2.11–2.12
- Quiz 4, page 2.50
- *ExamView® Assessment Suite*

Quick Start

Use QS Transparency 2.4 or write the following on the board.
Complete in the present.
1. Ellos siempre _____ más. (pedir)
2. El mesero nos _____. (servir)
3. Yo no _____ el pescado. (freír)
4. Tú _____ la misma cosa. (repetir)
5. Yo no _____ más. (seguir)

▶ TEACH
Core Instruction

Step 1 Read the explanation to the class.

Step 2 Call on students to read the example sentences aloud. This point should be rather easy.

▶ PRACTICE

Leveling EACH Activity

Easy Activities 7, 8, 9
Average–CHallenging Activities 7, 8, 9

Note: Activities 7, 8, and 9 are all Easy for students who are not having difficulty with the subjunctive verb forms. Those students who are still having problems with the verb forms will find them Average–Challenging.

CULTURA

Esta joven que anda con muletas acaba de salir de un centro médico en Trelew, Argentina. ¡Ojalá que se mejore pronto!

¡Ojalá! ¡Quizás! ¡Tal vez!

The expression **¡Ojalá!** or **¡Ojalá que!** comes from Arabic and it means *Would that . . .* Since the information that follows **ojalá** may or may not happen, it is followed by the subjunctive. The expressions **¡Quizás!** and **¡Tal vez!** mean *perhaps* or *maybe* and can also be followed by the subjunctive.

> **¡Ojalá que vengan!**
> **¡Quizás lleguen mañana!**
> **¡Tal vez estén aquí!**

Práctica

ESCUCHAR • HABLAR

7 Contesta con **quizás** según el modelo.

MODELO ¿Carla lo va a saber? →
¡Quizás lo sepa!

1. ¿Carla va a estar aquí?
2. ¿Va a ir al parque?
3. ¿Va a participar en la carrera?
4. ¿Va a salir primero?
5. ¿Va a romper un récord?
6. ¿Va a ganar un trofeo?

LEER • ESCRIBIR

8 Sigue el modelo.

MODELO tener cuidado →
¡Ojalá que tengan cuidado!

1. prestar atención
2. no tomar una decisión ridícula
3. ponerse el casco
4. llevar rodilleras
5. no tener ningún accidente
6. no ir al hospital

Comunicación

9 Trabaja con un(a) compañero(a). Los dos van a hablar de eventos que quieren que ocurran durante su vida. Introduzcan sus ideas con **¡ojalá!**

Differentiation

Many activities can serve as diagnostic tools. If students have problems with these activities, it indicates they do not know the subjunctive verb forms. If this is the case, it is suggested that you go over the forms again on pages 8–9. Slower paced students will need quite a bit more practice.

Answers

7
1. ¡Quizás esté aquí!
2. ¡Quizás vaya al parque!
3. ¡Quizás participe en la carrera!
4. ¡Quizás salga primero!
5. ¡Quizás rompa un récord!
6. ¡Quizás gane un trofeo!

El subjuntivo de los verbos de cambio radical

1. Verbs that have a stem change in the present indicative also have a stem change in the present subjunctive.

E → IE			
cerrar			
yo	cierre	nosotros(as)	cerremos
tú	cierres	*vosotros(as)*	*cerréis*
Ud., él, ella	cierre	Uds., ellos, ellas	cierren

O → UE			
encontrar			
yo	encuentre	nosotros(as)	encontremos
tú	encuentres	*vosotros(as)*	*encontréis*
Ud., él, ella	encuentre	Uds., ellos, ellas	encuentren

2. The verbs **preferir** (e → ie), **dormir** (o → ue), and **pedir** (e → i) have a stem change in every person of the present subjunctive.

	E → IE, I	O → UE, U	E → I
	preferir	**dormir**	**pedir**
yo	prefiera	duerma	pida
tú	prefieras	duermas	pidas
Ud., él, ella	prefiera	duerma	pida
nosotros(as)	prefiramos	durmamos	pidamos
vosotros(as)	*prefiráis*	*durmáis*	*pidáis*
Uds., ellos, ellas	prefieran	duerman	pidan

HABLAR • ESCRIBIR

 Contesta.
1. ¿Dónde quieres que yo me siente?
2. ¿Es importante que yo no pierda el juego?
3. ¿Quieres que yo vuelva temprano?
4. ¿Es posible que yo duerma aquí?
5. ¿Es necesario que yo se lo repita?

¡CUÍDATE BIEN!

cuarenta y tres **43**

Nota

- Other verbs with the **e → ie** stem change like **cerrar** are: **perder, sentarse, comenzar, empezar, pensar.**
- Other **o → ue** verbs like **encontrar** are: **acostarse, recordar, poder, volver.**
- **Sentir** is conjugated like **preferir.**
- Other verbs with the **e → i** stem change like **pedir** are: **repetir, freír, seguir, servir.**

Según los jóvenes, es importante que todos sigamos una dieta sana.

Gramática

Resources
- Workbook, pages 2.12–2.13
- Quiz 5, page 2.51
- *ExamView® Assessment Suite*

▶ TEACH
Core Instruction

Step 1 Have students repeat the forms of the verbs as you write them on the board or present them with PowerTeach.

Step 2 Remind students that if they pronounce the forms correctly, they will have no problem spelling them.

Note: The present indicative forms of stem-changing verbs were reviewed in the Quick Start activity on page 36.

Differentiation
Students with Auditory Impairments
Tell students to pay very close attention to the difference in sound between: **ie** and **e**; **ue** and **u**; **ie** and **ue**; **i** and **u**.

▶ PRACTICE

> **Leveling EACH Activity**
>
> **A**verage Activities 10, 11, 12

Activity ⑩ It is suggested that you go over this activity orally in class. Then have students write the activity.

Answers

⑧
1. ¡Ojalá que presten atención!
2. ¡Ojalá que no tomen una decisión ridícula!
3. ¡Ojalá que se pongan el casco!
4. ¡Ojalá que lleven rodilleras!
5. ¡Ojalá que no tengan ningún accidente!
6. ¡Ojalá que no vayan al hospital!

⑨ *Answers will vary.*

⑩ *Answers will vary but may include:*
1. Yo quiero que que tú te sientes _____.
2. Sí, (No, no) es importante que tú no pierdas el juego.
3. Sí, (No, no) quiero que tú vuelvas temprano.
4. Sí, (No, no) es posible que tú duermas aquí.
5. Sí, (No, no) es necesario que tú se lo repitas.

43

Activities ⑪ and ⑫ These activities can be gone over orally in class with or without previous presentation.

 ASSESS

Students are now ready to take Quiz 5 on page 2.51 of the TeacherTools booklet. If you prefer to create your own quiz, use the *ExamView®* *Assessment Suite.*

Resources

- Audio Activities TE, page 2.31
- Audio CD 2, Tracks 15–16
- Workbook, page 2.14
- Quiz 6, page 2.52
- *ExamView® Assessment Suite*

 TEACH
Core Instruction

Step 1 Have students open their books to page 44 and lead them through the explanation.

Step 2 Have them repeat all the example sentences after you.

Conexiones

Point out to students some problems non-English speakers have when learning English. They have great difficulty contrasting *as many as* and *as much as*. They are told to think of "count nouns," nouns that can have a numeral before them (like *dollars),* and "non-count nouns," words that cannot be preceded by a numeral (like *money).* You use *as many as* with "count nouns," for example, *She has as many dollars as I have.* You use *as much as* with "non-count nouns"— *She has as much money as I have.* It sounds easy but it's not easy for many non-English speakers.

 VIDEO Want help with the subjunctive? Watch **Gramática en vivo.**

Práctica

LEER • ESCRIBIR

⑪ Sigue el modelo.

MODELO **Quiere que tú lo cierres.** →
Quiere que nosotros lo cerremos.

1. Quiere que te sientes aquí.
2. Quiere que tú pierdas.
3. Quiere que tú lo encuentres.
4. Quiere que tú vuelvas pronto.
5. Quiere que duermas aquí.
6. Quiere que lo pidas.
7. Quiere que lo sigas.
8. Quiere que tú no lo repitas.

HABLAR • LEER • ESCRIBIR

⑫ Cambia el segundo verbo al verbo indicado.

1. Yo quiero que ellos lo cierren. (empezar, perder, encontrar, recordar, devolver, preferir, pedir, repetir)
2. Es posible que yo lo encuentre. (cerrar, perder, recordar, devolver, servir, pedir, repetir)
3. Es necesario que nosotros volvamos. (comenzar, sentarnos, recordar, dormir, seguir)

Comparación de igualdad

1. In Spanish you use **tanto... como** to compare quantities. Because **tanto** is an adjective, it has to agree with the noun it modifies.

Elena tiene tanta energía como yo.
Pero ella no tiene tantos accidentes como yo.

2. In Spanish you use **tan... como** to compare qualitites with either an adjective or adverb.

Él está tan enfermo como su amiga.
Él se va a curar tan rápido como ella.

3. The subject pronoun always follows the comparison of equality.

Él es tan bueno como tú.
Y tiene tanto dinero como yo.

Conexiones

El inglés
To compare equal quantities in English you use:
as much money as I
as many problems as I
To compare equal qualities you use:
as smart as she
as tall as he

GLENCOE Technology

Video in the Classroom

Gramática en vivo: *The Subjunctive* Enliven learning with the animated world of Professor Cruz! **Gramática en vivo** is a fun and effective tool for additional instruction and/or review.

Answers

⑪
1. Quiere que nosotros nos sentemos aquí.
2. Quiere que nosotros perdamos.
3. Quiere que nosotros lo encontremos.
4. Quiere que nosotros volvamos pronto.
5. Quiere que nosotros durmamos aquí.
6. Quiere que nosotros lo pidamos.
7. Quiere que nosotros lo sigamos.
8. Quiere que nosotros no lo repitamos.

Práctica

HABLAR

13 Personaliza. Da respuestas personales.
1. ¿Eres tan inteligente como tus amigos?
2. ¿Eres tan cómico(a) como tus amigos?
3. ¿Eres tan ambicioso(a) como tus amigos?
4. ¿Eres tan aficionado(a) a los deportes como tus amigos?
5. ¿Tienes tanta paciencia como tus amigos?
6. ¿Tienes tanto éxito como tus amigos?
7. ¿Tienes tanto trabajo como tus amigos?
8. ¿Tienes tantas ambiciones como tus amigos?

LEER • ESCRIBIR

14 Completa con **tan** o **tanto como**.
1. Ella corre en _____ carreras _____ yo.
2. Y ella va _____ rápido _____ yo.
3. Él puede levantar _____ pesas _____ yo.
4. Pero él no es _____ fuerte _____ yo.
5. Yo no hago _____ ejercicios _____ tú.
6. Yo no soy _____ aficionado(a) a los ejercicios físicos _____ tú.

CULTURA
Un grupo de gente mayor (de la tercera edad) está jugando voleibol en un gimnasio en Oaxaca, México.

Comunicación

15 Trabaja con un(a) compañero(a). Piensen en algunas personas que ustedes conocen que, en su opinión, tienen mucho en común o que tienen las mismas características físicas. Comparen a estas personas.

¡CUÍDATE BIEN!

Más práctica

- Workbook, p. 2.14
- StudentWorks™ Plus

Refrán

Can you guess what the following proverb means?

La mejor almohada es la conciencia sana.

¡Bravo!

You have now learned all the new vocabulary and grammar in this chapter. Continue to use and practice all that you know while learning more cultural information. **¡Vamos!**

cuarenta y cinco **45**

Gramática

▶ PRACTICE

Leveling EACH Activity

Easy Activity 13
Average Activity 14
CHallenging Activity 15

Activity 13 This activity can first be done orally with books closed. Students can also write the answers.

Activity 14 This activity may be done with or without prior preparation.

Cultural Snapshot

(page 45) This volleyball group gets together several days a week. All team members are over 55 years old.

Refrán

Have students recite the proverb aloud. Then see if they can figure out its meaning, and encourage them to try to give an equivalent expression in English such as "A clean conscience is a good pillow." Students may be able to think of other expressions related to the same theme.

Answers

12
1. Yo quiero que ellos lo empiecen (pierdan, encuentren, recuerden, devuelvan, prefieran, pidan, repitan).
2. Es posible que yo lo cierre (pierda, recuerde, devuelva, sirva, pida, repita).
3. Es necesario que nosotros comencemos (nos sentemos, recordemos, durmamos, sigamos).

13
1. Sí, (No, no) soy tan inteligente como mis amigos.
2. Sí, (No, no) soy tan cómico(a) como mis amigos.
3. Sí, (No, no) soy tan ambicioso(a) como mis amigos.
4. Sí, (No, no) soy tan aficionado(a) a los deportes como mis amigos.
5. Sí, (No, no) tengo tanta paciencia como mis amigos.
6. Sí, (No, no) tengo tanto éxito como mis amigos.
7. Sí, (No, no) tengo tanto trabajo como mis amigos.
8. Sí, (No, no) tengo tantas ambiciones como mis amigos.

14
1. tantas, como
2. tan, como
3. tantas, como
4. tan, como
5. tantos, como
6. tan, como

15 *Answers will vary.*

...ión

...ivities TE, page 2.32
...2, Tracks 17–18

Quick Start

Use QS Transparency 2.5 or write the following on the board. Answer.

1. ¿Te sientes bien cuando tienes fiebre?
2. ¿Te sientes bien cuando tienes catarro?
3. ¿Vas a la consulta del médico cuando estás enfermo(a)?
4. ¿Te examina el médico?
5. A veces, ¿te da una receta?
6. ¿Vas a la farmacia con la receta?

▶ TEACH
Core Instruction

Step 1 Have students close their books. Ask them to listen and repeat as you read the conversation aloud or play Audio CD 2.

Step 2 Have students open their books. Call on volunteers to read the conversation in parts with as much expression as possible.

Step 3 Go over the **¿Comprendes?** activities on page 47.

GLENCOE 🔊 Technology

Online Learning in the Classroom

Have students use QuickPass code ASD7844c2 for additional conversation practice. Students can download audio files for the conversation to their computer and/or MP3 player and complete a self-check quiz.

UN ACCIDENTE

GLENCOE SPANISH
Why It Works!

No new material is used in the **Conversación** in order not to confuse students. The **Conversación** recombines only the vocabulary and grammar that students have already learned to understand and manipulate.

GLENCOE 🔊 Technology

You may wish to use the editable PowerPoint® presentation on PowerTeach to have students listen to and repeat the conversation. Additional activities are also provided.

¿Comprendes?

A Contesta según la información en la conversación.

1. ¿Qué hacía Enrique cuando se cayó?
2. ¿Qué le duele?
3. ¿Cómo está el tobillo?
4. ¿Qué crees? ¿Quiere Enrique que Catalina lo lleve a la sala de emergencia? ¿Le gusta la idea?
5. Según Catalina, ¿por qué debe ir Enrique a la sala de emergencia?
6. ¿Es posible que no tenga el tobillo quebrado?

B **Resumiendo** Cuenta todo lo que pasó en la conversación en tus propias palabras.

C **Prediciendo** Predice lo que va a pasar a Enrique y Catalina en la sala de emergencia. Prepara una conversación que tiene lugar en el hospital. Debes incluir a otros en la conversación como el médico o el enfermero. ¡Usa tanta imaginación posible!

VIDEO To see how one friend helps another after a skateboarding accident, watch **Diálogo en vivo**.

GeoVistas

To learn more about Panama, take a tour on pages SH44–SH45.

Entrada a la sala de emergencias en un hospital en la Ciudad de Panamá

CULTURA

EMERGENCIAS →

HOSPITAL PUNTA PACIFICA
Afiliado a Johns Hopkins Medicine International

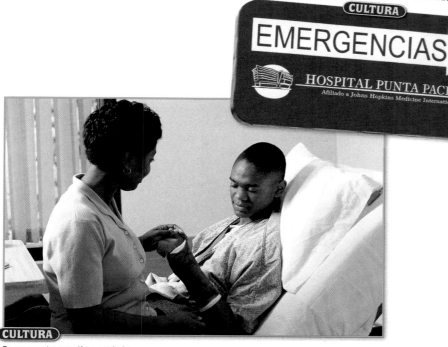

CULTURA
Es necesario que él se cuide bien.
Es posible que le duela mucho el brazo, ¿no?

¡CUÍDATE BIEN!

cuarenta y siete **47**

Answers

A
1. Hacía jogging cuando se cayó.
2. Le duele el tobillo.
3. Está muy hinchado.
4. No, Enrique no quiere que Catalina lo lleve a la sala de emergencia. No le gusta la idea.
5. Según Catalina, Enrique debe ir a la sala de emergencia porque le pueden tomar una radiografía y él sabrá si el tobillo está roto o torcido.
6. Sí, es posible que no tenga el tobillo quebrado.

B *Answers will vary.*

C *Answers will vary.*

Differentiation
Multiple Intelligences
Have **bodily-kinesthetic** students dramatize this conversation. Using the proper gestures and intonation, students can make it quite humorous. Seeing the dramatization also helps **visual-spatial** learners.

▶ PRACTICE

¿Comprendes?

A You may wish to allow students to look up the information in the conversation as they respond or you may wish to do this as a factual recall activity. Students can also write the answers to the questions.

B If a student is giving a review and appears to be having trouble, call on another to continue. You may also do this as a group activity and have each group present their conversation to the class.

GLENCOE Technology

Video in the Classroom
Diálogo en vivo In this episode, Vicky goes skateboarding. Ask students if they think she really hurt herself.

GeoVistas

Have students look at the map of Panama on page SH45. Have them locate the Panama Canal and look at the picture of the canal below. Ask students what geographic features they can observe that allow the canal to have been built in this location.

Resources

- Audio Activities TE, page 2.33
- Audio CD 2, Tracks 19–20

▶ TEACH
Core Instruction

Step 1 Have students read the **Estrategia de lectura** and do the **Antes de leer** activity silently.

Step 2 Call on a student to read several sentences aloud. Ask questions about what he or she read. If the pronunciation of the class is good, you can skip this step. Just have students read silently, go over the Reading Checks, and ask students a few more comprehension questions.

Step 3 Go over the **¿Comprendes?** activities.

Differentiation

There is no doubt that differently paced learners will produce language at different levels. Some techniques you may want to use to get the maximum from each group are:

- Ask a slower paced student three or four questions. He or she answers. The answers to your questions will provide an organized review.
- Call on a more able student to retell what the previous student just said, giving no help with guided questions.
- With no assistance, call on an advanced learner to retell the entire story in his/her own words.
- Ask some questions of a slower paced learner about what the previous student said.

Antes de leer

Dale una ojeada a la lectura y busca palabras que consideres desconocidas. No habrá muchas.

CULTURA

Están haciendo ejercicios aeróbicos en un gimnasio en Buenos Aires, Argentina.

✓ Reading Check

¿Qué hacen todos en el gimnasio?

Durante la lectura

Busca clarificaciones—si hay una palabra que no sabes, tal vez haya un sinónimo en la frase.

✓ Reading Check

¿Cuál es la ventaja de los parques?

ESTRATEGIA DE LECTURA

Adivinando Hay dos estrategias que te pueden ayudar a comprender lo que lees en español: reconocer o adivinar el significado de palabras aparentadas con una palabra inglesa y adivinar el significado de una palabra desconocida por medio del contexto en que se usa. Las otras palabras en la frase te pueden ayudar a determinar el significado de la palabra desconocida.

Vida activa y buena salud 🎧 ♻

Hoy en día el interés que tenemos en nuestra salud y forma física es fenomenal. Y este interés existe en España y Latinoamérica igual que en Estados Unidos.

Como es importante que uno haga ejercicios a lo menos tres veces a la semana, hay una gran proliferación de gimnasios. Estos gimnasios tienen muchos socios[1]. En el gimnasio hacen ejercicios aeróbicos y abdominales. Se estiran los brazos y las piernas. Hacen planchas. Algunos levantan pesas. ¡Todo para mantenerse en forma!

Además de los gimnasios los parques son inmensamente populares, y para ir a un parque no hay que ser socio o miembro. Un parque es un buen lugar para hacer jogging o correr unas vueltas. A muchos les gusta dar un paseo por el parque en bicicleta. Andar en bicicleta es una forma excelente de ejercicio. Otros se sientan en un lugar aislado del parque donde disfrutan del silencio y de la tranquilidad. Se relajan practicando yoga y meditando.

[1]socios *members*

CULTURA

El ciclista está haciendo ejercicios en un parque en Viña del Mar, Chile.

48 *cuarenta y ocho* **CAPÍTULO 2**

📷 Cultural Snapshot

(page 48) Viña del Mar is a rather upscale resort about ninety minutes from Santiago, just north of the port of Valparaiso.

GLENCOE 🖱 Technology

Online Learning in the Classroom

You may wish to have students use QuickPass code ASD7844c2 to develop their reading comprehension and writing skills. Students will be able to take a self-check quiz, which includes an essay.

Muchas ciudades tienen un maratón a lo menos una vez al año. Muchos maratones tienen un propósito benévolo[2] y atraen a muchos participantes. Además atraen a muchos espectadores que animan a los corredores que tienen que correr largas distancias.

Entre los jóvenes el patinaje en línea y el monopatín son muy apreciados. Tienen muchos aficionados. Pero, una advertencia[3]—al practicar estas formas de patinaje hay que tener mucho cuidado porque puedes lastimarte fácilmente. Siempre tienes que llevar casco y rodilleras. Nadie quiere que te hagas daño y que te encuentres en una sala de emergencia.

[2]propósito benévolo   *charitable purpose*   [3]advertencia   *warning*

¿Comprendes?

A **Categorizando** Completa la tabla según la información en la lectura.

actividades en un gimnasio	actividades en el parque	actividades durante un maratón	actividades populares entre los jóvenes

B **Personalizando** Contesta.
¿En qué actividades de la Actividad A participas? Explica por qué te gustan.

C **Analizando** Contesta.
¿Por qué son populares los gimnasios y los parques?

CULTURA
Los jóvenes están patinando en línea en Barcelona, España.

¡CUÍDATE BIEN!

Más práctica

Workbook, pp. 2.15–2.18
StudentWorks™ Plus

✓ **Reading Check**
¿Quiénes animan a los corredores en el maratón?

✓ **Reading Check**
¿Qué hay que tener al practicar el patinaje o el monopatín? ¿Por qué?

Después de leer

Prepara una lista de palabras aparentadas que encontraste en la lectura.

▶ PRACTICE

Pre-AP These cultural readings will develop the skills that students need to be successful on the reading and writing sections of the AP exam. Listening to these readings will also help prepare them for the auditory component.

GLENCOE SPANISH

Why It Works!

Note that as always in **¡Así se dice!,** readings are geared to the students' proficiency level in Spanish. This reading contains only material, vocabulary, and grammar that students have already learned. The only exceptions are the three footnoted vocabulary items.

Answers

A
actividades en un gimnasio: hacer ejercicios aeróbicos y abdominales, estirarse los brazos y las piernas, hacer planchas y levantar pesas
actividades en el parque: hacer jogging, correr unas vueltas, dar un paseo en bicicleta, practicar yoga
actividades durante un maratón: correr, animar a los corredores
actividades populares entre los jóvenes: practicar el patinaje en línea y el monopatín

B *Answers will vary.*

C *Answers will vary but may include:*
Son populares porque todo el mundo quiere mantenerse en forma.

LECTURA
UN POCO MÁS

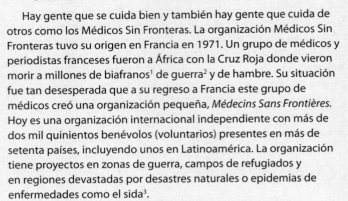

Resources

- Audio Activities TE, page 2.34
- Audio CD 2, Track 21

Teaching Options

You may wish to follow any one of the following procedures for the **Lectura—Un poco más.**

Independent reading Have students read the selection and do the post-reading activities as homework which you collect. This option is the least intrusive on class time and requires a minimum of teacher involvement.

Homework with in-class follow-up Assign the reading and post-reading activities as homework. Review and discuss the material in class the next day.

Intensive in-class activity This option includes a pre-reading vocabulary presentation, in-class reading and discussion, assignment of the activities for homework, and a discussion of the assignment in class the following day.

Conexiones

Have students find out more about the work of **Médicos Sin Fronteras** and present what they learn to the class. Ask them to consider how knowing a second language could be an advantage for someone doing this kind of work.

Antes de leer

Piensa en unas organizaciones benévolas o caritativas donde vives. ¿Qué tipo de trabajo hacen? ¿Has oído de Médicos Sin Fronteras, una famosa organización internacional?

Médicos Sin Fronteras

Hay gente que se cuida bien y también hay gente que cuida de otros como los Médicos Sin Fronteras. La organización Médicos Sin Fronteras tuvo su origen en Francia en 1971. Un grupo de médicos y periodistas franceses fueron a África con la Cruz Roja donde vieron morir a millones de biafranos[1] de guerra[2] y de hambre. Su situación fue tan desesperada que a su regreso a Francia este grupo de médicos creó una organización pequeña, *Médecins Sans Frontières.* Hoy es una organización internacional independiente con más de dos mil quinientos benévolos (voluntarios) presentes en más de setenta países, incluyendo unos en Latinoamérica. La organización tiene proyectos en zonas de guerra, campos de refugiados y en regiones devastadas por desastres naturales o epidemias de enfermedades como el sida[3].

Entre los benévolos hay médicos, cirujanos, enfermeros y técnicos. Hay también personas que se responsabilizan por los materiales que necesitan y la administración de los proyectos. Todos reciben muy poco dinero por el trabajo maravilloso que hacen.

En 1999 Médicos Sin Fronteras ganó el prestigioso Premio Nobel de la Paz.

[1]biafranos   *people from Biafra*   [3]sida   *AIDS*
[2]guerra   *war*

CAPÍTULO 2

GLENCOE Technology

Online Learning in the Classroom

You may wish to have students use QuickPass code ASD7844c2 to develop their reading comprehension and writing skills. Students will print and complete a review worksheet.

¿Comprendes?

Escoge.

1. Los Médicos Sin Fronteras _____.
   a. se cuidan bien
   b. cuidan de otros
   c. no tienen país
   d. son todos franceses

2. La organización Médicos Sin Fronteras tuvo su origen en _____.
   a. Francia
   b. Biafra, África
   c. la Cruz Roja
   d. una situación desesperada

3. ¿Quiénes establecieron la organización?
   a. miembros de la Cruz Roja
   b. un grupo internacional independiente
   c. un grupo de médicos y periodistas franceses
   d. un grupo de benévolos

4. Los biafranos morían _____.
   a. de un desastre natural
   b. de una epidemia
   c. de malnutrición y guerra
   d. a causa del calor

5. Por lo general, ¿quiénes toman refugio en los campos de refugiados?
   a. las víctimas de guerra
   b. los benévolos
   c. los enfermos
   d. los soldados

6. Los benévolos que trabajan con la organización _____.
   a. son todos personal médico
   b. tienen un salario
   c. reciben muy poco dinero
   d. viven de proyectos

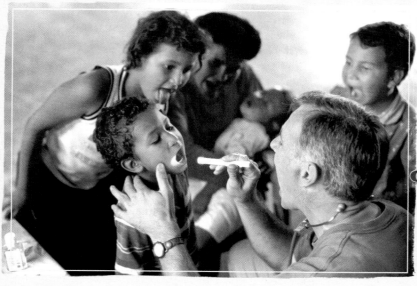

CULTURA
Un médico de la organización Médicos Sin Fronteras da atención médica a una familia hondureña después de un huracán.

¡CUÍDATE BIEN!

cincuenta y uno **51**

Answers

1. b
2. a
3. c
4. c
5. a
6. c

Prepárate para el examen
Self-check for achievement

Resources

- TPR Storytelling, pages 2.43–2.44
- Tests, pages 2.61–2.78
- Performance Assessment, Task 2, pages 2.79–2.80
- ExamView® Assessment Suite

✓ Self-check for achievement

This is a pre-test for students to take before you administer the chapter test. Note that each section is cross-referenced so students can easily find the material they feel they need to review. You may wish to use Self-Check Worksheet Transparency SC2 to have students complete this assessment in class or at home. You can correct the assessment yourself, or you may prefer to project the answers on the overhead in class using Self-Check Answers Transparency SC2A.

Differentiation

Slower Paced Learners

Have students work in pairs to complete the Self-Check in class. Once they have finished, call on individuals to give the correct answers as you review together.

Multiple Intelligences

To engage visual-spatial and bodily-kinesthetic learners, number from 1 to 40 on the board and call on a student to go to the board and write the correct answer (this may be done chronologically or you may allow students to choose the one they answer). Then have the student who wrote the first answer decide who will write the second, and so on, making sure to remind them not to pick the same person again.

52

Vocabulario

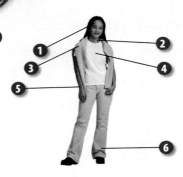

1 Identifica.

To review **Vocabulario 1**, turn to pages 32–33.

2 Corrige.

7. Es importante que uno lleve casco y rodilleras si levanta pesas.

8. A mucha gente le gusta andar en monopatín en el hospital.

9. Un maratón es una carrera de corta distancia.

10. Antes de correr, los corredores se estiran los dedos y los pies.

11. Cuando practicas yoga, haces muchas planchas.

3 Identifica.

12.

13.

14.

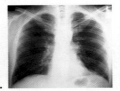

15.

To review **Vocabulario 2**, turn to pages 36–37.

4 Completa.

16. El niño se _____ el tobillo y lo tiene muy hinchado.

17. Se _____ la pierna y el cirujano ortopédico la tiene que poner en un yeso.

18. Los socorristas pusieron a la víctima en una camilla y la llevaron al hospital en _____.

19. José necesita ayuda para andar. Anda con _____.

CAPÍTULO 2

Answers

1

1. la frente
2. el cuello
3. el hombro
4. el pecho
5. la muñeca
6. el tobillo

2

7. Es importante que uno lleve casco y rodilleras si hace monopatín o patinaje en línea.
8. A mucha gente le gusta andar en monopatín en el parque.
9. Un maratón es una carrera de larga distancia.
10. Antes de correr, los corredores se estiran las piernas.
11. Cuando practicas yoga, liberas tu espíritu de tensiones.

3

12. la ambulancia
13. la silla de ruedas
14. la camilla
15. la radiografía

Gramática

⑤ Completa.

20. Es importante que nosotros _____ ejercicios. (hacer)
21. Es necesario que ellos nos _____. (acompañar)
22. Es posible que ella _____. (estar)
23. Es probable que yo _____. (ir)
24. Es imposible que tú lo _____. (saber)

⑥ Completa formando una frase.

25. Es necesario que...
26. Es posible que...
27. Es difícil que...

⑦ Completa.

28. ¡Ojalá _____ su equipo! (ganar)
29. ¡Quizás _____ ellos! (venir)
30. ¡Tal vez _____ (ellos) en el gimnasio! (estar)
31. ¡Ojalá _____ (tú) los resultados mañana! (tener)

⑧ Completa las frases con nosotros.

32. Ellos quieren que tú se lo pidas a Javier.
    Ellos quieren que nosotros...
33. Ella quiere que yo me siente aquí.
    Ella quiere que nosotros...

⑨ Completa con tan... como o tanto... como.

34. A veces los hospitales en las zonas rurales no son _____ buenos _____ los de las grandes ciudades.
35. Esta clínica es _____ moderna _____ la otra.
36. Ella tiene _____ paciencia _____ yo.
37. Yo hago _____ ejercicios _____ tú.

Cultura

⑩ Contesta.

38. ¿Por qué hay gimnasios que tienen muchos socios?
39. ¿Cuáles son algunas actividades atléticas que practica la gente en un parque?
40. ¿Qué propósito tienen muchos maratones?

 To review **el subjuntivo con expresiones impersonales,** turn to page 40.

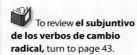 To review **ojalá, quizás, tal vez,** turn to page 42.

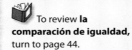 To review **el subjuntivo de los verbos de cambio radical,** turn to page 43.

To review **la comparación de igualdad,** turn to page 44.

To review this cultural information, turn to pages 48–49.

Differentiation

(continued)

This type of review activity is particularly appealing to interpersonal learners but will also benefit the class on the whole by promoting an inclusive, student-centered learning environment.

Slower Paced Learners

Encourage students who need extra help to refer to the book icons and review any section before answering the questions.

Pre-AP Students preparing for the AP exam may benefit from a set time limit when completing this Self-Check. This may also help to identify students with learning difficulties or slower paced students who need extra help.

GLENCOE Technology

Online Learning in the Classroom

You may wish to have students use QuickPass code ASD7844c2 for additional test preparation. They will be able to complete a self-check quiz for chapter review.

Answers

④
16. torció
17. rompió (quebró)
18. una ambulancia
19. muletas

⑤
20. hagamos
21. acompañen
22. esté
23. vaya
24. sepas

⑥
25–27. *Answers will vary.*

⑦
28. gane
29. vengan
30. estén
31. tengas

⑧
32. se lo pidamos a Javier.
33. nos sentemos aquí.

⑨
34. tan, como
35. tan, como
36. tanta, como
37. tantos, como

⑩
38. Todo el mundo quiere mantenerse en forma.
39. La gente hace jogging, corre unas vueltas, anda en bicicleta y practica yoga.
40. Tienen un propósito benévolo.

Prepárate para el examen

⭐ Tips for Success ·······

Encourage students to say as much as possible when they do these open-ended activities. Tell them not to be afraid to make mistakes, since the goal of the activities is real-life communication. If someone in the group makes an error, allow the others to politely correct him or her. Let students choose the activities they would like to do.

Tell students to feel free to elaborate on the basic theme and to be creative. They may use props, pictures, or posters if they wish.

Pre-AP These oral activities will give students the opportunity to develop and improve their speaking skills so that they may succeed on the speaking portion of the AP exam.

Note: You may want to use the rubric below to help students prepare their speaking activities.

Prepárate para el examen
✓ Practice for oral proficiency

1 Actividades atléticas
✓ *Discuss which sports you play*
Trabajen en grupos de tres o cuatro. Discutan todas las actividades atléticas en que participan ustedes. Determinen si tienen los mismos intereses o no.

2 Peligros
✓ *Talk about avoiding danger*
Las actividades atléticas pueden ser buenas para la salud pero cuando practicas ciertas actividades hay que tener cuidado de no lastimarte. ¿Cuáles son algunas cosas que debes hacer para evitar (no tener) accidentes?

3 Un accidente
✓ *Describe an accident you had when you were young*
Explica si tú eres propenso(a) a accidentes o si lo eras de niño(a). ¿Has tenido unos accidentes? Descríbelos. Si nunca has tenido un accidente explica como es posible que tengas tanta suerte.

4 Importante y necesario
✓ *Talk about what is important for you to do and what is necessary for you to do*
Completa una tabla como la de abajo y presenta la información a tu clase.

Es importante que yo	Y es necesario que yo
porque	

5 En la sala de emergencia
✓ *Helping someone out after an accident*
Estás en la sala de espera de la sala de emergencia en un hospital. Entran los padres con su hijo que ha tenido un accidente y se ha hecho daño. Los padres están nerviosos y solo hablan español. Ayúdalos.

EL DEPORTE LE PIDE MINERALES A TU CUERPO.

Villavicencio. Tu vida necesita minerales.

Scoring Rubric for Speaking

	4	3	2	1
vocabulary	extensive use of vocabulary, including idiomatic expressions	adequate use of vocabulary and idiomatic expressions	limited vocabulary marked with some anglicisms	limited vocabulary marked by frequent anglicisms that force interpretation by the listener
grammar	few or no grammatical errors	minor grammatical errors	some serious grammatical errors	serious grammatical errors
pronunciation	good intonation and largely accurate pronunciation with slight accent	acceptable intonation and pronunciation with distinctive accent	errors in intonation and pronunciation with heavy accent	errors in intonation and pronunciation that interfere with listener's comprehension
content	thorough response with interesting and pertinent detail	thorough response with sufficient detail	some detail, but not sufficient	general, insufficient response

Tarea

You have learned about many sports in Spanish. You have also learned about the parts of the body and physical fitness. Now you are going to write a research paper that discusses the physical benefits of some sports. Use the library and the Internet to find out more about how your body stays fit by doing each sport. Be sure to cite your sources.

Writing Strategy

Researching As you prepare to write your research paper, you will be consulting many sources for information. It is important that your sources be reliable, especially when they are found on the Internet. It is advisable to consult more than one source for any fact you present. If your two sources disagree, consult a third.

❶ Prewrite

- Before you begin your research, create a rough outline of your paper. This will help you identify the topics you need to research.

```
Título
A. El fútbol
   1. ¿Cómo se mantiene uno en forma jugando fútbol?
      a.
      b.
   2. ¿Cuáles son algunas desventajas o peligros del
      fútbol?
      a.
      b.
B. El jogging
   1. ¿Cómo se mantiene uno en forma haciendo
      jogging?
```

- As you research, fill the holes in your outline.

El andinista venezolano tiene todo el equipo necesario para escalar montañas.

❷ Write

- Use your outline as a guide while you write. It will ensure your information is organized and that nothing is omitted.
- It is very important to cite the sources you used to obtain information. This will add validity to your paper and it will also ensure that you do not plagiarize.

Evaluate

Your teacher will evaluate you on organization of information, correctness of grammar, and proper citation.

Pre-AP This **tarea** will give students the opportunity to develop and improve their writing skills so that they may succeed on the writing portion of the AP exam.

ABOUT THE SPANISH LANGUAGE

Note that the word **alpinista** is often used for *mountain climber*. In South America it is **andinista** for good reason. Ask students what this reason is.

Note: You may want to use the rubric below to help students prepare their writing tasks.

Scoring Rubric for Writing

	4	3	2	1
vocabulary	precise, varied	functional, fails to communicate complete meaning	limited to basic words, often inaccurate	inadequate
grammar	excellent, very few or no errors	some errors, but do not hinder communication	numerous errors interfere with communication	many errors, little sentence structure
content	thorough response to the topic	generally thorough response to the topic	partial response to the topic	insufficient response to the topic
organization	well organized, ideas presented clearly and logically	loosely organized, but main ideas present	some attempts at organization, but with confused sequencing	lack of organization

Resources

- Audio Activities TE,
  page 2.35–2.37
- Audio CD 2, Tracks 22–25
- Workbook, pages 2.19–2.20

Grammar Review

This page provides a quick "at a glance" summary of the grammar points students have learned in this chapter. The corresponding page numbers are also listed so that students can easily find each grammar point as it was presented.

Differentiation

Multiple Intelligences

You may want to call on **verbal-linguistic** and **logical-mathematical** learners for whom grammar often comes easily to explain the main concepts to their classmates in their own words. Having students explain the concepts in different ways may also help slower paced learners or students with learning difficulties.

Repaso del Capítulo ②

Gramática

- **El subjuntivo con expresiones impersonales** *(page 40)*
  The subjunctive is used after many impersonal expressions when it is not known if the information that follows will or will not take place.

  Es importante que tengas cuidado cuando levantas pesas.
  Es necesario que la niña lleve casco cuando anda en bicicleta.
  Es probable que ellos lleguen a tiempo.

- **¡Ojalá! ¡Quizás! ¡Tal vez!** *(page 42)*
  The expressions **¡Ojalá!, ¡Quizás!,** and **¡Tal vez!** are also followed by the subjunctive. Review the following sentences.

  ¡Ojalá no te hagas daño!
  Quizás vengan mañana.

- **El subjuntivo de los verbos de cambio radical** *(page 43)*
  Verbs that have a stem change in the present indicative also have a stem change in the present subjunctive.

cerrar		encontrar	
cierre	cerremos	encuentre	encontremos
cierres	cerréis	encuentres	encontréis
cierre	cierren	encuentre	encuentren

  Preferir and **sentir** (e → ie, i), **dormir** (o → ue, u), and **pedir, repetir, freír, seguir,** and **servir** (e → i, i) have a stem change in every person of the subjunctive. Review the following forms.

preferir		dormir		pedir	
prefiera	prefiramos	duerma	durmamos	pida	pidamos
prefieras	prefiráis	duermas	durmáis	pidas	pidáis
prefiera	prefieran	duerma	duerman	pida	pidan

- **Comparación de igualdad** *(page 44)*
  You use **tanto… como** to compare like quantities and **tan… como** to compare like qualities.

  Yo tengo tanta paciencia como mi padre.
  Anita hace tantos ejercicios como yo.

  La señora Mayo es tan simpática como la señora Hernández.
  Manolo corre tan rápido como tú.

CULTURA

Los jóvenes están haciendo jogging en Barcelona, España.

Juego There are a number of cognates in this list. See how many you and a partner can find. Who can find the most? Compare your list with those of your classmates.

Vocabulario

Identifying more parts of the body

la frente
el cuello
el hombro
el pecho
la muñeca
el tobillo
el dedo del pie

Talking about physical fitness

el gimnasio
el buzo
el casco
las rodilleras
los ejercicios
las planchas
las pesas
el movimiento
la respiración
el monopatín
el jogging
el/la corredor(a)
una carrera
de relevos
a campo traviesa
de larga distancia
una vuelta
un maratón
estirarse
patinar
en línea
practicar yoga
descansar
liberar

Talking about an accident

una herida
hinchado(a)
cortarse
torcerse
caerse
romperse, quebrarse
doler
hacerse daño

Talking about medical emergencies and a hospital

la ambulancia
el/la socorrista
la camilla
la sala de emergencia
la silla de ruedas
andar con muletas

Talking about medical care

el/la cirujano(a) ortopédico(a)
el/la enfermero(a)
una radiografía
un yeso
un hueso
los puntos, las suturas
una venda
reducir, acomodar

Other useful words and expressions

el espíritu
la tensión
lento(a)

Repaso del Capítulo 2

Vocabulary Review

The words and phrases in **Vocabulary 1** and **2** have been taught for productive use in this chapter. They are summarized here as a resource for both student and teacher. This list also serves as a convenient resource for the **Prepárate para el examen** activities on pages 52–55.

GLENCOE SPANISH

Why It Works!

This vocabulary reference list has not been translated into English for two reasons. First, it is recommended that students learn the new vocabulary through direct association with images on the **Vocabulario** pages. Second, all vocabulary is reintroduced in the chapter many times, and upon completion of the chapter students should be familiar with the meaning of all the words. If there are words that students still do not know, they can refer back to the vocabulary presentation in the chapter or the dictionary at the end of the book. If, however, it is your preference to give students the English translations, please refer to Vocabulary Transparency V2.1 or to the Chapter 2 PowerPoint® presentation on PowerTeach.

Don't forget the chapter project and cultural activities found on pages 28C–28D. Students have learned all the information that they will need to complete these engaging enrichment tasks.

Juego The cognates in this list are: **el gimnasio, los ejercicios, el movimiento, la respiración, el jogging, la distancia, un maratón, practicar yoga, liberar, la ambulancia, la emergencia, ortopédico(a), el espíritu, la tensión.**

Differentiation

Slower Paced Learners

Slower paced learners may benefit from creating their own visual dictionary of nouns and adjectives in this list. They can either draw their own depictions or use images from the Internet or magazines.

Every chapter of **¡Así se dice!** contains this review section of previously learned material. By recycling information from previous chapters, the cumulative review serves to remind students that they need to continue practicing what they have learned after finishing each chapter.

Activity 1 This activity reviews formal and informal commands. See pages 11, 13, SR30.

🎧 **Audio Script** *(CD 2, Track 26)*
1. Invita a Manolo y Sara.
2. Doblen a la derecha en la calle Príncipe.
3. No vayas a clase hoy. ¡Es sábado!
4. Lea usted el correo electrónico.
5. ¡No me dé tantos exámenes!
6. Ayúdenme, por favor.
7. Dámelo.
8. Permítanme asistir al concierto.

Activity 2 This activity reviews double object pronouns. See page R64.

Activity 3 This activity reviews double object pronouns with **se**. See page R64.

GLENCOE 🖱 Technology

Online Learning in the Classroom
You may wish to have students use QuickPass code ASD7844c2 for additional cumulative review. They will be able to complete a self-check quiz.

Repaso cumulativo

Repasa lo que ya has aprendido

These activities will help you review and remember what you have learned so far in Spanish.

 1 Escucha las frases. Indica en una tabla como la de abajo a quien habla el joven en cada frase.

a un(a) amigo(a)	a su profesor(a)	a sus padres

 2 Sigue el modelo.

MODELO —Son mis zapatos nuevos.
—¿Quién te los compró?

1. Es mi cámara nueva.
2. Es mi casco nuevo.
3. Son mis gafas nuevas.
4. Son mis esquís nuevos.
5. Son mis botas nuevas.

 3 Completa con los pronombres.

1. Yo le di los CDs a Anita.
   Yo _____ di a ella.
2. Carlos le devolvió el dinero a Juan.
   Carlos _____ devolvió a él.
3. Sara le dio las direcciones a usted.
   Sara _____ dio.
4. Yo le leí la receta a Susana.
   Yo _____ leí a ella.
5. Yo no le preparé la comida.
   Yo no _____ preparé.

Answers

 1
1. a un amigo
2. a sus padres
3. a un amigo
4. a su profesor
5. a su profesor
6. a sus padres
7. a un amigo
8. a sus padres

 2
1. ¿Quién te la compró?
2. ¿Quién te lo compró?
3. ¿Quién te las compró?
4. ¿Quién te los compró?
5. ¿Quién te las compró?

 3
1. se los
2. se lo
3. se las
4. se la
5. se la

Completa cada serie de frases en el presente, el pretérito y el imperfecto.

hablar

1. a. Yo _____ con Juan todos los días.

   b. Yo _____ con Juan ayer.

   c. Yo _____ mucho con Juan cuando éramos niños.

vender

2. a. Mi padre _____ carros.

   b. Ayer él _____ dos.

   c. Pero cuando yo era niño él no _____ carros.

escribir

3. a. Ahora nosotros le _____ un correo electrónico todos los días.

   b. Nosotros le _____ un correo electrónico el otro día.

   c. Nosotros le _____ correos electrónicos casi a diario cuando estaba en España.

hacer

4. a. No lo _____ yo.

   b. No lo _____ yo ayer.

   c. Yo no lo _____ nunca.

poner

5. a. ¿Por qué no _____ (tú) las maletas en la maletera?

   b. ¿Por qué no _____ (tú) las maletas en la maletera cuando fuiste al aeropuerto?

   c. Cada vez que hacías un viaje _____ las maletas en la maletera.

decir

6. a. Yo siempre _____ la verdad.

   b. Yo no te _____ una mentira. Fue la verdad.

   c. Yo nunca _____ mentiras—siempre la verdad.

poder

7. a. Ellos _____ hacerlo ahora.

   b. Ellos intentaron pero no _____ hacerlo.

   c. Ellos _____ hacerlo cuando eran más jóvenes.

CULTURA

El señor compraba el periódico cada día en el mismo quiosco en Buenos Aires, Argentina.

Activity This activity reviews present, preterite, and imperfect verb forms. See pages R7, R17, R29, R31, R43–R44.

Conexiones

Geography

You may wish to say to students: **Este señor lleva abrigo y bufanda. Está bien abrigado. En Buenos Aires, ¿qué mes será?** (note that **abrigo** and **bufanda** are new words). Students have learned about the reverse seasons.

GLENCOE Technology

Audio in the Classroom

The **¡Así se dice!** Audio Program for Chapter 2 has 26 activities, which afford students extensive listening and speaking practice.

Pre-AP To give students further open-ended oral and written practice, or to assess proficiency, go to AP Proficiency Practice Transparencies AP16 and AP29.

Answers

1. **a.** hablo
   b. hablé
   c. hablaba
2. **a.** vende
   b. vendió
   c. vendía

3. **a.** escribimos
   b. escribimos
   c. escribíamos
4. **a.** hago
   b. hice
   c. hacía

5. **a.** pones
   b. pusiste
   c. ponías
6. **a.** digo
   b. dije
   c. decía

7. **a.** pueden
   b. pudieron
   c. podían

Chapter Overview
Pasajes de la vida

● Scope and Sequence

Topics
- Weddings
- Baptisms
- Birthdays
- Funerals

Culture
- **Quinceañera** celebrations
- Wedding ceremonies and customs throughout the Spanish-speaking world
- *El hermano ausente en la cena de Pascua* by Abraham Valdelomar

Functions
- How to talk about passages of life: weddings, baptisms, birthdays, and funerals
- How to read a poem by the Peruvian writer Abraham Valdelomar

Structure
- The subjunctive to express wishes
- The subjunctive to express emotions
- Possessive pronouns

● Planning Guide

	required	recommended	optional
Vocabulario 1 *(pages 64–67)* El matrimonio La recepción	✓		
Vocabulario 2 *(pages 68–71)* El bautizo El cumpleaños El velorio El cementerio, El camposanto	✓		
Gramática *(pages 72–77)* El subjuntivo con deseos El subjuntivo con expresiones de emoción Los pronombres posesivos	✓		
Conversación *(pages 78–79)* ¿Habrá una boda?		✓	
Lectura cultural *(pages 80–83)* Celebraciones y ritos de pasaje		✓	
Literatura *(pages 84–87)* El hermano ausente en la cena de Pascua			✓
Prepárate para el examen *(pages 88–91)*			✓
Repaso cumulativo *(pages 94–95)*			✓

Correlations to National Foreign Language Standards

Page numbers in light print refer to the Student Edition. Page numbers in bold print refer to the Teacher Edition.	
Communication Standard 1.1 Interpersonal	pp. **62–63, 66, 68, 69, 70,** 73, **74,** 75, **81, 82, 83, 86, 87,** 90
Communication Standard 1.2 Interpretive	pp. **64,** 66, **67,** 67, **68,** 70, 71, **71,** 73, **73,** 74, 75, **75,** 77, **78,** 79, **79,** 80, **80,** 81, **81,** 82, 83, **84,** 85, **85,** 86, **86,** 87, 89, **89,** 94, **95**
Communication Standard 1.3 Presentational	pp. **60C, 60D, 64,** 67, 70, **71, 75, 79, 80, 81, 82, 84, 87, 88,** 90, 91, **92, 93**
Cultures Standard 2.1	pp. **60D,** 62–63, **62–63, 65, 69,** 79, 80–82, 83, 89, 90
Cultures Standard 2.2	pp. **60D,** 62, 67, **67, 68, 77, 85**
Connections Standard 3.1	pp. **60C, 60D,** 64, 69, **69,** 71, **71,** 72, **72, 85,** 86
Connections Standard 3.2	pp. **65,** 66, 68, **69,** 71, **74,** 77, **77,** 79, **79,** 83, **83,** 86, 87
Comparisons Standard 4.1	pp. 64, 68, 72, 76, **92,** 93
Comparisons Standard 4.2	pp. **60D, 61,** 62, **62, 65, 66,** 80, **82,** 83, 86
Communities Standard 5.1	pp. **65,** 66, 70, **82, 88, 90, 92**
Communities Standard 5.2	pp. 68, **69,** 79, **79,** 83, **83**

To read the ACTFL Standards in their entirety, see the front of the Teacher Edition.

Student Resources

Print
Workbook *(pp. 3.3–3.14)*
Audio Activities *(pp. 3.15–3.19)*
Pre-AP Workbook, Chapter 3

Technology
● StudentWorks™ Plus
■ ¡Así se dice! Vocabulario en vivo
■ ¡Así se dice! Gramática en vivo
■ ¡Así se dice! Diálogo en vivo
■ ¡Así se dice! Cultura en vivo
◗ Vocabulary PuzzleMaker
QuickPass glencoe.com

Teacher Resources

Print
TeacherTools, Chapter 3
Workbook TE *(pp. 3.3–3.14)*
Audio Activities TE *(pp. 3.17–3.34)*
Quizzes 1–5 *(pp. 3.37–3.42)*
Tests *(pp. 3.44–3.64)*
Performance Assessment, Task 3 *(pp. 3.65–3.66)*

Technology
♨ Quick Start Transparencies 3.1–3.5
♨ Vocabulary Transparencies V3.1–V3.5
∩ Audio CD 3
● *ExamView® Assessment Suite*
● TeacherWorks™ Plus
● PowerTeach
■ ¡Así se dice! Video Program
◗ Vocabulary PuzzleMaker
QuickPass glencoe.com

Chapter Project

Un anuncio

Students will work individually to design a birth announcement for themselves in Spanish.

1. Before students begin designing their announcements, you may wish to decide what medium they will use, or allow them to choose the medium. For example, you may prefer to have students complete their invitations by hand on cardstock or construction paper or use photo paper and design them on the computer.

2. Students should include at least three visual elements. Their announcements should be easy to read and visually appealing, arranged in a way that is pleasing and inviting to view.

3. Students should include all pertinent information that would appear on a birth announcement (name, date, size, etc.) and at least two sentences. To add a fun touch to the project, have students use copies of their own baby photos for one of their visual elements.

4. Once students have acquired the necessary information and decided on the images they will use, have them sketch the layout of their invitations to be handed in along with first drafts of the text. After you check their work, have them correct it and submit the final versions.

Scoring Rubric for Project

	1	3	5
Evidence of planning	Draft and layout are not provided.	Draft and layout are provided, but draft is not corrected.	Layout and corrected draft are provided.
Use of illustrations	Announcement contains no visual elements and is not visually appealing.	Announcement contains one or two visual elements and is somewhat visually appealing.	Announcement contains three or more visual elements and is visually appealing.
Presentation	Announcement contains little of the required elements.	Announcement contains some of the required elements.	Announcement contains all the required elements.

Culture

● Ojo de Dios

Every culture has different traditions to help welcome a new baby into the world. To bring a child a long and healthy life, the Huichol Indians in the Jalisco region of Mexico use two sticks and yarn to make an **Ojo de Dios.** When a child is born, the father creates the central eye of the weaving. One additional layer is added each year until the child is five years old. The four points of the **Ojo de Dios** represent the four natural elements: earth, fire, air, and water. The Huichol people believe that the design of the eye has the power to heal and protect and will watch over the newborn baby as he or she grows. The **Ojo de Dios** is a fairly simple craft project that you may wish to have students create as an in-class project or as an assignment completed at home.

● Mariachi

Mariachi bands exemplify traditional Mexican music. While its presence can be traced as far back as the sixteenth century, **mariachi** music was born in Jalisco, Mexico, in the rural countryside. In the nineteenth century these musical groups included a harp, one or two violins, some form of guitar, and voices. Over the years the makeup of the **mariachi** band has changed slightly and now includes five different instruments: the **guitarrón, vihuela,** guitar, violins, and trumpets. The **guitarrón** and **vihuela** give **mariachi** music its distinctive sound. The **guitarrón** is a small-scaled acoustic bass, while the **vihuela** is a high-pitched 5-string guitar. Both instruments are produced in Jalisco, Mexico. The wardrobe of modern-day **mariachi** musicians was developed in the 1930s and is based on the **charro,** the Mexican cowboy. The costume includes a large-brimmed **sombrero,** boots, short jacket, snug trousers, bow tie, and a wide belt. The jacket and trousers are ornately decorated with shiny metal buttons or detailed embroidery. **Mariachis** play at various occasions including weddings, birthdays, funerals, baptisms, and civic celebrations and are hired to serenade women with sweet, romantic songs. Historically these groups were made up of men exclusively, but many modern-day groups outside Mexico include women. There is an annual **mariachi** festival each September in Guadalajara, Mexico, at which groups from all over the world come to play and celebrate **mariachi** music.

50-Minute Lesson Plans

	Objective	Present	Practice	Assess/Homework
Day 1	Talk about weddings	Chapter Opener, pp. 60–61 (5 min.) Introducción al tema, pp. 62–63 (10 min.) Core Instruction/Vocabulario 1, pp. 64–65 (20 min.)	Activities 1–3, p. 66 (15 min.)	Student Workbook Activities A–C, pp. 3.3–3.4 *QuickPass* Vocabulary Practice
Day 2	Talk about weddings	Quick Start, p. 64 (5 min.) Review Vocabulario 1, pp. 64–65 (10 min.)	Activities 4–5, p. 67 (10 min.) Estudio de palabras, p. 67 (5 min.) Total Physical Response, p. 64 (5 min.) Audio Activities A–D, pp. 3.17–3.19 (15 min.)	Student Workbook Activities D–E, p. 3.4 *QuickPass* Vocabulary Practice
Day 3	Talk about baptisms, birthdays, and funerals	Core Instruction/Vocabulario 2, pp. 68–69 (15 min.) Video, Vocabulario en vivo (10 min.)	Activities 1–3, p. 70 (15 min.)	Quiz 1, p. 3.37 (10 min.) Student Workbook Activities A–B, p. 3.5 *QuickPass* Vocabulary Practice
Day 4	Talk about baptisms, birthdays, and funerals	Quick Start, p. 68 (5 min.) Review Vocabulario 2, pp. 68–69 (10 min.)	Activities 4–7, pp. 70–71 (20 min.) Audio Activities E–I, pp. 3.20–3.22 (15 min.)	Student Workbook Activities C–D, p. 3.5 *QuickPass* Vocabulary Practice
Day 5	The subjunctive to express wishes	Core Instruction/Gramática, El subjuntivo con deseos, p. 72 (15 min.)	Activities 1–6, pp. 73–74 (25 min.)	Quiz 2, p. 3.38 (10 min.) Student Workbook Activities A–B, p. 3.6 *QuickPass* Grammar Practice
Day 6	The subjunctive to express wishes	Quick Start, p. 72 (5 min.) Review Gramática, El subjuntivo con deseos, p. 72 (5 min.)	Activities 5–6, p. 74 (10 min.) InfoGap, p. SR4 (10 min.) Audio Activities A–D, pp. 3.22–3.24 (20 min.)	Student Workbook Activities C–D, pp. 3.6–3.7 *QuickPass* Grammar Practice
Day 7	The subjunctive to express emotions	Quick Start, p. 74 (5 min.) Core Instruction/Gramática, El subjuntivo con expresiones de emoción, p. 74 (10 min.)	Activities 7–9, p. 75 (15 min.) Audio Activities E–F, pp. 3.24–3.25 (10 min.)	Quiz 3, p. 3.39 (10 min.) Student Workbook Activities A–C, pp. 3.7–3.8 *QuickPass* Grammar Practice
Day 8	Possessive pronouns	Quick Start, p. 76 (5 min.) Core Instruction/Gramática, Los pronombres posesivos, p. 76 (15 min.)	Activities 10–12, p. 77 (10 min.) Audio Activities G–I, pp. 3.25–3.26 (10 min.)	Quiz 4, p. 3.40 (10 min.) Student Workbook Activities A–D, pp. 3.8–3.10 *QuickPass* Grammar Practice
Day 9	Develop reading and listening comprehension skills	Core Instruction/Conversación, p. 78 (20 min.) Video, Diálogo en vivo (10 min.)	¿Comprendes? B–C, p. 79 (10 min.)	Quiz 5, p. 3.41 (10 min.) ¿Comprendes? A, p. 79 *QuickPass* Conversation
Day 10	Discuss celebrating life passages	Core Instruction/Lectura cultural, pp. 80–82 (20 min.) Video, Cultura en vivo (5 min.)	¿Comprendes? A–B, p. 83 (10 min.)	Listening Comprehension Test, pp. 3.59–3.61 (15 min.) ¿Comprendes? C–E, p. 83 *QuickPass* Reading Practice
Day 11	Read a poem by Abraham Valdelomar	Core Instruction, Vocabulario, p. 84 (5 min.) Core Instruction/Literatura, pp. 85–86 (25 min.)	Vocabulario, Práctica, p. 85 (5 min.) ¿Comprendes? A–C, p. 87 (15 min.)	¿Comprendes? D–E, p. 87 *QuickPass* Reading Practice
Day 12	Read a poem by Abraham Valdelomar	Review Literatura, pp. 85–86 (10 min.)	¿Comprendes? D–E, p. 87 (10 min.) Prepárate para el examen, pp. 88–89 (20 min.)	Prepárate para el examen, Practice for written proficiency, p. 91
Day 13	Chapter review	Repaso del Capítulo 3, pp. 92–93 (15 min.)	Prepárate para el examen, Practice for oral proficiency, p. 90 (20 min.)	Test for Writing Proficiency, p. 3.64 (15 min.) Review for chapter test
Day 14	Chapter 3 Tests (50 min.) Reading and Writing Test, pp. 3.49–3.56 Literature Test, pp. 3.57–3.58		Speaking Test, p. 3.62 Test for Oral Proficiency, p. 3.63	

90-Minute Lesson Plans

	Objective	Present	Practice	Assess/Homework
Block 1	Talk about weddings	Chapter Opener, pp. 60–61 (5 min.) Introducción al tema, pp. 62–63 (15 min.) Quick Start, p. 64 (5 min.) Core Instruction/Vocabulario 1, pp. 64–65 (20 min.)	Activities 1–5, pp. 66–67 (20 min.) Estudio de palabras, p. 67 (5 min.) Total Physical Response, p. 00 (5 min.) Audio Activities A–D, pp. 3.17–3.19 (15 min.)	Student Workbook Activities A–E, pp. 3.3–3.4 *QuickPass* Vocabulary Practice
Block 2	Talk about baptisms, birthdays, and funerals	Quick Start, p. 68 (5 min.) Core Instruction/Vocabulario 2, pp. 68–69 (20 min.) Video, Vocabulario en vivo (10 min.)	Activities 1–7, pp. 70–71 (25 min.) Audio Activities E–I, pp. 3.20–3.22 (20 min.)	Quiz 1, p. 3.37 (10 min.) Student Workbook Activities A–D, p. 3.5 *QuickPass* Vocabulary Practice
Block 3	The subjunctive to express wishes	Quick Start, p. 72 (5 min.) Core Instruction/Gramática, El subjuntivo con deseos, p. 72 (15 min.)	Activities 1–6, pp. 73–74 (25 min.) InfoGap, p. SR4 (10 min.) Foldables, p. 67 (10 min.) Audio Activities A–D, pp. 3.22–3.24 (15 min.)	Quiz 2, p. 3.38 (10 min.) Student Workbook Activities A–D, pp. 3.6–3.7 *QuickPass* Grammar Practice
Block 4	The subjunctive to express emotions Possessive pronouns	Quick Start, p. 74 (5 min.) Core Instruction/Gramática, El subjuntivo con expresiones de emoción, p. 74 (10 min.) Quick Start, p. 76 (5 min.) Core Instruction/Gramática, Los pronombres posesivos, p. 76 (15 min.)	Activities 7–9, p. 75 (15 min.) Activities 10–12, p. 77 (10 min.) Audio Activities E–I, pp. 3.24–3.26 (20 min.)	Quiz 3, p. 3.39 (10 min.) Student Workbook Activities A–C, pp. 3.7–3.8 Student Workbook Activities A–D, pp. 3.8–3.10 *QuickPass* Grammar Practice
Block 5	Discuss celebrating life passages	Core Instruction/Conversación, p. 78 (20 min.) Video, Diálogo en vivo (10 min.) Core Instruction/Lectura cultural, pp. 80–82 (20 min.)	¿Comprendes? A–C, p. 79 (10 min.) ¿Comprendes? A–B, p. 83 (10 min.)	Quizzes 4–5, pp. 3.40–3.41 (20 min.) ¿Comprendes? C–E, p. 83 Prepárate para el examen, Practice for written proficiency, p. 91 *QuickPass* Conversation, Reading Practice
Block 6	Read a poem by Abraham Valdelomar	Core Instructiona, Vocabulario, p. 84 (10 min.) Core Instruction/Literatura, pp. 85–86 (15 min.)	Práctica, p. 85 (5 min.) ¿Comprendes? A–C, p. 87 (15 min.) Prepárate para el examen, Practice for oral proficiency, p. 90 (30 min.)	Listening Comprehension Test, pp. 3.59–3.61 (15 min.) ¿Comprendes? D–E, p. 87 Prepárate para el examen, pp. 88–89 *QuickPass* Reading Practice

Block 7	Chapter 3 Tests (50 min.)
	    Reading and Writing Test, pp. 3.49–3.56
	    Literature Test, pp. 3.57–3.58
	    Speaking Test, p. 3.62
	    Test for Oral Proficiency, p. 3.63
	    Test for Writing Proficiency, p. 3.64
	Chapter Project, p. 60C (40 min.)			

Preview

In this chapter, students will learn the vocabulary they need to discuss the various celebrations that accompany each rite of passage. Students will use the subjunctive to express wishes and emotions. They will also learn the possessive pronouns. To continue their literary studies, students will read a poem by Abraham Valdelomar that deals with a holiday meal.

Pacing

It is important to note that once you reach **¡Bravo!** in the chapter, there is no more new material for the students to learn. The rest of the chapter recycles what has already been covered. The suggested pacing listed here leaves two to three days for review, assessment, and enrichment activities such as the chapter project.

Vocabulario 1	1–2 days
Vocabulario 2	1–2 days
Gramática	2–3 days
Conversación	1 day
Lectura cultural	1 day
Literatura	1 day

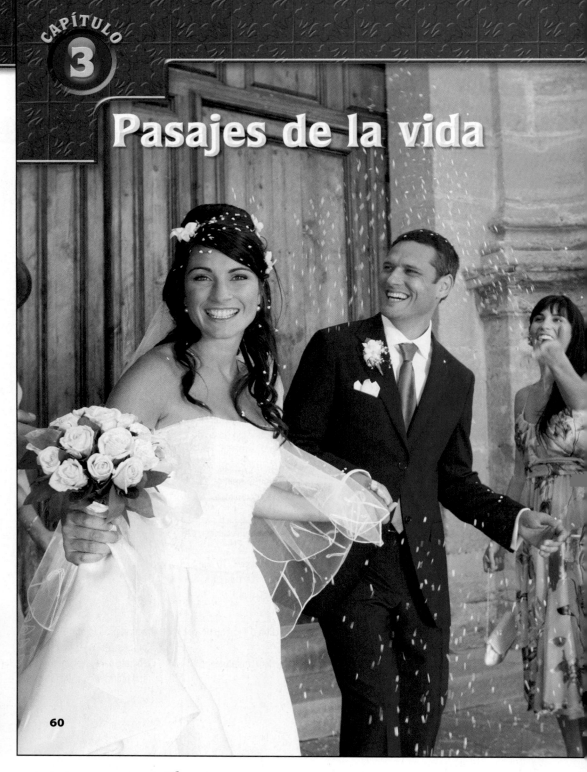

Pasajes de la vida

60

Teacher Works Plus™

The **¡Así se dice!** TeacherWorks™ Plus CD-ROM is an all-in-one planner and resource center. You may wish to use several of the following features as you plan and present the Chapter 3 material: Interactive Teacher Edition, Interactive Lesson Planner with Calendar, and Point and Click Access to Teaching Resources including Hotlinks to the Internet and Correlations to the National Standards.

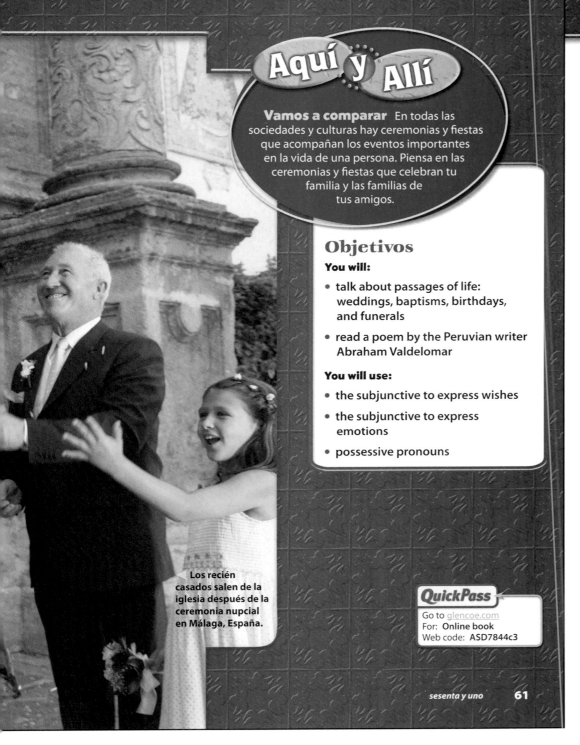

Aquí y Allí

Vamos a comparar En todas las sociedades y culturas hay ceremonias y fiestas que acompañan los eventos importantes en la vida de una persona. Piensa en las ceremonias y fiestas que celebran tu familia y las familias de tus amigos.

Objetivos

You will:

- talk about passages of life: weddings, baptisms, birthdays, and funerals
- read a poem by the Peruvian writer Abraham Valdelomar

You will use:

- the subjunctive to express wishes
- the subjunctive to express emotions
- possessive pronouns

Los recién casados salen de la iglesia después de la ceremonia nupcial en Málaga, España.

QuickPass

Go to glencoe.com
For: **Online book**
Web code: **ASD7844c3**

Introducción al tema

▶ PRESENT

Introduce the theme of the chapter by having students look at the photographs on these pages. Lead a discussion about the people and events seen here. Have them determine if there is anything they see that is the same as or different from what might take place in the United States. Once you have presented both **Vocabulario** sections, you may want to return to these pages and read the information that accompanies each photograph. Once students are fully acquainted with the vocabulary and grammar of the chapter, you may wish to come back to these pages and ask the questions that go with each photo.

📷 Cultural Snapshot

México *(page 62)* You may wish to review information about **el Día de los Muertos** from Chapter 5 of **¡Así se dice!** Level 2. Have students tell what they remember about this festival. **¿Es un disfraz una máscara? ¿Cuándo lleva la gente un disfraz o una máscara? ¿En qué país es muy popular el Día de los Muertos?**

Estados Unidos, República Dominicana *(page 62)* Many parties that are given to celebrate the **quinceañera** are quite extravagant. The day a young woman turns fifteen is important in all Spanish-speaking countries, as well as in all the Latino communities within the United States. It is more popular than the "sweet sixteen." **¿Qué hay el día que una joven latina**

Introducción al tema

Pasajes de la vida

Los pasajes de la vida son los eventos importantes que tienen lugar en la vida de todos nosotros desde el momento de nuestro nacimiento hasta la muerte. En este capítulo tendrás la oportunidad de observar unos de los ritos que acompañan los pasajes de la vida en las sociedades latinas.

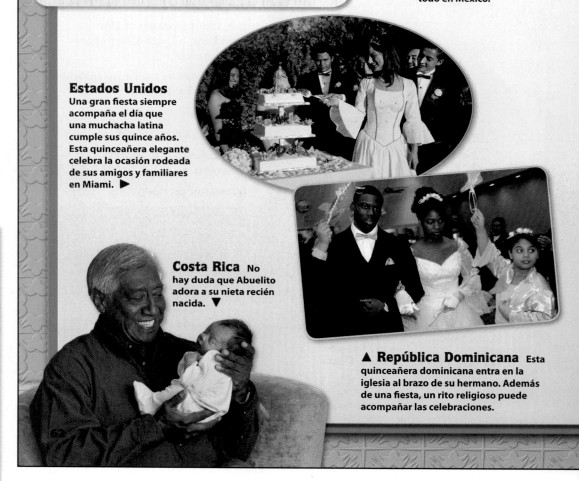

◄ México Es una máscara o disfraz que se lleva durante las celebraciones para el Día de los Muertos en varios países latinos—sobre todo en México.

Estados Unidos Una gran fiesta siempre acompaña el día que una muchacha latina cumple sus quince años. Esta quinceañera elegante celebra la ocasión rodeada de sus amigos y familiares en Miami. ▶

Costa Rica No hay duda que Abuelito adora a su nieta recién nacida. ▼

▲ República Dominicana Esta quinceañera dominicana entra en la iglesia al brazo de su hermano. Además de una fiesta, un rito religioso puede acompañar las celebraciones.

cumple sus quince años? ¿Quiénes asisten a la fiesta? A veces, ¿hay un rito religioso como parte de las celebraciones?

Costa Rica *(page 62)* Currently about 20 per cent of Spanish families have at least one grandparent living in the home. Grandparents in Spain and other Hispanic countries are playing an active role in the lives of their grandchildren. **¿Viven muchos abuelos en la misma casa que sus nietos en Estados Unidos? ¿Piensas que la influencia de los abuelos es algo importante aquí? ¿Con qué frecuencia ves a tus abuelos? ¿Se llevan ustedes bien?**

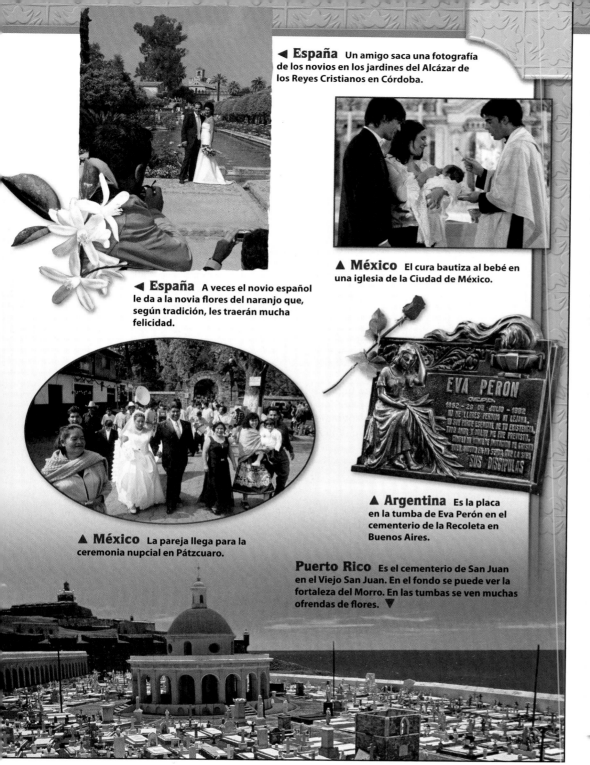

◄ **España** Un amigo saca una fotografía de los novios en los jardines del Alcázar de los Reyes Cristianos en Córdoba.

▲ **México** El cura bautiza al bebé en una iglesia de la Ciudad de México.

◄ **España** A veces el novio español le da a la novia flores del naranjo que, según tradición, les traerán mucha felicidad.

▲ **Argentina** Es la placa en la tumba de Eva Perón en el cementerio de la Recoleta en Buenos Aires.

▲ **México** La pareja llega para la ceremonia nupcial en Pátzcuaro.

Puerto Rico Es el cementerio de San Juan en el Viejo San Juan. En el fondo se puede ver la fortaleza del Morro. En las tumbas se ven muchas ofrendas de flores. ▼

España *(page 63)* In Spain, as well as in other Spanish-speaking countries, it is common for the bridal party to go to a beautiful park to have wedding pictures taken. Orange petals have a beautiful odor and according to tradition they bring good luck. **¿Dónde están los novios? ¿Qué está sacando un amigo? ¿A quién le da flores del naranjo el novio? ¿Por qué?**

México *(page 63 right)* **¿Quién bautiza al bebé? ¿Quiénes están con el bebé?**

México *(page 63 left)* In small towns in Mexico and other countries, it is common for guests to walk with the bride and groom to the church or town hall. They frequently walk together to a nearby park for photographs. **Describe a las personas en la foto.**

Argentina *(page 63)* Many family mausoleums have a bronze plaque for each member of the family interred there. This commemorative plaque is for Eva Perón, the powerful first lady of Argentina from 1946 until her death in 1952. **¿Quién es Eva Perón?**

Puerto Rico *(page 63)* As seen in this cemetery in San Juan, Puerto Rico, many grave sites are above ground. **¿Dónde está el cementerio? ¿Es similar a los cementerios donde vives tú?**

Vocabulario 1   presentación

Resources

- Vocabulary Transparencies V3.2–V3.3
- Audio Activities TE, pages 3.17–3.19
- Audio CD 3, Tracks 1–4
- Workbook, pages 3.3–3.4
- Quiz 1, page 3.37
- *ExamView® Assessment Suite*

Quick Start

Use QS Transparency 3.1 or write the following on the board.
Prepara una lista de todos tus parientes en español.

▶ TEACH
Core Instruction

Step 1 Present the vocabulary with books closed using Vocabulary Transparencies V3.2–V3.3.

Step 2 Have students repeat words once or twice. Intersperse with questions that make students use the new words. Examples are: **¿Quién se casa? ¿Dónde tiene lugar la ceremonia? ¿Les sorprende a todos que la pareja se case?**

Differentiation
Multiple Intelligences

Bodily-kinesthetic learners may find it helpful to act out an important life event. You may wish to have students enact a wedding. **La novia entra en la iglesia (el ayuntamiento, la senagoga, el hall). Los novios intercambian los anillos de boda. Ellos firman el registro de matrimonio. Los invitados les dan la enhorabuena a los recién casados. Los recién casados abren sus regalos.**

64

El matrimonio

La pareja se casa.
La ceremonia tiene lugar en la iglesia.
No le sorprende a nadie que ellos se casen.
Todos sus amigos esperan que pasen muchos años juntos.
Y todos quieren que sean felices.

Nota

- Another commonly used word for **anillo** is **sortija**.
- **El novio/La novia** can mean both *fiancé (fiancée)* and *groom/bride*. **Los novios** are the bride and groom.
- **El padrino** can mean *godfather* as well as *best man.*

Durante la ceremonia nupcial, el novio y la novia intercambian los anillos de boda.

Total Physical Response (TPR)

(Student 1), **ven acá.**
Arréglate la corbata.
(Student 2), **ven acá.**
Ponte el velo.
(Student 1), **toma un anillo.**
Pon el anillo en la mano izquierda de *(Student 2).*
Y ahora, *(Student 2),* **toma un anillo.**

Pon el anillo en la mano izquierda de *(Student 1).*
(Student 1) **y** *(Student 2),* **firmen el registro de matrimonio.**
(Student 1), **corta la torta de boda.**
(Student 2), **dale de comer una rebanada de torta a** *(Student 1).*

el ayuntamiento
la alcaldesa

el registro de matrimonio

Esta pareja se casa por (el, lo) civil.
Se casan en el ayuntamiento.
La alcaldesa los casa.

Durante la ceremonia civil es necesario
que los novios firmen el registro de
matrimonio.

La recepción

el anuncio nupcial

¡Enhorabuena!

Ana Cristina y Antonio

UNIÉNDONOS CON AMOR Y POR SIEMPRE CON
LA BENDICIÓN DE NUESTROS PADRES

Delia Aurora Aparicio de Loís
Carlos Estuardo Loís Rosado

Elena Marisel Gutiérrez de Ochoa
César David Ochoa Hernández

DESEAMOS COMPARTIR EL MOMENTO EN QUE
REAFIRMAREMOS NUESTRO AMOR INVITÁNDOLES A LA
CEREMONIA RELIGIOSA QUE SE REALIZARÁ EL DÍA VIERNES 25
DE MAYO A LAS 7.30 DE LA NOCHE EN LA IGLESIA
SAN FRANCISCO DE ASÍS CASTILLA 842 · SAN MIGUEL

SEVILLA, MAYO

AL CULMINAR LA CEREMONIA
LES ESPERAMOS EN LOS SALONES
DE LA VICARIA.

Hay una recepción en honor de los novios (recién casados).
Hay una cena (un banquete, un bufé).
Los novios reciben muchos regalos.

QuickPass
Go to glencoe.com
For: **Vocabulary practice**
Web code: **ASD7844c3**

▶ PRACTICE

Leveling EACH Activity

Easy Activities 1, 2
Average Activity 2 **Expansión**, Activity 4
CHallenging Activities 3, 5

Activity ❶

🎧 **Audio Script**

1. a. El novio y la novia forman la pareja que se casa.
b. El padrino y la dama de honor forman la pareja que se casa.

2. a. El novio escoge a la dama de honor.
b. La novia escoge a la dama de honor.

3. a. El traje de novia tiene un velo.
b. Los anillos de boda tienen un velo.

4. a. La ceremonia civil tiene lugar en la iglesia.
b. La ceremonia civil tiene lugar en el ayuntamiento.

5. a. Hay una cena o banquete durante la ceremonia nupcial.
b. Hay una cena o banquete durante la recepción después de la ceremonia.

Activities ❷ and ❸ These activities can be gone over orally in class first. They can also be done as paired activities.

 Cultural Snapshot

(page 66) You may wish to ask: **Aquí en Estados Unidos, ¿van muchas parejas a la iglesia en una limusina? A veces, ¿llegan en una limusina antigua?**

ESCUCHAR

❶ Escucha. Escoge la frase correcta. Usa una tabla como la de abajo para indicar tus respuestas.

a	b

HABLAR • ESCRIBIR

❷ Personaliza. Da respuestas personales.
1. ¿Has asistido una vez a una boda?
2. ¿Quiénes se casaron?
3. ¿Cómo se vistió la novia?
4. ¿Fue una ceremonia religiosa o civil?
5. ¿Dónde tuvo lugar la boda?
6. ¿Quiénes fueron el padrino y la dama de honor?
7. ¿Había un banquete?
8. ¿Fuiste a la recepción?

EXPANSIÓN

Ahora, sin mirar las preguntas, cuenta la información en tus propias palabras. Si no recuerdas algo, un(a) compañero(a) te puede ayudar.

LEER • HABLAR

❸ Con un(a) compañero(a) de clase, mira el anuncio nupcial. Hablen juntos haciendo y contestando preguntas sobre la información en el anuncio.

Ana Cristina y Antonio

UNIÉNDONOS CON AMOR Y POR SIEMPRE CON LA BENDICIÓN DE NUESTROS PADRES

Delia Aurora Aparicio de Lois
Carlos Estuardo Lois Rosado

Elena Marisel Gutiérrez de Ochoa
César David Ochoa Hernández

DESEAMOS COMPARTIR EL MOMENTO EN QUE REAFIRMAREMOS NUESTRO AMOR INVITÁNDOLES A LA CEREMONIA RELIGIOSA QUE SE REALIZARÁ EL DÍA VIERNES 25 DE MAYO A LAS 7.30 DE LA NOCHE EN LA IGLESIA SAN FRANCISCO DE ASÍS CASTILLA 842 - SAN MIGUEL.

SEVILLA, MAYO

AL CULMINAR LA CEREMONIA LES ESPERAMOS EN LOS SALONES DE LA VICARIA.

CULTURA
Los recién casados salen de la iglesia en Madrid y van a su recepción en una limusina antigua.

Answers

❶
1. a 3. a 5. b
2. b 4. b

❷ *Answers will vary but may include:*
1. Sí, he asistido (una vez) a una boda. (No, no he asistido nunca a una boda.)
2. ___ y ___ se casaron.
3. La novia llevó un traje de novia blanco y un velo.
4. Fue una ceremonia religiosa (civil).
5. La boda tuvo lugar en la iglesia (en el ayuntamiento).
6. El padrino fue ___ y la dama de honor fue ___.
7. Sí, (No, no) había un banquete.
8. Sí, (No, no) fui a la recepción.

❸ *Answers will vary, but students should use as many words as possible from Vocabulario 1 to talk about the information in the wedding announcement.*

LEER • ESCRIBIR

④ Completa con una palabra apropiada.

1. Una boda religiosa tiene lugar en una _____ o un templo.
2. Una _____ suele llevar un velo.
3. Un novio y una novia forman una _____.
4. Una boda civil tiene lugar en el _____.
5. En los países hispanos, el _____ casa a una pareja en una ceremonia civil.
6. Durante la ceremonia civil los novios tienen que _____ el registro nupcial.
7. Después de la ceremonia nupcial hay una _____.

Comunicación

⑤ En tus propias palabras describe una boda a la que asististe.

Estudio de palabras

casarse Ellos van a casarse en junio.
el casamiento El casamiento tendrá lugar en la iglesia.
los casados Los recién casados están muy contentos.

alegrarse Ellos se alegran de ver a todos sus amigos.
alegre Todos están muy alegres (contentos).
la alegría Hay mucha alegría.

Escribe con el contrario.

1. Ellos *se entristecen*.
2. Todos están *tristes*.
3. Se ve que hay mucha *tristeza*.
4. Ellos van a *divorciarse*.
5. No sé cuándo tendrá lugar *el divorcio*.
6. Sé que los recién *divorciados* están contentos.

FOLDABLES®
Study Organizer

POCKET BOOK
See page SH23 for help with making this foldable. Use this foldable to categorize the vocabulary and information you have learned that is related to passages of life. Make a pocket book for each passage of life that you study. Each time you read something about a passage of life, make a card and file it in the appropriate pocket book.

CULTURA

Los recién casados con sus familiares y amigos delante de la catedral en Jerez de la Frontera en España

PASAJES DE LA VIDA

sesenta y siete **67**

Writing Development

You may wish to have students write a composition based on the answers to the questions in Activity 2.

Activity ④ This activity should be written and then gone over in class.

Estudio de palabras

Call on students to read a new word and the sentence that illustrates its meaning and usage. You may also wish to have students write the activity before going over it in class.

 Cultural Snapshot

(page 67) Jerez de la Frontera is famous for its vineyards, which produce the grapes used in making sherry—**jerez** in Spanish. Jerez de la Frontera is also known for the skill of its purebred Carthusian horses—a breed created from a cross between the native Andalusian workhorse and the Arabian horse.

GLENCOE ● Technology

You may wish to use the editable PowerPoint® presentation on PowerTeach for additional vocabulary instruction and practice.

Answers

④
1. iglesia
2. novia
3. pareja
4. ayuntamiento
5. alcalde
6. firmar
7. recepción

⑤ *Answers will vary, but students should use as many words as possible from* Vocabulario 1 *to talk about a wedding they attended.*

Estudio de palabras

1. Ellos se alegran.
2. Todos están alegres.
3. Se ve que hay mucha alegría.
4. Ellos van a casarse.
5. No sé cuándo tendrá lugar el casamiento.
6. Sé que los recién casados están contentos.

▶ ASSESS

Students are now ready to take Quiz 1 on page 3.37 of the TeacherTools booklet. If you prefer to create your own quiz, use the *ExamView*® Assessment Suite.

Vocabulario 2   presentación

🎧 VIDEO To practice your new words, watch Vocabulario en vivo.

 Quick Start

Use QS Transparency 3.2 or write the following on the board.

Contesta.
1. ¿Cuándo naciste?
2. ¿Cuántos años tienes?
3. ¿Cuál es la fecha de tu cumpleaños?
4. ¿Cuántos años vas a cumplir?

▶ TEACH
Core Instruction

Step 1 Have students close their books. Present the vocabulary using Vocabulary Transparencies V3.4–V3.5.

Step 2 Have students repeat each word once or twice after you or Audio CD 3. Then have them build up to repeating entire sentences. Ask leveled questions to encourage all students to use the new vocabulary.

Step 3 Have students open their books and read the new material for reinforcement.

Differentiation
Multiple Intelligences

After you have presented the vocabulary with the overhead transparencies, engage **visual-spatial**, **verbal-linguistic**, and **interpersonal** learners by having students look at the

El bautizo

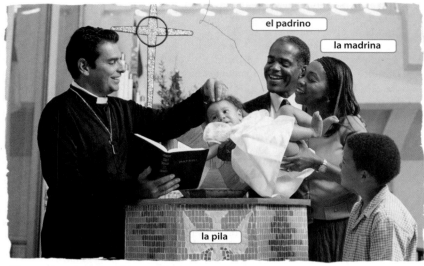

el padrino
la madrina
la pila

El cura bautiza al recién nacido.

El cumpleaños

En otras partes

Bizcocho often refers to a sponge cake or several types of cookies. It is probably safe to say the word **pastel** is the most common for **un pastel de cumpleaños, de boda,** but in many areas you will also hear **torta, tarta.** In Mexico, **una torta** is a sandwich.

las velas
el pastel, el bizcocho, la torta

Anita nació el ocho de noviembre.
Hoy cumple dieciséis años.
Ella está contenta que todas sus amigas vengan a celebrar su cumpleaños con ella.
Se alegra de que todas ellas se diviertan.

68   *sesenta y ocho*   CAPÍTULO 3

photographs on pages 68 and 69 and work with a partner to make up questions to ask the class. Or you may prefer to ask students to say anything they can about the photographs using complete sentences.

Cultura

Explain to students that in Spanish-speaking families a special celebration, called a **quinceañera,** is held when a girl turns fifteen. This term can refer to either the party or the girl whose birthday it is. **Quinceañera** celebrations are usually very elaborate. Ask the class if they can think of other similar celebrations (sweet sixteen, bar mitzvah/bat mitzvah).

El velorio

una esquela

Ha fallecido el señor

José Hernández

Falleció el día lunes 29-10-09. Su viuda, María Eugenia; sus hijas: Eugenia, Saeli; su yerno, Miguel González; su nieto, Mikel; su hermano, Constantino y señora; sus cuñados, sobrinos, demás familiares y amigos, invitan al acto del sepelio que se efectuará hoy a las 4:00 pm, en el Cementerio del Este.

El cortejo fúnebre partirá desde la Capilla CENTRAL de Funeraria Vallés.

Caracas, 30 de septiembre de 2009

el ataúd

Los amigos y familiares del difunto asisten al velorio.

El cementerio, El camposanto

la viuda del difunto

El cortejo fúnebre llega al cementerio.
El entierro tiene lugar en el cementerio.

Nota

- **El entierro** is often referred to as **el sepelio.** The corresponding verbs are **enterrar** and **sepultar.**
- The most common term is **la esquela** but you will also see and hear **el obituario.**

Learning from Realia

(page 69) Have students look at the **esquela** and identify the words for relatives they have already learned. New ones are: **yerno**—son-in-law; **cuñados**—brothers and sisters-in-law.

Explain to students that the verb **se efectuará** is used in formal announcements. Less formal ways to express the same idea are: **tendrá lugar, será.**

Additional Vocabulary

You may wish to give the word **el féretro** in addition to **el ataúd.**

Cultura

In small villages, particularly rural ones, it is still common to see the funeral cortège walk behind the casket. Cars are used in cities but, rather than go in a procession, people very often go on their own and meet outside the church before the service begins. They then enter the church behind the coffin and immediate family members.

Differentiation

Multiple Intelligences

Visual-spatial learners will enjoy designing a social events page for their school newspaper. The page should include at least one of each kind of event: wedding, birth, birthday, death. Graphics can be included in the form of clip art or actual photos. **Interpersonal** learners would enjoy doing this as a paired or small group activity.

GLENCOE Technology

Video in the Classroom

Vocabulario en vivo Watch and listen to Nora as she discusses how people celebrate some important moments in their lives in the Spanish-speaking world.

Teaching Options

Another way to reinforce the new vocabulary is to bring in Spanish-language newspapers and have students work in pairs to search for obituaries and wedding and birth announcements. The pairs can then report back to the class on what they found.

69

QuickPass

Go to glencoe.com
For: **Vocabulary practice**
Web code: ASD7844c3

▶ PRACTICE

Leveling EACH Activity

Easy Activities 1, 2
Average Activity 2 **Expansión**,
　Activities 3, 5, 6, 7
CHallenging Activity 4

Activity ❶

🎧 Audio Script

1. El bautizo tiene lugar en una iglesia.
2. El recién nacido bautiza al cura.
3. Tu cumpleaños se celebra en la fecha en que naciste.
4. Mucha gente tiene un pastel con velas para celebrar un cumpleaños.
5. La persona que celebra su cumpleaños recibe muchos regalos.
6. El entierro tiene lugar en la iglesia.
7. Una esquela avisa de un matrimonio.
8. El difunto es una persona muerta.

Activity ❷ This activity can be gone over orally in class calling on individuals at random, or you may have students do this as a paired activity.

Activity ❸ This activity should be prepared and then gone over in class.

ESCUCHAR

❶ Escucha y determina si la información que oyes es correcta o no. Usa una tabla como la de abajo para indicar tus respuestas.

correcta	incorrecta

ESCUCHAR • HABLAR • ESCRIBIR

❷ Personaliza. Da respuestas personales.
1. ¿Cuándo es tu cumpleaños?
2. ¿Cuándo naciste?
3. ¿Te preparan un pastel para tu cumpleaños?
4. ¿Cuántas velas habrá en tu próximo pastel?
5. ¿Te darán una fiesta para tu cumpleaños?
6. ¿Quiénes asistirán a la fiesta?
7. ¿Recibirás muchos regalos?
8. ¿Cuántos años cumplirás?

(EXPANSIÓN)

Ahora, sin mirar las preguntas, cuenta la información en tus propias palabras. Si no recuerdas algo, un(a) compañero(a) te puede ayudar.

LEER • ESCRIBIR

❸ Da otra palabra o expresión que significa la misma cosa.
1. un pastel
2. alegre
3. el obituario
4. el cementerio
5. el entierro
6. un cadáver, una persona muerta

Misa y Agradecimiento

Con motivo de cumplirse Diez y Ocho años de la partida de nuestra amada e inolvidable

JULIA MARÍA HERNÁNDEZ
(Q.E.P.D.)

Sus familiares Victor Lucena, sus hijas Cristina, Eucari, Miligros, Gregoria; sus nietos, bisnietos y amigos invitan para compartir su recuerdo a las misas de los dias 9 de Noviembre y 10 de Noviembre a las 6:00 p.m. en la Iglesia de Nuestra Señora de la Chiquinquirá, Av. Andrés Bello, La Florida.

Caracas, 9 de Noviembre de 2009

🍀 Comunidades

❹ En un grupo hagan una encuesta sobre los diferentes ritos que acompañan los pasajes de la vida de los miembros de su comunidad. ¿Varían los ritos o celebraciones según la etnia de las personas? ¿Son muchos de índole religiosa? Preparen una lista de las celebraciones y el (los) grupo(s) que las celebra(n). Presenten sus resultados a la clase.

Answers

❶
1. correcta
2. incorrecta
3. correcta
4. correcta
5. correcta
6. incorrecta
7. incorrecta
8. correcta

❷ *Answers will vary but may include:*
1. Mi cumpleaños es el _____ de _____.
2. Nací el _____ de _____.
3. Sí, me preparan un pastel para mi cumpleaños.
4. Habrá _____ velas en mi próximo pastel.
5. Sí, (No, no) me darán una fiesta para mi cumpleaños.
6. Todos mis amigos y mis parientes asistirán a la fiesta.
7. Sí, (No, no) recibiré muchos regalos.
8. Cumpliré _____ años.

❸
1. una torta (un bizcocho)
2. contento(a), (feliz)
3. la esquela
4. el camposanto
5. el sepelio
6. un difunto

❹ *Answers will vary, but students should use as many words as possible from Vocabulario 1 and 2 to talk about rites of passage.*

LEER • ESCRIBIR

⑤ Completa con una palabra apropiada.

1. El _____ bautiza al recién _____ en la _____.
2. El agua está en una _____.
3. Los _____ están presentes durante el bautizo.
4. Se le murió el esposo. Ella es _____.
5. Antes de ir al cementerio, los amigos y familiares del _____ asisten al velorio.
6. El _____ fúnebre llega al cementerio para el sepelio.
7. La novia lleva un traje de novia y un _____.
8. Hay _____ en un pastel de cumpleaños.

GeoVistas

To learn more about Chile, take a tour on pages SH52–SH53.

CULTURA

El camposanto en el desierto de Atacama en Poconchile, Chile

ESCRIBIR

⑥ Completa con la letra que falta.

1. el cemente__io
2. el velo__io
3. el entie__o
4. el obitua__io
5. el cu__a
6. la __ecepción
7. la pa__eja
8. ¡Enho__abuena!
9. la ce__emonia
10. lo entie__an en un ataúd

Ha fallecido el señor

José Hernández

Falleció el día lunes 29-10-09. Su viuda, María Eugenia; sus hijas: Eugenia, Saeli; su yerno, Miguel González; su nieto, Mikel; su hermano, Constantino y señora; sus cuñados, sobrinos, demás familiares y amigos, invitan al acto del sepelio que se efectuará hoy a las 4:00 pm, en el Cementerio del Este.

El cortejo fúnebre partirá desde la Capilla CENTRAL de Funeraria Vallés.

Caracas, 30 de septiembre de 2009

⊛ Comunicación

⑦ Con un(a) compañero(a) de clase hablen juntos haciendo y contestando preguntas sobre la información en la esquela.

PASAJES DE LA VIDA

setenta y uno **71**

Answers

⑤
1. cura, nacido, iglesia
2. pila
3. padrinos
4. viuda
5. difunto
6. cortejo
7. velo
8. velas

⑥
1. r
2. r
3. rr
4. r
5. r
6. r
7. r
8. r
9. r
10. rr

⑦ *Answers will vary.*

GLENCOE ⊛ Technology

Online Learning in the Classroom

Have students use QuickPass code ASD7844c3 for additional vocabulary practice. They can download audio files of all vocabulary to their computer and/or MP3 player. They will have access to online flashcards and eGames. Students can print and complete the **Vocabulario 1** and **2** Review Worksheet.

Differentiation
Advanced Learners

Have advanced learners use the given words and the related words from Activity 3 in original sentences.

Activity ⑤ This activity should be prepared and then gone over in class.

Activity ⑥ First have students fill in the missing letters. Then have them close their books, and give them the words as a dictation. This will help them distinguish the **r** sound from the **rr** sound.

📷 Cultural Snapshot

(page 71) This humble cemetery is in northern Chile in the Atacama Desert—the driest desert in the world.

GeoVistas

Have students locate the Atacama Desert on the map on page SH53. Then have students use pages SH52 and SH53 to come up with ideas for a poster or computerized slideshow based on demographic, historical, geographic, or cultural information about Chile. They may work individually, in pairs, or in small groups. Then have them give brief presentations to the class.

▶ ASSESS

Students are now ready to take Quiz 2 on page 3.38 of the TeacherTools booklet. If you prefer to create your own quiz, use the *ExamView® Assessment Suite.*

Resources

- Audio Activities TE, pages 3.22–3.24
- Audio CD 3, Tracks 10–13
- Workbook, pages 3.6–3.7
- Quiz 3, page 3.39
- ExamView® Assessment Suite

Quick Start

Use QS Transparency 3.3 or write the following on the board.

Parea las palabras relacionadas.

1. esperar   **a.** la preferencia
2. desear   **b.** el temor
3. preferir   **c.** el deseo
4. insistir   **d.** el mandato
5. mandar   **e.** la esperanza
6. temer   **f.** la insistencia

▶ TEACH
Core Instruction

Step 1 As you go over the first paragraph in the explanation, emphasize that the important question is whether or not the action in the clause is real. This makes the use of the subjunctive more meaningful, logical, and easy.

Step 2 Have students think of the meaning of each word or expression in Item 2 and analyze whether or not the information that will follow each one is definitely real.

Step 3 Call on individuals to read the example sentences.

✿ Conexiones

El inglés

Ask students if they use these subjunctive forms in English. If they do not, ask how they express the same idea.

✿ Conexiones

El inglés

The subjunctive is now rarely used in English. With many of these expressions, however, many speakers of English continue to use the subjunctive.

They insist that he do it.
I prefer that she know.

El subjuntivo con deseos

1. You already know that the subjunctive is used in a clause that follows the verb **querer** because even though someone wants another person to do something, it is not certain that he or she will really do it. The information in the clause is not factual. It may or may not happen and for this reason you must use the subjunctive.

> **Quiero que mis amigos vayan a la fiesta.**

2. For the same reason, the subjunctive is used in clauses introduced by each of the following expressions, since the information in the dependent clause is not definite.

desear	mandar *(to order)*
esperar	temer *(to fear)*
preferir	tener miedo de
insistir en	

> **Espero que no lleguen tarde.**
> **¿Insistes en que yo se lo diga?**
> **Tengo miedo de que él no me haga caso**
> **(que no me preste atención).**

CULTURA

Quiero que mi amigo suba conmigo en esta montaña rusa en el parque de atracciones en el Bosque de Chapultepec en México. Espero que no tenga miedo pero la verdad es que temo que le dé miedo.

⭐ Tips for Success

The basic concept for students to understand is that the subjunctive is used when we do not know if the action will take place. If we know that it is or will be a reality, the indicative is used. If students understand this, it will not be necessary for them to memorize lists of expressions that are followed by the subjunctive.

Indicative: factual, objective, stands alone, independent.

Subjunctive: subjective, not factual, cannot stand alone, may or may not happen.

Práctica

ESCUCHAR • HABLAR

 1 Conversa con un(a) compañero(a) según el modelo.

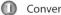 MODELO ¿Hacerlo? →
—¿Quién? ¿Yo?
—Sí, él prefiere que tú lo hagas.

1. ¿Aceptar la invitación?
2. ¿Asistir a la ceremonia?
3. ¿Comprar el regalo?
4. ¿Ir con él?
5. ¿No decir nada a nadie?

HABLAR • ESCRIBIR

2 Imagina que tienes unos amigos que se van a casar. Contesta.

1. ¿Prefieres que ellos se casen?
2. ¿Esperas que ellos sean felices?
3. ¿Deseas que te inviten a la boda?
4. ¿Deseas que ellos tengan una vida larga juntos?
5. ¿Temes que sea posible que tengan algunos problemas?

CULTURA

El escaparate de una tienda para novias en Barcelona, España

Comunicación

 3 Con un(a) compañero(a), discutan lo que ustedes quieren que sus amigos hagan y lo que prefieren que no hagan.

HABLAR • ESCRIBIR

4 Personaliza. Da respuestas personales.

1. ¿Insiste el/la profesor(a) en que ustedes le presten atención?
2. ¿Insiste en que ustedes escuchen cuando él/ella habla?
3. ¿Insiste en que ustedes hagan sus tareas?
4. ¿Insiste en que ustedes sepan las reglas de gramática?
5. ¿Insiste en que ustedes lleguen a clase a tiempo?

PASAJES DE LA VIDA

setenta y tres **73**

▶ PRACTICE

Leveling EACH Activity

Easy Activity 2
Average Activities 1, 4, 6
CHallenging Activities 3, 5

⭐ Tips for Success ·······

- The photo caption on page 72 reinforces the grammar concept being learned. Have students look for the use of the subjunctive as they read the caption.
- Notice how Activities 1, 2, and 4 concentrate on one particular form of the subjunctive. Activity 5 on page 74 makes students use many different forms.

Activities ①, ②, ③, ④ These activities can be gone over orally in class. They can then be written for homework.

GLENCOE 🖰 Technology

Online Learning in the Classroom

Have students use QuickPass code ASD7844c3 for additional grammar practice. They can review each grammar point with an eGame. They can also review all grammar points by doing the self-check quiz, which integrates the new vocabulary and grammar.

Answers

①
1. —¿Quién? ¿Yo? / —Sí, él prefiere que tú aceptes la invitación.
2. —¿Quién? ¿Yo? / —Sí, él prefiere que tú asistas a la ceremonia.
3. —¿Quién? ¿Yo? / —Sí, él prefiere que tú compres el regalo.
4. —¿Quién? ¿Yo? / —Sí, él prefiere que tú vayas con él.
5. —¿Quién? ¿Yo? / —Sí, él prefiere que tú no digas nada a nadie.

②
1. Sí, prefiero que ellos se casen.
2. Sí, espero que ellos sean felices.
3. Sí, deseo que me inviten a la boda.
4. Sí, deseo que ellos tengan una vida larga juntos.
5. Sí, temo que sea posible que tengan algunos problemas.

③ *Answers will vary, but students should use the correct form of the subjunctive of the verbs of their choosing after* querer *and* preferir.

④
1. Sí, el/la profesor(a) insiste en que nosotros le prestemos atención.
2. Sí, insiste en que nosotros escuchemos cuando él/ella habla.
3. Sí, insiste en que nosotros hagamos nuestras tareas.
4. Sí, insiste en que nosotros sepamos las reglas de gramática.
5. Sí, insiste en que nosotros lleguemos a clase a tiempo.

73

Activity ❺ This activity should be prepared first and then gone over in class.

ASSESS

Students are now ready to take Quiz 3 on page 3.39 of the TeacherTools booklet. If you prefer to create your own quiz, use the *ExamView® Assessment Suite*.

Resources

- Audio Activities TE, pages 3.24–3.25
- 🎧 Audio CD 3, Tracks 14–15
- Workbook, pages 3.7–3.8
- Quiz 4, page 3.40
- ● *ExamView® Assessment Suite*

🕐 Quick Start

Use QS Transparency 3.4 or write the following on the board.
Parea las palabras relacionadas.
1. triste
2. alegrarse
3. sorprender
4. gustar
5. sentir

a. el gusto
b. el sentimiento
c. entristecer, la tristeza
d. la alegría
e. la sorpresa

TEACH
Core Instruction

Explain to students that this is one of the few cases in which the subjunctive is used to express something that really took place. The use of the subjunctive is, however, logical because the information is introduced by a subjective idea, an emotion.

InfoGap

The *InfoGap* activity will allow students to practice in pairs.

CARTELERA DE CINE

AMOR CIEGO
(Todo público)

San Pedro 5	2-4:30-6:45-9:15 p.m.	*¢1.100 **¢600
Internacional 3	2-4:30-6:45-9:15 p.m	*¢1.100 **¢600
Cariari 6	2-4:30-6:45-7-9:15 p.m.	*¢1.100 **¢600
Cinemark	1:20-4:05-7:20-9:55 p.m.	*¢1.300 **¢1.000

LOS OTROS
(May. de 16 años)

San Pedro 4	2-4-7-9 p.m.	*¢1.100 **¢600

MONSTER, INC
(Todo público)

San Pedro 2	9 p.m. (inglés)	*¢1.200 **¢600
San Pedro 2	1:15-3:10-5:05-7 p.m.	*¢1.200 **¢600
Internacional 2	11:25-3:20-5:15-7:10-9:05 p.m.	*¢1.100 **¢600
Cariari 5	1:25-3:20-5:15-7:10-9:05 p.m.	*¢1.100 **¢600
Cinemark	1:25-3:40-6:45-9 p.m.	*¢1.300 **¢1.000
Cinemark	2-4:15 p.m. (inglés)	*¢1.300 **¢1.000

InfoGap For more practice with the subjunctive used to express wishes and emotions, do Activity 3 on page SR4 at the end of this book.

74 *setenta y cuatro*

LEER • ESCRIBIR
❺ Completa con la forma apropiada del verbo.

Yo no sé lo que vamos a hacer esta noche. Pablo quiere que nosotros __1__ (ir) al cine. Él insiste en que nosotros __2__ (ver) la película en el cine Apolo. Carlota teme que mañana __3__ (ser) el último día. Tiene miedo de que ellos __4__ (cambiar) las películas los sábados. Y tú, ¿quieres que nosotros __5__ (ir) al cine o que __6__ (hacer) otra cosa? ¿Qué me dices? Que Felipe quiere que ustedes __7__ (quedarse) en casa. ¿Por qué? Ah, él quiere que todo el grupo __8__ (ir) a su casa. Él prefiere que nosotros __9__ (escuchar) música y que __10__ (bailar). ¡Buena idea!

🌀 Comunicación

❻ Trabaja con un(a) compañero(a). Cada uno(a) de ustedes va a preparar una lista de características que ustedes quieren, prefieren o esperan que tenga su mejor amigo(a). Luego comparen sus listas y determinen las características que ustedes dos buscan en su mejor amigo(a).

El subjuntivo con expresiones de emoción

1. The subjunctive is used in a clause that is introduced by a verb or expression that conveys an emotion. Study the following sentences.

> **Me alegro de que él esté.**
> **Pero siento que su hermano no pueda asistir.**

One can argue that the information in the clause is factual. Such may be the case. Why then is the subjunctive used? It is used because the information in the clause is very subjective. I may be happy that he is here, but someone else may not be. I am sorry that his brother cannot attend, but someone else may be glad.

2. The following are verbs and expressions that convey emotion. They are all followed by the subjunctive.

alegrarse de	gustar
estar contento(a), triste	sentir
sorprender	ser una lástima (pena)

Answers

❺
1. vayamos
2. veamos
3. sea
4. cambien
5. vayamos
6. hagamos
7. se queden
8. vaya
9. escuchemos
10. bailemos

❻ *Answers will vary.*

📰 Learning from Realia

Use the schedule in **Cartelera de cine** as a prompt for students to create a conversation about the schedule of shows. They should be able to discuss their preferences for movies, times, and locations with a partner and present the conversations to the class.

Práctica

ESCUCHAR · HABLAR · ESCRIBIR

 Contesta según se indica sobre una boda.

1. ¿Te sorprende que ellos se casen? (sí)
2. ¿Le sorprende a Elena que ellos se casen? (no)
3. ¿Te sorprende que ellos te inviten a la boda? (sí)
4. ¿Le sorprende a Elena que ellos la inviten a la fiesta? (no)
5. ¿Estás contento(a) que José reciba una invitación? (sí)
6. ¿Está contenta Julia que él reciba una invitación? (no)
7. ¿Siente Julia que José asista a la fiesta? (no)

HABLAR · ESCRIBIR

 Completa.

1. Me alegro de que ellos...
2. Sentimos mucho que...
3. Es una pena que...
4. ¿Te sorprende que...
5. Ellos están contentos que...
6. Me gusta que...

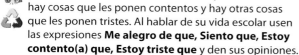
Comunicación

 Trabaja con un(a) compañero(a). Van a hablar de su escuela y de su vida escolar. Es cierto que en la escuela hay cosas que les ponen contentos y hay otras cosas que les ponen tristes. Al hablar de su vida escolar usen las expresiones **Me alegro de que, Siento que, Estoy contento(a) que, Estoy triste que** y den sus opiniones.

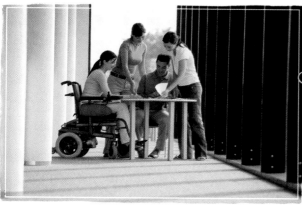

CULTURA

La señorita se va a casar y entra en la iglesia al brazo de su padre en Ajijic, México.

CULTURA

¡Qué pena! Es una lástima que los amigos tengan que pasar el fin de semana estudiando. Pero me sorprende que estén tan alegres.

setenta y cinco **75**

▶ PRACTICE

Leveling EACH Activity

Easy Activity 7
Average–CHallenging
  Activities 8, 9

Differentiation

Advanced Learners

After you have gone over the **Práctica** activities on page 75, have students make up original sentences using the expressions in Item 2 on page 74.

Slower Paced Learners

Ask slower paced learners to repeat the original sentences from above and to explain why they take the subjunctive.

⭐Tips for Success ·······

Have students look for the uses of the subjunctive in the caption that accompanies the photograph at the bottom of page 75. Ask them to explain why the subjunctive is used here.

·······························

Cultural Snapshot

(page 75) Ajijic is a pleasant community on Lake Chapala not far from Guadalajara. Lake Chapala is Mexico's largest inland body of water but, unfortunately, it is quite polluted.

▶ ASSESS

Students are now ready to take Quiz 4 on page 3.40 of the TeacherTools booklet. If you prefer to create your own quiz, use the *ExamView®* *Assessment Suite.*

Answers

7

1. Sí, me sorprende que ellos se casen.
2. No, a Elena no le sorprende que ellos se casen.
3. Sí, me sorprende que ellos me inviten a la boda.
4. No, a Elena no le sorprende que ellos la inviten a la fiesta.
5. Sí, estoy contento(a) que José reciba una invitación.
6. No, Julia no está contenta que él reciba una invitación.
7. No, Julia no siente que José asista a la fiesta.

8 *Answers will vary.*

9 *Answers will vary.*

Teaching Options

Ask students to write a few sentences expressing their feelings about certain issues or events and share them with the class. Create a master list to post as a resource for others.

75

Resources

- Audio Activities TE, pages 3.25–3.26
- Audio CD 3, Tracks 16–18
- Workbook, pages 3.8–3.10
- Quiz 5, page 3.41
- ExamView® Assessment Suite

Quick Start

Use QS Transparency 3.5 or write the following on the board.

Completa con un adjetivo posesivo.

1. Nosotros vivimos en los suburbios. ___ casa está en una calle tranquila.
2. Yo tengo un cuarto de dormir y mi hermano tiene un cuarto de dormir. ___ cuarto es más grande que ___ cuarto.
3. ¿Tienes una mascota? ¿Cómo se llama ___ mascota?
4. Ustedes tienen una casa nueva, ¿no? ¿Cuál es ___ nueva dirección?

▶ TEACH

Core Instruction

Step 1 Have students point to themselves as they say a form of **el mío,** have them look directly at a friend as they say a form of **el tuyo,** point to themselves and look at a friend as they say a form of **el nuestro,** and point to a friend as they say a form of **el suyo.**

Step 2 Have students repeat after you the possessive pronouns in Item 2.

Step 3 Spend more time on Item 3. Explain and give many examples of the different meanings of **el suyo, la suya, los suyos,** and **las suyas.** Then ask students to give examples.

76

CULTURA

Les sorprende a la joven y a su amigo que haya una mesa libre en el café.

¿Te acuerdas?

You have already learned the possessive adjectives.

mi	mis
tu	tus
su	sus
nuestro(a)	nuestros(as)
vuestro(a)	*vuestros(as)*

Los pronombres posesivos

1. A possessive pronoun replaces a noun that is modified by a possessive adjective.

> mi carro → el mío
> mi casa → la mía
> mis amigos → los míos

Note that the possessive pronoun must agree in number and gender with the noun it replaces. Possessive pronouns are accompanied by definite articles.

2. Study the following.

POSSESSIVE PRONOUNS

> el mío, la mía, los míos, las mías
> el tuyo, la tuya, los tuyos, las tuyas
> el nuestro, la nuestra, los nuestros, las nuestras
> *el vuestro, la vuestra, los vuestros, las vuestras*
> el suyo, la suya, los suyos, las suyas

> Yo tengo mis regalos, no los tuyos.
> Y él tiene sus regalos, no los nuestros.

3. Since the forms of **el suyo** can refer to so many different people, the meaning of **el suyo** is not always clear.

> Elena tiene el suyo.   *Elena has hers.*
> Elena tiene el de él.   *Elena has his.*

Whenever it is unclear to whom the possessive pronoun refers, a prepositional phrase replaces it for clarification.

EL SUYO	LA SUYA	LOS SUYOS	LAS SUYAS
el de Ud.	la de Ud.	los de Ud.	las de Ud.
el de él	la de él	los de él	las de él
el de ella	la de ella	los de ella	las de ella
el de Uds.	la de Uds.	los de Uds.	las de Uds.
el de ellos	la de ellos	los de ellos	las de ellos
el de ellas	la de ellas	los de ellas	las de ellas

4. Note that the definite article is often omitted after the verb **ser.** The article can be used, however, for emphasis.

> Estos libros son de Marta. Son suyos. No son míos.
> Estos son los míos y aquellos son los tuyos.

76 *setenta y seis*

CAPÍTULO 3

Differentiation

Students with Learning Difficulties

You may wish to spend more time on Item 3. Understanding how to use the forms of **el suyo** can be challenging for students with learning difficulties. Review the possessive adjectives **su** and **sus,** and explain that just like these adjectives, the forms of **el suyo** agree with the thing possessed, not with the subject who possesses it. Read the examples and give them others. Then go on to explain the chart. Use **el de Ud.** as an example. Point out that in each case, the first word (**el**) refers to the thing owned, and the last word **Ud.** refers to the person who owns it. Again, give several examples.

Práctica

ESCUCHAR • HABLAR

10 Practica con un(a) compañero(a) según el modelo.

MODELO mi casa y tu casa →
la mía y la tuya

1. mi carro y tu carro
2. mi maleta y la maleta de Enrique
3. tu boleto y mis boletos
4. la lista de Elena y tu lista
5. nuestras ideas y las ideas de ustedes
6. mis profesores y los profesores de mi hermano

ESCUCHAR • HABLAR • ESCRIBIR

11 Sigue el modelo.

MODELO ¿Tienes tu boleto? →
¡Ojalá tenga el mío!

1. ¿Tienes tu carro?
2. ¿Tienes nuestras maletas?
3. ¿Tienes tu pasaporte?
4. ¿Tienes mi pasaporte también?
5. ¿Tienes la dirección de Elena?
6. ¿Tienes el número del móvil de José?

LEER • ESCRIBIR

12 Emplea el pronombre posesivo en cada frase.

1. *Mi dama de honor* fue mi madre y *la dama de honor de Alicia* fue su mejor amiga.
2. *Mi ceremonia* tuvo lugar en la iglesia y *tu ceremonia* tuvo lugar en el ayuntamiento.
3. *Nuestra recepción* fue en un salón de banquetes y *la recepción de María y Carlos* fue en un restaurante.
4. *Tu cumpleaños* es el doce y *mi cumpleaños* es el trece del mismo mes.

Refrán

Can you guess what the following proverb means?

El casado casa quiere.

¡Bravo!

You have now learned all the new vocabulary and grammar in this chapter. Continue to use and practice all that you know while learning more cultural information. ¡Vamos!

CULTURA

El joven lleva a los perros a pasear por un parque en Buenos Aires. Todos estos perros no son suyos. Son de sus clientes.

setenta y siete **77**

Answers

Gramática

Tips for Success ....

Let students visualize the meaning of possessive pronouns by doing the following. Give a book to a boy, a girl, two boys, and two girls. Point to the boy holding the book and say **el de él;** point to the girl and say **el de ella,** and so on.

Give a book to a boy or girl, tell him or her to pretend to be the teacher and say **el de usted.**

PRACTICE

Leveling EACH Activity

Easy Activity 10
Average Activity 11
CHallenging Activity 12

Activity 12 This activity should be prepared and then gone over in class.

Cultural Snapshot

(page 77) This park is located in the lovely Recoleta neighborhood of Buenos Aires. Have students read the photo caption and find the possessive pronouns.

ASSESS

Students are now ready to take Quiz 5 on page 3.41 of the TeacherTools booklet. If you prefer to create your own quiz, use the *ExamView® Assessment Suite.*

Refrán

Have students recite the proverb aloud. Then see if they can figure out its meaning: "Married people want a home of their own."

Conversación

Resources
- Audio Activities TE, page 3.27
- Audio CD 3, Tracks 19–20

▶ TEACH

Core Instruction

Step 1 Have students close their books. Read the conversation to them or play Audio CD 3.

Step 2 Have the class repeat each line after you or the audio CD.

Step 3 Call on two students to read the conversation with as much expression as possible.

Step 4 After presenting the conversation, go over the **¿Comprendes?** activities. If students can answer the questions with relative ease, move on. Students should not be expected to memorize the conversation.

Differentiation

Multiple Intelligences

Ask a **verbal-linguistic** or advanced learner to summarize the conversation in his or her own words. Ask other class members whether they have anything to add to the summary given.

Teaching Options

If students are having few problems with pronunciation or comprehension, you can skip Steps 1 and 2 of the Core Instruction and just have students read the conversation aloud with as much expression as possible before going over the **¿Comprendes?** activities on page 79.

78

QuickPass

Go to glencoe.com
For: **Conversation practice**
Web code: **ASD7844c3**

¿Habrá una boda?

Adela	¿Te sorprende que se casen Cecilia y Enrique?
Carolina	De ninguna manera. Ya hace mucho tiempo que están saliendo juntos.
Adela	Hacen una buena pareja. Espero que sean felices y que tengan una buena vida.
Carolina	Yo también. Cecilia quiere que yo la ayude a escoger su traje de novia.
Adela	No compré el mío. Cuando me casé llevé el de mi mamá. A propósito, ¿vas a ser la dama de honor?
Carolina	No lo creo. Cecilia quiere que su madre sirva de dama de honor.
Adela	¿Cuándo será la boda? ¿Han fijado una fecha?
Carolina	¡Por supuesto! Dentro de poco van a enviar las invitaciones.

GLENCOE SPANISH

Why It Works!

Note that this conversation uses only vocabulary and grammar students have already learned. It also reinforces recently learned material. Have students look for all the examples of the subjunctive in the conversation.

GLENCOE Technology

Online Learning in the Classroom

Have students use QuickPass code ASD7844c3 for additional conversation practice. Students can download audio files for the conversation to their computer and/or MP3 player and complete a self-check quiz.

¿Comprendes?

A Identifica quien lo dice.

	Adela	Carolina
1. Es posible que le sorprenda que Cecilia y Enrique se casen.		
2. No le sorprende que Cecilia y Enrique se casen.		
3. Va a ayudar a Cecilia a escoger su traje de novia.		
4. No compró un traje de novia. Llevó el de su madre.		
5. Cecilia quiere que su madre sea la dama de honor.		
6. La pareja va a enviar las invitaciones dentro de poco.		

B Contesta.

1. ¿Por qué no le sorprende a Carolina que Cecilia y Enrique se casen?
2. ¿Qué esperan Adela y Carolina?
3. ¿Qué quiere Cecilia que haga Carolina?
4. ¿Por qué no compró un traje de novia Adela?
5. ¿Quién va a servir de dama de honor en la boda?
6. ¿Han fijado los novios una fecha para la boda?

C **Resumiendo** Con un(a) compañero(a) de clase discutan lo que aprendieron de la boda de Cecilia y Enrique según la conversación de Adela y Carolina.

Fidel Antonio Sánchez Rodríguez
María Eugenia Acosta Ardila

Filadelfo García Martínez
María del Refugio Martínez Lara

María Carolina y Alonso

Participan el enlace matrimonial de sus hijos y tienen el honor de invitarles a la ceremonia religiosa que se celebrará el día 22 de diciembre del presente en punto de las 18:30 horas, en la Capilla de Nuestra Señora del Rosario; Templo de Santo Domingo ubicada en calle 5 de Mayo y 4 Poniente, Centro Histórico

Puebla, Pue. Diciembre de 2010.

PASAJES DE LA VIDA

setenta y nueve **79**

▶ PRACTICE

¿Comprendes?

A Have students complete their charts and report back to the class.

B You may wish to allow students to refer back to the conversation for the answers or you may wish to do this as a factual recall activity.

Differentiation

Advanced Learners

For Activity C, you may want to call on an advanced learner first. Then call on another student to give a resumé of the one given by the first student.

Pre-AP Listening to this conversation on audio CD will help students develop the skills that they need to be successful on the listening portion of the AP exam.

GLENCOE ◉ Technology

You may wish to use the editable PowerPoint® presentation on PowerTeach to have students listen to and repeat the conversation. Additional activities are also provided.

GLENCOE ◉ Technology

Video in the Classroom

Diálogo en vivo In this episode, Vicky works as a wedding videographer. Ask students their opinion: Is the mother of the bride correct in saying that it's Vicky's fault that her daughter called off the wedding?

VIDEO To view a family planning a wedding, watch **Diálogo en vivo.**

Answers

A

1. Adela
2. Carolina
3. Carolina
4. Adela
5. Carolina
6. Carolina

B

1. Hace mucho tiempo que están saliendo juntos.
2. Esperan que Cecilia y Enrique sean felices y que tengan una buena vida.
3. Cecilia quiere que Carolina la ayude a escoger su traje de novia.
4. Adela no compró un traje de novia porque cuando se casó llevó el de su mamá.
5. La madre de Cecilia va a servir de dama de honor en la boda.
6. Sí, los novios han fijado una fecha para la boda.

C *Answers will vary, but students should use the vocabulary and the correct form of the verbs from the conversation.*

▶ TEACH
Core Instruction

Step 1 Have students read the **Antes de leer** and look at the photographs that accompany the **Lectura.**

Step 2 It is up to your discretion as to how thoroughly you wish students to know the information. You may wish to have students learn the material thoroughly enough that they can retell it in their own words—in other words, transfer from a receptive skill (read) to a productive skill (speak and/or write). In this case, you may wish to call on a student to read a few sentences aloud. Then stop and ask questions that other students answer. Questions should include the Reading Check questions.

Step 3 Have students do the **¿Comprendes?** activities on page 83. You may wish to have them do the activities as homework and then go over them in class, or you may prefer to do them in class.

LECTURA CULTURAL

Celebraciones y ritos de pasaje 🎧♻️

Antes de leer

Piensa en celebraciones y ritos de pasaje en tu familia. ¿Cómo celebra tu familia? ¿Cuáles son algunas tradiciones o costumbres típicas?

✓ **Reading Check**

¿Qué tipo de relación existe entre los padrinos y la familia del bebé?

Los pasajes de la vida empiezan con el nacimiento y terminan con la muerte o el fallecimiento de la persona. Casi todos los pasajes de la vida van acompañados de una ceremonia y en muchas ocasiones de una celebración. La mayoría de las ceremonias son de índole[1] religiosa.

El bautizo En los países hispanos donde la tradición católica es bastante fuerte, la primera ceremonia o rito de pasaje es el bautizo. Antes del bautizo los padres del bebé escogen a miembros de la familia o amigos íntimos para servir de padrinos. Una relación casi parentesca existe entre los padrinos y la familia del bebé. Esta relación empieza con la ceremonia del bautizo y perdura durante toda la vida. Se espera que los padrinos puedan ayudar a su ahijado(a) en el futuro y si es necesario sustituir a los padres naturales en el caso de la muerte, por ejemplo.

[1]índole   *kind, sort*

CULTURA
El cura bautiza al bebé en una iglesia en México. Los padres y los padrinos están muy orgullosos.

GLENCOE 🖱 Technology

Online Learning in the Classroom
You may wish to have students use QuickPass code ASD7844c3 to develop their reading comprehension and writing skills. Students can take a self-check quiz, which includes an essay.

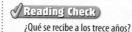

Otros ritos A los seis o siete años de edad el niño o la niña católica recibe su primera comunión. Tanto para los católicos como para los protestantes la confirmación tiene lugar entre los doce y catorce años. Un joven judío recibe su bar mitzvah a los trece años. Para la muchacha es el bat mitzvah o el bas mitzvah. Una fiesta o cena suele² seguir cada una de estas ceremonias religiosas.

✓ Reading Check

¿Qué se recibe a los trece años?

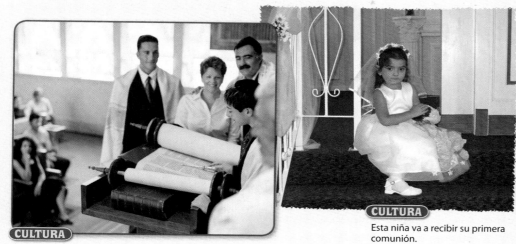

CULTURA

Un joven judío recibe su bar mitzvah en una sinagoga en la Ciudad de México. Durante la ceremonia lee del *Torá*.

CULTURA

Esta niña va a recibir su primera comunión.

El matrimonio La edad legal para contraer matrimonio varía de un país a otro. Hoy en día en España y Latinoamérica las parejas no se están casando tan jóvenes como antes. Los novios pueden casarse por la Iglesia o por (el, lo) civil. En algunos países el matrimonio civil es obligatorio. Durante la ceremonia civil en el ayuntamiento, los novios, acompañados de los testigos³, tienen que firmar el registro nupcial. La ceremonia religiosa puede tener lugar el mismo día o uno o dos días después. Para la ceremonia religiosa los convidados (invitados) toman sus asientos en la iglesia donde esperan la llegada de la novia que entra al brazo de su padre. La procesión nupcial consiste en la dama de honor, el padrino y los pajes. No siempre, pero en muchas ocasiones, la madre de la novia sirve de dama de honor y el padre del novio sirve de padrino. Los pajes suelen ser niños—en muchas ocasiones sobrinos de los novios. Durante la ceremonia los novios intercambian alianzas (anillos de matrimonio).

²suele *tends to*   ³testigos *witnesses*

✓ Reading Check

Típicamente, ¿quiénes sirven de dama de honor y padrino?

ochenta y uno **81**

Lectura

GLENCOE SPANISH

Why It Works!

This **Lectura,** like all others in **¡Así se dice!,** contains only Spanish that students have already learned, with the exception of the four footnoted vocabulary words. The **Lectura** is easy because it is at the students' proficiency level. Students are not encumbered with unknown lexical and grammatical items.

Comparaciones

Have students research a life event in another country and create a poster that compares and contrasts the event in that country with the event in the United States. Encourage students to use both illustrations and text in their posters. Ask them to present their finding to the class, using the poster as a visual aid.

Pre-AP This cultural reading will develop the skills that students need to be successful on the reading and writing sections of the AP exam. Listening to this reading will also help prepare them for the auditory component.

Heritage Speakers

Ask heritage speakers in your class to discuss how their own families practice these customs. Encourage students to ask them questions.

LECTURA CULTURAL

Después de la ceremonia hay una recepción con una gran cena o bufé. Todos los invitados bailan al ritmo de una orquesta o al son de un DJ. Todos los presentes les dan la enhorabuena a los recién casados.

CULTURA

El joven baila con su madre durante la recepción que sigue la ceremonia nupcial en Panamá.

Con motivo de cumplirse un mes del fallecimiento en la paz del Señor de nuestra querida:

ALICIA LARES DE ZAMORA
(Q.E.P.D.)

Su esposo, Oscar Zamora Conde; sus hijos: Alicia, María Elena, Virginia, Cynthia y Oscar Zamora Lares; sus hijos políticos: Juan Santaella y Dina Grisanti de Zamora; sus nietos: Héctor y Juan Bernardo Santaella Zamora, María Antonia Santaella de Zamora, María Villamil, Diego Bautista Urbaneja Zamora, María Virginia Olivo Zamora, María Fernanda Olivo Z. de Domínguez y María Carolina Olivo Z. de Ramírez, Cynthia Lander Zamora, Carina, Oscar Miguel y Bernardo Zamora Grisanti; sus bisnietos: Zamora Ripley, Zamora Tellería, Zamora Presilla, Febres-Cordero Zamora, Isaac Ríos; sobrinos nietos, primos y demás familiares agradecemos a todas aquellas personas que nos acompañaron y a las que nos han expresado su solidaridad en tan dolorosos momentos. Así mismo, invitamos a participar en una misa que, por el eterno descanso de su alma, se ofrecerá mañana **lunes 12 de noviembre a las 6:30 p.m. en la capilla del Instituto Cumbres de Caracas, calle Tauro de la urbanización Santa Paula.**

Caracas, 11 de noviembre de 2009

✓ Reading Check

¿Qué hacen los amigos y parientes del difunto después de la misa?

Siguen los pasajes. Los hijos tienen hijos. Los nietos crecen[4]. Hay aniversarios de boda—bodas de plata y bodas de oro. Y un día llega el último pasaje—la muerte.

El sepelio En los países hispanos el velorio en casa era tradicional, con el cuerpo presente. Hoy en día el velorio en casa es menos frecuente. En el caso de un difunto católico hay una misa en la iglesia. Después de la misa los amigos y parientes del difunto forman un cortejo para ir al cementerio donde se efectúa el entierro o el sepelio—frecuentemente en la tumba familiar. Se publica una esquela en el periódico avisando del fallecimiento del difunto.

[4]crecen *grow up*

82 *ochenta y dos*

CAPÍTULO 3

Answers

A
1. Los pasajes de la vida empiezan con el nacimiento y terminan con la muerte.
2. (correcta)
3. Hay mucha tradición católica en los países hispanos.
4. El bautizo es una ceremonia para el recién nacido.
5. Los padres del bebé escogen a los padrinos antes del bautizo.

82

B *Answers will vary but may include:*
Una relación casi parentesca que perdura durante toda la vida existe entre los padrinos y la familia del bebé. Se espera que los padrinos puedan ayudar a su ahijado(a) en el futuro y si es necesario sustituir a los padres naturales en el caso de la muerte, por ejemplo.

C
1. La edad legal para contraer matrimonio varía de un país a otro.
2. No, no se están casando tan jóvenes como antes.
3. Las parejas pueden casarse por la iglesia o por (el, lo) civil.
4. La ceremonia religiosa tiene lugar en la iglesia.
5. La ceremonia civil tiene lugar en el ayuntamiento.
6. La novia entra en la iglesia con su padre.
7. Con frecuencia, la novia escoge a su madre como dama de honor.
8. El novio escoge a su padre.
9. Los niños suelen ser los pajes.

¿Comprendes?

A Confirmando información Corrige las frases erróneas.

1. Los pasajes de la vida empiezan con la muerte y terminan con el nacimiento.
2. Un rito o ceremonia acompaña casi todos los pasajes de la vida.
3. Hay muy poca tradición católica en los países hispanos.
4. El bautizo es una ceremonia para el recién casado.
5. Los padres del bebé escogen a los padrinos después del bautizo.

B Analizando Analiza la importancia de los padrinos en la vida del recién nacido.

C Recordando hechos Contesta.

1. ¿Cuál es la edad legal para contraer matrimonio en los países hispanos?
2. ¿Se casan muy jóvenes los españoles y latinoamericanos?
3. ¿Cómo pueden casarse las parejas?
4. ¿Dónde tiene lugar la ceremonia religiosa?
5. ¿Dónde tiene lugar la ceremonia civil?
6. ¿Con quién entra en la iglesia la novia?
7. Con frecuencia, ¿a quién escoge la novia como dama de honor?
8. ¿A quién escoge el novio como padrino?
9. ¿Quiénes suelen ser los pajes?
10. ¿Qué intercambian los novios durante la ceremonia nupcial?

D Comparando y contrastando Compara unas costumbres tradicionales hispanas sobre las bodas con las costumbres de tu familia.

E Organizando Pon las siguientes oraciones en el orden apropiado.

1. El cortejo fúnebre sale para el camposanto.
2. A veces hay un velorio con el cuerpo presente.
3. El sepelio tiene lugar en el camposanto.
4. Según la tradición católica, hay una misa en la iglesia.

VIDEO To visit a famous cemetery in Argentina, watch **Cultura en vivo.**

CULTURA

Un camposanto en la Ciudad de Guatemala

Cultura

Aquí vemos una boda que tiene lugar en México. Como en muchas bodas latinas, los pajes son sobrinos de los novios. Un grupo de mariachis están ayudando a los novios a celebrar después de la ceremonia nupcial.

ochenta y tres **83**

▶ PRACTICE

¿Comprendes?

⭐Tips for Success ·······

These activities follow the same order in which the material is presented in the **Lectura.** You can intersperse the activities as follows:
El bautizo–A and B
El matrimonio–C and D
El sepelio–E

A You may wish to do this as a paired activity.
B This can be done as an entire class discussion or in individual groups.
C You may wish to allow students to look up answers or you may prefer to do this as a factual recall activity.
E Have students put this in order before going over it in class.

Comunidades

If you have students in class from many different ethnic backgrounds, there can be many interesting discussions concerning Activity D. Encourage the discussions to be in Spanish, if possible.

GLENCOE Technology

Video in the Classroom

Cultura en vivo In this episode, students will learn about la Recoleta, a famous cemetery in Buenos Aires, Argentina. Ask students if they know of a cemetery in the United States that has similar national importance. If so, how are the cemeteries the same? How are they different?

Answers

10. Los novios intercambian alianzas (anillos de matrimonio).

D *Answers will vary but may include:*
En algunos países la ceremonia civil en el ayuntamiento es obligatorio. No es obligatorio en Estados Unidos: las parejas pueden casarse o en la iglesia o en el ayuntamiento. En los países hispanos la ceremonia religiosa puede tener lugar el mismo día o uno o dos días después pero en Estados Unidos por lo general si una pareja se casa por (el, lo) civil, no hay ceremonia religiosa y vice versa (si hay ceremonia religiosa no hay ceremonia civil). Otra costumbre en los países hispanos es la de la madre de la novia sirviendo de dama de honor y del padre del novio sirviendo de padrino. En Estados Unidos, por lo general la novia escoge a su mejor amiga como dama de honor y el novio escoge a su mejor amigo como padrino.

E *The correct order is: 2, 4, 1, 3.*

Resources

- Audio Activities TE, pages 3.30–3.31
- Audio CD 3, Tracks 23–24
- Literature Test, page 3.55
- ExamView® Assessment Suite

Preview

Starting in Chapter 3, each chapter of ¡Así se dice! Level 3 has a literary section. Most literary selections are by well-known Latin American or Spanish writers. Some selections are poetry and others are prose.

It is up to the discretion of the teacher if you wish to do all or any of these literary works. The difficulty level of each selection is also indicated: 1 is difficult; 4 is quite easy.

Difficulty Level
3

Vocabulario

▶ **TEACH**

Core Instruction

If you wish to do the **Literatura** in depth, present the new words and their definitions. You may also wish to give students sentences using the new words.

Ellos tienen mucho afán de tener éxito.
El pintor pinta con un pincel.
Mucha gente pone miel en su té.
La criada limpia la casa y lava el lavado entre otras tareas domésticas.
No oigo lo que está diciendo porque está musitando.
Él piensa mucho en el antaño, en lo que ya ha pasado.

No hay nadie en el restaurante.
Hay muchas mesas vacías.
Acaso lo veo.

El hermano ausente en la cena de Pascua

de Abraham Valdelomar

▲ Ayacucho, Perú, ciudad en que murió Abraham Valdelomar en 1919

Vocabulario

el afán un deseo fuerte
el pincel un instrumento que se usa para pintar
la miel una sustancia dulce del néctar de las flores
la criada una persona que hace tareas domésticas por un salario
musitar murmurar
antaño de tiempos pasados
vacío(a) no ocupado, libre
acaso quizás

84 *ochenta y cuatro*   CAPÍTULO 3

Teaching Options

If you plan to merely expose students to this poem, have students study the vocabulary on their own and write the **Práctica** activity that follows.

Differentiation

Advanced Learners

Have advanced learners use the new words in original sentences. Or, have them ask questions using these words and calling on other students to answer.

Slower Paced Learners

Help slower paced learners by asking them *yes/no* questions using the words.

Práctica

Completa con una palabra apropiada.

1. No hay nada en el vaso. Está _____.
2. Tengo mucho _____ de ayudar a los menos afortunados.
3. Mucha gente pone _____ en su té en vez de azúcar.
4. El artista que pinta usa un _____.
5. _____ limpia la casa y recibe un sueldo.
6. No son cosas de hoy. Son cosas de _____.
7. No oigo bien lo que dice porque siempre _____.

INTRODUCCIÓN

Abraham Valdelomar (1888–1919) nació en Ica, Perú y murió en Ayacucho. Escribió cuentos regionales y poesías. Uno de los temas favoritos de su poesía es la vida familiar.

La laguna de Huacachina en Ica, Perú, ciudad natal de Abraham Valdelomar

CULTURA

PRACTICE

Have students complete the **Práctica** activity and go over it orally in class.

Cultural Snapshot

(page 84) Ayacucho is at an altitude of 8,987 feet in the Andes. The town has a very colonial look. Many of its inhabitants are indigenous people who speak Quechua as their first language and continue to wear many traditional costumes.

(page 85) Ica is a bustling town in Peru's richest wine-growing area. The Laguna de Huacachina is just three miles outside of town. This area was hard hit by an earthquake in 2007.

Introducción

You may wish to have students read the **Introducción** silently. Then ask: **¿Cuáles son unos ejemplos de la vida familiar?**

Conexiones

La geografía

Have students locate Ica and Ayacucho on the map of Peru on page SH51. Ask students what they can learn about these two cities just from looking at the map.

Answers

1. vacío
2. afán
3. miel
4. pincel
5. La criada
6. antaño
7. musita

▶ TEACH
Core Instruction

Step 1 Have students read the **Estrategia.** Discuss how using what they already know or have experienced will help students relate to, appreciate, and understand the poem.

Step 2 Have students read the **Antes de leer.** Lead a short discussion about **lo que le trae mucha felicidad a una madre y lo que le puede traer tristeza y pena.** Have students give as many examples as possible in their discussion.

Step 3 Have students read the poem to themselves.

Step 4 Play the recording as students follow along in their books.

Step 5 Have students read the **Durante la lectura** and discuss the answers to the questions.

Step 6 Call on a student to read one **estrofa** aloud. Ask questions about each **estrofa** before going on to the next one.

Step 7 Read the **Después de leer.** You may wish to have students share their opinions with the class.

⭐ Tips for Success ·······

A. Paraphrase the first **estrofa** or have an advanced learner do it.
En el comedor hay una mesa antigua. Sobre la mesa hay un mantel blanco. En la pared hay un cuadro. No se sabe quién es el artista. Es de un pintor anónimo. Hay también una alacena. Todo en el comedor está igual. No ha cambiado nada.

Estrategia

Usando lo ya experimentado Al leer muchas obras literarias debes identificarte con las palabras del autor, reflexionando sobre algo que tú mismo(a) ya has vivido. Tus experiencias personales tendrán una influencia en como percibes la situación del narrador.

Antes de leer

Reflexiona sobre el amor que tiene una madre por su hijo(a). No hay amor más sincero que el amor maternal. Piensa en lo que le trae mucha felicidad a la madre. Piensa también en lo que le puede traer tristeza y pena.

Durante la lectura

¿Qué información te da el título del poema? ¿Qué tendrá que ver con el estado de ánimo de la madre?

Después de leer

Forma tus opiniones sobre las razones del estado de ánimo de la madre.

86

El hermano ausente en la cena de Pascua 🎧

La misma mesa antigua y holgada[1], de nogal[2]
y sobre ella la misma blancura del mantel
y los cuadros de caza[3] de anónimo pincel
y la oscura alacena[4], todo, todo está igual…

5 Hay un sitio vacío en la mesa hacia el cual
mi madre tiende a veces su mirada de miel
y se musita el nombre del ausente; pero él
hoy no vendrá a sentarse en la mesa pascual.

La misma criada pone, sin dejarse sentir,
10 la suculenta vianda[5] y el plácido manjar[6]
pero no hay la alegría ni el afán de reír[7]

que animaran antaño la cena familiar;
y mi madre que acaso algo quiere decir,
ve el lugar del ausente y se pone a llorar.

---

[1] holgada *cómoda*
[2] nogal *tipo de madera*
[3] caza *hunting*
[4] alacena *cupboard*
[5] vianda *comida*
[6] manjar *meal*
[7] reír *laugh*

CULTURA
Un comedor en una casa de Perú

CAPÍTULO 3

B. Dramatize the following for **Estrofa 2** or have a student do it.
1. Show an empty chair.
2. Stare at the empty chair.
3. Murmur a name.
4. Put up your hands as you utter the name and look puzzled.

C. Ask questions about **Estrofas 3** and **4.**
¿Quién sirve la comida?

¿Es una criada nueva?
¿Qué sirve?
¿Hay mucha alegría?
¿Ríe la gente?
En el pasado, ¿había alegría? ¿Reía la gente?
¿Hacia dónde mira la madre?
¿Qué hace al ver el lugar?
¿Por qué?

¿Comprendes?

A **Parafraseando** ¿Cómo lo dice el poeta?
1. La misma mesa vieja y cómoda, de madera
2. y sobre la mesa el mismo mantel blanco
3. y las pinturas de caza de un artista desconocido
4. mi madre fija de vez en cuando su mirada dulce
5. pero no hay la felicidad ni el fuerte deseo de reír

B **Describiendo** Describe el comedor de la familia.

C **Recordando hechos** Contesta.
1. ¿Qué hay en la mesa?
2. ¿Quién mira hacia el sitio vacío?
3. ¿Qué se musita?
4. ¿Vendrá él hoy?

D **Explicando** Contesta.
¿Por qué es tan diferente esta cena familiar de las de antaño?

E **Llegando a conclusiones** Contesta.
¿Dónde estará el hermano ausente?

CULTURA
¿Es en esta casa que vive la familia que celebra la cena de Pascua?

PASAJES DE LA VIDA

ochenta y siete **87**

Literatura

▶ PRACTICE

¿Comprendes?

A Have students prepare this activity before going over it in class.

B and C Have students do these activities without looking up the answers.

D and E Encourage students to have animated discussions and use their imagination.

Teaching Options

If a student has experienced such a holiday dinner, he or she may want to talk about it. You may ask a question such as, **¿Hay alguien que pueda identificarte con la escena que nos presenta el autor en este poema?** Such a question does not force a student to talk about an unpleasant situation if he or she does not want to.

Pre-AP This reading will develop the skills that students need to be successful on the reading and writing sections of the AP exam. Listening to this reading will also help prepare them for the auditory component.

Answers

A
1. La misma mesa antigua y holgada, de nogal
2. y sobre la mesa la misma blancura del mantel
3. y los cuadros de caza de anónimo pincel
4. mi madre tiende a veces su mirada de miel
5. pero no hay la alegría y el afán de reír

B *Answers will vary but may include:*
En el comedor de la familia hay una vieja mesa de madera con un mantel blanco. Hay también cuadros de caza de un artista desconocido y una alacena oscura.

C
1. Hay un mantel blanco en la mesa.
2. La madre mira hacia el sitio vacío.
3. Se musita el nombre del ausente.
4. No, no vendrá hoy.

D *Answers will vary but may include:*
Esta cena es tan diferente de las de antaño porque el hermano no está y no hay alegría.

E *Answers will vary but may include:*
El hermano estará muerto. Tuvo un accidente y se murió.

87

Prepárate para el examen
Self-check for achievement

Resources

- Tests, pages 3.49–3.64
- Performance Assessment, Task 3, pages 3.65–3.66
- ExamView® Assessment Suite

✔ Self-check for achievement

This is a pre-test for students to take before you administer the chapter test. Note that each section is cross-referenced so students can easily find the material they feel they need to review. You may wish to use Self-Check Worksheet Transparency SC3 to have students complete this assessment in class or at home. You can correct the assessment yourself, or you may prefer to project the answers on the overhead in class using Self-Check Answers Transparency SC3A.

Differentiation

Slower Paced Learners

- Have students work in pairs to complete the Self-Check in class. This will allow them to check their answers through collaborative learning. Once they have finished, call on individuals to give the correct answers as you review together.
- Encourage students who need extra help to refer to the book icons and review any section before answering the questions.

To review **Vocabulario 1** and **Vocabulario 2,** turn to pages 64–65 and 68–69.

Vocabulario

1 **Completa con la palabra apropiada.**

1. Muchos trajes de novia tienen _____.
2. La novia y el novio son una _____.
3. Ellos quieren una ceremonia religiosa y van a casarse en la _____.
4. Durante la ceremonia nupcial los novios intercambian _____ de boda.
5. Una ceremonia civil tiene lugar en el _____.
6. Después de la ceremonia nupcial hay una _____.
7. Todos les dicen «_____» a los recién casados.
8. Durante la recepción hay un _____.
9. Un recién nacido católico recibe el _____.
10. El _____ bautiza al niño.
11. El _____ fúnebre va de la iglesia al cementerio.
12. El _____ tiene lugar en el cementerio.

Gramática

2 **Sigue el modelo.**

MODELO   desear / hacerlo →
         Deseo que tú lo hagas.

13. esperar / saberlo
14. preferir / tenerlo
15. insistir en / leerlo
16. temer / recordarlo
17. tener miedo de / perderte

To review **el subjuntivo con deseos,** turn to page 72.

3 **Completa con la forma apropiada del verbo.**

18. El profesor insiste en que nosotros _____. (aprender)
19. Yo espero que ustedes _____ buenos resultados. (tener)
20. Ellos desean que nosotros _____ felices. (ser)
21. Él prefiere que tú _____ conmigo. (ir)
22. Tememos que ellos _____ enfermos. (estar)

Answers

1

1. un velo
2. pareja
3. iglesia
4. anillos
5. ayuntamiento
6. recepción
7. Enhorabuena
8. cena (banquete, bufé)
9. bautizo
10. cura
11. cortejo
12. entierro (sepelio)

2

13. Espero que tú lo sepas.
14. Prefiero que tú lo tengas.
15. Insisto en que tú lo leas.
16. Temo que tú lo recuerdes.
17. Tengo miedo de que tú te pierdas.

3

18. aprendamos
19. tengan
20. seamos
21. vayas
22. estén

4 Completa las siguientes frases.

23. Me sorprende que tú _____.
24. Ellos se alegran de que nosotros _____.
25. Yo siento que ellos _____.
26. Ella está contenta que tú _____.
27. Es una lástima que yo _____.

5 Emplea el pronombre posesivo apropiado.

28–29. *Mi carro* es nuevo y *tu carro* es viejo.
30–31. *Nuestros amigos* pueden asistir pero *los amigos de José* no quieren asistir.
32–33. Yo he recibido *mi invitación*. ¿Has recibido *tu invitación*?
34–35. Tenemos *nuestros regalos* pero no tenemos *los regalos de ustedes*.

Cultura

6 Corrige las frases falsas.

36. La mayoría de las celebraciones o ritos que marcan los pasajes de la vida son de índole civil.
37. El bautizo es una ceremonia hebrea y el bat mitzvah es una ceremonia cristiana.
38. La edad legal para contraer matrimonio es la misma en todos los países hispanos.

7 Contesta.

39. En los países hispanos ¿dónde se casan muchas parejas?
40. ¿Cuál es el último pasaje de la vida?

PASAJES DE LA VIDA

To review **el subjuntivo con expresiones de emoción,** turn to page 74.

To review **los pronombres posesivos,** turn to page 76.

To review this cultural information, turn to pages 80–82.

Differentiation

Multiple Intelligences

To engage **visual-spatial** and **bodily-kinesthetic** learners, number from 1 to 40 on the board and call on a student to go to the board and write the correct answer (this may be done chronologically or you may allow students to choose the question they answer). Then have the student who wrote the first answer decide who will write the second, and so on, making sure that all students get called on at least once. This type of review activity is particularly appealing to **interpersonal** learners but will also benefit the class on the whole by promoting an inclusive, student-centered learning environment.

Pre-AP Students preparing for the AP exam may benefit from a set time limit when completing this Self-Check. This may also help to identify students with learning difficulties or slower paced students who need extra help. Be sure to review the correct answers to ensure that all students complete the Self-Check.

GLENCOE 🔍 Technology

Online Learning in the Classroom

You may wish to have students use QuickPass code ASD7844c3 for additional test preparation. They will be able to complete a self-check quiz for chapter review.

Answers

4 *Answers will vary, but students should use the correct form of the subjunctive.*

5
28. El mío
29. el tuyo
30. Los nuestros
31. los suyos
32. la mía
33. la tuya
34. los nuestros
35. los suyos

6
36. La mayoría de las celebraciones o ritos que marcan los pasajes de la vida son de índole religiosa.
37. El bautizo es una ceremonia cristiana y el bat mitzvah es una ceremonia hebrea.

38. La edad legal para contraer matrimonio en los países hispanos varía de un país a otro.

7
39. En los países hispanos muchas parejas se casan en la iglesia.
40. El último pasaje de la vida es la muerte.

89

Prepárate para el examen ✓
Practice for oral proficiency

⭐Tips for Success ·······

Encourage students to say as much as possible when they do these open-ended activities. Tell them not to be afraid to make mistakes, since the goal of the activities is real-life communication. If someone in the group makes an error, allow the others to politely correct him or her. Let students choose the activities they would like to do.

Tell students to feel free to elaborate on the basic theme and to be creative. They may use props, pictures, or posters if they wish.

·······························

Pre-AP These oral activities will give students the opportunity to develop and improve their speaking skills so that they may succeed on the speaking portion of the AP exam.

Note: You may want to use the rubric below to help students organize their speaking activities.

---

1 **Una boda**

✓ *Discuss weddings you have attended*

Trabaja con un(a) compañero(a). Cada uno(a) de ustedes va a describir una boda a la que has asistido. Luego comparen las dos bodas. ¿Había algunas diferencias entre las dos? ¿Cuáles eran las diferencias?

2 **Mi boda**

✓ *Talk about the type of wedding you prefer*

¿Has pensado alguna vez en tu boda? ¿Qué tipo de boda quieres tener? ¿Prefieres una gala o algo sencillo?

3 **Pasajes de la vida**

✓ *Discuss passages of life*

Con un grupo de compañeros, discute los ritos o ceremonias de pasajes de vida que ustedes han experimentado. ¿Han tenido experiencias diferentes? ¿Juega la religión un papel (rol) importante en estas ceremonias? ¿Juega su ascendencia cultural o étnica un papel en las ceremonias?

4 **Una fiesta**

✓ *Describe a celebration*

Describe tu fiesta favorita. ¿Qué celebra o conmemora? ¿Cuáles son algunas cosas que hacen los invitados durante la fiesta? ¿Hay ciertas costumbres tradicionales? ¿Cúales son? ¿Son étnicas o religiosas?

5 **Los deseos de mis padres**

✓ *Discuss what your parents want you to do*

Trabajen en grupos de cuatro y discutan lo que desean sus padres que ustedes hagan. Comparen los resultados y determinen si sus padres tienen los mismos deseos.

CULTURA

Decoraciones de Navidad en Madrid

Scoring Rubric for Speaking

	4	3	2	1
vocabulary	extensive use of vocabulary, including idiomatic expressions	adequate use of vocabulary and idiomatic expressions	limited vocabulary marked with some anglicisms	limited vocabulary marked by frequent anglicisms that force interpretation by the listener
grammar	few or no grammatical errors	minor grammatical errors	some serious grammatical errors	serious grammatical errors
pronunciation	good intonation and largely accurate pronunciation with slight accent	acceptable intonation and pronunciation with distinctive accent	errors in intonation and pronunciation with heavy accent	errors in intonation and pronunciation that interfere with listener's comprehension
content	thorough response with interesting and pertinent detail	thorough response with sufficient detail	some detail, but not sufficient	general, insufficient response

Tarea

In as much detail as possible, describe either your dream wedding or your ideal eighteenth birthday party. In addition to describing the scene, you should also discuss your hopes and wishes as well as your emotions. Your goal will be to create a description that is so vivid that the reader feels as if he or she is present at the event.

Writing Strategy

Visualizing A vivid description should draw the reader into the writer's world. In order to recreate this world, you must first have an image of it in your head. Before you begin to write, take some time to imagine the picture you want to capture and relay to the reader.

Close your eyes and visualize the scene that you will translate into words. Think about everything that your senses might perceive during this special occasion in your life.

- Who will be there and why? What are they wearing, saying, and doing?
- What emotions are you feeling and why?
- What is the atmosphere like? How does the scene appear and what is the mood?
- What is happening? How do you react, respond, or feel as a result of your surroundings?
- What do you hope will happen? Who do you hope will be there? What do you wish to occur?

❶ Prewrite

First use the diagram to help you decide what you would like to include in your description. Then, as you consider the different aspects of your description, think of more specific questions, such as:

❷ Write

- Set the stage by identifying the event and describing the scene that surrounds it.
- Write about the event in chronological order, focusing on those aspects that will interest the reader.
- Remember to incorporate new vocabulary that you have learned from the chapter.
- Be sure to show your understanding of the use of the subjunctive to express wishes and emotions.

Evaluate

Your teacher will evaluate you on your ability to write a vivid description as well as on the correct use of vocabulary and grammar.

PASAJES DE LA VIDA

Pre-AP This **tarea** will give students the opportunity to develop and improve their writing skills so that they may succeed on the writing portion of the AP exam.

Note: You may want to use the rubric below to help students organize their writing task.

Scoring Rubric for Writing

	4	3	2	1
vocabulary	precise, varied	functional, fails to communicate complete meaning	limited to basic words, often inaccurate	inadequate
grammar	excellent, very few or no errors	some errors, do not hinder communication	numerous errors interfere with communication	many errors, little sentence structure
content	thorough response to the topic	generally thorough response to the topic	partial response to the topic	insufficient response to the topic
organization	well organized, ideas presented clearly and logically	loosely organized, but main ideas present	some attempts at organization, but with confused sequencing	lack of organization

Resources

- Audio Activities TE, pages 3.32–3.33
- Audio CD 3, Tracks 25–27
- Workbook, page 3.14

Grammar Review

This page provides a quick "at a glance" summary of the grammar points students have learned in this chapter. The corresponding page numbers are also listed so that students can easily find each grammar point as it was presented.

Differentiation

Multiple Intelligences

You may want to call on **verbal-linguistic** and **logical-mathematical** learners for whom grammar often comes easily to explain the main concepts to their classmates in their own words. Having students explain the concepts in different ways may also help slower paced learners or students with learning difficulties.

Repaso del Capítulo ③

Gramática

- **El subjuntivo con deseos** *(page 72)*
  The subjunctive is used in clauses introduced by each of the following expressions, since the information in the dependent clause is not definite.

desear	mandar
esperar	temer
preferir	tener miedo de
insistir en	

  Espero que no lleguen tarde.

- **El subjuntivo con expresiones de emoción** *(page 74)*
  The subjunctive is used in a clause that is introduced by a verb or expression that conveys an emotion.

  Me alegro de que él esté.

  The following are verbs and expressions that convey emotion.

alegrarse de	gustar
estar contento(a), triste	sentir
sorprender	ser una lástima (pena)

- **Los pronombres posesivos** *(page 76)*
  A possessive pronoun replaces a noun modified by a possessive adjective. As with any pronoun, it must agree in number and gender with the noun it modifies.

  el mío, la mía, los míos, las mías
  el tuyo, la tuya, los tuyos, las tuyas
  el nuestro, la nuestra, los nuestros, las nuestras
  el vuestro, la vuestra, los vuestros, las vuestras
  el suyo, la suya, los suyos, las suyas

CULTURA

Estas jóvenes chilenas están contentas que no haya más clases hoy y que puedan disfrutar de un rato libre.

There are a number of cognates in this list. See how many you and a partner can find. Who can find the most? Compare your list with those of your classmates.

Vocabulario

Talking about a wedding

la ceremonia	la iglesia	el/la recién casado(a)	el velo
el anuncio nupcial	el cura	la dama de honor	el anillo de boda
el matrimonio, el casamiento	la novia	el padrino	casarse
la boda	el novio	el paje	
	la pareja	el traje de novia	

Talking about a civil ceremony

la ceremonia civil	el ayuntamiento	firmar
el registro de matrimonio	el alcalde, la alcaldesa	por (el, lo) civil

Talking about a wedding reception

una recepción	un banquete,	un regalo	¡Enhorabuena!
una cena	un bufé	en honor de	

Talking about a baptism

el bautizo	el padrino	la pila
el recién nacido	la madrina	bautizar

Talking about a birthday party

el cumpleaños	el bizcocho	la vela	cumplir... años
el pastel	la torta, la tarta	nacer	celebrar

Talking about a funeral

una esquela, un obituario	el ataúd	el cementerio, el camposanto	el entierro, el sepelio
el velorio	la viuda del difunto	el cortejo fúnebre	

Other useful words and expressions

los pasajes de la vida	alegre	esperar
la alegría	alegrarse	intercambiar
	sorprender	tener lugar

The words listed below come from this chapter's literary selection, *El hermano ausente en la cena de Pascua*. They were selected to become part of your active vocabulary because of their relatively high frequency.

el afán	la criada	vacío(a)
el pincel	musitar	acaso
la miel	antaño	

Don't forget the chapter project and cultural activities found on pages 60C–60D. Students have learned all the information that they will need to complete these engaging enrichment tasks.

Juego The cognates in this list are: **la ceremonia, el anuncio nupcial, el matrimonio, la dama de honor, civil, el registro, una recepción, un banquete, un bufé, en honor de, el bautizo, celebrar, un obituario, el cementerio, el cortejo fúnebre.**

Vocabulary Review

The words and phrases in **Vocabulario 1** and **2** have been taught for productive use in this chapter. They are summarized here as a resource for both student and teacher. This list also serves as a convenient resource for the **Prepárate para el examen** activities on pages 88–91.

GLENCOE SPANISH

Why It Works!

This vocabulary reference list has not been translated into English for two reasons. First, it is recommended that students learn the new vocabulary through direct association with images on the **Vocabulario** pages. Second, all vocabulary is reintroduced in the chapter many times, and upon completion of the chapter students should be familiar with the meaning of all the words. If there are words that students still do not know, they can refer back to the vocabulary presentation in the chapter or the dictionary at the end of the book. If, however, it is your preference to give students the English translations, please refer to Vocabulary Transparency V3.1 or to the Chapter 3 PowerPoint® presentation on PowerTeach.

Differentiation

Slower Paced Learners

Slower paced learners may benefit from creating their own visual dictionary of words in this list. They can either draw their own depictions or use images from the Internet or magazines.

Repaso cumulativo

Every chapter of ¡Así se dice! contains this review section of previously learned material. By recycling information from previous chapters, the cumulative review serves to remind students that they need to continue practicing what they have learned after finishing each chapter.

Activity 1 This activity reviews family vocabulary. See the Spanish-English/English-Spanish dictionary at the end of this book.

🎧 **Audio Script** *(CD 3, Track 28)*
1. Antonio López es el esposo de Ana López.
2. Los López, Ana y Antonio, tienen tres nietos.
3. Elisa López es hija única.
4. Marisa López es la sobrina de Ana López.
5. Los López tienen dos mascotas.
6. Juan López es el hijo de Marisa y Carlos López.
7. Maja es la hermana de Chispa.
8. Juan y Elisa son los primos de Ana y Antonio López.

Activity 2 This activity reviews possessive adjectives. See the Grammar Review, page SR15.

Activity 3 This activity reviews vocabulary needed to set a table at home. See the Spanish-English/English-Spanish dictionary at the end of this book.

Activity 4 This activity reviews informal commands. See the Grammar Review, page SR30.

94

Repaso cumulativo

Repasa lo que ya has aprendido

These activities will help you review and remember what you have learned so far in Spanish.

La familia López
Carlos
Marisa
Ana
Antonio
Juan
Elisa
Maja
Chispa

 1 **Escucha las frases.** Indica si cada frase es correcta según lo que ves en el dibujo.

 2 **Completa con el adjetivo posesivo.**
1. El otro hijo de mi padre es _____ hermano.
2. El hermano de mi padre es _____ tío y _____ hijos son _____ primos.
3. El esposo de mi tía Sandra es Alejandro. _____ esposo es _____ tío.
4. ¿Quieres que yo vaya a _____ casa esta tarde? ¿Dónde está _____ casa? Es necesario que tú me dés el número de _____ móvil.
5. Nosotros vivimos en San Luis. _____ casa tiene dos pisos y alrededor de _____ casa tenemos un jardín. _____ jardín es muy bonito.
6. Susana va a visitar a _____ abuelos. _____ abuelos viven bastante lejos de aquí y siempre están contentos de ver a _____ querida nieta.

 3 **Contesta.**
Dentro de poco tu familia va a comer. Una tarea tuya es la de poner la mesa. ¿Qué vas a poner en la mesa?

4 **Completa con el mandato de tú.**
1. _____ más. (comer)
2. _____ la sal. (pasar)
3. _____ el postre. (servir)
4. _____ la mesa. (poner)
5. _____ conmigo a la cocina. (venir)
6. _____ los platos. (lavar)
7. _____ la mesa. (limpiar)

Answers

1
1. correcta
2. incorrecta
3. incorrecta
4. incorrecta
5. correcta
6. correcta
7. incorrecta
8. incorrecta

2
1. mi
2. mi, sus, mis
3. Su, mi
4. tu, tu, tu
5. Nuestra, nuestra, Nuestro
6. sus, Sus, su

3 *Answers will vary but may include:*
Voy a poner en la mesa los platos, los tenedores, los cuchillos, las cucharitas, las cucharas, las tazas, los platillos, los vasos y las servilletas.

4
1. Come
2. Pasa
3. Sirve
4. Pon
5. Ven
6. Lava
7. Limpia

5 Pon las frases de la Actividad 4 en la forma negativa.

 6 Cambia a la forma negativa.
1. Levántate.
2. Acuéstate.
3. Háblame.
4. Dámelo.
5. Pásamelo.
6. Dímelo.

 7 Prepara una lista de ingredientes que lleva el arroz con pollo.

 8 Personaliza. Da respuestas personales.
1. ¿Has estado en la Florida?
2. Si has estado en la Florida, ¿qué ciudades has visitado en este estado?
3. Si no has estado en la Florida, ¿cuál es otro estado que has visitado?
4. ¿Has conocido a mucha gente?
5. ¿Has vuelto a visitar a tus amigos?

9 Escoge del banco de palabras y completa.

abierto	vuelto	dicho
hecho	puesto	visto

1. Nosotros hemos _____ el viaje.
2. ¿Quién ha _____ la puerta?
3. ¿Dónde has _____ los boletos?
4. Ellos no han _____.
5. Yo he _____ la exposición en el museo.
6. ¿Quién te ha _____ tal cosa?

CULTURA
La Plaza Mayor en el Viejo Madrid

PASAJES DE LA VIDA

95

Repaso cumulativo

Activity 5 This activity reviews the negative of the familiar command. See page 13.

Activity 6 This activity reviews the negative of the formal command. See page 11.

Activity 7 This activity reviews the recipe for Arroz con pollo and the related vocabulary. See page 16.

Activity 8 This activity reviews the present perfect tense. See page R66.

Activity 9 This activity reviews the present perfect tense. See page R66.

Pre-AP To give students further open-ended oral or written practice, or to assess proficiency, go to AP Proficiency Practice Transparency AP14.

GLENCOE Technology

Audio in the Classroom
The ¡Así se dice! Audio Program for Chapter 3 has 28 activities, which afford students extensive listening and speaking practice.

Online Learning in the Classroom
You may wish to have students use QuickPass code ASD7844c3 for additional cumulative review. They will be able to complete a self-check quiz.

Answers

5
1. No comas más.
2. No pases la sal.
3. No sirvas el postre.
4. No pongas la mesa.
5. No vengas conmigo a la cocina.
6. No laves los platos.
7. No limpies la mesa.

6
1. No te levantes.
2. No te acuestes.
3. No me hables.
4. No me los des.
5. No me lo pases.
6. No me lo digas.

7
el pollo, el arroz, el aceite de oliva, las cebollas, los tomates, los pimientos, los pimientos morrones, los chorizos, los guisantes congelados, el ajo, el consomé de pollo y el azafrán o bujol

8
1. Sí, (No, no) he estado en la Florida.
2. He visitado _____ y _____.
3. He visitado _____.
4. Sí (No, no) he conocido a mucha gente.
5. Sí, (No, no) he vuelto a visitar a mis amigos.

9
1. hecho
2. abierto
3. puesto
4. vuelto
5. visto
6. dicho

Chapter Overview
Quehaceres

● Scope and Sequence

Topics
- The hair salon
- Washing clothes
- Mailing letters and packages
- The bank

Culture
- European currency
- Hair salons, Laundromats, and banks in Spanish-speaking countries
- *El mensajero de San Martín*

Functions
- How to talk about errands
- How to discuss preparing for a trip through Andalusia
- How to read a short story from Argentina

Structure
- The subjunctive with expressions of doubt
- The subjunctive with adverbial clauses
- The pluperfect, conditional perfect, and future perfect tenses

● Planning Guide

	required	recommended	optional
Vocabulario (*pages 100–103*) La peluquería La lavandería El correo El banco	✔		
Gramática (*pages 104–111*) El subjuntivo con expresiones de duda El subjuntivo en cláusulas adverbiales Otros tiempos compuestos	✔		
Conversación (*pages 112–113*) ¡Tanto que hacer!		✔	
Lectura cultural (*pages 114–115*) Los preparativos para un viaje		✔	
Literatura (*pages 116–123*) El mensajero de San Martín			✔
Prepárate para el examen (*pages 124–127*)			✔
Repaso cumulativo (*pages 130–131*)			✔

Correlations to National Foreign Language Standards

Page numbers in light print refer to the Student Edition. Page numbers in bold print refer to the Teacher Edition.	
Communication Standard 1.1 Interpersonal	pp. **98–99, 102,** 104, **105,** 107, **109, 110,** 111, **113, 114, 122, 123,** 126
Communication Standard 1.2 Interpretive	pp. 102, **102,** 103, **103,** 104, 106, 107, **107,** 109, 110, **112,** 113, 114, **114,** 115, **115,** 118, 119, **119, 120, 121,** 123, **123,** 125, **125,** 131, **131**
Communication Standard 1.3 Presentational	pp. **96C, 100, 103, 105,** 106, **112,** 113, **113, 122, 123, 124,** 126, 127, **128, 129**
Cultures Standard 2.1	pp. **96C, 96D,** 98, **98–99,** 99, 104, 106, 107, 110, 113, 114, 115, 127
Cultures Standard 2.2	pp. **96D,** 98, **98,** 99, 109, **109,** 113, 114, **114,** 115, **117,** 125
Connections Standard 3.1	pp. **96C, 96D, 97, 109,** 115, **115,** 117, **117,** 118, **123**
Connections Standard 3.2	pp. 100, **100, 103,** 105, **105, 108,** 109, 110, **110,** 111, **111,** 113, **113,** 118–122, 123
Comparisons Standard 4.1	pp. **101,** 102, 106, **109, 119, 128,** 129
Comparisons Standard 4.2	pp. **96D,** 97, **97, 99,** 113, 114, **114,** 117, 119, 127
Communities Standard 5.1	pp. **96C, 96D,** 102, 107, **113,** 115, **124, 126, 128**
Communities Standard 5.2	pp. 100, **100,** 105, **105,** 106, **108,** 109, 110, **110,** 113, **113, 115**

To read the ACTFL Standards in their entirety, see the front of the Teacher Edition.

Student Resources

Print

Workbook *(pp. 4.3–4.12)*
Audio Activities *(pp. 4.13–4.17)*
Pre-AP Workbook, Chapter 4

Technology

- StudentWorks™ Plus
- ¡Así se dice! Vocabulario en vivo
- ¡Así se dice! Gramática en vivo
- ¡Así se dice! Diálogo en vivo
- ¡Así se dice! Cultura en vivo
- Vocabulary PuzzleMaker
- **QuickPass** glencoe.com

Teacher Resources

Print

TeacherTools, Chapter 4
    Workbook TE *(pp. 4.3–4.12)*
    Audio Activities TE *(pp. 4.15–4.32)*
    Quizzes 1–4 *(pp. 4.35–4.39)*
    Tests *(pp. 4.42–4.64)*
    Performance Assessment, Task 4 *(pp. 4.65–4.66)*

Technology

- Quick Start Transparencies 4.1–4.4
- Vocabulary Transparencies V4.1–V4.3
- Audio CD 4
- *ExamView® Assessment Suite*
- TeacherWorks™ Plus
- PowerTeach
- ¡Así se dice! Video Program
- Vocabulary PuzzleMaker
- **QuickPass** glencoe.com

Chapter Project

Una tira cómica

Students will work individually and in small groups to create a comic strip about errands and chores.

1. Divide the class into groups of three or four and have each group generate ideas for a comic strip. Since this is a collaborative project, each member of the group will be responsible for drawing several scenes. Students will work together on the arrangement of the story and illustrations.

2. Students should work as a team to come up with an original story related to errands and chores, including information about the characters. Groups should then choose a title for their comic strip according to the story. Although the students may work together to decide the overall visual elements of the comic strip, each member should create a different section.

3. Each group member will be responsible for illustrating an equal number of scenes and will also include any accompanying text. The text should be related to the pictures, and the illustrations should be bright and colorful. Each student should hand in a sketch of his or her scenes, along with an initial draft of the text.

4. After checking the sketches and drafts or having students peer edit them, have students correct any mistakes individually and then work together on the final draft. Students should submit their original sketches and drafts with their final versions.

Expansion: Students could also perform skits based on the stories told in their comic strips. Remind them to use appropriate polite gestures and expressions when they perform the skits.

Scoring Rubric for Project

	1	3	5
Evidence of planning	Draft and sketches are not provided.	Draft and sketches are provided, but draft is not corrected.	Sketches and corrected draft are provided.
Use of illustrations	Illustrations are unidentifiable or unrelated to text.	Illustrations are identifiable but lack color and do not fully relate to text.	Illustrations are identifiable, colorful, and fully relate to text.
Presentation	Comic strip contains little of the required elements.	Comic strip contains some of the required elements.	Comic strip contains all the required elements.

Culture

● Día de la Raza

The voyage of Christopher Columbus to the New World is remembered in the United States during the month of October. This is a controversial holiday for many because of the treatment of the indigenous people that followed Spain's occupation of South and Central America. So instead of celebrating Columbus Day, most Hispanic countries celebrate **Día de la Raza** on October 12. **Día de la Raza** celebrates the Hispanic heritage of Latin America and the birth of the first **latinoamericanos** with the arrival of the Spanish colonists. Festivities on this day may include parades, dances, bullfights, and plenty of food and music. The celebration goes by different names: in Spain, it is called **Día de la Hispanidad;** in Venezuela, **Día de la Resistencia Indígena;** and in Costa Rica, **Día de las Culturas.**

● Tango

While most people think of a type of dance when they see or hear the word, **tango** was a type of music before it was a popular ballroom dance. **Tango** music originated among the European immigrants in Argentina during the late nineteenth century. It was the music of the lower class. However, after **tango** music had been further refined and gained popularity in Europe in the early 1900s, Argentina's upper class also started to accept this new form of music and dance. By the end of World War I, the **tango** had international popularity. It is typically performed by a sextet referred to as an **orquesta típica,** comprised of two violins, piano, double bass and two **bandoneones,** an instrument similar to an accordion produced in Germany.

Some **tango** music is too complex for dancing—one of the most famous **tango** singers, Carlos Gardel, produced music that was meant for listening rather than dancing. But there is plenty of **tango** dance music, most of which was produced between the mid-1930s and the late 1950s during a period known as the Golden Age. Much of this music is still played today in dancehalls and ballrooms, but **tango** music has continued to evolve. Contemporary versions infuse more modern instrumentation with the traditional structure of **tango** music. Students can investigate the various forms of contemporary **tango** using Internet resources and list American movies and television shows they have seen in which the **tango** is danced.

50-Minute Lesson Plans

	Objective	Present	Practice	Assess/Homework
Day 1	Talk about running errands	Chapter Opener, pp. 96–97 (5 min.) Introducción al tema, pp. 98–99 (10 min.) Core Instruction/Vocabulario, pp. 100–101 (15 min.)	Activities 1–3, p. 102 (15 min.) InfoGap, p. SR5 (5 min.)	Student Workbook Activities A–C, pp. 4.3–4.4 **QuickPass** Vocabulary Practice
Day 2	Talk about running errands	Quick Start, p. 100 (5 min.) Review Vocabulario, pp. 100–101 (5 min.) Video, Vocabulario en vivo (10 min.)	Activities 4–5, p. 103 (10 min.) Estudio de palabras, p. 103 (5 min.) Total Physical Response, p. 101 (5 min.) Audio Activities A–D, pp. 4.15–4.18 (10 min.)	Student Workbook Activities D–F, pp. 4.4–4.5 **QuickPass** Vocabulary Practice
Day 3	The subjunctive with expressions of doubt	Quick Start, p. 104 (5 min.) Core Instruction/Gramática, El subjuntivo con expresiones de duda, p. 104 (10 min.) Video, Gramática en vivo (5 min.)	Activities 1–5, p. 105 (10 min.) Audio Activities A–D, pp. 4.18–4.19 (10 min.)	Quiz 1, p. 4.35 (10 min.) Student Workbook Activities A–C, p. 4.6 **QuickPass** Grammar Practice
Day 4	The subjunctive with adverbial clauses	Quick Start, p. 106 (5 min.) Core Instruction/Gramática, El subjuntivo en cláusulas adverbiales, p. 106 (10 min.)	Activities 6–9, pp. 106–107 (15 min.) Audio Activities E–F, p. 4.20 (10 min.)	Quiz 2, p. 4.36 (10 min.) Student Workbook Activities A–C, p. 4.7 **QuickPass** Grammar Practice
Day 5	The pluperfect, conditional perfect, and future perfect tenses	Core Instruction/Gramática, Otros tiempos compuestos, p. 108 (15 min.) Video, Cultura en vivo (10 min.)	Activities 10–13, pp. 109–110 (15 min.)	Quiz 3, p. 4.37 (10 min.) Student Workbook Activities A–B, p. 4.8 **QuickPass** Grammar Practice
Day 6	The pluperfect, conditional perfect, and future perfect tenses	Quick Start, p. 108 (5 min.) Review Gramática, Otros tiempos compuestos, p. 108 (10 min.) Video, Gramática en vivo (10 min.)	Activities 14–17, pp. 110–111 (15 min.) Audio Activities G–L, pp. 4.21–4.23 (10 min.)	Student Workbook Activities C–D, pp. 4.9–4.10 **QuickPass** Grammar Practice
Day 7	Develop reading and listening comprehension skills	Core Instruction/Conversación, p. 112 (20 min.) Video, Diálogo en vivo (10 min.)	¿Comprendes? A–B, p. 113 (10 min.)	Quiz 4, p. 4.38 (10 min.) ¿Comprendes? C, p. 113 **QuickPass** Conversation
Day 8	Discuss preparing for a trip through Andalusia	Core Instruction/Lectura cultural, p. 114 (20 min.)	¿Comprendes? A–B, p. 115 (15 min.)	Listening Comprehension Test, pp. 4.59–4.61 (15 min.) ¿Comprendes? C, p. 115 **QuickPass** Reading Practice
Day 9	Read a short story from Argentina	Core Instruction/Vocabulario, p. 116 (5 min.) Core Instruction/Literatura, pp. 117–122 (30 min.)	Vocabulario, Práctica, p. 116 (5 min.) ¿Comprendes? A–B, p. 123 (10 min.)	¿Comprendes? C–E, p. 123 **QuickPass** Reading Practice
Day 10	Read a short story from Argentina	Review Literatura, pp. 117–122 (10 min.)	¿Comprendes? C–E, p. 123 (10 min.) Prepárate para el examen, pp. 124–125 (20 min.)	Prepárate para el examen, Practice for written proficiency, p. 127 **QuickPass** Reading Practice
Day 11	Chapter review	Repaso del Capítulo 4, pp. 128–129 (15 min.)	Prepárate para el examen, Practice for oral proficiency, p. 126 (20 min.)	Test for Writing Proficiency, p. 4.64 (15 min.) Review for chapter test
Day 12	Chapter 4 Tests (50 min.) Reading and Writing Test, pp. 4.47–4.54 Literature Test, pp. 4.55–4.57 Speaking Test, p. 4.62 Test for Oral Proficiency, p. 4.63			

90-Minute Lesson Plans

	Objective	Present	Practice	Assess/Homework
Block 1	Talk about running errands	Chapter Opener, pp. 96–97 (5 min.) Introducción al tema, pp. 98–99 (15 min.) Quick Start, p. 100 (5 min.) Core Instruction/Vocabulario, pp. 100–101 (15 min.)	Activities 1–5, pp. 102–103 (20 min.) Estudio de palabras, p. 103 (5 min.) Total Physical Response, p. 101 (5 min.) InfoGap, p. SR5 (5 min.) Audio Activities A–D, pp. 4.15–4.18 (15 min.)	Student Workbook Activities A–F, pp. 4.3–4.5 **QuickPass** Vocabulary Practice
Block 2	The subjunctive with expressions of doubt The subjunctive with adverbial clauses	Quick Start, p. 104 (5 min.) Core Instruction/Gramática, El subjuntivo con expresiones de duda, p. 104 (10 min.) Video, Gramática en vivo (10 min.) Core Instruction/Gramática, El subjuntivo en cláusulas adverbiales, p. 106 (10 min.)	Activities 1–5, p. 105 (15 min.) Activities 6–9, pp. 106–107 (15 min.) Audio Activities A–F, pp. 4.18–4.20 (15 min.)	Quiz 1, p. 4.35 (10 min.) Student Workbook Activities A–C, p. 4.6 Student Workbook Activities A–C, p. 4.7 **QuickPass** Grammar Practice
Block 3	The pluperfect, conditional perfect, and future perfect tenses	Quick Start, p. 108 (5 min.) Core Instruction/Gramática, Otros tiempos compuestos, p. 108 (10 min.) Video, Cultura en vivo (10 min.) Video, Gramática en vivo (10 min.)	Activities 10–17, pp. 109–111 (25 min.) Audio Activities G–L, pp. 4.21–4.23 (10 min.)	Quizzes 2–3, pp. 4.36–4.37 (20 min.) Student Workbook Activities A–D, pp. 4.8–4.10 **QuickPass** Grammar Practice
Block 4	Discuss preparing for a trip through Andalusia	Core Instruction/Conversación, p. 112 (20 min.) Video, Diálogo en vivo (10 min.) Core Instruction/Lectura cultural, p. 114 (20 min.)	¿Comprendes? A–C, p. 113 (15 min.) ¿Comprendes? A–C, p. 115 (15 min.)	Quiz 4, p. 4.38 (10 min.) **QuickPass** Conversation, Reading Practice
Block 5	Read a short story from Argentina	Core Instruction/Vocabulario, p. 116 (5 min.) Core Instruction/Literatura, pp. 117–122 (30 min.)	Vocabulario, Práctica, p. 116 (5 min.) ¿Comprendes? A–E, p. 123 (20 min.) Prepárate para el examen, Practice for oral proficiency 1–3, p. 126 (15 min.)	Listening Comprehension Test, pp. 4.59–4.61 (15 min.) **QuickPass** Reading Practice
Block 6	Chapter Review	Repaso del Capítulo 4, pp. 128–129 (15 min.)	Prepárate para el examen, pp. 124–125 (20 min.) Prepárate para el examen, Practice for oral proficiency 4–5, p. 126 (15 min.) Prepárate para el examen, Practice for written proficiency, p. 127 (30 min.)	Literature Test, pp. 4.55–4.57 (10 min.) Review for chapter test

Block 7	Chapter 4 Tests (50 min.)
	    Reading and Writing Test, pp. 4.47–4.54
	    Speaking Test, p. 4.62
	    Test for Oral Proficiency, p. 4.63
	    Test for Writing Proficiency, p. 4.64
	Chapter Project, p. 96C (40 min.)			

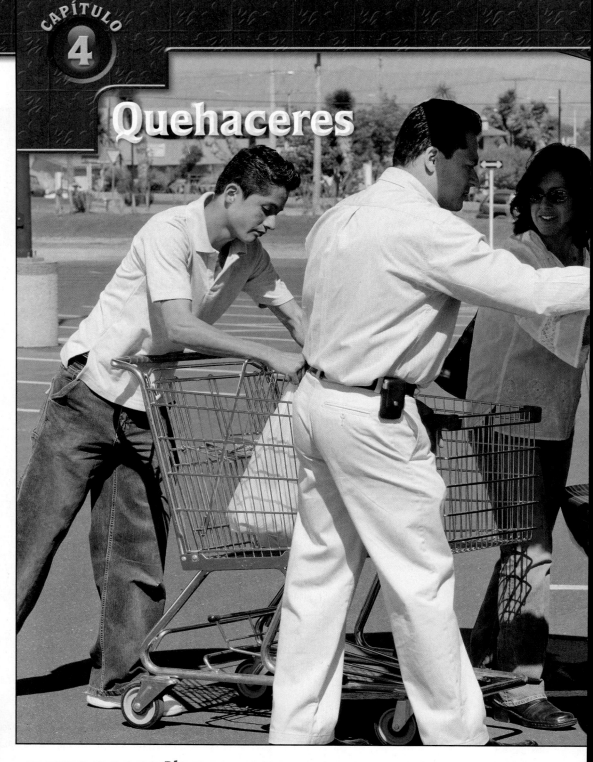

Preview

In this chapter, students will learn the basic vocabulary they need to do some routine errands and chores. They will learn these topics by joining a group of Spanish students who have a lot to do before leaving on a trip to Andalusia. Students will also read an Argentine story about the routine chore of carrying a message before e-mail or even mail service. Students will use the subjunctive with expressions of doubt and adverbial clauses. They will also learn to use the pluperfect and conditional perfect tenses and to recognize the future perfect.

Pacing

It is important to note that once you reach **¡Bravo!** in the chapter, there is no more new material for the students to learn. The rest of the chapter recycles what has already been covered. The suggested pacing listed here leaves two to three days for review, assessment, and enrichment activities such as the chapter project.

Vocabulario	1–2 days
Gramática	2–3 days
Conversación	1 day
Lectura cultural	1 day
Literatura	1 day

Quehaceres

TeacherWorks *Plus*

The **¡Así se dice!** TeacherWorks™ Plus CD-ROM is an all-in-one planner and resource center. You may wish to use several of the following features as you plan and present the Chapter 4 material: Interactive Teacher Edition, Interactive Lesson Planner with Calendar, and Point and Click Access to Teaching Resources including Hotlinks to the Internet and Correlations to the National Standards.

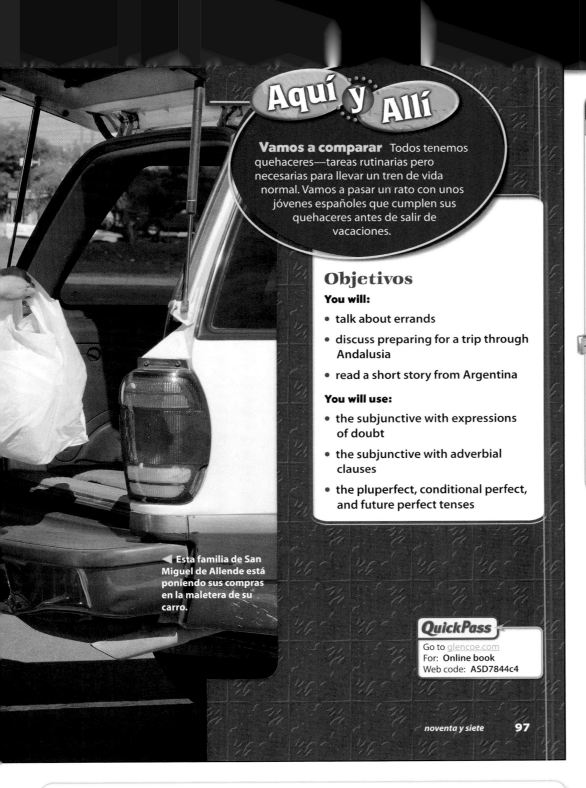

Aquí y Allí

Vamos a comparar Todos tenemos quehaceres—tareas rutinarias pero necesarias para llevar un tren de vida normal. Vamos a pasar un rato con unos jóvenes españoles que cumplen sus quehaceres antes de salir de vacaciones.

Objetivos

You will:

- talk about errands
- discuss preparing for a trip through Andalusia
- read a short story from Argentina

You will use:

- the subjunctive with expressions of doubt
- the subjunctive with adverbial clauses
- the pluperfect, conditional perfect, and future perfect tenses

◀ Esta familia de San Miguel de Allende está poniendo sus compras en la maletera de su carro.

QuickPass

Go to glencoe.com
For: **Online book**
Web code: **ASD7844c4**

Cultural Comparison
Students will join a group of young Spaniards as they go about their chores to prepare for a trip to Andalusia. They will also learn the task of getting a message from one place to another before the advent of mail service or e-mail. This sometimes took a degree of heroism.

Cultural Snapshot
Have students look at this photograph and consider whether or not it could have been taken in the United States. Although there are differences in lifestyles from one country to another, there are also many similarities these days.

Quia **Quia Interactive Online Student Edition** found at quia.com allows students to complete activities online and submit them for computer grading for instant feedback or teacher grading with suggestions for what to review. Students can also record speaking activities, listen to chapter audio, and watch the videos that correspond with each chapter. As a teacher you are able to create rosters, set grading parameters, and post assignments for each class. After students complete activities, you can view the results and recommend remediation or review. You can also add your own customized activities for additional student practice.

Introducción al tema

> ### PRESENT

Introduce the theme of the chapter by having students look at the photographs on these pages. Later, once you have presented the **Vocabulario** section, you may want to return to these pages. Students will be able to read and understand the written information and answer any corresponding questions. Encourage students to also refer back to these photographs as they learn more about daily tasks and chores in Spain and Latin America.

Cultural Snapshot

Nicaragua *(page 98)* ¿Es una peluquería unisex para señores y señoras? ¿Hay peluquerías unisex donde vives?

México *(page 98)* Stands that sell a variety of merchandise, particularly food, are very common in all areas of Latin America. **¿Dónde está este puesto de comida? ¿Es conveniente comer en un puesto como este cuando uno está apresurado y no tiene mucho tiempo? ¿Hay muchos puestos de comida donde vives?**

España *(page 98)* The ornate Palacio de Telecomunicaciones on the Plaza de Cibeles in central Madrid was built in 1918. **¿Cómo se llama este edificio? ¿De qué sirve? ¿Hay una casa de correos tan bonita y elegante como esta cerca de donde vives?**

Introducción al tema
Quehaceres

Mira las fotos para familiarizarte con el tema de este capítulo—los quehaceres. Pero, ¿qué son los quehaceres? Como indica la palabra misma son las tareas que tenemos que hacer—ir al banco, a la lavandería, a la peluquería, etc.

▲ **Nicaragua** Hoy en día la mayoría de las peluquerías son unisex como esta que vemos en un centro comercial en Managua.

México Cuando uno tiene muchos quehaceres, a veces no tiene tiempo para comer y se aprovecha de un puesto de comida como este en la Ciudad de México. Puede comer algo muy rápido y no perder tiempo. ▶

España ¿Es un palacio? Pues, sí y no. Es el Palacio de Telecomunicaciones en Madrid. Sirve de casa de correos. Es un lugar elegante adonde ir para echar una carta, ¿no? ▼

98

Puerto Rico Las instrucciones que salen en la pantalla de un cajero automático te facilitan el uso de la máquina. ▶

▲ **Argentina** A veces las lavanderías, que se llaman también lavaderos, están abiertas de noche como esta en Buenos Aires.

▲ **España** Es muy conveniente hacer tus transacciones bancarias en el cajero automático como las hace esta joven en Madrid.

◀ **Europa** El euro es la moneda de todos los países de la Unión Europea. Si viajas por España tienes que cambiar tus dólares en euros.

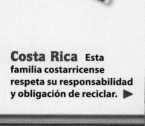

Costa Rica Esta familia costarricense respeta su responsabilidad y obligación de reciclar. ▶

99

Puerto Rico *(page 99)* ¿Cómo debes insertar tu tarjeta en el cajero automático? ¿Qué es la cinta magnética?

Argentina *(page 99)* ¿Hace calor en muchas lavanderías? ¿Hace calor porque hay muchas máquinas? En esta lavandería o lavandero, ¿hay un ventilador?

España *(page 99)* ¿Hay una fila larga delante del cajero automático? ¿Dónde está este? ¿Qué se puede hacer en un cajero automático?

Europa *(page 99)* ¿Cuál es la moneda de los países de la Unión Europea? ¿Cuál es la moneda de Estados Unidos?

Costa Rica *(page 99)* ¿Está poniendo la familia sus reciclables en la maletera de su carro?

Quick Start

Use QS Transparency 4.1 or write the following on the board.

Contesta.

1. ¿A qué hora te levantas?
2. ¿Quién se viste de una manera más elegante? ¿Tú o tu prima?
3. ¿Te lavas las manos antes o después de comer?
4. ¿A qué hora se acuestan tú y tu hermano?
5. ¿Te duermes enseguida o no?
6. En tu familia, ¿quién se levanta muy temprano?

▶ TEACH
Core Instruction

You may wish to follow some of the suggestions given in previous chapters for the presentation of the new vocabulary.

Differentiation
Multiple Intelligences

For **bodily-kinesthetic** learners, you may wish to have students dramatize the following: **apresurado, un corte de pelo, ir a la lavandería, poner la ropa en la lavadora, abrir un paquete de detergente, poner el detergente en la lavadora, planchar, poner un sello en una tarjeta, contar el dinero, escribir un cheque.**

100

La peluquería

José está muy apresurado.
Tiene mucho que hacer.

un corte de pelo

un recorte

José va a la peluquería.
El peluquero no le hizo un corte de pelo.
José quería solo un recorte.

La lavandería

la ropa sucia (para lavar), el lavado

José está en la lavandería automática.
Pone su ropa sucia en la lavadora.

la secadora

el detergente, el jabón en polvo

una camisa arrugada

Luego él añade un paquete de jabón en polvo.

Cuando la ropa sale de la secadora está muy arrugada.
Pero José la va a planchar.

100 *cien*

GLENCOE 🖰 Technology

Video in the Classroom

Vocabulario en vivo Watch and listen to Nora as she explains the chores she has to do.

El correo

el buzón

María fue al correo.
No tuvo que esperar en fila porque ya había puesto los sellos en la tarjeta.
Por eso la echó enseguida en el buzón.

la tarjeta postal

Saludos de México

el sobre

el sello, la estampilla

No se puede echar una carta sin sellos.

El banco

el dinero en efectivo

los billetes

el suelto

una moneda

el cajero automático

CAJA MADRID

Es posible depositar y retirar fondos electrónicamente.

Es necesario endosar un cheque antes de cobrarlo.
No puedes pagar con cheque sin que tengas una cuenta corriente.
Es necesario mantener un saldo (una cantidad de dinero en la cuenta).

Tasa de interés 5%

Susana pide un préstamo estudiantil para pagar la matrícula universitaria.
Un préstamo estudiantil es un préstamo a largo plazo, no a corto plazo.
La tasa de interés de un préstamo a largo plazo es más baja.

101

ABOUT THE SPANISH LANGUAGE

You may wish to explain to students that **el suelto** is *change*—meaning small coins rather than bills. **El cambio** is *change* in the general sense: **¿Tienes cambio de diez dólares? Cambiar** can also be *change* of one currency to another, for example from dollars to euros or pesos. **La vuelta,** sometimes **el vuelto,** is *change* one gets when paying a bill.

GLENCOE Technology

You may wish to use the editable PowerPoint® presentation on PowerTeach for additional vocabulary instruction and practice.

Total Physical Response (TPR)

(Student 1), **ven acá.**
Tienes mucha ropa sucia. Ponla en la lavadora.
Abre un paquete de jabón en polvo.
Pon el detergente en la lavadora.
Quita la ropa de la lavadora.

(Student 2), **ven acá.**
Toma el sobre.
Pon un sello en el sobre.
Escribe la dirección en el sobre.
Ve al buzón.
Echa la carta en el buzón.

(Student 3), **ven acá.**
Abre la chequera.
Quita un cheque de la chequera.
Escribe el cheque.
Deduce la cantidad del cheque de tu saldo.

▶ PRACTICE

Leveling EACH Activity

Easy Activities 1, 2, 3
Average Activities 4, 5

Activity ❶

🎧 Audio Script

1. José tiene el pelo muy largo y por eso necesita solo un recorte.
2. No puedes enviar una carta o una tarjeta sin que le pongas un sello.
3. El lavado es la ropa limpia.
4. Después de lavar la ropa en la lavadora, la pones en la secadora.
5. Se lava el pelo con jabón en polvo.
6. El suelto consiste en monedas.
7. Los billetes y las monedas son dinero en efectivo.
8. Uno siempre pide un préstamo cuando no necesita dinero.

Activity ❷ This activity can be done orally in class with books closed asking questions of students at random or as a paired activity.

Activity ❸ This activity can be done without preparation.

Go to glencoe.com
For: Vocabulary practice
Web code: ASD7844c4

¡Así se dice!

Habría de is a useful expression that means *I was supposed to.*
> **Habría de ir al banco y no fui.**

ESCUCHAR

❶ Escucha y determina si la información que oyes es correcta o no. Usa una tabla como la de abajo para indicar tus respuestas.

correcta	incorrecta

HABLAR · ESCRIBIR

❷ Personaliza. Da respuestas personales.

1. ¿Tienes muchos quehaceres?
2. ¿Cuándo vas a la peluquería?
3. ¿Lavas tu propia ropa sucia, o la lava otra persona? ¿Quién?
4. ¿Mandas cartas de vez en cuando?
5. ¿Envías muchos correos electrónicos?
6. ¿Te importa que tu camisa o pantalón esté arrugado?
7. ¿Tienes una cuenta corriente en el banco?
8. ¿Tienes una tarjeta de crédito?

EXPANSIÓN

Ahora, sin mirar las preguntas, cuenta la información en tus propias palabras. Si no recuerdas algo, un(a) compañero(a) te puede ayudar.

Nota

El cambio is a general word that means *change* or *exchange*. **El suelto** is *loose change*. **El vuelto,** sometimes **la vuelta,** is *change from a sale.*

LEER

❸ Escoge la frase correcta.

1. a. Un préstamo estudiantil es para pagar la matrícula y otros gastos universitarios.
   b. Un préstamo estudiantil es para comprar un carro.
2. a. Una hipoteca es un préstamo para comprar una casa. Una hipoteca es un préstamo a corto plazo.
   b. Una hipoteca es un préstamo para comprar una casa. Una hipoteca es un préstamo a largo plazo.
3. a. La tasa de interés es más baja para un préstamo a largo plazo.
   b. La tasa de interés es más baja para un préstamo a corto plazo.
4. a. Es necesario endosar un cheque.
   b. Es necesario endosar el dinero en efectivo.
5. a. Cuando necesitas dinero lo depositas en el banco.
   b. Cuando necesitas dinero lo retiras del banco.

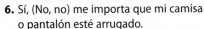

Answers

❶
1. incorrecta
2. correcta
3. incorrecta
4. correcta
5. incorrecta
6. correcta
7. correcta
8. incorrecta

❷
1. Sí, (No, no) tengo muchos quehaceres.
2. Voy a la peluquería cuando necesito un corte (recorte) de pelo.
3. Lavo mi propia ropa sucia. (____ lava mi ropa sucia.)
4. Sí, mando cartas de vez en cuando. (No, no mando cartas.)
5. Sí, (No, no) envío muchos correos electrónicos.

6. Sí, (No, no) me importa que mi camisa o pantalón esté arrugado.
7. Sí, (No, no) tengo una cuenta corriente en el banco.
8. Sí, (No, no) tengo una tarjeta de crédito.

❸
1. a	3. a	5. b
2. b	4. a	

LEER • ESCRIBIR

4 Completa con la palabra apropiada.

1. Los billetes y las monedas son ____.
2. Solo tengo billetes y necesito una moneda para el parquímetro. ¿Tienes ____?
3. Hay que ____ un cheque antes de cobrarlo.
4. Puedes depositar o ____ fondos electrónicamente.
5. Es necesario mantener un ____ en la cuenta corriente.
6. Por lo general la ropa que sale de la secadora está bastante ____ y es posible que la quieras ____.

5 Rompecabezas

Indica la expresión «intrusa».

1. a. poner sellos en la tarjeta
   b. echar una carta en el buzón
   c. buscar un cajero automático
   d. mandar una tarjeta postal

2. a. pedir un préstamo
   b. depositar fondos
   c. endosar un cheque
   d. ir por un corte de pelo

3. a. lavar la ropa sucia
   b. ir al correo
   c. añadir el detergente
   d. tener ropa arrugada

Estudio de palabras

cortar El barbero le corta el pelo.
el corte Tiene el pelo muy largo. Necesita un corte.
el recorte Le corta un poco. Le da solo un recorte.
corto Ahora tiene el pelo corto.

lavar Voy a lavar la ropa.
el lavado Tengo mucha ropa sucia. Tengo mucho lavado.
la lavadora Lo voy a lavar en la lavadora.
la lavandería Hay muchas lavadoras en la lavandería.

Completa con las palabras apropiadas.

1. No tengo el pelo ____. Lo tengo muy largo. No hay duda que necesito ____. Tendré que ir a la peluquería donde el peluquero me puede ____ el pelo.
2. Catalina es una estudiante universitaria. Vive en el dormitorio. Cuando tiene mucha ropa sucia, o sea mucho ____, no lo puede ____ en el dormitorio porque en el dormitorio no hay ____. Catalina tiene que ir a ____.

QUEHACERES

Más práctica

☐ Workbook, pp. 4.3–4.5
◉ StudentWorks™ Plus

CULTURA
Este banco está en una esquina de la ciudad de Punta Arenas en la Patagonia chilena.

DETERGENTE
AUTOMÁTICAS

MAYOR PODER CONTRA LAS MANCHAS DIFÍCILES

FÓRMULA SIN FOSFATOS

20 DOSIS

2,700Kg

InfoGap For more practice using your new vocabulary, do Activity 4 on page SR5 at the end of this book.

ciento tres **103**

Activity 4 Have students prepare this activity and then go over it in class.

Activity 5 Have students explain why the expression is **intrusa**.

Estudio de palabras

Have students prepare the **Estudio de palabras** activity before going over it in class. You may wish to call on students to read the words aloud and the sentences that convey their meaning.

Differentiation

Advanced learners

Have advanced learners make up additional sentences using the new words from **Estudio de palabras**.

Learning from Realia

(page 103) Ask students what they think **las manchas difíciles** means.

Cultural Snapshot

(page 103) Punta Arenas is in Patagonia in southern Chile. It is Patagonia's most important and prosperous city with a population of some 110,000. Punta Arenas is located on the Straits of Magellan. Its cold and gusty winds are almost constant.

▶ ASSESS

Students are now ready to take Quiz 1 on page 4.35 of the TeacherTools booklet. If you prefer to create your own quiz, use the *ExamView® Assessment Suite.*

Answers

4
1. dinero en efectivo
2. suelto
3. endosar
4. retirar
5. saldo
6. arrugada, planchar

5
1. c
2. d
3. b

Estudio de palabras

1 corto, un corte, cortar

2 lavado, lavar, lavadoras, la lavandería

QuickPass
Go to glencoe.com
For: Grammar practice
Web code: ASD7844c4

Quick Start

Use QS Transparency 4.2 or write the following on the board.

Completa en el presente.

1. ¿Lo _____ o lo _____ (tú)? (creer, dudar)
2. Yo lo _____ pero ellos lo _____. (creer, dudar)
3. Nosotros _____ que sí y él _____ que no. Él _____ de todo. (creer, creer, dudar)
4. Y ustedes, ¿lo _____ o lo _____? (creer, dudar)

▶ **TEACH**

Core Instruction

Step 1 It is suggested that you read Item 1 to the students and write the example sentences on the board or use the PowerPoint® presentation on PowerTeach.

Step 2 Give students a few minutes to study the expressions that denote doubt and those that denote certainty.

Differentiation

Advanced Learners

Explain to advanced learners that when asking a question with an expression of doubt or certainty, the speaker can decide whether to use the subjunctive or indicative. The form the speaker chooses indicates his or her opinion. The indicative indicates certainty. Subjunctive conveys doubt.

104

Lavado en seco
Lavandería y Lavamático
Katty

El subjuntivo con expresiones de duda

1. The subjunctive is always used after verbs or expressions that imply doubt or uncertainty.

   Dudo que él vaya por un corte de pelo.
   No creo que vaya por un corte de pelo.

2. If the verb or expression implies certainty, however, it is followed by a verb in the indicative, rather than in the subjunctive. The verb is frequently in the future tense.

   No dudo que él irá a la peluquería.
   Creo que él irá a la peluquería.

3. Study the following verbs and expressions of doubt and certainty.

DOUBT → SUBJUNCTIVE	CERTAINTY → INDICATIVE
dudar	no dudar
es dudoso	no es dudoso
no estar seguro(a)	estar seguro(a)
no creer	creer
no es cierto	es cierto

CULTURA

¿Crees que las motos son populares entre los jóvenes en España? Las motos estacionadas aquí están en una calle de Málaga.

⭐ **Tips for Success** ··········

- It is recommended that you go over the grammar activities in class before they are assigned for homework.
- Have students find the implementation of the grammar rule in the captions that accompany the photographs on pages 104–105.

Answers

1. Creo que cuesta mucho asistir a la universidad. (No creo que cueste mucho asistir a la universidad.)
2. No creo que hoy en día la gente escriba y envíe muchas cartas. (Creo que hoy en día la gente escribe y envía muchas cartas.)
3. Creo que la gente recibe y envía muchos correos electrónicos. (No creo que la gente reciba y envíe muchos correos electrónicos.)

Práctica

VIDEO Want help with the subjunctive with emotions, wishes, and doubts? Watch **Gramática en vivo.**

LEER • HABLAR • ESCRIBIR

1 Expresa tu opinión con **creo** o **no creo**. Usa el indicativo o subjuntivo como necesario.

1. Cuesta mucho asistir a la universidad.
2. Hoy en día la gente escribe y envía muchas cartas.
3. La gente recibe y envía muchos correos electrónicos.
4. Las bicicletas contaminan el aire.
5. Sirven comida excelente en la cafetería.
6. Ellas son más inteligentes que ellos.

ESCUCHAR • HABLAR

2 Conversa con un(a) compañero(a) según el modelo.

MODELO   —**Creo que iré por un corte de pelo.**
—**No, Martín. No creo que vayas por un corte de pelo.**

1. Creo que tendré una manicura.
2. Creo que les mandaré una tarjeta postal.
3. Creo que llevaré el lavado a la lavandería.
4. Creo que me queda bastante dinero.
5. Creo que tengo el suelto exacto.

LEER • ESCRIBIR

3 Introduce con **creo** o **dudo** y haz los cambios necesarios.

1. Mi mejor amigo(a) se casa pronto.
2. Me invita a la recepción.
3. La recepción será en un gran hotel.
4. La orquesta tocará música clásica.
5. Yo le regalo un carro.
6. Los novios viajan a Cancún.

CULTURA

Creo que esta pareja en Oaxaca, México, se va a casar.

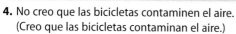

4 Habla con un(a) amigo(a) y dile todo lo que crees que harás mañana y todo lo que dudas que hagas mañana.

5 Trabajen en grupos de cuatro o cinco. Hablen de todo lo que creen que sucederá (ocurrirá) en sus vidas y lo que dudan o no creen que suceda (ocurra). Si es posible, expliquen por qué.

QUEHACERES

ciento cinco **105**

105

Quick Start

Use QS Transparency 4.3 or write the following on the board.

Cambia al condicional.
1. Ellos lo sabrán.
2. ¿Quién se lo oirá?
3. Ellos no hablarán así.
4. Yo podré hacerlo.
5. Tendremos que hacerlo.

▶ TEACH
Core Instruction

Step 1 Have students read aloud in unison the conjunctions and model sentences in Item 1.

Step 2 Explain to students once again that the subjunctive is used because what follows the conjunction may or may not happen.

▶ PRACTICE

Leveling EACH Activity

Easy Activity 6
Average Activities 8, 9,
   Activity 8 **Expansión**
CHallenging Activity 7

Activity 6 You can ask questions of students at random. It is also suggested that you do this activity orally with books closed.

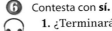

CULTURA

Estos policías vigilan para que no se cometan crímenes en las calles de Málaga, España.

El subjuntivo en cláusulas adverbiales

The subjunctive is used after the following conjunctions because the information that they introduce is not necessarily real. It may or may not occur.

para que	*so that*
de modo que	*so that, in such a way that*
de manera que	*so that, in such a way that*
con tal de que	*provided that*
sin que	*unless, without*
a menos que	*unless*

Marta no irá a menos que vayas tú.
Yo les voy a escribir para que sepan lo que está pasando.
Él no podrá pagar la matrícula a menos que le den un
   préstamo estudiantil.

Práctica

ESCUCHAR • HABLAR • ESCRIBIR

6 Contesta con **sí**.

1. ¿Terminará el trabajo con tal de que tú lo ayudes?
2. ¿Te lo explicará de modo que lo entiendas?
3. ¿Pedirás un préstamo sin que ellos lo sepan?
4. ¿Lo lavarás para que esté muy limpio?
5. ¿Tendrás que ir al banco para que te cambien los billetes grandes?

Comunidades

7 Un servicio de suma importancia que tiene que proveer un municipio a sus ciudadanos es el de la seguridad. Cada ciudad o pueblo tiene su departamento policial. En muchas ciudades de España y Latinoamérica hay policías de turismo sobre todo en los cascos históricos que frecuentan los turistas. Están para su seguridad y también para contestar sus preguntas o ayudarles con cualquier problema. En grupos de cuatro, discutan las obligaciones y responsabilidades que tienen los policías en su municipio y el trabajo que hacen. Presenten los resultados a la clase.

Activity 7 This activity is geared toward advanced learners.

Answers

6
1. Sí, terminará el trabajo con tal de que yo lo ayude.
2. Sí, me lo explicará de modo que lo entienda.
3. Sí, pediré un préstamo sin que ellos lo sepan.
4. Sí, lo lavaré para que esté muy limpio.
5. Sí, tendré que ir al banco para que me cambien los billetes grandes.

7 *Answers will vary.*

LEER • ESCRIBIR

 8 Completa con la forma apropiada del verbo indicado.

1. El profesor presenta la lección de modo que todos nosotros _____. (comprender)
2. Él sabe que nadie va a entender a menos que él la _____ de una manera clara. (presentar)
3. Explica todo de manera que _____ bien claro. (estar)
4. Nos enseña de manera que todos (nosotros) _____ aprender más. (querer)
5. Él ayudará a sus alumnos con tal de que le _____ atención. (prestar)
6. No te ayudará sin que _____ un esfuerzo. (hacer)

EXPANSIÓN

Ahora, sin mirar las preguntas, cuenta la información en tus propias palabras. Si no recuerdas algo, un(a) compañero(a) te puede ayudar.

CULTURA

Este profesor en Caracas, Venezuela, ¿presenta la lección de manera que sus alumnos la entiendan?

 Comunicación

9 Dile a un(a) compañero(a) lo que vas a hacer después de las clases. Tu compañero(a) te va a preguntar por qué. Explícale por qué usando algunas de las expresiones siguientes: **para que, de modo que, de manera que, con tal de que, sin que, a menos que.**

QUEHACERES

ciento siete **107**

Gramática

Activity 8 It is suggested that you allow students to prepare this activity before going over it in class.

⭐ **Tips for Success** ·······

Have students read the captions to the photographs on these pages. The captions reinforce the grammatical concept being learned.

··

GLENCOE **Technology**

Online Learning in the Classroom

Have students use QuickPass code ASD7844c4 for additional grammar practice. They can review each grammar point with an eGame. They can also review all grammar points by doing the self-check quiz, which integrates the chapter vocabulary with the new grammar.

▶ **ASSESS**

Students are now ready to take Quiz 3 on page 4.37 of the TeacherTools booklet. If you prefer to create your own quiz, use the *ExamView® Assessment Suite.*

Answers

8

1. comprendamos
2. presente
3. esté
4. queramos
5. presten
6. hagas

9 *Answers will vary.*

107

Quick Start

Use QS Transparency 4.4 or write the following on the board.

Completa con el presente del verbo haber.

1. Yo _____ terminado.
2. ¿Quién _____ hecho la cama?
3. Nosotros _____ hecho la cama.
4. ¡Increíble! Tú _____ llegado a tiempo.
5. ¿_____ vuelto ellos?

▶ TEACH
Core Instruction

Step 1 Since students already know the forms of the past participle, the imperfect, and the conditional, they should find the formation of these tenses quite easy.

Step 2 To teach the use of the pluperfect, have students think of the numbers *one* and *two*. Number *one* represents an action that began and ended in the past prior to a second action in the past, number *two*. Both are past actions, but *one* began and ended before *two* started. Action *one* is expressed with the pluperfect; action *two* with the preterite.

Step 3 Following Step 2, write *one* over **había salido** and **habían terminado** and *two* over **él llegó** and **nosotros empezamos.**

108

¿Te acuerdas?

Remember the following verbs have an irregular past participle.

decir	dicho
hacer	hecho
ver	visto
escribir	escrito
romper	roto
poner	puesto
volver	vuelto
morir	muerto
abrir	abierto
cubrir	cubierto

Step 4 Since the conditional perfect is used the same in both Spanish and English, it should be quite easy for students to understand.

Step 5 Because of its extremely low frequency of use, the future perfect is present solely for recognition.

Otros tiempos compuestos
El pluscuamperfecto, el condicional perfecto y el futuro perfecto

1. The pluperfect tense is formed by using the imperfect of the verb **haber** and the past participle. The conditional perfect is formed by using the conditional of the verb **haber** and the past participle.

	pluscuamperfecto	condicional perfecto
	salir	volver
yo	había salido	habría vuelto
tú	habías salido	habrías vuelto
Ud., él, ella	había salido	habría vuelto
nosotros(as)	habíamos salido	habríamos vuelto
vosotros(as)	*habíais salido*	*habríais vuelto*
Uds., ellos, ellas	habían salido	habrían vuelto

2. The pluperfect is used the same way in Spanish as it is in English—to state an action in the past that was completed prior to another past action.

> **Yo ya había salido cuando él llegó.**
> **Ellos ya habían terminado cuando nosotros empezamos.**

3. The conditional perfect is used in Spanish, as it is in English, to state what would have taken place had something else not interfered or made it impossible.

> **Yo habría ido pero no pude porque tuve que trabajar.**
> **Yo te habría dado cambio pero no me lo pediste.**

4. The future perfect is a tense that is hardly ever used. It is formed by using the future of **haber** and the past participle. It expresses a future action completed prior to another future action.

	terminar	ver
yo	habré terminado	habré visto
tú	habrás terminado	habrás visto
Ud., él, ella	habrá terminado	habrá visto
nosotros(as)	habremos terminado	habremos visto
vosotros(as)	*habréis terminado*	*habréis visto*
Uds., ellos, ellas	habrán terminado	habrán visto

GLENCOE Technology

Video in the Classroom

Cultura en vivo In this episode, students will visit a hair salon in a fashionable neighborhood in Madrid. Ask students to pay close attention to signs on the outside of the salon. How much does it cost to get a haircut with wash and style?

Práctica

VIDEO To visit a **peluquería** in Madrid, watch **Cultura en vivo**.

Más práctica
- Workbook, pp. 4.8–4.10
- StudentWorks™ Plus

LEER • ESCRIBIR

10 Cambia cada frase al pluscuamperfecto.

1. José ha ido a la peluquería.
2. El peluquero le ha cortado el pelo.
3. José ha salido de la peluquería.
4. María ha estado en la lavandería.
5. Su amigo ha puesto la ropa sucia en la lavadora.
6. Yo he lavado el pantalón con detergente en agua fría.
7. Le he pedido suelto.
8. Elena ha solicitado un préstamo.

ESCUCHAR • HABLAR • ESCRIBIR

11 Haz una sola frase según el modelo.

MODELO   Ellos salieron. Yo salí después. →
          Ellos ya habían salido cuando yo salí.

1. Ellos fueron a la peluquería. Yo los llamé después.
2. Ellos pidieron un préstamo. Yo fui al banco después.
3. Ellos pagaron. Yo pagué después.
4. Ellos cambiaron su dinero. Yo cambié el mío después.
5. Ellos volvieron a casa. Yo los vi después.

HABLAR • ESCRIBIR

12 Completa la siguiente tabla para indicar las cosas que ya habías hecho cuando tenías solo ocho años.

Yo ya	cuando tenía ocho años.

CULTURA
Una peluquería en Pisco, una ciudad en el sur de Perú

CULTURA
¿Quién no habría querido tomar una foto de esta plaza tan bonita en Baños, Ecuador?

109

▶ PRACTICE

Leveling EACH Activity

Easy Activity 10
Average Activity 11
CHallenging Activity 12

Activity **11** You may wish to point out that **ya** (*already*) is used only in afffirmative sentences with the present and pluperfect. **Todavía no** (*not yet*) is used in negative sentences.

Activity **12** Have students make up as many sentences as possible. This activity can be done individually, in pairs, or in groups.

✿ Conexiones

La historia

(Pisco) General San Martín landed at Paracas Bay in 1821 to fight for Peru's freedom from Spanish rule, and he made his headquarters near the Plaza de Armas in Pisco.

📷 Cultural Snapshot

(page 109 top) Pisco is a coastal town in southern Peru very near the Paracas Peninsula. The area is known for its fisheries and vineyards. Unfortunately, Pisco suffered severe damage during an earthquake in 2007.

(page 109 bottom) Baños is a popular tourist destination in Ecuador. It is known for its thermal baths whose waters come directly from the Tungarahua volcano.

Answers

10
1. José había ido a la peluqería.
2. El peluquero le había cortado el pelo.
3. José había salido de la peluquería.
4. María había estado en la lavandería.
5. Su amigo había puesto la ropa sucia en la lavadora.
6. Yo había lavado el pantalón con detergente en agua fría.
7. Le había pedido suelto.
8. Elena había solicitado un préstamo.

11
1. Ellos ya habían ido a la peluquería cuando yo los llamé.
2. Ellos ya habían pedido un préstamo cuando yo fui al banco.
3. Ellos ya habían pagado cuando yo pagué.
4. Ellos ya habían cambiado su dinero cuando yo cambié el mío.
5. Ellos ya habían vuelto a casa cuando yo los vi.

12 *Answers will vary.*

▶ PRACTICE
(continued)

Leveling EACH Activity

Easy Activity 13
Average Activities 14, 16
CHallenging Activities 15, 17

Activity 13 This activity can be done orally in class with books closed calling on students at random or it can be done as a paired activity.

Activity 15 Have students make up as many sentences as possible. This activity can be done individually, in pairs, or in groups.

GLENCOE Technology

Video in the Classroom
Gramática en vivo: *Compound tenses* Enliven learning with the animated world of Professor Cruz! **Gramática en vivo** is a fun and effective tool for additional instruction and/or review.

GLENCOE Technology

You may wish to use the editable PowerPoint® presentation on PowerTeach for additional grammar instruction and practice.

CULTURA

¿Por qué no habrían jugado los niños a la pelota en esta calle peatonal de Estepona, España?

ESCUCHAR • HABLAR

13 Contesta según el modelo indicando lo que habrías hecho pero no pudiste.

MODELO —¿Se lo habrías dicho?
—Sí, se lo habría dicho pero no pude.

1. ¿Habrías ido?
2. ¿Le habrías hablado?
3. ¿Les habrías ayudado?
4. ¿Lo habrías visto?
5. ¿Le habrías dicho algo?
6. ¿Habrías hecho algo?

LEER • ESCRIBIR

14 Completa con el condicional perfecto.

1. Ellos _____ pero no tenían hambre. (comer)
2. Ellos _____ algo pero no tenían sed. (tomar)
3. Ellos _____ pero no tenían sueño. (dormir)
4. Nosotros lo _____ pero no teníamos bastante dinero. (comprar)
5. Nosotros lo _____ pero la verdad es que teníamos miedo. (hacer)
6. Nosotros le _____ algo pero no lo vimos. (decir)
7. Sé que tú _____ éxito pero no fuiste. (tener)
8. Tú _____ pero sonó el teléfono. (salir)

HABLAR • ESCRIBIR

15 Explica por qué completando la siguiente tabla.

	ido	
	asistido	
	jugado	
Yo sé que Tomás habría	salido	pero...
	estudiado	
	vuelto	
	estado	

Answers

13
1. Sí, habría ido pero no pude.
2. Sí, le habría hablado pero no pude.
3. Sí, les habría ayudado pero no pude.
4. Sí, lo habría visto pero no pude.
5. Sí, le habría dicho algo pero no pude.
6. Sí, habría hecho algo pero no pude.

14
1. habrían comido
2. habrían tomado
3. habrían dormido
4. habríamos comprado
5. habríamos hecho
6. habríamos dicho
7. habrías tenido
8. habrías salido

15 *Answers will vary.*

LEER • ESCRIBIR

16 Completa con el condicional perfecto y el pretérito.

1. Ellos _____ pero no _____ porque empezó a llover. (salir)
2. Nosotros _____ a la playa pero no _____ porque hacía mal tiempo. (ir)
3. Él me _____ el dinero pero no me lo _____ porque no lo tenía. (dar)
4. Yo te lo _____ pero no te lo _____ porque no sabía los resultados. (decir)
5. Ella _____ en la ciudad pero no _____ en la ciudad porque costaba demasiado. (vivir)

❀ Comunicación

17 Trabajen en grupos de tres o cuatro y comenten sobre lo que cada uno(a) de ustedes habría hecho pero no pudo porque tuvo que hacer otra cosa.

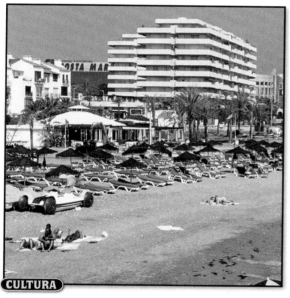

CULTURA

Me habría gustado pasar unos días en esta playa de la Costa del Sol en España.

QUEHACERES

Refrán

Can you guess what the following proverb means?

La ropa limpia no necesita jabón.

¡Bravo!

You have now learned all the new vocabulary and grammar in this chapter. Continue to use and practice all that you know while learning more cultural information. ¡Vamos!

Activity 16 It is suggested that you have students prepare this activity before going over it in class.

 Cultural Snapshot

(page 111) Marbella is a very popular and rather exclusive resort on the Costa del Sol.

▶ ASSESS

Students are now ready to take Quiz 4 on page 4.38 of the TeacherTools booklet. If you prefer to create your own quiz, use the *ExamView®️ Assessment Suite.*

Refrán

Proverbs, adages, idiomatic expressions, and other popular sayings provide a wealth of opportunities for students to learn about different cultural perspectives as well as perspectives shared by different cultures. They also serve to enrich students' overall understanding of language.

Have students recite the proverb aloud. Then have them give the literal translation. See if they can think of the context in which someone might say this. (You might respond with this proverb when someone is giving you a lot of excuses you didn't even ask for, making that person look guilty.) A similar English expression would be "Thou dost protest too much."

Answers

16   **17** *Answers will vary.*

1. habrían salido, salieron
2. habríamos ido, fuimos
3. habría dado, dio
4. habría dicho, dije
5. habría vivido, vivió

¡Bravo! The remaining pages of the chapter recycle information in a variety of ways, allowing students to build upon their newly acquired language skills as well as to keep track of their own progress. This format also ensures that students are not surprised by vocabulary or grammar that has not yet been introduced or studied.

Conversación

QuickPass

Go to glencoe.com
For: Conversation practice
Web code: ASD7844c4

Resources

- Audio Activities TE, pages 4.24–4.25
- Audio CD 4, Tracks 17–18

▶ TEACH
Core Instruction

Step 1 If the pronunciation of the class is satisfactory, you may wish to have students merely listen to the conversation on Audio CD 4.

Step 2 Then call on two students to read the conversation.

Step 3 Go over the **¿Comprendes?** activities.

Differentiation
Multiple Intelligences

Call on a pair of **bodily-kinesthetic** learners to act out the conversation for the class.

GLENCOE SPANISH

Why It Works!

In addition to containing no unfamiliar language, note that the new grammatical items of this chapter have been reintroduced in this short, natural conversation four times.

GLENCOE Technology

Online Learning in the Classroom

Have students use QuickPass code ASD7844c4 for additional conversation practice. Students can download audio files for the conversation to their computer and/or MP3 player and complete a self-check quiz.

¡TANTO QUE HACER!

112 *ciento doce*   CAPÍTULO 4

GLENCOE Technology

You may wish to use the editable PowerPoint® presentation on PowerTeach to have students listen to and repeat the conversation. Additional activities are also provided.

Answers

A *Answers will vary but may include:*
1. Julia está muy apresurada porque tiene mucho que hacer (antes de ir de viaje).
2. Habría de salir para Puerto Rico hoy.
3. No salió porque no había terminado todo su trabajo.
4. Va a salir mañana.
5. Tiene que ir a la lavandería para lavar su ropa sucia.

¿Comprendes?

A Contesta.

1. ¿Por qué está muy apresurada Julia?
2. ¿Cuándo habría de salir para Puerto Rico?
3. ¿Por qué no salió?
4. ¿Cuándo va a salir?
5. ¿Por qué tiene que ir a la lavandería?
6. ¿Por qué no va a ir a la peluquería?
7. ¿Por qué es importante que ella vaya al banco?
8. ¿Por qué no le importa que salga su ropa arrugada de la secadora?

B Analizando Contesta.

1. Isabel es una amiga buena. ¿Por qué? ¿Tienes un(a) amigo(a) como ella? ¿Lo (La) aprecias?
2. De todas las cosas que tiene que hacer Julia, una es muy importante. ¿Cuál es? ¿Por qué?

C Personalizando ¿Tienes quehaceres que son similares a los de Julia? ¿Cuáles?

VIDEO To watch some busy friends run errands in Argentina, watch **Diálogo en vivo.**

FOLDABLES®
Study Organizer

MINIBOOK
See page SH28 for help with making this foldable. Use this foldable to talk about errands. On each page, illustrate someone running an errand. Under each illustration, write about what each person is doing.

CULTURA

¿Cuáles son algunos servicios que ofrece esta lavandería en la Ciudad de Panamá? Se pone una colcha en la cama y es importante no manchar el mantel de café o salsa de tomate cuando tomas o comes algo. ¿Qué significarán «colcha» y «mancha»?

ciento trece **113**

Conversación

Differentiation

Multiple Intelligences
Visual-spatial learners might enjoy creating their own cartoon strips. They can either imitate these characters or create new ones. They may want to share their cartoons with others in the class.

▶ PRACTICE

¿Comprendes?

A It is suggested that you ask the questions orally with books closed. Call on students at random to respond.
B Have an open discussion. Encourage students to say as much as they can.
C This activity can be done as a paired or group activity.

 Comunicación

Presentational, Interpretive
Have students write a list of their typical chores. Have a student or a group of students poll the class for their answers, create a chart with the results, and then present the results to the class in Spanish, if possible. Have the class interpret the results.

GLENCOE Technology

Video in the Classroom
Diálogo en vivo In this episode, Francisco gets a haircut as Claudia runs errands. Ask students to tell which gestures and facial expressions indicate how Claudia, Francisco, and Chiquitín feel about Francisco's new look.

Answers

6. No va a ir a la peluquería porque tiene que ir al banco.
7. Es importante que ella vaya al banco porque no tiene bastante dinero para el viaje.
8. No le importa que salga su ropa arrugada de la secadora porque la va a poner en su mochila.

B *Answers will vary but may include:*

1. Isabel es una amiga buena porque quiere ayudar a Julia. Le dice que le lavará su ropa sucia. Sí, (No, no) tengo un(a) amigo(a) como ella.

2. Es muy importante que vaya al banco porque no tiene bastante dinero para el viaje.

⭐ Tips for Success ··········

Have students read the photo caption on page 113 to help them learn the unknown words in the window. **Plisar** means *to pleat.*

113

Resources

■ Audio Activities TE,
  pages 4.26–4.28
🎧 Audio CD 4, Tracks 19–21

▶ TEACH
Core Instruction

Step 1 Have students read the **Antes de leer** aloud or silently. This section helps with comprehension by introducing students to the information they will be reading about.

Step 2 Since the paragraphs are quite short, you may wish to call on a student to read a paragraph. You may also want to ask some questions such as:

¿Qué decidieron hacer Gregorio y unos amigos?

¿Qué región querían visitar?

¿De qué habían visto fotos?

¿Por cuánto tiempo habían ocupado España los árabes?

Step 3 You may wish to call on a student to give a review of a paragraph in his or her own words.

⭐ Tips for Success ·······

You may wish to tell students that the final paragraph contains several important details. To be able to remember the details, they should read the paragraph slowly and quite possibly more than once.

✿ Cultura

The information in the last paragraph is very useful for anyone traveling. Ask students if they have ever used an ATM. If they have, they will note some similarities. Ask them what the similarities are.

114

Antes de leer

Todos tenemos una lista de quehaceres típicos. Pero, piensa en unas cosas especiales que tienes que hacer en poco tiempo si decides salir por unas semanas.

✓ **Reading Check**

¿Quiénes ocuparon España y por cuánto tiempo?

✓ **Reading Check**

¿Qué tienen que hacer Gregorio y Maricarmen antes de salir?

✓ **Reading Check**

¿Cómo se puede cambiar dólares en otras monedas en el extranjero?

114   *ciento catorce*

Los preparativos para un viaje 🎧♻

Gregorio y unos amigos de su colegio en Madrid decidieron hacer un viaje por el sur de España—por Andalucía. Querían visitar Andalucía porque habían visto muchas fotografías de los famosos monumentos de los musulmanes: la Mezquita de Córdoba, la Alhambra de Granada y el Alcázar de Sevilla. De sus cursos de historia ya sabían que los árabes habían ocupado España por unos ocho siglos de 711 a 1492.

Como les quedan solo unos días antes de salir para Andalucía, cada uno tiene muchos quehaceres. Gregorio tiene el pelo bastante largo y quiere ir a la peluquería. Sabe que en agosto va a hacer mucho calor en Andalucía y sin duda van a pasar unos días en una playa de la Costa del Sol. Es mejor tener el pelo corto si va a ir al mar, ¿no?

Maricarmen tiene un montón de ropa sucia que tiene que llevar a la lavandería. Es una tarea que no le gusta nada pero no importa si sus pantalones, blusas y camisetas salen arrugadas porque todo se arrugará de nuevo en su mochila.

¡El dinero! Todos tienen que ir al banco porque sin dinero no se puede hacer nada. Pero en el banco todo es muy conveniente porque se puede usar el cajero automático a menos que uno no tenga una cuenta corriente.

¡Un detalle importante para ti! Si algún día decides viajar al extranjero[1] puedes usar el cajero automático para cambiar dinero. En España entras la cantidad de euros que quieres y en México la cantidad de pesos. Te saldrán los euros o pesos. Se convierten en dólares que enseguida se retiran electrónicamente de tu cuenta corriente. Es una transacción sencilla a menos que no tengas suficiente saldo en tu cuenta. ¡Cuidado!

[1]extranjero   *abroad*

CULTURA

Una vista de Córdoba

Pre-AP This cultural reading will develop the skills that students need to be successful on the reading and writing sections of the AP exam. Listening to this reading will also help prepare them for the auditory component.

📷 Cultural Snapshot

(page 114) This is the beautiful bell tower to the Mezquita de Córdoba, which today is a cathedral.

¿Comprendes?

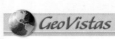
Más práctica
Workbook, p. 4.11
StudentWorks™ Plus

A Analizando Contesta.

1. ¿Por qué tiene que ir a la peluquería Gregorio?
2. ¿Por qué tiene que ir a la lavandería Maricarmen?
3. ¿Por qué no le importa que salga su ropa arrugada?
4. ¿Por qué tienen que ir todos al banco?
5. ¿Por qué será muy conveniente?

B Explicando Explica como puedes usar el cajero automático si viajas a un país extranjero donde no se usan dólares.

C Conectando con la historia Contesta.

Haz unas investigaciones sobre la enorme influencia de los árabes (los musulmanes) en la historia de España.

GeoVistas
To learn more about Spain, take a tour on pages SH40–SH41.

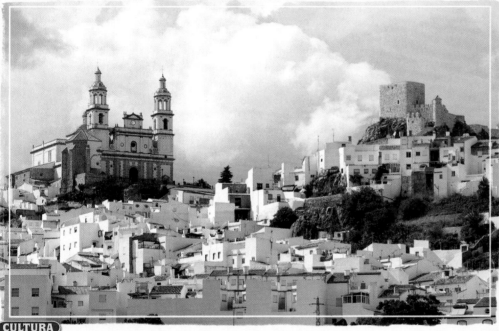

CULTURA
Una vista de Olvera, un pueblo pequeño cerca de la ciudad de Cádiz en Andalucía

QUEHACERES

ciento quince **115**

▶ PRACTICE

¿Comprendes?

A You may wish to ask these questions orally and have students respond without looking up the information.
B Have students be as detailed as possible.
C If you have students do this research project, you may wish to have them hand in what they wrote for extra credit.

Comunicación

Interpersonal
Have students work in pairs and make up a conversation about changing money at an ATM.

Cultural Snapshot

(page 115) Olvera is a lovely small town in the province of Cádiz. The area around Olvera is known for its production of olive oil.

GeoVistas

Have students look at the map of Spain on page SH41. Ask them to locate Cádiz and Córdoba. To reinforce the geography of Spain, you may wish to ask them to indicate the general location of Andalucía by pointing to it on the map.

Answers

A *Answers will vary but may include:*
1. Gregorio tiene que ir a la peluquería porque tiene el pelo bastante largo y quiere que el peluquero le corte el pelo.
2. Maricarmen tiene que ir a la lavandería porque tiene mucho lavado.
3. No le importa que salga su ropa arrugada porque se arrugará de nuevo en su mochila.
4. Todos tienen que ir al banco porque necesitan dinero.

5. Será muy conveniente porque se puede usar el cajero automático.

B *Answers will vary but may include:*
Puedo entrar la cantidad de euros en España o la cantidad de pesos en México y me salen los euros o pesos. Se convierte la cantidad en dólares que se retiran enseguida de mi cuenta corriente.

C *Answers will vary.*

Resources

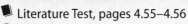

- Literature Test, pages 4.55–4.56
- *ExamView® Assessment Suite*

Preview

Starting in Chapter 3, each chapter of ¡Así se dice! Level 3 has a literary section. Most literary selections are by well-known Latin American or Spanish writers. Some selections are poetry and others are prose.

It is up to the discretion of the teacher if you wish to do all or any of these literary works. The difficulty level of each selection is also indicated from 1 to 4. 1 is difficult; 4 is quite easy.

Difficulty Level
4

Vocabulario
Core Instruction

You may wish to go over the definitions orally in class or you may wish to just have students read them on their own as homework. This will depend upon how in-depth you plan to present the literature selection.

Literatura

El mensajero de San Martín

de autor anónimo

▲ Una vista del Parque Nacional Torres del Paine en Chile

Vocabulario

el despacho   la oficina

un puñado   cantidad pequeña que cabe en la mano

el ejército   un grupo de soldados o militares

la choza   una casa muy humilde

apoderarse de   hacerse dueño de una cosa por la fuerza

encargar   poner una cosa al cuidado de otro; darle la responsabilidad a alguien de hacer algo

huir (huye)   escapar

sujetar   dominar a alguien

Práctica

Expresa de otra manera.
1. No quiero mucho. Necesito *solo un poco.*
2. Era imposible *dominar* al caballo.
3. Él *se hizo dueño* de todo el territorio.
4. ¿Por qué no pudo *escapar*?
5. Salió de su *oficina* apresuradamente.
6. Entró *el grupo de soldados.*
7. Hay *casas humildes* en los barrios pobres.

116   *ciento dieciséis*   CAPÍTULO 4

Answers

1. Necesito un puñado.
2. Era imposible sujetar al caballo.
3. Él se apoderó de todo el territorio.
4. ¿Por qué no pudo huir?
5. Salió de su despacho apresuradamente.
6. Entró el ejército.
7. Hay chozas en los barrios pobres.

INTRODUCCIÓN

Hay muchos quehaceres que la gente tenía que hacer casi a diario que hoy no tenemos que hacer casi nunca. Muchos de nosotros no vamos ni al correo para comprar sellos porque nos comunicamos casi exclusivamente por correo electrónico, mensaje de texto y mensaje instantáneo. Pero una vez era un mensajero el que tenía que viajar a pie o a caballo para transportar una comunicación. Y así fue el caso del joven Miguel quien se encargó de servir de mensajero al general San Martín.

FONDO HISTÓRICO

El general José de San Martín luchó por la independencia de Sudamérica. Era un hombre de mucha experiencia militar. San Martín ya había luchado en las guerras contra Napoleón en España y sabía que era imposible invadir Perú sin tomar la ruta que pasa por Chile. En 1817 cruzó la cordillera con su Ejército de los Andes y derrotó a (salió victorioso contra) los españoles en la batalla de Chacabuco. Esta derrota de las fuerzas españolas permitió al ejército de San Martín entrar triunfante en Santiago de Chile.

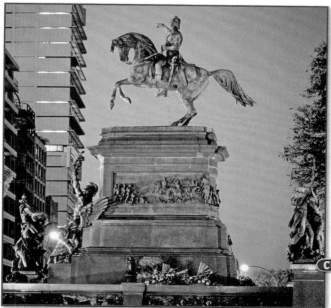

CULTURA
Monumento al libertador General San Martín en la Plaza San Martín en Buenos Aires

QUEHACERES

ciento diecisiete **117**

Introducción

You may wish to have students read the **Introducción** silently. Then ask them questions about it.

Fondo histórico

Have students read this information. It will give them the background they need to better understand the reading.

 Conexiones

La historia

If any students are taking a course in world history, you may wish to have them give some additional information.

 Cultural Snapshot

(page 117) San Martín is the national hero of Argentina.

▶ TEACH

Core Instruction

Step 1 Have students read the **Estrategia.** This is an important strategy when reading literary works that deal with characters. The more the reader can identify with the character(s) the more interesting the selection will be and the easier it will be to follow.

Step 2 You may wish to have students read the **Antes de leer** silently or you may wish to use it as a springboard for class discussion.

Step 3 You may wish to divide this reading into three or four equal segments.

Step 4 You may wish to ask the following key questions: **¿Dónde y cómo se va aumentando el suspenso del cuento? ¿Qué va a hacer el joven Miguel? ¿Qué crees? ¿Quiénes se pusieron sospechosos del Miguel? Miguel hizo algo que no habría debido hacer. ¿Qué hizo? ¿Qué hizo Miguel cuando el coronel le preguntó si llevaba una carta?**

Step 5 You may have students consider the **Durante la lectura** on their own or you may wish to use it as a springboard for open discussion.

Estrategia

Identificándose con los personajes Al leer un cuento hay que fijarte en la personalidad, el comportamiento y las acciones de los protagonistas. Poder precisar las razones por su conducta y acciones en muchas ocasiones te permitirá entender y seguir el desarrollo del argumento del cuento.

Antes de leer

Reflexiona sobre tu reacción personal si algún día te encuentras en una situación que te hace salir de casa para hacer algo patriótico y peligroso.

fusilarán *they will shoot*

arrieros *los que guardan animales*
halló *he found*
abogado *lawyer*

CULTURA
Lo viejo y lo moderno en Santiago de Chile

El mensajero de San Martín

El general don José de San Martín leía unas cartas en su despacho. Terminada la lectura, se volvió para llamar a un muchacho de unos dieciséis años que esperaba de pie junto a la puerta.

—Voy a encargarte una misión difícil y honrosa. Te conozco bien; tu padre y tres hermanos tuyos están en mi ejército y sé que deseas servir a la patria. ¿Estás resuelto a servirme?

—Sí, mi general, sí—contestó el muchacho.

—Debes saber que en caso de ser descubierto te fusilarán°—continuó el general.

—Ya lo sé, mi general.

—Muy bien. Quiero enviarte a Chile con una carta que no debe caer en manos del enemigo. ¿Has entendido, Miguel?

—Perfectamente, mi general—respondió el muchacho.

Dos días después, Miguel pasaba la cordillera de los Andes en compañía de unos arrieros°.

Llegó a Santiago de Chile; halló° al abogado° Rodríguez, le entregó la carta y recibió la respuesta, que guardó en su cinturón secreto.

—Mucho cuidado con esta carta—le dijo también el patriota chileno.

—Eres realmente muy joven; pero debes ser inteligente y buen patriota.

Miguel volvió a ponerse en camino lleno de orgullo°. Había hecho el viaje sin dificultades, pero tuvo que pasar por un pueblo cerca del cual se hallaba una fuerza realista al mando del coronel Ordóñez.

Alrededor se extendía el hermoso paisaje chileno. Miguel se sintió impresionado por aquel cuadro mágico; pero algo inesperado vino a distraer su atención.

Dos soldados, a quienes pareció sospechoso° ese muchacho que viajaba solo y en dirección a las sierras, se acercaron a él a galope. En la sorpresa del primer momento, Miguel cometió la imprudencia° de huir.

—¡Hola!—gritó uno de los soldados sujetándole el caballo por las riendas°.—¿Quién eres y adónde vas?

Miguel contestó humildemente que era chileno, que se llamaba Juan Gómez y que iba a la hacienda de sus padres.

Lo llevaron sin embargo a una tienda de campaña donde se hallaba, en compañía de varios oficiales, el coronel Ordóñez.

—Te acusan de ser agente del general San Martín—dijo el coronel.—¿Qué contestas a eso?

Miguel habría preferido decir la verdad, pero negó la acusación.

—Oye, muchacho,—añadió el coronel—más vale que confieses francamente, así quizá puedas evitarte el castigo°, porque eres muy joven. ¿Llevas alguna carta?

—No—contestó Miguel, pero cambió de color y el coronel lo notó.

Dos soldados se apoderaron del muchacho, y mientras el uno lo sujetaba, el otro no tardó en hallar el cinturón con la carta.

—Bien lo decía yo—observó Ordóñez, mientras abría la carta. Pero en ese instante Miguel, con un movimiento brusco, saltó como un tigre, le arrebató° la carta de las manos y la arrojó en un brasero° allí encendido.

—Hay que convenir en que eres muy valiente—dijo Ordóñez. —Aquél que te ha mandado sabe elegir su gente. Ahora bien, puesto que eres resuelto, quisiera salvarte y lo haré si me dices lo que contenía la carta.

—No sé, señor.

—¿No sabes? Mira que tengo medios de despertar tu memoria.

—No sé, señor. La persona que me dio la carta no me dijo nada.

orgullo *pride*

sospechoso *suspicious*

imprudencia *mistake*

riendas *reins*

castigo *punishment*

arrebató *grabbed*
arrojó en un brasero *tossed it in a brasier*

Durante la lectura

Para seguir la acción, presta atención a los detalles. Identifícate con las acciones de Miguel y reflexiona sobre lo que tú habrías hecho en la misma situación.

Teaching Options

- You may wish to have students read the selection silently, aloud, or in some combination of the two.
- There are many sections that contain dialogue. You may wish to assign parts and have students read in pairs, each one taking the role of a different person. You can change pairs frequently. Parts needed are indicated below. A narrator can read the background information. Speakers needed are: *page 118* narrator, el general San Martín, and el joven Miguel; *page 119* narrator, un soldado, el joven Miguel, and el coronel Ordóñez; *page 120* el coronel Ordóñez, narrator, and el joven Miguel; *page 121* narrator and el coronel Ordóñez; *page 122* narrator and un soldado

ABOUT THE SPANISH LANGUAGE

Students may not know what a **brasero** is. If no one knows, explain to students that it was a receptacle in which people burned wood or charcoal. It was frequently placed beneath the table in the main room or quarters and people put their feet near it to stay warm.

▶ TEACH

Core Instruction

You may wish to ask the following key questions: **Explica lo que significa: «El coronel admiró en secreto al niño pero no lo demostró.» Explica por qué lo admiró.**

 Cultural Snapshot

(page 120) This house in the Palermo section of Buenos Aires is a replica of the house in which San Martín died in Boulogne-sur-mer in northern France in 1850. After many internal political conflicts and fierce disagreements with Simón Bolívar, San Martín left South America in 1822 and never returned.

El coronel meditó un momento.

—Bien—dijo—te creo. ¿Podrías decirme al menos de quien era y a quien iba dirigida?

—No puedo, señor.

—¿Y por qué no?

—Porque he jurado°.

jurado *sworn*

El coronel admiró en secreto al niño pero no lo demostró. Abriendo un cajón de la mesa, tomó un puñado de monedas de oro.

—¿Has tenido alguna vez una moneda de oro?—preguntó a Miguel.

—No, señor—contestó el muchacho.

—Bueno, pues, yo te daré diez. ¿Entiendes? Diez de éstas, si me dices lo que quiero saber. Y eso, con sólo decirme dos nombres. Puedes decírmelo en voz baja—continuó el coronel.

—No quiero, señor.

—A ver—ordenó—unos cuantos azotes° bien dados a este muchacho.

azotes *lashes*

CULTURA

Es la réplica de la casa en que vivió San Martín durante su exilio en el norte de Francia. La casa se encuentra en la zona de Palermo en Buenos Aires.

CULTURA

Un corral en Villa Tehuelches, Chile

You may wish to ask the following key questions to help students understand the passage. ¿Era verdad que muchos soldados simpatizaban con el general San Martín? ¿Estaban de acuerdo con él? ¿Querían ellos la libertad también? ¿Qué pueden decir de los dos hermanos? ¿Qué piensan? ¿Va a cambiar la suerte del joven Miguel? ¿Por qué sí o no?

En presencia de Ordóñez, de sus oficiales y de muchos soldados, dos de éstos lo golpearon sin piedad. El muchacho apretó los dientes para no gritar. Sus sentidos comenzaron a turbarse° y luego perdió el conocimiento°.

—Basta—dijo Ordóñez—enciérrenlo por esta noche. Mañana confesará.

Entre los que presenciaron los golpes se encontraba un soldado chileno que, como todos sus compatriotas, simpatizaba con la causa de la libertad. Tenía dos hermanos, agentes de San Martín, y él mismo esperaba la ocasión favorable para abandonar el ejército real. El valor del muchacho le llenó de admiración.

A medianoche el silencio más profundo reinaba en el campamento. Los fuegos estaban apagados y sólo los centinelas° velaban con el arma en el brazo.

Miguel estaba en una choza, donde lo habían dejado bajo cerrojo°, sin preocuparse° más de él.

Entonces, en el silencio de la noche, oyó un ruido como el de un cerrojo corrido° con precaución. La puerta se abrió despacio y apareció la figura de un hombre. Miguel se levantó sorprendido.

turbarse *to become confused*
perdió el conocimiento *he lost consciousness*

centinelas *guardias*

cerrojo *lock*
preocuparse *worry*
corrido *opened, unbolted*

▶ TEACH

Core Instruction

Step 1 You may wish to ask students ¿Qué es un centinela? If it appears students do not know what a **centinela** is, explain it. You may also wish to ask: ¿Cómo podía huir el joven Miguel?

Step 2 You may wish to have students share their personal opinions and reactions to the reading.

Step 3 Have students discuss the **Después de leer** question.

Writing Development

Before discussing **Después de leer** in class, you may wish to have students write a paragraph in Spanish explaining their opinion. Be sure they give details to support what they say.

Differentiation

Multiple Intelligences

You may wish to have **bodily-kinesthetic** learners work together and prepare a skit about *El mensajero de San Martín*.

Cultural Snapshot

(page 122) The statue seen here is across the street from the house seen on page 120.

Una estatua del general San Martín con sus nietas en el parque de Palermo en Buenos Aires.

—¡Quieto!—murmuró una voz.—¿Tienes valor para escapar?

De repente Miguel no sintió dolores, cansancio°, ni debilidad; estaba ya bien, ágil y resuelto a todo. Siguió al soldado y los dos andaban como sombras° por el campamento dormido, hacia un corral donde se hallaban los caballos del servicio. El pobre animal de Miguel permanecía ensillado° aún y atado a un poste.

—Éste es el único punto por donde puedes escapar,—dijo el soldado—el único lugar donde no hay centinelas. ¡Pronto, a caballo y buena suerte!

El joven héroe obedeció°, despidiéndose de su generoso salvador con un apretón de manos y un ¡Dios se lo pague! Luego, espoleó° su caballo sin perder un minuto y huyó en dirección a las montañas.

Huyó para mostrar a San Martín, con las heridas de los golpes que habían roto sus espaldas, cómo había sabido guardar un secreto y servir a la patria.

cansancio *tiredness*

sombras *shadows*

ensillado *saddled*

obedeció *obeyed*

espoleó *he spurred*

122 *ciento veintidós*

CAPÍTULO 4

Answers

A

1. San Martín envió al joven a Chile con una carta que no debía caer en manos del enemigo.
2. Fue a Santiago de Chile.
3. La guardó en su cinturón secreto.
4. Huyó.
5. Lo llevaron a una tienda de campaña donde se hallaba el coronel Ordóñez. Le acusaron de ser agente del general San Martín.
6. Le arrebató la carta de las manos del coronel y la arrojó en un brasero.
7. Trataron de hacerle confesar por darle al muchacho unos azotes (por golpearlo).
8. Ordónez le ofreció a Miguel diez monedas de oro.
9. Un soldado chileno ayudó a Miguel.
10. Huyó en su caballo.

B *Answers will vary but may include:*
Cuando los soldados golpearon a Miguel, apretó los dientes para no gritar. Sus sentidos comenzaron a turbarse y luego perdió el conocimiento.

C *Answers will vary but may include:*
Cuando el coronel dijo que Miguel era agente del general San Martín, Miguel negó la acusación.

¿Comprendes?

A Recordando hechos Contesta.
1. ¿Qué misión le encargó San Martín al joven Miguel?
2. ¿Adónde fue Miguel?
3. ¿Dónde guardó la respuesta a la carta que le dio el abogado?
4. Al llegar los dos soldados enemigos, Miguel hizo algo erróneo, algo que no habría debido hacer. ¿Qué hizo?
5. ¿Adónde llevaron a Miguel y de qué le acusaron?
6. ¿Qué hizo Miguel cuando uno de los soldados halló su cinturón secreto?
7. ¿Cómo trataron de hacerle confesar?
8. ¿Qué le ofreció Ordóñez a Miguel para convencerle a hablar?
9. ¿Quién ayudó a Miguel?
10. ¿Cómo huyó Miguel?

B Describiendo Describe como el autor presenta la severidad con la que golpearon al pobre Miguel.

C Resumiendo Da un resumen de todo lo que hizo el joven Miguel para demostrar su heroísmo.

D Personalizando Acabas de leer sobre el heroísmo de un joven chileno. A tu juicio, ¿qué es una persona heroica? Escribe tu percepción personal del heroísmo.

E Analizando El clímax de un cuento es el punto de mayor interés o suspenso en el cuento. Para ti, ¿cuál es el clímax de este cuento?

Después de leer

Piensa en todo lo que hizo Miguel y determina si tú lo consideras un héroe o no. ¿Por qué?

CULTURA

La tumba de San Martín en la Catedral Metropolitana de Buenos Aires

---

▶ PRACTICE

¿Comprendes?

A It is suggested that you ask these questions orally with books closed and call on students to answer without looking up the information.

B This can be done as a group or paired activity.

C You may also wish to have students prepare a written summary.

D This activity can be done as an entire class discussion.

E You may wish to provide students with the following information.

✿ Conexiones

Elementos de un cuento o de una novela

- **la exposición** El autor empieza dándoles a sus lectores los datos necesarios para entender la acción de la obra. Por ejemplo, les da una descripción del ambiente o del tiempo.
- **el desarrollo** Es la introducción del asunto de la obra, es decir, las acciones de los personajes y sus motivos.
- **el suspenso** El autor introduce un elemento de tensión dramática—una especie de anticipación de lo que va a pasar.
- **el punto decisivo** Es algo que cambia la dirección de la obra.
- **el clímax** Es el momento culminante, el resultado del punto decisivo.
- **el desenlace** Es la parte que presenta las consecuencias finales.

Answers

Dijo que no llevaba carta. Entonces no dijo nada cuando el coronel le preguntaba de quien era la carta y a quien iba dirigida. No aceptó las diez monedas que le ofreció Ordóñez. Apretó los dientes para no gritar cuando los soldados lo golpearon. Y cuando el soldado chileno vino para ayudarlo a escapar, no sintió dolores; era resuelto a todo.

D *Answers will vary.*

E *Answers will vary.*

Pre-AP This reading will develop the skills that students need to be successful on the reading and writing sections of the AP exam.

Prepárate para el examen
Self-check for achievement

Resources

- Tests, pages 4.47–4.64
- Performance Assessment, Task 4, pages 4.65–4.66
- ExamView® Assessment Suite

✅ Self-check for achievement

This is a pre-test for students to take before you administer the chapter test. Note that each section is cross-referenced so students can easily find the material they feel they need to review. You may wish to use Self-Check Worksheet Transparency SC4 to have students complete this assessment in class or at home. You can correct the assessment yourself, or you may prefer to project the answers on the overhead in class using Self-Check Transparency SC4A.

Differentiation

Slower Paced Learners

Have students work in pairs to complete the Self-Check in class. Once they have finished, call on individuals to give the correct answers as you review together.

 To review **Vocabulario,** turn to pages 100–101.

 To review **el subjuntivo con expresiones de duda,** turn to page 104.

 To review **el subjuntivo en cláusulas adverbiales,** turn to page 106.

Vocabulario

1 Identifica.

1.   2.   3.

4.   5.

2 Completa con una palabra apropiada.

6. El peluquero le hace un _____ de pelo. No lo quiere muy corto.

7. El muchacho pone su ropa sucia en la _____.

8. Él tiene solo billetes grandes; necesita _____.

9–10. Se puede _____ y _____ fondos de una cuenta bancaria. Se puede hacer estas transacciones electrónicamente.

11. Un _____ estudiantil te puede ayudar a pagar la matrícula y otros gastos universitarios.

Gramática

3 Introduce la frase con no y haz los cambios necesarios.

12. Creo que él vendrá.

13. Dudo que él esté.

14. Creo que Susana lo conoce.

15. Dudo que él sea más inteligente que su hermana.

16. José cree que yo iré.

4 Completa con la forma apropiada del verbo indicado.

17. Él no podrá terminar el trabajo a menos que tú le _____. (ayudar)

18. Tenemos que mandarles un correo electrónico para que _____ lo que está pasando. (saber)

Answers

1
1. la peluquería (un corte de pelo)
2. el buzón
3. los sellos (las estampillas)
4. el jabón en polvo (el detergente)
5. el dinero en efectivo (los billetes)

2
6. recorte
7. lavadora
8. suelto
9. depositar
10. retirar
11. préstamo

3
12. No creo que él venga.
13. No dudo que él está.
14. No creo que Susana lo conozca.
15. No dudo que él es más inteligente que su hermana.
16. José no cree que yo vaya.

4
17. ayudes
18. sepan
19. pueda
20. vayamos

19. No le voy a molestar de manera que él _____ terminar con sus quehaceres. (poder)

20. Yo creo que él irá con tal de que nosotros _____ también. (ir)

5 **Completa con el pluscuamperfecto.**

21. Ella ya _____ cuando nosotros llegamos. (salir)
22. Ellos lo _____ y yo no lo sabía. (ver)
23. Ellos no sabían que yo le _____. (hablar)
24. Él ya te lo _____ cuando me lo dijo a mí. (decir)

6 **Contesta y completa.**

25–26. ¿Habrías ido?
Sí, _____ pero no pude porque _____.
27–28. ¿Habrían hecho ellos el trabajo?
Sí, lo _____ pero no pudieron porque _____.
29–30. ¿Habrían ustedes comido algo?
Sí, (nosotros) _____ algo pero no comimos nada porque _____.
31–32. ¿Lo habría hecho Enrique?
Sí, lo _____ pero no lo hizo porque _____.
33–34. ¿Lo habrían comprado ustedes? Sí, lo _____ pero no lo compramos porque _____.

7 **Escoge la forma apropiada del verbo.**

35. Tengo un montón de cosas que hacer sin que nadie me _____.
   a. ayuda   b. ayude
36. Él _____ hoy para Puerto Rico pero no pudo porque tenía mucho que hacer.
   a. habría salido b. había salido
37. Gregorio y un grupo de amigos ya _____ que iban a hacer un viaje a Andalucía.
   a. habrían decidido b. habían decidido
38. Quiere ir a la peluquería para que el peluquero le _____ el pelo.
   a. corte   b. corta

Cultura

8 **Contesta.**

39. ¿Por qué quieren ir a Andalucía Gregorio y sus amigos?
40. ¿Cuáles son algunos monumentos famosos que van a ver en Andalucía?

Preparate para el examen

To review **el pluscuamperfecto,** turn to page 108.

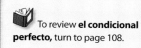
To review **el condicional perfecto,** turn to page 108.

CULTURA
Plaza de España, Sevilla

To review this cultural information, turn to page 114.

Differentiation

Slower Paced Learners

Encourage students who need extra help to refer to the book icons and review any section before answering the questions.

Pre-AP Students preparing for the AP exam may benefit from a set time limit when completing this Self-Check. This may also help to identify students with learning difficulties or slower paced students who need extra help.

 Cultural Snapshot

(page 125) The grandiose Plaza de España was constructed in 1929 as Spain's center piece for the 1929 World's Fair.

GLENCOE Technology

Online Learning in the Classroom

You may wish to have students use QuickPass code ASD7844c4 for additional test preparation. They will be able to complete a self-check quiz for chapter review.

Answers

5
21. había salido
22. habían visto
23. había hablado
24. había dicho

6
25. habría ido
26. *Answers will vary.*
27. habrían hecho
28. *Answers will vary.*
29. habríamos comido
30. *Answers will vary.*
31. habría hecho
32. *Answers will vary.*
33. habríamos comprado
34. *Answers will vary.*

7
35. b
36. a
37. b
38. a

8
39. Gregorio y sus amigos quieren ir a Andalucía porque nunca habían visto los famosos monumentos de los árabes que habían ocupado España por unos ocho siglos.
40. Algunos monumentos famosos que van a ver en Andalucía son la Mezquita de Córdoba, la Alhambra de Granada y el Alcázar de Sevilla.

Prepárate para el examen

Tips for Success ....

Encourage students to say as much as possible when they do these open-ended activities. Tell them not to be afraid to make mistakes, since the goal of the activities is real-life communication. If someone in the group makes an error, allow the others to politely correct him or her. Let students choose the activities they would like to do.

Tell students to feel free to elaborate on the basic theme and to be creative. They may use props, pictures, or posters if they wish.

Pre-AP These oral activities will give students the opportunity to develop and improve their speaking skills so that they may succeed on the speaking portion of the AP exam.

Note: You may want to use the rubric below to help students prepare their speaking activities.

Prepárate para el examen
Practice for oral proficiency

1 Algunos quehaceres
✔ *Discuss chores or duties you like and dislike*
Todos tenemos quehaceres. Algunos son tareas que nos gusta hacer y otros son tareas que no nos gusta hacer. Habla con un(a) compañero(a) de clase de sus quehaceres. Compárenlos y den las opiniones que tienen de ellos.

2 Una tabla de quehaceres
✔ *Talk about chores*
Toma los quehaceres mencionados en la Actividad 1 y organízalos en una tabla con los siguientes subtítulos. Preséntalos a la clase.

siempre	con frecuencia	nunca	me gusta	no me gusta

3 En mi futuro
✔ *Discuss what you may or may not do in the future*
Habla con un(a) compañero(a) de clase. Dile todo lo que crees que harás algún día y todo lo que dudas que hagas. Sigue hablando de un(a) hermano(a) o buen(a) amigo(a) y di lo que crees que él o ella hará o no hará.

CULTURA
¿Habría sido necesario ir a recoger tu ropa de esta lavandería en Málaga?

4 Lo habría hecho pero no pude
✔ *Talk about what you would have done but couldn't*
No hay duda que hay cosas que te habría gustado hacer pero no las hiciste porque por una razón u otra no pudiste. Di todas las cosas que habrías hecho y explica por qué no pudiste hacerlas.

5 Preparativos para un viaje—muchos quehaceres
✔ *Talk about preparing for a trip*
Antes de salir por una semana o más hay que organizar muchas cosas. Imagina que por un motivo u otro vas a pasar una semana fuera de casa. Explica todo lo que tienes que hacer antes de salir.

126 *ciento veintiséis*   CAPÍTULO 4

Scoring Rubric for Speaking				
	4	**3**	**2**	**1**
vocabulary	extensive use of vocabulary, including idiomatic expressions	adequate use of vocabulary and idiomatic expressions	limited vocabulary marked with some anglicisms	limited vocabulary marked by frequent anglicisms that force interpretation by the listener
grammar	few or no grammatical errors	minor grammatical errors	some serious grammatical errors	serious grammatical errors
pronunciation	good intonation and largely accurate pronunciation with slight accent	acceptable intonation and pronunciation with distinctive accent	errors in intonation and pronunciation with heavy accent	errors in intonation and pronunciation that interfere with listener's comprehension
content	thorough response with interesting and pertinent detail	thorough response with sufficient detail	some detail, but not sufficient	general, insufficient response

126

Tarea

Write a personal letter to a close friend or family member describing your experience living with a host family while studying abroad in a Spanish-speaking country. Discuss some memorable things that you did there, using vocabulary and grammar from this chapter.

Writing Strategy

Composing a personal letter Although the guidelines for writing a personal letter are not as strict as those of a formal letter, establishing a logical structure will make it easier to organize your thoughts while also making your message more enjoyable to the reader. The overall structure of a letter generally follows the basic pattern of starting with an introduction that describes the setting and sets the tone, followed by the body of the letter in which you use detailed descriptions to expand on different themes, then ending with a brief conclusion that ties everything together.

❶ Prewrite

- Before you compile the details that you wish to include in your letter, create an informal outline with the following headings.
    - I.   Introduction
    - II. Things I have done and things I would have done but couldn't
    - III. My daily or weekly routine
    - IV. My host family and what it's like to live with them
    - V.   How my host family compares with my family at home
    - VI. Conclusion

❷ Write

- Be sure to begin your letter with the date and the proper greeting (**Querido(a)** _____,).
- As you write, stick to language that you already know and try to incorporate as much vocabulary from this chapter as possible.
- Before signing off, don't forget the closing (**Atentamente, Besitos, Un abrazo, etc.**)

Evaluate

Your teacher will evaluate you based on your ability to incorporate appropriate vocabulary and correct grammar, as well as on the logical structure of your letter, the overall quality of the content, and the completeness of information.

Pre-AP This **tarea** will give students the opportunity to develop and improve their writing skills so that they may succeed on the writing portion of the AP exam.

Note: You may want to use the rubric below to help students prepare their writing task.

Scoring Rubric for Writing

	4	3	2	1
vocabulary	precise, varied	functional, fails to communicate complete meaning	limited to basic words, often inaccurate	inadequate
grammar	excellent, very few or no errors	some errors, do not hinder communication	numerous errors interfere with communication	many errors, little sentence structure
content	thorough response to the topic	generally thorough response to the topic	partial response to the topic	insufficient response to the topic
organization	well organized, ideas presented clearly and logically	loosely organized, but main ideas present	some attempts at organization, but with confused sequencing	lack of organization

Grammar Review

This page provides a quick "at a glance" summary of the grammar points students have learned in this chapter. The corresponding page numbers are also listed so that students can easily find each grammar point as it was presented.

Differentiation

Multiple Intelligences

You may want to call on **verbal-linguistic** and **logical-mathematical** learners for whom grammar often comes easily to explain the main concepts to their classmates in their own words. Having students explain the concepts in different ways may also help slower paced learners or students with learning difficulties.

Repaso del Capítulo ④

Gramática

- **El subjuntivo con expresiones de duda** *(page 104)*

  The subjunctive is always used after expressions that imply doubt or uncertainty. Review the following examples.

  Dudo que él lo haga.
  No creo que él lo haga.

  If the statement implies certainty, however, the indicative rather than the subjunctive is used. The verb is frequently in the future tense.

  No dudo que él lo hará.
  Creo que él lo hará.

- **El subjuntivo en cláusulas adverbiales** *(page 106)*

  The subjunctive is used after the following conjunctions: **para que, de modo que, de manera que, con tal de que, sin que, a menos que.**

  Marta irá con tal de que tú vayas.
  Marta no irá a menos que vayas tú.

- **El pluscuamperfecto, el condicional perfecto y el futuro perfecto** *(page 108)*

  Review the following forms of the pluperfect, conditional perfect, and future perfect.

	pluperfect	conditional perfect	future perfect
	salir	hacer	volver
yo	había salido	habría hecho	habré vuelto
tú	habías salido	habrías hecho	habrás vuelto
Ud., él, ella	había salido	habría hecho	habrá vuelto
nosotros(as)	habíamos salido	habríamos hecho	habremos vuelto
vosotros(as)	*habíais salido*	*habríais hecho*	*habréis vuelto*
Uds., ellos, ellas	habían salido	habrían hecho	habrán vuelto

The pluperfect is used to state what had happened in the past prior to another event. The conditional perfect is used to express what would have happened. The future perfect is very seldom used.

Yo había salido y ellos llegaron después.
Yo lo habría comprado pero no lo compré porque iba a costar demasiado.

There are a number of cognates in this list. See how many you and a partner can find. Who can find the most? Compare your list with those of your classmates.

Vocabulario

Talking about the hair salon

la peluquería	un corte de pelo	corto(a)
el/la peluquero(a)	un recorte	cortar

Talking about the laundromat

la lavandería	el jabón en polvo,	la secadora	planchar
la ropa sucia (para	el detergente	arrugado(a)
lavar), el lavado	la lavadora	lavar

Talking about the post office

el correo	el sobre	el buzón
la tarjeta postal	el sello, la	echar una carta
la carta	estampilla	

Talking about the bank

el banco	la cuenta corriente	el préstamo	cobrar
el dinero en efectivo	el saldo	a largo (corto)	depositar
los billetes	el cajero automático	plazo	retirar
la moneda	los fondos	la tasa de interés	
el suelto		endosar	

Other useful words and expressions

la matrícula	apresurado(a)
universitaria	habría de + *infinitivo*

 The words listed below come from this chapter's literary selection, *El mensajero de San Martín*. They were selected to become part of your active vocabulary because of their relatively high frequency.

el despacho	la choza	huir
un puñado	apoderarse de	sujetar
el ejército	encargar	

Don't forget the chapter project and cultural activities found on pages 96C–96D. Students have learned all the information that they will need to complete these engaging enrichment tasks.

 The cognates in this list are: **el detergente, la estampilla, el banco, depositar, universitaria.**

Vocabulary Review

The words and phrases in the **Vocabulario** section have been taught for productive use in this chapter. They are summarized here as a resource for both student and teacher. This list also serves as a convenient resource for the **Prepárate para el examen** activities on pages 124–127.

Differentiation

Slower Paced Learners

Slower paced learners may benefit from creating their own visual dictionary of nouns and adjectives in this list. They can either draw their own depictions or use images from the Internet or magazines.

Every chapter of ¡Así se dice! contains this review section of previously learned material. By recycling information from previous chapters, the cumulative review serves to remind students that they need to continue practicing what they have learned after finishing each chapter.

Activity 1 This activity reviews how to order food at a restaurant. See page R60 and the dictionaries at the end of this book.

Audio Script *(CD 4, Track 25)*
1. No hay mesas libres en el café.
2. Los amigos leyeron el menú.
3. El mesero escribió la orden.
4. La señora comió ensalada.
5. Es un café al aire libre.

Activity 2 This activity reviews the preterite forms of irregular verbs. See page R31.

Activity 3 This activity reviews the preterite forms of irregular verbs. See page R31.

CULTURA

Peatones en una calle de La Palma en las islas Canarias

130 *ciento treinta*

Repaso cumulativo

Repasa lo que ya has aprendido

These activities will help you review and remember what you have learned so far in Spanish.

 1 Escucha las frases. Indica si la frase describe el dibujo o no.

 2 Parea el infinitivo con el pretérito.

1. decir	a. estuve
2. poner	b. fui
3. estar	c. anduve
4. venir	d. puse
5. tener	e. quise
6. querer	f. dije
7. hacer	g. vine
8. andar	h. tuve
9. ir	i. hice

 3 Completa con el pretérito del verbo indicado.
1. Yo _____ muchos quehaceres. (tener)
2. Ellos _____ mucho pero no me _____. (hacer, ayudar)
3. Yo _____ que él no vendría pero ustedes _____ que vendría. (decir, decir)
4. Yo no _____ hacerlo y no _____ hacerlo. (querer, poder)
5. Tú lo _____ con cuidado, ¿no? (hacer)

CAPÍTULO 4

Answers

1
1. no
2. sí
3. no
4. no
5. sí

2
1. f
2. d
3. a
4. g
5. h
6. e
7. i
8. c
9. b

3
1. tuve
2. hicieron, ayudaron
3. dije, dijeron
4. quise, pude
5. hiciste
6. fui, fue
7. vinieron, pusieron
8. estuvimos

6. Yo _____ y ella _____ también. (ir, ir)

7. Ellos _____ en carro y _____ todo su equipaje en la maletera. (venir, poner)

8. Ellos no saben por qué no _____ nosotros. (estar)

 Cambia cada frase al pretérito.

1. Ellos hablan.
2. Mis hermanos trabajan.
3. Los niños comen.
4. Ellos beben leche.
5. Mis abuelos no viven aquí.
6. Ellos me escriben.
7. Los alumnos leen mucho.
8. Ellos oyen las noticias.

Los mochileros pasaron unos días fantásticos en Oaxaca, México.

 Trabaja con un(a) amigo(a). Cada uno dirá lo que hizo la semana pasada. Comparen lo que hicieron y decidan quién tuvo la semana más interesante.

 Escoge el artículo apropiado.

1. _____ leche es buena para la salud.
   a. El   b. La
2. _____ coche es nuevo.
   a. El   b. La
3. _____ clase es grande.
   a. El   b. La
4. ¿Dónde está _____ jabón en polvo?
   a. el   b. la
5. Es necesario endosar _____ cheque.
   a. el   b. la
6. Ellos viven en _____ ciudad.
   a. el   b. la
7. Están decorando _____ árbol de Navidad.
   a. el   b. la
8. _____ traje de novia es muy bonito.
   a. El   b. La

Activity 4 This activity reviews the preterite form of verbs. See page R29.

Activity 5 This activity reviews the preterite form of verbs. See pages R29 and R31.

Activity 6 This activity reviews definite articles. See page SR12.

 Cultural Snapshot

(page 131) Oaxaca is a beautiful colonial town in southern Mexico. It is a popular tourist destination.

Pre-AP To give students further open-ended oral or written practice, or to assess proficiency, go to AP Proficiency Practice Transparency AP9.

GLENCOE Technology

Audio in the Classroom

The **¡Así se dice!** Audio Program for Chapter 4 has 25 activities, which afford students extensive listening and speaking practice.

Online Learning in the Classroom

You may wish to have students use QuickPass code ASD7844c4 for additional cumulative review. They will be able to complete a self-check quiz.

Answers

1. Ellos hablaron.
2. Mis hermanos trabajaron.
3. Los niños comieron.
4. Ellos bebieron leche.
5. Mis abuelos no vivieron aquí.
6. Ellos me escribieron.
7. Los alumnos leyeron mucho.
8. Ellos oyeron las noticias.

 Answers will vary.

1. b
2. a
3. b
4. a
5. a
6. b
7. a
8. a

Chapter Overview
¿Buenos o malos modales?

● Scope and Sequence

Topics
- Courtesies
- Manners

Culture
- Typical greetings throughout Spanish-speaking countries
- Typical gestures used among many Spanish speakers
- *El conde Lucanor* by Don Juan Manuel

Functions
- How to discuss manners
- How to compare manners in Spanish-speaking countries to manners in the U.S.

Structure
- The imperfect subjunctive
- The subjunctive vs. the infinitive
- Suffixes

● Planning Guide

	required	recommended	optional
Vocabulario *(pages 136–139)* Saludos Despedidas Comportamiento	✓		
Gramática *(pages 140–145)* El imperfecto del subjuntivo Subjuntivo o infinitivo Sufijos	✓		
Conversación *(pages 146–147)* ¡Un pequeño malentendido!		✓	
Lectura cultural *(pages 148–151)* ¿Buen comportamiento o mal comportamiento?		✓	
Literatura *(pages 152–155)* El conde Lucanor			✓
Prepárate para el examen *(pages 156–159)*			✓
Repaso cumulativo *(pages 162–163)*			✓

Correlations to National Foreign Language Standards

Page numbers in light print refer to the Student Edition. Page numbers in bold print refer to the Teacher Edition.	
Communication Standard 1.1 Interpersonal	pp. **132C, 134–135,** 138, **138,** 143, **154, 155,** 158
Communication Standard 1.2 Interpretive	pp. **136,** 138, 139, **139,** 141, **141,** 143, **143,** 145, **146,** 147, 148, 149, 150, 151, **151, 153,** 154, **154,** 155, 157, **157,** 158, 162, **163**
Communication Standard 1.3 Presentational	pp. **132C, 132D, 136, 137,** 142, **146, 148, 150, 155, 156,** 159, **160**
Cultures Standard 2.1	pp. **132D,** 134–135, **134–135, 137, 139,** 142, 148–150, **150,** 151, 157, 158
Cultures Standard 2.2	pp. **132D, 142, 143, 144, 152,** 155, 162
Connections Standard 3.1	pp. **132D,** 138, **138,** 139, 152
Connections Standard 3.2	pp. 136, **136,** 137, 140, 142, **142,** 145, **145,** 147, **147,** 153–154, 155
Comparisons Standard 4.1	pp. 137, 140, 149, 150, **150,** 151, **160,** 161
Comparisons Standard 4.2	pp. **132D,** 133, **133, 134,** 147, **147,** 148, **149,** 153, 154, 158
Communities Standard 5.1	pp. **132C,** 147, 150, **158,** 159, **160**
Communities Standard 5.2	pp. 136, **136,** 142, **142, 146,** 147, **147**

To read the ACTFL Standards in their entirety, see the front of the Teacher Edition.

Student Resources

Print

Workbook *(pp. 5.3–5.14)*
Audio Activities *(pp. 5.15–5.21)*
Pre-AP Workbook, Chapter 5

Technology

- StudentWorks™ Plus
- ¡Así se dice! Vocabulario en vivo
- ¡Así se dice! Gramática en vivo
- ¡Así se dice! Diálogo en vivo
- ¡Así se dice! Cultura en vivo
- Vocabulary PuzzleMaker
- **QuickPass** glencoe.com

Teacher Resources

Print

TeacherTools, Chapter 5
    Workbook TE *(pp. 5.3–5.14)*
    Audio Activities TE *(pp. 5.17–5.36)*
    Quizzes 1–5 *(pp. 5.39–5.44)*
    Tests *(pp. 5.46–5.67)*
    Performance Assessment, Task 5 *(pp. 5.69–5.70)*

Technology

- Quick Start Transparencies 5.1–5.4
- Vocabulary Transparencies V5.1–V5.3
- Audio CD 5
- *ExamView® Assessment Suite*
- TeacherWorks™ Plus
- PowerTeach
- ¡Así se dice! Video Program
- Vocabulary PuzzleMaker
- **QuickPass** glencoe.com

Chapter Project

Una escena de telenovela

Students will work individually and in groups to prepare and perform a soap-opera scene dealing with the theme of good and bad manners.

1. Divide students into groups of four to six and have them choose a name for their soap opera and assign roles to each group member. Students will work together to create an outline of their scene and develop a rough draft of the scene's script. Along with the group's outline, individual students should submit a draft of his or her role to be checked or peer edited and revised accordingly. Corrected drafts should be turned in on the day of the group's performance.

2. Each group should include all roles equally when drafting a script and should incorporate three or more props or visual aids related to the theme of good and bad manners in the scene. Although it is important for the groups to prepare and practice their scenes in advance, they may use note cards for prompting. In this case, you may wish to remind them that reading word for word from their note cards will result in a lower score. If students have access to Spanish-language television, invite them to watch a few **telenovelas** and try to imitate the melodrama in their own scenes.

3. You may wish to have the groups perform in class or record their scenes outside of class for in-class viewing. If you have access to video equipment, record the in-class performances to share with parents or other Spanish classes.

4. Remind students to stick to the theme of good and bad manners. Encourage them to have fun with this project and to keep in mind that soap operas are often characterized by high drama and suspense.

Scoring Rubric for Project

	1	3	5
Evidence of planning	Draft of script is not provided.	Draft of script is provided but is not corrected.	Corrected draft of script is provided.
Use of visual aids	Soap opera contains no visual aids related to manners.	Soap opera contains few visual aids related to manners.	Soap opera contains several visual aids related to manners.
Presentation	Soap opera contains little of the required elements.	Soap opera contains some of the required elements.	Soap opera contains all the required elements.

Culture

● Día de los Santos Inocentes

In many Spanish-speaking countries, December 28 is **Día de los Santos Inocentes,** a day to play tricks and practical jokes on others. In some cities in Spain, newspapers and television newscasts will report false stories (e.g, a new planet has been discovered or everyone whose license plate ends with a nine must report to the police). One of the most common jokes is to make up a story that convinces a friend to part with money or some object of value. The friend who gets fooled may receive some candy or little treat in exchange but must also withstand joking and name-calling for the rest of the day for falling for the trick. Students can compare this day with April Fool's Day in the United States; they might enjoy writing their own **Día de los Santos Inocentes** news stories in Spanish.

● Reggaetón

Most of the types of music that have come out of Latin America have been influenced by music from other cultures. Modern music from Latin America is no exception. **Reggaetón** is a newer form of Latin music that has pulled from a variety of musical sources to create a unique sound. Jamaican reggae is a primary influence, but American hip-hop and other genres of Latin music, such as **merengue** and **salsa,** are also evident. The main characteristic of **reggaetón** is its driving drum-machine track, called "dem bow" in reference to the Jamaican song that first made the rhythm—an interplay between a steady 4/4 beat and a syncopated beat of 3 + 3 + 2—popular. Although its lyrics are more often rapped than sung, **reggaetón** is distinguishable from hip-hop by this distinctive rhythm. **Reggaetón** has its roots in Panama, but gained popularity in Puerto Rico during the 1990s, first among urban youth and eventually throughout the country; most **reggaetón** stars are now from Puerto Rico. Today **reggaetón** can be found all over Latin America and even around the world. Some major U.S. cities with large Hispanic populations (e.g., New York City and Los Angeles) have **reggaetón**-only radio stations.

50-Minute Lesson Plans

	Objective	Present	Practice	Assess/Homework
Day 1	Talk about manners	Chapter Opener, pp. 132–133 (5 min.) Introducción al tema, pp. 134–135 (10 min.) Core Instruction/Vocabulario, pp. 136–137 (10 min.) Video, Vocabulario en vivo (10 min.)	Activities 1–4, p. 138 (15 min.)	Student Workbook Activities A–D, pp. 5.3–5.4 *QuickPass* Vocabulary Practice
Day 2	Talk about manners	Quick Start, p. 136 (5 min.) Review Vocabulario, pp. 136–137 (10 min.)	Activities 5–7, p. 139 (10 min.) Estudio de palabras, p. 139 (5 min.) Total Physical Response, p. 137 (5 min.) Audio Activities A–F, pp. 5.17–5.20 (15 min.)	Student Workbook Activities E–G, p. 5.4 *QuickPass* Vocabulary Practice
Day 3	The imperfect subjunctive	Core Instruction/Gramática, El imperfecto del subjuntivo, p. 140 (15 min.)	Activities 1–3, p. 141 (15 min.) Audio Activities A–D, pp. 5.21–5.23 (10 min.)	Quiz 1, p. 5.39 (10 min.) Student Workbook Activities A–D, pp. 5.5–5.6 *QuickPass* Grammar Practice
Day 4	The imperfect subjunctive	Quick Start, p. 140 (5 min.) Review Gramática, El imperfecto del subjuntivo, p. 140 (10 min.) Video, Gramática en vivo (10 min.)	Activities 4–6, pp. 141–142 (10 min.) InfoGap, p. SR6 (5 min.)	Quiz 2, p. 5.40 (10 min.) Student Workbook Activities E–H, pp. 5.6–5.7 *QuickPass* Grammar Practice
Day 5	The subjunctive vs. the infinitive	Quick Start, p. 143 (5 min.) Core Instruction/Gramática, Subjuntivo o infinitivo, p. 143 (10 min.)	Activities 7–9, p. 143 (15 min.) Audio Activities E–G, pp. 5.23–5.24 (10 min.)	Quiz 3, p. 5.41 (10 min.) Student Workbook Activities A–C, p. 5.8 *QuickPass* Grammar Practice
Day 6	Suffixes	Quick Start, p. 144 (5 min.) Core Instruction/Gramática, Sufijos, p. 144 (15 min.)	Activities 10–14, pp. 144–145 (20 min.)	Quiz 4, p. 5.42 (10 min.) Student Workbook Activity A, p. 5.9 *QuickPass* Grammar Practice
Day 7	Develop reading and listening comprehension skills	Core Instruction/Conversación, p. 146 (20 min.) Video, Cultura en vivo (10 min.)	¿Comprendes? A–B, p. 147 (10 min.)	Quiz 5, p. 5.43 (10 min.) ¿Comprendes? C–E, p. 147 *QuickPass* Conversation
Day 8	Compare manners in Spanish-speaking countries to manners in the United States	Core Instruction/Lectura cultural, pp. 148–150 (20 min.)	¿Comprendes? A–C, p. 151 (15 min.)	Listening Comprehension Test, pp. 5.63–5.64 (15 min.) ¿Comprendes? D–E, p. 151 *QuickPass* Reading Practice
Day 9	Read a famous episode from *El conde Lucanor*	Core Instruction/Vocabulario, p. 152 (5 min.) Core Instruction/Literatura, pp. 153–154 (20 min.)	Vocabulario, Práctica 1–4, pp. 152–153 (15 min.) Comprendes? A–B, p. 155 (10 min.)	¿Comprendes? D, p. 155 *QuickPass* Reading Practice
Day 10	Read a famous episode from *El conde Lucanor*	Review Literatura, pp. 153–154 (10 min.)	¿Comprendes? C–D, p. 155 (15 min.) Prepárate para el examen, pp. 156–157 (25 min.)	Prepárate para el examen, Practice for written proficiency, p. 159 *QuickPass* Reading Practice
Day 11	Chapter review	Repaso del Capítulo 5, pp. 160–161 (15 min.)	Prepárate para el examen, Practice for oral proficiency, p. 158 (20 min.)	Test for Writing Proficiency, p. 5.67 (15 min.) Review for chapter test

Day 12	Chapter 5 Tests (50 min.)
	    Reading and Writing Test, pp. 5.51–5.58
	    Literature Test, pp. 5.59–5.61
	    Speaking Test, p. 5.65
	    Test for Oral Proficiency, p. 5.66			

90-Minute Lesson Plans

	Objective	Present	Practice	Assess/Homework
Block 1	Talk about manners	Chapter Opener, pp. 132–133 (5 min.) Introducción al tema, pp. 134–135 (15 min.) Quick Start, p. 136 (5 min.) Core Instruction/Vocabulario, pp. 136–137 (10 min.) Video, Vocabulario en vivo (10 min.)	Activities 1–7, pp. 138–139 (20 min.) Estudio de palabras, p. 139 (5 min.) Total Physical Response, p. 137 (5 min.) Audio Activities A–F, pp. 5.17–5.20 (15 min.)	Student Workbook Activities A–G, pp. 5.3–5.4 **QuickPass** Vocabulary Practice
Block 2	The imperfect subjunctive	Quick Start, p. 140 (5 min.) Core Instruction/Gramática, El imperfecto del subjuntivo, p. 140 (15 min.) Video, Gramática en vivo (10 min.)	Activities 1–6, pp. 141–142 (20 min.) InfoGap, p. SR6 (5 min.) Foldables, p. 142 (5 min.) Audio Activities A–D, pp. 5.21–5.23 (20 min.)	Quiz 1, p. 5.39 (10 min.) Student Workbook Activities A–H, pp. 5.5–5.7 **QuickPass** Grammar Practice
Block 3	The subjunctive vs. the infinitive Suffixes	Quick Start, p. 143 (5 min.) Core Instruction/Gramática, Subjuntivo o infinitivo, p. 143 (10 min.) Quick Start, p. 144 (5 min.) Core Instruction/Gramática, Sufijos, p. 144 (10 min.)	Activities 7–9, p. 143 (15 min.) Activities 10–14, pp. 144–145 (15 min.) Audio Activities E–G, pp. 5.23–5.24 (20 min.)	Quizzes 2–3, pp. 5.40–5.41 (20 min.) Student Workbook Activities A–C, p. 5.8 Student Workbook Activity A, p. 5.9 **QuickPass** Grammar Practice
Block 4	Discuss holidays celebrated in Spanish-speaking countries	Core Instruction/Conversación, p. 146 (20 min.) Video, Cultura en vivo (10 min.) Core Instruction/Lectura cultural, pp. 148–150 (20 min.)	¿Comprendes? A–C, p. 147 (10 min.) ¿Comprendes? A–C, p. 151 (10 min.)	Quizzes 4–5, pp. 5.42–5.43 (20 min.) ¿Comprendes? D–E, p. 147 ¿Comprendes? D–E, p. 151 **QuickPass** Conversation, Reading Practice
Block 5	Read a famous episode from *El conde Lucanor*	Core Instruction/Vocabulario, p. 152 (5 min.) Core Instruction/Literatura, pp. 153–154 (20 min.)	Vocabulario, Práctica 1–4, pp. 152–153 (15 min.) ¿Comprendes? A–D, p. 155 (20 min.) Prepárate para el examen, Practice for oral proficiency 1–3, p. 158 (15 min.)	Listening Comprehension Test, pp. 5.63–5.64 (15 min.) **QuickPass** Reading Practice
Block 6	Chapter review	Repaso del Capítulo 5, pp. 160–161 (15 min.)	Prepárate para el examen, pp. 156–157 (20 min.) Prepárate para el examen, Practice for oral proficiency 4–5, p. 158 (15 min.) Prepárate para el examen, Practice for written proficiency, p. 159 (30 min.)	Literature Test, pp. 5.59–5.61 (10 min.) Review for chapter test

Block 7	Chapter 5 Tests (50 min.)
	    Reading and Writing Test, pp. 5.51–5.58
	    Speaking Test, p. 5.65
	    Test for Oral Proficiency, p. 5.66
	    Test for Writing Proficiency, p. 5.67
	Chapter Project, p. 132C (40 min.)			

Preview

In this chapter, students will explore customs that are considered good manners in Hispanic cultures. They will observe that not all societies have the same set rules for how to act politely. In addition to learning the vocabulary necessary to discuss manners, students will learn the imperfect subjunctive and the use of the infinitive versus the subjunctive. They will also learn the use and meaning of suffixes. Students will read an episode from *El conde Lucanor* in which even the people of the eleventh century had their opinions about how things should be done.

Pacing

It is important to note that once you reach **¡Bravo!** in the chapter, there is no more new material for the students to learn. The rest of the chapter recycles what has already been covered. The suggested pacing listed here leaves two to three days for review, assessment, and enrichment activities such as the chapter project.

Vocabulario	1–2 days
Gramática	2–3 days
Conversación	1 day
Lectura cultural	1 day
Literatura	1 day

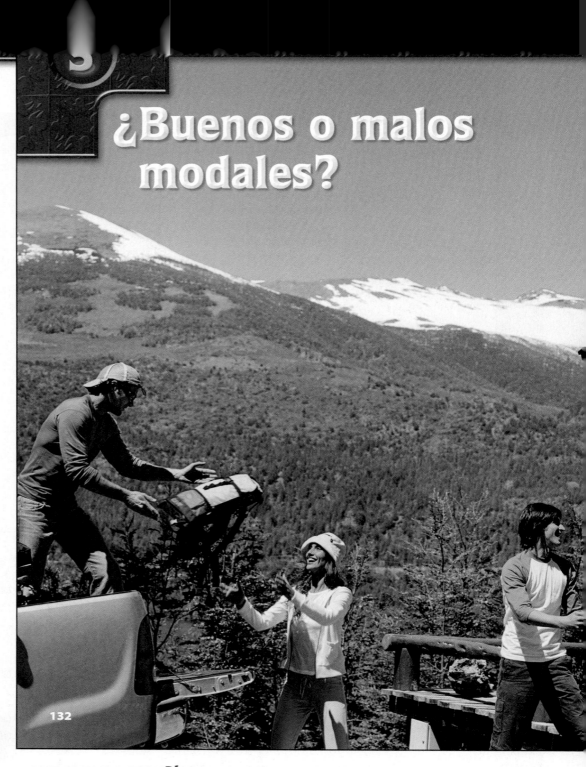

¿Buenos o malos modales?

132

TeacherWorks^Plus

The **¡Así se dice!** TeacherWorkst™ Plus CD-ROM is an all-in-one planner and resource center. You may wish to use several of the following features as you plan and present the Chapter 5 material: Interactive Teacher Edition, Interactive Lesson Planner with Calendar, and Point and Click Access to Teaching Resources including Hotlinks to the Internet and Correlations to the National Standards.

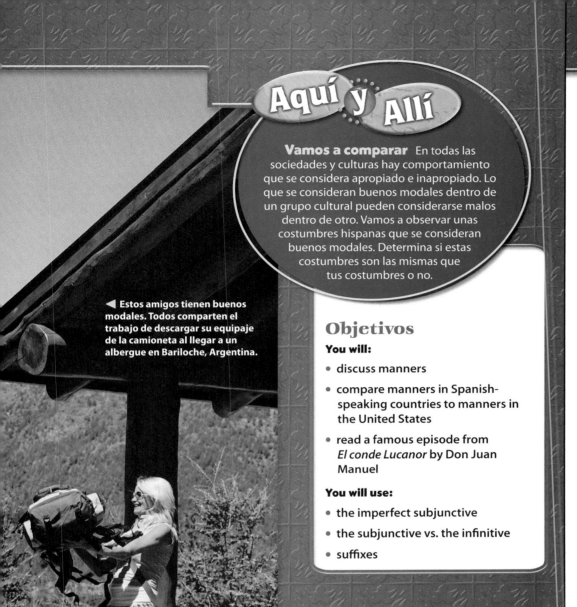

Aquí y Allí

Vamos a comparar En todas las sociedades y culturas hay comportamiento que se considera apropiado e inapropiado. Lo que se consideran buenos modales dentro de un grupo cultural pueden considerarse malos dentro de otro. Vamos a observar unas costumbres hispanas que se consideran buenos modales. Determina si estas costumbres son las mismas que tus costumbres o no.

◄ Estos amigos tienen buenos modales. Todos comparten el trabajo de descargar su equipaje de la camioneta al llegar a un albergue en Bariloche, Argentina.

Objetivos

You will:

- discuss manners
- compare manners in Spanish-speaking countries to manners in the United States
- read a famous episode from *El conde Lucanor* by Don Juan Manuel

You will use:

- the imperfect subjunctive
- the subjunctive vs. the infinitive
- suffixes

QuickPass

Go to glencoe.com
For: **Online book**
Web code: ASD7844c5

ciento treinta y tres **133**

Quia Interactive Online Student Edition found at quia.com allows students to complete activities online and submit them for computer grading for instant feedback or teacher grading with suggestions for what to review. Students can also record speaking activities, listen to chapter audio, and watch the videos that correspond with each chapter. As a teacher you are able to create rosters, set grading parameters, and post assignments for each class. After students complete activities, you can view the results and recommend remediation or review. You can also add your own customized activities for additional student practice.

Introducción al tema

▶ PRESENT

Introduce the theme of the chapter by having students look at the photographs on these pages. Later, once you have presented the **Vocabulario** section, you may want to return to these pages. Students will be able to read and understand the written information and answer any corresponding questions. Encourage students to also refer back to these photographs as they learn more about manners in Spain and Latin America.

Cultural Snapshot

Estados Unidos *(page 134)* ¿Qué hacen los muchachos en esta fotografía en Estados Unidos? Y, ¿qué hacen las muchachas? ¿Son de influencia latina estas costumbres?

México *(page 134)* ¿Cuándo se dan los amigos un besito en las mejillas?

Introducción al tema

¿Buenos o malos modales?

En este capítulo vas a estudiar unas costumbres de cortesía y lo que se consideran buenos o malos modales en las culturas latinas. Al mirar estas fotos, observa si hay unas cosas que tú también sueles hacer cuando saludas a un(a) amigo(a) o si te despides de un(a) amigo(a).

NO SE PEMITE EL USO DEL MOVIL

▲ **Estados Unidos** Estos jóvenes están en Estados Unidos. Observa que los muchachos se dan la mano y las muchachas se dan un besito en las mejillas. Es una costumbre latina que están adoptando muchos estadounidenses.

México Los amigos se dan un besito en esta plaza en San Miguel de Allende. ¿Qué piensas? ¿Se están saludando o se están despidiendo el uno de la otra? ▶

134

▲ **Argentina** Estas muchachas en Buenos Aires se dan el besito típico cuando se saludan y también cuando se despiden.

▲ **México** Los dos señores se dan el abrazo típico con unas palmadas en la espalda.

Ecuador En todas partes cuidar de los parques y jardines se considera buen comportamiento como indica este aviso en un parquecito de Baños. ▶

Las flores y las plantas son el alma de la tierra
¡Cuídalas! ¡No las Mates!

▲ **España** Estos jóvenes están conversando en un pueblo de España. Los españoles, igual que los latinoamericanos, suelen tocar a sus amigos y mantenerse cerca los unos de los otros cuando hablan juntos— y no es necesario que estén enamorados.

Panamá A mucha gente hispanohablante le gusta una conversación animada. Pero estos jóvenes en un cine en la Ciudad de Panamá no quieren que sus vecinos hablen durante la película. Con un gesto el joven les dice que se callen. ▼

Argentina *(page 135)* ¿Se da un besito en Argentina también?

México *(page 135)* ¿Quiénes se dan un abrazo? Describe un típico abrazo.

Ecuador *(page 135)* ¿Tiene que ver con el cuido y mantenimiento de los jardines el aviso? ¿Dónde está el aviso?

Panamá *(page 135)* ¿Dónde están los jóvenes? ¿Qué les gusta a muchos hispanohablantes? ¿Quieren estos jóvenes que la gente hable durante la película?

España *(page 135)* Cuando estos jóvenes hablan, ¿hay mucha distancia entre ellos?

135

Resources

- 📀 Vocabulary Transparencies V5.2–V5.3
- 📕 Audio Activities TE, pages 5.17–5.20
- 🎧 Audio CD 5, Tracks 1–6
- 📕 Workbook, pages 5.3–5.4
- 📕 Quiz 1, page 5.39
- 💿 *ExamView® Assessment Suite*

🕐 Quick Start

Use QS Transparency 5.1 or write the following on the board.
Escribe una lista de las partes del cuerpo que sabes en español.

▶ TEACH
Core Instruction

Step 1 Present vocabulary first with books closed using Vocabulary Transparencies V5.2–V5.3.

Step 2 You may wish to read each sentence to students once or twice and then ask questions such as: **¿Estaban sentados los amigos? ¿Dónde? ¿Quién llegó? ¿Qué hicieron todos cuando el invitado llegó? ¿Por qué se levantaron o se pusieron de pie?**

Differentiation
Multiple Intelligences

You may wish to have **bodily-kinesthetic** learners dramatize many of the actions in this vocabulary section.

📷 Cultural Snapshot

(page 136) These photographs were taken in Marbella, Spain.

Vocabulario
presentación

Saludos

Todos estaban sentados en la sala.
Llegó un invitado.

Cuando el invitado llegó, todos se levantaron.
Saludaron al recién llegado.
Para ser corteses, todos se pusieron de pie.

Un joven le dio la mano.
Es probable que los jóvenes y el invitado no se conozcan bien.
Pero no importa. Se da la mano a un amigo igual que a un conocido.

136 *ciento treinta y seis*   CAPÍTULO 5

GLENCOE 🖱 Technology

Video in the Classroom

Vocabulario en vivo Watch and listen to Nora as she explains manners in the Spanish-speaking world.

GLENCOE 🖱 Technology

You may wish to use the editable PowerPoint® presentation on PowerTeach for additional vocabulary instruction and practice.

Despedidas

la mejilla

Las dos jóvenes se dieron un besito.
Se dieron un besito en cada mejilla.

Los dos jóvenes se dieron un abrazo.
Se abrazaron cuando se despidieron.
Los dos jóvenes son amigos.

Jaime me invitó a cenar.
Cuando llegó la cuenta, no quería que yo pagara.
Insistió en que yo no pagara.
Él quería pagar porque me había invitado.

En otras partes

You will also hear **portarse,** as well as **comportarse,** in quite a few areas of Latin America.

Comportamiento

El chico no se había comportado bien.
Su madre se enfadó.
Se enfadó porque el chico no se
   comportaba bien.
Lo castigaba porque quería que tuviera
   buenos modales.

137

 Cultura

Choose students to come to the front of the class and act out the customs for saying good-bye. Ask them if they feel comfortable saying good-bye in this way. Is this something they do often or not?

 Comunicación

Presentational

You may wish to choose two outgoing students to make up and present a skit based on the picture at the bottom of page 137. Have them incorporate their new vocabulary into the script.

Total Physical Response (TPR)

(Student 1) **y** *(Student 2),* **vengan aquí, por favor.**

(Student 1) **y** *(Student 2),* **siéntense, por favor.**

(Student 3), **entra.**

(Student 1) **y** *(Student 2),* **levántense.**

(Student 3), **dale la mano a** *(Student 1).*

Ahora *(Student 3),* **dale la mano a** *(Student 2).*

Y ahora, siéntense todos.

Gracias.

(Student 1), **ven acá, por favor.**

Dramatiza todo lo que le digo.

Dale un besito a alguien.

Dale un abrazo a alguien.

Indícale a alguien que no quieres que pague.

Indícale a alguien que estás enfadado(a).

QuickPass

Go to glencoe.com
For: **Vocabulary practice**
Web code: **ASD7844c5**

▶ PRACTICE

Leveling EACH Activity

Easy Activites 1, 2, 3, 5, 7
Average Activity 6
CHallenging Activity 4,
   Activity 6 **Expansión**

Activity ❶

🎧 **Audio Script**

1. ¿Ellos se levantaron?
   a. Sí, levantaron la mano.
   b. Sí, se pusieron de pie.
2. ¿Por qué se enfadó la madre?
   a. Porque el niño tenía bue-
      nos modales.
   b. Porque el niño se com-
      portó mal.
3. ¿Se dieron un besito?
   a. Sí, en el brazo.
   b. Sí, en las mejillas.
4. Cuando se vieron los dos
   señores, ¿qué hicieron?
   a. Se abrazaron.
   b. Se sorprendieron.
5. ¿Por qué no quería que tú
   pagaras la cuenta?
   a. Porque él me había invi-
      tado a cenar.
   b. Porque insistió en que yo
      pagara.

Activities ❷ and ❸ These
activities can be done orally
with books closed calling on
students at random to respond.
They can also be done as
paired activities.

Activity ❹ Students will use
previously learned material
doing this activity.

 GeoVistas

Have students turn to page
SH53 and locate Uruguay on
the map. Ask them to point
out and name the capital.
Then ask them to compare
Uruguay's size with that of
neighboring countries.

ESCUCHAR

❶ Escucha. Escoge la frase correcta. Usa una tabla como la de
abajo para indicar tus respuestas.

a	b

ESCUCHAR • HABLAR

❷ Contesta con **sí.**
   1. ¿Se levantaron todos de la mesa?
   2. ¿Se levantaron cuando otros llegaron?
   3. ¿Algunos se dieron la mano?
   4. ¿Algunos se dieron un besito?
   5. ¿Se besaron en la mejilla?
   6. ¿Se abrazaron los señores?

HABLAR • ESCRIBIR

❸ Personaliza. Da respuestas personales.
   1. Cuando estás sentado(a) y llega otra persona, ¿te
      levantas?
   2. Cuando ves a un(a) amigo(a), ¿le das la mano?
   3. Si eres un muchacho, ¿le das un abrazo a un amigo?
   4. Si eres una muchacha, ¿le das un besito a una amiga?
   5. Si tú invitas a alguien a ir a una película, ¿pagas?
   6. Si estás haciendo cola y alguien se pone delante de
      ti, ¿te enfadas?
   7. ¿Quiénes se conocen mejor? ¿Los amigos o los
      conocidos?

🌐 GeoVistas

To learn more about
Uruguay, take a tour on
pages SH52–SH53.

 Comunicación

❹ Dile a un(a) amigo(a) lo que haces que consideras
buenos modales. Sigue diciéndole lo que consideras
malos modales. ¿Cuáles son algunos comportamientos
que te enfadan?

CULTURA
El señor ayuda a una señora
ciega a subir al taxi en su
pueblo en Uruguay.

138   *ciento treinta y ocho*   **CAPÍTULO 5**

Answers

❶
1. b   2. b   3. b   4. a   5. a

❷
1. Sí, todos se levantaron de la mesa.
2. Sí, se levantaron cuando otros llegaron.
3. Sí, algunos se dieron la mano.
4. Sí, algunos se dieron un besito.
5. Sí, se besaron en la mejilla.
6. Sí, los señores se abrazaron.

❸
1. Sí (No), cuando estoy sentado(a) y llega otra persona,
   (no) me levanto.
2. Sí (No), cuando veo a un(a) amigo(a), (no) le doy
   la mano.
3. Sí, (No, no) le doy un abrazo a un amigo.
4. Sí, (No, no) le doy un besito a una amiga.
5. Sí (No), si invito a alguien a ir a una película, (no) pago.
6. Sí (No), si estoy haciendo cola, y alguien se pone
   delante de mí, (no) me enfado.

LEER • ESCRIBIR

5 Da una palabra relacionada.
1. abrazar
2. besar
3. invitar
4. el brazo
5. el comportamiento

ESCRIBIR

6 Da la palabra cuya definición sigue.
1. una persona que acaba de llegar
2. un beso pequeño
3. una parte de la cara
4. un niño

EXPANSIÓN

Usa cada expresión en una frase original.

7 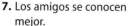 Juego Cambia una letra en cada palabra para formar una palabra nueva.
1. chino
2. casa
3. cuesta
4. sano
5. cuanto

Estudio de palabras

el amor El amor es una cosa divina.

enamorarse Los jóvenes se están enamorando.

enamorado(a) Ellos están enamorados y se van a casar.

malentender Ellos no lo entendieron bien. Lo malentendieron.

el malentendido Tenían un pequeño malentendido, pero nada serio.

Completa con la palabra apropiada.
Se ve el _____ en su cara. No hay duda que se están _____ si no están ya _____. Es evidente que no hay ningún _____ entre ellos.

Más práctica

▪ Workbook, pp. 5.3–5.4
⊕ StudentWorks™ Plus

Conexiones

La sociología
Los hablantes de todas las lenguas tienen sus gestos particulares. Aquí tienes dos que usan muchos hispanohablantes.

¡Estupendo!

¡Cuidado! ¡Mucho ojo!

Vocabulario

Activities 5 and 6 These activities can be prepared and then gone over in class. Call on several students to give their original sentences from Activity 6.

Estudio de palabras

Have students read each new word and the sentence that illustrates its meaning and usage. Then go over the activity.

Differentiation

Advanced Learners

Have advanced learners make up additional original sentences using the words from the **Estudio de palabras**.

Cultura

Heritage Speakers

Have students read the information in the **Conexiones** box. If you have heritage speakers in class, you may wish to ask them to demonstrate some other commonly used gestures. Ask the rest of the class if they are familiar with these gestures. If not, ask them to demonstrate the gesture they would use to communicate the same concept. Remind them that the gestures cannot be offensive.

¿BUENOS O MALOS MODALES?   *ciento treinta y nueve* **139**

Answers

7. Los amigos se conocen mejor.

4 *Answers will vary.*

5
1. un abrazo
2. un besito
3. un(a) invitado(a)
4. abrazar, un abrazo
5. comportarse

6
1. un(a) recién llegado(a)
2. un besito
3. la mejilla
4. un chico

7 *Answers will vary but may include:*
1. chico
2. cara (cama, cada, casi, caso, cosa)
3. cuenta
4. mano
5. cuando

Estudio de palabras
1. amor
2. enamorando
3. enamorados
4. malentendido

QuickPass

Go to glencoe.com
For: **Grammar practice**
Web code: **ASD7844c5**

Resources

- Audio Activities TE, pages 5.21–5.23
- Audio CD 5, Tracks 7–11
- Workbook, pages 5.5–5.7
- Quizzes 2 and 3, pages 5.40–5.41
- ExamView® Assessment Suite

 Quick Start

Use QS Transparency 5.2 or write the following on the board.

Completa con el imperfecto.

1. Yo lo ____. (saber)
2. Ellos siempre ____ bien. (salir)
3. Yo le ____ con frecuencia. (hablar)
4. Nosotros nunca ____ la misma cosa. (comer)
5. Tú ____ todos los domingos, ¿no? (ir)
6. Ellos siempre ____ al mismo tiempo. (llegar)

⭐Tips for Success

You may wish to quickly review the preterite on pages 130 and 131 before giving the explanation for the formation and use of the imperfect subjunctive.

▶ TEACH
Core Instruction

Step 1 Have students read Items 1–5 silently.

Step 2 Write the verb paradigms of **hablar, comer,** and **pedir** on the board and have the students say them aloud.

Step 3 Have the class say the forms of the irregular verbs in unison, making sure that their pronunciation is exact.

140

¿Te acuerdas?

Remember that the preterite tense was reviewed in the previous chapter. See pages 130–131.

¡Ojo!

Quisiera and **pudiera** can be used on their own to express *would like* and *could*.
Quisiera ir con ellos.
Nosotros **pudiéramos.**

El imperfecto del subjuntivo

1. The imperfect subjunctive of all verbs is formed by dropping the **-on** from the ending of the third person plural, **ellos(as),** form of the preterite tense of the verb.

PRETERITE	hablaron	comieron	pidieron	tuvieron	dijeron
STEM	hablar-	comier-	pidier-	tuvier-	dijer-

2. To this stem, you add the following endings: -a, -as, -a, -amos, -*ais,* -an.

	hablar	comer	pedir	tener	decir
yo	hablara	comiera	pidiera	tuviera	dijera
tú	hablaras	comieras	pidieras	tuvieras	dijeras
Ud., él, ella	hablara	comiera	pidiera	tuviera	dijera
nosotros(as)	habláramos	comiéramos	pidiéramos	tuviéramos	dijéramos
vosotros(as)	*hablarais*	*comierais*	*pidierais*	*tuvierais*	*dijerais*
Uds., ellos, ellas	hablaran	comieran	pidieran	tuvieran	dijeran

3. The same rules that apply to the use of the present subjunctive apply to the use of the imperfect subjunctive. The tense of the verb in the main clause determines whether the present or imperfect subjunctive must be used in the dependent clause. If the verb of the main clause is in the present or future tense, the present subjunctive is used in the dependent clause.

Quiero que ellos se **comporten** bien.
Será necesario que **tengan** buenos modales.

4. If the verb of the main clause is in the preterite, imperfect, or conditional, the imperfect subjunctive must be used in the dependent clause.

Él habló así para que **comprendiéramos.**
Me sorprendió que ellos no se **dieran** la mano.
Ella no quería que yo **pagara.**
Sería imposible que él no lo **supiera.**

5. The following is the sequence of tenses for using the present and imperfect subjunctive.

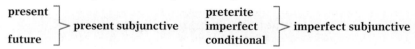

present / future ⟩ present subjunctive

preterite / imperfect / conditional ⟩ imperfect subjunctive

⭐Tips for Success

Remind students that if they pronounce a word correctly, they will spell it correctly. Have them pronounce each of these verb forms clearly.

Answers

1
1. Él quería que yo lo tuviera.
2. Él quería que yo lo supiera.
3. Él quería que yo lo comprara.
4. Él quería que yo lo hiciera.
5. Él quería que yo lo devolviera.
6. Él quería que yo lo leyera.
7. Él quería que yo lo comiera.
8. Él quería que yo lo escribiera.

Práctica

Más práctica
■ Workbook, pp. 5.5–5.7
● StudentWorks™ Plus

ESCUCHAR • HABLAR • ESCRIBIR

1 Sigue el modelo para hacer una frase completa.

MODELO invitarlo →
Él quería que yo lo invitara.

1. tenerlo
2. saberlo
3. comprarlo
4. hacerlo
5. devolverlo
6. leerlo
7. comerlo
8. escribirlo
9. ponerlo
10. buscarlo
11. decirlo
12. pedirlo

HABLAR

2 Contesta con **sí** o **no** según tu opinión.

1. ¿Te sorprendería que tus amigos te dieran la mano?
2. ¿Te sorprendería que una amiga te diera un besito en la mejilla?
3. ¿Te sorprendería que tus amigos se levantaran para saludarte?
4. ¿Te sorprendería que ellos se abrazaran?
5. ¿Te sorprendería que tus amigos tuvieran buenos modales?
6. ¿Te sorprendería que ellos se comportaran bien?
7. ¿Te sorprendería que hubiera un mal entendido entre tus amigos?

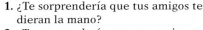

CULTURA
Abuelita quería que su nieta le diera la mano para ayudarla a bajarse del metro.

Comunicación

3 Trabajen en grupos pequeños y hablen de todo lo que les gustaría, lo que no les gustaría o lo que les sorprendería que pasara. Si es posible expliquen por qué.

ESCUCHAR • HABLAR • ESCRIBIR

4 Contesta según el modelo.

MODELO hablar español →
El profesor insistió en que habláramos español.

1. hablar mucho
2. pronunciar bien
3. llegar a clase a tiempo
4. aprender la gramática
5. escribir composiciones
6. leer novelas
7. trabajar mucho
8. hacer nuestras tareas

Nota
Verbs with **y** are spelled the same as those with **j**.
leyera   dijera
oyera   trajera

InfoGap For more practice using the imperfect subjunctive, do Activity 5 on page SR6 at the end of this book.

¿BUENOS O MALOS MODALES?

ciento cuarenta y uno **141**

▶ PRACTICE

Leveling EACH Activity

Easy Activities 1, 2
Average Activity 4
CHallenging Activity 3

Note: Please note that we have labeled these activities E, A, CH in comparison to one another. Given the nature of these structure points, however, many students will not find them truly easy.

Activities 1, 2, and 4 It is suggested that you first go over these activities orally in class with books closed. Call on students at random to respond. It is also suggested that you call on more able students for the first few items in each activity.

ABOUT THE SPANISH LANGUAGE

If you have a rather advanced group, you may wish to give them the alternate form of the imperfect subjunctive for recognition purposes only.

hablase, hablases, hablase, hablásemos, hablaseis, hablasen

tuviese, tuvieses, tuviese, tuviésemos, tuvieseis, tuviesen

dijese, dijeses, dijese, dijéremos, dijereis, dijeren

Answers

9. Él quería que yo lo pusiera.
10. Él quería que yo lo buscara.
11. Él quería que yo lo dijera.
12. Él quería que yo lo pidiera.

2
1. Sí, (No, no) me sorprendería que mis amigos me dieran la mano.
2. Sí, (No, no) me sorprendería que una amiga me diera un besito en

la mejilla.
3. Sí, (No, no) me sorprendería que mis amigos se levantaran para saludarme.
4. Sí, (No, no) me sorprendería que ellos se abrazaran.
5. Sí, (No, no) me sorprendería que mis amigos tuvieran buenos modales.

6. Sí, (No, no) me sorprendería que ellos se comportaran bien.
7. Sí, (No, no) me sorprendería que hubiera un mal entendido entre mis amigos.

3 *Answers will vary.*

4 El profesor insistió en que:
1. habláramos mucho.
2. pronunciáramos bien.
3. llegáramos a clase a tiempo.
4. aprendiéramos la gramática.
5. escribiéramos composiciones.
6. leyéramos novelas.
7. trabajáramos mucho.
8. hiciéramos nuestras

VIDEO Want help with the imperfect subjunctive? Watch **Gramática en vivo.**

▶ PRACTICE (continued)

Leveling EACH Activity

CHallenging Activities 5, 6

Activities **5** and **6** These activities should be prepared as homework before going over them in class.

Cultural Snapshot

(page 142) Such traditional dress is not very common today. One may see it worn, however, during certain cultural heritage celebrations.

GLENCOE **Technology**

Video in the Classroom

Gramática en vivo: *The imperfect subjunctive* Enliven learning with the animated world of Professor Cruz! **Gramática en vivo** is a fun and effective tool for additional instruction and/or review.

▶ ASSESS

Students are now ready to take Quizzes 2 and 3 on pages 5.40–5.41 of the TeacherTools booklet. If you prefer to create your own quiz, use the *ExamView® Assessment Suite.*

CULTURA

El entrenador insistió en que los miembros de su equipo jugaran bien.

FOLDABLES®
Study Organizer

LARGE SENTENCE STRIPS
See page SH31 for help with making this foldable. Use this foldable to practice using the imperfect subjunctive with a partner. On the front of each strip, use the verbs **querer, insistir, esperar,** and **dudar** to write a sentence in the present tense. Then have your partner rewrite each sentence on the back of each strip using the imperfect subjunctive. When you're finished, switch roles.

CULTURA

La familia de la novia insistió en que ella tuviera una boda tradicional en Ibiza, una de las islas Baleares de España.

142

LEER • ESCRIBIR

5 Completa con la forma apropiada del verbo indicado.

1. Yo tenía miedo de que ellos no _____ a tiempo. (llegar)
2. Estaban contentos que tú _____ para ayudarles. (estar)
3. No me sorprendió que ellos _____. (casarse)
4. Tenían miedo de que yo no _____ asistir a la recepción. (poder)
5. Durante la ceremonia civil, fue necesario que la pareja _____ el registro de matrimonio. (firmar)

ESCRIBIR

6 Escribe la frase de nuevo. Haz los cambios necesarios.

1. Ella quiere que yo llegue a tiempo.
   Ella quería _____.
2. Ella insiste en que seas cortés.
   Ella insistió _____.
3. Ella insistirá en que lo hagas correctamente.
   Ella insistiría _____.
4. Ella duda que ellos tengan razón.
   Ella dudó _____.
5. Ella quiere que hablemos con nuestros padres.
   Ella quería _____.

Subjuntivo o infinitivo

Más práctica
☐ Workbook, p. 5.8
◉ StudentWorks™ Plus

1. If the subject of the main clause is different from the subject of the dependent clause, the subjunctive is used.

MAIN CLAUSE		DEPENDENT CLAUSE
¿Tú quieres	que	yo vaya?
Nosotros preferimos	que	ustedes se lo digan.
Era necesario	que	tú lo supieras.

2. If there is no change of subject, the infinitive is used.

¿Tú quieres **ir**?
Preferimos **decírselo**.
Era necesario **saberlo**.

Práctica

ESCUCHAR • HABLAR • ESCRIBIR

7 Contesta con **sí**. Presta atención a los sujetos.
1. ¿Quieres decírselo?
2. ¿Quieres que yo se lo diga?
3. ¿Quieres sentarte?
4. ¿Quieres que ellos se sienten?
5. ¿Prefieres salir con ellos?
6. ¿Prefieres que yo salga con ellos?
7. ¿Prefieres pagar?
8. ¿Prefieres que ellos paguen?

ESCRIBIR

8 Forma frases.

MODELO   yo / esperar / él / ir →
                  Yo espero que él vaya.

1. yo / esperar / ustedes / venir pronto
2. yo / esperar / venir
3. ellos / esperar / nosotros / llegar
4. nosotros / esperar / tú / divertirte
5. yo / esperar / divertirme

CULTURA
¿Quieres dar un paseo por los bonitos jardines del Palacio Real en Madrid?

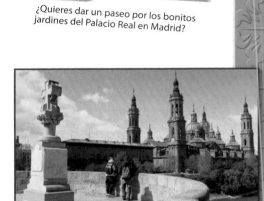

CULTURA
Estos jóvenes esperan pasar un buen día en Zaragoza, España. Están mirando la vista de la Basílica de Nuestra Señora del Pilar desde el puente de Piedra sobre el río Ebro.

Comunicación

9 Pregúntale a tu compañero(a) lo que él o ella quiere hacer este fin de semana. Después, pregúntale lo que sus padres quieren que él o ella haga. Decidan si ustedes quieren hacer las mismas cosas que sus padres quieren que hagan o no.

¿BUENOS O MALOS MODALES?

ciento cuarenta y tres   **143**

Cultural Snapshot

(page 143 top) The Palacio Real stands on the same spot as Madrid's first Arab fortress. The Royal Palace with its 2,800 rooms was commissioned in the early eighteenth century by Felipe IV.
(page 143 bottom) Zaragoza, capital of the province of Aragón and the Ciudad Autónoma, was founded by the Romans in 25 B.C. The beautiful Basílica del Pilar was named in honor of Spain's patron saint, la Virgen del Pilar. The present building dates from the seventeenth and eighteenth centuries and is known for its eleven domes.

Resources

■ Audio Activities TE, page 5.24
◎ Audio CD 5, Tracks 12–13
■ Workbook, page 5.8
■ Quiz 4, page 5.42
◉ ExamView® Assessment Suite

Quick Start

Use QS Transparency 5.3 or write the following on the board.
Completa con un infinitivo.
1. Yo debo ___.
2. Queremos ___.
3. Ellos tienen que ___.
4. ¿Acabas de ___?
5. ¿Prefieren ustedes ___?
6. Vamos a ___.

▶ TEACH

Core Instruction

As you go over Item 1, have students look at the examples. Point out that they will always use **que** before the subjunctive.

▶ PRACTICE

Leveling EACH Activity

Easy Activity 7
Average Activity 8
CHallenging Activity 9

Differentiation

Multiple Intelligences

To assist **visual-spatial** learners, have students put up two fingers when there is a change of subject and just one finger when there is no change of subject.

Gramática

Resources

- Workbook, page 5.9
- Quiz 5, page 5.43
- ExamView® Assessment Suite

Quick Start

Use QS Transparency 5.4 or write the following on the board.

Da el contrario.

1. bueno
2. alto
3. pequeño
4. viejo
5. limpio
6. ambicioso
7. interesante

▶ TEACH

Core Instruction

Have students read aloud the explanation given here as well as the examples. This point should be quite easy for almost all students.

▶ PRACTICE

Leveling EACH Activity

Easy Activities 10, 11, 12, 13, 14

Activities ⑩, ⑪, ⑫ You may wish to go over these activities orally in class before students write them.

GLENCOE Technology

You may wish to use the editable PowerPoint® presentation on PowerTeach for additional grammar instruction and practice.

En otras partes

Diminutive endings can vary in different parts of the Spanish-speaking world. The two most common are probably **-ito** and **-illo**, but you will also hear **-ico**.

CULTURA

Una casita bellísima en Cadaqués, España

Cultural Snapshot

(page 144) Cadaqués, on the Catalonian coast near the French border, was Dalí's home and continues to be popular among artists and literati.

Sufijos

1. A suffix is an ending you add to a word. You can add the suffixes **-ito** or **-illo** to a Spanish noun to form what is called the "diminutive" form of the noun. The meaning of the diminutive may refer to the actual physical size or it may convey a favorable emotional quality on the part of the speaker.

la casa	la casita	la chica	la chiquita
el beso	el besito	el perro	el perrito

2. If the noun ends in **-n** or the vowel **-e**, the suffix **-cito** is added.

el ratón	el ratoncito
el café	el cafecito

3. You can add the suffix **-ísimo** to an adjective to convey the meaning *very* or *most*. Remember that the adjective must agree with the noun it modifies.

un joven guapísimo	una joven guapísima
unos jóvenes guapísimos	unas jóvenes guapísimas

Note that an adjective that ends in a vowel drops the vowel before adding **-ísimo**.

bueno → buenísimo
grande → grandísimo

Práctica

LEER • ESCRIBIR

⑩ Da la forma diminutiva.

1. el vaso
2. la casa
3. el beso
4. el perro
5. el plato
6. el amigo
7. la abuela
8. el hijo
9. la botella
10. la caja

LEER • ESCRIBIR

⑪ Da la forma diminutiva.

1. el coche
2. el café
3. el parque
4. el ratón
5. la calle
6. el limón

Answers

⑩
1. el vasito
2. la casita
3. el besito
4. el perrito
5. el platito
6. el amiguito
7. la abuelita
8. el hijito
9. la botellita
10. la cajita

⑪
1. el cochecito
2. el cafecito
3. el parquecito
4. el ratoncito
5. la callecita
6. el limoncito

LEER • ESCRIBIR

 Emplea **-ísimo** con el adjetivo.

1. Es una comida buena.
2. Son animales grandes.
3. Es una lección difícil.
4. Tienen dos niños preciosos.
5. Tiene una prima bella.

⑬ **Trabalenguas** Lee con cuidado. ¡Diviértete!

1. Abuelita toma un cafecito y un platito de pastelitos en su cafecito favorito en el parquecito.
2. Los amiguitos juegan con su perrito en el jardincito de su casita.
3. Los gatitos y los perritos son animalitos preciosísimos.

⑭ **Juego** Work in groups. Make up as many words with **-ito**, **-ico**, **-illo** as possible in two minutes. See who wins.

CULTURA
Un cochecito en Sevilla

Refrán

Can you guess what the following proverb means?

A chico pajarillo, chico nidillo.

¡Bravo!

You have now learned all the new vocabulary and grammar in this chapter. Continue to use and practice all that you know while learning more cultural information. ¡Vamos!

GLENCOE **Technology**

Online Learning in the Classroom

Have students use QuickPass code ASD7844c5 for additional grammar practice. They can review each grammar point with an eGame. They can also review all grammar points by doing the self-check quiz, which integrates the chapter vocabulary with the new grammar.

▶ ASSESS

Students are now ready to take Quiz 5 on page 5.43 of the TeacherTools booklet. If you prefer to create your own quiz, use the *ExamView® Assessment Suite.*

Refrán

Proverbs, adages, idiomatic expressions, and other popular sayings provide a wealth of opportunities for students to learn about different cultural perspectives as well as perspectives shared by different cultures. They also serve to enrich students' overall understanding of language.

Have students recite the proverb aloud. Then see if they can give the literal translation: "Little bird, little nest." Ask them what this means.

¡Bravo! The remaining pages of the chapter recycle information in a variety of ways, allowing students to build upon their newly acquired language skills as well as to keep track of their own progress. This format also ensures that students are not surprised by vocabulary or grammar that has not yet been introduced or studied.

Answers

1. Es una comida buenísima.
2. Son animales grandísimos.
3. Es una lección dificilísima.
4. Tienen dos niños preciosísimos.
5. Tiene una prima bellísima.

⑭ *Answers will vary.*

QuickPass

Go to glencoe.com
For: **Conversation practice**
Web code: **ASD7844c5**

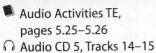

Resources

- Audio Activities TE, pages 5.25–5.26
- Audio CD 5, Tracks 14–15

▶ TEACH

Core Instruction

Step 1 If the pronunciation of the class is good, you may have them listen to the conversation once on Audio CD 5, Tracks 14–15.

Step 2 Call on students to read the conversation aloud.

Step 3 Do the **¿Comprendes?** activities.

Differentiation

Advanced Learners

Have more able or advanced learners work in pairs or small groups to make up their own conversation concerning a variety of **malentendidos**. You may wish to have a contest in which the class determines which pair or group made up the most original **malentendido**.

146 *ciento cuarenta y seis*   CAPÍTULO 5

GLENCOE Technology

Online Learning in the Classroom

Have students use QuickPass code ASD7844c5 for additional conversation practice. Students can download audio files for the conversation to their computer and/or MP3 player and complete a self-check quiz.

¿Comprendes?

VIDEO To learn about a Mexican custom, watch Cultura en vivo.

A Contesta según la información en la conversación.
1. ¿Quiénes hablan?
2. ¿Cómo se llama la prima de Yolanda?
3. ¿Quién la vio?
4. ¿Cómo la describió?
5. ¿Qué cree Bill?
6. ¿Por qué cree tal cosa?

B Explicando Contesta.
1. ¿Qué le explica Yolanda a Bill?
2. ¿Puede ella convencer a Bill?
3. ¿Qué cree Yolanda?

C Llegando a conclusiones ¿Qué piensas? ¿Estás de acuerdo con Bill o con Yolanda?

D Interpretando El título de la conversación es «¡Un pequeño malentendido!» ¿Por qué lleva tal título?

E Analizando How do such **malentendidos culturales** take place? Have you ever experienced one?

¿Qué crees? ¿Tiene razón Bill o hay un malentendido?

¿BUENOS O MALOS MODALES?

ciento cuarenta y siete **147**

Conversación

Heritage Speakers

If you have heritage students in class, have them indicate if they have ever encountered a misunderstanding that was culturally based. Have them explain the misunderstanding. You can ask non-heritage speakers the same question and have students tell where and under what circumstances the misunderstanding took place.

▶ PRACTICE

¿Comprendes?

A and **B** These activities can be done as oral activities with books closed. You can call on volunteers to respond.
C This activity can be done as a group discussion.
D and **E** These activities can be done as individual, paired, or group activities.

GLENCOE 🔍 Technology

Video in the Classroom

Cultura en vivo In this episode, students learn about the Day of the Dead celebrations in Mexico. Ask students if there are any similarities between the Day of the Dead and a holiday that they celebrate.

Pre-AP Listening to this conversation on audio CD will help students develop the skills that they need to be successful on the listening portion of the AP exam.

Answers

A
1. Bill y Yolanda hablan.
2. La prima de Yolanda se llama Julia.
3. Bill la vio.
4. Dijo que es una belleza.
5. Bill cree que Julia está enamorada de él.
6. Lo cree porque ella lo besó dos veces.

B
1. Yolanda le explica a Bill que estos besitos no tienen importancia. Julia lo besó en cada mejilla como señal de cariño y amistad.
2. No, ella no puede convencer a Bill.
3. Yolanda cree que es Bill que se está enamorando de Julia.

C *Answers will vary but may include:* Estoy de acuerdo con Yolanda. Bill no quiere comprender la costumbre porque está enamorado de Julia.

D *Answers will vary but may include:* Lleva este título porque Bill ha malentendido los besos que Julia lo había dado.

E *Answers will vary.*

LECTURA CULTURAL

Resources

- Audio Activities TE, pages 5.27–5.31
- Audio CD 5, Tracks 16–20

▶ TEACH

Core Instruction

Step 1 Have students read the **Antes de leer** section and look at the photographs that accompany the **Lectura**.

Step 2 It is up to your discretion as to how thoroughly you wish students to know the information. You may wish to have students learn the material thoroughly enough that they can retell it in their own words, that is transfer from a receptive skill (read) to a productive skill (speak and/or write). In this case it is suggested you call on a student to read a few sentences aloud. Then stop and ask questions that other students can answer.

Teaching Options

Alternatively, you may wish to split the class in groups and have each group read a different section of the **Lectura**. Then have groups report what they have learned to the rest of the class.

Antes de leer

Con tus compañeros, discute las convenciones de cortesía que se practican en tu familia y en tu comunidad.

✓ Reading Check

El mundo hispano goza de muchas influencias culturales diferentes. ¿Cuáles son algunas?

¿Buen comportamiento o mal comportamiento?

Costumbres diferentes Cada cultura tiene sus propias tradiciones y costumbres. Además cada sociedad tiene sus convenciones de cortesía que dictan lo que son buenos y malos modales. Si uno quiere relacionarse bien con gente de otras culturas tiene que aprender y entender sus tradiciones sociales. Y siempre hay que tomar en cuenta que «diferente» no es sinónimo de «inferior» ni «superior» porque cada sociedad tiene distintas normas de buen comportamiento.

Ya sabes que el mundo hispano es muy grande, y no hay una sola cultura hispana. Los muchos países que componen el mundo hispano gozan de¹ muchas influencias culturales diferentes—indígena, español-mediterránea, africana. Y ahora vamos a explorar algunos modales que se consideran buenos o malos en casi todas las naciones hispanohablantes.

Si una persona o un grupo de personas está sentado en un café, una oficina o aun en casa y llega otra persona, todos suelen levantarse y darle la mano al recién llegado para saludarlo. Es una costumbre que se practica igual entre los jóvenes.

¹gozan de   *enjoy*

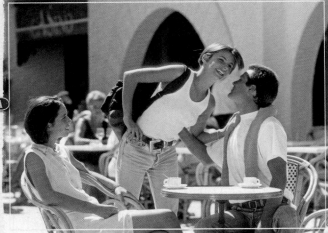

CULTURA
Un besito entre amigos en la mejilla no es señal de amor.

El abrazo El abrazo es otra costumbre muy hispana. Son los hombres que se conocen bien que se abrazan. Un señor rodea a un amigo con los brazos mientras le da unos golpes en la espalda. Los hombres se abrazan así cuando se encuentran[2] o cuando se despiden[3] el uno del otro.

El besito Las mujeres no se abrazan. Se dan un besito. Le dan el besito a una amiga o a un amigo que conocen bien. Dan el besito en cada mejilla, y la verdad es que las mejillas y los labios no se tocan. El besito va al aire. El abrazo o el besito es una señal de cariño y amistad entre amigos y parientes y nada más.

«Tú» y «usted» Hay que tener mucho cuidado con el uso de «tú» y «usted» y no hay siempre normas claras porque el uso de «tú» y «usted» puede variar de un país a otro o de una clase social a otra. El uso de «tú» se llama «el tuteo», y hablar con alguien en la forma de «tú» es «tutearlo». ¿Cuándo puedes tutear a una persona? Pues, es casi siempre aceptable tutear a una persona que tiene la misma edad que tú. En otras circunstancias debes esperar a que el individuo con quien hablas te invite a tutearlo. En general se tutea entre amigos, parientes y jóvenes. En los otros casos se usa «usted».

El voseo Ya sabes que el plural de «tú» en España es «vosotros». En Latinoamérica es «ustedes». Pero hay que señalar algo importantísimo. No en todas partes, pero en muchas partes de Latinoamérica en vez de decir «tú» la gente usa «vos», llamado «el voseo». Algunos ejemplos del voseo son:

Vos estás bien.
Vos podés hacerlo.
Vos tenés tiempo.
¿Vos te sentís mejor?
¿A qué hora vos te acostás?

[2]se encuentran *they meet*
[3]se despiden *they take leave*

✓ **Reading Check**
¿Cuándo se abrazan los hombres?

✓ **Reading Check**
¿Cuándo es aceptable tutear a una persona?

✓ **Reading Check**
¿Qué es «el voseo»?

CULTURA
Un saludo típico entre dos amigas en San Juan de Puerto Rico

¿BUENOS O MALOS MODALES?

ciento cuarenta y nueve **149**

★**Tips for Success** ·······
Before reading the paragraph about **tú** and **usted**, you may wish to call on a student to tell what he or she already knows about the formal and informal usage of these subject pronouns.
··

ABOUT THE SPANISH LANGUAGE

There is the assumption among some Spanish speakers that **voseo** is used only in less-than-sophisticated conversation. This is a misconception. In the Southern Cone, for example, the **voseo** is used among people of all educational and socioeconomic levels in all types of conversation. The **voseo** is also used in varying degrees in quite a few other areas of Latin America. **Voseo** appears in many dialogues, in advertisements, and in literary pieces.

✿ **Comparaciones** ●

Have students create a Venn diagram to compare and contrast manners and customs in the United States to those in Latin America and/or Spain. Then have them present their diagram to the class.

Cultura

- Have students discuss the titles they almost always use when speaking English. Ask them if they differ from the titles used in Spanish.
- Have students give the English equivalents to the terms **amigos** and **conocidos**. Then have them discuss how they interpret the meaning of *friend* versus *acquaintance*.

Heritage Speakers

Have heritage speakers give their reactions to the information in this **Lectura**. Ask them if they think there are some other items dealing with manners or behavior that students should know.

GLENCOE Technology

Online Learning in the Classroom

You may wish to have students use QuickPass code ASD7844c5 to develop their reading comprehension and writing skills. Students will be able to take a self-check quiz, which includes an essay.

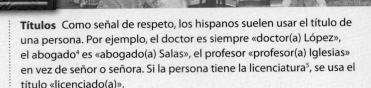

Títulos Como señal de respeto, los hispanos suelen usar el título de una persona. Por ejemplo, el doctor es siempre «doctor(a) López», el abogado[4] es «abogado(a) Salas», el profesor «profesor(a) Iglesias» en vez de señor o señora. Si la persona tiene la licenciatura[5], se usa el título «licenciado(a)».

CULTURA

Observa el uso de títulos en este aviso delante de un despacho (oficina) en la isla de Vieques, Puerto Rico. ¿De qué será la abreviatura **Lcda.?**

> Lcda. Aurora Padilla Morales
> Abogada-Notario
> Servicios Notariales
> Casos Civiles y Criminales

Reading Check

¿Cuál es la diferencia entre un amigo y un conocido?

Amigos o conocidos En unas culturas la gente se refiere a casi todos los que conocen como «amigos». Pero no es así en las culturas latinas. Un «amigo» es «un amigo»—una persona a quien conoces bien y en quien tienes confianza. Una persona a quien conoces pero no muy bien es un «conocido». En las culturas latinas uno tiene muchos conocidos y menos amigos. En otras culturas uno tiene muchos amigos y menos conocidos.

Reading Check

¿Cuál es una diversión que les gusta a muchos hispanohablantes?

Conversaciones y tertulias Para mucha gente hispanohablante no hay nada mejor que una buena conversación animada en que todos ofrecen sus opiniones o ideas con mucho entusiasmo. Si buscas la palabra «tertulia» en un diccionario bilingüe, es posible que encuentres la definición *party,* pero es en realidad una reunión de personas que se juntan con frecuencia. ¿Para qué? Para pasarlo bien pero aún más importante para conversar.

[4]abogado   *lawyer*
[5]licenciatura   *degree more or less equivalent to a master's degree*

CULTURA

Varias tertulias en un restaurante de un pueblecito vasco. Estos mismos señores se reúnen habitualmente para conversar de todo.

Answers

A *Answers will vary but may include:*
Es importante tomar en cuenta que «diferente» no es sinónimo de «inferior» ni «superior» porque cada cultura tiene sus propias tradiciones y costumbres y si uno quiero relacionarse bien con gente de otras culturas tiene que aprender y comprender sus tradiciones sociales.

¿Comprendes?

A **Analizando** Contesta.

¿Por qué es importante tomar en cuenta que «diferente» no es sinónimo de «inferior» ni «superior»?

B **Recordando hechos** Contesta.

¿Cuáles son tres culturas que tienen una influencia en las culturas hispanas?

C **Describiendo** Describe.

1. lo que hacen los hispanos cuando están sentados y llega(n) otra(s) persona(s)
2. un abrazo entre hombres
3. el besito que se dan los hispanos

D **Explicando**

1. Explica la diferencia entre el uso de «tú» y «usted». Explica también por qué es importante distinguir entre el uso de «tú» y «usted».
2. Explica lo que es «el voseo».

E **Confirmando información** Escoge según lo que has aprendido sobre las costumbres hispanas.

Más práctica
- Workbook, pp. 5.10–5.12
- StudentWorks™ Plus

CULTURA

Tommy Robredo y Martina Hingis practican buena conducta y buenos modales durante un partido de tenis en una playa de España.

	buenos modales	malos modales
1. no usar el título de la persona con quien hablas		
2. invitar a una persona a hacer algo y no pagar		
3. quedarse sentado(a) cuando llega alguien		
4. tutear a una persona que no conoces bien		
5. darle un besito a una amiga en las mejillas		

¿BUENOS O MALOS MODALES? *ciento cincuenta y uno* **151**

PRACTICE

¿Comprendes?

A This activity can be done as a complete class discussion. It is a very important topic in today's world.

B You may wish to call on students to explain how it is that these three cultural groups have influenced the Hispanic cultures.

C and **D** These activities can also be written.

Answers

B
Tres culturas que tienen una influencia en las culturas hispanas son las culturas indígena, español-mediterránea y africana.

C
1. Los hispanos se levantan cuando llega(n) otra(s) persona(s) y le(s) dan la mano para saludarla(s).
2. Un abrazo es una costumbre muy hispana. Los hombres que se conocen bien se abrazan: un señor rodea a un amigo con los brazos mientras le da unos golpes en la espalda.
3. Las mujeres se dan el besito. Le dan el besito a un(a) amigo(a) que conocen bien. Dan el besito en cada mejilla. Es una señal de cariño y amistad.

D
1. Puedes tutear a los amigos, parientes, jóvenes y personas que tienen la misma edad que tú. Es importante distinguir entre el uso de «tú» y «usted» para demostrar buenos modales y no ofender a nadie.
2. «El voseo» es usar el sujeto «vos» en vez de «tú»; se usa en muchas partes de Latinoamérica.

E
1. malos modales
2. malos modales
3. malos modales
4. malos modales
5. buenos modales

151

Literatura

El conde Lucanor
de don Juan Manuel

Preview

Starting in Chapter 3, each chapter of **¡Así se dice!** Level 3 has a literary section. Most literary selections are by well-known Latin American or Spanish writers. Some selections are poetry and others are prose.

It is up to the discretion of the teacher if you wish to do all or any of these literary works. The difficulty level of each selection is also indicated from 1 to 4. 1 is difficult; 4 is quite easy.

Difficulty Level
4–3

Vocabulario
Core Instruction

Step 1 Call on students to read the new words and their definitions.

Step 2 Have students study the new vocabulary and write the **Práctica** activities.

Tips for Success ....

Although the Spanish in this reading is not in the original fourteenth century language, it still has long sentences typical of the old style. For this reason, the information in the **Estrategia** will be very helpful for students.

▲ El pueblo medieval de Pedraza cerca de Segovia

Estrategia

Simplificando el texto Cuando lees una obra literaria antigua, es necesario simplificar el lenguaje porque el estilo ha cambiado mucho durante los siglos. Una sola frase puede ser larga y contener mucha información. Una estrategia importante es la de dividir las frases en segmentos más cortos mientras lees. Esto te ayuda a seguir el texto y recordar los detalles.

Vocabulario

la villa   ciudad, población

los demás   otras personas

el apodo   otro nombre que toma una persona o que se le da a la persona

el mozo   el joven

el provecho   el beneficio

sabio(a)   muy inteligente

mejorar   hacer mejor

suceder   ocurrir, pasar, tener lugar

olvidar   no recordar

hacerle caso   prestar atención

Práctica

1 Parea los contrarios.
   1. los demás
   2. una villa
   3. mejorar
   4. suceder

   a. no pasar nada
   b. un pueblo pequeño
   c. empeorar
   d. nosotros mismos

2 Usa cada palabra de la Actividad 1 en una frase original.

3 Da otra palabra o expresión.
   1. ciudad o población
   2. no tener en la memoria
   3. un muchacho
   4. prestar atención; fijarse en
   5. de mucha inteligencia
   6. los otros (refiriéndose a gente)

152 *ciento cincuenta y dos*

CAPÍTULO 5

 Cultural Snapshot

(page 152) Pedraza, some 19 miles northeast of Segovia, continues to maintain some of its sixteenth-century village charm in spite of some recent development. The village is completely circled by walls. From the village there are superb views of the Guadarrama Mountains.

 **Answers**

1
1. d   3. c
2. b   4. a

2 *Answers will vary.*

3
1. la villa   4. hacerle caso
2. olvidar   5. sabio(a)
3. un mozo   6. los demás

④ Expresa de otra manera.

1. Tenemos que proteger los derechos de *los otros.*
2. ¿Qué *pasa*?
3. Tienes que *prestarle atención* porque es *muy inteligente.*
4. Él tiene *varios nombres.*
5. Hay que sacar *beneficio* de la oportunidad.

INTRODUCCIÓN

El autor de *El conde Lucanor* es don Juan Manuel (1282–1349?), el sobrino del rey Alfonso X que tenía el apodo Alfonso X el Sabio. El plan del libro es sencillo. El conde Lucanor consulta a su consejero Patronio cada vez que tiene que enfrentar una situación difícil. Patronio le relata un cuento que le puede servir de guía al conde en la decisión que tiene que tomar. La moraleja del cuento se resume al final en unos versos cortitos.

El conde Lucanor 🎧

Capítulo XXIV

De lo que conteció° a un buen hombre con su hijo

En una ocasión ocurrió que el conde Lucanor le hablaba a Patronio, su consejero, y le dijo que estaba muy ansioso sobre una cosa que quería hacer. Estaba ansioso porque sabía que no importaba que lo hiciera o que no lo hiciera, habría quien lo criticara. El conde Lucanor quería que Patronio le diera consejos y Patronio le relató el siguiente cuento.

Ocurrió que un labrador bueno y honrado tenía un hijo joven y muy inteligente pero cada vez que el padre quería hacer algo para mejorar su hacienda° el hijo le contaba un montón de cosas negativas que podrían suceder. Después de un tiempo el buen labrador se puso enfadado porque sabía que estaba sufriendo daños en su negocio° porque siempre le hacía caso a lo que le decía su hijo. Por fin decidió que tenía que enseñarle una lección.

El buen hombre y su hijo eran labradores que vivían cerca de una villa. Un día fueron al mercado de la villa para comprar algunas cosas que necesitaban. Los dos se pusieron de acuerdo° que llevarían un asno para cargar° las compras. Los dos iban al mercado a pie y el asno no llevaba ninguna carga. Encontraron a unos hombres que volvían de la villa. Estos hombres empezaron a hablar entre sí°. El labrador oyó que decían que no les parecía muy prudente que los dos iban a pie mientras el asno andaba descargado. El padre le preguntó a su hijo lo que pensaba de los comentarios de

conteció *sucedió*

hacienda *estate, income*

negocio *business*

se pusieron de acuerdo *agreed*
cargar *carry, load*

entre sí *among themselves*

¿BUENOS O MALOS MODALES?

ciento cincuenta y tres **153**

▶ TEACH
Core Instruction

Step 1 After students read the **Antes de leer** section, ask them if it is easy to please all people at all times. Tell them to think about this as they read.

Step 2 Pick out paragraphs or sections that you consider particularly important and have students read them aloud.

Step 3 Pick out sections that you just want students to read silently either in class or at home. One or two students can be called on to give a synopsis in Spanish of the material that was read silently.

Step 4 You may wish to ask the following comprehension questions: **¿Por qué le habló el conde Lucanor al consejero, Patronio? ¿Contestó Patronio relatándole un cuento? ¿Cómo eran el labrador y su hijo? ¿Por qué se puso enfadado el padre con su hijo? ¿Qué tenía que enseñarle? ¿Adónde fueron un día el padre y su hijo? ¿Por qué decidieron llevar su asno? ¿Llevaba cargo el asno? ¿Qué dijo un grupo de hombres que pasaban? ¿Qué pensaba el hijo de lo que decían los hombres?**

Antes de leer

Es casi imposible tomar decisiones y hacer cosas sin que nadie te critique. ¿Es posible que tengas un amigo o pariente que casi siempre está en contra de lo que quieres hacer? Piensa en tal persona al leer este capítulo de El conde Lucanor.

---

④
1. Tenemos que proteger los derechos de los demás.
2. ¿Qué sucede?
3. Tienes que hacerle caso porque es sabio(a).
4. Él tiene apodos.
5. Hay que sacar provecho de la oportunidad.

▶ TEACH

Core Instruction

Step 1 As students read this page, have them discuss the ideas presented in the **Durante la lectura** section.

Step 2 You may wish to ask the following key questions: ¿Qué problema tiene el padre con su hijo? ¿Por qué se enfadó el padre con su hijo? ¿Qué hizo el padre para enseñarle una lección a su hijo?

Step 3 As an entire group, have the class discuss their conclusions in the **Después de leer** section. If they can relate the conclusion to their personal lives, have them give examples how.

Differentiation

Advanced Learners

Call on advanced learners to discuss the **moraleja** in their own words.

Durante la lectura

Identifica el problema que tiene el padre con su hijo. No olvides de que lo que sucede en el cuento tiene lugar en el siglo XIV. ¿Podría suceder hoy?

Al leer fíjate en lo que hace o dice el hijo que le enfada al padre.

tierno *tender*

CULTURA

Un burro con su carga de canastas en Segovia. Es una escena poco frecuente hoy en día.

fiel *faithful*

no dejes *don't stop*

aquellos hombres. El hijo dijo que le parecía que decían la verdad. Entonces el buen hombre mandó a su hijo que subiera en el (al) asno.

Seguían por el camino cuando encontraron a otros hombres que al verlos dijeron que no les parecía normal que un labrador viejo y cansado anduviera a pie (caminara) y que un joven fuerte anduviera montado en el asno. Una vez más el padre le preguntó a su hijo lo que pensaba de lo que decían estos. El hijo creyó que tenían razón y el padre mandó a su hijo que se bajara del asno para que él lo subiera.

A poca distancia encontraron una vez más a otros hombres. Estos dijeron que el buen hombre hacía muy mal porque él estaba acostumbrado a las fatigas del trabajo y él, y no el hijo pequeño y tierno°, debía andar a pie. El buen hombre le preguntó a su hijo qué le parecía de esto que aquellos hombres decían. El mozo contestó que estaba de acuerdo con ellos. Entonces el padre mandó a su hijo que él también subiera al asno de manera que ninguno de los dos anduviera a pie.

Después de poco encontraron a otros hombres que comenzaron a decir que aquella bestia en que iban era tan flaca que era cruel que los dos caballeros anduvieran montados en ella.

El padre le habló a su hijo:

—Mi hijo, ¿qué quieres que yo haga para que nadie me critique? Ya ves que todos nos han criticado—si los dos vamos a pie, si tú vas a pie, si yo voy a pie o si ninguno de los dos va a pie. Y cada vez que nos han criticado tú has estado de acuerdo con lo que decían. Espero que esto te sirva de lección. No puedes hacer nada que les parezca bien a todos. Hay que hacer lo que te sea conveniente con tal de que no sea malo. No puedes tener miedo de que alguien te critique porque la gente siempre habla de las cosas de los demás. Hay que aceptar el «lo que dirán».

—Y tú, señor conde, tienes que considerar el daño o el provecho que puedes sacar de algo. Si no tienes total confianza en lo que quieres hacer, debes buscar el consejo de gente inteligente y fiel°. Y si no encuentras tal consejero debes esperar a lo menos un día y una noche antes de resolver lo que quieres hacer. Y no dejes nunca de hacer lo que quieres hacer por miedo de lo que puede decir la gente de ello.

La moraleja es:

Por miedo a lo que dirá la gente, no dejes° de hacer lo que más apropiado y conveniente te parece ser.

Answers

A

1. Cada vez que quería hacer algo para mejorar su hacienda el hijo le contaba un montón de cosas negativas que podrían suceder.
2. Decidió que tenía que enseñarle una lección porque estaba sufriendo daños en su negocio porque siempre le hacía caso a lo que le decía su hijo.
3. El labrador y su hijo vivían cerca de una villa.

¿Comprendes?

A **Recordando hechos** Contesta.
1. ¿Cuál fue el problema que tenía el buen labrador con su hijo?
2. ¿Por qué decidió que tenía que enseñarle una lección?
3. ¿Dónde vivían el labrador y su hijo?
4. ¿Adónde iban? ¿Por qué?
5. ¿Sobre qué se pusieron de acuerdo los dos?

B **Describiendo** Describe lo que pasó cuando...
1. ninguno de los dos iba en el asno.
2. solo el hijo iba en el asno.
3. solo el padre iba en el asno.
4. los dos iban en el asno.

C **Analizando** Discute.
1. el por qué de los comentarios de los cuatro grupos de hombres que el padre y el hijo encontraron
2. la razón por la cual el padre se enfadó con su hijo

D **Resumiendo**
En tus propias palabras da un resumen de la conclusión del cuento.

Después de leer

Piensa en los consejos y la moraleja del cuento. ¿Estás de acuerdo con la conclusión o no? ¿La puedes relacionar con tu propia vida? ¿Cómo?

> **PRACTICE**

¿Comprendes?

A and **B** You may wish to have students answer these activities as factual recall or you may wish to permit them to look up the information. This activity may be prepared as homework.

C This activity can be done in pairs or small groups. It can also be prepared as homework.

D This activity can be written as a composition or prepared as homework.

Pre-AP This reading will develop the skills that students need to be successful on the reading and writing sections of the AP exam. Listening to this reading will also help prepare them for the auditory component.

CULTURA

Cuadro de un mercado en Segovia por Edward Angelo Goodall—siglo XIX

¿BUENOS O MALOS MODALES?

ciento cincuenta y cinco **155**

Answers

4. Iban al mercado de la villa para comprar algunas cosas que necesitaban.
5. Se pusieron de acuerdo que llevarían un asno para cargar las compras.

B

1. Encontraron a unos hombres que decían que no les parecía muy prudente que los dos iban a pie mientras el asno andaba descargada.

2. Encontraron a otros hombres que dijeron que no les parecía normal que un labrador viejo y cansado anduviera a pie y que un joven fuerte anduviera montado en el asno.
3. Encontraron a otros hombres que dijeron que el buen hombre hacía muy mal porque él estaba acostumbrado a las fatigas del trabajo y él, y no el hijo pequeño y tierno, andaba en el asno.

4. Encontraron a otros hombres que dijeron que el asno era tan flaco que era cruel que los dos caballeros anduvieran montados en ella.

C *Answers will vary.*

D *Answers will vary.*

155

Resources

- Tests, pages 5.51–5.68
- Performance Assessment, Task 5, pages 5.69–5.70
- ExamView® Assessment Suite

✔ Self-check for achievement

This is a pre-test for students to take before you administer the chapter test. Note that each section is cross-referenced so students can easily find the material they feel they need to review. You may wish to use Self-Check Worksheet Transparency SC5 to have students complete this assessment in class or at home. You can correct the assessment yourself, or you may prefer to project the answers on the overhead in class using Self-Check Answers Transparency SC5A.

Differentiation

Slower Paced Learners

Have students work in pairs to complete the Self-Check in class. Once they have finished, call on individuals to give the correct answers as you review together.

To review **Vocabulario,** turn to pages 136–137.

Vocabulario

1 **Completa.**

1. Ellos no se quedaron sentados. Se _____.
2. Ellas se dieron un besito en la _____.
3. Dos señores que son amigos se dan _____ cuando se ven.
4. Él siempre se comporta bien. Tiene buenos _____.
5. Los dos están _____ y se van a casar pronto.

2 **Da otra palabra o expresión.**

6. ponerse de pie   8. darse un abrazo
7. darse la mano   9. salir y decir «adiós»

Gramática

3 **Completa.**

10. Era necesario que ellos _____. (levantarse)
11. Me sorprendió que tú no le _____ la mano. (dar)
12. A mi parecer, sería imposible que él no _____ nada del asunto. (saber)
13. Ellos no querían que yo _____. (pagar)
14. Yo no lo haría a menos que lo _____ tú. (hacer)
15. Ellos salieron sin que nadie los _____. (ver)
16. Ella preferiría que Uds. no se lo _____ a nadie. (decir)
17. Me gustaría que él le _____ el regalo a mi hermano. (dar)

To review **el imperfecto del subjuntivo,** turn to page 140.

4 **Escribe de nuevo.**

18. Yo espero que tú lo hagas.
    Yo esperaba que _____.
19. Ellos quieren que yo vaya.
    Ellos querían que _____.
20. Ellos prefieren que lo sepamos.
    Ellos preferirían que _____.

Answers

1

1. levantaron (pusieron de pie)
2. mejilla
3. un abrazo (la mano)
4. modales
5. enamorados

2

6. levantarse
7. saludarse
8. abrazarse
9. despedirse

3

10. se levantaran
11. dieras
12. supiera
13. pagara
14. hicieras
15. viera
16. dijeran
17. diera

4

18. tú lo hicieras
19. yo fuera
20. lo supiéramos
21. vinieran
22. asistieras a la fiesta

21. Es imposible que vengan.
    Sería imposible que _____.
22. Insisto en que asistas a la fiesta.
    Insistí en que _____.

5 **Completa.**
23. Es necesario que nosotros le _____. (hablar)
24. Es necesario _____ con él. (hablar)
25. Ellos no quieren que tú lo _____. (hacer)
26. Y ellos no lo quieren _____ tampoco. (hacer)
27. Es importante _____ a tiempo. (llegar)
28. Prefiero _____ ahora. (salir)

6 **Da la palabra apropiada usando un sufijo.**
29. mi hijo querido
30. una casa pequeña
31. un coche pequeño
32. nuestro perro adorable
33. un café pequeño

7 **Emplea -ísimo con el adjetivo.**
34. Tengo dos cursos aburridos.
35. Es una muchacha guapa.

Cultura

8 **¿Sí o no?**
36. En los países hispanos todos se quedan sentados cuando llega o entra otra persona.
37. En las sociedades hispanas las mujeres siempre se abrazan cuando se encuentran.
38. En las sociedades hispanas los señores y las señoras que se conocen bien se dan un besito en la mejilla cuando se encuentran.
39. En los países hispanos son solo los mayores que se levantan cuando llega otra persona.
40. El voseo se usa en muy pocos países.

¿BUENOS O MALOS MODALES?

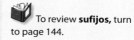
To review **subjuntivo o infinitivo,** turn to page 143.

To review **sufijos,** turn to page 144.

To review this cultural information, turn to pages 148–150.

CULTURA

Los jóvenes se encontraron y se saludaron en un centro comercial en San Juan, Puerto Rico. ¿Son amigos o conocidos?

ciento cincuenta y siete **157**

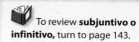
Differentiation
Slower Paced Learners
Encourage students who need extra help to refer to the book icons and review any section before answering the questions.

Pre-AP Students preparing for the AP exam may benefit from a set time limit when completing this Self-Check. This may also help to identify students with learning difficulties or slower paced students who need extra help. Be sure to review the correct answers to ensure that all students complete the Self-Check.

GLENCOE Technology

Online Learning in the Classroom
You may wish to have students use QuickPass code ASD7844c5 for additional test preparation. They will be able to complete a self-check quiz for chapter review.

Answers

5
23. hablemos
24. hablar
25. hagas
26. hacer
27. llegar
28. salir

6
29. mi hijito
30. una casita
31. un cochecito
32. nuestro perrito
33. un cafecito

7
34. aburridísimos
35. guapísima

8
36. no
37. no
38. sí
39. no
40. no

⭐ Tips for Success ....

Encourage students to say as much as possible when they do these open-ended activities. Tell them not to be afraid to make mistakes, since the goal of the activities is real-life communication. If someone in the group makes an error, allow the others to politely correct him or her. Let students choose the activities they would like to do.

Tell students to feel free to elaborate on the basic theme and to be creative. They may use props, pictures, or posters if they wish.

Pre-AP These oral activities will give students the opportunity to develop and improve their speaking skills so that they may succeed on the speaking portion of the AP exam.

Note: You may want to use the rubric below to help students organize their speaking activities.

1 Buenos y malos modales
✅ *Discuss good and bad manners*
Trabajen en grupos de cuatro. Den algunos ejemplos de lo que ustedes consideran buenos y malos modales.

2 Diferencias
✅ *Discuss some customs that are different*
Discute con un(a) compañero(a) de clase algunas diferencias entre costumbres sociales hispanas y costumbres que son «típicas» aquí en Estados Unidos. ¿Cuáles son algunas reglas de cortesía que existen en España y Latinoamérica que no existen aquí y viceversa?

3 Entrevista
✅ *Interview a classmate*
Si en tu escuela hay alumnos de unos países latinos, entrevístalos para determinar cuáles son algunas costumbres de cortesía y ejemplos de buenos modales que ellos practican que no se practican aquí y viceversa.

4 Mi querida familia
✅ *Discuss what your family would like you to do*
Habla con un(a) compañero(a) de clase. Dile todo lo que tu familia quisiera que tú hicieras. A tu parecer, ¿son exigentes (estrictos) o no? ¿Quisiera la familia de tu compañero(a) que él/ella hiciera más o menos las mismas cosas?

5 Un(a) niño(a) mal educado(a)
✅ *Describe an ill-behaved child*
Describe el comportamiento de un(a) niño(a) mal educado(a). Sé lo más original posible.

CULTURA

Un saludo tailandés típico. El saludo se llama *wai* y es un aspecto importante de la cultura tailandesa.

Scoring Rubric for Speaking

	4	3	2	1
vocabulary	extensive use of vocabulary, including idiomatic expressions	adequate use of vocabulary and idiomatic expressions	limited vocabulary marked with some anglicisms	limited vocabulary marked by frequent anglicisms that force interpretation by the listener
grammar	few or no grammatical errors	minor grammatical errors	some serious grammatical errors	serious grammatical errors
pronunciation	good intonation and largely accurate pronunciation with slight accent	acceptable intonation and pronunciation with distinctive accent	errors in intonation and pronunciation with heavy accent	errors in intonation and pronunciation that interfere with listener's comprehension
content	thorough response with interesting and pertinent detail	thorough response with sufficient detail	some detail, but not sufficient	general, insufficient response

Tarea

You have been asked to interview several people and then write a short essay for an upcoming program on manners around the world. Your short essay should focus not only on what are considered good and bad manners in your home, school, and community, but also on what you have learned about proper conduct in Spanish-speaking cultures. Be sure to incorporate vocabulary and grammar learned in this chapter.

Writing Strategy

Conducting an interview Interviewing a variety of individuals about a given topic can help to make your writing more authentic and convincing because it allows you to present several different perspectives while comparing and contrasting them with your own. By using multiple perspectives to elaborate on your theme, you provide the reader with more than one option, thus increasing the chances that he or she will relate to what you have written. Always prepare your questions ahead of time, and as you do so, think about the person you will be interviewing. It is also very important to take good notes during the interview process.

❶ Prewrite

- Decide whom you will be interviewing and arrange to meet them at a convenient time and place. Inform them that you will be asking what they think constitutes good and bad manners and what they know about manners around the world.
- Prepare at least five good questions for each separate interview.

❷ Write

- As you piece together the different elements of your short essay, think about the vocabulary you will be using.
- When considering how you are going to use the chapter's main grammar points, you should keep in mind that you will need to use other previously learned grammatical structures in order for your essay to be informative and meaningful.

Evaluate

Your teacher will evaluate you based on the proper use of vocabulary, correctness of grammar, logical structure, and completeness of information.

Pre-AP This **tarea** will give students the opportunity to develop and improve their writing skills so that they may succeed on the writing portion of the AP exam.

Note: You may want to use the rubric below to help students organize their writing task.

Scoring Rubric for Writing

	4	3	2	1
vocabulary	precise, varied	functional, fails to communicate complete meaning	limited to basic words, often inaccurate	inadequate
grammar	excellent, very few or no errors	some errors, do not hinder communication	numerous errors interfere with communication	many errors, little sentence structure
content	thorough response to the topic	generally thorough response to the topic	partial response to the topic	insufficient response to the topic
organization	well organized, ideas presented clearly and logically	loosely organized, but main ideas present	some attempts at organization, but with confused sequencing	lack of organization

Grammar Review

This page provides a quick "at a glance" summary of the grammar points students have learned in this chapter. The corresponding page numbers are also listed so that students can easily find each grammar point as it was presented.

Differentiation

Multiple Intelligences

You may want to call on **verbal-linguistic** and **logical-mathematical** learners for whom grammar often comes easily to explain the main concepts to their classmates in their own words. Having students explain the concepts in different ways may also help slower paced learners or students with learning difficulties.

Repaso del Capítulo 5

Gramática

- **El imperfecto del subjuntivo** *(page 140)*

  If the verb of the main clause is in the present or future tense, the present subjunctive is used in the dependent clause. If the verb of the main clause is in the preterite, imperfect, or conditional, the imperfect subjunctive is used in the dependent clause.

  Será imposible que él no lo sepa.
  Sería imposible que él no lo supiera.

  Él habla así para que comprendamos.
  Él habló así para que comprendiéramos.

  Ellos no quieren que él hable así.
  Ellos no querían que él hablara así.

- **Subjuntivo o infinitivo** *(page 143)*

  When there is no change of subject, the infinitive is used.

  Yo quiero ir. Y ellos no quieren que yo vaya.

- **Sufijos** *(page 144)*

  You add the suffixes **-ito** or **-illo** to a noun to form the diminutive form of the noun.

  la casa   la casita   la chica   la chiquita

  If the noun ends in **-n** or the vowel **-e,** the suffix **-cito** is added.

  el ratón   el ratoncito

  To express *very* or *most,* add the suffix **-ísimo** to an adjective.

  un joven guapísimo
  una joven guapísima

CULTURA

Este jovencito trabaja de mesero en un café en Buenos Aires y da un servicio buenísimo.

Juego There are a number of cognates in this list. See how many you and a partner can find. Who can find the most? Compare your list with those of your classmates.

Vocabulario

Discussing manners

el/la recién llegado(a)	el comportamiento	despedirse	comportarse
el/la invitado(a)	la mejilla	ponerse de pie	enfadarse
un besito	cortés	darse la mano	
un abrazo	formal	besar	
los modales	saludar(se)	abrazarse	

Other useful words and expressions

el/la conocido(a)	el amor	castigar
el/la chico(a)	enamorarse	¡Cuidado!
el malentendido	malentender	¡Mucho ojo!

 The words listed below come from this chapter's literary selection, *El conde Lucanor*. They were selected to become part of your active vocabulary because of their relatively high frequency.

la villa	el provecho	olvidar
los demás	sabio(a)	hacerle caso
el apodo	mejorar	
el/la mozo(a)	suceder	

¿BUENOS O MALOS MODALES?

ciento sesenta y uno **161**

 Don't forget the chapter project and cultural activities found on pages 132C–132D. Students have learned all the information that they will need to complete these engaging enrichment tasks.

Juego The cognates in this list are: **el/la invitado(a), formal.**

Repaso del Capítulo 5

Vocabulary Review

The words and phrases in the **Vocabulario** section have been taught for productive use in this chapter. They are summarized here as a resource for both student and teacher. This list also serves as a convenient resource for the **Prepárate para el examen** activities on pages 156–159.

GLENCOE SPANISH

Why It Works!

This vocabulary reference list has not been translated into English for two reasons. First, it is recommended that students learn the new vocabulary through direct association with images on the **Vocabulario** pages. Second, all vocabulary is reintroduced in the chapter many times, and upon completion of the chapter students should be familiar with the meaning of all the words. If there are words that students still do not know, they can refer back to the vocabulary presentation in the chapter or the dictionary at the end of the book. If, however, it is your preference to give students the English translations, please refer to Vocabulary Transparency V5.1 or to the Chapter 5 PowerPoint® presentation on PowerTeach.

161

Every chapter of ¡Así se dice! contains this review section of previously learned material. By recycling information from previous chapters, the cumulative review serves to remind students that they need to continue practicing what they have learned after finishing each chapter.

Activity 1 This activity reviews vocabulary related to traveling by train or airplane. See pages R24–R25.

🎧 **Audio Script** *(CD 5, Track 24)*

1. Los pasajeros compran los boletos en la ventanilla.
2. El joven tiene que facturar su equipaje.
3. El revisor revisa los billetes.
4. Ella va al mostrador de la línea aérea.
5. Marisol hace un viaje internacional.
6. El vuelo sale a tiempo.
7. Ellos tienen que pasar por el control de seguridad.
8. Van a bajarse en la próxima parada.

Activity 2 This activity reviews vocabulary related to traveling by plane or train. See pages R24–R25.

Activity 3 This activity reviews vocabulary related to traveling by train. See page R25.

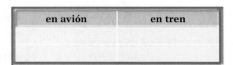

Repaso cumulativo

Repasa lo que ya has aprendido

These activities will help you review and remember what you have learned so far in Spanish.

 1 Escucha las frases. Indica en una tabla como la de abajo si describe un viaje en avión o en tren.

en avión	en tren

 2 Forma frases.

1. pasajeros / los / equipaje / el / facturan / el / en / mostrador
2. sale / número / vuelo / el / cincuenta / destino / con / a / Caracas
3. pasajeros / esperan / vuelo / los / salida / la / su / de
4. tienen / pasar / que / pasajeros / por / control / el / seguridad / de / los
5. necesario / tener / es / embarque / de / una / antes de / abordar / tarjeta / avión / el

 3 Identifica.

CULTURA

Dos AVES en la estación de Santa Justa en Sevilla, España

Answers

1
1. en tren
2. en avión
3. en tren
4. en avión
5. en avión
6. en avión
7. en avión
8. en tren

2
1. Los pasajeros facturan el equipaje en el mostrador.
2. El vuelo número cincuenta sale con destino a Caracas.
3. Los pasajeros esperan la salida de su vuelo.
4. Los pasajeros tienen que pasar por el control de seguridad.
5. Es necesario tener una tarjeta de embarque antes de abordar el avión.

3
1. los pasajeros
2. el vagón (el coche, el tren)
3. el andén
4. la vía

Parea los contrarios.

1. procedente de	**a.** la llegada
2. aterrizar	**b.** abordar
3. tarde	**c.** despegar
4. la salida	**d.** a tiempo
5. desembarcar	**e.** con destino a
6. sencillo	**f.** de ida y vuelta

 Parea los sinónimos.

1. el boleto	**a.** con un retraso
2. la tarjeta de embarque	**b.** de ida y regreso
3. con una demora	**c.** el billete
4. embarcar	**d.** el coche
5. el vagón	**e.** el pasabordo
6. de ida y vuelta	**f.** abordar

 Completa con un verbo apropiado en el presente.

1. Los pasajeros _____ un viaje en tren.
2. Yo _____ mi ropa en mi mochila.
3. El tren _____ del andén cinco.
4. Estamos en la estación de ferrocarril y no necesitamos un carrito porque _____ solamente dos mochilas.
5. Los pasajeros _____ cola delante de la ventanilla.
6. Ellos _____ su equipaje en la maletera del carro.

 Pon las frases de la Actividad 6 en el pretérito.

8 **Describe todo lo que ves en los dibujos sobre un fin de semana que la familia Núñez pasó en el camping.**

¿BUENOS O MALOS MODALES?

ciento sesenta y tres **163**

Activity 4 This activity reviews vocabulary related to traveling by plane or train. See pages R24–R25.

Activity 5 This activity reviews vocabulary related to traveling by plane or train. See pages R24–R25.

Activity 6 This activity reviews vocabulary related to traveling by plane or train and present tense verbs. See pages R7, R17, R24–R25.

Activity 7 This activity reviews vocabulary related to traveling by plane or train and verbs in the preterite tense. See pages R24–R25, R29, R31.

Activity 8 This activity reviews uses of verbs in the present tense. See pages R7, R17, R19.

Pre-AP To give students further open-ended oral or written practice, or to assess proficiency, go to AP Proficiency Practice Transparency 10.

GLENCOE Technology

Audio in the Classroom
The ¡Así se dice! Audio Program for Chapter 5 has 24 activities, which afford students extensive listening and speaking practice.

Online Learning in the Classroom
You may wish to have students use QuickPass code ASD7844c5 for additional cumulative review. They will be able to complete a self-check quiz.

Answers

4	**5**	**6**	**7**	**8**
1. e	**1.** c	**1.** hacen	**1.** hicieron	*Answers will vary.*
2. c	**2.** e	**2.** pongo	**2.** puse	
3. d	**3.** a	**3.** sale	**3.** salió	
4. a	**4.** f	**4.** traemos	**4.** trajimos	
5. b	**5.** d	**5.** hacen	**5.** hicieron	
6. f	**6.** b	**6.** ponen	**6.** pusieron	

Planning for Chapter 6

Chapter Overview
Viajes

● Scope and Sequence

Topics
- Air travel
- Train travel
- Car travel and rental

Culture
- A trip to Bolivia
- *Temprano y con sol* by Emilia Pardo Bazán

Functions
- How to discuss several modes of transportation
- How to talk about a trip to Bolivia
- How to read a short story by the Spanish author Emilia Pardo Bazán

Structure
- The subjunctive with conjugations of time
- The subjunctive to express suggestions and advice
- Irregular nouns

● Planning Guide

	required	recommended	optional
Vocabulario 1 *(pages 168–171)* En el aeropuerto	✓		
Vocabulario 2 *(pages 172–175)* La estación de tren (ferrocarril) La agencia de alquiler	✓		
Gramática *(pages 176–181)* El subjuntivo con conjunciones de tiempo El subjuntivo con verbos especiales Sustantivos irregulares	✓		
Conversación *(pages 182–183)* ¡Qué lío!		✓	
Lectura cultural *(pages 184–185)* ¡A Bolivia ya!		✓	
Literatura *(pages 186–191)* Temprano y con sol			✓
Prepárate para el examen *(pages 192–195)*			✓
Repaso cumulativo *(pages 198–199)*			✓

Correlations to National Foreign Language Standards

Page numbers in light print refer to the Student Edition. Page numbers in bold print refer to the Teacher Edition.	
Communication Standard 1.1 Interpersonal	pp. **166–167**, **169**, **173**, 175, **175**, **179**, **185**, **191**, 194
Communication Standard 1.2 Interpretive	pp. **168**, 170, **170**, **171**, 174, **174**, 175, **175**, 176, 177, **178**, 179, **179**, 181, **182**, 183, **183**, 184, **184**, 185, **186**, **187**, 188, **188**, 189, **189**, 190, **190**, 191, 193, **193**, 198, **199**
Communication Standard 1.3 Presentational	pp. **164C**, **169**, **173**, 175, **177**, **179**, **182**, **186**, **189**, 191, **191**, **192**, 194, **196**, **197**
Cultures Standard 2.1	pp. **164D**, 169, 174, 175, **175**, 183, **183**, 184, 193, 194, 195
Cultures Standard 2.2	pp. **164C**, **164D**, 166–167, **166–167**, 175, **177**, 180, 183, 184, 185, **185**, 188, **190**, 191, 193
Connections Standard 3.1	pp. **164C**, **164D**, 184, **184**, 188
Connections Standard 3.2	pp. 172, **172**, 173, 181, **181**, 183, **183**, 185, **185**, 188–190, 191
Comparisons Standard 4.1	pp. **168**, 173, **173**, 176, 178, 180, **181**, **183**, **196**, 197
Comparisons Standard 4.2	pp. **164D**, 165, **165**, **166**, **173**
Communities Standard 5.1	pp. **164C**, **164D**, 177, **192**, **194**, **196**
Communities Standard 5.2	pp. 172, **172**, **173**, 183, **183**, 185, **185**

To read the ACTFL Standards in their entirety, see the front of the Teacher Edition.

Student Resources

Print

Workbook *(pp. 6.3–6.14)*
Audio Activities *(pp. 6.15–6.20)*
Pre-AP Workbook, Chapter 6

Technology

- StudentWorks™ Plus
- ¡Así se dice! Vocabulario en vivo
- ¡Así se dice! Gramática en vivo
- ¡Así se dice! Diálogo en vivo
- ¡Así se dice! Cultura en vivo
- Vocabulary PuzzleMaker
- **QuickPass** glencoe.com

Teacher Resources

Print

TeacherTools, Chapter 6
    Workbook TE *(pp. 6.3–6.14)*
    Audio Activities TE *(pp. 6.17–6.33)*
    Quizzes 1–5 *(pp. 6.37–6.42)*
    Tests *(pp. 6.44–6.66)*
    Performance Assessment, Task 6 *(pp. 6.67–6.68)*

Technology

- Quick Start Transparencies 6.1–6.5
- Vocabulary Transparencies V6.1–V6.5
- Audio CD 6
- *ExamView® Assessment Suite*
- TeacherWorks™ Plus
- PowerTeach
- ¡Así se dice! Video Program
- Vocabulary PuzzleMaker
- **QuickPass** glencoe.com

Chapter Project

Una guía de viaje

Students will work individually and in groups to create a travel guide in Spanish for various regions throughout the Spanish-speaking world.

1. Divide the class into groups according to the following regions: **España, México, Centroamérica, el Caribe, Colombia y Venezuela, los países andinos (Bolivia, Ecuador y Perú)**, and **el Cono sur (Argentina, Chile, Paraguay y Uruguay)**. If a group's region includes four or more countries, each member of the group should focus on one country. If a group's region includes three or fewer countries, the group should assign specific areas within those countries to individuals. Groups should discuss what they would like to include in their travel guide (attractions, transportation, etc.) and work individually on each part.

2. Each member of the group will be responsible for creating at least two pages of the guide. Each page should include at least two visual elements, in addition to essential information related to the theme of travel. Students should check more than one source to verify that information is accurate. Students should submit a sketch of the layout of their pages and a rough draft of the text to be corrected and then handed in along with the final version.

3. Students will work with their groups to assemble the final version of their travel guide. They should then plan to present their travel guides to the rest of the class.

Expansion: Have each group prepare a quiz in advance for their classmates to take after the presentation. The quizzes may then be used as the basis for a test on the information the students learned.

Scoring Rubric for Project

	1	3	5
Evidence of planning	Draft and layout are not provided.	Draft and layout are provided, but draft is not corrected.	Layout and corrected draft are provided.
Use of illustrations	Travel guide contains no visual elements.	Travel guide contains few visual elements.	Travel guide contains several visual elements.
Presentation	Travel guide contains little of the required elements.	Travel guide contains some of the required elements.	Travel guide contains all the required elements.

Culture

● Día de los Reyes

In most Hispanic countries, December 25th does not mark the end of the holiday season. There is another day which calls for celebration—**Día de los Reyes.** This holiday, celebrated on January 6th, marks the day on which the Three Kings arrived in Bethlehem to present gifts to the infant Jesus, so it is a day on which people in Spanish-speaking countries give gifts, too. Traditionally, on the night before **Día de los Reyes** children set out their shoes for the Three Kings to fill with gifts. Often children will put grass or hay in their shoes as a snack for the Kings' camels. This tradition varies slightly from culture to culture. In some countries, shoeboxes are used instead of shoes or the shoes may be left under the children's beds. In Puerto Rico, **Día de los Reyes** is a national holiday—businesses close and festivities are held celebrating the occasion. **Día de los Reyes** does not replace Christmas in Hispanic countries. Children receive a few gifts on December 25th, but they receive the majority of their gifts on January 6th. The day concludes with a celebratory dinner with family and friends and a dessert of **rosca de Reyes,** an oval- or round-shaped sweet bread decorated with fruits to symbolize the jewels found on the Three Kings' lavish garments. Baked inside the **rosca de Reyes** is a small porcelain figurine. Whoever finds the figurine in his or her piece is crowned king or queen. If there are heritage speakers in the class, ask whether or not they celebrate this holiday and to share some of their traditions with the class.

● Mambo

Like many forms of music from Latin America, **mambo** was a modification of the traditional **danzón.** (The **danzón,** derived from European music brought to Latin America by colonists, has an ABAC or ABACA structure that contains an introduction [A], principal theme or melody [B], and a trio featuring strings [C].) In Cuba in 1938 Cachoa Lopéz wrote a song called "Mambo" in which he added African folk rhythms to the end of **danzón** (thus, an ABACD structure). This new form was not as popular as others in Cuba and caught on slowly elsewhere until the 1940s, when bandleader Perez Prado marketed his music as **mambo. Mambo** retained international popularity during the 1950s and 1960s, particularly in New York City. Of course, with a new form of music, grew a new form of dance—and due to the music's syncopated beat, a very difficult dance. **Mambo** is danced on the second beat of the measure, not the first. This means that dancers hold on the first beat (downbeat) and make the first step on beat two (offbeat). The weight change and bend in the knee while dancing the steps create the hip motion that is one of the chief characteristics of **mambo.** The **mambo** dance craze hit its peak in the mid-1950s. In New York City, the popular spot for **mambo** dancing was the Palladium Ballroom, where the city's best dancers would perform elaborate demonstrations.

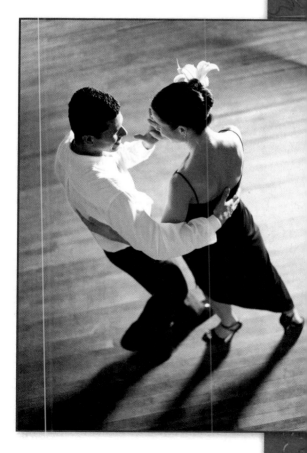

50-Minute Lesson Plans

	Objective	Present	Practice	Assess/Homework
Day 1	Talk about the airport	Chapter Opener, pp. 164–165 (5 min.) Introducción al tema, pp. 166–167 (10 min.) Core Instruction/Vocabulario 1, pp. 168–169 (20 min.)	Activities 1–3, p. 170 (15 min.)	Student Workbook Activities A–D, pp. 6.3–6.4 QuickPass Vocabulary Practice
Day 2	Talk about the airport	Quick Start, p. 168 (5 min.) Review Vocabulario 1, pp. 168–169 (10 min.)	Activities 4–5, p. 171 (10 min.) Estudio de palabras, p. 171 (5 min.) Total Physical Response, p. 169 (5 min.) Audio Activities A–D, pp. 6.17–6.19 (15 min.)	Student Workbook Activities E–H, pp. 6.4–6.5 QuickPass Vocabulary Practice
Day 3	Talk about the train station and renting a car	Core Instruction/Vocabulario 2, pp. 172–173 (15 min.) Video, Vocabulario en vivo (10 min.)	Activities 1–4, p. 174 (15 min.)	Quiz 1, p. 6.37 (10 min.) Student Workbook Activities A–C, pp. 6.6–6.7 QuickPass Vocabulary Practice
Day 4	Talk about the train station and renting a car	Quick Start, p. 172 (5 min.) Review Vocabulario 2, pp. 172–173 (5 min.)	Activities 5–7, p. 175 (15 min.) Estudio de palabras, p. 175 (10 min.) Foldables, p. 175 (5 min.) Audio Activities E–H, pp. 6.20–6.22 (10 min.)	Student Workbook Activities D–E, p. 6.7 QuickPass Vocabulary Practice
Day 5	The subjunctive with conjugations of time	Quick Start, p. 176 (5 min.) Core Instruction/Gramática, El subjuntivo con conjunciones de tiempo, p. 176 (10 min.)	Activities 1–4, pp. 176–177 (10 min.) InfoGap, p. SR7 (5 min.) Audio Activities A–C, pp. 6.23–6.24 (10 min.)	Quiz 2, p. 6.38 (10 min.) Student Workbook Activities A–D, pp. 6.8–6.9 QuickPass Grammar Practice
Day 6	The subjunctive to express suggestions and advice	Quick Start, p. 178 (5 min.) Core Instruction/Gramática, El subjuntivo con verbos especiales, p. 178 (15 min.)	Activities 5–7, p. 179 (10 min.) Audio Activities D–E, pp. 6.24–6.25 (10 min.)	Quiz 3, p. 6.39 (10 min.) Student Workbook Activities A–C, pp. 6.9–6.10 QuickPass Grammar Practice
Day 7	Irregular nouns	Quick Start, p. 180 (5 min.) Core Instruction/Gramática, Sustantivos irregulares, p. 180 (15 min.)	Activities 8–9, p. 181 (10 min.) Audio Activities F–G, pp. 6.25–6.26 (10 min.)	Quiz 4, p. 6.40 (10 min.) Student Workbook Activities A–B, p. 6.10 QuickPass Grammar Practice
Day 8	Develop reading and listening comprehension skills	Core Instruction/Conversación, p. 182 (15 min.) Video, Diálogo en vivo (10 min.)	¿Comprendes? A–C, 183 (15 min.)	Quiz 5, p. 6.41 (10 min.) QuickPass Conversation
Day 9	Talk about a trip to Bolivia	Core Instruction/Lectura cultural, p. 184 (15 min.) Video, Cultura en vivo (10 min.)	¿Comprendes? A–B, p. 185 (10 min.)	Listening Comprehension Test, pp. 6.61–6.63 (15 min.) ¿Comprendes? C–D, p. 185 QuickPass Reading Practice
Day 10	Read a short story by the Spanish author Emilia Pardo Bazán	Core Instruction/Vocabulario, p. 186 (5 min.) Core Instruction/Literatura, pp. 187–190 (25 min.)	Vocabulario, Práctica 1–2, p. 187 (10 min.) ¿Comprendes? A–B, p. 191 (10 min.)	¿Comprendes? C–D, p. 191 QuickPass Reading Practice
Day 11	Read a short story by the Spanish author Emilia Pardo Bazán	Review Literatura, pp. 187–190 (10 min.)	¿Comprendes? C–D, p. 191 (15 min.) Prepárate para el examen, pp. 192–193 (25 min.)	Prepárate para el examen, Practice for written proficiency, p. 195 QuickPass Reading Practice
Day 12	Chapter review	Repaso del Capítulo 6, pp. 196–197 (15 min.)	Prepárate para el examen, Practice for oral proficiency, p. 194 (20 min.)	Test for Writing Proficiency, p. 6.66 (15 min.) Review for chapter test
Day 13	Chapter 6 Tests (50 min.) Reading and Writing Test, pp. 6.49–6.57 Literature Test, pp. 6.59–6.60		Speaking Test, p. 6.64 Test for Oral Proficiency, p. 6.65	

90-Minute Lesson Plans

	Objective	Present	Practice	Assess/Homework
Block 1	Talk about the airport	Chapter Opener, pp. 164–165 (5 min.) Introducción al tema, pp. 166–167 (15 min.) Quick Start, p. 168 (5 min.) Core Instruction/Vocabulario 1, pp. 168–169 (20 min.)	Activities 1–5, pp. 170–171 (20 min.) Estudio de palabras, p. 171 (5 min.) Total Physical Response, p. 169 (5 min.) Audio Activities A–D, pp. 6.17–6.19 (15 min.)	Student Workbook Activities A–H, pp. 6.3–6.5 **QuickPass** Vocabulary Practice
Block 2	Talk about the train station and renting a car	Quick Start, p. 172 (5 min.) Core Instruction/Vocabulario 2, pp. 172–173 (15 min.) Video, Vocabulario en vivo (10 min.)	Activities 1–7, pp. 174–175 (20 min.) Estudio de palabras, p. 175 (10 min.) Foldables, p. 175 (5 min.) Audio Activities E–H, pp. 6.20–6.22 (15 min.)	Quiz 1, p. 6.37 (10 min.) Student Workbook Activities A–E, pp. 6.6–6.7 **QuickPass** Vocabulary Practice
Block 3	The subjunctive with conjugations of time The subjunctive to express suggestions and advice	Quick Start, p. 176 (5 min.) Core Instruction/Gramática, El subjuntivo con conjunciones de tiempo, p. 176 (15 min.) Core Instruction/Gramática, El subjuntivo con verbos especiales, p. 178 (15 min.)	Activities 1–4, pp. 176–177 (15 min.) InfoGap, p. SR7 (5 min.) Activity 5, p. 179 (5 min.) Audio Activities A–D, pp. 6.23–6.24 (20 min.)	Quiz 2, p. 6.38 (10 min.) Student Workbook Activities A–D, pp. 6.8–6.9 Student Workbook Activities A–B, p. 6.9 **QuickPass** Grammar Practice
Block 4	The subjunctive to express suggestions and advice Irregular nouns	Quick Start, p. 178 (5 min.) Review Gramática, El subjuntivo con verbos especiales, p. 178 (10 min.) Quick Start, p. 180 (5 min.) Core Instruction/Gramática, Sustantivos irregulares, p. 180 (15 min.)	Activities 6–7, p. 179 (10 min.) Activities 8–9, p. 181 (15 min.) Audio Activities E–G, pp. 6.25–6.26 (20 min.)	Quiz 3, p. 6.39 (10 min.) Student Workbook Activity C, p. 6.10 Student Workbook Activities A–B, p. 6.10 **QuickPass** Grammar Practice
Block 5	Talk about a trip to Bolivia	Core Instruction/Conversación, p. 182 (15 min.) Core Instruction/Lectura cultural, p. 184 (15 min.) Video, Cultura en vivo (10 min.)	¿Comprendes? A–C, p. 183 (15 min.) ¿Comprendes? A–C, p. 185 (10 min.)	Quizzes 4–5, pp. 6.40–6.41 (20 min.) ¿Comprendes? D, p. 185 **QuickPass** Conversation, Reading Practice
Block 6	Read a short story by the Spanish author Emilia Pardo Bazán	Core Instruction/Vocabulario, p. 186 (5 min.) Core Instruction/Literatura, pp. 187–190 (25 min.)	Vocabulario, Práctica 1–2, p. 187 (10 min.) ¿Comprendes? A–D, p. 191 (20 min.) Prepárate para el examen, Practice for oral proficiency 1–2, p. 194 (15 min.)	Listening Comprehension Test, pp. 6.61–6.63 (15 min.) **QuickPass** Reading Practice
Block 7	Chapter review	Repaso del Capítulo 6, pp. 196–197 (15 min.)	Prepárate para el examen, pp. 192–193 (20 min.) Prepárate para el examen, Practice for oral proficiency 3–4, p. 194 (10 min.) Prepárate para el examen, Practice for written proficiency, p. 195 (30 min.)	Test for Writing Proficiency, p. 6.66 (15 min.) Review for chapter test
Block 8	Chapter 6 Tests (50 min.) 　Reading and Writing Test, pp. 6.49–6.57 　Literature Test, pp. 6.59–6.60 　Speaking Test, p. 6.64 　Test for Oral Proficiency, p. 6.65 Chapter Project, p. 164C (40 min.)			

Viajes

164

Preview

In this chapter, students will discuss various modes of transportation. To do this they will review vocabulary from ¡Así se dice! Levels 1 and 2 and learn new expressions needed when travel plans have to change. Students will read about a trip through parts of Bolivia. They will also read a short story by the famous Spanish writer Emilia Pardo Bazán about a train trip taken by two youngsters. Students will learn to use the subjunctive with conjunctions of time and with clauses following expressions of advice, recommendations, and suggestions. They will also learn irregular nouns.

Pacing

It is important to note that once you reach **¡Bravo!** in the chapter, there is no more new material for the students to learn. The rest of the chapter recycles what has already been covered. The suggested pacing listed here leaves two to three days for review, assessment, and enrichment activities such as the chapter project.

Vocabulario 1	1–2 days
Vocabulario 2	1–2 days
Gramática	2–3 days
Conversación	1 day
Lectura cultural	1 day
Literatura	1 day

Teacher Works Plus

The **¡Así se dice!** TeacherWorks™ Plus CD-ROM is an all-in-one planner and resource center. You may wish to use several of the following features as you plan and present the Chapter 6 material: Interactive Teacher Edition, Interactive Lesson Planner with Calendar, and Point and Click Access to Teaching Resources including Hotlinks to the Internet and Correlations to the National Standards.

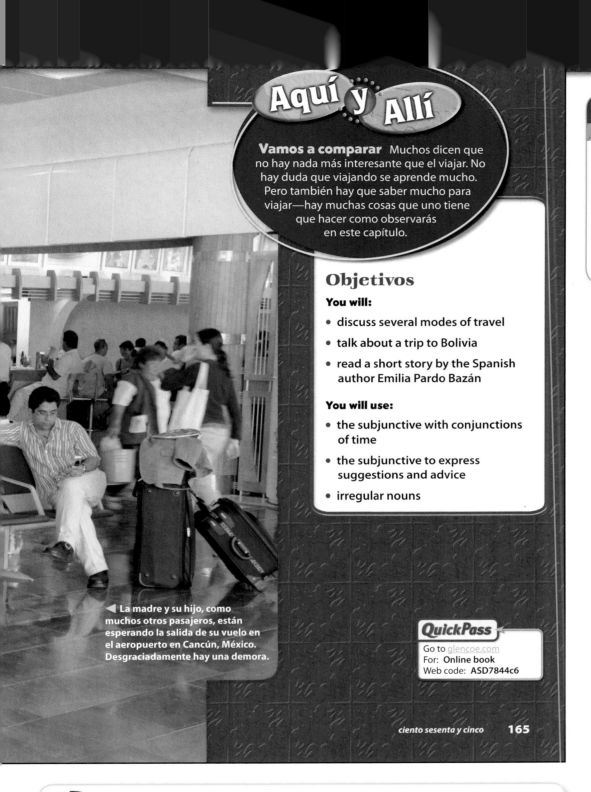

Aquí y Allí

Vamos a comparar Muchos dicen que no hay nada más interesante que el viajar. No hay duda que viajando se aprende mucho. Pero también hay que saber mucho para viajar—hay muchas cosas que uno tiene que hacer como observarás en este capítulo.

Objetivos

You will:

- discuss several modes of travel
- talk about a trip to Bolivia
- read a short story by the Spanish author Emilia Pardo Bazán

You will use:

- the subjunctive with conjunctions of time
- the subjunctive to express suggestions and advice
- irregular nouns

◀ La madre y su hijo, como muchos otros pasajeros, están esperando la salida de su vuelo en el aeropuerto en Cancún, México. Desgraciadamente hay una demora.

QuickPass

Go to glencoe.com
For: **Online book**
Web code: **ASD7844c6**

Quia Interactive Online Student Edition found at quia.com allows students to complete activities online and submit them for computer grading for instant feedback or teacher grading with suggestions for what to review. Students can also record speaking activities, listen to chapter audio, and watch the videos that correspond with each chapter. As a teacher you are able to create rosters, set grading parameters, and post assignments for each class. After students complete activities, you can view the results and recommend remediation or review. You can also add your own customized activities for additional student practice.

Introducción al tema
▶ PRESENT

Introduce the theme of the chapter by having students look at the photographs on these pages. Have them look at the people and places and determine what is the same or different from what they see in the United States. Once you have completed the vocabulary presentation, have students return to these pages and read the information that accompanies each photograph. Once students are fully acquainted with the vocabulary and grammar of the chapter, you may wish to return to these pages and ask the questions that go with each photo.

Cultural Snapshot

República Dominicana *(page 166)* In addition to the main airport in Santo Domingo that caters to business travelers and people returning home for visits, there are several other international airports on the island. Since the Dominican Republic has become an important tourist destination, there are many charter flights full of vacationers, particularly from the United States and Europe. **¿Qué tiene este señor de negocios en el aeropuerto? ¿Tiene que hacer un viaje aunque tiene la pierna quebrada? ¿Quién le ayuda? ¿Lo empuja la señorita en una silla de ruedas?**

Introducción al tema
Viajes

Cada día hay miles de personas que están viajando. Hay muchos motivos para hacer un viaje—vacaciones, negocios, visitas familiares, etc. Como vas a observar en este capítulo, hay más de una manera de viajar y de vez en cuando es necesario cambiar de planes al último momento.

▲ **República Dominicana** Este señor tiene que hacer un viaje importante y no importa que tenga una pierna quebrada. Una agente de la línea aérea le puede ayudar en el aeropuerto.

◀ **Guatemala** Estas dos jóvenes están de vacaciones en Guatemala. Acaban de visitar las famosas ruinas en Tikal y ahora están llegando al aeropuerto de Santa Elena.

España ¿Es una cafetería en un parque tropical? No. Está en la sala de espera de la estación de ferrocarril Atocha en Madrid. ▶

166

Guatemala *(page 166)* The small airport of Santa Elena is near the famous Mayan ruins of Tikal. **¿Están de vacaciones estas dos señoritas o están haciendo un viaje de negocios? ¿Qué acaban de visitar las amigas? ¿Qué aeropuerto usan los turistas que visitan las ruinas de Tikal?**

España *(page 166)* Atocha, close to the Prado Museum, is the major train station in Madrid. Large and modern, it serves **trenes de cercanías** and **trenes de largo recorrido**. **¿Dónde está la cafetería? ¿Qué es Atocha?**

El Salvador TACA, una línea aérea centroamericana, como todas las líneas aéreas, tiene etiquetas que los pasajeros pueden poner en su equipaje. La etiqueta es muy importante porque tiene la dirección del pasajero. Nunca se sabe si una maleta se va a perder o extraviar.

▲ **Puerto Rico** El maletero en el aeropuerto Luis Muñoz Marín en San Juan ayuda a los pasajeros con su equipaje.

◄ **Argentina** Es un tren de cercanías en Buenos Aires. El tren está completo. Hay unos pasajeros de pie.

Panamá El tren está en la estación de ferrocarril en la Ciudad de Panamá. Es el tren que corre a lo largo de las orillas del Canal de Panamá. ▼

167

El Salvador *(page 167)* TACA, a consortium of airlines from several Central American countries, has its home base in San Salvador. **¿Qué es TACA? ¿Qué pueden hacer los pasajeros con la etiqueta? ¿Por qué es importante poner una etiqueta en cada maleta y en cada pieza de equipaje de mano?**

Puerto Rico *(page 167)* **¿Quién ayuda a los pasajeros? ¿Con qué les ayuda?**

Argentina *(page 167)* Argentina no longer has long distance train service, but there are several lines that serve Buenos Aires and the outskirts. There is also minimal service in some other areas of the country. **¿Es este un tren de cercanías o de largo recorrido? ¿Está completo el tren? ¿Están todos los pasajeros asentados?**

Panamá *(page 167)* This is the train station in Panama City. Students read about the train service between Panama City and Colón along the Panama Canal in **¡Así se dice!** Level 2. The train serves commuters and tourists. There is one train a day in each direction. **¿Dónde está el tren? ¿Por dónde corre el tren en su recorrido entre Panamá y Colón?**

Vocabulario 1 presentación

Quick Start

Use QS Transparency 6.1 or write the following on the board.
Escribe cuántas palabras posibles sobre un viaje en avión.

▶ TEACH
Core Instruction

Step 1 Have students close their books. Present the vocabulary using Vocabulary Transparencies V6.2–V6.3.

Step 2 Have students open their books and read the vocabulary. To give students practice using the new words, ask questions such as: **¿Qué indica adonde está facturado el equipaje—el talón o la etiqueta? ¿Qué lleva la etiqueta? ¿Qué lleva el talón? Si vas a facturar equipaje, ¿hay un límite de peso?**

Teaching Options

Before introducing the vocabulary, have students recall words they have already learned about train and air travel from **¡Así se dice!** Levels 1 and 2. In addition, let students peruse pages 168 and 169 and indicate words they recognize.

En el aeropuerto

El talón indica hasta donde está facturado el equipaje—el destino.
La etiqueta lleva el nombre y la dirección del pasajero.
Hay un límite de peso. Una maleta no puede pesar más de 22 kilos.
No puede exceder el límite.

Los vuelos a Barcelona y a Pamplona no hacen escala.
Son vuelos sin escala.
Un vuelo directo hace escala antes de continuar a su destino.

El vuelo no está completo.
Hay unos asientos disponibles.

El vuelo no va a salir debido a un problema técnico (mecánico).
La línea tendrá que confirmar a los pasajeros en otro vuelo.

La pareja perdió su vuelo.
El vuelo ya había salido antes de que ellos llegaran a la puerta de salida.

168 *ciento sesenta y ocho*

CAPÍTULO 6

GLENCOE Technology

You may wish to use the editable PowerPoint® presentation on PowerTeach for additional vocabulary instruction and practice.

ABOUT THE SPANISH LANGUAGE

Ask students if they remember the meaning of the verb **perder** from the sports lesson in **¡Así se dice!** Level 1. **Los dos equipos quieren ganar pero un equipo tiene que perder. Los Osos pierden.** Ask them what they think **perder** means in this new context—**perder el vuelo**. If they cannot get it, give them the meaning *to miss*.

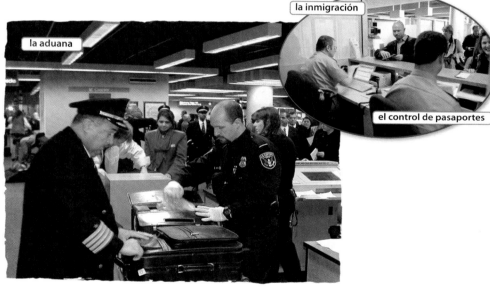

el reclamo de equipaje

la correa

Los pasajeros podrán reclamar (recoger) su equipaje facturado cuando lleguen a su destino.
El equipaje del vuelo 125 está llegando en la correa F.
Los pasajeros están reclamando (recogiendo) su equipaje.
Tienen que esperar hasta que vean sus maletas en la correa.

la inmigración

la aduana

el control de pasaportes

Los pasajeros en un vuelo internacional tienen que pasar por el control de pasaportes.
Tienen que pasar por la aduana también.

¡Así se dice!

¡Qué lío! is a fun expression you can use when nearly everything seems to go wrong. It means *What a mess!*

Differentiation

Advanced Learners

Call on advanced learners. Using overhead transparencies V6.2–V6.3, have them take the role of teacher and ask questions about the photographs on the transparencies.

Slower Paced Learners

Call on less able students. Using overhead transparencies V6.2–V6.3, have them give the Spanish word for any item they can.

 Comunicación

Interpersonal, Presentational

Have students work in pairs to present this role play to the class: You are in the baggage claim area and your bags do not appear. You show the employee (your partner) your claim tickets, but he or she knows nothing about your luggage. Discuss the problem together and find a solution.

En otras partes
Some other words you may hear for **la correa** are **la banda** and **el carrusel.**

Total Physical Response (TPR)

(Student), **ven acá, por favor.**
Acabas de llegar al aeropuerto de Miami.
Haz cola delante del control de pasaportes.
Muestra tu pasaporte al agente.
Ve a recoger tu equipaje.

Busca la correa en que va a llegar tu equipaje.
Mira las maletas que pasan.
Crees ver la tuya. Tómala.
Mira la etiqueta o el talón.
No, no es tuya.
Ponla en la carrea.

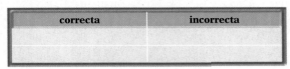
▶ PRACTICE

Leveling EACH Activity

Easy Activities 1, 2, 4
Average Activities 3, 5

Activity ❶

🎧 Audio Script

1. El talón indica para donde está facturada una maleta.
2. La etiqueta identifica de quien es la maleta—a quien pertenece.
3. Cuando viajas en avión no importa cuanto pesan tus maletas.
4. Un vuelo directo no hace escala.
5. Cuando el vuelo está completo no hay más asientos disponibles.
6. Han anulado el vuelo y va a salir pronto.
7. De vez en cuando un vuelo no sale a tiempo porque hay un problema mecánico.
8. Después de un vuelo el equipaje de los pasajeros llega en una correa.

Activity ❷ Students can say the word and then write it.

Activity ❸ You can go over this activity orally in class with books closed and call on students at random to respond. Answers can then be written as a homework assignment.

Differentiation

Multiple Intelligences

After doing Activity 3, call on a **verbal-linguistic** student to retell all the information in his or her own words. You can also have students write a summary of the activity.

170

 ESCUCHAR

❶ Escucha y determina si la información que oyes es correcta o no. Usa una tabla como la de abajo para indicar tus respuestas.

correcta	incorrecta

HABLAR • ESCRIBIR

❷ Identifica.

1.

2.

3.

4.

5.

6.

HABLAR • ESCRIBIR

❸ Contesta sobre un viaje en avión.

1. ¿Qué información hay en una etiqueta?
2. ¿Cuántos kilos no puede exceder una maleta sin que el pasajero tenga que pagar un suplemento?
3. ¿Hace un vuelo directo una escala antes de llegar a su destino final?
4. ¿Qué tienen que hacer las líneas aéreas si anulan un vuelo?
5. ¿Te gustaría más tener un asiento en la ventanilla o en el pasillo?
6. ¿Por dónde tienen que pasar los pasajeros que llegan en un vuelo internacional?
7. Como siempre hay una fila larga en el control de seguridad, ¿es posible perder tu vuelo si no llegas al aeropuerto bastante temprano?

Answers

❶
1. correcta
2. correcta
3. incorrecta
4. incorrecta
5. correcta
6. incorrecta
7. correcta
8. correcta

❷
1. el talón
2. la correa
3. la ventanilla
4. los asientos (las plazas)
5. la etiqueta
6. la maleta

❸
1. En una etiqueta hay el nombre y la dirección del pasajero.
2. Una maleta no puede exceder 22 kilos.
3. Sí, un vuelo directo hace una escala antes de llegar a su destino final.
4. Cuando las líneas aéreas anulan un vuelo tienen que confirmar a los pasajeros en otro vuelo.
5. Me gustaría más tener un asiento en la ventanilla (el pasillo).

Más practica

⬛ Workbook, pp. 6.3–6.5
StudentWorks™ Plus

LEER

4 Parea los sinónimos.

1. completo
2. anulado
3. una demora
4. el asiento
5. reclamar

a. recoger
b. lleno
c. la plaza
d. cancelado
e. un retraso

LEER • ESCRIBIR

5 Identifica donde.

1. donde puedes verificar (chequear) las salidas y llegadas de los vuelos
2. de donde salen los vuelos
3. donde llega el equipaje que descargan del avión después de un vuelo
4. donde inspeccionan el equipaje de los pasajeros que llegan en vuelos internacionales
5. donde revisan los pasaportes de los pasajeros internacionales

LLEGADAS   SALIDAS

Estudio de palabras

disponer Ellos disponen de muchas oportunidades.

disponible Hay muchas oportunidades disponibles.

disposición Ellos tienen muchas oportunidades a su disposición.

pasar José, favor de pasar la sal.
Pásame la sal, por favor.

el paso El niño tomó su primer paso.

el pasillo En el avión hay asientos en el pasillo y en la ventanilla.

el pase Él tiene un pase para poder entrar en la zona restringida.

Contesta. Da respuestas personales.

1. ¿Cuáles son algunas actividades disponibles en tu escuela?
2. ¿Cuáles son algunas ventajas o cosas beneficiosas que tú crees tener a tu disposición?
3. A veces para ser cortés, ¿le permites a alguien pasar delante de ti?
4. ¿Hay muchos pasillos en tu escuela?
5. ¿Necesitas un pase para poder entrar en tu escuela?

Activities 4 and 5 You may also want to have students use each word in an original sentence.

Estudio de palabras

Call on students to read the new word and the sentence that uses it in context.

Give students two minutes to look at the activity, and then ask the questions. Call on volunteers to respond.

GLENCOE Technology

Online Learning in the Classroom

Have students use QuickPass code ASD7844c6 for additional vocabulary practice. They can download audio files of all vocabulary to their computer and/or MP3 player. They will also have access to online flashcards and eGames.

▶ ASSESS

Students are now ready to take Quiz 1 on page 6.37 of the TeacherTools booklet. If you prefer to create your own quiz, use the *ExamView® Assessment Suite*.

Answers

6. Los pasajeros que llegan en un vuelo internacional tienen que pasar por el control de pasaportes y por la aduana.
7. Sí, es posible perder tu vuelo so no llegas al aeropuerto bastante temprano.

4

1. b   4. c
2. d   5. a
3. e

5

1. la pantalla
2. la puerta de salida
3. la correa
4. la aduana
5. el control de pasaportes

Estudio de palabras

Answers will vary.

Vocabulario 2 presentación

Resources

- Vocabulary Transparencies V6.4–V6.5
- Audio Activities TE, pages 6.20–6.22
- Audio CD 6, Tracks 5–8
- Workbook, pages 6.6–6.7
- Quiz 2, page 6.38
- *ExamView® Assessment Suite*

Quick Start

Use QS Transparency 6.2 or write the following on the board.
Escribe cuántas palabras posibles sobre un viaje en tren.

▶ TEACH
Core Instruction

You may wish to refer to suggestions from previous chapters for the presentation of the new vocabulary.

Teaching Options

Have students peruse page 172 and determine the vocabulary they recognize from **¡Así se dice!** Levels 1 and 2.

En otras partes

In addition to **las afueras,** the word **los alrededores** is frequently used.

La estación de tren (ferrocarril)

El tren de cercanías va a los suburbios—a las afueras de una ciudad.

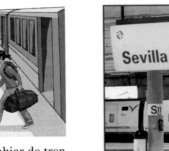

cambiar de tren, transbordar

Los pasajeros tienen que cambiar de tren en Sevilla.
En Sevilla tienen que bajar(se) del tren de cercanías y tomar el tren de largo recorrido.

172

El tren de largo recorrido enlaza ciudades grandes pero no muy cercanas.

GLENCOE Technology

Video in the Classroom

Vocabulario en vivo Watch and listen to Nora as she discusses various modes of transportation.

La agencia de alquiler

un mapa

Beatriz quiere alquilar (rentar, arrendar) un coche (un carro).
Quiere un coche con transmisión manual.

los seguros contra todo riesgo

el contrato

Rafaela firma el contrato.
Declinó los seguros porque tiene su propia póliza.
La tarifa incluye kilometraje ilimitado.
La agente le da un mapa.

el tanque lleno

el retrovisor

los limpiaparabrisas

el neumático

una abolladura

un rayón

Rafaela verifica (chequea) la condición del vehículo antes de aceptarlo.
Hay que devolver el carro a la agencia con el tanque lleno.

En otras partes

Alquilar is universally understood, but **rentar** and **arrendar** are used in many areas of Latin America.

Tips for Success

Give students two minutes to think of words they already learned about a car in **¡Así se dice!** Level 2.

En otras partes

The noun forms for these verbs are: **el alquiler, la renta, el arrendamiento.**

ABOUT THE SPANISH LANGUAGE

At a rental agency a map for a city and its area is **un plano. Un mapa** gives major highways and covers a larger geographical area.

Comunicación

Interpersonal, Presentational
Have students make up two conversations—in the rental office and inspecting the vehicle. Have them present their conversations to the class. Encourage students to make their conversations humorous.

Teaching Options

Have students create a crossword puzzle and/or word scramble with clues of the new vocabulary presented in this chapter. Have them exchange with each other or distribute to the class.

Comparaciones

Have students research train travel in Spanish-speaking countries and compare and contrast it with train travel in the U.S. They could consider price, comfort, availability, efficiency, and ease of booking a ticket. Ask volunteers to present their findings to the class, and suggest that they prepare some type of visual to enhance their presentation.

▶ PRACTICE

Leveling EACH Activity

Easy Activities 1, 2, 3
Average Activity 6
CHallenging Activities 4, 5, 7

Activity ①

🎧 **Audio Script**

1. ¿Cuál es el tren que enlaza una ciudad con los pueblos en sus alrededores?
   a. el tren de largo recorrido
   b. el tren de alta velocidad
   c. el tren de cercanías

2. ¿Qué debes consultar si no sabes a qué hora va a salir el tren?
   a. el horario
   b. la demora
   c. la agencia

3. ¿Tienen que cambiar de tren?
   a. Sí, lo han anulado.
   b. Sí, tienen que transbordar.
   c. Sí, tienen que hacer escala.

4. ¿Qué tiene que firmar una persona que alquila un vehículo?
   a. una etiqueta
   b. un mapa
   c. un contrato

5. ¿Por qué declinó los seguros el cliente?
   a. El kilometraje está incluido.
   b. Son seguros contra todo riesgo.
   c. Tiene su propia póliza.

6. Si estás conduciendo un carro y quieres pasar otro vehículo, ¿en qué debes mirar?
   a. el neumático
   b. el limpiaparabrisas
   c. el retrovisor

Activity ② Students can say and write each word.

Activities ③ and ④ These activities can be prepared and then gone over in class.

ESCUCHAR

① Escucha. Escoge la respuesta correcta. Usa una tabla como la de abajo para indicar tus respuestas.

a	b	c

HABLAR • ESCRIBIR

② Identifica.

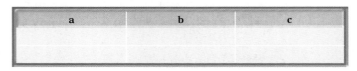

1.

2.

3.

4.

5.

6.

LEER

③ Parea los contrarios.

1. de cercanías   a. el centro
2. las afueras   b. aceptar
3. transmisión manual c. vacío
4. declinar   d. de largo recorrido
5. lleno   e. transmisión automática

HABLAR • ESCRIBIR

④ ¡Te toca a ti! Usa cada palabra de la Actividad 3 en una frase original.

CULTURA

Las señoras están sacando sus billetes de una máquina automática de ventas y al mismo tiempo están verificando la hora de salida de su tren.

174 ciento setenta y cuatro

CAPÍTULO 6

Answers

①	②	③
1. c	1. el horario	1. d
2. a	2. el rayón	2. a
3. b	3. el mapa	3. e
4. c	4. el tanque	4. b
5. c	5. el neumático	5. c
6. c	6. el retrovisor	

④ Answers will vary.

⭐ **Tips for Success** ·······

Have students read the caption that accompanies the photos, since they expand on the theme and vocabulary of the chapter.

HABLAR • ESCRIBIR

5 Contrasta. Explica la diferencia entre un tren de largo recorrido y un tren de cercanías.

LEER

6 Indica si la información es correcta o no.
1. Debes mirar en el retrovisor antes de rebasar otro carro.
2. Mucha gente va a una agencia de alquiler para comprar un carro.
3. Si una persona no tiene un permiso de conducir, no puede arrendar un carro.
4. Después de un accidente o choque, es posible que el carro tenga unos rayones y abolladuras.
5. No debes conducir un carro si no tienes una póliza de seguros.

FOLDABLES Study Organizer

PAPER FILE FOLDER
See page SH29 for help with making this foldable. Use this study organizer to talk about travel with a partner. Label each tab with the name of a city or country you would like to visit. Describe how you would travel to each destination, who you would travel with, and what you would do there.

Comunicación

7 Con un(a) compañero(a), habla de los trenes que hay donde vives. ¿Hay un tren de cercanías? ¿Y un tren de largo recorrido? ¿Tienen muchos usuarios o no?

¿Has viajado en tren alguna vez? Describe tus experiencias.

Estudio de palabras

acercarse a El tren se acerca a la estación.
cerca La estación está cerca del centro.
las cercanías Las cercanías están cerca de la ciudad.
cercano(a) El tren de cercanías sirve los pueblos cercanos.

1 Da los contrarios.
1. lejos de
2. lejano
3. las lejanías
4. alejarse de

2 Usa cada palabra de la Actividad 1 en una frase original.

CULTURA

Los jóvenes están esperando el tranvía en Bilbao, Euskadi. El tranvía, que es un medio de transporte popular en muchas ciudades de Europa y Latinoamérica, se está acercando a la estación.

VIAJES

ciento setenta y cinco **175**

Activity 5 This activity can be done in pairs.

Activity 6 This activity should be prepared and then gone over in class.

Differentiation

Advanced Learners

To make Activity 6 more challenging, have advanced students correct the wrong information.

Comunicación

Interpersonal

When partners do Activity 7, encourage them to say as much as possible. Tell them not to be afraid to make mistakes, since the goal here is real-life communication.

Cultural Snapshot

(page 175) The País Vasco is more commonly called Euskadi today. The Basque language is euskadera. There is a great deal of strong nationalist feeling in this area of Spain.

Estudio de palabras

You may refer to suggestions given in previous chapters for the **Estudio de palabras.**

Dictado You may give a dictation using forms of these words:
1. Yo me acerqué y él se acercó también.
2. Las cercanías son las regiones cercanas. Las regiones que están cerca.
3. Me alejé y ellos se alejaron también.
4. Ella no se alejó.
5. Las lejanías son las regiones lejanas—las regiones que están lejos.

Answers

5 *Answers will vary but may include:*
Un tren de largo recorrido enlaza ciudades grandes pero no muy cercanas y un tren de cercanías va a los suburbios (a las afueras) de una ciudad.

6
1. sí   3. sí   5. sí
2. no   4. sí

7 *Answers will vary.*

Estudio de palabras

1
1. cerca de
2. cercano
3. las cercanías
4. acercarse a

2 *Answers will vary.*

QuickPass

Go to glencoe.com
For: **Grammar practice**
Web code: ASD7844c6

Quick Start

Use QS Transparency 6.3 or write the following on the board.
Escribe cuántas palabras sepas en español sobre un carro.

▶ TEACH
Core Instruction

Step 1 Have students read the explanations as well as the example sentences and expressions.

Step 2 Point out how logical the use of the subjunctive is:

know fact: indicative
unknown but possible fact: subjunctive

ABOUT THE SPANISH LANGUAGE

It is recommended that you only tell students the rule given here. There is, however, a tendency with **después de que** (and **desde que**) to sometimes use the imperfect subjunctive (just as with **antes que**) even when the action is in the past.

▶ PRACTICE

Leveling EACH Activity

Easy Activities 1, 2

Average Activity 2 **Expansión**, Activities 3, 4

176

CULTURA

La pobre pareja perdió su tren porque ya había salido antes de que ellos llegaran a la estación en Sitges.

El subjuntivo con conjunciones de tiempo

1. The subjunctive is used with adverbial conjunctions of time when the verb of the main clause conveys a future time, since it is uncertain if the action in the adverbial clause will really take place. When the verb in the main clause is in the past, however, the indicative is used because the action of the clause has already taken place and is a reality.

FUTURO
Ella nos hablará cuando lleguemos.

PASADO
Ella nos habló cuando llegamos.

2. Some frequently used adverbial conjunctions of time that follow the same pattern are:

cuando	*when*	hasta que	*until*
en cuanto	*as soon as*	después de que	*after*
tan pronto como	*as soon as*		

3. The conjunction **antes de que**, *before*, is an exception. **Antes de que** is always followed by the subjunctive. The imperfect subjunctive is used after **antes de que** when the verb of the main clause is in the past or in the conditional.

Ellos saldrán antes de que nosotros lleguemos.
Ellos salieron antes de que nosotros llegáramos.
Ellos saldrían antes de que nosotros llegáramos.

Práctica

ESCUCHAR • HABLAR • ESCRIBIR

① Contesta según se indica. Presta atención a la forma del segundo verbo.

1. ¿Pasará Julia unos días en La Paz cuando esté en Bolivia? (sí)
2. ¿Arrendará su hermana un jeep en cuanto lleguen a La Paz? (no)
3. ¿Esperará hasta que salgan para el lago Titicaca? (sí)
4. ¿Inspeccionará Julia el jeep antes de que salgan de la agencia? (sí)
5. ¿Devolverá el jeep después de que vuelvan de su excursión a Titicaca? (sí)

Answers

①

1. Sí, Julia pasará unos días en La Paz cuando esté en Bolivia.
2. No, su hermana no arrendará un jeep en cuanto lleguen a La Paz.
3. Sí, esperará hasta que salgan para el lago Titicaca.
4. Sí, Julia inspeccionará el jeep antes de que salgan de la agencia.
5. Sí, devolverá el jeep después de que vuelvan de su excursión a Titicaca.

ESCUCHAR • HABLAR • ESCRIBIR

2 Contesta según se indica. Presta atención a la forma del segundo verbo.

1. Julia ha vuelto de Bolivia. ¿Pasó ella unos días en La Paz cuando estaba en Bolivia? (sí)
2. ¿Arrendó su hermana un jeep en cuanto llegaron a La Paz? (no)
3. ¿Esperó ella hasta que salieron para el lago Titicaca? (sí)
4. ¿Inspeccionó Julia el jeep antes de que salieran de la agencia? (sí)
5. ¿Devolvió el jeep a la agencia después de que volvieron de su excursión a Titicaca? (sí)

EXPANSIÓN

Ahora, sin mirar las preguntas, cuenta la información en tus propias palabras. Si no recuerdas algo, un(a) compañero(a) te puede ayudar.

LEER • ESCRIBIR

3 Completa con la forma apropiada del verbo indicado.
1. Ellos quieren salir en cuanto _____. (poder)
2. Van a salir cuando Carlos _____. (volver)
3. Luego tendrán que esperar hasta que él _____ las maletas en el baúl del carro. (poner)
4. Ellos salieron en cuanto _____. (poder)
5. Salieron en cuanto él _____. (volver)

LEER • ESCRIBIR

4 Completa con la forma apropiada del verbo indicado.
1. Ellos estarán aquí antes de que yo _____. (salir)
2. Ellos estuvieron aquí antes de que yo _____. (salir)
3. Yo lo sabré antes de que ustedes lo _____. (saber)
4. Yo lo sabía antes de que ustedes lo _____. (saber)
5. Ella me lo dirá antes de que yo te _____. (ver)
6. Ella me lo dijo antes de que yo te _____. (ver)

CULTURA Unos excursionistas en su SUV viajando por los Andes en Bolivia

VIAJES

Más práctica
Workbook, pp. 6.8–6.9
StudentWorks™ Plus

CULTURA Una vista del lago Titicaca no muy lejos de La Paz, Bolivia

InfoGap For more practice with the subjunctive used with conjunctions of time, do Activity 6 on page SR7 at the end of this book.

Activities 1 and 2 These activities can be done orally with books closed, calling on students at random. After going over the activities orally, students can write them.

Activities 3 and 4 These activities can be written and then gone over in class.

Differentiation

Advanced Learners
You may wish to call on more able students to make up original sentences using: **hasta que, tan pronto como, después de que,** and **antes de que.**

 Cultural Snapshot

(page 176) Sitges is a lovely beach resort just south of Barcelona. The **tren de cercanías** offers frequent service between Barcelona and Sitges. *(page 177 top)* Lake Titicaca is the highest navigable lake in the world. According to legend it is the birthplace of one of history's greatest empires. In the middle of the lake, Manco Capac and Mama Oello, the children of the Sun, came forth from a sacred rock located on the tip of the Isla del Sol where the Inca Empire started.

InfoGap
The InfoGap activity will allow students to practice in pairs.

ASSESS

Students are now ready to take Quiz 3 on page 6.39 of the TeacherTools booklet. If you prefer to create your own quiz, use the *ExamView® Assessment Suite.*

Answers

2
1. Sí, ella pasó unos días en La Paz cuando estaba en Bolivia.
2. No, su hermana no arrendó el jeep en cuanto llegaron a La Paz.
3. Sí, ella esperó hasta que salieron para el lago Titicaca.
4. Sí, Julia inspeccionó el jeep antes de que salieran de la agencia.
5. Sí, devolvió el jeep a la agencia después de que volvieron de su excursión a Titicaca.

3
1. puedan
2. vuelva
3. ponga
4. pudieron
5. volvió

4
1. salga
2. saliera
3. sepan
4. supieran
5. vea
6. viera

Resources

- Audio Activities TE, pages 6.24–6.25
- Audio CD 6, Tracks 12–13
- Workbook, pages 6.9–6.10
- Quiz 4, page 6.40
- ExamView® Assessment Suite

Quick Start

Use QS Transparency 6.4 or write the following on the board.

Usa las siguientes expresiones en una frase original.

1. pagar el peaje
2. cambiar de carril
3. adelantar
4. llegar a un cruce
5. llenar el tanque
6. cambiar la llanta

▶ TEACH
Core Instruction

It is up to the discretion of the teacher as to how thoroughly you wish to present this grammar point. Although the subjunctive is still frequently used following these verbs, it is becoming quite common to use the infinitive. Students will hear and see the infinitive frequently. **Le pedí venir a visitamos. Le ruego estudiar más. Nos pidieron no hacerlos. Les aconsejé llegar a tiempo. Te recomiendo no decir nada.**

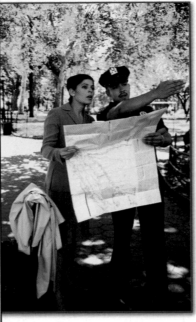

▲ El agente de policía le dice a la señora que siga derecho.

El subjuntivo con verbos especiales

1. Some verbs state or imply a command, advice, or suggestion. Such verbs are followed by the subjunctive because, even though we ask, tell, advise, or suggest that someone do something, it is not certain that the person will actually do it.

2. Some frequently used verbs that state or imply a command, an order, advice, or a suggestion are:

decir	*to tell*	exigir	*to demand*
escribir	*to write*	aconsejar	*to advise*
pedir	*to ask, request*	recomendar	*to recommend*
rogar	*to beg, plead*	sugerir	*to suggest*
mandar	*to order*		

3. Observe and analyze the following sentences.

Te digo que no llegues tarde.
Te dije que no llegaras tarde.

Les aconsejo que salgan juntos.
Les aconsejé que salieran juntos.

These verbs often take an indirect object pronoun in the main clause. The indirect object of the main clause is the subject of the dependent clause.

4. Note that the subjunctive follows the verbs **decir** and **escribir** only when they imply a command. If someone is simply giving information, the subjunctive is not used. Observe the following sentences.

Ella me dice que viene mañana.
She tells me that she's coming tomorrow.

Ella me dice que venga mañana.
She tells me to come tomorrow.

Cultural Snapshot

(page 179 top) As one can see on this lovely colonial street, La Paz, the highest capital city in the world, has many steep climbs.

Práctica

HABLAR

⑤ Contesta.

1. ¿Le recomiendas a Julia que alquile un jeep?
2. ¿Les aconsejas a tus amigos que no hagan muchos ejercicios en cuanto lleguen a La Paz?
3. ¿Te rogó tu amigo que lo esperaras en el aeropuerto?
4. ¿Te sugirió que llegaras temprano al aeropuerto?

CULTURA
Vista de una calle pintoresca en La Paz

ESCUCHAR • HABLAR

 ⑥ Sigue el modelo.

 MODELO —¿Qué les pidió Pedro?
esperar
—Él nos pidió que esperáramos.

1. no salir sin él
2. ir en metro
3. comprar los boletos para el avión
4. llegar temprano

LEER • ESCRIBIR

⑦ Forma oraciones con **que.**

1. su abuela le escribe / ser bueno
2. su abuela le escribe / estar bien
3. su abuela le escribe / tratar bien a su hermanita
4. su abuela le escribe / querer verlo
5. su abuela le escribe / cuidarse

CULTURA
Abuelita vive en Santo Domingo y está muy contenta cuando sus nietos le escriben y le dicen todo lo que están haciendo. Abuelita les dice que le escriban muy a menudo.

VIAJES

ciento setenta y nueve **179**

---

⑤
1. Sí, (No, no) le recomiendo a Julia que alquile un jeep.
2. Sí, (No, no) les aconsejo a mis amigos que no hagan muchos ejercicios en cuanto lleguen a La Paz.
3. Sí (No), mi amigo (no) me rogó que lo esperara en el aeropuerto.
4. Sí, (No, no) me sugirió que llegara temprano al aeropuerto

⑥ *All answers will begin with Él nos pidió…*
1. que no saliéramos sin él.
2. que fuéramos en metro.
3. que compráramos los boletos para el avión.
4. que llegáramos temprano.

⑦ *All answers will begin with Su abuela le escribe…*
1. que sea bueno.
2. que esté bien.
3. que trate bien a su hermanita.
4. que quiere verlo.
5. que se cuide.

Gramática

▶ PRACTICE

Leveling EACH Activity

Easy Activity 5
Average Activity 6
CHallenging Activity 7

⭐ Tips for Success ·······

It is recommended that you go over these grammar activities once in class before they are assigned for homework.

···

Activity ⑤ You can do this activity with books closed and call on students at random.

Activity ⑥ You can have students work in pairs to do this activity.

Activity ⑦ You may wish to give students two minutes to look over the activity to decide which verb form they want to use. Then go over the exercise orally and have students write it for homework.

Differentiation
Multiple Intelligences

Have **verbal-linguistic** students look at the photo of a grandmother in Santo Domingo. Have them pretend it is their grandmother and give information about her and what she tells (or probably would tell) them to do.

▶ ASSESS

Students are now ready to take Quiz 4 on page 6.40 of the TeacherTools booklet. If you prefer to create your own quiz, use the *ExamView® Assessment Suite.*

179

Resources

- Audio Activities TE, pages 6.25–6.26
- Audio CD 6, Tracks 14–15
- Workbook, page 6.10
- Quiz 5, page 6.41
- *ExamView® Assessment Suite*

 **Quick Start**

Use QS Transparency 6.5 or write the following on the board.

Completa con el o la.

1. ___ universidad
2. ___ postre
3. ___ clase
4. ___ coche
5. ___ deporte
6. ___ carne

▶ TEACH
Core Instruction

Merely have students read the words. The only way they will be able to give the correct gender of these nouns is by using them. This is one of those points that we "learn by doing."

 Cultural Snapshot

(page 180 top) This beach is in Troncones, Mexico, a small ecological beach community on the Pacific Ocean, northwest of Acapulco.

GLENCOE 🔊 Technology

You may wish to use the editable PowerPoint® presentation on PowerTeach for additional grammar instruction and practice.

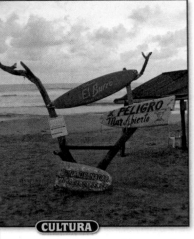

CULTURA

Las aguas del mar abierto pueden ser turbulentas y peligrosas.

Sustantivos irregulares

1. Feminine nouns that begin with a stressed **a** or the silent **h** followed by a stressed **a** take the masculine definite article **el** or the indefinite article **un**. The reason such nouns take the articles **el** and **un** is that it would be difficult to pronounce the two vowels—**la a, una a**—together. Since the nouns are feminine, the plural articles **las** and **unas** are used and any adjective modifying the noun is in the feminine form.

el agua	las aguas	*water(s)*
el/un águila	las águilas	*eagle(s)*
el/un área	las áreas	*area(s)*
el/un arma	las armas	*weapon(s)*
el/un hacha	las hachas	*ax(es)*
el/un ala	las alas	*wing(s)*
el hambre		*hunger*

El agua limpia es buena para la salud.
Las aguas turbulentas del mar pueden ser peligrosas.

2. There are several nouns in Spanish that end in **a** but are masculine. These are nouns derived from Greek roots. They take the definite article **el** and the indefinite article **un.**

el clima	el poema
el día	el programa
el drama	el sistema
el mapa	el telegrama
el planeta	el tema

3. Note that the noun **la mano** is irregular. Even though **la mano** ends in **o**, it is feminine—**la mano**. **La foto** is also used as a shortened version of **la fotografía**. The noun **radio** can be either **la radio** or **el radio**.

CULTURA

¿Cuántos alumnos han levantado la mano? El aula es moderna, ¿no?

Práctica

ESCUCHAR • HABLAR

 8 Contesta según se indica.

1. ¿Cuál es el arma que lleva don Quijote? (la lanza)
2. ¿Has leído los poemas de Rubén Darío? (no)
3. ¿Dónde pasaste el día? (en la escuela)
4. En clase, ¿qué tienes que levantar cuando tienes una pregunta? (la mano)
5. ¿Cuál es el tema de este capítulo? (los problemas que podemos encontrar cuando viajamos)
6. ¿Se envían muchos telegramas hoy en día? (no)

LEER • ESCRIBIR

9 Completa con el artículo definido.
1. _____ agua es buena para la salud.
2. Vamos a necesitar _____ mapa porque no somos de aquí y no conocemos _____ área.
3. El aire debajo de _____ alas del avión levanta el avión cuando despega.
4. _____ sistema de ferrocarriles en España es muy bueno.
5. Creo que _____ águila tiene _____ ala rota.
6. _____ hambre es _____ problema número uno en varias partes del mundo.
7. _____ aguas del Mediterráneo son más calmas que _____ aguas del Atlántico.
8. Tenemos que proteger _____ planeta Tierra.

Refrán

Can you guess what the following proverb means?

Todos los caminos conducen a Roma.

¡Bravo!

You have now learned all the new vocabulary and grammar in this chapter. Continue to use and practice all that you know while learning more cultural information. ¡Vamos!

CULTURA
Un ave exótica en una selva tropical de Ecuador

ciento ochenta y uno **181**

Gramática

▶ PRACTICE

Leveling EACH Activity

Easy Activity 8
Average Activity 9

⭐ Tips for Success ·······

Have students read these activities, go over them orally in class, write them for homework, and go over them orally once again. The more they hear these nouns with the correct article, the better!

·······································

▶ ASSESS

Students are now ready to take Quiz 5 on page 6.41 of the TeacherTools booklet. If you prefer to create your own quiz, use the *ExamView®* *Assessment Suite.*

Refrán

Proverbs, adages, idiomatic expressions, and other popular sayings provide a wealth of opportunities for students to learn about different cultural perspectives as well as perspectives shared by different cultures.

Have students recite the proverb aloud. Then see if they can figure out the equivalent expression in English: "All roads lead to Rome." Ask what they think this proverb means.

¡Bravo! The remaining pages of the chapter recycle information in a variety of ways, allowing students to build upon their newly acquired language skills as well as to keep track of their own progress.

Answers

 8
1. El arma que lleva don Quijote es la lanza.
2. No, no he leído los poemas de Rubén Darío.
3. Pasé el día en la escuela.
4. En clase, tengo que levantar la mano cuando tengo una pregunta.
5. El tema de este capítulo es los problemas que podemos encontrar cuando viajamos.
6. No, no se envían muchos telegramas hoy en día.

9
1. El
2. un, el
3. las
4. El
5. el, un
6. El, el
7. Las, las
8. el

Resources

- Audio Activities TE, pages 6.26–6.27
- Audio CD 6, Tracks 16–17

GLENCOE SPANISH

Why It Works!

No new material is used in the **Conversación** in order not to confuse students. The **Conversación** recombines only the vocabulary and grammar that students have already learned to understand and manipulate.

▶ TEACH
Core Instruction

Step 1 Have students close their books. Read the conversation to them or play Audio CD 6.

Step 2 Have the class repeat each line after you or the audio CD.

Step 3 Call on two students to read the conversation with as much expression as possible.

Step 4 After presenting the conversation, go over the **¿Comprendes?** activities. If students can answer the questions with relative ease, move on. Students should not be expected to memorize the conversation.

Teaching Options

If students are feeling quite at ease with the language, you may just have them read the conversation silently and then work in pairs to present little skits.

¡Qué lío!

Anita	Tengo malas noticias.
Mara	¿Qué? Dime.
Anita	Hay un problema mecánico y han anulado nuestro vuelo pero nos han confirmado en otro.
Mara	¿Cuándo sale?
Anita	¿Quieres que yo te lo diga? En cuatro horas.
Mara	¡Cuatro horas! Y además, ¿quién sabe si habrá otra demora? ¿Qué vamos a hacer cuando lleguemos tan tarde a Barcelona? Vamos a perder nuestro tren para Tarragona, ¿no?
Anita	Sí, el último tren sale antes de que llegue nuestro vuelo. Y además sería necesario ir del aeropuerto a la estación de tren.
Mara	¡Qué lío! En ese caso tendremos que buscar un hotel, ¿no?
Anita	No. No quiero tener que ir a un hotel.
Mara	Ni yo tampoco. ¿Por qué no alquilamos un coche? ¿Qué te parece?
Anita	¡Buena idea! Pero tenemos que pedir un mapa en la agencia de alquiler porque no conocemos el área.

182 *ciento ochenta y dos* **CAPÍTULO 6**

Differentiation
Advanced Learners

Ask advanced learners to make up a similar conversation and perform it for the class. Have other students answer questions to demonstrate whether they understood the conversation.

GLENCOE Technology

Online Learning in the Classroom

Have students use QuickPass code ASD7844c6 for additional conversation practice. Students can download audio files for the conversation to their computer and/or MP3 player and complete a self-check quiz.

¿Comprendes?

A Completa según la información en la conversación.
1. Anita tiene _____.
2. Han anulado el vuelo porque _____.
3. La línea aérea ha confirmado a Anita y a Mara _____.
4. El vuelo sale _____.
5. Ellas van a llegar _____.
6. Van a perder _____.
7. Lo van a perder porque _____.
8. Ninguna de las dos quiere _____.
9. Deciden que van a _____.

B **Resumiendo** Cuenta toda la información en la conversación en tus propias palabras.

C **Analizando** Contesta.
 ¿Por qué deciden Anita y Mara que deben alquilar un coche?

 VIDEO To take an interesting flight from Argentina to Venezuela, watch **Diálogo en vivo.**

Cultura

Si algún día decides rentar un vehículo en un país extranjero, es necesario inspeccionar bien el carro para determinar si tiene abolladuras o rayones y que el agente los anote. ¿Por qué? Porque, cuando devuelvas el vehículo, el agente lo inspeccionará por cualquier daño que encuentre.

BIZA
Rent a Car
Calle Lirios 14, Col. Bugambilias Puebla, Pue.

- Entrega a domicilio
- Kilometraje libre
- Mejoramos cualquier presupuesto
- Tarifas especiales a empresas
- Servicio los 365 días del año

Contamos con las mejores marcas

Tels.: (222)
244-3434 • 750-6277 • 413-3838

VIAJES

ciento ochenta y tres **183**

Conversación

 PRACTICE

¿Comprendes?

A You may allow students to look up the information or you may wish to do this as a factual recall activity.

Writing Development
After students give an oral summary in Activity B, you may wish to have students write a summary of the conversation.

Cultura
Have students read the **Cultura** note. It is important information for those planning to rent a vehicle in Spain or Latin America.

Learning from Realia
Entrega means:
a. entrance
b. intrigue
c. delivery
The English word *domicile* is related to the Spanish word **a domicilio.** Ask students what other expression in Spanish means **a domicilio.** How does this ad express "unlimited kilometers"? How does the ad state that their price cannot be beat? When does the agency close?

GLENCOE Technology

Video in the Classroom
Diálogo en vivo In this episode, Julián prepares for a flight from Argentina to Venezuela. Have students consult a physical map of South America to see if there might be any other viable modes of transportation between these two countries. Have them tell why or why not.

183

Resources

- 📙 Audio Activities TE, pages 6.28–6.29
- 🎧 Audio CD 6, Tracks 18–19

▶ **TEACH**

Core Instruction

Step 1 Have students read the **Antes de leer** and look at the photographs that accompany the **Lectura**.

Step 2 It is up to your discretion as to how thoroughly you wish students to know the information. You may wish to have students learn the material so they can retell it in their own words—transfer from a receptive skill (read) to a productive skill (speak and/ or write). In this case, call on a student to read a few sentences aloud, and ask questions for students to answer.

Step 3 Have students do the **¿Comprendes?** activities, either in class or as homework.

Differentiation

Reaching All Learners

Differently paced learners will produce language at different levels. Some techniques to get the maximum from each group are:

- Ask a slower paced student three or four *yes/no* questions. The answers to your questions will provide an organized review.
- Call on a more able student to retell what the previous student just said.
- Call on an advanced learner to retell the entire story in his or her own words.
- Ask questions of a slower paced learner about what the advanced learner said.

184

LECTURA CULTURAL

¡A Bolivia ya! 🎧 ♻️

Antes de leer

Antes de leer esta lectura sobre un viaje que van a hacer unas amigas a Bolivia, piensa en lo que ya sabes de los efectos de la altitud.

✓ **Reading Check**
¿Por qué tendrás que tener cuidado cuando desembarques del avión?

✓ **Reading Check**
¿Por qué tiene que ser muy larga la pista?

✓ **Reading Check**
¿Dónde viven los quechua y los aymara?

🌐 *GeoVistas*
To learn more about Bolivia, take a tour on pages SH50–SH51.

¿Quieres hacer un viaje algún día a Bolivia? No hay duda que sería una experiencia estupenda. Pero hay unas cosas interesantes que debes saber antes de llegar. ¡Número uno! La palabra «alto» es importante.

Hasta el aeropuerto que sirve La Paz se llama «El Alto». Lleva este nombre porque es el aeropuerto comercial más alto del mundo a una altura de 13.450 pies o 4.100 metros. A estas alturas hay menos oxígeno que al nivel del mar. Por eso, tendrás que tener cuidado cuando desembarques del avión. No es raro que un recién llegado tenga dificultad en respirar por la falta de oxígeno, pero el aeropuerto siempre tiene tanques de oxígeno disponibles.

Durante el aterrizaje tendrás una vista magnífica de La Paz porque está a 1.000 metros más abajo del aeropuerto. Parece estar en un cráter, y la belleza del claro cielo azul paceño es inolvidable—sobre todo en el invierno.

Y cuando salgas, tendrás otra experiencia que no vas a olvidar. Tu avión despegará de una de las pistas más largas del mundo. A esta altura el aire tiene muy poca densidad por falta de oxígeno y es difícil sostener el peso del avión. Así tiene que alcanzar una gran velocidad para poder despegar y continuar subiendo.

Cuando estés en Bolivia tienes que ir al lago Titicaca en la frontera entre Bolivia y Perú. Una vez más la palabra «alto». El lago Titicaca es el lago navegable más alto del mundo. A lo largo de las orillas[1] peruanas viven los quechua y a las orillas bolivianas los aymara. Estos grupos indígenas vestidos en trajes tradicionales cultivan papas y habichuelas y pescan trucha en sus barquitos o balsas de junco[2].

[1] orillas *shores*
[2] junco *reed*

CULTURA
Plaza Murillo en La Paz

184 *ciento ochenta y cuatro*

📷 **Cultural Snapshot**

(page 184) Plaza Murillo is the historical center of La Paz. It gets its name from General Murillo, one of the heroes of Bolivia's independence. The cathedral, government palace, and congress are on the plaza.

🌐 *GeoVistas*

Ask students to turn to the map of Bolivia on page SH51 and locate La Paz and Lake Titicaca. In what part of Bolivia are the mountains? How is Bolivia different geographically from Peru and Ecuador? *(Bolivia is land locked.)*

¿Comprendes?

A Recordando hechos Contesta.

1. ¿Cuál es el aeropuerto comercial más alto del mundo?
2. ¿Por qué tienen problemas unos recién llegados?
3. ¿Qué hay siempre a su disposición en el aeropuerto?
4. ¿Cómo es la pista en el aeropuerto de La Paz?
5. Durante el aterrizaje, ¿dónde parece estar La Paz?

B Identificando Identifica.

1. los aymara
2. los quechua

C Analizando Contesta.

1. ¿Por qué lleva el nombre «El Alto» el aeropuerto que sirve La Paz?
2. ¿Por qué pueden muchos recién llegados tener dificultad en respirar?
3. ¿Por qué tiene que ser tan larga la pista en el aeropuerto El Alto?

D Describiendo Describe.

1. la vista de la ciudad de La Paz desde la ventanilla de un avión
2. el lago Titicaca

VIDEO To take a trip through another Andean country, watch **Cultura en vivo.**

CULTURA
Una familia indígena en su balsa de junco en el lago Titicaca

CULTURA
Una joven con su alpaca en la isla del Sol en el lago Titicaca

185

PRACTICE

¿Comprendes?

B One student can give a description to the entire class or students can work in pairs.
C This critical thinking activity can be done as an entire class discussion.
D You may wish to have students write their descriptions.

ABOUT THE SPANISH LANGUAGE

There is not conformity of opinion about the pluralization of the names of American indigenous groups. Certain groups such as **los mayas** and **los aztecas** take an **-s** in the plural. With many other groups such as **los aymara, los quechua, los quiché,** and **los chibcha,** it is more common not to add **-s.** Names of groups will be seen both ways.

 Cultural Snapshot

(page 185 top) These are the typical **balsas de junco** that the indigenous peoples use for transportation on Lake Titicaca. *(page 185 bottom)* The small, yet spectacular isla del Sol is the birthplace of the Incas.

GLENCOE Technology

Video in the Classroom
Cultura en vivo In this episode, students will take a journey by train to Machu Picchu. You may wish to have students research this ancient, fortified city. Ask them to compare and contrast what they learn about the Incas with what they know about Native American history in the United States.

Answers

A

1. Es el aeropuerto que sirve La Paz. Se llama «El Alto».
2. Tienen problemas en respirar por la falta de oxígeno.
3. Siempre hay tanques de oxígeno.
4. Es una de las pistas más largas del mundo.
5. La Paz parece estar en un cráter.

B

1. Los aymara son los indios que viven a lo largo de las orillas bolivianas del lago Titicaca.
2. Los quechua son los indios que viven a lo largo de las orillas peruanas del lago Titicaca.

C

1. Es el aeropuerto comercial más alto del mundo.

2. A estas alturas hay menos oxígeno que al nivel del mar.
3. A esta altura el aire tiene muy poca densidad y es difícil sostener el peso del avión. La pista tiene que ser tan larga porque el avión tiene que alcanzar una gran velocidad para poder despegar y subir.

D *Answers will vary.*

Literatura

Temprano y con sol

de Emilia Pardo Bazán

▲ La Coruña, la provincia
natal de Pardo Bazán
en Galicia

Resources

📖 Literature Test, page 6.59
💿 ExamView® Assessment Suite

Preview

Starting in Chapter 3, each chapter of **¡Así se dice!** Level 3 has a literary section. Most literary selections are by well-known Latin American or Spanish writers.

The difficulty level of each selection is also indicated: 1 is difficult; 4 is quite easy.

Difficulty Level
3–2

Teaching Options

This literary selection is optional. You may wish to do it with the entire class or certain groups, or you may wish to assign it as homework for extra credit. You may also prefer to omit it.

Vocabulario

▶ **TEACH**

Core Instruction

Step 1 Call on students to read a new word and its definition.

Step 2 You may wish to ask some questions to enable students to use the new words. Some examples are: **¿Tiene tu amigo(a) muchas manías? ¿Conoces unas familias que tengan criada? ¿Cuál es uno de los cinco sentidos? ¿Tienes novio(a)? ¿Cuáles son otras palabras que significan «mozo»? ¿Tienes reloj? ¿Qué hora indica tu reloj ahora? ¿Hay pizzerias que entregan la pizza a casa (a domicilio)? ¿Se echó a correr el niño porque algo le asustó? ¿Te van a avisar de lo que pasa?**

Vocabulario

la manía preocupación exagerada; deseo desordenado

la criada señora que trabaja haciendo tareas domésticas por dinero

el oído el aparato que sirve para la audición, que nos permite oír

el/la novio(a) amigo con quien uno sale con frecuencia y a quien le expresa cariño

el mozo el joven, el muchacho

el reloj aparato que nos indica la hora

entregar dar

echar a empezar a, ponerse a

avisar informarle a alguien de algo; dejarle a uno saber algo

186 *ciento ochenta y seis*

CAPÍTULO 6

Differentiation

Advanced Learners

Have advanced learners use the new words in original sentences.

Slower Paced Learners

Help slower paced learners by asking them *yes/no* questions using the new words.

 Cultural Snapshot

(page 186) La Coruña is a port city in the northwestern corner of Spain. Galicia is known for its craggy mountains, valleys, and distinctive estuaries called **rías**. The **rías** in the north are known as the **Rías Altas** and those along the southwest are known as the **Rías Bajas.** La Coruña is a point of departure for the **Rías Altas.**

Práctica

1 Completa con una palabra apropiada.

1. No sé la hora porque mi _____ no anda.
2. No quería que nadie oyera lo que me decía. Así es que lo murmuró en mi _____.
3. Él tiene muchas _____. A veces yo no comprendo lo que hace.
4. Hace tiempo que los _____ están saliendo. Creo que se están enamorando.
5. Mucha gente de las clases altas pagan a una _____ para limpiar la casa.
6. El hijo de los López es un buen _____.

2 Expresa de otra manera.

1. Lo necesitan. ¿Cuándo se lo vas a *dar*?
2. El niño tenía miedo y *se puso a* correr.
3. Es necesario que lo sepan. ¿Por qué no les *informan* de lo que está pasando?
4. Es *un muchacho* inteligente y simpático.
5. Es *una obsesión* que tiene.

▲ Emilia Pardo Bazán (1852–1921), una ilustre autora española

Introducción

Emilia Pardo Bazán, la condesa de Pardo Bazán, es considerada una de los novelistas más importantes de la literatura española. Nació en La Coruña, Galicia, de una familia aristócrata. Fue una mujer culta de gran curiosidad intelectual y talento creativo.

Su obra incluye varias novelas psicológicas y regionales. En dos de sus novelas importantes estudia y describe la decadencia de la aristocracia gallega.

Pardo Bazán cultivó el cuento también y se le considera una maestra de este género literario.

Literatura

▶ PRACTICE

Activities 1 and 2 These activities can be completed individually and then gone over in class.

Introducción

You may wish to ask the following questions about the **Introducción**.

¿Tenía Emilia Pardo Bazán un título aristocrático? ¿Cuál? ¿Tiene fama de ser una escritora importante? ¿Escribió novelas o poesía? ¿Dónde nació ella? ¿Qué significa «fue una mujer culta»? ¿Qué estudia unas de sus novelas? ¿En qué otro género literario se considera a Pardo Bazán una maestra?

TEACH
Core Instruction

Step 1 Have students read the **Estrategia.** Explain that this is an important reading strategy. Many novels and short stories from both Spain and Latin America do not follow a chronological order. It is, therefore, extremely important when reading to always focus on the sequencing of the author.

Step 2 Have students read the **Antes de leer** and answer the question.

Step 3 Have students read the selection in sections, either silently or aloud. Ask them questions such as the following as you finish each section. ¿Qué manía tenían los dos chicos? ¿Dónde se encontraban los chicos? ¿Cuándo? ¿Cómo se llamaban los chicos? ¿Qué siempre quería hacer Currín?

Step 4 Have students read the **Durante la lectura** and discuss the answers to the questions.

Teaching Options

It is up to your discretion as to how thoroughly you wish students to know the information. You may wish to have students learn the material thoroughly enough that they can retell it in their own words—in other words, transfer from a receptive skill (read) to a productive skill (speak and/or write). In this case, you may wish to call on students to take turns reading a few sentences aloud. Then stop and ask questions that other students answer.

Antes de leer

Al reflexionar sobre tu niñez, ¿siempre lo haces en orden cronológico?

duros *antiguas monedas españolas*

dando una patada *stamping her feet*

Estrategia

Identificando la secuencia El argumento de una novela o cuento no sigue siempre un orden cronológico o sea, el orden en que ocurren los eventos. Así es el caso en este cuento de Pardo Bazán. Al leer tal obra es importante determinar la verdadera secuencia de los eventos.

Temprano y con sol

El empleado que vendía billetes en la oficina de la estación quedó sorprendido al oír una voz infantil que decía:

—¡Dos billetes, de primera clase, para París!…

Miró a una niña de once o doce años, de ojos y pelo negros, con un rico vestido de color rojo y un bonito sombrerillo. De la mano traía a un niño casi de la misma edad que ella, el cual iba muy bien vestido también. El chico parecía confuso; la niña muy alegre. El empleado sonrió y murmuró paternalmente:

—¿Directo, o a la frontera? A la frontera son ciento cincuenta pesetas, y…

—Aquí está el dinero—contestó la niña, abriendo su bolsa. El empleado volvió a sonreír y dijo:

—No es bastante.

—¡Hay quince duros° y tres pesetas!—exclamó la niña.

—Pero no es suficiente. Si no lo creen, pregunten ustedes a sus papás.

El niño se puso rojo, y la niña, dando una patada° en el suelo, gritó:

—¡Bien… , pues… , dos billetes más baratos!

—¿A una estación más próxima? ¿Escorial; Ávila?…

—¡Ávila, sí… , Ávila!…—respondió la niña.

Vaciló el empleado un momento; luego entregó los dos billetes. Subieron los dos chicos al tren y, al verse dentro del coche, comenzaron a bailar de alegría.

CULTURA

La bella ciudad amurallada de Ávila, España

 Cultural Snapshot

(page 188) Avila is surrounded by perfectly preserved medieval walls that average 40 feet in height and 10 feet in width. Avila, at 3,700 feet elevation, is the highest city on the Iberian Peninsula. Because of its pure air, there are many swallows and storks. Avila is home to Santa Teresa de Avila who founded the Order of the Carmelitas descalzas.

¿Cómo empezó aquel amor apasionado? Pues comenzó del modo más simple e inocente. Comenzó por la manía de los dos chicos de formar colecciones de sellos.

El papá de Finita y la mamá de Currín, ya enviudados° los dos, apenas° se conocían, aunque vivían en el mismo edificio. Currín y Finita, en cambio, se encontraban siempre en la escalera, cuando iban a la escuela.

Una mañana, al bajar la escalera, Currín notó que Finita llevaba un objeto, un libro rojo, ¡el álbum de sellos! Quería verlo. La colección estaba muy completa y contenía muchos sellos de varios países. Al ver un sello muy raro de la república de Liberia, exclamó Currín:

—¿Me lo das?
—Toma—respondió Finita.
—Gracias, hermosa—contestó Currín.
Finita se puso roja y muy alegre.
—¿Sabes que te he de decir una cosa?—murmuró el chico.
—Anda, dímela.
—Hoy no.

Ya era tarde y la criada que acompañaba a Finita la llevó a la escuela. Currín se quedó admirando su sello y pensando en Finita. Currín era un chico de carácter dulce, aficionado a los dramas tristes, a las novelas de aventuras y a la poesía. Soñaba con° viajes largos a países desconocidos. Verdad es que, aquella noche, soñó que Finita y él habían hecho una excursión a una tierra lejana.

Al día siguiente, nuevo encuentro en la escalera. Currín tenía unos sellos que iba a dar a Finita. Finita sonrió y se acercó a Currín, con misterio, diciendo:

—Dime lo que me ibas a decir ayer…
—No era nada…
—¡Cómo nada!—exclamó Finita, furiosa.—¡Qué idiota! Nada, ¿eh?

Currín se acercó al oído de la niña y murmuró:
—Sí, era algo…. Quería decirte que eres… ¡muy guapita!
Al decir esto, echó a correr escalera abajo.

Currín escribía versos a Finita y no pensaba en otra cosa más que en ella. Al fin de la semana eran novios.

Cierta tarde creyó el portero del edificio que soñaba. ¿No era aquélla la señorita Finita? ¿Y no era aquél el señorito Currín? ¿Y no subían los dos a un coche que pasaba? ¿Adónde van? ¿Deberé avisar a los padres?

—Oye—decía Finita a Currín, cuando el tren se puso en marcha.—Ávila, ¿cómo es? ¿Muy grande? ¿Bonita, lo mismo que París?

—No—respondió Currín.—Debe de ser un pueblo de pesca°.

VIAJES

enviudados *widowed*
apenas *scarcely*

Durante la lectura
Reflexiona sobre tu niñez y contesta las siguientes preguntas. ¿Recuerdas cuando eras niño(a)? ¿Imaginabas que tenías novio(a)? ¿Quién era? ¿Cómo se conocieron?

Soñaba con *He dreamed of*

pueblo de pesca *fishing village*

ciento ochenta y nueve **189**

Differentiation
Multiple Intelligences
- Call on **bodily-kinesthetic** learners to dramatize the following:
  De la mano traía a un niño.
  El chico parecía confuso; la niña muy alegre.
  El empleado sonrió y murmuró.
  La niña dio una patada en el suelo.
- Call on **bodily-kinesthetic** learners to dramatize (using words) or merely mime what took place on the staircase.
- Call on two **bodily-kinesthetic** learners to act out the conversation between Finita and Currín.

Slower Paced Learners
Slower paced learners may benefit from more frequent pauses in the reading to check for comprehension.

Advanced Learners
Ask the following of more able students: **¿Por qué vació un momento el empleado antes de entregarles los billetes?**

Teaching Options
- Either read to students or call on a student with good pronunciation and intonation to read the reaction of **el portero**. (For placement—**Cierta tarde creyó…**)
- Call on two individuals to read the conversation between Finita and Currín that continues on page 190.

Tips for Success
- Call on three individuals to take part in the dialogue on page 188. Hearing a dialogue makes it come alive and helps students understand better.
- Have students answer the following questions so you can better evaluate their level of understanding.

¿Adónde fueron los niños?
¿Cómo estaban vestidos?
¿Adónde querían ir los dos niños?
¿Por qué no pudieron ir allí?
¿Adónde decidieron ir?

▶ TEACH
Core Instruction

Step 1 Have the class read **Después de leer** and discuss as an entire group their opinions and reactions.

Step 2 Call on a student to tell what happened to Currín and Finita when they arrived in Ávila.

Step 3 Do the **¿Comprendes?** activities as a class or individually to go over together in class.

Cultural Snapshot

(page 190) The Arco de Triunfo is one of Paris' most famous monuments located in the center of the Etoile.

(page 191) The El Escorial, completed in 1584, was the dream of Felipe II. In the foothills of the Sierra de Guadarrama, it is just thirty minutes away from Madrid. It is part monastery, palace, and mausoleum.

CULTURA

El famoso Arco de Triunfo en el París de los años 1920

—Yo quiero ver París; y también quiero ver las pirámides de Egipto.

—Sí… —murmuró Currín,— pero… ¿y el dinero?

—¿El dinero?—contestó Finita.—Eres tonto. ¡Se puede pedir prestado°!

pedir prestado *borrow*

—¿Y a quién?

—¡A cualquier persona!

—¿Y si no nos lo quieren dar?

empeñar *pawn*
abrigo *overcoat*

—Yo tengo mi reloj que empeñar°. Tú también. Y puedo empeñar mi abrigo° nuevo. Si escribo a papá, nos enviará dinero.

—Tu papá estará furioso… ¡No sé qué haremos!

—Pues voy a empeñar mi reloj y tú puedes empeñar el tuyo. ¡Qué bien vamos a divertirnos en Ávila! Me llevarás al café… y al teatro… y al paseo….

Cuando llegaron a Ávila, salieron del tren. La gente salía y los novios no sabían a dónde dirigirse.

—¿Por dónde se va a Ávila?—preguntó Currín a un mozo que no les hizo caso. Por instinto se encaminaron a una puerta, entregaron sus billetes y, cogidos por un solícito agente de hotel, se metieron en el coche, que los llevó al Hotel Inglés.

Entretanto el gobernador de Ávila recibió un telegrama mandando la captura de los dos enamorados. Los fugitivos fueron llevados a Madrid, sin pérdida de tiempo. Finita fue internada en un convento y Currín quedó en una escuela, de donde no fueron permitidos salir en todo el año, ni aun los domingos.

Como consecuencia de aquella tragedia, el papá de Finita y la mamá de Currín llegaron a conocerse muy bien, y creció su mutua admiración de día en día. Aunque no tenemos noticias exactas, creemos que Finita y Currín llegaron a ser… hermanastros.

▶ Después de leer

¿Qué opinión tienes de este cuento? ¿Te parece verosímil o no? ¿Tiene un final feliz? ¿Por qué?

190 *ciento noventa*

CAPÍTULO 6

¿Comprendes?

A **Parafraseando** Parea.

1. dio una sonrisa
2. dijo en voz muy baja
3. como un padre
4. de un niño
5. suficiente
6. tonto
7. solícito
8. entregar

a. murmuró
b. estúpido
c. paternalmente
d. sonrió
e. dar
f. infantil
g. diligente
h. bastante

B **Recordando hechos** Contesta.

1. ¿Qué compraba la niña? ¿Dónde?
2. ¿Adónde quería ir?
3. ¿Qué no tenía la niña?
4. ¿Para dónde sacó los billetes?
5. ¿Cómo se pusieron los dos niños cuando subieron al tren?
6. ¿Qué coleccionaban los niños?
7. ¿Dónde vivían ellos?
8. ¿Se conocían sus padres?
9. ¿Habían enviudado sus padres?

C **Describiendo** Describe.

1. Da una descripción de Finita.
2. Da una descripción de Currín.

D **Interpretando** El final del cuento dice: «Aunque no tenemos noticias exactas, creemos que Finita y Currín llegaron a ser… hermanastros». Explica como será posible esto.

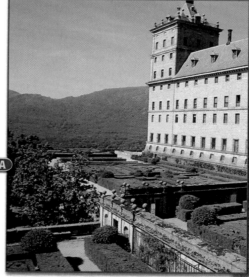

CULTURA
El Escorial

VIAJES

ciento noventa y uno **191**

▶ PRACTICE

¿Comprendes?

A After going over the entire selection, you may wish to challenge students to do this as a factual recall activity.

D You may wish to have students do this critical thinking activity in pairs or small groups.

Writing Development

For Activity C, you may wish to have students write a paragraph describing each one to give them practice in writing descriptive compositions.

Differentiation

Advanced Learners

As an expansion of Activity A, you may wish to have more advanced students use the words in the second column in original sentences.

Slower Paced Learners

You may wish to have students do the **¿Comprendes?** activities in pairs so students can help each other.

Pre-AP This reading will develop the skills that students need to be successful on the reading and writing sections of the AP exam.

Answers

A
1. d
2. a
3. c
4. f
5. h
6. b
7. g
8. e

B
1. La niña compraba dos billetes de primera clase. Los compraba en la oficina de una estación de tren.
2. Quería ir a París.
3. No tenía bastante dinero.
4. Sacó los billetes para Ávila.
5. Se pusieron muy alegres.
6. Coleccionaban sellos.

7. Vivían en el mismo edificio.
8. Sí, sus padres se conocían pero apenas.
9. Sí, sus padres habían enviudado.

C *Answers will vary but may include:*
1. Finita tenía once o doce años y tenía los ojos negros y el pelo negro. Tenía ropa muy bonita y un reloj. Tenía criada.
2. Currín tenía la misma edad que Finita. Era un chico de carácter dulce, aficionado a los dramas tristes, a las novelas de aventuras y a la poesía. Soñaba con viajes largos a países deconocidos.

D
Sus padres se casaron.

191

Prepárate para el examen
Self-check for achievement

Resources

- Tests, pages 6.49–6.66
- Performance Assessment, Task 6, pages 6.67–6.68
- *ExamView® Assessment Suite*

☑ Self-check for achievement

This is a pre-test for students to take before you administer the chapter test. Note that each section is cross-referenced so students can easily find the material they feel they need to review. You may wish to use Self-Check Worksheet Transparency SC6 to have students complete this assessment in class or at home. You can correct the assessment yourself, or you may prefer to project the answers on the overhead in class using Self-Check Answers Transparency SC6A.

Differentiation

Slower Paced Learners

Have students work in pairs to complete the Self-Check in class. This will allow them to check their answers through collaborative learning. Once they have finished, call on individuals to give the correct answers as you review together.

Vocabulario

1 **Indica si la información es correcta o no.**

1. Un vuelo internacional despega en un país y aterriza en otro.
2. La línea aérea ha anulado el vuelo. Sale a tiempo.
3. Ellos perdieron su vuelo porque llegaron tarde al aeropuerto.
4. Los pasajeros pueden reclamar su equipaje en inmigración.
5. No somos de aquí y necesitamos un mapa.
6. Las abolladuras son el resultado de un accidente.

2 **Escoge.**

7. (La maleta, El talón) indica hasta donde está facturado el equipaje.
8. Un vuelo entre Miami y Lima con una escala en Guayaquil es un vuelo (sin escala, internacional).
9. El avión no va a salir porque (hay una demora, está anulado).
10. El vuelo está completo y no hay asientos (disponibles, en la fila).
11. Los pasajeros (hacen, reclaman) su equipaje después del vuelo.
12. No soy de aquí y no conozco la región. Tendré que consultar (mi contrato, el mapa).
13. ¿Ha tenido este carro un accidente? Mira este (retrovisor, rayón).
14. Si alquilas un carro lo tienes que (reclamar, devolver) con el tanque lleno.

To review **Vocabulario 1** and **Vocabulario 2,** turn to pages 168–169 and 172–173.

Gramática

3 **Completa con la forma apropiada del verbo.**

15. Él me habló en cuanto me _____. (ver)
16. Él me hablará en cuanto me _____. (ver)
17. Ellos saldrán después de que nosotros _____. (llegar)
18. Ellos salieron después de que nosotros _____. (llegar)

To review **el subjuntivo con conjunciones de tiempo,** turn to page 176.

Answers

1
1. sí
2. no
3. sí
4. no
5. sí
6. sí

2
7. El talón
8. internacional
9. está anulado
10. disponibles
11. reclaman
12. el mapa
13. rayón
14. devolver

3
15. vio
16. vea
17. lleguemos
18. llegamos
19. sepa
20. supiera
21. paguen
22. pagaron
23. pueda
24. podía
25. vuelva
26. volví

19. Tú lo sabrás antes de que lo _____ yo. (saber)
20. Tú lo sabías antes de que lo _____ yo. (saber)
21. Él no comprará el billete hasta que ustedes lo _____. (pagar)
22. Él no compró el billete hasta que ustedes lo _____. (pagar)
23. Marta volverá a casa en cuanto _____. (poder)
24. Marta volvió a casa en cuanto _____. (poder)
25. Te llamaré tan pronto como _____ del aeropuerto. (volver)
26. Te llamé tan pronto como _____ del aeropuerto. (volver)

4 Completa.
27. Él me dijo que (yo) _____. (salir)
28. Ellos te dirán que lo _____. (hacer)
29. Ella nos aconseja que _____ atención. (prestar)
30. Yo les pedí que _____ a tiempo. (llegar)
31. Mi abuela me dice que _____ enferma pero no sabe lo que tiene. (estar)

5 Completa con el artículo definido.
32. Levanta _____ mano si tienes una pregunta.
33. No puedes beber _____ agua. No es potable.
34. Tenemos que proteger _____ planeta Tierra.
35. ¿Vas a ver _____ programa?
36. _____ aves tienen alas.

Cultura

6 Contesta.
37. ¿Qué es El Alto?
38. ¿Por qué tiene dificultad en respirar mucha gente que acaba de llegar a La Paz?
39. ¿Cuál es el lago navegable más alto del mundo?
40. ¿Quiénes viven a las orillas de este lago?

 To review **el subjuntivo con verbos especiales,** turn to page 178.

To review **sustantivos irregulares,** turn to page 180.

To review this cultural information, turn to page 184.

CULTURA

Laguna Verde y el volcán Licancabur en Bolivia

VIAJES

Answers

4
27. saliera
28. hagan
29. prestemos
30. llegaran
31. está

5
32. la
33. el
34. el
35. el
36. Las

6
37. El Alto es el aeropuerto comercial más alto del mundo. Está en La Paz, Bolivia.
38. Mucha gente que acaba de llegar a La Paz tiene dificultad en respirar porque hay menos oxígeno que al nivel del mar.
39. El lago navegable más alto del mundo es el lago Titicaca.
40. A las orillas peruanas viven los quechua y a las orillas bolivianas viven los aymara.

⭐ Tips for Success ·······

Encourage students to say as much as possible when they do these open-ended activities. Tell them not to be afraid to make mistakes, since the goal of the activities is real-life communication. If someone in the group makes an error, allow the others to politely correct him or her. Let students choose the activities they would like to do.

Tell students to feel free to elaborate on the basic theme and to be creative. They may use props, pictures, or posters if they wish.

Pre-AP These oral activities will give students the opportunity to develop and improve their speaking skills so that they may succeed on the speaking portion of the AP exam.

Note: You may want to use the rubric below to help students organize their speaking activities.

1 **En el aeropuerto**
❧ Check in at the airport
Imagínate que estás en el aeropuerto. Estás saliendo para una ciudad latinoamericana. Tienes que facturar tu equipaje, conseguir (obtener) tu tarjeta de embarque, etc. Ten una conversación con el/la agente de la compañía de aviación (tu compañero[a]).

2 **Un vuelo anulado**
❧ Get help when a flight's been cancelled
Trabajen en grupos de tres. Dos de ustedes son pasajeros y uno(a) es el/la agente de la línea aérea. El/La agente acaba de informarles que han anulado su vuelo. Tengan una conversación con el/la agente para determinar lo que va a hacer la línea aérea para acomodarlos.

3 **En una agencia de alquiler**
❧ Rent a car
Quieres alquilar un carro. Estás en la agencia. Ten una conversación con el/la empleado(a) de la agencia (tu compañero[a]).

4 **¿Qué tal el viaje?**
❧ Tell what you did before and after your trip
Imagínate que has hecho un viaje con unos amigos. Di todo lo que tú o ellos hicieron antes de que salieran y di todo lo que hiciste o hicieron todos ustedes en cuanto volvieron a casa.

CULTURA
Estos pasajeros están para salir en un vuelo del aeropuerto de la Ciudad de México.

Scoring Rubric for Speaking

	4	3	2	1
vocabulary	extensive use of vocabulary, including idiomatic expressions	adequate use of vocabulary and idiomatic expressions	limited vocabulary marked with some anglicisms	limited vocabulary marked by frequent anglicisms that force interpretation by the listener
grammar	few or no grammatical errors	minor grammatical errors	some serious grammatical errors	serious grammatical errors
pronunciation	good intonation and largely accurate pronunciation with slight accent	acceptable intonation and pronunciation with distinctive accent	errors in intonation and pronunciation with heavy accent	errors in intonation and pronunciation that interfere with listener's comprehension
content	thorough response with interesting and pertinent detail	thorough response with sufficient detail	some detail, but not sufficient	general, insufficient response

Tarea

You have recently been hired as a part-time travel agent for a local travel agency that specializes in booking and planning vacations to Spain and Latin America, and your first major assignment is to create a newsletter to be sent out to customers that will give them advice on traveling and tips on how to have a successful trip.

Writing Strategy

Creating a newsletter A newsletter from a travel agency serves two main purposes: first, to provide customers with useful information about their upcoming travel experience, and second, to promote the continued use of services offered by the company. Your newsletter should be clear and concise, as well as useful and inviting to your reader. In addition to including informative details, you should also think about style or layout, making sure that your newsletter is as visually appealing as it is easy to understand.

❶ Prewrite

- Give the travel agency a catchy name. Then choose three popular travel destinations in the Spanish-speaking world that you would like to visit and make them the focus of your newsletter.
- Use the diagram for each of your destinations to help you decide which ones to talk about when discussing the three different subtopics of this chapter: traveling by plane, by train, and by car. You should also include additional information about the main tourist attractions, hotel accommodations, and typical cuisine of each area, as well as any tips or advice

that travelers to each destination might find useful.

- Once you have filled in your diagram, you may find it necessary to eliminate some details because you do not want to overwhelm the reader with too much information. Remember that you want your newsletter to be both informative and enjoyable.

❷ Write

- Before you begin arranging the final version, write each part of your newsletter separately. Once you have written all of the parts, read over each of them to check for correct spelling and grammar, proper use of vocabulary, and the completeness as well as the usefulness of information.
- In addition to using vocabulary from the textbook, be sure to incorporate the main grammar points from this chapter—the subjunctive with conjunctions of time and the subjunctive to express commands, orders, advice, and suggestions.

Evaluate

Your teacher will evaluate you based on the style or design of your newsletter, the proper use of vocabulary, the correctness of spelling and grammar, and the completeness and usefulness of information.

Prepárate para el examen

Pre-AP This **tarea** will give students the opportunity to develop and improve their writing skills so that they may succeed on the writing portion of the AP exam.

Note: You may want to use the rubric below to help students organize their writing task.

Scoring Rubric for Writing				
	4	**3**	**2**	**1**
vocabulary	precise, varied	functional, fails to communicate complete meaning	limited to basic words, often inaccurate	inadequate
grammar	excellent, very few or no errors	some errors, do not hinder communication	numerous errors interfere with communication	many errors, little sentence structure
content	thorough response to the topic	generally thorough response to the topic	partial response to the topic	insufficient response to the topic
organization	well organized, ideas presented clearly and logically	loosely organized, but main ideas present	some attempts at organization, but with confused sequencing	lack of organization

Repaso del Capítulo 6

Resources

- Audio Activities TE, pages 6.30–6.32
- Audio CD 6, Tracks 20–23
- Workbook, pages 6.13–6.14

Grammar Review

This page provides a quick "at a glance" summary of the grammar points students have learned in this chapter. The corresponding page numbers are also listed so that students can easily find each grammar point as it was presented.

Differentiation

Multiple Intelligences

You may want to call on **verbal-linguistic** and **logical-mathematical** learners for whom grammar often comes easily to explain the main concepts to their classmates in their own words. Having students explain the concepts in different ways may also help slower paced learners or students with learning difficulties.

Gramática

- **El subjuntivo con conjunciones de tiempo** *(page 176)*

  Adverbial conjunctions of time such as **cuando, en cuanto, tan pronto como, hasta que,** and **después de que** are followed by the indicative when the action is in the past and by the subjunctive when it is in the future.

PASADO	FUTURO
Ella nos habló cuando llegamos.	Ella nos hablará cuando lleguemos.

  Note that the conjunction **antes de que** is always followed by the subjunctive.

  Ellos saldrán antes de que lleguemos.
  Ellos salieron antes de que nosotros llegáramos.

- **El subjuntivo con verbos especiales** *(page 178)*

  Verbs that state or imply a command, advice, or suggestion are followed by the subjunctive. Note also that they are usually used with an indirect object pronoun.

  Ellos te dicen que lo hagas.
  Ellos me aconsejaron que (yo) lo hiciera también.
  Ellos nos sugirieron a todos que lo hiciéramos.

- **Sustantivos irregulares** *(page 180)*

  Feminine nouns that begin with a stressed **a (ha)** take the masculine definite article **el** or the indefinite article **un** for the sake of pronunciation. However, they are feminine.

el/un águila	las águilas
el/un hacha	las hachas

  Many nouns that end in **-ma** have a Greek root and they are masculine—**el poema, el drama, el tema, el clima.** Note also that **el planeta** is masculine.

  Remember that **la mano** and **la foto** are feminine. **Radio** can be either **la radio** or **el radio.**

CULTURA

Un Águila imperial de España

Juego There are a number of cognates in this list. See how many you and a partner can find. Who can find the most? Compare your list with those of your classmates.

Vocabulario

Getting around an airport

el aeropuerto	el peso	el reclamo de	la inmigración
la maleta	la correa	equipaje	la aduana
el equipaje	la pantalla	el control de	pesar
el talón	la puerta de salida	pasaportes	reclamar, recoger
la etiqueta			

Talking about flights

un vuelo	una demora	la ventanilla	anular
directo	un asiento, una	la fila	confirmar
sin escala	plaza	completo(a)	hacer escala
el destino	el pasillo	disponible	perder el vuelo

Getting around a train station

la estación de tren	el tren	cercano(a)	cambiar de tren,
(ferrocarril)	de cercanías	enlazar	transbordar
	de largo recorrido		

Talking about renting a car

la agencia de	los seguros	un rayón	firmar
alquiler	contra todo riesgo	una abolladura	aceptar
el/la agente	la tarifa	ilimitado(a)	declinar
el contrato	el kilometraje	alquilar, rentar,	incluir
la póliza	el mapa	arrendar	verificar, chequear

Identifying some car parts

la transmisión	el retrovisor	el neumático
manual	los limpiaparabrisas	el tanque

Other useful words and expressions

los suburbios, las	acercarse a	¡Qué lío!
afueras	debido a	

 The words listed below come from this chapter's literary selection, *Temprano y con sol*. They were selected to become part of your active vocabulary because of their relatively high frequency.

la manía	el/la novio(a)	entregar
la criada	el/la mozo	echar a
el oído	el reloj	avisar

Don't forget the chapter project and cultural activities found on pages 164C–164D. Students have learned all the information that they will need to complete these engaging enrichment tasks.

Juego The cognates in this list are: **el aeropuerto, el control, los pasaportes, la inmigración, reclamar, directo, el destino, completo(a), confirmar, la estación de tren, la agencia, el/la agente, el contrato, la póliza, la tarifa, el kilometraje, el mapa, rentar, aceptar, declinar, verificar, chequear, la transmisión manual, el tanque, los suburbios, la manía, avisar.**

Vocabulary Review

The words and phrases in **Vocabulario 1** and **2** have been taught for productive use in this chapter. They are summarized here as a resource for both student and teacher. This list also serves as a convenient resource for the **Prepárate para el examen** activities on pages 192–195.

GLENCOE SPANISH

Why It Works!

This vocabulary reference list has not been translated into English for two reasons. First, it is recommended that students learn the new vocabulary through direct association with images on the **Vocabulario** pages. Second, all vocabulary is reintroduced in the chapter many times, and upon completion of the chapter students should be familiar with the meaning of all the words. If there are words that students still do not know, they can refer back to the vocabulary presentation in the chapter or the dictionary at the end of the book. If, however, it is your preference to give students the English translations, please refer to Vocabulary Transparency V6.1 or to the Chapter 6 PowerPoint® presentation on PowerTeach.

Differentiation

Slower Paced Learners

Slower paced learners may benefit from creating their own visual dictionary of words from this list. They can either draw their own depictions or use images from the Internet or magazines.

Every chapter of ¡Así se dice! contains this review section of previously learned material. By recycling information from previous chapters, the cumulative review serves to remind students that they need to continue practicing what they have learned after finishing each chapter.

Activity 1 This activity reviews distinguishing the past, present, and future tenses. See pages R7, R29, R31, R43, SR32.

🎧 **Audio Script** *(CD 6, Track 24)*
1. ¿A qué hora saliste de la escuela esta mañana?
2. Yo fui con Carlos a la fiesta ayer.
3. ¿Cuándo será la boda de Teresa y Paco?
4. Yo estoy muy enferma hoy.
5. Ellos volvieron a casa muy tarde ayer.
6. Nosotros pasábamos los veranos en la playa con nuestros abuelos.
7. ¿Cuándo vas a ir a visitar a los parientes?
8. Tú tomas el autobús cada mañana, ¿no?

Activity 2 This activity reviews the future and conditional tenses. See pages SR32–SR33, SR37.

Activity 3 This activity reviews the future and conditional tenses. See pages SR32–SR33, SR37.

Repaso cumulativo

Repasa lo que ya has aprendido

These activities will help you review and remember what you have learned so far in Spanish.

 1 Escucha las frases. Indica en una tabla como la de abajo si la acción ocurre en el pasado, el presente o el futuro.

en el pasado	en el presente	en el futuro

 2 Cambia el futuro al condicional.
1. Iré en avión.
2. Ellos tomarán el tren.
3. ¿Pondrás el equipaje en la maletera?
4. Haremos el viaje juntos.
5. ¿Llegarán ustedes a tiempo?
6. ¿No comerás durante el vuelo?
7. No subiré la escalera.
8. Tomaré el ascensor.

 3 Contesta.
1. Algún día, ¿irás a México?
2. ¿Pasarás unos días en la capital?
3. ¿Visitarás el museo de Antropología?
4. ¿Harás una excursión a Xochimilco?
5. ¿Verás los jardines flotantes?

CULTURA
La Torre Latinoamericana en la Ciudad de México

Answers

 1
1. en el pasado
2. en el pasado
3. en el futuro
4. en el presente
5. en el pasado
6. en el pasado
7. en el futuro
8. en el presente

 2
1. Iría en avión.
2. Ellos tomarían el tren.
3. ¿Pondrías el equipaje en la maletera?
4. Haríamos el viaje juntos.
5. ¿Llegarían ustedes a tiempo?
6. ¿No comerías durante el vuelo?
7. No subiría la escalera.
8. Tomaría el ascensor.

 3
1. Sí, (No, no) iré a México.
2. Sí, (No, no) pasaré unos días en la capital.
3. Sí, (No, no) visitaré el museo de Antropología.
4. Sí, (No, no) haré una excursión a Xochimilco.
5. Sí, (No, no) veré los jardines flotantes.

4 Completa con el condicional.

1. Él lo _____ pero yo no lo _____. (hacer)
2. Ellos lo _____ pero tú no lo _____. (saber)
3. Nosotros lo _____ pero ellos no lo _____. (decir)
4. Yo _____ pero mi hermano no _____. (salir)
5. Yo sé que tú lo _____ pero yo no lo _____. (devolver)

5 Parea el infinitivo con el participio pasado.

1. hacer   **a.** abierto
2. decir   **b.** puesto
3. poner   **c.** vuelto
4. volver   **d.** cerrado
5. romper   **e.** visto
6. abrir   **f.** comido
7. cerrar   **g.** hecho
8. vivir   **h.** roto
9. comer   **i.** dicho
10. ver   **j.** vivido

6 Contesta según el modelo.

MODELO   —¿Lo habrían hecho ustedes?
               —Sí, lo habríamos hecho pero no pudimos.

1. ¿Habrían ido ustedes?
2. ¿Se lo habrías dicho a José?
3. ¿Habría vuelto tu hermano?
4. ¿Habrías firmado el contrato?
5. ¿Ella te habría devuelto el dinero?

7 Completa la siguiente tabla.

infinitivo	participio presente	participio pasado
hablar		
	comiendo	
		recibido
abrir		
		vuelto
pedir		
	leyendo	

VIAJES

Activity 4 This activity reviews the conditional tense. See pages SR32–SR33, SR37.

Activity 5 This activity reviews past participles. See page R66.

Activity 6 This activity reviews the conditional perfect tense. See page 108.

Activity 7 This activity reviews present and past participles. See pages R66, 108.

Pre-AP To give students further open-ended oral or written practice, or to assess proficiency, go to AP Proficiency Practice Transparencies AP21 and AP23.

GLENCOE Technology

Audio in the Classroom
The ¡Así se dice! Audio Program for Chapter 6 has 24 activities, which afford students extensive listening and speaking practice.

Answers

4
1. haría, haría
2. sabrían, sabrías
3. diríamos, dirían
4. saldría, saldría
5. devolverías, devolvería

5
1. g   6. a
2. i   7. d
3. b   8. j
4. c   9. f
5. h   10. e

6
1. Sí, habríamos ido pero no pudimos.
2. Sí, se lo habría dicho a José pero no pude.
3. Sí, mi hermano habría vuelto pero no pudo.
4. Sí, habría firmado el contrato pero no pude.
5. Sí, ella me habría devuelto el dinero pero no pudo.

7
hablando, hablado
comer, comido
recibir, recibiendo
abriendo, abierto
volver, volviendo
pidiendo, pedido
leer, leído

Chapter Overview
Arte y literatura

● Scope and Sequence

Topics
- Art
- Literature

Culture
- Don Quijote and Sancho Panza
- *La liberación del peón* by Diego Rivera
- *No sé por qué piensas tú* by Nicolás Guillén

Functions
- How to discuss fine art and literature
- How to talk about a mural by the Mexican artist Diego Rivera
- How to read a sonnet by the Spaniard Federico García Lorca
- How to read a poem by the Cuban poet Nicolás Guillén

Structure
- The present perfect and pluperfect subjunctive
- **Si** clauses
- Adverbs ending in **-mente**

● Planning Guide

	required	recommended	optional
Vocabulario 1 (pages 204–207) El arte	✔		
Vocabulario 2 (pages 208–211) La literatura	✔		
Gramática (pages 212–217) El subjuntivo Cláusulas con **si** Los adverbios que terminan en **-mente**	✔		
Conversación (pages 218–219) ¡Ojalá que tuviera el talento!		✔	
Lectura cultural (pages 220–223) Las artes		✔	
Literatura (pages 224–225) *No sé por qué piensas tú*			✔
Prepárate para el examen (pages 226–229)			✔
Repaso cumulativo (pages 232–233)			✔

● Correlations to National Foreign Language Standards

Page numbers in light print refer to the Student Edition. Page numbers in bold print refer to the Teacher Edition.	
Communication Standard 1.1 Interpersonal	pp. **202–203, 206,** 207, **207, 211,** 215, **219, 223,** 228
Communication Standard 1.2 Interpretive	pp. 206, **208,** 210, **210, 212,** 213, **213,** 215, 217, **218,** 219, **219,** 220, **220,** 221, **221, 222,** 223, **224,** 225, **225,** 227, **227,** 228, 232, 233, **233**
Communication Standard 1.3 Presentational	pp. **200C, 200D, 205, 209,** 210, 211, **211, 215,** 216, **218, 222, 223, 225, 226,** 228, 229, **230, 231**
Cultures Standard 2.1	pp. **200D,** 223
Cultures Standard 2.2	pp. **200C, 200D,** 202–203, **202–203, 204, 205,** 207, **207, 208, 211,** 220–222, **221,** 223, 227, 231
Connections Standard 3.1	pp. **200C, 200D,** 202–203, **204, 205,** 207, **207, 208, 209,** 214, **214,** 220, **220, 221,** 223, 224, **224,** 225
Connections Standard 3.2	pp. 208, **208, 209,** 211, **211,** 215, **215,** 217, **217,** 221, **221,** 225
Comparisons Standard 4.1	pp. **209,** 214, **217, 230,** 231
Comparisons Standard 4.2	pp. 201, **201, 214**
Communities Standard 5.1	pp. **200C, 207, 209,** 210, **226, 228, 230**
Communities Standard 5.2	pp. **205,** 208, **208,** 211, **211,** 215, **215,** 221, **221,** 228
To read the ACTFL Standards in their entirety, see the front of the Teacher Edition.	

● Student Resources

Print

Workbook *(pp. 7.3–7.14)*
Audio Activities *(pp. 7.15–7.21)*
Pre-AP Workbook, Chapter 7

Technology

- ◉ StudentWorks™ Plus
- ▬ ¡Así se dice! Vocabulario en vivo
- ▬ ¡Así se dice! Gramática en vivo
- ▬ ¡Así se dice! Diálogo en vivo
- ▬ ¡Así se dice! Cultura en vivo
- ✎ Vocabulary PuzzleMaker
- **QuickPass** glencoe.com

● Teacher Resources

Print

TeacherTools, Chapter 7
 Workbook TE *(pp. 7.3–7.14)*
 Audio Activities TE *(pp. 7.17–7.34)*
 Quizzes 1–4 *(pp. 7.37–7.41)*
 Tests *(pp. 7.44–7.64)*
 Performance Assessment, Task 7 *(pp. 7.65–7.66)*

Technology

- ⬓ Quick Start Transparencies 7.1–7.4
- ⬓ Vocabulary Transparencies V7.1–V7.5
- ∩ Audio CD 7
- ◉ *ExamView® Assessment Suite*
- ◉ TeacherWorks™ Plus
- ◉ PowerTeach
- ▬ ¡Así se dice! Video Program
- ✎ Vocabulary PuzzleMaker
- **QuickPass** glencoe.com

Chapter Project

Una exposición de arte y literatura

Students will work individually to create a poster board presenting the life and works of a famous Hispanic artist or writer. The projects can then form part of an exhibition on art and literature of the Spanish-speaking world.

1. To ensure that students focus on writers and artists of merit, you may wish to have them choose from a prepared list of important artistic and literary figures. As students conduct independent research on the artist or writer of their choice, remind them to cite all sources of information and to always check more than one source to verify that the information is correct.

2. Poster boards must include at least three visual elements and should display a title that is eye-catching and easy to read. The poster board should include only relevant information and be clearly written or typed. Each student should submit a sketch of the layout of his or her poster, along with a draft of the Spanish text describing the life and works of the writer or artist. Once their drafts have been checked or peer edited, students should revise them and hand the drafts and sketches in with their final versions.

3. Have students present their poster boards in class for further oral practice. You may wish to allow them to create PowerPoint® presentations to aid in reporting the information they found.

Expansion: You may wish to hold an art and literature exhibition with the completed projects, as an in-class or after-school activity. For example, students could attend the exposition during class and then hold small conversations about what they liked and disliked, and/or parents and Spanish-speakers from the community could be invited to attend the exposition during the evening.

Scoring Rubric for Project

	1	3	5
Evidence of planning	Draft and layout are not provided.	Draft and layout are provided, but draft is not corrected.	Layout and corrected draft are provided.
Use of illustrations	Poster board contains no visual elements.	Poster board contains few visual elements.	Poster board contains several visual elements.
Presentation	Poster board contains little of the required elements.	Poster board contains some of the required elements.	Poster board contains all the required elements.

Culture

● Carnaval

In Hispanic countries, **Carnaval** is a grand celebration that takes place in late February or
early March to mark the beginning of the
Lenten fast before Easter. This tradition was
brought to Latin America by the Spaniards who
celebrated **Carnaval** in their home country.
Carnaval festivities vary from country to country
and even locally, but typically, the celebration
lasts for several days, includes plenty of music,
dancing, food, and fun, and features a parade
with ornate floats and costumed marchers. The
costumes may be representations of animals or
the traditional dress of that region. In some
areas a **Carnaval** queen is selected to reign over
the parade and other festivities. You may wish
to have students further research the festivities
of a Hispanic city or region and create a presentation with their findings.

● Chachachá

It is not often that the creation of a new musical genre
can be attributed to one single person; the creation of
the **chachachá** may in fact be the single instance of this.
Cuban composer Enrique Jorrín is credited with the
creation of **chachachá** in the late 1940s. His modification of the traditional **dazón** led to melodies that were
less syncopated than those of the **mambo,** and therefore
easier to dance to. The name **chachachá** was derived
from the sound the dancers' feet made as they grazed
the floor on three successive beats. This new rhythm
inspired other composers and band leaders to be more
creative with the **danzones** of the time. All variations of
the **chachachá** (or cha-cha, as it is more commonly
referred to in the dance world) remained highly popular
through the 1950s. It is the most recent dance to be
incorporated into the Latin family. The simplicity of its
movements has allowed the cha-cha to remain popular
with amateur dancers while retaining its status as a professional ballroom dance. Ask students if anyone can
demonstrate the cha-cha for the class. If no one knows
the steps, share the graphic on this page with students
and have fun as everyone tries to follow the steps. After
trying the steps, ask if students enjoy this type of dancing more than others.

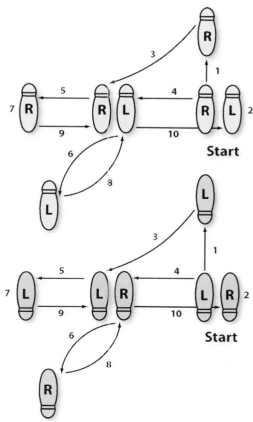

50-Minute Lesson Plans

	Objective	Present	Practice	Assess/Homework
Day 1	Talk about art	Chapter Opener, pp. 200–201 (5 min.) Introducción al tema, pp. 202–203 (10 min.) Core Instruction/Vocabulario 1, pp. 204–205 (20 min.)	Activities 1–3, p. 206 (15 min.)	Student Workbook Activities A–D, pp. 7.3–7.4 **QuickPass** Vocabulary Practice
Day 2	Talk about art	Quick Start, p. 204 (5 min.) Review Vocabulario 1, pp. 204–205 (10 min.)	Activities 4–5, p. 207 (10 min.) Estudio de palabras, p. 207 (5 min.) Total Physical Response, p. 205 (5 min.) Audio Activities A–D, pp. 7.17–7.19 (15 min.)	Student Workbook Activities E–H, pp. 7.4–7.5 **QuickPass** Vocabulary Practice
Day 3	Talk about literature	Core Instruction/Vocabulario 2, pp. 208–209 (15 min.) Video, Vocabulario en vivo (10 min.)	Activities 1–4, p. 210 (15 min.)	Quiz 1, p. 7.37 (10 min.) Student Workbook Activities A–B, pp. 7.5–7.6 **QuickPass** Vocabulary Practice
Day 4	Talk about literature	Quick Start, p. 208 (5 min.) Review Vocabulario 2, pp. 208–209 (5 min.) Video, Diálogo en vivo (10 min.)	Activities 5–7, pp. 210–211 (15 min.) Audio Activities E–G, pp. 7.19–7.21 (15 min.)	Student Workbook Activities C–D, p. 7.6 **QuickPass** Vocabulary Practice
Day 5	The present perfect and pluperfect subjunctive	Quick Start, p. 212 (5 min.) Core Instruction/Gramática, El subjuntivo, p. 212 (15 min.)	Activities 1–3, p. 213 (10 min.) Audio Activities A–C, pp. 7.21–7.22 (10 min.)	Quiz 2, p. 7.38 (10 min.) Student Workbook Activities A–F, pp. 7.7–7.8 **QuickPass** Grammar Practice
Day 6	**Si** clauses	Quick Start, p. 214 (5 min.) Core Instruction/Gramática, Cláusulas con **si**, p. 214 (10 min.) Video, Gramática en vivo (5 min.)	Activities 4–7, p. 215 (10 min.) Audio Activities D–E, pp. 7.23–7.24 (10 min.)	Quiz 3, p. 7.39 (10 min.) Student Workbook Activities A–C, p. 7.9 **QuickPass** Grammar Practice
Day 7	Adverbs ending in **-mente**	Core Instruction/Gramática, Los adverbios que terminan en **-mente**, p. 216 (10 min.)	Activities 8–9, p. 217 (10 min.) Foldables, p. 217 (5 min.) Audio Activities F–H, pp. 7.24–7.25 (15 min.)	Quiz 4, p. 7.40 (10 min.) Student Workbook Activities A–B, p. 7.10 **QuickPass** Grammar Practice
Day 8	Develop reading and listening comprehension skills	Core Instruction/Conversación, p. 218 (20 min.)	¿Comprendes? A–C, p. 219 (20 min.) InfoGap, SR8 (10 min.)	**QuickPass** Conversation
Day 9	Discuss fine art and literature	Core Instruction/Lectura cultural, pp. 220–222 (20 min.) Video, Cultura en vivo (5 min.)	¿Comprendes? A–C, p. 223 (10 min.)	Listening Comprehension Test, pp. 7.59–7.61 (15 min.) ¿Comprendes? D–G, p. 223 **QuickPass** Reading Practice
Day 10	Read a poem by the Cuban poet Nicolás Guillén	Core Instruction/Literatura, pp. 224–225 (15 min.)	¿Comprendes? A–B, p. 225 (10 min.) Prepárate para el examen, pp. 226–227 (25 min.)	¿Comprendes? C, p. 225 Prepárate para el examen, Practice for written proficiency, p. 229 **QuickPass** Reading Practice
Day 11	Chapter review	Repaso del Capítulo 7, pp. 230–231 (15 min.)	Prepárate para el examen, Practice for oral proficiency, p. 228 (20 min.)	Test for Writing Proficiency, p. 7.64 (15 min.) Review for chapter test

Day 12	Chapter 7 Tests (50 min.)
	    Reading and Writing Test, pp. 7.49–7.56
	    Literature Test, pp. 7.57–7.58
			Speaking Test, p. 7.62
			Test for Oral Proficiency, p. 7.63	

90-Minute Lesson Plans

	Objective	Present	Practice	Assess/Homework
Block 1	Talk about art	Chapter Opener, pp. 200–201 (5 min.) Introducción al tema, pp. 202–203 (10 min.) Quick Start, p. 204 (5 min.) Core Instruction/Vocabulario 1, pp. 204–205 (20 min.)	Activities 1–5, pp. 206–207 (20 min.) Estudio de palabras, p. 207 (5 min.) Total Physical Response, p. 205 (10 min.) Audio Activities A–D, pp. 7.17–7.19 (15 min.)	Student Workbook Activities A–H, pp. 7.3–7.5 *QuickPass* Vocabulary Practice
Block 2	Talk about literature	Quick Start, p. 208 (5 min.) Core Instruction/Vocabulario 2, pp. 208–209 (20 min.) Video, Vocabulario en vivo (10 min.) Video, Diálogo en vivo (10 min.)	Activities 1–7, pp. 210–211 (20 min.) Audio Activities E–G, pp. 7.19–7.21 (15 min.)	Quiz 1, p. 7.37 (10 min.) Student Workbook Activities A–D, pp. 7.5–7.6 *QuickPass* Vocabulary Practice
Block 3	The present perfect and pluperfect subjunctive **Si** clauses	Quick Start, p. 212 (5 min.) Core Instruction/Gramática, El subjuntivo, p. 212 (15 min.) Core Instruction/Gramática, Cláusulas con **si**, p. 214 (15 min.)	Activities 1–3, p. 213 (15 min.) Activities 4–5, p. 215 (10 min.) InfoGap, p. SR8 (5 min.) Audio Activities A–D, pp. 7.21–7.23 (15 min.)	Quiz 2, p. 7.38 (10 min.) Student Workbook Activities A–F, pp. 7.7–7.8 Student Workbook Activities A–B, pp. 7.9 *QuickPass* Grammar Practice
Block 4	**Si** clauses Adverbs ending in **-mente**	Quick Start, p. 214 (5 min.) Review Gramática, Cláusulas con **si**, p. 214 (10 min.) Video, Gramática en vivo (10 min.) Core Instruction/Gramática, Los adverbios que terminan en **-mente**, p. 216 (15 min.)	Activities 6–7, p. 215 (10 min.) Activities 8–9, p. 217 (10 min.) Foldables, p. 216 (5 min.) Audio Activities E–H, pp. 7.24–7.25 (15 min.)	Quiz 3, p. 7.39 (10 min.) Student Workbook Activity C, p. 7.9 Student Workbook Activities A–B, p. 7.10 *QuickPass* Grammar Practice
Block 5	Discuss fine art and literature	Core Instruction/Conversación, p. 218 (15 min.) Core Instruction/Lectura cultural, pp. 220–222 (20 min.) Video, Cultura en vivo (10 min.)	¿Comprendes? A–C, p. 219 (15 min.) ¿Comprendes? A–D, p. 223 (20 min.)	Quiz 4, p. 7.40 (10 min.) ¿Comprendes? E–G, p. 223 Prepárate para el examen, Practice for written proficiency, p. 229 *QuickPass* Conversation, Reading Practice
Block 6	Develop reading comprehension skills	Core Instruction/Literatura, pp. 224–225 (15 min.)	¿Comprendes? A–C, p. 225 (15 min.) Prepárate para el examen, pp. 226–227 (20 min.) Prepárate para el examen, Practice for oral proficiency, p. 228 (25 min.)	Listening Comprehension Test, pp. 7.59–7.61 (15 min.) Review for chapter test *QuickPass* Reading Practice
Block 7	Chapter 7 Tests (50 min.) Reading and Writing Test, pp. 7.49–7.56 Literature Test, pp. 7.57–7.58 Speaking Test, p. 7.62 Test for Oral Proficiency, p. 7.63 Test for Writing Proficiency, p. 7.64 Chapter Project, p. 200C (40 min.)			

Arte y literatura

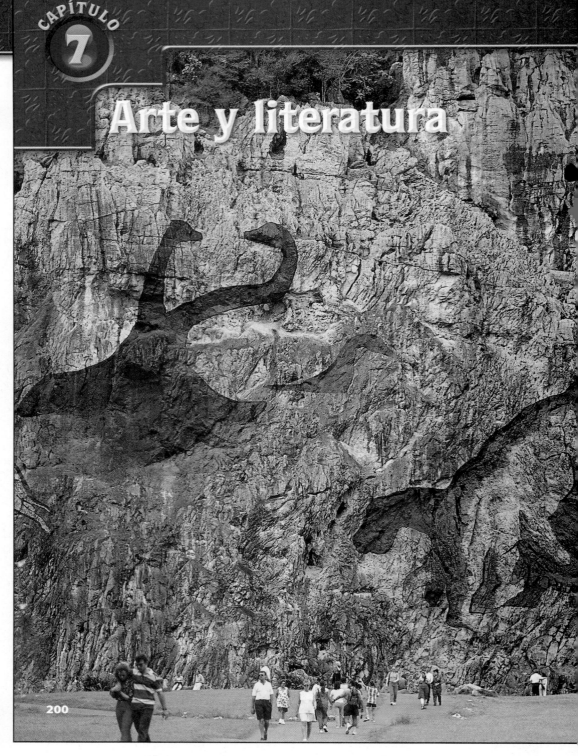

200

Preview

In this chapter, students will learn the basic vocabulary they need to discuss and read about fine arts and literature. They will discuss the painting *La liberación del peón* by the famous Mexican artist Diego Rivera. They will also learn the fine line between art, music, and poetry by reading García Lorca's poem *Canción de jinete.* In addition, students will read a poem *No sé por qué piensas tú* by the Cuban poet Nicolás Guillén. Students will use the present and pluperfect subjunctive and **si** clauses. They will also learn to form adverbs with **-mente**.

Pacing

It is important to note that once you reach **¡Bravo!** in the chapter, there is no further new material for the students to learn. The rest of the chapter recycles what has already been covered. The suggested pacing listed here leaves two to three days for review, assessment, and enrichment activities such as the chapter project.

Vocabulario 1	1–2 days
Vocabulario 2	1–2 days
Gramática	2–3 days
Conversación	1 day
Lectura cultural	1 day
Literatura	1 day

TeacherWorks^{Plus}

The **¡Así se dice!** TeacherWorks™ Plus CD-ROM is an all-in-one planner and resource center. You may wish to use several of the following features as you plan and present the Chapter 7 material: Interactive Teacher Edition, Interactive Lesson Planner with Calendar, and Point and Click Access to Teaching Resources including Hotlinks to the Internet and Correlations to the National Standards.

Aquí y Allí

Vamos a comparar La gente del mundo hispanohablante aprecia mucho la literatura y las artes plásticas. No es raro que durante una fiesta alguien se levante para recitar una poesía bonita. ¿Consideras importantes las artes? ¿Te interesan mucho?

SPOTLIGHT ON CULTURE

Cultural Comparison
Students will learn about art and literature in the Spanish-speaking world and will discuss the importance of art and literature in their own lives.

Objetivos

You will:

- discuss fine art and literature
- talk about a mural by the Mexican artist Diego Rivera
- read a sonnet by the Spaniard Federico García Lorca
- read a poem by the Cuban poet Nicolás Guillén

You will use:

- the present perfect and pluperfect subjunctive
- **si** clauses
- adverbs ending in **-mente**

◀ Mural de tema prehistórico en Pinar del Río, Cuba

QuickPass

Go to glencoe.com
For: **Online book**
Web code: **ASD7844c7**

doscientos uno **201**

Qüia **Quia Interactive Online Student Edition** found at quia.com allows students to complete activities online and submit them for computer grading for instant feedback or teacher grading with suggestions for what to review. Students can also record speaking activities, listen to chapter audio, and watch the videos that correspond with each chapter. As a teacher you are able to create rosters, set grading parameters, and post assignments for each class. After students complete activities, you can view the results and recommend remediation or review. You can also add your own customized activities for additional student practice.

Introduce the theme of the chapter by having students look at the photographs on these pages. Lead a discussion about the art seen here. Are students familiar with any of the works of art, artists, or the poet shown here? Ask if they can name some famous Hispanic artists and writers. Once you have completed the vocabulary presentation, have students return to these pages and read the information that accompanies each photograph. Later, when students are fully acquainted with the vocabulary and grammar of the chapter, you may wish to come back to these pages and ask the questions that go with each photo.

Cultural Snapshot

España *(page 202)* This art museum in Catalonia is adjacent to the Bishop's Palace. It is known for its mixed collection of ancient and modern art.

Colombia *(page 202)* Fernando Botero was born in Medellín in 1932. He is known for his figures of **personajes voluminosos** in both his paintings and statues. Some of his statues are gigantic and have been exhibited outdoors in many cities of the world. **¿De dónde es Fernando Botero? ¿Qué tipo de artista es?**

Introducción al tema
Arte y literatura

Mira las fotos para averiguar lo mucho que tiene que ofrecer el mundo hispanohablante en cuanto a las artes visuales y literarias.

▲ **España** Un manuscrito antiguo en el Museo de Arte en Girona

▲ **Colombia** El famoso escultor y pintor colombiano Fernando Botero

México La casa de Frida Kahlo en Coyoacán, un suburbio de la Ciudad de México, es hoy un museo. ▼

202

México *(page 202)* Frida Kahlo was born in Coyoacán in 1910. She died in Mexico City in 1954. She had a life of much suffering and pain after a horrendous trolley accident on her way home from school. In spite of this, she was a prolific artist with a personal, somewhat surrealistic style, much of which is quite autobiographical. She was married for many years to the famous muralist Diego Rivera. **¿Dónde está la casa de Frida Kahlo? ¿Qué es Coyoacán? ¿Qué es su casa hoy? ¿Qué hay en el patio o jardín de la casa?**

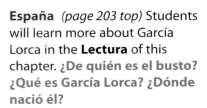

◀ **España** El busto del renombrado poeta andaluz Federico García Lorca en el jardín de su casa natal en Fuentevaqueros en la provincia de Granada.

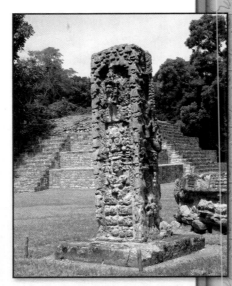

▲ **Honduras** Una estela en las magníficas ruinas mayas de Copán

▲ **España** Una joven en el museo de la Fundación Joan Miró en Barcelona

España Las fallas es una fiesta que tiene lugar en marzo en Valencia. Se hacen figuras de cartón de personajes conocidos que se exhíben por una semana por toda la ciudad. Estas figuras se llaman «ninots» en valenciano. La noche del 19 de marzo se queman y a la medianoche los fuegos iluminan la ciudad entera. El «ninot» que vemos aquí es del artista surrealista Salvador Dalí. ▼

203

España *(page 203 top)* Students will learn more about García Lorca in the **Lectura** of this chapter. **¿De quién es el busto? ¿Qué es García Lorca? ¿Dónde nació él?**

España *(page 203 middle)* Joan Miró, known for his surreal paintings and ceramics, was born in Barcelona in 1893. He died in Palma de Mallorca in 1983. Miró himself founded *la Fundació Joan Miró* in 1975. **¿Sus obras son abstractas o figurativas?**

Honduras *(page 203)* An **estela** is a vertical column (sometimes a pedestal) in stone and usually has a funereal inscription. **¿Dónde está esta estela? ¿De quiénes son las ruinas en Copán?**

España *(page 203 bottom)* This is a **ninot** of Dalí, the famous ultra-surrealist artist born in Figueres, Spain. He died in the town of his birth in 1989. Some of his most famous works are housed in a museum of his name in Saint Petersburg, Florida. **¿Qué son las fallas? ¿Cuándo tienen lugar? ¿Qué se exhíbe por toda la ciudad? ¿Qué pasa la noche del 19 de marzo?**

Quick Start

Use QS Transparency 7.1 or write the following on the board.

Escoge la palabra apropiada.

tocó vio oyó asistió compró

1. Elena ___ un concierto.
2. Él ___ en la banda.
3. El joven ___ una exposición de arte.
4. Ella ___ a la fiesta.
5. Ella ___ las entradas.

▶ TEACH

Core Instruction

Step 1 You may wish to borrow some supplies from the art department to use as props in presenting the vocabulary from this section.

Step 2 You may wish to bring in pieces of art or use the Glencoe **Museo de Arte** overhead transparencies to give students additional examples when learning terms such as **obra abstracta, obra figurativa, naturaleza muerta, estatua, cerámica.**

Differentiation

Multiple Intelligences

Have **bodily-kinesthetic** learners act out setting up an easel, putting brushes in oil paints, applying paint to canvas, molding a statue or ceramic piece, etc.

204

Vocabulario 1 presentación

El arte

La pintura

la pintora, la artista
el lienzo
el caballete
las acuarelas

La artista pone el lienzo en un caballete. Pinta con un pincel.

el óleo
el pincel
una naturaleza muerta

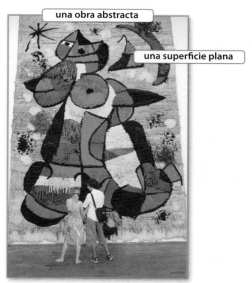

una obra abstracta
una superficie plana

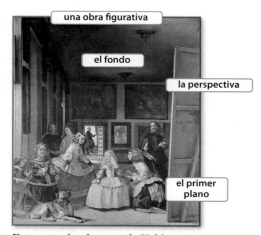

una obra figurativa
el fondo
la perspectiva
el primer plano

Es un cuadro famoso de Velázquez.
En el fondo hay una puerta abierta.
En el primer plano vemos al artista mismo.
Tiene su pincel en la mano.
Vemos también la parte trasera del caballete.

204 *doscientos cuatro*

Cultural Snapshot

(page 204 bottom left) This wall hanging, titled *The Foundation Tapestry,* was created by Joan Miro in 1979. It is located in the Miró Museum in Barcelona.

(page 204 bottom right) Velázquez painted his famous *Las meninas* in 1656. A very unique feature of the painting is that it shows Velázquez himself at the easel painting Felipe IV and Mariana de Austria who are reflected in a mirror in the background. In the foreground we see the **infantas** or "princesses" with their dog and the pages.

La escultura

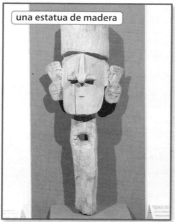

el taller

el escultor

la estatua, la escultura

el cincel

El escultor talla con un cincel.
Trabaja en un taller.

una estatua de bronce

una estatua de madera

una cerámica
de yeso

ARTE Y LITERATURA

doscientos cinco **205**

⭐ **Tips for Success** ·······

If you have one or more students who are especially interested in art, you may wish to let them help in the presentation of this material.

···

Differentiation
Multiple Intelligences

• You may wish to have **visual-spatial** learners look through the Glencoe **Museo de Arte** transparencies for a work of art that they like by a Hispanic artist. Have them research the painting and give a report to the class.

• **Auditory-musical** learners might enjoy creating a melody that relates to each type of art—abstract, realistic, and still life. They could sing or play an instrument of their choice. Invite the class to discuss how music relates to art.

❁ Comunidades

You may wish to plan a field trip to any museum within a reasonable distance that has a collection of art from Spain or Latin America. Have students write a brief report on what was their favorite work of art and why.

📷 Cultural Snapshot

(page 205 bottom left) This bronze statue of **el oso y el madroño** (strawberry tree), Madrid's official symbol, is at Puerta del Sol square.
(page 205 bottom right) This ceramic statue by Roy Lichtenstein is in Barcelona.

Total Physical Response (TPR)

(Student), **ven acá, por favor.**
Toma el lienzo.
Estira el lienzo en el caballete.
Vas a pintar algo. Toma el pincel.
Pon el pincel en los óleos.

Aplica el color en el lienzo.
Aléjate del caballete.
Estudia tu cuadro.
Aplica un poquito más pintura.

PRACTICE

Leveling EACH Activity

Easy Activities 1, 3
Average Activities 2, 4
CHallenging Activity 5

Activity 1

Audio Script

1. El pintor usa un pincel y el escultor usa un cincel.
2. Hay una diferencia entre óleos y acuarelas.
3. La escultora no puede trabajar si no tiene caballete.
4. Hay mucha acción en una naturaleza muerta.
5. El primer plano de un cuadro está al fondo.
6. Una cerámica es de bronce.

Activity 2 It is suggested you go over this activity first orally in class calling on students at random. Students can then do the activity in pairs or write it as a homework assignment.

Activity 3 You may wish to have students categorize these words before going over them in class.

GLENCOE SPANISH

Why It Works!

Note that we give students ample opportunity to practice their new vocabulary so that they will be able to remember their new words and use them with relative ease.

Cultural Snapshot

(page 206) Calella de Palafrugell is a pretty fishing village on the Costa Brava north of Barcelona.

QuickPass
Go to glencoe.com
For: **Vocabulary practice**
Web code: **ASD7844c7**

ESCUCHAR

1 Escucha y determina si la información que oyes es correcta o no. Usa una tabla como la de abajo para indicar tus respuestas.

correcta	incorrecta

HABLAR • ESCRIBIR

2 Contesta sobre el trabajo de los artistas.

1. ¿En qué pone el artista el lienzo?
2. ¿Con qué aplica el artista los óleos al lienzo?
3. ¿Con qué talla un escultor?
4. ¿Qué materias puede usar el escultor?
5. ¿Dónde trabajan un artista y un escultor?
6. ¿Es una cerámica de yeso, de madera o de bronce?

LEER • ESCRIBIR

3 Categoriza las palabras.

	pintura	escultura
1. el cincel		
2. el pincel		
3. el lienzo		
4. el bronce		
5. el caballete		
6. tallar		
7. pintar		
8. una superficie plana		
9. acuarelas y óleos		
10. cerámicas		

CULTURA

El artista está pintando una vista playera en Calella de Palafrugell en la Costa Brava de España.

Answers

1

1. correcta
2. correcta
3. incorrecta
4. incorrecta
5. incorrecta
6. incorrecta

2

1. El artista pone el lienzo en el caballete.
2. El artista aplica los óleos al lienzo con un pincel.
3. Un escultor talla con un cincel.
4. El escultor puede usar el bronce, la madera o el yeso.
5. Un artista y un escultor trabajan en un taller.
6. Una cerámica es de yeso.

3

1. escultura
2. pintura
3. pintura
4. escultura
5. pintura
6. escultura
7. pintura
8. pintura
9. pintura
10. escultura

LEER

4 ¿Sí o no? Determina si la información es correcta o no.

1. Una obra de arte figurativa presenta una interpretación literal o realista de la materia que pinta el artista.
2. La materia que pinta el artista es el tema o motivo de la obra.
3. Dos medios que emplean los pintores son la acuarela y el óleo. Hay un tercero—el acrílico.
4. Un artista nunca pinta sobre una superficie plana (llana).
5. La perspectiva es la representación de los objetos en tres dimensiones—alto, ancho, profundidad—sobre una superficie plana.
6. Una naturaleza muerta tiene mucha acción y movimiento.

Comunicación

5 Trabaja con un(a) compañero(a) y en sus propias palabras describan las diferencias entre un cuadro abstracto, un cuadro figurativo y una naturaleza muerta. Por lo general, ¿qué tipo de cuadro les atrae más?

Estudio de palabras

pintar El artista pinta.
el pintor El que pinta es pintor.
la pintura El pintor usa pintura.
pintoresco Ella pinta una escena pintoresca.

Completa el párrafo.
El ____ ____. Aplica la ____ al lienzo con un pincel. ____ una escena ____.

Conexiones

Las Bellas Artes
Frida Kahlo es una de las más renombradas artistas del siglo veinte. Su padre era de ascendencia judío-húngara y su madre una señora mexicana quien persuadió a su esposo ser fotógrafo. La madre dio a sus hijas una educación tradicional mexicana pero Frida siempre tenía cierto espíritu rebelde. Decidió estudiar arte. Un día al regresar a casa el camión (bus) que tomaba chocó con un tranvía. Frida recibió numerosas heridas y sufrió de profundos dolores durante toda su vida. Pero su sufrimiento no la prohibió producir una obra cautelosa (grande).

CULTURA
Una galería del famoso museo Guggenheim en Bilbao, España

ARTE Y LITERATURA

Vocabulario 1

Differentiation
Advanced Students
You may wish to go over Activity 4 once and then call on advanced students to correct any wrong statements.

Comunicación

Interpersonal
Activity 5 When having students do a completely open-ended activity, they are functioning as if they were communicating in a real-life situation. It is normal for learners to make a few mistakes. For this reason, you may decide not to interrupt and correct errors. This is up to your discretion.

Estudio de palabras
You may wish to use suggestions from previous chapters to present the **Estudio de palabras** section.

Conexiones

El arte
You may wish to have certain students do additional research on the extraordinary life of the renowned Frida Kahlo. Students may also bring in a book of her many **autorretratos,** which often show her in indigenous dress.

Cultural Snapshot
(page 207) This Guggenheim Museum, a modern architectural gem, is one of Europe's most renowned museums. You may wish to show students the photo of the museum in **¡Así se dice!** Level 1, on pages 262 and 263.

Answers

4
1. sí 4. no
2. sí 5. sí
3. sí 6. no

5 *Answers will vary, but students should use as many words as possible from Vocabulario 1 to talk about the differences between abstract, realistic, and still life paintings.*

Estudio de palabras

1. pintor
2. pinta
3. pintura
4. Pinta
5. pintoresca

VIDEO To practice your new words, watch **Vocabulario en vivo.**

Quick Start

Use QS Transparency 7.2 or write the following on the board.
Completa con el pretérito.
1. El autor ___ el libro. (escribir)
2. La artista ___ el cuadro. (pintar)
3. Ellos ___ la estatua de madera. (tallar)
4. Yo ___ el lienzo en el caballete. (poner)
5. Yo ___ los poemas. (leer)

▶ PRESENT

Core Instruction

Step 1 After presenting the vocabulary using Vocabulary Transparencies V7.4–V7.5 or having students read the information on each page, you may ask questions such as the following: ¿Qué es *El Quijote*? ¿Qué es una novela? ¿Quiénes son los protagonistas de una novela? ¿Qué es el argumento? ¿En qué se divide una novela?

Step 2 As you present this vocabulary you may wish to ask: ¿Cuál es más corto: un cuento o una novela? ¿Cuál tiene más capítulos, un cuento o una novela? ¿Es el cuento prosa o poesía? Y, ¿una novela? ¿Son el cuento y la novela del mismo género literario?

La literatura

La novela

Es una novela famosa, *El Quijote*.
La novela es una forma literaria narrativa.
Don Quijote y Sancho Panza son los protagonistas de la novela.
Los protagonistas son los personajes más importantes de la obra.

La novela *El Quijote* tiene lugar en La Mancha.
La acción en la novela es el argumento.
El lugar y el ambiente en que se desarrolla el argumento es La Mancha.

208

 Un libro se divide en capítulos.

GLENCOE Technology

Video in the Classroom
Vocabulario en vivo Watch and listen to Nora as she discusses literature and art.

⚘ Conexiones

La literatura
As you introduce this vocabulary, you may wish to first take a few minutes and have students discuss in English what they have learned in their English classes concerning the characteristics of a novel, short story, and poem. Then progress by teaching the Spanish terms here.

El cuento

Es un libro de cuentos de Horacio Quiroga.
Un cuento es más corto que una novela.
Un cuento, igual que una novela, es prosa.

Si yo tuviera talento, escribiría un cuento.

La poesía

el poeta

La poesía es un género literario.
El poeta escribe poesías.

Verde que te quiero verde.
Verde viento. Verdes ramas.
El barco sobre la mar
y el caballo en la montaña.
Sobre el rostro del aljibe,
se mecía la gitana.
Verde carne, pelo verde,
con ojos de fría plata.
Un carámbano de luna
la sostiene sobre el agua.

Verde que te quiero verde.
Verde viento. Verdes ramas.
¿No veis la herida que tengo
desde el pecho a la garganta?
Dejadme subir al menos
hasta las altas barandas,
¡dejadme subir!, dejadme
hasta las verdes barandas.
Barandales de la luna
por donde retumba el agua.
F. García Lorca

Cada línea de un poema es un verso.
Cada serie de versos es una estrofa.
Muchos poemas o poesías tienen rima,
pero no todos.

ARTE Y LITERATURA

doscientos nueve **209**

Teaching Options

Check students' understanding of the literature terms by having them use a triple Venn diagram as a pre-writing tool for a short paragraph that compares and contrasts the three literary genres mentioned here.

⭐Tips for Success

Hold up a page that contains a poem. Point to **un verso** and **una estrofa.** Read the words that rhyme and then say **la rima.** Ask: **¿Tienen rima todos los poemas o poesías?**

Heritage Speakers

Ask heritage speakers to read aloud any Spanish-language poems they are familiar with or to report on any Spanish-language books they particularly like.

Differentiation

Multiple Intelligences

Verbal-linguistic learners may want to read the excerpt from *El Quijote* that is in ¡Así se dice! Level 2, pages 359 to 361. They could then report back to the class about what Cervantes was trying to portray through the characters and adventures in his book.

ABOUT THE SPANISH LANGUAGE

There is sometimes confusion about the use of the words **poesía** and **poema. Poesía** is the term for the literary genre, poetry. **La poesía** is used with **poesía lírica, poesía épica,** etc. **Una poesía,** however, can also be a poem, more often a short poem. **Un poema** is a poem that is quite a bit longer such as **un poema épico.**

GLENCOE 💿 Technology

You may wish to use the editable PowerPoint® presentation on PowerTeach for additional vocabulary instruction and practice.

QuickPass
Go to glencoe.com
For: **Vocabulary practice**
Web code: **ASD7844c7**

▶ PRACTICE

Leveling EACH Activity

Easy Activities 1, 4, 5, 6
Average Activities 2, 3
CHallenging Activity 4
   Expansión, Activity 7

Activities ❶ and ❹ These activities can be gone over orally with books closed, calling on students at random to respond. Students can then also work in pairs.

Activities ❷ and ❸ You may wish to give students a few minutes to look over these activities. Then go over them in class and have students write the answers for homework.

Differentiation

Advanced Learners

To expand on Activity 5, have advanced learners tell the class in Spanish about works they have read. To ensure that other students are paying attention, you can then call on slower paced learners to answer some questions about what they heard.

GLENCOE Technology

Online Learning in the Classroom

Have students use QuickPass code ASD7844c7 for additional vocabulary practice. They can download audio files of all vocabulary to their computer and/or MP3 player. They will have access to online flashcards and eGames. Students can print and complete the **Vocabulario 1** and **2** Review Worksheet.

210

CULTURA
Un azulejo en la puerta de Bisagra en Toledo, España

ESCUCHAR • HABLAR

❶ Contesta sobre un género literario.
  1. ¿Es una novela prosa o poesía?
  2. ¿En qué se divide una novela?
  3. ¿Tiene personajes una novela?
  4. ¿Quiénes son los personajes más importantes?
  5. ¿Es una novela más larga o más corta que un cuento?
  6. ¿Tiene un cuento un argumento igual que una novela?

LEER • ESCRIBIR

❷ Identifica.
  1. los personajes más importantes de una novela
  2. la acción en una novela
  3. donde se desarrolla o sucede la acción de la novela
  4. forma literaria a la cual pertenecen la novela y el cuento

LEER • ESCRIBIR

❸ Completa con palabras apropiadas.
  La __1__ y la prosa son dos géneros literarios. Cada línea de un poema es un __2__ y cada serie de versos es una __3__. Muchas __4__ tienen __5__ pero no todas.

HABLAR

❹ Personaliza. Da respuestas personales.
  1. ¿Prefieres la poesía o la prosa?
  2. ¿Prefieres leer una novela o un cuento?
  3. ¿Lees mucho?
  4. ¿Cuál es tu novela favorita?
  5. ¿Quién es tu novelista favorito(a)?
  6. ¿Quién es tu poeta favorito(a)?
  7. ¿Prefieres mirar un cuadro o leer un libro?

EXPANSIÓN

Trabaja con un(a) compañero(a). Compartan sus respuestas y compárenlas.

LEER • ESCRIBIR

❺ Completa.

	novelas que he leído	cuentos que he leído	poesías que he leído
en inglés			
en español			

Answers

❶
1. Una novela es prosa.
2. Una novela se divide en capítulos.
3. Sí, una novela tiene personajes.
4. Los personajes más importantes son los protagonistas.

5. Una novela es más larga que un cuento.
6. Sí, un cuento tiene un argumento igual que una novela.

❷
1. los protagonistas
2. el argumento
3. el lugar, el ambiente
4. la prosa (la narrativa)

❸
1. poesía
2. verso
3. estrofa
4. poesías
5. rima

❹
1. Prefiero la poesía (la prosa).
2. Prefiero leer una novela (un cuento).
3. Sí, (No, no) leo mucho.

LEER

6 Escoge. Indica tus preferencias en cada categoría de uno a tres. Uno—te gusta mucho, tres—no te gusta.

	1	2	3
1. novelas románticas			
2. novelas históricas			
3. novelas de ficción, novelas ficticias			
4. novelas policíacas			
5. novelas de ciencia-ficción			
6. biografías			
7. autobiografías			

 VIDEO To watch a performance of a scene from *Don Quijote,* watch **Diálogo en vivo.**

Más práctica

- Workbook, pp. 7.5–7.6
- StudentWorks™ Plus

Comunicación

7 Trabajando en grupos de tres o cuatro, van a preparar una encuesta. Cada grupo informará a los otros grupos los resultados de su grupo al completar el cuestionario en la Actividad 6. Luego van a compilar los resultados y determinar el orden de las preferencias de todos los miembros de la clase.

CULTURA
La biblioteca de El Escorial, un palacio y monasterio cerca de Madrid, construido en el siglo dieciséis.

ARTE Y LITERATURA

doscientos once **211**

Answers

4. Mi novela favorita es ____.
5. Mi novelista favorito(a) es ____.
6. Mi poeta favorito(a) es ____.
7. Prefiero mirar un cuadro (leer un libro).

5 *Answers will vary.*

6 *Answers will vary.*

7 *Answers will vary.*

▶ **ASSESS**

Students are now ready to take Quiz 2 on page 7.38 of the TeacherTools booklet. If you prefer to create your own quiz, use the *ExamView® Assessment Suite.*

Vocabulario 2

Activity 6 To make this activity more challenging, you can have students give reasons for their choices.

Comunicación

Interpersonal, Presentational, Interpretive

Activity 7 is a group activity that will particularly interest **interpersonal** and **logical-mathematical** learners. It is suggested that you limit the time students spend on compiling the results.

GLENCOE Technology

Video in the Classroom

Diálogo en vivo In this episode, Alberto and Claudia attend literature class. Ask students why the teacher thinks Alberto's outfit is perfect for him to play the role of Don Quijote. If they are not familiar with the story of Don Quijote, have them research this famous Spanish novel.

Cultural Snapshot

(page 210) Explain that **azulejos** are a typical form of Spanish painted, tin-glazed, ceramic tile work. Have interested students research their origin and use over the centuries and the role they play in the architectural designs of many buildings in Spain.

(page 211) The austere monastery El Escorial was constructed under the direction of Felipe II between 1563 and 1584. The library has some 40,000 rare manuscripts and ancient books including the diary of Santa Teresa de Ávila.

211

QuickPass

Go to glencoe.com
For: **Grammar practice**
Web code: ASD7844c7

El subjuntivo
Presente perfecto, pluscuamperfecto

1. The present perfect subjunctive is formed by using the present subjunctive of the auxiliary verb **haber** and the past participle. Study the following forms.

	hablar	comer	vivir
yo	haya hablado	haya comido	haya vivido
tú	hayas hablado	hayas comido	hayas vivido
Ud., él, ella	haya hablado	haya comido	haya vivido
nosotros(as)	hayamos hablado	hayamos comido	hayamos vivido
vosotros(as)	hayáis hablado	hayáis comido	hayáis vivido
Uds., ellos, ellas	hayan hablado	hayan comido	hayan vivido

¿Te acuerdas?

You reviewed the irregular past participles in the previous chapter on page 199.

2. The present perfect subjunctive is used when the action in a dependent clause that takes the subjunctive occurred before the action in the main clause.

Has venido.	Me alegro de que hayas venido.
Lo han visto.	Dudo que lo hayan visto.
Lo hemos hecho.	Es imposible que lo hayamos hecho.

3. The pluperfect subjunctive is formed with the imperfect subjunctive of the verb **haber** and the past participle.

	hablar	comer	vivir
yo	hubiera hablado	hubiera comido	hubiera vivido
tú	hubieras hablado	hubieras comido	hubieras vivido
Ud., él, ella	hubiera hablado	hubiera comido	hubiera vivido
nosotros(as)	hubiéramos hablado	hubiéramos comido	hubiéramos vivido
vosotros(as)	hubierais hablado	hubierais comido	hubierais vivido
Uds., ellos, ellas	hubieran hablado	hubieran comido	hubieran vivido

4. The pluperfect subjunctive is used after a verb in the past tense or conditional when the action of the verb in the subjunctive occurred prior to the action in the main clause.

Estaba convencido de que ellos lo habían hecho.
Pero me sorprendió que ellos lo hubieran hecho.
Me dijeron que él lo había dicho.
Nunca habría (yo) creído que él lo hubiera dicho.

212 *doscientos doce*

Resources

- Audio Activities TE, pages 7.21–7.22
- Audio CD 7, Tracks 8–10
- Workbook, pages 7.7–7.8
- Quiz 3, page 7.39
- *ExamView® Assessment Suite*

Quick Start

Use QS Transparency 7.3 or write the following on the board.
Escribe a lo menos cinco cosas que has hecho este año.

▶ TEACH
Core Instruction

Step 1 Read to students or have students read the explanations in Items 1 and 2 about the present perfect subjunctive. Then go over the conjugations and sample sentences. See if students can guess the equivalent in English (something *has happened*). Explain that the present perfect subjunctive is used to talk about action that has taken place before the action in the main clause. Point out that the present perfect subjunctive, like the present subjunctive, follows impersonal expressions and expressions of emotion, desire, opinion, and doubt.

Step 2 Read to students or have students read the explanations in Items 3 and 4 about the pluperfect, or past perfect, subjunctive and the verb forms. See if students can guess the equivalent in English (something *had happened*). It is action that had taken place before another past action.

212

GLENCOE 🖰 Technology

Online Learning in the Classroom
Have students use QuickPass code ASD7844c7 for additional grammar practice. They can review each grammar point with an eGame. They can also review all grammar points by doing the self-check quiz, which integrates the chapter vocabulary with the new grammar.

GLENCOE 🖰 Technology

You may wish to use the editable PowerPoint® presentation on PowerTeach for additional grammar instruction and practice.

Práctica

Más práctica

Workbook, pp. 7.7–7.8
StudentWorks™ Plus

ESCUCHAR • HABLAR

1 Contesta.

1. ¿No crees que ellos hayan llegado?
2. ¿Es posible que hayan salido tarde?
3. Es imposible que se hayan perdido, ¿no?
4. Es raro que Roberto no te haya llamado, ¿no?
5. ¿Temes que les haya pasado algo?
6. ¿Es posible que ellos te hayan llamado y que no haya sonado tu móvil?

> No puedo creer que no hayan llegado todavía. Es posible que me hayan enviado un mensaje.

LEER • ESCRIBIR

2 Completa la siguiente tarjeta postal con el presente perfecto del subjuntivo.

Querida Susana,

¿Es posible que ya __1__ (terminar) tus vacaciones? No creo que los quince días __2__ (pasar) tan rápido. Espero que tú lo __3__ (pasar) bien en México y que __4__ (divertirse). Me alegro de que __5__ (tener) la oportunidad de visitar la casa de Diego Rivera y Frida Kahlo en Coyoacán. Y me alegro de que __6__ (poder) visitar el país de tus abuelos.

LEER • ESCRIBIR

3 Completa con el pluscuamperfecto del subjuntivo.

1. Francamente yo dudaba que él lo _____. (hacer)
2. Y él dudaba que yo lo _____. (hacer)
3. ¿Cómo era posible que nadie le _____ nada? (decir)
4. Me sorprendió que ustedes no _____ el trabajo. (terminar)
5. Estaba contento que tú _____ la exposición. (ver)

CULTURA

Entrada principal al museo Frida Kahlo en Coyoacán, México. Es en esta casa que nació la famosa artista.

ARTE Y LITERATURA

doscientos trece **213**

Answers

1

1. No, no creo que ellos hayan llegado.
2. Sí, es posible que hayan salido tarde.
3. Sí, es imposible que se hayan perdido.
4. Sí, es raro que Roberto no me haya llamado.
5. Sí, (No, no) temo que les haya pasado algo.
6. Sí, (No, no) es posible que ellos hayan llamado y que no haya sonado mi móvil.

2

1. hayan terminado
2. hayan pasado
3. hayas pasado
4. te hayas divertido
5. hayas tenido
6. hayas podido

3

1. hubiera hecho
2. hubiera hecho
3. hubiera dicho
4. hubieran terminado
5. hubieras visto

Resources

- Audio Activities TE, pages 7.23–7.24
 Audio CD 7, Tracks 11–12
- Workbook, page 7.9
- Quiz 4, page 7.40
- ExamView® Assessment Suite

Quick Start

Use QS Transparency 7.4 or write the following on the board.
Pon los siguientes verbos en el futuro y el condicional.

1. yo / ir
2. ellos / decirlo
3. tú / devolverlo
4. nosotros / salir
5. él / saberlo

▶ **TEACH**
Core Instruction

Step 1 Have students read the explanations in Items 1 and 2.

Step 2 Have students repeat the model sentences.

Step 3 You may wish to write the sequence of tenses on the board and have students give more examples.

**Tips for Success** ·······

Have students read the photo caption, as it reinforces the new grammar point.

···

 Cultural Snapshot

(page 214) La Boca was once an area of Buenos Aires inhabited by recent immigrants mostly from Italy. Today most of the original inhabitants have moved on, but La Boca remains a picturesque port area popular with artists and tourists.

214

Cláusulas con si

1. Si *(If)* clauses are used to express a contrary-to-fact condition. For these clauses, there is a very definite sequence of tenses. Study the following examples.

> **Si tengo bastante dinero, haré el viaje.**
> *If I have enough money, I will take the trip.*
>
> **Si tuviera bastante dinero, haría el viaje.**
> *If I had enough money, I would take the trip.*
>
> **Si yo hubiera tenido bastante dinero, yo habría hecho el viaje.**
> *If I had had enough money, I would have taken the trip.*

2. Note that the sequence of tenses for **si** clauses is the following:

MAIN CLAUSE	SI CLAUSE
future	present indicative
conditional	imperfect subjunctive
conditional perfect	pluperfect subjunctive

GeoVistas

To learn more about Argentina, take a tour on pages SH52–SH53.

CULTURA
Si yo pudiera ir a Buenos Aires, me encantaría visitar el barrio artístico de La Boca.

214 *doscientos catorce*   CAPÍTULO 7

 GeoVistas

Have students turn to pages SH52–SH53 and find Argentina on the map. Ask them to locate Buenos Aires and name two things they learn about the city from the map. Then have them read the **Gente** paragraph on page SH53. Ask whether the immigration history of Argentina and the United States is similar and, if so, how.

Práctica

HABLAR

4 Personaliza. Da respuestas personales.
1. Si tienes el dinero, ¿comprarás el cuadro?
2. Si tuvieras el dinero, ¿comprarías el cuadro?
3. Si hubieras tenido el dinero, ¿habrías comprado el cuadro?
4. Si vas a Puerto Rico, ¿visitarás el Museo de Arte en San Juan?
5. Si fueras a Puerto Rico, ¿visitarías el Museo de Arte en San Juan?
6. Si hubieras ido a Puerto Rico, ¿habrías visitado el Museo de Arte en San Juan?

LEER • ESCRIBIR

5 Completa con las formas apropiadas del verbo.
1. **tener**
   Ellos irán si _____ el tiempo.
   Yo también iría si _____ el tiempo.
   Yo sé que tú habrías ido si _____ el tiempo.
2. **dar**
   Yo lo compraré si alguien me _____ el dinero.
   Y él también lo compraría si alguien le _____ el dinero.
   ¿Uds. lo habrían comprado si alguien les _____ el dinero?
3. **ir**
   Yo iré a Córdoba si _____ a España.
   Él iría a Córdoba si _____ a España.
   Yo sé que nosotros habríamos ido a Córdoba si _____ a España.

HABLAR • ESCRIBIR

6 Personaliza. Da respuestas personales.
1. Si alguien te diera mil dólares, ¿qué comprarías?
2. Si tú pudieras hacer un viaje, ¿adónde irías?
3. Si tú estudias mucho, ¿qué notas recibirás?
4. Si tú hubieras estado en España, ¿qué ciudades habrías visitado?

Comunicación

7 Trabaja con un(a) compañero(a). Dile todo lo que harías si tuvieras más tiempo. Luego él o ella dirá lo que él o ella haría.

ARTE Y LITERATURA

doscientos quince **215**

CULTURA
Museo de Arte en San Juan, Puerto Rico

InfoGap For more practice with **si** clauses, do Activity 7 on page SR8 at the end of this book.

VIDEO Want help with the present perfect and pluperfect subjunctive? Watch **Gramática en vivo.**

Más práctica
Workbook, p. 7.9
StudentWorks™ Plus

Gramática

Answers

4
1. Sí (No), si tengo el dinero, (no) compraré el cuadro.
2. Sí (No), si tuviera el dinero, (no) compraría el cuadro.
3. Sí (No), si hubiera tenido el dinero, (no) habría comprado el cuadro.
4. Sí (No), si voy a Puerto Rico, (no) visitaré el Museo de Arte en San Juan.
5. Sí (No), si fuera a Puerto Rico, (no) visitaría el Museo de Arte en San Juan.
6. Sí (No), si hubiera ido a Puerto Rico, (no) habría visitado el Museo de Arte en San Juan.

5
1. tienen, tuviera, hubieras tenido
2. da, diera, hubiera dado
3. voy, fuera, hubiéramos ido

6 Answers will vary.

7 Answers will vary.

PRACTICE

Leveling EACH Activity

Easy Activity 4
Average Activities 5, 6
CHallenging Activity 7

Teaching Options

Activity 4
a. You can ask these questions with books closed and call on students at random to respond.
b. You can have students answer with **no** and tell what they would do.

Activity 5 Have students prepare this activity before going over it in class.

Activity 6 Have students give as many different answers as they can.

Differentiation

Advanced Learners
Have students who have a grasp of the grammar and who are creative think up sentences beginning with **si** that describe the many things they would like to have happen or wish had happened. They could also make up questions using **si** clauses and call on others to answer.

GLENCOE Technology

Video in the Classroom
Gramática en vivo: *The present perfect and pluperfect subjunctive* Enliven learning with the animated world of Professor Cruz!
Gramática en vivo is a fun and effective tool for additional instruction and/or review.

215

Resources

- Audio Activities TE, pages 7.24–7.25
- 🎧 Audio CD 7, Tracks 13–15
- Workbook, page 7.10
- ⊙ ExamView® Assessment Suite

▶ TEACH

Core Instruction

This grammar point is quite easy so students should have little or no difficulty understanding and using it.

¡Ojo! Learners frequently forget to drop the **-mente** from any adverbs that precede the last one. This rule always applies to written Spanish but does not necessarily apply to spontaneous speech.

📷 Cultural Snapshot

(page 216) This section of Córdoba was the Jewish quarter of the city before the Inquisition. It is still called **la judería.**

FOLDABLES®
Study Organizer

CATEGORY BOOK

See page SH21 for help with making this foldable. Use this study organizer to practice forming adverbs with a partner. On the front of each tab, write an adjective. Then pass the foldable to your partner who will, on the back of each strip, rewrite the adjective in the form of an adverb. When you're finished, switch roles.

Los adverbios que terminan en -mente

1. An adverb modifies a verb, an adjective, or another adverb. In Spanish, many adverbs end in **-mente**. To form an adverb from an adjective that ends in **-e** or a consonant, you simply add **-mente** to the adjective. Study the following.

ADJECTIVE	+ -mente	ADVERB
enorme		enormemente
reciente		recientemente
principal		principalmente
general		generalmente

2. To form an adverb from an adjective that ends in **-o**, add **-mente** to the feminine **-a** form of the adjective.

FEMININE ADJECTIVE	+ -mente	ADVERB
sincera		sinceramente
cariñosa		cariñosamente

3. When more than one adverb ending in **-mente** modifies a verb, only the last adverb carries the **-mente** ending. Study the following.

> Él habló lenta y claramente.
> Yo se lo digo honesta y sinceramente.

CULTURA

Córdoba es realmente una ciudad pintoresca.

Práctica

ESCUCHAR • HABLAR • ESCRIBIR

8 Forma adverbios.

1. triste
2. puntual
3. elegante
4. rápido
5. respetuoso

6. humilde
7. loco
8. discreto
9. rico
10. posible

ESCUCHAR • HABLAR • ESCRIBIR

9 Contesta según el modelo.

MODELO ¿Cómo habla Ramón? (lento / claro) →
Ramón habla lenta y claramente.

1. ¿Cómo responde Luisa? (sincero / honesto)
2. ¿Cómo enseña la profesora? (claro / cuidadoso)
3. ¿Cómo se viste ella? (sencillo / elegante)
4. ¿Cómo conduce Pepe? (rápido / peligroso)
5. ¿Cómo se porta el niño? (cortés / respetuoso)

Refrán

Can you guess what the following proverb means?

Allá va Sancho con su rocín.

CULTURA
El niño mira atentamente al payaso que trabaja energéticamente en una plaza de Granada.

¡Bravo!

You have now learned all the new vocabulary and grammar in this chapter. Continue to use and practice all that you know while learning more cultural information. ¡Vamos!

ARTE Y LITERATURA

doscientos diecisiete **217**

▶ PRACTICE

Leveling EACH Activity

Easy Activity 8
Average Activity 9

Activities 8 and 9 Students can go over these activities orally in class and then write them for homework.

★Tips for Success ·······

Have students read the photo caption and identify the adverbs. As an expansion, have them give other adverbs that could describe the actions in the photograph.

Refrán

Have students recite the proverb aloud. Although there is not an exact equivalent in English, encourage students to think of expressions related to the same theme, such as "like two peas in a pod." Ask in what context they hear this expression.

¡Bravo! The remaining pages of the chapter recycle information in a variety of ways, allowing students to build upon their newly acquired language skills as well as to keep track of their own progress. This format also ensures that students are not surprised by vocabulary or grammar that has not yet been introduced or studied.

Answers

8

1. tristemente
2. puntualmente
3. elegantemente
4. rápidamente
5. respetuosamente
6. humildemente
7. locamente
8. discretamente
9. ricamente
10. posiblemente

9

1. Luisa responde sincera y honestamente.
2. La profesora enseña clara y cuidadosamente.
3. Ella se viste sencilla y elegantemente.
4. Pepe conduce rápida y peligrosamente.
5. El niño se porta cortés y respetuosamente.

217

Resources

- Audio Activities TE, page 7.26
- Audio CD 7, Tracks 16–17

▶ TEACH

Core Instruction

Step 1 Have students close their books and listen to the conversation on Audio CD 7.

Step 2 As soon as students have listened to the conversation, ask them some questions about what they heard (without having read the conversation). ¿Le gustaría a Elena ser artista? ¿Cuál es el problema que tiene? ¿Tiene Carlos mucho talento? ¿Aprecie él el arte? etc.

Step 3 Call on pairs to read the conversation aloud. Encourage them to speak with as much expression as possible and to use facial expressions and gestures to help convey the meaning. See if students are then better able to answer the questions from Step 2.

Step 4 Go over the ¿Comprendes? activities.

Differentiation

Multiple Intelligences

Have **bodily-kinesthetic** learners role play a conversation with a friend in which they discuss what famous writer or artist they would like to be and why. Ask for pairs to volunteer to present their role plays to the class.

¡Ojalá que tuviera el talento!

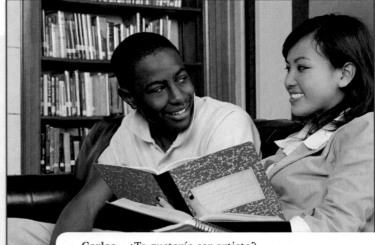

Carlos	¿Te gustaría ser artista?
Elena	Me gustaría si tuviera algún talento, pero no lo tengo.
Carlos	Ni yo tampoco. Y es una pena porque aprecio mucho el arte.
Elena	Yo también. Pero creo que tú eres aún más aficionado que yo.
Carlos	Creo que he heredado mi afición a las artes de mi madre. Si ella no se hubiera dedicado la vida a una carrera de medicina, le habría gustado ser escritora.
Elena	¿A ella le gusta leer?
Carlos	Mucho. No puedes imaginar cuántas novelas lee en un mes. Con tantos pacientes no sé cómo tiene el tiempo.
Elena	Hablando de novelas me hace pensar en algo que me pasó en una librería en Guatemala.
Carlos	Dime.
Elena	Es un cuento real. Una joven le pidió al empleado que le recomendara una novela.
Carlos	¿Y?
Elena	Él le preguntó qué tipo de novela quería y ella respondió «buena literatura». El empleado no quería ser descortés pero empezó a reír y dijo que lo que es buena literatura para uno no lo es para otro.
Carlos	El empleado tenía razón. No importa que sea una novela, una poesía o un cuadro, yo sé si me gusta o no. Y es posible que lo que a mí me gusta no te guste a ti. ¡Así es!

GLENCOE Technology

Online Learning in the Classroom

Have students use QuickPass code ASD7844c7 for additional conversation practice. Students can download audio files for the conversation to their computer and/or MP3 player and complete a self-check quiz.

¿Comprendes?

A Identifica quién según la información en la conversación.

	Carlos	Elena
1. Le gustaría ser artista pero no puede porque no tiene talento artístico.		
2. Aprecia mucho el arte, aún más que el/la otro(a).		
3. Su madre habría querido ser escritora si no se hubiera dedicado a la medicina.		
4. Había estado en una librería en Guatemala.		

B Contesta según la información en la conversación.
1. ¿Qué pidió una joven en una librería de Guatemala?
2. ¿Qué tipo de novela quería?
3. ¿Por qué se rió el empleado?
4. ¿Estás de acuerdo con lo que dijo él?

C Personalizando ¿Cuál es tu reacción al episodio en la librería en Guatemala?

CULTURA

La librería en Antigua, Guatemala, donde tuvo lugar la conversación sobre «la buena literatura»

ARTE Y LITERATURA

doscientos diecinueve **219**

Conversación

▶ PRACTICE

¿Comprendes?

A Have students try to identify the speaker without referring back to the conversation.
B You may wish to do this as a factual recall activity.
C This activity can also be done as a group discussion.

Differentiation

Advanced Learners

Before doing Activity C, you may wish to call on an advanced learner to give an account of the episode in the bookstore in his or her own words.

Slower Paced Learners

Ask slower paced learners *yes/no* questions about the summary they just heard.

Pre-AP Listening to this conversation on audio CD will help students develop the skills that they need to be successful on the listening portion of the AP exam.

Answers

A
1. Elena
2. Carlos
3. Carlos
4. Elena

B
1. Una joven en una librería de Guatemala pidió que el empleado le recomendara una novela.
2. Quería «buena literatura».
3. El empleado se rió porque lo que es buena literatura para uno no lo es para otro.
4. Sí, (No, no) estoy de acuerdo con lo que dijo él.

C *Answers will vary.*

LECTURA
CULTURAL

Resources

- Audio Activities TE, pages 7.27–7.30
- Audio CD 7, Tracks 18–21

▶ TEACH
Core Instruction

Step 1 Have the class discuss the **Antes de leer** questions.

Step 2 As soon as students have read the first half of the first paragraph, you may have the class discuss **¿Comprendes?** Activity A.

Step 3 Ask: **¿Cuáles son unas razones de la Revolución mexicana?**

Step 4 Have students respond to the Reading Checks either silently or orally.

Step 5 You may wish to ask the following additional comprehension questions. **¿A quiénes vemos en el primer plano del fresco? ¿Qué están cortando? ¿Quién está atado con las cuerdas? ¿Qué se ve a lo lejos? ¿Qué está ardiendo? ¿Qué nos indica la hacienda en llamas? ¿Quién ha recibido su castigo?**

Teaching ● Options

Because of the nature of this reading, you may wish to have all students read the entire selection. If not, you may want to divide it and have one group focus on Diego Rivera and his art and the other on Federico García Lorca and his poetry.

Antes de leer

¿Cómo afectan tu vida el arte y la literatura? ¿Te interesan? ¿Te importan? ¿Cómo y por qué?

✓ Reading Check

¿Cómo era la vida mexicana durante la época en que vivía Diego Rivera?

Las artes 🎧♻

El arte y la literatura están estrechamente relacionadas con la vida porque es la vida misma o la percepción de la vida la que inspira la obra de muchos artistas y escritores. Vamos a tomar como ejemplo la obra del famoso muralista mexicano Diego Rivera. Para comprender su obra hay que saber algo sobre la realidad de la vida mexicana durante la época en que vivía. A principios del siglo veinte reinaban en México la inquietud e inestabilidad políticas. Los peones pobres trataban de mejorar su vida. Querían liberarse de los terratenientes corruptos que los trataban muy mal. En 1911 cayó la dictadura de Porfirio Díaz y estalló (empezó) la Revolución mexicana que duró hasta 1921. Fue durante esta época que vivió Diego Rivera, y lo que vio le inspiró a representar en arte la valiente lucha del peón mexicano.

CULTURA
El famoso pintor y muralista Diego Rivera (1886–1957)

220 *doscientos veinte*

CAPÍTULO 7

⭐ Tips for Success ·········

Have students discuss the photograph. They can use the vocabulary from Vocabulario 1 of this chapter.

La liberación del peón *La liberación del peón* es un fresco sobre yeso. En el primer plano vemos a un grupo de tristes soldados revolucionarios. Están cortando las cuerdas¹ con que está atado² un peón muerto. Tienen una manta para cubrirle el cuerpo desnudo y azotado³. A lo lejos en el fondo se ven las llamas⁴ de una hacienda que está ardiendo⁵. La hacienda en llamas nos indica que el dueño (propietario) de la hacienda que tenía la responsabilidad de la muerte del pobre peón ya ha recibido su castigo⁶. Y ahora, silenciosa y tristemente, los soldados hacen lo que pueden por su compañero caído.

¹cuerdas *ropes*
²atado *tied*
³azotado *beaten*

⁴llamas *flames*
⁵ardiendo *burning*
⁶castigo *punishment*

VIDEO To learn about artisans from Venezuela, watch **Cultura en vivo.**

✓ **Reading Check**
¿A quién cuidan los soldados?
¿Por qué están muy tristes?

CULTURA
La liberación del peón de Diego Rivera

ARTE Y LITERATURA

doscientos veintiuno **221**

Differentiation

Multiple Intelligences

Many **visual-spatial** students learn better when they can visualize what they are reading about. As you go over this paragraph about *La liberación del peón*, point to or have students point to the exact part of the painting that is being described in each sentence.

🍀 *Conexiones*

La historia

Have students research what was happening in Mexico during Diego Rivera's lifetime.

Show some examples of his works and have a class discussion about which part of the culture and history of Mexico and its people he was highlighting. How do his paintings reveal his viewpoints?

▶ TEACH
Core Instruction

Step 1 Have students give the adjectives that describe each of the following: **Córdoba, la jaca, la luna, el camino.**

Step 2 You may want to intersperse **¿Comprendes?** Activities D, E, and F as you are presenting this page.

Teaching Options

You can do any or all of the activities outlined below.

1. Have students listen to the recording of the poem. Tell them to close their eyes as they listen.
2. Have students listen to the recording again as they read along.
3. Call on a student with good pronunciation to read the poem aloud.

GLENCOE Technology

Online Learning in the Classroom

You may wish to have students use QuickPass code ASD7844c7 to develop their reading comprehension and writing skills. Students will be able to take a self-check quiz, which includes an essay.

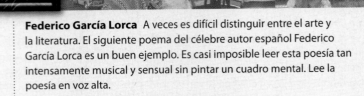

Federico García Lorca A veces es difícil distinguir entre el arte y la literatura. El siguiente poema del célebre autor español Federico García Lorca es un buen ejemplo. Es casi imposible leer esta poesía tan intensamente musical y sensual sin pintar un cuadro mental. Lee la poesía en voz alta.

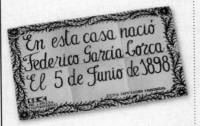

> ### Canción de jinete[7]
>
> Córdoba
> Lejana y sola.
>
> Jaca[8] negra, luna grande,
> y aceitunas en mi alforja[9].
> Aunque sepa los caminos
> yo nunca llegaré a Córdoba.
>
> Por el llano[10], por el viento,
> jaca negra, luna roja.
> La muerte me está mirando
> desde las torres de Córdoba.
>
> ¡Ay qué camino tan largo!
> ¡Ay mi jaca valerosa!
> ¡Ay que la muerte me espera,
> antes de llegar a Córdoba!
>
> Córdoba.
> Lejana y sola.

CULTURA

Murales dedicados a las obras de Federico García Lorca en su pueblo natal de Fuentevaqueros en Granada

Ahora que has leído la poesía piensa en el cuadro mental que viste. ¿Qué animal viste? ¿Qué había en la alforja? ¿Qué había en el cielo? ¿Era grande o no? ¿Iluminaba el camino? ¿Qué viste en el fondo de tu cuadro mental?

García Lorca (1898–1936) vivía en Andalucía cuando estalló la horrible Guerra Civil española en 1936. El joven escritor, artista y músico murió en este mismo año cuando tenía solo treinta y ocho años. Todavía queda vaga y misteriosa la causa de su muerte pero se cree que fue la Guardia Civil quien lo mató. ¿Te parece que el autor presumía su trágico fin al escribir esta poesía?

[7]jinete *(horse) rider*
[8]Jaca *pony*
[9]alforja *saddle bag*
[10]llano *plain*

Pre-AP This cultural reading will develop the skills that students need to be successful on the reading and writing sections of the AP exam. Listening to this reading will also help prepare them for the auditory component.

¿Comprendes?

Más práctica
Workbook, pp. 7.11–7.12
StudentWorks™ Plus

A Explicando y analizando Explica en tus propias palabras el significado de la siguiente frase: «El arte y la literatura están estrechamente relacionadas con la vida porque es la vida misma o la percepción de la vida la que inspira la obra de muchos artistas y escritores».

B Recordando hechos Contesta.
1. ¿Cómo fue la situación política en México durante la vida de Diego Rivera?
2. ¿Quiénes querían mejorar su vida?
3. ¿De quiénes querían liberarse?
4. ¿Cuándo estalló la Revolución mexicana?

C Describiendo Describe lo que ves en *La liberación del peón*. ¿Qué sentimientos surgen en ti al mirar el cuadro?

D Visualizando Lee de nuevo *Canción de jinete* y completa lo siguiente sobre tu cuadro mental.
1. la persona en tu cuadro
2. el animal
3. el cielo
4. los ruidos
5. el camino
6. el paisaje

E Personalizando Explica como te sientes al leer esta poesía. ¿Cuál es el elemento de misterio?

F Interpretando Contesta.
1. ¿Qué emoción evoca en ti el pensar en una jaca negra galopeando por un llano ventoso durante una noche oscura bajo una luna llena?
2. Para ti, ¿qué simboliza la luna llena?
3. ¿Quién habla en la poesía? ¿Adónde va? ¿Dónde está? ¿Cómo es?
4. ¿Cuándo llegará a Córdoba? ¿Por qué?
5. Llama a su jaca «valerosa». ¿Quién es realmente el valiente? ¿Por qué?

G Intrepretando ¿Cuál es tu opinión? ¿Presumía García Lorca su trágico fin al escribir esta poesía unos nueve años antes de su muerte?

CULTURA
La torre de la Mezquita de Córdoba

ARTE Y LITERATURA

doscientos veintitrés **223**

▶ PRACTICE

¿Comprendes?

A You may wish to do this as an entire class discussion.
B Call on students to respond without looking up the answers.
C This can be done as a group activity.
D You may wish to have the entire class listen to responses. Call on other students if they wish to add information.
E This activity can be done as an entire class discussion. Students may have different ideas.

Writing Development
You may also want to have students write a short composition to answer Activity E.

Differentiation
Slower Paced Learners
You may want to do Activity F with the entire class. This will enable slower paced students to hear interpretations they may not have been able to think of on their own.

G You may wish to have students work in small groups.

Answers

A *Answers will vary but may include:* Muchos artistas y escritores se inspiran de la vida para crear sus obras.

B
1. Durante la vida de Diego Rivera reinaban en México la inquietud e inestabilidad políticas.
2. Los peones querían mejorar su vida.
3. Querían liberarse de los terratenientes corruptos que los trataban muy mal.
4. La Revolución mexicana estalló en 1911.

C *Answers will vary.*

D
1. un jinete
2. una jaca negra
3. una luna grande y roja
4. el viento
5. muy largo
6. el llano

E *Answers will vary.*

F
1. *Answers will vary.*
2. *Answers will vary.*
3. El jinete habla. Va a Córdoba. Está en el camino. *Answers will vary.*
4. Nunca llegará a Córdoba porque la muerte lo espera.
5. El jinete es realmente el valiente. *Answers will vary.*

G *Answers will vary.*

Resources

- Audio Activities TE, page 7.31
- Audio CD 7, Track 22
- Literature Test, page 7.57
- ExamView® Assessment Suite

Preview

Starting in Chapter 3, each chapter of **¡Así se dice!** Level 3 has a literary section. Most literary selections are by well-known Latin American or Spanish writers.

It is up to the discretion of the teacher if you wish to do all or any of these literary works. The difficulty level of each selection is also indicated from 1 to 4. 1 is difficult; 4 is quite easy.

Difficulty Level
4

Introducción

You may wish to have students read the **Introducción** silently and then ask them questions about it such as: **¿Dónde nació Nicolás Guillén? ¿Qué tienen muchas poesías de Guillén? ¿De qué otros asuntos habla Guillén en su poesía?**

 Conexiones

La historia

Have students read **Fondo histórico.** You may wish to ask the following comprehension questions: **¿Quién era Fulgencio Batista? ¿Por qué temía el pueblo el ejército cubano?** Ask whether students have studied this time period in World History class. Have them brainstorm what they already know about Cuba. Ask them what dictator took over after Batista. Then have them research Cuba during Guillén's life to gain an understanding of how Cuba came to be the way it is today.

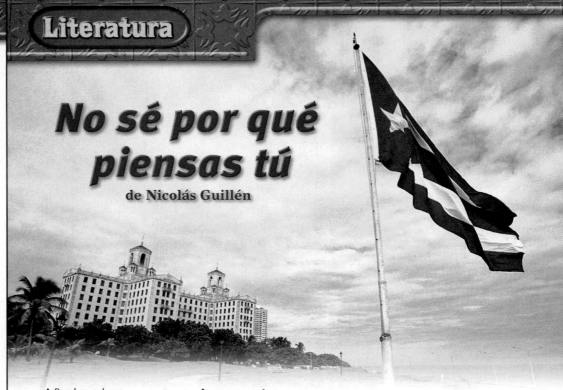

No sé por qué piensas tú

de Nicolás Guillén

▲ Bandera cubana delante del Hotel Nacional en la Habana

▲ Nicolás Guillén

INTRODUCCIÓN

Nicolás Guillén (1902–1989) nació en Camagüey, Cuba, de sangre española y africana. Es el más conocido de los poetas cubanos, sobre todo por su poesía negroide. Muchas poesías de Guillén tienen el ritmo sensual y musical africano de uno de los bailes típicos de Cuba, el son, tal como:

> **¡Mayombe—bombe—mayombé!**
> **¡Mayombe—bombe—mayombé!**
> **¡Mayombe—bombe—mayombé!**

En otras poesías Guillén habla de sus preocupaciones sociales, raciales y humanas—sobre todo la explotación socioeconómica de los de ascendencia africana.

FONDO HISTÓRICO

No te será difícil leer esta poesía tierna y emotiva porque el autor emplea un lenguaje sencillo. Pero antes de leer la poesía tienes que saber algo sobre el fondo histórico.

El jefe del gobierno cubano, Fulgencio Batista, era un dictador cruel. La población civil, o sea el pueblo, odiaba[1] y temía al ejército porque era el ejército que tenía el deber de imponer la política opresiva e injusta del dictador.

[1]odiaba *hated*

 **GeoVistas**

Have students turn to pages SH46–SH47 and find the map of Cuba. Ask them to locate La Habana. What symbol tells them that this is the capital? Then have them locate Camagüey, the town where Nicolás Guillén was born.

No sé por qué piensas tú

No sé por qué piensas tú
soldado, que te odio yo,
si somos la misma cosa
yo,
5   tú

Tú eres pobre, lo soy yo:
soy de abajo, lo eres tú;
¿de dónde has sacado tú,
soldado, que te odio yo?

10   Me duele que a veces tú
te olvides de quién soy yo;
caramba, si yo soy tú,
lo mismo que tú eres yo.

Pero no por eso yo
15   he de[1] malquererte, tú;
si somos la misma cosa,
yo,
tú,
no sé por qué piensas tú
20   soldado, que te odio yo.

Ya nos veremos yo y tú
juntos en la misma calle,
hombro con hombro, tú y yo,
sin odios ni yo ni tú
25   pero sabiendo tú y yo,
a donde vamos yo y tú...
¡No sé por qué piensas tú,
soldado, que te odio yo!

[1]he de *I am supposed to*

CULTURA

Una vista de La Habana, Cuba

GeoVistas

To learn more about Cuba,
take a tour on pages
SH46–SH47.

¿Comprendes?

A **Interpretando** En tu opinión ¿qué quiere decir el autor cuando dice…
1. «somos la misma cosa»?
2. «soy de abajo, lo eres tú»?

B **Interpretando** A veces el poeta dice «yo y tú» y otras veces dice «tú y yo». ¿Es posible que tenga una razón para cambiar la posición de los pronombres? ¿Cuál será?

C **Analizando** Contesta.
1. ¿Qué dice el hablante para tratar de convencer al soldado que no lo odia?
2. Según lo que has aprendido sobre el fondo histórico o el ambiente político en que tiene lugar la poesía, ¿por qué sería posible que la persona quien habla lo odiara?

ARTE Y LITERATURA

doscientos veinticinco **225**

Literatura

▶ TEACH
Core Instruction

Step 1 You may wish to have the class listen to the recording of this poem on Audio CD 7. You may have students close their books as they listen and then listen a second time as they follow along in their books.

Step 2 Have students read the **Estrategia**. Discuss why it is often helpful to read a poem aloud.

Step 3 Call on a student to read one **estrofa** aloud. Ask questions about each **estrofa** before going on to the next one.

Step 4 Have students establish ¿Quién es el *tú* en el verso «¡No sé por qué piensas tú, soldado, que te odio yo!»? ¿Quién es el *yo*?

Step 5 Ask questions such as: ¿Qué tienen los dos en común? ¿Qué se espera para el futuro?

Step 6 Go over the ¿Comprendes? activities.

▶ PRACTICE
¿Comprendes?

A Have students give as many interpretations as they can.

B You may have to assist some groups by asking: ¿Es posible que tenga algo que ver con la igualdad?

✓ Writing Development
For Activity C, you may wish to have students write their answers as a composition.

Estrategia

Leyendo en voz alta Lee el poema en voz alta a un(a) compañero(a). El oírlo te ayudará a identificarte mejor con los sentimientos y el estado de ánimo de la persona que habla.

225

Prepárate para el examen
Self-check for achievement

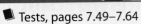

Resources

■ Tests, pages 7.49–7.64
■ Performance Assessment, Task 7, pages 7.65–7.66
🔘 ExamView® Assessment Suite

✅ Self-check for achievement

This is a pre-test for students to take before you administer the chapter test. Note that each section is cross-referenced so students can easily find the material they feel they need to review. You may wish to use Self-Check Worksheet Transparency SC7 to have students complete this assessment in class or at home. You can correct the assessment yourself, or you may prefer to project the answers on the overhead in class using Self-Check Answers Transparency SC7A.

Differentiation

Slower Paced Learners

• Have students work in pairs to complete the Self-Check in class. This will allow them to check their answers through collaborative learning. Once they have finished, call on individuals to give the correct answers as you review together.

• Encourage students who need extra help to refer to the book icons and review any section before answering the questions.

226

📖 To review **Vocabulario 1** and **Vocabulario 2,** turn to pages 204–205 and 208–209.

226   *doscientos veintiséis*

Vocabulario

1 Identifica.

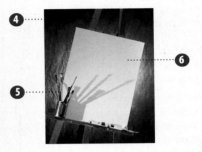

❶ Yo he nacido en esos llanos de la estepa castellana,
❷ donde había unos ⌐cristianos¬ ❸
que vivían como ⌐hermanos¬
en república cristiana.

❹ .....
❻
❺ .....

2 Completa.

7. El artista pone el lienzo en un _____.
8. Muchos artistas pintan en un _____.
9. Los escultores tallan con un _____.
10–11. Los escultores pueden tallar estatuas o esculturas de _____ o de _____.
12. La _____ es la representación de los objetos en tres dimensiones sobre una superficie llana.
13. Dos medios que emplean los artistas son acuarelas y _____.
14. Una novela se divide en _____.
15. _____ es el personaje más importante de una novela.
16. _____ es la acción o lo que tiene lugar en una novela.
17–18. Cada línea de una poesía es un _____ y una serie de estos es una _____.

CAPÍTULO 7

Answers

1
1. un verso
2. una estrofa
3. el rima
4. el caballete
5. el pincel
6. el lienzo

2
7. caballete
8. lienzo
9. cincel
10. bronce
11. madera
12. perspectiva
13. óleos
14. capítulos

15. El protagonista
16. El argumento
17. verso
18. estrofa

3
19. hayan visto
20. haya gustado
21. haya podido
22. hayan tenido

4
23. Si ellos pueden, visitarán a sus abuelos.
24. Si ellos pudieran, visitarían a sus abuelos.
25. Si ellos hubieran podido, habrían visitado a sus abuelos.

Gramática

3 **Completa con el presente perfecto del subjuntivo.**

19. Es posible que ellos _____ la exposición de las estatuas de Fernando Botero. (ver)
20. Me alegro de que a ti te _____ la exposición. (gustar)
21. Es una lástima que yo no _____ ir. (poder)
22. Dudo que ellos _____ la misma oportunidad. (tener)

4 **Sigue el modelo.**

MODELO   yo / tener tiempo / ir →
Si yo tengo tiempo, iré.
Si yo tuviera tiempo, iría.
Si yo hubiera tenido tiempo, habría ido.

23–25. ellos / poder / visitar a sus abuelos
26–28. tú / prometer hacerlo / yo / no decir nada
29–31. yo / ir / hacer el trabajo

5 **Forma el adverbio.**

32. elegante
33. franco
34. cordial
35. sencillo

Cultura

6 **Contesta.**

36. ¿Qué tipo de obra refleja la realidad con más precisión—una obra figurativa o una obra abstracta?
37. ¿Cómo fue la situación política mexicana durante la vida de Diego Rivera?
38. ¿Cuáles son algunas cosas que puedes ver en su cuadro *La liberación del peón*?
39. ¿Cuáles son algunas cosas que puedes visualizar al leer la poesía *Canción de jinete* de García Lorca?
40. ¿Cómo murió García Lorca?

CULTURA

Un mural en un edificio de la Universidad Autónoma de México

ARTE Y LITERATURA

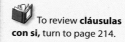

To review **el presente perfecto del subjuntivo,** turn to page 212.

To review **cláusulas con si,** turn to page 214.

To review **los adverbios que terminan en -mente,** turn to page 216.

To review this cultural information, turn to pages 220–222.

Differentiation

Multiple Intelligences

To engage **visual-spatial** and **bodily-kinesthetic** learners, number 1 to 40 on the board and call on a student to go to the board and write the correct answer (this may be done chronologically or students may choose the one they answer). Then have the student who wrote the first answer decide who will write the second, and so on, making sure that all students participate. This type of review activity appeals to **interpersonal** learners but will also benefit the class on the whole by promoting an inclusive, student-centered learning environment.

Pre-AP Students preparing for the AP exam may benefit from a set time limit when completing this Self-Check. This may also help to identify students with learning difficulties or slower paced students.

GLENCOE Technology

Online Learning in the Classroom

You may wish to have students use QuickPass code ASD7844c7 for additional test preparation. They can complete a self-check quiz for chapter review.

doscientos veintisiete **227**

Answers

26. Si tú prometes hacerlo, yo no diré nada.
27. Si tú prometieras hacerlo, yo no diría nada.
28. Si tú hubieras prometido hacerlo, yo no habría dicho nada.
29. Si yo voy, haré el trabajo.
30. Si yo fuera, haría el trabajo.
31. Si yo hubiera ido, yo habría hecho el trabajo.

5

32. elegantemente
33. francamente
34. cordialmente
35. sencillamente

6

36. Una obra figurativa refleja la realidad con más precisión.

37. Durante la vida de Diego Rivera había en México la inquietud e instabilidad políticas.
38. Puedes ver los tristes soldados revolucionarios que cortan las cuerdas con que está atado un peón muerto y que tienen una manta para cubrirle el cuerpo. También puedes ver en el fondo

las llamas de la hacienda que está ardiendo.
39. Puedes visualizar el jinete sobre su jaca negra, la luna grande y roja en el cielo y el paisaje llano.
40. Murió en circunstancias misteriosas pero se cree que fue el Guardia Civil quien lo mató.

Tips for Success ·······

Encourage students to say as much as possible when they do these open-ended activities. Tell them not to be afraid to make mistakes, since the goal of the activities is real-life communication. If someone in the group makes an error, allow the others to politely correct him or her. Let students choose the activities they would like to do.

Tell students to feel free to elaborate on the basic theme and to be creative. They may use props, pictures, or posters if they wish.

Pre-AP These oral activities will give students the opportunity to develop and improve their speaking skills so that they may succeed on the speaking portion of the AP exam.

Note: You may want to use the rubric below to help students prepare their speaking activities.

1 ¿El arte o la literatura?
✓ *Discuss fine art and literature*
Trabajen en grupos de cuatro. Discutan si son más aficionados al arte o a la literatura. Den sus razones. Determinen los resultados. ¿Comparten ustedes las mismas opiniones o no? Entre el grupo, ¿hay uno o más que tenga talento artístico? Discutan el talento.

2 Lecturas
✓ *Discuss what you like to read*
Trabaja con un(a) compañero(a). Hablen de las cosas que les gusta leer. Si es posible que haya cosas que no les gusta leer, identifíquenlas.

3 El arte
✓ *Talk about preferences in art*
Discute el arte con un(a) compañero(a). ¿Eres muy aficionado(a) al arte o no? ¿Prefieres obras de arte figurativo o de arte abstracto? Explica tu preferencia.

4 Mi cuadro favorito
✓ *Talk about your favorite painting*
En el Internet, busca unos cuadros. De todos los cuadros que miras decide cuál es tu favorito. Descríbelo de la manera más detallada posible. Explica por qué has escogido este cuadro.

5 Mi novela o cuento favorito
✓ *Talk about your favorite novel or short story*
De todas las novelas o cuentos que has leído, ¿cuál es tu favorito(a)? Da una sinopsis de tu obra favorita.

6 Si tuvieras un millón de dólares…
✓ *Discuss what you would do*
Piensa en todo lo que harías si tuvieras un millón de dólares. Prepara una lista. Compara tu lista con la de otros miembros de la clase. ¿Hay muchos que harían las mismas cosas? Piensa en tu lista y decide si te indica algo sobre tu personalidad o el tipo de persona que eres. ¿A qué conclusiones has llegado?

CULTURA
Artistas del futuro estudiando en México

Scoring Rubric for Speaking				
	4	**3**	**2**	**1**
vocabulary	extensive use of vocabulary, including idiomatic expressions	adequate use of vocabulary and idiomatic expressions	limited vocabulary marked with some anglicisms	limited vocabulary marked by frequent anglicisms that force interpretation by the listener
grammar	few or no grammatical errors	minor grammatical errors	some serious grammatical errors	serious grammatical errors
pronunciation	good intonation and largely accurate pronunciation with slight accent	acceptable intonation and pronunciation with distinctive accent	errors in intonation and pronunciation with heavy accent	errors in intonation and pronunciation that interfere with listener's comprehension
content	thorough response with interesting and pertinent detail	thorough response with sufficient detail	some detail, but not sufficient	general, insufficient response

Tarea

Write a critique of a poem or work of art. Discuss the scene/setting and the images created by the artist or the author, as well as the emotions and feelings evoked by the artwork or poem.

Writing Strategy

Critiquing Writing a critique of a work of art or of literature does not so much involve criticizing as it does using a critical eye to describe the way in which different elements or aspects of the work function together to give an overall impression. When critiquing a painting or a poem, it often helps to begin with objective information and observations. Then gradually move to subjective statements such as what you like about the work, what the work means to you, why you think the work is important, etc.

① Prewrite

• Choose the poem or work of art that you would like to critique. Take a few moments to reflect upon the author or artist, the title, and the historical context in which the work was created.

• Use the diagram to help you structure the details you wish to include.

lo objetivo

título, autor o artista, contexto histórico, técnica, materiales, estructura, ambiente

imágenes, personajes, objetos, colores, tono

emociones y sentimientos

→ interpretación personal

lo subjetivo

ARTE Y LITERATURA

• Check your compiled information for correct spelling and proper use of vocabulary before you begin the first draft.

② Write

• Start off your critique by mentioning the most objective details, such as title and artist or author, historical context, technique, materials used, structure, setting or scene, etc.

• Next describe the different elements of the artwork or poem; then discuss the emotions or feelings evoked by those elements.

• Conclude with your own interpretation and personal reaction.

• Reread what you have written. Double check to see that you have used correct vocabulary, and, if you have not already done so, look for ways to incorporate at least two of the chapter's grammar points.

• Once you have revised your first draft, write the final version.

Evaluate

Your teacher will evaluate you based on correct spelling, proper use of vocabulary and grammar, logical structure, and completeness of information.

Pre-AP This **tarea** will give students the opportunity to develop and improve their writing skills so that they may succeed on the writing portion of the AP exam.

Note: You may want to use the rubric below to help students prepare their writing task.

	Scoring Rubric for Writing			
	4	**3**	**2**	**1**
vocabulary	precise, varied	functional, fails to communicate complete meaning	limited to basic words, often inaccurate	inadequate
grammar	excellent, very few or no errors	some errors, do not hinder communication	numerous errors interfere with communication	many errors, little sentence structure
content	thorough response to the topic	generally thorough response to the topic	partial response to the topic	insufficient response to the topic
organization	well organized, ideas presented clearly and logically	loosely organized, but main ideas present	some attempts at organization, but with confused sequencing	lack of organization

Repaso del Capítulo 7

Resources

- Audio Activities TE, pages 7.32–7.33
- Audio CD 7, Tracks 23–24
- Workbook, pages 7.13–7.14

Grammar Review

This page provides a quick "at a glance" summary of the grammar points students have learned in this chapter. The corresponding page numbers are also listed so that students can easily find each grammar point as it was presented.

Differentiation

Multiple Intelligences

You may want to call on **verbal-linguistic** and **logical-mathematical** learners for whom grammar often comes easily to explain the main concepts to their classmates in their own words. Having students explain the concepts in different ways may also help slower paced learners or students with learning difficulties.

Gramática

- **Presente perfecto y pluscuamperfecto del subjuntivo** *(page 212)*

  The present perfect subjunctive is formed by using the present subjunctive of **haber** and the past participle. The pluperfect subjunctive is formed with the imperfect subjunctive of **haber** and the past participle.

	hablar	
	present perfect	**pluperfect**
yo	haya hablado	hubiera hablado
tú	hayas hablado	hubieras hablado
Ud., él, ella	haya hablado	hubiera hablado
nosotros(as)	hayamos hablado	hubiéramos hablado
vosotros(as)	*hayáis hablado*	*hubierais hablado*
Uds., ellos, ellas	hayan hablado	hubieran hablado

  Note that the present perfect or pluperfect subjunctive is used when the action in the dependent clause occurred prior to the action in the main clause.

  > **Dudo que ellos lo hayan visto.**
  > *I doubt that they have seen it.*

  > **Me sorprendió que ellos hubieran hecho tal cosa.**
  > *It surprised me that they had (would have) done such a thing.*

- **Cláusulas con si** *(page 214)*

  The sequence of tenses for **si** clauses is as follows.

MAIN CLAUSE	SI CLAUSE
future	present indicative
conditional	imperfect subjunctive
conditional perfect	pluperfect subjunctive

  > **Si tengo bastante dinero, haré el viaje.**
  > **Si tuviera bastante dinero, haría el viaje.**
  > **Si yo hubiera tenido bastante dinero, yo habría hecho el viaje.**

- **Los adverbios que terminan en -mente** *(page 216)*

  To form an adverb from an adjective that ends in **-e** or a consonant, add **-mente** to the adjective. If an adjective ends in **-o**, add **-mente** to the feminine **-a** form of the adjective.

enorme	→	enormemente	principal →	principalmente
sincera	→	sinceramente		

Vocabulario

Talking about painting

el arte	la pintura	una naturaleza	pintoresco(a)
el/la artista, el/la	el óleo	muerta	plano(a)
pintor(a)	la acuarela	una superficie	pintar
el lienzo	el cuadro	la perspectiva	
el caballete	una obra figurativa	el primer plano	
el pincel	(abstracta)	el fondo	

Talking about sculpture

el/la escultor(a)	la escultura, la	una cerámica de
el taller	estatua	yeso
	de bronce (de	el cincel
	madera)	tallar

Talking about literature and poetry

la literatura	el capítulo	el cuento	la rima
el género	los personajes	la poesía	dividirse
la obra	el/la protagonista	el/la poeta	desarrollarse
la prosa (la	el argumento	el poema	
narrativa)	el lugar	el verso	
la novela	el ambiente	la estrofa	

Other useful words and expressions

el talento	trasero(a)

CULTURA
Una obra del escultor Agustín Ibarrola «Los cubos de la memoria» en Llanes, Asturias. ¿Presentó claramente su motivo el artista?

ARTE Y LITERATURA

doscientos treinta y uno **231**

Vocabulary Review

The words and phrases in **Vocabulario 1** and **2** have been taught for productive use in this chapter. They are summarized here as a resource for both student and teacher. This list also serves as a convenient resource for the **Prepárate para el examen** activities on pages 226–229.

GLENCOE SPANISH

Why It Works!

This vocabulary reference list has not been translated into English for two reasons. First, it is recommended that students learn the new vocabulary through direct association with images on the **Vocabulario** pages. Second, all vocabulary is reintroduced in the chapter many times, and upon completion of the chapter students should be familiar with the meaning of all the words. If there are words that students still do not know, they can refer back to the vocabulary presentation in the chapter or the dictionary at the end of the book. If, however, it is your preference to give students the English translations, please refer to Vocabulary Transparency V7.1 or to the Chapter 7 PowerPoint® presentation on PowerTeach.

Differentiation

Slower Paced Learners

Slower paced learners may benefit from creating their own visual dictionary of words in this list. They can either draw their own depictions or use images from the Internet or magazines.

Every chapter of ¡Así se dice! contains this review section of previously learned material. By recycling information from previous chapters, the cumulative review serves to remind students that they need to continue practicing what they have learned.

⭐Tips for Success ·······

These activities help you determine how much your students are retaining. You may want to skip some of the activities if your students do not need them. It is suggested, however, that you do the audio activity.

···

Activity 1 This activity reviews good and bad manners and behaviors. See pages 136, 137.

🎧 **Audio Script** *(CD 7, Track 25)*
1. Alguien llegó y todos se levantaron.
2. Se dieron la mano.
3. El niño puso los codos en la mesa mientras comía.
4. Él me invitó a cenar. Por eso yo pagué.
5. Todos se quedaron sentados cuando llegó otra persona.

Activity 2 This activity reviews object pronouns. See pages R53, R64.

Activity 3 This activity reviews comparative and superlative constructions. See pages 44, SR16, SR17.

232

Repaso cumulativo

Repasa lo que ya has aprendido

These activities will help you review and remember what you have learned so far in Spanish.

 1 Escucha las frases. Indica en una tabla como la de abajo si cada frase representa buenos o malos modales.

buenos modales	malos modales

 2 Escribe cada frase de nuevo con pronombres de complemento.
1. Compré *el traje de baño*.
2. ¿Pusiste *los boletos* en la maleta?
3. Él me vendió *el carro*.
4. Yo te devolví *el dinero*.
5. Ella me enseñó *las fotografías*.
6. Vimos *los cuadros* ayer.
7. Yo he leído *la novela* dos veces.
8. *Le* mandé *el correo electrónico* a Susana.
9. El médico *le* dio *los medicamentos a Felipe*.
10. El profesor *les* explicó *la lección*.

CULTURA
La muchacha lee claramente en voz alta delante de su clase en una escuela en Trinidad, Cuba.

3 Completa con el comparativo o el superlativo.
1. Gabriel García Márquez es ____ conocido ____ muchos autores contemporáneos.
2. Es posible que él sea ____ conocido ____ todos.
3. Me gusta ____ la obra de Velázquez ____ la de Murillo.
4. El Museo de Antropología en la Ciudad de México es ____ grande ____ el Palacio de Bellas Artes.
5. Creo que es ____ grande ____ todos los museos del país.
6. La obra de García Lorca es ____ extensa ____ la obra de Antonio Machado.

Answers

 1
1. buenos modales
2. buenos modales
3. malos modales
4. malos modales
5. malos modales

 2
1. Lo compré.
2. ¿Los pusiste en la maleta?
3. Él me lo vendió.
4. Yo te lo devolví.
5. Ella me las enseñó.
6. Los vimos ayer.
7. Yo la he leído dos veces.
8. Se lo mandó (a Susana).

9. El médico se los dio (a Felipe).
10. El profesor se la explicó.

 3
1. más, que
2. el más, de
3. más, que
4. más, que
5. el más, de
6. más, que

Contesta según la información.

José tiene trece años. Sara tiene ocho.
Y Elena tiene diecisiete.

1. ¿Quién es menor que José?
2. ¿Quién es mayor que José?
3. ¿Quién es el/la menor?
4. ¿Quién es el/la mayor?
5. ¿Quiénes son mayores que Sara?

 Completa con el comparativo o superlativo.

1. Esta novela es buena pero a mi parecer esa es _____. No sé cuál es _____ mejor _____ todas.
2. El comportamiento de este niño es malo pero el comportamiento de su hermano es aún _____. Es posible que el suyo sea _____ todos.

 Haz lo siguiente.

1. Prepara una lista de todos los artículos de ropa (las prendas de vestir) que conoces.
2. Prepara una lista de expresiones que necesitas si vas de compras en una tienda de ropa.

 Conversa. Con un(a) compañero(a) prepara una conversación que tiene lugar en una tienda de ropa.

◀ ¿Qué piensas? ¿Es uno de estos hermanos menor que el otro? O, ¿es posible que sean gemelos?

ARTE Y LITERATURA

doscientos treinta y tres **233**

Activity 4 This activity reviews the irregular comparisons **mayor** and **menor**. See page SR17.

Activity 5 This activity reviews the irregular comparative forms of **bueno** and **malo**. See page SR17.

Activity 6 This activity reviews vocabulary and expressions pertaining to clothing and clothes shopping. See page R38.

Activity 7 This activity reviews vocabulary and expressions pertaining to clothing and clothes shopping. See page R38.

GLENCOE Technology

Audio in the Classroom

The **¡Así se dice!** Audio Program for Chapter 7 has 25 activities, which afford students extensive listening and speaking practice.

Online Learning in the Classroom

You may wish to have students use QuickPass code ASD7844c7 for additional cumulative review. They will be able to complete a self-check quiz.

Answers

1. Sara es menor que José.
2. Elena es mayor que José.
3. Sara es la menor.
4. Elena es la mayor.
5. José y Elena son mayores que Sara.

5
1. mejor, la, de
2. peor, el peor de

1. *Answers will vary but should include as many articles of clothing as possible from the vocabulary students have learned thus far.*
2. *Answers will vary but should include as many expressions as possible having to do with shopping in a clothing store.*

 Answers will vary, but students should use as much vocabulary and as many expressions as possible having to do with clothing and clothes shopping.

Chapter Overview
Latinos en Estados Unidos

● Scope and Sequence

Topics
- History of Latinos in the United States
- Spanish speakers in the United States
- Spanish television and press in the United States

Culture
- Street festivals in the U.S. honoring Latino heritage and culture
- *A Julia de Burgos* by Julia de Burgos

Functions
- How to talk about the history of Spanish-speakers in the U.S.
- How to discuss the experience of Latinos in the U.S.
- How to read a poem by the Puerto Rican poet Julia de Burgos

Structure
- The subjunctive with **aunque**
- The subjunctive with **-quiera**
- Definite and indefinite articles (special uses)
- Apocopated adjectives

● Planning Guide

	required	recommended	optional
Vocabulario (*pages 238–241*) La televisión La prensa	✓		
Gramática (*pages 242–249*) El subjuntivo con **aunque** El subjuntivo con **-quiera** Usos especiales del artículo definido Uso especial del artículo indefinido Adjetivos apocopados	✓		
Conversación (*pages 250–251*) Los medios han cambiado		✓	
Lectura cultural (*pages 252–255*) Latinos en Estados Unidos		✓	
Literatura (*pages 256–259*) A Julia de Burgos			✓
Prepárate para el examen (*pages 260–263*)			✓
Repaso cumulativo (*pages 266–267*)			✓

● Correlations to National Foreign Language Standards

Page numbers in light print refer to the Student Edition. Page numbers in bold print refer to the Teacher Edition.	
Communication Standard 1.1 Interpersonal	pp. **234C, 236–237, 239,** 243, **243, 251, 259,** 262
Communication Standard 1.2 Interpretive	pp. **238, 240,** 242, 243, **243,** 244, 246, 247, **250,** 251, **251,** 252, 253, 254, 255, **256,** 258, 259, 261, **261,** 262, 266, **267**
Communication Standard 1.3 Presentational	pp. **234C, 234D, 237,** 240, **249, 250, 252, 253, 260,** 262, 263, **264**
Cultures Standard 2.1	pp. **234C, 234D,** 236–237, **237,** 252–254, **254,** 258, 259
Cultures Standard 2.2	pp. **234D, 236,** 236–237, 251, **253,** 259
Connections Standard 3.1	pp. **234D,** 237, **237, 243,** 245, 246, **246,** 249, 252–254, **254,** 255, **255,** 257, 259, 261, 263
Connections Standard 3.2	pp. 241, **241,** 242, **248,** 249, **249,** 253, **253,** 258, 259
Comparisons Standard 4.1	pp. 236, **239,** 245, 248, **249, 264,** 265
Comparisons Standard 4.2	pp. 235, **235,** 251, 252–254, 258, 259, 261, 262
Communities Standard 5.1	pp. **234C, 238, 239,** 246, 251, **253, 260, 262, 264**
Communities Standard 5.2	pp. 241, **241,** 251, 253, **253,** 262

To read the ACTFL Standards in their entirety, see the front of the Teacher Edition.

● Student Resources

Print

Workbook *(pp. 8.3–8.10)*
Audio Activities *(pp. 8.11–8.15)*
Pre-AP Workbook, Chapter 8

Technology

- StudentWorks™ Plus
- ¡Así se dice! Vocabulario en vivo
- ¡Así se dice! Gramática en vivo
- ¡Así se dice! Diálogo en vivo
- ¡Así se dice! Cultura en vivo
- Vocabulary PuzzleMaker
- **QuickPass** glencoe.com

● Teacher Resources

Print

TeacherTools, Chapter 8
    Workbook TE *(pp. 8.3–8.10)*
    Audio Activities TE *(pp. 8.13–8.27)*
    Quizzes 1–4 *(pp. 8.31–8.35)*
    Tests *(pp. 8.38–8.58)*
    Performance Assessment, Task 8 *(pp. 8.59–8.60)*

Technology

- Quick Start Transparencies 8.1–8.4
- Vocabulary Transparencies V8.1–V8.3
- Audio CD 8
- *ExamView® Assessment Suite*
- TeacherWorks™ Plus
- PowerTeach
- ¡Así se dice! Video Program
- Vocabulary PuzzleMaker
- **QuickPass** glencoe.com

Chapter Project

Un perfil demográfico

Students will work individually and in small groups to create a presentation that provides a demographic profile of a specific Hispanic group living in the United States.

1. Divide students into groups of three or four and assign a different Hispanic American population to each one. Group members will work together to determine the demographic elements they would like to research and present, such as age, occupation, and housing. Groups should make sure to distribute the work evenly. Students should be reminded to cite all sources and to always check more than one source to verify that the information is correct.

2. Each student will be responsible for designing and presenting a portion of the group's presentation. Each group presentation should incorporate at least three visual elements, one of which must be some kind of graph. Students should submit a draft of the text they will use, to be checked or peer edited, then corrected and handed in with the final version.

3. Students will work with their groups in order to put together the final version of their demographic profile as well as their visual aids before presenting the profile to the class.

Expansion: To add another degree of difficulty, you may wish to have each group prepare a short quiz for their classmates to take after the presentation. The students' quizzes may then be used as the basis for a test on the information that was presented.

Technology Expansion: If students have access to the software, you might have them convert their presentations to PowerPoint®. Encourage them to use animation features to enliven the presentation. Students could share the presentations with their social studies classes.

Scoring Rubric for Project

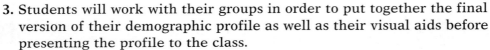

	1	3	5
Evidence of planning	No draft is provided.	Draft is provided but is not corrected.	Corrected draft is provided.
Visual elements	No visual elements are present.	Some visual elements are present.	Several visual elements are present.
Presentation	Demographic profile contains little of the required elements.	Demographic profile contains some of the required elements.	Demographic profile contains all the required elements.

Culture

● Día de los Niños

Throughout Mexico and most of Latin America, April 30 is known as **Día de los Niños**—a day to draw attention to the well-being of children and their importance in society. This holiday began in Mexico in 1925 and is now celebrated not only throughout Latin America but also in parts of the United States where, since 1996, the day has expanded to include **Día de los Libros,** which helps promote literacy in children, no matter what language they speak. Many U.S. cities organize activities, often in conjunction with a local library, to celebrate **Día de los Niños/Día de los Libros.** Some activities for this day may include reading bilingual books, singing songs in Spanish and English, and making crafts. Have students search the Internet to find a U.S. city that celebrates this special day and report on what types of festivities take place.

● Tejano

The region now known as Texas was originally part of the area conquered by the Spanish during the fifteenth century. People who inhabited this region were known as **tejanos**—Texans born of Hispanic heritage. Today the term not only refers to people, but also to a specific type of music. Alice, Texas, is known as the birthplace of **tejano** music since that is where the first **tejano** record label was created in the 1940s—however, forms of **tejano** music had been around long before then. **Tejano** music has been influenced by traditional Mexican and Latin American sounds; German, Polish, and Czech polka and waltz; and rock, blues, and country western. Early **tejano** instruments included drum, **bajo sexto,** 12-string bass guitar, and accordion; as the form evolved, other instruments—such as electric guitar, brass horns, and synthesizers—found a place in the band. **Tejano** is quite popular in Mexico and other Latin America countries while its popularity in the United States outside Texas has been more limited to cities with large Hispanic populations. One breakthrough **tejano** artist was Selena Quintanilla, who won major awards including the Grammy before her tragic death. Have students research current winners of the annual Tejano Music Awards, listen to some of the songs, and discuss how their growing knowledge of Spanish will help them to appreciate **tejano** lyrics.

Planning for Chapter 8

50-Minute Lesson Plans

	Objective	Present	Practice	Assess/Homework
Day 1	Talk about Spanish television and press in the United States	Chapter Opener, pp. 234–235 (5 min.) Introducción al tema, pp. 236–237 (10 min.) Core Instruction/Vocabulario, pp. 238–239 (20 min.)	Activities 1–3, p. 240 (15 min.)	Student Workbook Activities A–C, pp. 8.3–8.4 **QuickPass** Vocabulary Practice
Day 2	Talk about Spanish television and press in the United States	Quick Start, p. 238 (5 min.) Review Vocabulario, pp. 238–239 (10 min.) Video, Vocabulario en vivo (10 min.)	Activity 4, p. 240 (5 min.) Estudio de palabras, p. 241 (5 min.) Audio Activities A–E, pp. 8.13–8.15 (15 min.)	Student Workbook Activities D–E, p. 8.4 **QuickPass** Vocabulary Practice
Day 3	The subjunctive with **aunque**	Quick Start, p. 242 (5 min.) Core Instruction/Gramática, El subjuntivo con **aunque**, p. 242 (10 min.)	Activities 1–3, pp. 242–243 (10 min.) InfoGap, p. SR9 (5 min.) Audio Activities A–B, 8.16 (10 min.)	Quiz 1, p. 8.31 (10 min.) Student Workbook Activities A–C, p. 8.5 **QuickPass** Grammar Practice
Day 4	The subjunctive with **-quiera**	Core Instruction/Gramática, El subjuntivo con **-quiera**, p. 244 (15 min.)	Activities 4–5, p. 244 (15 min.) Audio Activity C, p. 8.17 (10 min.)	Quiz 2, p. 8.32 (10 min.) Student Workbook Activities A–B, p. 8.6 **QuickPass** Grammar Practice
Day 5	Definite and indefinite articles (special uses)	Core Instruction/Gramática, Usos especiales del artículo definido, p. 245 (15 min.)	Activities 6–8, p. 246 (15 min.) Foldables, p. 240 (10 min.) Audio Activity D, p. 8.17 (10 min.)	Student Workbook Activities A–B, pp. 8.6–8.7 **QuickPass** Grammar Practice
Day 6	Definite and indefinite articles (special uses)	Quick Start, p. 247 (5 min.) Review Gramática, Usos especiales del artículo definido, p. 245 (5 min.) Core Instruction/Gramática, Uso especial del artículo indefinido, p. 247 (5 min.)	Activities 9–10, p. 246 (10 min.) Activities 11–13, p. 247 (15 min.) Audio Activities E–F, pp. 8.17–8.18 (10 min.)	Student Workbook Activity A, p. 8.7 **QuickPass** Grammar Practice
Day 7	Apocopated adjectives	Core Instruction/Gramática, Adjetivos apocopados, p. 248 (15 min.)	Activities 14–16, pp. 248–249 (25 min.)	Quiz 3, p. 8.33 (10 min.) **QuickPass** Grammar Practice
Day 8	Develop reading and listening comprehension skills	Core Instruction/Conversación, p. 250 (20 min.)	¿Comprendes? A–D, p. 251 (20 min.)	Quiz 4, p. 8.34 (10 min.) ¿Comprendes? E, p. 251 **QuickPass** Conversation
Day 9	Talk about the history of Spanish speakers in the United States	Core Instruction/Lectura cultural, pp. 252–254 (20 min.) Video, Cultura en vivo (10 min.)	¿Comprendes? A, p. 255 (5 min.)	Listening Comprehension Test, pp. 8.53–8.55 (15 min.) ¿Comprendes? B–C, p. 255 **QuickPass** Reading Practice
Day 10	Read a poem by the Puerto Rican poet Julia de Burgos	Core Instruction/Vocabulario, p. 256 (5 min.) Core Instruction/Literatura, pp. 257–258 (20 min.)	Vocabulario, Práctica, p. 256 (5 min.) ¿Comprendes? A–D, p. 259 (20 min.)	**QuickPass** Reading Practice
Day 11	Read a poem by the Puerto Rican poet Julia de Burgos	Review Literatura, pp. 257–258 (10 min.)	¿Comprendes? E–F, p. 259 (15 min.) Prepárate para el examen, pp. 260–261 (25 min.)	Prepárate para el examen, Practice for written proficiency, p. 263 **QuickPass** Reading Practice
Day 12	Chapter review	Repaso del Capítulo 8, pp. 264–265 (15 min.)	Prepárate para el examen, Practice for oral proficiency, p. 262 (20 min.)	Test for Writing Proficiency, p. 8.58 (15 min.) Review for chapter test
Day 13	Chapter 8 Tests (50 min.) Reading and Writing Test, pp. 8.43–8.50 Literature Test, pp. 8.51–8.52		Speaking Test, p. 8.56 Test for Oral Proficiency, p. 8.57	

90-Minute Lesson Plans

	Objective	Present	Practice	Assess/Homework
Block 1	Talk about Spanish television and press in the United States	Chapter Opener, pp. 234–235 (5 min.) Introducción al tema, pp. 236–237 (10 min.) Quick Start, p. 238 (5 min.) Core Instruction/Vocabulario, pp. 238–239 (15 min.) Video, Vocabulario en vivo (10 min.)	Activities 1–4, p. 240 (20 min.) Estudio de palabras, p. 241 (10 min.) Audio Activities A–E, pp. 8.13–8.15 (15 min.)	Student Workbook Activities A–E, pp. 8.3–8.4 **QuickPass** Vocabulary Practice
Block 2	The subjunctive with **aunque** The subjunctive with **-quiera**	Quick Start, p. 242 (5 min.) Core Instruction/Gramática, El subjuntivo con **aunque**, p. 242 (10 min.) Core Instruction/Gramática, El subjuntivo con -**quiera**, p. 244 (10 min.)	Activities 1–3, pp. 242–243 (15 min.) InfoGap, p. SR9 (10 min.) Activities 4–5, p. 244 (10 min.) Audio Activities A–C, pp. 8.16–8.17 (20 min.)	Quiz 1, p. 8.31 (10 min.) Student Workbook Activities A–C, p. 8.5 Student Workbook Activities A–B, p. 8.6 **QuickPass** Grammar Practice
Block 3	Definite and indefinite articles (special uses)	Core Instruction/Gramática, Usos especiales del artículo definido, p. 245 (15 min.) Core Instruction/Gramática, Uso especial del artículo indefinido, p. 247 (10 min.)	Activities 6–10, p. 246 (20 min.) Activities 11–13, pp. 247–249 (15 min.) Audio Activities D–F, pp. 8.17–8.18 (20 min.)	Quiz 2, p. 8.32 (10 min.) Student Workbook Activities A–B, pp. 8.6–8.7 Student Workbook Activity A, p. 8.7 **QuickPass** Grammar Practice
Block 4	Apocopated adjective Develop reading and listening comprehension skills	Core Instruction/Gramática, Adjetivos apocopados, p. 248 (15 min.) Core Instruction/Conversación, p. 250 (20 min.)	Activities 14–16, pp. 248–249 (25 min.) ¿Comprendes? A–D, p. 251 (20 min.) Foldables, p. 240 (10 min.)	¿Comprendes? E, p. 251 **QuickPass** Grammar Practice, Conversation
Block 5	Talk about the history of Spanish speakers in the United States	Core Instruction/Lectura cultural, pp. 252–254 (25 min.) Video, Cultura en vivo (10 min.)	¿Comprendes? A–C, p. 255 (20 min.) Prepárate para el examen, Practice for oral proficiency 1–2, p. 262 (15 min.)	Quizzes 3–4, pp. 8.33–8.34 (20 min.) **QuickPass** Reading Practice
Block 6	Read a poem by the Puerto Rican poet Julia de Burgos	Core Instruction/Vocabulario, p. 256 (5 min.) Core Instruction/Literatura, pp. 257–258 (25 min.)	Vocabulario, Práctica, p. 256 (5 min.) ¿Comprendes? A–F, p. 259 (25 min.) Prepárate para el examen, Practice for oral proficiency 3–4, p. 262 (15 min.)	Listening Comprehension Test, pp. 8.53–8.55 (15 min.) **QuickPass** Reading Practice
Block 7	Chapter review	Repaso del Capítulo 8, pp. 264–265 (20 min.)	Prepárate para el examen, pp. 260–261 (25 min.) Prepárate para el examen, Practice for written proficiency, p. 263 (30 min.)	Literature Test, pp. 8.51–8.52 (15 min.) Review for chapter test
Block 8	Chapter 8 Tests (50 min.) Reading and Writing Test, pp. 8.43–8.50 Speaking Test, p. 8.56 Test for Oral Proficiency, p. 8.57 Test for Writing Proficiency, p. 8.58 Chapter Project, p. 234C (40 min.)			

Preview

In this chapter, students will learn about the origins of the some fourty-four million Latinos living in the United States and their impact on this nation's economics, marketing, media, and culture. To do this, students will learn vocabulary related to certain historical events and the modern media. They will continue to learn new uses of the subjunctive as well as apocopated (short-ened) adjectives and special uses of definite and indefinite articles.

Pacing

It is important to note that once you reach **¡Bravo!** in the chapter, there is no more new material for the students to learn. The rest of the chapter recycles what has already been covered. The suggested pacing listed here leaves two to three days for review, assessment, and enrichment activities such as the chapter project.

Vocabulario	1–2 days
Gramática	2–3 days
Conversación	1 day
Lectura cultural	1 day
Literatura	1 day

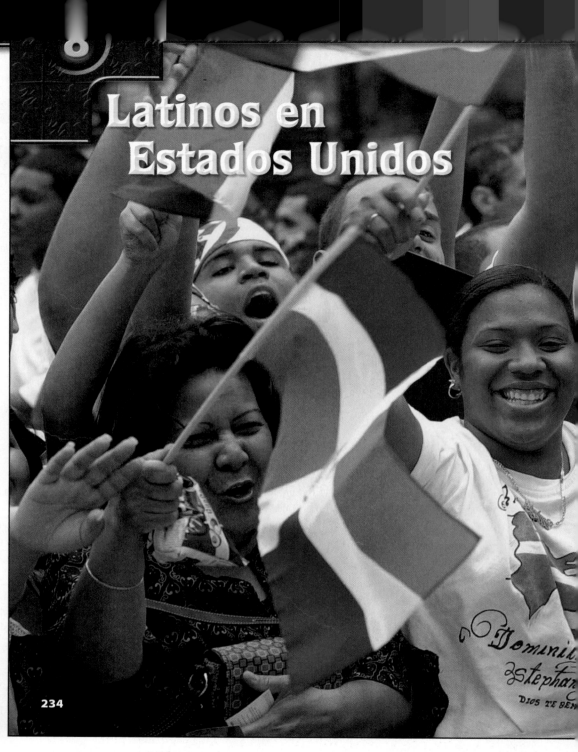

Latinos en Estados Unidos

234

TeacherWorks *Plus*™

The **¡Así se dice!** TeacherWorks™ Plus CD-ROM is an all-in-one planner and resource center. You may wish to use several of the following features as you plan and present the Chapter 8 material: Interactive Teacher Edition, Interactive Lesson Planner with Calendar, and Point and Click Access to Teaching Resources including Hotlinks to the Internet and Correlations to the National Standards.

Vamos a comparar Hoy en día la población latina consta de más de cuarenta y cuatro millones de personas. Los latinos o hispanos en Estados Unidos vienen de todos los países hispanohablantes y viven en todas partes de Estados Unidos. Se ve la influencia hispana o latina en muchos aspectos de la vida estadounidense.

Objetivos

You will:

- talk about the history of Spanish speakers in the United States
- read a poem by the Puerto Rican poet Julia de Burgos

You will use:

- the subjunctive with **aunque**
- the subjunctive with **-quiera**
- definite and indefinite articles (special uses)
- apocopated adjectives

◄ Hay un gran desfile para celebrar el día de los dominicanos en la Ciudad de Nueva York.

SPOTLIGHT ON CULTURE

Cultural Comparison

Students will learn that when speaking of Latinos or Hispanics in the United States, one is not speaking of a singular, homogenous group. Latinos come from different places for different reasons. The many areas of origin do not share all the same ethnic or cultural patterns.

QuickPass

Go to glencoe.com
For: **Online book**
Web code: **ASD7844c8**

doscientos treinta y cinco **235**

 Quia Interactive Online Student Edition found at quia.com allows students to complete activities online and submit them for computer grading for instant feedback or teacher grading with suggestions for what to review. Students can also record speaking activities, listen to chapter audio, and watch the videos that correspond with each chapter. As a teacher you are able to create rosters, set grading parameters, and post assignments for each class. After students complete activities, you can view the results and recommend remediation or review. You can also add your own customized activities for additional student practice.

Introducción al tema

▶ PRESENT

Introduce the theme of the chapter by having students look at the photographs on these pages. Lead a discussion about the many Hispanic communities depicted. Later, once you have presented the **Vocabulario** section, you may want to return to these pages. Students will be able to read and understand the written information and answer any corresponding questions.

Cultural Snapshot

Nueva York *(page 236)* When Alex Rodríguez was born in Washington Heights, New York, the primary demography of the area was Puerto Rican. Today it is Dominican. **¿Qué es Alex Rodríguez? ¿Dónde nació? ¿De dónde eran sus padres? Además de vivir en Nueva York, ¿dónde ha vivido Alex Rodríguez? ¿Cuánto dinero donó él a la Universidad de Miami? ¿Para qué lo donó?**

Florida *(page 236)* In addition to many Latino groups, Florida has a very large population of Brazilians, Haitians, and people from the English-speaking islands of the West Indies. **¿En qué idioma se dan las instrucciones electorales en el estado de la Florida?**

California *(page 236)* **¿Sabes quién es Frida Kahlo? ¿Has visto la película sobre su vida? ¿Cómo se llama la película? ¿Qué actriz jugó el papel de Frida?**

Introducción al tema
Latinos en Estados Unidos

No importa adonde vayas en Estados Unidos no hay duda que podrás observar la influencia latina. Hoy hay más de cuarenta y cuatro millones de hispanos o latinos en Estados Unidos. Aunque vienen de todos los países latinos, el grupo mayoritario son de ascendencia mexicana.

▲ Nueva York Alex Rodríguez, el famoso beisbolista de los Yanquis de Nueva York, nació en Washington Heights de padres dominicanos. Ha vivido también en la República Dominicana y Miami, Florida. Rodríguez donó 3,9 millones de dólares a la Universidad de Miami para la construcción de un estadio de béisbol.

◀ Florida Como en muchas ciudades de Estados Unidos, las instrucciones en los centros electorales se dan en inglés y español. En este centro electoral en Miami son también en criollo, el idioma de los haitianos.

California Salma Hayek juega el papel de Frida Kahlo en la película *Frida*. ▼

▲ Florida Este azulejo español está en la entrada de un restaurante en Ybor City en Tampa.

236

Florida *(page 236)* Cuban influence has been strong in Ybor City, Tampa, since 1868 when Ybor and several others established cigar factories. Ybor City has many restaurants and is quite popular with tourists. **¿Está en España este azulejo español? ¿Dónde está?**

Florida Se venden camisetas durante el Carnaval de la Calle Ocho en la Pequeña Habana en Miami. ▶

◀ **California** Jaime Escalante se considera uno de los educadores más famosos de Estados Unidos. Él nació en La Paz, Bolivia, pero pasó la mayor parte de su carrera como profesor de cálculo en una escuela secundaria en East Los Angeles. Su vida se dramatizó en la película *Stand and Deliver*.

Texas Estatua en honor de los conquistadores españoles en San Antonio ▶

▲ **California** Una celebración para el Cinco de Mayo en la calle Olvera en East Los Angeles

237

Florida *(page 237)* Calle Ocho is the center of the section of Miami known as La Pequeña Habana. Although the Cuban influence is still dominant, there are now restaurants and shops of various Latino origins. **¿Qué se está vendiendo aquí durante el carnaval? ¿Dónde?**

California *(page 237 middle)* Jaime Escalante taught in a high school in East Los Angeles with a heavily impoverished Mexican American population. **¿Quién es Jaime Escalante? ¿Dónde nació él? ¿Dónde enseño? ¿Qué enseñó? ¿En qué se dramatiza su vida?**

California *(page 237 bottom)* **El Cinco de Mayo** commemorates the victory of the Mexicans against the French in the Battle of Puebla. **¿Dónde tiene lugar esta celebración?**

Comunicación

Presentational

You may wish to divide students into small groups to research cities in the United States that have been significantly influenced by their Latino communities. Have them report what they learn to the class.

Vocabulario · presentación 🎧

🕐 Quick Start

Use QS Transparency 8.1 or write the following on the board.
Escribe a lo menos cuatro palabras sobre cada uno de los siguientes deportes.
    el béisbol
    el básquetbol
    el fútbol

▶ TEACH
Core Instruction

Step 1 You may wish to have students read the sentences that accompany each photo and ask questions such as: **¿Qué es una emisora? ¿Cuál es una de las emisoras importantes de televisión en Estados Unidos? ¿A qué se dedica Univisión? ¿Es una emisora también una estación de televisión?**

Step 2 This is the first chapter in which students are introduced to new words through definitions. Call on a student to read the new word and its definition. You may also wish to use the new word in a sentence. **¿Quieres darle una ojeada a la revista? ¿Hay luchas horribles durante una guerra? ¿Luchan los soldados en una guerra? ¿Es el sacerdote una persona religiosa o laïca?**

La televisión

una emisora de televisión

Univisión es una emisora de televisión.
Una emisora es una empresa o compañía.
Se dedica a emisiones de radio y televisión.

una emisión televisiva, un programa de televisión

Una emisora es también una estación de televisión, como el canal (la cadena) 7, por ejemplo.
Hay muchas emisoras latinas en Estados Unidos.
Aunque están en Estados Unidos, emiten los programas en español.

un ancla

El ancla (noticiero) da las noticias.
Quienquiera que lo escuche dice que es un buen noticiero.
Tiene reportajes interesantes.

Heritage Speakers

If you have heritage speakers in class, have them identify their favorite Spanish-language channels, anchors, and TV programs. Have them tell something about each.

La prensa

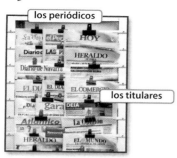

los periódicos

los titulares

los libros de bolsillo

la revista

la publicidad, la promoción, la propaganda

La periodista escribe para el periódico.
Los artículos llevan titulares.
Una revista tiene mucha publicidad.
La televisión y la prensa son medios de comunicación.

Más vocabulario

una ojeada mirada rápida

una guerra una serie de luchas o batallas

los soldados los que luchan en las batallas durante una guerra

el sacerdote un cura o padre religioso (católico)

acomodado(a) adinerado, rico, que tiene dinero

ilustre famoso

apoderarse de tomar el poder por fuerza, tomar el control

darse cuenta de llegar a saber, comprender

sobrepasar exceder

tomar en cuenta considerar

lograr obtener (conseguir) lo que se desea

otorgar dar

invertir dar fondos monetarios, hacer inversiones

doscientos treinta y nueve **239**

Vocabulario

Vocabulario

🎴 Comunicación

Interpersonal

Ask students to work in pairs, asking each other the following personal questions. **¿Qué periódico lees? ¿Qué revistas lees? ¿Qué programas de televisión te gustan? ¿Escuchas de vez en cuando la radio?**

ABOUT THE SPANISH LANGUAGE

You will hear both **los medios** and **la media** meaning *media.*

GLENCOE 🖱 Technology

You may wish to use the editable PowerPoint® presentation on PowerTeach for additional vocabulary instruction and practice.

🎴 Comunidades

- You may wish to have students view some Spanish-language TV programs in class or at home.
- You may wish to have students listen to a Spanish-language radio station. Ask them to pay particular attention to the advertisements. Are the businesses and events that are promoted the same as those on local English-language stations? If not, ask them what new things they learned about their community.
- You may wish to have students research the Spanish-speaking media that exists in your community. Have them use the following categories: television stations, radio stations, magazines, and newspapers.

▶ PRACTICE

Leveling EACH Activity

Easy Activities 1, 2
Average Activities 3, 4

Activity ❶ You may wish to give students a few minutes to look over the words and then do the exercise in class.

Activity ❷ It is suggested that you do this as an entire class activity. Call on members of the class at random to answer questions. You may also wish to have students write the answers to the questions for homework.

Activities ❸ and ❹ It is suggested that students prepare these activities before going over them in class.

⭐ Tips for Success ·······

The more students hear and use the new vocabulary, the more they will be able to use it at ease and to retain it.

··

GLENCOE ⬉ Technology

Online Learning in the Classroom

Have students use QuickPass code ASD7844c8 for additional vocabulary practice. They can download audio files of all vocabulary to their computer and/or MP3 player. They will also have access to online flashcards and eGames.

QuickPass
Go to glencoe.com
For: **Vocabulary practice**
Web code: **ASD7844c8**

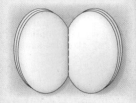

FOLDABLES
Study Organizer

FORWARD-BACKWARD BOOK
See page SH22 for help with making this foldable. Use this study organizer to talk to a partner about television and the press. Write **La televisión** on the cover and inside list your favorite television programs. On the other cover, write **La prensa** and inside list your favorite magazines and newspapers. Share your book with your partner and explain why these programs and publications are your favorites. When you're finished, switch roles.

HABLAR • ESCRIBIR
❶ Da una(s) palabra(s) relacionada(s).
1. las noticias
2. guerrero
3. emitir
4. la televisión
5. el periódico
6. la inversión
7. el ojo
8. cómodo

HABLAR
❷ Personaliza. Da respuestas personales.
1. ¿Cuál es tu canal de televisión favorito?
2. ¿Hay emisoras que emiten en español donde vives?
3. ¿Quién es tu ancla favorito(a)?
4. ¿Hay mucha publicidad en la televisión?
5. ¿Interrumpe las emisiones la publicidad?
6. ¿Qué periódico lees?
7. ¿Qué medio prefieres? ¿La televisión o la prensa?
8. ¿Das una ojeada al periódico todos los días?
9. ¿Lees los titulares?
10. ¿Encabeza o introduce un artículo el titular?

LEER • ESCRIBIR
❸ Completa con la palabra o expresión apropiada.
1. Es necesario _____ todas las opiniones disponibles antes de tomar una decisión.
2. Si quieren que el proyecto tenga éxito tendrán que _____ mucho dinero.
3. Espero que ellos tengan éxito y que _____ realizar su objetivo.
4. Él tiene mucho dinero. Es bastante _____.
5. Los dos grupos quieren _____ del mismo territorio y no hay duda que van a luchar.
6. No tienes que leerlo detenida y detalladamente. Es suficiente darle una _____.

LEER • ESCRIBIR
❹ Expresa de otra manera.
1. Ella es una poeta *famosa*.
2. Había una *serie de batallas*.
3. Van a *darle* un premio.
4. Es de una familia *adinerada*.
5. No debes *exceder* el límite.
6. Debes *considerar* todas las opciones que tienes a tu disposición.
7. Quieren *tomar control* de la ciudad *por fuerza*.
8. Es *un programa de televisión*.

240 *doscientos cuarenta*   **CAPÍTULO 8**

Answers

❶
1. noticiero
2. la guerra
3. la emisora, la emisión
4. televisivo
5. el/la periodista
6. invertir
7. la ojeada
8. acomodado

❷
1. Mi canal de televisión favorito es el canal _____.
2. Sí, (No, no) hay emisoras que emiten en español donde vivo.
3. Mi ancla favorito(a) es _____.
4. Sí, hay mucha publicidad en la televisión.

5. Sí, la publicidad interrumpe las emisiones.
6. Leo _____.
7. Prefiero la televisión (la prensa).
8. Sí, (No, no) doy una ojeada al periódico todos los días.
9. Sí, (No, no) leo los titulares.
10. Sí, el titular encabeza o introduce un artículo.

Estudio de palabras

conquistar Los españoles conquistaron a los indígenas americanos.

el conquistador Los españoles eran los conquistadores.

la conquista La conquista española tuvo lugar en el siglo dieciséis.

colonizar Los españoles colonizaron gran parte de las Américas.

el colonizador Los españoles eran los colonizadores.

la colonia Ellos establecieron muchas colonias.

colonial Las zonas coloniales de las ciudades son pintorescas.

1 Completa.
1. Francisco Pizarro fue el _____ de Perú.
2. Francisco Pizarro _____ Perú y Hernán Cortés _____ México.
3. La _____ era muy cruel.
4. Los sacerdotes españoles establecieron _____ en California.
5. Ellos _____ muchas partes del sudoeste de Estados Unidos.
6. Muchas ciudades latinoamericanas tienen barrios o cascos _____.

2 Contesta sobre la época de la conquista. Fíjate en las palabras aparentadas.
1. ¿Llegaron los conquistadores españoles a las Américas durante el siglo XVI?
2. ¿Vinieron los sacerdotes con los conquistadores?
3. Después de los conquistadores, ¿llegaron los colonizadores?
4. ¿Establecieron ellos colonias?
5. ¿Había luchas entre los españoles y los indígenas?

CULTURA
Misión al norte de San Diego, California

Estudio de palabras

You may wish to call on one student to read the new word and another to read the sentence that defines it. Go over the activities orally in class and then have students write them for homework.

GLENCOE Technology

Video in the Classroom
Vocabulario en vivo Watch and listen to Nora as she discusses the rich history of Spanish speakers in the world and in the Latino community in the United States.

▶ ASSESS

Students are now ready to take Quiz 1 on page 8.31 of the TeacherTools booklet. If you prefer to create your own quiz, use the *ExamView® Assessment Suite.*

Answers

 3
1. tomar en cuenta
2. invertir
3. logren
4. acomodado
5. apoderarse
6. ojeada

4
1. ilustre
2. guerra
3. otorgarle
4. acomodada
5. sobrepasar
6. tomar en cuenta
7. apoderarse
8. una emisión

Estudio de palabras

1
1. conquistador
2. conquistó, conquistó
3. conquista
4. colonias
5. colonizaron
6. coloniales

2
1. Sí, los conquistadores españoles llegaron a América durante el siglo XVI.
2. Sí, los sacerdotes vinieron con los conquistadores.
3. Sí, después de los conquistadores llegaron los colonizadores.
4. Sí, ellos establecieron colonias.
5. Sí, había luchas entre los españoles y los indígenas.

Resources

- Audio Activities TE, page 8.16
- Audio CD 8, Tracks 6–7
- Workbook, page 8.5
- Quiz 2, page 8.32
- ExamView® Assessment Suite

Quick Start

Use QS Transparency 8.2 or write the following on the board.

Completa en el pretérito.

1. Ellos ___ a la playa. (ir)
2. Ellos ___ mucho tiempo allí. (pasar)
3. Yo ___ en el mar. (nadar)
4. José ___ en el agua. (esquiar)
5. Nosotros ___ en un chiringuito. (comer)
6. Yo ___ paella y mi amigo ___ un pescado frito. (pedir, pedir)

⭐Tips for Success

Reinforce how logical the use of the subjunctive can be. If the information after **aunque** is a reality, you use the indicative. If it is merely a possibility you use the subjunctive.

▶ PRACTICE

Leveling EACH Activity

Easy Activities 1, 2
Average Activity 3

Activity ① This activity can be done as an entire class or as a pair or group activity. It is important, however, that all students hear the correct answers.

Conexiones

El mercado

¿Qué es un mercado? Es cualquier lugar adonde vayamos a comprar algo. Pero el término «el mercado» tiene otro significado. El mercado incluye todos los consumidores, o sea, todos los eventuales compradores de un producto. Como todos no queremos comprar el mismo producto, el mercado tiene segmentos. Algunos ejemplos son los jóvenes, la gente mayor, los hombres, las mujeres, los latinos.

El subjuntivo con **aunque**

The conjunction **aunque** (*although*) may be followed by the subjunctive or the indicative depending upon the meaning of the sentence.

> **Ellos van a salir aunque llueva.**
> **Ellos van a salir aunque llueve.**

In the first example the subjunctive is used to indicate that it is not raining now, but they will go out even if it does rain. In the second example, the indicative is used to indicate that it is raining and they will go out even though it is indeed raining.

Práctica

ESCUCHAR • HABLAR • ESCRIBIR

① Contesta según el modelo.

MODELO —Hace mucho calor. ¿Vas a jugar?
—Sí, voy a jugar aunque hace mucho calor.

1. No tienes entrada. ¿Vas al concierto?
2. Podría llover. ¿Vas a salir?
3. No entiendes español. ¿Vas a escuchar el programa?
4. Elena no tiene dinero. ¿Va a hacer el viaje?
5. Es posible que ella no tenga dinero. ¿Va a hacer el viaje?
6. Es posible que haya tráfico. ¿Quieres ir en carro?
7. El avión te cuesta más. ¿Quieres ir en avión?
8. Es posible que el bus tarde más tiempo. ¿Vas a tomar el bus?

CULTURA
Monumento a la Revolución en la Ciudad de México

Answers

①
1. Sí, voy al concierto aunque no tengo entrada.
2. Sí, voy a salir aunque pueda llover.
3. Sí, voy a escuchar el programa aunque no entiendo español.
4. Sí, Elena va a hacer el viaje aunque no tiene dinero.
5. Sí, ella va a hacer el viaje aunque no tenga dinero.
6. Sí, quiero ir en carro aunque haya tráfico.
7. Sí, quiero ir en avión aunque me cuesta más.
8. Sí, voy a tomar el bus aunque tarde más tiempo.

LEER · ESCRIBIR

2 Escoge según el contexto.

1. Hoy en día las noticias son malas pero el ancla tiene que dar las noticias aunque (sean, son) malas.
2. Ellos hablan muy bien el español pero contestan en inglés aunque (hablan, hablen) español.
3. Yo no sé si la profesora nos va a dar una tarea pero voy a salir aunque nos (da, dé) una.
4. Se sabe que él tiene mucho dinero pero aunque (es, sea) muy acomodado, es bastante tacaño. No le gusta gastar su dinero.
5. Es posible que él no lo sepa. Pero aunque no lo (sabe, sepa) no le voy a decir nada.
6. El público se opone. Sin embargo el oficial va a seguir con su plan aunque todos (están, estén) en contra.

Más práctica

■ Workbook, p. 8.5
⊕ StudentWorks™ Plus

InfoGap For more practice using the subjunctive with **aunque,** do Activity 8 on page SR9 at the end of this book.

CULTURA
Una empresa latina cubriendo las noticias en Chicago

 Comunicación

3 Trabaja con un(a) compañero(a) de clase. Los dos van a discutir unas cosas que van a hacer aunque ocurra algo que lo haga difícil. Luego discutan unas cosas que van a hacer aunque saben que va a ser muy difícil hacerlas. En ambos casos, expliquen por qué.

LATINOS EN ESTADOS UNIDOS

doscientos cuarenta y tres **243**

Answers

2

1. son
2. hablan
3. dé
4. es
5. sepa
6. están

3 *Answers will vary.*

Gramática

Activity 2 You can go over this activity in class without previous preparation.

Activity 3 When having students do an open-ended activity that has no learning prompts, they are actually communicating as if they were in a real-life situation. In such a situation, it is normal for learners to make a few mistakes. For this reason, you may decide not to interrupt and correct each error a student makes. This is up to your discretion.

 Conexiones

Las carreras

The information presented in the **Conexiones** box on page 242 is important for students who may plan to major in business (**el comercio**).

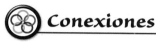

Online Learning in the Classroom

Have students use QuickPass code ASD7844c8 for additional grammar practice. They can review each grammar point with an eGame. They can also review all grammar points by doing the self-check quiz, which integrates the chapter vocabulary with the new grammar.

▶ ASSESS

Students are now ready to take Quiz 2 on page 8.32 of the TeacherTools booklet. If you prefer to create your own quiz, use the *ExamView® Assessment Suite.*

243

Resources

- Audio Activities TE, page 8.17
- Audio CD 8, Track 8
- Workbook, page 8.6
- ExamView® Assessment Suite

▶ **TEACH**
Core Instruction

This grammatical point is quite easy and should not be very difficult for most students.

⭐ **Tips for Success** ....

Have students read the photo caption to reinforce the new grammar concept.

▶ **PRACTICE**

Leveling EACH Activity

Easy Activity 4
Average Activity 5

Activity 4 This activity can be done orally in class with books closed. Call on students at random to answer.

Activity 5 This activity can be gone over once in class and then written as a homework assignment.

📷 **Cultural Snapshot**

(page 244) Ibiza is one of the Balearic islands. It is not as large as Mallorca and it has many quaint beaches. It is a favorite spot for artists and the international jet set.

244

El subjuntivo con -quiera

Many words are made indefinite by adding **-quiera**. Such words are followed by the subjunctive. **Quiera** is the same as the *ever* in *whoever, wherever.*

quienquiera	cuandoquiera	dondequiera
comoquiera	cualquiera	adondequiera

Quienquiera que sea, no nos podrá resolver el problema.
Adondequiera que vayas, oirás el español.

CULTURA

Adondequieras que vayas en las islas Baleares tendrás vistas fabulosas.

Práctica

ESCUCHAR • HABLAR • ESCRIBIR

4 Contesta.
  1. ¿Irás cuandoquiera que salgan ellos?
  2. ¿Estarás de acuerdo con cualquier idea que tenga él?
  3. ¿Los acompañarás adondequiera que vayan?
  4. ¿Se lo dirás a quienquiera que te escuche?
  5. ¿Lo podrás hacer dondequiera que estés?

LEER • ESCRIBIR

5 Completa con la forma apropiada del verbo.
  1. Te prometo que te ayudaré con cualquier problema que _____. (tener)
  2. Te daré ayuda cuandoquiera que la _____. (necesitar)
  3. Adondequiera que (nosotros) _____ no veremos nada más bello. (ir)
  4. Quienquiera que lo _____ hecho, debe confesar. (haber)
  5. Comoquiera que ellos lo _____, saldrá bien. (hacer)

244 *doscientos cuarenta y cuatro*   CAPÍTULO 8

Usos especiales del artículo definido

1. Unlike English, the definite article must be used in Spanish with all general or abstract nouns. Compare the Spanish and English in the following examples.

La leche es buena para la salud.
Milk is good for the health.

Los programas de televisión pueden ser educativos.
Television programs can be educational.

El amor es una cosa divina.
Love is a divine thing.

2. The definite article must be used with the title of a person when talking about the person. The article is not used when addressing the person.

La doctora González es dentista.
Buenos días, Doctora González.

El licenciado Ugarte es periodista.
Buenas tardes, Licenciado Ugarte.

3. The definite article, rather than the indefinite article, is used with quantities, weights, and measures.

El biftec está a 500 pesos el kilo.
Steak is 500 pesos a kilo.

Los huevos cuestan 1,50 la docena.
Eggs cost 1.50 a dozen.

4. When the definite article is used with the days of the week, it means *on*.

Lunes es el primer día de la semana.
Monday is the first day of the week.

Él sale el sábado.
He leaves on Saturday.

Ella no trabaja los domingos.
She doesn't work on Sundays.

5. The definite article is used with the season in a general sense.

El verano es una estación de calor.
   but
Hace calor en (el) verano.
Julio es un mes de verano.

 Conexiones

Las matemáticas
Los huevos están a 1,17 euros la media docena. El tipo de cambio actual es 1,48 euros a un dólar. Calcula cuánto cuesta media docena de huevos. Luego calcula cuánto costaría una docena.

▶ TEACH
Core Instruction

The information given for the use of the definite article is quite straightforward. It is suggested that rather than relying on a great deal of explanation or on an English translation, students should practice the grammar point in order to develop an "ear" for its use.

GLENCOE Technology

You may wish to use the editable PowerPoint® presentation on PowerTeach for additional grammar instruction and practice.

► PRACTICE

Leveling EACH Activity

Easy Activities 6, 7
Average Activities 8, 9, 10

Activities ⑥–⑩ It is suggested that you go over these activities orally in class before assigning them as homework.

Carreras This **Carrera** section is useful for students who like to write and may be considering a career in advertising.

CULTURA

Manny Díaz, el alcalde de Miami, da una entrevista a un ancla latina.

Carreras

¿Te interesaría tratar de identificar a los consumidores que necesitarían o comprarían cierto producto? Si contestas que sí, es posible que una carrera en marketing te interese. Y una función importante del marketing es la publicidad y la promoción, porque es necesario convencer a los consumidores (al mercado) que deben comprar cierto producto. ¿Te gusta escribir un mensaje en pocas palabras—un mensaje interesante que atrae mucha atención? Si tienes tal talento, debes considerar una carrera en la publicidad. Y como el mercado hispanohablante es tan grande, el español te puede ayudar.

Práctica

HABLAR

⑥ Personaliza. Da respuestas personales.

1. ¿Cuáles son los vegetales y frutas que te gustan?
2. ¿Cuáles son los deportes que te gustan?
3. ¿Cuáles son los cursos que te interesan?

LEER • ESCRIBIR

⑦ Completa.

1. _____ guerra es una cosa horrible.
2. _____ periodistas trabajan para un periódico y _____ anclas para emisoras de televisión.
3. _____ tigres y _____ leones son animales salvajes pero _____ perros y _____ gatos son animales domésticos.
4. A _____ niños les gusta _____ leche. _____ leche y _____ legumbres son buenas para la salud.
5. _____ verano es mi estación favorita pero mi amiga prefiere _____ primavera.

LEER • HABLAR • ESCRIBIR

⑧ Completa con el artículo cuando necesario.

—Buenos días. ¿Está ___1___ doctor Salas, por favor?
—Sí, ___2___ señora. ¿De parte de quién?
—De parte de ___3___ señora Ochoa.
—Un momentito, ___4___ Señora Ochoa. ___5___ doctor Salas estará con usted en un momento.
—Buenos días, ___6___ Doctor Salas.

HABLAR • ESCRIBIR

⑨ Contesta.

1. ¿Qué días de la semana tienes clases?
2. ¿Cuál es tu día favorito?
3. ¿Qué día es hoy?
4. ¿Cuáles son los días laborales, los días que tenemos que trabajar?

HABLAR

⑩ Con un(a) compañero(a) prepara una conversación según el modelo.

MODELO una lata de atún / 10 pesos →
—¿Cuál es el precio del atún?
—10 pesos la lata.

1. una docena de huevos / 1 euro
2. un kilo de tomates / 500 pesos
3. una botella de agua mineral / 3 quetzales
4. un frasco de mayonesa / 50 pesos

Answers

⑥ *Answers will vary.*

⑦
1. La
2. Los/Las, los/las
3. Los, los, los, los
4. los, la, La, las, Las
5. El, la

⑧
1. el 3. la 5. El
2. –   4. –   6. –

⑨
1. Tengo clases el ___, el ___, etc.
2. Mi día favorito es ___.
3. Hoy es ___.
4. Los días laborales son ___.

⑩
1. ¿Cuál es el precio de los huevos? / 1 euro la docena.
2. ¿Cuál es el precio de los tomates? / 500 pesos el kilo.
3. ¿Cuál es el precio del agua mineral? / 3 quetzales la botella.
4. ¿Cuál es el precio de la mayonesa? / 50 pesos el frasco.

Uso especial del artículo indefinido

1. In Spanish, unlike English, the indefinite article is omitted after the verb **ser** when the noun that follows is not modified.

> **La señora Dávila es periodista.**
> **Don Luis es profesor.**

2. The indefinite article is used, however, in the same way as in English if the noun is modified.

> **Sandra Cisneros es una autora conocida.**
> **Es una autora que ha tenido mucha fama.**
> **Es una autora de mucho renombre.**

Práctica

HABLAR

 Contesta.

1. ¿Es profesor el señor Gómez?
2. ¿Es un profesor bueno?
3. ¿Era poeta García Lorca?
4. ¿Era un poeta famoso?
5. ¿Es artista Isabel?
6. ¿Es una artista que ha tenido exposiciones de sus cuadros?

LEER • ESCRIBIR

 Completa con el artículo indefinido cuando necesario.

1. El señor Fernández es _____ periodista.
2. El señor Fernández es _____ periodista conocido que escribe para el *Miami Herald*.
3. Carlos es _____ alumno que estudia mucho.
4. El señor López es _____ cocinero.
5. Es _____ cocinero excelente.

CULTURA

La famosa escritora latina Sandra Cisneros da una conferencia durante un festival de libros en Los Ángeles.

Comunicación

 Trabaja con un(a) compañero(a) de clase. Cada uno(a) pensará en una persona que conoce. Dirá qué es y luego dará uno o más detalles. Túrnense. Pueden usar las siguientes palabras.

profesor(a)	**actor, actriz**	**médico(a)**	**dentista**
futbolista	**periodista**	**beisbolista**	**ancla**
artista	**escritor(a)**		

Resources

- Audio Activities TE, page 8.18
- Audio CD 8, Track 11
- Workbook, page 8.7
- Quiz 3, page 8.33
- *ExamView® Assessment Suite*

Quick Start

Use QS Transparency 8.4 or write the following on the board.

Da la palabra apropiada.

1. jugador de fútbol
2. cuida a los enfermos
3. enseña
4. pinta cuadros
5. escribe para el periódico
6. toca instrumentos musicales
7. vende medicamentos

▶ TEACH
Core Instruction

This point is quite easy and should not pose a challenge to most students.

▶ PRACTICE

Leveling EACH Activity

Easy Activities 11, 12
Average Activity 13

Activities 12 **and** 13 It is suggested that you go over these activities once in class and then have students write them.

▶ ASSESS

Students are now ready to take Quiz 3 on page 8.33 of the TeacherTools booklet. If you prefer to create your own quiz, use the *ExamView® Assessment Suite*.

Answers

 11

1. Sí (No), el señor Gómez (no) es profesor.
2. Sí, (No, no) es un profesor bueno.
3. Sí, García Lorca era poeta.
4. Sí, era un poeta famoso.
5. Sí (No), Isabel (no) es artista.
6. Sí, (No, no) es una artista que ha tenido exposiciones de sus cuadros.

12

1. –
2. un
3. un
4. –
5. un

13 *Answers will vary.*

▶ TEACH
Core Instruction

This is another grammar point that, once briefly explained to students, should be reinforced through substantial practice in order to develop their "ear" for its use. The more students hear and use it, the better they will understand and know it.

★ Tips for Success ·······

You may wish to review all of the ordinal numbers. Students have learned them all, but not in a consecutive list. Remind students that only **primero** and **tercero** are shortened.

primero, segundo, tercero, cuarto, quinto, sexto, séptimo, octavo, noveno, décimo

▶ PRACTICE

Leveling EACH Activity

Easy Activity 14
Average Activities 15, 16

📰 Learning from Realia

(page 248) Have students look at these postcards displaying the names of two U.S. cities. Ask them to explain how the grammar point taught on this page is demonstrated.

248

Adjetivos apocopados

1. Several adjectives in Spanish have a shortened form when they precede a singular masculine noun. The **-o** ending is dropped.

bueno	El Universal es un **buen** periódico. Es un periódico bueno.
malo	No es un **mal** periódico. No es un periódico malo.
primero	No estamos en el **primer** semestre. Estamos en el segundo.
tercero	Estamos en el **tercer** año de español.

2. Alguno and **ninguno** also drop the **-o** before a masculine singular noun.

Algún día lo vamos a saber.
No hay **ningún** problema.

3. Ciento is shortened to **cien** before a masculine or a feminine noun.

Hay más de **cien** periódicos y **cien** emisoras en español.

4. Grande becomes **gran** when it precedes a singular masculine or feminine noun. The form **gran** conveys the meaning of *great* or *famous.* **Grande** after the noun almost always means *big* or *large.*

una **gran** mujer y un **gran** hombre

5. Santo becomes **San** before a masculine saint's name unless the name begins with **To-** or **Do-**.

San Pedro	**Santo Domingo**	**Santa María**
San Diego	**Santo Tomás**	**Santa Teresa**

Práctica

HABLAR
14 Contesta.

1. En tu opinión, ¿cuál es un buen canal de televisión donde tú vives?
2. ¿Conoces una buena emisora en español?
3. En tu opinión, ¿cuál es un buen periódico y cuál es una buena revista?
4. ¿Fue Cervantes un gran autor?
5. ¿Es *El Quijote* una gran novela?

248 *doscientos cuarenta y ocho* CAPÍTULO 8

Answers

14

1. En mi opinión, un buen canal de televisión donde vivo es ____.
2. Sí, (No, no) conozco una buena emisora en español.
3. En mi opinión, un buen periódico es ____ y una buena revista es ____.
4. Sí, Cervantes fue un gran autor.
5. Sí, *El Quijote* es una gran novela.
6. Sí, el español es el primer idioma de muchos latinos en Estados Unidos.
7. Sí, San Diego es una ciudad en California.
8. Sí, Santo Domingo es la capital de la República Dominicana.

6. ¿Es el español el primer idioma de muchos latinos en Estados Unidos?
7. ¿Es San Diego una ciudad en California?
8. ¿Es Santo Domingo la capital de la República Dominicana?

LEER • ESCRIBIR

 Completa con la forma apropiada del adjetivo.

1. **primero**
   Es la _____ vez que el equipo gana el _____ partido.
2. **tercero**
   Tienes que doblar a la derecha en la _____ bocacalle y el edificio que buscas es el _____ edificio a mano izquierda.
3. **grande**
   Nueva York es una _____ ciudad y es también una ciudad _____.
4. **alguno, ninguno**
   ¡Ojalá que _____ día él no tenga _____ problema!
5. **ciento**
   La novela tiene más de _____ páginas pero no tiene _____ capítulos.
6. **malo**
   Es una _____ situación. Él ha invertido mucho dinero en un _____ negocio.
7. **ninguno**
   Desgraciadamente él no tiene _____ experiencia.

Conexiones

La geografía

 Da la información.

1. la capital de Puerto Rico
2. la capital de El Salvador
3. la capital de Costa Rica
4. la capital de la República Dominicana
5. tres ciudades de California que llevan los nombres de santos

Refrán

Can you guess what the following proverb means?

Aunque duela, salga la muela.

¡Bravo!

You have now learned all the new vocabulary and grammar in this chapter. Continue to use and practice all that you know while learning more cultural information. ¡Vamos!

Answers

⑮
1. primera, primer
2. tercera, tercer
3. gran, grande
4. algún, ningún
5. cien, cien
6. mala, mal
7. ninguna

⑯
1. San Juan
2. San Salvador
3. San José
4. Santo Domingo
5. *Answers will vary but may include:*
   San Diego, San Francisco, San José, Santa Mónica, San Bernardino, San Luis Obispo, San Clemente, San Fernando, Santa Bárbara, San Juan Capistrano, Santa Ana

---

Gramática

Activity ⑮ This activity can be done as a complete class activity calling on students at random to respond.

Activity ⑯ It is suggested that you go over this activity once orally and then have students write it for homework.

Differentiation

Slower Paced Learners
You may wish to review words such as **el programa, el diagrama, el drama, el sistema, el poema, el planeta.**

Advanced Learners
Have advanced learners make up original sentences using adjectives in the apocopated form.

▶ ASSESS

Students are now ready to take Quiz 4 on page 8.34 of the TeacherTools booklet. If you prefer to create your own quiz, use the *ExamView® Assessment Suite.*

Refrán

Have students recite the proverb aloud. Then see if they can figure out its meaning, and encourage them to try to give an equivalent expression in English such as "No pain, no gain."

¡Bravo!
The remaining pages of the chapter recycle information in a variety of ways, allowing students to build upon their newly acquired language skills as well as to keep track of their own progress. This format also ensures that students are not surprised by vocabulary or grammar that has not yet been introduced or studied.

Resources

- Audio Activities TE, pages 8.18–8.19
- Audio CD 8, Tracks 12–13

▶ TEACH

Core Instruction

Step 1 Have students close their books and listen to the conversation using Audio CD 8.

Step 2 Call on two students to read the conversation aloud using as much intonation as possible.

Step 3 Go over the ¿Comprendes? activities.

Differentiation

Multiple Intelligences

You may wish to invite **verbal-linguistic** learners to read the conversation aloud with as much expression as possible. Then call on **bodily-kinesthetic** learners to act out the conversation for the class. They do not have to recite it from memory. Encourage them to ad-lib and say anything that makes sense.

No new material is used in the **Conversación** in order not to confuse students. The **Conversación** recombines only the vocabulary and grammar that students have already learned to understand and manipulate. This conversation reintroduces the grammar presented in this chapter five times.

250 *doscientos cincuenta*   CAPÍTULO 8

¿Comprendes?

A Prepara una lista de tipos de emisiones televisivas.

B Explica.
Explica lo que son Univisión y Telemundo.

C Contesta según la información en la conversación.
1. ¿Qué está aumentando en los medios en Estados Unidos?
2. ¿Por qué están invirtiendo dinero en la publicidad en español muchas compañías estadounidenses?
3. ¿Por qué es interesante que una ciudad como Washington, D.C., tenga unos veinticuatro periódicos publicados en español?

D Resumiendo En tus propias palabras resume toda la información sobre los medios en español.

E ¡En tu tiempo libre!
Como hay tantas emisoras de televisión y radio en español aquí en Estados Unidos tienes una oportunidad de practicar tu español y divertirte al mismo tiempo. Escucha un programa de radio en español o mira un programa de televisión. Luego dile a la clase lo que oíste o viste. ¿Qué tipo de programa fue? ¿Te gustó? ¿Lo entendiste fácilmente?

Comunidades

¿Hay emisoras de televisión hispanas donde vives? ¿Cuántas? ¿Cuáles son? ¿Hay periódicos o revistas en español? ¿Cuáles?

◀ Publicidad en español en la ciudad de Chicago

▶ PRACTICE

¿Comprendes?

A and **C** Have students prepare these activities before going over them in class.
B Have students answer without previous preparation.
D Have students speak on their own without preparing. If a student begins to get flustered, let another student continue.

Comunicación

Interpersonal
Have students work in pairs and tell each other if they watch TV often or not. If so, have them tell the names of their favorite programs.

Pre-AP Listening to this conversation on audio CD will help students develop the skills that they need to be successful on the listening portion of the AP exam.

Answers

A *Answers will vary but may include:*
noticieros, debates, telenovelas, filmes, juegos infantiles, emisiones deportivas

B
Univisión y Telemundo son dos emisoras de televisión latinos.

C
1. El número de emisoras que emiten en español está aumentando en Estados Unidos.
2. Muchas compañías estadounidenses están invirtiendo dinero en la publicidad en español porque quieren que sus productos lleguen al enorme mercado latino.
3. Es interesante porque Washington, D.C., no se considera una ciudad con una gran población hispana.

D *Answers will vary.*

E *Answers will vary.*

Resources

- Audio Activities TE, pages 8.19–8.22
- Audio CD 8, Tracks 14–15

▶ TEACH
Core Instruction

Step 1 To prepare students for the reading, discuss the **Antes de leer** questions in class.

Step 2 Have students listen to the reading on Audio CD 8 or follow along in their books as you read to them. Or, you may prefer to have students take turns reading aloud.

Step 3 Ask students the Reading Check questions after each corresponding section.

Step 4 Have students do the **¿Comprendes?** activities on page 255.

Teaching Options

- You may also wish to have the entire class read all of the **Lectura** or you may wish to divide it into logical parts, assigning each part to a different group. Each group will report to the others concerning what they learned. Logical divisions are: **Los mexicanoamericanos, Los puertorriqueños, Los cubanoamericanos,** and **Los nuevos inmigrantes.**

- You may wish to occasionally have students paraphrase some expressions or sentences from the **Lectura.** Some examples are: **salió victorioso en una guerra → ganó una guerra; como consecuencia → por consiguiente; España**

Antes de leer

Antes de leer esta lectura, piensa en tus antepasados y contesta las siguientes preguntas: ¿De dónde vinieron tus antepasados? ¿De qué país inmigraron? ¿Cuándo? ¿Por qué?

✓ **Reading Check**

¿Dónde establecieron colonias los españoles?

CULTURA

Las calles Diez y Once en el centro de Los Ángeles

✓ **Reading Check**

¿Cuáles son los diferentes grupos de mexicanoamericanos?

Latinos en Estados Unidos 🎧 ♻

Todo el mundo sabe que los españoles exploraron y colonizaron la mayor parte de Centroamérica y Sudamérica. Menos conocido es el hecho de que los españoles también exploraron y colonizaron gran parte de la América del Norte. En 1512 Juan Ponce de León, el gobernador de Puerto Rico, llegó a la Florida. Poco después Lucas Vázquez de Ayllón fundó una colonia en la Carolina del Sur mientras Álvaro Núñez Cabeza de Vaca exploraba todo el sudoeste desde Tampa, Florida, hasta el golfo de California.

También vinieron sacerdotes que establecieron misiones que a través de los años dieron sus nombres a pueblos y ciudades como San Antonio, Santa Fe, San Diego y tantas más. Los españoles llegaron a lo que hoy es Estados Unidos mucho antes de que los ingleses fundaran su primera colonia en Jamestown en 1607. Hubo otra ola de inmigración española en 1936 cuando estalló la horrible Guerra Civil española.

Los mexicanoamericanos Ya sabemos que el grupo más grande de latinos o hispanos en Estados Unidos son los mexicanoamericanos. Viven en todas partes del país aunque se concentran en los estados del suroeste entre Texas y California—territorio que una vez fue mexicano. Muchos de ellos nacieron allí antes de que el territorio pasara a manos de Estados Unidos. Luego, después de la Revolución mexicana hubo otra ola de inmigración de gente que salía de México por razones políticas y económicas. Hoy también vienen muchos mexicanos en busca de trabajo con la esperanza de lograr una vida mejor para sus familias.

Entre los inmigrantes más recientes hay quienes que no se consideran formalmente mexicanoamericanos porque en muchos casos no se establecen permanentemente en Estados Unidos. Dentro de la comunidad mexicanoamericana hay una gran diversidad social, económica, lingüística y política. Una gran mayoría de los mexicanoamericanos mantienen elementos de la cultura mexicana y la lengua española. Se sienten participantes en dos culturas igualmente importantes—la mexicana y la estadounidense.

252 *doscientos cincuenta y dos*

CAPÍTULO 8

cedió Puerto Rico a Estados Unidos → España dio Puerto Rico a Estados Unidos; otorgándoles a los puertorriqueños → dándoles a los puertorriqueños; la gran migración no se realizó hasta → la gran migración no tuvo lugar (no fue) hasta; el mayor motivo → el motivo principal (más importante); la mayoría → la mayor parte; se establecieron → se instalaron; en zonas → en regiones.

Los puertorriqueños En 1899 Estados Unidos salió victorioso en una guerra con España. Como consecuencia de esta guerra Cuba ganó su independencia y España cedió Puerto Rico a Estados Unidos. En 1917 el presidente Woodrow Wilson firmó el *Jones Act* otorgándoles a los puertorriqueños la ciudadanía estadounidense. Puerto Rico sigue siendo un Estado Asociado[1] de Estados Unidos. La gran migración hacia el «continente» no se realizó hasta después de la Segunda Guerra mundial. El mayor motivo por esta migración fue económico. Muchos puertorriqueños salieron de su querida Isla del Encanto en busca de trabajo. La mayoría de ellos se establecieron en el nordeste, sobre todo en zonas urbanas de Nueva York y Nueva Jersey. Mucha gente de ascendencia puertorriqueña sigue viviendo en el nordeste pero hoy en día están en todas partes con comunidades bastante numerosas en Illinois, Texas y la Florida.

[1]Estado Asociado   *Commonwealth*

VIDEO To learn about a Latino tradition in the United States, watch **Cultura en vivo.**

✓ **Reading Check**

¿Por qué son ciudadanos de Estados Unidos los puertorriqueños?

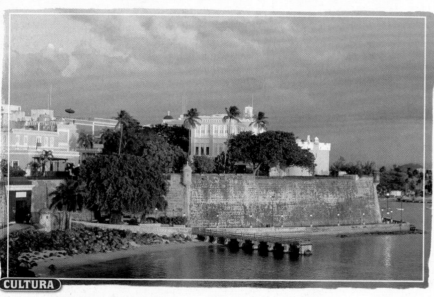

CULTURA
El Morro en San Juan de Puerto Rico

Heritage Speakers

As you go over each section of the **Lectura,** have any heritage speakers who belong to the cultural group being discussed relate some of their own experiences to the class.

GLENCOE 🔍 **Technology**

Video in the Classroom

Cultura en vivo In this episode, students will attend a **quinceañera.** Ask them if their families have any comparable coming-of-age celebrations.

Cultural Snapshot

(page 253) El Morro, built by the Spaniards as a fortress, surrounds almost all of Old San Juan. The section seen here was the original gateway to the city, and the beautiful building is the governor's mansion.

GLENCOE 🔍 **Technology**

Online Learning in the Classroom

You may wish to have students use QuickPass code ASD7844c8 to develop their reading comprehension and writing skills. Students will be able to take a self-check quiz, which includes an essay.

253

GeoVistas

Have students turn to pages SH54–SH55 and look at the map of the United States. Have students locate the states mentioned in this **Lectura** and ask them why they think these places have such large Latino populations. Then have students read the material and look at the photos on these pages. You may wish to ask questions such as: ¿Cuáles son los eventos u ocasiones de los desfiles que se ven en las fotos?

LECTURA CULTURAL

Los cubanoamericanos Desde 1868 ha habido colonias cubanas en Estados Unidos. En ese año Vicente Martínez Ybor trasladó su fábrica de tabacos de La Habana a Cabo Cayo, *Key West* en inglés. Poco después otros tabaqueros lo siguieron y se establecieron en Tampa en un barrio que todavía hoy se llama Ybor City. Pero la gran migración de los cubanos empezó en 1959 cuando los guerrilleros bajo Fidel Castro dieron fin a la dictadura de Fulgencio Batista y establecieron en Cuba un gobierno marxista. Muchos cubanos, sobre todo los más acomodados, decidieron abandonar su patria y tomar el duro camino del exilio. Muchos de ellos se dirigieron a Nueva Jersey y la Florida. Aún hoy muchas partes de la ciudad de Miami siguen siendo otra versión de La Habana.

Reading Check
¿Tuvieron motivos diferentes los cubanos que se establecieron en Tampa en el siglo diecinueve que los cubanos que vinieron en los años sesenta del siglo pasado?

Los nuevos inmigrantes Sigue llegando gente de muchas partes de Latinoamérica añadiendo a la población latina o hispana de este país. Dentro de poco los dominicanos van a sobrepasar la población puertorriqueña en la Ciudad de Nueva York.

La mayoría de los recién llegados—dominicanos, colombianos, ecuatorianos, venezolanos, centroamericanos—vienen por motivos económicos o políticos. A causa de una serie de guerras y conflictos, muchos nicaragüenses, guatemaltecos y salvadoreños han tenido que tomar el camino del exilio.

La comunidad latina de Estados Unidos es una vasta comunidad heterogénea que ha contribuido y sigue contribuyendo con su arte, su talento y su sabor al bienestar y al progreso de la nación entera.

GeoVistas
To learn more about Latinos in the United States, take a tour on pages SH54–SH55.

Reading Check
¿A qué contribuye la comunidad latina?

CULTURA
Desfile en la avenida de las Américas en Nueva York para celebrar el Día de la Independencia de la República Dominicana

Answers

A *Answers will vary.*

B

1. El grupo mayoritario de latinos en Estados Unidos son los mexicanoamericanos.
2. Viven en todas partes del país pero se concentran en los estados del suroeste entre Texas y California.
3. Muchos de ellos nacieron allí (en el suroeste) antes de que el territorio pasara a manos de Estados Unidos.
4. Hubo otra gran ola de inmigración mexicana después de la Revolución mexicana.
5. Entre los inmigrantes más recientes de México hay unos que no se consideran mexicanoamericanos porque en muchos casos no se establecen permanentemente en Estados Unidos.

¿Comprendes?

A Resumiendo En tus propias palabras resume la información histórica sobre los españoles en la América del Norte.

B Recordando hechos Contesta.
1. ¿Cuál es el grupo mayoritario de latinos en Estados Unidos?
2. ¿Dónde viven?
3. ¿Dónde nacieron muchos de ellos?
4. ¿Cuándo hubo otra gran ola de inmigración mexicana?
5. Entre los inmigrantes más recientes de México, ¿por qué hay unos que no se consideran mexicanoamericanos?

C Explicando Explica.
1. como es que los puertorriqueños son ciudadanos estadounidenses
2. por qué había grandes migraciones de puertorriqueños hacia el «continente»
3. donde se establecieron la mayoría de los puertorriqueños
4. cuando empezó la gran migración de cubanos a Estados Unidos y por qué
5. de donde vienen los nuevos inmigrantes
6. las razones por las cuales los nuevos inmigrantes deciden venir a Estados Unidos

Más práctica
Workbook, pp. 8.8–8.9
StudentWorks™ Plus

Conexiones

El inglés
¿Cuáles son algunas palabras que se usan en inglés que son de origen español? Y, ¿cuáles son algunos lugares geográficos en Estados Unidos que tienen nombres españoles? Presenta tu información a la clase.

CULTURA Un restaurante latino en Hialeah, Florida

LATINOS EN ESTADOS UNIDOS

doscientos cincuenta y cinco **255**

Lectura

▶ PRACTICE
¿Comprendes?
A Students can also write their summary.
B You may wish to do this as a factual recall activity or allow students to look up the answers.
C All of the items in this activity can serve as topics for classroom discussion.

Pre-AP This cultural reading will develop the skills that students need to be successful on the reading and writing sections of the AP exam. Listening to this reading will also help prepare them for the auditory component.

Conexiones
Have students give answers to the questions in the **Conexiones** box on page 255 of the Student Edition.

Answers

C
1. Los puertorriqueños son ciudadanos estadounidenses porque después de la guerra en 1899 España cedió Puerto Rico a Estados Unidos y en 1917 el presidente Wilson firmó el *Jones Act* otorgándoles a los puertorriqueños la ciudadanía estadounidense.
2. Había grandes migraciones de puertorriqueños hacia el «continente» porque muchos puertorriqueños salieron de Puerto Rico en busca de trabajo.
3. La mayoría de los puertorriqueños se establecieron en el nordeste, sobre todo en zonas urbanas de Nueva York y Nueva Jersey.
4. La gran migración de los cubanos empezó en 1959 cuando los guerrilleros bajo Fidel Castro dieron fin a la dictadura de Fulgencio Batista y establecieron en Cuba un gobierno marxista.
5. Los nuevos inmigrantes vienen de muchas partes de Latinoamérica.
6. Los nuevos inmigrantes deciden venir a Estados Unidos por motivos económicos o políticos.

255

A Julia de Burgos

de Julia de Burgos

Resources

- Audio Activities TE, pages 8.23–8.24
- Audio CD 8, Track 16
- Literature Test, page 8.51
- *ExamView® Assessment Suite*

Preview

Starting in Chapter 3, each chapter of ¡**Así se dice!** Level 3 has a literary section. Most literary selections are by well-known Latin American or Spanish writers. Some selections are poetry and others are prose.

It is up to the discretion of the teacher if you wish to do all or any of these literary works. The difficulty level of each selection is also indicated from 1 to 4. 1 is difficult; 4 is quite easy.

Difficulty Level
2

Vocabulario

▶ TEACH

Core Instruction

Step 1 Call on students to read the new words and their definitions.

Step 2 Assign the **Práctica** activity.

Differentiation

Advanced Learners

Call on advanced learners to use the new words in original sentences.

▶ PRACTICE

It is suggested that you have students prepare this activity before going over it in class.

▲ Universidad de Puerto Rico en Río Piedras

Vocabulario

el amo dueño, propietario

el corazón órgano vital que impulsa la sangre

el cura sacerdote

la cifra número, dígito

mentir no decir la verdad, decir mentiras

olfatear percibir olores y aromas

alzarse levantarse

Práctica

Completa con una palabra apropiada.

1. _____ bendice a los que asisten a Misa.
2. El número 10 es una _____ y el número 5 es otra.
3. _____ es un órgano musculoso. Es también un órgano vital.
4. Te voy a decir la verdad. Te prometo que no voy a _____.
5. Yo no sé quién es el _____ del negocio.
6. Ella _____ antes de empezar a hablar a su público.

 Cultural Snapshot

(page 256) The prestigious Universidad de Puerto Rico has two major campuses: one in Río Piedras in San Juan and the other in Mayagüez on the east coast.

Answers

1. El cura
2. cifra
3. El corazón
4. mentir
5. amo
6. se alza (se alzó)

INTRODUCCIÓN

Julia de Burgos era poeta, dramaturga y educadora puertorriqueña. Era también feminista y una activista política. Nació en Carolina, Puerto Rico, en 1914. Era de una familia grande y pobre pero sus padres insistieron en que sus hijos recibieran una educación buena. Desde niña Julia mostró una gran inteligencia. Ella estudió en la Universidad de Puerto Rico donde recibió el Certificado de Maestra.

Mientras ejercía su profesión de maestra primaria, se dedicaba también a la poesía. En 1940 ella fue a Nueva York donde dio recitales de sus poesías a los puertorriqueños que residían en esta gran ciudad. Salió de Estados Unidos y fue a vivir en Cuba donde continuó a dedicarse a la poesía. En Cuba se descubrió que sufría de cáncer, lo que afectó negativamente a su producción literaria.

Dejó Cuba y se estableció una vez más en Nueva York. Además de sufrir de un cáncer mortífero tuvo una vida turbulenta—varios matrimonios fracasados, problemas psicológicos y una adicción al alcohol. Falleció (murió) trágicamente en Nueva York en 1953 a los 39 años.

CULTURA

Mural de Julia de Burgos en el barrio de East Harlem en la Ciudad de Nueva York

CULTURA

Capitolio Nacional en La Habana, Cuba

Estrategia

Hojeando Antes de leer este poema, dale una ojeada, o sea, léelo rápidamente. Fíjate en el título y determina a quién le estará hablando el poeta. Después de hojearlo, reflexiona sobre su mensaje principal. Luego léelo de nuevo prestando atención a todos los detalles.

Introducción

You may wish to intersperse comprehension questions about the life of Julia de Burgos—a life that was quite sad and tragic.

▶ TEACH
Core Instruction

Step 1 Have students read the **Estrategia**.

Step 2 Then have them scan the poem, trying to get as much meaning as possible.

Teaching Options

Because of the difficulty level of this selection, you may wish to skip it with slower paced learners.

▶ TEACH
Core Instruction

Step 1 Have students look at the sidenotes before they read the poem again.

Step 2 You may also want to have students look at the **¿Comprendes?** activities before studying the poem in depth. It will help them look for important details.

Step 3 It is suggested that you call on a student to read an **estrofa** with as much expression as possible. Then discuss each **estrofa**.

Teaching Options

In order to aid student comprehension, you may wish to ask them the following questions in English and have them respond in Spanish.

How does Julia de Burgos say the following?
1. You are cold and false.
2. but I spill out my heart
3. You are a **señora** who puts on airs.
4. I am a real woman.
5. You use makeup.
6. I don't use makeup. I'm natural.
7. You are submissive and have restraints.
8. I am as free as can be.

Antes de leer

Basado en lo que sabes de la vida de Julia de Burgos, piensa en lo que serían sus reacciones ante las injusticias e hipocresías sociales.

Durante la lectura

Presta atención al tono del poema. ¿Qué emociones te sientes? ¿Qué dice la poeta de las mujeres?

Después de leer

Reflexiona sobre el «tú» y el «yo» en el poema. ¿A cuál te simpatizas más?

¹se tiende *spreads out*
²muñeca *doll*
³destello *sparkle*
⁴miel *honey*
⁵te rizas *curl*
⁶casera *homemaker*
⁷atada a los prejuicios *tied to the prejudices*
⁸desbocado *runaway*
⁹alhajas *jewels*
¹⁰clavada *stuck*
¹¹duelo *sorrow, grief*
¹²alborotadas *excited, noisy*
¹³cenizas *ashes*
¹⁴tea *torch*
¹⁵pecados *sins*

258

A Julia de Burgos 🎧

Ya las gentes murmuran que yo soy tu enemiga
porque dicen que en verso doy al mundo mi yo.
Mienten, Julia de Burgos. Mienten, Julia de Burgos.
La que se alza en mis versos no es tu voz: es mi voz
5   porque tú eres ropaje y la esencia soy yo;
y el más profundo abismo se tiende¹ entre las dos.

Tú eres fría muñeca² de mentira social,
y yo, viril destello³ de la humana verdad.
Tú, miel⁴ de cortesanas hipocresías; yo no;
10   que en todos mis poemas desnudo el corazón.

Tú eres como tu mundo, egoísta; yo no;
que en todo me lo juego a ser lo que soy yo.
Tú eres solo la grave señora señorona; yo no,
yo soy la vida, la fuerza, la mujer.

15   Tú eres de tu marido, de tu amo; yo no;
yo de nadie, o de todos, porque a todos, a
todos en mi limpio sentir y en mi pensar me doy.
Tú te rizas⁵ el pelo y te pintas; yo no;
a mí me riza el viento, a mí me pinta el sol.

20   Tú eres dama casera⁶, resignada, sumisa,
atada a los prejuicios⁷ de los hombres; yo no;
que yo soy Rocinante corriendo desbocado⁸
olfateando horizontes de justicia de Dios.

Tú en ti misma no mandas;
25   a ti todos te mandan; en ti mandan tu esposo, tus
padres, tus parientes, el cura, el modista,
el teatro, el casino, el auto, las alhajas⁹,
el banquete, el champán, el cielo
y el infierno, y el que dirán social.
30   En mí no, que en mí manda mi solo corazón,
mi solo pensamiento; quien manda en mí soy yo.

Tú, flor de aristocracia; y yo, la flor del pueblo.
Tú en ti lo tienes todo y a todos se lo debes,
mientras que yo, mi nada a nadie se la debo.
35   Tú, clavada¹⁰ al estático dividendo ancestral,
y yo, un uno en la cifra del divisor social
somos el duelo¹¹ a muerte que se acerca fatal.

Cuando las multitudes corran alborotadas¹²
dejando atrás cenizas¹³ de injusticias quemadas,
40   y cuando con la tea¹⁴ de las siete virtudes,
tras los siete pecados¹⁵, corran las multitudes,
contra ti, y contra todo lo injusto y lo inhumano,
yo iré en medio de ellas con la tea en la mano.

Answers

 A
1. Está hablando de sí misma.
2. la mentira social, miel de cortesanas hipocresías, egoísta, Tú te rizas el pelo y te pintas, flor de aristocracia
3. Dice que es la escencia, el viril destello de la humana verdad, que desnuda el corazón, que no es egoísta, es la vida, la fuerza, la mujer.
4. Se refiere a lo que dicen los otros (lo que dice la sociedad) de ella.

B *Answers will vary but may include:*
1. «Ropaje» simboliza las cosas que los otros ven, o sea, el personaje que la autora le presenta al público; «esencia» simboliza lo que los otros no ven, o sea, como realmente es ella.
2. Simboliza el control que exige la sociedad (el público) en ella.
3. Simboliza la persona que verdaderamente es ella pero la que no ve el público.
4. Simboliza la sinceridad con que escribe.

5. Simboliza las esfuerzas que hace para presentarse bien al público aunque realmente prefiere ser más natural.
6. Simboliza las esfuerzas que hace para presentarse bien al público aunque realmente prefiere ser más natural.
7. Simboliza que ella no se controla sino que los otros la controlan.
8. Simboliza que es su corazón que la controla.

¿Comprendes?

A **Analizando** Contesta.

1. Cuando Julia de Burgos escribe, ¿de quién está hablando en sus versos? ¿De sí misma o de otras?
2. ¿Qué alusiones hace la autora a la hipocresía y falsedad de la sociedad?
3. ¿Cómo expresa Julia de Burgos que ella nunca es hipócrita?
4. ¿A qué se refiere la poeta al decir «el que dirán social»?

B **Interpretando** ¿Qué simboliza… ?

1. «ropaje y la esencia»
2. «fría muñeca de mentira social»
3. «destello de la humana verdad»
4. «en todos mis poemas desnudo el corazón»
5. «tú te rizas el pelo… a mí me riza el viento»
6. «te pintas; yo no… a mí me pinta el sol»
7. «tú en ti misma no mandas»
8. «en mí manda mi solo corazón»
9. «tú, flor de aristocracia; y yo; la flor del pueblo»

C **Identificando**

1. Identifica todos los elementos feministas en el poema.
2. Identifica todas las alusiones al esnobismo.

D **Comparando** Compara todas las características del «tú» y del «yo».

E **Criticando** Critica y da tus opiniones sobre la siguiente interpretación del poema. «Es el conflicto entre ‹la mujer interior› libre y ‹la mujer exterior› sujeta a las restricciones y limitaciones sociales».

F **Personalizando** Contesta.

1. ¿Es posible que conozcas a una «tú»? Describe a esa persona.
2. ¿Es posible que conozcas a una «yo»? Describe a esa persona.
3. ¿Qué opiniones tienes de cada una de esas personas?

CULTURA

Una exhibición de cerámicas en la Galería Taller Boricua en el Centro Cultural Julia de Burgos en East Harlem en la Ciudad de Nueva York

Literatura

▶ PRACTICE

¿Comprendes?

A – **F** These activities can serve as interesting class discussions about the poem. You may wish to present these activities as you present each section of the poem. You may also wish to have students write all or some of these activities.

Answers

9. «Flor de aristocracia» simboliza que es muy popular con los ricos y los célebres porque sigue las demandas de la sociedad; «flor del pueblo» simboliza su sencillez y humildad.

C *Answers will vary but may include:*

1. «viril», «en todo me lo juego a ser lo que soy yo», «yo soy la vida, la fuerza», «yo de nadie», «a mí me riza el viento, a mí me pinta el sol», «yo soy Rocinante corriendo desbocado olfateando horizontes de justicia de Dios», «en mi manda mi solo corazón, mi solo pensamiento; quien manda en mí soy yo», «mi nada a nadie se la debo», «un uno en la cifra del divisor social», «contra todo lo injusto y lo inhumano yo iré en medio de ellas con la tea en la mano»

2. «las gentes murmuran», «fría muñeca de mentira social», «miel de cortesanas hipocresías», «egoísta», «Tú te rizas el pelo y te pintas», «el modista», «el teatro», «el casino», «las alhajas», «el banquete», «el champán», «flor de aristocracia», «estático dividendo ancestral»

D *Answers will vary.*

E *Answers will vary.*

F *Answers will vary.*

259

Resources

- Tests, pages 8.43–8.58
- Performance Assessment,
  Task 8, pages 8.59–8.60
- *ExamView® Assessment Suite*

✓ Self-check for achievement

This is a pre-test for students to take before you administer the chapter test. Note that each section is cross-referenced so students can easily find the material they feel they need to review. You may wish to use Self-Check Worksheet Transparency SC8 to have students complete this assessment in class or at home. You can correct the assessment yourself, or you may prefer to project the answers on the overhead in class using Self-Check Answers Transparency SC8A.

Differentiation

Slower Paced Learners

Have students work in pairs to complete the Self-Check in class. Once they have finished, call on individuals to give the correct answers as you review together.

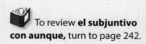 To review **Vocabulario,** turn to pages 238–239.

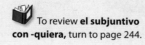 To review **el subjuntivo con aunque,** turn to page 242.

To review **el subjuntivo con -quiera,** turn to page 244.

Vocabulario

1 **Da una palabra relacionada.**
1. conquistar
2. emitir
3. guerrero
4. cómodo
5. ojo

2 **Da la palabra cuya definición sigue.**
6. un cura
7. dar, conceder
8. considerar, tomar en consideración
9. famoso
10. el que escribe para un periódico
11. los que luchan en una guerra
12. el que da o anuncia las noticias en la televisión
13. exceder
14. llegar a saber
15. tomar el poder
16. lo que interrumpe los programas de televisión

Gramática

3 **Escribe una sola frase con aunque.**
17. Van a salir. Y está lloviendo.
18. Van a salir. Y parece que va a llover.
19. El lo terminará. Y sabemos que va a ser difícil.
20. Él lo terminará. No se sabe si será difícil o no.
21. El profesor enseñará. Y no le pagan bien.
22. El profesor enseñará. Y parece que no van a pagarle bien.

4 **Completa.**
23–24. Quienquiera que _____ (ser) (tú) y adondequiera que _____ (ir), date cuenta de las consecuencias de tus acciones.

260 *doscientos sesenta*

CAPÍTULO 8

Answers

1
1. la conquista (el conquistador)
2. la emisora (la emisión)
3. la guerra
4. acomodado(a)
5. una ojeada

2
6. un sacerdote
7. otorgar
8. tomar en cuenta
9. ilustre
10. el periodista
11. los soldados
12. el ancla
13. sobrepasar

14. darse cuenta de
15. apoderarse de
16. la publicidad (la promoción, la propaganda)

3
17. Van a salir aunque está lloviendo.
18. Van a salir aunque llueva.

19. Él lo terminará aunque va a ser difícil.
20. Él lo terminará aunque sea difícil.
21. El profesor enseñará aunque no le pagan bien.
22. El profesor enseñará aunque no le pague bien.

5 Completa con el artículo definido cuando necesario.

25–26. Tenemos clases ____ lunes pero yo no fui a la escuela ____ lunes pasado.

27. ____ profesor González es un profesor excelente.

28. Buenos días, ____ Doctora Amaral.

29. ____ paciencia es una virtud.

30. Los tomates están a cincuenta ____ kilo.

31–32. En algunos calendarios ____ domingo es el primer día de la semana y en otros ____ lunes es el primer día de la semana.

6 Escribe cada frase de nuevo añadiendo los detalles adicionales.

33. Ella es escritora. (buena y famosa)

34. Don José es periodista. (que escribe para el *Miami Herald*)

35. El doctor García es médico. (en el Hospital Metropolitano)

7 Completa con la forma apropiada del adjetivo.

36. Es un ____ canal de televisión. (bueno)

37. Hay más de ____ páginas en este libro. (ciento)

Cultura

8 ¿Sí o no?

38. Muchos mexicanoamericanos nacieron en tierra que una vez fue territorio mexicano.

39. Después de la guerra, en 1899, Cuba cedió Puerto Rico a Estados Unidos.

40. La gran migración de cubanoamericanos tuvo lugar después de la derrota del dictador Fulgencio Batista cuando Fidel Castro estableció un gobierno marxista.

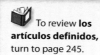

To review **los artículos definidos,** turn to page 245.

To review **los artículos indefinidos,** turn to page 247.

To review **los adjetivos apocopados,** turn to page 248.

To review this cultural information, turn to pages 252–254.

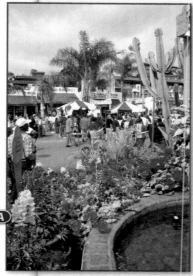

CULTURA
Celebración para el Cinco de Mayo en Old Town Historic State Park en San Diego, California

Prepárate para el examen

Differentiation

Slower Paced Learners

Encourage students who need extra help to refer to the book icons and review any section before answering the questions.

Pre-AP Students preparing for the AP exam may benefit from a set time limit when completing this Self-Check. This may also help to identify students with learning difficulties or slower paced students who need extra help.

GLENCOE Technology

Online Learning in the Classroom

You may wish to have students use QuickPass code ASD7844c8 for additional test preparation. They will be able to complete a self-check quiz for chapter review.

LATINOS EN ESTADOS UNIDOS

doscientos sesenta y uno **261**

Answers

4
23. seas
24. vayas

5
25. los
26. el
27. El
28. –
29. La
30. el
31. –
32. –

6
33. Ella es una escritora buena y famosa.
34. Don José es un periodista que escribe para el *Miami Herald*.
35. El doctor García es un médico en el Hospital Metropolitano.

7
36. buen
37. cien

8
38. sí
39. no
40. sí

Tips for Success ·······

Encourage students to say as much as possible when they do these open-ended activities. Tell them not to be afraid to make mistakes, since the goal of the activities is real-life communication. If someone in the group makes an error, allow the others to politely correct him or her. Let students choose the activities they would like to do.

Tell students to feel free to elaborate on the basic theme and to be creative. They may use props, pictures, or posters if they wish.

··

Pre-AP These oral activities will give students the opportunity to develop and improve their speaking skills so that they may succeed on the speaking portion of the AP exam.

Note: You may want to use the rubric below to help students prepare their speaking activities.

Prepárate para el examen ✓
Practice for oral proficiency

1 Comunidades
✓ *Interview Latinos in your community*

Trabajen en grupos pequeños. Van a hacer una encuesta. Entrevisten a alumnos en la escuela o a personas que viven en su ciudad o pueblo. Si hay muchos latinos en su comunidad determinen de dónde son. Organicen los resultados de su encuesta y preparen una tabla indicando el número de habitantes de cada grupo—desde el más numeroso hasta el menos numeroso. Si no hay latinos en la comunidad, identifiquen otros grupos étnicos que viven en la comunidad.

CULTURA

Residentes de un barrio latino en Chicago llamado el «Pueblo Pequeño» mirando el desfile para celebrar el Día de la Independencia mexicana

2 Nuestros antepasados
✓ *Discuss your ancestors*

En grupos pequeños, hablen de donde vienen o de donde vinieron sus antepasados. Si posible, discutan los motivos que tenían los que emigraron a Estados Unidos. ¿Tenían muchos los mismos motivos?

3 Costumbres y tradiciones latinas
✓ *Interview Latino students about their customs and traditions*

Si hay alumnos latinos en la clase de español o en la escuela, habla con ellos de sus costumbres y tradiciones ¿Tienen todos las mismas costumbres y tradiciones o son diferentes aunque todos son latinos?

4 No me importa. Lo voy a hacer.
✓ *Talk about what you will do even if it is difficult*

Eres una persona que persevera mucho. Eres tenaz. Di todo lo que vas a hacer aunque pase algo que haga difícil lo que quieres hacer.

Scoring Rubric for Speaking

	4	3	2	1
vocabulary	extensive use of vocabulary, including idiomatic expressions	adequate use of vocabulary and idiomatic expressions	limited vocabulary marked with some anglicisms	limited vocabulary marked by frequent anglicisms that force interpretation by the listener
grammar	few or no grammatical errors	minor grammatical errors	some serious grammatical errors	serious grammatical errors
pronunciation	good intonation and largely accurate pronunciation with slight accent	acceptable intonation and pronunciation with distinctive accent	errors in intonation and pronunciation with heavy accent	errors in intonation and pronunciation that interfere with listener's comprehension
content	thorough response with interesting and pertinent detail	thorough response with sufficient detail	some detail, but not sufficient	general, insufficient response

Tarea

Write a biographical sketch of a famous Hispanic American who is no longer living. Your biography should include important data that will provide the reader with a snapshot of the person's life and an overview of his or her contributions to society (why he or she is considered a famous historical figure).

Writing Strategy

Biography Writing a biographical sketch involves presenting information about a person's life in a clear, concise, and orderly fashion. Although it is necessary to remain objective when telling another's life story, it is also important to carefully select the facts that you wish to present, because a biography is not just a summary of an individual's life but also a celebration of his or her life accomplishments.

❶ Prewrite

As you begin compiling data, arrange the information in chronological order. It may also be helpful to research the person's life in terms of distinct phases or stages, such as birth, childhood, youth, marriage, parenthood, old age, and death.

You may wish to use the following graphic timeline to organize your information and ideas.

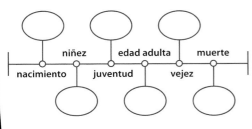

niñez   edad adulta   muerte

nacimiento   juventud   vejez

- You should also think about ways to incorporate **aunque** with the subjunctive and/or indicative, as well as the subjunctive with **-quiera,** into your writing.
- Before you begin your biographical sketch, try to estimate how many paragraphs you are going to write and which information you are going to include in each one.

❷ Write

- As you compose your biographical sketch, be sure to structure your writing in a logical fashion. Use transitions to ensure that your writing flows smoothly.
- Be cautious not to plagiarize or copy information word-for-word. You should cite any sources used.
- Do not attempt to translate from English to Spanish.
- Don't be afraid to use the dictionary, but at the same time, don't overuse it. Whenever possible, stick to vocabulary and grammar that you already know.
- After you finish the rough draft, revise it and write the final version. Double check for any unnecessary errors or avoidable mistakes.

Evaluate

Your teacher will evaluate you based on proper use of vocabulary, correct spelling and grammar, logical structure, and completeness and appropriateness of information.

Pre-AP This **tarea** will give students the opportunity to develop and improve their writing skills so that they may succeed on the writing portion of the AP exam.

Note: You may want to use the rubric below to help students prepare their writing task.

Scoring Rubric for Writing

	4	3	2	1
vocabulary	precise, varied	functional, fails to communicate complete meaning	limited to basic words, often inaccurate	inadequate
grammar	excellent, very few or no errors	some errors, do not hinder communication	numerous errors interfere with communication	many errors, little sentence structure
content	thorough response to the topic	generally thorough response to the topic	partial response to the topic	insufficient response to the topic
organization	well organized, ideas presented clearly and logically	loosely organized, but main ideas present	some attempts at organization, but with confused sequencing	lack of organization

Repaso del Capítulo 8

Resources

■ Audio Activities TE, pages 8.24–8.26
◠ Audio CD 8, Tracks 17–18
■ Workbook, page 8.10

Grammar Review

This page provides a quick "at a glance" summary of the grammar points students have learned in this chapter. The corresponding page numbers are also listed so that students can easily find each grammar point as it was presented.

Differentiation

Multiple Intelligences

You may want to call on **verbal-linguistic** and **logical-mathematical** learners for whom grammar often comes easily to explain the main concepts to their classmates in their own words. Having students explain the concepts in different ways may also help slower paced learners or students with learning difficulties.

Gramática

- ### El subjuntivo con aunque *(page 242)*

  The conjunction **aunque** *(although)* may be followed by the subjunctive or the indicative depending upon the meaning of the sentence.

Ellos van a salir aunque llueva.	*They are going out even though it may rain.*
Ellos van a salir aunque llueve.	*They are going out even though it is raining.*

- ### El subjuntivo con -quiera *(page 244)*

  Many words are made indefinite by adding **-quiera**. Such words are followed by the subjunctive. **Quiera** is the same as the *ever* in *whoever, wherever.*

quienquiera	cuandoquiera	dondequiera
comoquiera	cualquiera	adondequiera

  Quienquiera que sea, no nos podrá resolver el problema.

- ### Usos especiales del artículo definido *(page 245)*

  The definite article must be used with all general or abstract nouns, with a title (except in direct address), with quantities, and with days of the week to express the meaning *on.*

La leche es buena para la salud.	*Milk is good for the health.*
La doctora González es dentista.	*Dr. González is a dentist.*
El biftec está a 900 pesos el kilo.	*Steak is 900 pesos a kilo.*
Él sale el sábado.	*He leaves on Saturday.*
Ella trabaja los viernes.	*She works on Fridays.*

- ### Uso especial del artículo indefinido *(page 247)*

  The indefinite article is omitted after the verb **ser** when the noun that follows is not modified. The indefinite article is used if the noun is modified.

  La señora Dávila es periodista.
  Sandra Cisneros es una autora conocida.

- ### Adjetivos apocopados *(page 248)*

  Some adjectives in Spanish have a shortened form when they precede a singular masculine noun.

un buen libro	**el tercer mes**

  Some adjectives have a shortened form when they precede a masculine or feminine noun.

una gran mujer	**cien personas**

▲ La leche es importante para los niños, como vemos en este envase de leche en Guadalajara, México.

uego There are a number of cognates in this list. See how many you and a partner can find. Who can find the most? Compare your list with those of your classmates.

Vocabulario

Talking about the Spanish conquest of the Americas

el sacerdote	la colonia	la lucha, la batalla	luchar
el conquistador	la guerra	colonial	colonizar
la conquista	el soldado	conquistar	establecer
el colonizador			

Talking about the news media

los medios de comunicación	el ancla, el/la noticiero(a)	la prensa	el artículo
la emisora de televisión	el canal, la cadena	el periódico	el/la radio
	las noticias	el titular	emitir
la emisión televisiva, el programa de televisión	la publicidad, la propaganda, la promoción	la revista	
		el/la periodista	
		el reportaje	

Other useful words and expressions

una ojeada	acomodado(a)	sobrepasar	otorgar
el libro de bolsillo	ilustre	tomar en cuenta	invertir
la empresa, la compañía	apoderarse de	lograr	
	darse cuenta de		

 The words listed below come from this chapter's literary selection, *A Julia de Burgos.* They were selected to become part of your active vocabulary because of their relatively high frequency.

el amo	la cifra	olfatear
el corazón	mentir	alzarse
el cura		

Repaso del Capítulo ⑧

Vocabulary Review

The words and phrases in the **Vocabulario** section have been taught for productive use in this chapter. They are summarized here as a resource for both student and teacher. This list also serves as a convenient resource for the **Prepárate para el examen** activities on pages 260–263.

GLENCOE SPANISH

Why It Works!

This vocabulary reference list has not been translated into English for two reasons. First, it is recommended that students learn the new vocabulary through direct association with images on the **Vocabulario** pages. Second, all vocabulary is reintroduced in the chapter many times, and upon completion of the chapter students should be familiar with the meaning of all the words. If there are words that students still do not know, they can refer back to the vocabulary presentation in the chapter or the dictionary at the end of the book. If, however, it is your preference to give students the English translations, please refer to Vocabulary Transparency V8.1 or to the Chapter 8 PowerPoint® presentation on PowerTeach.

Don't forget the chapter project and cultural activities found on pages 234C–234D. Students have learned all the information that they will need to complete these engaging enrichment tasks.

 uego The cognates in this list are: **el conquistador, la conquista, el colonizador, la colonia, el soldado, la batalla, colonial, conquistar, colonizar, los medios de comunicación, la televisión, televisiva, el programa, el canal, la publicidad, la promoción, el artículo, el/la radio, la compañía.**

Every chapter of ¡Así se dice! contains this review section of previously learned material. By recycling information from previous chapters, the cumulative review serves to remind students that they need to continue practicing what they have learned after finishing each chapter.

Activity 1 This activity reviews past, present, and future verb tenses. See pages R7, R17, R19, R29, R31, R43–R44.

🎧 **Audio Script** *(CD 8, Track 19)*
1. El tren salió a las ocho.
2. Los invitados van a llegar a las ocho.
3. ¿Te levantas a la misma hora cada día?
4. Durante los inviernos, Adela iba a las montañas a esquiar, pero yo trabajaba.
5. ¿Por qué dijiste tal cosa?
6. Los mozos ayudaron a los pasajeros con su equipaje.
7. Este fin de semana, vamos a la playa donde tomaremos el sol y nadaremos.
8. Mis hermanos fueron al parque ayer para jugar al fútbol con sus amigos.
9. El año que viene iremos a Salamanca para estudiar allí.
10. Todos los alumnos entraban en clase a las ocho.

Activity 2 This activity reviews the uses of the imperfect versus the preterite. See pages R29, R31, R43–R44, R54.

Activity 3 This activity reviews the imperfect. See pages R43–R44.

Repaso cumulativo
Repasa lo que ya has aprendido

These activities will help you review and remember what you have learned so far in Spanish.

 1 Escucha las frases. Indica en una tabla como la de abajo si la acción de cada frase tiene lugar en el pasado, el presente o el futuro.

pasado	presente	futuro

 2 Completa con la forma apropiada del pretérito o del imperfecto.
1. Él _____ a México el año pasado. (ir)
2. Él _____ a México cada año. (ir)
3. Ella me lo _____ solo una vez. (decir)
4. Ella siempre _____ la misma cosa. (decir)
5. Ellos nos _____ muy a menudo. (visitar)
6. Ellos nos _____ el enero pasado. (visitar)
7. Yo lo _____ ayer. (ver)
8. Yo lo _____ con frecuencia. (ver)

3 Escribe las siguientes frases en el pasado.
1. Hace muy buen tiempo.
2. El sol brilla en el cielo.
3. Todos están contentos.
4. El bebé tiene solo dos meses.
5. Es adorable.
6. Tiene ojos grandes y una sonrisa adorable.

CULTURA
Una plaza en Guadalajara, México

Answers

1
1. pasado
2. futuro
3. presente
4. pasado
5. pasado
6. pasado
7. futuro
8. pasado
9. futuro
10. pasado

2
1. fue
2. iba
3. dijo
4. decía
5. visitaban
6. visitaron
7. vi
8. veía

3
1. Hacía muy buen tiempo.
2. El sol brillaba en el cielo.
3. Todos estaban contentos.
4. El bebé tenía solo dos meses.
5. Era adorable.
6. Tenía ojos grandes y una sonrisa adorable.

Repaso cumulativo

 4 Completa en el pasado.

1. Yo _____ con José cuando tú me _____. (hablar, interrumpir)
2. Él _____ sus tareas cuando yo _____. (hacer, salir)
3. Ellos _____ en México cuando _____ la noticia. (estar, recibir)
4. Yo _____ durmiendo cuando _____ mi móvil. (estar, sonar)
5. ¿Qué _____ tú cuando ellos _____? (hacer, llegar)

5 Da el artículo definido apropiado.

1. _____ mano
2. _____ mapa
3. _____ planeta
4. _____ tierra
5. _____ clase
6. _____ arma
7. _____ armas
8. _____ dramas
9. _____ agua
10. _____ águilas

6 Trabaja con un(a) compañero(a). Inventen una conversación basada en los dibujos.

LATINOS EN ESTADOS UNIDOS

doscientos sesenta y siete **267**

Activity 4 This activity reviews using the preterite and imperfect tenses in the same sentence. See pages R29, R31, R43–R44, R54.

Activity 5 This activity reviews agreement of nouns and definite articles. See page SR13.

Activity 6 This activity reviews vocabulary related to the beach. See page R24.

Pre-AP To give students further open-ended oral or written practice, or to assess proficiency, go to AP Proficiency Practice Transparency AP11.

GLENCOE Technology

Audio in the Classroom
The ¡Así se dice! Audio Program for Chapter 8 has 19 activities, which afford students extensive listening and speaking practice.

Online Learning in the Classroom
You may wish to have students use QuickPass code ASD7844c8 for additional cumulative review. They will be able to complete a self-check quiz.

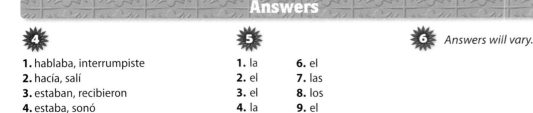

Answers

4
1. hablaba, interrumpiste
2. hacía, salí
3. estaban, recibieron
4. estaba, sonó
5. hacías, llegaron

5
1. la
2. el
3. el
4. la
5. la
6. el
7. las
8. los
9. el
10. las

6 *Answers will vary.*

267

Chapter Overview
Historia de la comida latina

● Scope and Sequence

Topics
- Food and food preparation
- History of food

Culture
- Various foods popular throughout Spain and Latin America
- Arabic influence in Latin cuisine
- *Oda a la alcachofa* by Pablo Neruda

Functions
- How to identify more foods
- How to describe food preparation
- How to discuss the history of foods from Europe and the Americas
- How to read a poem by the Chilean poet Pablo Neruda

Structure
- The passive voice
- Relative pronouns
- Expressions of time with **hace** and **hacía**

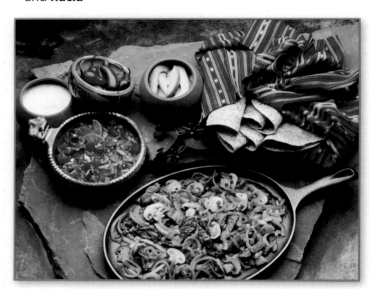

● Planning Guide

	required	recommended	optional
Vocabulario *(pages 272–275)* Más legumbres y hortalizas La carne Las especias	✓		
Gramática *(pages 276–281)* La voz pasiva Los pronombres relativos Expresiones de tiempo con **hace** y **hacía**	✓		
Conversación *(pages 282–283)* ¡¿Los tomates son venenosos?!		✓	
Lectura cultural *(pages 284–287)* Historia de la comida		✓	
Literatura *(pages 288–291)* *Oda a la alcachofa*			✓
Prepárate para el examen *(pages 292–295)*			✓
Repaso cumulativo *(pages 298–299)*			✓

Correlations to National Foreign Language Standards

Page numbers in light print refer to the Student Edition.	Page numbers in bold print refer to the Teacher Edition.
Communication Standard 1.1 Interpersonal	pp. **270–271, 281, 286, 291,** 294
Communication Standard 1.2 Interpretive	pp. **272, 273,** 274, **274, 275, 276,** 277, **278, 280, 282,** 283, 284, **284,** 285, 286, 287, 289, **289,** 290, 291, 293, **293,** 294, 298, **299**
Communication Standard 1.3 Presentational	pp. **268C, 272, 273,** 275, **277, 281, 284, 285, 287, 288,** 290, **291, 292,** 293, **293,** 295, **296, 297**
Cultures Standard 2.1	pp. **268D,** 279
Cultures Standard 2.2	pp. **268D,** 270–271, **270–271,** 275, **277, 278,** 283, 284–286, **285, 286,** 287, 288, 289, 291, 293, 294, 295
Connections Standard 3.1	pp. **268C, 268D,** 278, **278, 282,** 284–286, **286,** 287, 289
Connections Standard 3.2	pp. 272, **272,** 281, **281,** 283, **286,** 287, 289–290, 291
Comparisons Standard 4.1	pp. **268C,** 276, 278, **279,** 280, **281,** 283, **285, 296,** 297
Comparisons Standard 4.2	pp. **268C, 268D, 269,** 269, **278,** 284–286, 287, 293, 294, 295
Communities Standard 5.1	pp. **268C,** 275, **286, 294,** 295, **296**
Communities Standard 5.2	pp. 272, **272, 273, 286,** 287

To read the ACTFL Standards in their entirety, see the front of the Teacher Edition.

Student Resources

Print

Workbook *(pp. 9.3–9.14)*
Audio Activities *(pp. 9.15–9.18)*
Pre-AP Workbook, Chapter 9

Technology

- StudentWorks™ Plus
- ¡Así se dice! Vocabulario en vivo
- ¡Así se dice! Gramática en vivo
- ¡Así se dice! Diálogo en vivo
- ¡Así se dice! Cultura en vivo
- Vocabulary PuzzleMaker
- **QuickPass** glencoe.com

Teacher Resources

Print

TeacherTools, Chapter 9
   Workbook TE *(pp. 9.3–9.14)*
   Audio Activities TE *(pp. 9.17–9.28)*
   Quizzes 1–5 *(pp. 9.31–9.36)*
   Tests *(pp. 9.38–9.57)*
   Performance Assessment, Task 9 *(pp. 9.59–9.60)*

Technology

- Quick Start Transparencies 9.1–9.4
- Vocabulary Transparencies V9.1–V9.3
- Audio CD 9
- *ExamView® Assessment Suite*
- TeacherWorks™ Plus
- PowerTeach
- ¡Así se dice! Video Program
- Vocabulary PuzzleMaker
- **QuickPass** glencoe.com

Chapter Project

Una cultura plurilingüe

Students will work individually and in small groups to research cultures that speak a Romance language other than Spanish. They will compare their findings to their own and Hispanic culture, and then present their findings and teach some of the language to the class.

1. Divide the class into small groups and assign each group one of the Romance languages to investigate: French, Italian, Latin, Portuguese, and Romanian. Group members will work together to list cooking-related items that they believe are common to their three cultures and assign three of these items to each member.

2. For each assigned item: Students should provide the item's name in English, Spanish, and the third language, find an image of the item, label the image in all three languages, and write three sentences in Spanish based on their cultural research about the item stressing cross-cultural comparisons. Remind students to cite all sources and to always check more than one source to verify that their information is correct.

3. The group will decide how they would like to present their work (poster boards, handouts, computer). Each student will be responsible for project his or her part of the presentation. Students should submit their images and a draft of the text they will use, to be checked or peer edited, then corrected and handed in with the final version.

4. Students should return to their groups in order to put together the final version of their project and plan the presentation they will give to the class.

Expansion: You may wish to have each group prepare a short quiz for their classmates to take after their presentation. The groups' quizzes may then be used as the basis for a test on the information that was presented.

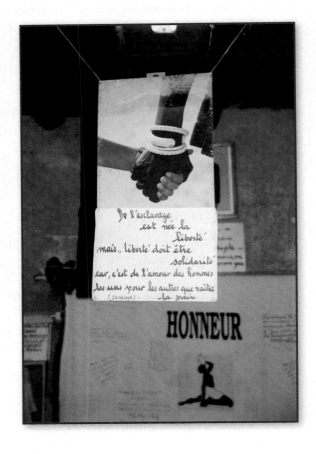

Scoring Rubric for Project

	1	3	5
Evidence of planning	No draft is provided.	Draft is provided but is not corrected.	Corrected draft is provided.
Visual elements	No visual elements are present.	Some visual elements are present.	All visual elements are present.
Presentation	Presentation contains little of the required elements.	Presentation contains some of the required elements.	Presentation contains all the required elements.

Culture

● Cinco de Mayo

It is a common misconception, especially in the United States, that **Cinco de Mayo** is Mexico's Independence Day. An important day in Mexican history, the fifth of May is actually the anniversary of the Battle of Puebla, fought on that day in 1862, between the Mexican militia and the French army for control of Mexico. The Mexican militia at Puebla hoped to hold off the French just long enough for reinforcements to arrive in Mexico City. But the militia was able to do more than that—they defeated the French army, which greatly outnumbered them! The victory was so inspiring that it helped Mexico to eventually defeat the French.

Mexicans celebrate **Cinco de Mayo** with patriotic parades, mock battles, dances, fireworks, music, and food. Most of the celebrations take place in the state of Puebla and Mexico City. Festivities take place elsewhere as well, particularly in areas of the United States with large Mexican American populations. **Cinco de Mayo** is a day to celebrate the heritage, culture, and patriotism of people of Mexican descent. Some feel that the holiday has become over-commercialized. Have students think about ways in which they may have seen **Cinco de Mayo** made more commercial in their own, or other, communities.

● Merengue

Most of the music that has come out of Latin America is music for dancing. **Merengue** is no exception. This particular style of music originated in the Dominican Republic and is considered the national dance music there. In the 1850s, it was sung in rural parts of the country with guitar and hand-percussion accompaniment but was not accepted by the upper class due to its often lewd and vulgar lyrics. In the 1930s, the status of **merengue** was elevated during Rafael Trujillo's presidential campaign, when **merengue** musicians accompanied him while visiting parts of the country. Once he became president, Trujillo continued to integrate **merengue** into the mainstream. Important band leaders were commissioned to write **merengue** songs in honor of Trujillo, and the radio station owned by his brother played **merengue** on air.

The traditional **merengue** band, **conjunto típico,** is made up of an accordion, a **tambora** (two-sided drum), and a **güira** (metal grater). During its rise in popularity, the instruments of the **merengue** band changed slightly to match the contemporary Big Band trend. This **orquesta merengue** added a horn section, piano, timbales, hi-hat, conga, bass, and backup singers. Although various instruments have been added or replaced during its history, the **tambora** and **güira** are the focal instruments that make **merengue** what it is.

50-Minute Lesson Plans

	Objective	Present	Practice	Assess/Homework
Day 1	Talk about food and food preparation	Chapter Opener, pp. 268–269 (5 min.) Introducción al tema, pp. 270–271 (10 min.) Core Instruction/Vocabulario, pp. 272–273 (15 min.)	Activities 1–4, p. 274 (15 min.) InfoGap, p. SR10 (5 min.)	Student Workbook Activities A–D, pp. 9.3–9.4 **QuickPass** Vocabulary Practice
Day 2	Talk about food and food preparation	Quick Start, p. 272 (5 min.) Review Vocabulario, pp. 272–273 (5 min.) Video, Vocabulario en vivo (10 min.)	Activities 5–7, p. 275 (10 min.) Total Physical Response, p. 273 (5 min.) Audio Activities A–C, pp. 9.17–9.18 (15 min.)	Student Workbook Activities E–G, pp. 9.4–9.5 **QuickPass** Vocabulary Practice
Day 3	The passive voice	Quick Start, p. 276 (5 min.) Core Instruction/Gramática, La voz pasiva, p. 276 (10 min.)	Activities 1–4, p. 277 (15 min.) Audio Activities A–D, pp. 9.19–9.20 (10 min.)	Quiz 1, p. 9.31 (10 min.) Student Workbook Activities A–F, pp. 9.5–9.7 **QuickPass** Grammar Practice
Day 4	Relative pronouns	Quick Start, p. 278 (5 min.) Core Instruction/Gramática, Los pronombres relativos, p. 278 (10 min.)	Activities 5–8, p. 279 (15 min.)	Quizzes 2–3, pp. 9.32–9.33 (20 min.) Student Workbook Activities A–B, pp. 9.7–9.8 **QuickPass** Grammar Practice
Day 5	Expressions of time with **hace** and **hacía**	Quick Start, p. 280 (5 min.) Core Instruction/Gramática, Expresiones de tiempo con **hace** y **hacía**, p. 280 (10 min.)	Activities 9–11, pp. 280–281 (15 min.) Audio Activities E–F, p. 9.21 (10 min.)	Quiz 4, p. 9.34 (10 min.) Student Workbook Activities A–B, p. 9.8 **QuickPass** Grammar Practice
Day 6	Develop reading and listening comprehension skills	Core Instruction/Conversación, p. 282 (20 min.)	¿Comprendes? A–D, p. 283 (20 min.)	Quiz 5, p. 9.35 (10 min.) **QuickPass** Conversation
Day 7	Discuss various foods popular throughout Spain and Latin America	Core struction/Lectura cultural, pp. 284–286 (20 min.) Video, Cultura en vivo (5 min.)	¿Comprendes? A–C, p. 287 (10 min.)	Listening Comprehension Test, pp. 9.53–9.54 (15 min.) ¿Comprendes? D–F, p. 287 **QuickPass** Reading Practice
Day 8	Read a poem by the Chilean poet Pablo Neruda	Core Instruction/Literatura, pp. 288–290 (20 min.)	¿Comprendes? A–B, p. 291 (10 min.) Prepárate para el examen, pp. 292–293 (20 min.)	¿Comprendes? C–E, p. 291 Prepárate para el examen, Practice for written proficiency, p. 295 **QuickPass** Reading Practice
Day 9	Chapter review	Repaso del Capítulo 9, pp. 296–297 (15 min.)	Prepárate para el examen, Practice for oral proficiency, p. 294 (20 min.)	Test for Writing Proficiency, p. 9.57 (15 min.) Review for chapter test
Day 10	Chapter 9 Tests (50 min.) Reading and Writing Test, pp. 9.43–9.53 Literature Test, pp. 9.51–9.52 Speaking Test, p. 9.55 Test for Oral Proficiency, p. 9.56			

90-Minute Lesson Plans

	Objective	Present	Practice	Assess/Homework
Block 1	Talk about food and food preparation	Chapter Opener, pp. 268–269 (5 min.) Introducción al tema, pp. 270–271 (10 min.) Quick Start, p. 272 (5 min.) Core Instruction/Vocabulario, pp. 272–273 (15 min.) Video, Vocabulario en vivo (10 min.)	Activities 1–7, pp. 274–275 (20 min.) InfoGap, p. SR10 (5 min.) Total Physical Response, p. 273 (5 min.) Audio Activities A–C, pp. 9.17–9.19 (15 min.)	Student Workbook Activities A–G, pp. 9.3–9.5 **QuickPass** Vocabulary Practice
Block 2	The passive voice Relative pronouns	Quick Start, p. 276 (5 min.) Core Instruction/Gramática, La voz pasiva, p. 276 (15 min.) Core Instruction/Gramática, Los pronombres relativos, p. 278 (15 min.)	Activities 1–4, p. 277 (20 min.) Activities 5–6, p. 279 (10 min.) Audio Activities A–D, pp. 9.19–9.20 (15 min.)	Quiz 1, p. 9.31 (10 min.) Student Workbook Activities A–F, pp. 9.5–9.7 Student Workbook Activities A–B, pp. 9.7–9.8 **QuickPass** Grammar Practice
Block 3	Relative pronouns Expressions of time with **hace** and **hacía**	Quick Start, p. 278 (5 min.) Review Gramática, Los pronombres relativos, p. 278 (10 min.) Quick Start, p. 280 (5 min.) Core Instruction/Gramática, Expresiones de tiempo con **hace** y **hacía,** p. 280 (10 min.)	Activities 7–8, p. 279 (10 min.) Activities 9–11, pp. 280–281 (15 min.) Audio Activities E–F, p. 9.21 (15 min.)	Quizzes 2–3, pp. 9.32–9.33 (20 min.) Student Workbook Activities A–B, p. 9.8 **QuickPass** Grammar Practice
Block 4	Discuss various foods popular throughout Spain and Latin America	Core Instruction/Conversación, p. 282 (20 min.) Core Instruction/Lectura cultural, pp. 284–286 (20 min.) Video, Cultura en vivo (5 min.)	¿Comprendes? A–D, p. 283 (15 min.) ¿Comprendes? A–C, p. 287 (10 min.)	Quizzes 4–5, pp. 9.34–9.35 (20 min.) ¿Comprendes? D–F, p. 287 Prepárate para el examen, Practice for written proficiency, p. 295 **QuickPass** Conversation, Reading Practice
Block 5	Read a poem by the Chilean poet Pablo Neruda	Core Instruction/Literatura, pp. 288–290 (15 min.)	¿Comprendes? A–C, p. 291 (15 min.) Prepárate para el examen, pp. 292–293 (20 min.) Prepárate para el examen, Practice for oral proficiency, p. 294 (25 min.)	Listening Comprehension Test, pp. 9.53–9.54 (15 min.) ¿Comprendes? D–E, p. 291 Review for chapter test **QuickPass** Reading Practice

Block 6	Chapter 9 Tests (50 min.)
	    Reading and Writing Test, pp. 9.43–9.50
	    Literature Test, pp. 9.51–9.52
	    Speaking Test, p. 9.55
	    Test for Oral Proficiency, p. 9.56
	    Test for Writing Proficiency, p. 9.57
	Chapter Project, p. 268C (40 min.)			

Preview

In this chapter, students will identify more foods in Spanish and will be able to talk about food preparation. They will learn about the influences and history of foods from Spain and Latin America—the combination of products indigenous to the Americas and those imported by the Spaniards, including those introduced by the Arabs into Spain. They will also read a poem by the famous Chilean poet Pablo Neruda—*Oda a una alcachofa.* Students will learn the passive voice, relative pronouns, and time expressions with **hace** and **hacía.**

Pacing

It is important to note that once you reach **¡Bravo!** in the chapter, there is no more new material for the students to learn. The rest of the chapter recycles what has already been covered. The suggested pacing listed here leaves two to three days for review, assessment, and enrichment activities such as the chapter project.

Vocabulario	1–2 days
Gramática	2–3 days
Conversación	1 day
Lectura cultural	1 day
Literatura	1 day

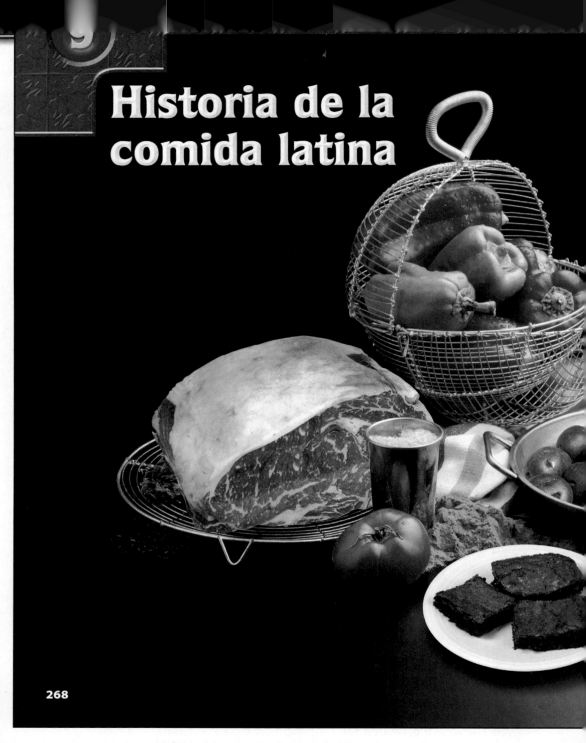

Historia de la comida latina

268

Teacher Works *Plus*

The **¡Así se dice!** TeacherWorks™ Plus CD-ROM is an all-in-one planner and resource center. You may wish to use several of the following features as you plan and present the Chapter 9 material: Interactive Teacher Edition, Interactive Lesson Planner with Calendar, and Point and Click Access to Teaching Resources including Hotlinks to the Internet and Correlations to the National Standards.

Caption: Comestibles—unos tienen su origen en Europa y otros en las Américas.

Aquí y Allí

Vamos a comparar Cuando comemos algo es raro que pensemos en el origen, o sea, en la historia de lo que estamos comiendo. La historia de la comida es muy interesante. Vamos a ver las influencias históricas entre unos platos que se comen en Estados Unidos y en los países hispanos.

Objetivos

You will:

- identify more foods
- describe food preparation
- discuss the history of foods from Europe and the Americas
- read a poem by the famous Chilean poet Pablo Neruda

You will use:

- the passive voice
- relative pronouns
- expressions of time with **hace** and **hacía**

QuickPass

Go to glencoe.com
For: **Online book**
Web code: **ASD7844c9**

CAPÍTULO 9

SPOTLIGHT ON CULTURE

Cultural Comparison
Students will better appreciate foods by learning their origins, history, and influences and by comparing foods they are accustomed to eating with foods popular in Spain and Latin America.

doscientos sesenta y nueve **269**

Quia Interactive Online Student Edition found at quia.com allows students to complete activities online and submit them for computer grading for instant feedback or teacher grading with suggestions for what to review. Students can also record speaking activities, listen to chapter audio, and watch the videos that correspond with each chapter. As a teacher you are able to create rosters, set grading parameters, and post assignments for each class. After students complete activities, you can view the results and recommend remediation or review. You can also add your own customized activities for additional student practice.

269

Introduce the theme of the chapter by having students look at the photographs on these pages. Lead a discussion about the foods seen here. Have students brainstorm about the origins of some of these foods. Then ask them to name some famous Hispanic dishes. Once you have completed the vocabulary presentation, have students return to these pages and read the information that accompanies each photograph. Later, when students are fully acquainted with the vocabulary and grammar of the chapter, you may wish to come back to these pages and ask the questions that go with each photo.

Cultural Snapshot

Guatemala *(page 270)* Guatemala is known for its delicious tropical fruits. Today Guatemala also produces a wide variety of vegetables that are for sale in U.S. stores. **¿Qué está vendiendo este señor? ¿Qué es un mango? ¿Dónde se cultivan los mangos?**

España *(page 270 top)* The **alcachofa** was introduced into Spain by the Arabs. A popular dish in Spain is **alcachofas salteadas,** artichoke hearts sautéed in garlic and olive oil. **¿Qué tipo de legumbre es la alcachofa? ¿Cómo son sus hojas? ¿Cuál es el origen de la palabra** *alcachofa*? **¿Quiénes introdujeron la alcachofa en España?**

Introducción al tema
Historia de la comida latina

El tema de este capítulo, «La historia de la comida», tiene unos hechos interesantes y sorprendentes. Mira estas fotos y adivina si sabes dónde tienen su origen estos comestibles.

▲ **Guatemala** Este señor está vendiendo mangos, una deliciosa fruta que se cultiva en muchas regiones tropicales de las Américas.

◀ **España** La alcachofa es una legumbre verde. Tiene hojas, algunas de ellas espinosas. La palabra «alcachofa», como casi todas las palabras que empiezan en al-, es del árabe. Los árabes introdujeron las alcachofas en España.

España Los olivares de Andalucía producen muchas olivas o aceitunas de que se produce el famoso aceite español. ▼

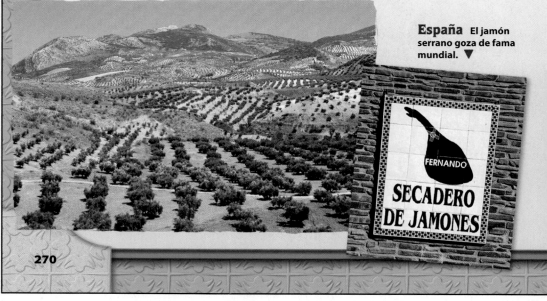

España El jamón serrano goza de fama mundial. ▼

FERNANDO
SECADERO DE JAMONES

270

España *(page 270 bottom)* Spain is one of the world's largest producers of olive oil. Olive oil is used in the preparation of many dishes. The cured hams, particularly **el jamón serrano,** are delicious and preferred by many. **¿Qué producen los olivares? ¿Están en Andalucía estos olivares? ¿Qué se produce de las aceitunas u olivas?**

▲ **Perú** Aquí vemos un campo de maíz en la región de Arequipa. Como se ve, el maíz no es siempre amarillo. Un campo de maíz en México y Centroamérica es «una milpa». ¿Crees que se come más maíz en las Américas o en Europa?

▲ **Perú** Estas papas de varios colores están en un supermercado de Estados Unidos pero vienen de Perú. ¿Sabes quiénes son los primeros cultivadores de papas?

◀ **Venezuela** La familia está disfrutando de un bufé grande que tiene una selección variada de comida de muchas influencias.

Ecuador Los tomates, como vas a aprender, tienen una historia muy interesante. Los tomates, igual que las habichuelas o los frijoles que se ven aquí, se cultivan en Ecuador. La agricultura es una industria importante del país. ▼

Perú *(page 271 left)* Potatoes of many colors have been cultivated in Peru since long before the arrival of the Spaniards. Potato is a staple in the high Andean regions and **chuño** is a form of treated potato that is frozen in the ground and baked by the sun. **¿Se venden papas peruanas en los supermercados de Estados Unidos? ¿Quiénes eran los primeros cultivadores de las papas?**

Perú *(page 271 right)* **¿Tiene varios colores el maíz? ¿Hay muchos granos de maíz en una mazorca? ¿Qué es una milpa? ¿Dónde? ¿Dónde se come más maíz?**

Venezuela *(page 271)* **¿Qué es un bufé?**

Ecuador *(page 271)* Many Latin American countries, including Ecuador, have economies based very much on agriculture. Produce from all over Latin America is readily available throughout the United States. **¿Dónde se cultivan estos tomates, habichuelas o frijoles? ¿Son hortalizas los tomates? ¿Qué son?**

Vocabulario

presentación

VIDEO To practice your new words, watch **Vocabulario en vivo.**

Quick Start

Use QS Transparency 9.1 or write the following on the board.

Da a lo menos tres de cada uno de los siguientes.

frutas vegetales carnes condimentos

▶ TEACH
Core Instruction

Step 1 You may wish to use suggestions given in previous chapters for the presentation of the words and sentences.

Step 2 When presenting the vocabulary, intersperse questions such as: **¿Se corta la berenjena en rodizas? ¿Se rebozan las rodajas? ¿Se rebozan en huevo batido y pan rallado? ¿Se fríen las rodajas en una sartén? ¿Se fríen en aceite de oliva? ¿En qué se corta le berenjena?**

Teaching Options

There are many single words on this page for students to learn. You may wish to have students merely study them on their own. If, however, there are students in the class who need help with pronunciation, you may want to have them repeat each word after you or Audio CD 9 at least once.

Más legumbres y hortalizas

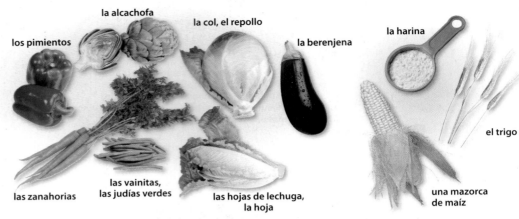

los pimientos
la alcachofa
la col, el repollo
la berenjena
la harina
el trigo
las zanahorias
las vainitas, las judías verdes
las hojas de lechuga, la hoja
una mazorca de maíz

el huerto

En un huerto se cultivan legumbres (hortalizas) o frutas.
Un huerto es más pequeño que una huerta.

la viña
la vid
las uvas

La carne

el cordero
la carne de res
el cerdo

Las especias

el cilantro
el orégano

272

Differentiation

Multiple Intelligences

Logical-mathematical learners, as well as others, may benefit from putting all the foods they remember in Spanish into a chart divided by categories. You could turn this into a game with a set time period to see who can name the most foods.

GLENCOE 🖱 Technology

Video in the Classroom

Vocabulario en vivo Watch and listen to Nora as she shops at a market to prepare for a special meal.

la rodaja

el huevo batido

el pan rallado

Se rebozan las rodajas de berenjena en huevo batido y pan rallado.

el/la sartén

Después se fríen en una sartén con aceite de oliva.

El que prepara la comida o cocina es el cocinero.
El cocinero que elabora algo delicioso debe estar muy orgulloso.

la olla

Se hierve el arroz en una olla.

Los comensales son los que se sientan a la mesa para comer juntos.

el picadillo, la carne picada

Se rellenan los pimientos de carne picada.

273

Total Physical Response (TPR)

(Student), **ven acá, por favor.**
Me vas a indicar como haces las siguientes cosas.
Cultivas un huerto.
Elaboras una comida.
Cortas algo.
Cortas una berenjena en rodazas.
Miras las rodajas.

Bates un huevo.
Rebozas las rodajas de berenjena en huevo batido y pan rallado.
Pones les rodajas en una sartén.
Fríes las berenjenas.
Rellenas una olla de agua.
Hierves el agua.
Picas la carne.
Rellenas un pimiento de carne picada.

PRACTICE

Leveling EACH Activity

Easy Activities 1, 2, 3, 6
Average Activities 4, 5, 7

Activity ❶
🎧 Audio Script
1. el lugar donde se cultivan o plantan legumbres o frutas
2. la carne de una oveja
3. una legumbre de color de naranja
4. una legumbre que puede ser de color verde, rojo, amarillo o naranja
5. el lugar donde hay muchas vides que producen uvas
6. los que se sientan a la mesa para comer juntos
7. un vegetal u hortaliza verde que tiene hojas
8. una hierba aromática que sirve de condimento

Activity ❷ It is suggested you do this activity as an oral activity with books closed calling on students at random.

Differentiation
Advanced Learners
You may wish to have advanced learners use each word or expression in Activity 3 in an original sentence.

Teaching Options
Another way to reinforce new vocabulary is to use the photographs as a springboard for asking questions that require students to answer with their new words. For example, for the photograph on page 274, ask: **¿De qué están rellenas las enchiladas? Y, ¿de qué están cubiertas? (cebolla picada y cilantro)**

QuickPass
Go to glencoe.com
For: **Vocabulary practice**
Web code: **ASD7844c9**

ESCUCHAR
❶ Escoge la palabra apropiada del banco de palabras.

la zanahoria	el pimiento	la lechuga
el huerto	la especia	el cordero
la viña	los comensales	

HABLAR
❷ Contesta.
1. ¿Se puede cultivar frutas y vegetales en un huerto?
2. ¿Qué fruta producen las vides en una viña?
3. ¿Es la manzana una fruta tropical o no?
4. El cilantro es una hierba que se usa mucho en la cocina latina. ¿Conoces el cilantro? ¿Te gusta su sabor?
5. ¿Pones orégano en tu pizza?
6. ¿Se puede rebozar muchos mariscos y pescados en pan rallado antes de freírlos?

CULTURA
Una enchilada de carne y una enchilada de queso

LEER • ESCRIBIR
❸ Da otra palabra.
1. las vainitas
2. las legumbres
3. preparar la comida
4. el biftec
5. la carne picada

LEER • ESCRIBIR
❹ Completa con una palabra apropiada.
1. _____ es el producto que resulta del trigo molido (ground).
2. _____ y _____ son especias.
3. Se corta la berenjena en _____ antes de freírla.
4. Se reboza la berenjena en _____ y _____ antes de freírla.
5. Se _____ los pimientos de carne picada o de queso.

InfoGap For more practice using your new vocabulary, do Activity 9 on page SR10 at the end of this book.

Answers

❶
1. el huerto
2. el cordero
3. la zanahoria
4. el pimiento
5. la viña
6. los comensales
7. la lechuga
8. la especia

❷
1. Sí, se puede cultivar frutas y vegetales en un huerto.
2. Producen uvas.
3. No, la manzana no es una fruta tropical.
4. Sí, (No, no) conozco el cilantro. Sí, (No, no) me gusta su sabor.
5. Sí, (No, no) pongo orégano en mi pizza.
6. Sí, se puede rebozar muchos mariscos y legumbres en pan rallado antes de freírlos.

❸
1. las judías verdes
2. las hortalizas
3. cocinar
4. la carne de res
5. el picadillo

❹
1. La harina
2. El orégano, el cilantro

LEER • ESCRIBIR

5 Corrige la información falsa.
   1. Se hierve el agua en una sartén.
   2. Los que preparan la comida son los camareros.
   3. Los que comen juntos son los meseros.
   4. El que elabora algo que sale riquísimo (delicioso) debe estar deprimido.
   5. Una huerta es más pequeña que un huerto.

CULTURA
Se sirve muy buena pizza en este restaurante de Buenos Aires.

6 Rompecabezas

Trata de identificar tantos comestibles que puedas usando las letras en la frase siguiente. Puedes usar la misma letra más de una vez. Compara tu lista con las de tus compañeros.

¡Vamos al Restaurante Valladolid para cenar!

✿ Comunidades

7 Si hay unos alumnos latinos en la clase de español o algunos latinos que viven en tu comunidad, pregúntales las palabras que ellos usan para los diferentes comestibles. Los nombres cambian mucho de una región a otra. Aquí tienes solo un ejemplo: **judías verdes, ejotes, vainitas, habichuelas y chauchas.**

HISTORIA DE LA COMIDA LATINA

doscientos setenta y cinco **275**

FOLDABLES®
Study Organizer

SINGLE PICTURE FRAME
See page SH27 for help with making this foldable. Use this study organizer to practice talking about food with a partner. Draw a picture of a meal that includes some of the ingredients and foods you just learned about. Pass the foldable to your partner who will identify the ingredients of the meal and explain how they are prepared. Take turns.

Vocabulario

Answers

3. rodajas
4. huevo batido, pan rallado
5. rellenan

5
1. Se hierve el agua en una olla.
2. Los que preparan la comida son los cocineros.
3. Los que comen juntos son los comensales.
4. El que elabora algo que sale riquísimo (delicioso) debe estar orgulloso.

5. Un huerto es más pequeño que una huerta.

6 *Answers will vary but may include:* uvas, pan rallado, carne de res, cilantro, col, repollo, cordero, cerdo, mariscos, salsa, pollo, oliva, aceite, cilantro, especias.

7 *Answers will vary.*

QuickPass

Go to glencoe.com
For: Grammar practice
Web code: ASD7844c9

Resources

- Audio Activities TE, pages 9.19–9.20
- Audio CD 9, Tracks 4–7
- Workbook, pages 9.5–9.7
- Quiz 3, page 9.33
- ExamView® Assessment Suite

 Quick Start

Use QS Transparency 9.2 or write the following on the board.

Completa con el adjetivo de nacionalidad.

1. paella ___ (valenciano)
2. aceite ___ (español)
3. comida ___ (español)
4. pizza ___ (italiano)
5. vegetales ___ (japonés)
6. salchicha ___ (alemán)
7. salsa ___ (mexicano)

▶ **TEACH**

Core Instruction

Step 1 As you contrast the active and passive voice, call on some students to give additional examples in English.

Step 2 This **se** construction is a review since it was taught in Level 2.

Step 3 It is up to the discretion of the teacher to what degree you wish to emphasize the true passive. Since it is not frequently used, you may wish to present it more for recognition than for production.

¿Te acuerdas?

You have already learned the **se** construction to express the passive voice.

CULTURA

Se venden periódicos de todas partes del mundo hispano en este quiosco en la Ciudad de México.

La voz pasiva

1. The following are examples of sentences in the active and passive voice.

ACTIVE   *The chef prepared the food.*
            The servers served the meal.

PASSIVE   *The food was prepared by the chef.*
             The meal was served by the servers.

Note that the subject in a sentence in the active voice becomes what is called the "agent" (by whom it was done).

2. In Spanish, the passive voice is most frequently expressed by using the pronoun **se**, especially when the agent is not expressed.

Se venden legumbres en la verdulería.
Se vende carne en la carnicería.
Se comen muchos frijoles en México.
Se usa mucho aceite de oliva en España.

3. This **se** construction is also used when the subject is indefinite.

¿Cómo se dice en español?
How does one say it in Spanish?
How is it said in Spanish?

Se habla español en muchos países.
They speak Spanish in many countries.
Spanish is spoken in many countries.

4. The true passive is much less commonly used in Spanish than in English. In Spanish, the active voice is preferred. When used, the true passive is formed by using the verb **ser** and the past participle followed by **por.**

ACTIVE   **Los moros conquistaron España en el siglo ocho.**

PASSIVE   **España fue conquistada por los moros en el siglo ocho.**

5. The true passive is frequently found in a shortened form in headlines.

Casa destruida por huracán
Niño herido en accidente de automóvil

GLENCOE Technology

Online Learning in the Classroom

Have students use QuickPass code ASD7844c9 for additional grammar practice. They can review each grammar point with an eGame. They can also review all grammar points by doing the self-check quiz, which integrates the chapter vocabulary with the new grammar.

GLENCOE Technology

You may wish to use the editable PowerPoint® presentation on PowerTeach for additional grammar instruction and practice.

Práctica

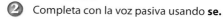
ESCUCHAR • HABLAR

① Contesta.
1. ¿Se abre o se cierra la tienda por la mañana?
2. ¿Qué idioma se habla en México?
3. ¿Se oye mucho español en la ciudad de Miami?
4. ¿Cómo se dice *vegetable* en español?

LEER • ESCRIBIR

② Completa con la voz pasiva usando **se**.
1. _____ vegetales y frutas en un huerto. (cultivar)
2. _____ mucho pescado en las regiones cerca de la costa. (comer)
3. _____ las rodajas de berenjena en huevos batidos y pan rallado. (rebozar)
4. _____ las alcachofas en una olla. (hervir)
5. _____ la carne con arroz y habichuelas. (servir)
6. _____ el bacón en una sartén. (freír)
7. _____ las compras en una bolsa. (poner)
8. _____ pan en la panadería y _____ dulces y tortas en la pastelería. (vender)

HORARIO DE LUNES A VIERNES		
Mañanas	09.30	13.30
Tardes	16.30	20.00
Sábados	10.00	13.00

CULTURA
El horario indica a qué hora se abre y a qué hora se cierra el negocio.

③ **Juego** Trabajando en grupos, hagan tantas frases que puedan con las siguientes expresiones.

se habla   se oye   se come   se dice   se cierra
se escribe   se venden   se abre   se ven

ESCUCHAR • HABLAR • ESCRIBIR

④ Sigue el modelo.

MODELO   La comida fue preparada por el cocinero. →
         El cocinero preparó la comida.

1. España fue conquistada por los árabes.
2. España fue invadida por los árabes en el siglo ocho.
3. Los árabes fueron expulsados por los españoles en el siglo quince.
4. La mayor parte de Latinoamérica fue colonizada por España.
5. La novela fue escrita por Gabriel García Márquez.
6. La cocinera fue admirada por sus clientes.

SE PROHIBE
EJERCER EL COMERCIO EN ESTE LUGAR, LA PERSONA QUE SEA SORPRENDIDA SERA CONSIGNADA A LA AUTORIDAD COMPETENTE

CULTURA
Un aviso fuerte sobre algo que se prohíbe en la Ciudad de México

HISTORIA DE LA COMIDA LATINA   *doscientos setenta y siete*   **277**

Answers

①
1. Se abre la tienda por la mañana.
2. Se habla español en México.
3. Sí, se oye mucho español en la ciudad de Miami.
4. Se dice «legumbre» («hortaliza») en español.

②
1. Se cultivan
2. Se come
3. Se rebozan
4. Se hierven
5. Se sirve
6. Se fríe
7. Se ponen
8. Se vende, se venden

③ *Answers will vary.*

④
1. Los árabes conquistaron España.
2. Los árabes invadieron España en el siglo ocho.
3. Los españoles expulsaron a los árabes en el siglo quince.
4. España colonizó la mayor parte de Latinoamérica.
5. Gabriel García Márquez escribió la novela.
6. Sus clientes admiraron a la cocinera.

Resources

- Audio Activities TE, page 9.21
- Audio CD 9, Track 8
- Workbook, pages 9.7–9.8
- Quiz 4, page 9.34
- ExamView® Assessment Suite

Quick Start

Use QS Transparency 9.3 or write the following on the board.
Escribe una frase con cada expresión.
1. ir al restaurante
2. leer el menú
3. servir
4. pedir la cuenta
5. dejar una propina

▶ TEACH
Core Instruction

Step 1 Read each item to the class and go over it before you move on to the next item.

Step 2 Call on students to read the sample sentences in each item. Be sure to encourage students to ask questions.

Differentiation
Advanced Learners

Ask advanced learners to give additional sentences using relative pronouns and adjectives.

⭐ Tips for Success ·······

- The most important relatives from the viewpoint of usage are the pronoun **lo que** and the adjective **cuyo**. Students should, however, be able to recognize the **el que** forms.

- Have students read the captions that accompany each photo, since they reinforce the new grammatical point.

278

CULTURA

Este joven cuyo padre es dueño de una cafetería en Córdoba, España, está preparando churros.

GeoVistas

To learn more about Mexico, take a tour on pages SH42–SH43.

CULTURA

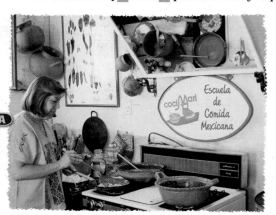

La cocinera María Solarzano es la que tiene una escuela culinaria de cocina tradicional mexicana en San Miguel de Allende.

Los pronombres relativos

1. The pronouns **el que, la que, los que,** and **las que** are equivalent to the English *the one who (that)* or *the ones who (that)*. They can be used as subjects or objects and they can replace either persons or things.

> De todas mis recetas, la que preparo ahora es mi favorita.
> *Of all my recipes, the one I am preparing now is my favorite.*

> De todos mis hermanos, es José el que tiene más talento.
> *Of all my brothers, Joe is the one who has the most talent.*

2. The relative pronoun often introduces a sentence. Note the sequence of tenses in the following sentences.

> El que habla ahora es mi hermano. *(present / present)*
> La que hablará mañana es mi hermana. *(future / present)*
> Los que hablaron ayer fueron mis primos. *(preterite / preterite)*

3. **Lo que** is a neuter relative pronoun that replaces a general or abstract idea rather than a specific antecedent.

> Lo que le hace falta a este plato es más sal.
> *What this dish needs is more salt.*

> No sé lo que están haciendo en la cocina.
> *I don't know what they are doing in the kitchen.*

4. The relative adjective **cuyo** is equivalent to the English *whose*. **Cuyo** agrees with the noun it modifies.

> Es la señora cuyos hijos son los dueños del restaurante.
> El cocinero cuyas recetas prefiero trabaja aquí.

278 *doscientos setenta y ocho* CAPÍTULO 9

📷 Cultural Snapshot

(page 278 top) Ask if anyone remembers reading about **churros** as a breakfast food in Spain. Ask a student to describe them.
(page 278 bottom) Many of the world's most famous kitchens these days have female chefs. This is a relatively new phenomenon.

GeoVistas

Have students turn to pages SH42–SH43 and locate the map of Mexico. Ask students to find the capital and ask them if there are any similarities between the capital's name and the name of the U.S. capital. Have them describe the Mexican food they see on page SH43.

Práctica

LEER • HABLAR • ESCRIBIR

5 Sigue el modelo.

MODELO   don Pedro / hablar / con el dueño →
El que habla con el dueño es don Pedro.
El que hablará con el dueño es don Pedro.
El que habló con el dueño fue don Pedro.

1. la cocinera / preparar / la comida
2. los comensales / comer / la comida
3. los campesinos / cultivar / las legumbres
4. el dueño / pagar / el salario
5. mis primas / llegar / tarde

LEER • ESCRIBIR

6 Completa.

1. De todos los vegetales _____ prefiero es el repollo.
2. De todas las frutas _____ me gusta más es la manzana.
3. De todos mis profesores _____ me enseñó más fue el señor Centeno.
4. _____ salieron fueron los primeros en llegar.

HABLAR

7 Completa. Da respuestas personales.

1. Lo que necesito es _____.
2. Lo que quiero es _____.
3. Lo que me gusta es _____.
4. Lo que prefiero es _____.
5. Lo que ellos me dicen es _____.

LEER • ESCRIBIR

8 Completa.

1. El restaurante _____ nombre se me escapa es fabuloso.
2. Es el cocinero _____ recetas han ganado premios.
3. Es la señora _____ vides producen las mejores uvas.
4. Es una cocinera _____ fama es mundial.
5. La señora _____ hijo está hablando ahora es la directora de la escuela.

CULTURA

Las que están tocando instrumentos y cantando delante de su escuela son estudiantes del Liceo 7 en Providencia, una zona de Santiago de Chile.

Más práctica

Workbook, pp. 9.7–9.8
StudentWorks™ Plus

Gramática

▶ PRACTICE

Leveling EACH Activity

Easy Activity 7
Average Activities 5, 6, 8

⭐ Tips for Success ·······

You may wish to allow students to look over these activities for a few minutes and then go over them orally in class before having students write them for homework.

Cultural Snapshot

(page 279) Note that a **liceo** is a term used for a secondary school, particularly in **el Cono sur.**

▶ ASSESS

Students are now ready to take Quiz 4 on page 9.34 of the TeacherTools booklet. If you prefer to create your own quiz, use the *ExamView® Assessment Suite.*

HISTORIA DE LA COMIDA LATINA   *doscientos setenta y nueve*   **279**

Answers

5

1. La que prepara la comida es la cocinera. La que preparará la comida es la cocinera. La que preparó la comida fue la cocinera.
2. Los que comen la comida son los comensales. Los que comerán la comida son los comensales. Los que comieron la comida fueron los comensales.

3. Los que cultivan las legumbres son los campesinos. Los que cultivarán las legumbres son los campesinos. Los que cultivaron las legumbres fueron los campesinos.
4. El que paga el salario es el dueño. El que pagará el salario es el dueño. El que pagó el salario fue el dueño.

5. Las que llegan tarde son mis primas. Las que llegarán tarde son mis primas. Las que llegaron tarde fueron mis primas.

6

1. el que   3. el que
2. la que   4. Los que

7 *Answers will vary.*

8

1. cuyo
2. cuyas
3. cuyas
4. cuya
5. cuyo

279

Resources

■ Audio Activities TE, page 9.21
🎧 Audio CD 9, Track 9
■ Workbook, page 9.8
■ Quiz 5, page 9.35
◉ ExamView® Assessment Suite

Quick Start

*Use QS Transparency 9.4 or write
the following on the board.*
**Escribe todo lo que necesitas
para poner la mesa.**

▶ TEACH
Core Instruction

Step 1 Students have already
learned the **hace** construction
with the present. This is, however, a point that needs frequent reinforcement.

Step 2 You may wish to add
additional information to the
illustrative sentences to demonstrate what intervened.
Hacía cinco años que ellos se
conocían cuando por una
razón u otra no se vieron más.
Hacía mucho tiempo que él lo
sabía y por fin me lo dijo.

▶ PRACTICE

Leveling EACH Activity

Easy Activity 9
Average Activities 10, 11

Activity ⑨ This activity can
be done orally with books
closed calling on students at
random to respond.

¿Te acuerdas?

You have already learned
the time expression with
hace in the present tense.

Expresiones de tiempo con hace y hacía

1. The present tense is used with **hace** to express an action
that began in the past and continues into the present.
English uses the present perfect.

> **¿Hace cúanto tiempo que estás aquí?**
> *How long have you been here?*
>
> **Hace dos años que estoy aquí.**
> *I have been here for two years.*

2. The imperfect tense is used with **hacía** to express something
that had been going on for some time before something else
intervened. You will note from the following examples that
in English the pluperfect tense is used.

> **Hacía cinco años que ellos se conocían.**
> *They had known each other for five years.*
>
> **Hacía mucho tiempo que él lo sabía.**
> *He had known it for a long time.*

Práctica

HABLAR

⑨ Personaliza. Da respuestas personales.

1. ¿Hace cuántos años que vives en la misma casa?
2. ¿Tienes una mascota? ¿Tienen tus primos una
mascota? ¿Hace cuánto tiempo que tú o tus primos
tienen una mascota?
3. ¿Tienes un móvil? ¿Hace cuánto tiempo que tienes
tu móvil?
4. ¿Tienes novio(a)? ¿Hace cuánto tiempo que sales
con él o ella?

El muchacho quiere a su
perro. Hace cinco años que
tiene su perro.

⭐ Tips for Success ··············

The more students hear these expressions, the more successful they will be in
using them. You may wish to ask the following questions about the photo.
**¿Hace mucho tiempo que el muchacho
quiere a su mascota? ¿Hace cuánto
tiempo que la tiene? ¿Tienes una
mascota? ¿Qué tienes? ¿Hace cuánto
tiempo que lo/la tienes?**

Answers

⑨

1. Hace ___ años que vivo en la misma casa.
2. Sí, (No, no) tengo una mascota. Sí (No), mis
primos (no) tienen una mascota. Hace ___ años
(meses, semanas, etc.) que tengo (que mis primos
tienen) una mascota.
3. Sí, (No, no) tengo un móvil. Hace ___ años
(meses, semanas, etc.) que tengo un móvil.
4. Sí, (No, no) tengo novio(a). Hace ___ años
(meses, semanas, etc.) que salgo con él (ella).

LEER • ESCRIBIR • HABLAR

10 Completa cada pregunta y luego contéstala.

1. ¿Hace cuánto tiempo que tú _____ aquí? (estar)
2. ¿Hace cuánto tiempo que tú _____ a esta escuela? (asistir)
3. ¿Hace cuánto tiempo que tú _____ a tu mejor amigo(a)? (conocer)
4. ¿Hace cuánto tiempo que tú _____ español? (estudiar)
5. ¿Hace cuánto tiempo que Enrique _____ con Sandra? (salir)
6. ¿Hace una hora que _____ aquel señor? (hablar)

LEER • ESCRIBIR

11 Completa con la forma apropiada del verbo indicado.

1. Hacía dos años que ellos _____ allí cuando tuvieron que mudarse. (vivir)
2. Hacía cinco años que ellos se _____ antes de casarse. (conocer)
3. Hacía solo cinco días que él _____ enfermo cuando se murió. (estar)
4. Hacía mucho tiempo que ellos lo _____ sin que dijeran nada a nadie. (saber)
5. Hacía a lo menos dos años que ella _____ en el mismo restaurante. (trabajar)

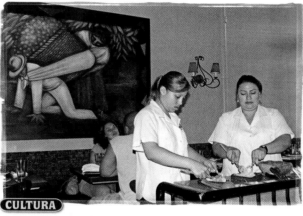

CULTURA

Las dos meseras están preparando guacamole. Hace muchos años que trabajan en este restaurante en Guadalajara, México.

HISTORIA DE LA COMIDA LATINA

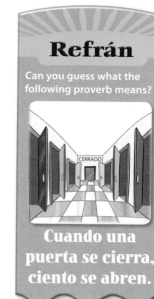

Refrán

Can you guess what the following proverb means?

CERRADO

Cuando una puerta se cierra, ciento se abren.

¡Bravo!

You have now learned all the new vocabulary and grammar in this chapter. Continue to use and practice all that you know while learning more cultural information. ¡Vamos!

doscientos ochenta y uno **281**

Gramática

Activities 10 and 11 These activities can be gone over in class and then assigned for homework.

⭐Tips for Success

Have students work in small groups. Vary ability levels. Have students make up and respond to as many personal questions using the **hace** expression as possible.

▶ ASSESS

Students are now ready to take Quiz 5 on page 9.35 of the TeacherTools booklet. If you prefer to create your own quiz, use the *ExamView® Assessment Suite.*

Refrán

Proverbs, adages, idiomatic expressions, and other popular sayings provide a wealth of opportunities for students to learn about different cultural perspectives as well as perspectives shared by different cultures. They also serve to enrich students' overall understanding of language.

Have students recite the proverb aloud. Then see if they can figure out its meaning, and encourage them to try to give an equivalent expression in English: "When one door closes, another one opens." Ask in what context this expression is used.

¡Bravo!
The remaining pages of the chapter recycle information in a variety of ways, allowing students to build upon their newly acquired language skills as well as to keep track of their own progress.

Answers

10

1. estás; Hace _____ (horas, minutos, etc.) que estoy aquí.
2. asistes; Hace _____ (años, meses, etc.) que asisto a esta escuela.
3. conoces; Hace _____ (años, meses, etc.) que conozco a mi mejor amigo(a).
4. estudias; Hace _____ años que estudio español.
5. sale; Hace _____ (semanas, meses, años, etc.) que Enrique sale con Sandra.
6. habla; Sí, (No, no) hace una hora que habla aquel señor.

11

1. vivían
2. conocían
3. estaba
4. sabían
5. trabajaba

281

QuickPass

Go to glencoe.com
For: **Conversation practice**
Web code: ASD7844c9

Resources

- Audio Activities TE, pages 9.22–9.23
- 🎧 Audio CD 9, Tracks 10–11

▶ TEACH
Core Instruction

Step 1 Have students close their books and listen to Audio CD 9.

Step 2 Do not ask specific questions. Just ask students which foods were involved in the historical information to see if they listened.

Step 3 Call on students to read the conversation aloud. You may wish to break it into three sections.

Step 4 After each section, ask comprehension questions.

⭐Tips for Success

Many students are not good listeners. Tell them they are going to hear a conversation in which there are several historical items of interest. Tell them to pay particular attention to these items. This guidance will help them succeed in understanding the conversation.

Cultural Snapshot

(page 282) This market is in Málaga, Spain.

282

¡¿Los tomates son venenosos?!

Felipe Joe, ¿qué crees? ¿La papa? ¿Es de Europa o de las Américas?

Joe ¡La papa! Es de Europa. Mi familia es de ascendencia irlandesa y comemos muchas papas.

Felipe Y Teresa. ¿De dónde será el tomate?

Teresa Pues, el tomate también tiene que ser de Europa. Yo lo sé porque mi familia es italiana y en Italia preparamos muchas salsas a base de tomates.

Felipe Les voy a decir una cosa. Ninguno de los dos tiene razón. Están equivocados.

Joe ¡Increíble! ¿Nos estás diciendo que la papa y el tomate son de las Américas?

Felipe Sí. Y lo que es muy interesante es que hasta el siglo veinte había muchos europeos que creían que los tomates eran venenosos y no los comían por nada.

Teresa Felipe, me estás tomando el pelo. No es posible que una vez en Italia no se comieran tomates.

Felipe No. No te estoy tomando el pelo. Es la pura verdad. Y, en su vida, ¿han comido papas azules o negras?

Teresa Nunca.

Felipe Pues, los primeros que cultivaban las papas eran los incas en las regiones frías del altiplano andino y siguen produciéndolas en una gran variedad de colores.

Joe Lo encuentro difícil creer que se estaban comiendo papas en los Andes antes de que las comieran mis antepasados en Irlanda.

 Conexiones

La historia

In the ancient ruins of Peru and Chile, archaeologists have found potato remains that date back to 500 B.C. The Incas grew and ate them and also worshipped them. They even buried potatoes with their dead and stashed potatoes in concealed bins for use in case of war or famine. The Incas called the potato **papas,** as they do today. The Spanish conquistadors first encountered the potato when they arrived in Peru in 1532 in search of gold. Have students research the potato or another food of their choice and write a conversation using the format of the conversation about tomatoes.

¿Comprendes?

A Identifica según la información en la conversación.
1. los errores que cometieron Joe y Teresa
2. información sobre la ascendencia de Joe y Teresa

B Describiendo Da algunos detalles sobre estas hortalizas.
1. los tomates
2. las papas

C Analizando Contesta.
1. ¿Por qué creían Joe y Teresa que Felipe les estaba tomando el pelo?
2. ¿Te sorprendió la información sobre las papas y los tomates? ¿Por qué?

¡Así se dice!

Tomarle el pelo a alguien is a fun expression that is equivalent to the English expression *to pull someone's leg.*

 Cultura

D ¿Cuáles son algunos productos que se usan con frecuencia en la elaboración de platos étnicos de tu grupo cultural?

CULTURA

Ya sabes que se dice «cacahuates» en muchas partes de Latinoamérica y «maní» en Puerto Rico. Nota que se dice «maní» en Argentina también.

▶ PRACTICE

¿Comprendes?

All of these activities can be done as class discussions. They can also be written.

¡Así se dice!

You may wish to give students some more examples with this expression. **No puede ser. Me estás tomando el pelo. No me tomes el pelo. Te aseguro. No es verdad. Te estaba tomando el pelo.**

ABOUT THE SPANISH LANGUAGE

Cacahuetes rather than **cacahuates** is said in Spain.

Pre-AP Listening to this conversation on audio CD will help students develop the skills that they need to be successful on the listening portion of the AP exam.

Answers

A
1. Joe creía que las papas eran de Europa y Teresa creía que los tomates también eran de Europa.
2. Joe es de ascendencia irlandesa y Teresa es de ascendencia italiana.

B
1. Hasta el siglo pasado había muchos europeos que creían que los tomates eran venenosos y no los comían por nada.
2. Los primeros que cultivaban las papas eran los incas en las regiones frías del altiplano andino y las tienen de una gran variedad de colores.

C
1. Joe creía que Felipe le estaba tomando el pelo porque lo encuentra difícil creer que se estaban comiendo papas en los Andes antes de que las comieran sus antepasados en Irlanda. Teresa creía que Felipe le estaba tomando el pelo porque no cree que sea posible que una vez en Italia no comieran tomates.
2. *Answers will vary but may include:* Sí, la información sobre las papas y los tomates me sorprendió porque creía que estas legumbres eran de Europa.

D *Answers will vary.*

LECTURA CULTURAL

Resources

- Audio Activities TE, pages 9.24–9.26
- Audio CD 9, Tracks 12–13

▶ TEACH
Core Instruction

Step 1 If you wish to present this selection thoroughly with all students, you may follow suggestions given in previous chapters.

Step 2 Have students make a list of indigenous and imported products as they read **Un taco de carne.**

Step 3 Have students answer the following questions when reading **Las especias. ¿Por qué necesitaban especias los españoles? ¿Dónde estaban las especias? ¿Costaban mucho? ¿Adónde iban para encontrar especias? ¿Llegó Colón a la India? ¿Adónde llegó? ¿Quiénes recibían sal por el trabajo que hacían? ¿De dónde viene la palabra «salario»? ¿Cuál es una definición de «salario»? ¿Cuál es otra palabra en español que significa «salario»?**

Teaching Options

You may wish to break this selection into sections and have each group do a section. Each group must report to the others about what they learned. Logical breaks are each page or each subhead.

Antes de leer

Piensa en todo lo que te gusta comer. ¿Jamás pensado en el origen de los comestibles?

Reading Check

¿Cómo es que el taco de carne es una combinación de dos civilizaciones?

Historia de la comida 🎧 ♻

Vamos a darle una ojeada a la interesante historia de la comida. Se sabe que la comida de las Américas tiene muchas influencias indígenas y españolas. Y no se puede olvidar que en la comida española hay influencia del Medio Oriente porque España estuvo bajo el dominio de los árabes por unos ocho siglos. Los nombres mismos de varios comestibles como la berenjena y la alcachofa son de origen árabe. Más adelante leeremos de la aceptación de estas legumbres en la cocina de las Américas, pero antes vamos a considerar la importancia de la historia de unas comidas muy sencillas.

Un taco de carne Vamos a observar las interesantes influencias en un simple taco. El taco de carne es una combinación de tortilla de maíz y carne de res con tomate y lechuga. Y es también una combinación de dos civilizaciones y culturas.

La tortilla de maíz es de las Américas. Hacía siglos que los indígenas de México—los mayas y aztecas—estaban comiendo tortillas de maíz antes de que llegaran los españoles. La tortilla era de maíz porque no había trigo. Los que introdujeron el trigo a las Américas fueron los españoles. También trajeron ganado. Antes de la llegada de los españoles no había vacas, ovejas y caballos en las Américas.

▲ Tacos suaves de carne

Pre-AP This cultural reading will develop the skills that students need to be successful on the reading and writing sections of the AP exam. Listening to this reading will also help prepare them for the auditory component.

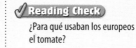

Los tomates Es verdad que los españoles trajeron muchos productos, pero también encontraron muchos productos nuevos en América. Los españoles no conocían el maíz, ni la papa, ni el tomate. Eran los indígenas americanos los que cultivaban el tomate. Luego los españoles lo introdujeron en Europa donde lo cultivaban pero solo como decoración. ¿Te parecería posible que ellos tuvieran miedo a los tomates? Pues, así era. Ellos creían que eran venenosos y que si los comieran, morirían. En Inglaterra y Norteamérica no se comían tomates hasta el siglo diecinueve.

Las especias El mismo descubrimiento de las Américas por parte de los europeos se debe a la comida. Cristóbal Colón salió de España en busca de una nueva ruta a Asia porque en Asia había especias. En aquel entonces[1] las especias eran necesarias para conservar la comida. Muchas personas en Europa se estaban muriendo de hambre porque no tenían especias. Eran muy caras porque venían de Asia por tierra—en caravanas—y los viajes de Asia a Europa duraban años. Colón creía que por mar podría llegar al Oriente en menos tiempo. Quería ir a la India porque sabía que allí estaban las especias que buscaba pero sabemos que Colón nunca llegó a la India. Llegó a las Indias—en las Américas.

—«Favor de pasar la sal». —¡Qué cosa más sencilla! La sal. Pero había una vez que la gente se estaba luchando por sal. Pagaban a los soldados romanos con sal y de allí viene la palabra «salario». Y, ¿cuál es la palabra en inglés?

[1]En aquel entonces *At that time*

✓ Reading Check
¿Para qué usaban los europeos el tomate?

▲ Tumbet—un plato mallorquín tradicional

✓ Reading Check
En sus viajes, ¿qué buscaba Colón? ¿Por qué?

CULTURA
Un gran surtido de especias incluyendo el azafrán en un mercado en Granada, España

HISTORIA DE LA COMIDA LATINA

doscientos ochenta y cinco **285**

Differentiation
Multiple Intelligences
Visual-spatial learners learn better from visual representations than from written text alone. Assign them to create a wall calendar of foods with a different Spanish food illustrated for each month of the year. Work with the technology people in your building to print out copies of these calendars and sell them to students and adults at a moderate price. Use the funds collected to sponsor a Hispanic "food feast" for the foreign language classes.

Teaching Options
Have students look at the photos for this reading and describe the foods they see. Have them read the signs in the bottom photo on page 285 and ask what they think **molido** *(ground)* means.

GLENCOE Technology
Online Learning in the Classroom
You may wish to have students use QuickPass code ASD7844c9 to develop their reading comprehension and writing skills. Students will be able to take a self-check quiz, which includes an essay.

Lectura

▶ TEACH

Core Instruction

Step 1 Have students make a list of dishes made with some ingredients of Arab origin.

Step 2 After all the discussion about this **Lectura,** ask students which of the foods or dishes they have eaten and whether they liked them.

Step 3 Have students do the **¿Comprendes?** activities. Note that they can be done orally in class in pairs, small groups, or with the entire class, or as written activities.

Differentiation

Advanced Learners

Call on advanced students or students interested in history to give any information they remember about the Moors or Arabs in Spain.

Heritage Speakers

Ask heritage speakers in the class or from the community to speak in Spanish about the origins and different types of Hispanic foods. Encourage them to talk about foods they like and dislike. If possible, they could bring samples of some foods to class for students to taste.

286

LECTURA CULTURAL

Reading Check
¿Cómo es que hay influencia árabe en la comida latina?

▲ Artefacto mochica de un señor comiendo maíz, Perú

La influencia árabe Ahora vamos a volver a la influencia árabe en la cocina latina. La berenjena y la alcachofa son dos hortalizas que fueron introducidas en España por los moros (árabes). La berenjena, igual que en España, es muy apreciada en todo Latinoamérica. Se puede cortarla simplemente en rodajas y freírla o rebozarla en huevo batido y harina o pan rallado antes de echarla a la sartén. También se puede rellenarla de queso o de picadillo—carne picada de cerdo o vaca. Las recetas son muy parecidas en casi todos los países. En Chile la berenjena rellena con picadillo es muy popular. En Venezuela se comen berenjenas con vainitas. El plato se sirve ligeramente fría o a la temperatura ambiente[2]. En la República Dominicana está riquísimo el caviar de berenjena. Es una mezcla de trozos de berenjena pelada con cebolla, pimiento dulce, tomates, cilantro y vinagre todo bien mezclado. Se sirve con hojas de lechuga o galletas saladas.

Las alcachofas no son tan apreciadas en Latinoamérica. Sin embargo la autora de un libro interesantísimo sobre la cocina latinoamericana encontró una receta chilena para preparar alcachofas con una salsa besamel[3] y queso parmesano rallado. ¡Qué coincidencia que ella la encontrara en Chile! El poema que vamos a leer, *Oda a la alcachofa,* fue escrita por el famoso poeta chileno Pablo Neruda.

[2]temperatura ambiente *room temperature*

[3]besamel *bechamel (una salsa de crema)*

▲ Un plato de alcachofas rellenas de queso de parmesana

286 *doscientos ochenta y seis*

CAPÍTULO 9

Answers

A *Answers will vary.*

B
ingredientes americanos: la tortilla de maíz, los tomates
ingredientes europeos: la carne de res, el trigo

C
productos de origen indígena: el maíz, las papas, los tomates

productos de origen europeo: el trigo, el ganado (la carne de res y el cordero)

D
1. Creían que los tomates eran venenosos y si comían tomates iban a morir.
2. Dos legumbres que los moros introdujeron en España son la berenjena y la alcachofa.

3. Se puede cortarlas simplemente en rodajas y freírlas o rebozarlas en huevo batido y pan rallado antes de echarlas a la sartén. También se puede rellenarlas con queso o con picadillo. Se comen también con vainitas en Venezuela. En la República Dominicana hay el caviar de

¿Comprendes?

A **Comparando y contrastando** Discute las diferentes influencias en la cocina española y la cocina latinoamericana. ¿Cómo es que existían estas influencias? ¿Cuáles eran las razones históricas?

VIDEO To learn about Latino food in the United States, watch **Cultura en vivo.**

B **Analizando** Completa el siguiente diagrama con información sobre un sencillo taco de carne.

ingredientes americanos	ingredientes europeos

C **Categorizando** Completa la siguiente tabla.

productos de origen indígena	productos de origen europeo

D **Recordando hechos** Contesta.
1. ¿Qué creían los europeos de los tomates?
2. ¿Cuáles son dos legumbres que los moros introdujeron en España?
3. ¿Cuáles son varias maneras en que se preparan las berenjenas?
4. ¿Cuál de estas dos legumbres es más apreciada en Latinoamérica—la berenjena o la alcachofa?
5. ¿En qué país encontró la autora de un libro sobre la cocina latinoamericana una receta para preparar alcachofas?

E **Analizando** Contesta.
1. ¿Cómo es que el mismo descubrimiento por parte de los españoles o europeos tenía que ver con la comida?
2. ¿Cuál es la derivación de la palabra *salary*?

F **Personalizando** ¿Qué hechos aprendiste en esta lectura que te sorprendieron?

doscientos ochenta y siete **287**

▶ PRACTICE

¿Comprendes?

A This activity can be done as a class discussion activity.

B and **C** Have students fill in the charts and then go over them in class.

D It is suggested you do this as a factual recall activity and not permit students to look up answers.

E Students can do this as a paired activity.

F This activity can be done as a class discussion. You may also want students to prepare a short composition on this topic.

Teaching Options

If you only have a group read a section of the **Lectura,** have them do only the corresponding activity.

Differentiation

Advanced Learners
Slower Paced Learners

Many types of learners like competitions. Have students make up all types of *true/false* statements about the information in the **Lectura.** Students can say if the statement is correct or make up the correct answer. All types of students can be actively involved. Advanced learners will make up more complex sentences. Slower students will make up easier, shorter ones, but they are all using language on their own.

 Cultural Snapshot

(page 286 left) Note the ear of corn on this Incan urn.

287

Answers

berenjena, una mezcla de trozos de berenjena pelada con cebolla, pimiento dulce, tomates, cilantro y vinagre todo bien mezclado. Se sirve con hojas de lechuga o galletas saladas.
4. La berenjena es más apreciada que la alcachofa en Latinoamérica.

5. La encontró en Chile.

E
1. Tenía que ver con la comida porque Colón buscaba una nueva ruta a Asia porque en Asia había especias. Colón quería ir a India por las especias pero nunca llegó a la India; llegó a las Indias—en las Américas.
2. La palabra *salary* viene de la palabra **sal**. Los soldados romanos recibían su pago en sal y de allí viene la palabra «salario».

F *Answers will vary.*

Oda a la alcachofa
de Pablo Neruda

▲ Una escultura de
Pablo Neruda en
una playa de Isla
Negra, Chile

Literatura

Resources

- Audio Activities TE,
  pages 9.27–9.28
- Audio CD 9, Track 13
- Literature Test, page 9.51
- *ExamView® Assessment Suite*

Preview

Starting in Chapter 3, each chapter of **¡Así se dice!** Level 3 has a literary section. Most literary selections are by well-known Latin American or Spanish writers. Some selections are poetry and others are prose.

It is up to the discretion of the teacher if you wish to do all or any of these literary works. The difficulty level of each selection is also indicated: 1 is difficult; 4 is quite easy.

Difficulty Level
2

Introducción

You may wish to have students read the **Introducción** silently. Then ask comprehension questions about Neruda. You may wish to add that this poetry collection includes a poem titled *Oda al tomate.* Advanced students, or students interested in literature, may want to read this other poem and write or give a report comparing and contrasting it to the poem here.

INTRODUCCIÓN

Pablo Neruda nació en Chile en 1904. Además de ser maestro Neruda sirvió como cónsul chileno en varias ciudades españolas e hispanoamericanas.

Neruda se considera uno de los mejores poetas de todos los tiempos. Muchas de sus poesías surrealistas no son de fácil comprensión. Pero también hay en la obra de Neruda «el poeta realista, fotógrafo del cielo» como él mismo se llamó.

En la oda que sigue, *Oda a la alcachofa* tomada de sus *Odas elementales,* observarás un estilo sencillo y conciso de pocas palabras. El poeta se inspira en temas concretos y humildes y los poemas de esta fase de su creación van dirigidos a la persona sencilla.

Note: The poem *Oda a la alcachofa* by Pablo Neruda is not in itself difficult, but it does contain a fair amount of seldom-used vocabulary as seen in the footnotes. We rate it high average in difficulty level. It is a poem that many students could enjoy because of the way in which Neruda humanizes the **alcachofa.**

Oda a la alcachofa 🎧

La alcachofa
de tierno corazón
se vistió de guerrero[1],
erecta, construyó
5 una pequeña cúpula,
se mantuvo
impermeable
bajo
sus escamas[2],
10 a su lado
los vegetales locos
se encresparon[3],
se hicieron
zarcillos[4], espadañas[5],
15 bulbos conmovedores[6],
en el subsuelo
durmió la zanahoria
de bigotes[7] rojos,
la viña
20 resecó[8] los sarmientos[9]

por donde sube el vino,
la col
se dedicó
a probarse faldas,
25 el orégano
a perfumar el mundo,
y la dulce
alcachofa
allí en el huerto,
30 vestida de guerrero,
bruñida[10]
como una granada,
orgullosa,
y un día
35 una con otra
en grandes cestos
de mimbre[11], caminó
por el mercado
a realizar su sueño[12]:
40 la milicia.

[1]guerrero *warrior*
[2]escamas *scales*
[3]se encresparon *curled up*
[4]zarcillos *tendrils*
[5]espadañas *bullrushes*
[6]conmovedores *moving, touching*
[7]bigotes *moustaches*
[8]resecó *dried out*
[9]sarmientos *vine shoots*
[10]bruñida *polished*
[11]mimbre *wicker*
[12]sueño *dream*

Visualizando Al leer, visualiza lo que está describiendo el poeta. Trata de hacer un cuadro mental de los distintos lugares por los cuales pasa la alcachofa.

Antes de leer

Antes de leer esta oda piensa en una alcachofa. Tanto mejor si has comido una. Si no, mira las fotografías que acompañan la oda para enterarte de la apariencia y composición de esta hortaliza.

◀ Una alcachofa

Una granada ▼

HISTORIA DE LA COMIDA LATINA   *doscientos ochenta y nueve* **289**

▶ **TEACH**
Core Instruction

Step 1 Discuss the **Estrategia** with the class. Explain that they will understand the poem better if they stop to visualize, or see in their minds, what the places look like.

Step 2 Discuss the **Antes de leer.** Ask students whether they have ever eaten an artichoke. If so, how was it prepared? Did they like it? (See the Tips for Success below.)

Step 3 Have students listen to the recording on Audio CD 9 two times, first with their books closed and a second time as they follow along in their books.

Step 4 Then call on individuals to read aloud about ten lines at a time, with as much expression as possible. Follow each reading with questions.

⭐**Tips for Success** ·······

If some students have never seen an artichoke, have students look carefully at the photos on pages 289 and 290, or better yet bring an artichoke to class. Cut it in half to show students the interior. Show how the leaves are taken off when eaten and how the heart remains to be eaten last. Knowing what the artichoke looks like should help students understand its warrior look in the garden in spite of its tender heart.

▶ TEACH
Core Instruction

Step 1 Have students read the **Durante la lectura** and **Después de leer.** You may wish to have them discuss their reactions to each one in class.

Step 2 Have students figure out who the **mariscales** are and what caused the "explosion." Have them concentrate on the way María treated the **alcachofa** and what she did with it when she got it home. How does the warrior **alcachofa** end its career?

Differentiation
Multiple Intelligences

- You may want to ask **verbal-linguistic** students to write their own "ode" to their favorite Hispanic food. They should describe the food and also how it is prepared and eaten. They should be able to use similes and metaphors to associate things with the food they have chosen.
- **Bodily-kinesthetic** learners will enjoy making up a pantomime skit that begins in the garden and ends in María's kitchen. Have them perform the skit for the class.

▶ Durante la lectura

Fíjate en la descripción que nos da el poeta de una alcachofa. ¿Habla el poeta de la alcachofa como si fuera una persona? Además, determina en cuántos lugares tiene lugar la acción.

▶ Después de leer

¿Cómo explicas el uso del verbo «se vistió» a principios de la oda y «desvestimos» al final de la oda?

En hileras[13]
nunca fue tan
   marcial
como en la feria,
los hombres
45   entre las legumbres
con sus camisas
   blancas
eran
mariscales
de las alcachofas,
50   las filas apretadas[14],
las voces de
   comando,
y la detonación
de una caja que cae,
pero
55   entonces
viene
María
con su cesto,
escoge
60   una alcachofa,
no le teme,
la examina, la
   observa
contra la luz como si
   fuera un huevo,

la compra,
65   la confunde
en su bolsa
con un par de
   zapatos,
con un repollo y una
   botella
70   de vinagre
hasta
que entrando a la
   cocina
la sumerge en la
   olla.

Así termina
75   en paz
esta carrera
del vegetal armado
que se llama
   alcachofa,
luego
80   escama por escama
desvestimos
la delicia
y comemos
la pacífica pasta
85   de su corazón verde.

[13] En hileras *In military file*
[14] apretadas *squashed, tightly packed*

Answers

 A

1. Se viste de guerrero, es erecta, impermeable, bruñida, orgullosa, marcial; está en filas apretadas y está armado.
2. Tiene escamas.
3. Compara la alcachofa a la zanahoria y a la col. La zanahoria durmió y la col se dedicó a probarse faldas.
4. Tiene lugar en el huerto, en el mercado y en la cocina de María.
5. Su sueño es la milicia.

 B

1. b
2. b
3. a
4. a

¿Comprendes?

A **Analizando** Indica.
1. los atributos marciales o militares de la alcachofa
2. lo que tiene la alcachofa que la hace bien armada
3. legumbres a las que compara Neruda la alcachofa
4. tres lugares en que tiene lugar el poema
5. el sueño de la alcachofa

B **Analizando e interpretando** Escoge.
1. ¿Por qué diría el poeta que la col se dedicó a probarse faldas?
   a. Porque la col se compone de muchas hojas.
   b. Porque la col tiene la forma de una falda.
2. ¿Por qué diría el poeta que el orégano se dedicó a perfumar el mundo?
   a. El orégano es un perfume.
   b. El orégano tiene un olor fuerte y distintivo.
3. ¿Quiénes serán los marciales en el mercado?
   a. las alcachofas mismas
   b. los que trabajaban en el mercado
4. La palabra «detonación» añade al ambiente militar. ¿A qué se refiere la detonación?
   a. al ruido que hizo una caja que cayó
   b. a las voces de comando

C **Interpretando** ¿Cuál es el elemento de paz que introduce el poeta a la escena?

D **Describiendo** Contesta.
1. ¿Qué hace María con la alcachofa? ¿Cómo la trata? ¿Dónde la pone? ¿Qué más tiene en su bolsa?
2. ¿Qué hace María con la alcachofa en la cocina?
3. ¿Qué hacemos antes de comer una alcachofa? ¿Qué parte de la alcachofa comemos? ¿Cómo es?

E **Interpretando**
1. Un crítico ha dicho que Neruda es un gran virtuoso de las imágenes. El poeta representa las cosas en toda su humanidad. ¿Crees que Neruda humaniza a la alcachofa? Si contestas que sí, ¿cuáles son los elementos o rasgos humanos que encuentras en la alcachofa?
2. ¿Cuáles son los sentimientos que tienes hacia la alcachofa? ¿Por qué?

CULTURA

La entrada a la casa de Pablo Neruda en Isla Negra

Literatura

▶ PRACTICE

¿Comprendes?

A Allow students to prepare this activity before going over it in class.

B You may wish to do this activity without previous preparation.

C This can be used as a class discussion.

D It is suggested you do this activity orally with books closed and call on students at random.

E This activity should be discussed in class and then written as a composition.

Cultural Snapshot

(page 291) Pablo Neruda's main home was this one on Isla Negra. He also had another beautiful home in Valparaiso. Students may want to research to learn more about these places.

Answers

C

Cuando en casa de María se come la alcachofa.

D

1. María escoge la alcachofa, la examina, la observa contra la luz como si fuera un huevo y la compra. La pone en su bolsa. En su bolsa tiene también un par de zapatos, un repollo y una botella de vinagre.

2. En la cocina María sumerge la alcachofa en una olla.

3. Antes de comer una alcachofa sacamos las escamas. Comemos el corazón. Es muy tierno.

E

1. *Answers will vary but may include:* La alcachofa se viste de guerrero, tiene un corazón tierno, tiene un sueño (la milicia), parece orgullosa, es como un soldado.

2. *Answers will vary.*

291

Prepárate para el examen
Self-check for achievement

Resources

- Tests, pages 9.43–9.57
- Performance Assessment, Task 9, pages 9.59–9.60
- ExamView® Assessment Suite

✔ Self-check for achievement

This is a pre-test for students to take before you administer the chapter test. Note that each section is cross-referenced so students can easily find the material they feel they need to review. You may wish to use Self-Check Worksheet Transparency SC9 to have students complete this assessment in class or at home. You can correct the assessment yourself, or you may prefer to project the answers on the overhead in class using Self-Check Answers Transparency SC9A.

Differentiation

Slower Paced Learners

Have students work in pairs to complete the Self-Check in class. Then call on individuals to give the correct answers as you review together.

Multiple Intelligences

To engage **visual-spatial** and **bodily-kinesthetic** learners, number 1 to 40 on the board and call on a student to go to the board and write the correct answer (this may be done chronologically or you may allow students to choose the one they answer). Then have the student who wrote the first answer decide who will write the second, and so on, making sure to remind them not to pick the same person again.

292

 To review **Vocabulario,** turn to pages 272–273.

To review **la voz pasiva,** turn to page 276.

Vocabulario

1 Identifica.

1.   2.   3.

4.   5.   6.

7.   8.

2 Completa.

9. El orégano es _____.
10. Se cultivan legumbres y frutas en _____.
11. Otra palabra que significa «col» es «_____».
12. Hay vides en _____.
13–14. Cortas la berenjena en _____ y las _____ en huevo batido y pan rallado.
15. La carne de una vaca es _____.
16. Cuando uno hace algo bueno debe estar _____.
17. Son los _____ los que se sientan a una mesa para comer juntos.

Gramática

3 Completa.

18. _____ abr_ la tienda a las nueve de la mañana.
19. Las puertas _____ cierr_ a las ocho de la noche.
20. _____ habl_ español en México y Panamá.
21. España _____ invadida _____ los árabes en el siglo ocho.
22. Los países del continente sudamericano _____ colonizados _____ los españoles y los portugueses.

Answers

1
1. el pimiento
2. la berenjena
3. la alcachofa
4. el trigo
5. la col (el repollo)
6. el maíz
7. las uvas
8. las judías verdes (las vainitas)

2
9. una especia
10. un huerto
11. el repollo
12. una viña
13. rodajas
14. rebozas
15. la carne de res
16. orgulloso
17. comensales

3
18. Se, e
19. se, an
20. Se, a
21. fue, por
22. fueron, por

4
23. El que
24. Las que
25. los que
26. Los que
27. fueron
28. lo que
29. lo que
30. cuya

4 Completa con el pronombre relativo.

23. _____ habla ahora es el dueño del restaurante.

24–25. _____ preparan la comida son las cocineras y _____ se sientan juntos para comer la comida son los comensales.

26–27. _____ llegaron primero _____ mis primos.

28. No hago siempre _____ debo hacer.

29. No nos importa _____ dice él.

30. Es mi amigo _____ hermana acaba de ganar el gran premio.

5 Contesta.

31. ¿Hace cuánto tiempo que vives en la misma casa?

32. ¿Hace cuánto tiempo que estudias español?

33. ¿Hace mucho tiempo que se conocen tú y tu mejor amigo(a)?

6 Completa.

34. _____ ocho siglos que los árabes estuvieron en España cuando los españoles los expulsaron.

35. _____ solamente un mes que su padre estaba enfermo cuando se murió.

Cultura

7 Identifica.

36. dos productos de origen europeo

37. dos productos de origen americano

8 Contesta.

38. ¿Por qué no comían tomates los europeos?

39. ¿Cómo refleja el sencillo taco de carne la historia de la comida?

40. ¿Cómo es que hay influencias del Medio Oriente en la cocina española?

To review **los pronombres relativos**, turn to page 278.

To review **hace** and **hacía**, turn to page 280.

To review this cultural information, turn to pages 284–286.

HISTORIA DE LA COMIDA LATINA

Differentiation

Slower Paced Learners

Encourage students who need extra help to refer to the book icons and review any section before answering the questions.

Pre-AP Students preparing for the AP exam may benefit from a set time limit when completing this Self-Check. This may also help to identify students with learning difficulties or slower paced students who need extra help.

GLENCOE Technology

Online Learning in the Classroom

You may wish to have students use QuickPass code ASD7844c9 for additional test preparation. They will be able to complete a self-check quiz for chapter review.

Answers

5

31. Hace _____ años que vivo en la misma casa.

32. Hace _____ años que estudio español.

33. Sí (No, no), hace mucho tiempo que mi mejor amigo(a) y yo nos conocemos.

6

34. Hacía

35. Hacía

7

36. *Answers will vary but should include two of the following:* el trigo, el ganado, la carne de res, el cordero.

37. *Answers will vary but should include two of the following:* el maíz, las papas, los tomates.

8

38. No comían tomates porque creían que eran venenosos y que morirían si los comieran.

39. El sencillo taco de carne refleja la historia de la comida porque es la combinación de dos civilizaciones—la civilización americana y la civilización europea.

40. Hay influencias del Medio Oriente en la cocina española porque los árabes invadieron España e introdujeron varios comestibles como la berenjena y la alcachofa.

Prepárate para el examen
Practice for oral proficiency

⭐ Tips for Success ....

Encourage students to say as much as possible when they do these open-ended activities. Tell them not to be afraid to make mistakes, since the goal of the activities is real-life communication. If someone in the group makes an error, allow the others to politely correct him or her. Let students choose the activities they would like to do.

Tell students to feel free to elaborate on the basic theme and to be creative. They may use props, pictures, or posters if they wish.

Pre-AP These oral activities will give students the opportunity to develop and improve their speaking skills so that they may succeed on the speaking portion of the AP exam.

Note: You may want to use the rubric below to help students prepare their speaking activities.

---

1 Comunidades
✓ *Talk about food in the United States*
Imagínate que estás viajando por un país latinoamericano y alguien te pregunta lo que se come aquí en Estados Unidos—lo que consideras una típica comida norteamericana. Se dice que no es muy fácil contestar esta pregunta. ¿Cómo la contestarías?

2 La comida étnica
✓ *Describe some ethnic meals from your family background*
Trabajen en grupos pequeños. Comparen y contrasten algunas comidas que comen en casa que tienen influencia de sus orígenes étnicos. ¿Hay muchas diferencias entre lo que comen ustedes? ¿Hay algunos platos que les interesan a todos?

3 Hace mucho tiempo que lo hago.
✓ *Talk about some things you have been doing for a long time*
Trabaja con un(a) compañero(a) de clase. Describan algunas cosas que ustedes hacen desde ya hace mucho tiempo—desde su niñez. Decidan lo que tienen en común.

CULTURA
Este joven cubano tiene una rebanada de pizza en cada mano.

4 Yo en la cocina
✓ *Discuss your talent or lack of talent in the kitchen*
¿Eres un(a) buen(a) cocinero(a) o no? Si por una razón u otra tuvieras que preparar una comida, ¿qué prepararías? Y, ¿cómo la prepararías? Da la receta.

5 No me tomes el pelo.
✓ *Talk about pulling someone's leg*
Piensa en algunas cosas que les dices a tus amigos o parientes cuando quieres tomarles el pelo. Dile a un(a) compañero(a) de clase lo que les dices. ¿Tienes el talento de convencerles que les estás hablando en serio o saben tus amigos enseguida lo que estás haciendo?

Scoring Rubric for Speaking

	4	3	2	1
vocabulary	extensive use of vocabulary, including idiomatic expressions	adequate use of vocabulary and idiomatic expressions	limited vocabulary marked with some anglicisms	limited vocabulary marked by frequent anglicisms that force interpretation by the listener
grammar	few or no grammatical errors	minor grammatical errors	some serious grammatical errors	serious grammatical errors
pronunciation	good intonation and largely accurate pronunciation with slight accent	acceptable intonation and pronunciation with distinctive accent	errors in intonation and pronunciation with heavy accent	errors in intonation and pronunciation that interfere with listener's comprehension
content	thorough response with interesting and pertinent detail	thorough response with sufficient detail	some detail, but not sufficient	general, insufficient response

Tarea

To celebrate the cultural exchange between Spain and the Americas, a popular Hispanic food magazine is going to publish the best article on any Latin American or Spanish dish that combines ingredients from both worlds. Based on your own research and on information presented in the textbook, write a short essay about a dish that mixes Old World and New World elements.

Writing Strategy

Thesis statement One thing all essays have in common is a thesis statement in which you present the main theme, explain the purpose of your essay, and tie everything together. In a sense, the thesis statement is like a road map that guides the reader by telling him or her what to expect. As with an outline, it is a good idea to compose your thesis statement before writing your essay to help organize your ideas and ensure that you do not stray off topic.

❶ Prewrite

- Conduct preliminary research to choose a dish that blends ingredients from the Americas with those introduced by Spanish colonizers. Use the following list to help you find the dish that will be the focus of your essay.

PRODUCTOS DE LAS AMÉRICAS	PRODUCTOS TRAÍDOS POR LOS ESPAÑOLES
el aguacate	el ajo
el cacahuate (maní)	la almendra
el cacao	el arroz
el calabacín	el azúcar
la calabaza	la cabra
el camote (batata, papa dulce)	la cebolla

el chile (ají)	el cerdo
el frijol	la gallina
el girasol	la harina de trigo
el maíz	la lechuga
el pavo (guajalote)	el limón
la papa	la manzana
la papaya	la naranja
el pimiento	la oliva (aceituna)
la piña	la oveja
la quinoa	el queso
el tomate	la uva
la vainilla	la vaca
la yuca (casava)	la zanahoria

- Once you have chosen your dish, you will need to research the history and background of the dish, as well as of the ingredients.
- Make an outline of the different parts of your essay and write your thesis statement.

❷ Write

- Be careful not to plagiarize and remember to cite your sources.
- Do not attempt to translate from English to Spanish. Whenever possible, stick to vocabulary and grammar that you already know.
- Use the following grammar points learned in this chapter: both forms of the passive voice, two different relative pronouns, and at least one expression of time with **hace** or **hacía.**

Evaluate

Your teacher will evaluate you on proper use of vocabulary, correct spelling and grammar, logical structure, clarity of expression, and overall content and style.

HISTORIA DE LA COMIDA LATINA

doscientos noventa y cinco **295**

Pre-AP This **tarea** will give students the opportunity to develop and improve their writing skills so that they may succeed on the writing portion of the AP exam.

Note: You may want to use the rubric below to help students prepare their writing task.

Scoring Rubric for Writing

	4	3	2	1
vocabulary	precise, varied	functional, fails to communicate complete meaning	limited to basic words, often inaccurate	inadequate
grammar	excellent, very few or no errors	some errors, do not hinder communication	numerous errors interfere with communication	many errors, little sentence structure
content	thorough response to the topic	generally thorough response to the topic	partial response to the topic	insufficient response to the topic
organization	well organized, ideas presented clearly and logically	loosely organized, but main ideas present	some attempts at organization, but with confused sequencing	lack of organization

Repaso del Capítulo 9

Grammar Review

This page provides a quick "at a glance" summary of the grammar points students have learned in this chapter. The corresponding page numbers are also listed so that students can easily find each grammar point as it was presented.

Differentiation

Multiple Intelligences

You may want to call on **verbal-linguistic** and **logical-mathematical** learners for whom grammar often comes easily to explain the main concepts to their classmates in their own words. Having students explain the concepts in different ways may also help slower paced learners or students with learning difficulties.

Gramática

- **La voz pasiva** *(page 276)*
  In Spanish, the passive voice is most frequently expressed by using the pronoun **se**. This **se** construction is also used when the subject is indefinite and the agent is not mentioned.

  > **Se venden legumbres en la verdulería.**
  > **Se habla español en muchos países.**

  The true passive is not frequently used in Spanish. The active voice is preferred.

  > ACTIVE **Los moros conquistaron España en el siglo ocho.**
  > PASSIVE **España fue conquistada por los moros en el siglo ocho.**

- **Los pronombres relativos** *(page 278)*
  The pronouns **el que, la que, los que,** and **las que** can be used as a subject or object and they can replace either a person or a thing.

  > **De todos mis hermanos es José el que tiene más talento.**
  > *Of all my brothers Joe is the one who has the most talent.*

  Note the sequence of tenses in the following sentences.

  > **El que habla ahora es mi hermano.** *(present / present)*
  > **La que hablará mañana es mi hermana.** *(future / present)*
  > **Los que hablaron ayer fueron mis primos.** *(preterite / preterite)*

  Lo que is a neuter relative pronoun.

  > **Lo que le hace falta a este plato es más sal.**
  > *What this dish needs is more salt.*

  Cuyo is an adjective equivalent to the English *whose* and agrees with the noun it modifies.

  > **Es la señora cuyos hijos son los dueños del restaurante.**
  > **El cocinero cuyas recetas prefiero trabaja en este restaurante.**

- **Expresiones de tiempo con hace y hacía** *(page 280)*
  The present tense is used with **hace** to express an action that began in the past and continues into the present. English uses the present perfect.

  > **Hace dos años que estoy aquí.**   *I have been here for two years.*

  The imperfect tense is used with **hacía** to express what had been going on before something else happened.

  > **Hacía mucho tiempo que él lo sabía.**   *He had known it for a long time.*

CULTURA

Un azulejo con la figura de un señor musulmán en la fachada de una casa en Ronda, España

There are a number of cognates in this list. See how many you and a partner can find. Who can find the most? Compare your list with those of your classmates.

Vocabulario

Identifying more foods

las legumbres, las hortalizas	el pimiento	la carne	unas especias
la zanahoria	la alcachofa	la carne de res	el orégano
la col, el repollo	una mazorca de maíz	el cordero	el cilantro
las vainitas, las judías verdes	las hojas de lechuga, la hoja	el cerdo	el trigo
la berenjena		el picadillo, la carne picada	la harina
			las uvas

Talking about food preparation

el/la cocinero(a)	el pan rallado	la olla	rellenar
la rodaja	el aceite de oliva	cocinar	hervir
el huevo batido	el/la sartén	freír	rebozar

Other useful words and expressions

la viña	la huerta	cultivar
la vid	los comensales	
el huerto	orgulloso(a)	

HISTORIA DE LA COMIDA LATINA

doscientos noventa y siete **297**

Vocabulary Review

The words and phrases in the **Vocabulario** section have been taught for productive use in this chapter. They are summarized here as a resource for both student and teacher. This list also serves as a convenient resource for the **Prepárate para el examen** on pages 292–295.

GLENCOE SPANISH

Why It Works!

This vocabulary reference list has not been translated into English for two reasons. First, it is recommended that students learn the new vocabulary through direct association with images on the **Vocabulario** pages. Second, all vocabulary is reintroduced in the chapter many times, and upon completion of the chapter students should be familiar with the meaning of all the words. If there are words that students still do not know, they can refer back to the vocabulary presentation in the chapter or the dictionary at the end of the book. If, however, it is your preference to give students the English translations, please refer to Vocabulary Transparency V9.1 or to the Chapter 9 PowerPoint® presentation on PowerTeach.

Differentiation

Slower Paced Learners

Slower paced learners may benefit from creating their own visual dictionary of nouns and adjectives in this list. They can either draw their own depictions or use images from the Internet or magazines.

Don't forget the chapter project and cultural activities found on pages 268C–268D. Students have learned all the information that they will need to complete these engaging enrichment tasks.

 The cognates in this list are: **el orégano, el cilantro, oliva, la viña, cultivar.**

 Cultural Snapshot

(page 297) This is a typical Andalusian olive grove.

Every chapter of ¡Así se dice!
contains this review section of
previously learned material.
By recycling information from
previous chapters, the cumulative review serves to remind
students that they need to continue practicing what they
have learned after finishing
each chapter.

Activity 1 This activity
reviews vocabulary related to
art and literature. See pages
204–205, 208–209.

🎧 **Audio Script** (CD 9, Track 14)

1. Es una cerámica de bronce.
2. Los protagonistas son los
   personajes más importantes
   de una obra.
3. Muchos poemas tiene rima,
   pero no todos.
4. Hay una diferencia entre
   óleos y acuarelas.
5. Si yo tuviera dinero,
   compraría el cuadro.
6. Una novela es más larga que
   un cuento.
7. Si tuviera más talento, pintaría
   una naturaleza muerta.
8. En Salamanca hay una
   biblioteca llena de obras
   literarias famosas.
9. Cada serie de versos es una
   estrofa.
10. Si fueran a España, visitarían
    el museo del Prado.

Activity 2 This activity
reviews vocabulary related to
food and food preparation. See
pages R37, 4–5, 272.

Activity 3 This activity
reviews food vocabulary and
grammar used to express like,
dislike, and want. See pages
R37, R46, 4–5.

Activity 4 This activity
reviews food and restaurant
vocabulary. See pages R37,
R60, 4–5.

298

Repaso cumulativo

Repasa lo que ya has aprendido

These activities will help you review and remember
what you have learned so far in Spanish.

 Escucha las frases. Indica en una tabla como la de
abajo si la frase se refiere al arte o a la literatura.

arte	literatura

 Haz una lista de los ingredientes que pondrías en una
buena ensalada.

 Personaliza. Da respuestas personales.

1. ¿Cuáles son los comestibles que te gustan?
2. ¿Cuáles son algunos comestibles que no te gustan?
3. ¿Cómo te gusta la carne de res? ¿Casi cruda, a
   término medio o bien hecha?
4. ¿Te gustan más los mariscos o el pescado?
5. ¿Te gusta el postre?
6. ¿Cuáles son tus postres favoritos?
7. ¿Qué comes para el desayuno?
8. ¿Qué comes para el almuerzo?
9. ¿A qué hora desayunas?
10. ¿A qué hora almuerzas?

 Usa cada palabra en una frase original.

el primer plato   *el postre*   *la sobremesa*

el segundo plato   *el cuchillo*   *el tenedor*

el servicio   *el menú*   *la cuenta*

la cuchara

298   *doscientos noventa y ocho*   CAPÍTULO 9

Answers

1. arte   6. literatura
2. literatura   7. arte
3. literatura   8. literatura
4. arte   9. literatura
5. arte   10. arte

 Answers will vary but may include: En una buena ensalada
pondría lechuga, tomates, cebollas, pepinos, pimientos y aguacate.

3

1. Los comestibles que me gustan son ____.
2. Algunos comestibles que no me gustan son ____.
3. Me gusta la carne de res casi cruda (a término medio, bien
   hecha).

Completa en el presente y el pretérito.

1. Los meseros _____ la comida. (servir)
2. Yo _____ un biftec a término medio. (pedir)
3. El mesero me lo _____ como yo lo _____. (servir, pedir)
4. Tú _____ el pescado pero nosotros no lo _____. (freír, freír)
5. Él _____ todo y yo no _____ nada. (repetir, repetir)

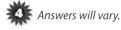 **Crea una historia sobre la familia Suárez según los dibujos. Luego preséntala a la clase.**

HISTORIA DE LA COMIDA LATINA

 Activity 5 This activity reviews using verbs in the present and past tenses. See pages R7, R17, R29, R31.

Activity 6 This activity reviews family vocabulary, home vocabulary, and food shopping vocabulary. See pages R2, R36–R37.

GLENCOE Technology

Audio in the Classroom

The ¡Así se dice! Audio Program for Chapter 9 has 14 activities, which afford students extensive listening and speaking practice.

Online Learning in the Classroom

You may wish to have students use QuickPass code ASD7844c9 for additional cumulative review. They will be able to complete a self-check quiz.

Pre-AP To give students further open-ended oral or written practice, or to assess proficiency, go to AP Proficiency Practice Transparency AP28.

Answers

4. Me gustan más los mariscos. (Me gusta más el pescado.)
5. Sí, (No, no) me gusta el postre.
6. Mis postres favoritos son _____.
7. Para el desayuno como _____.
8. Para el almuerzo como _____.
9. Desayuno a las _____.
10. Almuerzo a la(s) _____.

4 *Answers will vary.*

5
1. sirven, sirvieron
2. pido, pedí
3. sirve, pido; sirvió, pedí
4. fríes, freímos; freíste, freímos
5. repite, repito; repitió, repetí

6 *Answers will vary, but students should use as much vocabulary as possible having to do with families, free time activities, vegetables and fruits, and shopping. They should also use any expressions they have learned that would be used in a market.*

Chapter Overview
Carreras

● Scope and Sequence

Topics
- Careers
- Job applications and interviews
- Second language and the job market

Culture
- Shopping on Calle Florida in Buenos Aires
- Mezquita de Cordoba and other Arabic influences throughout Spain
- *Un día de éstos* by Garbriel García Márquez

Functions
- How to talk about professions and occupations
- How to have a job interview
- How to discuss the importance of learning a second language
- How to read a short story by the Colombian novelist Gabriel García Márquez

Structure
- **Por** and **para**
- The subjunctive with relative clauses

● Planning Guide

	required	recommended	optional
Vocabulario (*pages 304–309*) Profesiones Oficios	✔		
Gramática (*pages 310–317*) **Por** y **para** **Por** y **para** con expresiones de tiempo **Por** y **para** con el infinitivo Otros usos de **por** y **para** El subjuntivo en cláusulas relativas	✔		
Conversación (*pages 318–319*) Solicitando un puesto		✔	
Lectura cultural (*pages 320–321*) Una lengua importante		✔	
Literatura (*pages 322–327*) *Un día de éstos*			✔
Prepárate para el examen (*pages 328–331*)			✔
Repaso cumulativo (*pages 334–335*)			✔

Correlations to National Foreign Language Standards

Page numbers in light print refer to the Student Edition. Page numbers in bold print refer to the Teacher Edition.	
Communication Standard 1.1 Interpersonal	pp. **300C, 302–303, 305, 307,** 308, **308, 317, 319, 320, 321, 327,** 330
Communication Standard 1.2 Interpretive	pp. **300C, 304,** 306, 307, 308, **309,** 311, **312, 313,** 315, 317, **318,** 319, 320, 321, 324, **324,** 327, **327,** 329, **329,** 330, 334, **335**
Communication Standard 1.3 Presentational	pp. **300C, 305,** 307, **307, 318, 320, 321, 322, 325, 328,** 331, **332**
Cultures Standard 2.1	pp. **300D,** 302–303
Cultures Standard 2.2	pp. **300D,** 307, **311, 312,** 315, 320, **322,** 330, **330**
Connections Standard 3.1	pp. **300C, 300D, 302–303, 320,** 322, **322,** 323, 324, 329, 330
Connections Standard 3.2	pp. 304, **304,** 305, **307, 316,** 317, **317,** 319, **319,** 321, **321,** 324–326, 327
Comparisons Standard 4.1	pp. 304, 305, 310, 313, 320, **332,** 333
Comparisons Standard 4.2	pp. 301, **301,** 316, 320, 321, 330
Communities Standard 5.1	pp. **300C,** 302–303, 307, 308, 311, 315, 321, **323,** 327, 330, **330, 332**
Communities Standard 5.2	pp. 304, **304, 316,** 317, 319, **319,** 321, **321**

To read the ACTFL Standards in their entirety, see the front of the Teacher Edition.

Student Resources

Print

Workbook *(pp. 10.3–10.12)*
Audio Activities *(pp. 10.13–10.16)*
Pre-AP Workbook, Chapter 10

Technology

- StudentWorks™ Plus
- ¡Así se dice! Vocabulario en vivo
- ¡Así se dice! Gramática en vivo
- ¡Así se dice! Diálogo en vivo
- ¡Así se dice! Cultura en vivo
- Vocabulary PuzzleMaker
- **QuickPass** glencoe.com

Teacher Resources

Print

TeacherTools, Chapter 10
    Workbook TE *(pp. 10.3–10.12)*
    Audio Activities TE *(pp. 10.15–10.30)*
    Quizzes 1–3 *(pp. 10.33–10.36)*
    Tests *(pp. 10.38–10.57)*
    Performance Assessment, Task 10 *(pp. 10.59–10.62)*

Technology

- Quick Start Transparencies 10.1–10.3
- Vocabulary Transparencies V10.1–V10.3
- Audio CD 10
- *ExamView® Assessment Suite*
- TeacherWorks™ Plus
- PowerTeach
- ¡Así se dice! Video Program
- Vocabulary PuzzleMaker
- **QuickPass** glencoe.com

Chapter Project

Una entrevista de trabajo

Students will work in pairs to plan and perform a job interview for a position in which knowledge of Spanish would be beneficial.

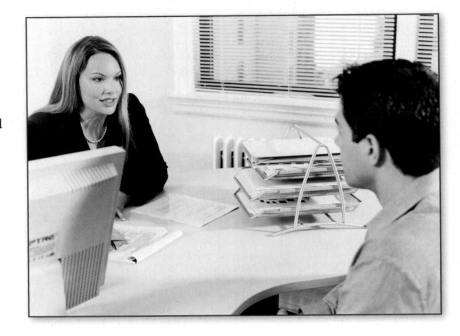

1. Divide the class into pairs. Have each pair choose an appropriate profession for which knowledge of Spanish would be useful and decide who will play the roles of interviewer and interviewee. Students should work together to create a script that will serve as a guideline for the performance of their interview.

2. Each student will submit a draft of the entire script, to be checked or peer edited, then revised and turned in with the final version. Students should prepare for their interview by practicing several times. Each interview performance should incorporate at least three visual aids or props. You may wish to allow students to use note cards for prompting, but remind them that reading directly from their note cards will result in a lower score.

3. To add an element of improvisation and to check for comprehension, ask additional follow-up questions or have members of the class do so. If you have access to video equipment, record the students' performances and play them back to allow students to critique their own and classmates' interviews. They can discuss the importance of interviewing skills in the real world and the importance of mastering Spanish for certain professions.

Expansion: This project could be combined with the writing assignment for this chapter on page 331, which is to create a résumé or curriculum vitae. In this case, students could exchange roles and interview each other for their dream job.

Scoring Rubric for Project

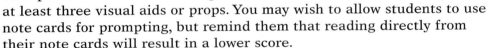
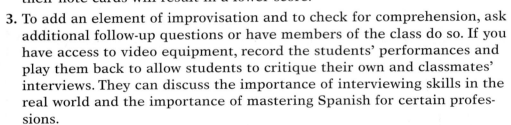

	1	3	5
Evidence of planning	Draft of script is not provided.	Draft of script is provided but is not corrected.	Corrected draft of script is provided.
Use of props or visual aides	Interview uses no props or visual aids.	Interview uses one or two props or visual aids.	Interview uses several props or visual aids.
Presentation	Interview contains little of the required elements.	Interview contains some of the required elements.	Interview contains all the required elements.

Culture

● Inti Raymi

Every June 24th, hundreds of thousands of visitors flock to Cuzco, Peru to witness **Inti Raymi,** the Festival of the Sun. The second-largest festival in South America, this celebration includes a week of parades, music, and dancing that culminates in an ancient Incan religious ceremony honoring the sun, **Inti Raymi,** that is performed by more than five hundred actors. The ceremony begins in Cuzco in front of the Santo Domingo church, which was built over the remains of the ancient Inca Temple of the Sun. Here Sapa Inca (the Inca Emperor) gives an invocation to the crowd and is then carried on a golden throne in a procession of elaborately costumed high priests, officials of the court, and nobles to the ancient fortress of Sacsayhuamán, two kilometers from Cuzco. When the procession reaches Sacsayhuamán, Sapa Inca climbs to a high altar so everyone in the crowd can see him. There a llama is sacrificed (in a realistic simulation) and the high priest raises the heart to ensure the fertility of the earth. The priests then examine the bloodstains to see the future of the Inca. At dusk, large stacks of straw are set on fire as the procession returns to Cuzco. **Inti Raymi** marks the winter solstice in Peru and the start of a new year for the sun. Have students research other celebrations or rituals throughout the world that mark the summer or winter solstice.

● La música andina

Although the European conquest of the sixteenth century introduced Spanish and African cultural influences that have since affected its music, Latin America possessed indigenous sounds—one was Andean music. Andean music comes from countries that were once inhabited by the Incas—Chile, Peru, Argentina, Ecuador, and Bolivia. One element that distinguishes this music from other Latin American genres is its unique instrumentation. Traditional woodwind instruments used in Andean music are the **quena,** a notched-end flute, **zampoñas,** or panpipes, and the **tarka,** a vertical flute. Drums, represented by **tambar** or **bombo,** are used to drive the rhythm. The Spanish affected this musical form by introducing stringed instruments to the Incas, resulting in the use of the harp and the invention of the **charango**, a small 10-string guitar made from the shell of an armadillo. During the 1960s there was a revitalization of Andean music that led to the creation of **nueva canción.** This new form of music contained lyrics charged with social and political issues and would take on the role of protest music for decades to come. Andean music remains widely available and musical groups who perform this traditional musical can be found all over the world. Have students research names of popular Andean music artists or samples of Andean music.

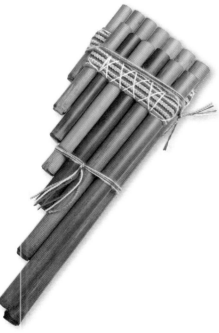

50-Minute Lesson Plans

	Objective	Present	Practice	Assess/Homework
Day 1	Talk about professions and occupations	Chapter Opener, pp. 300–301 (5 min.) Introducción al tema, pp. 302–303 (10 min.) Core Instruction/Vocabulario, pp. 304–305 (15 min.)	Activities 1–5, pp. 306–307 (20 min.)	Student Workbook Activities A–D, pp. 10.3–10.4 *QuickPass* Vocabulary Practice
Day 2	Talk about professions and occupations	Quick Start, p. 304 (5 min.) Review Vocabulario, pp. 304–305 (5 min.) Video, Vocabulario en vivo (10 min.)	Activities 6–10, pp. 307–308 (15 min.) Estudio de palabras, p. 309 (5 min.) Audio Activities A–F, pp. 10.15–10.18 (10 min.)	Student Workbook Activities E–G, pp. 10.4–10.5 *QuickPass* Vocabulary Practice
Day 3	**Por** and **para**	Quick Start, p. 310 (5 min.) Core Instruction/Gramática, **Por** y **para**, p. 310 (10 min.) Core Instruction/Gramática, **Por** y **para** con expresiones de tiempo, p. 312 (5 min.)	Activities 1–2, p. 311 (10 min.) Activities 3–4, p. 312 (10 min.)	Quiz 1, p. 10.33 (10 min.) *QuickPass* Grammar Practice
Day 4	**Por** and **para**	Quick Start, p. 314 (5 min.) Core Instruction/Gramática, **Por** y **para** con el infinitivo, p. 313 (10 min.) Core Instruction/Gramática, Otros usos de **por** y **para**, p. 314 (10 min.)	Activities 5–6, pp. 313–314 (10 min.) Activities 7–9, pp. 315–316 (10 min.) Audio Activity A, p. 10.19 (5 min.)	Student Workbook Activities A–B, pp. 10.6–10.7 *QuickPass* Grammar Practice
Day 5	The subjunctive with relative clauses	Core Instruction/Gramática, El subjuntivo en cláusulas relativas, p. 316 (10 min.) Video, Gramática en vivo (10 min.)	Activities 10–11, p. 317 (10 min.) Audio Activities B–C, pp. 10.19–10.20 (10 min.)	Quiz 2, p. 10.34 (10 min.) Student Workbook Activities A–B, p. 10.8 *QuickPass* Grammar Practice
Day 6	Develop reading and listening comprehension skills	Core Instruction/Conversación, p. 318 (20 min.) Video, Diálogo en vivo (10 min.)	¿Comprendes? A–B, p. 319 (10 min.)	Quiz 3, p. 10.35 (10 min.) ¿Comprendes? C, p. 319 *QuickPass* Conversation
Day 7	Discuss the importance of learning a second language	Core Instruction/Lectura cultural, p. 320 (15 min.) Video, Cultura en vivo (10 min.)	¿Comprendes? A–B, p. 321 (10 min.)	Listening Comprehension Test, pp. 10.53–10.54 (15 min.) ¿Comprendes? C, p. 321 *QuickPass* Reading Practice
Day 8	Read a short story by the Colombian novelist Gabriel García Márquez	Core Instruction/Vocabulario, p. 322 (5 min.) Core Instruction/Literatura, pp. 323–326 (30 min.)	Vocabulario, Práctica, p. 323 (5 min.) ¿Comprendes? A–B, p. 327 (10 min.)	¿Comprendes? C–D, p. 327 *QuickPass* Reading Practice
Day 9	Read a short story by the Colombian novelist Gabriel García Márquez	Review Literatura, pp. 323–326 (10 min.)	¿Comprendes? C–D, p. 327 (15 min.) Prepárate para el examen, pp. 328–329 (25 min.)	Prepárate para el examen, Practice for written proficiency, p. 331 *QuickPass* Reading Practice
Day 10	Chapter review	Repaso del Capítulo 10, pp. 332–333 (15 min.)	Prepárate para el examen, Practice for oral proficiency, p. 330 (20 min.)	Test for Writing Proficiency, p. 10.57 (15 min.) Review for chapter test

Day 11	Chapter 10 Tests (50 min.)
	  Reading and Writing Test, pp. 10.43–10.49
	  Literature Test, pp. 10.50–10.52
	  Speaking Test, p. 10.55
	  Test for Oral Proficiency, p. 10.56			

90-Minute Lesson Plans

	Objective	Present	Practice	Assess/Homework
Block 1	Talk about professions and occupations	Chapter Opener, pp. 300–301 (5 min.) Introducción al tema, pp. 302–303 (10 min.) Quick Start, p. 304 (5 min.) Core Instruction/Vocabulario, pp. 304–305 (15 min.) Video, Vocabulario en vivo (10 min.)	Activities 1–10, pp. 306–308 (20 min.) Estudios de palabras, p. 309 (5 min.) Audio Activities A–F, pp. 10.15–10.18 (20 min.)	Student Workbook Activities A–G, pp. 10.3–10.5 *QuickPass* Vocabulary Practice
Block 2	**Por** and **para**	Quick Start, p. 310 (5 min.) Core Instruction/Gramática, **Por** y **para**, p. 310 (20 min.) Core Instruction/Gramática, **Por** y **para** con expresiones de tiempo, p. 312 (10 min.) Core Instruction/Gramática, **Por** y **para** con el infinitivo, p. 313 (15 min.)	Activities 1–2, p. 311 (10 min.) Activities 3–4, p. 312 (10 min) Activities 5–6, pp. 313–314 (10 min.)	Quiz 1, p. 10.33 (10 min.) *QuickPass* Grammar Practice
Block 3	**Por** and **para** The subjunctive with relative clauses	Quick Start, p. 314 (5 min.) Core Instruction/Gramática, Otros usos de **por** y **para**, p. 314 (15 min.) Core Instruction/Gramática, El subjuntivo en cláusulas relativas, p. 316 (15 min.) Video, Gramática en vivo (10 min.)	Activities 7–9, pp. 315–316 (15 min.) Activities 10–11, p. 317 (15 min.) Audio Activities A–C, pp. 10.19–10.20 (15 min.)	Student Workbook Activities A–B, pp. 10.6–10.7 Student Workbook Activities A–B, p. 10.8 *QuickPass* Grammar Practice
Block 4	Discuss the importance of learning a second language	Core Instruction/Conversación, p. 318 (15 min.) Video, Diálogo en vivo (10 min.) Core Instruction/Lectura cultural, p. 320 (20 min.) Video, Cultura en vivo (10 min.)	¿Comprendes? A–B, p. 319 (5 min.) ¿Comprendes? A–C, p. 321 (10 min.)	Quizzes 2–3, pp. 10.34–10.35 (20 min.) ¿Comprendes? C, p. 319 *QuickPass* Conversation, Reading Practice
Block 5	Read a short story by the Colombian novelist Gabriel García Márquez	Core Instruction/Vocabulario, p. 322 (5 min.) Core Instruction/Literatura, pp. 323–326 (30 min.)	Vocabulario, Práctica, p. 323 (5 min.) ¿Comprendes? A–D, p. 327 (20 min.) Prepárate para el examen, Practice for oral proficiency 1–3, p. 330 (15 min.)	Listening Comprehension Test, pp. 10.53–10.54 (15 min.) *QuickPass* Reading Practice
Block 6	Chapter Review	Repaso del Capítulo 10, pp. 332–333 (15 min.)	Prepárate para el examen, pp. 328–329 (20 min.) Prepárate para el examen, Practice for oral proficiency 4–5, p. 330 (15 min.) Prepárate para el examen, Practice for written proficiency, p. 331 (30 min.)	Literature Test, pp. 10.50–10.52 (10 min.) Review for chapter test

Block 7	Chapter 10 Tests (50 min.)
	  Reading and Writing Test, pp. 10.43–10.49
	  Speaking Test, p. 10.55
	  Test for Oral Proficiency, p. 10.56
	  Test for Writing Proficiency, p. 10.57
	Chapter Project, p. 300C (40 min.)			

Preview

In this chapter, students will learn the basic vocabulary to discuss careers and trades. They will also learn the importance of knowing Spanish and/or another language in today's globalized business world. Students will read a short story by the famous Colombian writer García Márquez about a dentist and a politician. They will also learn the uses of **por** and **para** and the subjunctive in relative clauses.

Pacing

It is important to note that once you reach **¡Bravo!** in the chapter, there is no more new material for the students to learn. The rest of the chapter recycles what has already been covered. The suggested pacing listed here leaves two to three days for review, assessment, and enrichment activities such as the chapter project.

Vocabulario	1–2 days
Gramática	2–3 days
Conversación	1 day
Lectura cultural	1 day
Literatura	1 day

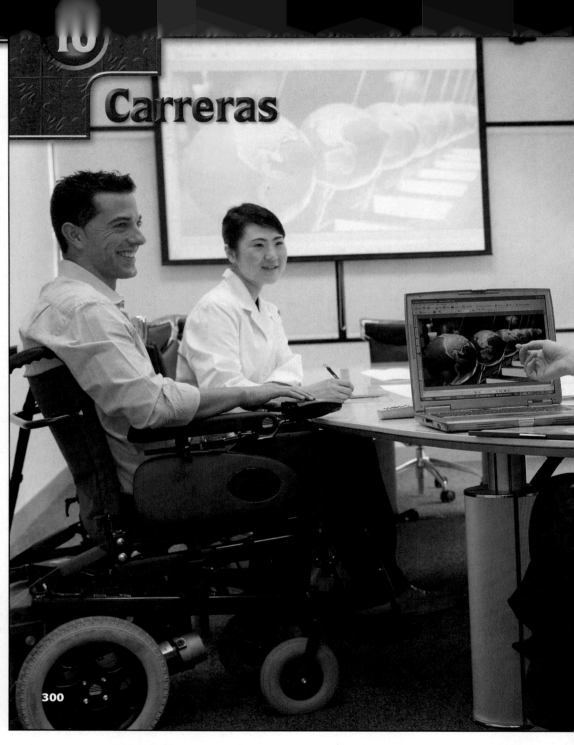

Carreras

300

TeacherWorks Plus

The **¡Así se dice!** TeacherWorks™ Plus CD-ROM is an all-in-one planner and resource center. You may wish to use several of the following features as you plan and present the Chapter 10 material: Interactive Teacher Edition, Interactive Lesson Planner with Calendar, and Point and Click Access to Teaching Resources including Hotlinks to the Internet and Correlations to the National Standards.

Vamos a comparar Vamos a observar el impacto y la importancia de la globalización en Estados Unidos igual que en el mundo hispanohablante. Vamos a explorar también las oportunidades profesionales disponibles para el que tenga un conocimiento del español.

Cultural Comparison
Students will observe people of many nationalities working for multinational enterprises in all parts of the world.

Objetivos

You will:

- talk about professions and occupations
- have a job interview
- discuss the importance of learning a second language
- read a short story by the famous Colombian writer Gabriel García Márquez

You will use:

- **por** and **para**
- the subjunctive in relative clauses

◀ **El personal de esta empresa española en el Parque Tecnológico de San Sebastián es de muchas nacionalidades. Como muchas empresas multinacionales tienen que reclutar personal que hable una variedad de idiomas.**

QuickPass

Go to glencoe.com
For: **Online book**
Web code: **ASD7844c10**

trescientos uno **301**

QUIA **Quia Interactive Online Student Edition** found at quia.com allows students to complete activities online and submit them for computer grading for instant feedback or teacher grading with suggestions for what to review. Students can also record speaking activities, listen to chapter audio, and watch the videos that correspond with each chapter. As a teacher you are able to create rosters, set grading parameters, and post assignments for each class. After students complete activities, you can view the results and recommend remediation or review. You can also add your own customized activities for additional student practice.

Introducción al tema

▶ PRESENT

Introduce the theme of the chapter by having students look at the photographs on these pages. Once you have completed the vocabulary presentation, have students return to these pages and read the information that accompanies each photograph. Once students are fully acquainted with the vocabulary and grammar of the chapter, you may wish to come back to these pages and ask the questions that go with each photo.

Cultural Snapshot

California *(page 302)* ¿Quién es el alcalde de Los Ángeles?

México *(page 302)* ¿Está en la Ciudad de México el banco? ¿Es una sucursal de un banco estadounidense? ¿Tienen muchos bancos estadounidenses sucursales en países hispanohablantes? ¿Tienen muchos bancos extranjeros sucursales en Estados Unidos?

Argentina *(page 302)* ¿Están participando estos ejecutivos en una teleconferencia? Los ejecutivos que están sentados en la mesa, ¿están en Buenos Aires? ¿Trabajan para una empresa multinacional en Argentina? El señor que está en la pantalla, ¿dónde está su oficina? ¿Trabajan todos con la misma empresa?

Introducción al tema
Carreras

El tema de este capítulo son carreras y oficios— el trabajo que se puede hacer con y sin preparación universitaria. Explorará también unas profesiones y oficios en los cuales el conocimiento del español te beneficiará.

▲ **California** Antonio Villaraigosa, alcalde de Los Ángeles

◀ **México** Una sucursal de un banco estadounidense en la Ciudad de México

Argentina Ejecutivos de una empresa multinacional en Buenos Aires participan en una teleconferencia con sus colegas en su oficina en Nueva York. El señor en la pantalla está usando su español en su oficina en Estados Unidos. ▼

302

ABOGADOS
Pablo Rojo Platero
ENGLISH SPOKEN LAWYERS
PROPERTY ADVISER

▲ **España** Los abogados tienen clientes anglohablantes en su bufete en Madrid. Aunque ellos hablan inglés, ¿lo dominan bien?

▲ **Miami Beach** Estos dos policías están usando su español mientras ayudan a un joven latino.

Dental Assistant Needed
Spanish Speaking
No Experience Necessary

▲ **San Antonio** Están buscando un asistente dental que hable español. Y no es necesario que tenga experiencia.

▲ **Miami** Un congreso (una convención) donde están reclutando candidatos que hablen español para una variedad de empleos

Nueva York Esta guía en las Naciones Unidas habla con turistas y visitantes de todas partes del mundo. ▶

303

España *(page 303)* ¿Cómo se sabe que estos abogados españoles tienen clientes que hablan inglés? ¿Qué indica que no dominan perfectamente el inglés?

Miami *(page 303 middle left)* ¿Qué se reclutan en este congreso? ¿Qué tienen que hablar los candidatos? ¿Qué tipo de empleos hay?

Nueva York *(page 303)* ¿Dónde trabaja esta guía? ¿Con quiénes trabaja? ¿Qué tiene que hablar?

Resources

- Vocabulary Transparencies V10.2–V10.3
- Audio Activities TE, pages 10.15–10.18
- Audio CD 10, Tracks 1–6
- Workbook, pages 10.3–10.5
- Quiz 1, page 10.33
- *ExamView® Assessment Suite*

Quick Start

Use QS Transparency 10.1 or write the following on the board.

Usa cada palabra en una frase original.

1. el profesor
2. el médico
3. el enfermero
4. el mesero
5. el cocinero
6. el asistente de vuelo

▶ TEACH

Core Instruction

Step 1 Have students either read or repeat these words once.

Step 2 You may wish to give students sentences using each word or have them use each word in a sentence.

Step 3 You may wish to have students listen to the sentences using Audio CD 10.

Step 4 Have students give another word or expression for each of the following: una compañía, un comerciante, un propietario, empleados del gobierno, una solicitud, el departamento de personal, el candidato, un empleo.

Profesiones

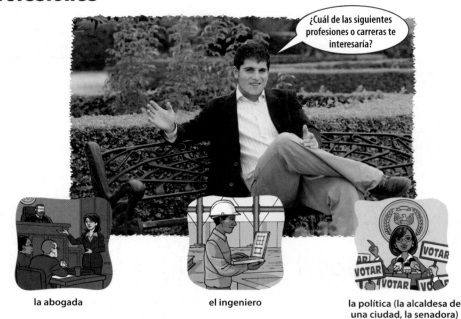

¿Cuál de las siguientes profesiones o carreras te interesaría?

la abogada   el ingeniero   la política (la alcaldesa de una ciudad, la senadora)

Oficios

¿Cuál de los siguientes oficios te interesaría?

el plomero, el fontanero

la albañil

Nota

Los nombres de muchas profesiones y oficios son palabras afines: asistente, ejecutivo, arquitecto, dentista, farmacéutico, programador de computadoras (informática); electricista, carpintero, mecánico(a), plomero (fontanero).

304 *trescientos cuatro*   CAPÍTULO 10

Los comerciantes trabajan para una
compañía (empresa, sociedad).
Los comerciantes se llaman también
hombres o mujeres de negocios.
Los comerciantes pueden ser también
dueños de una tienda.

Los contables preparan
estados financieros.

No puedo trabajar a tiempo completo.
Quiero un trabajo a tiempo parcial.

un anuncio
(clasificado)

Elena es una estudiante universitaria.
Lee los anuncios clasificados.
No puede ni quiere trabajar cuarenta
horas por semana.

Los funcionarios trabajan en
una oficina gubernamental
(de gobierno).

una solicitud
(aplicación) de
empleo

El señor está en la oficina del departamento de personal.
Se dice también «el servicio de recursos humanos».
El señor ha llenado una solicitud de empleo.
El candidato (aspirante) está teniendo una entrevista.
Está buscando un puesto que le pague bien.

Tips for Success

Have students look at the photos, make up questions about them, and ask other members of the class.

Comunicación

Presentational

Divide the class into several groups. Have each group create a matching activity pairing vocabulary related to jobs with a description of each job. Have each group present their activity to the rest of the class.

GLENCOE Technology

You may wish to use the editable PowerPoint® presentation on PowerTeach for additional vocabulary instruction and practice.

Nota

En español, la palabra
general **oficina** cambia
según la profesión.
- el bufete del abogado
- el consultorio (la consulta)
  del médico
- el gabinete del dentista

trescientos cinco **305**

▶ PRACTICE

Leveling EACH Activity

Easy Activities 1, 2, 6, 7
Average Activities 5, 8,
  Activity 7 **Expansión**
CHallenging Activities 3, 4

Activity ①

🎧 **Audio Script**

1. los que cuidan de las muelas (los dientes)
2. los que trabajan para una empresa o son dueños de establecimientos que tienen como meta u objetivo la compra y venta de mercancías
3. los que cuidan y curan a los enfermos
4. los que preparan y analizan los datos y estados financieros de una empresa
5. los que tienen empleos gubernamentales
6. los que conciben y ejecutan la construcción de un edificio
7. los que hacen o venden cosas de madera

Activity ② This activity can be done orally with books closed calling on students at random to respond.

Activity ③ You may wish to have students prepare this activity before going over it in class.

CULTURA
El pintor está pintando un cuadro del paisaje de la Costa Brava en España.

CULTURA
¿Qué expresión tiene en la cara este niño en el gabinete del dentista?

① Escucha y escoge de la lista la profesión que se describe.

los médicos	los contables
los arquitectos	los funcionarios
los comerciantes	los farmacéuticos
los carpinteros	los alcaldes
los ejecutivos	los dentistas

HABLAR

② Contesta. ¿A quién necesitas si…
1. tienes que reparar tu carro?
2. tienes un problema legal?
3. no te sientes bien, estás enfermo(a)?
4. el agua está goteando (saliendo) de la lavadora?
5. te duele una muela?
6. tienes una receta del médico?

HABLAR • ESCRIBIR

③ Aquí tienes una lista de otras profesiones u oficios que conoces. Con un(a) compañero(a), describe el trabajo que hace cada uno(a).
1. el/la empleado(a) en una tienda
2. el/la mesero(a)
3. el/la agricultor(a)
4. el/la profesor(a)
5. el/la recepcionista
6. el/la asistente(a) de vuelo
7. el/la cocinero(a)
8. el/la pintor(a)
9. el/la mecánico(a)
10. el/la enfermero(a)

④ **Juego** Piensa en un oficio o profesión. Tu compañero(a) te puede hacer hasta tres preguntas para ayudarle a adivinar o acertar el oficio o la profesión en que estás pensando. Túrnense.

Answers

①
1. los dentistas
2. los comerciantes
3. los médicos
4. los contables
5. los funcionarios
6. los arquitectos
7. los carpinteros

②
1. Necesito un mecánico.
2. Necesito un abogado.
3. Necesito un médico.
4. Necesito un plomero (fontanero).
5. Necesito un dentista.
6. Necesito un farmacéutico.

③ *Answers will vary but may include:*

1. El/La empleado(a) en una tienda ayuda a los clientes en la tienda.
2. El/La mesero(a) les sirve a los clientes en un restaurante.
3. El/La agricultor(a) siembra los campos y cultiva las legumbres en una finca.
4. El/La profesor(a) enseña.
5. El/La recepcionista les da su llave a los huéspedes en un hotel.
6. El/La asistente(a) de vuelo les sirve la comida a los pasajeros en un avión.
7. El/La cocinero(a) prepara los platos en un restaurante.
8. El/La pintor(a) pinta cuadros.
9. El/La mecánico(a) repara los carros.
10. El/La enfermero(a) ayuda al médico y les toma la tensión arterial a los pacientes.

ESCUCHAR • HABLAR

5 Contesta sobre una visita a un departamento de recursos humanos.

1. Anita está en una oficina del departamento de recursos humanos. ¿Estará buscando ella un puesto con la compañía?
2. ¿Es posible que ella esté un poco nerviosa?
3. ¿Quiere ella un trabajo que sea interesante y que le pague bien?
4. ¿Va a tener ella una entrevista?
5. ¿Debe Anita tener una carta de recomendación?
6. ¿Tendrá ella que llenar una solicitud de trabajo?

SE NECESITAN
CARPINTEROS
FINISHERS Y PINTORES
CON LICENCIA DE CONDUCIR VÁLIDA
Y EXPERIENCIA EN CARPINTERIA
Necesita documentos
legales para trabajar.
Salario basado en experiencia
703-699-6998
Llamar de 8-5pm

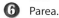 LEER

6 Parea.

1. el departamento
2. recursos humanos
3. un puesto
4. el candidato
5. anuncios

a. un trabajo, un empleo
b. el aspirante
c. el servicio
d. clasificados
e. personal

 ESCUCHAR • HABLAR

7 Contesta según se indica.

1. ¿Juan busca trabajo? (sí)
2. ¿Qué ha leído? (un anuncio en el periódico)
3. ¿Qué compañía está reclutando (buscando) empleados? (Bancomar)
4. ¿Adónde va Juan? (al departamento de recursos humanos de Bancomar)
5. ¿Qué tiene que llenar? (una solicitud de empleo)
6. ¿A quién le da la solicitud? (a la recepcionista)
7. ¿Qué va a tener? (una entrevista)

(EXPANSIÓN)

Ahora, sin mirar las preguntas, cuenta la información en tus propias palabras. Si no recuerdas algo, un(a) compañero(a) te puede ayudar.

 LEER • ESCRIBIR

8 Completa con una palabra apropiada.

1. Juan está buscando trabajo pero no quiere trabajar cuarenta horas por semana. Está buscando trabajo _____.
2. El que trabaja cuarenta horas por semana trabaja _____.
3. Su padre le dice que lea los _____ en el periódico.

FOLDABLES
Study Organizer

ENVELOPE FOLD
See page SH30 for help with making this foldable. Use this study organizer to talk about professions and occupations with a partner. On each tab, describe the work that is done at a particular job. Then pass the foldable to your partner who will use the clues to identify the professions or occupations. When you're finished, switch roles.

CARRERAS

trescientos siete **307**

Activity 5 This activity can also be done orally with books closed calling on students at random to respond.

Activity 6 This activity can be done without previous preparation.

Differentiation

Advanced Learners

Call on advanced learners to use the words from Activity 6 in original sentences.

Activity 8 You can go over this activity first in class and then have students write it for homework.

Comunicación

Interpersonal, Presentational

You may wish to have students work in pairs to find an ad for a job in a local Spanish-language newspaper or magazine. Next, have them prepare a two-minute conversation in which one of them plays the role of the interviewer and the other plays the role of the job candidate. Have them present their short conversation in front of the class.

Cultural Snapshot

(page 306 top) Calella de Palafrugell is a small, attractive fishing village on the Costa Brava north of Barcelona.

Answers

4 *Answers will vary.*

5

1. Sí, ella estará buscando un puesto con la compañía.
2. Sí, es posible que ella esté un poco nerviosa.
3. Sí, ella quiere un trabajo que sea interesante y que le pague bien.
4. Sí, ella va a tener una entrevista.

5. Sí, Anita debe tener una carta de recomendación.
6. Sí, ella tendrá que llenar una solicitud de trabajo.

6

1. c   3. a   5. d
2. e   4. b

7

1. Sí, Juan busca trabajo.
2. Ha leído un anuncio en el periódico.
3. Bancomar está reclutando (buscando) empleados.

4. Juan va al departamento de recursos humanos de Bancomar.
5. Tiene que llenar una solicitud de empleo.
6. Le da la solicitud a la recepcionista.
7. Va a tener una entrevista.

8

1. a tiempo parcial
2. a tiempo completo
3. anuncios clasificados

▶ PRACTICE (continued)

Leveling EACH Activity

Average Activity 9

CHallenging Activity 10

Activity ❾ This activity can also be done orally with books closed calling on students at random to respond.

Activity ❿ When having students do an open-ended activity with no learning prompts, they are communicating as if they were in in a real-life situation. In such a situation, it is normal for learners to make a few mistakes. For this reason, you may decide not to interrupt and correct each error a student makes. This is up to your discretion.

GLENCOE SPANISH

Why It Works!

Note that in **¡Así se dice!** students are given ample opportunity to use their new words so that they become an active part of their vocabulary.

InfoGap

This *InfoGap* activity will allow students to practice in pairs. This will help interpersonal learners, who learn well through interaction and collaboration. The activity should be very manageable since all vocabulary and grammar are familiar to them.

InfoGap For more practice using your new vocabulary, do Activity 10 on page SR11 at the end of this book.

HABLAR

❾ Personaliza. Da respuestas personales.

1. ¿Trabajas o has trabajado alguna vez?
2. ¿Dónde?
3. ¿Por qué trabajas o no trabajas?
4. ¿Recibes un sueldo (salario)?
5. ¿Qué haces con el dinero que ganas?
6. Si no trabajas y no recibes un sueldo, ¿de dónde recibes dinero? ¿Te dan tus padres una semana o una mesada?
7. Si recibes dinero cada mes (mensualmente), ¿recibes una semana o una mesada?

EXPANSIÓN

Ahora, sin mirar las preguntas, cuenta la información en tus propias palabras. Si no recuerdas algo, un(a) compañero(a) te puede ayudar.

 Comunicación

❿ Trabaja con un(a) compañero(a). Vas a tener una entrevista para un trabajo a tiempo parcial. Uno(a) será el/la candidato(a) y el/la otro(a) será el/la empleado(a) en el departamento de personal. Pueden dar la entrevista dos veces cambiando de rol.

CULTURA

La empleada vende libros y materiales escolares en esta librería en Guadalajara, México.

308 *trescientos ocho*

CAPÍTULO 10

Answers

❾

1. Sí, (No, no) trabajo. / Sí, (No, no) he trabajado.
2. Trabajo (He trabajado) en ___.
3. (No) Trabajo porque ___.
4. Sí, (No, no) recibo un sueldo (salario).
5. *Answers will vary.*
6. Recibo dinero de ___. Mis padres (no) me dan un semana o una mesada.
7. Recibo una mesada.

❿ *Answers will vary.*

Estudio de palabras

comerciar negociar comprando y vendiendo

el comercio el acto de vender y comprar; una tienda o almacén

el/la comerciante persona que se dedica a la compra y venta de mercancías; individuo que es propietario de un comercio

comercial relativo al comercio o a los comerciantes

vender traspasarle (darle) algo a alguien por un precio convenido

el/la vendedor(a) persona que vende algo; dependiente o empleado en una tienda

la venta acción y efecto de vender

1 Da lo contario.
   1. comprar
   2. la compra
   3. el/la comprador(a)

2 Completa.
   1. Una tienda de departamentos es una empresa _____.
   2. El _____ puede ser un almacén o tienda y el propietario de tal empresa es _____.
   3. Los joyeros _____ joyas: pulseras o brazaletes de oro y plata, anillos de diamantes y esmeraldas, etc. Son _____ que se dedican a la compra y _____ de joyas.
   4. Mi prima trabaja en una agencia de automóviles. Ella es _____ de carros pero yo no sé la marca que _____ aunque sé que es una marca japonesa.
   5. Ellos van a mudarse (cambiar de casa) y tienen su casa en _____.

CULTURA

La comerciante tiene un comercio o negocio exitoso vendiendo rosas en un puesto durante una fiesta en Barcelona.

CARRERAS

trescientos nueve **309**

Más práctica
Workbook, pp. 10.3–10.5
StudentWorks™ Plus

Vocabulario

Estudio de palabras

Call on students to read each new word and its definition. Have them prepare the activities and then go over them in class. These activities can be done orally or they can be written.

GLENCOE Technology

Online Learning in the Classroom

Have students use QuickPass code ASD7844c10 for additional vocabulary practice. They can download audio files of all vocabulary to their computer and/or MP3 player. They will have access to online flashcards and eGames. Students can print and complete the **Vocabulario** Review Worksheet.

▶ ASSESS

Students are now ready to take Quiz 1 on page 10.33 of the Chapter 10 TeacherTools booklet. If you prefer to create your own quiz, you may want to use the Chapter 10 question bank on the *ExamView®* *Assessment Suite* or you may prefer to create your own questions in your choice of format.

Estudio de palabras

1 1. vender
    2. la venta
    3. el/la vendedor(a)

2 1. comercial
    2. comercio, el/la comerciante
    3. venden, los comerciantes, la venta
    4. vendedora, vende
    5. venta

 QuickPass

Go to glencoe.com
For: Grammar practice
Web code: ASD7844c10

Resources
 ExamView® Assessment Suite

Quick Start

Use QS Transparency 10.2 or write
the following on the board.
Prepara una sinopsis de
tiempos.
(yo) hablar (tú) comer
(ellos) vivir
presente
pretérito
imperfecto
futuro
condicional
presente del subjuntivo
imperfecto del subjuntivo

▶ TEACH
Core Instruction

Step 1 Have students read
Items 1 through 5 silently.

Step 2 Call on individuals to
read the explanatory material
aloud and have all students
repeat the model sentences
aloud in unison.

Step 3 Explain to students
that the more they practice
using **por** and **para,** the easier
it will be. You may wish to
explain to them that it is a
very tricky grammar point that
often gives non-native Spanish
speakers trouble and occasionally challenges native speakers. Again, this is a grammar
point that requires practice to
train a speaker's ear.

CULTURA

Los hermanos fueron de compras
en la Ciudad de México. Querían
comprar un regalo para su mamá y
se lo van a dar mañana.

Por y para

1. The prepositions **por** and **para** have very specific uses
   in Spanish. They are not interchangeable. These two
   prepositions are often translated into English as *for*. Such
   a translation is quite restrictive because these two words
   express many ideas in addition to *for*.

2. The preposition **para** is used to indicate destination or
   purpose.

   El avión salió para Bogotá.
   The plane left for Bogota.

   Este regalo es para María.
   This gift is for Mary.

   Ella estudia para abogada.
   She is studying to be a lawyer.

3. The preposition **por,** in contrast to **para,** is more circuitous.
   Rather than expressing a specific destination, **por** conveys
   the meanings *through, by,* and *along.*

   Ellos viajaron por la América del Sur.
   They traveled through South America.

   Su barco pasó por las costas de las islas Galápagos.
   Their boat passed by the shores of the Galápagos Islands.

   El ladrón entró en la casa por la ventana.
   The thief entered the house through the window.

4. **Por** also has the meanings *on behalf of, in favor of,* and
   instead of. Observe and analyze the difference in meaning in
   the following sentences.

   Le compré el regalo para mi madre.
   *I bought the gift for my mother. (I'm going to give the gift
   to my mother.)*

   Compré el regalo por mi madre.
   *I bought the gift for my mother. (The gift is for another
   person, but my mother could not go out to buy it so I went
   for her.)*

5. The preposition **por** is used after the verbs **ir, mandar,
   volver,** and **venir** in order to show the reason for the errand.

   El joven fue a la tienda por pan.
   The young man went to the store for bread.

   Ellos mandaron por el médico.
   They sent for the doctor.

☆ Tips for Success

The following type of chart helps some
students to understand **por** and **para.**
para is used to introduce something
quite direct
→|
por is used to introduce something
rather circuitous in comparison to direct

You can use this drawing to illustrate
other aspects of **por** and **para.**
para → Bogotá **para** → la costa
⟳ por la ciudad
⟳ por la costa

Práctica

HABLAR

① Contesta.

1. ¿Va a salir para Quito Josefa?
2. ¿Va a viajar por Ecuador?
3. ¿Va a andar por el casco antiguo Josefa?
4. ¿Va a comprar regalos para sus parientes?
5. Algunos amigos quieren que ella les compre unas cerámicas ecuatorianas y le han dado el dinero para comprarlas. ¿Va Josefa a comprar las cerámicas por ellos?

EXPANSIÓN

Ahora, sin mirar las preguntas, cuenta la información en tus propias palabras. Si no recuerdas algo, un(a) compañero(a) te puede ayudar.

LEER • ESCRIBIR

② Completa sobre un día en Buenos Aires.

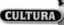

1. Hoy yo salí _____ el mercado a las ocho de la mañana.
2. Julia no pudo ir así que yo fui _____ ella.
3. Cuando salí del mercado, di un paseo _____ el centro de la ciudad.
4. Pasé _____ las tiendas de la calle Florida.
5. Entré en una de las tiendas y le compré un regalo _____ mi madre. Se lo voy a dar a ella mañana.
6. Cuando volví a casa, el hijo de Julia vino _____ las cosas que yo le había comprado en el mercado.

EXPANSIÓN

Ahora, sin mirar las frases, cuenta la información en tus propias palabras. Si no recuerdas algo, un(a) compañero(a) te puede ayudar.

CULTURA

La gente andaba por la Plaza de Armas en Quito, Ecuador.

CULTURA

La joven «comerciante» te venderá una bolsa para las compras en la calle Florida en Buenos Aires.

CARRERAS

trescientos once **311**

▶ PRACTICE

Leveling EACH Activity

Easy Activity 1
Average Activity 2
CHallenging Activity 1
Expansión, Activity 2
Expansión

Activities ① and ② Since students need a great deal of practice using **por** and **para,** it is suggested that you have students go over these activities in class, prepare them at home, and then go over them again in class.

☆ Tips for Success ·······

To reinforce **por** and **para,** have students read the captions that accompany the photos on pages 310–311.

··

📷 Cultural Snapshot

(page 310) These shoppers are on the famous Reforma in Mexico City. The Reforma is referred to as the Champs Elysées of Mexico City.

(page 311 bottom) La calle Florida is a pedestrian-only shopping street in downtown Buenos Aires.

Answers

①

1. Sí (No), Josefa (no) va a salir para Quito.
2. Sí, (No, no) va a viajar por Ecuador.
3. Sí (No), Josefa (no) va a andar por el casco antiguo.
4. Sí, (No, no) va a comprar regalos para sus parientes.
5. Sí (No), Josefa (no) va a comprar las cerámicas por ellos.

②

1. para
2. por
3. por
4. por
5. para
6. por

Resources

ExamView® Assessment Suite

▶ TEACH

Core Instruction

Use the chart with arrows again.

para	para
→| el día ocho	→| diciembre

↻ por el noche
↻ por diciembre

▶ PRACTICE

Leveling EACH Activity

Easy Activity 3
Average Activity 4

Activity ❸ This activity can be done orally in class.

Activity ❹ This activity should be prepared and then gone over in class.

Differentiation

Advanced Learners

Call on several advanced learners to recall the historical information in Activity 4 in their own words.

312

Por y para con expresiones de tiempo

1. The preposition **para** is used to indicate a deadline.

> **Ellos tienen que terminar el trabajo para el día ocho.**
> *They have to finish the work by the eighth.*

2. Por, in contrast to **para,** is used to define a period of time.

> **Los directores van a estar aquí por una semana.**
> *The directors are going to be here for a week.*

3. Por is also used to express an indefinite time.

> **Creo que ellos van a volver por diciembre.**
> *I think they are going to return around December.*

Práctica

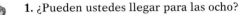

HABLAR

❸ Contesta.

1. ¿Pueden ustedes llegar para las ocho?
2. ¿Será posible tener los resultados para mañana?
3. ¿Por cuánto tiempo podrán ustedes quedarse aquí?
4. La última vez que ustedes vinieron, estuvieron por dos semanas, ¿no?
5. ¿Piensan ustedes volver otra vez por Pascuas?

LEER • ESCRIBIR

❹ Completa.

Los árabes salieron del Norte de África __1__ España en el siglo ocho. Invadieron España en el año 711, y estuvieron en el país __2__ unos ocho siglos. Viajaron __3__ toda la península ibérica. Por eso, si uno hace un viaje __4__ España verá la influencia de los árabes en casi todas partes del país. Pero si uno viaja __5__ Andalucía en el sur del país, visitará sin duda la famosa Alhambra de Granada, el Alcázar de Sevilla y la Mezquita de Córdoba, tres monumentos famosos de los árabes. __6__ mañana yo tengo que preparar un informe sobre la influencia musulmana en España __7__ mi clase de español. Así que yo fui hoy a la biblioteca __8__ los libros que me hacían falta.

CULTURA

La gran Mezquita de Córdoba es una joya arquitectónica de los moros que estuvieron en España por ocho siglos.

Answers

❸

1. Sí, (No, no) podemos llegar para las ocho.
2. Sí, (No, no) será posible tener los resultados para mañana.
3. Podremos quedarnos aquí por ____.
4. Sí, (No, no) estuvimos por dos semanas.
5. Sí, (No, no) pensamos volver otra vez por Pascuas.

❹
1. para
2. por
3. por
4. por
5. por
6. Para
7. para
8. por

 Cultural Snapshot

(page 312) The Mezquita de Córdoba was built between the eighth and tenth centuries. It is one of the earliest and most beautiful examples of Moorish architecture in Spain. There are 850 columns of granite, marble, jasper, and onyx. Today the Mezquita is a Christian cathedral.

Por y para con el infinitivo

1. When followed by an infinitive, **para** expresses purpose and means *in order to*.

> **Tengo que ir a la biblioteca para hacer investigaciones.**
> *I have to go to the library (in order) to do research.*

2. When **por** is followed by an infinitive, it expresses what remains to be done.

> **Me queda mucho por hacer.**
> *I still have a lot to do.*

3. The expression **estar para** means *to be about to* or *to be ready to*.

> **Ellos están para salir pero no sé lo que van a hacer porque está para llover.**
> *They are about (ready) to leave, but I don't know what they are going to do because it's about to rain.*

4. The expression **estar por** means *to be inclined to*. It does not mean that the action will definitely take place.

> **Estoy por salir porque hace buen tiempo.**
> *I'm in the mood to go out because the weather is nice.*

Práctica

HABLAR

5 Contesta.

1. ¿Vas a ir a tu cuarto para escribir tu currículum vitae?
2. ¿Lo has terminado o te queda mucho por hacer?
3. ¿A qué hora estarás listo(a) para salir?
4. ¿Estás por ir de compras o por ver un filme?
5. ¿Estás listo(a) para empezar a trabajar?

CULTURA

Estos jóvenes se preparan para muchas carreras diferentes en la biblioteca de la Universidad de Málaga en España.

trescientos trece **313**

Resources

ExamView® Assessment Suite

▶ TEACH
Core Instruction

Have students read Items 1–4 and the model sentences aloud.

▶ PRACTICE

Leveling EACH Activity

Easy Activity 5
Average Activity 6

Activities **5** and **6** You may wish to use suggestions given for previous activities.

GLENCOE Technology

Online Learning in the Classroom

Have students use QuickPass code ASD7844c10 for additional grammar practice. They can review each grammar point with an eGame. They can also review all grammar points by doing the self-check quiz, which integrates the chapter vocabulary with the new grammar.

Answers

5

1. Sí, (No, no) voy a ir a mi cuarto para escribir mi currículum vitae.
2. Lo he terminado. (Me queda mucho por hacer.)
3. Estaré listo(a) para salir a la(s) ____.
4. Estoy por ir de compras (ver un filme).
5. Sí, (No, no) estoy listo(a) para empezar a trabajar.

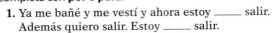

Quick Start

Use QS Transparency 10.3 or write the following on the board.

Prepara una sinopsis de tiempos.

   (yo) decir (ellos) ir
   (nosotros) tener

presente
pretérito
imperfecto
futuro
condicional
presente del subjuntivo
imperfecto del subjuntivo

▶ TEACH
Core Instruction

You may wish to have students make up more examples of these uses of **por** and **para**. Examples could be: **Para niño, sabe mucho. Para joven, ha viajado mucho. Ellos lucharon por la independencia, el respeto, una mejor vida. Me pagó por el regalo, la ayuda, el servicio. Yo lo tomé por español, presidente, hombre importante. Las papas, zanahorias, vegetales se venden por kilo. La carne y el pescado se venden por kilo.**

⭐ Tips for Success ....

To reinforce the use of **por** and **para,** have students read the captions to the photos on pages 314–315.

··

314

CULTURA

Para comprar localidades (entradas) para el teatro tienes que hacer cola delante de la taquilla como hacen estos madrileños.

CULTURA

En el famoso mercado La Boquería en Barcelona las patatas se venden por kilo.

314

LEER • ESCRIBIR

6 Completa con **por** o **para.**

1. Ya me bañé y me vestí y ahora estoy _____ salir. Además quiero salir. Estoy _____ salir.
2. ¡Ay, pero mira! Está _____ llover.
3. Tendré que subir _____ mi paraguas.
4. Quiero ir al cine y _____ ir al cine tendré que tomar un taxi porque no hay bus que pase _____ el cine.
5. Me pregunto si tendré que hacer cola _____ comprar las entradas.
6. Estoy _____ divertirme. Al salir del cine voy a visitar uno de los mesones en Cuchilleros.
7. Trabajé todo el día y todavía me queda mucho _____ hacer.

Otros usos de **por** y **para**

1. Para is used to express a comparison.

   Para cubano él habla muy bien el inglés.
   For a Cuban, he speaks English very well.

   Para norteamericano Roberto habla muy bien el español.
   For an American, Robert speaks Spanish very well.

2. Por is used to express means, manner, or motive.

   La carta llegó por correo.
   The letter arrived by mail.

   Los soldados lucharon por la libertad de su país.
   The soldiers fought for the freedom of their country.

3. Por is used to express *in exchange for.*

   Él me pagó cien dólares por el trabajo que hice.
   He paid me a hundred dollars for the work I did.

   Él cambió euros por dólares.
   He exchanged euros for dollars.

4. Por is also used to express an opinion or estimation.

   Yo lo tomé por francés, pero es español.
   I took him for French, but he is Spanish.

5. Por is used to indicate measure or number.

   Las papas se venden por kilo.
   Potatoes are sold by the kilo.

   Este avión vuela a 1.000 kilómetros por hora.
   This plane flies 1,000 kilometers per hour.

CAPÍTULO 10

Answers

6
1. para, por
2. para
3. por
4. para, por
5. para
6. por
7. por

Práctica

LEER • ESCRIBIR

7 Completa con **por** o **para**.

1. _____ español, el señor Lugones habla muy bien el francés.
2. _____ argentina, la señora Caravallo sabe mucho de Estados Unidos.
3. Ella vino a Miami en avión. Dijo que el avión volaba a más de mil kilómetros _____ hora.
4. Ella cambió sus pesos _____ dólares antes de salir de Argentina.
5. La primera vez que yo conocí a la señora Caravallo, yo la tomé _____ italiana. La verdad es que ella es de ascendencia italiana pero hace años que su familia vive en Argentina.
6. La señora Caravallo sabe que a mí me gustan mucho los zapatos argentinos. Ella me trajo dos pares. No quería que yo le pagara pero yo le di el dinero _____ los zapatos.

EXPANSIÓN

Ahora, sin mirar las frases, cuenta la información en tus propias palabras. Si no recuerdas algo, un(a) compañero(a) te puede ayudar.

ESCUCHAR • HABLAR

8 Contesta usando una expresión con **por** o **para**.

1. ¿Cuál es el destino del tren? ¿Córdoba?
2. ¿A quién vas a darle los regalos? ¿A tu prima?
3. Cuando vendiste tu bicicleta, ¿te dieron cien dólares?
4. Es mexicano pero habla muy bien el inglés, ¿verdad?
5. ¿Cuándo piensas venir? ¿En junio?
6. ¿Te queda mucho o poco trabajo?
7. ¿Cuándo lo terminarás? ¿La semana que viene?
8. Ellos pasaron mucho tiempo en España, ¿verdad?

CULTURA

Para una estación vieja, está en muy buenas condiciones, ¿no?

CARRERAS

trescientos quince **315**

▶ PRACTICE

Leveling EACH Activity

Easy Activity 7
Average–CHallenging
Activities 8, 9
CHallenging Activity 7
Expansión

Activities 7, 8, and 9 You may wish to go over these activities in class, have students prepare them at home, and then go over them once again in class. The more students are able to hear **por** and **para** being used, the more accurately they will use them.

▶ ASSESS

Students are now ready to take Quiz 2 on page 10.34 of the TeacherTools booklet. If you prefer to create your own quiz, use the *ExamView®* *Assessment Suite.*

Answers

7
1. Para
2. Para
3. por
4. por
5. por
6. por

8
1. Sí, el tren va para Córdoba.
2. Sí, los regalos son para ella.
3. Sí, me dieron cien dólares por mi bicicleta.
4. Sí, para mexicano habla muy bien el inglés.
5. Sí, pienso venir por junio.
6. Me queda mucho (poco) por hacer.
7. Sí, lo terminaré para la semana que viene.
8. Sí, estuvieron allí por mucho tiempo.

Gramática

Gramática

LEER • ESCRIBIR

9 Cambia cada frase usando **por** o **para**.

1. Hay un montón de trabajo *que tengo que* terminar.
2. Los chicos van ahora *en la dirección de* la ciudad.
3. Nos gusta viajar *en* Colombia.
4. Subimos al tren *con destino a* Granada.
5. Voy al mercado *en busca de* carne.
6. Tengo que estar allí *no más tarde de* las tres.
7. Estaremos en Cali *durante* siete días.
8. Andan *en* el parque.
9. Mis padres lo pagaron *en vez de* mí.
10. Papá no podía asistir, así que yo fui *en lugar de* él.
11. *A pesar de que es* rico, no es generoso.

El subjuntivo en cláusulas relativas

1. A relative clause describes or modifies a noun. If the noun refers to a definite person or thing, the indicative is used in the relative clause. If the noun refers to an indefinite person or thing, the subjunctive is used in the relative clause.

   Están buscando un asistente que hable español.
   Yo conozco a un asistente ejecutivo que habla español.

   Note that the a **personal** is omitted before an indefinite person.

2. The subjunctive can also be used in a relative clause that modifies a superlative or negative antecedent when the speaker or writer wishes to imply exaggeration.

   No hay persona que pinte como ella.
   Es el mejor libro que se haya escrito.

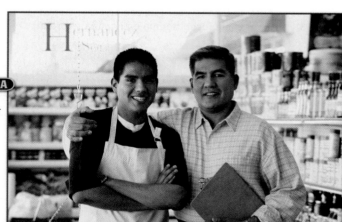

CULTURA
Para el padre, no hay nadie que trabaje mejor que su hijo.

316   *trescientos dieciséis*

TEACH
Core Instruction

Step 1 Have students read Items 1 and 2 aloud. Then call on individual students to read the example sentences.

Step 2 Have students complete the following statements:
Están buscando ___ que hable español. (un médico, un carpintero, un dentista, un plomero, etc.) **No hay persona que ___ como ella.** (pinte, hable, trabaje, cante, aprenda, comprenda)

Resources
- Audio Activities TE, pages 10.19–10.20
- Audio CD 10, Tracks 8–9
- Workbook, page 10.8
- Quiz 3, page 10.35
- ExamView® Assessment Suite

GLENCOE Technology

You may wish to use the editable PowerPoint® presentation on PowerTeach for additional grammar instruction and practice.

Video in the Classroom

Gramática en vivo: *The subjunctive with adverbial and adjective clauses* Enliven learning with the animated world of Professor Cruz! **Gramática en vivo** is a fun and effective tool for additional instruction and/or review.

Nota

The **a personal** is never used after the verb **tener**.
Tengo un amigo que habla español y francés.

Answers

9
1. por
2. para
3. por
4. para
5. por
6. para
7. por
8. por
9. por
10. por
11. Para

10
1. Sí, (No, no) quiero un puesto que me pague bien.
2. Sí, (No, no) quiero un puesto que me permita viajar.
3. Sí, (No, no) quiero trabajar en una oficina que esté cerca de mi casa.
4. Sí, tengo un puesto que me paga bien. (No, no tengo un puesto que me paga bien.)
5. Sí, tengo un puesto que me permite viajar. (No, no tengo un puesto que me permite viajar.)
6. Sí, trabajo en una oficina que está cerca de mi casa. (No, no trabajo en una oficina que está cerca de mi casa.)

Práctica

VIDEO Want more help with the subjunctive? Watch **Gramática en vivo.**

Más práctica

📘 Workbook, p. 10.8
💻 StudentWorks™ Plus

ESCUCHAR • HABLAR

10 Contesta.

1. ¿Quieres un puesto que te pague bien?
2. ¿Quieres un puesto que te permita viajar?
3. ¿Quieres trabajar en una oficina que esté cerca de tu casa?
4. ¿Tienes un puesto que te paga bien?
5. ¿Tienes un puesto que te permite viajar?
6. ¿Trabajas en una oficina que está cerca de tu casa?

ESCUCHAR • HABLAR • ESCRIBIR

11 Sigue el modelo.

MODELO ser de aquí →
    —Buscamos un abogado que sea de aquí.
    —¿Ah, sí? Conozco a un abogado que es de aquí.

1. conocer las leyes del estado
2. poseer una licencia profesional
3. ser honesto
4. poder trabajar los fines de semana
5. tener mucha experiencia
6. hablar español

Quiero un puesto que me permita viajar por el mundo hispanohablante.

CARRERAS

Refrán

Can you guess what the following proverb means?

Por el pan baila el perro, que no por el dueño.

¡Bravo!

You have now learned all the new vocabulary and grammar in this chapter. Continue to use and practice all that you know while learning more cultural information. ¡Vamos!

trescientos diecisiete **317**

Gramática

▶ PRACTICE

Leveling EACH Activity

Easy Activity 10
Average Activity 11

Activity 10 This activity can be done orally with books closed calling on students at random.

Activity 11 This activity can be done as a paired activity in the form of a short conversation. You can also have students write the conversations.

▶ ASSESS

Students are now ready to take Quiz 3 on page 10.35 of the TeacherTools booklet. If you prefer to create your own quiz, use the *ExamView® Assessment Suite.*

Refrán

Have students recite the proverb aloud and give its literal translation. Then see how many other proverbs they can think of that include the word *dog*.

¡Bravo! The remaining pages of the chapter recycle information in a variety of ways, allowing students to build upon their newly acquired language skills as well as to keep track of their own progress. This format also ensures that students are not surprised by vocabulary or grammar that has not yet been introduced or studied.

Answers

11

1. Buscamos un abogado que conozca las leyes del estado. ¿Ah, sí? Conozco a un abogado que conoce las leyes del estado.
2. Buscamos un abogado que posea una licencia profesional. ¿Ah, sí? Conozco a un abogado que posee una licencia profesional.
3. Buscamos un abogado que sea honesto. ¿Ah, sí? Conozco a un abogado que es honesto.
4. Buscamos un abogado que pueda trabajar los fines de semana. ¿Ah, sí? Conozco a un abogado que puede trabajar los fines de semana.
5. Buscamos un abogado que tenga mucha experiencia. ¿Ah, sí? Conozco a un abogado que tiene mucha experiencia.
6. Buscamos un abogado que hable español. ¿Ah, sí? Conozco a un abogado que habla español.

317

Resources

- Audio Activities TE, pages 10.20–10.21
- Audio CD 10, Tracks 10–11

▶ TEACH
Core Instruction

You may wish to follow suggestions given in previous chapters for the presentation of this conversation.

GLENCOE SPANISH

Why It Works!

In addition to introducing no unknown Spanish, this short conversation reinforces **por** and **para** four times and subjunctive in relative clauses two times.

Differentiation
Multiple Intelligences

To engage **bodily-kinesthetic** learners, call on students to come to the front of the room and dramatize the conversation using gestures, facial expressions, and proper intonation.

Visual-spatial learners might also enjoy creating their own cartoon strips. They can either imitate these characters or create new ones. They may want to share their cartoons with others in the class.

GLENCOE Technology

You may wish to use the editable PowerPoint® presentation on PowerTeach to have students listen to and repeat the conversation. Additional activities are also provided.

GLENCOE Technology

Online Learning in the Classroom

Have students use QuickPass code ASD7844c10 for additional conversation practice. Students can download audio files for the conversation to their computer and/or MP3 player and complete a self-check quiz.

SOLICITANDO UN PUESTO

318 *trescientos dieciocho*

CAPÍTULO 10

¿Comprendes?

VIDEO To discuss career paths, watch **Diálogo en vivo.**

A Contesta según la información en la conversación.

1. ¿Qué tipo de trabajo está buscando Patricia?
2. ¿Quiere trabajar a tiempo completo?
3. ¿Qué ha visto Jaime?
4. ¿Puede aceptar Patricia un puesto que requiera un conocimiento del inglés? ¿Por qué?
5. ¿Qué opinión tienen sus amigos anglohablantes de su inglés?

B Resumiendo Cuéntale a un(a) compañero(a) toda la información sobre Patricia.

C Analizando Contesta.

1. Usa la imaginación. Decide por qué sería imposible que Patricia trabajara a tiempo completo.
2. ¿Qué hace Jaime para ayudar a Patricia a buscar trabajo?

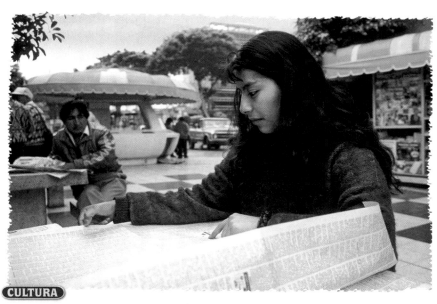

CULTURA

La joven está buscando un puesto y está leyendo los anuncios clasificados en un periódico en Lima, Perú.

trescientos diecinueve **319**

Conversación

▶ PRACTICE

¿Comprendes?

A This activitiy can be done orally in class. You may or may not wish to have students look up the answers.

B You may also wish to have students write the summary.

✿ Comunicación

Interpersonal

You may wish to have students work in pairs and ask each other the following questions. **¿Quieres trabajar a tiempo parcial? ¿Puedes trabajar a tiempo parcial o no? ¿Por qué no puedes trabajar? Si quieres y puedes trabajar, ¿qué tipo de trabajo buscas?** Then have one member of the team summarize the answers and present them to the class.

GLENCOE 🖰 Technology

Video in the Classroom
Diálogo en vivo In this episode, our friends in Argentina contemplate their future careers. Ask students what careers interest them in which they can use Spanish.

Pre-AP Listening to this conversation on audio CD will help students develop the skills that they need to be successful on the listening portion of the AP exam.

Answers

A

1. Está buscando un puesto a tiempo parcial que le interese y que le pague bien.
2. No, no quiere trabajar a tiempo completo.
3. Ha visto un anuncio para vendedor o vendedora en una tienda de departamentos.
4. Sí, Patricia puede aceptar un puesto que requiera un conocimiento del inglés porque hace tres años que estudia inglés.
5. Sus amigos anglohablantes le dicen que para mexicana habla muy bien.

B *Answers will vary but may include:*

Patricia está buscando un puesto a tiempo parcial para ganar un poco de dinero extra. Posiblemente le interesaría trabajar como vendedora en una tienda de departamentos. Hace tres años que estudia inglés y para mexicana lo habla muy bien. Va a llamar por una entrevista.

C

1. *Answers will vary.*
2. Cree que lo importante es que ella habla inglés.

Resources

- Audio Activities TE, page 10.22
- Audio CD 10, Tracks 12–13

▶ TEACH
Core Instruction

Step 1 This reading is quite easy and you may wish to have the class read it silently.

Step 2 Once students are finished reading, have them make up questions to ask one another.

Carreras Have students research on the Internet the need for multilingual employees in different career fields. In which fields is it helpful to speak another language? Why? Is there a difference in the salaries offered to bilingual and monolingual candidates?

Antes de leer

¿Conoces a alguien que usa el español en su trabajo? ¿Qué hace esta persona?

✓ Reading Check

Hoy en día, ¿qué está teniendo más y más importancia?

✓ Reading Check

¿Qué es una empresa multinacional?

Una lengua importante

No hay duda que el conocimiento de otro idioma te puede beneficiar en muchas carreras. En el mundo de globalización en que vivimos el comercio internacional tiene más y más importancia. En tal mundo, no es suficiente solo exportar nuestros productos al extranjero. Las grandes empresas de todas partes del mundo han llegado a ser multinacionales. Quiere decir que tienen instalaciones o sucursales[1] y filiales[2] en muchos países del mundo. Es posible que algún día trabajes con una compañía estadounidense y que tu oficina esté en Caracas, Panamá o Madrid. O es posible que trabajes con una compañía española o latinoamericana y que tu oficina esté en Miami, Los Ángeles o Chicago.

Es posible que el español en sí no sea una carrera. Pero el español con otra especialización te dará una ventaja tremenda. Si te especializas en la contabilidad, el marketing o la informática y conoces bien el español, podrás trabajar con una de las muchas empresas multinacionales. El español y tu otra especialización te ayudarán a encontrar un trabajo que te pague bien y que te dé la oportunidad de viajar y ver el mundo.

En esta época de globalización es posible que te sea necesario saber otro idioma—un tercer idioma. Una vez más el haber estudiado español te ayudará porque una vez que dominas un idioma es mucho más fácil adquirir otro. No te olvides: sigue con tus estudios del español porque te abrirá puertas interesantes y es posible que te dé oportunidades inesperadas.

[1]sucursales *branches*
[2]filiales *affiliates*

CULTURA

Una compañía estadounidense entrega carga a todas partes del mundo.

GLENCOE ◈ Technology

Online Learning in the Classroom

You may wish to have students use QuickPass code ASD7844c10 to develop their reading comprehension and writing skills. Students will be able to take a self-check quiz, which includes an essay.

¿Comprendes?

Más práctica
Workbook, pp. 10.9–10.10
StudentWorks™ Plus

VIDEO To learn about careers in the Spanish-speaking world, watch **Cultura en vivo.**

A Explicando Explica.
1. lo que es el comercio internacional
2. lo que es la globalización
3. como es posible que quizás trabajes para una empresa española y tu oficina esté en Estados Unidos
4. la importancia del español aunque no sea una carrera en sí
5. por qué el español te podrá ayudar a aprender un tercer idioma

CULTURA
Edificios modernos de empresas internacionales en una zona comercial de Madrid—Campo de las Naciones

B Personalizando Da respuestas personales.
1. ¿Has observado unas influencias de la globalización en tu propia vida? ¿Cuáles?
2. ¿Piensas seguir con tus estudios del español?
3. ¿Te gustaría tener un trabajo que te pagara bien y que te permitiera viajar y ver el mundo? ¿Por qué?

C Pronosticando consecuencias o resultados Contesta.
¿Tienes una idea de lo que quisieras ser de adulto? ¿Hay una profesión u oficio que te interese? ¿Es posible que el español te ayude en tu carrera?

trescientos veintiuno **321**

▶ PRACTICE

¿Comprendes?

A You may wish to have students write these explanations before going over them in class.

B and **C** Have students share their personal responses to these questions as a group discussion.

Writing Development
You may also wish to have students write Activity C as a composition.

GLENCOE ☜ Technology

Video in the Classroom
Cultura en vivo In this episode, students will learn about a small village in Venezuela that has produced many major league baseball players. Ask students if they know the names of any players from Venezuela or any other Latin American countries.

Pre-AP This cultural reading will develop the skills that students need to be successful on the reading and writing sections of the AP exam. Listening to this reading will also help prepare them for the auditory component.

Answers

A
1. El comercio internacional es el comercio entre las grandes empresas de todas partes del mundo.
2. La globalización es el mundo en que el comercio internacional tiene más y más importancia y en que las grandes empresas han llegado a ser multinacionales.
3. Es posible porque las grandes empresas tienen instalaciones o sucursales y filiales en el extranjero. Una empresa española puede tener un sucursal o un filial en Estados Unidos.
4. El español es importante porque con otra especialización te dará una ventaja tremenda.
5. El español te podrá ayudar a aprender un tercer idioma porque una vez que dominas un idioma es mucho más fácil adquirir otro.

B *Answers will vary but may include:*
1. Sí, (No, no) he observado influencias de la globalización en mi propia vida.
2. Sí, (No, no) pienso seguir con mis estudios del español.
3. Sí, (No, no) me gustaría tener un trabajo que me pagara bien y que me permitiera viajar y ver el mundo porque _____.

C *Answers will vary.*

Literatura

Resources

- Audio Activities TE, pages 10.26–10.30
- Audio CD 10, Track 18
- Literature Test, pages 10.50–10.51
- ExamView® Assessment Suite

Preview

Starting in Chapter 3, each chapter of ¡Así se dice! Level 3 has a literary section. Most literary selections are by well-known Latin American or Spanish writers. Some selections are poetry and others are prose.

It is up to the discretion of the teacher if you wish to do all or any of these literary works. The difficulty level of each selection is also indicated from 1 to 4. 1 is difficult; 4 is quite easy.

Difficulty Level
3

Vocabulario
Core Instruction

Step 1 Have a student read a new word and another read its definition.

Step 2 Go over the **Práctica** activity.

Differentiation
Advanced Learners

Have more advanced students make up some original sentences after doing the **Práctica** activity.

Un día de éstos
de Gabriel García Márquez

▲ Una vista del pintoresco distrito colonial de la ciudad de Cartagena en la costa caribeña de Colombia

Vocabulario

el/la madrugador(a) el que se levanta temprano por la mañana

la muñeca la parte del cuerpo donde se articula la mano con el brazo

una lágrima una gotita de agua que sale de los ojos cuando uno llora

enjuto(a) flaco

sordo(a) que no puede oír, que ha perdido el sentido del oído

hinchado(a) extendido, inflado

apresurarse tener prisa; ir rápido

amanecer empezar a aparecer la luz del día

GeoVistas

To learn more about Colombia, take a tour on pages SH48–SH49.

CAPÍTULO 10

Cultural Snapshot

(page 322) Cartagena, Colombia, was founded in 1533 on a site inhabited by the indigenous Caribs. It is a beautiful city known for its Spanish colonial architecture and it is on UNESCO's list of world heritage sites. Recently Cartagena has expanded dramatically and its modern sections have many high-rises.

GeoVistas

Have students turn to pages SH48–SH49 and locate the map of Colombia. Ask them to find the capital and name it. You may also wish to ask students to identify some geographical similarities between Colombia and its neighbor, Venezuela.

Práctica

Completa con una palabra apropiada.

1. Él se cayó y se le torció el tobillo. Tiene el tobillo muy _____.
2. Ella no se levanta hasta las diez de la mañana. No es _____.
3. Tienes que hablarle en voz más alta porque es bastante _____.
4. Don Quijote es _____, no Sancho Panza.
5. Tienen que estar en el gabinete del dentista en cinco minutos. Tienen que _____ para no llegar tarde.
6. Ella patinaba y se cayó. Cree que tiene la _____ torcida.
7. Está llorando tanto que se le están saliendo _____.
8. Un madrugador todavía está despierto cuando _____.

INTRODUCCIÓN

Gabriel García Márquez es uno de los escritores más importantes de las letras hispanas. Es el más brillante exponente de la tendencia literaria contemporánea denominada «realismo mágico».

García Márquez nació en Arataca, Colombia, en 1928. En la universidad estudió periodismo y leyes. Ha sido periodista en Barranquilla, Bogotá y Cartagena. Él escribió cuentos cortos para los periódicos donde trabajaba. Ahora escribe novelas y ya ha escrito muchas. Entre sus muchas novelas dos que son popularísimas son *Cien años de soledad* y *El amor en los tiempos del cólera*.

En 1982, García Márquez recibió el premio Nobel de Literatura.

El cuento que sigue «Un día de éstos» es de su obra *Los funerales de la Mamá Grande*. Los dos protagonistas ejercen profesiones muy distintas. Uno es dentista y el otro es político. ¡A ver como se comportan!

FONDO HISTÓRICO

Antes de leer este cuento hay que conocer el fondo histórico. En 1948 el candidato liberal y laborista para presidente de Colombia fue asesinado. Este suceso produjo un clima de terror por todo el país. La lucha entre liberales y conservadores fue acompañada de mucha violencia. En una sola década, han perdido la vida más de 300.000 personas.

CULTURA

El famoso autor colombiano recibe el premio Nobel de Literatura en Estocolmo, Suecia.

Introducción

You may wish to ask students some comprehension questions about the life of Gabriel García Márquez.

Note: Students will learn a great deal more about García Márquez in ¡**Así se dice!** Level 4.

Heritage Speakers

If you have any students in class who are from Colombia, have them present some background information to the class about the current social and political climate of the country.

Answers

1. hinchado
2. madrugadora
3. sordo(a)
4. enjuto
5. apresurarse
6. muñeca
7. lágrimas
8. amanece

▶ TEACH
Core Instruction

Step 1 Have students read the **Estrategia.** Tell them it is important to monitor their comprehension not because the selection is difficult, but because it contains quite a few details.

Step 2 Before beginning to read a page, have students take a quick look at the sidenotes.

Step 3 You may wish to have students read some paragraphs silently and some aloud. If students seem to have some trouble understanding, ask them questions.

Step 4 Explain to students that when they read, some information is more important than other information. An example is a sentence such as: **Después de las ocho hizo una pausa... de la casa vecina.**

Step 5 Starting at the bottom of the page, call on one student to take the part of the son and the other the part of the dentist. Have them continue to read the dialogue sections aloud. When you get to the bottom of page 325, call on another student to read the part of the **alcalde.**

Estrategia

Monitoreando tu comprensión Monitoreando tu comprensión significa que siempre estás verificando si comprendes lo que estás leyendo. Si de vez en cuando no crees que estés entendiendo, hazte preguntas sobre las ideas principales, los personajes y eventos. Si no puedes contestar tu pregunta, repasa el texto. Lee con más cuidado y si es necesario pídele ayuda a alguien.

vidriera *drawer*
dentadura postiza *set of false teeth*
yeso *plaster*

cargadores *suspenders*

fresa *drill*
pulir *polish*

gallinazos *buzzards*
caballete *chimney cowl*

Durante la lectura

Fíjate en las emociones fuertes que tiene el dentista. ¿Por qué las tiene?

CULTURA

Se levanta el sol cuando amanece y se pone el sol cuando atardece. Aquí vemos una bonita puesta del sol sobre el mar Mediterráneo.

Un día de éstos 🎧

El lunes amaneció tibio y sin lluvia. Don Aurelio Escovar, dentista sin título y buen madrugador, abrió su gabinete a las seis. Sacó de la vidriera° una dentadura postiza° montada aún en el molde de yeso° y puso sobre la mesa un puñado de instrumentos que ordenó de mayor a menor, como en una exposición. Llevaba una camisa a rayas, sin cuello, cerrada arriba con un botón dorado, y los pantalones sostenidos con cargadores° elásticos. Era rígido, enjuto con una mirada que raras veces correspondía a la situación, como la mirada de los sordos.

Cuando tuvo las cosas dispuestas sobre la mesa rodó la fresa° hacia el sillón de resortes y se sentó a pulir° la dentadura postiza. Parecía no pensar en lo que hacía, pero trabajaba con obstinación, pedaleando en la fresa incluso cuando no se servía de ella.

Después de las ocho hizo una pausa para mirar el cielo por la ventana y vio dos gallinazos° pensativos que se secaban al sol en el caballete° de la casa vecina. Siguió trabajando con la idea de que antes del almuerzo volvería a llover. La voz destemplada de su hijo de once años lo sacó de su abstracción.

—Papá.

—¿Qué?

—Dice el alcalde que si le sacas una muela.

—Dile que no estoy aquí.

Estaba puliendo un diente de oro. Lo retiró a la distancia del brazo y lo examinó con los ojos a medio cerrar. En la salita de espera volvió a gritar su hijo.

—Dice que sí estás porque te está oyendo.

El dentista siguió examinando el diente. Sólo cuando lo puso en la mesa con los trabajos terminados, dijo:

—Mejor.

Volvió a operar la fresa. De una cajita de cartón donde guardaba las cosas por hacer, sacó un puente° de varias piezas y empezó a pulir el oro.

—Papá.

—¿Qué?

Aún no había cambiado de expresión.

—Dice que si no le sacas la muela te pega un tiro°.

Sin apresurarse, con un movimiento extremadamente tranquilo, dejó de pedalear en la fresa, la retiró del sillón y abrió por completo la gaveta° inferior de la mesa. Allí estaba el revólver.

—Bueno—dijo. —Dile que venga a pegármelo.

Hizo girar el sillón hasta quedar de frente a la puerta, la mano apoyada en el borde de la gaveta. El alcalde apareció en el umbral°. Se había afeitado la mejilla izquierda, pero en la otra, hinchada y dolorida, tenía una barba de cinco días. El dentista vio en sus ojos marchitos muchas noches de desesperación. Cerró la gaveta con la punta de los dedos y dijo suavemente:

—Siéntese.

—Buenos días—dijo el alcalde.

—Buenos—dijo el dentista.

Mientras hervían los instrumentos, el alcalde apoyó el cráneo en el cabezal de la silla y se sintió mejor. Respiraba un olor glacial. Era un gabinete pobre: una vieja silla de madera, la fresa de pedal y una vidriera con pomos de loza°.

puente *dental bridge*

te pega un tiro *he'll shoot you*

gaveta *drawer*

umbral *doorway*

pomos de loza *small porcelain bottles*

CULTURA
Una callecita de Cartagena, Colombia, que termina, o muere, en las orillas del mar Caribe

CARRERAS

Differentiation
Multiple Intelligences

To help **bodily-kinesthetic** learners, call on students to dramatize the meaning of the following: **El dentista siguió examinando el diente. Volvió a operar la fresa. Te paga un tiro. Dejó de pedalear la fresa y abrió por completa la gaveta inferior de la mesa.**

El alcalde apareció en el umbral. Se había afeitada la mejilla izquierda. Tenía la otra (mejilla) hinchada y dolorita. Cerró la gaveta con la punta de los dedos.

▶ TEACH
Core Instruction

Step 1 Read to the students: «El alcalde sintió un crujido...» to «El dentista le dio un trapo limpio.»

Step 2 Be sure the students reading the part of the dentist and the mayor use the proper intonation and expression.

Differentiation
Multiple Intelligences

Call on a **bodily-kinesthetic** learner to dramatize what you are saying.

---

cancel de tela *cloth screen*

cautelosa *cautious, careful*

escupidera *spittoon, cuspidor*
aguamanil *washstand*

cordal inferior *bottom wisdom tooth*
gatillo *forceps*
se aferró *clung to, grasped*
riñones *kidneys*

muertos *deaths (you have caused)*
crujido *crackle, creak*

sudoroso *sweaty*
jadeante *panting*
guerrera *military jacket*
a tientas *groping*
trapo *rag*
cielo raso desfondado *chipped ceiling*
telaraña *spider web*
araña *spider*
haga buches *rinse*

red *screen*
misma vaina *same difference*

Frente a la silla, una ventana con un cancel de tela° hasta la altura de un hombre. Cuando sintió que el dentista se acercaba el alcalde afirmó los talones y abrió la boca.

Don Aurelio Escovar le movió la cara hacia la luz. Después de observar la muela dañada, ajustó la mandíbula con una cautelosa° presión de los dedos.

—Tiene que ser sin anestesia—dijo.

—¿Por qué?

—Porque tiene un absceso.

El alcalde lo miró a los ojos. —Está bien—dijo, y trató de sonreír. El dentista no lo correspondió. Llevó a la mesa de trabajo la cacerola con los instrumentos hervidos y los sacó del agua con unas pinzas frías, todavía sin apresurarse. Después rodó la escupidera° con la punta del zapato y fue a lavarse las manos en el aguamanil°. Hizo todo sin mirar al alcalde. Pero el alcalde no lo perdió de vista.

Era un cordal inferior°. El dentista abrió las piernas y apretó la muela con el gatillo° caliente. El alcalde se aferró° a las barras de la silla, descargó toda su fuerza en los pies y sintió un vacío helado en los riñones°, pero no soltó un suspiro. El dentista sólo movió la muñeca. Sin rencor, más bien con una amarga ternura, dijo:

—Aquí nos paga veinte muertos°, teniente.

El alcalde sintió un crujido° de huesos en la mandíbula y sus ojos se llenaron de lágrimas. Pero no suspiró hasta que no sintió salir la muela. Entonces la vio a través de las lágrimas. Le pareció tan extraña a su dolor, que no pudo entender la tortura de sus cinco noches anteriores.

Inclinado sobre la escupidera, sudoroso°, jadeante°, se desabotonó la guerrera° y buscó a tientas° el pañuelo en el bolsillo del pantalón. El dentista le dio un trapo° limpio.

—Séquese las lágrimas—dijo.

El alcalde lo hizo. Estaba temblando. Mientras el dentista se lavaba las manos, vio el cielo raso desfondado° y una telaraña° polvorienta con huevos de araña° e insectos muertos. El dentista regresó secándose las manos.

—Acuéstese—dijo—y haga buches° de agua de sal.

El alcalde se puso de pie, se despidió con un displicente saludo militar, y se dirigió a la puerta estirando las piernas, sin abotonarse la guerrera.

—Me pasa la cuenta—dijo.

—¿A usted o al municipio?

El alcalde no lo miró. Cerró la puerta, y dijo, a través de la red° metálica:

—Es la misma vaina°.

Answers

A

1. El alcalde quiere que el dentista le saque una muela.
2. Su hijo se lo dice al dentista.
3 El dentista no lo quiere hacer.
4. Va a pegarle un tiro si no le saca la muela.
5. Tomó un revólver.
6. Tenía que sacarle la muela sin anestesia porque tiene un absceso.

B *Answers will vary but may include:*

1. El dentista es un hombre sin mucha emoción. Es rígido y enjuto con una mirada que raras veces corresponde a la situación. No le presta atención a su hijo. Se fija en su trabajo. No mira al alcalde y no le habla mucho. Hace todo de manera tranquilo sin apresurarse.
2. El gabinete del dentista es pobre. Tiene una vieja silla de madera, la fresa de pedal y una vidriera

¿Comprendes?

A **Recordando hechos** Contesta.
1. ¿Quién quiere que el dentista le saque una muela?
2. ¿Quién se lo dice al dentista?
3. ¿Cómo reacciona el dentista?
4. ¿Qué hará el alcalde si el dentista no le saca la muela?
5. ¿Qué saca el dentista de una gaveta antes de que entre en el gabinete el alcalde?
6. Según el dentista, ¿por qué era necesario sacarle la muela sin anestesia?

B **Describiendo** Describe.
1. al dentista
2. el gabinete del dentista
3. al alcalde mientras el dentista le sacaba la muela

C **Interpretando** Interpreta el significado de la conversación entre el dentista y el alcalde sobre el pago de la cuenta.

D **Analizando** Contesta sobre el estilo del autor.

¿Qué acciones introduce el autor en el cuento para hacerles sentir a sus lectores la tensión fuerte que existe entre el alcalde y el dentista?

Después de leer

¿Cuáles son tus reacciones ante la actitud y comportamiento del dentista?

Carreras

Si te interesa la odontología (ser dentista), prepara una lista de todos los términos relacionados con este campo que se encuentran en el cuento.

CULTURA
Una clínica dental en Palma de Mallorca

CARRERAS *trescientos veintisiete* **327**

PRACTICE

¿Comprendes?
A You may wish to do this activity as factual recall.
B Students can also write their descriptions.

Differentiation
Advanced Learners
C Call on advanced learners to give oral answers to this activity.
D Students can also write their analysis in this activity.

Comunicación

Interpersonal
Use the following questions to generate a class discussion.
¿Pueden simpatizar con el dentista? ¿Tiene compasión por él? ¿Por qué sí o por qué no?

Answers
con pomos de loza. Frente a la silla hay una ventana con un cancel de tela. Tiene el cielo raso desfondado y hay una telaraña polvorienta.
3. El alcalde se aferró a las barras de la silla y descargó toda su fuerza en los pies pero no soltó un suspiro. Sus ojos se llenaron de lágrimas pero no suspiró hasta que no sintió salir la muela.

C *Answers will vary.*

D *Answers will vary but may include:*
El alcalde dice que va a pegarle un tiro si el dentista no le saca la muela. El dentista saca su revólver y le dice a su hijo que diga al alcalde que venga a pegárselo. El dentista hace todo sin mirar al alcalde y no le habla mucho, pero el alcalde no pierde de vista al dentista. El dentista no le da anestesia al alcalde y parece que goza del dolor

que experimenta el alcalde porque dice con una amarga ternura que «paga veinte muertos». El alcalde se despidió del dentista con un displicente saludo militar.

Prepárate para el examen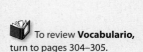
Self-check for achievement

Resources

- Tests, pages 10.43–10.57
- Performance Assessment, Task 10, pages 10.59–10.60
- ExamView® Assessment Suite

✔ Self-check for achievement

This is a pre-test for students to take before you administer the chapter test. Note that each section is cross-referenced so students can easily find the material they feel they need to review. You may wish to use Self-Check Worksheet Transparency SC10 to have students complete this assessment in class or at home. You can correct the assessment yourself, or you may prefer to project the answers on the overhead in class using Self-Check Answers Transparency SC10A.

Differentiation

Slower Paced Learners

Have students work in pairs to complete the Self-Check in class. Once they have finished, call on individuals to give the correct answers as you review together.

Multiple Intelligences

To engage **visual-spatial** and **bodily-kinesthetic** learners, number from 1 to 40 on the board and call on a student to go to the board and write the correct answer (this may be done chronologically or you may allow students to choose the one they answer). Have the student who wrote the first answer decide who will write the second, and so on.

328

Vocabulario

To review Vocabulario, turn to pages 304–305.

1 Completa.

1–2. Otras palabras que se refieren a una oficina son _____ y _____.

3–4. Una _____ diseña un puente y un _____ lo construye.

5. Los _____ trabajan para el gobierno.

6. Para ser _____ hay que poder diseñar programas para la computadora.

7. El jefe de la administración de una ciudad se llama «el _____».

8. _____ va a preparar los medicamentos para la receta que le da Anita.

9. Su padre es representante de ventas y se dedica a la _____ de varias mercancías mexicanas.

10. Otra palabra que significa «empresa» es _____.

11. _____ hace cosas de madera.

12. Hay un problema con las luces en mi casa. Tengo que llamar un _____.

13. Se puede decir el departamento de personal o de _____.

14–15. Antes de que una empresa te ofrezca un puesto es necesario tener una _____ y llenar una _____.

16. El entrevistador le ha dicho al _____ que es necesario hablar inglés y español.

17. En los periódicos hay _____ para los que buscan trabajo.

18. Trabajar cuarenta horas por semana es trabajar _____.

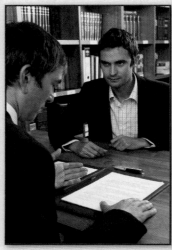

▲ El candidato tiene una entrevista en el departamento de recursos humanos de la empresa.

Gramática

To review por and para, turn to pages 310, 312, 314.

2 Completa con por o para.

19. El tren sale _____ Barcelona.

20. Tenemos que estar allí _____ el día diez.

21. Vamos a estar _____ unos ocho días.

22. Después de terminar nuestro trabajo vamos a viajar _____ el país.

23–24. _____ norteamericano habla muy bien el español pero nadie lo toma _____ hispanohablante.

25–26. Yo compré el regalo _____ mi madre que quiere dárselo a mi hermana. El regalo es _____ mi hermana.

328 *trescientos veintiocho*

To review Vocabulario, turn to pages 304–305.

To review por and para, turn to pages 310, 312, 314.

Answers

1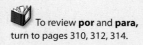

1. el bufete (el gabinete)
2. el consultorio (la consulta)
3. arquitecta
4. ingeniero
5. funcionarios
6. programador de computadoras
7. alcalde
8. El farmacéutico
9. venta
10. la sociedad (la compañía)
11. El (Un) carpintero
12. electricista
13. recursos humanos
14. entrevista
15. solicitud de empleo
16. candidato (aspirante)
17. anuncios clasificados
18. a tiempo completo

2

19. para
20. para
21. por
22. por
23. Para
24. por
25. por
26. para

3 Completa con por o para.

27. El cielo está muy nublado. Está _____ llover.
28. Estoy _____ divertirme. ¿Qué podemos hacer?
29. Ellos han llamado _____ ayuda.
30. Siempre está trabajando y le queda mucho _____ hacer.
31. Los huevos se venden _____ docena.
32. Él quiere darme dólares _____ euros.

4 Completa.

33. Están buscando asistentes que _____ español. (hablar)
34. ¿Por qué? Ya tienen muchos asistentes que _____ español. (hablar)
35. Su padre trabaja con una compañía que _____ sucursales en otros países. (tener)
36. ¿Conoces una compañía que _____ oficinas en México? (tener)

Cultura

5 Contesta.

37. ¿Qué es una compañía multinacional?
38. ¿Qué significa el mundo de globalización?
39–40. ¿Cuáles son dos maneras en que el español te podrá beneficiar en tu vida profesional?

CULTURA
Empleadas de una empresa
estadounidense en Lima, Perú

📖 To review **por** and **para**, turn to pages 310, 312, 314.

📖 To review **el subjuntivo en cláusulas relativas,** turn to page 316.

📖 To review this cultural information, turn to page 320.

Preparate para el examen ✓

Differentiation
(continued)

This type of review activity is particularly appealing to **inter-personal** learners but will also benefit the class on the whole by promoting an inclusive, student-centered learning environment.

Slower Paced Learners
Encourage students who need extra help to refer to the book icons and review any section before answering the questions.

Pre-AP Students preparing for the AP exam may benefit from a set time limit when completing this Self-Check. This may also help to identify students with learning difficulties or slower paced students who need extra help.

GLENCOE 🖱 Technology

Online Learning in the Classroom
You may wish to have students use QuickPass code ASD7844c10 for additional test preparation. They will be able to complete a self-check quiz for chapter review.

Answers

3
27. para
28. por
29. por
30. por
31. por
32. por

4
33. hablen
34. hablan
35. tiene
36. tenga

5
37. *Answers will vary but may include:*
Una compañía multinacional es una empresa que tiene sucursales o filiales al extranjero.

38. *Answers will vary but may include:*
La globalización es el mundo en que el comercio tiene más y más importancia. Las grandes empresas de todas partes del mundo han llegado a ser multinacionales.

39–40. *Answers will vary but may include:*
El español con otra especialización como la contabilidad, el marketing o la informática te podrá ayudar a encontrar un empleo con una empresa multinacional que te pague bien y que sea interesante. El español te dará la oportunidad de viajar y ver el mundo.

Prepárate para el examen ✓
Practice for oral proficiency

⭐ Tips for Success ·······

Encourage students to say as much as possible when they do these open-ended activities. Tell them not to be afraid to make mistakes, since the goal of the activities is real-life communication. If someone in the group makes an error, allow the others to politely correct him or her. Let students choose the activities they would like to do.

Tell students to feel free to elaborate on the basic theme and to be creative. They may use props, pictures, or posters if they wish.

·····································

Pre-AP These oral activities will give students the opportunity to develop and improve their speaking skills so that they may succeed on the speaking portion of the AP exam.

📷 Cultural Snapshot

(page 330) Cuenca is known for its **casas colgadas** or *hanging houses*. Cuenca is situated in an area of dramatic gorges and cliffs.

Note: You may want to use the rubric below to help students prepare their speaking activities.

1 Profesiones de interés
✓ *Talk about professions and occupations*
Trabaja con un(a) compañero(a). Hablen de las profesiones u oficios en que tendrían interés. Expliquen por qué les interesaría cierta profesión.

2 Una entrevista
✓ *Interview a job candidate*
Eres un(a) empleado(a) en una agencia de empleos. Un(a) compañero(a) es un(a) candidato(a) para un puesto. Tú vas a darle una entrevista. Pregúntale sobre sus estudios, experiencia, aptitudes personales, talentos artísticos, etc. Luego cambien de rol.

3 Un nuevo alumno hispano
✓ *Talk about career possibilities*
El/La consejero(a) de orientación *(guidance counselor)* de tu escuela te ha pedido ayudar a un(a) estudiante hispanohablante que acaba de llegar de un país latinoamericano. Quiere que le hagas preguntas para determinar una carrera que le interese. Luego quiere que le expliques todo lo que tiene que hacer para prepararse para esa carrera.

4 Un trabajo ideal
✓ *Describe an ideal job*
Piensa en lo que tú considerarías un trabajo ideal o algo que a ti te gustaría hacer. Describe tu trabajo ideal a un(a) compañero(a). Luego cambien de rol.

5 ¡Seguir con el español! ¿Por qué?
✓ *Discuss the importance of studying Spanish*
Tú y un(a) compañero(a) van a hablarles a los alumnos en una clase del primer año de español. Les van a decir por qué deben continuar con sus estudios del español. Les van a explicar por qué es muy importante el estudio del español. Traten de ser creativos y usen su sentido de humor.

CULTURA

¿Te interesaría pintar como esta artista en la Plaza Mayor en Cuenca, España?

Scoring Rubric for Speaking

	4	3	2	1
vocabulary	extensive use of vocabulary, including idiomatic expressions	adequate use of vocabulary and idiomatic expressions	limited vocabulary marked with some anglicisms	limited vocabulary marked by frequent anglicisms that force interpretation by the listener
grammar	few or no grammatical errors	minor grammatical errors	some serious grammatical errors	serious grammatical errors
pronunciation	good intonation and largely accurate pronunciation with slight accent	acceptable intonation and pronunciation with distinctive accent	errors in intonation and pronunciation with heavy accent	errors in intonation and pronunciation that interfere with listener's comprehension
content	thorough response with interesting and pertinent detail	thorough response with sufficient detail	some detail, but not sufficient	general, insufficient response

Tarea

Imagine yourself in ten years applying for your "dream job." By then, you will have received further education in some area of specialization and will probably have acquired related work experience. Now that the job for which you have been preparing has become available, you must create a résumé (**currículum vitae**) that will show why you are a strong candidate for the position.

Writing Strategy

Persuasiveness When creating a résumé, your primary focus should be on how the job for which you are applying matches up with your background and your career goals. Since applying for a job is a formal process, it is always important to keep your audience in mind and to adhere to certain conventions or rules of professional communication. In order to convince the employer that you are indeed a highly qualified candidate, your writing—both in content and in form—should be persuasive.

❶ Prewrite

- Begin by reflecting on what life will be like for you in ten years. Decide on a career that will suit your interests and that will draw upon your education and your work experience.
- Create a timeline or basic chronology of the jobs you will have worked and the training you will have received by then, making sure they relate in some way to the career you have chosen.

- You may also wish to make a list of additional information to be included in your résumé, such as a statement of your objectives, evidence of community service, and other personal achievements that will make your résumé stand out.

❷ Write

- Although there are many different styles, most effective résumés contain information that is categorized under various headings. Within each category, the information is listed in reverse chronological order (starting with the most recent).
- The following headings may serve as a guideline: **Datos personales, Formación académica, Experiencia profesional, Idiomas, Informática, Otros datos (Servicio comunitario, Cualidades, Otras habilidades, Actividades, Intereses).**
- Be sure to narrow things down so that all information can fit on a single page. When describing your accomplishments, avoid unnecessary repetition and use strong or active verbs that will grab the reader's attention.
- When generating facts about your future self, feel free to be creative but also remember to take this assignment seriously and to view it as an opportunity to gain further practice for upcoming "real-world" situations.

Evaluate

Your teacher will evaluate you on proper use of vocabulary, correct spelling and grammar, completeness of information, and quality of content and style.

Pre-AP This **tarea** will give students the opportunity to develop and improve their writing skills so that they may succeed on the AP exam.

Note: You may want to use the rubric below to help students prepare their writing task.

Scoring Rubric for Writing				
	4	**3**	**2**	**1**
vocabulary	precise, varied	functional, fails to communicate complete meaning	limited to basic words, often inaccurate	inadequate
grammar	excellent, very few or no errors	some errors, do not hinder communication	numerous errors interfere with communication	many errors, little sentence structure
content	thorough response to the topic	generally thorough response to the topic	partial response to the topic	insufficient response to the topic
organization	well organized, ideas presented clearly and logically	loosely organized, but main ideas present	some attempts at organization, but with confused sequencing	lack of organization

Repaso del Capítulo 10

Grammar Review

This page provides a quick "at a glance" summary of the grammar points students have learned in this chapter. The corresponding page numbers are also listed so that students can easily find each grammar point as it was presented.

Differentiation

Multiple Intelligences

You may want to call on **verbal-linguistic** and **logical-mathematical** learners for whom grammar often comes easily to explain the main concepts to their classmates in their own words. Having students explain the concepts in different ways may also help slower paced learners or students with learning difficulties.

Cultural Snapshot

(page 332) The Galapagos Islands are 960 kilometers off the coast of Ecuador. The archipelago is made up of thirteen large islands, six small islands, and more than forty islets. The Galapagos Islands are a habitat for a great variety of species—one of the most famous being the gigantic tortoise.

Gramática

- **Por y para** *(pages 310, 312, and 314)*

  The prepositions **por** and **para** have very specific uses.

  Para is used to represent a destination, purpose or reason, or readiness. It can also express a comparison or a deadline.

  > Salen **para** Madrid.
  > El paquete es **para** María.
  > Estudia **para** ingeniero.
  > Están **para** salir.
  > **Para** cubano, habla bien el inglés.
  > Tiene que terminar **para** el día ocho.

  Por, on the other hand, is more circuitous. It expresses *through, by, on behalf of, instead of,* and *in exchange for.* It expresses the reason for an errand, a period of time, indefinite time, means, manner, an opinion, or estimation. **Por** is also used to indicate a measure or number.

  > Viajaron **por** España.
  > Entró **por** la ventana.
  > Compré el regalo **por** María.
  > Voy **por** agua.
  > Estuvieron **por** dos semanas.
  > Estarán **por** Navidad.
  > Lo toman **por** cubano, pero no lo es.
  > Estamos **por** *(in the mood)* salir.
  > Me dio pesos **por** dólares.
  > Se venden **por** kilo.
  > Ya tengo mucho **por** hacer.

- **Subjuntivo en cláusulas relativas** *(page 316)*

  When a relative clause modifies an indefinite antecedent, the subjunctive is used in the clause. If the antecedent is definite the indicative is used.

  > Estamos buscando alguien que **tenga** experiencia en ventas.
  > Conozco a alguien que **tiene** experiencia en ventas.

CULTURA

El barco pasa por la costa de las islas Galápagos en Ecuador.

There are a number of cognates in this list. See how many you and a partner can find. Who can find the most? Compare your list with those of your classmates.

Vocabulario

Talking about offices and office personnel

la oficina	médico	ejecutivo(a)	la empresa, la
el bufete del	el gabinete del	el/la ejecutivo(a)	sociedad, la
abogado	dentista	el/la programador(a)	compañía
el consultorio (la	el/la contable	de computadoras	el estado financiero
consulta) del	el/la asistente(a)	(informática)	

Identifying some government workers

el gobierno	el/la senador(a)	el/la funcionario(a)
el/la político(a)	el/la alcalde(sa)	gubernamental
		(de gobierno)

Talking about businesspeople

el/la comerciante	el hombre (la mujer)	el/la dueño(a)	el/la vendedor(a)
	de negocios		

Identifying some professions

la carrera	el/la arquitecto(a)	el/la abogado(a)	el/la farmacéutico(a)
la profesión	el/la ingeniero(a)	el/la dentista	

Identifying some trades

el oficio	el/la plomero(a),	el/la carpintero(a)
el/la electricista	el/la fontanero(a)	el/la albañil

Talking about job opportunities

un puesto	el servicio de	el/la estudiante	el currículum vitae,
el anuncio	recursos humanos	universitario(a)	el currículo
(clasificado)	el/la candidato(a),	la solicitud	un trabajo
el departamento	el/la aspirante	(aplicación) de	a tiempo completo
de personal,	la entrevista	empleo	a tiempo parcial

Other useful words and expressions

llenar

The words listed below come from this chapter's literary selection, *Un día de éstos*. They were selected to become part of your active vocabulary because of their relatively high frequency.

el/la madrugador(a)	enjuto(a)	apresurarse
la muñeca	sordo(a)	amanecer
una lágrima	hinchado(a)	

Vocabulary Review

The words and phrases in the **Vocabulario** section have been taught for productive use in this chapter. They are summarized here as a resource for both student and teacher. This list also serves as a convenient resource for the **Prepárate para el examen** activities on pages 328–331.

GLENCOE SPANISH

Why It Works!

This vocabulary reference list has not been translated into English for two reasons. First, it is recommended that students learn the new vocabulary through direct association with images on the **Vocabulario** pages. Second, all vocabulary is reintroduced in the chapter many times, and upon completion of the chapter students should be familiar with the meaning of all the words. If there are words that students still do not know, they can refer back to the vocabulary presentation in the chapter or the dictionary at the end of the book. If, however, it is your preference to give students the English translations, please refer to Vocabulary Transparency V10.1 or to the Chapter 10 PowerPoint® presentation on PowerTeach.

Don't forget the chapter project and cultural activities found on pages 300C–300D. Students have learned all the information that they will need to complete these engaging enrichment tasks.

The cognates in this list are: **la oficina, el/la médico(a), el/la dentista, el/la asistente(a) ejecutivo(a), el/la ejecutivo(a), el/la programador(a) de computadoras, la compañía, el/la político(a), el/la senador(a), gubernamental, la carrera, la profesión, el/la arquitecto(a), el/la electricista, el/la plomero(a), el/la carpintero(a), clasificado, el servicio de recursos humanos, el/la candidato(a), el/la estudiante universitario(a), la aplicación de empleo, el currículum vitae, completo, parcial.**

Every chapter of ¡Así se dice! contains this review section of previously learned material. By recycling information from previous chapters, the cumulative review serves to remind students that they need to continue practicing what they have learned after finishing each chapter.

Activity 1 This activity reviews the use of the present, past, and future tenses of verbs. See pages R7, R17, R19, R29, R31, R43–R44, SR32.

🎧 **Audio Script** *(CD 10, Track 19)*

1. Anita nació el ocho de noviembre.
2. Mañana celebrará su día especial con todas sus amigas.
3. Ella está contenta que todas sus amigas vengan a celebrar su cumpleaños.
4. Mi tío murió el jueves.
5. El entierro tendrá lugar en el cementerio cerca de su casa.
6. El profesor nos devolverá nuestros exámenes pronto.
7. Espero recibir una nota muy buena.
8. Recibí una nota muy alta en el último examen.

Activity 2 This activity reviews the use of most verb tenses learned to this point. See pages R54, 140.

Activity 3 This activity reviews irregular verbs in the present tense. See page R7 and the verb charts at the end of this book.

334

Repaso cumulativo

Repasa lo que ya has aprendido

These activities will help you review and remember what you have learned so far in Spanish.

 Escucha las frases. Indica en una tabla como la de abajo si la acción toma lugar en el pasado, el presente o el futuro.

en el pasado	en el presente	en el futuro

2 Completa con el verbo **hablar**. Fíjate en las expresiones adverbiales para determinar el tiempo del verbo que necesitas.

1. Hace tres años que yo _____ español.
2. Pero yo no _____ español cuando era niño(a).
3. Yo le _____ a él ayer y _____ con él esta mañana.
4. No, no le _____ mañana.
5. Yo le _____ si pudiera pero nunca contesta su móvil ni sus correos electrónicos.
6. Yo le _____ antes de que llegue.
7. Yo le _____ antes de que llegara.

3 Personaliza. Da respuestas personales.

1. ¿Quién eres?
2. ¿Cuántos años tienes?
3. ¿A qué hora sales para la escuela?
4. ¿Conoces a mucha gente?
5. ¿Sabes mucho?
6. ¿Haces mucho trabajo?
7. ¿Conduces un carro?
8. ¿Siempre dices la verdad?
9. ¿Cómo vas a la escuela?
10. ¿Dónde estás ahora?

▲ El joven hace sus tareas en la biblioteca después de las clases.

Answers

1
1. en el pasado
2. en el futuro
3. en el presente
4. en el pasado
5. en el futuro
6. en el futuro
7. en el presente
8. en el pasado

 2
1. hablo
2. hablaba
3. hablé, hablaré (hablé)
4. hablaré
5. hablaría
6. hablaré
7. hablé

 3
1. Soy _____.
2. Tengo _____ años.
3. Salgo para la escuela a las _____.
4. Sí, (No, no) conozco a mucha gente.
5. Sí, (No, no) sé mucho.
6. Sí, (No, no) hago mucho trabajo.
7. Sí, (No, no) conduzco un carro.

Completa con el pretérito o imperfecto.

1. El lo hace ahora y lo _____ ayer.
2. Ellos lo dicen y siempre lo _____.
3. Yo voy con frecuencia pero no _____ mucho cuando era joven.
4. Abuelita me habla ahora y me _____ ayer también.
5. ¿Él da muchas fiestas? Sí, y como sabes, siempre _____ fiestas.

Completa para formar frases.

1. Quiero que tú _____.
2. Es necesario que ellos _____.
3. Prefiero que ustedes _____.
4. Te aconsejamos que _____.
5. Es importante que ella _____.
6. Yo le hablaré cuando _____.
7. Tú lo verás antes de que _____.
8. Esperaremos aquí hasta que ellos _____.

Completa para formar frases.

1. Quería que tú _____.
2. Fue necesario que ellos _____.
3. Preferiría que ustedes _____.
4. Te aconsejaríamos que _____.
5. Fue importante que ella _____.
6. Yo le hablé cuando _____.
7. Tú lo viste antes de que _____.
8. Esperaríamos hasta que ellos _____.

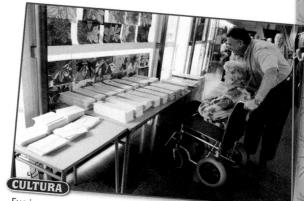

CULTURA

Fue importante que la señora supiera para quien votaba durante las elecciones para el Parlamento de Cataluña.

Activity 4 This activity reviews the use of preterite and imperfect verbs. See pages R29, R31, R43–R44, R54.

Activity 5 This activity reviews the use of the present subjunctive. See pages 40, 72, 140.

Activity 6 This activity reviews the use of the imperfect subjunctive. See page 140.

GLENCOE Technology

Audio in the Classroom

The **¡Así se dice!** Audio Program for Chapter 10 has 19 activities, which afford students extensive listening and speaking practice.

Online Learning in the Classroom

You may wish to have students use QuickPass code ASD7844c10 for additional cumulative review. They will be able to complete a self-check quiz.

Pre-AP To give students further open-ended oral or written practice, or to assess proficiency, go to AP Proficiency Practice Transparency AP12.

Answers

8. Sí, (No, no) digo siempre la verdad.
9. Voy a la escuela en carro (en bus, a pie).
10. Estoy en _____.

1. hizo	4. habló
2. decían	5. daba
3. iba	

5 *Answers will vary.*

6 *Answers will vary.*

Student Resources

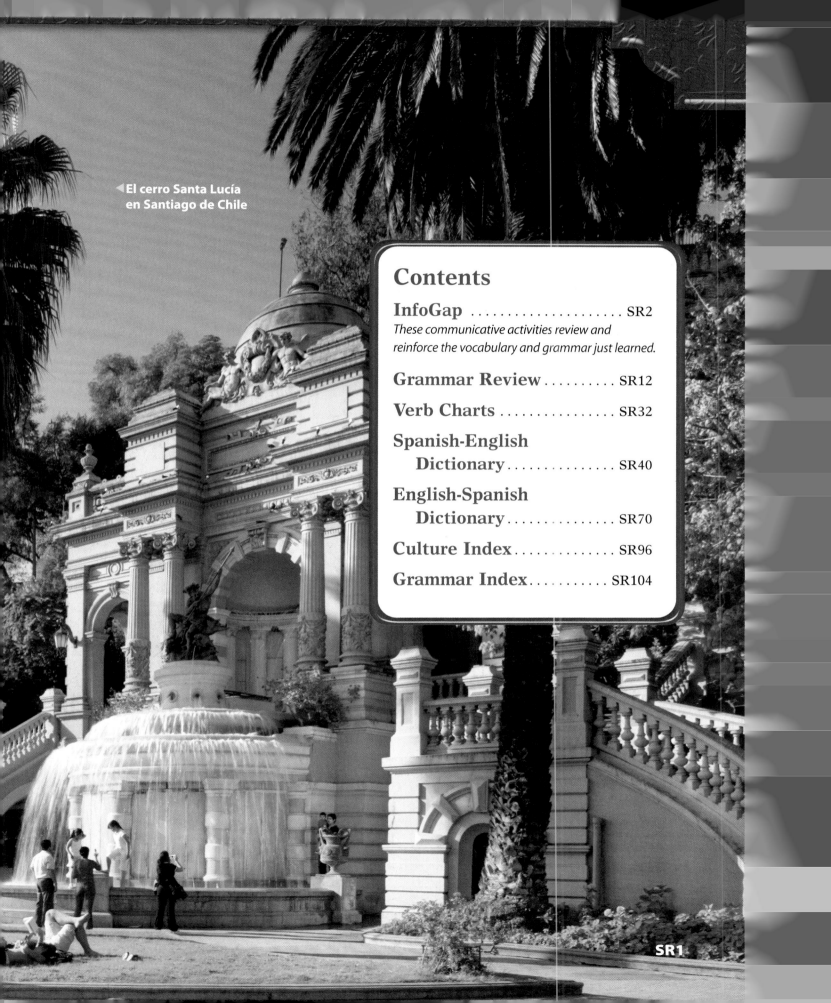

El cerro Santa Lucía
en Santiago de Chile

Contents

InfoGap

Activity 1

InfoGap

Alumno A Ask your partner the following questions. Correct answers are in parentheses.

1. ¿Qué quiere Marisa que su primo haga? (*Marisa quiere que su primo se acueste.*)

2. ¿Qué quieren sus amigos que Marta haga? (*Sus amigos quieren que Marta salga este fin de semana.*)

3. ¿Qué quieres que hagamos esta noche? (*Quiero que miremos la tele esta noche.*)

4. ¿Qué quiere la madre de Diego que él haga? (*La madre de Diego quiere que él limpie la casa.*)

Alumno A Answer your partner's questions based on the cues below.

1. jugar tenis

2. preparar la comida

3. conducir con cuidado

4. decir la verdad

Alumno B Answer your partner's questions based on the cues below.

1. acostarse

2. salir este fin de semana

3. mirar la tele

4. limpiar la casa

Alumno B Ask your partner the following questions. Correct answers are in parentheses.

1. ¿Qué quieren los padres que sus hijos hagan?
   (*Los padres quieren que sus hijos jueguen tenis.*)

2. ¿Qué quieres que yo haga?
   (*Quiero que tú prepares la comida.*)

3. ¿Qué quiere Olivia que su hermana haga?
   (*Olivia quiere que su hermana conduzca con cuidado.*)

4. ¿Qué quiere el profesor que sus alumnos hagan?
   (*El profesor quiere que sus alumnos digan la verdad.*)

Activity 2

Alumno A Answer your partner's questions based on the photo below.

Alumno A Ask your partner the following questions. Correct answers are in parentheses.

1. ¿Qué se ha cortado la joven?
   (La joven se ha cortado el dedo.)

2. ¿Ella está en la ambulancia?
   (No, ella no está en la ambulancia.)

3. ¿Ella se ha hecho mucho daño?
   (No, ella no se ha hecho mucho daño.)

4. ¿Qué le pone la enfermera?
   (La enfermera le pone una venda.)

Alumno B Answer your partner's questions based on the photos below.

Alumno B Ask your partner the following questions. Correct answers are in parentheses.

1. ¿Qué se ha torcido el joven?
   (El joven se ha torcido el tobillo.)

2. ¿Habla el joven con los socorristas?
   (No, el joven no habla con los socorristas.)

3. ¿Con quién habla el joven?
   (El joven habla con la médica.)

4. ¿Está en una silla de ruedas?
   (Sí, está en una silla de ruedas.)

InfoGap

Alumno A Ask your partner the following questions. Correct answers are in parentheses.

1. ¿Qué quieres?
   (Quiero que [tú] vayas conmigo a la fiesta de cumpleaños de mi prima.)

2. ¿Qué mandan tus padres?
   (Mis padres mandan que yo asista al bautizo de mi sobrino.)

3. ¿Qué siente tu madre?
   (Mi madre siente que mis abuelos no puedan asistir a su fiesta de cumpleaños.)

4. ¿Qué te sorprende?
   (Me sorprende que mi hermana se case pronto.)

Alumno A Answer **no** to your partner's questions based on the cues below.

1. a la escuela

2. caminar

3. casarse

4. solo(a)

Alumno B Answer your partner's questions based on the cues below.

1. tú / ir conmigo a la fiesta de cumpleaños de mi prima

2. yo / asistir al bautizo de mi sobrino

3. mis abuelos / no poder asistir a su fiesta de cumpleaños

4. mi hermana / casarse pronto

Alumno B Ask your partner the following questions. Correct answers are in parentheses.

1. ¿Insisten tus padres en que vayas al cine?
   (No, mis padres insisten en que yo vaya a la escuela.)

2. ¿Prefieres que tus amigas tomen el bus?
   (No, prefiero que mis amigas caminen.)

3. ¿Estás contento(a) que tu hermano se gradúe?
   (No, estoy contento[a] que mi hermano se case.)

4. ¿Desean tus padres que estudies con tus amigos? (No, mis padres desean que estudie solo[a].)

Activity 4

InfoGap

Alumno A Answer your partner's questions based on the pictures below.

Alumno A Ask your partner the following questions. Correct answers are in parentheses.

1. ¿Dónde está César?
   (César está en la lavandería.)

2. ¿Pone su ropa sucia en la lavadora o saca su ropa?
   (Pone su ropa sucia en la lavadora.)

3. ¿Dónde está Anita?
   (Anita está en el correo.)

4. ¿Qué hace allí?
   (Echa su tarjeta en el buzón.)

Alumno B Answer your partner's questions based on the pictures below.

1–2.

3–4.

Alumno B Ask your partner the following questions. Correct answers are in parentheses.

1. ¿Dónde trabaja Alonso?
   (*Alonso trabaja en una peluquería.*)

2. ¿Con qué paga el cliente, con dinero en efectivo o con cheque?
   (*El cliente paga con dinero en efectivo.*)

3. ¿Dónde está Gloria?
   (*Gloria está enfrente del cajero automático.*)

4. ¿Dónde está Susana, en el banco o en el correo?
   (*Susana está en el banco.*)

InfoGap

Activity 5

Alumno A Ask your partner the following questions. Correct answers are in parentheses.

1. ¿Qué era necesario?
   (Era necesario que todos se pusieran de pie.)

2. ¿Qué quería la profesora?
   (La profesora quería que los alumnos sacaran notas buenas.)

3. ¿Qué te sorprendió?
   (Me sorprendió que Juan no llegara a tiempo.)

4. ¿Qué es una lástima?
   (Es una lástima que nosotros perdamos la película.)

Alumno A Answer your partner's questions based on the cues below.

1. yo / levantarme temprano

2. la cocinera / freír el pescado

3. ellos / estudiar toda la noche

4. yo / pagar la cuenta

Alumno B Answer your partner's questions based on the cues below.

1. todos / ponerse de pie

2. los alumnos / sacar notas buenas

3. Juan / no llegar a tiempo

4. nosotros / perder la película

Alumno B Ask your partner the following questions. Correct answers are in parentheses.

1. ¿Qué quería tu madre?
   (Mi madre quería que yo me levantara temprano.)

2. ¿En qué insistió el cliente?
   (El cliente insistió en que la cocinera friera el pescado.)

3. ¿Qué será necesario?
   (Será necesario que ellos estudien toda la noche.)

4. ¿Qué dudó tu hermana?
   (Mi hermana dudó que yo pagara la cuenta.)

Activity 6

Alumno A Ask your partner the following questions. Correct answers are in parentheses.

1. ¿Cuándo podrás reclamar tu equipaje?
(Podré reclamar mi equipaje cuando llegue a mi destino.)

2. ¿Cuándo hablarás con Marta?
(Hablaré con Marta antes de que cambie de tren.)

3. ¿Cuándo saldrás?
(Saldré tan pronto como pueda.)

4. ¿Cuándo alquilaste el carro?
(Alquilé el carro en cuanto llegué al aeropuerto.)

Alumno A Answer your partner's questions based on the cues below.

1. antes de que / salir de la agencia

2. cuando / tener bastante dinero

3. después de que / encontrar la información

4. en cuanto / sentirme mejor

Alumno B Answer your partner's questions based on the cues below.

1. cuando / llegar a mi destino

2. antes de que / cambiar de tren

3. tan pronto como / poder

4. en cuanto / llegar al aeropuerto

Alumno B Ask your partner the following questions. Correct answers are in parentheses.

1. ¿Cuándo inspeccionarás el jeep?
(Inspeccionaré el jeep antes de que salga de la agencia.)

2. ¿Cuándo viajarás?
(Viajaré cuándo tenga bastante dinero.)

3. ¿Cuándo devolviste el libro?
(Devolví el libro después de que encontré la información.)

4. ¿Cuándo practicarás el esquí acuático?
(Practicaré el esquí acuático en cuanto me sienta mejor.)

Activity 7

Alumno A Ask your partner the following questions. Correct answers are in parentheses.

Alumno A Use the cues below to answer your partner's questions.

1. Si tienes bastante tiempo, ¿qué harás?
(*Si tengo bastante tiempo, escribiré una novela.*)

2. Si ellos te hubieran preguntado, ¿qué habrías hecho?
(*Si ellos me hubieran preguntado, les habría dicho la verdad.*)

3. Si viajaras a Costa Rica, ¿qué harías?
(*Si viajara a Costa Rica, iría a la playa.*)

4. Si tienes bastante dinero, ¿qué harás? (*Si tengo bastante dinero, compraré un cuadro famoso.*)

1. eliminar la pobreza

2. ver más exposiciones

3. ir a la estación de esquí

4. celebrar

Alumno B Use the cues below to answer your partner's questions.

1. escribir una novela

2. decirles la verdad

3. ir a la playa

4. comprar un cuadro famoso

Alumno B Ask your partner the following questions. Correct answers are in parentheses.

1. Si fueras presidente(a), ¿qué harías?
(*Si fuera presidente[a], eliminaría la pobreza.*)

2. Si hubieras tenido más tiempo, ¿qué habrías hecho?
(*Si hubiera tenido más tiempo, habría visto más exposiciones.*)

3. Si nieva, ¿qué harás?
(*Si nieva, iré a la estación de esquí.*)

4. Si hubieras ganado el partido, ¿qué habrías hecho?
(*Si hubiera ganado el partido, habría celebrado.*)

Alumno A Ask your partner the following questions. Correct answers are in parentheses.

1. ¿Vas a salir?
(Sí, voy a salir aunque es tarde.)

2. ¿Vas a esquiar?
(Sí, voy a esquiar aunque no haya nieve.)

3. ¿Vas a decirle la verdad?
(Sí, voy a decirle la verdad aunque es difícil.)

4. ¿Vas a ir a la fiesta?
(Sí, voy a ir a la fiesta aunque vaya solo[a].)

Alumno A Answer your partner's questions with **sí** and the conjunction **aunque** based on the information provided.

1. No sabes si tienes el libro.

2. Es temprano.

3. No sabes si tienes que ir a pie.

4. Ya sabes que es caro.

Alumno B Answer your partner's questions with **sí** and the conjunction **aunque** based on the information provided.

1. Es tarde.

2. No sabes si habrá nieve.

3. Ya sabes que va a ser difícil.

4. No sabes si vas a ir solo(a).

Alumno B Ask your partner the following questions. Correct answers are in parentheses.

1. ¿Vas a estudiar?
(Sí, voy a estudiar aunque no tenga el libro.)

2. ¿Vas a despertarse?
(Sí, voy a despertarme aunque es temprano.)

3. ¿Vas a ir a la escuela?
(Sí, voy a ir a la escuela aunque tenga que ir a pie.)

4. ¿Vas a comprar el billete?
(Sí, voy a comprar el billete aunque es caro.)

InfoGap

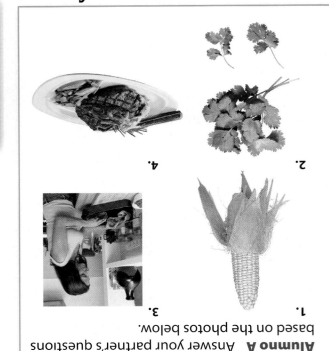

Alumno A   Ask your partner the following questions. Correct answers are in parentheses.

1. ¿Qué quisieras comer?
   (Quisiera comer una alcachofa.)

2. ¿Qué hace la cocinera, reboza las rodajas o hierve el arroz?
   (La cocinera hierve el arroz.)

3. ¿Qué especia se cultiva en este huerto?
   (Se cultiva el orégano en este huerto.)

4. ¿Quiénes son ellos, los comensales o los cocineros?
   (Son los comensales.)

Alumno A   Answer your partner's questions based on the photos below.

Alumno B   Answer your partner's questions based on the photos below.

1.

3.

2.

4.

Alumno B   Ask your partner the following questions. Correct answers are in parentheses.

1. ¿Qué necesitas, una zanahoria o una mazorca de maíz?
   (Necesito una mazorca de maíz.)

2. ¿Cuál es la especia que se usa?
   (Se usa el cilantro.)

3. ¿Prepara la cocinera la carne picada o el arroz?
   (Prepara la carne picada.)

4. ¿Qué pediste?
   (Pedí la carne de res.)

Activity 10

Alumno A Ask your partner the following questions. Correct answers are in parentheses.

1. ¿Raúl es ingeniero o político?
   (Raúl es ingeniero.)

2. ¿Está llenando una solicitud de empleo o está leyendo los anuncios clasificados?
   (Elena está leyendo los anuncios clasificados.)

3. ¿Para qué profesión estudió Leonora?
   (Leonora estudió para ser abogada.)

4. ¿Felipe es funcionario o plomero?
   (Felipe es plomero.)

Alumno A Answer your partner's questions based on the pictures below.

1.

Diana

2.

Alejandra

3.

4.

Miguel

Alumno B Ask your partner the following questions. Correct answers are in parentheses.

1. ¿Diana es contable o política?
   (Diana es política.)

2. ¿Alejandra es albañil o comerciante?
   (Alejandra es albañil.)

3. ¿Es una solicitud de empleo o un anuncio clasificado?
   (Es una solicitud de empleo.)

4. ¿Miguel es funcionario o comerciante?
   (Miguel es comerciante.)

Alumno B Answer your partner's questions based on the pictures below.

1.

Raúl

3.

Lenora

2.

Elena

4.

Felipe

Grammar Review

Nouns and articles

Nouns and definite articles

A noun is the name of a person, place, or thing. Unlike English, all nouns in Spanish have a gender—either masculine or feminine. Almost all nouns that end in **-o** are masculine and almost all nouns that end in **-a** are feminine. Note that the definite article **el** is used with masculine nouns. The definite article **la** is used with feminine nouns.

MASCULINE	FEMININE
el muchacho	la muchacha
el libro	la escuela
el curso	la sala

Nouns that end in **-e** can either be masculine or feminine. It is necessary for you to learn the gender.

MASCULINE	FEMININE
el padre	la madre
el restaurante	la carne
el nombre	la leche
el norte	la gente
el billete	la nube

Many nouns that end in **-e** and refer to a person can be either masculine or feminine.

el cliente	la cliente
el paciente	la paciente

It is also necessary to learn the gender of nouns that end in a consonant.

el comedor	la flor
el animal	la capital
el jamón	la mujer

Note, however, that nouns that end in **-ción, -dad, -tad** are always feminine.

la habitación	la universidad	la dificultad

Irregular nouns

There are not very many irregular nouns in Spanish. The ones you have learned so far are:

la mano   **el problema**   **la foto** (*from* **la fotografía**)

The following nouns end in **-a** but they are masculine.

el clima	**el planeta**
el día	**el poema**
el drama	**el programa**
el mapa	**el telegrama**

The following nouns end in **-a** or **-ha** and they are feminine. Because of the difficulty pronouncing the two **a** sounds together they take the articles **el** and **un** in the singular. All other articles and adjectives are feminine.

el águila	**las águilas**
el agua	**las aguas**
el arma	**las armas**
el hacha	**las hachas**
el hambre	

Plural of nouns

To form the plural of nouns you add **-s** to nouns that end in a vowel. You add **-es** to nouns that end in a consonant. Note, too, that the definite articles **el** and **la** become **los** and **las** in the plural.

MASCULINE PLURAL	FEMININE PLURAL
los libros	**las novelas**
los cuartos	**las casas**
los coches	**las carnes**
los comedores	**las flores**

Nouns that end in **-z** change the **-z** to **-c** and add **-es.**

el lápiz   **los lápices**

Nouns that end in **-ción** drop the accent in the plural.

la estación	**las estaciones**
la conversación	**las conversaciones**

For special uses of the definite article, see page 245 in Chapter 8 of *¡Así se dice!* Level 3.

Indefinite articles

The indefinite articles are *a, an,* and *some* in English. They are **un, una, unos,** and **unas** in Spanish. Note that the indefinite article, like the definite article, must agree with the noun it modifies in both gender (masculine or feminine) and number (singular or plural).

<table>
<tr><td></td><td>SINGULAR</td><td colspan="2">PLURAL</td></tr>
<tr><td>**un** alumno</td><td>**una** alumna</td><td>**unos** alumnos</td><td>**unas** alumnas</td></tr>
<tr><td>**un** café</td><td>**una** clase</td><td>**unos** cafés</td><td>**unas** clases</td></tr>
<tr><td>**un** árbol</td><td>**una** flor</td><td>**unos** árboles</td><td>**unas** flores</td></tr>
</table>

For special uses of the indefinite article, see pages 247 in Chapter 8 of *¡Así se dice!* Level 3.

Contractions

The prepositions **a** *(to, at)* and **de** *(of, from)* contract (combine) with the definite article **el** to form one word, **al** or **del.** There is no contraction with **la, los,** or **las.**

> **Voy al mercado; no vuelvo del mercado.**
> **Es el dinero del empleado, no del cliente.**

A personal

Remember that whenever a person is the direct object of the verb, it must be preceded by **a.** This **a personal** also contracts with **el.**

> **Conozco a Juan.**
> **Pero no conozco al hermano de Juan.**

Nouns and adjectives

Agreement of nouns and adjectives

An adjective is a word that describes a noun. An adjective must agree in gender (masculine or feminine) and number (singular or plural) with the noun it describes or modifies.

Adjectives that end in **-o** have four forms, the same as nouns that end in **-o.**

	SINGULAR	PLURAL
MASCULINE	**el muchacho simpático**	**los muchachos simpáticos**
FEMININE	**la muchacha simpática**	**las muchachas simpáticas**

Adjectives that end in **-e** have only two forms—singular and plural.

	SINGULAR	PLURAL
MASCULINE	**el alumno inteligente**	**los alumnos inteligentes**
FEMININE	**la alumna inteligente**	**las alumnas inteligentes**

Adjectives that end in a consonant have only two forms—singular and plural. Note that the plural ends in **-es.**

	SINGULAR	PLURAL
MASCULINE	**un curso fácil**	**dos cursos fáciles**
FEMININE	**una tarea fácil**	**dos tareas fáciles**

Adjectives of nationality

Adjectives of nationality that end in a consonant have four forms. Observe the following.

un joven francés   **unos jóvenes franceses**
una joven francesa   **unas jóvenes francesas**

Note that adjectives of nationality that end in **-s** or **-n (inglés, japonés, tailandés, alemán, catalán)** drop the written accent in all forms except the masculine singular.

Possessive adjectives

A possessive adjective tells who owns or possesses something—*my* book and *your* pencil. Like other adjectives in Spanish, possessive adjectives agree with the noun they modify. Note that only **nuestro** and *vuestro* have four forms.

MASCULINE SINGULAR	FEMININE SINGULAR	MASCULINE PLURAL	FEMININE PLURAL
mi tío	**mi tía**	**mis tíos**	**mis tías**
tu tío	**tu tía**	**tus tíos**	**tus tías**
su tío	**su tía**	**sus tíos**	**sus tías**
nuestro tío	**nuestra tía**	**nuestros tíos**	**nuestras tías**
vuestro tío	*vuestra tía*	*vuestros tíos*	*vuestras tías*

Since **su** can refer to many different people, it is often accompanied by a phrase that gives clarification.

su familia

la familia de Juan   la familia de él
la familia de María   la familia de ella
la familia de Juan y María   la familia de ellos
          la familia de usted
          la familia de ustedes

Demonstrative adjectives

Until recently the demonstrative pronoun *(this one, that one, these, those)* had to carry a written accent to differentiate it from a demonstrative adjective. That is no longer the case and the pronouns are the same as the adjectives.

In Spanish there are three demonstrative adjectives (pronouns): **este** *(this)*, **ese** *(that)*, and **aquel** *(that, farther away)*. Each of the demonstratives has four forms and must agree in gender and number with the nouns it modifies or replaces.

MASCULINE SINGULAR	FEMININE SINGULAR	MASCULINE PLURAL	FEMININE PLURAL
este libro	**esta chaqueta**	**estos libros**	**estas chaquetas**
ese libro	**esa chaqueta**	**esos libros**	**esas chaquetas**
aquel libro	**aquella chaqueta**	**aquellos libros**	**aquellas chaquetas**

Suffixes

The suffixes **-ito**, **-ico**, and **-illo** can be added to nouns to convey the meaning *small*. They sometimes add an element of endearment.

> **Mamá y su hijito**
> **Quiere mucho a su abuelita.**
> **Es un chiquito (chiquillo).**

When a noun ends in **-e** or a consonant **–cito** is added.

> **mi cochecito**
> **un ratoncito**

-ísimo

The suffix **–ísimo** adds a superlative element to an adjective.

> **¡Buenísimo!**
> **Fue una experiencia fabulosísima.**

Comparative and superlative

Regular forms

You use the comparative *(more, -er)* and the superlative *(most, -est)* to compare people or things.

To form the comparative in Spanish you use **más** (or **menos**) before the adjective, adverb, or noun. The comparative is followed by **que: más… que.**

> **Él es más inteligente que los otros.**
> **Ella es más ambiciosa que los otros.**

Note that the comparative is followed by the subject pronoun or a negative word.

> más alto que yo (tú, él, nosotros)
>
> más alto que nadie

To form the superlative you use the definite article with **más**. Note that **de** follows the superlative: **el (la) más... de.**

> Él es el más ambicioso de todos.
>
> Ella es la alumna más inteligente de todos.

Irregular forms

The adjectives **bueno** and **malo** as well as the adverbs **bien** and **mal** have irregular comparative and superlative forms.

	COMPARATIVE	SUPERLATIVE
bueno	mejor	el/la mejor
malo	peor	el/la peor
bien	mejor	el/la mejor
mal	peor	el/la peor

> Él es mejor jugador que su hermano.
>
> Pero su hermana Teresa es la mejor jugadora de los tres.
>
> La verdad es que ella juega mejor que nadie.
>
> Ella juega mejor que yo.

(El) mayor and **(el) menor** are also comparative and superlative forms. They most often refer to age and sometimes size.

> Mi hermano menor tiene trece años.
>
> Y mi hermana mayor tiene diecisiete.
>
> La Ciudad de México tiene el mayor número de habitantes.

Comparison of equality

To compare things that have equal qualities (*as . . . as*) you use **tan... como** in Spanish. Note that **tan** can precede an adjective or an adverb.

> Ella es tan inteligente como sus hermanos.
>
> Sus hermanos son tan inteligentes como ella.
>
> Ella habla tan rápido como los otros.

To compare equal quantities (*as much . . . as, as many . . . as*) you use **tanto... como.** Since **tanto** is an adjective it must agree with the noun it modifies.

> Él tiene tanta paciencia como su hermana.
>
> Susana no tiene tantos primos como yo.

Note that the subject pronouns follow **como.**

Formation of adverbs

An adverb is formed by adding **-mente** to the feminine form of the adjective.

maravillosa	maravillosamente
clara	claramente
enorme	enormemente
fácil	fácilmente

If more than one adverb is used only the last one in the series has **-mente**.

Él habló clara y cómicamente.

Pronouns

A pronoun is a word that replaces a noun. Review the forms of the pronouns that you have learned so far.

SUBJECT PRONOUNS	DIRECT OBJECT PRONOUNS	INDIRECT OBJECT PRONOUNS	REFLEXIVE PRONOUNS	PREPOSITIONAL PRONOUNS
yo	me	me	me	mí
tú	te	te	te	ti
Ud., él, ella	lo, la	le	se	Ud., él, ella
nosotros(as)	nos	nos	nos	nosotros(as)
vosotros(as)	*os*	*os*	*os*	*vosotros(as)*
Uds., ellos, ellas	los, las	les	se	Uds., ellos, ellas

Remember that an object pronoun comes right before the conjugated form of the verb.

Ella me ve.   **Ella nos habla.**   **Ella lo ha escrito.**

The direct object pronoun is the direct receiver of the action of the verb. The indirect object is the indirect receiver of the action of the verb.

The direct object pronouns **lo, la, los, las** can refer to a person or a thing.

Ellos tiraron la pelota.   **Ellos la tiraron.**

Ellos vieron a sus amigos.   **Ellos los vieron.**

The indirect object pronouns **le, les** refer most frequently to people. They are often accompanied by a prepositional phrase for clarification.

Ella le habló { a él / a ella. / a usted. }   **Yo les hablé** { a ellos. / a ellas. / a ustedes. }

Note that the prepositional pronouns **mí** and **ti** form one word with **con**.

Yo voy contigo y tú vas conmigo.

Double object pronouns

When there are two object pronouns in the same sentence, the indirect object pronoun always precedes the direct object pronoun.

> **Él me lo dijo.**
>
> **Nuestros padres nos los dan.**
>
> **¿Quién te lo dio?**

The indirect object pronouns **le** and **les** change to **se** when used with a direct object pronoun (**lo, la, los, las**).

> **El profesor se lo explica muy bien.**
>
> **¿Quién se las compró?**

Se is often accompanied by a prepositional phrase to clarify its meaning.

> **Yo se lo di**
> - a usted.
> - a él.
> - a ella.
> - a ustedes.
> - a ellos.
> - a ellas.

Position of object pronouns

The object pronouns always precede the conjugated form of the verb.

> **José me vio.**
>
> **El profesor se lo explicó a ustedes.**
>
> **Ellos no lo han hecho.**

With the progressive tenses or the infinitive the pronouns can either come before the helping verb or can be added to the present participle or the infinitive.

> **Ellos nos están ayudando.** **Ella te lo va a explicar.**
>
> **Ellos están ayudándonos.** **Ella va a explicártelo.**
>
> **Ella se la está vendiendo a ellos.** **Ellos nos quieren ayudar.**
>
> **Ella está vendiéndosela a ellos.** **Ellos quieren ayudarnos.**

Note that in order to maintain the same stress you add a written accent mark to the present participle with either one or two pronouns. You add an accent to the infinitive with two pronouns only.

The object pronouns are added to an affirmative command. They precede the negative command.

AFFIRMATIVE	NEGATIVE
Háblame.	**No me hables.**
Dáselo.	**No se lo des.**
Invítelos usted.	**No los invite.**
Díganmelo.	**No me lo digan.**

Note that in order to maintain the same stress, you add a written accent to the command with a pronoun.

Possessive Pronouns

The possessive pronoun is used to replace a noun that is modified by a possessive adjective. The possessive pronoun must agree in number and gender with the noun it replaces. In almost all cases the possessive pronoun is accompanied by the appropriate definite article.

el mío	**la mía**	**los míos**	**las mías**
el tuyo	**la tuya**	**los tuyos**	**las tuyas**
el suyo	**la suya**	**los suyos**	**las suyas**
el nuestro	**la nuestra**	**los nuestros**	**las nuestras**
el vuestro	*la vuestra*	*los vuestros*	*las vuestras*

Since the pronoun **el suyo** can refer to so many things it is often clarified by a prepositional phrase:

el suyo		la suya		los suyos		las suyas	
el	de usted	la	de usted	los	de usted	las	de usted
	de ustedes		de ustedes		de ustedes		de ustedes
	de él		de él		de él		de él
	de ellos		de ellos		de ellos		de ellos
	de ella		de ella		de ella		de ella
	de ellas		de ellas		de ellas		de ellas

Yo tengo mi boleto, no el tuyo.

¿Dónde están tus maletas? No veo las tuyas; veo solo las de José.

Su carro está en el garaje y el nuestro está en la calle.

You will note that after the verb **ser,** the definite article is often omitted.

Aquella casa es nuestra.

¿Es suya esta cámara?

The definite article can be used, however, to give emphasis.

¿Aquel paquete? Es el mío. No es el tuyo.

Relative pronouns

The pronoun **que** introduces a clause that modifies a noun. **Que** can be used to replace a person or thing and can be either the subject or object of the clause.

> **El señor que habla es de aquí.**
> **El libro que está en la mesa es mío.**
> **El señor que vimos anoche es de aquí.**
> **El libro que escribió el señor es interesante.**

Que can also be used after a preposition but only when it refers to a thing.

> **Leí el libro de que hablas.**

A quien(es) can replace **que** only when it refers to a person and is the direct object of the clause.

> **El señor que (a quien) conocimos es de aquí.**

The pronoun **quien** must be used after a preposition when it refers to a person.

> **La persona (a quien, de quien, con quien) habla él es mi prima.**

The longer pronouns **el que, la que, los que,** and **las que** may be used as a subject or object of a clause and can refer to a person or a thing. They often convey the meaning *the one (ones) that* or *the one (ones) who.*

> **El que llega es mi hermano.**
> **(De todos los libros) el que lees es mi favorito.**
> **Las que están hablando ahora son mis primas.**

Lo que is a neuter pronoun which replaces a general or abstract idea rather than a specific antecedent.

> **Lo que necesito es más dinero.**
> **No sé lo que está diciendo.**

Cuyo is equivalent to the English *whose.* It is an adjective and agrees with the noun it modifies.

> **El señor cuya hija habla ahora es el director de la compañía.**
> **La señora cuyos documentos tienes va a viajar a Chile.**

Negative expressions

To make a sentence negative, you merely put **no** before the verb or before the object pronoun that precedes the verb.

> **El gato no está en el jardín.**
> **No lo veo.**

Review the following affirmative and negative expressions.

AFFIRMATIVE	NEGATIVE
algo	**nada**
alguien	**nadie**
siempre	**nunca**

> **Nadie está aquí.**

Note that in Spanish, unlike in English, more than one negative word can be used in the same sentence.

> **No ves a nadie.**
> **Ellos nunca hablan a nadie de nada.**

The negative of **también** is **tampoco.**

> **A Juan le gusta. A mí también.**
> **A Juan no le gusta. Ni a mí tampoco.**

Verbs such as interesar, aburrir, gustar

Note the construction with verbs such as **interesar** and **aburrir.**

> **La historia me interesa.**
> **Me interesa la historia.** } *History interests me.*

> **Los deportes no les aburren.**
> **No les aburren los deportes.** } *Sports don't bore them.*

Gustar functions the same as **interesar** and **aburrir.** It conveys the meaning *to like,* but it literally means *to please.*

Me			**Me**		
Te			**Te**		
Le	} gusta el helado.		**Le**	} gustan los vegetales.	
Nos			**Nos**		
Les			**Les**		

Expressions with the infinitive

The infinitive is the form of the verb that ends in **-ar, -er,** or **-ir.** The infinitive often follows another verb.

> **Ellos quieren salir.**
> **Yo debo estudiar más.**
> **Me gusta leer.**

Three very common expressions that are followed by the infinitive are **tener que** *(to have to)*, **ir a** *(to be going to)*, and **acabar de** *(to have just)*.

> **Tengo que trabajar y estudiar más.**
> **Y voy a trabajar y estudiar más.**
> **Acabo de recibir una nota mala.**

You can use the expression **favor de** followed by an infinitive to ask someone in a polite way to do something.

> **Favor de escribir tu nombre.**
> **Favor de ayudarme.**

Note that the object pronoun is added to the infinitive.

Ser and estar

Spanish has two verbs that mean *to be.* They are **ser** and **estar** and each one has distinct uses.

Ser

You use **ser** to express a characteristic, where someone or something is from, or what something is made of.

> **Él es guapo. Es inteligente también.**
> **Ellos son de Nuevo México.**
> **Su casa es de adobe.**

Estar

You use **estar** to express a condition or location.

> **Él está muy cansado y está triste también.**
> **Madrid está en España.**
> **Sus amigos están en Madrid.**

Saber and conocer

Both **saber** and **conocer** mean *to know.*

Saber means to know a fact or to have information about something. With an infinitive it expresses to know how to do something.

> **Yo sé su número de teléfono.**
> **Sabemos que ella va a viajar.**
> **Todos saben usar el Internet.**

Conocer means *to know* in the sense of *to be familiar with.* It is used with people or complex, abstract concepts.

> **Yo conozco a su amigo, Tadeo.**
> **Ellos conocen bien la historia de España.**

Reflexive verbs

When the subject is both the doer and receiver of the action of the verb, you have to use a reflexive pronoun with the verb. Study the following examples of the reflexive construction.

REFLEXIVE	NONREFLEXIVE
Ella se levanta.	**Ella levanta al niño.**
Él se divierte.	**Él divierte a sus amigos.**
Me cepillo.	**Cepillo a mi perro.**

When the reflexive is followed by an article of clothing or a part of the body, you use a definite article in Spanish. (In English the possessive adjective is used.)

> **Me lavo la cara y las manos.**
> **Ella tiene frío y se pone el suéter.**

Verbs tenses

See the charts on page SR32 for the verb forms you have learned.

Verb tense usage

Present

You use the present tense to state what is taking place now or what always takes place.

> **Hablamos español.**
> **Juegan fútbol en el otoño.**
> **Siempre hacen la misma cosa.**

You can also use the present tense to express a future action.

> **Salen mañana.**
> **Vamos a México en julio.**

Preterite

You use the preterite to express an action that began and ended at a specific time in the past.

> **Ellos salieron la semana pasada.**
> **Nosotros llegamos ayer.**
> **Los árabes invadieron España en 711.**

Imperfect

You use the imperfect to describe a continuous, habitual action in the past. The time at which the action began or ended is not important.

> **Ellos siempre hacían la misma cosa.**
> **Yo los veía de vez en cuando.**
> **Ellos iban a España con frecuencia porque tenían una casa allí.**

You use the imperfect to describe things in the past.

> **Él era joven.**
> **Tenía solo dos años.**
> **Hacía buen tiempo.**
> **Su hermana era muy simpática.**

You use the imperfect to reminisce about past events.

> **Cuando yo era niño vivíamos en Puerto Rico y siempre celebrábamos el Día de los Reyes. Yo recuerdo bien que recibíamos nuestros regalos el seis de enero.**

You use the imperfect with verbs to express mental activities or emotions in the past.

> **Él lo creía.**
> **Querían hacerlo.**
> **Estaban contentos.**

Time expressions with hace, hacía

Hace is used with the present tense to express an action that began in the past and continues into the present.

> **¿Cuánto tiempo hace que estás en México?**
> **Hace dos años que asistimos a la misma escuela.**

Hacía is used with the imperfect tense to express an action that had been going on until something else occurred.

> **Hacía cinco años que ellos trabajaban en Puerto Rico cuando fueron a España.**
> **Hacía mucho tiempo que lo sabíamos.**

Future

The true future *will* is used less frequently in Spanish than in English.

> **Le hablaré a él mañana.**
> **Volverán la semana que viene.**

The present tense and the **ir a** + infinitive construction are often used to convey the future.

> **Le hablo a él mañana.**   **Le voy a hablar mañana.**
> **Vuelven la semana que viene.**   **Van a volver la semana que viene.**

Conditional

You use the conditional in Spanish the same as in English. It tells what would or could happen.

> **¿Iría él?**   **Sí, él iría.**
> **¿Lo sabrían ellos?**   **Sí, ellos lo sabrían.**
> **¿Estarías contento?**   **Sí, yo estaría contento.**

Present perfect

The present perfect is used to describe an action without reference to a specific past time. It is accompanied by time expressions such as **ya, todavía no, jamás, nunca.**

> **Nunca hemos hecho tal cosa.**
> **En mi vida he tenido dos accidentes.**
> **Todavía no han llegado.**

Pluperfect tense

The pluperfect tense is used to describe a past action that had actually taken place prior to another past action.

> **Ellos ya habían salido cuando nosotros llegamos.**
> **Lo había aprendido muchos años antes de empezar la secundaria.**

Future perfect

The future perfect is very seldom used. It conveys an action in the future that was completed prior to another future action.

> **Ellos lo habrán discutido antes de hablar con nosotros.**

Conditional Perfect

The conditional perfect is used the same in Spanish as in English to explain what would have happened had something else not made it impossible.

> **Habríamos ido pero no pudimos porque no tuvimos bastante dinero.**
> **Él lo habría sabido pero nadie se lo dijo.**

Progressive tense

The progressive tense is formed by using the verb **estar** (or **ir, seguir**) and the present participle. You use the progressive to indicate that the action is actually taking place.

> **Estamos pasando tiempo en la playa.**
> **Estoy mirando a los niños.**
> **Están nadando en el mar.**

Subjunctive

You use the subjunctive in a dependent clause. As the word *subjunctive* implies, it is used to express a subjective action that is not necessarily a fact. It may or may not take place. So far you have learned the following uses of the subjunctive.

You use the subjunctive in a clause introduced by an expression of desire.

> **Quiero que ellos salgan ahora.**
> **Ellos quieren que estudiemos y que tengamos éxito.**
> **¿Prefieres que yo espere aquí?**
> **Él insiste en que tú lo sepas.**

You use the subjunctive following many impersonal expressions.

> **Es importante que lleguemos a tiempo.**
> **Es necesario que ellos lo sepan.**
> **Es mejor que tú lo hagas.**

The subjunctive follows the expressions **ojalá, quizás,** and **tal vez.**

> **¡Ojalá vengan a la fiesta!**
> **¡Quizá(s) vayan!**
> **¡Tal vez lo sepan!**

You use the subjunctive after an expression of doubt. The indicative is used with certainty.

CERTAINTY	DOUBT
Creo que les va a gustar.	**No creo que les guste.**
No dudo que vendrán.	**Dudo que vengan.**
Es cierto que lo saben.	**No es cierto que lo sepan.**

You use the subjunctive after expressions of emotion.

> **Estoy contento que ellos asistan.**
> **¡Qué pena que su padre esté enfermo!**
> **Siento que ellos no lo sepan.**

You use the subjunctive after expressions of advice, request, etc. Note that such expressions are used with an indirect object.

> *Te* **pido que lo hagas.**
> *Les* **aconsejamos** *a ustedes* **que presten atención.**

You use the subjunctive with any word that has **-quiera.**

> **Quienquiera que seas y adondequiera que vayas y cuandoquiera que llegues**

You use the subjunctive in adverbial expressions introduced by **de manera que,**
para que.

> **Los padres trabajan duro para que sus hijos tengan una buena vida.**
> **El profesor habla claramente de manera que entendamos.**

The subjunctive is used after **aunque** (*even though*) when it is not known if the
information that follows will take place. The indicative is used when the action is real
or definite.

> **Saldremos aunque llueva.** (*even though it may rain*)
> **Saldremos aunque está lloviendo.** (*even though it is raining*)

The subjunctive is used in a relative clause that modifies an indefinite antecedent. The
indicative is used if the antecedent is definite. Note that the **a personal** is omitted
with an indefinite noun.

> **Buscamos un contable que tenga experiencia.**
> **Conocemos a un contable que tiene experiencia.**

Sequence of tenses with the subjunctive

The present subjunctive is used in any clause that requires the subjunctive when the
verb in the main clause is in the present or future tense. The imperfect subjunctive is
used when the verb in the main clause is in the preterite, imperfect, or conditional.

MAIN CLAUSE	DEPENDENT CLAUSE
present future → **que** (present subjunctive)	preterite imperfect → **que** (imperfect subjunctive) conditional
Quiero que él venga. **Querrán que él venga.**	**No quiso que él viniera.** **Quería que él viniera.** **Querría que él viniera.**
Es importante que ellos lo sepan. **Será importante que ellos lo sepan.**	**Fue importante que ellos lo supieran.** **Era importante que ellos lo supieran.** **Sería importante que ellos lo supieran.**
Te pido que lo hagas. **Te pediré que lo hagas.**	**Te pidió que lo hicieras.** **Te pedía que lo hicieras.** **Te pediría que lo hicieras.**
Busco una secretaria que hable español. **Buscaré una secretaria que hable español.**	**Busqué una secretaria que hablara español.** **Buscaba una secretaria que hablara español.** **Buscaría una secretaria que hablara español.**

Subjunctive with adverbial expressions of time

The subjunctive is used with an adverbial conjunction of time when it is not known if the action will really take place. If the action in the adverbial clause of time actually took place the indicative is used.

> **Voy a esperar hasta que lleguen ellos.**
> **Espera aquí hasta que lleguen.**　　　　**Esperé hasta que llegaron.**
> **Esperaría hasta que llegaran.**

Note, however, that the conjunction **antes de que** is always followed by the subjunctive. If the verb in the main clause is in the past, the imperfect subjunctive is used.

> **Ellos llegarán antes de que nosotros salgamos.**
> **Ellos llegaron antes de que nosotros saliéramos.**

Present perfect subjunctive

You use the present perfect subjunctive in a clause that requires the subjunctive when the action would be prior to the action of the main verb.

> **Espero que hayan llegado.**
> **Dudamos que él lo haya hecho.**
> **Estamos contentos que todo haya salido bien.**

Pluperfect subjunctive

You use the pluperfect subjunctive in any clause introduced by a verb in the past when the action in the dependent clause would have take place prior to the action in the main clause.

> **Yo dudaba mucho que él lo hubiera sabido.**
> **Estaría contento que hubieras tenido más éxito.**
> **Habríamos salido aunque hubiera llovido.**

Si clauses

Si clauses are referred to as contrary-to-fact clauses. The most comon sequence of tenses for **si** clauses follows:

MAIN CLAUSE	SI CLAUSE
future	present indicative
conditional	imperfect subjunctive
conditional perfect	pluperfect subjunctive

Yo iré si tengo bastante dinero.
Yo iría si tuviera bastante dinero.
Yo habría ido si hubiera tenido bastante dinero.

Passive voice with se

The pronoun **se** is used to express something being done without saying by whom.

Se habla español en México.
{ *Spanish is spoken in Mexico.*
One speaks Spanish in Mexico.
They speak Spanish in Mexico. }

¿A qué hora se abre el restaurante?
Se sirven comidas mexicanas y peruanas.

Passive voice with ser

The true passive voice is used less frequently in Spanish than in English.

La ciudad fue invadida por el ejército.
El edificio fue destruido por un incendio.

Active voice is more commonly used than passive voice.

El ejército invadió la ciudad.
El incendio destruyó el edificio.

Imperative (commands)

You use the subjunctive form of the verb for all formal (**usted, ustedes**) commands and the negative familiar (**tú**) command.

Hable Ud.	**No hable Ud.**	**Hablen Uds.**	**No hablen Uds.**	**No hables.**
Coma Ud.	**No coma Ud.**	**Coman Uds.**	**No coman Uds.**	**No comas.**

You use the **usted** form of the present indicative for the familiar (**tú**) command.

Habla.
Come.

Note that you add the object pronouns to affirmative commands. The pronouns come before the negative command.

AFFIRMATIVE	NEGATIVE
Prepárelo.	**No lo prepare.**
Escríbanlo Uds.	**No lo escriban Uds.**
Háblame.	**No me hables.**

There are no irregular formal commands. You will find any irregular familiar (**tú**) commands in the following verb charts.

Por y para

The prepositions **por** y **para** have very specific uses.

Para is used to represent a destination, purpose, reason, or readiness. It can also express a comparison or a deadline.

>**Salen para Madrid.**
>**El paquete es para María.**
>**Estudia para ingeniero.**
>**Están para salir.**
>**Para cubano, habla bien el inglés.**
>**Tiene que terminar para el día ocho.**

Por, on the other hand, is more circuitous. It expresses *through, by, on behalf of, instead of,* and *in exchange for.* It expresses the reason for an errand, a period of time or indefinite time, means, manner, as well as an opinion or estimation. **Por** is also used to indicate a measure or number.

>**Viajaron por España.**
>**Entró por la ventana.**
>**Compré el regalo por María.**
>**Voy por agua.**
>**Estuvieron por dos semanas.**
>**Estarán por Navidad.**
>**Lo toman por cubano, pero no lo es.**
>**Estamos por** *(in the mood)* **salir.**
>**Me dio pesos por dólares.**
>**Se venden por kilos.**
>**Ya tengo mucho por hacer.**

Verb Charts

REGULAR VERBS			
INFINITIVO	**hablar** *to speak*	**comer** *to eat*	**vivir** *to live*
PARTICIPIO PRESENTE	hablando	comiendo	viviendo
PARTICIPIO PASADO	hablado	comido	vivido

Simple Tenses

INDICATIVO

	hablar	comer	vivir
PRESENTE	hablo hablas habla hablamos *habláis* hablan	como comes come comemos *coméis* comen	vivo vives vive vivimos *vivís* viven
IMPERFECTO	hablaba hablabas hablaba hablábamos *hablabais* hablaban	comía comías comía comíamos *comíais* comían	vivía vivías vivía vivíamos *vivíais* vivían
PRETÉRITO	hablé hablaste habló hablamos *hablasteis* hablaron	comí comiste comió comimos *comisteis* comieron	viví viviste vivió vivimos *vivisteis* vivieron
FUTURO	hablaré hablarás hablará hablaremos *hablaréis* hablarán	comeré comerás comerá comeremos *comeréis* comerán	viviré vivirás vivirá viviremos *viviréis* vivirán
CONDICIONAL	hablaría hablarías hablaría hablaríamos *hablaríais* hablarían	comería comerías comería comeríamos *comeríais* comerían	viviría vivirías viviría viviríamos *viviríais* vivirían

REGULAR VERBS *(continued)*			
SUBJUNTIVO	**hablar** *to speak*	**comer** *to eat*	**vivir** *to live*
PRESENTE	hable hables hable hablemos *habléis* hablen	coma comas coma comamos *comáis* coman	viva vivas viva vivamos *viváis* vivan
IMPERFECTO	hablara hablaras hablara habláramos *hablarais* hablaran	comiera comieras comiera comiéramos *comierais* comieran	viviera vivieras viviera viviéramos *vivierais* vivieran

Compound Tenses			
INDICATIVO			
PRESENTE PERFECTO	he hablado has hablado ha hablado hemos hablado *habéis hablado* han hablado	he comido has comido ha comido hemos comido *habéis comido* han comido	he vivido has vivido ha vivido hemos vivido *habéis vivido* han vivido
PLUSCUAM-PERFECTO	había hablado habías hablado había hablado habíamos hablado *habíais hablado* habían hablado	había comido habías comido había comido habíamos comido *habíais comido* habían comido	había vivido habías vivido había vivido habíamos vivido *habíais vivido* habían vivido
FUTURO PERFECTO	habré hablado habrás hablado habrá hablado habremos hablado *habréis hablado* habrán hablado	habré comido habrás comido habrá comido habremos comido *habréis comido* habrán comido	habré vivido habrás vivido habrá vivido habremos vivido *habréis vivido* habrán vivido
CONDICIONAL PERFECTO	habría hablado habrías hablado habría hablado habríamos hablado *habríais hablado* habrían hablado	habría comido habrías comido habría comido habríamos comido *habríais comido* habrían comido	habría vivido habrías vivido habría vivido habríamos vivido *habríais vivido* habrían vivido

Verb Charts

VERB CHARTS

REGULAR VERBS (continued)

SUBJUNTIVO

PRESENTE PERFECTO	haya hablado	haya comido	haya vivido
	hayas hablado	hayas comido	hayas vivido
	haya hablado	haya comido	haya vivido
	hayamos hablado	hayamos comido	hayamos vivido
	hayáis hablado	*hayáis comido*	*hayáis vivido*
	hayan hablado	hayan comido	hayan vivido
PLUSCUAM-PERFECTO	hubiera hablado	hubiera comido	hubiera vivido
	hubieras hablado	hubieras comido	hubieras vivido
	hubiera hablado	hubiera comido	hubiera vivido
	hubiéramos hablado	hubiéramos comido	hubiéramos vivido
	hubierais hablado	*hubierais comido*	*hubierais vivido*
	hubieran hablado	hubieran comido	hubieran vivido

Stem-changing verbs (-ar and -er verbs)

INFINITIVO	empezar (e→ie) *to begin*	perder (e→ie) *to lose*	recordar (o→ue) *to remember*	volver (o→ue) *to return*
INDICATIVO				
PRESENTE	empiezo	pierdo	recuerdo	vuelvo
	empiezas	pierdes	recuerdas	vuelves
	empieza	pierde	recuerda	vuelve
	empezamos	perdemos	recordamos	volvemos
	empezáis	*perdéis*	*recordáis*	*volvéis*
	empiezan	pierden	recuerdan	vuelven
SUBJUNTIVO				
PRESENTE	empiece	pierda	recuerde	vuelva
	empieces	pierdas	recuerdes	vuelvas
	empiece	pierda	recuerde	vuelva
	empecemos	perdamos	recordemos	volvamos
	empecéis	*perdáis*	*recordéis*	*volváis*
	empiecen	pierdan	recuerden	vuelvan

e→ie
Other verbs conjugated like **empezar** and **perder** are: **cerrar, comenzar, sentar(se), despertar(se), recomendar, pensar, defender, entender, querer, encender.**

o→ue
Other verbs conjugated like **recordar** and **volver** are: **acordar, almorzar, contar, costar, probar, encontrar, mostrar, soñar, acostar(se), devolver, mover, poder, jugar (u→ue).**

Stem-changing verbs (-ir verbs)

INFINITIVO	preferir (e→ie, i) to prefer	dormir (o→ue, u) to sleep	pedir (e→i, i) to ask for
PARTICIPIO PRESENTE	prefiriendo	durmiendo	pidiendo
INDICATIVO			
PRESENTE	prefiero prefieres prefiere preferimos *preferís* prefieren	duermo duermes duerme dormimos *dormís* duermen	pido pides pide pedimos *pedís* piden
PRETÉRITO	preferí preferiste prefirió preferimos *preferisteis* prefirieron	dormí dormiste durmió dormimos *dormisteis* durmieron	pedí pediste pidió pedimos *pedisteis* pidieron
SUBJUNTIVO			
PRESENTE	prefiera prefieras prefiera prefiramos *prefiráis* prefieran	duerma duermas duerma durmamos *durmáis* duerman	pida pidas pida pidamos *pidáis* pidan

e→ie, i

Other verbs conjugated like **preferir** are: **sentir(se), sugerir, mentir, divertir(se), advertir, invertir.**

o→ue

Another verb conjugated like **dormir** is **morir.**

e→i, i

Other verbs conjugated like **pedir** are: **repetir, servir, seguir, vestirse, freír, reír, sonreír, despedir(se).**

VERB CHARTS

IRREGULAR VERBS

PARTICIPIO PASADO	**abrir** *to open* abierto					

PRETÉRITO	**andar** *to walk* anduve	anduviste	anduvo	anduvimos	*anduvisteis*	anduvieron

PRESENTE	**conocer** *to know, to be familiar with* conozco	conoces	conoce	conocemos	*conocéis*	conocen

PARTICIPIO PASADO	**cubrir** *to cover* cubierto					

	dar *to give*					
PRESENTE	doy	das	da	damos	*dais*	dan
PRETÉRITO	di	diste	dio	dimos	*disteis*	dieron
SUBJUNTIVO: PRESENTE	dé	des	dé	demos	*deis*	den

	decir *to say*					
PARTICIPIO PRESENTE	diciendo					
PARTICIPIO PASADO	dicho					
PRESENTE	digo	dices	dice	decimos	*decís*	dicen
PRETÉRITO	dije	dijiste	dijo	dijimos	*dijisteis*	dijeron
FUTURO	diré	dirás	dirá	diremos	*diréis*	dirán
CONDICIONAL	diría	dirías	diría	diríamos	*diríais*	dirían
IMPERATIVO FAMILIAR	di					

PARTICIPIO PASADO	**devolver** *to return (bring back)* devuelto					

PARTICIPIO PASADO	**escribir** *to write* escrito					

	estar *to be*					
PRESENTE	estoy	estás	está	estamos	*estáis*	están
PRETÉRITO	estuve	estuviste	estuvo	estuvimos	*estuvisteis*	estuvieron
SUBJUNTIVO: PRESENTE	esté	estés	esté	estemos	*estéis*	estén

PARTICIPIO PASADO	**freír** *to fry* frito					

IRREGULAR VERBS (continued)

haber *to have (in compound tenses)*

PRESENTE	he	has	ha	hemos	*habéis*	han
PRETÉRITO	hube	hubiste	hubo	hubimos	*hubisteis*	hubieron
IMPERFECTO	había	habías	había	habíamos	*habíais*	habían
FUTURO	habré	habrás	habrá	habremos	*habréis*	habrán
CONDICIONAL	habría	habrías	habría	habríamos	*habríais*	habrían
SUBJUNTIVO: PRESENTE	haya	hayas	haya	hayamos	*hayáis*	hayan

hacer *to do, to make*

PARTICIPIO PASADO	hecho					
PRESENTE	hago	haces	hace	hacemos	*hacéis*	hacen
PRETÉRITO	hice	hiciste	hizo	hicimos	*hicisteis*	hicieron
FUTURO	haré	harás	hará	haremos	*haréis*	harán
CONDICIONAL	haría	harías	haría	haríamos	*haríais*	harían
IMPERATIVO FAMILIAR	haz					

ir *to go*

PARTICIPIO PRESENTE	yendo					
PRESENTE	voy	vas	va	vamos	*vais*	van
PRETÉRITO	fui	fuiste	fue	fuimos	*fuisteis*	fueron
IMPERFECTO	iba	ibas	iba	íbamos	*ibais*	iban
SUBJUNTIVO: PRESENTE	vaya	vayas	vaya	vayamos	*vayáis*	vayan
IMPERATIVO FAMILIAR	ve					

morir *to die*

PARTICIPIO PASADO	muerto

oír *to hear*

PRESENTE	oigo	oyes	oye	oímos	*oís*	oyen

poder *to be able to*

PARTICIPIO PRESENTE	pudiendo					
PRETÉRITO	pude	pudiste	pudo	pudimos	*pudisteis*	pudieron
FUTURO	podré	podrás	podrá	podremos	*podréis*	podrán
CONDICIONAL	podría	podrías	podría	podríamos	*podríais*	podrían

poner *to put*

PARTICIPIO PASADO	puesto					
PRESENTE	pongo	pones	pone	ponemos	*ponéis*	ponen
PRETÉRITO	puse	pusiste	puso	pusimos	*pusisteis*	pusieron
FUTURO	pondré	pondrás	pondrá	pondremos	*pondréis*	pondrán

IRREGULAR VERBS *(continued)*

querer *to want*

PRETÉRITO	quise	quisiste	quiso	quisimos	*quisisteis*	quisieron
FUTURO	querré	querrás	querrá	querremos	*querréis*	querrán
CONDICIONAL	querría	querrías	querría	querríamos	*querríais*	querrían

romper *to break*

PARTICIPIO PASADO	roto

saber *to know (how)*

PRESENTE	sé	sabes	sabe	sabemos	*sabéis*	saben
PRETÉRITO	supe	supiste	supo	supimos	*supisteis*	supieron
FUTURO	sabré	sabrás	sabrá	sabremos	*sabréis*	sabrán
CONDICIONAL	sabría	sabrías	sabría	sabríamos	*sabríais*	sabrían
SUBJUNTIVO: PRESENTE	sepa	sepas	sepa	sepamos	*sepáis*	sepan

ser *to be*

PRESENTE	soy	eres	es	somos	*sois*	son
PRETÉRITO	fui	fuiste	fue	fuimos	*fuisteis*	fueron
IMPERFECTO	era	eras	era	éramos	*erais*	eran
SUBJUNTIVO: PRESENTE	sea	seas	sea	seamos	*seáis*	sean
IMPERATIVO FAMILIAR	sé					

tener *to have*

PRESENTE	tengo	tienes	tiene	tenemos	*tenéis*	tienen
PRETÉRITO	tuve	tuviste	tuvo	tuvimos	*tuvisteis*	tuvieron
FUTURO	tendré	tendrás	tendrá	tendremos	*tendréis*	tendrán
CONDICIONAL	tendría	tendrías	tendría	tendríamos	*tendríais*	tendrían
IMPERATIVO FAMILIAR	ten					

traer *to bring*

PRESENTE	traigo	traes	trae	traemos	*traéis*	traen
PRETÉRITO	traje	trajiste	trajo	trajimos	*trajisteis*	trajeron

venir *to come*						
PARTICIPIO PRESENTE	viniendo					
PRETÉRITO	vine	viniste	vino	vinimos	*vinisteis*	vinieron
FUTURO	vendré	vendrás	vendrá	vendremos	*vendréis*	vendrán
CONDICIONAL	vendría	vendrías	vendría	vendríamos	*vendríais*	vendrían
IMPERATIVO FAMILIAR	ven					
ver *to see*						
PARTICIPIO PASADO	visto					
PRESENTE	veo	ves	ve	vemos	*veis*	ven
PRETÉRITO	vi	viste	vio	vimos	*visteis*	vieron
IMPERFECTO	veía	veías	veía	veíamos	*veíais*	veían
volver *to return*						
PARTICIPIO PASADO	vuelto					

Verb Charts

VERB CHARTS

Spanish-English Dictionary

The Spanish-English Dictionary contains all productive and receptive vocabulary from ¡**Así se dice!** Levels 1, 2, and 3. The locator numbers following each productive entry indicate the chapter and vocabulary section in which the word is introduced (e.g., 3.2 means Chapter 3, Vocabulary 2). Level 1 chapter/section numbers are light print (3.2); Level 2 numbers are *italic (3.2)*; Level 3 chapter/section numbers are **bold (3.2)**. LP refers to the Level 1 **Lecciones preliminares.** If no locator follows an entry, the word or expression is receptive.

A

a at; to
  a eso de las tres (cuatro, diez, etc.) at around three (four, ten, etc.) o'clock
  a fines de at the end of
  a la una (a las dos, a las tres...) at one o'clock (two o'clock, three o'clock), LP
  a lo lejos in the distance
  a lo menos at least
  a menos que unless
  a menudo often
  a pesar de in spite of
  a pie on foot, 3.2
  ¡A propósito! By the way!, 8.2
  ¿a qué hora? at what time?, LP
  a solas alone
  a tiempo on time, 10.2; *1.2*
  a veces at times, sometimes, 6.1; *1.2*
  a ver let's see
abajo down; below
de abajo below
(ir) para abajo (to go) down
abandonar el cuarto to check out (hotel), 7
el **abismo** abyss
la **abolladura** dent, **6.2**
el **abono** fertilizer
abordar to board, 10.2; *1.2*
abordo aboard, on board, 10.2; *1.2*
abotonarse to button
abrazarse to hug (someone), **5**
el **abrazo** hug, **5**
abreviado(a) abbreviated, shortened
abrigado(a) wrapped up
el **abrigo** coat

abril April, LP
abrir to open, 4.2
abrochado(a) fastened, 10.2; *1.2*
el/la **abuelo(a)** grandfather, grandmother, 2.1
los **abuelos** grandparents, 2.1
abundoso(a) abundant
aburrido(a) boring, 1.2
aburrir to bore
acá here, 11.2; *2.2*
acabar de to have just (done something), 4.2
la **academia** school
acaso perhaps, **3 (Lit.)**
  por si acaso just in case
acceder to access
el **accidente** accident, *11.2;* **2.2**
el **aceite** oil, *4*
  el aceite de oliva olive oil, *9*
la **aceituna** olive, 4.2
el **acento** accent
la **aceptación** acceptance, success
aceptar to accept, **6.2**
la **acera** sidewalk, *8.1*
acercarse to approach
acomodado(a) wealthy, well-off, **8**
acomodar to set (bone), *11.2;* **2.2**
aconsejar to advise
acontecer to happen
acordarse (ue) to remember
  ¿Te acuerdas? Do you remember?
acostarse (ue) to go to bed, *11.1; 2.1*
acostumbrarse to get used to
el **acotamiento** shoulder (road), *9.1*
la **actividad** activity
actual present-day, current
actuar to act, to take action
la **acuarela** watercolor, **7.1**
acudir to go to

acuerdo: de acuerdo okay, agreed; **estar de acuerdo con** to agree with, to be in agreement
adelantar(se) to pass (car), *9.1*
adelante ahead
  ir hacia adelante to move forward, ahead
además furthermore, what's more; besides
además de in addition to, besides
¡Adiós! Good-bye., LP
adivinar to guess
adjunto: el documento adjunto attached file, *6.1*
admitir to admit
¿adónde? (to) where?, 3.2
la **aduana** customs, **6.1**
la **advertencia** warning
advertir (ie) to warn
aérea: la línea aérea airline, 10.1; *1.1*
aeróbico(a) aerobic
el **aerodeslizador** hovercraft, hydrofoil
el **aeropuerto** airport, 10.1; *1.1;* **6.1**
el **afán** strong wish, desire, **3 (Lit.)**
afeitarse to shave
afición: tener (mucha) afición a to be (very) fond of
aficionado(a): ser aficionado(a) a to like, to be a fan of
el/la **aficionado(a)** fan, 5.1
el/la **afiliado(a)** member, affiliate
afine: la palabra afine cognate
afirmar to dig in
afortunados: los menos afortunados the less fortunate, the needy
las **afueras** suburbs, 2.2; outskirts, **6.2**
agarrar velocidad to pick up speed

la **agencia** agency
  la agencia de alquiler car rental agency, **6.2**
el/la **agente** agent, 10.1; *1.1*; **6.2**
la **aglomeración** big city
agosto August, LP
agradable pleasant, friendly, agreeable, 6.1
agrario(a) agrarian
agresivo(a) aggressive
agrícola agricultural
el **agua** *(f.)* water, 4.1
  el agua corriente running water
  el agua mineral (con gas) (sparkling) mineral water, 4.2
el **aguacate** avocado, *10; 1*
el **águila** *(f.)* eagle
el **aguinaldo** Christmas gift, *5.2*
el/la **ahijado(a)** godchild
ahora now
el **aire** air
  al aire libre open-air, outdoor, 7.2
el **aire acondicionado** air conditioning, *7*
aislado(a) isolated
el **ají** chili pepper
el **ajo** garlic, *10; 1*
al to the, on the, in the
  al aire libre open-air, outdoor, 7.2
  al borde mismo de right on the edge of
  al contrario on the contrary
  al lado de beside, next to, 2.2
la **alacena** cupboard
el **albañil** mason, **10**
la **alberca** swimming pool, *7.1*
el **albergue juvenil** youth hostel, *7*
la **albóndiga** meatball, 4.2
el **álbum** album
la **alcachofa** artichoke, **9**
  las alcachofas salteadas sautéed artichokes
el/la **alcalde(sa)** mayor, *3.1*
alcanzar to reach
la **alcoba** bedroom
la **aldea** small village
alegrarse to rejoice, *3.1*
alegre happy, 6.1; *3.1*
la **alegría** happiness, joy, **3.1**
alejarse de to go away from
alemán(ana) German
los **alemanes** Germans
la **alfombrilla** mouse pad, *6.1*
el **álgebra** *(f.)* algebra
algo something; anything, 8.2

¿Algo más? Anything else?, 9.2
alguien someone, somebody, 8.2
algunos(as) some
el **alimento** food
las **alitas** wings, *10; 1*
allá over there, 9.1
allí there
el **alma** *(f.)* soul
las **almejas** clams, *4*
la **almohada** pillow, *7*
el **almuerzo** lunch, 4.1
  tomar el almuerzo to have lunch, 4.1
¡Aló! Hello! *(on the phone)*
alpino: el esquí alpino downhill skiing
alquilar to rent, 7.1; *3.2*; **6.2**
alrededor de around, 2.2
los **alrededores** outskirts, surroundings
altivo(a) arrogant
alto(a) tall, 1.1; high, 3.1; upper
  la clase alta upper class
  la nota alta high grade, 3.1
la **altura** altitude
el/la **alumno(a)** student, 1.2
alzarse to rise **8**
amanecer to dawn, **10 (Lit.)**
amargo(a) bitter
amarillo(a) yellow, 5.1
la **ambición** ambition
ambicioso(a) hardworking, 1.2
el **ambiente** atmosphere, environment, *7.2*
la **ambulancia** ambulance, *11.2*; **2.2**
la **América del Sur** South America
americano(a) American
el/la **amigo(a)** friend, 1.1
la **amistad** friendship
el **amo(a)** owner, **8**
el **amor** love, *5*
amurallado(a) walled
anaranjado(a) orange *(color)*, 5.1
ancho(a) wide, broad, *8.1*
el **ancla** anchor *(television)*, **8**
andar to go, to walk; to ride, *3.2*
  andar a caballo to ride a horse, *3.2*
  andar en bicicleta to ride a bike, *11.1*; **2.1**
el **andén** *(railway)* platform, *3.1*
andino(a) Andean, of the Andes

angosto(a) narrow, *8.1*
la **angustia** distress, anguish
el **anillo de boda** wedding ring, *3.1*
animado(a) lively
el **animal** animal
animar to cheer (somebody, something) on; to liven up
ánimo: estado de ánimo frame of mind
anoche last night, 7.1
anónimo(a) anonymous
el **anorak** anorak, ski jacket, *7.2*
anotar to note
ansioso(a) anxious, worried
los **anteojos de sol** sunglasses, *7.1*
el/la **antepasado(a)** ancestor
el **antepecho** parapet
anterior previous, *6.1*
antes de before, *3.2*
antes de que before (doing something)
los **antibióticos** antibiotics
antiguo(a) ancient, old, *8.1*; former
  el casco (barrio) antiguo the old city, *8.1*
antipático(a) unpleasant, not nice 1.1
los **antojitos** snacks, nibbles, 4.2
anular to cancel
anunciar to announce
el **anuncio** announcement, **10**
  el anuncio clasificado classified ad, **10**
añadir to add, *10; 1*
el **año** year, LP
  el Año Nuevo New Year
  el año pasado last year, 7.1
  ¿Cuántos años tiene? How old is he (she)?, 2.1
  cumplir… años to be (turn) . . . years old; **3.2**
apagado(a) put out, extinguished
apagar to turn off, *6.1*
el **aparato** device
aparcar to park, *8.1*
aparentado(a) related
la **apariencia** appearance, looks
  ¿Qué apariencia tiene? What does he (she) look like?
el **apartamento** apartment, 2.2
  la casa de apartamentos apartment house
el **apartamiento** apartment, 2.2
aparte apart, on the side
apenas scarcely, hardly
apetecer to feel like, to crave
apetito: ¡Buen apetito! Bon appétit! Enjoy your meal!

Spanish-English Dictionary

aplaudir to applaud, to clap, 5.1

el **aplauso** applause, 5.1
   recibir aplausos to be applauded, 5.1

la **aplicación de empleo** job application, **10**

aplicar to apply

apoderarse de to take by force, **4** (Lit.)

el **apodo** nickname, **5** (Lit.)

apoyar to lean, to support

apreciado(a) appreciated, liked

aprender to learn, 4.2

apresurado(a) hurried, **4**

apresurarse to be in a hurry, **10** (Lit.)

apretar to clench

el **apretón de manos** handshake

apropiado(a) appropriate

aproximadamente approximately

aquel(la) that, 9.1

aquí here, 9.1
   Aquí (lo, la, etc.) tienes. Here it (they) is (are).

árabe Arabic

aragonés(esa) from Aragon (Spain)

el **árbol** tree, 2.2
   el árbol de Navidad Christmas tree, 5.2

el **arcén** shoulder (road), 9.1

el **archivo** file, 6.1

el **área** (f.) area

la **arena** sand, 7.1

argentino(a) Argentine

el **argumento** plot, **7.2**

árido(a) dry, arid

la **aritmética** arithmetic

el **arma** (f.) weapon

armar to put up (tent), 11.2; 2.2

el **armario** closet, 7

la **arqueología** archeology

el/la **arquitecto(a)** architect, **10**

arrendamiento: la agencia de arrendamiento car rental agency

arrendar (ie) to rent, **6.2**

la **arroba** the @ sign, 6.1

el **arroyo** brook

el **arroz** rice, 4.1

arrugado(a) wrinkled, **4**

el **arte** art, 1.2; **7.1**

arterial: la tensión arterial blood pressure, 6.2

la **artesanía** crafts, 9.2

el **artículo** article, **8**

el/la **artista** artist, **7.1**

asar to grill, to roast, 10; **1**

la **ascendencia** heritage, background

el **ascensor** elevator, 7

asegurar to assure

asegurarse to make sure

así thus, so, in this way

el **asiento** seat, 10.1; 1.1; **6.1**
   el número del asiento seat number, 10.1; 1.1

asignar to assign, 6.2

la **asistencia médica** medical care

el/la **asistente(a) ejecutivo(a)** executive assistant, **10**

el/la **asistente(a) de vuelo** flight attendant, 10.2; 1.2

asistir a to attend, 8.1

el **asno** donkey

el **aspa** (f.) sail (windmill)

el/la **aspirante** (job) candidate, **10**

astuto(a) astute, smart

el **asunto** business, affair

atacar to attack

atado(a) tied

el **ataúd** coffin, **3.2**

la **atención** attention
   ¡Atención! Careful!
   prestar atención to pay attention, 3.1

el **aterrizaje** landing, 10.2; 1.2

aterrizar to land, 10.2; 1.2

el/la **atleta** athlete

las **atracciones** rides (amusement park), 8.1
   el parque de atracciones amusement park, 8.1

atraer to attract

atrapar to catch, 5.2

atrás: hacia atrás backwards

el **atributo** attribute, positive feature

el **atún** tuna, 9.2

aumentar to grow, to increase, to enlarge

aun even

aún still

aunque although, even though

el **auricular** (phone) receiver, 6.2

ausente absent

el/la **ausente** absent, missing person

auténtico(a) authentic, real

el **autobús** bus, 8.1; 8.1
   perder el autobús to miss the bus, 8.1

automático(a) automatic, 10.1; 1.1
   el distribuidor automático boarding pass kiosk, 10.1; 1.1; automatic dispenser, 3.1

la **autopista** highway, 9.1

el/la **autor(a)** author

autoservicio self-serve

la **autovía** highway, 9.1

avanzado(a) difficult, 7.2; advanced

avaro(a) stingy

la **avenida** avenue, 8.1

la **aventura** adventure

la **avería** breakdown

averiado(a) broken-down

el **avión** airplane, 10.1; 1.1

la **avioneta** small plane, light aircraft

avisar to advise, **6** (Lit.)
   avisar de to notify, to announce

ayer yesterday, 7.1
   ayer por la tarde yesterday afternoon, 7.1

la **ayuda** help, assistance

ayudar to help, 10.1; 1.1

el **ayuntamiento** city hall, **3.1**

el **azafrán** saffron

el **azúcar** sugar

azul blue, 2.1

el **azulejo** glazed tile, floor tile

B

el **bache** pothole

el **bacón** bacon, 4.1; 7

el/la **bailador(a)** dancer

bailar to dance, 5.2

bajar to go down, 7.2; to download, 6.2

bajar(se) to get off (train), 3.2

la **bajeza** baseness

bajo(a) short, 1.1; low, 3.1; poor, lower-class
   la nota baja low grade, 3.1

el **balcón** balcony

el **balneario** seaside resort, beach resort, 7.1

el **balón** ball, 5.1

el **baloncesto** basketball, 5.2

el **banco** bank, 4

la **banda** band, 8.1; 5.2; lane (highway)

la **banda municipal** municipal band, *5.2*

la **bandeja de entradas** inbox *(e-mail), 6.1*

la **bandeja de enviados** sent mailbox *(e-mail), 6.1*

la **bandera** flag

el **banquete** banquet, **3.1**

el **bañador** swimsuit, *7.1*

bañarse to take a bath, to bathe oneself

la **bañera** bathtub, *7*

el **baño** bath; bathroom

el cuarto de baño bathroom, *2.2; 7*

el **bar (bas/bat) mitzvah** bar (bas/bat) mitzvah

barato(a) inexpensive, cheap, *9.1*

Todo te sale más barato. It's all a lot cheaper (less expensive)., *9.1*

la **barba** beard

la **barbacoa** barbecue

barbaridad: ¡Qué barbaridad! That's awful!

¡Bárbaro! Great!, Awesome!, *5.2*

el **barbero** barber

el **barco** boat

el **barquito** small boat, *7.1*

la **barra** bar *(soap),* 11.2; *2.2;* counter, bar *(restaurant)*

la barra de jabón bar of soap, 11.2; *2.2*

la **barra de herramientas** toolbar, *6.1*

el **barrio** neighborhood, area, quarter, district, *8.1*

basado(a) en based on

base: a base de composed of

la **base** base, *5.2*

el **básquetbol** basketball, *5.2*

la cancha de básquetbol basketball court, *5.2*

¡Basta! That's enough!

bastante rather, quite, *1.2;* enough

el **bastón** ski pole, *7.2*

la **batalla** battle, **8**

el **bate** bat, *5.2*

el/la **bateador(a)** batter, *5.2*

batear to hit, to bat, *5.2*

batear un jonrón to hit a home run, *5.2*

el **batido** shake, smoothie, *4.2*

el huevo batido scrambled egg, **9**

el **baúl** trunk *(car),* 10.1; *1.1*

bautizar to baptize, **3.2**

el **bautizo** baptism, **3.2**

el **bebé** baby

beber to drink, *4.1*

la **bebida** beverage, drink, *4.1*

el **béisbol** baseball, *5.2*

el/la beisbolista baseball player, *5.2*

el campo de béisbol baseball field, *5.2*

el/la jugador(a) de béisbol baseball player, *5.2*

la **belleza** beauty

bello(a) beautiful

bendecir to bless

la **benzina** gas(oline)

la **berenjena** eggplant, **9**

besar to kiss, **5**

el **besito** little kiss (usually on the cheek), **5**

el **beso** kiss

la **bestia** beast, animal

los **biafranos** people from Biafra

la **biblioteca** library

la **bicicleta** bicycle, *2.2*

andar en bicicleta to ride a bike, *11.1; **2.1***

bien well, fine, LP

bien educado(a) polite, well-mannered, *6.1*

bien hecho(a) well-done *(meat),* **4**

estar bien to be (feel) well, fine, *6.2*

Muy bien. Very well., LP

el **bienestar** well-being

la **bienvenida: dar la bienvenida** to greet, to welcome

bienvenido(a) welcome

el **bife** beef

el **biftec** steak, **4**

el **billete** ticket, 10.1; *1.1;* bill, **4**

el billete de ida y vuelta round-trip ticket, *3.1*

el billete electrónico e-ticket, 10.1; *1.1*

el billete sencillo one-way ticket, *3.1*

la **biología** biology

el/la **biólogo(a)** biologist

el **bizcocho** cake, *5.1; **3.2***

blanco(a) white, *5.1*

la **blancura** whiteness

blando(a) soft

bloquear to block, *5.1*

el **blue jean** jeans, *9.1*

la **blusa** blouse, *3.1*

la **boca** mouth, *6.2*

la **boca del metro** subway entrance, *8.1*

la **bocacalle** intersection, *9.1*

el **bocadillo** sandwich, *4.1*

los **bocaditos** snacks

la **boda** wedding, **3.1**

la **bodega** grocery store

la **boletería** ticket window, 7.2; *3.1*

el **boleto** ticket, 7.2; *3.1*

el boleto de ida y regreso round-trip ticket, *3.1*

el boleto electrónico e-ticket, 10.1; *1.1*

el boleto sencillo one-way ticket, *3.1*

el **bolígrafo** pen, 3.1

el **bolívar** bolivar *(currency of Venezuela)*

la **bolsa de dormir** sleeping bag, 11.2; *2.2*

bolsillo: el libro de bolsillo paperback, *3.1; **8***

la **bombilla** *(drinking)* container

los **bombones** candy

bonito(a) pretty, *1.1*

el **borde** side *(of a street, sidewalk);* edge

al borde mismo de right on the edge of

borrador: el botón borrador delete key, *6.1*

borrar to delete, *6.1*

el **bosque** woods

la **bota** boot, *7.2*

botar to throw out

botar la casa por la ventana to splurge

el **bote** can, *9.2*

la **botella** bottle, *9.2*

el **botón** button, key *(computer),* *6.1*

el botón borrador delete key, *6.1*

el botón regresar (retroceder) back button, *6.1*

Brasil Brazil

brasileño(a) Brazilian

bravo(a) rough, stormy

el **brazo** arm, *11.1; **2.1***

brillar to shine

bronce: de bronce bronze *(adj.),* 8.2; **7.1**

bronceador(a): la loción bronceadora suntan lotion, *7.1*

bucear to go snorkeling, *7.1;* to scuba dive

el **buceo** snorkeling, *7.1;* scuba diving

buen good, LP

estar de buen humor to be in a good mood, *6.1*

Hace buen tiempo. The weather is nice., LP

tener un buen sentido de humor to have a good sense of humor, *6.1*

Spanish-English Dictionary

bueno(a) good, 1.1; Hello!
(on the phone)
  Buenas noches. Good
    evening., LP
  Buenas tardes. Good
    afternoon., LP
  Buenos días. Good
    morning., Hello., LP
  sacar notas buenas to get
    good grades, 3.1
el **bufé** buffet, **3.1**
el **bufete del abogado** lawyer's
    office, **10**
la **bufetería** dining car, *3.2*
el **burrito** burrito
el **bus** bus
  el bus escolar school bus,
    3.2
  perder el autobús to miss
    the bus, 8.1
  tomar el autobús to take
    the bus
  busca: en busca de seeking,
    in search of
  buscar to look for, to seek,
    3.2
el **buzo** sweat suit, warm-ups,
    11.1; 2.1
el **buzón** mailbox, **4**

--- C ---

el **caballero** gentleman
  el caballero andante knight
    errant
el **caballete** easel, *7.1*
el **caballo** horse, *3.2*
  andar a caballo to ride a
    horse, *3.2*
  montar a caballo to go
    horseback riding, *8.2*
  caber to fit
la **cabeza** head, 6.2; *2.1*
  tener dolor de cabeza to
    have a headache, 6.2
el **cabezal** headrest
la **cabina de mando** cockpit
    (airplane)
la **cabina de peaje** tollbooth, *9.1*
el **cacahuate** peanut, 8.1
el **cacahuete** peanut
la **cacerola** saucepan, *10; 1*
el **cacique** leader, chief
  cada each, every, 2.2
  caer to fall
  caerse to fall, *11.2; 2.2*
el **café** café, 4.2; coffee, 4.1; *7*
la **cafetería** cafeteria, 4.1

  el coche cafetería dining
    car, *3.2*
la **caída** drop
  la llamada caída dropped
    call *(cell phone)*, 6.2
la **caja** cash register, 3.2; box
el/la **cajero(a)** cashier, teller
el **cajero automático** ATM, **4**
el **cajón** box
la **calavera** skull, *5.1;* sweet cake
    made for the Day of the
    Dead
los **calcetines** socks, 5.1
la **calculadora** calculator, 3.1
el **caldo** broth
  caliente hot, 4.1
  el chocolate caliente hot
    chocolate, 4.1
la **calle** street, *8.1*
  la calle de sentido único
    one-way street, *9.1*
  calmo(a) calm, 6.1
el **calor** heat
  Hace calor. It's hot., LP
  tener calor to be hot, 11.1;
    2.1
  calzar to wear, to take *(shoe
    size)*, 9.1
  ¿Qué número calzas?
    What size shoe do you
    wear (take)?, 9.1
la **cama** bed, 2.2; *7*
  guardar cama to stay in
    bed *(illness)*, 6.2
  hacer la cama to make the
    bed, *7*
  quedarse en la cama to
    stay in bed, 11.1; *2.1*
la **cámara digital** digital
    camera, *7.1; 6.2*
el/la **camarero(a)** server, waiter
    (waitress), *4; (hotel)*
    housekeeper, *7*
los **camarones** shrimp, 4.2
  cambiar to change, *3.2; 6.2*
  cambio: en cambio on the
    other hand
el **camello** camel, *5.2*
la **camilla** stretcher, *11.2; 2.2*
  caminar to walk, *5.1*
la **caminata: dar una caminata**
    to take a hike, 11.2; *2.2*
el **camino** road
  ponerse en camino to set
    off
  tomar el camino to set out
    for
el **camión** bus *(Mexico), 8.1;*
    truck, *9.2*

la **camisa** shirt, 3.1
  **la camisa de manga corta
    (larga)** short- (long-)
    sleeved shirt, 9.1
la **camiseta** T-shirt, 5.1
el **campamento** camp
la **campana** bell tower
la **campanada** peal of the bell
el/la **campeón(ona)** champion
el/la **campesino(a)** farmer,
    peasant, *8.2*
el **camping** camping, 11.2; *2.2;*
    campsite
  ir de camping to go
    camping, 11.2; *2.2*
el **campo** field, 5.1; *8.2;* country,
    countryside, *8.2*
  el campo de béisbol
    baseball field, 5.2
  el campo de fútbol soccer
    field, 5.1
  la carrera a campo traviesa
    cross-country race, *11.1;*
    2.1
  la casa de campo country
    house, *8.2*
el **camposanto** cemetery, *5.1;* **3.2**
  canadiense Canadian
el **canal** lane *(highway)*
la **canasta** basket, 5.2
la **cancha** court, 5.2
  **la cancha de básquetbol
    (tenis)** basketball *(tennis)*
    court, 5.2
  la cancha de voleibol
    volleyball court, 7.1
la **candela** candle
el **cangrejo de río** crayfish
  cansado(a) tired, 6.1
el/la **cantante** singer, 8.1
  cantar to sing, 8.1
la **cantidad** quantity, amount,
    number of
la **cantina** cafeteria
el **cañón** canyon, *3.2*
la **capital** capital
el **capítulo** chapter, **7.2**
el **capó** hood *(car)*, 9.2
la **cara** face, 6.1
la **característica** feature, trait
  ¡Caramba! Good heavens!
el **carbón** coal
el/la **candidato(a)** candidate, **10**
el **cardo** thorn
  cargado(a) thrown (over one's
    shoulders); loaded
el **Caribe** Caribbean
  el mar Caribe Caribbean
    Sea

el **cariño** affection
cariñoso(a) adorable, affectionate; 2.1
caritativo(a) charitable
la **carne** meat, 4.1; *4;* **9**
   la carne de res beef, *4;* **9**
   la carne picada ground meat, **9**
el **carnet** driver's license, *9.2*
el **carnet de identidad** ID card, 10.2; *1.2*
la **carnicería** butcher shop
caro(a) expensive, 9.1
la **carpa** tent, 11.2; *2.2*
   armar (montar) una carpa to put up a tent, 11.2; *2.2*
la **carpeta** folder, 3.2; *6.1*
la **carrera** race, *11.1;* **2.1;** career, **10**
   la carrera a campo traviesa cross-country race, *11.1;* **2.1**
   la carrera de larga distancia long-distance race, *11.1;* **2.1**
   la carrera de relevos relay race, *11.1;* **2.1**
la **carretera** highway, *9.1*
el **carril** lane *(highway)*, *9.1*
el **carrito** shopping cart, 9.2
el **carro** car, 2.2; *9.2*
   en carro by car
la **carta** letter, **4**
la **casa** house, 2.2
   la casa de apartamentos apartment building, 2.2
   la casa de campo country house, *8.2*
   en casa at home
   regresar a casa to go home, 3.2
el **casamiento** marriage, **3.1**
casarse to get married, **3.1**
el **casco** helmet, 7.2; *11.1;* **2.1**
el **casco antiguo** the old city, *8.1*
casi almost, practically, 8.2; *4*
   casi crudo rare *(meat),* *4*
el caso case
   hacer caso pay attention
castaño(a) brown, chestnut *(eyes, hair),* 2.1
castigar to punish, **5**
el **castillo** castle
la **casucha** shack
catarro: tener catarro to have a cold, 6.2
el/la **cátcher** catcher, 5.2
la **catedral** cathedral
la **categoría** category
catorce fourteen, LP
el **caucho** tire

causa: a causa de because of, on account of
cautivar to captivate, to charm
la **cazuela** saucepan, pot, *10;* **1**
el **CD** CD
la **cebolla** onion, 9.2; *10;* **1**
ceder to cede, to hand over
celebrar to celebrate, *5.2;* **3.2**
el **celular** cell phone, *6.1*
el **cementerio** cemetery, *5.1;* **3.2**
la **cena** dinner, 4.1; **3.1**
cenar to have dinner, 4.1
el **cenote** natural water well
el **centro** downtown, *8.1;* center
el **centro comercial** shopping center, mall, 9.1
cepillarse to brush, 11.1; *2.1*
   cepillarse los dientes to brush one's teeth, 11.1; *2.1*
el **cepillo** brush, 11.2; *2.2*
   el cepillo de dientes toothbrush, 11.2; *2.2*
las **cerámicas** ceramics, 9.2
cerca (de) near, 3.2
cercanías: el tren de cercanías suburban train, **6.2**
cercano(a) near, nearby, close, **6.2**
el **cerdo** pig, *8.2;* pork, **9**
   la chuleta de cerdo pork chop, *4;* **1**
el **cereal** cereal, 4.1
la **ceremonia** ceremony, **3.1**
   la ceremonia civil civil ceremony (wedding), **3.1**
cero zero, LP
cerrar (ie) to close, 11.2; *2.2*
la **cesta** basket
el **cesto** basket, 5.2
la **chacra** farm, *8.2*
el **champán** champagne
el **champú** shampoo, 11.2; *2.2*
¡Chao! Good-bye!, Bye!, LP
la **chaqueta** jacket, 9.1
   la chaqueta de esquí ski jacket, anorak, 7.2
las **chauchas** green beans
chico(a) little
   A chico pajarillo, chico nidillo. Little bird, little nest.
el/la **chico(a)** boy, girl **5**
chileno(a) Chilean
la **chimenea** fireplace, *5.2*
el **chipotle** jalapeño pepper
el **chiringuito** refreshment stand
el **chisme** rumor, gossip
el **choclo** corn
el **chocolate** chocolate, 4.1
   el chocolate caliente hot chocolate, 4.1

el **chorizo** Spanish sausage
la **choza** shack, **4 (Lit.)**
la **chuleta de cerdo** pork chop, *4;* **1**
el **churro** (type of) doughnut
ciego(a) blind
el/la **ciego(a)** blind man (woman)
el **cielo** sky, *5.2*
cien(to) one hundred, LP
la **ciencia** science, 1.2
cierto(a) true, certain, *6.1*
la **cifra** number, **8**
el **cilantro** cilantro, **9**
el **cincel** chisel, **7.1**
cinco five, LP
cincuenta fifty, LP
el **cine** movie theater, movies, 8.2
   ir al cine to go to the movies, 8.2
el **cinturón de seguridad** seat belt, 10.2; *1.2*
la **circunstancia** circumstance
el/la **cirujano(a) ortopédico(a)** orthopedic surgeon, *11.2;* **2.2**
la **ciudad** city, 2.2; *8.1*
civil: por (el, lo) civil civil, **3.1**
la **civilización** civilization
claro(a) clear
   claro que of course
la **clase** class *(school),* 1.2; class *(ticket),* 3.1
   en primera (segunda) clase first-class (second-class), *3.1*
   la sala de clase classroom, 3.1
clavar con una multa to give (someone) a ticket, *9.1*
la **clave de área** area code, *6.2*
clic: hacer clic to click *(computer),* *6.1*
el/la **cliente** customer, 9.2; **7**
el **clima** climate
la **clínica** clinic
cobrar to cash, **4**
la **cocción** cooking
cocer (ue) to cook, *10;* **1**
el **coche** car, *9.2;* train car, *3.1*
   el coche deportivo sports car, *9.2*
el **coche comedor (cafetería)** dining car, *3.2*
el **cochinillo asado** roast suckling pig
la **cocina** kitchen, 2.2; *10;* **1;** stove, *10;* **1;** cooking, cuisine
cocinar to cook, *10;* **1**
el/la **cocinero(a)** cook, *10;* **1**
el **cocodrilo** crocodile

Spanish-English Dictionary

el **código** code

el **codo** elbow, 11.1; *2.1*

cogido(a) picked up, taken

la **col** cabbage, **9**

la **cola** cola (soda), 4.1; line *(of people)*, 10.2; *1.2*

    hacer cola to wait in line, 10.2; *1.2*

el **colegio** secondary school, high school

el **colgador** hanger, *7*

colgar (ue) to hang up

la **colina** hill

la **colocación** placement

colocar to place, to put

colombiano(a) Colombian, *1.2*

la **colonia** colony, **8**

colonial colonial, **8**

el **colonizador** colonizer, **8**

colonizar to colonize, **8**

el **color** color, 5.1

    de color marrón brown, 5.1

    ¿De qué color es? What color is it?

el **comando** command

combinado: el plato combinado combination plate

el **comedor** dining room, 2.2

    el coche comedor dining car, *3.2*

el/la **comensal** diner, **9**

comenzar (ie) to begin

comer to eat, 4.1

    dar de comer a to feed

el/la **comerciante** businessperson, **10**

los **comestibles** food, *4*

cometer to make (mistake); to commit

cómico(a) funny, comical, 1.1

la **comida** meal, 4.1; food

como like, as; since

¿cómo? How?; What?, 1.1

    ¿Cómo es él? What's he like? What does he look like?, 1.1

    ¿Cómo está… ? How is … ?

    ¡Cómo no! Sure! Of course!

cómodo(a) comfortable

comoquiera however

el/la **compañero(a)** companion

la **compañía** company, **8**

comparar to compare

el **compartimiento superior** overhead bin, 10.2; *1.2*

compartir to share

completar to complete, to fill in

completo(a) full, *3.2*; **6.1**

componer to compose, to make up

el **comportamiento** behavior, conduct, 6.1; **5**

comportarse to behave, **5**

la **composición** composition

la **compra** purchase, 9.2

el/la **comprador(a)** shopper, customer

comprar to buy, 3.2

compras: ir de compras to shop, to go shopping, 9.1

comprender to understand, 4.2; to include

la **comprensión** understanding

la **computadora** computer, 3.2; **6.1**

comunicarse to communicate with each other

la **comunión** communion

con with

    con frecuencia often

    con retraso (una demora) late, delayed, 10.2; *1.2*

el **concierto** concert, 8.1

el **conde** count

el **condimento** condiment, *10*; **1**

el **condominio** condominium

conducir to drive, 9.2; to lead

la **conducta** conduct, behavior, 6.1

    tener buena conducta to be well-behaved, 6.1

el/la **conductor(a)** driver, *9.2*

conectado(a) on-line, connected

conectar to connect

la **conexión** connection

confeccionar to make, to prepare, *5.1*

la **conferencia** lecture

confesar to confess, to tell the truth

confiabilidad reliability

confiable reliable, trustworthy

confiar to entrust

la **confirmación** confirmation

confirmar to confirm (seat on a flight), **6.1**

conforme: estar conforme to agree, to be in agreement

confortar to soothe

confundir to mix in, to confuse

congelado(a) frozen, 9.2

los productos congelados frozen food, 9.2

el **congelador** freezer, *10*; **1**

el **conjunto** band, musical group, 8.1

conmovedor(a) moving

conocer to know, to be familiar with, 9.1; to meet

conocido(a) known

el/la **conocido(a)** acquaintance, **5**

el **conocimiento** knowledge

el **conquistador** conqueror

conquistar to conquer, **8**

consecuencia: por consecuencia as a result, consequently

el/la **consejero(a)** counselor

el **consejo** advice

considerar to consider

consiguiente: por consiguiente consequently

el **consomé** bouillon, consommé

la **consonante** consonant

constar (de) to consist of, to be made up of

la **consulta del médico** doctor's office, 6.2; **10**

consultar to consult

el **consultorio** doctor's office, 6.2; **10**

el/la **consumidor(a)** consumer

el/la **contable** accountant, **10**

contagioso(a) contagious

la **contaminación del aire** air pollution

contaminar to pollute

contar (ue) to tell, to count

contemporáneo(a) contemporary

el **contenido** contents

contento(a) happy, 6.1

contestar to answer, 3.1

continental: el desayuno continental Continental breakfast, *7*

el **continente** continent

continua: la línea continua solid line *(road)*, *9.1*

continuar to continue

contra against

contraer matrimonio to get married

contrario(a) opposite; opposing

    al contrario on the contrary

    el equipo contrario opposing team, 7.1

contrastar to contrast

el **contrato** contract, **6.2**

contribuir to contribute

el **control de pasaportes** passport inspection, **6.1**

el **control de seguridad** security (checkpoint), 10.2; *1.2*

    pasar por el control de seguridad to go through security, 10.2; *1.2*

convencer to convince

convenir (ie) to admit

la **conversación** conversation

conversar to converse

el **convertible** convertible, *9.2*

convertir (ie, i) to convert, to transform

la **copa: la Copa Mundial** World Cup

la **copia** copy, *6.1*

    la copia dura hard copy, *6.1*

el **corazón** heart, **8**

la **corbata** tie, *9.1*

el **cordero** lamb, *4*; **9**

la **cordillera** mountain chain, range

la **corona** wreath, *5.1*

el **corral** corral, *8.2*

la **correa** conveyor belt, *6.1*

el/la **corredor(a)** runner *11.1*; *2.1*

el **correo** mail, *4*

el **correo electrónico** e-mail, *3.2*; *6.1*

correr to run, *5.2*

corresponder to respond

corrido(a) opened

cortar to cut off, *6.2*; to cut, to chop, *10*; *1*

    cortar en pedacitos to cut in small pieces, to dice, *10*; *1*

    cortar en rebanadas to slice, *10*; *1*

    Estás cortando. You're breaking up. *(telephone)*, *6.2*

    Se nos cortó la línea. We've been cut off. *(telephone)*, *6.2*

cortarse to cut oneself, *11.2*; **2.2**

el **corte de pelo** haircut, *4*

el **cortejo fúnebre** funeral procession, *3.2*

cortés polite, *5*

cortesano(a) of the court, courtly

la **cortesía** courtesy

corto(a) short, *9.1*; **4**

    de manga corta short-sleeved, *9.1*

el **pantalón corto** shorts, *5.1*

la **corvina** corbina, drumfish

la **cosa** thing, *3.1*

la **cosecha** harvest, *8.2*

cosechar to harvest, *8.2*

cosmopolita cosmopolitan

la **costa** coast

costar (ue) to cost, *9.1*

    ¿Cuánto cuesta? How much does it cost?, *3.2*

costarricense Costa Rican

la **costumbre** custom

el **cráneo** skull, *5.1*

crear to create

crecer to grow

creer to believe, to think

    creo que sí (que no) I (don't) think so, *4.2*

la **crema dental** toothpaste, *11.2*; *2.2*

la **crema solar** suntan lotion, *7.1*

el/la **criado(a)** housekeeper; maid, **3 (Lit.)**

cristiano(a) Christian

criticar to criticize

el **cruce** crosswalk, pedestrian crossing, *8.1*; intersection, *9.1*

crudo(a) raw, *8.1*

    casi crudo rare *(meat)*, *4*

    los vegetales crudos raw vegetables, crudités, *8.1*

cruzar to cross; to intersect, *9.1*

el **cuaderno** notebook, *3.1*

la **cuadra** *(city)* block, *9.1*

el **cuadro** painting, *8.2*; **7.1**

¿cuál? which? what?, LP

    ¿Cuál es la fecha de hoy? What is today's date?, LP

¿cuáles? which ones? what?

cualquier(a) any

cualquier otro(a) any other

cualquiera whichever, whatever

cuando when, *3.1*

¿cuándo? when?, *3.2*

cuanto: en cuanto as soon as; **en cuanto a** in terms of, as far as . . . is concerned

¿cuánto? how much?

    ¿A cuánto está(n). . . ? How much is (are) . . . ?, *9.2*

    ¿Cuánto es? How much is it (does it cost)?, LP

¿cuántos(as)? how many?, *2.1*

    ¿Cuántos años tiene? How old is he (she)?, *2.1*

cuarenta forty, LP

el **cuarto** room, *2.2*; *7*; quarter

el **cuarto de baño** bathroom, *2.2*; *7*

el **cuarto de dormir** bedroom, *2.2*

el **cuarto sencillo (doble)** single (double) room, *7*

y cuarto quarter-past (the hour), LP

cuatro four, LP

cuatrocientos(as) four hundred, *9.2*

el/la **cubano(a)** Cuban

el/la **cubanoamericano(a)** Cuban American

cubierto(a) covered; indoor

cubrir to cover

la **cuchara** tablespoon, *4*

la **cucharada** tablespoonful

la **cucharadita** teaspoonful

la **cucharita** teaspoon, *4*

el **cuchillo** knife, *4*

el **cuello** neck, *11.1*; **2.1**; collar

la **cuenca** basin *(river)*

la **cuenta** check *(restaurant)*, *4.2*; *4*; account

    la cuenta corriente checking account, **4**

    darse cuenta de to realize, **8**

    por su cuenta on its own

    tomar en cuenta to take into account, **8**

el **cuento** story, *7.2*

el **cuerdo** string

el **cuerpo** body, *11.1*; *2.1*

la **cueva** cave

¡Cuidado¡ Look out! Watch out!, *5*

    con (mucho) cuidado (very) carefully

    tener cuidado to be careful, *9.1*

cuidadoso(a) careful

cuidar to take care of, to care for

    ¡Cuídate! Take care of yourself!

la **culpa** blame, guilt

cultivar to work *(land)*; to grow, *8.2*; **9**

culto(a) cultured

la **cultura** culture

el **cumpleaños** birthday, *8.1*; *3.2*

cumplir. . . años to be (turn) . . . years old

    cumplir un sueño to fulfill a wish, to make a wish come true

la **cuota** toll

la **cúpula** dome

el **cura** priest, *3.1*

curarse to get better, to recover

Spanish-English Dictionary

el **currículo** curriculum vitae

el **currículum vitae** résumé, curriculum vitae, **10**

el **curso** class, course, 1.2

cuyo(a) whose

— D —

la **dama de honor** maid of honor, **3.1**

el **daño** harm

  hacerse daño to harm oneself, to get hurt, *11.2;* **2.2**

dar to give, 3.1

  dar de comer a to feed

  dar la vuelta to turn around, *9.1*

  dar un examen (una prueba) to give a test, 3.1

  dar una caminata to take a hike, 11.2; **2.2**

  dar una fiesta to throw a party, 8.1

darse cuenta de to realize

darse la mano to shake hands, *5*

datar to date *(time)*

los **datos** data, facts

de of, from, LP

  ¿de dónde? from where?, 1.1

  de manera que so that, in such a way that

  de modo que so that, in such a way that

  De nada. You're welcome., LP

  ¿De parte de quién, por favor? Who's calling, please?, *6.2*

  ¿de qué nacionalidad? what nationality?, 1.1

  de vez en cuando from time to time, 10.2; *1.2*

  No hay de qué. You're welcome., LP

debajo de below, underneath, 10.2; *1.2*

deber should, 4.2; to owe

el **deber** duty

debido a owing to, **6.1**

la **debilidad** weakness

decidir to decide

decir to say, to tell

la **decisión** decision

  tomar una decisión to make a decision

declinar to decline, **6.2**

decorar to decorate, 5.2

dedicado(a) devoted

el **dedo** finger, 11.1; *2.1*

el **dedo del pie** toe, *11.1;* **2.1**

deducirse to deduct

el **defecto** defect

defender (ie) to defend

definido(a) definite

dejar to leave (something), *4;* to let, to allow

  dejar con to put an end to

  dejar de to stop, to give up

  dejar un mensaje to leave a message, *6.2*

  dejar una propina to leave a tip, *4*

del of the, from the

delante de in front of, 2.2

delantero(a) front *(adj.)*, 8.1

delgado(a) thin

demás (the) rest

  los demás other people, **5 (Lit.)**

demasiado too *(adv.)*, too much

la **demora** delay, 10.2; *1.2;* **6.1**

  con una demora late, 10.2; *1.2*

denominado(a) named, designated

la **densidad** density

dental: el tubo de crema dental tube of toothpaste, 11.2; *2.2*

dentífrica: la pasta dentífrica toothpaste

dentro de within

  dentro de poco soon, shortly thereafter, 10.2; *1.2*

el **departamento** apartment, 2.2

  el departamento de orientación guidance office

  el departamento de personal human resources (personnel) department, **10**

  el departamento de recursos humanos human resources department, **10**

el/la **dependiente(a)** salesperson, employee, 9.1

el **deporte** sport, 5.1

  el deporte de equipo team sport

  el deporte individual individual sport

deportivo(a) *(related to)* sports

  el coche deportivo sports car, *9.2*

depositar to deposit, **4**

deprimido(a) sad, depressed, 6.1

derecho straight (ahead), *9.1*

derecho(a) right, 11.1; *2.1*

  a la derecha on the right, *9.1*

derrocar to bring down

la **derrota** defeat

derrotar to defeat

desafortunadamente unfortunately

desagradable unpleasant, not nice

desaparecer to disappear

desarrollarse to develop, **7.2**

el **desastre** disaster

desastroso(a) disastrous, catastrophic

el **desayuno** breakfast, 4.1; *7*

  el desayuno americano American breakfast, *7*

  el desayuno continental Continental breakfast, *7*

  tomar el desayuno to have breakfast, 4.1

desbodado(a) runaway

descansar to rest, *11.1;* **2.1**

el **descapotable** convertible, *9.2*

descargar to download, *6.2;* to unload

descargado(a) carrying no load

descolgar (ue) (el auricular) to unhook (the telephone receiver), *6.2*

desconocido(a) unknown

desconsolado(a) very sad

descortés(esa) discourteous, rude

describir to describe

la **descripción** description

el **descubrimiento** discovery

el **descuento** discount

desde since; from

desear to want, to wish, 4.2

  ¿Qué desean tomar? What would you like *(to eat, drink)?*, 4.2

desembarcar to deplane, disembark, 10.2; *1.2*

desembocar to lead, to go (from one street into another), to come out onto

el **deseo** wish, desire

desesperado(a) desperate

desfilar to walk (in a parade or procession), *5.1*

el **desfile** parade, *5.2*

desgraciadamente unfortunately

deshuesado(a) deboned

el **desierto** desert

desinflada: la llanta desinflada flat tire, *9.2*

desnudar to strip, to lay bare

desnudo(a) naked

el **despacho** office, **4 (Lit.)**

despacio slow, slowly, *9.1*

despedirse (i, i) to say good-bye to, to take leave, **5**

despegar to take off *(plane)*,*10.2; 1.2*

el **despegue** takeoff *(plane)*, *10.2; 1.2*

despertarse (ie) to wake up, *11.1; 2.1*

después (de) after, *3.1;* later

después de que after (doing something)

destemplado(a) sharp, unpleasant

el/la **destinatario(a)** addressee, recipient, *6.1*

el **destino** destination, *3.1;* **6.1**

con destino a (going) to; for, *10.2; 1.2*

las **desventajas** disadvantages

desvestir (i, i) to undress

el **detalle** detail

detenidamente thoroughly

el **detergente** detergent, **4**

detrás de in back of, behind, *2.2*

devolver (ue) to return (something), *5.2*

el **día** day

Buenos días. Good morning., LP

el Día de los Muertos Day of the Dead, *5.1*

el Día de los Reyes Epiphany (January 6), *5.1*

hoy en día nowadays

¿Qué día es hoy? What day is it today?, LP

el **diablo** devil

el **diagnóstico** diagnosis

el **diálogo** dialogue

diario(a) daily

a diario on a daily basis

la rutina diaria daily routine, *11.1; 2.1*

el **diario** daily newspaper

el **dibujo** drawing, illustration

diciembre December, LP

el **dictado** dictation

dictar to dictate

diecinueve nineteen, LP

dieciocho eighteen, LP

dieciséis sixteen, LP

diecisiete seventeen, LP

el **diente** clove (of garlic)

los **dientes** teeth, 11.1; *2.1*

cepillarse (lavarse) los dientes to brush one's teeth, 11.1; *2.1*

la **dieta** diet

diez ten, LP

de diez en diez by tens

la **diferencia** difference

diferente different, *9.2*

difícil difficult, *1.2*

la **dificultad** difficulty

sin dificultad easily

difunto(a) dead, deceased, *5.1*

el/la **difunto(a)** deceased, dead person, *5.1*

¡Diga! Hello! *(on the phone)*

¡Dígame! Hello! *(on the phone)*

dinámico(a) dynamic, 6.1

el **dinero** money, 3.2

el dinero en efectivo cash, **4**

dirán: el «lo que dirán» what people might say

la **dirección** address, *6.1;* direction

la dirección de correo electrónico (e-mail) e-mail address, *6.1*

las **direccionales** turn signals, *9.2*

dirigirse to head toward

el **disco** record

discreto(a) discrete

diseñar to design

el **disfraz** disguise, costume, *5.1*

disfrutar (de) to enjoy

displicente indifferent

disponderse to prepare (to do something)

disponible available, **6.1**

dispuesto(a) disposed, laid out

distancia: de larga distancia long-distance *(race), 11.1;* **2.1**

distinguir to distinguish

distinto(a) different

distraer to distract

el **distribuidor automático** boarding pass kiosk, 10.1; *1.1;* ticket dispenser, *3.1*

el **distrito** district, area, section

divertido(a) fun, funny, amusing

divertir (ie, i) to amuse, 11.2; *2.2*

divertirse (ie, i) to have a good time, to have fun, 11.2; *2.2*

dividirse to divide, to separate, **7.2**

divino(a) divine, heavenly

doblar to turn, *9.1*

doble: el cuarto doble double (hotel room), **7**

dobles doubles *(tennis), 5.2*

doce twelve, LP

la **docena** dozen

el **documento adjunto** attached file, *6.1*

el **dólar** dollar

doler (ue) to ache, to hurt, 6.2; *11.2;* **2.2**

Le (me, etc.) duele mucho. It hurts him (me, etc.) a lot., *11.2;* **2.2**

Me duele(n)… My . . . ache(s)., 6.2

el **dolor** pain, ache, 6.2

tener dolor de cabeza to have a headache, 6.2

tener dolor de estómago to have a stomachache, 6.2

tener dolor de garganta to have a sore throat, 6.2

el **domenical** Sunday newspaper

domesticado(a) domesticated

dominar to speak very well

el **domingo** Sunday, LP

dominicano(a) Dominican

la República Dominicana Dominican Republic

el **dominio** rule

el **dominó** dominos

donde where

¿dónde? Where?, 1.1

¿de dónde? from where?, 1.1

dondequiera wherever

dorado(a) golden, (made of) gold

dormir (ue, u) to sleep

la bolsa de dormir sleeping bag, 11.2; *2.2*

el cuarto de dormir bedroom, 2.2

el saco de dormir sleeping bag, 11.2; *2.2*

dormirse (ue, u) to fall asleep, 11.1; *2.1*

el **dormitorio** bedroom, 2.2

dos two

doscientos(as) two hundred, *9.2*

el **drama** drama

driblar to dribble, 5.2

la **ducha** shower, 11.1; *2.1*

Spanish-English Dictionary

tomar una ducha to take a shower, 11.1; *2.1*

la **duda** doubt

  sin duda without a doubt, doubtless

  duele(n): Me duele(n)... My . . . hurts (aches)., 6.2

  Me duele que... It hurts me that . . .

el **duelo** duel

el/la **dueño(a)** owner, **10**

  dulce sweet, *5.1*

  el pan dulce pastry, *7*

el **dulce** sweet

  durante during, 3.2

  durar to last

  duro(a) hard, difficult, 1.2

  la copia dura hard copy, *6.1*

el **DVD** DVD, 3.2

E

la **ebullición** boiling

  echar to throw, to expel

  echar a to start to (do something), **6** (Lit.)

  echar una carta to mail a letter, **4**

  económico(a) inexpensive

  ecuatoriano(a) Ecuadoran, 1.1

la **edad** age

  la Edad Media Middle Ages

el **edificio** building, 2.2

la **educación** education

  la educación física physical education, 1.2

  educado(a) mannered

  estar bien (mal) educado(a) to be polite (rude), 6.1

  efectuarse to take place

  egoísta selfish, egotistical

el/la **ejecutivo(a)** executive, **10**

el **ejemplo** example

  por ejemplo for example

los **ejercicios** exercises, 11.1; **2.1**

  ejercicios de respiración breathing exercises, *11.1;* **2.1**

  hacer ejercicios to exercise, *11.1;* **2.1**

el **ejército** army, **4** (Lit.)

los **ejotes** green beans

  el the *(m. sing.)*, 1.1

él he, 1.1

elaborar to make, to produce, *5.1*

electrónico electronic, 10.1; *1.1*

  el boleto (billete) electrónico e-ticket, 10.1; *1.1*

  el correo electrónico e-mail, 3.2; *6.1*

el **elefante** elephant

  elegante elegant, fancy

  elegir (i, i) to elect, to pick

  elemental elementary

  ella she, 1.1

  ellos(as) they, 1.2

el **elote** corn

el **e-mail** e-mail, *6.1*

  embarcar to board, 10.2; *1.2*

  embargo: sin embargo however, nevertheless

el **embarque** boarding, 10.1; *1.1*

el **embotellamiento** traffic jam

  emergencia: la sala de emergencia emergency room, *11.2;* **2.2**

la **emisión televisiva** television program, **8**

la **emisora de televisión** television station, **8**

  emitir to broadcast, **8**

  emocionante moving; exciting

  emotivo(a) emotional, sensitive

la **empanada** meat pie, 4.2

  empeorar to make worse, to worsen

  empezar (ie) to begin, 5.1

el/la **empleado(a)** salesperson, employee, 3.2

la **empresa** company, **8**

  empujar to push

  en in; on; at

  en casa at home

  enamorado(a) in love

el/la **enamorado(a)** sweetheart

  enamorado(a) de in love with

  enamorarse to fall in love, **5**

  encaminarse to head toward

  encantar to love, to adore, *6.2*

el **encanto** enchantment

  encargar to put in charge, **4** (Lit.)

  encargarse to take it upon oneself

  encender (ie) to light, *5.2*

  encerrar (ie) to enclose; to lock up

  encestar to make a basket *(basketball)*, 5.2

la **enchilada** enchilada

  encima: por encima de above, over, 5.2

  encontrar (ue) to find, to encounter

  encontrarse (ue) to be found; to meet

el **encuentro** encounter, meeting

la **encuesta** survey

  endosar endorse, **4**

el/la **enemigo(a)** enemy

  energético(a) energetic, 6.1

la **energía** energy, 6.1

  enero January, LP

  enfadado(a) angry, mad, 6.1

  enfadar to make angry, 6.1

  enfadarse to get angry, **5**

la **enfermedad** illness

el/la **enfermero(a)** nurse, 6.2; *11.2;* **2.2**

  enfermo(a) ill, sick, 6.2

el/la **enfermo(a)** sick person, patient

  enfrente de in front of

  ¡Enhorabuena! Congratulations!, **3.1**

  enjuto(a) thin, skinny, **10** (Lit.)

  enlatado(a) canned

  enlazar to connect, **6.2**

  enojado(a) angry, mad, annoyed, 6.1

  enojar to make angry, to annoy, 6.1

  enorme enormous

la **ensalada** salad, 4.1

  enseguida right away, 4.2

  enseñar to teach, 3.1

  entender (ie) to understand, 8.2

  entero(a) entire, whole

  enterrado(a) buried, *5.1*

  enterrar (ie) to bury

el **entierro** burial, *3.2*

  entonces then

  en aquel entonces at that time

la **entrada** ticket, 8.1; entrée *(meal);* entrance

  entradas: la bandeja de entradas e-mail inbox, *6.1*

  entrar to enter, to go into, 5.1

  entrar en línea to go online, *6.1*

  entre between, among

  entregar to hand over, to deliver, **6** (Lit.)

el/la **entrenador(a)** coach, manager

entretanto meanwhile

la **entrevista** interview, **10**

el/la **entrevistador(a)** interviewer

entusiasmado(a) enthusiastic

el **entusiasmo** enthusiasm, 6.1

enviados: la bandeja de enviados sent mailbox, *6.1*

enviar to send, 3.2

el **episodio** episode

la **época** times, period

el **equilibrio** balance

el **equipaje** luggage, baggage, 10.1; *1.1;* **6.1**

el equipaje de mano hand luggage, carry-on bags, 10.2; *1.2*

el **equipo** team, 5.1; equipment

el deporte de equipo team sport

la **equitación** horseback riding, *8.2*

equivocado(a) mistaken, wrong

escala: hacer escala to stop over, to make a stop, **6.1**

la **escalera** stairs, staircase, *8.1*

la escalera mecánica escalator, *8.1*

el **escalope de ternera** veal cutlet, *10;* **1**

el **escaparate** store window, 9.1

la **escena** scene

escoger to choose

escolar *(adj.)* school

el bus escolar school bus, 3.2

los materiales escolares school supplies, 3.1

la tarifa escolar student fare

escribir to write, 4.2

el **escrito** document, paper

escrito(a) written

el/la **escritor(a)** writer

escritorio: la pantalla de escritorio *(computer)* screen, *6.1*

escuchar to listen (to), 3.2

¿Me escuchas? Can you hear me? *(telephone),* 6.2

el **escudero** squire

la **escuela** school, 1.2

la escuela primaria elementary school

la escuela secundaria secondary school, high school, 1.2

el/la **escultor(a)** sculptor, *8.2;* **7.1**

la **escultura** sculpture, **7.1**

ese(a) that, that one

eso: a eso de at about *(time)*

por eso for this reason, that is why

esos(as) those

la **espalda** back, 11.1; *2.1*

espantable horrendous

España Spain

el **español** Spanish *(language);* person, 1.2

español(a) Spanish *(adj.)*

la **especia** spice, **9**

la **especialidad** specialty

especialmente especially

específico(a) specific

espectacular spectacular

el **espectáculo** show, spectacle

el/la **espectador(a)** spectator

el **espejo** mirror, 11.1; *2.1*

espera: la sala de espera waiting room, *3.1*

esperar to wait (for), 10.2; *1.2;* to hope; to expect, **3.1**

el **espíritu** mind, spirit, *11.1;* **2.1**

la **esplendidez** splendor

espontáneo(a) spontaneous

la **esposa** wife, 2.1

el **esposo** husband, 2.1

la **esquela** obituary, *3.2*

el **esqueleto** skeleton, *5.1*

el **esquí** ski; skiing, 7.2

el esquí acuático (náutico) waterskiing, 7.1

el esquí alpino downhill skiing

el esquí nórdico cross-country skiing

el/la **esquiador(a)** skier, 7.2

esquiar to ski, 7.2

esquiar en el agua to water-ski, 7.1

la **esquina** corner, *8.1*

¿Está... , por favor? Is . . . there, please?, *6.2*

establecer(se) to establish; to settle, **8**

el **establecimiento** establish, settling

el **establo** stable, *8.2;* manger

la **estación** season, LP; resort, 7.1; station, *3.1*

la estación de esquí ski resort, 7.2

la estación de ferrocarril (tren) railroad (train) station, *3.1;* **6.2**

la estación de metro subway (metro) station, *8.1*

la estación de servicio gas station, *9.2*

¿Qué estación es? What season is it?, LP

estacionar to park

la **estadía** stay

el **estadio** stadium

el **estado financiero** financial statement, **10**

Estados Unidos United States

estadounidense from the United States

estallar to break out, to explode

la **estampilla** stamp, **4**

la **estancia** ranch, *8.2*

estar to be, 3.1

¿Está... ? Is . . . there?, 6.2

estar bien to feel fine, 6.2

estar cansado(a) to be tired, 6.1

estar contento(a) (triste, nervioso[a], etc.) to be happy (sad, nervous, etc.), 6.1

estar de buen (mal) humor to be in a good (bad) mood, 6.1

estar enfermo(a) to be sick, 6.2

estar para (+ infinitivo) to be about to (do something)

la **estatua** statue, *8.2;* **7.1**

la **estatura** stature, height

este(a) this, this one, 9.1

el **este** east

estereofónico(a) stereo

el **estilo** style

estimado(a) esteemed

estirarse to stretch, 11.1; *2.1;* **2.1**

el **estómago** stomach, 6.2

el dolor de estómago stomachache, 6.2

estos(as) these

la **estrategía** strategy

estrechamente closely

estrecho(a) narrow, *8.1*

la **estrella** star

estremecerse to shake

el **estrés** stress, 6.2

la **estrofa** stanza, *7.2*

la **estructura** structure

el/la **estudiante** student

el/la estudiante universitario(a) university student, **10**

estudiantil: la tarifa estudiantil student fare

estudiar to study, 3.1

el **estudio** study

los estudios sociales social studies, 1.2

Spanish-English Dictionary

la **estufa** stove, 10; **1**
estupendo(a) terrific, stupendous
la **etiqueta** luggage identification tag, **6.1**
la **etnia** ethnicity, ethnic group
étnico(a) ethnic
el **euro** euro (currency of most of the countries of the European Union)
Europa Europe
el **evento** event
evitar to avoid
el **examen** test, exam, 3.1
 el examen físico physical, 6.2
examinar to examine, 6.2
exceder to go over (speed limit)
excelente excellent
la **excepción** exception
la **excursión** excursion, outing
el/la **excursionista** hiker
exigente demanding
exigir to demand, to require
existir exist
el **éxito** success, 6.1
 tener éxito to succeed, to be successful, 6.1
exótico(a) exotic
experimentar to try, to try out; to experience
el/la **experto(a)** expert, 7.2
explicar to explain
el/la **explorador(a)** explorer
la **exposición de arte** art show, exhibition, 8.2
la **expresión** expression
extenderse (ie) to extend
extranjero(a) foreign
 al extranjero abroad
extraño(a) strange
extraordinario(a) extraordinary

la **fábrica** factory
fabuloso(a) fabulous
fácil easy, 1.2
la **factura** bill
facturar el equipaje to check luggage, 10.1; 1.1
la **falda** skirt, 3.1
el **fallecimiento** death, demise
falso(a) false
la **falta** lack
faltar to lack, not to have, 6.1

Le falta paciencia. He (She) has no patience., 6.1
la **familia** family, 2.1
familiar (related to) family
los **familiares** family members
famoso(a) famous
la **fantasía** fantasy
fantástico(a) fantastic
el/la **farmacéutico(a)** druggist, pharmacist
la **farmacia** pharmacy, drugstore, 6.2
el **favor** favor
 Favor de (+ infinitivo). Please (do something)., 11.2; 2.2
 por favor please, LP
favorito(a) favorite
febrero February, LP
la **fecha** date, LP
 ¿Cuál es la fecha de hoy? What is today's date?, LP
fecundo(a) prolific
la **felicidad** happiness
feliz happy, 5.2
 ¡Felices Pascuas! Happy Easter!
 ¡Feliz Hanuka! Happy Hanukkah!, 5.2
 ¡Feliz Navidad! Merry Christmas!, 5.2
feo(a) unattractive, ugly, 1.1
la **feria** festival, fair, 5.1; fairground
ferrocarril: la estación de ferrocarril train station, railroad station, 3.1, **6.2**
festivo: el día festivo holiday
la **fiebre** fever, 6.2
 tener fiebre to have a fever, 6.2
fiel loyal, faithful
la **fiesta** party, 8.1; holiday, 5.1
 dar una fiesta to throw a party, 8.1
 la fiesta de las luces festival of lights (Hanukkah), 5.2
fijarse to pay attention to, to concentrate on
fijo(a) fixed, unchanging
la **fila** line (of people); row (of seats), **6.1**
 estar en fila to wait in line
el **film** film, movie
el **filme** film, movie, 8.2
el **fin** end; death
 en fin in short
 el fin de semana weekend, 7.1

por fin finally
final: al final de at the end of
la **finca** farm, 8.2
fines: a fines de at the end of
fingir to pretend
firmar to sign, **3.1**
físico(a) physical
 la apariencia física physical appearance, looks
 la educación física physical education, 1.2
flaco(a) thin
el **flan** flan, custard, 4.1
la **flauta** flute
la **flecha** arrow
flexible open-minded, flexible, 6.1
la **flor** flower, 2.2
el **foco** center, focal point
la **fogata** bonfire, campfire
fondo background, **7.1**
 al fondo to the bottom
los **fondos** funds, money, **4**
el/la **fontanero(a)** plumber, **10**
la **forma** form, piece, 10.2; 1.2; shape
 la forma de identidad piece of ID, 10.2; 1.2
formal formal, **5**
formar to form, to make up; to put together
el **formulario** form
forzado(a) forced
la **foto(grafía)** photo, 7.1
la **fractura** fracture
el **francés** French, 1.2
el **franciscano** Franciscan
franco(a) frank, sincere, candid
el **frasco** jar, 9.2
la **frase** sentence
la **frazada** blanket, 7
frecuencia: con frecuencia often, frequently
frecuentemente frequently
freír (i, i) to fry, 4; **1**
los **frenos** brakes, 9.2
la **frente** forehead, 11.1; **2.1**
frente a in front of
fresco(a) cool, LP; fresh
 Hace fresco. It's cool (weather)., LP
los **frijoles** beans, 4.1
el **frío** cold
frío(a) cold, 4.2
 Hace frío. It's cold (weather)., LP
 tener frío to be cold, 11.1; 2.1

frito(a) fried

las patatas (papas) fritas
french fries, *4.1*

frontal: la página frontal
home page, *6.1*

la **frontera** border

la **fruta** fruit, *9.2*

el puesto de frutas fruit
stand, *9.2*

la **frutería** fruit stand, *9.2*

el **fuego** flame, heat, *10;* **1**

a fuego lento on low heat,
10; **1**

los **fuegos artificiales** fireworks,
5.2

la **fuente** fountain

fuera de outside

fuerte strong; substantial

las **fuerzas** (armed) forces

fumar: la señal de no fumar
no-smoking sign, *10.2; 1.2*

el/la **funcionario(a)**
gubernamental (de
gobierno) government
official, **10**

fundar to found

el **fútbol** soccer, *5.1*

el campo de fútbol soccer
field, *5.1*

el fútbol americano
football

el/la **futbolista** soccer player

el **futuro** future

el **gabinete del dentista** dentist's
office, **9**

las **gafas para el sol** sunglasses,
7.1

el **galán** elegant man,
heartthrob

gallardo(a) brave, dashing

las **galletas** crackers, *8.1*

la **gallina** hen, *8.2*

galope: a galope galloping

la **gamba** shrimp, prawn

el **ganado** cattle, livestock, *8.2*

ganar to win, *5.1;* to earn

ganas: tener ganas de to feel
like

el **garaje** garage, *2.2*

la **garganta** throat, *6.2*

el dolor de garganta sore
throat, *6.2*

la **garita de peaje** tollbooth, *9.1*

el **gas: el agua mineral con gas**
carbonated (sparkling)
mineral water, *4.2*

la **gaseosa** soda, carbonated
drink, *4.1*

la **gasolina** gas

la **gasolinera** gas station, *9.2*

gastar to spend; to waste

el **gasto** expense

el/la **gato(a)** cat, *2.1;* jack *(car), 9.2*

la **gaveta** drawer

el/la **gemelo(a)** twin, *2.1*

general general

en general in general

por lo general usually, as a
rule

generalmente usually,
generally

el **género** genre, **7.2**

generoso(a) generous

la **gente** people, *9.1*

la **geografía** geography

la **geometría** geometry

la **gesticulación** gesture

el **gigante** giant

el **gimnasio** gym(nasium), *11.1;*
2.1

girar to turn, to swivel

la **gitanilla** little gypsy

el **globo** balloon

el/la **gobernado(a)** governor

el **gobierno** government, **10**

el **gol** goal, *5.1*

meter un gol to score a
goal, *5.1*

el **golpe** blow; pat (on the back)

golpear to hit *(ball), 5.2*

la **goma** tire, *9.2*

gordo(a) fat

el **gorro** ski hat, *7.2*

gozar de to enjoy

grabar to record

Gracias. Thank you., LP

dar gracias a to thank

Mil gracias.
Thanks a million.

gracioso(a) funny, *1.1*

la **gramática** grammar

gran, grande big, large, *1.2*

la **grandeza** greatness, grandeur

el **granero** barn, *8.2*

la **granja** farm, *8.2*

gratis for free

gratuito(a) free

grave serious

gris gray, *5.1*

gritar to yell, to shout

el **grupo** group, *8.1*

la **guagua** bus *(Puerto Rico,*
Cuba), 8.1

el **guante** glove, *5.2*

la **guantera** glove compartment,
9.2

guapo(a) attractive, good-
looking, *1.1*

guardar to guard, *5.1;* to save,
to keep, *6.1*

guardar cama to
stay in bed *(illness), 6.2*

la **guardería** shelter

guatemalteco(a) Guatemalan,
1.1

la **guerra** war, **8**

el **guerrero** warrior

la **guía** guidebook

la guía telefónica phone
book, *6.2*

guiar to guide

el **guisante** pea, *9.2*

la **guitarra** guitar

gustar to like, to be pleasing
to, *5.1*

el **gusto** pleasure; like; taste

Mucho gusto. Nice *(It's a*
pleasure) to meet you.

H

haber to have *(in compound*
tenses)

haber de (+ infinitivo) to
have to (do something)

las **habichuelas** beans

las habichuelas tiernas
green beans, string
beans

la **habitación** bedroom; hotel
room, *7*

el/la **habitante** inhabitant

el/la **hablante** speaker

hablar to speak, to talk, *3.1*

hablar en el móvil to talk
on the cell phone

hablar por teléfono to talk
on the phone

¿Hablas en serio? Are you
serious?

habría de (+ infinitivo)
I was supposed to (do
something), **4**

hace: Hace... años . . . years
ago

Hace buen tiempo. The
weather is nice., LP

¿Hace cuánto tiempo... ?
How long . . . ?

Hace fresco. It's cool
(weather)., LP

Hace frío. It's cold
(weather)., LP

Hace mal tiempo. The
weather is bad., LP

Hace (mucho) calor. It's
(very) hot *(weather).,* LP

Hace sol. It's sunny., LP

Hace viento. It's windy., LP

hacer to do, to make, *10.2; 1.2*

hacer clic to click
(computer), 6.1

Spanish-English Dictionary

hacer cola to stand (wait) in line, 10.2; *1.2*

hacer ejercicios to exercise, *11.1;* **2.1**

hacer jogging to go jogging, *11.1;* **2.1**

hacer la cama to make the bed, *7*

hacer la maleta to pack, *10.1;* *1.1*

hacer planchas to do push-ups, *11.1;* **2.1**

hacer un viaje to take a trip, *10.1;* *1.1*

hacerle caso to pay attention, **5** (Lit.)

hacerse daño to hurt oneself, *11.2;* **2.2**

el **hacha** *(f.)* ax

hacia toward

hacia atrás backwards

la **hacienda** ranch, *8.2*

el **hall** concourse *(train station),* *3.1*

hallar to find

el **hambre** *(f.)* hunger

Me muero de hambre. I'm starving., *4*

tener hambre to be hungry, *4.1*

la **hamburguesa** hamburger, *4.1*

el **Hanuka** Hanukkah, *5.2*

¡Feliz Hanuka! Happy Hanukkah!, *5.2*

la **harina** flour, *9*

hasta until; up to; as far as; even

¡Hasta luego! See you later!, LP

¡Hasta mañana! See you tomorrow!, LP

¡Hasta pronto! See you soon!, LP

hasta que until

hay there is, there are, *2.2*

hay que it's necessary to (do something), one must, *10.2;* *1.2*

Hay sol. It's sunny., LP

No hay de qué. You're welcome., LP

¿Qué hay? What's new (up)?

la **hazaña** achievement

hebreo(a) Jewish, Hebrew, *5.2*

el **hecho** fact

hecho(a): bien hecho(a) well-done *(meat),* *4*

el **helado** ice cream, *4.1*

el **heno** hay, *8.2*

la **herida** wound, injury, *11.2;* **2.2**

el/la **herido(a)** injured person

el/la **hermanastro(a)** stepbrother, stepsister, *2.1*

el/la **hermano(a)** brother, sister, *2.1*

hermoso(a) beautiful

el **héroe** hero

la **heroína** heroine

herramientas: la barra de herramientas toolbar, *6.1*

hervir (ie, i) to boil, *10;* **1**

el **hielo** ice, *7.2*

el patinaje sobre el hielo ice-skating, *7.2*

la **hierba** grass, *8.2*

las **hierbas** herbs

el **hígado** liver

higiénico: el rollo de papel higiénico roll of toilet paper, *11.2;* **2.2**

el/la **hijo(a)** son, daughter, child, *2.1*

el/la hijo(a) único(a) only child, *2.1*

los **hijos** children, *2.1*

hinchado(a) swollen, *11.2;* **2.2**

hincharse to get swollen, to swell

hispano(a) Hispanic

hispanohablante Spanish-speaking

el/la **hispanohablante** Spanish speaker

la **historia** history, *1.2*

el/la **historiador(a)** historian

la **hoja** sheet (of paper), *3.1;* leaf (of lettuce), *9*

hojear to skim, to scan

¡Hola! Hello!, LP

el **hombre** man

el **hombro** shoulder, *11.1;* **2.1**

honesto(a) honest

honor: en honor de in honor of, *3.1*

honrado honest, upright

honroso(a) honorable

la **hora** hour; time, *10.1;* *1.1*

¿a qué hora? at what time?, LP

la hora de embarque boarding time, *10.1;* *1.1*

la hora de salida departure time, *10.1;* *1.1*

¿Qué hora es? What time is it?, LP

el **horario** *(train)* schedule, timetable, *3.1*

el **horizante** horizon

el **horno** oven, *10;* **1**

el **horno de microondas** microwave oven, *10;* **1**

la **hortaliza** vegetable, *9*

hospedarse to stay in a hotel, *7*

el **hospital** hospital

el **hostal** hostel, small (inexpensive) hotel, *7*

el **hotel** hotel, *7*

hoy today, LP

¿Cuál es la fecha de hoy? What's today's date?, LP

hoy en día nowadays

¿Qué día es hoy? What day is it today?, LP

la **huerta** orchard, *8.2;* *9*

el **huerto** vegetable garden, *9*

el **hueso** bone, *5.1;* **2.2**

el/la **huésped(a)** guest, *7*

el **huevo** egg, *4.1;* *7*

el huevo batido scrambled egg, *9*

los huevos pasados por agua soft-boiled eggs

los huevos revueltos scrambled eggs, *7*

huir to flee, **4** (Lit.)

humanitario(a) humanitarian

humano(a) human, *11.1;* *2.1*

el ser humano human being

humilde humble

el **humor** mood; humor

estar de buen (mal) humor to be in a good (bad) mood, *6.1*

tener un buen sentido de humor to have a good sense of humor, *6.1*

el **huso horario** time zone

I

el **icono** icon, *6.1*

ida y vuelta (regreso): un boleto (billete) de ida y vuelta (regreso) round-trip ticket, *3.1*

la **idea** idea

la **identidad** identification, *10.2;* *1.2*

el **carnet de identidad**
ID card, 10.2; *1.2*

identificar to identify

el **idioma** language

la **iglesia** church, **3.1**

igual que as well as; like; just as

iluminar to light up, to illuminate, *5.2*

ilustre illustrious, distinguished, **8**

la **imagen** picture, image

impaciente impatient, 6.1

impar odd *(numeric)*

impermeable waterproof

el **impermeable** raincoat

imponer to impose

importa: No importa. It doesn't matter.

la **importancia** importance

importante important

imposible impossible

la **impresora** printer, *6.1*

imprimir to print, *6.1*

el **impuesto** tax

incluir to include, **6.2**
¿Está incluido el servicio? Is the tip included?, 4.2

incluso even

incomodar to inconvenience

increíble incredible

indicar to indicate

indígena native, indigenous, 9.2

el/la **indígena** indigenous person

individual: el deporte individual individual sport

individuales singles *(tennis)*, 5.2

índole character, nature

industrializado(a) industrialized

inesperado(a) unexpected

la **inestabilidad** instability

infantil childlike

inferior bottom

el **infierno** hell

la **infinidad** infinity

la **influencia** influence

la **información** information, 3.2

la **informática** information technology

el **informe** report

el/la **ingeniero(a)** engineer, **10**

el **inglés** English, 1.2

la **Inglaterra** England

el **ingrediente** ingredient

inhóspito(a) inhospitable, desolate

inicial: la página inicial home page, *6.1*

inicio: la página de inicio home page, *6.1*

inmenso(a) immense

la **inmigración** immigration, **6.1**

el **inodoro** toilet, *7*

inolvidable unforgettable

la **inquietud** restlessness, agitation

insertar to insert, *3.1*

inspeccionar to inspect

inteligente intelligent, 1.2

intercambiar to exchange, **3.1**

el **interés** interest

interesante interesting, 1.2

interesar to interest, 5.1

las **intermitentes** turn signals, *9.2*

el **Internet** Internet, 3.2; *6.1*
navegar el Internet to surf the Net, 3.2; *6.1*

interurbano(a) city-to-city

intervenir (ie) to intervene

íntimo(a) close

la **introducción** introduction

introducir to insert, *6.2*

invertir (ie, i) to invest, **8**

el **invierno** winter, LP

la **invitación** invitation

el/la **invitado(a)** guest

invitar to invite

ir to go, 3.2
ir a (+ infinitivo) to be going to (do something), 4.1
ir a casa to go home, 3.2
ir a pie to go on foot, 3.2
ir al cine to go to the movies, 8.2
ir de camping to go camping, 11.2; *2.2*
ir de compras to go shopping, 9.1

irlandés(esa) Irish

la **isla** island

el **istmo** isthmus

italiano(a) Italian

izquierdo(a) left, 11.1; *2.1*
a la izquierda to the left, *9.1*

el **jabón** soap, 11.2; *2.2*
la barra (pastilla) de jabón bar of soap, 11.2; *2.2*
el jabón en polvo powdered detergent, **4**

jamás never

el **jamón** ham, 4.1

el **sándwich de jamón y queso** ham and cheese sandwich, 4.1

el **jardín** garden, 2.2

el/la **jardinero(a)** outfielder, 5.2

jogging: hacer jogging to go jogging, *11.1*; **2.1**

el **jonrón** home run
batear un jonrón to hit a home run

joven young

el/la **joven** young person, 1.1

la **joya** jewel, piece of jewelry

judío(a) Jewish, *5.2*

las **judías verdes** green beans, 9.2; **9**

el **juego** game, 5.1

el **jueves** Thursday, LP

el/la **jugador(a)** player, 5.1

jugar (ue) to play, 5.1
jugar (al) fútbol (béisbol, básquetbol) to play soccer (baseball, basketball), 5.1

el **jugo** juice, 4.1
el jugo de naranja orange juice, 4.1; *7*

el **juguete** toy

juicio: a tu juico in your opinion

julio July, LP

junio June, LP

junto a next to

juntos(as) together

el **kilo** kilo(gram) (2.2 lbs.), 9.2

el **kilometraje** mileage, **6.2**

el **kilómetro** kilometer

L

la the *(f. sing.)*, 1.1; it, her *(pron.)*

el **labio** lip

laborable: el día laborable working day

el **laboratorio** laboratory

laborioso(a) hardworking

el/la **labrador(a)** farm worker

labrar to work *(land)*, 8.2

el **lacón** bacon, *7*

lácteo(a): productos lácteos dairy products

el **lado** side
al lado de beside, next to, 2.2

ladrar to bark

el **lago** lake

Spanish-English Dictionary

la **lágrima** tear, **10** (Lit.)
la **lámpara** lamp, 2.2
la **langosta** lobster, *4*
la **lanza** lance
el/la **lanzador(a)** pitcher, 5.2
lanzar to kick, to throw, 5.1
el **lapicero** ballpoint pen
el **lápiz** pencil, 3.1
largo(a) long, 5.1
  a lo largo de along
  el tren de largo recorrido long-distance train, **6.2**
las the (f. pl.); them (pron.)
lástima: ser una lástima to be a shame
lastimarse to harm oneself, to get hurt
la **lata** can, 9.2
latino(a) Latino
Latinoamérica Latin America
el/la **latinoamericano(a)** Latin American
el **lavabo** washbasin, sink, *7*
el **lavado** laundry, *4*
la **lavadora** washing machine, *4*
la **lavandería** laundromat, *4*
el **lavaplatos** dishwasher, **10; 1**
lavar to wash, 11.2; **2.2; 4**
lavarse to wash oneself, 11.1; *2.1*
  lavarse el pelo (la cara, las manos) to wash one's hair (face, hands), 11.1; *2.1*
  lavarse los dientes to clean (brush) one's teeth, 11.1; *2.1*
le to him, to her; to you (formal) (pron.)
la **lección** lesson
la **leche** milk, 4.1
  el café con leche coffee with milk, café au lait
el **lechón asado** roast suckling pig
la **lechuga** lettuce, 4.1
  la hoja de lechuga leaf of lettuce, *9*
la **lectura** reading
leer to read, 4.2
la **legumbre** vegetable, 4.1; **9**
lejano(a) distant (from); far-off
lejos (de) far (from), 3.2
  a lo lejos in the distance
la **lengua** language
lentamente slowly
lento(a) slow, 11.1; **2.1;** low (heat), 10; **1**

  a fuego lento on low heat, 10; **1**
el **león** lion
les to them; to you (formal) (pron.)
la **letra** letter (of alphabet)
las **letras** literature
levantar to raise, 3.1; to clear, 4; to lift, 11.1; **2.1**
  levantar la mano to raise one's hand, 3.1
  levantar la mesa to clear the table, 4
  levantar pesas to lift weights, 11.1; **2.1**
levantarse to get up, 11.1; *2.1*
la **ley** law
la **leyenda** legend
liberar to free, to rid, 11.1; **2.1**
la **libertad** freedom
la **libra** pound (weight)
libre free, unoccupied, 4.2; *3.2*
  al aire libre outdoor, open-air
  el tiempo libre spare time, 8.1
la **librería** bookstore
la **libreta de direcciones** (e-mail) address book, 6.1
el **libro** book, 3.1
  el libro de bolsillo paperback, 3.1; **8**
la **licencia** driver's license, 9.2
el **líder** leader
el **lienzo** canvas, 7.1
la **liga** league
  las Grandes Ligas Major Leagues
ligeramente lightly
ligero(a) light
el **límite de velocidad** speed limit
el **limón** lemon
la **limonada** lemonade
los **limpiaparabrisas** windshield wipers, 6.2
limpiar to clean, *7*
limpio(a) clean, *7*
lindo(a) beautiful
la **línea** (telephone) line, 6.2; (road) line, 9.1
  línea continua solid line, 9.1
  Se nos cortó la línea. We've been cut off. (phone), 6.2
línea: en línea online, 6.1
  entrar en línea to go online, 6.1

la **línea aérea** airline, 10.1; *1.1*
lío: ¡Qué lío! What a mess!, **6.1**
la **liquidación** sale, 9.1
listo(a) ready
la **litera** bunk
la **literatura** literature, 7.2
la **llama** llama
la **llamada** (telephone) call, 6.2
  la llamada perdida (caída) dropped call (cell phone), 6.2
llamar to call, 11.2; **2.2**
llamarse to call oneself, to be called, named, 11.1; *2.1*
  Me llamo… My name is . . . , 11.1; *2.1*
el **llano** plains
la **llanta** tire, *9.2*
  la llanta de repuesto (recambio) spare tire, 9.2
la **llave** key, *7*
  la llave magnética magnetic key, *7*
la **llegada** arrival, 3.1
llegar to arrive, 4.1
llenar to fill, 9.2; **10**
lleno(a) de full of, 6.1
llevar to carry; to wear, 3.1; to take; to bear; to have
llorar to cry
llover (ue) to rain
  Llueve. It's raining., LP
lluvioso(a) rainy
lo it, him, you (formal) (pron.)
lo que what, that which
la **loción bronceadora** suntan lotion, sunblock, 7.1
loco(a) crazy
el **lodo** mud
lógico(a) logical
lograr to achieve, to get, **8**
la **loncha** slice (ham)
la **lonja** slice (ham)
el **loro** parrot
los them (m. pl.) (pron.)
el **lote** lot
las **luces** lights, 5.2; headlights, 9.2
  la fiesta de las luces festival of lights (Hanukkah), 5.2
la **lucha** battle, fight, **8**
luchar to fight, **8**
luego later, LP; then, 3.2
  ¡Hasta luego! See you later!, LP
el **lugar** place; setting, 7.2

en lugar de instead of
tener lugar to take place, **3.1**
lujoso(a) luxurious
el **lunes** Monday, LP
la **luz** light, *5.2*
la luz roja red light, *9.1*

la **madera** wood
de madera wooden, **7.1**
la **madrastra** stepmother, 2.1
la **madre** mother, 2.1
los **madrileños** citizens of Madrid
la **madrina** godmother, **3.2**
el/la **madrugador(a)** early riser, 11.1; *2.1;* **10 (Lit.)**
los **maduros** ripe bananas
el/la **maestro(a)** teacher; master
magnético(a) magnetic, *7*
magnífico(a) magnificent, splendid
Magos: los Reyes Magos the Three Wise Men, *5.2*
el **maíz** corn, 9.2
la mazorca de maíz ear of corn, **9**
mal bad
estar de mal humor to be in a bad mood, *6.1*
Hace mal tiempo. The weather is bad., LP
mal educado(a) ill-mannered, rude, *6.1*
el **malecón** boardwalk (seafront)
malentender (ie) to misunderstand, **5**
el **malentendido** misunderstanding, **5**
los **males** the evil (things), the ills
la **maleta** suitcase, 10.1; *1.1;* **6.1**
hacer la maleta to pack, 10.1; *1.1*
la **maletera** trunk *(of a car),* 10.1; *1.1*
malicioso(a) malicious
malo(a) bad, 1.2
sacar notas malas to get bad grades, 3.1
malquerer (ie) to dislike
mamá mom, mommy
mandar to send
el **mandato** command
la **mandíbula** jaw
el **mando** command, charge
la cabina de mando cockpit

manejar to drive
la **manera** manner, way
de ninguna manera in no way, by no means
manga: de manga corta (larga) short- *(long-)* sleeved, 9.1
el **maní** peanut, 8.1
la **manía** habit, obsession, **6 (Lit.)**
la **mano** hand, 3.1
el equipaje de mano carry-on luggage, 10.2; *1.2*
levantar la mano to raise one's hand, 3.1
manso(a) gentle
la **manta** blanket, *7*
el **mantel** tablecloth, *4*
mantener (ie) to maintain
mantenerse en forma to stay in shape
la **mantequilla** butter, 4.1; *7*
la **manzana** apple, 9.2; (city) block, *9.1*
mañana tomorrow, LP
¡Hasta mañana! See you tomorrow!, LP
la **mañana** morning
de la mañana A.M.
por la mañana in the morning
el **mapa** map, **6.2**
la **máquina** machine
la **maquinaría** machinery, equipment
el **mar** sea, ocean, 7.1
el mar Caribe Caribbean Sea
el **maratón** marathon, *11.1;* **2.1**
marcar to score, 5.1; to dial, *6.2*
marcar el número to dial the number, *6.2*
marcar un tanto to score a point, 5.1
la **marcha** march
en marcha working
marchar to march
marchito(a) withered, shriveled
el **marido** husband, 2.1
el **marinero** sailor
el **mariscal** marshal
los **mariscos** shellfish, seafood, *4*
marrón: de color marrón brown, 5.1
el **martes** Tuesday, LP
marzo March, LP
mas but
más more, 9.1
¡Qué... más... ! What a . . . !

la **máscara** mask, *5.1*
la máscara de oxígeno oxygen mask, 10.2; *1.2*
la **mascota** pet, 2.1
matar to kill
las **matemáticas** mathematics, math, 1.2
los **materiales escolares** school supplies, 3.1
la **matrícula universitaria** university degree, *4*
el **matrimonio** marriage, **3.1**
el **mausoleo** mausoleum, *5.1*
máximo(a) highest, top
la velocidad máxima speed limit, top speed
mayo May, LP
la **mayonesa** mayonnaise, 9.2
mayor older, 2.1
hacerse mayor to grow older
el/la **mayor** the oldest, 2.1; the greatest
la **mayoría** majority
mayoritario(a) *(related to)* majority
mazorca: la mazorca de maíz ear of corn, **9**
me me *(pron.)*
mediano(a) medium, medium-size
la **medianoche** midnight
el **medicamento** medicine, 6.2
la **medicina** medicine, 6.2
el/la **médico(a)** doctor, 6.2
la **medida** measurement
las **medidas** measures
el **medio** means; ways; middle
a término medio medium *(meat), 4*
el medio de transporte means of transport, *8.1*
medio(a) half; middle
la clase media middle class
y media half-past (the hour), LP
el **mediodía** noon
el **Medio Oriente** Middle East
medios: los medios de comunicación media, **8**
la **mejilla** cheek, *5*
los **mejillones** mussels, *4*
mejor better
el/la **mejor** the best
mejorar to make better, **5 (Lit.)**
menor younger, 2.1; lesser
el/la **menor** the youngest, 2.1; the least
la **menora** menorah, *5.2*
menos less, 9.1
a lo menos at least

Spanish-English Dictionary

menos cuarto a quarter to (the hour)

el **mensaje** message, *6.2*

   el mensaje de texto text message

   el mensaje instantáneo instant message

el/la **mensajero(a)** messenger

mentir (ie, i) to lie, **8**

la **mentira** deceit, lie

el **menú** menu, *4.2; 4*

menudo: a menudo often

el **mercado** market, *9.2*

la **mercancía** merchandise

la **merienda** snack, *4.2*

la **mermelada** jam, marmalade, *7*

el **mes** month, *LP*

la **mesa** table, *2.2; 4*

   levantar la mesa to clear the table, *4*

   poner la mesa to set the table, *4*

   quitar la mesa to clear the table, *4*

la **mesada** monthly allowance

el/la **mesero(a)** waiter (waitress), server, *4.2; 4*

la **meseta** meseta, plateau

la **mesita** table, *2.2; 4*

el **mesón** old-style bar, tavern

meter to put, to place

   meter un gol to score a goal, *5.1*

el **metro** subway, metro, *8.1;* meter

   la boca del metro subway station entrance, *8.1*

   la estación de metro subway station, *8.1*

el **metrópoli** metropolis, big city

mexicano(a) Mexican, *1.2*

la **mezcla** mixture

mi my

mí me

el **miedo** fear

   tener miedo to be afraid, *7.2*

la **miel** honey, **3 (Lit.)**

el/la **miembro(a)** member, *2.1*

mientras while, *5.2*

el **miércoles** Wednesday, *LP*

la **migración** migration

mil (one) thousand, *9.2*

el **millón** million, *9.2*

el/la **millonario(a)** millionaire

mimado(a) spoiled *(person)*

el **mimo** mime, *8.1*

la **mina** mine

el **minuto** minute

¡Mira! Look!, *3.1*

la **mirada** gaze, look

   tener la mirada fijada to keep one's eyes fixed on

mirar to look at, *3.2*

mirarse to look at oneself, *11.1; 2.1*

la **misa** mass

la **miseria** poverty

la **misión** mission

mismo(a) same, *1.2;* own; very

misterioso(a) mysterious

mixto(a) co-ed

la **mochila** backpack, knapsack, *3.1*

el/la **mochilero(a)** backpacker, hiker, *11.2; 2.2*

   viajar de mochilero to go backpacking, hiking

la **moda** fashion

los **modales** manners, *6.1; 5*

   tener buenos (malos) modales to have good (bad) manners, to be well-behaved (rude), *6.1*

moderno(a) modern

modesto(a) inexpensive

el/la **modista** fashion designer

el **modo** way

molestar to bother, to annoy, *6.1*

la **molestia** nuisance, trouble, bother

el **molino de viento** windmill

el **monasterio** monastery

la **moneda** coin, *9.1; 4*

el **mono** monkey

el **monopatín** skateboard, *11.1; 2.1*

el **monstruo** monster

la **montaña** mountain, *7.2*

   la montaña rusa roller coaster, *8.1*

montañoso(a) mountainous

montar to put up *(tent)*, *11.2; 2.2;* to ride, *8.2*

   montar a caballo to go horseback riding, *8.2*

el **montón** bunch, heap

el **monumento** monument

la **moraleja** moral

mórbido(a) morbid

morder (ue) to bite

moreno(a) dark-haired, brunette, *1.1*

morir (ue, u) to die, *4*

el **morrón** sweet red pepper

el **mostrador** (ticket) counter, *10.1; 1.1*

mostrar (ue) to show, *10.2; 1.2*

el **motivo** theme; reason, motive

el **móvil** cell phone, *3.2; 6.1*

el **movimiento** movement, *11.1; 2.1*

el **mozo** bellhop, *7;* young boy, lad, **5 (Lit.)**

el **MP3** MP3 player, *3.2; 6.2*

la **muchacha** girl, *1.1*

el **muchacho** boy, *1.1*

mucho a lot, many, much, *2.2;* very, *LP*

   Hace mucho calor (frío). It's very hot (cold)., *LP*

   Mucho gusto. Nice to meet you., *1.2*

   ¡Mucho ojo! Careful!, **5**

mudarse to move

los **muebles** furniture, *2.2*

la **muela** molar

la **muerte** death

muerto(a) dead

el/la **muerto(a)** dead person, deceased, *5.1*

   el Día de los Muertos the Day of the Dead, *5.1*

la **mujer** wife, *2.1*

la **mula** mule

las **muletas** crutches, *11.2; 2.2*

   andar con muletas to walk on crutches, *11.2; 2.2*

la **multa** fine, *9.1*

mundial: la Copa Mundial World Cup

el **mundo** world

   todo el mundo everyone

la **muñeca** wrist, *11.1; 2.1*

el **mural** mural

el/la **muralista** muralist

el **muro** wall

el **museo** museum, *8.2*

la **música** music, *1.2*

el/la **músico(a)** musician, *8.1*

musitar to murmur, whisper, **3 (Lit.)**

el **muslo** thigh, *10; 1*

muy very, *LP*

   muy bien very well, *LP*

N

nacer to be born, **3.2**

el **nacimiento** birth

nacional national

la **nacionalidad** nationality, 1.1

¿de qué nacionalidad? what nationality?, 1.1

nada nothing, not anything, 8.2

De nada. You're welcome., LP

Nada más. Nothing else., 9.2

Por nada. You're welcome., LP; for no reason

nadar to swim, 7.1

nadie nobody, not anybody, 8.2

la **nafta** gasoline

la **naranja** orange (*fruit*), 4.1

la **narrativa** narrative, 7.2

natal pertaining to where someone was born

la **naturaleza** nature

la naturaleza muerta still life, **7.1**

navegar la red (el Internet) to surf the Web (the Internet), 3.2; *6.1*

la **Navidad** Christmas, *5.2*

el árbol de Navidad Christmas tree, *5.2*

¡Feliz Navidad! Merry Christmas!

necesario: Es necesario. It's necessary., *11.2;* **2.2**

necesitar to need, 3.2

negar (ie) to deny

negativo(a) negative

el **negocio** store, business

el hombre (la mujer) de negocios businessman (woman), **10**

negro(a) black, 2.1

negroide negroid

nervioso(a) nervous, 6.1

el **neumático** tire, *9.2;* **6.2**

nevado(a) snowy, snow-covered

nevar (ie) to snow, 7.2

Nieva. It's snowing., LP

la **nevera** refrigerator, *10;* **1**

ni neither, nor

Ni idea. No idea.

nicaragüense Nicaraguan

el/la **nieto(a)** grandson, granddaughter, grandchild, 2.1

la **nieve** snow, 7.2

ninguno(a) none, not any

de ninguna manera in no way, by no means

la **niñez** childhood

el/la **niño(a)** boy, girl, child, 6.2

el **nivel** level

no no

No hay de qué. You're welcome., LP

no obstante nevertheless

la **noche** night, evening

Buenas noches. Good evening., LP

esta noche tonight, 4.1

por la noche in the evening

la **Nochebuena** Christmas Eve, *5.2*

la **Nochevieja** New Year's Eve

nombrar to name

el **nombre** name, 2.1

la **noria** Ferris wheel, *8.1*

la **norma** norm, standard

normal normal, 6.2

el **norte** north

norteamericano(a) American, North American, 1.1

nos us (*pron.*)

nosotros(as) we

la **nota** grade, mark, 3.1

sacar notas buenas (malas) to get good (bad) grades, 3.1

las **noticias** news, piece of news, **8**

el **noticiero** news report, program

el/la **noticiero(a)** newscaster, **8**

novecientos(as) nine hundred, 9.2

la **novela** novel

el/la **novelista** novelist

noventa ninety, LP

la **novia** bride, **3.1;** girlfriend **6** (Lit.)

noviembre November, LP

el **novio** groom, **3.1;** boyfriend, **6** (Lit.)

los **novios** sweethearts

la **nube** cloud, 7.1

nublado(a) cloudy, 7.1

nuestro(a) our

nueve nine, LP

nuevo(a) new, 1.1

de nuevo again

el **número** shoe size, 9.1; number, 10.1; *1.1*

el número del asiento seat number, 10.1; *1.1*

el número de teléfono telephone number, 6.2

el número del vuelo flight number, 10.1; *1.1*

¿Qué número calzas? What size shoe do you wear (take)?, 9.1

nunca never, not ever, 8.2

nupcial nuptial, wedding, **3.1**

o or

el **obituario** obituary, **3.2**

el **objetivo** objective

obligatorio(a) required, obligatory

la **obra** work; work of art

la obra abstracta abstract work (of art), **7.1**

la obra figurativa figurative work (of art), **7.1**

observar to observe, to notice

el **obstáculo** obstacle

obstinado(a) obstinate, stubborn, 6.1

occidental western

el **océano** ocean

ochenta eighty, LP

ocho eight, LP

ochocientos(as) eight hundred, 9.2

octubre October, LP

ocupado(a) occupied, 4.2; *3.2*

ocurrir to happen

la **oda** ode

el **odio** hatred

el **oeste** west

la **oficina** office, *8.1;* **9**

ofrecer to offer

la **ofrenda** offering, *5.1*

el **oído** ear, **6** (Lit.)

oír to hear, 8.1

Ojalá que... Would that . . . , I hope . . . , *11.2;* **2.2**

la **ojeada** glance, **8**

dar una ojeada to take a look at

¡Ojo! Watch out! Be careful!

¡Mucho ojo! Careful!, **5**

el **ojo** eye, 2.1

tener mucho ojo to be very careful

tener ojos azules (castaños, verdes) to have blue (brown, green) eyes, 2.1

la **ola** wave, 7.1

el **óleo** oil paint, **7.1**

olfatear to sniff, to smell, **8**

oliva: el aceite de oliva olive oil, **9**

la **olla** pot, *10;* **1**

olvidar to forget, **5** (Lit.)

once eleven, LP

la **onza** ounce

opinar to think, to have an opinion

la **opinión** opinion

oponerse to be opposed

Spanish-English Dictionary

la **oportunidad** opportunity
el/la **opresor(a)** oppressor
oprimir to press, to push *(button, key)*, 6.1
opuesto(a) opposite
la **oración** sentence
el **orden** order
la **orden** order *(restaurant)*, 4.2
el **ordenador** computer, 3.2; 6.1
ordenar to order; to arrange
el **orégano** oregano, 9
la **orfebrería** craftsmanship in precious metals
organizar to organize, to set up
el **órgano** organ
orgulloso(a) proud, 9
oriental eastern
el **origen** origin, background
originarse to come from
las **orillas** banks, shores
a orillas de on the shores of
el **oro** gold
la **orquesta** orchestra, band
la **orquídea** orchid
ortopédico(a): el/la cirujano(a) ortopédico(a) orthopedic surgeon, 11.2; 2.2
oscuro(a) dark
el **otoño** autumn, fall, LP
otorgar to give, to grant, 8
otro(a) other, another
otros(as) others
el **oxígeno** oxygen
la máscara de oxígeno oxygen mask, 10.2; 1.2
¡Oye! Listen!, 1.2

P

paceño(a) of, from La Paz
pacer to graze, 8.2
la **paciencia** patience, 6.1
paciente patient *(adj.)*, 6.1
el/la **paciente** patient, 6.2
el **padrastro** stepfather, 2.1
el **padre** father, 2.1
los **padres** parents, 2.1
el **padrino** best man, 3.1; godfather, 3.2
pagar to pay, 3.2
la **página** page
la página de inicio (inicial, frontal) home page, 6.1
el **pago** pay, wages
el **país** country

el **paisaje** landscape
la **paja** straw, 5.2
el **pájaro** bird
el **paje** page, 3.1
la **palabra** word
la palabra afine cognate
el **palacio** palace
la **palma** palm tree
la **paloma** pigeon
la **palta** avocado
el **pan** bread
el pan dulce pastry, 7
el pan rallado bread crumbs, 9
el pan tostado toast, 4.1; 7
la **panadería** bakery
el **panecillo** roll, 4.1; 7
el **panqueque** pancake
la **pantalla** screen, 6.1
la pantalla de escritorio (computer) screen, monitor, 6.1
el **pantalón** pants, 3.1
el pantalón corto shorts, 5.1
el pantalón largo long pants, 9.1
la **panza** belly
el **pañuelo** handkerchief
la **papa** potato, 4.1
las papas fritas french fries, 4.1
el **papel** paper, 3.1; role
la hoja de papel sheet of paper, 3.1
el rollo de papel higiénico roll of toilet paper, 11.2; 2.2
el **paquete** package, 9.2
par even *(numeric)*
el **par** pair, 9.1
el par de zapatos pair of shoes, 9.1
para for; in order to
el **parabrisas** windshield, 9.1
la **parada** stop, station, 3.2
la parada de autobús bus stop, 8.1
el **parador** inn
el **paraguas** umbrella
el **paraíso** paradise
parar(se) to stop, 9.1
parear to match
parecer to seem, to look like
a mi (tu, su) parecer in my (your, his) opinion
¿Qué te parece? What do you think?

parecido(a) similar
la **pareja** couple, 3.1
parentesco(a): una relación parentesca a relationship of kinship
el/la **pariente** relative, 2.1
el **parking** parking lot, 8.1
el **parque** park, 11.2; 2.2
el parque de atracciones amusement park, 8.1
parquear to park
el **parqueo** parking lot, 8.1
el **parquímetro** parking meter, 9.1
el **párrafo** paragraph
la **parrilla** grill, 10; 1
la **parte** part; place
¿De parte de quién, por favor? Who's calling, please?, 6.2
en muchas partes in many places
la mayor parte the greatest part, the most
participar to participate, to take part in
el **partido** game, 5.1
el **pasabordo** boarding pass
pasado(a) last, 7.1
el año pasado last year, 7.1
la semana pasada last week, 7.1
el **pasaje de la vida** life passage, 3
el/la **pasajero(a)** passenger, 10.1; 1.1
el **pasaporte** passport, 10.2; 1.2
pasar to pass, to go, 5.2; to spend *(time)*, 7.1; to pass *(car)*, 9.1
pasar un rato to spend some time
pasarlo bien to have a good time, to have fun, 11.2; 2.2
pasar por el control de seguridad to go through security, 10.2; 1.2
¿Qué pasa? What's going on? What's happening?
¿Qué te pasa? What's the matter (with you)?
la **Pascua (Florida)** Easter
pascual *(related to)* Easter
el **paseo** avenue, walk, 8.1
dar un paseo to take a walk
dar un paseo en bicicleta to take a (bike) ride

el **pasillo** aisle, 10.2; *1.2;* **6.1**

la **pasta dentífrica** toothpaste

el **pastel** cake, 8.1; **3.2**

la **pastilla** bar *(soap)*

los **patacones** slices of fried plantain

patada: dar una patada to stamp

la **patata** potato, 4.1

las patatas fritas french fries, 4.1

el **patín** ice skate, 7.2

el/la **patinador(a)** ice-skater, 7.2

el **patinaje** skating, 7.2; *11.1;* **2.1**

el patinaje en línea in-line skating, *11.1;* **2.1**

el patinaje sobre hielo ice-skating, 7.2

patinar to skate, to go skating, 7.2; *11.1;* **2.1**

patinar en línea to go in-line skating, *11.1;* **2.1**

patinar sobre el hielo to ice-skate, 7.2

la **patria** country, fatherland

patrón patron, 5.1

el/la santo(a) patrón(ona) patron saint, 5.1

patronal pertaining to a patron saint, 5.1

pausado(a) slow, deliberate

pavimentado(a) paved

el **pavimento** pavement

el **peaje** toll, *9.1*

la cabina (garita) de peaje tollbooth, *9.1*

el/la **peatón(ona)** pedestrian, *8.1*

peatonal *(related to)* pedestrians, *8.1*

el **pecho** chest, *11.1;* **2.1**

la **pechuga (de pollo)** (chicken) breast, *10;* **1**

el **pedacito** little piece, *10;* **1**

pedalear to pedal

el **pedazo** piece

pedir (i, i) to ask for, to request, 4

peinarse to comb one's hair, *11.1;* **2.1**

el **peine** comb, *11.2;* **2.2**

pelar to peel, *10;* **1**

la **película** movie, film, 8.2

el **peligro** danger

peligroso(a) dangerous

pelirrojo(a) redheaded, 1.1

el **pelo** hair, 2.1

tener el pelo rubio (castaño, negro) to have blond (brown, black) hair, 2.1

la **pelota** ball *(baseball, tennis),* 5.2

la pelota vasca jai alai

la **peluquería** hair salon, 4

el/la **peluquero(a)** hair stylist, 4

la **pena** pain, sorrow; pity

¡Qué pena! What a shame!, 5.1

pendiente steep

el **pendiente** incline

el **pensamiento** thought

pensar (ie) to think, 5.1

pensar en to think about

¿Qué piensas? What do you think?, 5.1

el **peón** peasant, farm laborer, 8.2

peor worse

el/la **peor** worst

el **pepino** cucumber, *10;* **1**

pequeño(a) small, little, 1.2

la **percha** hanger, 7

percibir to perceive

perder (ie) to lose, 5.1; to miss, 8.1

perder el vuelo to miss the flight, **6.1**

perdida: la llamada perdida dropped call *(cell phone),* 6.2

la **pérdida** loss

perdón pardon me, excuse me

perdurar to last, to endure

la **peregrinación** pilgrimage

perezoso(a) lazy, 1.2

el **periódico** newspaper, *3.1;* **8**

el/la **periodista** journalist, **8**

permanecer to remain

permiso: Con permiso. Excuse me., 10.1; *1.1*

el **permiso de conducir** driver's license, 9.2

permitir to permit

pero but

el/la **perro(a)** dog, 2.1

la **persona** person

el **personaje** character *(in a novel, play),* **7.2**

la **personalidad** personality, 6.1

la **perspectiva** perspective, **7.1**

pertenecer to belong

peruano(a) Peruvian

la **pesa** weight, *11.1;* **2.1**

levantar pesas to lift weights, *11.1;* **2.1**

pesar to weigh, **6.1**

a pesar de in spite of

la **pescadería** fish market

el **pescado** fish, 4.1

pescar to fish

el **peso** peso *(monetary unit of several Latin American countries);* weight, **6.1**

picada: la carne picada ground meat, **9**

el **picadillo** ground meat, **9**

picar to nibble on; to chop; to mince, *10;* **1**

picaresco(a) picaresque

el/la **pícher** pitcher, 5.2

el **pico** mountain top, peak, 7.2

el **pie** foot, 5.1; *2.1*

a pie on foot, 3.2

de pie standing

piedad: sin piedad mercilessly

la **piedra** stone

la **pierna** leg, 11.1; *2.1*

la **pieza** bedroom; piece; part

la **pila** swimming pool; baptismal font, **3.2**

el **pimentón** pepper *(vegetable)*

la **pimienta** pepper *(spice),* 4

el **pimiento** bell pepper, 9.2; *10;* **1**

el **pin** PIN

el **pincel** paintbrush, **3 (Lit.)**

el **pinchazo** flat tire, *9.2*

los **pinchitos** kebabs, 4.2

pintado(a) painted

pintar to paint, **7.1**

el/la **pintor(a)** painter, artist, 8.2; **7.1**

pintoresco(a) picturesque, **7.1**

la **pintura** paint, **7.1**

las **pinzas** tongs

la **piña** pineapple, 9.2

la **piscina** swimming pool, 7.1

el **piso** floor, 2.2; apartment *(Spain)*

la **pista** ski slope, 7.2; runway, 10.2; *1.2;* lane *(highway)*

la pista de patinaje ice-skating rink, 7.2

la **pizca** pinch

la **pizza** pizza, 4.1

placentero(a) pleasant

el **plan** structure, layout

la **plancha de vela** windsurfing; sailboard, 7.1

practicar la plancha de vela to windsurf, to go windsurfing, 7.1

planchar to iron, 4

planchas: hacer planchas to do push-ups, *11.1;* **2.1**

planear to plan

el **planeta** planet

plano: el primer plano foreground, **7.1**

el **plano** map, *9.1*

plano(a) flat, **7.1**

la **planta** plant, 2.2

la **plata** silver

Spanish-English Dictionary

el **plátano** banana, 9.2
el **platillo** home plate, 5.2; saucer, 4
el **plato** dish (food); plate, 4; course (meal)
la **playa** beach, 7.1
la **plaza** square, plaza, 8.1; seat (train, plane), 3.2; **6.1**
el/la **plomero(a)** plumber, **10**
la **pluma** (fountain) pen
la **población** population
pobre poor
el/la **pobre** poor boy (girl)
poco(a) a little; few, 2.2
   dentro de poco soon; shortly thereafter
   un poco más a little more
poder (ue) to be able, 5.1
el **poema** poem, **7.2**
la **poesía** poetry, poem, **7.2**
el/la **poeta** poet, **7.2**
el/la **policía** police officer
policíacas: novelas policíacas mysteries, detective fiction
el/la **político(a)** politician, **10**
la **póliza** policy, **6.2**
el **pollo** chicken, 4.1; 10; 1
polvoriente dusty
poner to put, to place, to set, 10.2; 1.2; to make (someone something)
   poner al fuego to heat, 10; 1
   poner la mesa to set the table, 4
   poner unos puntos (unas suturas) to give (someone) stitches, 11.2; **2.2**
ponerse to put on (clothes), 11.1; 2.1; to become, to turn
   ponerse de pie to stand up, 5
   ponerse en marcha to start moving
popular popular
por for, by
   por ejemplo for example
   por encima de over, 5.2
   por eso that's why, for this reason
   por favor please, LP
   por fin finally
   por hora per hour
   por la mañana in the morning
   por la noche at night, in the evening
   por la tarde in the afternoon

por lo general in general
Por nada. You're welcome., LP; for no reason
¿por qué? why?, 3.2
¡Por supuesto! Of course!
los **porotos** green beans
porque because, 3.2
el/la **porrista** cheerleader
portátil: la computadora portátil laptop computer
el/la **porteño(a)** person from Buenos Aires
la **portería** goal line, 5.1
el/la **portero(a)** goalie, 5.1
portugués(esa) Portuguese
poseer to possess
posible possible
positivo(a) positive
el **postre** dessert, 4.1
practicar to practice (sport)
   practicar la plancha de vela (la tabla hawaiana) to go windsurfing (surfing), 7.1
   practicar yoga to do yoga, 11.1; **2.1**
el **precio** price, 9.1
precolombino(a) pre-Columbian
la **preferencia** preference
preferir (ie, i) to prefer, 5.2; 4
el **prefijo del país** country code, 6.2
la **pregunta** question, 3.1
preguntar to ask (a question)
el **premio** prize, award
prender to turn on, 6.1
la **prensa** press, 8
preparar to prepare; to get ready
la **prepa(ratoria)** high school
presenciar to witness, to attend
presentar to introduce
los **presentes** those present, the attendees
el **préstamo** loan, **4**
   el préstamo a corto (largo) plaza short- (long-) term loan, 4
prestar: prestar atención to pay attention, 3.1
presumir to predict
el **pretendiente** suitor
primario(a): la escuela primaria elementary school
la **primavera** spring, LP
primero(a) first, LP

el primer plano foreground, **7.1**
el primero de enero (febrero, etc.) January (February, etc.) 1, LP
en primera clase first class, 3.2
el/la **primo(a)** cousin, 2.1
la **princesa** princess
principal main
el/la **principiante** beginner, 7.2
prisa: de prisa fast, hurriedly
   a toda prisa with full speed
privado(a) private, 2.2
probable probable, likely
probarse (ue) to try on
el **problema** problem
   No hay problema. No problem.
procedente de coming, arriving from, 10.2; 1.2
el **procedimiento** step (recipe)
la **procesión** procession, parade, 5.1
producir to produce
el **producto** product; food, 9.2
   los productos congelados frozen food, 9.2
la **profesión** profession, occupation, **10**
profesional professional
el/la **profesor(a)** teacher, 1.2
profundo(a) deep
el **programa de televisión** television program, **8**
el/la **programador(a) de computadoras** computer programmer, **10**
prohibido(a) forbidden, 9.1
prometer to promise
la **promoción** (sales) promotion, **8**
el **pronombre** pronoun
pronto: ¡Hasta pronto! See you soon!, LP
la **propaganda** advertising, **8**
propenso(a) prone to
la **propina** tip (restaurant), 4
propio(a) own, 5.1
propósito: ¡A propósito! By the way . . . , 8.2
   propósito benévelo charitable purpose
la **prosa** prose, **7.2**
el/la **protagonista** protagonist, **7.2**
protectora: la loción protectora sunblock
el **provecho** benefit, **5** (Lit.)
próximo(a) next, 3.2

la **prueba** test, exam, 3.1
publicar to publish
la **publicidad** advertising, **8**
el **público** audience
el **pueblo** town
el **puente** bridge
la **puerta** gate *(airport)*, 10.2; *1.2*; door, *9.2*
   la puerta de salida gate *(airport)*, 10.2; *1.2*; **6.1**
   la puerta delantera (trasera) front (back) door (bus)
el **puerto** port
puertorriqueño(a) Puerto Rican, 1.1
pues well
el **puesto** market stall, 9.2; position, **10**
puesto que since
los **pulmones** lungs
pulsar to press *(button, key)*, *6.1*
la **pulsera** bracelet
el **pulso: tomar el pulso** to take (someone's) pulse, *6.2*
la **punta de los dedos** fingertips
el **punto** point; dot *(Internet)*, *6.1*; stitch, *11.2*; **2.2**
   poner puntos (a alguien) to give (somebody) stitches, *11.2*; **2.2**
puntual punctual
el **puñado** handful, **4 (Lit.)**
el **pupitre** desk, 3.1

Q

que that; who
¿qué? what? how?, LP
   ¿a qué hora? at what time?, LP
   ¿de qué nacionalidad? what nationality?
   No hay de qué. You're welcome., LP
   ¿Qué desean tomar? What would you like (to eat)?, 4.2
   ¿Qué día es hoy? What day is it today?, LP
   ¿Qué hay? What's new (up)?
   ¿Qué hora es? What time is it?, LP
   ¡Qué lío! What a mess!, **6.1**
   ¿Qué… más… ! What a . . . !
   ¿Qué pasa? What's going on? What's happening?, 3.1
   ¡Qué pena! What a shame!, 5.1

¿Qué tal? How are things? How are you?, LP
¿Qué tal le gustó? How did you like it? *(formal)*
¿Qué tiempo hace? What's the weather like?, LP
quebrarse (ie) to break, *11.2*; **2.2**
quedar (bien) to fit, to look good on, 9.1
   Esta chaqueta no te queda bien. This jacket doesn't fit you., 9.1
quedar(se) to remain, to stay, *11.1*; **2.1**
quemarse to burn, *10*; **1**
querer (ie) to want, to wish, 5.1; to love
querido(a) dear, beloved
el **queso** cheese, 4.1
   el sándwich de jamón y queso ham and cheese sandwich, 4.1
el **quetzal** quetzal *(currency of Guatemala)*
¿quién? who?, 1.1
   ¿De parte de quién, por favor? Who's calling, please?, *6.2*
¿quiénes? who? *(pl.)*, 1.2
quince fifteen, LP
la **quinceañera** fifteen-year-old girl
quinientos(as) five hundred, 9.2
el **quiosco** kiosk, newsstand, *3.1*
quisiera I'd like
quitar la mesa to clear the table, *4*
quitarse to take off *(clothes)*, *11.1*; **2.1**
quizá(s) maybe, perhaps, 7.2

R

el **racimo** bunch *(grapes)*
el/la **radio** radio
la **radiografía** X ray, *11.2*; **2.2**
   Le toman (hacen) una radiografía. They're taking an X ray of him (her)., *11.2*; **2.2**
la **raja** slice *(melon)*
la **rama** branch
el **rancho** ranch, *8.2*
la **ranura** slot, *6.2*
rápidamente quickly
rápido(a) fast
la **raqueta** *(tennis)* racket, 5.2
raro(a) rare
el **rascacielos** skyscraper, *8.1*
el **rato** time, while

   pasar un rato to spend some time
el **ratón** mouse, *6.1*
rayas: a rayas striped
el **rayón** scratch, **6.2**
la **raza** breed
la **razón** reason
   tener razón to be right
el/la **realista** realist
realista royalist
realizarse to happen, to come to pass
rebajar to lower *(prices)*, 9.1
la **rebanada** slice *(bread)*, *10*; **1**
   cortar en rebanadas to slice, *10*; **1**
rebasar to pass *(car)*, 9.1
rebozar to coat (with batter), **9**
la **recámara** bedroom, 2.2
recambio: la rueda (llanta) de recambio spare tire, *9.2*
la **recepción** front desk *(hotel)*, *7*; reception, *3.1*
el/la **recepcionista** hotel clerk, *7*
el/la **receptor(a)** catcher, 5.2
la **receta** prescription, *6.2*; recipe, *10*; **1**
recetar to prescribe, *6.2*
recibir to receive, 4.1; to catch
   recibir aplausos to be applauded, 5.1
recién recently, newly
   los recién casados newlyweds, *3.1*
   el/la recién llegado(a) person who has just arrived, **5**
   el/la recién nacido(a) newborn, *3.2*
reciente recent
reclamar to claim, *6.1*
el **reclamo de equipaje** baggage claim, *6.1*
recoger to collect, to gather, pick up *6.1*
recomendar (ie) to recommend
reconocer to recognize
recordar (ue) to remember
el **recorrido** trip, route
   el tren de largo recorrido long-distance train, *6.2*
el **recorte** trim, **4**
los **recuerdos** memories
recuperar to claim, to get back
la **red** the Web, *3.2*; *6.1*; net, 5.2
   navegar la red to surf the Web, *3.2*; *6.1*
   pasar por encima de la red to go over the net, 5.2
reducido(a) reduced

Spanish-English Dictionary

reducir to reduce; to set *(bone)*, 11.2; **2.2**
  reducir la velocidad to reduce speed, 9.1
reemplazar to replace
refacción: la rueda (llanta) de refacción spare tire
reflejar to reflect
reflexionar to think about, to reflect on
el **refresco** soft drink, 4.2
el **refrigerador** refrigerator, 10; **1**
refrito(a) refried
el **refugio** refuge
el **regalo** gift, present, 8.1; **3.1**
regatear to bargain, 9.2
el **régimen** diet
la **región** region
el **registro de matrimonio** wedding register, **3.1**
la **regla** rule
regresar to go back, to return, 3.2
  el botón regresar back button, back key, 6.1
  regresar a casa to go home, 3.2
regreso: el boleto de ida y regreso round-trip ticket, 3.1
regular regular, average
la **reina** queen
reinar to rule, reign; to prevail
reír (i, i) to laugh
relacionado(a) related
relacionar to relate, to connect
relacionarse to mix with, to have contact with
relevos: la carrera de relevos relay race, 11.1; **2.1**
religioso(a) religious
rellenar to fill, to put filling in, 9
el **reloj** watch, **6 (Lit.)**
el **rencor** resentment
rendir (i, i) honor to honor
renombrado(a) famous
rentar to rent, 7.1; *3.2*; **6.2**
repartido(a) distributed, split up among
repasar to review
el **repaso** review
repente: de repente suddenly, all of a sudden
repetir (i, i) to repeat, *4;* to have seconds *(meal), 4*
el **repollo** cabbage, **9**

el **reportaje** report, **8**
la **república** republic
  la República Dominicana Dominican Republic
repuesto: la rueda (llanta) de repuesto spare tire, 9.2
requerir (ie, i) to require
la **reserva** reservation
la **reservación** reservation, 7
reservar to reserve, 7
resfriado(a) stuffed up *(cold),* 6.2
el **resorte** spring (mechanical)
respetado(a) respected
respetar to respect
respetuoso(a) respectful
la **respiración** breathing, *11.1;* **2.1**
respirar to breathe
responsable responsible
la **respuesta** answer
el **restaurante** restaurant, *4*
resuelto(a) resolute, determined
resultar to turn out to be
resumirse to be summed up
retirar to withdraw, *4*
el **retraso** delay, 10.2; *1.2*
  con retraso late, 10.2; *1.2*
el **retrato** portrait
retroceder: el botón retrodecer back button, back key, 6.1
el **retrovisor** rearview mirror, **6.2**
la **reunión** meeting, get-together
reunirse to meet, to get together
revisar to check *(ticket),* 3.2
el/la **revisor(a)** conductor, 3.2
la **revista** magazine, *3.1;* **8**
revolver (ue) to stir, *10;* **1**
revueltos: los huevos revueltos scrambled eggs, 7
el **rey** king
  el Día de los Reyes Epiphany (January 6), 5.2
  los Reyes Magos the Three Wise Men, 5.2
rico(a) rich; delicious
  ¡Qué rico! How delicious!
rígido(a) stiff
la **rima** rhyme, **7.2**
el **rincón** corner
los **riñones** kidneys
el **río** river
el **risco** cliff, *3.2*

el **ritmo** rhythm
el **rito** rite
robar to steal
la **roca** rock, stone
el **rocín** donkey; nag
la **rodaja** slice *(lemon, cucumber);* **9**
rodar (ue) to roll
rodeado(a) surrounded
rodear con los brazos to put one's arms around
la **rodilla** knee, 11.1; **2.1**
la **rodillera** kneepad, *11.1;* **2.1**
rogar (ue) to beg
rojo(a) red, 5.1
  la luz roja red light, *9.1*
el **rol** role
el **rollo de papel higiénico** roll of toilet paper, 11.2; *2.2*
el **rompecabezas** puzzle
romperse to break, 11.2; **2.2**
  Se rompió la pierna. He (She) broke his (her) leg., *11.2;* **2.2**
la **ropa** clothing, 9.1
  la ropa para lavar dirty clothes, **4**
  la ropa sucia dirty clothes, **4**
la **ropaje** wardrobe
la **rosa** rose
rosado(a) pink, 5.1
roto(a) broken
el **rótulo** sign, *9.1*
rubio(a) blonde, 1.1
la **rueda** tire, 9.2
  la rueda de repuesto (recambio) spare tire, 9.2
  la silla de ruedas wheelchair, 11.2; **2.2**
el **ruido** noise
las **ruinas** ruins
la **ruta** route
la **rutina diaria** daily routine, 11.1; *2.1*

S

el **sábado** Saturday, LP
la **sábana** sheet, *7*
saber to know, 9.1
sabio(a) wise, **5 (Lit.)**
el **sabor** flavor, *10;* **1;** taste
sacar to get, 3.1; to take, 7.1
  sacar fotos to take pictures, 7.1

sacar notas buenas (malas) to get good (bad) grades, 3.1

el **sacerdote** priest, **8**

el **saco de dormir** sleeping bag, 11.2; *2.2*

el **sacrificio** sacrifice

la **sal** salt, *4*

la **sala** living room, 2.2

   la sala de clase classroom, 3.1

   la sala de emergencia emergency room, *11.2;* **2.2**

   la sala de espera waiting room, *3.1*

   salado(a) salty

el **saldo** sale, 9.1; (bank) balance, **4**

la **salida** departure, 10.1; *1.1;* exit, *9.1*

   la hora de salida time of departure, 10.1; *1.1*

   la puerta de salida gate *(airport),* 10.2; *1.2*

   salir to leave; to go out, 8.1; to turn out, to result

   Todo te sale más barato. Everything costs a lot less.; It's all a lot less expensive., 9.1

el **salón** room *(museum),* 8.2

la **salsa** sauce, gravy, *10;* **1;** dressing

   saltar to jump (over)

   salteado(a) sautéed

la **salud** health, 6.1

   saludar to greet, **5**

el **saludo** greeting, LP

   salvar to save

la **sandalia** sandal, 9.2

el **sándwich** sandwich, 4.1

   el sándwich de jamón y queso ham and cheese sandwich, 4.1

la **sangre** blood

   sano(a) healthy

el/la **santo(a)** saint

   el/la santo patrón(ona) patron saint, *5.1*

el **sarape** blanket

el/la **sartén** skillet, frying pan, *10;* **1**

   satisfacer to satisfy

el **sato** a type of dog from Puerto Rico

   sea: o sea or, in other words

la **secadora** dryer, **4**

   secarse to dry oneself

   seco(a) dry

   secundario(a): la escuela secundaria high school, 1.2

la **sed** thirst, 4.1

   tener sed to be thirsty, 4.1

---

el **sedán** sedan, *9.2*

   seguir (i, i) to follow, *4;* to continue, *9.1*

   según according to

   segundo(a) second

   en segunda clase second class *(ticket),* 3.1

   el segundo tiempo second half *(soccer),* 5.1

   seguramente surely, certainly

la **seguridad: el control de seguridad** security *(airport),* 10.2; *1.2*

   el cinturón de seguridad seat belt, 10.2; *1.2*

   seguro que certainly

   seguro(a) sure; safe

los **seguros contra todo riesgo** comprehensive insurance, **6.2**

   seis six, LP

   seiscientos(as) six hundred, *9.2*

   seleccionar to choose, *3.1*

el **sello** stamp, **4**

la **selva** jungle, forest

el **semáforo** traffic light, *8.1*

la **semana** week, LP; weekly allowance

   el fin de semana weekend, 7.1

   la semana pasada last week, 7.1

   sembrar (ie) to plant, to sow, *8.2*

   seminómada seminomad

el/la **senador(a)** senator, **10**

   sencillo(a) one-way, *3.1;* single *(hotel room),* 7; simple

   el billete (boleto) sencillo one-way ticket, *3.1*

   el cuarto sencillo single room, *7*

la **senda** path, *3.2*

   sentado(a) seated

   sentarse (ie) to sit down, 11.1; *2.1*

el **sentido** direction, *9.1;* sense, 6.1

   la calle de sentido único one-way street, *9.1*

   sentir (ie, i) to be sorry; to feel

   Lo siento mucho. I'm very sorry.

   sentirse (ie, i) to feel

la **señal** sign, 10.2; *1.2*

   la señal de no fumar no-smoking sign, 10.2; *1.2*

   señalar to point out

el **señor** sir, Mr., gentleman, LP

la **señora** Ms., Mrs., madam, LP

los **señores** Mr. and Mrs.

---

la **señorita** Miss, Ms., LP

el **sepelio** burial, **3.2**

   septiembre September, LP

   ser to be

el **ser** being

   los seres humanos human beings

   los seres vivientes living beings

   serio(a) serious, 1.1

   ¿Hablas en serio? Are you serious?

el **servicio** tip, 4.2; restroom, 10.2; *1.2;* service, *9.2*

   ¿Está incluido el servicio? Is the tip included?, 4.2

   la estación de servicio gas station, service station, *9.2*

la **servilleta** napkin, *4*

   servir (i, i) to serve, *4*

   servir de to serve as

   servirse (i, i) de to use

   sesenta sixty, LP

   setecientos(as) seven hundred, *9.2*

   setenta seventy, LP

   severo(a) harsh, strict

   si if

   sí yes, LP

   siempre always, 8.2

   siento: Lo siento mucho. I'm sorry. (That's too bad.), 5.1

la **sierra** mountain range

el/la **siervo(a)** slave, serf

la **siesta** nap

   siete seven, LP

el **siglo** century

el **significado** meaning

   significar to mean

   siguiente following

la **silla** chair, 2.2

   la silla de ruedas wheelchair, *11.2;* **2.2**

el **sillón** armchair

   similar similar

   simpático(a) nice, 1.1

   simpatizar con to sympathize with

   sin without

   sincero(a) sincere

   sino but rather

el **síntoma** symptom

el **sistema** system

el **sitio** space *(parking)*

el **sitio Web** Web site, *6.1*

el/la **snowboarder** snowboarder, 7.2

las **sobras** leftovers

   sobre on, on top of; about

   sobre todo above all, especially

el **sobre** envelope, **4**

Spanish-English Dictionary

la **sobremesa** dessert; after-dinner conversation

sobrepasar to surpass, **8**

la **sobrepoblación** overpopulation

sobrevivir to survive

sobrevolar (ue) to fly over

el/la **sobrino(a)** nephew, niece, 2.1

social social

    los estudios sociales social studies, 1.2

la **sociedad** society; company, corporation, **10**

el/la **socio(a)** member, partner

socorrer to help

el/la **socorrista** paramedic, 11.2; **2.2**

el **sofá** sofa, 2.2

el **sol** sun, 7.1

    Hace (Hay) sol. It's sunny., LP

    tomar el sol to sunbathe, 7.1

solamente only

solar: la crema solar suntan lotion, 7.1

solas: a solas alone

el **soldado** soldier, 8

soler (ue) to be used to, to do something usually

solicitar to apply for

la **solicitud de empleo** job application, **10**

solo only

solo(a) single; alone; lonely

soltar to release

el/la **soltero(a)** single, unmarried person

el **sombrero** hat

el **son** sound

sonar (ue) to ring, *6.1*

soñar to dream

el **sonido** sound

la **sonrisa** smile, 6.1

la **sopa** soup

soplar to blow *(wind)*

sordo(a) deaf, **10 (Lit.)**

sorprender to surprise, **3.1**

la **sorpresa** surprise, 4.1

sospechas: tener sospechas to be suspicious

sostener (ie) to support; to hold up

su his, her, their, your *(formal)*

suavemente softly

subir to go up, 7.2; to get on *(train, etc.),* 3.1

el **subsuelo** subsoil

subterráneo(a) underground

los **suburbios** suburbs, 2.2; **6.2**

suceder to happen, **5 (Lit.)**

el **suceso** event

sucio(a) dirty, 7

Sudamérica South America

sudamericano(a) South American

el **suegro** father-in-law

suele(n): *see* **soler**

el **suelo** ground, floor

el **suelto** change, **4**

el **sueño** dream

    tener sueño to be sleepy

la **suerte** luck

    ¡Buena suerte! Good luck!

    ¡Qué suerte tengo! How lucky I am!, 9.1

el **suéter** sweater, 11.1; *2.1*

sufrir to suffer

sugerir (ie, i) to suggest

sujetar to subject, to subdue, **4 (Lit.)**

sumergir to submerge, to immerse

sumiso(a) submissive, docile

la **superficie** surface, **7.1**

superior upper, top

    el compartimiento superior overhead bin *(airplane),* 10.2; *1.2*

el **supermercado** supermarket, 9.2

el **supiro** breath

el **sur** south

    la América del Sur South America

el **surfing** surfing, 7.1

surgir to come up with, to arise

el **surtido** assortment

sus their, your *(pl.)*

sustituir to substitute for

el **susto** fear

la **sutura** stitch, 11.2; **2.2**

suturar to give (someone) stitches

el **SUV** SUV, *9.2*

T

el **tabaquero** cigar maker

la **tabla** chart, table

la **tabla hawaiana** surfboard, 7.1

    practicar la tabla hawaiana to surf, to go surfing, 7.1

tacaño(a) stingy, cheap, *9.1*

el **taco** taco

la **tajada** slice *(ham, meat),* 9.2

tal such

    ¿Qué tal? How are things? How are you?, LP

    ¿Qué tal tu clase de español? How's your Spanish class?

    tal como such as

tal vez maybe, perhaps, 7.2

el **talento** talent, 7.2

la **talla** size, 9.1

    ¿Qué talla usas? What size do you take?, 9.1

tallar to carve, **7.1**

el **taller** workshop, **7.1**

el **talón** heel (of a shoe); luggage claim ticket, **6.1**

el **tamaño** size

también also, too, 1.2

el **tambor** drum

el **tamborín** small drum

tampoco either, neither

tan so

    tan… como as . . . as

    tan pronto como as soon as

el **tanque** gas tank, *9.2*; **6.2**

el **tanto** score, point, 5.1; clue, picture

    marcar un tanto to score a point, 5.1

tanto(a) so much

    tanto(a)… como as much . . . as

    tantos(as)… como as many . . . as

la **tapa** lid, *10;* **1**

tapar to cover *(pot)*

las **tapas** snacks, nibbles, 4.2

el **tapón** traffic jam

la **taquilla** box office, ticket window, 8.2

tardar: no tardar en not to take long (to do something)

tarde late, 10.2; *1.2*

la **tarde** afternoon

    ayer por la tarde yesterday afternoon, 7.1

    Buenas tardes. Good afternoon., LP

la **tarea** homework; task

la **tarifa** fare, *3.1*; price, **6.2**

la **tarjeta** card; pass

    la tarjeta de abordar boarding pass

    la tarjeta de crédito credit card, *3.1*

    la tarjeta de embarque boarding pass, 10.1; *1.1*

la **tarjeta postal** postcard, **4**
la **tarjeta telefónica** telephone card, *6.2*
la **tarta** cake, 8.1; ***3.2***
la **tasa de interés** interest rate, **4**
el **taxi** taxi, 10.1; *1.1*
el/la **taxista** taxi driver, 10.1; *1.1*
la **taza** cup, 4.1; *4*
te you *(fam. pron.)*
el **té** tea
el **teclado** keyboard, *6.1*
el/la **técnico(a)** technician
la **tecnología** technology
tejano(a) Texan
los **tejidos** fabrics, 9.2
la **tele** TV
telefónico(a) *(related to)* phone, *6.2*
la **guía telefónica** phone book, *6.2*
la **tarjeta telefónica** phone card, *6.2*
el **teléfono** telephone
hablar por teléfono to speak on the phone
el **número de teléfono** phone number, *6.2*
el **teléfono celular** cell phone, *6.1*
el **teléfono público** pay phone, *6.2*
la **telenovela** serial, soap opera
el **telesilla** chairlift, ski lift, 7.2
el **telesquí** ski lift, 7.2
la **televisión** television
el **tema** theme
temblar (ie) to tremble, to shake
tembloroso(a) trembling
la **temperatura** temperature, 7.2
temprano(a) early, 11.1; *1.2*
el **tenderete** market stall, 9.2
el **tenedor** fork, *4*
tener (ie) to have, 2.1
tener... años to be . . . years old, 2.1
tener calor (frío) to be hot (cold), 11.1; *2.1*
tener catarro to have a cold, 6.2
tener cuidado to be careful, *9.1*
tener dolor de... to have a(n) . . . -ache, 6.2
tener el pelo rubio (castaño, negro) to have blond (brown, black) hair, 2.1
tener éxito to be successful, 6.1
tener fiebre to have a fever, 6.2
tener ganas de to feel like

tener hambre to be hungry, 4.1
tener lugar to take place
tener miedo to be afraid, 7.2
tener ojos azules (castaños, verdes) to have blue (brown, green) eyes, 2.1
tener que to have to (do something), 4.1
tener sed to be thirsty, 4.1
el/la **teniente** deputy mayor
el **tenis** tennis, 5.2
la **cancha de tenis** tennis court, 5.2
jugar (al) tenis to play tennis, 5.2
los **tenis** sneakers, tennis shoes, 9.1
el/la **tenista** tennis player
la **tensión** tension, stress, 11.1; *2.1*
la **tensión arterial** blood pressure, 6.2
tercer(o)(a) third
terco(a) stubborn, 6.1
terminar to end, to finish
término: a término medio medium *(meat), 4*
el **término** term
la **ternera** veal, *10; 1*
el **escalope de ternera** veal cutlet, *10; 1*
la **ternura** tenderness
el/la **terrateniente** landowner
la **terraza** terrace, balcony
el **terremoto** earthquake
el **tesoro** treasure
ti you
tibio(a) lukewarm
el **ticket** ticket, 7.2
el **tiempo** weather, LP; half *(soccer),* 5.1
a tiempo on time, 10.2; *1.2*
a tiempo completo full-time, **10**
a tiempo parcial part-time, **10**
Hace buen (mal) tiempo. The weather is nice (bad)., LP
¿Qué tiempo hace? What's the weather like?, LP
el **segundo tiempo** second half *(soccer),* 5.1
la **tienda** store, 3.2
la **tienda de ropa** clothing store, 9.1
la **tienda de campaña** tent, 11.2; *2.2*
tierno(a) tender; affectionate
la **tierra** land, 8.2
el **tigre** tiger

los **timbales** small drums, kettledrums
el **timbre (sonoro)** ringtone, *6.2*
tímido(a) shy
el/la **tío(a)** uncle, aunt, 2.1
los **tíos** aunt and uncle, 2.1
el **tiovivo** merry-go-round, *8.1*
típico(a) typical
el **tipo** type, 6.1
el **tiquete** ticket, *9.1*
tirar to throw, 5.2
el **titular** headline, **8**
el **título** title; degree
la **toalla** towel, 7.1; *7*
el **tobillo** ankle, *11.1; **2.1***
el **tocadiscos** record player
tocar to touch, 5.1; to play *(musical instrument),* 8.1; *5.2*
¡Te toca a ti! It's your turn!
el **tocino** bacon, 4.1; *7*
todavía still; yet
todo(a) everything; all
sobre todo above all, especially
todo el mundo everyone, *5.2*
todos(as) everyone, 8.1; everything; all
en todas partes everywhere
tomar to take, 3.1; to have *(meal),* 4.1
tomar el almuerzo (el desayuno) to have lunch (breakfast), 4.1
tomar el bus to take the bus
tomar el pulso a alguien to take someone's pulse, 6.2
tomar el sol to sunbathe, 7.1
tomar en cuenta to take into account, **8**
tomar fotos to take pictures, 7.1
tomar la tensión arterial a alguien to take someone's blood pressure, 6.2
tomar un examen to take a test, 3.1
tomar una ducha to take a shower, 11.1; *2.1*
tomar una radiografía to take an X ray of someone, *11.2; **2.2***
el **tomate** tomato, 4.1
la **tonelada** ton
el **tono** dial tone, *6.2*
tontería: ¡Qué tontería! How silly! What nonsense!
las **tonterías** foolish things
tonto(a) foolish, crazy
torcerse (ue) to sprain, to twist, *11.2; **2.2***

Spanish-English Dictionary

Se torció el tobillo. He (She) sprained his (her) ankle., *11.2;* **2.2**

torcido(a) sprained, twisted

la **torre** tower

la **torta** cake, 4.1; **3.2;** sandwich

la **tortilla** tortilla

la **tos** cough, 6.2

tener tos to have a cough, 6.2

toser to cough, 6.2

la **tostada** tostada

las **tostadas** toast, 4.1

tostado(a) toasted

el pan tostado toast, 4.1; *7*

los **tostones** slices of fried plantain, 4.2

trabajar to work, 3.2; *8.2*

el **trabajo** work, **10**

tradicional traditional

traer to carry, to bring, to take, 10.1; *1.1*

el **tráfico** traffic, *8.1*

el **traje** suit

el **traje de baño** swimsuit, 7.1

el **traje de novia** wedding dress, **3.1**

tranquilo(a) calm, 6.1

transbordar to transfer *(trains), 3.2;* **6.2**

la **transmisión manual** manual transmission, **6.2**

el **tránsito** traffic

transporte: los medios de transporte means of transportation, *8.2*

tras behind

trasero(a) back, **7.1**

trasladar to move (something), to transfer

el **tratamiento** treatment

tratar to treat

tratar de to try to (do something)

tratar de desviar to try to dissuade

través: a través de through; over

la **travesía** crossing

traviesa: a campo traviesa cross-country *(race), 11.1;* **2.1**

el **trayecto** stretch (of road)

trece thirteen, LP

el **trecho** stretch *(distance)*

treinta thirty, LP

treinta y uno thirty-one, LP

el **tren** train, *3.1;* **6.2**

el tren de cercanías suburban train, **6.2**

el tren de largo recorrido long-distance train, **6.2**

tres three, LP

trescientos(as) three hundred, 9.2

el **trigo** wheat, *8.2;* **9**

triste sad, 6.1

la **tristeza** sadness, sorrow

el **trocito** little piece

la **trompeta** trumpet

las **tropas** troops

tropical tropical

el **trotamundos** globe-trotter

el **trozo** piece

la **trucha** trout

el **T-shirt** T-shirt

tu your *(sing. fam.)*

tú you *(sing. fam.)*

el **tubo de crema dental** tube of toothpaste, 11.2; *2.2*

la **tumba** grave, tomb, *5.1*

turbarse to be disturbed, to be altered

el **turismo** tourism

el/la **turista** tourist

tutear to use «tú» when addressing someone

u or *(used instead of **o** before words beginning with **o** or **ho**)*

Ud., usted you *(sing.) (formal)*

Uds., ustedes you *(pl.) (formal)*

último(a) last; final

un(a) a, an, 1.1

la **una** one o'clock, LP

único(a) only, 2.1; one-way, *9.1*

la calle de sentido único one-way street, *9.1*

el/la hijo(a) único(a) only child, 2.1

la **unidad** unit

el **uniforme** uniform, 3.1

la **universidad** university

universitario(a) *(related to)* the university, college; college student

uno one, LP

unos(as) some

urbano(a) urban, *8.1*

usar to use, 3.2; to wear *(size), 9.1*

¿Qué talla usas? What size do you wear (take)?, 9.1

el **uso** use

el/la **usuario(a)** user

la **uva** grape, 9.2; **9**

la **vaca** cow, *8.2*

las **vacaciones** vacation, 7.1

estar de vacaciones to be on vacation

vacante vacant

vacilar to hesitate

el **vacío** void, empty space

vacío(a) empty, *9.2;* **3 (Lit.)**

vagar to wander, to roam

el **vagón** train car, *3.1*

la **vainilla** vanilla

las **vainitas** green beans, **9**

Vale. It's a good idea.

más vale que... it is better that . . .

No vale. It's not worth it., 7.1

valeroso(a) brave

valiente brave, courageous, valiant

el **valle** valley

el **valor** bravery, valor

¡Vamos! Let's go!

varios(as) several

el **varón** man, boy

vasco(a) Basque

la pelota vasca jai-alai

el **vaso** glass, 4.1

el **váter** toilet, *7*

veces: a veces at times, sometimes, 6.1

el/la **vecino(a)** neighbor

el **vegetal** vegetable, 4.1

los vegetales crudos raw vegetables, crudités, 8.1

vegetariano(a) vegetarian, 4.1

veinte twenty, LP

veinticinco twenty-five, LP

veinticuatro twenty-four, LP

veintidós twenty-two, LP

veintinueve twenty-nine, LP

veintiocho twenty-eight, LP

veintiséis twenty-six, LP

veintisiete twenty-seven, LP

veintitrés twenty-three, LP

veintiuno twenty-one, LP

la **vela** candle, 8.1; *5.2;* **3.2**

vela: la plancha de vela windsurfing; sailboard, 7.1

velar to keep watch

el velo veil, **3.1**

la velocidad speed, *9.1*

la velocidad máxima speed limit, *9.1*

el velorio wake, **3.2**

la venda bandage, *11.2;* **2.2**

el/la vendedor(a) merchant, 9.2; **10**

vender to sell, 6.2

venenoso(a) poisonous

venezolano(a) Venezuelan

venir (ie) to come, 10.2; *1.2*

el verano (año, mes) que viene next summer (year, month), 8.2

la venta small hotel

las ventajas advantages

la ventanilla ticket window, 7.2, *3.1;* window *(plane),* 10.2; *1.2;* **6.1**

ventoso(a) windy

ver to see, 4.2

no tener nada que ver con not to have anything to do with

el verano summer, LP

el verbo verb

la verdad truth

Es verdad. That's true (right)., 9.1

¿Verdad? Right?

verdadero(a) real, true

verde green, 2.1

las judías verdes green beans, 9.2; **9**

la verdulería greengrocer (vegetable) store, 9.2

la verdura vegetable, 4.1

verificar to check, **6.2**

verosímil true-to-life

el verso verse, **7.2**

el vestido dress, 9.1

el vestido de novia wedding dress

vestirse (i, i) to get dressed, to dress, 4

la vez time

a veces at times, sometimes, 6.1; *1.2*

cada vez each time, every time

de vez en cuando from time to time, occasionally, 10.2; *1.2*

en vez de instead of

una vez más (once) again, one more time

la vía track, *3.1;* lane *(highway)*

viajar to travel

viajar en avión (tren) to travel by plane (train)

el viaje trip, voyage 10.1; *1.1*

hacer un viaje to take a trip, 10.1; *1.1*

la víctima victim

la vid grapevine, **9**

la vida life

el video video

viejo(a) old, 2.2

el viento wind, LP

Hace viento. It's windy., LP

el viernes Friday, LP

la villa small town, **5 (Lit.)**

el vinagre vinegar, **4**

el vino wine

la viña vineyard, **9**

el violín violin

la virtud virtue

visitar to visit, 8.2

la víspera de Año Nuevo New Year's Eve

la vista view; sight

perder la vista to lose sight of

la viuda (del difunto) widow, **3.2**

vivir to live, 4.1

vivo(a) lively

los vivos the living

la vocal vowel

el volante steering wheel, *9.2*

volar (ue) to fly

el volcán volcano

volcar to flip over

el voleibol volleyball, 7.1

la cancha de voleibol volleyball court, 7.1

volver (ue) to return, 5.1

volver a casa to go back (return) home, 8.1

volver a (+ infinitivo) to (do something) again

volverse to turn around

vosotros(as) you (pl.)

la voz voice

en voz alta aloud

el vuelo flight, 10.1; *1.1;* **6.1**

el número del vuelo flight number, 10.1; *1.1*

el vuelo directo direct flight, **6.1**

el vuelo sin escala non-stop flight, **6.1**

vuelta: un boleto (billete) de ida y vuelta round-trip ticket, *3.1*

la vuelta lap, *11.1;* **2.1**

Vuestra Merced Your Highness

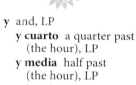

y and, LP

y cuarto a quarter past (the hour), LP

y media half past (the hour), LP

ya already

¡Ya voy! I'm coming!, 11.2; *2.2*

el yeso cast *(medical)*, 11.2; **2.2;** plaster, **7.1**

yo I; me

el yoga yoga, *11.1;* **2.1**

la zanahoria carrot, 9.2; *10;* **1**

las zapatillas (sports) shoes, sneakers, 5.1

los zapatos shoes, 9.1

la zona area, zone

el zoológico zoo, *8.1*

el zumo juice *(Spain)*

English-Spanish Dictionary

The English-Spanish Dictionary contains all productive and receptive vocabulary from ¡Así se dice! Levels 1, 2, and 3. The locator numbers following each productive entry indicate the chapter and vocabulary section in which the word is introduced (e.g., 3.2 means Chapter 3, Vocabulary 2). Level 1 chapter/section numbers are light print (3.2); Level 2 numbers are *italic (3.2)*; Level 3 chapter/section numbers are **bold (3.2)**. LP refers to the Level 1 **Lecciones preliminares.** If no locator follows an entry, the word or expression is receptive.

A

@ la arroba, *6.1*
a, an un(a), 1.1
able: to be able poder (ue), 5.1
aboard abordo (de), 10.2; *1.2*
about sobre; *(time)* a eso de
above por encima de, 5.2
  above all sobre todo
abroad al extranjero
abstract work (of art) la obra abstracta, **7.1**
to **accept** aceptar, **6.2**
accident el accidente, *11.2;* **2.2**
accompanied by acompañado(a) de, *3.2*
according to según
accountant el/la contable, **10**
ache el dolor, 6.2
to **ache** doler (ue), 6.2; *11.2;* **2.2**
  My . . . ache(s). Me duele(n)... , 6.2
to **achieve** lograr, **8**
acquaintance el/la conocido(a), **5**
activity la actividad
to **add** añadir, *10;* **1**
addition: in addition to además de
address la dirección, *6.1*
  address book la libreta de direcciones, *6.1*
  e-mail address la dirección de correo electrónico (e-mail), *6.1*
addressee el/la destinatario(a), *6.1*
adorable cariñoso(a), 2.1; adorable
advanced avanzado(a), **7.2**
advantage la ventaja
advertising la propaganda, la publicidad, **8**

to **advise** aconsejar; avisar, **6 (Lit.)**
afraid: to be afraid tener miedo, 7.2
after después (de), 3.1; *(time)* y; después de que
  It's ten after one. Es la una y diez., LP
afternoon la tarde
  Good afternoon. Buenas tardes., LP
  this afternoon esta tarde, 7.1
  yesterday afternoon ayer por la tarde, 7.1
again de nuevo
against contra
age la edad
agency la agencia
agent el/la agente, 10.1; *1.1;* **6.2**
ago: . . . years (months, etc.) ago hace... años (meses, etc.)
agricultural agrícola
air el aire
  open-air (outdoor) café (market) el café (mercado) al aire libre
air conditioning el aire acondicionado, **7**
airline la línea aérea, 10.1; *1.1*
airplane el avión, 10.1; *1.1*
airport el aeropuerto, 10.1; *1.1;* **6.1**
aisle el pasillo, 10.2; *1.2;* **6.1**
album el álbum
algebra el álgebra
all todo(a), 6.2; todos(as), 8.1
  above all sobre todo
to **allow** dejar
almost casi, 8.2; *4*
alone solo(a); a solas
already ya
also también, 1.2
although aunque
always siempre, 8.2
A.M. de la mañana
ambulance la ambulancia, *11.2;* **2.2**

American americano(a)
among entre
to **amuse** divertir (ie), 10.2; *1.2*
amusement park el parque de atracciones, *8.1*
  amusement park ride la atracción, *8.1*
amusing divertido(a)
anchor (television) el/la ancla, **8**
ancient antiguo(a), *8.1*
and y, LP
Andean andino(a)
angry enfadado(a), enojado(a), 6.1
  to get angry enfadarse, **5**
  to make angry enfadar, 6.1
animal el animal
ankle el tobillo, *11.1;* **2.1**
announcement el anuncio, **10**
to **annoy** molestar, enojar, 6.1
another otro(a)
answer la respuesta
to **answer** contestar, 3.1
any cualquier
  any other cualquier otro(a)
anybody alguien, 8.2
anything algo, 8.2
  Anything else? ¿Algo más?, 9.2
apartment el apartamento, el apartamiento, el departamento, 2.2; el piso
  apartment building la casa de apartamentos, 2.2
appearance la apariencia
to **applaud** aplaudir, 5.1
  to be applauded recibir aplausos, 5.1
applause el aplauso, 5.1
apple la manzana, 9.2
appreciated apreciado(a)
to **approach** acercarse de
April abril, LP
archeology la arqueología

architect el/la arquitecto(a), **10**

area la zona; el área (f.)

area code la clave de área, 6.2

Argentine argentino(a)

arithmetic la aritmética

arm el brazo, 11.1; 2.1

army el ejército, **4 (Lit.)**

around alrededor de, 2.2; (time) a eso de

arrival la llegada, 3.1

to **arrive** llegar, 4.1

arriving from procedente de, 10.2; 1.2

art el arte, 1.2; **7.1**

  art show (exhibition) la exposición de arte, 8.2

artichoke la alcachofa, **9**

  artichoke (sautéed) alcachofa salteada

article el artículo, **8**

artist el/la artista; el/la pintor(a), 8.2; **7.1**

as como

  as . . . as tan… como

  as many . . . as tantos(as)… como

  as much . . . as tanto(a)… como

  as soon . . . as en cuanto, tan pronto como

to **ask (a question)** preguntar

to **ask for** pedir (i, i), *4*

assign asignar, 6.2

assistance la ayuda

assistant: executive assistant el/la asistente(a) ejecutivo(a), **10**

at a, en

  at (@) sign la arroba, 6.1

  at around (time) a eso de

  at home en casa, 2.2

  at night por la noche; de noche

  at one o'clock (two o'clock, three o'clock . . .) a la una (a las dos, a las tres…), LP

  at times a veces, 6.1; 1.2

  at what time? ¿a qué hora?, LP

athlete el/la atleta

atmosphere el ambiente, **7.2**

attached file el documento adjunto, 6.1

to **attend** asistir a, 8.1

attention: to pay attention prestar atención, 3.1

attractive guapo(a), 1.1

August agosto, LP

aunt la tía, 2.1

  aunt and uncle los tíos, 2.1

author el/la autor(a)

automatic automático(a), 10.1; 1.1

  automatic dispenser el distribuidor automático, 3.1

autumn el otoño, LP

ATM el cajero automático, **4**

available disponible, 6.1

avenue la avenida, 8.1

average regular

avocado el aguacate, 10; **1;** la palta

Awesome! ¡Bárbaro!, 5.2

ax el hacha (f.)

back la espalda, 11.1; 2.1

back (adj.) trasero(a), **7.1**

  back button (key) el botón regresar (retroceder), 6.1

  back door la puerta trasera, 8.1

back: in back of detrás de, 2.2

background la ascendencia; el fondo, **7.1**

backpack la mochila, 3.1

backpacker el/la mochilero(a), 11.2; 2.2

backwards hacia atrás

bacon el tocino, el bacón, 4.1; 7; el lacón, 7

bad malo(a), 1.2; mal, LP

  The weather is bad. Hace mal tiempo., LP

  to be in a bad mood estar de mal humor, 6.1

  to get bad grades sacar notas malas, 3.1

baggage el equipaje, 10.1; 1.1

  baggage claim el reclamo de equipaje, 6.1

  baggage claim ticket el talón, 6.1

  carry-on baggage el equipaje de mano, 10.1; 1.1

bakery la panadería

balance el saldo, 4

balcony el balcón

ball (soccer, basketball) el balón, 5.1; (volleyball) el voleibol, 7.1; (baseball, tennis) la pelota, 5.2

  to hit the ball batear, 5.2; golpear, 5.2

  to kick (throw) the ball lanzar el balón, 5.1

balloon el globo

ballpoint pen el bolígrafo, 3.1; el lapicero, la pluma

banana el plátano, 9.2

  ripe bananas los maduros

band (music) la banda, 8.1; 5.2; el conjunto, 8.1

  city band la banda municipal, 5.2

bandage la venda, 11.2; **2.2**

bank el banco, **4**

banquet el banquete, 3.1

baptism el bautizo, 3.2

baptismal font la pila, 3.2

to **baptize** bautizar, 3.2

bar: bar of soap la barra de jabón, 11.2; 2.2; la pastilla de jabón

to **bargain** regatear, 9.2

barn el granero, 8.2

base (baseball) la base, 5.2

baseball el béisbol, 5.2

  baseball field el campo de béisbol, 5.2

  baseball game el juego (partido) de béisbol, 5.2

  baseball player el/la jugador(a) de béisbol, el/la beisbolista, 5.2

basket (basketball) el cesto, la canasta, 5.2

  to make a basket encestar, meter el balón en la cesta, 5.2

basketball el básquetbol, el baloncesto, 5.2

  basketball court la cancha de básquetbol, 5.2

bat el bate, 5.2

to **bat** batear, 5.2

bath el baño, 2.2; 7

bathing suit el bañador, el traje de baño, 7.1

bathroom el cuarto de baño, 2.2; 7

bathtub la bañera, 7

batter el/la bateador(a), 5.2

battle la lucha, la batalla, **8**

to **be** ser, 1.1; estar, 3.1

  to be able (to) poder (ue), 5.1

  to be about to (do something) estar para + infinitivo

  to be afraid tener miedo, 7.2

  to be applauded recibir aplausos, 8.1

  to be born nacer, 3.2

  to be called (named) llamarse, 11.1; 2.1

  to be careful tener cuidado, 9.1

English-Spanish Dictionary

to be cold (hot) tener frío (calor), 11.1; *2.1*

to be cut off cortar la linea (a alguien), *6.2*

to be familiar with conocer, 9.1

to be fine (well) estar bien, 6.2

to be going to (do something) ir a + infinitivo, 4.1

to be happy estar contento(a), alegre, 6.1

to be hungry tener hambre, 4.1

to be in a good (bad) mood estar de buen (mal) humor, 6.1

to be in the mood for estar por

to be pleasing (to someone) gustar, 5.1

to be ready to (do something) estar para + infinitivo

to be sad estar triste, deprimido(a), 6.1

to be sick estar enfermo(a), 6.2

to be sorry sentir (ie, i)

to be successful tener éxito, 6.1

to be thirsty tener sed, 4.1

to be tired estar cansado(a), 6.1

to be (turn) . . . years old cumplir... años, *3.2*

to be . . . years old tener... años, 2.1

to **be in a hurry** apresurarse, **10 (Lit.)**

beach la playa, 7.1

beach resort el balneario, 7.1

beans los frijoles, 4.1

  green beans (string beans) las judías verdes, 9.2; **9;** las vainitas, **9**

beautiful bello(a), hermoso(a)

because porque, 3.2

bed la cama, 2.2; *7*

  to go to bed acostarse (ue), 11.1; *2.1*

  to make the bed hacer la cama, *7*

  to stay in bed guardar cama, 6.2; quedarse en la cama, 11.1; *2.1*

bedroom el cuarto de dormir, la recámara, 2.2; la habitación, *7*; el dormitorio, la alcoba, la pieza

beef la carne de res, *4*; **9;** el bife

before antes de, 3.2

beforehand antes, 10.1; *1.1*

to **beg** rogar (ue)

to **begin** empezar (ie), 5.1; comenzar (ie)

beginner el/la principiante, 7.2

to **behave** comportarse, *5*

behaved: to be well-behaved tener buena conducta, 6.1

behavior la conducta, el comportamiento, 6.1; **5**

behind detrás de, 2.2

to **believe** creer

bell pepper el pimiento, 9.2; *10;* **1**

bell tower la campana

bellhop el mozo, *7*

to **belong** pertenecer

below debajo de, 10.2; *1.2*

benefit el provecho, *5* (Lit.)

beside al lado de, 2.2

besides además

best el/la mejor

best man el padrino, **3.1**

better mejor

between entre

beverage la bebida, el refresco, 4.1

bicycle la bicicleta, 2.2

  to ride a bicycle andar en bicicleta, 11.1; *2.1*

big gran, grande, 1.2

bike ride: to go for a bike ride dar un paseo en bicicleta

bike riding: to go bike riding andar en bicicleta, *11.1;* **2.1**

bill la factura; el billete, *4*

biologist el/la biólogo(a)

biology la biología

bird el pájaro

birthday el cumpleaños, 8.1; **3.2**

black negro(a), 2.1

blanket la manta, la frazada, *7*

block (city) la cuadra, la manzana, *9.1*

to **block** bloquear, 5.1

blond(e) rubio(a), 1.1

  to have blond hair tener el pelo rubio, 2.1

blood pressure la tensión arterial, 6.2

blouse la blusa, 3.1

to **blow (wind)** soplar

blue azul, 2.1

blue jeans el blue jean, 9.1

board: on board abordo (de), 10.2; *1.2*

to **board** embarcar, abordar, 10.2; *1.2*

boarding el embarque, 10.1; *1.1*

  boarding pass la tarjeta de embarque, 10.1; *1.1;* el pasabordo, la tarjeta de abordar

  boarding pass kiosk el distribuidor automático, 10.1; *1.1*

  boarding time la hora de embarque, 10.1; *1.1*

boat (small) el barquito, 7.1

body (human) el cuerpo (humano), 11.1; *2.1*

to **boil** hervir (ie, i), *10;* **1**

boiling la ebullición

bone el hueso, *5.1;* **2.2**

  to set the bone reducir, acomodar el hueso, *11.2;* **2.2**

book el libro, 3.1

boot la bota, 7.2

border la frontera

to **bore** aburrir

boring aburrido(a), 1.2

born: to be born nacer, **3.2**

to **bother** molestar, enfadar, enojar, 6.1

bottle la botella, 9.2

box office la taquilla, 8.2

boy el muchacho, 1.1; el niño, 6.2; el chico, *5;* el mozo, **5 (Lit.)**

boyfriend el novio, **6 (Lit.)**

brakes los frenos, 9.2

  to put on (apply) the brakes poner los frenos

brave valeroso(a)

Brazilian brasileño(a)

bread el pan

  bread crumbs el pan rallado, **9**

to **break** romper; romperse, quebrarse (ie), *11.2;* **2.2**

  He (She) broke his (her) leg. Se rompió (se quebró) la pierna., *11.2;* **2.2**

breakdown la avería

breakfast el desayuno, 4.1; *7*

    Continental breakfast el desayuno continental, *7*

    to have breakfast tomar el desayuno, 4.1; desayunarse

breaking: You're breaking up. (telephone) Estás cortando., *6.2*

breast *(chicken)* la pechuga, *10;* **1**

breathing la respiración, *11.1;* **2.1**

    breathing exercises los ejercicios de respiración, *11.1;* **2.1**

breed la raza

bride la novia, **3.1**

to **bring** traer, 10.1; *1.1*

to **bring down** derrocar

broad ancho(a), *8.1*

to **broadcast** emitir, **8**

broken roto(a); quebrado(a)

bronze *(adj.)* de bronce, 8.2; **7.1**

brother el hermano, 2.1

brown castaño(a), 2.1; de color marrón, 5.1

    to have brown eyes tener ojos castaños, 2.1

    to have brown hair tener el pelo castaño, 2.1

brunette moreno(a), 1.1

brush el cepillo, 11.2; **2.2**

    toothbrush el cepillo de dientes, 11.2; **2.2**

to **brush** cepillar, 11.1; **2.1**

    to brush one's hair cepillarse, 11.1; **2.1**

    to brush one's teeth cepillarse (lavarse) los dientes, 11.1; **2.1**

buffet el bufé, **3.1**

building el edificio, 2.2

bunk la litera

burial el entierro, el sepelio **3.2**

buried enterrado(a), *5.1*

to **burn** quemarse, *10;* **1**

burrito el burrito

to **bury** enterrar (ie)

bus el autobús, el camión, la guagua, *8.1;* el bus

    bus stop la parada de autobús (de camiones, de guaguas), *8.1*

    school bus el bus escolar, 3.2

    to miss the bus perder el autobús, 8.1

businessman el hombre de negocios, **10**

businessperson el/la comerciante, **10**

businesswoman la mujer de negocios, **10**

but pero

butcher shop la carnicería

butter la mantequilla, 4.1; *7*

button el botón, *6.1*

    back button el botón regresar (retroceder), *6.1*

    delete button el botón borrador, *6.1*

to **buy** comprar, 3.2

by por; en

    by plane (car, bus) en avión (carro, autobús)

    by tens de diez en diez

    By the way! ¡A propósito!, 8.2

Bye! ¡Chao!, LP

C

cabbage el repollo, la col, **9**

café el café, 4.2

    outdoor café el café al aire libre

cafeteria la cafetería, 4.1

cake la torta, 4.1; **3.2**; el bizcocho, *5.1;* **3.2**; el pastel, la tarta, 8.1; **3.2**

calculator la calculadora, 3.1

call (phone) la llamada, *6.2*

    dropped call la llamada perdida (caída), *6.2*

to **call** llamar, 11.2; **2.2**

    Who's calling, please? ¿De parte de quién, por favor?, *6.2*

calm calmo(a), tranquilo(a), *6.1*

camel el camello, *5.2*

camera la cámara, 7.1; *6.2*

    digital camera la cámara digital, 7.1; *6.2*

camping el camping, 11.2; **2.2**

    to go camping ir de camping, 11.2; **2.2**

can el bote, la lata, 9.2

Canadian canadiense

candidate el/la aspirante, el/la candidato(a), **10**

candle la vela, 8.1; *5.2;* **3.2**

canned enlatado(a)

canvas el lienzo, **7.1**

canyon el cañón, *3.2*

cap el gorro, 7.2

capital la capital

car el carro, 2.2; *9.2;* el coche, *9.2; (train)* el coche, el vagón, *3.1*

    dining car el coche comedor (cafetería), la bufetería, *3.1*

    sports car el coche deportivo, *9.2*

car rental agency la agencia de alquiler, *6.2*

carbonated drink la gaseosa, 4.1

card la tarjeta, 3.1; *6.2;* el carnet, 10.2; *1.2*

    credit card la tarjeta de crédito, 3.1

    ID card el carnet de identidad, 10.2; *1.2*

    phone card la tarjeta telefónica, *6.2*

career la carrera, **10**

careful: to be careful tener cuidado, *9.1*

    Careful! ¡Cuidado!, ¡Mucho ojo!, **5**

carefully con cuidado

Caribbean Sea el mar Caribe

carrot la zanahoria, *9.2; 10;* **1**

to **carry** llevar, 3.1; traer, 10.1; *1.1*

    carry-on luggage el equipaje de mano, 10.2; *1.2*

cart el carrito, *9.2;* **3.1**

to **carve** tallar, **7.1**

case: in case en caso de; por si acaso

cash register la caja, 3.2

cash el dinero en efectivo, **4**

to **cash** cobrar, **4**

cashier el/la cajero(a)

cast *(medical)* el yeso, 11.2; **2.2**

castle el castillo

cat el/la gato(a), 2.1

to **catch** atrapar, *5.2*

catcher el/la cátcher, el/la receptor(a), *5.2*

Catholic católico(a)

cattle el ganado, *8.2*

to **cause** causar

to **celebrate** celebrar, *5.2;* **3.2**

celebration la celebración

cell phone el móvil, 3.2, *6.1;* el celular, *6.1*

cemetery el cementerio, el camposanto, *5.1;* **3.2**

century el siglo

ceramics las cerámicas, *9.2*

cereal el cereal, 4.1

ceremony la ceremonia, **3.1**

    civil ceremony (wedding) la ceremonia civil, **3.1**

English-Spanish Dictionary

English-Spanish Dictionary

certain cierto(a), *6.1*

chair la silla, 2.2

chairlift el telesilla, el telesquí, 7.2

change (monetary) suelto, *4*

to **change** cambiar, *3.2;* **6.2**

   to change trains (transfer) transbordar, *3.2*

chapter el capítulo, 7.2

character el personaje, 7.2

charitable purpose el propósito benévolo

cheap barato(a), 9.1

   It's all a lot cheaper. Todo te sale más barato., 9.1

check (restaurant) la cuenta, 4.2; *4*

to **check (ticket)** revisar, *3.2;* **(facts)** verificar, **6.2**

to **check luggage** facturar el equipaje, 10.1; *1.1*

to **check out (hotel room)** abandonar el cuarto, *7*

checking account la cuenta corriente, *4*

cheek la mejilla, *5*

cheese el queso, 4.1

   ham and cheese sandwich el sándwich de jamón y queso, 4.1

chemistry la química

chest el pecho, 11.1; **2.1**

chicken el pollo, 4.1; *10;* **1**

   chicken breast la pechuga de pollo, *10;* **1**

   chicken thigh el muslo de pollo, *10;* **1**

   chicken wings las alitas de pollo, *10;* **1**

child el/la niño(a), 6.2

children los hijos, 2.1

Chilean chileno(a)

chili pepper el ají

chisel el cincel, 7.1

chocolate el chocolate, 4.1

   hot chocolate el chocolate caliente, 4.1

to **choose** escoger; seleccionar, *3.1*

chop: pork chop la chuleta de cerdo, *10;* **1**

to **chop** picar, *10;* **1**

Christian cristiano(a)

Christmas la Navidad, las Navidades, *5.2*

   Christmas Eve la Nochebuena, *5.2*

Christmas gift el aguinaldo, *5.2*

Christmas tree el árbol de Navidad, *5.2*

Merry Christmas! ¡Feliz Navidad!

church la iglesia, *3.1*

cilantro el cilantro, **9**

city la ciudad, 2.2; *8.1*

city hall el ayuntamiento, **3.1**

civil civil

   civil ceremony (wedding) la ceremonia civil, *3.1*

   por (el, lo) civil civil, *3.1*

civilization la civilización

to **claim** reclamar, **6.1**

clams las almejas, *4*

to **clap** aplaudir, 5.1

clarinet el clarinete

class (school) la clase; el curso, 1.2; **(ticket)** la clase, *3.1*

   first (second) class en primera (segunda) clase, *3.1*

classified ad anuncio clasificado, **10**

classroom la sala de clase, 3.1

clean limpio(a), *7*

to **clean** limpiar, *7*

to **clear the table** levantar, quitar la mesa, *4*

clerk el/la empleado(a), 3.1; el/la dependiente, 9.1

to **click (computer)** hacer clic, *6.1*

cliff el risco, *3.2*

climate el clima

close (to) cerca de

to **close** cerrar (ie), 11.2; **2.2**

closet el armario, *7*

clothes la ropa, 9.1

   dirty clothes la ropa para lavar, la ropa sucia *4*

clothes hanger la percha, el colgador, *7*

clothing la ropa, 9.1

   clothing store la tienda de ropa, 9.1

cloud la nube, 7.1

cloudy nublado(a), 7.1

clove (of garlic) el diente

coach el/la entrenador(a)

coast la costa

to **coat (with batter)** rebozar, **9**

code: area code la clave de área, *6.2*

   country code el prefijo del país, *6.2*

co-ed mixto(a)

coffee el café, 4.1; *7*

coffin el ataúd, **3.2**

cognate la palabra afine

coin la moneda, *9.1;* **4**

cola la cola, 4.1

cold el frío; frío(a), 4.2; **(illness)** el catarro, 6.2

   It's cold (weather). Hace frío., LP

   to be cold tener frío, 11.1; *2.1*

   to have a cold tener catarro, 6.2

to **collect** recoger, *6.1*

college la universidad

Colombian el/la colombiano(a), 1.2

colonial colonial, **8**

to **colonize** colonizar, **8**

colonizer el colonizador, **8**

colony la colonia, **8**

color el color, 5.1

comb el peine, 11.2; **2.2**

to **comb one's hair** peinarse, 11.1; *2.1*

to **come** venir (ie), 10.2; *1.2*

   I'm coming! ¡Ya voy!, 11.2; **2.2**

to **come out onto** desembocar

comical cómico(a), gracioso(a), 1.1

coming from procedente de, 10.2; *1.2*

companion el/la compañero(a)

company la compañía, la empresa, la sociedad, **8**

to **complete** completar

completely totalmente

composition la composición

computer la computadora, el ordenador, 3.2; *6.1*

   computer programmer el/la programador(a) de computadoras, **10**

concert el concierto, 8.1

concourse (train station) el hall, *3.1*

condiment el condimento, *10;* **1**

condo(minium) el condominio

conduct la conducta, el comportamiento, 6.1

conductor (train) el revisor, *3.2*

to **confirm (seat on a flight)** confirmar, **6.1**

Congratulations!
¡Enhorabuena!, **3.1**

to **connect** enlazar, **6.2**

connected conectado(a)

connection la conexión

consonant la consonante

to **consult** consultar

to **contain** contener (ie)

contemporary
contemporáneo

continent el continente

Continental breakfast
el desayuno continental, *7*

to **continue** continuar;
seguir (i, i), *9.1*

contract el contrato, **6.2**

contrary: on the contrary
al contrario

conversation la conversación

convertible el descapotable, el
convertible, *9.2*

conveyor belt la correa, **6.1**

to **convince** convencer

cook el/la cocinero(a), *10;* **1**

to cook cocinar, cocer (ue),
10; **1**

cooking la cocción

cool fresco(a), LP

It's cool (weather). Hace
fresco., LP

copy la copia, *6.1*

hard copy la copia dura, *6.1*

corn el maíz, *9.2;* el elote,
el choclo

ear of corn la mazorca de
maíz, **9**

corner la esquina, *8.1*

to **conquer** conquistar, **8**

corporation la sociedad, **10**

corral el corral, *8.2*

to **cost** costar (ue), *9.1*

How much does it cost?
¿Cuánto cuesta?, 3.2

Costa Rican costarricense

costume el disfraz, *5.1*

cough la tos, *6.2*

to have a cough tener tos, *6.2*

to **cough** toser, *6.2*

counter *(airline)* el mostrador,
10.1; 1.1

country el país; el campo, *8.2*

country code el prefijo
del país, *6.2*

country house la casa
de campo, *8.2*

Spanish-speaking countries
los países hispanohablantes

countryside el campo, *8.2*

couple la pareja, **3.1**

course el curso, *1.2*

court la cancha, *5.2*

basketball (tennis) court
la cancha de básquetbol
(tenis), *5.2*

volleyball court la cancha
de voleibol, *7.1*

courtesy la cortesía

cousin el/la primo(a), *2.1*

to **cover** cubrir, tapar

cow la vaca, *8.2*

crackers las galletas, *8.1*

crafts la artesanía, *9.2*

crazy loco(a)

credit card la tarjeta
de crédito, *3.1*

to **cross** cruzar, *9.1*

cross-country *(skiing)*
el esquí nórdico, *7.2;* *(race)*
la carrera a campo traviesa,
11.1; **2.1**

crosswalk el cruce, *8.1*

crutches las muletas, *11.2;* **2.2**

to walk on crutches andar
con muletas, *11.2;* **2.2**

Cuban el/la cubano(a)

Cuban American
el/la cubanoamericano(a)

cucumber el pepino, *10;* **1**

cuisine la cocina

culture la cultura

cup la taza, *4.1; 4*

curriculum vitae
el currículum vitae, **10**

custard el flan, *4.1*

custom la costumbre

customer el/la cliente, *9.2; 7*

customs la aduana, **6.1**

to **cut** cortar, *10;* **1**

to cut (up) in small pieces
cortar en pedacitos, *10;* **1**

cut off: We've been cut off.
(telephone) Se nos cortó la
línea., *6.2*

to **cut oneself** cortarse, *11.2;* **2.2**

cutlet: veal cutlet el escalope
de ternera, *10;* **1**

D

daily diario(a)

daily routine la rutina
diaria, *11.1;* **2.1**

dairy products los productos
lácteos

to **dance** bailar, *5.2*

danger el peligro

dangerous peligroso(a)

dark-haired moreno(a), *1.1*

data los datos

date la fecha, LP

What's today's date?
¿Cuál es la fecha
de hoy?, LP

daughter la hija, *2.1*

to **dawn** amanecer, **10 (Lit.)**

day el día, LP; fiesta, *5.1*

the Day of the Dead el Día
de los Muertos, *5.1*

patron saint's day la fiesta
patronal, *5.1*

What day is it (today)?
¿Qué día es hoy?, LP

dead muerto(a), difunto(a), *5.1*

**dead person, deceased
person** el/la muerto(a),
el/la difunto(a), *5.1*

deaf sordo(a), **10 (Lit.)**

dear querido(a)

death la muerte

deboned deshuesado(a)

December diciembre, LP

to **decide** decidir

to **decline** declinar, **6.2**

to **decorate** decorar, *5.2*

deep profundo(a)

definition la definición

delay el retraso, la demora,
10.2; 1.2; **6.1**

to **delete** borrar, *6.1*

delete key *(computer)*
el botón borrador, *6.1*

delicious delicioso(a); rico(a)

to **deliver** entregar, **6 (Lit.)**

to **demand** exigir

dent la abolladura, **6.2**

dentist's office la gabinete
del dentista, **9**

departure la salida, *10.1; 1.1*

departure gate la puerta
de salida, *10.2; 1.2;* **6.1**

departure time la hora
de salida, *10.1; 1.1*

to **depend** depender (ie) (de)

to **deplane** desembarcar, *10.2; 1.2*

to **deposit** depositar, **4**

to **describe** describir

description descripción

desert el desierto

desk el pupitre, *3.1*

desolate inhóspito(a)

dessert el postre, *4.1*

destination el destino, *3.1;* **6.1**

detergent el detergente, **4**

powdered detergent
el jabón en polvo, **4**

to **develop** desarrollarse, *7.2*

device el aparato

English-Spanish Dictionary

diagnosis el diagnóstico

to **dial** marcar el número, 6.2

dial tone el tono, 6.2

to **dice** cortar en pedacitos, 10; **1**

dictation el dictado

to **die** morir (ue, u), 4

diet la dieta

difference la diferencia

different diferente, 9.2

difficult difícil; duro(a), 1.2; avanzado(a), 7.2

difficulty la dificultad

digital camera la cámara digital, 7.1; 6.2

diner el/la comensal, 9

dining car el coche comedor (cafetería), la bufetería, 3.2

dining room el comedor, 2.2

dinner la cena, 4.1; **3.1**

  to have dinner cenar, 4.1

direction (road) sentido, 9.1

  in each direction en cada sentido, 9.1

directions las direcciones

dirty sucio(a), 7

disadvantage la desventaja

disagreeable desagradable

to **disappear** desaparecer

to **discover** descubrir

to **disembark** desembarcar, 1.2

disguise el disfraz, 5.1

dish el plato, 4

dishwasher el lavaplatos, 10; **1**

dispenser: automatic boarding pass dispenser el distribuidor automático, 10.1; 1.1

distance: long distance de larga distancia, 11.1; **2.1**

distinguished ilustre, 8

district el casco, el barrio, 8.1

to **dive** bucear, 7.1

to **divide** dividirse, 7.2

divine divino(a)

to **do** hacer, 10.2; 1.2

  to do homework hacer las tareas

  to do push-ups hacer planchas, 11.1; **2.1**

  to do yoga practicar yoga, 11.1; **2.1**

doctor el/la médico(a), 6.2

  doctor's office el consultorio, la consulta, 6.2; **10**

document el documento

  attached document el documento adjunto, 6.1

dog el/la perro(a), 2.1

dollar el dólar

Dominican dominicano(a)

  Dominican Republic la República Dominicana

door la puerta, 9.2

  front (back) door la puerta delantera (trasera)

dot (Internet) el punto, 6.1

double (room) un cuarto doble, 7

doubles (tennis) dobles, 5.2

doubt la duda

to **doubt** dudar

doughnut (type of) el churro

down: to go down bajar, 7.2

downhill skiing el esquí alpino, 7.2

to **download** bajar, descargar, 6.2

downtown el centro, 8.1

dozen la docena

drama el drama

drawing el dibujo

dream el sueño

dress el vestido, 9.1

to **dress** vestirse (i, i), 4

to **dribble** driblar (con el balón), 5.2

drink (beverage) la bebida, 4.1; el refresco, 4.2

to **drink** beber, 4.1

to **drive** conducir, manejar, 9.2

driver el/la conductor(a), 9.2

driver's license el permiso de conducir, la licencia, el carnet, 9.2

dropped call una llamada caída (perdida), 6.2

drugstore la farmacia, 6.2

dry seco(a)

dryer la secadora, 4

during durante, 3.2

DVD el DVD, 3.2

dynamic dinámico(a), 6.1

E

---

e-mail el correo electrónico, 3.2; 6.1; el e-mail

  e-mail address la dirección de correo electrónico (e-mail), 6.1

e-mail inbox la bandeja de entradas, 6.1

e-ticket el boleto (billete) electrónico, 10.1; 1.1

each cada, 2.2

eagle el águila (f.)

ear el oído, **6 (Lit.)**

early temprano, 11.1; 2.1

early riser el/la madrugador(a), 11.1; 2.1; **10 (Lit.)**

to **earn** ganar

easel el caballete, **7.1**

easily sin dificultad, 7.2

east el este

easy fácil, 1.2

to **eat** comer, 4.1

  to eat breakfast (lunch) tomar el desayuno (el almuerzo), 4.1

  to eat dinner cenar, 4.1

Ecuadoran ecuatoriano(a), 1.1

education la educación

  physical education la educación física, 1.2

egg el huevo, 4.1; **7**

scrambled eggs los huevos revueltos, 7; los huevos batidos, **9**

eggplant la berenjena, **9**

eight ocho, LP

eight hundred ochocientos(as), 9.2

eighteen dieciocho, LP

eighty ochenta, LP

either tampoco

elbow el codo, 11.1; 2.1

electronic electrónico(a), 10.1; 1.1

elementary school la escuela primaria

elevator el ascensor, 7

eleven once, LP

else: Anything else? ¿Algo más?, 9.2; **Nothing else.** Nada más., 9.2

emergency room la sala de emergencia, 11.2; **2.2**

employee el/la empleado(a), 3.2; el/la dependiente, 9.1

empty vacío(a), 9.2; **3 (Lit.)**

enchilada la enchilada

end el fin

  at the end (of) al final (de); a fines de

to **end** terminar

to **endorse** endosar, 4

energetic energético(a), 6.1

energy la energía, 6.1
engine el motor
engineer el/la ingeniero(a), **10**
English *(language)* el inglés, 1.2
to enjoy disfrutar; gozar
to enjoy oneself divertirse (ie, i), 11.2; *2.2*
enormous enorme
enough bastante; suficiente
to enter entrar, 5.1
enthusiasm el entusiasmo, 6.1
enthusiastic lleno(a) de entusiasmo, 6.1; entusiasmado(a)
entire entero(a)
entrance la entrada; *(subway)* la boca del metro, *8.1*
envelope el sobre, **4**
environment el ambiente, 7.2
Epiphany el Día de los Reyes, *5.2*
equal igual
escalator la escalera mecánica, *8.1*
especially especialmente; sobre todo
to establish estalecer(se), **8**
ethnic étnico(a)
euro el euro
European europeo(a)
even aun; hasta
even *(numeric)* par
evening la noche
Good evening. Buenas noches., LP
in the evening por la noche
yesterday evening anoche, 7.1
every cada, 2.2; todos(as)
every day (year) todos los días (años)
everybody todo el mundo *5.1;* todos(as), 8.1
everyone todo el mundo *5.1;* todos(as), 8.1
everything todo, 6.2
everywhere en todas partes
exactly exactamente
exam el examen, la prueba, 3.1
physical exam el examen físico, 6.2
to take an exam tomar un examen, 3.1
to examine examinar, 6.2
example: for example por ejemplo
to exceed exceder
excellent excelente

exception la excepción
to exchange intercambiar, **3.1**
Excuse me. Con permiso., 10.1; *1.1*
executive el/la ejecutivo(a), **10**
executive assistant el/la asistente(a) ejecutivo(a), **10**
exercise los ejercicios, 11.1; **2.1**
to exercise hacer ejercicios, 11.1; **2.1**
exhibition la exposición (de arte), 8.2
to exist existir
exit la salida, *9.1*
exotic exótico(a)
to expect esperar, **3.1**
expensive caro(a), 9.1
less expensive más barato, 9.1
expert el/la experto(a), 7.2
to explain explicar
expressway la autopista, la autovía, *9.1*
extraordinary extraordinario(a)
eye el ojo, 2.1
to have blue (green, brown) eyes tener ojos azules (verdes, castaños) 2.1

fabrics los tejidos, 9.2
fabulous fabuloso(a)
face la cara, 6.1
fact el hecho
fair la feria, 5.1
fall el otoño, LP
to fall caerse, *11.2;* **2.2**
to fall asleep dormirse (ue), 11.1; **2.1**
to fall in love enamorarse, **5**
false falso(a)
family la familia, 2.1
family *(adj.)* familiar
famous famoso(a)
fan el/la aficionado(a), 5.1
fantastic fantástico(a)
far lejos (de), 3.2
fare la tarifa, *3.1*
farm la finca, la granja, la chacra, 8.2
farmer el/la campesino(a), el peón, 8.2
farmhand el peón, 8.2
to fascinate fascinar

fast rápido(a)
fastened abrochado(a), 10.2; *1.2*
fat gordo(a)
father el padre, 2.1
favor el favor
favorite favorito(a)
fear el miedo
feature la característica
February febrero, LP
to feel sentirse (ie, i)
to feel like (doing something) tener ganas de + infinitivo
Ferris wheel la noria, *8.1*
fertilizer el abono
festival la feria, *5.1*
festival of lights (Hanukkah) la fiesta de las luces, *5.2*
fever la fiebre, 6.2
to have a fever tener fiebre, 6.2
few poco(a), pocos(as), 2.2
a few unos(as)
fewer menos
field el campo, *5.1;* *8.2*
baseball field el campo de béisbol, 5.2
soccer field el campo de fútbol, 5.1
fifteen quince, LP
fifteen-year-old girl la quinceañera
fifty cincuenta, LP
to fight luchar, **8**
figurative work (of art) la obra figurativa, **7.1**
file el archivo, *6.1;* el documento
attached file el documento adjunto, *6.1*
to fill llenar, *9.2;* **10;** *(put filling in)* rellenar, **9**
to fill up *(gas tank)* llenar el tanque, *9.2;* **6.2**
film el filme, la película, 8.2; el film
finally por fin
financial statement el estado financiero, **10**
to find encontrar (ue)
fine la multa, *9.1*
fine *(adj.)* bien, LP
to be fine estar bien, 6.2
finger el dedo, 11.1; *2.1*
to finish terminar
fire el fuego, *10;* **1**
fireplace la chimenea, 5.2
fireworks los fuegos artificiales, 5.2

English-Spanish Dictionary

first primero(a), LP
   first-class primera clase, *3.1*
   first of January el primero de enero, LP
fish el pescado, 4.1
fish market la pescadería
to **fit** quedar, 9.1
   This jacket doesn't fit you. Esta chaqueta no te queda bien., 9.1
five cinco, LP
five hundred quinientos(as), 9.2
flame el fuego, *10;* **1**
   on a low flame (heat) a fuego lento, *10;* **1**
flan el flan, 4.1
flat plano(a), **7.1**; *(tire)* el pinchazo, 9.2
flavor el sabor, *10;* **1**
to **flee** huir, **4 (Lit.)**
flight el vuelo, 10.1; *1.1;* **6.1**
   direct flight el vuelo directo, **6.1**
   flight attendant el/la asistente(a) de vuelo, 10.2; *1.2*
   flight number el número del vuelo, 10.1; *1.1*
   non-stop flight el vuelo sin escala, **6.1**
to **flip over** volcar
floor el piso, 2.2
flower la flor, 2.2
flute la flauta
to **fly** volar (ue)
folder la carpeta, 3.2; **6.1**
to **follow** seguir (i, i), *4*
following siguiente
food la comida, 4.1; los comestibles, *4;* el alimento
   frozen food los productos congelados, 9.2
foot el pie, 5.1; *2.1*
   on foot a pie, 3.2
football el fútbol americano
for por, para; con destino a, 10.2; *1.2*
   for example por ejemplo
forbidden prohibido(a), 9.1
foreground el primer plano, **7.1**
forehead la frente, 11.1; **2.1**
foreign extranjero(a)
to **forget** olvidar, **5 (Lit.)**
fork el tenedor, *4*

form una forma, 10.2; *1.2*
formal formal, **5**
former antiguo(a)
forty cuarenta, LP
fountain pen la pluma, 5.1
four cuatro, LP
four hundred cuatrocientos(as), 9.2
fourteen catorce, LP
fracture la fractura
free libre, 4.2; *3.2*
to **free** liberar, *11.1;* **2.1**
freezer el congelador, *10;* **1**
French el francés, 1.2; *(adj.)* francés(esa), *4*
french fries las papas (patatas) fritas, 4.1
frequently con frecuencia, frecuentemente
fresh fresco(a)
Friday el viernes, LP
fried frito(a)
friend el/la amigo(a), 1.1; el/la compañero(a)
friendly agradable, 6.1
from de, LP; desde
   from time to time de vez en cuando
   from where? ¿de dónde?, 1.1
front *(adj.)* delantero(a), **8.1**
   in front of delante de, 2.2
front desk *(hotel)* la recepción, *7*
front door *(car, bus)* la puerta delantera, **8.1**
frozen congelado(a), 9.2
   frozen food los productos congelados, 9.2
fruit la fruta, 9.2
fruit stand la frutería, el puesto de frutas, 9.2
to **fry** freír (i, i), *4;* **1**
frying pan el/la sartén, *10;* **1**
full completo(a), 3.2; **6.1**
full of lleno(a) de, 6.1
full-time a tiempo completo, **10**
fun: to have fun divertirse (ie, i), pasarlo bien, 11.2; **2.2**
funds los fondos, *4*
funeral procession el cortejo fúnebre, **3.2**
funny cómico(a); gracioso(a), 1.1; divertido(a)
furious furioso(a)
furniture los muebles, 2.2
future el futuro

G

game el juego; *(match)* el partido, 5.1
garage el garaje, 2.2
garden el jardín, 2.2
garlic el ajo, *10;* **1**
gasoline la gasolina, la nafta, la benzina
gas station la estación de servicio, la gasolinera, 9.2
gas tank el tanque, 9.2
gate *(airport)* la puerta de salida, 10.2; *1.2;* **6.1**
to **gather** recoger, **6.1**
general general
   generally, in general en general, por lo general
generous generoso(a)
genre el género, **7.2**
gentle manso(a)
gentleman el señor, LP
geography la geografía
geometry la geometría
German alemán(ana)
to **get** sacar, 3.1; lograr, **8**
   to get angry enfadarse, **5**
   to get good (bad) grades sacar notas buenas (malas), 3.1
to **get dressed** ponerse la ropa, 11.1; *2.1;* vestirse (i, i), *4*
to **get off** *(train, bus)* bajar(se), *3.2*
to **get on** *(train, bus)* subir, 3.1; *(plane)* abordar, 10.2; *1.2*
to **get together** reunirse
to **get up** levantarse, 11.1; *2.1*
gift el regalo, 8.1; **3.1**;
   Christmas gift el aguinaldo, *5.2*
girl la muchacha, 1.1; la niña, 6.2; la chica, **5**
   fifteen-year-old girl la quinceañera
girlfriend la novia, **6 (Lit.)**
to **give** dar, 3.1; otorgar, **8**
   to give an exam dar un examen (una prueba), 3.1
   to give back devolver (ue)
   to give (someone) stitches poner unos puntos (unas suturas) (a alguien)
   to give (throw) a party dar una fiesta, 8.1
   to give up renunciar

glance la ojeada, **8**
glass (drinking) el vaso, 4.1; *4*
glove el guante, 5.2
glove compartment
la guantera, *9.2*
to **go** ir, 3.2; pasar, 5.2; andar, *3.2*
Let's go! ¡Vamos!
to be going
(to do something)
ir a + infinitivo, 4.2
to go back regresar, 3.2;
volver (ue), 5.1
to go bike riding andar
en bicicleta, *11.1;* **2.1**
to go camping
ir de camping, 11.2; *2.2*
to go down bajar, 7.2
to go for a hike dar una
caminata, 11.2; *2.2*
to go home regresar a casa,
ir a casa, 3.2; volver (ue)
a casa, 8.1
to go horseback riding
andar a caballo, *3.2;*
montar a caballo, 8.2
to go ice-skating patinar
sobre el hielo, 7.2
to go in-line skating
patinar en línea, *11.1;* **2.1**
to go jogging hacer
jogging, *11.1;* **2.1**
to go on a trip hacer un
viaje
to go online entrar en
línea, *6.1*
to go out salir, 8.1
to go over the net pasar
por encima de la red, 5.2
to go rollerblading (inline
skating) patinar en línea,
11.1; **2.1**
to go scuba diving bucear
to go shopping
ir de compras, 9.1
to go skiing esquiar, 7.2
to go snorkeling bucear,
7.1
to go surfing practicar
la tabla hawaiana, 7.1
to go swimming nadar, 7.1
to go through pasar por,
10.2; *1.2*
to go to bed acostarse (ue),
11.1; *2.1*
to go to the movies
ir al cine, 8.2
to go up subir, 7.2
to go waterskiing esquiar
en el agua, 7.1
to go windsurfing practicar
la plancha de vela, 7.1

goal el gol, 5.1
to score a goal meter un gol,
5.1
goal line la portería, 5.1
goalie el/la portero(a), 5.1
godchild el/la ahijado(a)
godfather el padrino, *3.2*
godmother la madrina, *3.2*
going to con destino a, 10.2; *1.2*
gold el oro
good buen, LP; bueno(a), 1.1
to be in a good mood
estar de buen humor, 6.1
to get good grades
sacar notas buenas, 3.1
Good afternoon. Buenas
tardes., LP
Good evening. Buenas
noches., LP
Good morning. Buenos
días., LP
Good-bye. ¡Adiós!; ¡Chao!, LP
to say good-bye despedirse
(i, i), **5**
good-looking guapo(a),
bonito(a), 1.1
government el gobierno, **10**
government official
el/la funcionario(a)
gubernamental
(de gobierno), **10**
grade la nota, 3.1
high grade la nota alta, 3.1
low grade la nota baja, 3.1
to get good (bad) grades
sacar notas buenas
(malas), 3.1
grandchildren los nietos, 2.1
granddaughter la nieta, 2.1
grandfather el abuelo, 2.1
grandmother la abuela, 2.1
grandparents los abuelos, 2.1
grandson el nieto, 2.1
to **grant** otorgar, **8**
grape la uva, 9.2; **9**
grapevine la vid, **9**
grass la hierba, *8.2*
grave la tumba, *5.1*
gravy la salsa, *10;* **1**
gray gris, 5.1
to **graze** pacer, *8.2*
great gran, grande
Great! ¡Bárbaro!, 5.2
greater (greatest) part
(la) mayor parte
green verde, 2.1
green beans las judías verdes,
9.2; **9;** las vainitas, **9**
green pepper el pimiento, 9.2;
10; **1**

greengrocer
(vegetable) store
la verdulería, 9.2
to **greet** saludar, **5**
greeting el saludo, LP
grill la parrilla, *10;* **1**
to **grill** asar, *10;* **1**
groom el novio, *3.1*
ground el suelo
group (*musical*) el grupo,
el conjunto, 8.1
to **grow (*agriculture*)** cultivar,
8.2; **9**
to **guard** guardar, 5.1
Guatemalan guatemalteco(a),
1.1
to **guess** adivinar
guest el/la invitado(a); *(hotel)*
el/la cliente, el/la huésped(a),
7
guitar la guitarra, 8.1
guy el tipo, 6.1
gymnasium el gimnasio,
11.1; **2.1**

— **H** —

habit la manía, **6 (Lit.)**
hair el pelo, 2.1
to brush one's hair
cepillarse, 11.1; *2.1*
to comb one's hair
peinarse, 11.1; *2.1*
to have blond (brown, black)
hair tener el pelo rubio
(castaño, negro), 2.1
haircut el corte de pelo, *4*
hair salon la peluquería, *4*
hair stylist el/la peluquero(a),
4
half (*soccer*) el tiempo, 5.1
second half (*soccer*)
el segundo tiempo, 5.1
half past (*hour*) y media, LP
ham el jamón, 4.1
ham and cheese sandwich
el sándwich de jamón
y queso, 4.1
hamburger la hamburguesa,
4.1
hand la mano, 3.1
to raise one's hand levantar
la mano, 3.1
handful el puñado, **4 (Lit.)**
to **hand over** entregar, **6 (Lit.)**
handsome guapo(a), 1.1
hanger la percha, el colgador,
7
Hanukkah el Hanuka, *5.2*

English-Spanish Dictionary

to **happen** pasar; ocurrir; suceder, **5** (Lit.)
  What's happening?
    ¿Qué pasa?
happiness la alegría, **3.1**; la felicidad
happy alegre, 6.1; **3.1**; contento(a), 6.1; feliz, *5.2*
  Happy Hanukkah!
    ¡Feliz Hanuka!, *5.2*
hard difícil, duro(a), *1.2*
hard copy la copia dura, *6.1*
hardworking ambicioso(a), *1.2*
harvest la cosecha, *8.2*
to **harvest** cosechar, *8.2*
hat el sombrero; *(ski)* el gorro, *7.2*
to **have** tener (ie), *2.1*; haber *(in compound tenses)*
  to have a cold tener catarro, *6.2*
  to have a cough tener tos, *6.2*
  to have a fever tener fiebre, *6.2*
  to have a good time pasarlo bien, divertirse (ie, i), 11.2; *2.2*
  to have a headache tener dolor de cabeza, *6.2*
  to have a party dar una fiesta, *8.1*
  to have a snack tomar una merienda, *4.2*
  to have a sore throat tener dolor de garganta, *6.2*
  to have a stomachache tener dolor de estómago, *6.2*
  to have blond (brown, black) hair tener el pelo rubio (castaño, negro), *2.1*
  to have blue (brown, green) eyes tener ojos azules (castaños, verdes), *2.1*
  to have breakfast (lunch) tomar el desayuno (el almuerzo); *4.1*
  to have dinner cenar, *4.1*
  to have fun pasarlo bien, divertirse (ie, i), 11.2; *2.2*
  to have just (done something) acabar de + infinitivo, *4.2*
  to have to (do something) tener que, *4.1*
hay el heno, *8.2*
he él, *1.1*
head la cabeza, 6.2; *2.1*

headache: to have a headache tener dolor de cabeza, *6.2*
headlights las luces, *9.2*
headline el titular, **8**
health la salud, *6.1*
to **hear** oír, *8.1*
  ¿Can you hear me? (telephone)
    ¿Me escuchas?, *6.2*
heart el corazón, **8**
heat el calor; el fuego, 10; **1**
  on low heat a fuego lento, 10; **1**
to **heat** poner en el fuego, 10; **1**
heavy pesado(a)
heel (of a shoe) el talón
height la altura
Hello! ¡Hola!, LP; *6.2*; *(on the phone)* ¡Diga!, ¡Dígame!, ¡Alo!, ¡Bueno!
helmet el casco, 7.2; *11.1*; **2.1**
help la ayuda
to **help** ayudar, 10.1; *1.1*
hen la gallina, *8.2*
her *(f. sing.) (pron.)* la
  to her *(pron.)* le
her su(s)
here aquí, 9.1; acá, 11.2; *2.2*
  Here it (they) is (are).
    Aquí lo (la, los, etc.) tienes.
hero el héroe
heroine la heroína
Hi! ¡Hola!, LP
high alto(a), *3.1*
high school la escuela secundaria, 1.2; el colegio
highway la autopista, la autovía, la carretera, *9.1*
hike: to take (go for) a hike dar una caminata, 11.2; *2.2*
hiker el/la mochilero(a), 11.2; *2.2*
him *(m. sing.) (pron.)* lo
  to him *(pron.)* le
his su(s)
Hispanic hispano(a)
history la historia, *1.2*
to **hit** *(baseball)* batear; *(tennis, volleyball)* golpear, *5.2*
  to hit a home run batear un jonrón, *5.2*
holiday la fiesta, *5.1*
home la casa, 2.2; a casa; *3.2*
  at home en casa
  to go home regresar a casa, 3.2; volver (ue) a casa, 8.1

home page la página de inicio (inicial, frontal), *6.1*
home plate el platillo, *5.2*
home run el jonrón, *5.2*
  to hit a home run batear un jonrón, *5.2*
homework las tareas
honest honesto(a)
honor: in honor of en honor de, **3.1**
hood *(car)* el capó, *9.2*
to **hope** esperar, **3.1**
  I hope . . . Ojalá… , *11.2*; **2.2**
horse el caballo, *3.2*
horseback riding la equitación, *8.2*
  to go horseback riding andar a caballo, 3.2; montar a caballo, *8.2*
hospital el hospital
hostel: youth hostel el albergue juvenil, el hostal, *7*
hot: to be hot tener (ie) calor, *11.1*; **2.1**
  It's (very) hot (weather). Hace (mucho) calor., LP
hot caliente, *4.1*
hotel el hotel, *7*
  small (inexpensive) hotel el hostal, *7*
hotel clerk el/la recepcionista, *7*
hour la hora
house la casa, *2.2*
  apartment house la casa de apartamentos
  private house la casa privada, *2.2*
housekeeper la camarera, *7*; el/la criado(a), **3** (Lit.)
how? ¿cómo?, 1.1; ¿qué?, LP
  How are things going? ¿Qué tal?, LP
  How are you? ¿Qué tal?, LP; ¿Cómo estás?
  How much does it cost? ¿Cuánto cuesta?, *3.2*
  How much is (are) . . . ? ¿A cuánto está(n)… ?, *9.2*
  How much is it? ¿Cuánto es?, LP
  How old is he (she)? ¿Cuántos años tiene?, *2.1*
how long . . . ? ¿Hace cuánto tiempo... ?
how many? ¿cuántos(as)?, *2.1*
how much? ¿cuánto?, *3.1*

however comoquiera
hug el abrazo, **5**
to **hug (someone)** abrazarse, **5**
human humano(a), 11.1; *2.1*
human being el ser humano
human resources department el departamento de personal (de recursos humanos), **10**
humble humilde
humor: to have a good sense of humor tener un buen sentido de humor, 6.1
hundred cien(to, ta), LP
hunger el hambre (*f.*)
hungry: to be hungry tener hambre, 4.1
hurried apresurado(a), **4**
hurry: to be in a hurry apresurarse, **10 (Lit.)**
to **hurt** doler (ue), 6.2; *11.2; 2.2*
It hurts him (me, etc.) a lot. Le (Me, etc.) duele mucho., *11.2; 2.2*
My head (stomach, etc.) hurts. Me duele la cabeza (el estómago, etc.), *11.2; 2.2*
to **hurt (oneself)** hacerse daño, *11.2; 2.2*
husband el esposo, el marido, 2.1

I yo, 1.1
ice el hielo, 7.2
ice cream el helado, 4.1
ice skate el patín, 7.2
to **ice-skate** patinar sobre el hielo, 7.2
ice-skater el/la patinador(a), 7.2
ice-skating el patinaje sobre (el) hielo, 7.2
ice-skating rink la pista de patinaje, 7.2
icon el icono, *6.1*
ID card el carnet de identidad, 10.2; *1.2*
idea la idea
idealist el/la idealista
identification la identidad, 10.2; *1.2*
piece of identification la forma de identidad, 10.2; *1.2*
to **identify** identificar
if si
ill enfermo(a), 6.2
ill-mannered mal educado(a), 6.1
illness la enfermedad

illustrious ilustre, **8**
to **imagine** imaginar
immediately enseguida, 4.2; inmediatamente
immense inmenso
immigration la inmigración, **6.1**
impatient impaciente, 6.1
important importante
impossible imposible
in en
in back of detrás de, 2.2
in front of delante de, 2.2
in general por lo general
inbox (e-mail) la bandeja de entradas, *6.1*
incline pendiente
to **include** incluir, **6.2**
Is the tip included? ¿Está incluido el servicio?, 4.2
to **increase** aumentar
incredible increíble
to **indicate** indicar
indigenous indígena, 9.2
individual: individual sport el deporte individual
inexpensive barato(a), 9.1
influence la influencia
to **inform** informar
information la información, 3.2
ingredient el ingrediente
inhabitant el/la habitante
inhospitable inhóspito(a)
injured herido(a)
injury la herida, *11.2; 2.2*
in-line skating el patinaje en línea, *11.1; 2.1*
to go in-line skating patinar en línea, *11.1; 2.1*
inn el parador
to **insert** insertar, *3.1*; introducir, *6.2*
instead of en vez de
instrument el instrumento
insurance: comprehensive insurance los seguros contra todo riesgo, **6.2**
intelligent inteligente, 1.2
interest el interés
to **interest** interesar, 5.1
interesting interesante, 1.2
international internacional, 10.1; *1.1*
interest rate la tasa de interés, **4**
Internet el Internet, 3.2; *6.1*
to surf the Net navegar el Internet, 3.2; *6.1*
to **interrupt** interrumpir

to **intersect** cruzarse
intersection la bocacalle, el cruce, 9.1
interview la entrevista, **10**
to **interview** entrevistar
interviewer el/la entrevistador(a)
to **invest** invertir (ie, i), **8**
to **invite** invitar
Irish irlandés(esa)
to **iron** planchar, **4**
Is . . . there, please? ¿Está... , por favor?, *6.2*
island la isla
it lo, la
Italian italiano(a)

jack *(car)* el/la gato(a), 9.2
jacket la chaqueta, 9.1
ski jacket la chaqueta de esquí, el anorak, 7.2
jam la mermelada, *7*
January enero, LP
Japonese japonés(esa)
jar el frasco, 9.2
jeans el blue jean, 9.1
Jewish judío(a), hebreo(a), *5.2*
job application la aplicación (la solicitud) de empleo, **10**
jogging: to go jogging hacer jogging, *11.1; 2.1*
journalist el/la periodista, **8**
juice el jugo, el zumo, 4.1
orange juice el jugo de naranja, 4.1; *7*
July julio, LP
June junio, LP
just: to have just (done something) acabar de + infinitivo, 4.2
just as (like) igual que

kebabs los pinchitos, 4.2
to **keep** guardar, *6.1*
key la llave, *7*; *(computer)* el botón, *6.1*
back key el botón de regresar (retroceder), *6.1*
delete key el botón borrador, *6.1*
magnetic key la llave magnética, *7*
keyboard el teclado, *6.1*

English-Spanish Dictionary

to **kick** lanzar, *5.1*
kilogram el kilo, *9.2*
kilometer el kilómetro
kind la clase
king el rey
   the Three Kings (Wise Men) los Reyes Magos, *5.2*
kiosk *(newsstand)* el quiosco, *3.1; (ticket dispenser)* el distribuidor automático, *3.1*
kiss el beso; **(little, often on cheek)** el besito, *5*
to **kiss** besar, *5*
kitchen la cocina, *2.2; 10; 1*
knapsack la mochila, *3.1*
knee la rodilla, *11.1; 2.1*
kneepad la rodillera, *11.1; 2.1*
knife el cuchillo, *4*
to **know** saber; conocer, *9.1*
   to know how (to do something) saber, *9.1*

to **lack** faltar, *6.1*
   He/She lacks . . . Le falta… , *6.1*
lamb el cordero, *4; 9*
lamp la lámpara, *2.2*
land la tierra, *8.2*
to **land** aterrizar, *10.2; 1.2*
landing el aterrizaje, *10.2; 1.2*
landowner el/la terrateniente
landscape el paisaje
lane *(highway)* el carril, *9.1;* la pista, la vía, la banda, el canal
language la lengua
lap *(track)* la vuelta, *11.1; 2.1*
laptop computer la computadora portátil
large gran, grande, *1.2*
last pasado(a) *7.1;* último(a)
   last night anoche, *7.1*
   last week la semana pasada, *7.1*
   last year el año pasado, *7.1*
to **last** durar
late tarde; con retraso (una demora), *10.2; 1.2*
later luego, LP; más tarde; después
   See you later! ¡Hasta luego!, LP
Latin America Latinoamérica

Latin American latinoamericano(a)
Latino latino(a)
to **laugh** reír
laundromat la lavandería, *4*
laundry el lavado, *4*
lawyer's office el bufete del abogado, *10*
lazy perezoso(a), *1.2*
to **lead (from one street into another)** desembocar
leaf (of lettuce) una hoja de lechuga, *9*
league la liga
to **learn** aprender, *4.2*
least: at least a lo menos
to **leave** salir, *8.1*
to **leave (something)** dejar, *4*
   to leave a message dejar un mensaje, *6.2*
   to leave a tip dejar una propina, *4*
left izquierdo(a), *11.1; 2.1*
   to the left a la izquierda, *9.1*
leftovers las sobras
leg la pierna, *11.1; 2.1*
lemon el limón
lemonade la limonada
less menos, *9.1*
lesson la lección
to **let** dejar; permitir
letter la carta, *4*
letter (of alphabet) la letra
lettuce la lechuga, *4.1*
   leaf of lettuce la hoja de lechuga, *9*
lid la tapa, *10; 1*
to **lie** mentir (ie, i), *8*
life la vida
   life passage el pasaje de la vida, *3*
to **lift** levantar, *11.1; 2.1*
   to lift weights levantar pesas, *11.1; 2.1*
light la luz, *5.2*
   red light la luz roja, *9.1*
   traffic light el semáforo, *8.1*
to **light** encender (ie), *5.2*
to **light up** iluminar, *5.2*
lightly ligeramente
lights las luces, *5.2; (headlights)* las luces, *9.2*
   festival of lights (Hanukkah) la fiesta de las luces, *5.2*
like como

to **like** gustar, *5.1;* encantar, *6.2*
   What would you like (to eat)? ¿Qué desean tomar?, *4.2*
line *(of people)* la cola, *10.2; 1.2;* la fila
   to wait in line hacer cola, *10.2; 1.2;* estar en fila
line la línea, *6.2*
   solid line *(road)* la línea continua, *9.1*
to **line up** hacer cola, *10.2; 1.2*
lion el león
lip el labio
to **listen to** escuchar, *3.2*
   Listen! ¡Oye!, *1.2*
literary literario(a)
literature la literatura, *7.2;* las letras
little pequeño(a), *1.2*
   a little poco(a), *2.2*
to **live** vivir, *4.1*
livestock el ganado, *8.2*
living room la sala, *2.2*
loan el préstamo, *4*
   short- (long-) term loan el préstamo a corto (largo) plazo, *4*
lobster la langosta, *4*
logical lógico(a)
long largo(a), *5.1*
long-distance *(race)* de larga distancia, *11.1; 2.1*
long-sleeved de manga larga, *9.1*
Look! ¡Mira!, *3.1*
to **look at** mirar, *3.2*
to **look at oneself** mirarse, *11.1; 2.1*
to **look for** buscar, *3.2*
Look out! ¡Cuidado!, *5*
to **lose** perder (ie), *5.1*
lot: a lot mucho(a), LP; muchos(as), *2.1*
lotion: suntan lotion la crema solar, la loción bronceadora, *7.1*
low bajo(a), *3.1*
   low (heat), a fuego lento, *10; 1*
to **lower** *(price)* rebajar, *9.1*
love el amor, *5*
   in love with enamorado(a) de
   loved one el/la amado(a)
to **love** encantar, *6.2;* querer (ie)
   She loves the music. Le encanta la música.

luck: How lucky I am!
¡Qué suerte tengo!, 9.1
luggage el equipaje, 10.1; *1.1*;
6.1
  carry-on luggage el equipaje
de mano, 10.1; *1.1*
  luggage cart carrito, *3.1*
  luggage claim ticket,
el talón, **6.1**
  luggage identification tag
la etiqueta, **6.1**
  to check luggage facturar
el equipaje, 10.1; *1.1*
lunch el almuerzo, 4.1
  to have lunch tomar el
almuerzo, 4.1
luxurious lujoso(a)

M

mad enojado(a), enfadado(a),
6.1
Madam la señora, LP
made hecho(a)
magazine la revista, *3.1;* **8**
magnetic magnético(a), *7*
magnificent magnífico(a)
maid la camerera, *7;* el/la
criado(a), **3 (Lit.)**
  maid of honor la dama
de honor, **3.1**
mail el correo, *4*
  e-mail el correo
electrónico, *6.1*
to **mail a letter** echar una carta, *4*
mailbox el buzón, *4*
main principal
majority la mayoría;
mayoritario(a) *(adj.)*
to **make** hacer, 10.2; *1.2;*
confeccionar, elaborar, *5.1*
  to make a basket
(basketball) encestar, 5.2
  to make a stopover hacer
escala, **6.1**
  to make better mejorar,
5 (Lit.)
  to make the bed hacer
la cama, *7*
mall el centro comercial, 9.1
man el hombre
manners los modales, 6.1; **5**
  to have good (bad)
manners tener buenos
(malos) modales, 6.1
manual transmission
la transmisión manual, **6.2**
many muchos(as), 2.2
  as many . . . as tantos(as)…
como

how many? ¿cuántos(as)?,
2.1
map el plano, *9.1;* el mapa, **6.2**
marathon el maratón, *11.1;* **2.1**
March marzo, LP
mark la nota, 3.1
  bad (low) mark la nota
mala (baja), 3.1
  good (high) mark la nota
buena (alta), 3.1
  to get good (bad) marks
sacar notas buenas
(malas), 3.1
market el mercado, 9.2
  native market el mercado
indígena, 9.2
market stall el puesto,
el tenderete, 9.2
marmalade la mermelada, *7*
marriage el matrimonio,
el casamiento, **3.1**
married: to get married
casarse, **3.1**
mask la máscara, *5.1*
mason el albañil, **10**
to **match** parear
mathematics las matemáticas,
1.2
mausoleum el mausoleo, *5.1*
maximum máximo(a)
May mayo, LP
maybe quizá, quizás, tal vez,
7.2
mayonnaise la mayonesa, 9.2
mayor el/la alcalde(sa), **3.1**
me *(pron.)* me
  to (for) me a (para) mí
meal la comida, 4.1
to **mean** significar
means of transport el medio
de transporte, *8.1*
meat la carne, 4.1; *4;* **9**
  ground meat la carne
picada, el picadillo, **9**
meatball la albóndiga, 4.2
meat pie la empanada, 4.2
media los medios
de comunicación, **8**
medicine el medicamento,
la medicina, 6.2
medium *(meat)* a término
medio, *4*
medium-sized mediano(a)
to **meet** encontrarse (ue);
conocer
member el miembro, 2.1;
socio(a)
menorah la menora, *5.2*
menu el menú, 4.2; *4*

merchant el/la
vendedor(a), 9.2; **10**
Merry Christmas!
¡Feliz Navidad!
merry-go-round el tiovivo,
8.1
mess: What a mess! ¡Qué lío!,
6.1
message el mensaje, *6.2*
meter el metro
Mexican mexicano(a)
Mexican American
mexicanoamericano(a), 1.2
microwave oven el horno de
microondas, *10;* **1**
Middle Ages la Edad Media
midnight la medianoche
mile la milla
mileage el kilometraje, **6.2**
milk la leche, 4.1
million el millón, 9.2
  million dollars un millón
de dólares, 9.2
mime el mimo, *8.1*
to **mince** picar, *10;* **1**
mind el espíritu, *11.1;* **2.1**
mineral water el agua
mineral, 4.2
mirror el espejo, *11.1;* **2.1**
Miss señorita, LP
to **miss (the bus, the flight)**
perder (ie) (el autobús,
el vuelo), 8.1; **6.1**
misunderstand malentender
(ie), **5**
misunderstanding
el malentendido, **5**
mobile phone el móvil, 3.2,
6.1; el celular, *6.1*
modern moderno(a)
mom mamá
moment el momento
monastery el monasterio
Monday el lunes, LP
money el dinero, 3.2
monitor *(computer)*
la pantalla de escritorio, *6.1*
month el mes, LP
monument el monumento
mood el humor, 6.1
  to be in a good (bad) mood
estar de buen (mal)
humor, 6.1
moon la luna
more más, 9.1
morning la mañana
  Good morning. Buenos
días., LP
  in the morning por la
mañana; de la mañana

English-Spanish Dictionary

mother la madre, 2.1
motive el motivo
mountain la montaña, 7.2
mountaintop el pico, 7.2
mouse el ratón, *6.1*
mousepad la alfombrilla, *6.1*
mouth la boca, 6.2
to **move** mover (ue)
movement el movimiento, *11.1;* **2.1**
movie la película, el filme, 8.2; el film
movie theater el cine, 8.2
movies: to go to the movies ir al cine, 8.2
MP3 player el MP3, 3.2; *6.2*
Mr. el señor, LP
Mr. and Mrs. los señores
Mrs. la señora, LP
Ms. la señorita, la señora, LP
much mucho(a), LP
  as much . . . as tan… como, *11.2;* **2.2**
  How much is it (does it cost)? ¿Cuánto es?, LP; ¿Cuánto cuesta?, 3.2
mud el lodo
to **murmur** musitar, **3 (Lit.)**
museum el museo, 8.2
music la música, 1.2
musician el/la músico(a), 8.1
mussels los mejillones, 4
must deber
my mi
mysterious misterioso(a)

N

name el nombre, 2.1
  My name is . . . Me llamo… , 11.1; *2.1*
  What is your name? ¿Cómo te llamas?, 11.1; *2.1;* ¿Cuál es su nombre?
napkin la servilleta, 4
narrative la narrativa, **7.2**
narrow angosto(a), estrecho(a), *8.1*
national nacional
nationality la nacionalidad, 1.1
  what nationality? ¿de qué nacionalidad?, 1.1
native indígena, 9.2
native person el/la indígena
nature la naturaleza

near cerca de, 3.2; cercano(a), **6.2**
necessary necesario(a)
  It's necessary. Es necesario., *11.2;* **2.2**
  it's necesssary to (do something) hay que, 10.2; *1.2*
neck el cuello, *11.1;* **2.1**
necktie la corbata, 9.1
to **need** necesitar, 3.2
negative negativo(a)
neighbor el/la vecino(a)
neighborhood el casco, el barrio, *8.1*
neither tampoco
nephew el sobrino, 2.1
nervous nervioso(a), 6.1
net *(World Wide Web)* la red, 3.2; *6.1; (tennis),* 5.2
  to surf the Net navegar el Internet, 3.2; *6.1*
never nunca, 8.2; jamás
new nuevo(a), 1.1
  New Year el Año Nuevo
  New Year's Eve la Nochevieja, la víspera del Año Nuevo
newborn el/la recién nacido(a), **3.2**
newlyweds los recién casados, **3.1**
news la(s) noticia(s), **8**
newscaster el/la noticiero(a), **8**
newspaper el periódico, *3.1;* **8**
newsstand el quiosco, 3.1
next próximo(a), *3.2;* que viene, 8.2
  next stop la próxima parada, 3.2
  next summer (year, etc.) el verano (año, etc.) que viene, 8.2
next to al lado de, 2.2
Nicaraguan nicaragüense
nice simpático(a), 1.1; *(weather)* buen (tiempo)
  Nice to meet you. Mucho gusto., 1.2
  The weather is nice. Hace buen tiempo., LP
nickname el apodo, **5 (Lit.)**
niece la sobrina, 2.1
night la noche
  at night por la noche
  Good night. Buenas noches., LP

last night anoche, 7.1
nine nueve, LP
nine hundred novecientos(as), 9.2
nineteen diecinueve, LP
ninety noventa, LP
no no, LP; ninguno(a)
  by no means de ninguna manera
nobody nadie, 8.2
none ninguno(a)
noon el mediodía
no one nadie, 8.2
no-smoking sign la señal de no fumar, 10.2; *1.2*
normal normal, 6.2
north el norte
North American norteamericano(a), 1.1
not no, 1.2
notebook el cuaderno, 3.1
nothing nada, 8.2
  Nothing else. Nada más., 9.2
novel la novela
novelist el/la novelista
November noviembre, LP
now ahora
nowadays hoy en día
number el número, 10.1; *1.1;* la cifra, **8**
  flight number el número del vuelo, 10.1; *1.1*
  seat number el número del asiento, 10.1; *1.1*
  telephone number el número de teléfono, *6.2*
nuptial nupcial, **3.1**
nurse el/la enfermero(a), 6.2; *11.2;* **2.2**

O

obituary la esquela, el obituario, **3.2**
object el objeto
objective el objetivo
obligatory obligatorio(a)
to **observe** observar
obsession la manía, **6 (Lit.)**
obstinate obstinado(a), 6.1
occasionally de vez en cuando
occupation la profesión, **10**
occupied ocupado(a), 4.2; *3.2*
ocean el océano
o'clock: It's two o'clock. Son las dos., LP

October octubre, LP
odd *(numeric)* impar
of de, LP
    Of course! ¡Cómo no!; ¡Claro!
    of the del, de la
to **offer** ofrecer
offering la ofrenda, *5.1*
office la oficina, *8.1;* **9**; el despacho, **4 (Lit.)**
    doctor's office la consulta del médico, *6.2;* **10**
official: government official el/la funcionario(a) gubernamental (de gobierno), **10**
often con frecuencia, a menudo
oil el aceite, *4*
    olive oil el aceite de oliva, **9**
oil paint el óleo, **7.1**
okay de acuerdo
old viejo(a), *2.2;* antiguo(a), *8.1*
    How old is he (she)? ¿Cuántos años tiene?, *2.1*
    old city el casco (barrio) antiguo, *8.1*
older mayor, *2.1*
oldest el/la mayor, *2.1*
olive la aceituna, *4.2;* la oliva
on sobre; en
    on board abordo, *10.2;* *1.2*
    on foot a pie, *3.2*
    on the edge of al borde mismo de
    on time a tiempo, *10.2;* *1.2*
    on top of sobre
one uno; uno(a), LP
one hundred cien(to), LP
one thousand mil, *9.2*
one-way (ticket) el boleto (billete) sencillo, *3.1;* **(street)** la calle de sentido único, *9.1*
onion la cebolla, *9.2;* **10**; **1**
online: to go online entrar en línea, *6.1*
only único(a), *2.1;* solo; solamente
to **open** abrir, *4.2*
open-air al aire libre, *7.2*
open-minded flexible, *6.1*
opinion la opinión
opponents el equipo contrario, *7.1*
opposite el contrario
or o, u *(used instead of **o** in front of words beginning with **o** or **ho**)*
orange (color) anaranjado(a), *5.1*

orange (fruit) la naranja, *4.1*
    orange juice el jugo (zumo) de naranja, *4.1;* *7*
orchard la huerta, *8.2;* **9**
order (restaurant) la orden, *4.2*
to **order (restaurant)** pedir (i, i)
oregano el orégano, **9**
to **organize** organizar
origin el origen
orthopedic surgeon el/la cirujano(a) ortopédico(a), *11.2;* **2.2**
other otro(a)
    any other cualquier otro(a)
    other people los demás, **5 (Lit.)**
our nuestro(a), nuestros(as)
outdoor *(adj.)* al aire libre, *7.2*
outfielder el/la jardinero(a), *5.2*
outskirts los alrededores, las afueras, **6.2**
oven el horno, *10;* **1**
over por encima de, *5.2*
overhead bin el compartimiento superior, *10.2;* *1.2*
overpopulation la sobrepoblación
owing to debido a, *6.1*
own propio(a), *5.1*
owner el amo, **8 (Lit.)**; el/la dueño(a), **10**
oxygen mask la máscara de oxígeno, *10.2;* *1.2*

to **pack** hacer la maleta, *10.1;* *1.1*
package el paquete, *9.2*
page la página; el paje, **3.1**
    home page la página de inicio (inicial, frontal), *6.1*
pain el dolor, *6.2*
paint la pintura, **7.1**
to **paint** pintar, **7.1**
paintbrush el pincel, **3 (Lit.)**
painter el/la pintor(a), *8.2;* **7.1**
painting el cuadro, *8.2;* **7.1**; la pintura
pair el par, *9.1*
    pair of shoes el par de zapatos, *9.1*
pants el pantalón, *3.1*
    long pants el pantalón largo, *9.1*

paper el papel, *3.1*
    sheet of paper la hoja de papel, *3.1*
    toilet paper el papel higiénico, *11.2;* *2.2*
paperback (book) el libro de bolsillo, *3.1;* **8**
parade el desfile, *5.2*
    to walk in a parade desfilar, *5.1*
paramedic el/la socorrista, *11.2;* **2.2**
parents los padres, *2.1*
park el parque, *11.2;* **2.2**
to **park** aparcar, *8.1;* estacionar, parquear
parka el anorak, *7.2*
parking lot un parking, un parqueo, *8.1*
parking meter el parquímetro, *9.1*
part la parte
    the greatest part, the majority la mayor parte
part-time a tiempo parcial, **10**
party la fiesta, *8.1*
    to (have) throw a party dar una fiesta, *8.1*
to **pass** pasar, *5.2;* *(car)* adelantar(se), rebasar, pasar, *9.1*
passenger el/la pasajero(a), *10.1;* *1.1*
passport el pasaporte, *10.2;* *1.2*
    passport inspection el control de pasaportes, **6.1**
past el pasado
pastry el pan dulce, *7*
path la senda, *3.2*
patience la paciencia, *6.1*
patient *(noun)* el/la paciente, *6.2*
patient *(adj.)* paciente, *6.1*
patron saint el/la santo(a) patrón(ona), *5.1*
    patron saint's day la fiesta patronal, *5.1*
pavement el pavimento
to **pay** pagar, *3.2*
    to pay attention prestar atención, *3.1;* hacerle caso, **5 (Lit.)**
pay phone el teléfono público, *6.2*
pea el guisante, *9.2*
peaceful tranquilo(a), *6.1*
peak el pico, *7.2*
peanut el cacahuate, el maní, *8.1;* el cacahuete

English-Spanish Dictionary

peasant el campesino, el peón, *8.2*

pedestrian el/la peatón(ona), *8.1*

   pedestrian crossing el cruce peatonal, *8.1*

to **peel** pelar, *10;* **1**

pen el bolígrafo, *3.1;* el lapicero, la pluma

pencil el lápiz, *3.1*

people la gente, *9.1*

   other people los demás, **5 (Lit.)**

pepper *(spice)* la pimienta, *4;* *(bell pepper)* el pimiento, *9.2; 10;* **1**; el pimentón; el ají; el chipotle; el morrón

perhaps quizá, quizás, tal vez, *7.2;* acaso, *3* **(Lit.)**

to **permit** permitir

person la persona

   person who just arrived el/la recién llegado(a), **5**

personality la personalidad, *6.1*

perspective la perspectiva, *7.1*

Peruvian el/la peruano(a)

peso el peso

pet la mascota, *2.1*

pharmacist el/la farmacéutico(a)

pharmacy la farmacia, *6.2*

phone el teléfono

   cell phone el móvil, *3.2, 6.1;* el (teléfono) celular, *6.1*

   pay phone el teléfono público, *6.2*

   phone book la guía telefónica, *6.2*

   phone call la llamada telefónica, *6.2*

   phone card la tarjeta telefónica, *6.2*

   phone number el número de teléfono, *6.2*

   phone receiver el auricular, *6.2*

   public phone el teléfono público, *6.2*

   to pick up the phone descolgar (ue) el auricular, *6.2*

   to speak on the phone hablar por teléfono

photo(graph) la foto(grafía), *7.1*

   to take photos sacar (tomar) fotos, *7.1*

physical *(exam)* el examen físico, *6.2*

   physical education la educación física, *1.2*

physics la física

piano el piano

to **pick up** recoger, *6.1*

to **pick up** *(phone)* descolgar (ue) el auricular, *6.2*

to **pick up** *(speed)* agarrar velocidad

picture la foto(grafía); la imagen

   to take pictures sacar (tomar) fotos, *7.1*

picturesque pintoresco(a); **7.1**

piece el pedazo, el trozo (trocito)

   little piece el pedacito, *10;* **1**

pig el cerdo, *8.2;* el cochinillo, el lechón, el chancho

pillow la almohada, *7*

pinch la pizca

pineapple la piña, *9.2*

pink rosado(a), *5.1*

pitcher *(baseball)* el/la pícher, el/la lanzador(a), *5.2*

pizza la pizza, *4.1*

place el lugar, *7.2;* el sitio

to **plan** planear

plane el avión, *10.1; 1.1*

planet el planeta

plant la planta, *2.2*

to **plant** sembrar (ie), *8.2*

plantain: slices of fried plantain los tostones, *4.2;* los patacones

plaster el yeso, **7.1**

plate el plato, *4*

platform *(railway)* el andén, *3.1*

to **play** *(sport)* jugar (ue), *5.1;* *(musical instrument)* tocar, *8.1; 5.2*

   to play soccer (baseball, etc.) jugar (al) fútbol (béisbol, etc.), *5.1*

player el/la jugador(a), *5.1*

   baseball player el/la jugador(a) de béisbol, el/la beisbolista, *5.2*

plaza la plaza, *8.1*

pleasant agradable, *6.1;* placentero(a)

please por favor, LP; favor de (+ infinitivo), *11.2; 2.2*

pleasure: It's a pleasure to meet you. Mucho gusto.

plot el argumento, **7.2**

plumber el/la fontanero(a), el/la plomero(a), **10**

P.M. de la tarde, de la noche

poem el poema, **7.2**

poet el/la poeta, **7.2**

poetry la poesía, **7.2**

point el tanto, *5.1;* el punto

   to score a point marcar un tanto, *5.1*

to **point out** señalar

policy la póliza, **6.2**

polite bien educado(a), *6.1;* cortés, **5**

politician el/la político(a), **10**

polluted contaminado(a)

pollution la contaminación

pool la piscina, la alberca, *7.1;* la pila

poor pobre

popular popular

population la población

pork el cerdo, **9**

pork chop la chuleta de cerdo, *4;* **1**

portrait el retrato

Portuguese portugués(esa)

position el puesto, **10**

to **possess** poseer

possibility la posibilidad

possible posible

postcard la tarjeta postal, *4*

pot la olla, la cacerola, la cazuela *10;* **1**

potato la papa, la patata, *4.1*

   french fried potatoes las papas (patatas) fritas, *4.1*

pothole el bache

practically casi, *8.2*

to **practice** practicar

to **prefer** preferir (ie, i), *5.2;* *4*

to **prepare** preparar; confeccionar, *5.1*

to **prescribe** recetar, *6.2*

prescription la receta, *6.2*

present el regalo, *8.1*

   Christmas present el aguinaldo, *5.2*

to **present** presentar

president el/la presidente(a)

press la prensa, **8**

to **press** *(button)* oprimir, pulsar, *6.1*

pretty bonito(a), 1.1; hermoso(a)

previous anterior, 6.1

price el precio, 9.1; la tarifa, **6.2**

priest el cura, **3.1**; el sacerdote, 8

primary primario(a)

to **print** imprimir, 6.1

printer la impresora, 6.1

private privado(a), 2.2

probable probable

problem el problema

procession la procesión, 5.1

product el producto, 9.2

profession la profesión, 10

promotion (sales) la promoción, 8

prose la prosa, 7.2

protagonist la protagonista, **7.2**

proud orgulloso(a), **9**

public público(a)

Puerto Rican puertorriqueño(a), 1.1

pulse el pulso, 6.2

to **punish** castigar, 5

purchase la compra, 9.2

to **push (button)** oprimir, pulsar, 6.1

push-ups: to do push-ups hacer planchas, 11.1; **2.1**

to **put** poner, 10.2; 1.2; meter, 5.2

to **put in charge** encargar, **4 (Lit.)**

to **put on (clothes)** ponerse, 11.1; 2.1; (brakes) poner los frenos

to **put up (tent)** armar, montar, 11.2; 2.2

puzzle el rompecabezas

quarter (city) el casco, el barrio, 8.1; (time) el cuarto, LP

a quarter past (the hour) y cuarto, LP

question la pregunta, 3.1

to ask a question preguntar, 3.1

quickly rápidamente

quiet tranquilo(a), calmo(a), 6.1

quite bastante, 1.2

R

race la carrera, 11.1; **2.1**

cross-country race la carrera a campo traviesa, 11.1; **2.1**

long-distance race la carrera de larga distancia, 11.1; **2.1**

relay race la carrera de relevos, 11.1; **2.1**

racket la raqueta, 5.2

railroad el ferrocarril, 3.1

railroad platform el andén, 3.1

railroad station la estación de ferrocarril, 3.1; **6.2**

to **rain** llover (ue)

It's raining. Llueve., LP

raincoat impermeable

to **raise** levantar, 3.1

to raise one's hand levantar la mano, 3.1

ranch la hacienda, la estancia, el rancho, 8.2

rare (meat) casi crudo, 4

rate la tarifa; la tasa

rather bastante, 1.2

raw crudo(a), 8.1

raw vegetables los vegetales crudos, 8.1

reaction la reacción

to **read** leer, 4.2

reading la lectura

ready listo(a)

to **realize** darse cuenta de, 8

really realmente

rearview mirror el retrovisor, **6.2**

reason la razón, el motivo

to **receive** recibir, 4.1

receiver (telephone) el auricular, 6.2

reception la recepción, **3.1**

recipe la receta, 10; **1**

recipient el/la destinatario(a), 6.1

to **recognize** reconocer

to **recommend** recomendar (ie)

record el disco

red rojo(a), 5.1

red light la luz roja, 9.1

redheaded pelirrojo(a), 1.1

to **reduce (price)** rebajar, 9.1

to **reduce (speed)** reducir la velocidad, 9.1

reduced reducido(a)

refrigerator el refrigerador, la nevera, 10; **1**

region la región

to **rejoice** alegrarse, 3.1

relative el/la pariente, 2.1

relay: relay race la carrera de relevos, 11.1; **2.1**

reliability la confiabilidad

religious religioso(a)

to **remain** quedarse, 11.1; **2.1**

to **remember** recordar (ue)

to **rent** alquilar, rentar, 7.1; 3.2; **6.2**; arrendar (ie), **6.2**

to **repeat (take second helping)** repetir (i, i), 4

report el reportaje, 8

to **represent** representar

republic la república

Dominican Republic la República Dominicana

to **request** pedir (i, i), 4

to **require** exigir

required obligatorio(a)

reservation la reservación, 7; la reserva

to **reserve** reservar, 7

resort: seaside resort el balneario, 7.1

ski resort la estación de esquí, 7.2

rest lo demás

to **rest** descansar, 11.1; **2.1**

restaurant el restaurante, 4

restroom el servicio, 10.2; 1.2

result el resultado

résumé el currículum vitae, **10**

to **return** regresar, 3.2; volver (ue), 5.1; **to return (something)** devolver (ue), 5.2

review el repaso

to **review** repasar

rhyme la rima, **7.2**

rice el arroz, 4.1

rich rico(a)

to **rid** liberar, 11.1; **2.1**

ride: to go for a (bike) ride dar un paseo en bicicleta

to **ride (horse)** andar a caballo, 3.2; montar a caballo, 8.2; (bicycle) andar en bicicleta, 11.1; **2.1**

English-Spanish Dictionary

rides *(amusement park)* las atracciones, *8.1*

right derecho(a), 11.1; *2.1*

  right on the edge of al borde mismo de

  to the right a la derecha, *9.1*

  right: That's right! ¡Verdad!

  right away enseguida, 4.2

to **ring** sonar (ue), *6.1*

ringtone el timbre (sonoro), *6.2*

rink *(ice-skating)* la pista de patinaje, 7.2

to **rise** alzarse, **8**

rite el rito

river el río

roast asado(a)

  roast suckling pig el cochinillo asado, el lechón asado, el chancho asado

  to roast asar, *10;* **1**

roll *(bread)* el panecillo, 4.1; *7*

roll of toilet paper el rollo de papel higiénico, 11.2; *2.2*

rollerblading el patinaje en línea, *11.1;* **2.1**

rollerblading: to go rollerblading patinar en línea, *11.1;* **2.1**

roller coaster la montaña rusa, *8.1*

romantic romántico(a)

room el cuarto, 2.2; *7;* *(museum)* el salón, 8.2

  bathroom el cuarto de baño, 2.2; *7*

  bedroom el cuarto de dormir, la recámara, 2.2; el dormitorio, la habitación, la alcoba, la pieza

  classroom la sala de clase, 3.1

  dining room el comedor, 2.2

  emergency room la sala de emergencia, *11.2;* **2.2**

  living room la sala, 2.2

  restroom el servicio, 10.2; *1.2*

  single (double) room el cuarto sencillo (doble), *7*

  waiting room la sala de espera, *3.1*

round-trip *(ticket)* el boleto (billete) de ida y vuelta (regreso), *3.1*

routine la rutina, 11.1; *2.1*

  daily routine la rutina diaria, 11.1; *2.1*

row *(of seats)* la fila, **6.1**

rude mal educado(a), 6.1

ruins las ruinas

rule la regla

to **run** correr, 5.2

runner el/la corredor(a), *11.1;* **2.1**

running water el agua corriente

runway la pista, 10.2; *1.2*

rural rural

sad triste, deprimido(a), 6.1

saffron el azafrán

sailboard la plancha de vela, 7.1

saint el/la santo(a), *5.1*

  patron saint el/la santo(a) patrón(ona), *5.1*

salad la ensalada, 4.1

sale el saldo, la liquidación, 9.1

salesperson el/la empleado(a), 3.2; el/la dependiente(a), 9.1

salt la sal, *4*

salty salado(a)

same mismo(a), 1.2

sand la arena, 7.1

sandal la sandalia, 9.2

sandwich el sándwich, el bocadillo, 4.1; la torta

  ham and cheese sandwich el sándwich de jamón y queso, 4.1

satisfied satisfecho(a)

to **satisfy** satisfacer

Saturday el sábado, LP

sauce la salsa, *10;* **1**

saucepan la cacerola, la cazuela, la olla, *10;* **1**

saucer el platillo, *4*

sausage el chorizo

to **save** guardar, *6.1*

saxophone el saxófono

to **say** decir, *3.2*

  to say good-bye despedirse (i, i), **5**

scenery el paisaje

schedule *(train)* el horario, *3.1*

school la escuela, 1.2; el colegio; la academia

  elementary school la escuela primaria

  high school la escuela secundaria, 1.2; el colegio

school *(adj.)* escolar

  school bus el bus escolar, 3.2

  school supplies los materiales escolares, 3.1

science la ciencia, 1.2

score el tanto, 5.1

  to score a goal meter un gol, 5.1

  to score a point marcar un tanto, 5.1

scrambled: scrambled eggs los huevos revueltos, *7;* los huevos batidos, **9**

scratch el rayón, *6.2*

screen *(computer)* la pantalla de escritorio, *6.1;* la pantalla, **6.1**

scuba diving el buceo

  to go scuba diving bucear

sculptor el/la escultor(a), 8.2; **7.1**

sculpture la escultura, 8.2; **7.1**

sea el mar, 7.1

  Caribbean Sea el mar Caribe

seafood los mariscos, *4*

search: in search of en busca de

to **search** buscar, *3.2*

seaside resort el balneario, 7.1

season la estación, LP

  What season is it? ¿Qué estación es?, LP

seat el asiento, 10.1; *1.1;* **6.1;** la plaza, 3.2; **6.1**

  seat number el número del asiento, 10.1; *1.1*

seat belt el cinturón de seguridad, 10.2; *1.2*

second segundo(a), 5.1

  second-class segunda clase, *3.1*

  second half *(soccer)* el segundo tiempo, 5.1

secondary secundario(a), 1.2

security *(checkpoint)* el control de seguridad, 10.2; *1.2*

  to go through security pasar por el control de seguridad, 10.2; *1.2*

sedan el sedán, *9.2*

  four-door sedan el sedán a cuatro puertas, *9.2*

to **see** ver, 4.2

  let's see a ver

  See you later. ¡Hasta luego!, LP

  See you soon! ¡Hasta pronto!, LP

  See you tomorrow! ¡Hasta mañana!, LP

to **seem** parecer

  It seems to me . . . Me parece…

to **select** seleccionar, *3.1*

self-serve autoservicio

to **sell** vender, 6.2

senator el/la senador(a), **10**

to **send** enviar, 3.2; mandar

sense: sense of humor el sentido de humor, 6.1

  to have a good sense of humor tener un buen sentido de humor, 6.1

sent mailbox la bandeja de enviados, *6.1*

sentence la frase, la oración

September septiembre, LP

serious serio(a), 1.1

to **serve** servir (i, i), *4*

  to serve as servir (i, i) de

server el/la mesero(a), 4.2, *4;* el/la camarero(a), *4*

service el servicio, *9.2*

to **set** *(table)* poner la mesa, *4;* *(bone)* reducir, acomodar el hueso, 11.2; *2.2*

setting el lugar, 7.2

to **settle** establecer(se), **8**

seven siete, LP

seven hundred setecientos(as), *9.2*

seventeen diecisiete, LP

seventy setenta, LP

several varios(as)

shack la choza, **4 (Lit.)**; la casucha

shake *(drink)* el batido, 4.2

to **shake hands** darse la mano, **5**

shame: What a shame! ¡Qué pena!, 5.1

  to be a shame ser una lástima

shampoo el champú, 11.2; *2.2*

shape la forma

she ella, 1.1

sheet la sábana, *7*

sheet of paper la hoja de papel, 3.1

shellfish los mariscos, *4*

shirt la camisa, 3.1

  short- (long-) sleeved shirt la camisa de manga corta (larga), 9.1

shoe size el número, 9.1

  What size shoe do you wear (take)? ¿Qué número calzas?, 9.1

shoes las zapatillas, 5.1; los zapatos, 9.1

to **shop** ir de compras, 9.1

shopping cart el carrito, 9.2

shopping center el centro comercial, 9.1

short *(person)* bajo(a), 1.1; *(length)* corto(a), 9.1; *4*

short-sleeved de manga corta, 9.1

shorts el pantalón corto, 5.1

should deber, 4.2

shoulder *(road)* el acotamiento, el arcén, 9.1; *(body)* el hombro, 11.1; *2.1*

to **show** mostrar (ue), 10.2; *1.2*

shower la ducha, 11.1; *2.1*

  to take a shower tomar una ducha, 11.1; *2.1*

shrimp los camarones, 4.2

shy tímido(a)

sick enfermo(a), 6.2

sick person el/la enfermo(a)

side el lado

sidewalk la acera, 8.1

sign la señal, 10.2; *1.2; (road)* el rótulo, *9.1*

  no-smoking sign la señal de no fumar, 10.2; *1.2*

to **sign** firmar, *3.1*

similar similar

since desde; como

sincere sincero(a); franco(a)

to **sing** cantar, 8.1

singer el/la cantante, 8.1

single solo(a); *(room)* un cuarto sencillo, *7*

singles *(tennis)* individuales, 5.2

sink el lavabo, *7*

sir señor, LP

sister la hermana, 2.1

to **sit down** sentarse (ie), 11.1; *2.1*

site (Web site) el sitio, *6.1*

six seis, LP

six hundred seiscientos(as), *9.2*

sixteen dieciséis, LP

sixty sesenta, LP

size *(clothing)* la talla; *(shoes)* el número, 9.1

  What size *(clothing)* **do you wear (take)?** ¿Qué talla usas?, 9.1

  What size *(shoe)* **do you wear (take)?** ¿Qué número calzas?, 9.1

to **skate** patinar, 7.2; *11.1; 2.1*

  to ice-skate patinar sobre el hielo, 7.2

  to in-line skate (rollerblade) patinar en línea, *11.1; 2.1*

skateboard el monopatín, *11.1; 2.1*

skating el patinaje, 7.2; *11.1; 2.1*

skeleton el esqueleto, 5.1

ski el esquí, 7.2

  ski hat el gorro, 7.2

  ski jacket la chaqueta de esquí, el anorak, 7.2

  ski lift el telesilla, el telesquí, 7.2

  ski pole el bastón, 7.2

  ski resort la estación de esquí, 7.2

  ski slope la pista, 7.2

to **ski** esquiar, 7.2

  to water-ski esquiar en el agua, 7.1

skier el/la esquiador(a), 7.2

skiing el esquí, 7.2

  cross-country skiing el esquí nórdico

  downhill skiing el esquí alpino, 7.2

  waterskiing el esquí acuático (náutico), 7.1

skillet el/la sartén, *10; 1*

skinny enjuto(a), **10 (Lit.)**

skirt la falda, 3.1

skull el cráneo, la calavera, *5.1*

sky el cielo, 5.2

skyscraper el rascacielos, 8.1

to **sleep** dormir (ue, u)

  sleeping bag el saco (la bolsa) de dormir, 11.2; *2.2*

English-Spanish Dictionary

sleeved: short- (long-) sleeved de manga corta (larga), 9.1

slice la tajada, 9.2; la rebanada, 10; **1**; *(ham)* la lonja, la loncha; *(lemon, cucumber)* la rodaja, 9; *(melon)* la raja

to **slice** cortar en rebanadas, *10;* **1**

slope la pista, 7.2

slot la ranura, *6.2*

slow lento(a), *11.1;* **2.1**

slowly despacio, *9.1*

small pequeño(a), 1.2

to **smell** olfatear, **8**

smile la sonrisa, 6.1

smoking: no-smoking sign la señal de no fumar, 10.2; *1.2*

smoothie el batido, 4.2

snack la merienda; las tapas, los antojitos, 4.2; los bocaditos

sneakers las zapatillas, 5.1; los tenis, 5.2

to **sniff** olfatear, **8**

to **snorkel** bucear, *7.1*

snorkeling el buceo, *7.1*

snow la nieve, 7.2

to **snow** nevar (ie), 7.2

It's snowing. Nieva., LP

snowboarder el/la snowboarder, 7.2

so tan; **(thus)** así

so that para que, de modo que, de manera que

soap el jabón, 11.2; *2.2*

bar of soap la barra de jabón, 11.2; *2.2;* la pastilla de jabón

soap opera la telenovela

soccer el fútbol, 5.1

soccer field el campo de fútbol, 5.1

social studies los estudios sociales, 1.2

socks los calcetines, 5.1

soda la cola, la gaseosa, 4.1

sofa el sofá, 2.2

soft blando(a)

soft drink el refresco, 4.2

soldier el soldado, **8**

solid line *(road)* la línea continua, *9.1*

some algunos(as); unos(as)

someone alguien, 8.2

something algo

sometimes a veces, 6.1; *1.2;* de vez en cuando

son el hijo, 2.1

soon pronto, LP; dentro de poco, 10.2; *1.2*

as soon as en cuanto

See you soon! ¡Hasta pronto!, LP

sore throat: to have a sore throat tener dolor de garganta, 6.2

to **surprise** sorprender, *3.1*

sorry: to be sorry sentir (ie, i)

I'm sorry. Lo siento mucho., 5.1

soul el alma *(f.)*

soup la sopa

south el sur

South America la América del Sur, la Sudamérica

to **sow** sembrar (ie), *8.2*

space el espacio; *(parking)* el sitio (para estacionar)

Spain España

Spanish *(language)* el español, 1.2; *(person)* el/la español(a)

Spanish *(adj.)* español(a)

Spanish speaker el/la hispanohablante

Spanish-speaking hispanohablante

spare time el tiempo libre, 8.1

spare tire la rueda (llanta) de repuesto (recambio), *9.2;* de refacción

to **speak** hablar, 3.1

to speak on the phone hablar por teléfono

special especial

specialty la especialidad

spectator el/la espectador(a)

speed la velocidad, *9.1*

speed limit la velocidad máxima, *9.1;* el límite de velocidad

to **spend *(time)*** pasar, 7.1; *(money)* gastar

spice la especia; **9**

spirit el espíritu, *11.1;* **2.1**

to **splurge** botar la casa por la ventana

spoon *(tablespoon)* la cuchara, *4; (teaspoon)* la cucharita, *4*

sport el deporte, 5.1

individual sport el deporte individual

team sport el deporte de equipo

sports *(related to)* deportivo(a)

sports car el coche deportivo, *9.2*

to **sprain** torcerse (ue), *11.2;* **2.2**

He (She) sprained his (her) ankle. Se torció el tobillo., *11.2;* **2.2**

spring la primavera, LP

square *(town)* la plaza, *8.1*

stable el establo, *8.2*

stadium el estadio

stairs la escalera, *8.1*

stall *(market)* el puesto, el tenderete, 9.2

stamp la estampilla, el sello, **4**

to **stand in line** hacer cola, 10.2; *1.2;* estar en fila

to **stand up** ponerse de pie, **5**

standing de pie

stanza la estrofa, *7.2*

star la estrella

to **start to (do something)** echar a, **6 (Lit.)**

starving: I'm starving. Me muero de hambre., *4*

state el estado

station *(train)* la estación de ferrocarril (tren), *3.1;* **6.2;** *(subway)* la estación de metro, *8.1; (gas)* la estación de servicio, la gasolinera, *9.2*

statue la estatua, *8.2;* **7.1**

stay la estadía

to **stay** quedarse, *11.1;* **2.1**

to stay in bed *(illness)* guardar cama, 6.2; **to stay at home *(idleness)*** quedarse en la cama, 11.1; *2.1*

to **stay in a hotel** hospedarse, 7

steak el biftec, 4

steep pendiente

steering wheel el volante, 9.2

stepbrother el hermanastro, 2.1

stepfather el padrastro, 2.1

stepmother la madrastra, 2.1

stepsister la hermanastra, 2.1

still todavía

still life la naturaleza muerta, **7.1**

stingy tacaño(a), 9.1

to **stir** revolver (ue), 10; **1**

stitch el punto, la sutura, 11.2; **2.2**

  to give (someone) stitches poner unos puntos (unas suturas) (a alguien), 11.2; **2.2**

stomach el estómago, 6.2

  to have a stomachache tener dolor de estómago, 6.2

stone la piedra

stop la parada, 3.2

  next stop la próxima parada, 3.1

  to make a stopover hacer escala, **6.1**

to **stop** parar(se), 9.1

store la tienda, 3.2

story el cuento, **7.2**; la historia

stove la cocina, la estufa, 10; **1**

straight (ahead) derecho, 9.1

  to go straight (ahead) seguir (i, i) derecho, 9.1

straw la paja, 5.2

street la calle, 8.1

  one-way street la calle de sentido único, 9.1

stress el estrés, 6.2; las tensiones, 11.1; **2.1**

stretch (distance) el trecho

to **stretch** estirarse, 11.1; 2.1; **2.1**

stretcher la camilla, 11.2; **2.2**

string beans las judías verdes, 9.2

strong fuerte

stubborn obstinado(a), terco(a), 6.1

student el/la alumno(a), 1.2; el/la estudiante; (adj.) estudiantil, escolar, 3.1

  university student el/la estudiante universitario(a), **10**

study el estudio

  social studies los estudios sociales, 1.2

to **study** estudiar, 3.1

stuffed up (head cold) resfriado(a), 6.2

stupendous estupendo(a)

style el estilo

to **subject** sujetar, **4 (Lit.)**

suburbs las afueras, los suburbios, 2.2; **6.2**

subway el metro, 8.1

  subway entrance la boca del metro, 8.1

  subway station la estación de metro, 8.1

to **succeed** tener éxito, 6.1

success el éxito, 6.1

successful: to be successful tener éxito, 6.1

such tal

suddenly de repente

to **suffer** sufrir

sugar el azúcar

to **suggest** sugerir (ie, i)

suitcase la maleta, 10.1; 1.1; **6.1**

  to pack one's suitcase hacer la maleta, 10.1; 1.1

summer el verano, LP

sun el sol

to **sunbathe** tomar el sol, 7.1

Sunday el domingo, LP

sunglasses los anteojos de sol, las gafas para el sol, 7.1

sunny: It's sunny. Hace (Hay) sol., LP

suntan lotion la crema solar, la loción bronceadora, 7.1

supermarket el supermercado, 9.2

supplies: school supplies los materiales escolares, 3.1

supposed to: I was supposed to (do something) habría de (+ infinitivo), **4**

sure seguro(a)

to **surf** practicar la tabla hawaiana, 7.1

to **surf the Web (the Net)** navegar la red (el Internet), 3.2; **6.1**

surface la superficie, **7.1**

surfboard la tabla hawaiana, 7.1

surfing la tabla hawaiana, el surfing, 7.1

  to go surfing practicar la tabla hawaiana, el surfing, 7.1

surgeon:
  orthopedic surgeon el/la cirujano(a) ortopédico(a), 11.2; **2.2**

to **surpass** sobrepasar, **8**

surprise la sorpresa, 4.1

survey la encuesta

SUV el SUV, 9.2

sweat suit el buzo, 11.1; **2.1**

sweater el suéter, 11.1; 2.1

sweet dulce, 5.1

to **swim** nadar, 7.1

swimming pool la piscina, la alberca, 7.1; la pila

swimsuit el bañador, el traje de baño, 7.1

swollen hinchado(a), 11.2; **2.2**

symptom el síntoma

system el sistema

T-shirt la camiseta, 5.1; el T-shirt

table la mesa, la mesita, 2.2; 4

  to clear the table levantar, quitar la mesa, 4

  to set the table poner la mesa, 4

tablecloth el mantel, 4

tablespoon la cuchara, 4; (in recipe) la cucharada

taco el taco

to **take** tomar, 3.1; traer, 10.1; 1.1; sacar, 7.1

  to take (by force) apoderarse de, **4 (Lit.)**

  to take (size) usar, calzar, 9.1

  to take a bath bañarse

  to take a flight tomar un vuelo

  to take a hike dar una caminata, 11.2; **2.2**

  to take a shower tomar una ducha, 11.1; **2.1**

  to take a test tomar un examen, 3.1

  to take a trip hacer un viaje, 10.1; 1.1

  to take an X ray of someone tomar una radiografía, 11.2; **2.2**

  to take into account tomar en cuenta, **8**

  to take pictures (photos) sacar (tomar) fotos, 7.1

English-Spanish Dictionary

to take place tener lugar, **3.1**

to take someone's blood pressure tomar la tensión arterial, 6.2

to take someone's pulse tomar el pulso, 6.2

to take the (school) bus tomar el bus (escolar), 3.2

to **take off** *(airplane)* despegar, 10.2; *1.2; (clothes)* quitarse, 11.1; *2.1*

to **take out** sacar

taken ocupado(a), 4.2; *3.2*

takeoff el despegue, 10.2; *1.2*

talent el talento, **7.2**

to **talk** hablar, 3.1

to talk on a cell phone hablar en el móvil

to talk on the phone hablar por teléfono

tall alto(a), 1.1

tank *(car)* el tanque, *9.2*

taste el gusto

tax el impuesto

taxi el taxi, 10.1; *1.1*

taxi driver el/la taxista, 10.1; *1.1*

tea el té

to **teach** enseñar, 3.1

teacher el/la profesor(a), 1.2

team el equipo, 5.1

team sport el deporte de equipo

tear la lágrima, **10 (Lit.)**

teaspoon la cucharita, *4; (in recipe)* la cucharadita

teeth los dientes, 11.1; *2.1*

to brush one's teeth cepillarse (lavarse) los dientes, 11.1; *2.1*

telegram el telegrama

telephone el teléfono

pay telephone el teléfono público, *6.2*

(related to) **telephone** telefónico(a), *6.2*

telephone book la guía telefónica, *6.2*

telephone call la llamada telefónica, *6.2*

telephone card la tarjeta telefónica, *6.2*

telephone line la línea, *6.2*

telephone number el número de teléfono, *6.2*

telephone receiver el auricular, *6.2*

to pick up the telephone descolgar (ue) el auricular, *6.2*

to speak on the telephone hablar por teléfono

television la televisión, la tele

television program la emisión televisiva, el programa de televisión, **8**

television station la emisora de televisión, **8**

temperature la temperatura, 7.2

ten diez, LP

tennis el tenis, 5.2

tennis court la cancha de tenis, 5.2

tennis player el/la tenista, 5

tennis racket la raqueta, 5.2

tennis shoes los tenis, 9.1

to play tennis jugar (ue) (al) tenis, 5.2

tension la tensión, *11.1; 2.1*

tent la carpa, la tienda de campaña, 11.2; *2.2*

to put up a tent armar, montar la carpa (la tienda de campaña), 11.2; *2.2*

terrace la terraza

terrible terrible

test el examen, la prueba, 3.1

to give a test dar un examen (una prueba), 3.1

to take a test tomar un examen, 3.1

Texan tejano(a)

text message el mensaje de texto

Thank you. Gracias., LP

that aquel, aquella, 9.1; ese(a)

that *(one)* eso

the el, la, 1.1

their su(s)

them las, los

to them *(form. pl.) (pron.)* les

theme el tema

then luego, 3.2

there allí, allá, 9.1

Is . . . there? ¿Está… ?, *6.2*

there is, there are hay, 2.2

therefore por eso

these estos(as)

they ellos(as), 1.2

thigh el muslo, 10; **1**

thin flaco(a); delgado(a); enjuto(a), **10 (Lit.)**

thing la cosa, 3.1

to **think** pensar (ie), 5.1

What do you think? ¿Qué piensas?, 5.1

thirsty: to be thirsty tener sed, 4.1

thirteen trece, LP

thirty treinta, LP

thirty-one treinta y uno, LP

this este(a), 9.1

those aquellos(as), esos(as)

thousand mil, 9.2

three tres, LP

the Three Wise Men los Reyes Magos, *5.2*

three hundred trescientos(as), 9.2

throat la garganta, 6.2

to have a sore throat tener dolor de garganta, 6.2

to **throw** lanzar, tirar, 5.2

to throw (give) a party dar una fiesta, 8.1

Thursday el jueves, LP

thus así

ticket el boleto, el ticket, 7.2; *3.1;* la entrada, 8.1; el billete, 10.1; *1.1;* el tiquet(e); *(car)* la multa, *9.1*

e-ticket el boleto (billete) electrónico, 10.1; *1.1*

one-way ticket el boleto (billete) sencillo, *3.1*

round-trip ticket el boleto (billete) de ida y vuelta (regreso), *3.1*

to give (someone) a ticket clavar con una multa, *9.1*

ticket counter *(airport)* el mostrador, 10.1; *1.1*

ticket dispenser el distribuidor automático, *3.1*

ticket window la ventanilla, la boletería, 7.2, *3.1;* la taquilla, 8.2

tie la corbata, 9.1

tiger el tigre

time la hora, LP; 10.1; *1.1;* el tiempo, 8.1; la vez

  at times (sometimes) a veces, 6.1; *1.2*

  at what time? ¿a qué hora?, LP

  boarding time la hora de embarque, 10.1; *1.1*

  departure time la hora de salida, 10.1; *1.1*

  from time to time de vez en cuando, 10.2, *1.2*

  full-time a tiempo completo

  on time a tiempo, 10.2; *1.2*

  part-time a tiempo parcial

  spare time el tiempo libre, 8.1

  What time is it? ¿Qué hora es?, LP

timetable el horario, *3.1*

timid tímido(a)

tip el servicio, 4.2; la propina, **4**

  Is the tip included? ¿Está incluido el servicio?, 4.2

tire la llanta, la goma, el neumático, la rueda, 9.2; **6.2;** el caucho

  flat tire el pinchazo, 9.2

  spare tire la rueda (llanta) de repuesto (recambio), 9.2

tired cansado(a), 6.1

to a

toast las tostadas, el pan tostado, 4.1; *7*

today hoy, LP

  What day is it today? ¿Qué día es hoy?, LP

  What is today's date? ¿Cuál es la fecha de hoy?, LP

toe el dedo del pie, *11.1;* **2.1**

together juntos(as)

toilet el inodoro, el váter, *7*

toilet paper el papel higiénico, 11.2; *2.2*

  roll of toilet paper el rollo de papel higiénico, 11.2; *2.2*

toll el peaje, *9.1;* la cuota

tollbooth la cabina (garita) de peaje, *9.1*

tomato el tomate, 4.1

tomb la tumba, *5.1*

tomorrow mañana, LP

  See you tomorrow! ¡Hasta mañana!, LP

tonight esta noche, 4.1

too también, 1.2

toolbar la barra de herramientas, *6.1*

toothbrush el cepillo de dientes, 11.2; *2.2*

toothpaste la crema dental, 11.2; *2.2;* la pasta dentífrica

  tube of toothpaste el tubo de crema dental, 11.2; *2.2*

to **touch** tocar, 5.1

tourist el/la turista

toward hacia

towel la toalla, 7.1; *7*

town el pueblo; la villa, **5 (Lit.)**

town square la plaza, *8.1*

toy el juguete

track *(train)* la vía, *3.1*

traffic el tráfico, *8.1;* el tránsito

traffic jam el tapón

traffic light el semáforo, *8.1;* la luz roja, *9.1*

trail el camino; la senda, *3.2*

train el tren, *3.1;* **6.2**

  long-distance train el tren de largo recorrido, **6.2**

  suburban train el tren de cercanías, **6.2**

train car el coche, el vagón, *3.1*

train conductor el/la revisor, *3.2*

train station la estación de ferrocarril (tren), *3.1*

to **transfer** *(train)* transbordar, *3.2;* **6.2**

transmission: manual transmission la transmisión manual, **6.2**

transportation: means of transportation los medios de transporte, *8.2*

to **travel** viajar

tree el árbol, 2.2

trim el recorte, **4**

trip el viaje, 10.1; *1.1*

  to take a trip hacer un viaje, 10.1; *1.1*

trombone el trombono

truck el camión, *9.2*

true *(adj.)* verdadero(a); cierto(a), *6.1*

  That's true. Es verdad., 9.1

trunk *(car)* el baúl, la maletera, 10.1; *1.1*

truth la verdad

to **try** tratar de

tube el tubo, 11.2; *2.2*

Tuesday el martes, LP

tuna el atún, 9.2

to **turn** doblar, *9.1*

to **turn around** dar la vuelta, *9.1*

to **turn off** apagar, *6.1*

to **turn on** prender, *6.1*

to **turn . . . years old** cumplir… años, **3.2**

  turn signals las direccionales, *9.2*

TV la tele

twelve doce, LP

twenty veinte, LP

twenty-eight veintiocho, LP

twenty-five veinticinco, LP

twenty-four veinticuatro, LP

twenty-nine veintinueve, LP

twenty-one veintiuno, LP

twenty-seven veintisiete, LP

twenty-six veintiséis, LP

twenty-three veintitrés, LP

twenty-two veintidós, LP

twin el/la gemelo(a), 2.1

to **twist** torcerse, *11.2;* **2.2**

two dos, LP

two hundred doscientos(as), *9.2*

type el tipo, *6.1*

typical típico(a)

U

ugly feo(a), 1.1

unattractive feo(a), 1.1

uncle el tío, 2.1

under debajo de, 10.2; *1.2*

underneath debajo de, 10.2; *1.2*

to **understand** comprender, 4.2; entender (ie), 8.2

unfortunately desgraciadamente

to **unhook** *(telephone receiver)* descolgar (ue) el auricular, *6.2*

uniform el uniforme, *3.1*

United States Estados Unidos

  from the United States estadounidense

university la universidad

  university degree la matrícula universitaria, **4**

unless a menos que

unoccupied libre, 4.2; *3.2*

unpleasant antipático(a), 1.1; desagradable

until hasta, LP; hasta que

English-Spanish Dictionary

English-Spanish Dictionary

up: to go up subir, *7.2*
upper superior
urban urbano(a), *8.1*
us *(pl. pron.)* nos
to **use** usar, *3.2*

vacation las vacaciones, *7.1*
vanilla *(adj.)* de vainilla
various varios(as)
veal la ternera, *10; 1*
veal cutlet el escalope
de ternera, *10; 1*
vegetable la legumbre,
la verdura, el vegetal, *4.1; 9;*
la hortaliza, *9*
   vegetable garden el huerto, *9*
   vegetable store (greengrocer)
   la verdulería, *9.2*
vegetarian vegetariano(a), *4.1*
veil el velo, *3.1*
Venezuelan venezolano(a)
verse el verso, *7.2*
very muy, LP; mucho, LP
   It's very hot (cold). Hace
   mucho calor (frío)., LP
   Very well. Muy bien, LP
view la vista
vinegar el vinagre, *4*
vineyard la viña, *9*
violin el violín
to **visit** visitar, *8.2*
volcano el volcán
volleyball el voleibol, *7.1*
   volleyball court la cancha
   de voleibol, *7.1*
vowel la vocal

to **wait (for)** esperar, *10.2; 1.2*
   to wait in line hacer cola,
   10.2; 1.2; estar en fila
waiter (waitress)
el/la mesero(a), *4.2, 4;*
el/la camarero(a), *4*
waiting room la sala
de espera, *3.1*
wake el velorio, *3.2*

to **wake up** despertarse (ie),
11.1; 2.1
to **walk** caminar, *5.1;* andar
   to walk in a procession
   desfilar, *5.1*
to **want** querer (ie), *5.1;* desear,
4.2
war la guerra, **8**
warm-ups *(clothing)* el buzo,
11.1; **2.1**
to **warn** advertir (ie, i)
warning la advertencia
to **wash** lavar, *11.2; 2.2; 4*
to **wash oneself** lavarse, *11.1; 2.1*
   to wash one's hair (face,
   hands) lavarse el pelo
   (la cara, las manos), *11.1;*
   2.1
washbasin el lavabo, *7*
washing machine la lavadora, *4*
watch el reloj, *6* **(Lit.)**
to **watch** mirar, *3.2;* ver, *4.2*
Watch out! ¡Cuidado!, *5*
water el agua, *4.1*
   running water el agua
   corriente
   (sparkling) mineral water
   el agua mineral (con gas),
   4.2
watercolor la acuarela, *7.1*
waterskiing el esquí acuático
(náutico), *7.1*
   to water-ski esquiar
   en el agua, *7.1*
wave la ola, *7.1*
way la manera
   to lose one's way perder (ie)
   el camino
we nosotros(as)
wealthy acomodado(a), **8**
weapon el arma *(f.)*
to **wear** llevar, *3.1; (shoe size)*
calzar, *9.1; (clothing size)*
usar, *9.1*
weather el tiempo, LP
   It's cold (weather).
   Hace frío., LP
   It's cool (weather).
   Hace fresco., LP
   The weather is bad.
   Hace mal tiempo., LP
   The weather is nice.
   Hace buen tiempo., LP
   What's the weather like?
   ¿Qué tiempo hace?, LP

Web la red, *3.2;* **6.1**
   to surf the Web navegar
   la red, *3.2;* **6.1**
Web site el sitio Web, *6.1*
wedding la boda, *3.1*
wedding dress el traje
de novia, *3.1*
wedding register el registro
de matrimonio, *3.1*
wedding ring el anillo
de boda, *3.1*
Wednesday el miércoles, LP
week la semana, LP
   last week la semana pasada,
   7.1
weekend el fin de semana, *7.1*
to **weigh** pesar, **6.1**
weight la pesa, *11.1;* **2.1;**
(of something) el peso, **6.1**
weights: to lift weights
levantar pesas, *11.1;* **2.1**
welcome: You're welcome.
De nada., Por nada., No hay
de qué., LP
well bien, LP; pues
   Very well. Muy bien., LP
well-done *(meat)* bien
hecho(a), *4*
well-known renombrado(a)
well-mannered bien
educado(a), *6.1*
west el oeste
what ¿qué?, ¿cuál?, ¿cuáles?,
LP; ¿cómo?, *1.1*
   at what time? ¿a qué hora?,
   LP
   What a mess! ¡Qué lío!, **6.1**
   What a shame! ¡Qué pena!,
   5.1
   What day is it (today)?
   ¿Qué día es hoy?, LP
   What does he (she, it) look
   like? ¿Cómo es?, *1.1*
   What's happening?
   What's going on? ¿Qué
   pasa?, *3.1*
   What is he (she, it) like?
   ¿Cómo es?, *1.1*
   What is today's date?
   ¿Cuál es la fecha de hoy?,
   LP
   what nationality? ¿de qué
   nacionalidad?, *1.1*
   What's new (up)?
   ¿Qué hay?

What size *(clothing)* **do you wear (take)?** ¿Qué talla usas?, 9.1

What size shoe do you wear (take)? ¿Qué número calzas?, 9.1

What would you like (to eat)? ¿Qué desean tomar?, 4.2

What time is it? ¿Qué hora es?, LP

whatever cualquiera

wheat el trigo, 8.2; **9**

wheelchair la silla de ruedas, *11.2;* **2.2**

when cuando, 3.1

when? ¿cuándo?, 3.2

whenever cuandoquiera

where donde

where? ¿dónde?, 1.1; ¿adónde?, 3.2

from where? ¿de dónde?, 1.1

wherever dondequiera

which? ¿cuál?, LP; ¿cuáles?

whichever cualquiera

while mientras, 5.2

to **whisper** musitar, **3 (Lit.)**

white blanco(a), 5.1

who? ¿quién?, 1.1; ¿quiénes?, 1.2

Who's calling, please? ¿De parte de quién, por favor?, *6.2*

whoever quienquiera

whole entero(a)

whose cuyos(as)

why? ¿por qué?, 3.2

wide ancho(a), 8.1

widow la viuda, **3.2**

wife la esposa, la mujer, 2.1

to **win** ganar, 5.1

wind el viento, LP

window *(store)* el escaparate, 9.1; *(plane)* la ventanilla, 10.2; *1.2;* **6.1**

windshield el parabrisas, *9.1*

windshield wipers los limpiaparabrisas, **6.2**

windsurfing la plancha de vela, 7.1

to go windsurfing practicar la plancha de vela, 7.1

windy: It's windy. Hace viento., LP

wings las alitas, *10;* **1**

winter el invierno, LP

wise sabio(a), **5 (Lit.)**

the Three Wise Men los Reyes Magos, *5.2*

wish el afán, **3 (Lit.)**

to **wish** desear, 4.2

with con

to **withdraw** retirar, **4**

within dentro de

without sin, 7.2

woman la dama

wooden de madera, **7.1**

word la palabra

work el trabajo, **10;** *(art)* la obra

abstract work (of art) la obra abstracta, **7.1**

figurative work (of art) la obra figurativa, **7.1**

to **work** trabajar, 3.2; *(land)* cultivar, labrar, 8.2

workshop el taller, **7.1**

world el mundo

World Cup la Copa Mundial

worldwide mundial

worse peor

worst el/la peor

worth: It's not worth it. No vale., 7.1

Would that . . . Ojalá que… , *11.2;* **2.2**

wound la herida, *11.2;* **2.2**

wreath la corona, *5.1*

wrinkled arrugado(a), **4**

wrist la muñeca, *11.1;* **2.1**

to **write** escribir, 4.2

written escrito(a)

wrong erróneo(a)

X ray la radiografía, *11.2;* **2.2**

They're taking an X ray (of him or her). Le toman (hacen) una radiografía., *11.2;* **2.2**

year el año, LP

last year el año pasado, 7.1

to be turning . . . years old cumplir… años

to be . . . years old tener… años, 2.1

yellow amarillo(a), 5.1

yes sí, LP

yesterday ayer, 7.1

yesterday afternoon ayer por la tarde, 7.1

yesterday evening anoche, 7.1

yet aún; todavía

yoga el yoga, *11.1;* **2.1**

to do yoga practicar yoga, *11.1;* **2.1**

you tú; *(sing. form.)* usted; *(pl. form.)* ustedes; *(pl. fam.)* vosotros(as); *(fam. pron.)* ti; te; *(form. pron.)* le

You're welcome. De (Por) nada.; No hay de qué., LP

young person el/la joven, 1.1

younger menor, 2.1

youngest el/la menor, 2.1

your *(fam.)* tu(s); *(form.)* su(s)

It's your turn! ¡Te toca a ti!

youth hostel el albergue juvenil, el hostal, 7

zero cero, LP

zone la zona

zoo el zoológico, *8.1*

Culture Index

Numbers in light print indicate that the cultural reference was introduced in a prior level.
Numbers in bold print indicate that the cultural reference is introduced in Level 3.

A

B

C

Culture Index

Culture Index

Culture Index

Culture Index

N

O

Culture Index

Grammar Index

Grammar Index

Grammar Index

Credits

The McGraw-Hill Companies, Inc. would like to acknowledge the artists and agencies who participated in illustrating this program: Michael Arnold; Bill Dickson represented by Contact Jupiter; Glencoe/McGraw-Hill; Pat Lewis; Cedric Hohnstadt; Geo Parkin represented by American Artists Rep. Inc.; Mapping Specialists, Ltd.

Photo Credits

COVER i Chad Ehlers/ImageState; **iv** Colin Monteath/age fotostock; **ix** (l)Jack Hollingsworth/age fotostock, (r)Ken Welsh/age fotostock; **v** (l)Andrew Payti, (r)David H. Brennan; **vi** (l)The McGraw-Hill Companies, (r)Andrew Payti; **vii** Getty Images; **viii** Jeremy Woodhouse/age fotostock; **x** JUPITERIMAGES/PHOTOS.COM/Alamy Images; **xi** (l)The McGraw-Hill Companies, (r)Black Star/Alamy Images; **xii** (l)Miguel Ángel Muñoz/age fotostock; (r)James Darell/Photolibrary; **xiii** Blend Images/age fotostock; **xiv** David H. Brennan; **xv** (l)The McGraw-Hill Companies, (r)David H. Brennan; **xvi** Andrew Payti; **SH0** (t)Andrew Payti, (c)Yvonne Cadiz, (b)Scott Gries/Getty Images; **SH1** (tl)Fotosearch, (tr)Rebecca Smith, (b)Clasos Agencia International/CORBIS SYGMA; **SH2** Getty Images; **SH2–SH3** BananaStock/Jupiter Images; **SH3** Andersen Ross/age fotostock; **SH4** Siede Preis/Getty Images; **SH5** Brand X Pictures/age fotostock; **SH6** Bananastock/PictureQuest/Jupiter Images; **SH20** File Photo; **SH31** (t)Andrew Payti, (c)Gabriela Zamudio, (bl)Rebecca Smith, (br)Matthew Johnston/Alamy Images; **SH38–SH39** Colin Monteath/age fotostock; **SH40** (tl)Atlantide Phototravel/CORBIS, (tr)José Antonio Jiménez/age fotostock, (bl)Randa Bishop/ImageState, (br)Paul Hardy/CORBIS; **SH41** (t)Rafa Fierres/age fotostock, (c)FAN travelstock/Alamy Images, (b)Jorge Bai/Alamy Images; **SH42** (tl)SuperStock/age fotostock, (tr)Adalberto Ríos/age fotostock, (bl)Robert Fried/Alamy Images, (br)José Enrique Molina; **SH43** (tl)Kord.com/age fotostock, (tr)FoodCollection/age fotostock, (b)Keith Dannemiller/Alamy Images; **SH44** (tl)Ryan Fox/age fotostock, (tr)Macduff Everton/CORBIS, (bl)Jan Csernoch/Alamy Images, (br)Nik Wheeler/CORBIS; **SH45** (t)Ken Welsh/age fotostock, (b)Danny Lehman/CORBIS; **SH46** (tl)Passport Stock/age fotostock, (tr)Ken Welsh/age fotostock, (b)Alvaro Leiva/age fotostock; **SH47** (tl)Creatas/age fotostock, (tr)Mark Lewis/Getty Images, (bl)Chris Cheadle/age fotostock, (br)terry harris just greece photo library/Alamy Images; **SH48** (t)Mardagada/Alamy Images, (c)Sean Sprague/Alamy Images, (b)AFP PHOTO/Raul Arboleda/Getty Images; **SH49** (t)Paulo Fridman/CORBIS, (cl)GC Minerals/Alamy Images, (cr)Kevin Schafer/Stone/ Getty Images, (b)Andoni Canela/age fotostock; **SH50** (t)Robert Fried/Alamy Images, (c)Coco Dalfiono/age fotostock, (c)Tono Labra/age fotostock, (b)Bjanka Kadic/Alamy Images; **SH51** (t)Pictorial Press/Alamy Images, (b)Roberto Contini/age fotostock; **SH52** (tl)José Fusté Raga/age fotostock, (tr)Jordi Camí/age fotostock, (bl)Stockbyte/Alamy Images, (br)Digital Vision/Getty Images; **SH53** (t)Raymond Forbes/age fotostock, (bl)H. Fougfire/Iconotec/age fotostock, (br)Oliver Gerhard/Alamy Images; **SH54** (t)www.rekindlephoto.com/Don Despain/Alamy Images, (cl)Jeff Greenberg/age fotostock, (cr)StockAB/Alamy Images, (b)Kim Karpeles/Alamy Images; **SH55** (t)Richard Levine/Alamy Images, (c)Jeff Greenberg/age fotostock, (b)Visions of America, LLC/Alamy Images; **R0–R1** MELBA PHOTO AGENCY/Alamy Images; **R2** David H. Brennan; **R3** (tl)Frederico Gil, (tr)Steve Weinstein, (b)Saxpix.com/age fotostock; **R5** Danita Delimont/Alamy Images; **R6** Robert Fried/Alamy Images; **R8** David H. Wells/age fotostock; **R9** Andrew Payti; **R10–R11** DANI CARDONA/Reuters/CORBIS; **R12** (tl tr br)David H. Brennan, (bl)Frederico Gil; **R13** (tl)Design Pics./Alamy Images, (tr)Media Minds/Alamy Images, (b)Richard Hutchings; **R15** (t)CORBIS/age fotostock, (b)Elliot Nichol/Alamy Images; **R18** (t)Andrew Payti, (b)sergio pitamitz/age fotostock; **R19** VStock LLC/age fotostock; **R20** (l)Gen Nishino/Getty Images, (r)IT Stock Free/age fotostock; **R21** Steve Weinstein; **R22–R23** Jeff Curtes/CORBIS; **R24** (tl)Robert Fried/Alamy Images, (tr)The McGraw-Hill Companies, (cl)C. Squared Studios/Photodisc, (c)Doug Bryant/DDB Stock Photo, (cr)Timothy Fuller, (bl)J.D. Dallet/age fotostock, (br)ARCO/W. Dieterich/age fotostock; **R25** (tl)Andrew Payti, (tr)Rios Szalay/Sexto Sol/Getty Images, (c)Gonzalo Azumendi/age fotostock, (bl)Paco Ayala/age fotostock, (bc)ThinkStock/age fotostock, (br)Andrew Payti; **R26** Andrew Payti; **R28** Digital Vision/Alamy Images; **R29 R30 R31 R32** Andrew Payti; **R34–R35** Gabriel J. Jimenez/eStock Photo; **R36** (tl)Leonardo Diad Romero/age fotostock, (tr)Michael Silver/Alamy Images, (bl)blickwinkel/Alamy Images, (br)Kim Karpeles/Alamy Images; **R37** (l to r, t to b)(2)The McGraw-Hill Companies, (3)Burke/Triolo Producti/age fotostock, (4–13)Andrew Payti; **R38** David H. Brennan; **R39** Ken Welsh/age fotostock; **R40** Andrew Payti; **R41** David H. Brennan; **R42 R43 R44 R45 R46** Andrew Payti; **R48–R49** Eitan Simanor/Alamy Images; **R50** (tl tr)David H. Brennan, (c)Carlos Nieto/age fotostock, (bl)Maria E. Villalta, (br)Jose Fuste Raga/age fotostock; **R51** Kelli Drummer-Avendaño; **R52** David H. Brennan; **R53** The McGraw-Hill Companies; **R54** Ken Welsh/age fotostock; **R55 R56 R57** Andrew Payti; **R58–R59** R1/Alamy Images; **R60** (tl tr bl)David H. Brennan, (br)Melvyn Longhurst/Alamy Images; **R61** Andrew Payti; **R62** (t)Nancy R. Cohen/Getty Images, (b)Comstock/PunchStock; **R64** Thinkstock Images/age fotostock; **R65** Ingolf Pompe 7/Alamy Images; **R66 R67** Andrew Payti; **0–1** Kathy Tarantola/Index Stock Imagery; **2** (t)Robert Holmes/CORBIS, (cl)Peter M. Wilson/Alamy Images, (cr)Andrew Payti, (b)David R. Frazier Photolibrary, Inc./Alamy Images, (bl)LeighSmithImages/Alamy Images, (br)Kevin Foy/Alamy Images; **3** (tl)The McGraw-Hill Companies, (tr)Jeff Greenberg/Alamy Images, (c)Jeremy Hoare/Food And Drink Photos/age fotostock; **4** (t)CORBIS, (cl bl br)Alamy Images, (cr)age fotostock; **5** (l to r, t to b)(2)(7)(8)The McGraw-Hill Companies, (3)(4)(6)Alamy Images, (5)(9)age fotostock; **6** Kerri Galloway; **7** (t)Andrew Payti, (c)Getty Images, (b)Alamy Images; **8** Punchstock; **9** Andrew Payti; **10** age fotostock; **11** (l)Kelli Drummer-Avendaño, (r)Andrew Payti; **12** Lori Ernfridsson; **14** David H. Brennan; **15** Andrew Payti; **16** (l r)Alamy Images, (t border)Andrew Payti, (t border)Brand X Pictures/PunchStock, (t border)Digital Vision/PunchStock, (t border)Masterfile; **17** (l c)Andrew Payti, (r)The McGraw-Hill Companies, (t border)Andrew Payti, (t border)BananaStock/PunchStock, (t border)Brand X Pictures/PunchStock, (t border)CORBIS, (t border)Digital Vision/PunchStock, (t border)Don Tremain/Getty Images, (t border)The McGraw-Hill Companies; **18** Alamy Images; **19** (l)The McGraw-Hill Companies, (r)Andrew Payti; **20** (tl)Jupiterimages, (tr bl br)Getty Images, (cl)Ken Cavanagh/The McGraw-Hill Companies, (cr)CORBIS; **22** Andrew Payti; **23** Hill Street Sudios/Crystal Cartier/Getty Images; **26** Punchstock; **27** Andrew Payti; **28–29** Rafael Campillo/age fotostock; **30** (t)ImageSource/age fotostock, (c)The McGraw-Hill Companies, (bl)Ben Welsh/age fotostock, (br)Robert Fried/Alamy Images; **31** (tl)Wig Worland/Alamy Images, (tr)Lori Ernfridsson, (cl)Robert Fried/Alamy Images, (cr)Andrew Payti, (b)LOOK Die Bildagentur der Fotografen GmbH/Alamy Images; **32** (tl b)David H. Brennan, (tr)age fotostock; **33** (tl)Getty Images, (tc)Pixtal/age fotostock, (tr)David H. Brennan, (cl)Andrew Payti, (cr)Dennis MacDonald/age fotostock, (b)Kirby Lee/WireImage/Getty Images, **34** (tl tc)Getty Images, (tr)Gary He/The McGraw-Hill Companies, (b)Alamy Images; **35** Andrew Payti; **36** (tl tc tr)David H. Brennan, (b)Alamy Images; **37** David H. Brennan; **38** Andrew Payti; **39** Jeronimo Alba/age fotostock; **40** (t)Andrew Payti, (b)age fotostock; **42** Andrew Payti; **43** age fotostock; **45** Andrew Payti; **47** (l)Getty Images, (r)Andrew

CREDITS

Credits